Mike Meyers'

CompTIA A+®
Guide to Managing
and Troubleshooting PCs

Third Edition
(Exams 220-701 & 220-702)

Mike Meyers'

CompTIA A+®
Guide to Managing
and Troubleshooting PCs

Third Edition
(Exams 220-701 & 220-702)

Mike Meyers

New York Chicago San Fran
Lisbon London Madrid Mexico City
New Delhi San Juan Seoul Singapore Sydney

The McGraw·Hill Companies

Cataloging-in-Publication Data is on file with the Library of Congress

McGraw-Hill books are available at special quantity discounts to use as premiums and sales promotions, or for use in corporate training programs. To contact a representative, please e-mail us at bulksales@mcgraw-hill.com.

Mike Meyers' CompTIA A+® Guide to Managing and Troubleshooting PCs, Third Edition (Exams 220-701 & 220-702)

    234567890   WDQ WDQ   109876543210

ISBN: Book p/n 978-0-07-171381-8 and CD p/n 978-0-07-171383-2
of set 978-0-07-171380-1

MHID: Book p/n 0-07-171381-6 and CD p/n 0-07-171383-2
of set 0-07-171380-8

Sponsoring Editor
Timothy Green

Editorial Supervisor
Jody McKenzie

Project Editor
Laura Stone

Acquisitions Coordinator
Meghan Riley

Technical Editor
Christopher A. Crayton

Copy Editor
Malinda McCain

Proofreader
Paul Tyler

Indexer
Jack Lewis

Production Supervisor
James Kussow

Composition
Glyph International

Illustration
Glyph International

Art Director, Cover
Jeff Weeks

■ About the Author

Mike Meyers, lovingly called the "AlphaGeek" by those who know him, is the industry's leading authority on CompTIA A+ certification. He is the president and co-founder of Total Seminars, LLC, a provider of PC and network repair seminars, books, videos, and courseware for thousands of organizations throughout the world. Mike has been involved in the computer and network repair industry since 1977 as a technician, instructor, author, consultant, and speaker. Author of numerous popular PC books and videos, including the best-selling *CompTIA A+ Certification All-in-One Exam Guide*, Mike is also the series editor for the highly successful *Mike Meyers' Certification Passport* series, the *Mike Meyers' Computer Skills* series, and the *Mike Meyers' Guide to* series, all published by McGraw-Hill. As well as writing, Mike has personally taught (and continues to teach) thousands of students, including U.S. senators, U.S. Supreme Court justices, the United Nations, every branch of the U.S. Armed Forces, most branches of the Department of Justice, hundreds of corporate clients, academic students at every level, prisoners, and pensioners.

E-mail: michaelm@totalsem.com
Facebook: Mike Meyers (Houston, TX)
Twitter/Skype/most instant messaging clients: desweds
Web forums: www.totalsem.com/forums

About the Editor in Chief

Scott Jernigan wields a mighty red pen as Editor in Chief for Total Seminars. With a Master of Arts degree in Medieval History, Scott feels as much at home in the musty archives of London as he does in the warm computer glow of Total Seminars' Houston headquarters. After fleeing a purely academic life, he dove headfirst into IT, working as an instructor, editor, and writer. Scott has edited and contributed to dozens of books on computer literacy, hardware, operating systems, networking, and certification. His latest book is *Computer Literacy—Your Ticket to IC³ Certification*. Scott co-authored the best-selling *A+ Certification All-in-One Exam Guide*, Fifth Edition, and the *Mike Meyers' A+ Guide to Managing and Troubleshooting PCs* (both with Mike Meyers). He has taught computer classes all over the United States, including stints at the United Nations in New York and the FBI Academy in Quantico.

About the Technical Editor

Christopher A. Crayton (MCSE, MCP+I, CompTIA A+, CompTIA Network+) is an author, technical editor, technical consultant, security consultant, and trainer. Formerly a computer and networking instructor at Keiser College (2001 Teacher of the Year), Chris has also worked as network administrator for Protocol and at Eastman Kodak Headquarters as a computer and network specialist. Chris has authored several print and online books on topics ranging from CompTIA A+ and CompTIA Security+ to Microsoft Windows Vista. Chris has provided technical edits and reviews for many publishers, including McGraw-Hill, Pearson Education, Charles River Media, Cengage Learning, Wiley, O'Reilly, Syngress, and Apress.

Peer Reviewers

Thank you to the reviewers, past and present, who contributed insightful reviews, criticisms, and helpful suggestions that continue to shape this textbook.

Donat Forrest
Broward County Community College
Pembroke Pines, FL

Winston Maddox
Mercer County Community College
West Windsor, NJ

Brian Ives
Finger Lakes Community College
Canadaigua, NY

Rajiv Malkan
Montgomery College
Conroe, Texas

Farbod Karimi
Heald College
San Francisco, CA

Scott Sweitzer
Indiana Business College
Indianapolis, IN

Tamie Knaebel
Jefferson Community College
Louisville, KY

Randall Stratton
DeVry University
Irving, TX

Keith Lyons
Cuyahoga Community College
Parma, OH

Thomas Trevethan
CPI College of Technology
Virginia Beach, VA

■ Acknowledgments

Scott Jernigan, my Editor in Chief at Total Seminars and boon companion on many an evening, worked his usual magic pulling together this latest edition. My thanks, amigo!

My acquisitions editor, Tim Green, kept me on target to get this book done. Seriously. Who else could motivate me to work on the book while on vacation in Key West, Florida? The sun, the surf, the silliness…all dashed away by a phone call. But I'm not bitter, just happy the book is done and Tim will quit yelling at me.

To Chris Crayton. You went so far beyond the call of technical editor that you should have your very own unique title, like *über technical editor king*! Thank you for helping make this book happen.

To Ed Dinovo. Your contributions of words and ideas helped build this book into a much better work than it could have been without you. Thank you very much.

To Alec Fehl. You did an outstanding job on this new book, and it is always a pleasure working with you.

My in-house photographer and fellow geek, Michael Smyer, contributed in many ways. His gorgeous photographs grace most pages. His tirelessness in challenging me technically on almost every topic both irritated and frustrated me, but the book is much better because of it. Excellent work, Michael.

Ford Pierson, my in-house editor and illustrator, brought outrageous wit and skill to his contributions throughout the book. Plus he has a killer instinct in Counter-Strike that makes the gaming sessions all the better. Great job, Ford.

Aaron Verber came in at the last minute with his red pen to help with page proofs, showing a careful eye that Scott will adore. I look forward to many more projects with you, lad.

On the McGraw-Hill side, the crew once again demonstrated why McGraw-Hill is the best in show as a publisher. With excellent work and even better attitude, this book went smoothly together.

Laura Stone reprised her role as developmental editor for this edition, keeping me on my toes for every detail, fact, illustration, screen shot, and photograph—all this while bouncing the newly born and very cute Maleah on one knee. Laura, you're amazing and a joy to work with. Thanks!

To the copy editors, page proofers, and layout folks—Malinda McCain, Paul Tyler, Jack Lewis, Amarjeet Kumar, and all the folks at Glyph International—superb work in every facet. Thank you for being the best.

■ *To Intel, for making great CPUs—and to AMD, for keeping Intel on the ball.*

—Mike Meyers

ABOUT THIS BOOK

■ Important Technology Skills

Information technology (IT) offers many career paths, leading to occupations in such fields as PC repair, network administration, telecommunications, Web development, graphic design, and desktop support. To become competent in any IT field, however, you need certain basic computer skills.

Mike Meyers' CompTIA A+ Guide to Managing and Troubleshooting PCs *builds a foundation for success in the IT field by introducing you to fundamental technology concepts and giving you essential computer skills.*

Try This! *exercises apply core skills in a new setting.*

Key Terms, *identified in red, point out important vocabulary and definitions that you need to know.*

Tech Tip *sidebars provide inside information from experienced IT professionals.*

Cross Check *questions develop reasoning skills: ask, compare, contrast, and explain.*

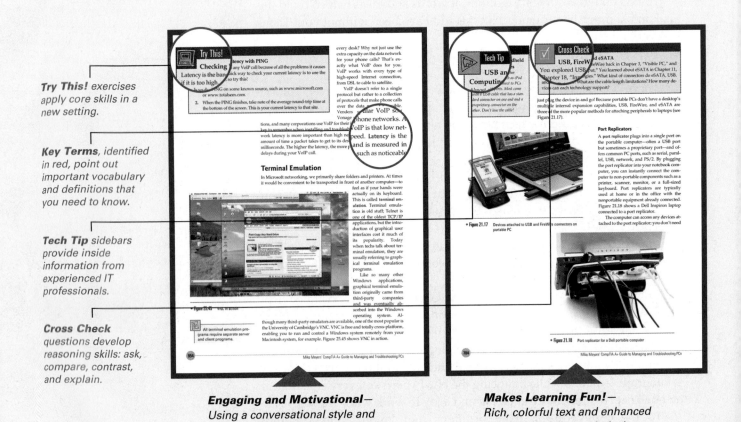

Engaging and Motivational—
Using a conversational style and proven instructional approach, the author explains technical concepts in a clear, interesting way using real-world examples.

Makes Learning Fun!—
Rich, colorful text and enhanced illustrations bring technical subjects to life.

Proven Learning Method Keeps You on Track

Mike Meyers' CompTIA A+ Guide to Managing and Troubleshooting PCs *is structured to give you comprehensive knowledge of computer skills and technologies. The textbook's active learning methodology guides you beyond mere recall and, through thought-provoking activities, labs, and sidebars, helps you develop critical-thinking, diagnostic, and communication skills.*

Effective Learning Tools

This pedagogically rich book is designed to make learning easy and enjoyable and to help you develop the skills and critical-thinking abilities that will enable you to adapt to different job situations and troubleshoot problems.

Mike Meyers' proven ability to explain concepts in a clear, direct, even humorous way makes these books interesting, motivational, and fun.

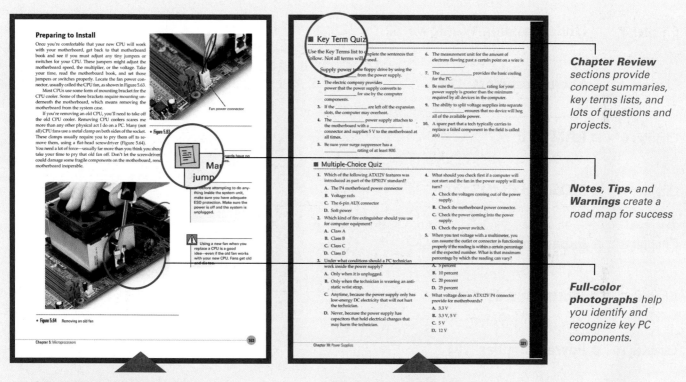

Chapter Review sections provide concept summaries, key terms lists, and lots of questions and projects.

Notes, **Tips**, and **Warnings** create a road map for success

Full-color photographs help you identify and recognize key PC components.

Offers Practical Experience—
Tutorials and lab assignments develop essential hands-on skills and put concepts in real-world contexts.

Robust Learning Tools—
Summaries, key terms lists, quizzes, essay questions, and lab projects help you practice skills and measure progress.

Each chapter includes:

- **Learning objectives** that set measurable goals for chapter-by-chapter progress

- **Try This!**, **Cross Check**, and **Tech Tip** sidebars that encourage you to practice and apply concepts in real-world settings

- **Notes**, **Tips**, and **Warnings** that guide you through difficult areas

- **Exam-driven organization** that divides chapters into Historical/Conceptual, Essentials, Practical Application, and Beyond A+ sections, making it easy to focus study time on the core and specialization areas of the exams

- Plenty of full-color **photographs** and **illustrations** that provide clear, up-close pictures of the technology, making difficult concepts easy to visualize and understand

- **Highlighted Key Terms**, **Key Terms lists**, and **Chapter Summaries** that provide you with an easy way to review important concepts and vocabulary

- **Challenging End-of-Chapter Quizzes** that inclu vocabulary-building exercises, multiple-choice questions, essay questions, and on-the-job lab projects

CONTENTS AT A GLANCE

CONTENTS

Chapter 5
■ Microprocessors 124

Chapter 6
■ RAM 176

Chapter 7
■ BIOS and CMOS 204

Chapter 11
▓ Hard Drive Technologies 324

Chapter 12
▓ Implementing Hard Drives 366

Chapter 13
▓ Removable Media 424

Chapter 17
■ Maintaining and Troubleshooting Windows 592

Chapter 18
■ Input/Output 650

Chapter 19
■ Video 678

Chapter 27
■ The Complete PC Tech 1006

Appendix A
■ Mapping to the CompTIA A+ Objectives 1026

Appendix B
■ About the CD-ROM 1046

■ Glossary 1049

■ Index 1087

I started writing computer books for the simple reason that no one wrote the kind of books I wanted to read. The books were either too simple (Chapter 1, "Using Your Mouse") or too complex (Chapter 1, "TTL Logic and Transistors"), and none of them provided a motivation for me to learn the information. I believed that there were geeky readers just like me who wanted to know *why* they needed to know the information in a computer book.

Good books motivate readers to learn what they are reading. For example, if a book discusses binary arithmetic but doesn't explain why I need to learn it, that's not a good book. Tell me that understanding binary makes it easier to understand how a CPU works or why a megabyte is different from a million bytes—then I get excited, no matter how geeky the topic. If I don't have a good motivation to do something, then I'm simply not going to do it (which explains why I haven't jumped out of an airplane!).

In this book, I teach you why you need to understand the technology that runs almost every modern business. You'll learn to build and fix computers, exploring every nook and cranny, and master the art of the PC tech. In the process, you'll gain the knowledge you need to pass the CompTIA A+ certification exams.

Enjoy, my fellow geek.

—Mike Meyers

The logo of the CompTIA Authorized Quality Curriculum (CAQC) program and the status of this or other training material as "Authorized" under the CompTIA Authorized Quality Curriculum program signifies that, in CompTIA's opinion, such training material covers the content of CompTIA's related certification exam.

The contents of this training material were created for the CompTIA A+® exams 220-701 and 220-702, covering CompTIA certification objectives that were current as of August 2009.

CompTIA has not reviewed or approved the accuracy of the contents of this training material and specifically disclaims any warranties of merchantability or fitness for a particular purpose.

CompTIA makes no guarantee concerning the success of persons using any such "Authorized" or other training material in order to prepare for any CompTIA certification exam.

■ How to Become CompTIA Certified

This training material can help you prepare for and pass a related CompTIA certification exam or exams. In order to achieve CompTIA certification, you must register for and pass a CompTIA certification exam or exams.

In order to become CompTIA certified, you must:

1. Select a certification exam provider. For more information please visit http://www.comptia.org/certifications/testprep/testingcenters.aspx.

2. Register for and schedule a time to take the CompTIA certification exam(s) at a convenient location.

3. Read and sign the Candidate Agreement, which will be presented at the time of the exam(s). The text of the Candidate Agreement can be found at http://www.comptia.org/certifications/testprep/policies/agreement.aspx.

4. Take and pass the CompTIA certification exam(s).

For more information about CompTIA's certifications, such as its industry acceptance, benefits or program news, please visit www.comptia.org/certification.

CompTIA is a not-for-profit information technology (IT) trade association. CompTIA's certifications are designed by subject matter experts from across the IT industry. Each CompTIA certification is vendor-neutral, covers multiple technologies and requires demonstration of skills and knowledge widely sought after by the IT industry.

To contact CompTIA with any questions or comments, please call (1) (630) 678 8300 or email questions@comptia.org.

For instructor and student resources, check out www.mhaplusolc.com. Students will find the chapter quizzes from the end of each chapter, and teachers can access instructor support materials.

■ Additional Resources for Teachers

Resources for teachers are provided via an Online Learning Center that maps to the organization of this textbook. This site includes the following:

- Answer keys to the end-of-chapter quizzes from this textbook

- Answer keys to the *Mike Meyers' CompTIA A+ Guide to Managing and Troubleshooting PCs Lab Manual, Third Edition* lab activities

- Instructor's Manual that contains learning objectives, classroom preparation notes, instructor tips, and a lecture outline for each chapter

- Engaging PowerPoint slides on the lecture topics (including full-color artwork from this book)

- Access to EZ Test online and test files that enable you to generate a wide array of tests. EZ Test features automatic grading, hundreds of practice questions, and a variety of question types and difficulty levels, enabling you to customize each test to maximize student progress

- LMS cartridges and other formats may also be available upon request; contact your sales representative

The Path of the PC Tech

"Of everything I've learned during my stint at Maximum PC, one lesson reigns supreme: The PC is what we make of it."

—George Jones, *Maximum PC*

In this chapter, you will learn how to

- **Explain the importance of gaining skill in managing and troubleshooting PCs**
- **Explain the importance of CompTIA A+ certification**
- **Describe how to become a CompTIA A+ Certified Technician**

Computers have taken over the world, or at least many professions. Everywhere you turn, a quick dig beneath the surface sawdust of construction, the grease of auto mechanics, and the hum of medical technology reveals one or more personal computers (PCs) working away, doing essential jobs. Because the PC evolved from novelty item to essential science tool to everyday object in a short period of time, there's a huge demand for a workforce that can build, maintain, troubleshoot, and repair PCs.

The Importance of Skill in Managing and Troubleshooting PCs

The people who work with computers—the **Information Technology (IT)** workforce—do such varied jobs as design hardware, write computer programs that enable you to do specific jobs on the PC, and create small and large groupings of computers—**networks**—so people can share computer resources. IT people built the Internet, one of the most phenomenal inventions of the 20th century. IT people maintain the millions of computers that make up the Internet. Computer technicians (or **PC techs**, as those of us in the field call each other) make up the core of the IT workforce. Without the techs, none of the other stuff works. Getting workers with skill in building, maintaining, troubleshooting, and fixing PCs is essential for success for every modern business.

In the early days of the personal computer, anyone who used a PC had to have skills as a PC tech. The PC was new, buggy, and prone to problems. You didn't want to rely on others to fix your PC when the inevitable problems arose. Today's PCs are much more robust and have fewer problems, but they're also much more complex machines. Today's IT industry, therefore, needs specialized workers who know how to make the machines run well.

Every profession requires specialized skills. For the most part, if you want to *get* or *keep* a job that requires those specialized skills, you need some type of **certification** or license. If you want a job fixing automobiles, for example, you get the *Automotive Service Excellence* (*ASE*) certification. If you want to perform companies' financial audits, you get your *Certified Public Accountant* (*CPA*) certification.

Nearly every profession has some criteria that you must meet to show your competence and ability to perform at a certain level. Although the way this works varies widely from one profession to another, all of them will at some point make you take an exam or series of exams. Passing these exams proves that you have the necessary skills to work at a certain level in your profession, whether you're an aspiring plumber, teacher, barber, or lawyer.

If you successfully pass these exams, the organization that administers those exams grants you certification. You receive some piece of paper or pin or membership card that you can show to potential clients or employers. This certification gives those clients or employers a level of confidence that you can do what you say you can do. Without this certification, either you will not find suitable work in that profession or no one will trust you to do the work.

The Importance of CompTIA A+ Certification

Microcomputers were introduced in the late 1970s, and for many years PC technicians did not have a universally recognized way to show clients or

employers that they know what to do under the hood of a personal computer. Sure, vendor-specific certifications existed, but the only way to get them was to get a job at an authorized warranty or repair facility first and then get the certification. Not that there's anything wrong with vendor-specific training; it's just that no single manufacturer has taken enough market share to make IBM training, for example, something that works for any job. (Then there is always that little detail of getting the job first before you can be certified....)

The software/networking side of our business has not suffered from the same lack of certifications. Due to the dominance of certain companies at one time or another (for example, Microsoft and Cisco), the vendor-specific certifications have provided a great way to get and keep a job. For example, Microsoft's *Microsoft Certified Systems Engineer* (*MCSE*) and Cisco's *Cisco Certified Internetwork Expert* (*CCIE*) have opened the doors for many.

But what about the person who runs around all day repairing printers, repartitioning hard drives, upgrading device drivers, and assembling systems? What about the PC hobbyists who want to be paid for their skills? What about the folks who, because they had the audacity to show that they knew the difference between CMOS and a command prompt, find themselves with a new title such as PC Support Technician or Electronic Services Specialist? On the other hand, how about the worst title of them all: "The Person Who Doesn't Get a Nickel Extra but Who Fixes the Computers"? CompTIA A+ certification fills that need.

What Is CompTIA A+ Certification?

CompTIA A+ certification is an industry-wide, vendor-neutral certification program developed and sponsored by the **Computing Technology Industry Association (CompTIA)**. The CompTIA A+ certification shows that you have a basic competence in supporting microcomputers. You achieve this certification by taking two computer-based, multiple-choice examinations. The tests cover what technicians should know after nine months of full-time PC support experience. CompTIA A+ certification enjoys wide recognition throughout the computer industry. To date, more than 800,000 technicians have become CompTIA A+ certified, making it the most popular of all IT certifications.

Who Is CompTIA?

CompTIA is a nonprofit industry trade association based in Oakbrook Terrace, Illinois. It consists of over 20,000 members in 102 countries. You'll find CompTIA offices in such diverse locales as Amsterdam, Dubai, Johannesburg, Tokyo, and São Paulo.

CompTIA provides a forum for people in these industries to network (as in meeting people), represents the interests of its members to the government, and provides certifications for many aspects of the computer industry. CompTIA sponsors A+, Network+, Security+, and other certifications. CompTIA works hard to watch the IT industry and constantly looks to provide new certifications to meet the ongoing demand from its membership. Check out the CompTIA Web site at **www.comptia.org** for details on the other certifications you can obtain from CompTIA.

Virtually every company of consequence in the IT industry is a member of CompTIA. Here are a few of the biggies:

Adobe Systems	AMD	Best Buy	Brother International
Canon	Cisco Systems	CompUSA	Fujitsu
Gateway	Hewlett-Packard	IBM	Intel
Kyocera	McAfee	Microsoft	NCR
Novell	Panasonic	Sharp Electronics	Siemens
Symantec	Toshiba	Total Seminars, LLC (that's my company)	Plus many thousands more

CompTIA began offering CompTIA A+ certification back in 1993. When it debuted, the IT industry largely ignored CompTIA A+ certification. Since that initial stutter, however, the CompTIA A+ certification has grown to become the de facto requirement for entrance into the PC industry. Many companies require CompTIA A+ certification for all of their PC support technicians, and the CompTIA A+ certification is widely recognized both in the United States and internationally. Additionally, many other certifications recognize CompTIA A+ certification and use it as credit toward their certifications.

The Path to Other Certifications

Most IT companies—big and small—see CompTIA A+ certification as the entry point to IT. From CompTIA A+, you have a number of certification options, depending on whether you want to focus more on hardware and operating systems or move into network administration (although these aren't mutually exclusive goals). The following three certifications are worth serious consideration:

- CompTIA Network+ certification
- Microsoft Certified Professional certifications
- Cisco certifications

CompTIA Network+ Certification

If you haven't already taken the CompTIA Network+ certification exam, make it your next certification. Just as CompTIA A+ certification shows you have solid competency as a PC technician, **CompTIA Network+ certification** demonstrates your skills as a network technician, including understanding of network hardware, installation, and troubleshooting. CompTIA's Network+ certification is a natural step for continuing toward your Microsoft or Cisco certifications. Take the CompTIA Network+: it's your obvious next certification.

Microsoft Certified Professional Certifications

Microsoft operating systems control a huge portion of all installed networks, and those networks need qualified support people to make them run. **Microsoft Certified Professional** certifications are a natural next step after the CompTIA certifications. They offer a whole slew of tracks and exams,

CompTIA A+ is the entry point to IT, though definitely not the only route for learning about computers and having certifications to prove that knowledge. Several certifications cover computer literacy or digital literacy, the phrase that means "what every person needs to know about computers to survive in the 21st century." The most popular computer literacy certification is Certiport's IC³ certification that tests on general computer knowledge; office productivity applications, such as Word and PowerPoint; and Internet applications such as Web browsing and e-mail.

CompTIA has a pre–CompTIA A+ exam (*not* a certification), called the *CompTIA Strata IT Technology exam,* that's geared a bit more to a user preparing to become a tech. It's designed to check basic knowledge levels for people getting into IT.

ranging from simple specializations in Windows Vista to numerous Microsoft Certified IT Professional (MCITP) certifications and beyond. You can find more details on Microsoft's learning Web site at www.microsoft .com/learning/en/us/certification/cert-overview.aspx.

Cisco Certification

Let's face it, Cisco routers pretty much run the Internet and most intranets in the world. A *router* is a networking device that controls and directs the flow of information over networks, such as e-mail messages, Web browsing, and so on. Cisco provides five levels of certification for folks who want to show their skills at handling Cisco products, such as the **Certified Cisco Network Associate (CCNA)**, plus numerous specialty certifications. See the Cisco certification Web site here for more details: www.cisco.com/web/learning/ le3/learning_career_certifications_and_learning_paths_home.html.

■ How Do I Become CompTIA A+ Certified?

You become CompTIA A+ certified, in the simplest sense, by taking and passing two computer-based, multiple-choice exams. No prerequisites are required for taking the CompTIA A+ certification exams (although there's an assumption of computer literacy, whether or not you have one of the computer literacy certifications). There is no required training course and no training materials to buy. You *do* have to pay a testing fee for each of the two exams. You pay your testing fees, go to a local testing center, and take the tests. You immediately know whether you have passed or failed. By passing both exams, you become CompTIA A+ certified. There are no requirements for professional experience. You do not have to go through an authorized training center. There are no annual dues. You pass; you're in. That's it. Now for the details.

> Previously, CompTIA offered a basic exam and then a choice of three different second exams. CompTIA reverted to the simpler two-exam format in 2009.

The Basic Exam Structure

CompTIA names the two exams introduced in 2009 as **CompTIA A+ 220-701 (Essentials)** and **CompTIA A+ 220-702 (Practical Application)**. It's common to refer to these two exams as the 2009 exams to differentiate them from older CompTIA exams. Although you may take either of the two exams first, I recommend taking the Essentials followed by the Practical Application. The Essentials exam concentrates on understanding terminology and technology, how to do fundamental tasks such as upgrading RAM, and basic Windows operating system support. The Practical Application exam builds on the Essentials exam, concentrating on advanced configuration and troubleshooting.

Both of the exams are extremely practical, with little or no interest in theory. All questions are multiple choice or "click on the right part of the picture" questions. The following is an example of the questions you will see on the exams:

Your laser printer is printing blank pages. Which item should you check first?

A. Printer drivers

B. Toner cartridge

C. Printer settings

D. Paper feed

The correct answer is B, the toner cartridge. You can make an argument for any of the others, but common sense (and skill as a PC technician) tells you to check the simplest possibility first.

The 2009 exams use a regular test format in which you answer a set number of questions and are scored based on how many correct answers you give, rather than the adaptive format used in years past. These exams have no more than 100 questions each. (Both exams have 100 questions each at the time of this writing.)

Be aware that CompTIA may add new questions to the exams at any time to keep the content fresh. The subject matter covered by the exams won't change, but new questions may be added periodically at random intervals. This policy puts stronger emphasis on understanding concepts and having solid PC-tech knowledge rather than trying to memorize specific questions and answers that may have been on the tests in the past. Going forward, no book or Web resource will have all the "right answers" because those answers will change constantly. Luckily for you, however, this book does not just teach you what steps to follow in a particular case but also explains how to be a knowledgeable tech who understands *why* you're doing those steps, so that when you encounter a new problem (or test question), you can work out the answer. Not only will this help you pass the exams, you'll also be a better PC tech!

To keep up to date, we monitor the CompTIA A+ exams for new content and update the special Tech Files section of the Total Seminars Web site (www.totalsem.com) with new articles covering subjects we believe may appear on future versions of the exams.

Windows-Centric

The CompTIA A+ exams are exclusively centered on the Microsoft Windows operating systems you would expect at a workstation or home. There are no Linux questions. There are no Macintosh OS X questions. You won't be asked about any version of Windows Server or Windows Mobile (used on smartphones and PDAs). Objectives in both exams clearly focus on the following operating systems:

- Windows 2000 Professional
- Windows XP Professional
- Windows XP Home
- Windows XP Media Center
- Windows Vista Home
- Windows Vista Home Premium
- Windows Vista Business
- Windows Vista Ultimate

Windows 7

CompTIA has the darnedest luck when it comes to the timing of new CompTIA A+ exams compared to releases of new Windows versions. CompTIA released the previous CompTIA A+ exams back in 2006, about four months before Microsoft released Windows Vista. It seems that once again CompTIA is caught missing a new operating system. Just a few months after CompTIA announced the 2009 updates to the CompTIA A+, Microsoft unveiled the next version of Windows: Windows 7.

Assuming CompTIA stays true to form, the chances of Windows 7 making it onto this version of the CompTIA A+ are very small. Adding Windows 7 is a major undertaking that would require CompTIA to change their clearly defined exam objectives. Don't worry about Windows 7. Structurally it is identical to Windows Vista. Even Microsoft has stated that Windows 7 is "a refined version of Windows Vista." If you know Vista, you will know Windows 7—and CompTIA isn't going to ask you about Windows 7 until the next update, probably around 2012.

Essentials (Exam 220–701)

The questions on the CompTIA A+ Essentials exam fit into one of six objectives. The number of questions for each objective is based on the percentages shown in Table 1.1.

The Essentials exam tests your knowledge of computer components, expecting you to be able to identify just about every common device on PCs, including variations within device types. Here's a list:

- Floppy drives
- Hard drives
- Optical drives
- Solid state drives
- Motherboards
- Power supplies
- CPUs
- RAM
- Monitors
- Input devices, such as keyboards, mice, and touchscreens
- Video and multimedia cards
- Network and modem cards
- Cables and connectors
- Heat sinks, fans, and liquid cooling systems
- Laptops and portable devices
- Printers
- Scanners
- Network switches, cabling, and wireless adapters
- Biometric devices

Table 1.1	Essentials (Exam 220-701) Objectives and Percentages	
Domain		**Percentage**
1.0 Hardware		27%
2.0 Troubleshooting, Repair, and Maintenance		20%
3.0 Operating Systems and Software		20%
4.0 Networking		15%
5.0 Security		8%
6.0 Operational Procedure		10%

The Essentials exam tests your ability to install, configure, and maintain all the standard technology involved in a personal computer. You need to be able to install and set up a hard drive, for example, and configure devices in Windows 2000, Windows XP, and Windows Vista. You have to understand drivers. You have to know your way around Windows and understand the tasks involved in updating, upgrading, and installing the operating systems. You need to know the standard diagnostic tools available in Windows—not only so you can fix problems, but also so you can work with higher-level techs to fix things.

You're tested on your knowledge of computer security, including identifying, installing, and configuring security hardware and software. You need to know security tools and diagnostic techniques for troubleshooting. You're not expected to know everything, just enough to be competent.

Finally, the Essentials exam puts a lot of emphasis on operational procedures, such as safety and environmental issues and also communication and professionalism. You need to know how to recycle and dispose of computer gear properly. You have to understand and avoid hazardous situations. The exam tests your ability to communicate effectively with customers and coworkers. You need to understand professional behavior and demonstrate that you have tact, discretion, and respect for others and their property.

Practical Application (Exam 220-702)

The CompTIA A+ 220-702 exam covers four objectives. Table 1.2 lists the objectives and percentages.

The Practical Application exam covers the same hardware and software as Essentials, but with a much more hands-on approach to determining the appropriate technology for a situation—running diagnostics and troubleshooting—rather than identification of hardware or operating system utilities. The exam tests your knowledge of computer components and programs so you can make informed recommendations to customers. You need to understand how all the technology should work, know the proper steps to figure out why something doesn't work, and then fix it.

The first domain, Hardware, provides a stark example of the difference in focus between the exams. Essentials talks about identifying names, purposes, and characteristics of various devices. The Practical Application exam, in contrast, goes into more depth, placing you in real-world scenarios where you must decide what to do. Every sub-objective in the Hardware objective starts with "Given a scenario" and then asks you to do something. Objective 1.1 says, for example, "Given a scenario, install, configure and maintain personal computer components." Objective 1.2 says, "Given a

Table 1.2	Practical Application (Exam 220-702) Objectives and Percentages	
Domain	**Percentage**
1.0 Hardware	38%
2.0 Operating Systems	34%
3.0 Networking	15%
4.0 Security	13%

scenario, detect problems, troubleshoot and repair/replace personal computer components." The other objectives follow suit.

Another big difference between the two exams is the treatment of the Operating Systems and Software objective in the Essentials exam versus Operating Systems in the Practical Application exam. Essentials tests you on how to use Windows and how to recognize the components, features, and basic utilities of the operating systems. The Practical Application exam goes much deeper. You need to understand intimately how to use the command line to manage the operating systems. You're expected to know all sorts of disk structures and run all the major disk management tools. Finally, the Practical Application exam grills you on operating system recovery tools and techniques so you can help customers get back up and running quickly.

> Even though the Practical Application exam does not specifically cover operational procedures, expect some questions about ethics, proper behavior in the workplace, ways to communicate with customers to get the most information in troubleshooting situations, and more.

How Do I Take the Exams?

Two companies, **Prometric** and **Pearson VUE**, administer the CompTIA A+ testing. There are thousands of Prometric and Pearson VUE testing centers across the United States and Canada, and the rest of the world. You may take the exams at any testing center. Both Prometric and Pearson VUE offer complete listings online of all available testing centers. You can select the closest training center and schedule your exams right from the comfort of your favorite Web browser:

> www.prometric.com
> www.vue.com

Alternatively, in the United States and Canada, call Prometric at 800-776-4276 or Pearson VUE at 877-551-PLUS (7587) to schedule the exams and to locate the nearest testing center. International customers can find a list of Prometric and Pearson VUE international contact numbers for various regions of the world on CompTIA's Web site at www.comptia.org.

You must pay for the exam when you call to schedule. Be prepared to sit on hold for a while. Have your Social Security number (or international equivalent) and a credit card ready when you call. Both Prometric and Pearson VUE will be glad to invoice you, but you won't be able to take the exam until they receive full payment.

If you have special needs, both Prometric and Pearson VUE will accommodate you, although this may limit your selection of testing locations.

How Much Does the Exam Cost?

The cost of the exam depends on whether you work for a CompTIA member or not. At this writing, the cost for non-CompTIA members is $168 (U.S.) for each exam. International prices vary, but you can check the CompTIA Web site for international pricing. Of course, the prices are subject to change without notice, so always check the CompTIA Web site for current pricing.

Very few people pay full price for the exam. Virtually every organization that provides CompTIA A+ training and testing also offers discount **vouchers**. You buy a discount voucher and then use the voucher number instead of a credit card when you schedule the exam. Vouchers are sold per exam, so you'll need two vouchers to take the two CompTIA A+ exams.

Total Seminars is one place to get discount vouchers. You can call Total Seminars at 800-446-6004 or 281-922-4166, or get vouchers via the Web site: www.totalsem.com. No one should ever pay full price for CompTIA A+ exams.

How to Pass the CompTIA A+ Exams

The single most important thing to remember about the CompTIA A+ certification exams is that CompTIA designed the Essentials exam to test the knowledge of a technician with only 500 hours experience (about three months) and the Practical Application exam to test the knowledge of a technician with only 1000 hours experience (about six months)—so keep it simple! The exams aren't interested in your ability to overclock DDR3 CAS timings in CMOS or whether you can explain the exact difference between the Intel ICH10 and the AMD 790 southbridges. Don't bother with a lot of theory—think in terms of practical knowledge and standards. Read the book, do whatever works for you to memorize the key concepts and procedures, take the practice exams on the CD in the back of the book, review any topics you miss, and you should pass with no problem.

 Those of you who just want more knowledge in managing and troubleshooting PCs can follow the same strategy as certification-seekers. Think in practical terms and work with the PC as you go through each chapter.

Some of you may be in or just out of school, so studying for exams is nothing novel. But if you haven't had to study for and take an exam in a while, or if you think maybe you could use some tips, you may find the next section valuable. It lays out a proven strategy for preparing to take and pass the CompTIA A+ exams. Try it. It works.

Obligate Yourself

The very first step you should take is to schedule yourself for the exams. Have you ever heard the old adage, "Heat and pressure make diamonds"? Well, if you don't give yourself a little "heat," you'll end up procrastinating and delay taking the exams, possibly forever. Do yourself a favor. Using the following information, determine how much time you'll need to study for the exams, and then call Prometric or Pearson VUE and schedule them accordingly. Knowing the exams are coming up makes it much easier to turn off the television and crack open the book. You can schedule an exam as little as a few weeks in advance, but if you schedule an exam and can't take it at the scheduled time, you must reschedule at least a day in advance or you'll lose your money.

Set Aside the Right Amount of Study Time

After helping thousands of techs get their CompTIA A+ certification, we at Total Seminars have developed a pretty good feel for the amount of study time needed to pass the CompTIA A+ certification exams. The following table provides an estimate to help you plan how much study time you must commit to the CompTIA A+ certification exams. Keep in mind that these are averages. If you're not a great student or if you're a little on the nervous side, add 10 percent; if you're a fast learner or have a good bit of computer experience, you may want to reduce the figures.

To use Table 1.3, just circle the values that are most accurate for you and add them up to get your estimated total hours of study time.

Table 1.3	Analyzing Skill Levels			
		Amount of Experience		
Tech Task	**None**	**Once or Twice**	**Every Now and Then**	**Quite a Bit**
Installing an adapter card	12	10	8	4
Installing and configuring hard drives	12	10	8	2
Installing modems and NICs	8	6	6	3
Connecting a computer to the Internet	8	6	4	2
Installing printers and scanners	4	3	2	1
Installing RAM	8	6	4	2
Installing CPUs	8	7	5	3
Fixing printers	6	5	4	3
Fixing boot problems	8	7	7	5
Fixing portable computers	8	6	4	2
Building complete systems	12	10	8	6
Using the command line	8	8	6	4
Installing/optimizing Windows	10	8	6	4
Using Windows 2000/XP	6	6	4	2
Using Windows Vista	10	8	4	2
Configuring NTFS permissions	6	4	3	2
Configuring a wireless network	6	5	3	2
Configuring a software firewall	6	4	2	1
Installing a sound card	2	2	1	0
Removing malware	4	3	2	0
Using OS diagnostic tools	8	8	6	4
Using a volt-ohm meter	4	3	2	1

To that value, add hours based on the number of months of direct, professional experience you have had supporting PCs, as shown in Table 1.4.

A total neophyte usually needs a little over 200 hours of study time. An experienced tech shouldn't need more than 60 hours.

Total hours for you to study: _____.

Table 1.4	Adding Up Your Study Time
Months of Direct, Professional Experience...	**To Your Study Time...**
0	Add 50
Up to 6	Add 30
6 to 12	Add 10
Over 12	Add 0

A Strategy for Study

Now that you have a feel for how long it's going to take, you're ready to develop a study strategy. I'd like to suggest a strategy that has worked for others who've come before you, whether they were experienced techs or total newbies. This book is designed to accommodate the different study agendas of these two groups of students. The first group is experienced techs who already have strong PC experience but need to be sure they're ready to be tested on the specific subjects covered by the CompTIA A+ exams. The second group is those with little or no background in the computer field. These techs can benefit from a more detailed understanding of the history and concepts that underlie modern PC technology, to help them remember the specific subject matter information they must know for the exams. I'll use the shorthand terms Old Techs and New Techs for these two groups. If you're not sure which group you fall into, pick a few chapters and go through some end-of-chapter questions. If you score less than 70%, go the New Tech route.

I have broken most of the chapters into four distinct parts:

- **Historical/Conceptual**   Topics that are not on the CompTIA A+ exams but will help you understand more clearly what is on the CompTIA A+ exams.

- **Essentials**   Topics that clearly fit under the CompTIA A+ Essentials exam domains.

- **Practical Application**   Topics that clearly fit under the CompTIA A+ Practical Application exam domains.

- **Beyond A+**   More advanced issues that probably will not be on the CompTIA A+ exams—yet.

 Not all chapters will have all four sections.

The beginning of each of these areas is clearly marked with a large banner that looks like this:

Historical/Conceptual

Those of you who fall into the Old Tech group may want to skip everything except the Essentials and Practical Application areas in each chapter. After reading those sections, jump immediately to the questions at the end of the chapter. The end-of-chapter questions concentrate on information in the Essentials and Practical Application sections. If you run into problems, review the Historical/Conceptual sections in that chapter. Note that you may need to skip back to previous chapters to get the Historical/Conceptual information you need for later chapters.

After going through every chapter as described, Old Techs can move directly to testing their knowledge by using the free practice exams on the CD-ROM that accompanies the book. Once you start scoring above 90%, you're ready to take the exams. If you're a New Tech—or if you're an Old Tech who wants the full learning experience this book can offer—start by reading the book, *the whole book,* as though you were reading a novel, from page one to the end without skipping around. Because so many computer terms and concepts build on each other, skipping around greatly increases the odds that you will become confused and end up closing the book and firing up

your favorite PC game. Not that I have anything against PC games, but unfortunately that skill is *not* useful for the CompTIA A+ exams!

Your goal on this first read is to understand concepts, the *whys* behind the *hows*. Having a PC nearby as you read is helpful so you can stop and inspect the PC to see a piece of hardware or how a particular concept manifests in the real world. As you read about floppy drives, for example, inspect the cables. Do they look like the ones in the book? Is there a variation? Why? It is imperative that you understand why you are doing something, not just how to do it on one particular system under one specific set of conditions. Neither the exams nor real life as a PC tech works that way.

If you're reading this book as part of a managing and troubleshooting PCs class rather than a certification-prep course, I highly recommend going the New Tech route, even if you have a decent amount of experience. The book contains a lot of details that can trip you up if you focus only on the test-specific sections of the chapters. Plus, your program might stress historical and conceptual knowledge as well as practical, hands-on skills.

The CompTIA A+ certification exams assume that you have basic user skills. The exams really try to trick you with questions on processes that you may do every day and not think much about. Here's a classic: "To move a file from the C:\DATA folder to the D:\ drive using Windows Explorer, what key must you hold down while dragging the file?" If you can answer that without going to your keyboard and trying a few likely keys, you're better than most techs! In the real world, you can try a few wrong answers before you hit on the right one, but for the exams, you have to *know* it. Whether Old Tech or New Tech, make sure you are proficient at user-level Windows skills, including the following:

- Recognizing all the components of the standard Windows desktop (Start menu, notification area, etc.)

- Manipulating windows—resizing, moving, and so on

- Creating, deleting, renaming, moving, and copying files and folders within Windows

- Understanding file extensions and their relationship with program associations

- Using common keyboard shortcuts/hotkeys

- Installing, running, and closing a Windows application

Any PC technician who has been around a while will tell you that one of the great secrets in the computer business is that there's almost never anything completely new in the world of computer technology. Faster, cleverer, smaller, wider—absolutely—but the underlying technology, the core of what makes your PC and its various peripheral devices operate, has changed remarkably little since PCs came into widespread use a few decades ago. When you do your initial read-through, you may be tempted to skip the Historical/Conceptual sections—don't! Understanding the history and technological developments behind today's PCs helps you understand why they work—or don't work—the way they do. Basically, I'm passing on to you the kind of knowledge you might get by apprenticing yourself to an older, experienced PC tech.

After you've completed the first read-through, go through the book again, this time in textbook mode. If you're an Old Tech, start your studying here. Try to cover one chapter at a sitting. Concentrate on the Essentials and Practical Application sections. Get a highlighter and mark the phrases and sentences that bring out major points. Be sure you understand how the pictures and illustrations relate to the concepts being discussed.

Once you feel you have a good grasp of the material in the book, you can check your knowledge by using the practice exams included on the CD-ROM in the back of the book. You can take these in Practice mode or Final mode. In Practice mode, you can use the Assistance window to get a helpful hint for the current questions, use the Reference feature to find the chapter that covers the question, check your answer for the question, and see an explanation of the correct answer. In Final mode, you answer all the questions and receive an exam score at the end, just like the real thing.

Both modes show you an overall grade, expressed as a percentage, as well as a breakdown of how well you did on each exam domain. The Review Questions feature lets you see what questions you missed and what the correct answers are. Use these results to guide further studying. Continue reviewing the topics you miss and taking additional exams until you are consistently scoring in the 90% range. When you get there, you are ready to pass the CompTIA A+ certification exams.

Study Tactics

Perhaps it's been a while since you had to study for a test. Or perhaps it hasn't, but you've done your best since then to block the whole experience from your mind. Either way, savvy test-takers know that certain techniques make studying for tests more efficient and effective.

Here's a trick used by students in law and medical schools who have to memorize reams of information: write it down. The act of writing something down (not typing, *writing*) in and of itself helps you to remember it, even if you never look at what you wrote again. Try taking separate notes on the material and re-creating diagrams by hand to help solidify the information in your mind.

Another oldie but goodie: Make yourself flash cards with questions and answers on topics you find difficult. A third trick: Take your notes to bed and read them just before you go to sleep. Many people find they really do learn while they sleep!

Contact

If you have any problems, any questions, or if you just want to argue about something, feel free to send an e-mail to the author—michaelm@totalsem.com—or to the editor—scottj@totalsem.com.

For any other information you might need, contact CompTIA directly at their Web site: www.comptia.org.

Chapter 1 Review

■ Chapter Summary

After reading this chapter and completing the exercises, you should understand the following about the path of the PC tech.

Explain the importance of gaining skill in managing and troubleshooting PCs

■ The IT workforce designs, builds, and maintains computers, computer programs, and networks. PC techs take care of personal computers, thus representing an essential component in that workforce. As PCs become more complex, the IT workforce needs specialized PC techs.

■ Certifications prove to employers that you have the necessary skills. If you want a job fixing automobiles, for example, you get the *Automotive Service Excellence* (*ASE*) certification. To be certified, you take and successfully pass exams. Then the organization that administers those exams grants you certification. This is particularly important for IT workers.

Explain the importance of CompTIA A+ certification

■ In the early days of the personal computer, you could get vendor-specific certifications, such as IBM Technician, but nothing general for PC techs. Worse, you often had to have a job at that company to get the vendor-specific certification. The software and networking side of IT doesn't have that issue. To prove skill in working with Windows, for example, you could become a Microsoft Certified Technology Specialist (MCTS).

■ CompTIA A+ certification is an industry-wide, vendor-neutral certification program that shows that you have a basic competence in supporting microcomputers. You achieve this certification by taking two computer-based, multiple-choice examinations. The tests cover what technicians should know after nine months of full-time PC support experience. CompTIA A+ certification enjoys wide recognition throughout the computer industry.

■ CompTIA is a nonprofit, industry trade association based in Oakbrook Terrace, Illinois. It consists of over 20,000 members in 102 countries. CompTIA provides a forum for people in these industries to network, represents the interests of its members to the government, and provides certifications for many aspects of the computer industry. CompTIA sponsors A+, Network+, Security+, and other certifications.

■ The CompTIA A+ certification is the de facto entry point to IT. From CompTIA A+, you have a number of certification options, depending on whether you want to focus more on hardware and operating systems or move into network administration. You can get CompTIA Network+ certification, for example, or go on to get Microsoft or Cisco certified. CompTIA Network+ certification is the most obvious certification to get after becoming CompTIA A+ certified.

Describe how to become a CompTIA A+ Certified Technician

■ You become CompTIA A+ certified, in the simplest sense, by taking and passing two computer-based, multiple-choice exams. No prerequisites are required for taking the CompTIA A+ certification exams. There is no required training course and no training materials to buy. You *do* have to pay a testing fee for each of the two exams.

■ The CompTIA exams introduced in 2009 are *220-701* (*Essentials*) and *220-702* (*Practical Application*). It's common to refer to these two exams as the 2009 exams to differentiate them from older CompTIA exams. Although you may take either of the two exams first, I recommend taking the Essentials, followed by the Practical Application.

■ Both of the exams are extremely practical, with little or no interest in theory. All questions are multiple choice or "click on the right part of the picture" questions. CompTIA may add new questions to the exams at any time to keep the content fresh, although the subject matter covered by the exams won't change.

■ Two companies, Prometric and Pearson VUE, administer the actual CompTIA A+ testing. You can schedule exam time and location via the Web site for either company, www.prometric.com or www.vue.com. Check CompTIA's Web site for international links.

- To achieve success with the CompTIA A+ certification exams, think in terms of practical knowledge. Read the book. Work through the problems. Work with computers. Take the practice exams. You should obligate yourself by scheduling your exams. This keeps you focused on study.

- Read the book all the way through once. Experienced techs should then concentrate on the test-specific sections to prepare for the exams. Less experienced techs should read the book all the way through again until everything makes sense.

- If you're reading this book as part of a managing and troubleshooting PCs class rather than a certification-prep course, I highly recommend going the New Tech route, even if you have a decent amount of experience. The book contains a lot of details that can trip you up if you focus only on the test-specific sections of the chapters.

■ Key Terms

certification *(1)*

Certified Cisco Network Associate (CCNA) *(4)*

CompTIA A+ 220-701 (Essentials) *(4)*

CompTIA A+ 220-702 (Practical Application) *(4)*

CompTIA A+ certification *(2)*

CompTIA Network+ certification *(3)*

Computing Technology Industry Association (CompTIA) *(2)*

Information Technology (IT) *(1)*

Microsoft Certified Professional (MCP) *(3)*

network *(1)*

PC tech *(1)*

Pearson VUE *(8)*

Prometric *(8)*

voucher *(8)*

www.comptia.org *(2)*

■ Key Term Quiz

Use the Key Terms list to complete the sentences that follow. Not all terms will be used.

1. You can lump together all the folks who design, build, program, and fix computers into the _____ workforce.

2. You can become CompTIA A+ certified by passing the _____ and CompTIA A+ 220-702 (Practical Application) exams.

3. A _____ gives clients and employers a level of confidence that you can do what you say you can do.

4. A casual term for a person who builds and maintains computers is _____.

5. Prometric and _____ administer the CompTIA A+ certification exams.

6. You can use a _____ when you schedule your exam to save some money.

7. Persons desiring to work in Windows-based networking should pursue _____ certification after completing their CompTIA certifications.

8. You can find the latest information about the CompTIA A+ certification exams here: _____.

9. Typically, techs who attain CompTIA A+ certification then pursue _____ to add to their computer credentials.

10. A grouping of computers that enables people to share resources is called a _____.

1. Which of the following is a vendor-specific certification? (Select all that apply.)

   A. Certified Cisco Network Associate

   B. CompTIA A+

   C. CompTIA Network+

   D. Microsoft Certified Systems Engineer

2. Which of the following certifications is the de facto requirement for entrance into the PC industry?

   A. Certified Cisco Network Associate

   B. CompTIA A+

   C. CompTIA Network+

   D. Microsoft Certified Systems Engineer

3. John loves the Internet and wants a career working on the machines that make the Internet work. He has completed both CompTIA A+ and Network+ certifications. Which of the following certifications would make a good next step?

   A. Certified Cisco Network Associate

   B. Certified Cisco Network Professional

   C. CompTIA Security+

   D. Microsoft Certified Systems Engineer

4. Which of the following exams focuses on installing, configuring, and maintaining all the standard technology involved in a personal computer?

   A. Certified Cisco Network Associate

   B. CompTIA A+ 220-701 (Essentials)

   C. CompTIA A+ 220-702 (Practical Application)

   D. Microsoft Certified Systems Engineer

5. At which of the following Web sites can you register to take the CompTIA A+ certification exams?

   A. www.comptia.org

   B. www.microsoft.com

   C. www.totalsem.com

   D. www.vue.com

6. How many exams must you pass to become CompTIA A+ certified?

   A. One

   B. Two

   C. Three

   D. Four

7. How much practical IT experience do you need to become CompTIA A+ certified?

   A. Six months

   B. One year

   C. Two years

   D. None

8. How many questions should you expect on the 220-702 Practical Application exam?

   A. 25

   B. 50

   C. 100

   D. The number of questions varies because the exams are adaptive.

9. The CompTIA A+ certification covers which of the following operating systems? (Select two.)

   A. Linux

   B. OS X

   C. Windows XP Media Center

   D. Windows Vista

10. What percentage of questions should you expect on operating systems in the 220-701 Essentials exam?

    A. 10%

    B. 15%

    C. 20%

    D. 25%

11. What percentage of questions should you expect on operating systems in the 220-702 Practical Application exam?

    A. 10%

    B. 13%

    C. 20%

    D. 34%

12. How much does it cost to take each exam (at the time of this book's publication)?

    A. $100 each

    B. $138 each

    C. $168 each

    D. $150 each

13. What percentage of questions should you expect on Windows 7 in the 220-702 Practical Application exam?

    A. 10%

    B. 13%

    C. 20%

    D. None

14. The 220-701 Essentials exam will *not* test you on which of the following computer components?

    A. Biometric devices

    B. Keyboards

    C. Printers

    D. Zip drives

15. What is CompTIA?

    A. A vendor-specific certification association

    B. A testing administration company

    C. A for-profit, industry trade corporation

    D. A nonprofit, industry trade association

■ Essay Quiz

1. Write a short essay on the benefits of certification in the field of computers. Include discussion on how the CompTIA certifications function within the broader category of computer certification. Why do you suppose people get certifications rather than (or in addition to) two- and four-year college degrees in IT?

Lab Project

• Lab Project 1.1

1 If you have access to the Internet, do some searching on computer certifications. Make a personal certification tree or pathway that maps out a series of certifications to pursue that might interest you. What certifications would be useful if you want to be a graphics designer, for example? What if you want to create computer games?

Operational Procedures

In this chapter, you will learn how to

■ **Present yourself with a proper appearance and professional manner**

■ **Talk to customers in a professional, productive manner**

■ **Work with PCs safely using the proper tools**

One of the interesting parts of teaching new techs is keeping up with the skills that get a tech a job and the issues that cause them to lose the jobs they get. To me, the number one reason techs fail to get or hold onto a job isn't lack of technical skill; it's lack of what CompTIA calls "operational procedures." Personally, I think a better name might be "life skills and basic safety," but it boils down to the same thing: nontechnical skills that technicians are famous for lacking.

I like to describe myself as a "nerd" and I consider it a compliment if you call me one. Nerds are smart and like to work with technology—these are the good aspects of nerd-dom. On the other hand, most people would think of the term nerd as an insult. Nerds are rarely portrayed in a positive manner in the media, and I think I know why. Nerds generally suffer from some pretty serious social weaknesses. These weaknesses are classics: bad clothing, shyness, and poor communication skills. This chapter covers some basic life skills to enable you to enjoy your nerdiness and yet function out in the real world. You'll learn how to dress, how to act, and how to communicate. After you're well on your way to the beginnings of social graces, we'll discuss some of the hazards (such as static electricity) you may run into in your job and the tools you can use to prevent problems. After all, nerds who cannot stay organized—or who break equipment or themselves—need to learn some tricks to keep everything organized and safe.

(left column — partially cut off)

to access a mi…
or with data…
learning pass…
for you. If y…
usual situatio…

It's funny…
John in accou…
The phone or…
Regardless of…
tech needs to…

Ethic of Recip…

would have t…
people's thin;…
touch anythir…
paper, or cub…
times, even v…

Dependabili…

Dependabilit…
don't mean t…
swerable for…
perform thos…
dependability…

The singl…
for job appoi…
a society whe…
call it the "A…
counted on s…
periences wh…
pointment is…
of money in l…

If you or…
there. Don't…
showing up…
Figure out if…
traffic. There…
early is on tir…
vent you fror…
as you know…
simple apolo;…

Responsil…
sponsible for…
pensive equi;…
there are bac…
even if this i…
make a backu…
to the data or…

Adaptability…

Adaptability…
within the sc…

The Professional Tech

A professional tech displays professionalism, which might seem a little trite if it weren't absolutely true. The tech presents a professional appearance and follows a proper ethical code. I call the latter the Traits of a Tech. Let's take a look at these two areas in more detail.

Appearance

Americans live in a casual society, and I think that's great, because I prefer dressing casually. The problem with casual is that perhaps our society is becoming *too* casual. New techs sometimes fail to appreciate that customers equate casual clothing with a casual attitude. You might think you're just fixing somebody's computer, but you're doing much more than that. You are saving precious family photos. You are keeping a small business in operation. This is serious stuff, and nobody wants an unclean, slovenly person doing these important jobs. Take a look at Figure 2.1. This is our resident illustrator (among other job descriptions), Ford Pierson, casually dressed to hang with his buddies.

I have a question for you. If you ran a small business and your primary file server died, leaving 15 employees with nothing to do, how would you feel about Ford as a tech coming into your office looking like this? I hope your answer would be "not too confident." Every company has some form of dress code for techs. Figure 2.2 shows Ford dressed in a fairly typical example, with a company polo shirt, khaki pants, and dark shoes (trust me on that score). Please also note that both his shirt and his pants are wrinkle free. All techs either know how to iron or know the location of the nearest cleaners.

While we are looking at this model of a man, do you appreciate that his hair is combed and his face is cleanly shaven? It's too bad I can't use scratch-and-sniffs, but if I did, you'd also notice that Professional Ford took a shower, used some deodorant, and brushed his teeth.

I hope that most of the people who read this smile quietly to themselves and say, "Well, of course." The sad truth tells me otherwise. Next time you look at a tech, ask yourself how many of these simple appearance and hygiene issues were missed. Then make a point not to be one of the unkempt techs.

The Traits of a Tech

When I was a Boy Scout in the United States, we learned something called The Boy Scout Creed, a list of traits that define the ethics of a Boy Scout. Even thought I haven't been a Boy Scout for a long time, I still have them memorized. "A Scout is trustworthy, loyal, helpful, friendly, courteous, kind, obedient, cheerful, thrifty, brave, clean, and reverent."

My goal here isn't a sales pitch for scouting in any form, but rather to give you an idea of what we are trying to achieve: a list of ethics that will help you be a better technician. The list you are about to see is my own creation, but it does a great job of covering the CompTIA A+ objectives. Let's

● **Figure 2.1**   Casual Ford

● **Figure 2.2**   Professional Ford

repair process. Every PC repair is to some degree a guessing game. No one knows all the possible problems that can go wrong with a computer. There is no universal PC repair manual to which you can refer to tell you how to fix computers. Good techs must be able to adapt to any situation, both technically and in the environment. For example, good techs should be able to fix most peripherals, even if they are not experts on that particular device. As you progress through the book, you'll discover that most devices fit into one family or another and that there are certain diagnostic/repair steps that you can at least try to enact a repair.

Adaptability isn't just for technical issues. PCs find themselves broken in the strangest places and ways. An adaptable tech doesn't have a problem if a computer sits at the top of a suspension bridge or behind a desk. An adaptable tech can work around mean dogs, broken water lines, and noisy little kids. (But there are some very important rules to dealing with kids. See later in this chapter.)

A technician has to be versatile. The best example of this is what I call the User Advocate. User Advocates are technicians who take the time to learn the processes of whatever organization they work for and look to create technology solutions for problems and inefficiencies. This also means a tech should be at least competent if not expert at all the computer applications used by the organization. When you combine your IT skills with an understanding of how the business works, you become amazingly versatile, quickly finding yourself with more responsibility and (hopefully) more money.

A big part of versatility is offering different repair options in certain situations. When there is more than one way to fix things, make sure the customer knows all the options, but also give them your recommendation. Tell them why you feel your recommendation is the best course of action, but give them knowledge necessary to make their own decision.

A tech's versatility isn't limited to IT skills. Woe to the tech who doesn't understand basic electrical wiring and building codes. I've had hundreds of repair scenarios where the fix was as simple as knowing how to turn on an electrical breaker or moving a PC away from an electrical motor. No, these aren't IT skills, but a versatile tech knows these problems exist.

Sensitivity

Sensitivity is the ability to appreciate another's feeling and emotions. Sensitivity requires observing others closely, taking time to appreciate their feelings, and acting in such a way that makes them feel comfortable. I've rarely felt that technicians I've met were good at sensitivity. The vast majority of nerds I know, including myself, tend to be self-centered and unaware of what's going on around them. Let me give you a few tips I've learned along the way.

Understand that the customer is paying for your time and skills. Also understand that your presence invariably means something is wrong or broken, and few things make users more upset than broken computers. When you are "on the clock," you need to show possibly very upset customers that you are giving their problem your full attention. To do this, you need to avoid distractions. If you get a personal call, let it roll over to voicemail. If you get a work-related call, politely excuse yourself, walk away for privacy, and keep the call brief. Never talk to coworkers in a place where

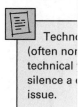

Techn
(often nor
technical
silence a
issue.

• **Figure 2.3**

your customer can hear. Never speak badly of a customer; you never know where you'll run into them next.

Last, be culturally sensitive. We live in a diverse world of races, religions, etiquettes, and traditions. If a customer's religious holiday conflicts with your work schedule, the customer wins. If the customer wants you to take off your shoes, take them off. If the customer wants you to wear a hat, wear one. When in doubt, always ask the customer for guidance.

■ Communication

When you deal with users, managers, and owners who are frustrated and upset because a computer or network is down and they can't work, your job requires you to take on the roles of detective and psychologist. Talking with frazzled and confused people and getting answers to questions about how the PC got into the state it's in takes skill. Communicating clearly and effectively is important. Plus, you need to follow the rules of tech-person decorum, acting with personal integrity and respect for the customer. Finally, use assertive communication to empathize with and educate the user. Great techs spend the time needed to develop these essential skills.

Assertive Communication

In many cases, a PC problem results from user error or neglect. As a technician, you must show users the error of their ways without creating anger or conflict. You do this by using assertive communication. **Assertive communication** isn't pushy or bossy, but it's also not the language of a pushover. Assertive communication first requires you to show the other person that you understand and appreciate the importance of his feelings. Use statements such as "I know how frustrating it feels to lose data" or "I understand how infuriating it is when the network goes out and you can't get your job done." Statements like these cool off the situation and let customers know you are on their side. Avoid using the word "you," as it can sound accusatory.

The second part of assertive communication is making sure you state the problem clearly without accusing the user directly: "Not keeping up with defragmenting your hard drive slows it down," or "Help me understand how the network cable keeps getting unplugged during your lunch hour." Last, tell the user what you need to prevent this error in the future. "Please call me whenever you hear that buzzing sound," or "Please check the company's approved software list before installing anything." Always use "I" and "me," and never make judgments. "I can't promise the keyboard will work well if it's always getting dirty" is much better than "Stop eating cookies over the keyboard, you slob!"

Respectful Communication

The final key in communicating with users revolves around **respect**. You don't do the user's job, but you should respect that job and person as an essential cog in the organization. Communicate with users the way you would

like them to communicate with you, were the roles reversed. Again, this follows the Ethic of Reciprocity.

Generally, IT folks are there to support the people doing a company's main business. You are there to serve their needs and, all things being equal, to do so at their convenience, not yours.

Don't assume the world stops the moment you walk in the door and that you may immediately interrupt their work to do yours. Although most customers are thrilled and motivated to help you the moment you arrive, this may not always be the case. Ask the magic question, "May I start working on the problem now?" Give customers a chance to wrap up, shut down, or do anything else necessary to finish their business and make it safe for you to do yours.

Engage the user with the standard rules of civil conversation. Take the time to listen. Don't interrupt customers as they describe a problem; just listen and take notes. You might hear something that leads to resolving the problem. Rephrase and repeat the problems back to the customer to verify you understand the issue ("So the computer is locking up three times a day?"). Use an even, nonaccusatory tone, and although it's okay to try to explain a problem if the user asks, never condescend and never argue.

Remain positive in the face of adversity. Don't get defensive if you can't figure something out quickly and the user starts hassling you. Remember that an angry customer isn't really angry with you—he's just frustrated—so don't take his anger personally. Take it in stride; smile, and assure him that computer troubleshooting sometimes takes a while.

Avoid letting outside interruptions take your focus away from the user and her computer problem. Things that break your concentration slow down the troubleshooting process immensely. Plus, customers will feel insulted if you start chatting on your cell phone with your significant other about a movie date later that night when you're supposed to be fixing their computers! You're not being paid to socialize, so turn those cell phones and pagers to vibrate. That's why the technogods created voicemail. Never take any call except one that is potentially urgent. If a call is potentially urgent, explain the urgency to the customer, step away, and deal with the call as quickly as possible.

If you discover that the user caused the problem, either through ignorance or by accident, don't minimize the importance of the problem, but don't be judgmental or insulting about the cause. We all screw up sometimes, and these kinds of mistakes are your job security. *You get paid because people make mistakes and machines break.* Chances are you'll be back at that workstation six months or a year later, fixing something else. By becoming the user's advocate and go-to person, you create a better work environment. If a mistaken action caused the problem, explain in a positive and supportive way how to do the task correctly and then have the user go through the process while you are there to reinforce what you said.

Eliciting Answers

Your job as a tech is to get the computer fixed, and the best way to start that process is to determine what the computer is doing or not doing. You must start by talking to the customer. Allow the customer to explain the problem fully while you record the information. Once the person has described the

situation, you must then ask questions. This process is called **eliciting answers**.

Although each person is different, most users with a malfunctioning computer or peripheral will be afraid and often defensive about the problem. To overcome this initial attitude, you need to ask the right questions *and* listen to the customer's answers. Then ask the proper follow-up questions.

Always avoid accusatory questions, because they won't help you in the least (Figure 2.4). "What did you do?" generally gets a confused or defensive "Nothing" in reply, which doesn't get you closer to solving the problem. First, ask questions that help clarify the situation. Repeat what you think is the problem after you've listened all the way through the user's story.

● **Figure 2.4**   Never accuse!

Follow up with fact-seeking questions. "When did it last work?" "Has it ever worked in this way?" "Has any software changed recently?" "Any new hardware?" Ask open-ended questions to narrow the scope ("What applications are running when the computer locks up?").

By keeping your questions friendly and factual, you show users that you won't accuse them or judge their actions (Figure 2.5). You also show them that you're there to help them. After the initial tension drops away, you'll often get more information: for instance, a recitation of something the user might have tried or changed. These clues can help lead to a quick resolution of the problem.

Remember that you may know all about computer technology, but the user probably does not. This means a user will often use vague and/or incorrect terms to describe a particular computer component or function. That's just the way it works, so don't bother to correct them. Wherever possible, avoid using jargon, acronyms, or abbreviations specific to computers. They simply confuse the already upset user and can make you sound like you're talking down to them. Just ask direct, factual questions in a friendly tone, using simple, non-jargon language to zero in on what the user was trying to accomplish and what happened when things went wrong. Use visual aids when possible. Point at the machine or go to a working PC to have the user show what went wrong or what she did or tried to do.

● **Figure 2.5**   Keeping it friendly

People do usually want to get a handle on what you are doing—in a simplified way. You don't want to overwhelm them, but don't be afraid to use simple analogies or concepts to give them an idea of what is happening. If you have the time (and the skills), use drawings, equipment, and other visual aids to make technical concepts more clear. If a customer is a closet tech and is really digging for answers—to the point that it's affecting your ability to do your job—compliment her initiative and then direct her to outside training opportunities. Better yet, tell her where she can get a copy of this book!

Docu

At the
day y
work
tomer
you r
clude

Follo

I call
confir
a chai
that f

■ S

Effec
blesh
thing
thoug
know
tools
lems

Ele

If you
do, y
static
charg
your
elect
happ
touch
hum
but I
tive p
work

An

ESD
elect
cret
same
the I
devi
the c

Chap

■ Key Term Quiz

Use the Key Terms list to complete the sentences that follow. Not all terms will be used.

1. Always place an expansion card or other computer part into a(n) _____ when it's not in use to protect against electrostatic discharge.

2. A few screwdrivers and an anti-static wrist strap should be in your _____.

3. An effective use of _____ means clearly stating a problem without accusing the user of creating that problem.

4. Accomplished computer techs should treat anything said to them as a personal confidence, not to be repeated to coworkers or bosses. A tech brings _____ to the job.

5. You should avoid learning _____ to other folks' computers so you don't get blamed if something happens to those computers.

6. Treating other people the way you want to be treated is an example of the _____.

7. A magnetic field interfering with electronics is _____.

8. A(n) _____ is a device that stops the flow of electricity.

9. To begin troubleshooting a computer problem, start by talking to the customer and allowing the customer to explain the problem fully, and then ask follow-up questions. This process is called _____.

10. A customer complains that he can hear music coming from his computer speakers, even though the computer's not playing any music. This is most likely caused by _____.

■ Multiple-Choice Quiz

1. While troubleshooting a fairly routine printing problem, the customer explains in great detail precisely what he was trying to do, what happened when he tried to print, and what he had attempted as a fix for the problem. At what point should you interrupt him?

   A. After he describes the first problem

   B. As soon as you understand the problem

   C. As soon as you have a solution

   D. Never

2. While manning the help desk, you get a call from a distraught user who says she has a blank screen. What would be a useful follow-up question? (Select two.)

   A. Is the computer turned on?

   B. Is the monitor turned on?

   C. Did you reboot?

   D. What did you do?

3. While manning the help desk, you get a call from Sharon in accounting. She's lost a file that she knows she saved to her hard drive. Which of the following statements would direct Sharon to open her My Documents folder in the most efficient and professional manner?

   A. Sharon, check My Documents.

   B. Sharon, a lot of programs save files to a default folder, often to a folder called My Documents. Let's look there first. Click on the Start button and move the mouse until the cursor hovers over My Documents. Then press the left mouse button and tell me what you see when My Documents opens.

   C. It probably just defaulted to My Docs. Why don't you open Excel or whatever program you used to make the file, and then open a document and point it to My Documents?

   D. Look, Sharon, I know you're a clueless noob when it comes to computers, but how could somebody lose a file? Just open up My Documents and look there for the file.

4. Al in marketing calls in for tech support, complaining that he has a dead PC. What is a good first question or questions to begin troubleshooting the problem?

   A. Did the computer ever work?

   B. When did the computer last work?

   C. When you say "dead," what do you mean? What happens when you press the power button?

   D. What did you do?

5. While manning the help desk, you get a call from Bryce in sales complaining that he can't print and every time he clicks on the network shared drive, his computer stops and freezes. He says he thinks it's his hard driver. What would be a good follow-up question or statement?

   A. Bryce, you're an idiot. Don't touch anything. I'll be there in five minutes.

   B. Okay, let's take this one step at a time. You seem to have two problems, one with printing and the second with the network shared drive, right?

   C. First, it's not a hard *driver*; it's a hard *drive*. It doesn't have anything to do with the network share or printing, so that's just not right.

   D. When could you last print?

6. When troubleshooting a software problem on Phoebe's computer and listening to her describe the problem, your beeper goes off. It's your boss. What would be an acceptable action for you to make?

   A. Excuse yourself, walk out of the cube, and use a cell phone to call your boss.

   B. Pick up Phoebe's phone and dial your boss's number.

   C. Wait until Phoebe finishes her description and then ask to use her phone to call your boss.

   D. Wait until Phoebe finishes her description, run through any simple fixes, and then explain that you need to call your boss on your cell phone.

7. While fixing a printing problem on Paul's computer, you check his e-mail out of curiosity to see if there are any interesting messages there. You notice several personal e-mails he has sent sitting in his Sent Items mail folder. Using the company computer for personal e-mail is against regulations, so what should you do?

   A. Leave the e-mail on the computer and notify your boss.

   B. Delete the e-mails from the computer and notify your boss.

   C. Delete the e-mails from the computer and remind Paul of the workplace regulations.

   D. You shouldn't be looking in his e-mail folders at all as it compromises your integrity.

8. Upon responding to a coworker's request for help, you find her away from her desk and Microsoft Excel on the screen with a spreadsheet open. How do you proceed?

   A. Go find the coworker and ask her to exit her applications before touching her computer.

   B. Exit Excel and save changes to the document and begin troubleshooting the computer.

   C. Exit Excel without saving changes to the document and begin troubleshooting the computer.

   D. Use the Save As command to save the file with a new name, exit Excel, and begin troubleshooting the computer.

9. You are solving a problem on Kate's computer that requires you to reboot several times. Upon each reboot, the logon screen appears and prompts you for a username and password before you can continue working. Kate has gone to another office to continue her work on another computer. How do you proceed?

   A. Call Kate, ask her for her password, type it in, and continue working on the problem.

   B. Insist that Kate stay with you and have her type the password each time it is needed.

   C. Call Kate and have her come in to type the password each time it is needed.

   D. Have Kate temporarily change her password for you to use as you work; then have her change it back when you are through.

10. You are working in a customer's home and his five-year-old child continues to scream and kick the back of your chair. What do you do?

   A. Ignore the child and finish your work as quickly as you can.

   B. Discipline the child as you see fit.

   C. Politely ask your client to remove the child from your work area.

   D. Tell your client you refuse to work under such conditions and leave the premises with the job half done.

11. After replacing a keyboard a user has spilled coffee on for the fifth time, what should you say to the user?

   A. I can't guarantee the new keyboard will work if it gets dirty.

   B. I can't guarantee the new keyboard will work if you continue to spill coffee on it.

   C. These keyboards are expensive. Next time we replace one because you spilled coffee, it's coming out of your paycheck.

   D. You need to be more careful with your coffee.

12. When is it appropriate to yell at a user?

   A. When he screws up the second time.

   B. When he interrupts your troubleshooting.

   C. When he screws up the fifth time.

   D. Never.

13. What's the best practice when working inside a system unit and installing and removing components?

   A. Wear an anti-static wrist strap.

   B. Touch a doorknob to ground yourself before going into the case.

   C. Place components on the motherboard to keep them grounded.

   D. Use plastic tools.

14. Which of the following tools would you find in a typical PC tech's toolkit? (Select two.)

   A. Phillips-head screwdriver

   B. Torx wrench

   C. Hammer

   D. File

15. What term describes the flow of a static electrical charge from a person to the inside of the PC?

   A. EMI

   B. ESD

   C. HDMI

   D. TTFN

■ Essay Quiz

1. Your worksite currently has no ESD protection. In fact, your supervisor doesn't feel that such protection is necessary. Write a proposal to purchase ESD protection equipment for the computer assembly/repair facility that will convince your supervisor that ESD protection is necessary and cost-effective in the long run. What kinds of protection will you recommend?

2. A friend is considering turning his computer hobby into a career and has asked your advice on outfitting himself as a freelance computer technician. What tools can you recommend to your friend?

3. A user phones you at your desk and reports that after pressing the power button on his computer and hearing the hard drive spin up, his screen remains blank. What questions can you ask to determine the problem?

Lab Projects

• Lab Project 2.1

Visit your local computer store or hardware store and purchase the items for a hardware tech toolkit.

You may want to include a variety of screwdrivers, anti-static wrist strap, tweezers, or other items.

• Lab Project 2.2

Visit your local computer store to observe how techs interact with people and how professionally they dress and appear. I suggest this not to judge the store's techs, but simply to watch and learn. How do the techs talk to customers? How do the customers react? How would you handle the same situation if you followed the guidelines in this chapter?

The Visible PC

chapter 3

"Gamepads do not good FPS controllers make."

—Will smith, *Maximum PC*

In this chapter, you will learn how to

■ **Describe how the PC works**

■ **Identify all the connectors and devices on a typical PC system unit**

■ **Discuss the major internal components of a PC**

Mastering the craft of a PC technician requires you to learn a lot of details about the many pieces of hardware in the typical PC. Even the most basic PC contains hundreds of discrete hardware components, each with its own set of characteristics, shapes, sizes, colors, connections, and so on. By the end of this book, you will be able to discuss all of these components in detail. This chapter takes you on a tour of a typical PC, starting with an overview of how computers work, and then examining both external connectors and internal components.

Remember the children's song that goes, "Oh, the leg bone connects to the thigh bone..."? Well, think of the rest of the chapter in that manner, showing you what the parts look like and giving you a rough idea about how they work and connect. In later chapters, you'll dissect all of these PC "leg bones" and "thigh bones" and get to the level of detail you need to install, configure, maintain, and fix computers. Even if you are an expert, do not skip this chapter! It introduces a large number of terms used throughout the rest of the book. Many of these terms you will know, but some you will not, so take some time and read it.

It is handy, although certainly not required, to have a PC that you can take the lid off of and inspect as you progress. Almost any old PC will help—it doesn't even need to work. So get thee a screwdriver, grab your PC, and see if you can recognize the various components as you read about them.

Historical/Conceptual

How the PC Works

You've undoubtedly seen a PC in action: a nice, glossy monitor displaying a picture that changes according to the actions of the person sitting in front of it, typing away on a keyboard and clicking on a mouse. Sound pours out of tiny speakers that flank the screen, and a box whirs happily beneath the table. The PC is a computer: a machine that enables you to do work, produce documents, play games, balance your checkbook, and look up the latest sports scores on the Internet.

Although the computer is certainly a machine, it's also **programming**: the commands that tell the computer what to do to get work done. These commands are just ones and zeros that the computer's hardware understands, enabling it to do amazing actions, such as perform powerful mathematic functions, move data (also ones and zeros), realize the mouse has moved, and put pretty icons on the screen. So a computer is a complex interaction between hardware and computer programming, created by your fellow humans.

Ever heard of Morse code? Morse code is nothing more than dots and dashes to those who do not understand it, but if you send dots and dashes (in the right order) to someone who understands Morse code, you can tell the recipient a joke. Think of programming as Morse code for the computer (Figure 3.1). You may not understand those ones and zeros, but your computer certainly does!

There's more to the ones and zeros than just programming. All of the data on the computer—the Web pages, your documents, your e-mail—is also stored as ones and zeros. Programs know how to translate these ones and zeros into a form humans understand.

Programming comes in two forms. First are the applications: the programs that get work done. Word processing programs, Web browsers, and e-mail programs are all considered applications. But applications need a main program to support them. They need a program that enables you to start and stop applications, copy/ move/delete data, talk to the hardware, and perform lots of other jobs. This program is called the operating system (OS). Microsoft Windows is the most popular OS today, but there are other computer operating systems, such as Apple Macintosh OS X and the popular (and free) Linux (Figure 3.2). Computer people lump operating systems and applications into the term **software** to differentiate them from the hardware of the computer.

Understanding the computer at this broad conceptual level—in terms of hardware, OS, and programs—can help you explain things

I know this. This is binary! It all makes sense now.

• **Figure 3.1**   Computer musing that a string of ones and zeros makes perfect sense.

• **Figure 3.2**   Typical OS X, Linux, and Windows interfaces

The CompTIA A+ certification exams only cover the Windows operating system, so you won't see much discussion of OS X or Linux in this book. Nevertheless, a good tech should possess a basic understanding of these two excellent operating systems.

to customers, but good techs have a much more fundamental appreciation and understanding of the complex interplay of all of the software and the individual pieces of hardware. In short, techs need to know the processes going on behind the scenes.

From the CompTIA A+ tech's perspective, the computer functions through four stages: input, processing, output, and storage. Knowing which parts participate in a particular stage of the computing process enables you to troubleshoot on a fundamental and decisive level.

Input

To illustrate this four-step process, let's walk through the steps involved in a fairly common computer task: preparing your taxes. [Insert collective groan here.] February has rolled around and, at least in the United States, millions of people install their favorite tax software, TurboTax from Intuit, onto their computers to help them prepare their taxes. After starting TurboTax, your first job is to provide the computer with data: essential information, such as your name, where you live, how much you earned, and how many dollars you gave to federal and state governments.

Various pieces of hardware enable you to input data, the most common of which are the keyboard and mouse. Most computers won't react when you say, "Hey you!"—at least not anywhere outside of a *Star Trek* episode. Although that day will come, for now you must use something decidedly more mechanical: a keyboard to type in your data. The OS provides a fundamental service in this process as well. You can bang on a keyboard all day and accomplish nothing unless the OS translates your keystrokes into code that the rest of your computer's hardware understands.

Processing

Next, the computer processes your data. After you place information in various appropriate "boxes" in TurboTax, the computer does the math for you. Processing takes place inside the system unit—the box under your desk (see Figure 3.3)—and happens almost completely at a hardware level, although that hardware functions according to rules laid out in the OS. Thus again you have a complex interaction between hardware and software.

The processing portion is the magical part—you can't see it happen. The first half of this book demystifies this stage, because good techs understand all of the pieces of the process. I won't go through the specific hardware involved in the processing stage here, because the pieces change according to the type of process.

Output

Simply adding up your total tax for the year is useless unless the computer shows you the result. That's where the third step—output—comes into play (Figure 3.4). Once the computer finishes processing data, it must put the information somewhere for you to inspect it. Often it places data on the monitor so you can see what you've just typed. It might send the data over to the printer if you tell it, so you can print out copies of your tax return to mail to the Internal Revenue Service (or whatever the Tax Man is called where you live). A hardware device does the actual printing, but the OS controls the printing process. Again, it's a fundamental interaction of hardware and software.

Storage

Once you've sent in your tax return, you most likely do not want all that work simply to disappear. What happens if the IRS comes back a couple of months later with a question about your return? Yikes! You need to keep permanent records and you need to keep a copy of the tax program. The fourth stage in the computing process is storage. A lot of devices are used in the storage process, the most visible of which are the external storage parts, such as a thumb drive or recordable CD discs (Figure 3.5).

The Art of the PC Technician

Using the four stages of the computing process—input, processing, output, and storage—to master how the PC works and, in turn, become a great technician requires that you understand all of the pieces of hardware and software involved *and* the interactions between them that make up the various stages. You have to know what the parts do,

• **Figure 3.3** Processing takes place somewhere in here!

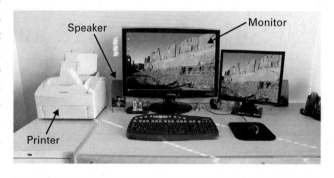

• **Figure 3.4** Output devices

• **Figure 3.5** Typical storage (CD-R discs)

in other words, and how they work together. The best place to start is with a real computer. Let's go through the process of inspecting a typical, complete PC, including opening up a few important pieces to see the components inside. Hopefully, you have a real computer in front of you right now that you may dismantle a bit. No two computers are exactly the same, so you'll see differences between your PC and the one in this chapter—and that's okay. You'll come to appreciate that all computers have the same main parts that do the same jobs even though they differ in size, shape, and color.

By the time you reach the end of this book, you'll have a deeper, more nuanced understanding of the interaction of hardware and software in the four-stage computing process. Just as great artists have mastered fundamental skills of their trade before creating a masterpiece, you'll have the fundamentals of the art of the computer technician and be on your road to mastery.

Essentials

■ The Complete PC

Sometimes I hate the term "personal computer." That term implies a single device, like a toaster. A typical PC is more than one device, and you need all of the parts (or at least most) to make the PC work. The most important part of the PC is the box that usually sits under your desk: the one that all of the other parts connect to, called the **system unit**. All of the processing and storage takes place in the system unit. All of the other parts of the PC—the printer, the keyboard, the monitor—connect to the system unit and are known collectively as **peripherals**. Figure 3.6 shows a typical desktop PC, with the system unit and peripherals as separate pieces.

Most computers have a standard set of peripherals to provide input and output. You'll see some variation in color, bells, and whistles, but here's the standard set.

- **Monitor** The big television thing that provides a visual output for the computer.

- **Keyboard** Keypad for providing keyed input. Based on a typewriter.

- **Mouse** Pointing device used to control a graphical pointer on the monitor for input.

- **Speakers/headphones** Speakers provide sound output.

- **Printer** Provides printed paper output.

A typical PC has all of these peripherals, but no law requires a PC to have them. Plenty of PCs may not have a printer. Some PCs don't have speakers. Some computers don't even have a keyboard, mouse, or monitor—but they tend to hide in unlikely places, such as the inside of a jet fighter or next to the engine in an automobile.

System unit   Peripherals

● **Figure 3.6**   Typical desktop computer with peripherals

Other PCs may have many more peripherals. Installing four or five printers on a single PC is easy, if you so desire. You'll also find hundreds of other types of peripherals, such as Web cameras and microphones, on many PCs. You add or remove peripherals depending on what you need from the system. The only limit is the number of connections for peripherals available on the system unit.

External Connections

Every peripheral connects to the system unit through one of the many types of ports. The back of a typical system unit (Figure 3.7) has many cables running from the system unit to the various peripherals. You may even have a few connectors in the front. All of these connectors and ports have their own naming conventions, and a good tech knows all of them. It's not acceptable to go around saying such things as "That's a printer port" or "That's a little-type keyboard connector." You need to be comfortable with the more commonly used naming conventions so you can say "That's a female DB-25" or "That's a USB connector."

Plugs, Ports, Jacks, and Connectors

Although PCs use close to 50 different types of connections, almost all fit into one of six major types: DIN, USB, FireWire, DB, RJ, and audio. Read the next paragraphs to get your terminology straight and then you can jump into the various connectors with gusto.

No one seems to use the terms *plug*, *port*, *jack*, or *connector* correctly, so let's get this right from the start. To connect one device to another, you need a cable containing the wires that make the connection. On each device, as well as on each end of the connecting cable, you need standardized parts to make that connection. Because these are usually electrical connections, one part needs to fit inside another to make a snug, safe connection.

A **plug** is a part with some type of projection that goes into a *port*. A **port** is a part that has some type of matching hole or slot that accepts the plug. You never put a port into a plug; it's always the other way around. The term **jack** is used as an alternative to port, so you may also put a plug into a jack. The term **connector** describes either a port or a plug. As you progress though this chapter and see the various plugs and ports, this will become clearer (Figure 3.8).

• **Figure 3.7**   Connections in the back of a PC

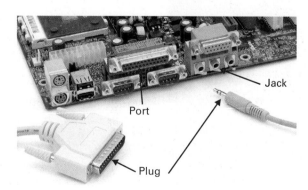

• **Figure 3.8**   Plug, port, and jack

• **Figure 3.9** DIN (top) and mini-DIN (bottom) connectors

Mini-DIN Connectors

Most PCs sport the European-designed **mini-DIN connectors**. The original DIN connector was replaced by mini-DIN a long time ago, so you'll only see mini-DIN connectors on your PC (see Figure 3.9 bottom). Older-style keyboards and mice plugged into DIN ports (Figure 3.9 top).

USB Connectors

Universal serial bus (USB) provides the most common general-purpose connection for PCs. You'll find USB versions of many devices, such as mice, keyboards, scanners, cameras, and printers. USB connections come in three sizes: A, B, and mini-B. The USB A connector's distinctive rectangular shape makes it easily recognizable (Figure 3.10).

You never see a USB B connector on your computer. USB B connectors are for the other end of the USB cable, where it attaches to the USB device (Figure 3.11).

The USB B connector's relatively large size makes it less than optimal for small devices such as cameras, so the USB folks also make the smaller mini-B–style connector shown in Figure 3.12.

USB has a number of features that make it particularly popular on PCs. First, USB devices are **hot-swappable**, which means you can insert or remove them without restarting your PC. Almost every other type of connector requires you to turn the system off, insert or remove the connector, and then turn the system back on. Hot-swapping completely eliminates this process.

Second, many USB devices get their electrical power through the USB connection, so they don't need batteries or a plug for an electrical outlet. You can even recharge some devices, such as cellular phones, by plugging them into a USB port (Figure 3.13).

FireWire Connectors

FireWire, also known as **IEEE 1394**, moves data at incredibly high speeds, making it the perfect connection for highly specialized applications such as

• **Figure 3.10** USB A connector and port

• **Figure 3.11** USB B connector

Mike Meyers' CompTIA A+ Guide to Managing and Troubleshooting PCs

• **Figure 3.12** USB mini-B connector

streaming video from a digital video camera onto a hard drive. FireWire consists of a special 6-wire connector, as shown in Figure 3.14, or a 9-wire connector for devices that need more speed and power. A smaller, 4-pin version is usually seen on peripherals. Like USB, FireWire devices are hot-swappable.

DB Connectors

Over the years, **DB connectors** have been used for almost any type of peripheral you can think of, with the exception of keyboards. They have a slight *D* shape, which allows only one proper way to insert a plug into the socket and makes it easier to remember what they're called. Technically, they're known as D-sub or **D-subminiature** connectors, but most techs call them DBs.

Each male DB plug has a group of small pins that connect to DB ports. Female DB plugs connect to male DB ports on the system unit. DB connectors in the PC world can have from 9 to 37 pins or sockets, although you rarely see a DB connector with more than 25 pins or sockets. Figure 3.15 shows an example. DB-type connectors are some of the oldest and most common connectors used in the back of PCs.

It wasn't that long ago that a typical PC used at least three or more different DB connectors. Over the past few years, the PC world has moved away from DB connectors. A typical modern system has only one or two, usually for video.

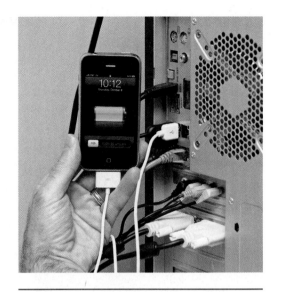

• **Figure 3.13** Cell phone charging via a USB connection

> **Tech Tip**
>
> **D-Subminiature Naming Scheme**
> *Each size D-sub connector—called the shell size—has a specific name in the D-sub manufacturing world. A two-row, 9-pin connector, for example, is officially a DE-9 connector rather than a DB-9. The E refers to the 9-pin shell size. Why all of the DA, DB, DC, DD, and DE connectors became DB-x in the world of personal computers is a mystery, but most techs simply call them DB connectors.*

• **Figure 3.14** FireWire connector and port   • **Figure 3.15** DB-25 connector and port

RJ Connectors

You have more than likely seen an **RJ connector**, whether or not you knew it by that name. The little plastic plug used to connect your telephone cord to the jack (techs don't use the word "port" to describe RJ connectors) is a classic example of an RJ plug. Modern PCs use only two types of RJ jacks: the RJ-11 and the RJ-45. The phone jack is an RJ-11. It is used almost exclusively for modems. The slightly wider RJ-45 jack is used for your network connection. Figure 3.16 shows an RJ-11 jack (top) and an RJ-45 jack (bottom).

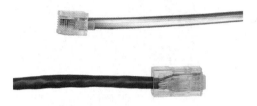

● **Figure 3.16**   RJ-11 (top) and RJ-45 (bottom)

Audio Connectors

Speakers and microphones connect to audio jacks on the system unit. The most common type of sound connector in popular use is the *1/8-inch* connector, also called a **mini-audio connector**. These small connectors have been around for years; they're just like the plug you use to insert headphones into a radio, music player, or similar device (Figure 3.17). Traditionally, you'd find the audio jacks on the back of the PC, but many newer models sport front audio connections as well.

Devices and Their Connectors

Now that you have a sense of the connectors, let's turn to the devices common to almost every PC to learn which connectors go with which device.

● **Figure 3.17**   Mini-audio jacks and plug

Cards Versus Onboard

All of the connectors on the back of the PC are just that: connectors. Behind those connectors are the actual devices that support whatever peripherals plug into those connectors. These devices might be built into the computer, such as a keyboard port. Others might be add-on expansion cards that a tech installed into the PC.

Most PCs have special **expansion slots** inside the system unit that enable you to add more devices on expansion cards. Figure 3.18 shows a typical card. If you want some new device and your system unit doesn't have that device built into the PC, you just go to the store, buy a card version of that

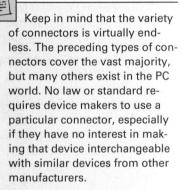

Keep in mind that the variety of connectors is virtually endless. The preceding types of connectors cover the vast majority, but many others exist in the PC world. No law or standard requires device makers to use a particular connector, especially if they have no interest in making that device interchangeable with similar devices from other manufacturers.

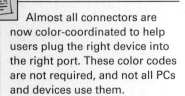

Almost all connectors are now color-coordinated to help users plug the right device into the right port. These color codes are not required, and not all PCs and devices use them.

Try This!

Feeling Your Way Around Connectors

Given that most PCs tend to sit on the floor under desks, a good PC tech learns to recognize most every PC connector by touch. This is a great exercise to do with a partner.

1. Look at all of the connectors on the back of any PC's system unit.

2. Turn the system unit around so you can no longer see the connections.

3. Try to identify the connectors by feel.

---

device, and snap it in. Later chapters of the book go into great detail on how to do this, but for now just appreciate that a device might be built in or it might come on a card.

Be careful handling cards. Touch the metal plate with the 90-degree bend and try to avoid touching any of the electronics. As mentioned in Chapter 2, "Operational Procedures," always put cards into an anti-static bag when moving them to prevent ESD.

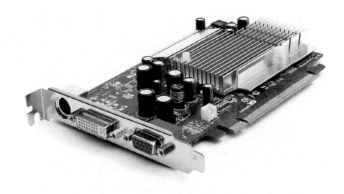

● **Figure 3.18**   Typical expansion card

Keyboard

Today's keyboards come in many shapes and sizes, but they always connect to your computer by either a mini-DIN port or a USB port. Many keyboards ship with an adapter so you can use either port. Most keyboard plugs and mini-DIN keyboard ports are colored purple (see Figure 3.19).

Monitor

A monitor connects to the video connector on the system unit. You'll usually see one of two types of video connectors: the older 15-pin female DB **Video Electronics Standards Association (VESA)** connector or the unique, **digital video interface (DVI)** connector. VESA connectors are colored blue, whereas DVI connectors are white. Many video cards have both types of connectors (see Figure 3.20) or two VESA or two DVI connectors. Video cards with two connectors support two monitors, a very cool thing to do!

The newest video connector is called **Hi-Definition Multimedia Interface (HDMI)**, shown in Figure 3.21. HDMI is still very new to the video scene and brings a number of enhancements, such as the ability to carry both video and sound on the same cable. Primarily designed for home theater, computers with HDMI connectors grow more common every year.

● **Figure 3.19**   Keyboard plug and port

Sound

The sound device in a computer performs two functions. First, it takes digital information and turns it into sound, outputting the sound through speakers. Second, it takes sound that is input through a microphone or some other audio source and turns it into digital data.

To play and record sounds, your sound device needs to connect to a set of speakers and a microphone or more. All PCs have at least two miniature audio jacks:

● **Figure 3.20**   Video card with (from left to right) S-Video, DVI, and VESA ports

● **Figure 3.21**   HDMI connector

● **Figure 3.22**   Typical bank of 1/8-inch audio jacks

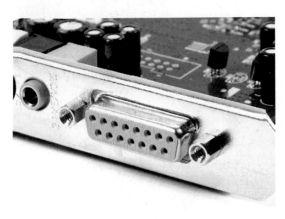

● **Figure 3.23**   Legacy joystick/MIDI port

Modern PCs have built-in network connections, but this is a fairly recent development. For many years, network devices only came on an expansion card, called a **network interface card (NIC)**. The term is so common that even built-in network connections—which most certainly are not cards—are still called NICs.

one for a microphone and another for stereo speakers. Better cards provide extra miniature audio jacks for surround sound. Figure 3.22 is a typical onboard soundcard showing six different 1/8-inch jacks. Four of these are for speakers and two are for input (such as microphones). The color scheme for sound connections is complex, but for now remember one color—green. That's the one you need to connect a standard pair of stereo speakers.

An older sound card may still provide a female 15-pin DB port that enables you to attach an electronic musical instrument interface or add a joystick to your PC (see Figure 3.23). These multi-function joystick/MIDI ports are rare today.

Adding more and more audio jacks to sound cards made the back of a typical sound card a busy place. In an effort to consolidate the various sound signals, the industry invented the **Sony/Philips Digital Interface Format (S/PDIF)** connection. S/PDIF comes in coaxial and optical versions. Figure 3.24 shows a motherboard with both (the coaxial connection is on the left). One S/PDIF connection replaces all of the mini-audio connections, assuming your surround speaker system also comes with an S/PDIF connection.

Network

Networks are groups of connected PCs that share information. The PCs most commonly connect via some type of cabling that usually looks like an extra-thick phone cable. A modern PC uses an RJ-45 connection to connect to the network. Figure 3.25 shows a typical RJ-45 network connector. Network connectors do not have a standard color.

Mouse

Most folks are pretty comfortable with the function of a mouse—it enables you to select graphical items on a graphical screen. A PC mouse has at least two buttons (as opposed to the famous one-button mouse that came with Apple Macintosh computers

S/PDIF

● **Figure 3.24**   S/PDIF connection

Mike Meyers' CompTIA A+ Guide to Managing and Troubleshooting PCs

● **Figure 3.25**   Typical network connection

● **Figure 3.26**   Mouse with mini-DIN connection

until recently), while a better mouse provides a scroll wheel and extra buttons. A mouse uses either a USB port or a dedicated, light-green mini-DIN connector (see Figure 3.26).

A variation of the mouse is a **trackball**. A trackball does the same job as a mouse, but instead of pushing it around like a mouse, the trackball stays in one place as you roll a ball with your fingers or thumb (Figure 3.27).

Modem

The old **modem** enables you to connect your PC to a telephone. Modems are another easily identifiable device in PCs as they have one or

● **Figure 3.27**   Trackball

Tech Tip

Serial Ports

External modems traditionally connected to a male 9-pin or 25-pin D-subminiature port on the system unit called a **serial port** *(shown in the following illustration). Although just about every external modem today connects to USB, a few computers still come with a serial port for legacy devices.*

Serial ports are one of the few connectors on modern systems that were also used in the first PCs more than 20 years ago.

• **Figure 3.28**   Internal modem

two RJ-11 jacks. One jack is to connect the modem to the telephone jack on the wall. If the modem has a second RJ-11 jack, it is for an optional telephone so you can use the phone line when the modem is not in use (see Figure 3.28).

Printer

For many years, printers only used a special connector called a **parallel port**. Parallel ports use a 25-pin female DB connector that's usually colored fuchsia (see Figure 3.29).

After almost 20 years of domination by parallel ports, most printers now come with USB ports, FireWire, Ethernet, and Wi-Fi 802.11 b/g/n connectivity options. Parallel ports are quickly fading away from the backs of most computers.

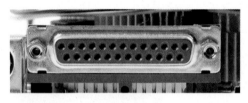

• **Figure 3.29**   Parallel port

Joystick

Joysticks weren't supposed to be used just for games (see Figure 3.30). When the folks at IBM added the 2-row, 15-pin female DB joystick connector to PCs, they envisioned joysticks as hard-working input devices, just as the mouse is today. Except in the most rare circumstances, however, the only thing a **joystick** does today is enable you to turn your PC into a rather expensive game machine. But is there a more gratifying feeling than easing that joystick over, pressing the Fire button, and watching an enemy fighter jet get blasted by a well-placed Sidewinder missile? I think not. Traditional joystick connecters are colored orange, but most joysticks today connect to USB ports.

• **Figure 3.30**   Joystick

eSATA

More and more PCs are showing up with eSATA ports like the one shown in Figure 3.31. The **eSATA** is a special connector for external hard drives and optical drives.

Plenty More!

Keep in mind that there are lots more devices and connectors out there. This section includes only the most common and the ones you're most likely to see. As you progress through this book, you'll see some less common connecters and where they are used.

• **Figure 3.31**   eSATA port

■ Inside the System Unit

Now that you've seen the devices that connect to the PC, it's time to open up the system unit to inspect the major internal components of a typical PC. A single PC is composed of thousands of discrete components. Although no one can name every tiny bit of electronics in a PC, a good technician should be able to name the major internal components that make up the typical PC. Let's open and inspect a system unit to see these components and gain at least a concept of what they do. In later chapters, you'll see all of these components in much more detail.

Case

The system unit's case is both the internal framework of the PC and the external skin that protects the internal components from the environment. Cases come in an amazing variety of styles, sizes, and colors. Figure 3.32 shows the front and back of a typical PC case. The front of the case holds the buttons for turning the system on and off, lights to tell you the status of the system, and doors for accessing removable media drives such as floppy, CD-ROM, and DVD drives. This system also provides USB, FireWire, and audio connections in the front for easy access if you want to use a device that needs these connections.

The back of the case holds the vast majority of the system unit connections. You will also notice the power supply—almost always at the top of the case—distinguished by its cooling fan and power plug. Note that one area of the back, the I/O area, holds all of the onboard connections (see Figure 3.33), while another area in the back contains slots for cards. Similarly, the case uses slots to enable access to the external connectors on cards installed in the system unit.

Opening a case is always…interesting. There's no standard way to open a case, and I'm convinced that the folks making system units enjoy some sick humor inventing new and complex ways to open them. In general,

• **Figure 3.32**   Case—front and back

You'll hear the PC case called the *enclosure*, especially at the more expensive end of the spectrum. Case, enclosure, and system unit are interchangeable terms.

● **Figure 3.33**   Onboard devices

you detach the sides of a case by removing a few screws in the back of the system unit, as shown in Figure 3.34. Use common sense and you won't have too many problems. Just don't lose track of your screws or where each one was inserted!

Once you've opened the case, take a look inside. You'll see metal framework, all kinds of cables, and a number of devices. As you inspect the devices, you may gently push cables to the side to get a better view. Don't forget to wear an anti-static wrist strap (attaching it to any handy metal part of the case) or touch the metal case occasionally to prevent ESD.

CPU

The **central processing unit (CPU)**, also called the **microprocessor**, performs all of the calculations that take place inside a PC. CPUs come in a variety of shapes and sizes, as shown in Figure 3.35.

● **Figure 3.34**   Opening a system unit

● **Figure 3.35**   Typical CPUs still in protective packaging

Modern CPUs generate a lot of heat and thus require a cooling fan and heat sink assembly to avoid overheating (see Figure 3.36). A heat sink is a big slab of copper or aluminum that helps draw heat away from the processor. The fan then blows the heat out into the case. You can usually remove this cooling device if you need to replace it, although some CPU manufacturers have sold CPUs with a fan permanently attached.

CPUs have a make and model, just like automobiles do. When talking about a particular car, for example, most people speak in terms of a Ford Taurus or a Toyota Camry. When they talk about CPUs, people say Intel Core i7 or AMD Phenom. Over the years, there have been only a few major CPU manufacturers, just as there are only a few major auto manufacturers. The two most common makes of CPUs used in PCs are AMD and Intel.

Although only a few manufacturers of CPUs have existed, those manufacturers have made hundreds of models of CPUs. Some of the more common models made over the past few years have names such as Core 2, Core i7, Celeron, Athlon, and Phenom.

Finally, CPUs come in a variety of packages. The package defines how the CPU looks physically and how it connects to the computer. Intel CPUs currently use a package type called *land grid array* (*LGA*), and AMD likes *pin grid array* (*PGA*). Every CPU package type has a number of versions and each type is designed to fit into a particular connection called a socket. Sockets have such names as Socket AM3 or Socket B. Figure 3.37 shows a CPU with its matching socket.

Chapter 5, "Microprocessors," goes into great detail on CPUs, but for now remember that every CPU has a make, a model, and a package type.

RAM

Random access memory (RAM) stores programs and data currently being used by the CPU. The maximum amount of programs and data that a piece of RAM can store is measured in units called *bytes*. Modern PCs have many millions, even billions, of bytes of RAM, so RAM is measured in units called *megabytes* (*MB*) or *gigabytes* (*GB*). An average PC will have from 1 to 4 GB of RAM, although PCs may have more or less RAM. Each piece of RAM is called a *stick*. One common type of stick found in today's PC is called a *dual inline memory module* (*DIMM*). Figure 3.38 shows two examples of DIMMs used in PCs.

Your PC takes only one type of DIMM, and you must know the type so you can add or replace RAM when needed. Chapter 6, "RAM," covers everything you need to know to work comfortably with RAM.

● **Figure 3.36**   CPU with fan

● **Figure 3.37**   CPU and matching socket

Some parts of your PC are much more sensitive to ESD than others. Your CPU and RAM are very sensitive to ESD. If you touch the metal parts of your CPU or RAM and you have even the tiniest amount of charge, you can destroy them.

● **Figure 3.38**   Two DIMMs

Motherboard

You can compare a motherboard to the chassis of an automobile. In a car, everything connects to the chassis either directly or indirectly. In a PC, everything connects to the motherboard either directly or indirectly. A **motherboard** is a thin, flat piece of circuit board, usually green or gold, and often slightly larger than a typical piece of notebook paper (see Figure 3.39).

A motherboard contains a number of special sockets that accept various PC components. The CPU and RAM, for example, plug directly into the motherboard. Other devices, such as floppy drives, hard drives, CD and DVD drives, connect to the motherboard sockets through short cables. Motherboards also provide onboard connectors for external devices such as mice, printers, joysticks, and keyboards.

All motherboards use multipurpose expansion slots in which you can add adapter cards. Different types of expansion slots exist for different types of cards (see Figure 3.40).

● **Figure 3.39**   Typical motherboard

Power Supply

The **power supply**, as its name implies, provides the necessary electrical power to make the PC operate. The power supply takes standard electrical power and converts it into power your PC can use. Most power supplies are about the size of a shoebox cut in half and are usually a gray or metallic color (see Figure 3.41).

A number of connectors lead out of the power supply. Every power supply provides special connectors to power the motherboard and a number of other general-use connectors that provide power to any device that needs electricity. Check out Chapter 10, "Power Supplies," for more information.

● **Figure 3.40**   Placing a card into an expansion slot

● **Figure 3.41**   Power supply

Floppy Drive

The **floppy drive** enables you to access removable floppy disks (diskettes). The floppy drive used in PCs today is a 3.5-inch floppy drive. Floppy drives only store a tiny amount of data and have all but disappeared from PCs.

The floppy drive's data connection to the computer is via a ribbon cable, which in turn connects to the motherboard. The connection to the motherboard is known as the *floppy drive controller* (Figure 3.42).

• **Figure 3.42**   Floppy drive connected to motherboard

Hard Drive

A **hard drive** stores programs and data that are not currently being used by the CPU. Although RAM storage is measured in megabytes and gigabytes, a PC's hard drive stores much more data than a typical PC's RAM—hundreds of gigabytes to *terabytes*. A terabyte is 1000 gigabytes.

An average PC has one hard drive, although most PCs accept more. Special PCs that need to store large amounts of data, such as a large corporation's main file-storage computer, can contain many hard drives—8 to 16 drives in some cases.

The two most common types of hard drives seen in today's PCs are the older *Parallel Advanced Technology Attachment* (*PATA*) and the more modern *Serial Advanced Technology Attachment* (*SATA*). PATA drives use a ribbon cable very similar to the one used by floppy drives, whereas SATA drives use a very narrow cable. Figure 3.43 shows a SATA drive (left) next to a PATA drive (right). Most motherboards come with connections for both types of drives.

Optical drives use the same PATA or SATA connections used with hard drives. Figure 3.44 shows a DVD drive sharing a single ribbon cable with a PATA hard drive—a common sight inside a PC.

Tech Tip

SCSI

A very few PCs use small computer system interface (SCSI) drives. SCSI drives are generally faster and more expensive, so they usually show up only in high-end PCs such as network servers or graphics workstations.

Optical Drives

Optical drives enable a computer to read one or more types of optical discs, such as CD, DVD, or Blu-ray Disc (Figure 3.45). CDs store around 700 MB

• **Figure 3.43**   SATA and PATA drives showing data connectors

• **Figure 3.44**   Hard drive and DVD drive

● Figure 3.45   Assorted optical discs

Chapter 13, "Removable Media," goes into great detail on the assorted discs and drive types.

and come in three varieties: CD-ROM (*read only memory*: you can't change the data on them), CD-R (*recordable*: you can change the data once), and CD-RW (*rewritable*: you can change the data on them over and over). DVDs store much more data—the smallest capacity DVDs store around 4 GB, enough for a Hollywood movie—and come in even more varieties: DVD-ROM, DVD+R, DVD-R, DVD+RW, and DVD-RW, just to name the more famous ones. Blu-ray Discs are popular for high-definition movies, but there are also Blu-ray Discs for storing data with capacities starting at 25 GB.

All of these optical discs require an optical drive that knows how to read them. If you want to do anything with a CD-RW disc, for example, you need a CD-RW drive. If you want to use a DVD+R disc, you need a DVD+R drive. Luckily, most optical drives support many different types of discs, and some support every common type of optical disc available. Figure 3.46 shows typical optical drives. Note that some of them advertise what disc types they use. Others give no clue whatsoever.

Know Your Parts

The goal of this chapter was to get you to appreciate the names and functions of the various parts of the PC: peripherals, connectors, and components. By starting with the Big Picture view, you may now begin breaking down the individual components on a chapter-by-chapter basis and truly understand at great depth how each component works and how it interconnects with the PC system as a whole.

● Figure 3.46   Optical drives

Chapter 3 Review

■ Chapter Summary

After reading this chapter and completing the exercises, you should understand the following about the visible PC.

Describe how the PC works

■ The two parts of the PC—hardware and software—work intimately together to enable you to do work.

■ The computer tech knows the four stages of computing: input, processing, output, and storage. Understanding how the various pieces of hardware and software interact in each stage enables you to master the art of the PC tech.

Identify all the connectors and devices on a typical PC system unit

■ Most computers have a standard set of peripherals to provide input and output. Typical devices include the monitor, keyboard, mouse, speakers, and printer.

■ PCs use many kinds of external connectors, but most fit into one of six major types: mini-DIN, USB, FireWire, DB, RJ, and mini-audio. A plug goes into a port or jack. Connectors are often identified by their shape (such as DB connectors that look like a capital D), by their gender (male or female), and by the number of pins. Most PCs have two round mini-DIN connectors, one for the keyboard and the other for the mouse.

■ Universal serial bus (USB) connectors come in three sizes, A, B, and mini-B. Many devices plug into USB ports, including keyboards and cameras. USB is hot-swappable, so you may insert or remove devices without restarting the computer.

■ Also known as IEEE 1394, the FireWire interface is perfect for high-speed devices such as digital video cameras. PCs rarely have built-in 4- or 6-wire FireWire connectors, so users typically purchase a FireWire adapter card.

■ DB connectors come in a variety of sizes, but only one shape. You'll find only a few DB connectors on modern PCs, primarily for printers and video.

■ The telephone jack is an RJ connector, called an RJ-11. Most network cards have a wider RJ-45 jack.

■ Speakers and microphones connect to mini-audio jacks. You'll always find these on the back of the system unit; newer models have connectors on the front as well.

■ Keyboards connect into either a dedicated mini-DIN keyboard port or a USB port. Monitors connect to VGA or DVI ports. Mice and trackballs use the mini-DIN or USB ports as well. Keeping with the same trend, printers come in one of two common varieties: those that plug into a DB-25 port and those that plug into a USB port. A joystick plugs into either a 15-pin female DB port or a USB port.

Discuss the major internal components of a PC

■ Everything fits inside or connects to the case, more technically called a system unit. The system unit provides the framework for buttons, lights, drives, access doors, and so forth. Opening the case is usually a matter of unscrewing screws and pulling one side open.

■ The central processing unit (CPU), also called the microprocessor or brain of the computer, has a make, a model, a speed, and a package. AMD and Intel are the two most common makers of CPUs. CPU speed is measured in megahertz (MHz) or gigahertz (GHz). The pin grid array (PGA) is the most common CPU package. A CPU cooling fan or heat sink is essential to dissipate the heat.

■ Random access memory (RAM) contains the current programs and data that the CPU is using. Most PC memory is installed on sticks called dual inline memory modules (DIMMs). RAM capacity is measured in megabytes (MB) or gigabytes (GB).

■ The motherboard contains soldered components, expansion slots, and sockets for the CPU, RAM, and other components. Expansion slots are connectors for expansion cards that enable optional devices to communicate with the PC.

- A floppy drive uses a ribbon cable to connect to the floppy drive controller on the motherboard. The most common type is the 3.5-inch floppy drive.

- Hard drives store programs and data that the CPU is not currently using. An average PC has one hard drive, although most PCs accept more. Most PCs use either PATA or SATA drives, both of which commonly connect to controllers built into the motherboard.

- Optical drives enable the computer to access optical discs. Some optical drives can record CDs, such as the compact disc-recordable (CD-R) or the compact disc-rewritable (CD-RW) drives. Most PCs now have digital versatile disc (DVD) drives that support capacities large enough for a full-length movie.

■ Key Terms

central processing unit (CPU) (52)
connector (43)
DB connector (45)
digital video interface (DVI) (47)
D-subminiature (45)
eSATA (51)
expansion slot (46)
FireWire (44)
floppy drive (55)
hard drive (55)
Hi-Definition Multimedia Interface (HDMI) (47)
hot-swappable (44)
IEEE 1394 (44)
jack (43)
joystick (50)
keyboard (42)
microprocessor (52)
mini-audio connector (46)
mini-DIN connector (44)
modem (49)
monitor (42)

motherboard (54)
mouse (42)
network interface card (NIC) (48)
optical drive (55)
parallel port (50)
peripherals (42)
plug (43)
port (43)
power supply (54)
printer (42)
programming (39)
random access memory (RAM) (53)
RJ connector (46)
serial port (49)
software (39)
Sony/Philips Digital Interface Format (S/PDIF) (48)
speakers (42)
system unit (42)
trackball (49)
universal serial bus (USB) (44)
Video Electronics Standards Association (VESA) (47)

■ Key Term Quiz

Use the Key Terms list to complete the sentences that follow. Not all terms will be used.

1. The monitor attaches to the video card with a 15-pin female DB connector called a(n) _____ connector.

2. If you install a DIMM stick, your computer will have more _____.

3. The _____ has a make, a model, a speed, and a package.

4. Two RJ-11 connectors identify the _____.

5. When attaching a peripheral, put the plug into the _____ or jack.

6. The _____ takes standard electrical power from a wall outlet and converts it to power your PC can use.

7. If an expansion card contains an RJ-45 jack, it is a(n) _____.

8. A 25-pin female DB connector with a printer attached to it is a(n) _____.

9. An internal storage device that typically holds 200 GB or more is a(n) _____.

10. The box that all the other components plug into is called the _____.

■ Multiple-Choice Quiz

1. Which of the following connections can replace all of the mini-audio jacks on a system unit?
   - A. FireWire
   - B. HDMI
   - C. S/PDIF
   - D. VESA

2. A modern keyboard generally connects to which of the following ports? (Select two.)
   - A. FireWire
   - B. Mini-DIN
   - C. USB
   - D. VESA

3. USB connectors come in which of the following sizes? (Select three.)
   - A. A
   - B. B
   - C. Mini-A
   - D. Mini-B

4. Which of the following devices attaches with a ribbon cable?
   - A. CPU
   - B. CD-ROM drive
   - C. RAM
   - D. Sound card

5. Which of the following devices measure(s) storage capacity in megabytes or gigabytes?
   - A. Floppy disk and hard drive
   - B. NIC
   - C. CPU
   - D. Modem

6. Which of the following devices has enough storage capacity to hold a movie?
   - A. CD-ROM
   - B. CD-R
   - C. CD-RW
   - D. DVD

7. Which of the following connector types enable you to plug a device into them and have the device function without your restarting the computer? (Select two.)
   - A. FireWire
   - B. Mini-DIN
   - C. Serial
   - D. USB

8. Which of the following ports would you most likely find built into a motherboard?
   - A. A keyboard port
   - B. A DVI port
   - C. An HDMI port
   - D. An RDA port

9. Which of the following connectors is used mostly for external hard drives?
   - A. PATA
   - B. eSATA
   - C. HDMI
   - D. PS/2

10. Which of the following ports can handle a connection from a monitor?
    - A. DVI
    - B. FireWire
    - C. Mini-DIN
    - D. USB

11. Which of the following ports enables a modern PC to connect to a network?

   A. Mini-audio

   B. Mini-DIN

   C. RJ-13

   D. RJ-45

12. Which of the following connectors is used for hard drives?

   A. Parallel

   B. SATA

   C. HDMI

   D. TTFN

13. Of the following, what do USB and FireWire connections have in common?

   A. Both are used for connecting keyboards

   B. Both support dual monitors

   C. Both support hot-swapping devices

   D. Both use D-subminiature connectors

14. Which devices enable you to select graphical items on a graphical screen? (Select two.)

   A. Modem

   B. Mouse

   C. Touchball

   D. Trackball

15. Which device traditionally used a 2-row, 15-pin DB connector (though current models connect through USB)?

   A. Joystick

   B. Keyboard

   C. Mouse

   D. Printer

■ Essay Quiz

1. Although serial and parallel ports have been around forever, newer and faster ports such as USB and FireWire are now available. At the same time, new computers have faster CPUs, more RAM, and larger-capacity hard drives. What factors do you think are driving the PC market for these improvements? Do you feel that you need to have the newest and the greatest PC? Why or why not?

2. Jason, one of your coworkers who knows nothing about computer hardware, needs to move his computer and will be responsible for reassembling it himself in his new office across town. What advice can you give him about disassembly steps that will help him reassemble the computer successfully? List at least five things Jason should do as he disassembles the computer, transports it, and reassembles it. Do shapes and colors help him?

3. A floppy drive was a standard component for personal computers from their beginning. Today, most manufacturers build PCs without a floppy drive. Would you want to purchase a PC without a floppy drive? Why or why not? If so, what kinds of alternative devices would you want your computer to have?

4. Hearing that you are taking a computer hardware course, Aunt Sally approaches you about helping her select a new computer. She wants to use the computer primarily for office applications, to track her budget, to receive and send e-mail, and to surf the Internet. What are you going to tell her about the kind of PC to buy? What peripherals should she purchase? Why?

Lab Projects

• Lab Project 3.1

Many personal computers do not normally include the relatively new eSATA port. Check the following three Web sites: www.dell.com, www.hp.com, and www.lenovo.com. Is an eSATA port standard built-in equipment on their new computers? If so, how many eSATA ports are included? If not, do the sites offer eSATA as an optional add-on?

• Lab Project 3.2

Find an advertisement for a new personal computer in a current newspaper or magazine and examine it to determine the following:

■ What make, model, and speed of CPU does it have?

■ How much RAM does it have?

■ What is the storage capacity of the hard drive?

■ Does it include a Blu-ray Disc, CD-RW, or DVD drive?

■ Does it come with a network interface card?

■ Is a monitor included? If so, what kind and size?

Understanding Windows

In this chapter, you will learn how to

- **Relate the history of Microsoft Windows**
- **Explain the Windows interface**
- **Identify the operating system folders of Windows 2000, XP, and Vista**
- **Describe the utilities in Windows essential to techs**

As a tech, you need to understand Windows at a level beyond that of regular users. This chapter introduces you to some of the more powerful aspects of Windows, such as NTFS and the Registry. Not only must techs run through the standard Windows features that everyone uses every day (Start button, Recycle Bin, and so on), they must also be comfortable drilling down underneath that user-friendly surface to get their hands a little dirty.

This chapter begins by introducing and organizing the many variations of Windows on the market today and helping you appreciate the difference between, for example, Windows XP Home and Windows Vista Ultimate. The chapter then takes you through the Windows interface in detail. The third section looks more closely at the techie aspects of Windows, including the structure of the OS. The fourth section provides an overview of the many utilities for techs available in Windows. The chapter closes in the "Beyond A+" section with a discussion of the versions of Windows not on the current CompTIA A+ exams, such as Windows 7 and non-desktop versions of Windows. Let's get started!

Historical/Conceptual

■ A Brief History of Microsoft Windows

Many users think of Windows as a monolithic thing, as *the* operating system (OS) for the PC (as opposed to the Macintosh), but as a tech you need to understand that Microsoft produces many varieties of the OS, each with specific tools, utilities, file structures, and interfaces. And you need to be able to navigate through any modern version of Windows fluidly.

Microsoft currently supports seven families of Windows, of which three concern the CompTIA A+ certified technician: Windows 2000, Windows XP, and Windows Vista. (I'll cover the other four families of Windows in the "Beyond A+" section of this chapter.) Within each of these families—my word, not Microsoft's—Windows comes in multiple versions. Here's the list for the top three:

Table 4.1	Versions of Windows on the CompTIA A+ Exams	
Windows Family	**Versions (32-bit)**	**Versions (64-bit)**
Windows 2000	■ Windows 2000 Professional ■ Windows 2000 Server	Nothing widely available
Windows XP	■ Windows XP Home ■ Windows XP Professional ■ Windows Media Center ■ Windows XP Tablet PC Edition[1]	■ Windows XP 64-bit version ■ Windows XP Professional x64 Edition
Windows Vista[2]	■ Windows Vista Home Basic ■ Windows Vista Home Premium ■ Windows Vista Business ■ Windows Vista Ultimate	■ Windows Vista Home Basic ■ Windows Vista Home Premium ■ Windows Vista Business ■ Windows Vista Ultimate

1 Windows XP Tablet PC Edition is not covered on the CompTIA A+ exams but is included here for completeness.
2 Microsoft has released two other versions of Windows Vista: Starter Edition and Enterprise. Vista Starter Edition is a simplified version of the operating system designed for the developing world and is not sold in developed countries. Vista Enterprise is a version of Vista Business designed for large-volume customers and is only sold to Microsoft's enterprise-level customers.

The problem of variety is compounded the minute you start working with older computers or talking with users or techs who've been in computers for a few years. You'll hear about Windows 95, for example, or Windows Me, or even Windows 3.*x*. Huh? What are these versions (Figure 4.1)? How do they fit in the picture?

This section outlines the history of Microsoft Windows and then takes an in-depth look at the differences among the many versions of Microsoft's flagship operating system. That way you can sort out the essentials for today's techs from the many varieties you'll hear about.

Microsoft entered the operating system game in the early 1980s with a command-line OS called Microsoft Disk Operating System, or MS-DOS. With a command-line OS, you interacted with the computer to run programs and save files and all the other computing functions by typing and

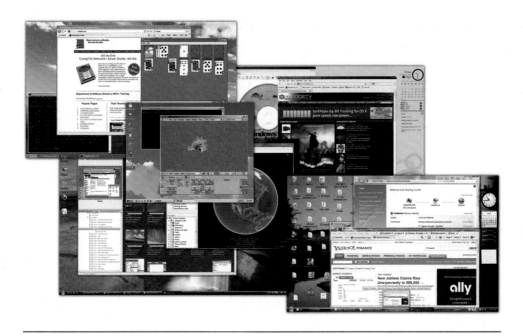

● **Figure 4.1** Lots of Windows!

then pressing the ENTER key on your keyboard. This whole typing thing worked for people who could memorize commands and such, but alternative operating systems, such as the Apple Macintosh, offered a visual interface, where you could interact with the computer by clicking on pictures. The time came for Microsoft to step up its game and produce a graphical user interface (GUI) where users could use a mouse to point and click.

Early Windows

Microsoft released several versions of Windows 3.1, with minor differences in name. Techs call the versions collectively Windows 3.x.

The earliest version of Windows, Microsoft Windows 1.0, dates from 1985 and was little more than a graphical overlay of the DOS command-line operating system. This overlay version of Windows went through a number of updates, ending with the first truly popular version of Windows, Windows for Workgroups version 3.1 (Figure 4.2).

In 1989, Microsoft offered a completely separate version of Windows called Windows NT. Windows NT was a true graphical operating system and was dramatically more powerful than the Windows overlay versions. Windows NT also cost more than other versions of Windows, however, and saw little adoption outside of servers and systems where users needed a lot of power. Windows NT went through a number of versions, culminating with Windows NT 4.0 in 1996 (Figure 4.3).

Comparing Windows NT to the old overlay versions of Windows is akin to comparing the first computer game you ever played to the games we play today: technically the same thing (a game), but that's about it. Windows NT had so many features that showing them all could take days, but one is important. NT came with a new way to organize hard drives and files, called the NT File System (NTFS). Before NTFS, all versions of Windows used an ancient file system

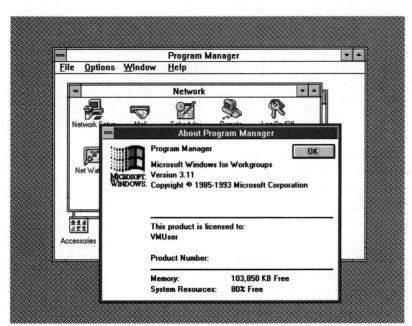

● **Figure 4.2** Windows for Workgroups

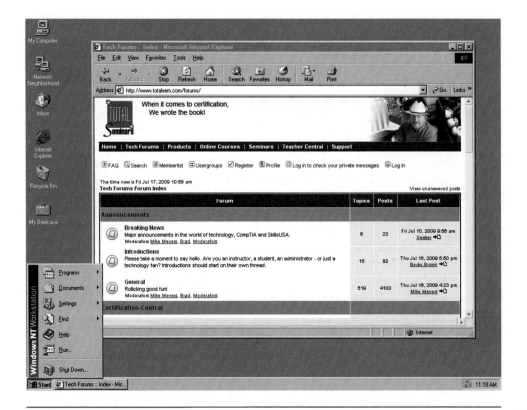

● **Figure 4.3**   Windows NT 4.0

called the file allocation table (FAT). FAT was great when first invented in
the late 1970s, but by the mid-80s it was showing its age. NTFS took care of a
number of problems, the biggest of which was security. FAT had no security. There was no way to control what people did with your files. NTFS was
built from the ground up with security in mind. We'll cover both FAT and
NTFS later in the book, but for now appreciate that only Windows NT had
NTFS.

It wasn't until 1995 that Microsoft dumped the overlay concept and introduced Windows 95, the first version of Windows for the standard user
that was also a full-blown operating system (Figure 4.4). Windows 95 offered many improvements over Windows 3.*x*, and eventually Microsoft released several upgraded versions as well, such as Windows 98, Windows 98
SE, and Windows Me. The upgraded versions continued to use the FAT file
system. Over the years, Windows has gone through massive changes and a
large number of improved versions. The later versions have nothing in common with earlier versions other than the name "Windows."

When we describe Windows
95, 98, 98 SE, and Me from a
historical standpoint, we lump
them all together, using the
term "Windows 9*x*."

Modern Windows

The vast majority of computers in the field today run one of the three modern families of Windows, so the CompTIA A+ certification focuses on those
as well: Windows 2000, Windows XP, and Windows Vista. But as you know
from Table 4.1 at the beginning of this chapter, just saying the name of a
Windows family doesn't do the varieties within that family justice. The trick
is to organize these versions in such a way to discover their similarities and

● **Figure 4.4** Windows 95—The Windows of your forefathers

differences. In this section, we'll look at versions of Windows 2000, XP, and Vista, as well as a few other versions of Windows, and see the differences in detail.

A great place to start is with the arrival of Windows 2000 in 2001. Throughout most of the 1990s, before Windows 2000 came along (followed very quickly by Windows XP), Windows was in a bit of a mess. Microsoft had two totally different operating systems—each called Windows—that it sold for two different markets. Microsoft sold the Windows 9*x* series for the home user and small office, and the much more powerful Windows NT series for corporate environments.

Essentials

Windows 2000

Windows 2000 was the first step toward changing this mess. It was based on the old Windows NT (including support for NTFS), but for the first time it included a great interface, provided support for dang near any program, and was substantially easier to use than the old Windows NT. Microsoft originally presented Windows 2000 as a replacement for Windows NT, but its stability and ease of use motivated many knowledgeable Windows 9*x* users to upgrade to Windows 2000. Windows 2000 started to appear as "the single Windows to replace all the other versions."

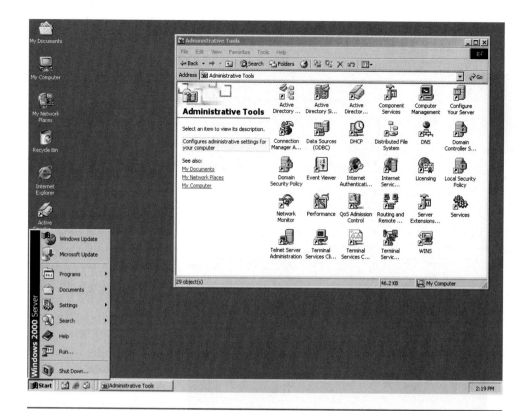

● **Figure 4.5** Windows 2000 Server

Windows 2000 came in two versions: Professional and Server. The CompTIA A+ exams do not cover Windows Server versions, but a good tech should at least know that these server versions exist. If you were to look at the Windows 2000 Server desktop, you'd be hard pressed to see any obvious differences from the Windows 2000 Professional version. Don't let Windows 2000 Server fool you (Figure 4.5). Windows Server is a heavy-duty version, loaded with extra software and features that make it superb for running an office server. Windows Server versions are also extremely expensive, costing on average of around $200 per computer that accesses the server.

> Windows 2000 was the last version of Windows to come in both Server and Professional versions. After the release of Windows XP, Microsoft introduced the next version of Windows Server as Server 2003. Windows Server 2008 is the latest version of Windows Server.

Windows XP

Windows XP came hot on the heels of Windows 2000. Under the hood, XP was basically the same as Windows 2000 but added a dramatically improved interface and a number of new features, such as a built-in CD writer. Microsoft also broke with the beauty of 2000's "one OS for everyone" idea. Microsoft visualized three types of users—professionals, home users, and media junkies—so Windows XP came in several versions, such as Windows XP Professional, Windows XP Home, and Windows XP Media Center.

Windows XP Professional

Microsoft Windows XP Professional is, in many people's opinions, the most versatile and therefore the most mainstream version of Windows XP. Microsoft tuned Windows XP Professional for office environments with

• Figure 4.9   Microsoft Media Center

Personal Video Recorder (PVR) program that enables you to watch and record television (you'll need a TV tuner card) and organize all of your media, from photos to music.

On the Microsoft Media Center Web site, Microsoft declares that the Windows XP Microsoft Media Center edition is based on Windows XP Professional; however, other than the Media Center program, Windows XP Media Center's capabilities are identical to those of Windows XP Home.

Windows Vista

Even though Windows 7 is available, Windows Vista is the latest version of Windows on the current CompTIA A+ exams. It's important to recognize Vista and know what choices you have when deciding which version of Vista you need for a particular PC. Windows has a number of versions of Vista, each geared toward a particular market segment. Let's look at the most common versions of Vista.

• Figure 4.10   Vista Home Premium Media Center

Windows Vista Home Basic

Windows Vista Home Basic is roughly equivalent to Windows XP Home. Microsoft gears it to home users not needing more advanced multimedia support.

Windows Vista Home Premium

Windows Vista Home Premium is the same as Windows Vista Home Basic, but it adds an upgraded Windows Media Center PVR application, similar to the one found in Windows XP Media Center (Figure 4.10).

Windows Vista Business

Windows Vista Business is the basic business version and has all the security, file-sharing, and access controls seen in Windows XP Professional.

Windows Vista Ultimate

Windows Vista Ultimate combines all of the features of every other Vista version and includes some other features, such as a game performance tweaker and DVD ripping capability (Figure 4.11).

You can determine your Windows version by right-clicking My Computer in Windows 2000 or XP, or Computer in Vista and Windows 7, and selecting Properties.

• **Figure 4.11**   Vista Ultimate

Enter 64-bit Windows

From roughly 1986 to around 2001, all CPUs were 32-bit. While we will save the big discussion of what 32-bit means for Chapter 5, "Microprocessors," for now let's keep it simple: a 32-bit CPU can only use a maximum of 4 gigabytes of RAM (2^{32} = 4,294,967,296). Starting in 2001 we began to see 64-bit CPUs that could accept more than 4 gigabytes. 64-bit CPUs are now extremely common.

    The leap from 32-bit to 64-bit processing has a number of advantages. The really big compelling reason to go from 32- to 64-bit is that 64-bit CPUs support more than 4 gigabytes of RAM. The more RAM you have, the more programs—and the bigger the programs—your system will run. Until fairly recently, not too many of us cared to go above 4 gigabytes of RAM. We didn't need the RAM and we didn't have a CPU that could run at 64 bits. My, how things have changed over the past few years!

    The 64-bit CPUs first showed up with the Intel Itanium back in 2001. At that time the only folks interested in 64-bit processing were large data centers and a few organizations that needed to crunch big numbers. To run a computer with an Itanium, you needed an operating system that worked with a 64-bit processor. Up to this point, every version of Windows only ran at 32-bit. Microsoft answered the call by creating special 64-bit versions of Windows 2000 and XP, but these 64-bit versions of Windows 2000 were very rare.

    In 2003, Advanced Micro Devices (AMD) started to ship the popular Athlon 64 CPU. This CPU could run in either 32-bit or 64-bit mode, making 64-bit a realistic option for most of us. Intel followed AMD around 2004 with

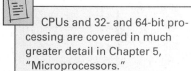

CPUs and 32- and 64-bit processing are covered in much greater detail in Chapter 5, "Microprocessors."

Remember for the exams that 32-bit CPUs can support up to 4 GB of RAM. In concept, 64-bit CPUs can support up to 16 *terabytes* of memory, although you certainly won't find that much memory in the typical PC.

Pentium 4 CPUs also capable of 32-bit or 64-bit processing. Since then, almost every CPU sold by Intel or AMD has the ability to run in either 32-bit or 64-bit mode. Moving from the 32-bit to the 64-bit world is easy, but only if you have a version of Windows to support 64-bit. Microsoft has multiple versions of Windows designed to support 64-bit CPUs.

Windows XP 64-bit Versions

The 64-bit-only version of Windows XP was called Windows XP 64-bit Edition (apparently Microsoft decided not to get cute when naming that one). Given that it only worked on Intel Itanium processors, the chance of your seeing this operating system is pretty small unless you decide to work in a place with powerful server needs. The Windows XP Professional x64 Edition is much more common, as it runs on any AMD or Intel processor that supports both 32 and 64 bits (Figure 4.12).

Windows XP 64-bit versions have had some impact, as they were the first stable Windows versions that truly supported 64-bit processing, but it was the introduction of Microsoft Vista that really started the move into the 64-bit world.

Windows Vista 64-bit Versions

Every one of the earlier listed Vista versions comes in both 32-bit and 64-bit versions. As we move into PCs with more than 4 gigabytes of RAM, it's important to make sure your version of Windows is a 64-bit version (Figure 4.13).

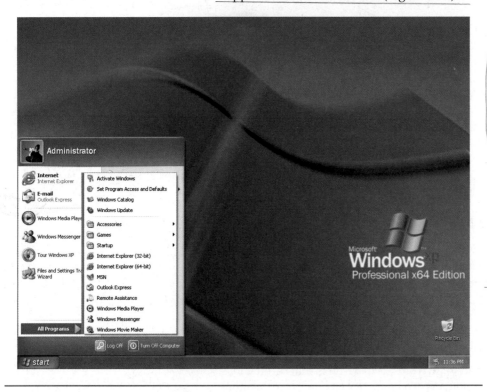

● **Figure 4.12** Windows XP Professional x64 Edition

Windows 7 is not on the CompTIA A+ exams, but you should still know it. Every version of Windows 7 comes in 32-bit and 64-bit on the same install disc.

Transitioning to 64-bit Windows

Techs use the x# terminology to describe a particular computer architecture, implying that there is some compatibility within that architecture. This matters because people need some comfort that the software they purchase will work properly with the computer they have. The transition from 32-bit versions of Windows to 64-bit versions of Windows requires a certain update in terminology.

x86 versus x64   Intel originally used numbers to name its CPUs, such as 8086, 80286, 80386, and so on. To talk about them collectively, the industry replaced the leading numbers with an *x* and kept the numbers that stayed consistent for all the processors, thus **x86** describes the Intel CPU

architecture for PCs. All the 32-bit versions of Windows were designed to run on x86 architecture.

The move to 64-bit CPUs and, equally importantly, to 64-bit versions of Windows required some sort of change in terminology. Microsoft and others picked up the x# terminology and changed it to market 64-bit-only versions of their software, branding the 64-bit software as **x64**. A consumer, therefore, could look at a product such as Windows XP Professional x64 Edition and very quickly know that the software was designed for 64-bit CPUs rather than 32-bit CPUs.

The two x# uses—x86 and x64—don't really compare, but that's okay. Computer people love the letter *X* almost as much as car manufacturers do.

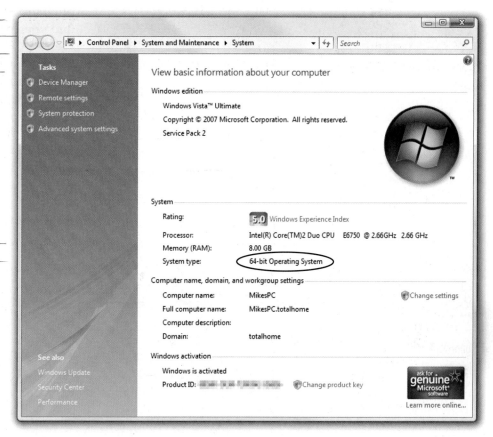

• **Figure 4.13** 64-bit Vista

Software Compatibility Transitions to updated architecture, such as the change from x86 to x64, create concern among users, because they fear that their old programs won't run or will run poorly, or that they'll have problems with compatibility down the road. Techs need to allay those fears by educating users properly. Here's the scoop in a nutshell.

Most of the 64-bit processors run either 32-bit or 64-bit versions of Windows without missing a beat. The 64-bit versions of Windows require a 64-bit CPU; they snicker at 32-bit (or x86) processors and refuse to play. Many companies have produced 64-bit versions of application software that only work with 64-bit Windows running with a 64-bit CPU. Great, right? But what about all those 32-bit applications out there working for a living? It gets interesting.

Windows Vista 64-bit versions support most 32-bit applications, sometimes without any user intervention and sometimes through explicit use of the Windows compatibility mode options. (Just for the record, you sometimes need to use Windows compatibility mode options to run older programs on Windows Vista 32-bit versions, so it's not just a function of 64-bit support for 32-bit apps.) Windows can try to emulate previous versions of Windows if an application balks at loading.

To run a program in an emulated version of Windows, you need to access the primary executable file that, when double-clicked, makes the

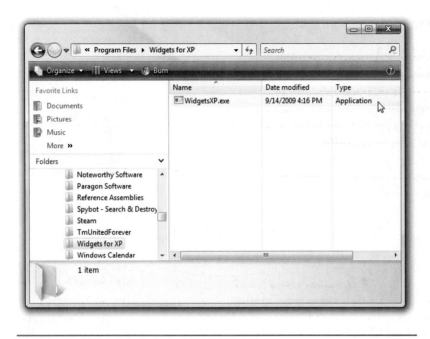

program run. We'll go through where to find your program files in the various versions of Windows later in this chapter, but a quick example should suffice here. A user has a custom program—called "Widgets for XP"—designed to take advantage of particular features in Windows XP Professional with Service Pack 2 installed and it doesn't work in Windows Vista. Open Computer and go to C:\Program Files\Widgets for XP and look for a file with the type listed as Application, such as WidgetsXP.exe (Figure 4.14). Right-click and select Properties.

On the Compatibility tab, you can select the checkbox next to *Run this program in compatibility mode for*: and select the OS of choice (Figure 4.15). In this case, we would select Windows XP (Service Pack 2) to provide optimal compati-bility for the application. Windows saves the configuration change and tries to open the program in compatibility mode each time the program loads.

• **Figure 4.14**   Finding an executable file

• **Figure 4.15**   Compatibility mode options

The Windows Interface

All versions of Windows share certain characteristics, configuration files, and general look and feel. Here's some good news: You'll find the same, or nearly the same, utilities in almost all versions of Windows, and once you master one version—both GUI and command-line interface—you'll pretty much have them all covered. This section covers the essentials: where to find things, how to maneuver, and what common utilities are available. Where versions of Windows differ in concept or detail, I'll point that out along the way. You'll get to the underlying structure of Windows in the subsequent two sections of this chapter. For now, let's look at the common user interface.

User Interface

Windows offers a set of utilities, or **interfaces**, that every user should know about—both how and why to access them. And since every user should know about them, certainly every CompTIA A+ certified tech should as well! Let's take a quick tour of the typical Windows GUI.

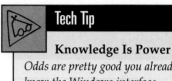

Tech Tip

Knowledge Is Power
Odds are pretty good you already know the Windows interface—but do you know what the CompTIA A+ calls all these parts? Don't skip this section!

Login

Logging into a Windows computer is something we all do but few of us take time to appreciate. Your user name and password define what you can do on your computer. Every version of Windows supports multiple users on a single machine, so the starting point for any tour of the Windows user interface starts with the **login screen**. Figure 4.16 shows the old, ugly, but very functional Windows 2000 login screen.

Microsoft improved the login screen in XP, creating a new type of login called the **Welcome screen** (Figure 4.17). If you're using Windows XP Home or Media Center, this is the only login screen you will see. Windows XP Professional also has the Welcome screen. If you're running a Windows XP Professional system that connects to a Windows domain, however, you go right back to the classic login screen (Figure 4.18).

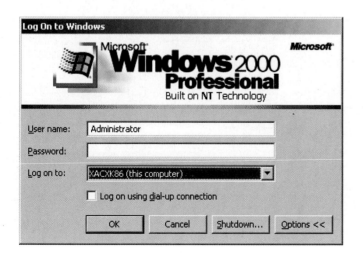

• **Figure 4.16**   Windows 2000 login screen

● **Figure 4.22** Transparency

💡 Vista Home Basic does not support Aero desktop.

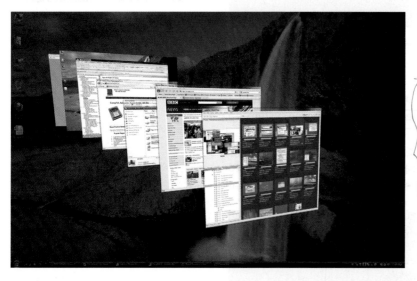

● **Figure 4.23** Flip 3D

Tech Tip

Upgrade Time!

If you can't run on the Aero desktop, you need to upgrade your system to meet the minimum requirements. This usually means a new video card or updated video card drivers. See Chapter 19, "Video," for details.

Microsoft claims makes the user experience more enjoyable and productive. I'm not going to get into an argument on the value of the Aero desktop, but it is an important part of the Windows Vista (and Windows 7) interface. Most of the Aero features are overly technical—even for the CompTIA A+ exams—but the end result is a faster, smoother desktop with two interesting features: transparency and Flip 3D. **Transparency**, as the name implies, gives an adjustable amount of transparency to the edges of your windowed programs, as you can see in Figure 4.22.

Flip 3D enables you to view and select all of your open Windows in a 3-D format as shown in Figure 4.23. It's actually very handy once you start using it.

Flip 3D is fun to use. Press the WINDOWS KEY-TAB key combination to start it. Keep pressing the key combination to cycle through the windows. When the window you want is in the forefront, release the keys, and that window will be the active window on your screen. Try WINDOWS KEY-TAB-SHIFT to scroll through your windows in the opposite direction.

To use the Aero desktop, you must have a video card that supports Aero. We'll save the in-depth discussion for Chapter 19, "Video," but for now here's what Microsoft says your video needs:

- DirectX 9 capability or better
- At least 128 megabytes of video RAM
- Windows Display Driver Model (WDDM) driver
- Pixel Shader version 2.0

Now that you know what you need (again, these will be covered in detail in Chapter 19, "Video"), here's the easy way. When you install Vista, the installer checks your video to determine if it can support Aero. If your video card is capable, Aero is turned on automatically.

On an installed system, press the WINDOWS KEY-TAB combination. If the Flip 3D appears, you have Aero. If it doesn't, Aero is not active.

To turn on Aero, right-click on your desktop and then select the Personalize menu option. Next, select Window Color and Appearance. If you see a screen that looks like Figure 4.24, you already have Aero running. If you see a screen that looks like Figure 4.25, select the Windows Aero color scheme to activate the Aero desktop.

If you're running Aero, note that the Window Color and Appearance screen shown in Figure 4.24 has a slider to adjust the transparency settings and a checkbox to turn transparency off completely.

There are a number of other features that, although not on the CompTIA A+ certification exams, you really should try. The WINDOWS KEY-T combination gives a preview of all minimized windows. ALT-TAB gives a preview of

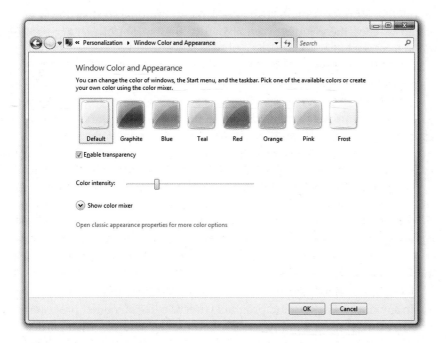

• **Figure 4.24** You've got Aero!

all running windows. Try Aero. It may not be the productivity tool Microsoft promises it to be, but it sure is fun.

Taskbar and Start Menu

The **taskbar** runs along the bottom of all Windows desktops and includes up to four sections (depending on the version of Windows and your configuration). Starting at the left side, these are the Start button, the Quick Launch toolbar, the running programs area, and the notification area. Although the taskbar by default sits at the bottom of the desktop, you can move it to either side or to the top of the screen.

One of the main jobs of the taskbar is to show the **Start button**, probably the most clicked button on all Windows systems. You can find the Start button on the far left end of the taskbar. Figure 4.26 shows the Start

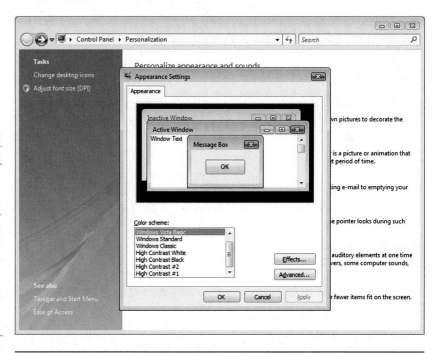

• **Figure 4.25** The lack of transparency and the flat window with no drop shadow show that Aero is not activated.

• **Figure 4.26** Three different Windows Start buttons

buttons for Windows 2000, Windows XP, and Windows Vista (in order). Click the Start button to bring up the Start menu, where you can see the applications installed on the system and start them. Now, move your mouse cursor onto the All Programs (Windows XP) or Programs (all other versions) menu item. When the All Programs/Programs menu appears, move the cursor to the Accessories menu. Locate the Notepad program and click it.

You have a lot of clicking to do in this chapter, so take a moment to reflect on what I call the General Rules of Clicking. With a few exceptions, these rules always apply, and they really help in manipulating the Windows interface to do whatever you need done:

■ Click menu items once to use them.
■ Click icons once to select them.
■ Click icons twice to use them.
■ Right-click anything and select Properties to see its properties.

Microsoft calls the area at the far right of the taskbar the *notification area*, but you might see it referred to on the CompTIA A+ certification exams as the *system tray*.

By default, Windows hides lesser-used menu options, so if you don't see Notepad, click the double down-arrows at the bottom of the Accessories menu to make Notepad appear.

Great! If you opened Notepad properly, you should see something like Figure 4.27, with Notepad displaying an untitled text page. Notice how Notepad shows up on the taskbar at the bottom of your screen. Most running programs appear on the taskbar in this way. Close the Notepad program by clicking on the button with the X in the upper-right corner of the Notepad window. Look again at the taskbar to see that Notepad no longer appears there.

Now look all the way to the right end of the taskbar. This part of the taskbar is known officially as the **notification area**, though many techs and the CompTIA A+ certification exams call it the **system tray**. You will at a minimum see the current time displayed in the system tray, and on most Windows systems you'll also see a number of small icons there. Figure 4.28 shows the system tray on my PC.

These icons show programs running in the background. Most programs run in a window. Background programs function like any other program except they do not use a window, simply because the nature of their particular jobs makes a window unnecessary. Thousands of programs like to run in the system tray: network status, volume controls, battery state (on laptops), and removable device status are just a few examples. What shows up on yours depends on your version of Windows, what hardware you use, and what background programs you have installed. Some of the icons in Figure 4.28, for example, include my antivirus program, a handy notification program for incoming Facebook and Twitter messages, and my UPS program.

Near the left end of the taskbar, next to the Start button, you will find the **Quick Launch toolbar** (Figure 4.29), a handy extra where you can select often-used programs with a single click. On Windows XP systems, the Quick Launch toolbar is not displayed on the taskbar by default, so before you can use this convenient feature, you must right-click the taskbar, select Properties, and check Show Quick Launch. To change the contents of the Quick Launch toolbar, simply drag icons onto or off of it.

The Many Faces of Windows Explorer

Windows Explorer enables you to manipulate files and folders stored on all the drives in or connected to your computer. Microsoft presents the tool in a variety of ways to help you focus quickly on what you want to accomplish. If you want to see the contents of an optical disc, for example, you can open **My Computer** (Windows 2000/XP) or **Computer** (Windows Vista/7) by double-clicking the icon on the desktop or selecting

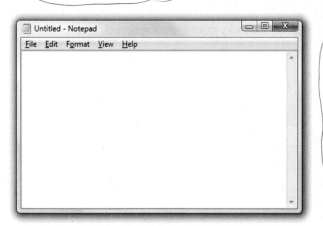

● **Figure 4.27** Notepad application (note the buttons in the upper-right corner)

● **Figure 4.28** System tray showing several icons and the time

● **Figure 4.29** Quick Launch toolbar

the icon from the Start menu to have Windows Explorer open with the drives displayed (Figure 4.30). To display the contents of a drive or folder, double-click it.

Windows Explorer in Windows 2000 has a fairly Spartan interface, whereas Windows XP offers a series of common tasks in a bar along the left side of the screen, as you can see in Figure 4.30. Windows Vista also offers tasks, but the options display in a bar below the location bar, near the top of the window (Figure 4.31).

When you access My Documents (Windows 2000/XP) or Documents (Windows Vista/7) by double-clicking the icon on the desktop or selecting from the Start menu, Windows opens Windows Explorer with your user folders displayed. Because your My Documents/Documents folder is

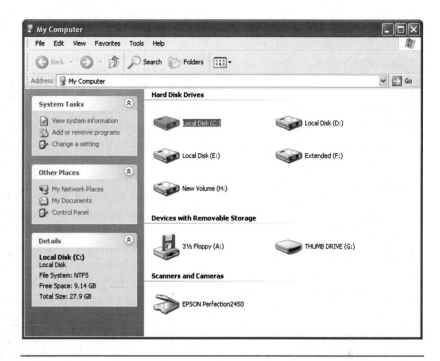

• Figure 4.30   Windows Explorer in Windows XP displaying the drives installed, as well as common tasks on the left

• Figure 4.31   Windows Explorer in Windows Vista displaying the drives installed and showing tasks

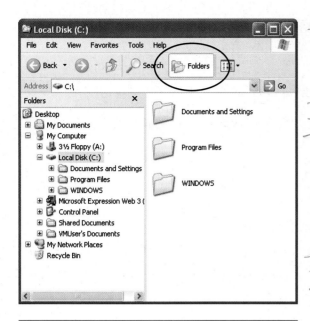

• **Figure 4.32** Windows Explorer in Windows XP with the Folders list toggled on

stored (by default) on the C: hard drive, Windows Explorer shows the contents of that drive, drilled down specifically to your folders.

The fact that one way to open Windows Explorer is to double-click My Computer or Computer, and another way to open Windows Explorer is to double-click My Documents or Documents—and the two methods show different contents initially—leads many users to assume that they have two distinct tools. That's simply not the case. Windows Explorer changes what's displayed to suit specific tasks preset by Microsoft, but it's a single tool that can point to different locations on your computer.

Even better, you can change the look of Windows Explorer by clicking a button. The Folders button in Windows 2000 and Windows XP toggles the **Folders list** on or off on the left (Figure 4.32). The Folders list is a tree menu that enables you to move the focus of Windows Explorer to different folders or drives. The Folders list replaces the common tasks bar in Windows XP. Note that the Folders list is enabled by default in Windows Vista no matter whether you open the tool through Computer or Documents.

In Windows Vista, you can alter the view of Windows Explorer in several ways. On the taskbar, you can click the down arrow next to Views to change the size of the icons, the details displayed, and more. You can turn off the Folders list if desired by clicking the down arrow next to Organize and then selecting Layout from the menu options.

The Folders list view makes copying and moving files and folders from one location to another very easy. The steps differ slightly when you copy to a folder on the same drive versus when you copy to a folder on a different drive, although the first step is the same: Select a folder in the Folders list, and the contents of that folder appear in the main pane on the right.

To move or copy a file from one folder to another folder on the same drive, click and hold a file or folder in the main pane and then drag the cursor over to any folder in the Folders list. A → symbol will appear in Windows Vista and 7, although not in Windows 2000 or XP. Release the mouse button, and you move that file or folder to the new folder. If you want to copy a file or folder rather than move it, press the CTRL key on your keyboard and then click and drag into the desired folder. The → symbol (if any) changes to a +; release the mouse button to copy the file or folder.

To copy or move a file from one folder to another folder on a different drive, click and hold a file or folder in the main pane and then drag the cursor over to any folder in the Folders list, and a + symbol will appear. Release the mouse button, and you'll make a copy of that file or folder in the new folder. If you want to move a file or folder rather than just copy it, press the SHIFT key on your keyboard and then click and drag into the desired folder. The + symbol changes to a → in Windows Vista/7 or just goes away in Windows 2000/XP; release the mouse button to move the file or folder.

Notice the differences in the icons displayed in Windows Explorer? Windows assigns different icons to different types of files, based on their **extensions**, the set of characters at the end of a filename, such as .EXE, .TXT, or .JPG. The oldest extensions, starting from back in the DOS era, are usually

Try This!

Practice Moving and Copying

If the Folders list option is new to you and you haven't done a lot of moving or copying files or folders, try this.

1. Open up My Computer or Computer and double-click on the C: drive.

2. Right-click in a blank spot and select New | Folder from the context menu. This will create a new folder named New Folder by default. The name of the New Folder is highlighted for changing when you first create it. If you click elsewhere, the folder gets the default New Folder name.

3. Select the folder and press F2 or right-click and select Rename from the options. Change the name to something other than New Folder, such as temp, tmp, practice, etc. The rest of this exercise assumes you named the new folder "temp."

4. Click the Folders button if necessary to display the Folders list on the left part of the Windows Explorer screen.

5. In the Folders list, select the temp folder. The contents of that folder should be blank in the main pane.

6. Select any other folder in the Folders list to change the focus of the main pane.

7. Hold down the CTRL key and then click and drag a file or folder from that new folder so that the cursor hovers over the temp folder and you see the + symbol. Release the mouse button and then select the temp folder to see the file or folder you just copied. Note that if you don't hold the CTRL key down, you'll move rather than copy the file.

8. Try this a few more times to increase your comfort level with copying.

9. Now move a file or folder from one folder to the temp folder and then back, verifying that you moved rather than just copied the file. Do *not* do this with any files or folders in the C:\ Windows folder! When you move a file in Vista, you'll see the → appear before you release the mouse button. In Windows 2000/ XP you won't see any symbol at all.

three characters, but current programs may use two-character extensions, such as .JS (JavaScript) or .AU (audio), or even four-character extensions, such as the ubiquitous .HTML for Web pages. In rare cases, a filename might actually have no extension.

As you look at these icons on your own screen, some of you might say, "But I don't see any extensions!" That's because Windows hides them by default. To see the extensions in 2000/XP, select Tools | Folder Options to open the Folder Options dialog box (Figure 4.33). Click the View tab and uncheck *Hide extensions for known file types*. In Vista, click on Organize | Folder and Search Options | View tab to see the same dialog box.

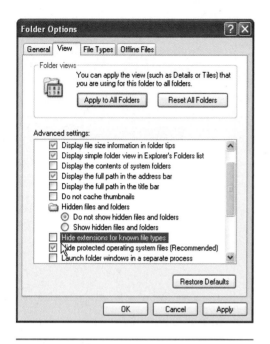

• **Figure 4.33**   Folder Options dialog box

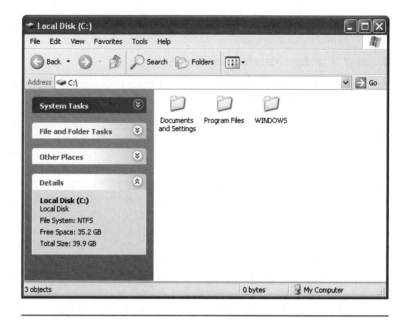

• **Figure 4.34**   Default My Computer view where many things are hidden

There are two other very handy settings under the View tab, but to see the results well, you need to be in the C: drive of My Computer, as shown in Figure 4.34.

Go back into the View tab under Folder Options, click the *Show hidden files and folders* radio button, and then uncheck *Hide protected operating system files*. Click the *Apply to Folders* button in Windows Vista, the *Apply to All Folders* button in Windows XP, or the Apply button in Windows 2000. Your C: drive should look like Figure 4.35 (it shows the Windows XP version) when you are finished. As before, when you return to examining the folder contents, you will see the file extensions, and possibly some previously hidden files.

Now that those files are visible, you have the awesome responsibility of keeping them safe. In general, the less you handle your vital system files, the better. You'll learn some ways to do useful things with files that were previously hidden, but unless you really know what you're doing, it's best to leave them alone. Before you turn a PC over to someone who isn't a trained PC tech, you'll probably want to hide those system files again.

Microsoft has tried to help users organize their files and folders through various user folders and subfolders that you access through Windows Explorer. The different operating systems offer different choices, so let's look at My Documents and the User's Files.

• **Figure 4.35**   My Computer displaying hidden files and folders

My Documents, My [Whatever]   All versions of Windows provide a special folder structure for each user account so users have their own places to store personal data. This folder grouping is called **My Documents** in Windows 2000 and XP. Many Windows programs take advantage of My Documents and by default store their files in the folder or in a subfolder.

Windows XP installations do not show My Documents on the desktop by default. On Windows XP, you can access it readily through the Start menu, or you can add it to your desktop. Right-click the desktop and select Properties to open the Display Properties dialog box. Select the Desktop tab, and then click on the Customize Desktop button to open the Desktop Items dialog box (Figure 4.36). On the General tab, select the checkbox next to My Documents, My Computer, or both, and then click OK to close the dialog box and make any selected icons appear on the desktop.

Windows XP adds a number of subfolders to My Documents: My Pictures (which offers filmstrip and thumbnail views of pictures you store there), My Music (which will fire up Media Player to play any file), My Videos (which, again, starts Media Player), and more. Figure 4.37 shows My Pictures, using the thumbnail view. Many applications have since jumped on the bandwagon and added their own My [*Whatever*] folders in My Documents. Before I retired my Windows XP machine, for example, I had My eBooks, My Web Sites, My Received Files, My Virtual Machines…My Goodness!

User's Files   Windows Vista takes the equivalent of My Documents to a whole new level with the **User's Files** option. (Although a Documents folder

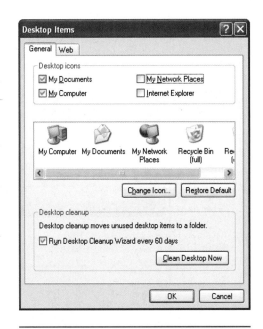

• **Figure 4.36**   XP Desktop Items dialog box

As with most tools in Windows, Microsoft gives you more than one way to accomplish tasks. In XP and Vista, try right-clicking the Start menu icon, selecting Properties, and choosing the Classic Start Menu radio button.

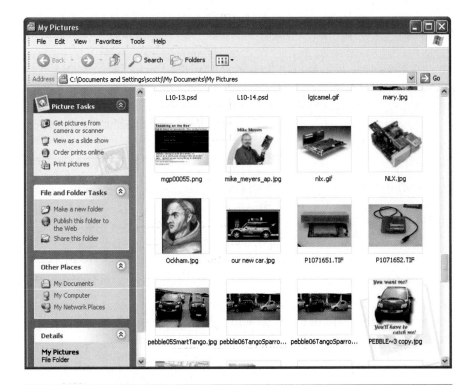

• **Figure 4.37**   My Pictures subfolder in My Documents

is available, it's designed literally for documents, such as text files.) Click on the Start menu and you'll see a folder option with the user name of the account that's currently logged into the computer. With that option, not only do you get all of the folders you get in Windows 2000/XP, but Vista also adds a number of other folders as well as interesting but important data such as your Internet Explorer favorites and copies of recent searches.

Just as with Windows XP, the user's folder does not show on the desktop by default. To see this folder, right-click on the desktop, select Personalize, and then click *Change desktop icons* on the left of the Personalization window. You'll see a Desktop Icon Setting dialog box where you can select the User's File option to display the personal files of the logged-in user account. Figure 4.38 shows the User's Files folder for my editor, with the Desktop Icon Settings dialog box in the background.

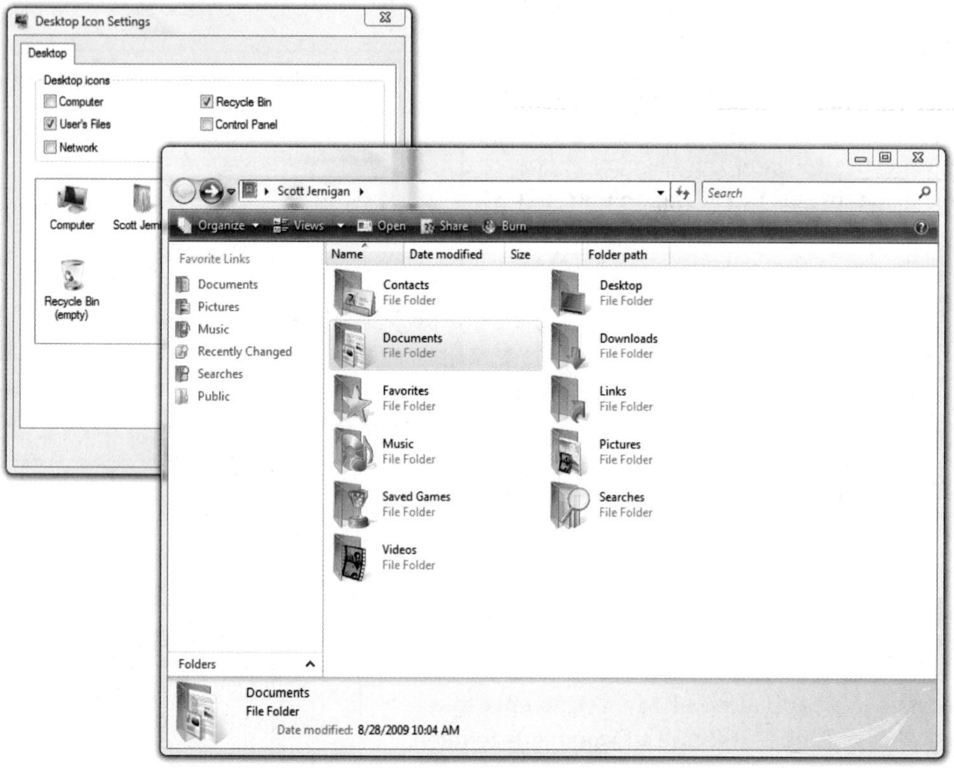

• **Figure 4.38** Typical user accounts folder in Windows Vista

No matter what your version of Windows decides to call it, My Documents/User's Files is an incredibly critical part of your computer's directory structure. Not only does this store your most personal (and important) documents, it also stores most of the personalization settings for each user. You'll see more of My Documents/User's Files in the next section.

✓ **Cross Check**

The Computing Process

While you're reading about the various interface features of Windows, now would be a good time to review the section "How the PC Works" in Chapter 3, "The Visible PC," and put things in context. What are the four functions of computing? With which function does the operating system interact? Why is that a trick question?

Recycle Bin

In Windows, a file is not erased when you delete it. Windows adds a level of protection in the form of a special folder called the **Recycle Bin**. When you delete a file in Windows, the file moves into the Recycle Bin. It stays there until you empty the Recycle Bin or restore the file, or until the Recycle Bin reaches a preset size and starts erasing its oldest contents.

To access the Recycle Bin's properties, right-click the icon and select Properties. The Recycle Bin's properties look different in different versions

of Windows, but they all work basically the same. Figure 4.39 shows the properties of a typical Windows XP Recycle Bin. Note that you set the amount of drive space to use for the Recycle Bin, 10 percent being the default amount. If a hard drive starts to run low on space, this is one of the first places to check.

My Network Places/Network

Systems tied to a network, either via a network cable or by a modem, have a folder called **My Network Places** in XP or simply **Network** in Vista (see Figure 4.40). This shows all the current network connections available to you. You'll learn about My Network Places in Chapter 23, "Local Area Networking."

Windows Sidebar

Windows Vista comes with a UI feature called the **Windows Sidebar**, a tool that sits on the desktop and enables small helper applications—called Microsoft Gadgets—to run. You can display a clock, for example, or a dynamic weather update. Vista comes with a handful of Gadgets, but developers have gone crazy with them, enabling you to add all sorts of useful tools, such as the Twitter feed and World of Warcraft search and realm status Gadgets in Figure 4.41.

Hot Keys

In Windows, you can use key combinations to go directly to various programs and places. Here's a reasonably extensive list of general-purpose commands

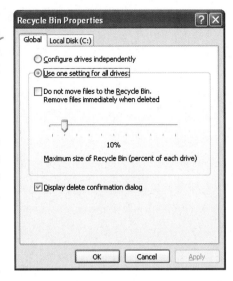

• **Figure 4.39** Windows XP Recycle Bin Properties

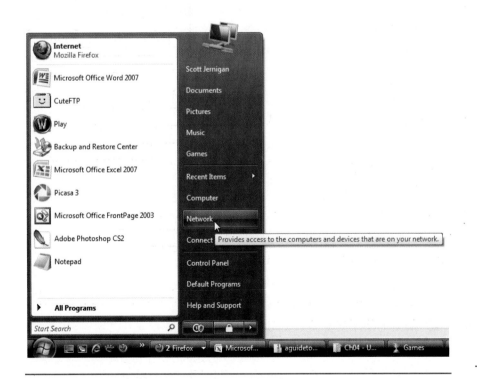

• **Figure 4.40** Network in Windows Vista

• **Figure 4.41** Windows Sidebar in action

for Windows. Be aware that some applications may change the use of these commands.

Function Keys

- **F1** Help
- **F2** Rename
- **F3** Search menu
- **F5** Refresh the current window
- **F6** Move among selections in current windows

Popular Hot Keys

- **CTRL-ESC** Open Start menu
- **ALT-TAB** Switch between open programs
- **ALT-F4** Quit program
- **CTRL-Z** Undo the last command
- **CTRL-A** Select all the items in the current window
- **SHIFT-DELETE** Delete item permanently
- **SHIFT-F10** Open a shortcut menu for the selected item (this is the same as right-clicking an object)
- **SHIFT** Bypass the automatic-run feature for optical media (by pressing and holding down the SHIFT key while you insert optical media)
- **ALT-SPACE** Display the main window's System menu (from this menu you can restore, move, resize, minimize, maximize, or close the window)
- **ALT-ENTER** Open the properties for the selected object

Working with Text

- **CTRL-C** Copy
- **CTRL-X** Cut
- **CTRL-V** Paste
- **CTRL-Z** Undo

I've covered only the most basic parts of the Windows desktop in this chapter. The typical Windows desktop includes many other parts, but for techs and for the CompTIA A+ certification exams, what you've learned here about the desktop is more than enough.

Windows Key Shortcuts

These shortcuts use the special Windows key:

- **WINDOWS KEY** Start menu
- **WINDOWS KEY-D** Show desktop
- **WINDOWS KEY-E** Windows Explorer
- **WINDOWS KEY-L** Locks the computer
- **WINDOWS KEY-TAB** Cycle through taskbar buttons (or Flip 3D with Windows Aero in Vista)
- **WINDOWS KEY-BREAK** Open the System Properties dialog box

Practical Application

■ Operating System Folders

The modern versions of Windows organize essential files and folders in a relatively similar fashion. All have a primary system folder for storing most Windows internal tools and files. All have a set of folders for programs and user files. All use a special grouping of files called the Registry to keep track of all the hardware loaded and the drivers that enable you to use that hardware. Finally, every version has a RAM cache file, enabling more robust access to programs and utilities. Yet once you start to get into details, you'll find some very large differences. It's very important for you to know in some detail the location and function of many common folders and their contents.

> The CompTIA A+ exams love to ask detailed questions about the locations of certain folders. Make sure you know this section!

System Folder

SystemRoot is the tech name given to the folder in which Windows has been installed. SystemRoot by default is C:\WINNT in Windows 2000, while Windows XP and Vista's SystemRoot defaults to C:\WINDOWS. Be warned, these are defaults but not always the case; during the installation process, you can change where Windows is installed.

It's handy to know about SystemRoot. You'll find it cropping up in many other tech publications, and you can specify it when adjusting certain Windows settings to make sure they work under all circumstances. When used as part of a Windows configuration setting, add percent signs (%) to the beginning and end like so: %SystemRoot%.

If you don't know where Windows is installed on a particular system, here's a handy trick. Get to a command prompt, type **cd %systemroot%**, and press ENTER. The prompt changes to the directory in which the Windows OS files are stored. Slick! See Chapter 15, "Working with the Command-Line Interface," for details on how to use the command prompt in Windows.

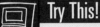 **Try This!**

Getting to a Command Prompt

Each version of Windows gives you several ways to access a command prompt, so depending on your version, try the steps below.

1. In Windows 2000 or Windows XP, go to Start | Run to open the Run dialog box.
2. Type **cmd** and press ENTER to open a command prompt.
3. Alternatively, go to Start | All Programs | Accessories | System Tools and select Command Prompt.

1. In Windows Vista, go to Start and type **cmd** into the Start Search text area. Press ENTER to open a command line.
2. Alternatively, go to Start | All Programs | Accessories and select Command Prompt.

The system folder contains many subfolders, too numerous to mention here, but CompTIA wants you to know the names of a number of these subfolders as well as what goes in them. Let's run through the subfolders you should recognize and define (these folders are in all versions of Windows):

■ **%SystemRoot%\FONTS** All of the fonts installed in Windows live here.

- **%SystemRoot%\Offline Files** When you tell your Web browser to save Web pages for offline viewing, they are stored in this folder. This is another folder that Windows automatically deletes if it needs the space.

- **%SystemRoot%\SYSTEM32** This is the *real* Windows! All of the most critical programs that make Windows run are stored here.

- **%SystemRoot%\Temp** Anytime Windows or an application running on Windows needs to create temporary files, they are placed here. Windows deletes these files automatically as needed, so never place an important file in this folder.

Program and Personal Document Folders

Windows has a number of important folders that help organize your programs and documents. They sit in the root directory at the same level as the system folder, and of course they have variations in name depending on the version of Windows. We'll assume that your computer is using a C: drive—a pretty safe assumption, although there actually is a way to install all of Windows on a second hard-drive partition.

C:\Program Files (All Versions)

By default, most programs install some or all of their essential files into a subfolder of the Program Files folder. If you installed a program, it should have its own folder in here. Individual companies decide how to label their subfolders. Installing Photoshop made by Adobe, for example, creates the Adobe subfolder and then an Adobe Photoshop subfolder within it. Installing Silverlight from Microsoft, on the other hand, only creates a Microsoft Silverlight folder with the program files within it. (Some programmers choose to create a folder at the root of the C: drive, bypassing Program Files altogether, but that's becoming increasingly rare.)

C:\Program Files (x86)

The 64-bit versions of Windows Vista and Windows 7 create two directory structures for program files. The 64-bit applications go into the C:\Program Files folder, whereas the 32-bit applications go into the C:\Program Files (x86) folder. The separation makes it easy to find the proper version of whatever application you seek.

Personal Documents

As you might expect, given the differences among the desktop names for personal document locations outlined earlier in the chapter, the personal folders for Windows 2000/XP and Windows Vista differ in location and name. Windows 2000 and Windows XP place personal folders in the Documents and Settings folder, whereas Windows Vista uses the Users folder. From there, they differ even more.

C:\Documents and Settings (2000 and XP) All of the personal settings for each user are stored here. All users have their own subfolders in Documents and Settings. In each user folder, you'll find another level of folders with

familiar names such as Desktop, My Documents, and Start Menu. These folders hold the actual contents of these items. Let's dive through these to see the ones you need to know for the CompTIA A+ exams.

- **\Documents and Settings\Default User (hidden)** All of the default settings for a user. For example, if the user doesn't specify a screensaver to use, Windows refers to this folder's settings to determine what screensaver it should use if needed.

- **\Documents and Settings\All Users** You can make settings for anyone who uses the computer. This is especially handy for applications: some applications are installed so all users may use them and some might be restricted to certain users. This folder stores information for any setting or application that's defined for all users on the PC.

- **\Documents and Settings\ Shared Documents (XP Only)** If you're using XP's Simple File Sharing, this is the only folder on the computer that's shared.

- **\Documents and Settings\ <User Name>** This folder stores all settings defined for a particular user (Figure 4.42).

Opening any user's folder reveals a number of even lower folders. Each of these stores very specific information about the user.

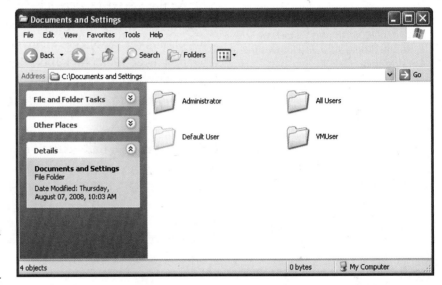

• **Figure 4.42** Contents of a typical \Documents and Settings folder in XP

- **\Documents and Settings\<User Name>\Desktop** This folder stores the files on the user's desktop. If you delete this folder, you delete all the files placed on the desktop.

- **\Documents and Settings\<User Name>\<User name's> Documents** This is the My Documents folder for that user.

- **\Documents and Settings\<User Name>\Application Data (hidden)** This folder stores information and settings used by various programs that the user has installed.

- **\Documents and Settings\<User Name>\Start Menu** This folder stores any customizations the user made to the Start menu.

> When you're looking at your own account folders, you'll see My Documents rather than <User name's> Documents in the \Documents and Settings\ <User Name> folder.

C:\Users (Vista) Vista dumps the old Documents and Settings for the Users folder. Functionally similar to Documents and Settings, there are a number of subfolders here that you need to know to pass the CompTIA A+ exams.

Vista and 7 make a special hidden folder called "Default User" that points to the User folder to support older applications.

Let's repeat the process, locating the same functions in their new locations.

- **\Users\Default (hidden)** and **\Users\All Users** All of these folders retain the same functions as in 2000/XP.
- **\Users\<User Name>** The big change takes place under each of the \Users\<User Name> folders. This folder still stores all settings defined for a particular user; however, this folder in Vista/7 is much more detailed than in 2000/XP (Figure 4.43). Luckily, you only need to know a few folders for the exams.
- **\Users\<User Name>\Desktop** Same as 2000/XP.
- **\Users\<User Name>\Documents** This is the Documents folder for that user. Compare the name of this folder to the one in Windows 2000/XP and know which is which.
- **\Users\<User Name>\Downloads** Microsoft's preferred download folder for applications to use. Most applications do use this folder but some do not.
- **\Users\<User Name>\Start Menu** Same as 2000/XP.

Be very careful here. Some of the folder name differences between 2000/XP and Vista/7 are subtle. Make sure you know the difference.

Any good tech knows the name and function of all the folders just listed. As a tech, you will find yourself manually drilling into these folders for a number of reasons. Users rarely go directly into any of these folders with Windows Explorer. That's a good thing since, as a technician, you need to appreciate how dangerous it is for them to do so. Imagine a user going into a \Users\<User Name>\Desktop folder and wiping out someone's desktop folders. Luckily, Windows protects these folders by using NTFS permissions, making it very difficult for users to destroy anything other than their own work.

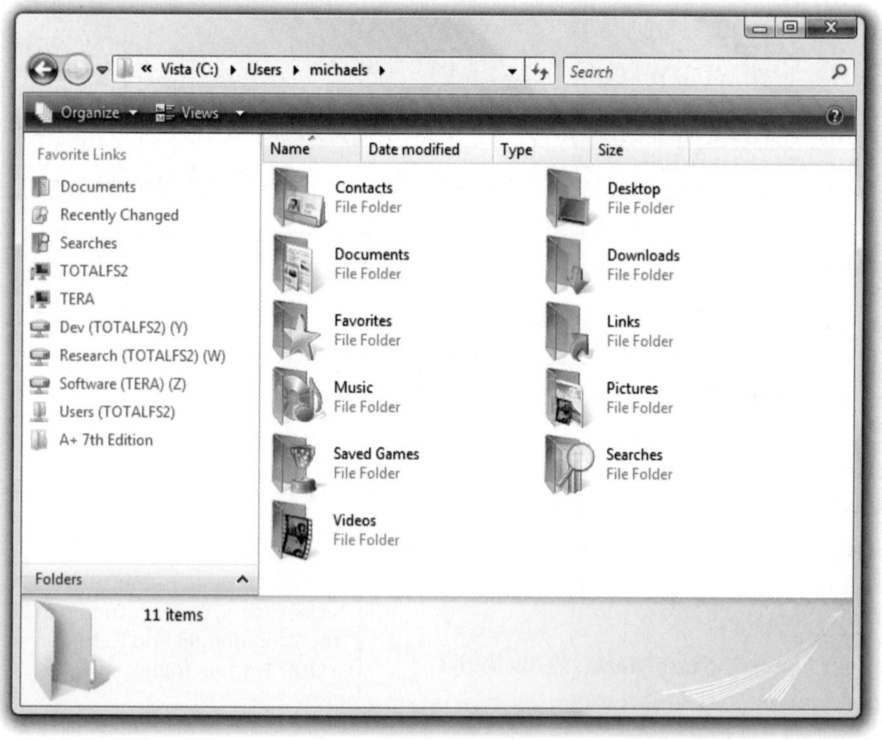

• **Figure 4.43** Contents of a typical \Users\<User Name>\ folder in Vista

Registry

The **Registry** is a huge database that stores everything about your PC, including information on all of the hardware in the PC, network information, user preferences, file types, and virtually anything else you might run into with Windows. Almost any form of configuration you do to a Windows system involves editing the Registry. Every version of Windows stores the numerous Registry files (called *hives*) in the \%SystemRoot%\System32\

config folder. Fortunately, you rarely have to access these massive files directly. Instead, you can use a set of relatively tech-friendly applications to edit the Registry.

The CompTIA A+ certification exams do not expect you to memorize every aspect of the Windows Registry. You should, however, understand the basic components of the Registry, know how to edit the Registry manually, and know the best way to locate a particular setting.

Accessing the Registry

Before you look in the Registry, let's look at how you access the Registry directly by using a Registry editor. Once you know that, you can open the Registry on your machine and compare what you see to the examples in this chapter.

Windows 2000 comes with two Registry editors: REGEDT32.EXE, shown in Figure 4.44, and the much older REGEDIT.EXE (Figure 4.45). You start either of these programs by going to a command prompt and typing its filename.

The reason for having two different Registry editors is long and boring, and explaining it would require a very dull 15-minute monologue (preferably with an angelic chorus singing in the background) about how the Registry worked in Windows 9x and Windows NT. Suffice it to say that in Windows 2000, only REGEDT32 is safe to use for actual editing, but you can use the older REGEDIT to perform searches, because REGEDT32's search capabilities are not very good.

Starting with Windows XP, Microsoft eliminated the entire two-Registry-editor nonsense by creating a new REGEDT32 that includes strong search functions. No longer are there two separate programs, but interestingly, entering either REGEDIT or REGEDT32 at a command prompt brings up the same program, so feel free to use either program name. We can also dispense with calling the Registry Editor by its filename and use its proper title.

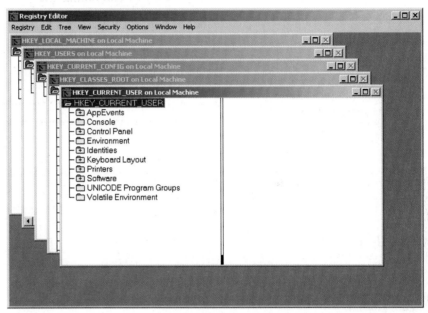

● **Figure 4.44**   REGEDT32 in Windows 2000

● **Figure 4.45**   REGEDIT in Windows 2000

Registry Components

The Registry is organized in a tree structure similar to the folders in the PC. Once you open the Registry Editor in Windows, you will see five main subgroups, or **root keys**:

- HKEY_CLASSES_ROOT
- HKEY_CURRENT_USER
- HKEY_USERS
- HKEY_LOCAL_MACHINE
- HKEY_CURRENT_CONFIG

When writing about keys and values, I'll use the expression *key = value*.

Try opening one of these root keys by clicking on the plus sign to its left; note that more subkeys are listed underneath. A subkey also has other subkeys, or *values*. Figure 4.46 shows an example of a subkey with some values. Notice that the Registry Editor shows keys on the left and values on the right, just as Windows Explorer shows directories on the left and files on the right.

The secret to understanding the Registry is to understand the function of the five root keys first. Each of these root keys has a specific function, so let's take a look at them individually.

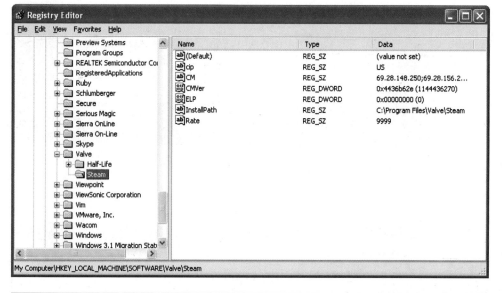

• **Figure 4.46**   Typical Registry keys and values

HKEY_CLASSES_ROOT

This root key defines the standard *class objects* used by Windows. A class object is a named group of functions that define what you can do with the object it represents. Pretty much everything that has to do with files on the system is defined by a class object.

For example, the Registry uses two class objects to define the popular MP3 sound file. If you search the Registry for the .MP3 file extension, you will find the first class object, which associates the .MP3 file extension with the name "Winamp.File" on this computer (Figure 4.47).

Ah, but what are the properties of Winamp.File? That's what the HKEY_CLASSES_ROOT root key is designed to handle. Search this section again for "Winamp.File" (or whatever it said in the value for your MP3 file) and look for a subkey called "open." This variable determines the **file association** (Figure 4.48), which is the Windows term for what program to use to open a particular type of file.

This subkey tells the system everything it needs to know about a particular software item, from which program to use to open a file, to the type of

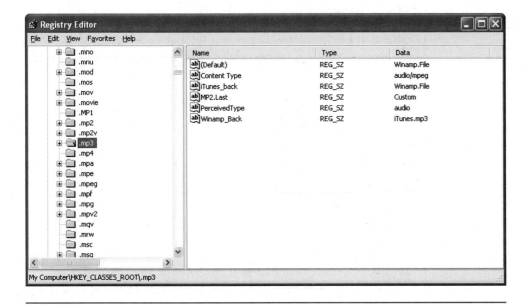

• **Figure 4.47** Association of .MP3 with Winamp

icon used to show the file, to what to show when you right-click on that file type. Although it is possible to change most of these settings in the Registry Editor, the normal way is to choose more user-friendly methods. In Windows XP, for example, you can right-click on a file and select Properties, and then click the Change button on the General tab to open the Open With dialog box (Figure 4.49). From there you can browse to select the program you want to use.

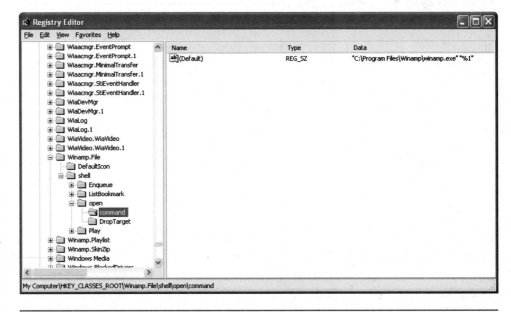

• **Figure 4.48** Winamp file settings

HKEY_CURRENT_USER and HKEY_USERS

Windows is designed to support more than one user on the same PC, storing personalized information such as desktop colors, screensavers, and the contents of the desktop for every user that has an account on the system. HKEY_CURRENT_USER stores the current user settings, and HKEY_USERS stores all of the personalized information for all users on a PC. While you certainly can change items such as the screensaver here, the better way is to right-click on the desktop and select Properties.

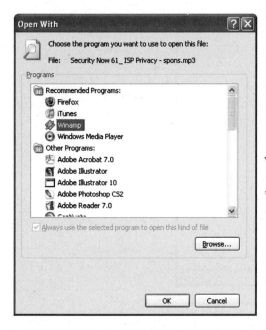

● **Figure 4.49**   Changing the file association the easy way

The default and recommended page-file size is 1.5 times the amount of installed RAM on your computer.

HKEY_LOCAL_MACHINE

This root key contains all the data for a system's non-user-specific configurations. This encompasses every device and every program in your PC. For example, Figure 4.50 shows the description of a DVD disc drive.

HKEY_CURRENT_CONFIG

If the values in HKEY_LOCAL_MACHINE have more than one option, such as two different monitors, this root key defines which one is currently being used. Because most people have only one type of monitor and similar equipment, this area is almost never touched.

Page File

Windows uses a portion of the hard drive as an extension of system RAM, through what's called a *RAM cache*. A RAM cache is a block of cylinders on a hard drive set aside as what's called a **page file**, *swap file*, or *virtual memory*. When the PC starts running out of real RAM because you've loaded too many programs, the system swaps programs from RAM to the page file, opening more space for programs currently active. All versions of Windows use a page file, so here's how one works.

Let's assume you have a PC with 4 GB of RAM. Figure 4.51 shows the system RAM as a thermometer with gradients from 0 to 4 GB. As programs load, they take up RAM, and as more and more programs are loaded (labeled A, B, and C in the figure), more RAM is used.

At a certain point, you won't have enough RAM to run any more programs (Figure 4.52). Sure, you could close one or more programs to make room for yet another one, but you can't keep all of the programs running simultaneously. This is where virtual memory comes into play.

● **Figure 4.50**   Registry information for a DVD drive

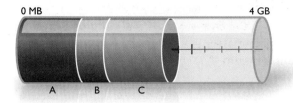

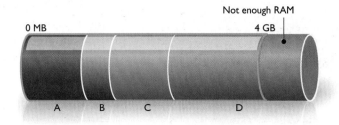

• **Figure 4.51**   A RAM thermometer showing that more
programs take more RAM

• **Figure 4.52**   Not enough RAM to load program D

Windows' virtual memory starts by creating a page file that resides somewhere on your hard drive. The page file works like a temporary storage box. Windows removes running programs temporarily from RAM into the page file so other programs can load and run. If you have enough RAM to run all your programs, Windows does not need to use the page file—Windows brings the page file into play only when insufficient RAM is available to run all open programs.

To load, Program D needs a certain amount of free RAM. Clearly, this requires that unloading some other program (or programs) from RAM without actually closing any programs. Windows looks at all running programs—in this case A, B, and C—and decides which program is the least used. That program is then cut out of or swapped from RAM and copied into the page file. In this case, Windows has chosen Program B (Figure 4.53). Unloading Program B from RAM provides enough RAM to load Program D (Figure 4.54).

It is important to understand that none of this activity is visible on the screen. Program B's window is still visible, along with those of all the other running programs. Nothing tells the user that Program B is no longer in RAM (Figure 4.55).

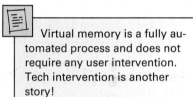

Virtual memory is a fully automated process and does not require any user intervention. Tech intervention is another story!

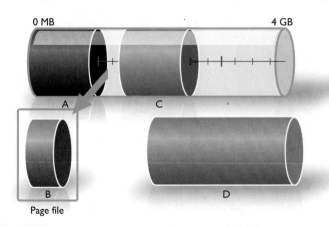

• **Figure 4.53**   Program B being unloaded from memory

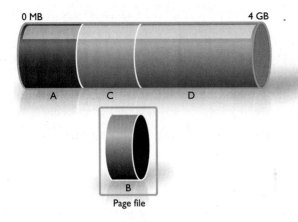

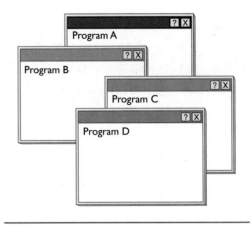

• **Figure 4.55** You can't tell whether a program is swapped or not.

• **Figure 4.54** Program B stored in the page file—room is made for Program D

If you have a second hard drive installed in your PC, you can often get a nice performance boost by moving your page file from the C: drive (the default) to the second drive. To move your page file in all versions of Windows, go to the Control Panel | System applet and select the Advanced tab in 2000/XP or Advanced system settings menu in Vista/7. This opens the System Properties dialog box. In the Performance section, click the Settings button to open the Performance Options dialog box. Select the Advanced tab, and then click the Change button in the Virtual Memory section. Select a drive from the list and give it a size or range, and you're ready to go.

Just don't turn virtual memory off completely. Although Windows can run without virtual memory, you will definitely take a performance hit.

So what happens if you click on Program B's window to bring it to the front? The program can't actually run from the page file; it must be loaded back into RAM. First, Windows decides which program must be removed from RAM, and this time Windows chooses Program C (Figure 4.56). Then it loads Program B into RAM (Figure 4.57).

Swapping programs to and from the page file and RAM takes time. Although no visual clues suggest that a swap is taking place, the machine slows down quite noticeably as Windows performs the swaps. The alternative (Figure 4.58) is far less acceptable. Page files are a crucial aspect of Windows operation.

Windows handles page files automatically, but occasionally you'll run into problems and need to change the size of the page file or delete it and let Windows re-create it automatically. The page file is PAGEFILE.SYS. You can often find it in the root directory of the C: drive, but again, that can be changed. Wherever it is, the page file is a hidden system file, which means in practice that you'll have to play with your folder-viewing options to see it.

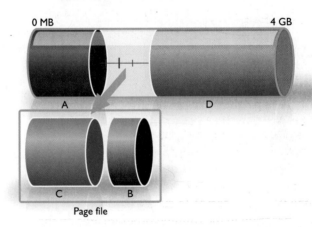

• **Figure 4.56** Program C is swapped to the page file.

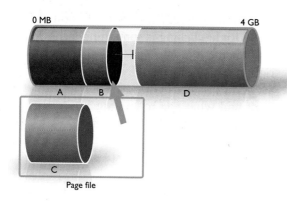

• **Figure 4.58**   The alternative to page files

• **Figure 4.57**   Program B is swapped back into RAM.

■ Tech Utilities

Windows offers a huge number of utilities that enable techs to configure the OS, optimize and tweak settings, install hardware, and more. The trick is to know where to go to find them. This section shows the six most common locations in Windows where you can access utilities: right-click, Control Panel, System Tools, command line, Administrative Tools, and the Microsoft Management Console. Note that these are locations for tools, not tools themselves, and you can access many tools from more than one of these locations. However, you'll see some of the utilities in many of these locations. Stay sharp in this section, as you'll need to access utilities to understand the inner workings of Windows in the next section.

Right-Click

Windows, being a graphical user interface OS, covers your monitor with windows, menus, icons, file lists—all kinds of pretty things you click on to do work. Any single thing you see on your desktop is called an *object*. If you want to open any object in Windows, you double-click on it. If you want to change something about an object, you right-click on it.

Right-clicking on an object brings up a small menu called the **context menu**, and it works on everything in Windows. In fact, try to place your mouse somewhere in Windows where right-clicking does *not* bring up a menu (there are a few places, but they're not easy to find). What you see on the little menu when you right-click varies dramatically depending on the item you decide to right-click. If you right-click a running program in the running program area on the taskbar, you'll see items that relate to a window, such as move, resize, and so on (Figure 4.59). If you right-click on your desktop, you get options for changing the appearance

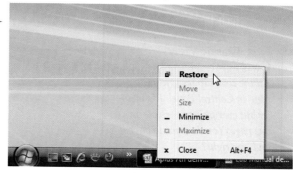

• **Figure 4.59**   Right-clicking on a program

• **Figure 4.65**   User Accounts window of the User Accounts applet

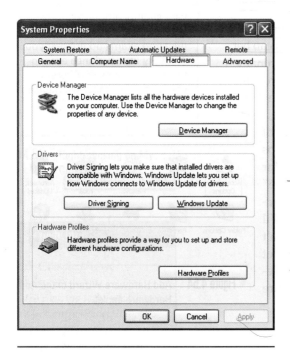

• **Figure 4.66**   Windows XP System applet with the Hardware tab selected

Device Manager many more times during the course of this book and your career as a PC tech.

There are many ways to get to the Device Manager—make sure you know all of them! The first way is to open the Control Panel and double-click the System applet icon. This brings up the System Properties dialog box. In 2000/XP, you access the Device Manager by selecting the Hardware tab and then clicking the Device Manager button. Figure 4.66 shows the Hardware tab of the System Properties dialog box in Windows XP. In Vista/7, the System dialog box has a direct connection to Device Manager (Figure 4.67).

You can also get to the System Properties dialog box in all versions of Windows by right-clicking My Computer/Computer and selecting Properties. From there, the path to the Device Manager is the same as when you access this dialog box from the Control Panel.

The second (and more streamlined) method is to right-click My Computer/Computer and select Manage. This opens a window called Computer Management, where you'll see Device Manager listed on the left side of the screen, under System Tools. Just click on Device Manager and it opens. You can also access Computer Management by opening the Administrative Tools applet in the Control Panel and then selecting Computer Management (Figure 4.68).

Holding down the WINDOWS key and pressing PAUSE is yet another way to get to the System Properties dialog box. Keyboard shortcuts are cool!

• **Figure 4.67** Windows Vista System applet with the Device Manager menu option circled

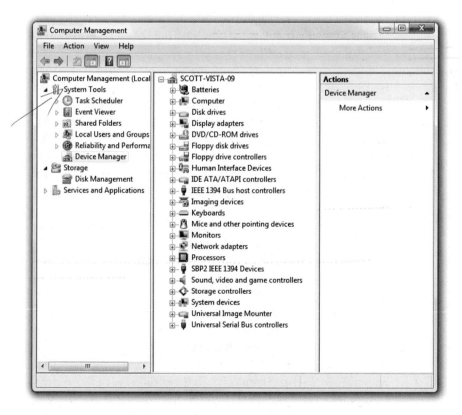

• **Figure 4.68** Device Manager in Computer Management

Why are there so many ways to open Device Manager? Well, remember that we're only looking at locations in Windows from which to open utilities, not at the actual utilities themselves. Microsoft wants you to get to the tools you need when you need them, and it's better to have multiple paths to a utility rather than just one.

The Device Manager displays every device that Windows recognizes, organized in special groups called *types*. All devices of the same type are grouped under the same type heading. To see the devices of a particular type, you must open that type's group. Figure 4.68 shows a Windows Vista Device Manager screen with all installed devices in good order—which makes us techs happy. If Windows detects a problem, the device has a red *X* or a black exclamation point on a yellow field, as in the case of the device in Figure 4.69.

A red *X* in Windows 2000 or XP means Windows (or you) disabled the device—right-click on the device to enable it. The tough one is the black exclamation point. If you see this, right-click on the device and select Properties. Read the error code in the Device Status pane, and then look up Microsoft Knowledge Base article 310123 to see what to do. There are around 40 different errors—nobody bothers to memorize them! (The knowledge base article is for Windows XP, but these error codes are the same in all versions of Windows.)

Vista and Windows 7 use the same icons and add one very handy one. If a device is working but you manually disable it, you get a down-arrow (Figure 4.70). Just as in previous versions, right-click the down-arrow and select Properties. You'll see a nice dialog box explaining the issue (Figure 4.71).

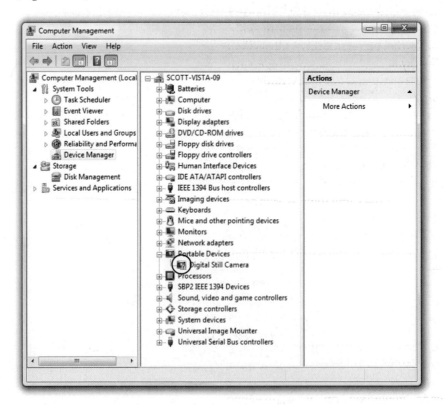

• **Figure 4.69** Problem device

The Device Manager isn't just for dealing with problems. It also enables you to update drivers with a simple click of the mouse (assuming you have a replacement driver on your computer). Right-click a device and select Update Driver from the menu to get the process started. Figure 4.72 shows the options in Windows Vista.

Make sure you can get to Device Manager! You will come back to it again and again in subsequent chapters, because it is the first tool you should access when you have a hardware problem.

System Tools

The Start menu offers a variety of tech utilities collected in one place: select Start | Programs | Accessories | System Tools. In the **System Tools** menu, you'll find commonly accessed tools such as System Information and Disk Defragmenter (Figure 4.73).

Many techs overlook memorizing how to find the appropriate Windows tool to diagnose problems, but nothing hurts your credibility with a client like fumbling around, clicking a variety of menus and applets, while mumbling, "I know it's around here somewhere." The CompTIA A+ certification exams therefore test you on a variety of paths to appropriate tools. One of those paths is Start | Programs | Accessories | System Tools. Windows XP has all the same tools as Windows 2000, plus a few more. Vista adds a few beyond XP. I'll say what version of Windows has the particular system tool.

Activate Windows (XP, Vista)

Windows XP unveiled a copy-protection scheme called **activation**. Activation is a process where your computer sends Microsoft a unique code generated on your machine based on the Install CD/DVD's

● **Figure 4.70** Hmm…could be a problem.

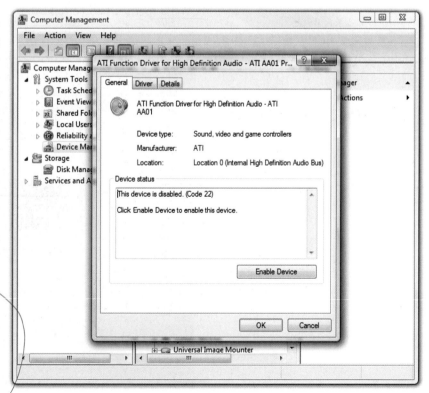

● **Figure 4.71** Problem device properties

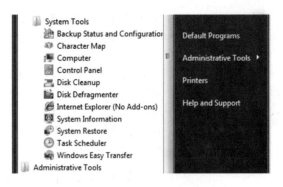

• **Figure 4.73**   System Tools menu options

• **Figure 4.72**   Selecting Update Driver Software in the Windows Vista Device Manager

Once you've activated Windows, this applet goes away.

product key and a number of hardware features, such as the amount of RAM, the CPU processor model, and other ones and zeros in your PC. Normally, activation is done at install time, but if you choose not to activate at install or if you make "substantial" changes to the hardware, you'll need to use the Activate Windows utility (Figure 4.74). With the Activate Windows utility, you can activate over the Internet or over the telephone.

Backup (2000, XP)

The Backup utility enables you to back up selected files and folders to removable media such as tape drives. Backing up is an important function

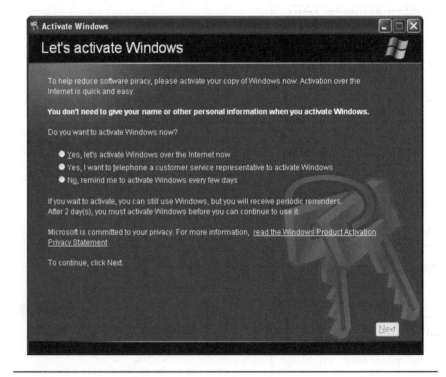

• **Figure 4.74**   Activate Windows

that's covered in detail in Chapters 16, "Securing Windows Resources," and 26, "Securing Computers."

Backup Status and Configuration (Vista, 7)

Vista and 7 do not enable you to back up files on your computer selectively. You can only back up personal data with the Backup Status and Configuration Tool or, if you have Vista Business, Ultimate, or Enterprise, perform a complete PC backup by using Windows Complete PC Backup. If you want to pick and choose the file to back up, you need to buy a third-party tool. Also, this tool only allows you to back up to optical media, a hard drive, or a networked drive.

 Neither Windows XP Home nor Windows XP Media Center Edition includes Backup during installation. You must install the Backup program from the Windows installation CD by running the \Valueadd\MSFT\Ntbackup\ NTbackup.msi program.

Character Map (All)

Ever been using a program only to discover you need to enter a strange character such as the euro character (€) but your word processor doesn't support it? That's when you need the Character Map. It enables you to copy any Unicode character into the Clipboard (Figure 4.75).

Disk Cleanup (All)

Disk Cleanup looks for unneeded files on your computer, which is handy when your hard drive starts to get full and you need space. You must run Disk Cleanup manually in Windows 2000, but Windows XP and Windows Vista start this program whenever your hard drive gets below 200 MB of free disk space.

Disk Defragmenter (All)

You use Disk Defragmenter to make your hard drive run faster—you'll see more details on this handy tool in Chapter 12, "Implementing Hard Drives." You can access this utility in the same way you access the Device Manager; you also find Disk Defragmenter in the Computer Management Console. A simpler method is to select Start | All Programs | Accessories | System Tools—you'll find Disk Defragmenter listed there. You can also right-click on any drive in My Computer or Computer, select Properties, and click the Tools tab, where you'll find a convenient Defragment Now button.

Files and Settings Transfer Wizard (Windows XP)

Suppose you have an old computer full of files and settings, and you just bought yourself a brand new computer. You want to copy everything from your old computer onto your new computer—what to do? Microsoft touts the Files and Settings Transfer Wizard as just the tool you need (Figure 4.76). This utility copies your desktop files and folders and, most conveniently, your settings from Internet Explorer and Outlook

• Figure 4.75   Character Map

• Figure 4.76   Files and Settings Transfer Wizard

Express; however, it won't copy over your programs, not even the Microsoft ones, and it won't copy settings for any programs other than IE and Outlook Express. If you need to copy everything from an old computer to a new one, you'll probably want to use a disk-imaging tool such as Norton Ghost.

Windows Easy Transfer (Windows Vista)

Vista's Windows Easy Transfer is an aggressively updated version of the Files and Settings Transfer Wizard. It does everything the older version does and adds the capability to copy user accounts and other settings (Figure 4.77).

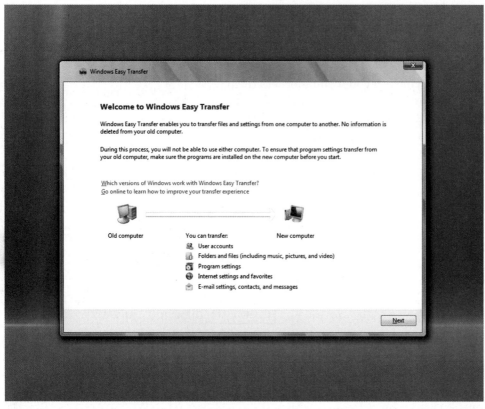

• **Figure 4.77** Windows Easy Transfer

Scheduled Tasks (All)

With the Scheduled Tasks utility, you can schedule any program to start and stop any time you wish. The only trick to this utility is that you must enter the program you want to run as a command on the command line, with all the proper switches. Figure 4.78 shows the configuration line for running the Disk Defragmenter program.

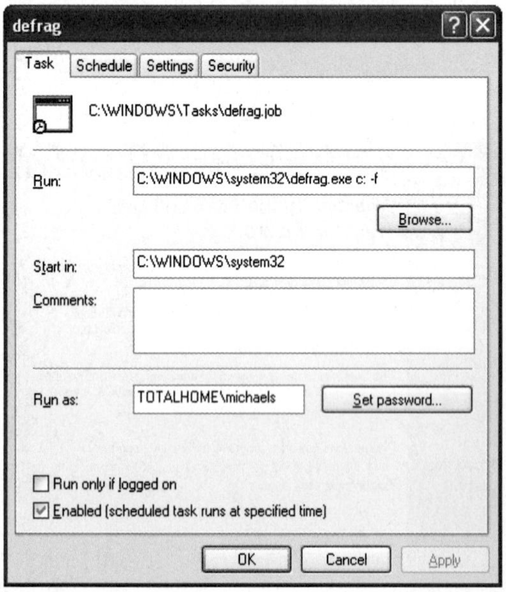

Security Center (Windows XP)

The Security Center is a one-stop location for configuring many security features on your computer. This tool is also in the Control Panel. Vista removes Security Center from System Tools. All of these security features, and many more, are discussed in detail in their related chapters.

System Information (All)

System Information is one of those tools that everyone (including the CompTIA A+ exams) likes to talk about, but it's uncommon to meet techs who say they actually use this tool. System Information shows tons of information about the hardware and software on your PC (Figure 4.79). You can also click on the Tools menu to use it as a launch point for a number of programs.

• **Figure 4.78** Scheduled Tasks utility

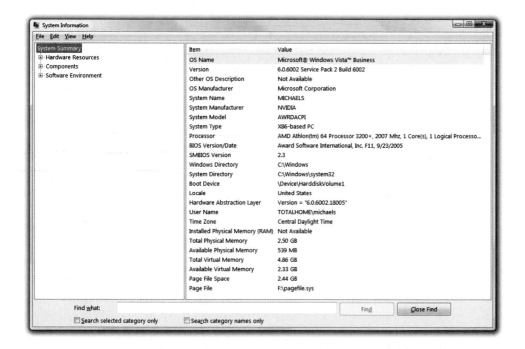

● **Figure 4.79** System Information

System Restore (XP, Vista)

System Restore is not only handy, it's also arguably the most important single utility you'll ever use in Windows when it comes to fixing a broken system. System Restore enables you to take a "snapshot"—a copy of a number of critical files and settings—and return to that state later (Figure 4.80). System Restore holds multiple snapshots, any of which you may restore to in the future.

Imagine you're installing some new device in your PC, or maybe a piece of software. Before you actually install, you take a snapshot and call it "Before Install." You install the device, and now something starts acting weird. You go back into System Restore and reload the previous snapshot, and the problem goes away.

System Restore isn't perfect. It only backs up a few critical items, and it's useless if the computer won't boot, but it's usually the first thing to try when something goes wrong—assuming, of course, you made a snapshot!

BitLocker (Vista Enterprise and Ultimate)

BitLocker is a tool to encrypt files, folders, or entire hard drives. It's a great way to make

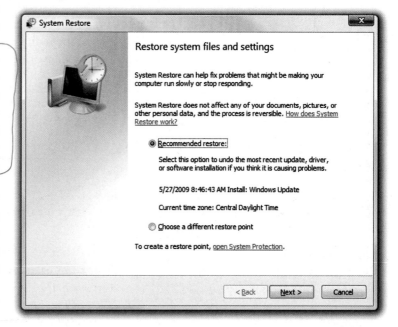

● **Figure 4.80** System Restore

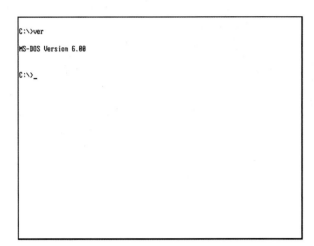

```
C:\>ver

MS-DOS Version 6.00


C:\>_
```

• **Figure 4.81**   DOS command prompt

📄 The command-line interface goes back to the early days of computing, but it continues to be an essential tool in all modern operating systems, including Linux, Mac OS X, and all versions of Windows. Chapter 15, "Working with the Command-Line Interface," goes into the command line in detail.

sure other people can't read your stuff, but it also makes data recovery risky. If you really want security, use BitLocker.

Command Line

The Windows command-line interface is a throwback to how Microsoft operating systems worked a long, long time ago when text commands were entered at a command prompt. Figure 4.81 shows the command prompt from DOS, the first operating system commonly used in PCs.

DOS is dead, but the command-line interface is alive and well in every version of Windows—including Windows 7. Every good tech knows how to access and use the command-line interface. It is a lifesaver when the graphical part of Windows doesn't work, and it is often faster than using a mouse if you're skilled at using it. An entire chapter is devoted to the command line, but let's look at one example of what the command line can do. First, you need to get there. In Windows XP, select Start | Run, and type **cmd** in the dialog box. Click OK and you get to a command prompt. In Windows Vista, you do the same thing in the Start | Start Search dialog box. Figure 4.82 shows a command prompt in Windows Vista.

Once at a command prompt, type **dir** and press ENTER on your keyboard. This command displays all the files and folders in a specific directory—probably your user folder for this exercise—and gives sizes and other information. DIR is just one of many useful command-line tools you'll learn about in this book.

Microsoft Management Console

One of the biggest complaints about earlier versions of Windows was the wide dispersal of the many utilities needed for administration and troubleshooting. Despite years of research, Microsoft could never find a place for all the utilities that would please even a small minority of support people. In a moment of sheer genius, Microsoft determined that the ultimate utility was one that the support people made for themselves! This brought on the creation of the amazing Microsoft Management Console.

The **Microsoft Management Console (MMC)** is simply a shell program in Windows that holds individual utilities called *snap-ins*. To start an MMC, select Start | Run or just Start, type **mmc**, and press ENTER to get a blank MMC. Blank MMCs aren't much to look at (Figure 4.83).

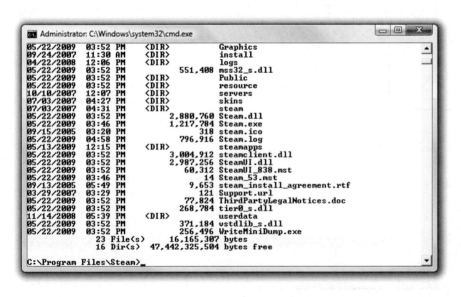

• **Figure 4.82**   Command prompt in Windows Vista

Mike Meyers' CompTIA A+ Guide to Managing and Troubleshooting PCs

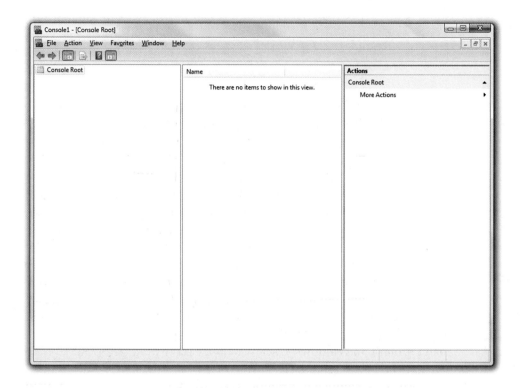

● **Figure 4.83** Blank MMC

You make a blank MMC console useful by adding snap-ins, which include most of the utilities you use in Windows. Even the good old Device Manager is a snap-in. You can add as many snap-ins as you like, and you have many to choose from. Many companies sell third-party utilities as MMC snap-ins.

For example, to add the Device Manager snap-in, open the blank MMC and select File | Add/Remove Snap-in (Console | Add/Remove Snap-in in Windows 2000). Here you will see a list of available snap-ins in Windows Vista (Figure 4.84). (Click the Add button in 2000/XP to open a similar screen.) Select Device Manager, and click the Add button to open a dialog box that prompts you to choose the local or a remote PC for the snap-in to work with. Choose Local Computer for

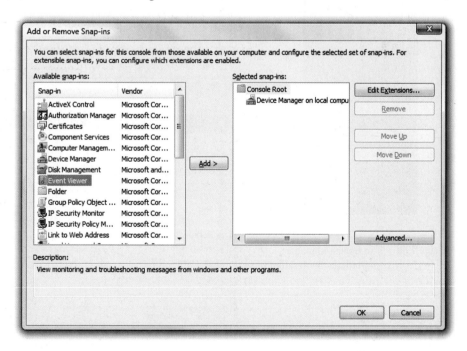

● **Figure 4.84** Available snap-ins

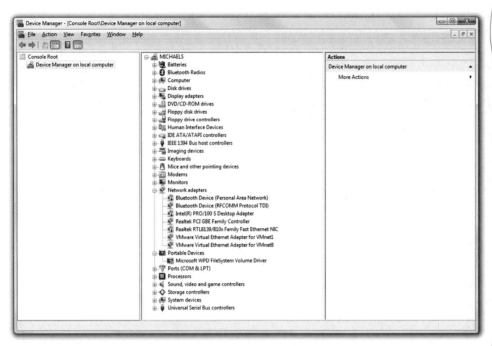

this exercise, and click the Finish button. Click the Close button to close the Add Standalone Snap-in dialog box, and then click OK to close the *Add or Remove Snap-ins* dialog box.

You should see Device Manager listed in the console. Click it. Hey, that looks kind of familiar, doesn't it (see Figure 4.85)?

Once you've added the snap-ins you want, just save the console under any name, anywhere you want. I'll save this console as Device Manager, for example, and drop it on my desktop (see Figure 4.86). I'm now just a double-click away from the Device Manager.

• **Figure 4.85**   Device Manager as a snap-in

• **Figure 4.86**   The Device Manager shortcut on the desktop

Administrative Tools

Windows combines the most popular snap-ins into an applet in the Control Panel called **Administrative Tools**. Open the Control Panel and open Administrative Tools (Figure 4.87).

• **Figure 4.87**   Administrative Tools

Administrative Tools is really just a folder that stores a number of pre-made consoles. As you poke through these, notice that many of the consoles share some of the same snap-ins—nothing wrong with that. Of the consoles in a standard Administrative Tools collection, the ones you'll spend the most time with are Computer Management, Event Viewer, Reliability and Performance (or just Performance in Windows 2000/XP), and Services.

The CompTIA A+ certification exams have little interest in some of these snap-ins, so this book won't cover them all. If I don't mention it, it's almost certainly not on the test!

Computer Management

The **Computer Management** applet is a tech's best buddy, or at least a place where you'll spend a lot of time when building or maintaining a system (Figure 4.88). You've already spent considerable time with two of its components: System Tools and Storage. Depending on the version of Windows, System Tools also offers System Information, Performance Logs and Alerts, Reliability and Performance, Device Manager, and more. Storage is where you'll find Disk Management.

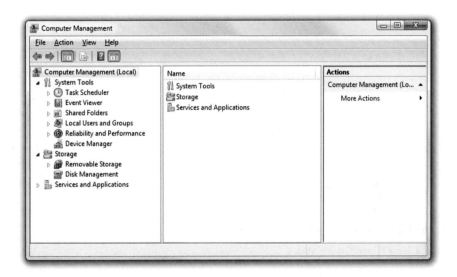

• **Figure 4.88**   Computer Management applet

Event Viewer

Event Viewer shows you at a glance what has happened in the last day, week, or more, including when people logged in and when the PC had problems (Figure 4.89). You'll see more of Event Viewer in Chapter 26, "Securing Computers."

Performance (Windows 2000/XP)

The **Performance** console consists of two snap-ins: System Monitor and Performance Logs and Alerts. You can use these for reading *logs*—files that record information over time. The System Monitor can also monitor real-time data (Figure 4.90).

Suppose you are adding a new cable modem

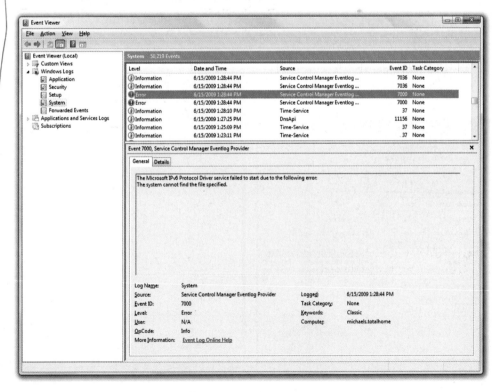

• **Figure 4.89**   Event Viewer reporting system errors

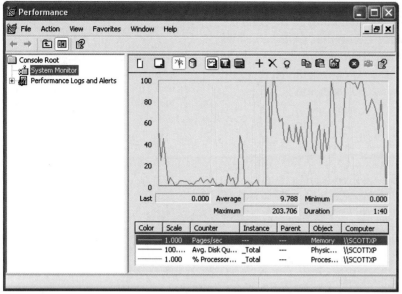

and you want to know just how fast you can download data. Click the plus sign (+) on the toolbar to add a counter. Click the *Use local computer counters* radio button, and then choose Network Interface from the Performance Object pull-down menu. Make sure the *Select counters from list* radio button is selected. Last, select Bytes Received/sec. The dialog box should look like Figure 4.91.

Click Add, and then click Close; probably not much is happening. Go to a Web site, preferably one where you can download a huge file. Start downloading and watch the chart jump; that's the real throughput (Figure 4.92).

Reliability and Performance Monitor (Windows Vista)

The **Reliability and Performance Monitor** in Windows Vista offers just about everything you can find in the Performance applet of older versions of Windows—although everything is monitored by default, so there's no need to add anything. In addition, it includes the Reliability Monitor. The Reliability Monitor enables you to see at a glance what's been done to the computer over a period of time, including software installations and uninstallations, failures of hardware or applications, and general uptime (Figure 4.93). It's a nice starting tool for checking a Vista machine that's new to you.

• **Figure 4.90**   System Monitor in action

You'll learn more about the Performance console in Chapter 17, "Maintaining and Troubleshooting Windows."

You'll learn more about the Reliability and Performance Monitor in Chapter 17.

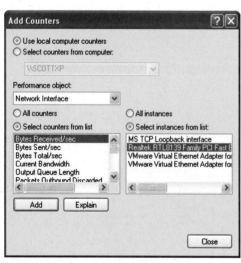

• **Figure 4.91**   Setting up a throughput test

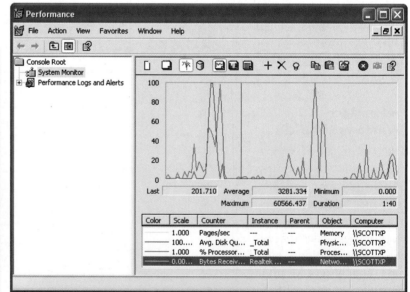

• **Figure 4.92**   Downloading with blazing speed

Services

Windows runs a large number of separate programs called **services**. The best way to visualize a service is to think of it as something that runs, yet is invisible. Windows comes with about 100 services by default, and they handle a huge number of tasks, from application support to network functions. You can use the Services applet to see the status of all services on the system, including services that are not running (Figure 4.94).

Right-click a service and select Properties to modify its settings. Figure 4.95 shows the properties for the Bluetooth support service. See the Startup type pull-down menu? It shows three options: Automatic, Manual, and Disabled. Automatic means it starts when the system starts, Manual means you have to come to this tab to start it, and Disabled prevents anything from starting it. Make sure you know these three settings, and also make sure you understand how to start, stop, pause, and resume services (note the four buttons below Startup Type).

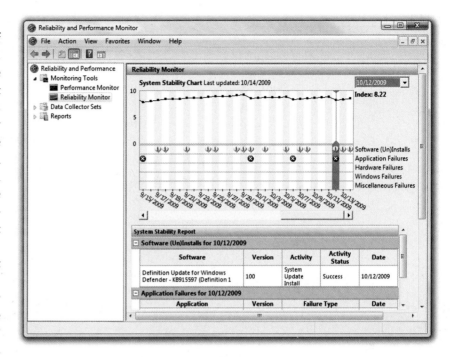

• **Figure 4.93**   The Reliability and Performance Monitor open to the Reliability Monitor screen

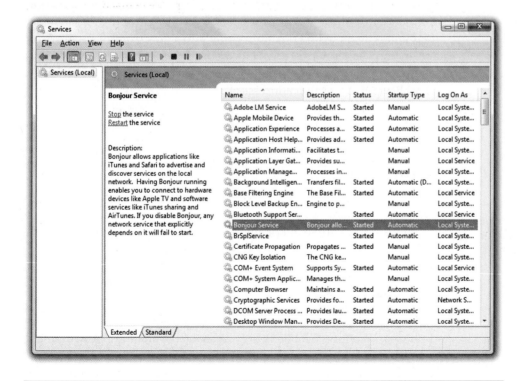

• **Figure 4.94**   Services applet

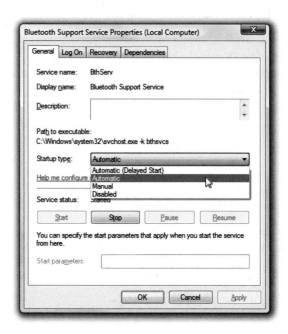

● **Figure 4.95**   Bluetooth support service properties

Beyond A+

Microsoft adds or tweaks utilities from one version of its flagship operating system to the next. Plus, tools often move from version to version. The Performance applet in Windows XP, for example, became the Reliability and Performance Monitor in Windows Vista. With Windows 7, Microsoft shifted things again, with Reliability going into a new Control Panel applet called Action Center. Go figure. Half the fun in migrating to a new OS is hunting down your favorite tools!

This Beyond A+ section addresses the several versions of Windows not on the CompTIA A+ exams: Windows 7, Windows Mobile, Windows XP Tablet PC Edition, and Windows Embedded.

Windows 7

Windows 7 came out just a few months after CompTIA announced the 220-701 and 220-702 exams, so it's not on those exams. However, the differences between Vista and 7 are so minor "under the hood" that it's safe to say if you know Vista, you know Windows 7 (Figure 4.96).

Windows Mobile

Windows Mobile is a very small version of Windows designed for PDAs and phones. Windows Mobile is only available as an Original Equipment Manufacturer (OEM) product, which means you buy the device and it comes with Windows Mobile—you can't buy some PDA or phone and then buy Windows Mobile separately.

• **Figure 4.96**   Windows 7

Windows XP Tablet PC Edition

A tablet PC is a laptop with a built-in touch screen. The idea behind a tablet PC is to drastically reduce, if not totally eliminate, the use of a keyboard (Figure 4.97). In some situations, tablet PCs have started to become popular. Windows XP Tablet PC Edition is Microsoft's operating solution for tablet PCs. Tablet PC Edition is still Windows XP, but it adds special drivers and applications to support the tablet.

 You'll see more of Windows XP Tablet PC Edition in Chapter 21, "Portable Computing."

Windows Vista comes with the tablet PC features built in, so there's no need for a special tablet version of Vista (or Windows 7, for that matter).

Windows Embedded

The world is filled with PCs in the most unlikely places. Everything from cash registers to the F-22 Raptor fighter plane contains some number of tiny PCs. These aren't the PCs you're used to seeing, though. They almost never have mice, monitors, keyboards, and the usual I/O you'd expect to see, but they are truly PCs, with a CPU, RAM, BIOS, and storage.

These tiny PCs need operating systems just like any other PC, and a number of companies make specialized OSs for embedded PCs. Microsoft makes Windows Embedded just for these specialized embedded PCs.

• **Figure 4.97**   Tablet PC

Chapter 4 Review

■ Chapter Summary

After reading this chapter and completing the exercises, you should understand the following about Microsoft Windows.

Relate the history of Microsoft Windows

■ Microsoft entered the operating system game in the early 1980s with a command-line OS called Microsoft Disk Operating System, or MS-DOS. With a command-line OS, you interacted with the computer to run programs, save files, and do all the other computing functions by typing and pressing the ENTER key on your keyboard.

■ The earliest versions of Windows were little more than a graphical overlay of the DOS command-line operating system. This overlay version of Windows went through a number of updates, ending with the first truly popular version of Windows, Windows for Workgroups version 3.1. The last versions are collectively referred to as Windows 3.x.

■ In 1989, Microsoft offered a completely separate version of Windows called Windows NT, a true graphical operating system that was dramatically more powerful than the Windows overlay versions. It cost a lot more, unfortunately, so did not see widespread adoption by regular users, only by business users. What set NT apart from other versions of Windows (including later consumer-oriented products) was its very secure file system, NTFS.

■ From 1995 through 2000, Microsoft offered consumers an alternative version of Windows that went through several updates, such as Windows 95 and Windows 98. Collectively these versions of Windows are called Windows 9x. All of these versions of Windows used forms of FAT for file systems, not the more secure NTFS.

■ Microsoft currently supports seven families of Windows, of which three concern the CompTIA A+ certified technician: Windows 2000, Windows XP, and Windows Vista. All can use the NTFS file system.

■ Windows 2000 came in two versions: Professional and Server. The CompTIA A+ exams do not cover Windows Server versions, but a good tech should at least know these server versions exist. If you were to look at the Windows 2000 Server desktop, you'd be hard pressed to see any obvious differences from the Windows 2000 Professional version.

■ Microsoft released several versions of the successor to Windows 2000, such as Windows XP Professional and Windows XP Home. Windows XP Professional provides full-blown data security, and it is the only version of Windows XP with the capability of logging into a special Windows Server–controlled domain. Windows XP Home is a stripped-down version of XP Professional, without some of the important security features, such as no access to the Encrypting File System. Windows XP Media Center offers features for the media junkie, such as a personal video recorder to capture television shows for later viewing.

■ Windows Vista comes in many flavors, such as Windows Vista Home Premium and Windows Vista Business. Windows Vista Ultimate combines all of the features of every other Vista version and includes some other features, such as a game performance tweaker and DVD ripping capability.

■ Windows XP and Windows Vista come in 64-bit versions to take advantage of the extra computing power and memory capacity available with modern 64-bit processors. A 32-bit operating system is limited to a mere 4 GB of RAM, whereas a 64-bit OS can have gobs more. The 64-bit versions of Windows XP saw some use, but the 64-bit versions of Vista took the 64-bit OS into the mainstream.

Explain the Windows interface

■ Every version of Windows supports multiple users on a single machine, so the starting point for any tour of the Windows user interface starts with the login screen. Windows 2000 has a straightforward login screen where you enter a user name and password. Windows XP offers the Welcome screen in addition to the standard login, where users can click an icon next to their user name to log in, although this feature is disabled in a domain environment. Windows Vista has a beefed-up Welcome screen that works in both a workgroup and a domain.

- The Windows desktop is the primary interface to the computer in every version of Windows. Windows Vista differs from previous versions of Windows with the use of transparencies and other nice features of the Windows Aero interface. Flip 3D enables users to quickly and visually cycle through open programs.

- Some of the important items on the desktop are the taskbar, Start button, Quick Launch toolbar, and notification area, or system tray. The taskbar shows running programs. The Start button gives you access to the Start menu where you can run installed applications. The Quick Launch toolbar enables you to select often-used programs with a single click, though it's not displayed by default in Windows XP. The notification area shows icons for applications running in the background, such as your antivirus software.

- My Computer in Windows 2000 and Windows XP and Computer in Windows Vista offer access to the files and folders on mass storage drives on the computer. To view the contents of any device, double-click its icon in My Computer/Computer. You can tell by a file's icon or extension—if you alter the default folder view to show file extensions—what type of file it is, such as a .JPG picture file.

- Windows Explorer is the main tool for observing and manipulating files on a system. The tool differs in some ways among the versions tested on the CompTIA A+ exams. Windows Explorer and My Computer/Computer are two facets of the same application in Windows XP and Windows Vista but two distinct applications in Windows 2000.

- When you delete a file in Windows, it moves into the Recycle Bin. It stays there until you empty the Recycle Bin or restore the file, or until the Recycle Bin reaches a preset size and starts erasing its oldest contents.

- Windows offers many useful keyboard key combinations for accomplishing common tasks. Some combinations work specifically with the operating system utilities, such as pressing the WINDOWS KEY and the PAUSE key to open the System applet. Other combinations work throughout most applications, such as CTRL-C to copy something and CTRL-V to paste whatever was copied.

Identify the operating system folders of Windows 2000, XP, and Vista

- SystemRoot is the tech name given to the folder in which Windows has been installed. SystemRoot by default is C:\WINNT in Windows 2000, while Windows XP and Vista's SystemRoot defaults to C:\WINDOWS.

- Most programs install some or all of their essential files into a subfolder of the Program Files folder. This folder is found almost always in the root of the same drive where you find the Windows system folder. Windows Vista 64-bit versions have a separate Program Files (x86) folder for 32-bit applications.

- Personal documents are stored by default in the Documents and Settings folder (Windows 2000 and Windows XP) or the Users folder in Windows Vista. Within the folder structure, you'll find folders for each user account and, within those user account folders, folders such as Desktop, Start Menu, and so on. Just as with Program Files, the Documents and Settings/Users folder will be on the same drive as the Windows system folder.

- The Registry is a database that stores everything about your PC, including information on all of the hardware in the PC, network information, user preferences, file types, and virtually anything else you might run into with Windows. The Registry is composed of several hives.

- You can access the Registry Editor by typing **regedt32** or **regedit** at the Start | Run menu or at the Start | Start Search dialog box, depending on the version of Windows.

- The Registry has five root keys that define various elements of Windows. HKEY_CLASSES_ROOT, for example, defines the standard class objects used by Windows. A class object is a named group of functions that define what you can do with the object it represents. A .JPG file is defined here, for example, as a type of image file associated with a specific program.

- Windows uses a portion of the hard drive as an extension of system RAM, through what's called a page file. A page file is a block of cylinders on a hard drive set aside as what's called a page file, swap file, or virtual memory. When the PC starts running out of real RAM because you've loaded too many programs, the system swaps programs from RAM to the page file, opening more space for programs currently active.

Describe the utilities in Windows essential to techs

- Windows offers many utilities that enable techs to configure the operating system, optimize and tweak settings, install hardware, and more. Six that techs use frequently are right-click, Control Panel, System Tools, command line, Administrative Tools, and the Microsoft Management Console.

- Right-clicking an object brings up the context menu for the object so you can act on it. One common right-click option is Properties.

- The Control Panel handles most of the maintenance, upgrade, and configuration aspects of Windows. The Control Panel contains many applets that are displayed either as a set or in categories in Windows XP or Windows Vista.

- The Device Manager enables techs to examine and configure all the hardware and drivers in a Windows PC. The Device Manager displays every device that Windows recognizes, organized in special groups called types. You can see resources used by devices and update drivers directly in Device Manager. Device Manager places an icon on top of any hardware device that's not functioning properly or is manually disabled. Device Manager is the first tool you should access when you have a hardware problem.

- The System Tools menu in the Start menu offers techs a one-stop shop for many handy utilities. You'll find Disk Defragmenter and Disk Cleanup here, for example. The Files and Settings Transfer Wizard in Windows XP or the Windows Easy Transfer tool in Windows Vista appears in this menu as well.

- The command-line interface enables you to type commands to the operating system. This can give you access to utilities and tools that often provide quicker results than graphical tools.

- The Microsoft Management Console (MMC) is simply a shell program in Windows that holds individual utilities called snap-ins. These snap-ins enable you to accomplish varying tech tasks. You can create custom MMCs or use ones preconfigured by Microsoft.

- The Administrative Tools in the Control Panel are preconfigured MMCs, such as Computer Management and Event Viewer. Users rarely need to access these MMCs, but techs know their Administrative Tools.

■ Key Terms

activation *(105)*
Administrative Tools *(112)*
Aero *(77)*
applets *(101)*
Computer *(80)*
Computer Management *(113)*
context menu *(99)*
Control Panel *(100)*
desktop *(76)*
Device Manager *(101)*
extensions *(82)*
file association *(94)*
Flip 3D *(78)*
Folders list *(82)*
interface *(75)*
login screen *(75)*
Microsoft Management Console (MMC) *(110)*
My Computer *(80)*
My Documents *(85)*
My Network Places *(87)*
Network *(87)*

notification area *(80)*
page file *(96)*
Performance *(113)*
Quick Launch toolbar *(80)*
Recycle Bin *(86)*
Registry *(92)*
Reliability and Performance Monitor *(114)*
root keys *(94)*
services *(115)*
Start button *(79)*
SystemRoot *(89)*
System Tools *(105)*
system tray *(80)*
taskbar *(79)*
transparency *(78)*
User's Files *(85)*
Welcome screen *(75)*
Windows Explorer *(80)*
Windows Sidebar *(87)*
x64 *(73)*
x86 *(72)*

Key Term Quiz

Use the Key Terms list to complete the sentences that follow. Not all terms will be used.

1. You can readily see programs running in the background by looking at the _____.

2. The _____ stores information about all the hardware, drivers, and applications on a Windows system.

3. The first place you should look on a PC with malfunctioning hardware is the _____.

4. Most tech tools in Windows can be found in _____.

5. The _____ in Windows offers a great spot for accessing favorite programs without resorting to the Start menu.

6. Jill accidentally deleted a critical file. Winona the tech assures her that the file is no doubt in the _____ and not lost forever.

7. Windows uses the _____ or swap file for virtual memory.

8. Windows Vista desktop uses _____ to enable transparency and Flip 3D.

9. You can use the login screen to log into a Windows 2000 computer, but Windows XP and Windows Vista offer the option of using the _____ to log in.

10. A file association is defined by its _____.

Multiple-Choice Quiz

1. What is the best way to access the Registry Editor in Windows XP?

   A. Start | Programs | DOS prompt icon. Type **EDIT**.

   B. Start | Programs | Registry Editor.

   C. Start | Run. Type **regedit32** and click OK.

   D. Start | Run. Type **regedt32** and click OK.

2. Windows XP provides a number of ready-made MMC snap-ins stored in the _____ applet in the Control Panel.

   A. System

   B. Network

   C. Administrative Tools

   D. MMC

3. Which of the following are part of the Windows desktop?

   A. Services, command line, applications

   B. Right-click, drag and drop, point and click

   C. Quick Launch toolbar, system tray, taskbar

   D. CPU, RAM, hard drive

4. The Microsoft Management Console holds individual utilities called what?

   A. Built-ins

   B. Snap-ins

   C. Applets

   D. MMCs

5. The folder in which Windows is installed is known generically as what?

   A. RootFolder

   B. WinRoot

   C. SystemRoot

   D. System32

6. What is the name of the virtual memory file in Windows 2000/XP?

   A. SWAP.SYS

   B. CACHE.VM

   C. SYSTEM.RAM

   D. PAGEFILE.SYS

7. How do you access a command prompt in Windows Vista?

   A. Start | Run, type **cmd** and press ENTER.

   B. Start | Run, type **dos** and press ENTER.

   C. Start | Start Search, type **cmd** and press ENTER.

   D. Start | Start Search, type **dos** and press ENTER.

8. What copy protection scheme is used in Windows Vista?

   A. Activation

   B. BitLocker

   C. Event Viewer

   D. Services

9. Which of the following operating systems use the Backup Status and Configuration tool to back up files and folders?

   A. Windows 2000

   B. Windows XP Home

   C. Windows XP Professional

   D. Windows Vista

10. Which key combination enables you to switch between loaded programs?

    A. ALT-ESC

    B. ALT-TAB

    C. CTRL-C

    D. CTRL-X

11. What is the benefit of 64-bit Windows over 32-bit Windows?

    A. Supports more hard drives

    B. Fewer lockups

    C. Supports more memory

    D. Supports more monitors

12. Which version of Windows provides multimedia support, such as a personal video recorder?

    A. Windows 2000 Professional

    B. Windows XP Home

    C. Windows XP Media Center

    D. Windows Vista Home Basic

13. For a user account called "Ethan," where would you expect to find the personal documents folder in a Windows Vista computer?

    A. C:\Ethan

    B. C:\Users\Ethan

    C. C:\Documents and Settings\Ethan

    D. C:\Windows\Ethan

14. What applet can you use to view the status of all services on a system?

    A. Character Map

    B. Performance Monitor

    C. Services

    D. System Information

15. What is the primary tool you use to observe and manipulate files on a computer?

    A. Registry

    B. Windows Aero

    C. Windows desktop

    D. Windows Explorer

■ Essay Quiz

1. Your department just added four new interns who will share two PCs running Windows XP. Your boss has decided that you're the person who should take the newbies under your wing and teach them about Windows. Write a brief essay on some essential Windows folders and interfaces that every *user* should know.

2. Your boss just got off the phone with the corporate headquarters and is in somewhat of a panic. She doesn't know the first thing about the Microsoft Management Console, but now every tech is going to be issued a custom MMC. Write a brief essay explaining the function of the MMC to help allay her worries.

3. A colleague has approached you with a serious problem. He was on tech support for his home PC, and the support person told him the only way to fix the problem he was having on his Windows XP Home PC was to edit the Registry manually. Then the tech scared him, saying that if he messed up, he could destroy his PC forever. Write a short essay discussing the Registry and the tools for editing it.

4. As part of your promotion, it is your responsibility to train the new techs your boss just hired. Write a brief essay describing the tools in the System Tools folder group.

Lab Projects

• Lab Project 4.1

Create your own MMC loaded with the snap-ins you use the most, or that you would like to experiment with. Add at least three snap-ins. Save the MMC on your desktop and give it an appropriate name.

• Lab Project 4.2

In a couple of places in the chapter, you got a taste of working with some of the more complex tools in Windows, such as the Event Viewer and Performance console. Go back through the text and reread those sections, and then do an Internet search for a how-to article. Then work with the tools.

Microprocessors

"MEGAHERTZ: This is a really, really big hertz."

—DAVE BARRY

In this chapter, you will learn how to

■ **Identify the core components of a CPU**

■ **Describe the relationship of CPUs and memory**

■ **Explain the varieties of modern CPUs**

■ **Install and upgrade CPUs**

For all practical purposes, the terms **microprocessor** and **central processing unit (CPU)** mean the same thing: it's that big chip inside your computer that many people often describe as the brain of the system. You know that CPU makers name their microprocessors in a fashion similar to the automobile industry: CPU names get a make and a model, such as Intel Core i7 or AMD Phenom II X4. But what's happening inside the CPU to make it able to do the amazing things asked of it every time you step up to the keyboard?

■ CPU Core Components

Although the computer might seem to act quite intelligently, comparing the CPU to a human brain hugely overstates its capabilities. A CPU functions more like a very powerful calculator than like a brain—but, oh, what a calculator! Today's CPUs add, subtract, multiply, divide, and move billions of numbers per second. Processing that much information so quickly makes any CPU look intelligent. It's simply the speed of the CPU, rather than actual intelligence, that enables computers to perform feats such as accessing the Internet, playing visually stunning games, or creating graphics.

A good PC technician needs to understand some basic CPU functions to support PCs, so let's start with an analysis of how the CPU works. If you wanted to teach someone how an automobile engine works, you would use a relatively simple example engine, right? The same principle applies here. Let's begin our study of the CPU with the granddaddy of all PC CPUs: the famous Intel 8088, invented in the late 1970s. Although this CPU first appeared over 25 years ago, it defined the idea of the modern microprocessor and contains the same basic parts used in even the most advanced CPUs today. Stick with me, my friend. Prepare to enter that little bit of magic called the CPU.

The Man in the Box

Let's begin by visualizing the CPU as a man in a box (Figure 5.1). This is one clever guy in this box. He can perform virtually any mathematical function, manipulate data, and give answers *very quickly*.

This guy is potentially very useful to us, but there's a catch—he lives closed up in a tiny box. Before he can work with us, we must come up with a way to exchange information with him (Figure 5.2).

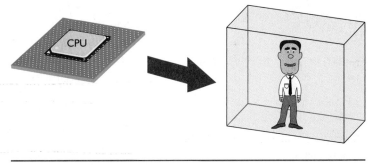

• **Figure 5.1**   Imagine the CPU as a man in a box

Imagine that we install a set of 16 light bulbs, 8 inside his box and 8 outside his box. Each of the 8 light bulbs inside the box connects to one of the 8 bulbs outside the box to form a pair. Each pair of light bulbs is always either on or off. You can control the 8 pairs of bulbs by using a set of 8 switches outside the box, and the Man in the Box can also control them by using an identical set of 8 switches inside the box. This light-bulb communication device is called the **external data bus (EDB)**.

Figure 5.3 shows a cutaway view of the external data bus. When either you or the Man in the Box flips a switch on, *both* light bulbs go on, and the switch on the other side is also flipped to the on position. If you

• **Figure 5.2**   How do we talk to the Man in the Box?

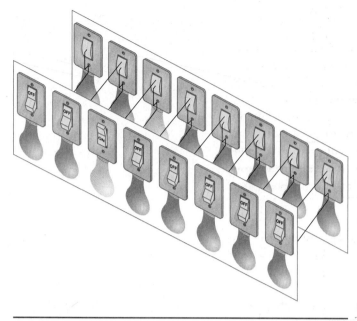

• **Figure 5.3** Cutaway of the external data bus—note that one light bulb pair is on

or the Man in the Box turns a switch off, the light bulbs on both sides are turned off, along with the other switch for that pair.

Can you see how this works? By creating on/off patterns with the light bulbs that represent different pieces of data or commands, you can send that information to the Man in the Box, and he can send information back in the same way—*assuming that you agree ahead of time on what the different patterns of lights mean.* To accomplish this, you need some sort of codebook that assigns meanings to the many patterns of lights that the external data bus might display. Keep this thought in mind while we push the analogy a bit more.

Before going any further, make sure you're clear on the fact that this is an analogy, not reality. There really is an external data bus, but you won't see any light bulbs or switches on the CPU. You can, however, see little wires sticking out of the CPU (Figure 5.4). If you apply voltage to one of these wires, you in essence flip the switch. Get the idea? So if that wire had voltage, and if a tiny light bulb were attached to the wire, that light bulb would glow, would it not? By the same token, if the wire had no power, the light bulb would not glow. That is why the switch-and-light-bulb analogy may help you picture these little wires constantly flashing on and off.

Now that the external data bus enables you to communicate with the Man in the Box, you need to see how it works by placing voltages on the wires. This brings up a naming problem. It's a hassle to say something like "on-off-on-off-on-on-off-off" when talking about which wires have voltage. Rather than saying that one of the external data bus wires is on or off, use the number 1 to represent on and the number 0 to represent off (Figure 5.5). That way, instead of describing the state of the lights as "on-off-on-off-on-on-off-off," I can instead describe them by writing "10101100."

In the world of computers, we constantly turn wires on and off. As a result, we can use this "1 and 0" or **binary** system to describe the state of these wires at any given moment. (See, and you just thought computer geeks spoke in binary to confuse normal people. Ha!) There's much more to binary numbering in the world of computing, but this is a great place to start. We will revisit the binary numbering system in greater detail in Chapter 8, "Expansion Bus."

• **Figure 5.4** Close-up of the underside of a CPU

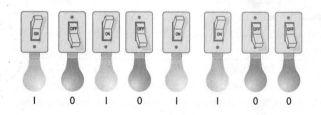

• **Figure 5.5** Here "1" means on, "0" means off.

Registers

The Man in the Box provides good insight into the workspace inside a CPU. The EDB gives you a way to communicate with the Man in the Box so you can give him work to do. But to do this work, he needs a worktable; in fact, he needs at least four worktables. Each of these four worktables has 16 light bulbs. These light bulbs are not in pairs; they're just 16 light bulbs lined up straight across the table. Each light bulb is controlled by a single switch, operated only by the Man in the Box. By creating on/off patterns like the ones on the EDB, the Man in the Box can use these four sets of light bulbs to work math problems. In a real computer, these worktables are called **registers** (Figure 5.6).

Registers provide the Man in the Box with a workplace for the problems you give him. All CPUs contain a large number of registers, but for the moment let's concentrate on the four most common ones: the *general-purpose registers*. Intel named them AX, BX, CX, and DX.

Great! We're just about ready to put the Man in the Box to work, but before you close the lid on the box, you must give the Man one more tool. Remember the codebook we mentioned earlier? Let's make one to enable us to communicate with him. Figure 5.7 shows the codebook we'll use. We'll give one copy to him and make a second for us.

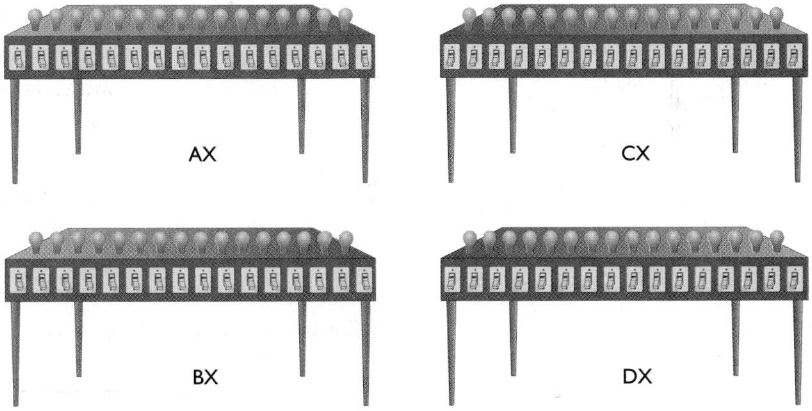

In this codebook, for example, 10000111 means *Move the number 7 into the AX register*. These commands are called the microprocessor's **machine language**. The commands listed in the figure are not actual commands; as you've probably guessed, I've simplified dramatically. The Intel 8088 CPU, invented in the late 1970s, actually used commands very similar to these, plus a few hundred others.

Here are some examples of real machine language for the Intel 8088:

10111010	The next line of code is a number. Put that number into the DX register.
01000001	Add 1 to the number already in the CX register.
00111100	Compare the value in the AX register with the next line of code.

By placing machine language commands—called *lines of code*—onto the external data bus one at a time, you can instruct the Man in the Box to do specific tasks. All of the machine language commands that the CPU understands make up the CPU's **instruction set**.

So here is the CPU so far: the Man in the Box can communicate with the outside world via the external data bus; he has four registers he can use to work on the problems you give him; and he has a codebook—the instruction set—so he can understand the different patterns (machine language commands) on the external data bus (Figure 5.8).

Tech Tip

General-Purpose Registers
The 8088 was the first CPU to use the four now famous AX–DX general-purpose registers, and they still exist in even the latest CPUs. (But they have a lot more light bulbs!)

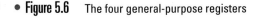

AX

CX

BX

DX

● **Figure 5.6**   The four general-purpose registers

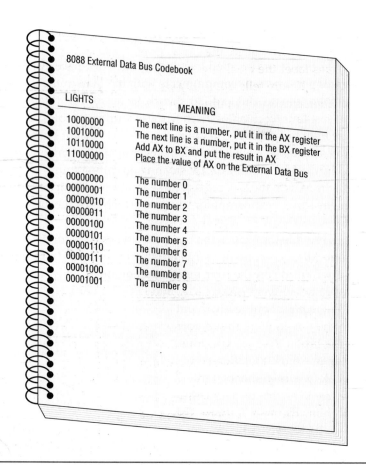

LIGHTS	MEANING
10000000	The next line is a number, put it in the AX register
10010000	The next line is a number, put it in the BX register
10110000	Add AX to BX and put the result in AX
11000000	Place the value of AX on the External Data Bus
00000000	The number 0
00000001	The number 1
00000010	The number 2
00000011	The number 3
00000100	The number 4
00000101	The number 5
00000110	The number 6
00000111	The number 7
00001000	The number 8
00001001	The number 9

8088 External Data Bus Codebook

• **Figure 5.7**   CPU codebook

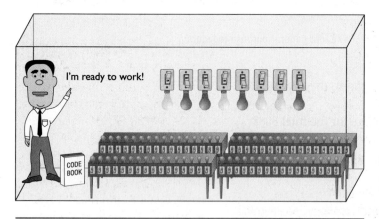

• **Figure 5.8**   The CPU so far

Clock

Okay, so you're ready to put the Man in the Box to work. You can send the first command by lighting up wires on the EDB. How does he know when you've finished setting up the wires and it's time to act?

Have you ever seen one of those old-time manual calculators with the big crank on one side? To add two numbers, you pressed a number key, the + key, and another number key, but then to make the calculator do the calculation and give you the answer, you had to pull down the crank. That was the signal that you had finished entering data and instructions and were ready for the calculator to give you an answer.

Well, a CPU also has a type of crank. To return to the Man in the Box, imagine there's a bell inside the box activated by a button on the outside of the box. Each time you press the button to sound the bell, the Man in the Box reads the next set of lights on the external data bus. Of course, a real

computer doesn't use a bell. The bell on a real CPU is a special wire called the **clock wire** (most diagrams label the clock wire CLK). A charge on the CLK wire tells the CPU that another piece of information is waiting to be processed (Figure 5.9).

For the CPU to process a command placed on the external data bus, a certain minimum voltage must be applied to the CLK wire. A single charge to the CLK wire is called a **clock cycle**. Actually, the CPU requires at least two clock cycles to act on a command, and usually more. Using the manual calculator analogy, you need to pull the crank at least twice before anything happens. In fact, a CPU may require hundreds of clock cycles to process some commands (Figure 5.10).

The maximum number of clock cycles that a CPU can handle in a given period of time is referred to as its **clock speed**. The clock speed is the fastest speed at which a CPU can operate, determined by the CPU manufacturer. The Intel 8088 processor had a clock speed of 4.77 MHz (4.77 million cycles per second), extremely slow by modern standards, but still a pretty big number compared to using a pencil and paper. CPUs today run at speeds in excess of 3 GHz (3 billion cycles per second).

1 hertz (1 Hz) = 1 cycle per second

1 megahertz (1 MHz) = 1 million cycles per second

1 gigahertz (1 GHz) = 1 billion cycles per second

Understand that a CPU's clock speed is its *maximum* speed, not the speed at which it *must* run. A CPU can run at any speed, as long as that speed does not exceed its clock speed. Manufacturers used to print the CPU's clock speed directly onto the CPU, but for the past few years they've used cryptic codes (Figure 5.11). As the chapter progresses you'll see why they do this.

The **system crystal** determines the speed at which a CPU and the rest of the PC operate. The system crystal is usually a quartz oscillator, very similar to the one in a wristwatch, soldered to the motherboard (Figure 5.12).

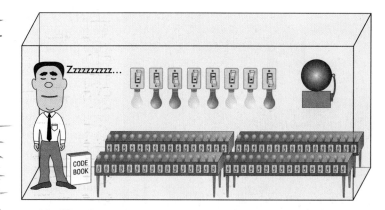

● **Figure 5.9** The CPU does nothing until activated by the clock.

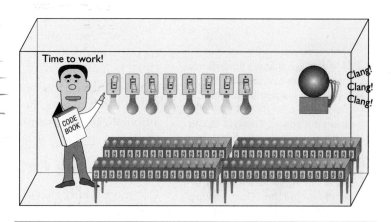

● **Figure 5.10** The CPU often needs more than one clock cycle to get a result.

● **Figure 5.11** Where is the clock speed?

• **Figure 5.12**   One of many types of system crystals

The quartz oscillator sends out an electric pulse at a certain speed, many millions of times per second. This signal goes first to a clock chip that adjusts the pulse, usually increasing the pulse sent by the crystal by some large multiple. (The folks who make motherboards could connect the crystal directly to the CPU's clock wire, but then if you wanted to replace your CPU with a CPU with a different clock speed, you'd need to replace the crystal too.) As long as the PC is turned on, the quartz oscillator, through the clock chip, fires a charge on the CLK wire, in essence pushing the system along.

Visualize the system crystal as a metronome for the CPU. The quartz oscillator repeatedly fires a charge on the CLK wire, setting the beat, if you will, for the CPU's activities. If the system crystal sets a beat slower than the CPU's clock speed, the CPU will work just fine, though at the slower speed of the system crystal. If the system crystal forces the CPU to run faster than its clock speed, it can overheat and stop working.

Before you install a CPU into a system, you must make sure that the crystal and clock chip send out the correct clock pulse for that particular CPU. In the not-so-old days, this required very careful adjustments. With today's systems, the motherboard talks to the CPU (at a very slow speed), the CPU tells the motherboard the clock speed it needs, and the clock chip automatically adjusts for the CPU, making this process now invisible.

> Aggressive users sometimes intentionally overclock CPUs by telling the clock chip to multiply the pulse faster than the CPU's designed speed. They do this to make slower (cheaper) CPUs run faster. This is a risky business that can destroy your CPU, but those willing to take that risk often do it. See the "Overclocking" section later in this chapter.

> Some motherboards enable you to override the default or automatic settings by changing a jumper or making a change in CMOS. A few enthusiasts' motherboards even enable you to make software changes to alter the speed of your CPU.

Back to the External Data Bus

One more reality check. We've been talking about tables with racks of light bulbs, but of course real CPU registers don't use light bulbs to represent on/ 1 and off/0. Registers are tiny storage areas on the CPU made up of microscopic semiconductor circuits that hold charges. It's just easier to imagine a light bulb lit up to represent a circuit holding a charge; when the light bulb is off, there is no charge.

Figure 5.13 is a diagram of a real 8088 CPU, showing the wires that comprise the external data bus and the single clock wire. Because the registers are inside the CPU, you can't see them in this figure.

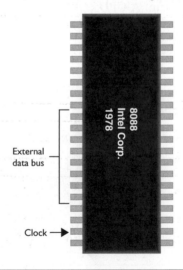

• **Figure 5.13**   Diagram of an Intel 8088 showing the external data bus and clock wires

Now that you have learned what components are involved in the process, try the following simple exercise to see how the process works. In this example, you tell the CPU to add 2 + 3. To do this, you must send a series of commands to the CPU; the CPU will act on each command, eventually giving you an answer. Refer to the codebook in Figure 5.7 to translate the instructions you're giving the Man in the Box into binary commands.

Did you try it? Here's how it works:

1. Place 10000000 on the external data bus (EDB).
2. Place 00000010 on the EDB.
3. Place 10010000 on the EDB.
4. Place 00000011 on the EDB.
5. Place 10110000 on the EDB.
6. Place 11000000 on the EDB.

When you finish step 6, the value on the EDB will be 00000101, the decimal number 5 written in binary.

Congrats! You just added 2 + 3 by using individual commands from the codebook. This set of commands is known as a **program**, which is a series of commands sent to a CPU in a specific order for the CPU to perform work. Each discrete setting of the external data bus is a line of code. This program, therefore, has six lines of code.

■ Memory

Now that you've seen how the CPU executes program code, let's work backward in the process for a moment and think about how the program code gets to the external data bus. The program itself is stored on the hard drive. In theory, you could build a computer that sends data from the hard drive directly to the CPU, but there's a problem—the hard drive is too slow. Even the ancient 8088, with its clock speed of 4.77 MHz, could conceivably process several million lines of code every second. Modern CPUs crank out billions of lines every second. Hard drives simply can't give the data to the CPU at a fast enough speed.

Computers need some other device that takes copies of programs from the hard drive and then sends them, one line at a time, to the CPU quickly enough to keep up with its demands. Because each line of code is nothing more than a pattern of eight ones and zeros, any device that can store ones and zeros eight-across will do. Devices that in any way hold ones and zeros that the CPU accesses are known generically as **memory**.

Many types of devices store ones and zeros perfectly well—technically even a piece of paper counts as memory—but computers need memory that does more than just store groups of eight ones and zeros. Consider this pretend program:

1. Put 2 in the AX register.
2. Put 5 in the BX register.
3. If AX is greater than BX, run line 4; otherwise, go to line 6.

4. Add 1 to the value in AX.

5. Go back to line 1.

6. Put the value of AX on the EDB.

This program has an IF statement, also called a *branch* by CPU makers. The CPU needs a way to address each line of this memory—a way for the CPU to say to the memory, "Give me the next line of code" or "Give me line 6." Addressing memory takes care of another problem: the memory must not only store programs but also store the result of the programs. If the CPU adds 2 + 3 and gets 5, the memory needs to store that 5 in such a way that other programs may later read that 5, or possibly even store that 5 on a hard drive. By addressing each line of memory, other programs will know where to find the data.

Memory and RAM

Memory must store not only programs but also data. The CPU needs to be able to read and write to this storage medium. Additionally, this system must enable the CPU to jump to *any* line of stored code as easily as to any other line of code. All of this must be done at or at least near the clock speed of the CPU. Fortunately, this magical device has existed for many years: **random access memory (RAM)**.

In Chapter 6, "RAM," the concept of RAM is developed in detail, so for now let's look at RAM as an electronic spreadsheet, like one you can generate in Microsoft Excel (Figure 5.14). Each cell in this spreadsheet can store only a one or a zero. Each cell is called a **bit**. Each row in the spreadsheet is eight bits across to match the external data bus of the 8088. Each row of eight bits is called a **byte**. In the PC world, RAM transfers and stores data to and from the CPU in byte-sized chunks. RAM is therefore arranged in byte-sized rows. Here are the terms used to talk about quantities of bits:

1	0	0	0	0	0	1	1
0	1	0	0	0	0	0	0
0	0	0	0	1	1	0	1
0	1	0	1	0	0	0	0
0	0	0	0	0	0	0	1
0	1	0	1	1	0	1	0
0	0	1	1	1	1	0	0
0	0	0	0	1	0	0	1
1	1	1	0	0	0	0	0
0	0	1	0	1	1	1	0
1	0	0	0	0	0	0	0
1	0	1	0	1	0	1	0

• **Figure 5.14**   RAM as a spreadsheet

- Any individual 1 or 0 = a bit
- 4 bits = a nibble
- 8 bits = a byte
- 16 bits = a word
- 32 bits = a double word
- 64 bits = a paragraph or quad word

The number of bytes of RAM varies from PC to PC. In earlier PCs, from around 1980 to 1990, the typical system would have only a few hundred thousand bytes of RAM. Today's systems often have billions of bytes of RAM.

Let's stop here for a quick reality check. Electronically, RAM looks like a spreadsheet, but real RAM is made of groups of semiconductor chips soldered onto small cards that snap into your computer (Figure 5.15). In Chapter 6, "RAM," you'll see how these groups of chips actually make

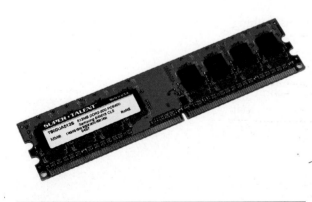

• **Figure 5.15**   Typical RAM

themselves look like a spreadsheet. For now, don't worry about real RAM and just stick with the spreadsheet idea.

The CPU accesses any one row of RAM as easily and as fast as any other row, which explains the "random access" part of RAM. Not only is RAM randomly accessible, it's also fast. By storing programs on RAM, the CPU can access and run them very quickly. RAM also stores any data that the CPU actively uses.

Computers use **dynamic RAM (DRAM)** for the main system memory. DRAM needs both a constant electrical charge and a periodic refresh of the circuits; otherwise, it loses data—that's what makes it dynamic rather than static in content. The refresh can cause some delays, because the CPU has to wait for the refresh to happen, but modern CPU manufacturers have clever ways to get by this issue, as you'll see when you read about the generations of processors later in this chapter.

Don't confuse RAM with mass storage devices such as hard drives and flash drives. You use hard drives and flash drives to store programs and data permanently. Chapter 11, "Hard Drive Technologies," Chapter 12, "Implementing Hard Drives," and Chapter 13, "Removable Media," discuss permanent storage in intimate detail.

Cross Check

RAM

You learned a few essentials about RAM in Chapter 3, "The Visible PC," so check back in that chapter and see if you can answer these questions. How is RAM packaged? Where do you install the PC's primary RAM, called the *system RAM*, in the system unit?

Address Bus

So far, the entire PC consists of only a CPU and RAM. But the CPU and the RAM need some connection so they can talk to each other. To do so, extend the external data bus from the CPU so it can talk to the RAM (Figure 5.16).

Wait a minute. This is not a matter of just plugging the RAM into the external data bus wires! RAM is a spreadsheet with thousands and thousands of discrete rows, and you only need to look at the contents of one row of the spreadsheet at a time, right? So how do you connect the RAM to the external data bus in such a way that the CPU can see any one given row but still give the CPU the capability to look at *any* row in RAM? We need some type of chip between the RAM and the CPU to make the connection. The CPU needs to be able to say which row of RAM it wants, and the chip should handle the mechanics of retrieving that row of data from the RAM and putting it on the external data bus. Wouldn't you know I just happen to have such a chip? This chip comes with many names, but for right now just call it the **memory controller chip (MCC).**

The MCC contains special circuitry so it can grab the contents of any single line of RAM and place that data or command on the external data bus. This in turn enables the CPU to act on that code (Figure 5.17).

Once the MCC is in place to grab any discrete byte of RAM, the CPU needs to be able to tell the MCC which line of code it needs. The CPU therefore gains a second set of wires, called the **address bus**, with which it can

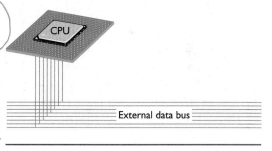

• **Figure 5.16**   Extending the EDB

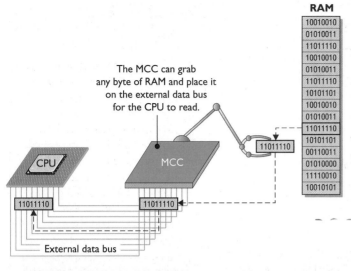

The MCC can grab any byte of RAM and place it on the external data bus for the CPU to read.

RAM

10010010
01010011
11011110
10010010
01010011
11011110
10101101
10010010
01010011
11011110
10101101
00110011
01010000
11110010
10010101

• **Figure 5.17**   The MCC grabs a byte of RAM.

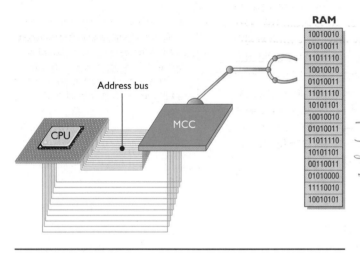

RAM

10010010
01010011
11011110
10010010
01010011
11011110
10101101
10010010
01010011
11011110
10101101
00110011
01010000
11110010
10010101

• **Figure 5.18**   Address bus

communicate with the MCC. Different CPUs have different numbers of wires (which, you will soon see, is very significant). The 8088 had 20 wires in its address bus (Figure 5.18).

By turning the address bus wires on and off in different patterns, the CPU tells the MCC which line of RAM it wants at any given moment. Every different pattern of ones and zeros on these 20 wires points to one byte of RAM. There are two big questions here. First, how many different patterns of on-and-off wires can exist with 20 wires? And second, which pattern goes to which row of RAM?

How Many Patterns?

Mathematics can answer the first question. Each wire in the address bus exists in only one of two states: on or off. If the address bus consisted of only one wire, that wire would at any given moment be either on or off. Mathematically, that gives you (pull out your old pre-algebra books) $2^1 = 2$ different combinations. If you have two address bus wires, the address bus wires create $2^2 = 4$ different combinations. If you have 20 wires, you would have 2^{20} (or 1,048,576) combinations. Because each pattern points to one line of code and each line of RAM is one byte, *if you know the number of wires in the CPU's address bus, you know the maximum amount of RAM that a particular CPU can handle.*

Because the 8088 had a 20-wire address bus, the most RAM it could handle was 2^{20} or 1,048,576 bytes. The 8088, therefore, had an *address space* of 1,048,576 bytes. This is not to say that every computer with an 8088 CPU had 1,048,576 bytes of RAM. Far from it! The original IBM PC only had a measly 64 kilobytes— but that was considered plenty back in the Dark Ages of Computing in the early 1980s.

Okay, so you know that the 8088 had 20 address wires and a total address space of 1,048,576 bytes. Although this is accurate, no one uses such an exact term to discuss the address space of the 8088. Instead you say that the 8088 had one *megabyte* (1 MB) of address space.

What's a "mega"? Well, let's get some terminology down. Dealing with computers means constantly dealing with the number of patterns a set of wires can handle. Certain powers of 2 have names used a lot in the computing world. The following list explains.

1 kilo = 2^{10} = 1,024 (abbreviated as "K")

1 kilobyte = 1,024 bytes (abbreviated as "KB")

1 mega = 2^{20} = 1,048,576 (abbreviated as "M")

1 megabyte = 1,048,576 bytes (abbreviated as "MB")

1 giga = 2^{30} = 1,073,741,824 (abbreviated as "G")

1 gigabyte = 1,073,741,824 bytes (abbreviated as "GB")

1 tera = 2^{40} = 1,099,511,627,776 (abbreviated as "T")

1 terabyte = 1,099,511,627,776 bytes (abbreviated as "TB")

1 kilo is *not* equal to 1,000 (one thousand)

1 mega is *not* equal to 1,000,000 (one million)

1 giga is *not* equal to 1,000,000,000 (one billion)

1 tera is *not* equal to 1,000,000,000,000 (one trillion)

(But they are pretty close!)

Tech Tip

Kilos

Of course, 1 kilo is equal to 1,000 when you talk in terms of the metric system. It also means 1,000 when you talk about the clock speed of a chip, so 1 KHz is equal to 1,000 Hz. When you talk storage capacity, though, the binary numbers kick in, making 1 KB = 1,024 bytes. Got it? This same bizarre dual meaning applies all the way up the food chain, so 1 MHz is 1,000,000 Hz, but 1 MB is 1,048,576 bytes; 1 GHz is 1 billion Hz, but 1 GB is 1,073,741,824 bytes; and so on.

Which Pattern Goes to Which Row?

The second question is a little harder: "Which pattern goes to which row of RAM?" To understand this, let's take a moment to discuss binary counting. In binary, only two numbers exist, 0 and 1, which makes binary a handy way to work with wires that turn on and off. Let's try to count in binary: 0, 1…what's next? It's not 2—you can only use zeros and ones. The next number after 1 is 10! Now let's count in binary to 1000: 0, 1, 10, 11, 100, 101, 110, 111, 1000. Try counting to 10000. Don't worry; it hardly takes any time at all.

Super; you now count in binary as well as any math professor. Let's add to the concept. Stop thinking about binary for just a moment and think about good old base 10 (regular numbers). If you have the number 365, can you put zeros in front of the 365, like this: 000365? Sure you can—it doesn't change the value at all. The same thing is true in binary. Putting zeros in front of a value doesn't change a thing! Let's count again to 1000 in binary. In this case, add enough zeros to make 20 places:

Bits and bytes are abbreviated differently. Bytes get a capital *B* whereas bits get a lowercase *b*. So for example, 4 KB is four kilobytes, but 4 Kb is four kilobits.

```
00000000000000000000
00000000000000000001
00000000000000000010
00000000000000000011
00000000000000000100
00000000000000000101
00000000000000000110
00000000000000000111
00000000000000001000
```

Hey, wouldn't this be a great way to represent each line of RAM on the address bus? The CPU identifies the first byte of RAM on the address bus with 00000000000000000000. The CPU identifies the last RAM row with 11111111111111111111. When the CPU turns off all of the address bus wires, it wants the first line of RAM; when it turns on all of the wires, it wants the 1,048,576th line of RAM. Obviously, the address bus also addresses all of the rows of RAM in between. So, by lighting up different patterns of ones and zeros on the address bus, the CPU can access any row of RAM it needs.

Modern CPUs

Modern CPUs retain the core structures of the Intel 8088, such as registers, instruction sets, and, of course, the **arithmetic logic unit (ALU)**—our friend, the Man in the Box. But in the decades of the personal computer, many manufacturers have risen to challenge Intel's dominance—some have even survived—and all processor makers have experimented with various processor shapes, connectors, and more. The amazing variety of modern CPUs presents unique challenges to a new tech. Which processors go on which motherboards? Can a motherboard use processors from two or more manufacturers? Aren't processors all designed for PCs and thus interchangeable?

This section maps out the modern processor scene. It starts with a brief look at the manufacturers so you know who the players are. Once you know who's making the CPUs, we'll go through the generations of CPUs in wide use today, starting with the Intel Pentium. All modern processors share fundamental technology first introduced by Intel in the Pentium CPU. I use the Pentium, therefore, to discuss the details of the shared technology, and then add specific bonus features when discussing subsequent processors.

Manufacturers

When IBM awarded Intel the contract to provide the CPUs for its new IBM PC back in 1980, it established for Intel a virtual monopoly on all PC CPUs. The other home-computer CPU makers of the time faded away: MOS Technology, Zilog, Motorola—no one could compete directly with Intel. Over time, other competitors have risen to challenge Intel's market-segment share dominance. In particular, a company called Advanced Micro Devices (AMD) began to make clones of Intel CPUs, creating an interesting and rather cutthroat competition with Intel that lasts to this day.

Intel

Intel Corporation thoroughly dominated the personal computer market with its CPUs and motherboard support chips. At nearly every step in the evolution of the PC, Intel has led the way with technological advances and surprising flexibility for such a huge corporation. Intel CPUs—and more specifically, their instruction sets—define the personal computer. Intel currently produces a dozen or so models of CPU for both desktop and portable computers. Most of Intel's desktop processors are sold under the Celeron, Pentium, and Core brands. Their very low-power portable/smart phone chips are branded Atom; their high-end workstation/server ones are called Xeon.

AMD

You can't really talk about CPUs without mentioning Advanced Micro Devices—the Cogswell Cogs to Intel's Spacely Sprockets. AMD makes

---

Tech Tip

Intel Core Branding

As we go to print, Intel has announced a simplified naming scheme for the majority of its new processors, all under the Core brand name. The Core i3, Core i5, and Core i7 processor names quickly relay where the processor fits in relation to other Core processors. The Core i7 will offer more power than the Core i5, for example. My guess is that they'll keep the Atom processor line separate and distinct from the Core family.

superb CPUs for the PC market and provides competition that keeps Intel on its toes. Like Intel, AMD doesn't just make CPUs, but their CPU business is certainly the part that the public notices. AMD has made CPUs that clone the function of Intel CPUs. If Intel invented the CPU used in the original IBM PC, how could AMD make clone CPUs without getting sued? Well, chipmakers have a habit of exchanging technologies through cross-license agreements. Way back in 1976, AMD and Intel signed just such an agreement, giving AMD the right to copy certain types of CPUs.

The trouble started with the Intel 8088. Intel needed AMD to produce CPUs. The PC business was young back then, and providing multiple suppliers gave IBM confidence in their choice of CPUs. Life was good. But after a few years, Intel had grown tremendously and no longer wanted AMD to make CPUs. AMD said, "Too bad. See this agreement you signed?" Throughout the 1980s and into the 1990s, AMD made pin-for-pin identical CPUs that matched the Intel lines of CPUs (Figure 5.19). You could yank an Intel CPU out of a system and snap in an AMD CPU—no problem!

In January 1995, after many years of legal wrangling, Intel and AMD settled and decided to end the licensing agreements. As a result of this settlement, AMD chips are no longer compatible with sockets or motherboards made for Intel CPUs—even though in some cases the chips look similar. Today, if you want to use an AMD

● **Figure 5.19** Identical Intel and AMD 486 CPUs from the early 1990s

CPU, you must purchase a motherboard designed for AMD CPUs. If you want to use an Intel CPU, you must purchase a motherboard designed for Intel CPUs. So you now have a choice: Intel or AMD. You'll look at both brands as you learn more about modern processors in this chapter.

CPU Packages

One of the many features that make PCs attractive is the ability for users (okay, maybe advanced users) to replace one CPU with another. If you want a removable CPU, you need your CPUs to use a standardized package with a matching standardized socket on the motherboard. CPUs have gone through many packages, with manufacturers changing designs like snakes shedding skins. The fragile little DIP package of the 8088 (Figure 5.20) gave way to rugged slotted processors in the late 1990s (Figure 5.21), which have in turn given way to CPUs using the now prevalent grid array packaging.

● **Figure 5.20** The dual inline pin package of the Intel 8088

● **Figure 5.21** An AMD Athlon Slot A processor

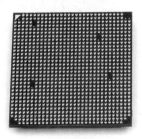 

• **Figure 5.22**   Samples of PGA packages

The grid array package has been popular since the mid-1980s. The most common form of grid array is the pin grid array (PGA). PGA CPUs are distinguished by their square shape with many—usually hundreds—of tiny pins (Figure 5.22).

Collectively, Intel and AMD have used close to 100 variations of the PGA package over the years for hundreds of CPU models with such names as staggered-PGA, micro-PGA, ball grid array (which uses tiny balls instead of pins), and land grid array (which uses flat pads instead of pins). Other varieties of PGA CPUs are based on the number of pins sticking out of the CPU.

The CPUs snap into special sockets on the motherboard, with each socket designed to match the pins (or balls or pads) on the CPU. To make CPU insertion and removal easier, these sockets—officially called **zero insertion force (ZIF) sockets**—use a small arm on the side of the socket (Figure 5.23) or a cage that fits over the socket (Figure 5.24) to hold the CPU in place. ZIF sockets are universal and easily identified by their squarish shape.

The first generations of sockets used a numbering system that started with Socket 1 and went through Socket 8. Because of the hassle of trying to remember how many pins went with each type of socket, CPU makers started giving all sockets a name based on the number of pins. Most sockets today have names like Socket 1366 and Socket 775 to reflect the number of pins.

• **Figure 5.23**   ZIF socket with arm on side

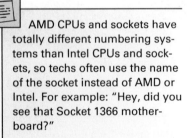

Although there are many types of PGA packages, most techs just call them all "PGA."

AMD CPUs and sockets have totally different numbering systems than Intel CPUs and sockets, so techs often use the name of the socket instead of AMD or Intel. For example: "Hey, did you see that Socket 1366 motherboard?"

• **Figure 5.24**   ZIF socket with cage over the top

It's very important to know the more common CPU/socket types. As you go through each type of CPU in this chapter, pay attention to the socket types used by those particular CPUs.

The Pentium CPU: The Early Years

Since the advent of the 8088 way back in the late 1970s, CPU makers have made many improvements. As technology has progressed from the 8088 to the most current CPUs, the sizes of the external data bus, address bus, and registers have grown dramatically. The clock speeds at which CPUs run have kept pace, getting faster and faster with each successive generation of processor. The 1980s were an exciting time for CPU technology. The 8088 CPU was supplanted by a series of improved processors with names such as 80286, 80386, and 80486 (Figure 5.25). These CPU families incorporated wider buses, increasingly higher clock speeds, and other improvements.

In the early 1990s, Intel unveiled the Pentium CPU. Although no longer manufactured, the original Pentium CPU was the first Intel CPU to contain all of the core functions that define today's modern CPUs.

The Pentium retained the core features of the 8088 and subsequent processors, although the clock was much faster, the address bus and external data bus were wider, and the registers had more bits. You'll also see a number of other improvements that simply didn't exist on the original 8088.

• **Figure 5.25**   Old CPUs

Many of the CPU features attributed here to the Pentium actually appeared earlier, but the Pentium was the first CPU to have *all* of these features.

The Rise of 32-bit Processing

The old 8088 had 16-bit registers, an 8-bit EDB, and a 20-bit address bus. Old operating systems (such as DOS and early versions of Windows) were written to work on the 8088. Over the years, later CPUs gradually increased their address buses and general-purpose register sizes to 32 bits, allowing much more powerful operating systems (such as Linux, Windows XP, and Windows Vista) to work with the Pentium to process larger numbers at a single time and to address up to $2^{32} = 4,294,967,296 = 4$ gigabytes of RAM (see Figure 5.26). Running 32-bit operating systems on 32-bit hardware is called *32-bit processing*.

Both AMD and Intel now make 64-bit processors that address up to $2^{64} = 18,446,744,073,709,551,616$ bytes of RAM. To take advantage of this larger address bus, a 64-bit version of the operating system must be used. You'll learn more about 64-bit processors later in this chapter.

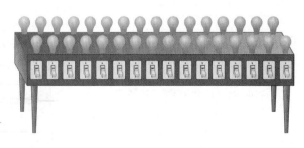

• **Figure 5.26**   A 32-bit register

Pipelining

Remember earlier when we talked about pulling the crank multiple times to get an answer out of the CPU? This is because to get a command from the

EDB, do the calculation, and then get the answer back out on the EDB, the CPU takes at least four steps (each of these steps is called a *stage*):

1. **Fetch**   Get the data from the EDB.
2. **Decode**   Figure out what type of command needs to be done.
3. **Execute**   Perform the calculation.
4. **Write**   Send the data back onto the EDB.

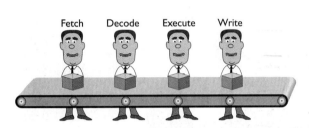

- **Figure 5.27**   Simple pipeline

Smart, discrete circuits inside your CPU handle each of these stages. In early CPUs, when a command was placed on the EDB, each stage did its job and the CPU handed back the answer before starting the next command, requiring at least four clock cycles to process a command. In every clock cycle, three of the four circuits sat idle. Today, the circuits are organized in a conveyer-belt fashion called a **pipeline**. With pipelining, each stage does its job with each clock-cycle pulse, creating a much more efficient process. The CPU has multiple circuits doing multiple jobs, so let's add pipelining to the Man in the Box analogy. Now, it's *Men* in the Box (Figure 5.27)!

Pipelines keep every stage of the processor busy on every click of the clock, making a CPU run more efficiently without increasing the clock speed. Note that at this point, the CPU has four stages: fetch, decode, execute, and write—a four-stage pipeline. No CPU ever made has fewer than four stages, but advancements in caching have increased the number of stages over the years. Current CPU pipelines contain many more stages, up to 20 in some cases.

Pipelining isn't perfect. Sometimes a stage hits a complex command that requires more than one clock cycle, forcing the pipeline to stop. Your CPU tries to avoid these stops, called *pipeline stalls*. The decode stage tends to cause the most pipeline stalls; certain commands are complex and therefore harder to decode than other commands. The Pentium used two decode stages to reduce the chance of pipeline stalls due to complex decoding.

Pipelining certainly helped the Pentium run more efficiently, but there's another issue: the execute stage. The inside of the CPU is composed of multiple chunks of circuitry to handle the many types of calculations your PC needs to do. For example, one part, the *integer unit*, handles integer math: basic math for numbers with no decimal point. A perfect example of integer math is $2 + 3 = 5$. The typical CPU spends more than 90 percent of its work doing integer math. But the Pentium also had special circuitry to handle complex numbers, called the **floating point unit (FPU)**. With a single pipeline, only the integer unit or the floating point unit worked at any execution stage. Worse yet, floating point calculation often took many, many clock cycles to execute, forcing the CPU to stall the pipeline until the floating point finished executing the complex command (Figure 5.28).

To keep things moving, the folks at Intel gave the Pentium two pipelines: one main, do-everything pipeline and one that only handled integer math. Although this didn't *stop* pipeline stalls, a second pipeline kept running when the main one stalled (see Figure 5.29).

Tech Tip

Lengthening Pipelines

After the Pentium, pipelines kept getting longer, reaching up to 20 stages in the Pentium 4. Since then, Intel and AMD have kept CPU pipelines around 12 stages (although this could change again).

You'll see the integer unit referred to as the arithmetic logic unit (ALU) in many sources. Either term works.

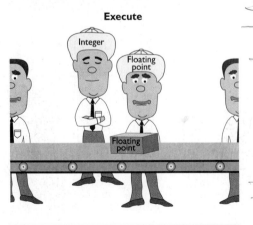

- **Figure 5.28**   Bored integer unit

Mike Meyers' CompTIA A+ Guide to Managing and Troubleshooting PCs

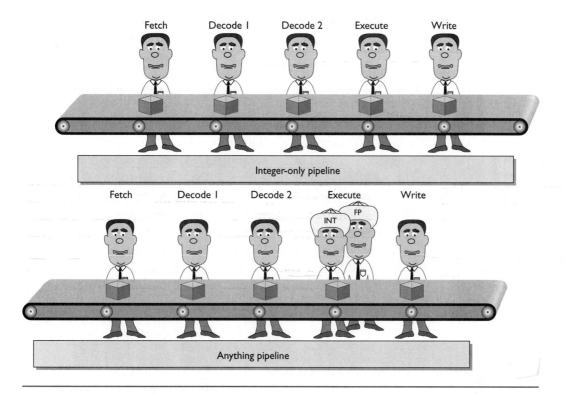

Integer-only pipeline

Anything pipeline

• **Figure 5.29**   The Pentium dual pipeline

The two pipelines on the old Pentium were so successful that Intel and AMD added more and more pipelines to subsequent CPUs. Most CPUs today have around eight pipelines, although there's tremendous variance from CPU to CPU.

> One of the biggest differences between equivalent AMD and Intel processors is the pipelines. AMD tends to go for lots of short pipelines, whereas Intel tends to go with just a few long pipelines.

CPU Cache

When you send a program to the CPU, you actually run lots of little programs all at the same time. Okay, let's be fair here: *you* didn't send all of these little programs—you just started your Web browser or some other program. The moment you double-clicked that icon, Windows started sending lots of programs to the CPU. Each of these programs breaks down into some number of little pieces, called *threads*, and data. Each thread is a series of instructions designed to do a particular job with the data.

Take a look at Figure 5.30. It shows four programs in RAM: a Web browser, Solitaire, an image-editing program, and an e-mail

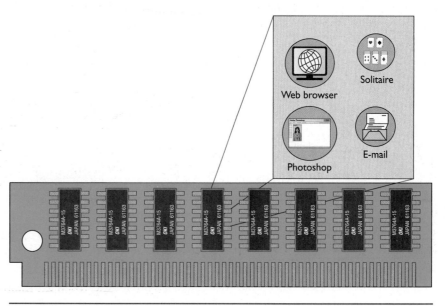

• **Figure 5.30**   Four programs in RAM

program. Note they are not the same size. Some programs need more RAM than others.

Modern CPUs don't execute instructions sequentially, first doing step 1, then step 2, and so on; but rather process all kinds of instructions. Most applications have certain instructions and data that get reused, sometimes many times.

Pipelining CPUs work fantastically well as long as the pipelines stay filled with instructions. Because the CPU runs faster than the RAM can supply it with code, you'll always get pipeline stalls—called **wait states**—because the RAM can't keep up with the CPU. To reduce wait states, the Pentium came with built-in, very high-speed RAM called **static RAM (SRAM)**. This SRAM would preload as many instructions as possible and would also keep copies of already run instructions and data in the hope that the CPU would need to work on them again (see Figure 5.31). SRAM used in this fashion is called a **cache**.

The SRAM cache inside the CPU was tiny, only about 16 KB, but it improved performance tremendously. In fact, it helped so much that many

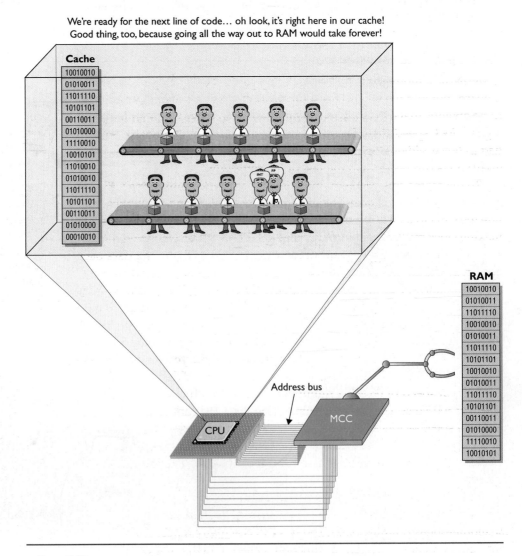

• **Figure 5.31**   RAM cache

Mike Meyers' CompTIA A+ Guide to Managing and Troubleshooting PCs

motherboard makers began adding a cache directly to the Pentium motherboards. These caches were much larger, usually around 128 to 512 KB. When the CPU looked for a line of code, it first went to the built-in cache; if the code wasn't there, the CPU went to the cache on the motherboard. The cache on the CPU was called the *L1 cache* because it was the one the CPU first tried to use. The cache on the motherboard was called the *L2 cache*, not because it was on the motherboard but because it was the second cache the CPU checked. Later, engineers took this cache concept even further and added the L2 cache onboard the CPU. Some CPUs even include three caches: an L1, an L2, and an L3 cache.

The Pentium was capable of *branch prediction*, a process whereby the CPU attempted to anticipate program branches before they got to the CPU itself. An IF statement provides a nice example of this: "If the value in the AX register = 5, stop running this code and jump to another memory location." Such a jump would make all of the data in the cache useless. The Pentium could recognize a branch statement. Using a counter that kept a record about the direction of the previous branch, the CPU would guess which way the branch was going to go and make sure that side of the branch was in its cache. The counter wasn't perfect, but it was right more often than it was wrong.

You'll hear caches referred to as Level 1, Level 2, and Level 3 for L1, L2, and L3 cache, respectively. Any of the terms are acceptable.

Tech Tip

It's Not Just Size That Matters
It's tempting to ask why processor manufacturers didn't just include bigger L1 caches instead of making onboard L1 and L2 caches. The answer is that a very small L1 and a larger L2 are much more efficient than a single fast L1.

Clock Speed and Multipliers

In the earliest motherboards, the clock chip pushed every chip on the motherboard, not just the CPU. This setup worked great for a while until it became obvious that CPU makers (really Intel) could make CPUs with a much higher clock speed than the rest of the chips on the motherboard. So Intel had a choice: either stop making faster CPUs or come up with some way to make CPUs run faster than the rest of the computer.

To overcome this problem, Intel developed clock-multiplying CPUs. A **clock-multiplying CPU** takes the incoming clock signal and multiplies it inside the CPU to let the internal circuitry of the CPU run faster. The secret to making clock multiplying work is caching. CPUs with caches spend the majority of their clock cycles performing calculations and moving data back and forth within the caches, not sending any data on the external buses.

All modern CPUs are clock multipliers. So in reality, every CPU now has two clock speeds: the speed that it runs internally and the speed that it runs when talking on the address bus and the external data bus. Multipliers run from 2× up to almost 30×! Multipliers do not have to be whole numbers. You can find a CPU with a multiplier of 6.5× just as easily as you would find one with a multiplier of 7×. A late-generation Pentium would have an external speed of 66 MHz multiplied by 4.5× for an internal speed of 300 MHz. The Intel Pentium 4 3.06-GHz CPU runs at an external speed of 133 MHz with a 23× multiplier to make—yes, you've got it—3.06 GHz. Without the invention of multiplying, modern CPUs would be nowhere near their current blazing speeds.

The clock speed and the multiplier on Pentium CPU systems had to be manually configured via jumpers or DIP switches on the motherboard (Figure 5.32). Today's CPUs actually report to the motherboard through a function called CPUID (CPU identifier), and the speed and multiplier are set automatically.

Clock multiplying first surfaced during the reign of the Intel 80486 CPUs. The first clock multipliers exactly doubled the clock speed, resulting in the term *clock doubling*. This term is used interchangeably with *clock multiplying*, even though modern CPUs multiply far more than just times two.

• **Figure 5.32** DIP switch on an old motherboard

For years, users pushed for faster and faster CPU clock speeds, because clock speed was considered the most important way to differentiate one CPU from another. By 2003, advancements in caching, pipelining, and many other internal aspects of the CPU made clock speed an inaccurate way to compare one CPU to another. CPU makers give their processors model numbers—nothing more than marketing names—to tell one processor from another. The Intel Core Duo T2300, for example, actually runs at 1.66 GHz (166 MHz external speed with a 10× multiplier). If you want to know the speed of a particular processor, you must go to the CPU maker's Web site or other source.

CPU Voltages

In the simplest sense, a CPU is a collection of *transistors*, tiny electrical switches that enable the CPU to handle the binary code that makes up programs. Transistors, like other electrical devices, require a set voltage to run properly. Give a transistor too much and you fry it, too little and it doesn't work. For the first ten years of the personal computer, CPUs ran on 5 volts of electricity, just like every other circuit on the motherboard. To increase the complexity and capability with new generations of CPUs, microprocessor developers simply increased the number of transistors. But eventually they altered this strategy to increase the efficiency of the CPUs and keep the size down to something reasonable.

Intel and AMD discovered that by reducing the amount of voltage used, you could reduce the size of the transistors and cram more of them into the same space. Intel released the Pentium, for example, that required only 3.3 volts. AMD responded with its versions of the Pentium-class CPUs with even lower voltages.

Motherboard manufacturers had to scramble to adapt to the changing CPU landscape by creating motherboards that could handle multiple voltages of CPUs. All of the logic circuits still ran at 5 volts, so manufacturers started installing a **voltage regulator module (VRM)** that damped down voltages specifically for the CPUs.

Because the new and improved motherboards handled many CPU voltages, initially techs had to install a VRM specific to the CPU. As manufacturers got better at the game and built VRMs into the motherboards, techs just had to change jumpers or flip switches rather than install a VRM (Figure 5.33).

Getting the voltage right on today's CPUs is no longer a concern. Just as for clock speed and multipliers, today's CPUs tell the motherboard the voltage they need automatically. The integrated VRMs take care of the rest (Figure 5.34).

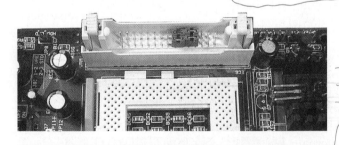

• **Figure 5.33**   Volt regulator module

The feature set of the early Pentium CPUs beats at the heart of every subsequent processor. Newer processors have a 64-bit data bus, 32-bit or larger address bus, 32-bit or larger registers, multiple pipelines, and two or three levels of cache. All run at some multiple of the system clock. So, now that you have the scoop on the Pentium, you're ready to check out subsequent CPU models.

Original Pentium

The Pentium is not a new chip; it's been around since 1990, and the last versions of the Pentium chip were discontinued in 1995. The original Pentium was the springboard for the Pentium Pro, probably the most important CPU ever made, and thus it makes sense to start there. The rest of this chapter looks at all of the popular CPUs developed since the Pentium and describes how they've built on this legacy CPU (Figure 5.35).

AMD made a competitor to the Pentium called the AMD K5. The AMD K5 was pin-compatible with the Pentium, but to keep Intel from suing them, AMD made the K5 very different on the inside, using a totally new (at least for Intel) method of processing. The AMD K5 had some success but was rather quickly upstaged by better AMD CPUs.

Pentium Pro

In 1995, Intel released the next generation of CPU, the Pentium Pro, often called the P6. The Pentium Pro was a huge CPU with a distinctive, rectangular PGA package (Figure 5.36). The P6 had the same bus and register sizes as the Pentium, but three new items made the P6 more powerful than its predecessor: quad pipelining, dynamic processing, and an on-chip L2 cache. These features carried on into every CPU version that followed, so many people consider the Pentium Pro to be the true "Father of the Modern CPU."

• **Figure 5.34**   Typical motherboard voltage regulators

Superscalar Execution

The P6 had four pipelines, twice as many as the Pentium. These pipelines were deeper and faster. With this many pipelines, the P6 was guaranteed to always, no matter what, run at least two instructions at the same time. The ability to execute more than one instruction in any one clock cycle is called *superscalar execution*.

• **Figure 5.35**   An early Pentium

• **Figure 5.36**   Pentium Pro

Out-of-Order Processing/Speculative Execution

From time to time, a CPU must go to system memory to access code, no matter how good its cache. When a RAM access takes place, the CPU must wait a few clock cycles before processing. Sometimes the wait can be 10 or 20 clock cycles. System memory is dynamic RAM and needs to be refreshed (charged up) periodically, causing further delays. When the P6 was forced into wait states, it took advantage of the wait to look at the code in the pipeline to see if it could run any commands while the wait states were active. If it found commands it could process that were not dependent on the data being fetched from DRAM, it ran these commands out of order, a feature called *out-of-order processing*. After the DRAM returned with the code, it rearranged the commands and continued processing.

The P6 improved on the Pentium's branch prediction by adding a far more complex counter that would predict branches with a better than 90-percent success rate. With the combination of out-of-order processing and the chance of a branch prediction so high, the CPU could grab the predicted side of the branch out of the cache and run it out of order in one pipeline, even before running the branch itself. This was called *speculative execution*.

On-Chip L2 Cache

The P6 had both an L1 and an L2 cache on the CPU. Because the L2 cache was on the chip, it ran almost as fast as the L1 cache (Figure 5.37). Be careful with the term "on-chip." Just because the L2 cache was on the chip, that doesn't mean it was built into the CPU. The CPU and the L2 cache shared the same package, but physically they were separate.

The inclusion of the L2 cache on the chip gave rise to some new terms to describe the connections between the CPU, MCC, RAM, and L2 cache. The address bus and external data bus (connecting the CPU, MCC, and RAM) were lumped into a single term called the **frontside bus**, and the connection between the CPU and the L2 cache became known as the **backside bus**.

Figure 5.38 shows a more modern configuration, labeling the important buses. Note that the external data bus and address bus are there, but the chipset provides separate address buses and external data buses—one set just for the CPU and another set for the rest of the devices in the PC. No official name has been given to the interface between the RAM and the chipset. On the rare occasions when they discuss it, most techs simply call it the *RAM interface*.

• Figure 5.37 A P6 opened to show separate CPU and L2 cache (*photo courtesy of Intel*)

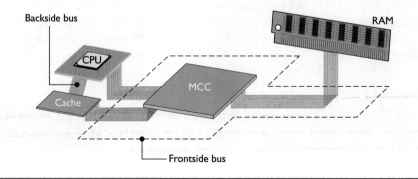

• Figure 5.38 Frontside and backside buses

The Pentium Pro had a unique PGA case that fit into a special socket, called Socket 8. No other CPU used this type of socket. The Pentium Pro made strong inroads in the high-end server market, but its high cost made it unacceptable for most people's desktop computers.

Although the Pentium Pro never saw a large volume of sales compared with the Pentium, many people in the industry consider it the most important chip ever created by Intel. Its feature set was the prototype for all CPUs designed ever since.

Later-Generation Pentium-Class CPUs

Intel's usual game plan in the rough-and-tumble business of chip making is to introduce a new CPU and simultaneously declare all previous CPUs obsolete. That did not happen with the Pentium Pro, however, because Intel never really developed the P6 for most users. It was to be the CPU for powerful, higher-end systems. This kept the Pentium as the CPU of choice for all but the most power-hungry systems.

While the Pentium Pro languished on the high end for several years, Intel and AMD developed new Pentium-class CPUs that incorporated a series of powerful improvements, some of which were taken from the Pentium Pro. These improvements required that they be regarded as a new family of CPUs, which I call the "later-generation Pentium-class CPUs" (Figure 5.39). Although certainly some profound differences exist between these CPUs, they all have three groups of similar improvements: multimedia extensions (MMX), increased multipliers/clocks, and improved processing.

Later-generation Pentiums were pin-compatible with earlier Pentiums, but included a large number of improvements. The most important improvement was increases in multipliers, and therefore clock speeds, but other improvements also took place—some borrowed from the P6 and some developed just for this new breed of Pentium.

• **Figure 5.39**   Later-generation Pentium

MMX

In 1996, Intel added a new enhancement to its Pentium CPU, called **multimedia extensions (MMX)**, in response to the large number of programs with heavy graphics needs coming out at this time. MMX was designed to work with large graphics by calculating on large chunks of data and performing vector math (vector math is needed to handle graphical issues such as spinning a 3D object). MMX was not heavily supported by the folks who wrote graphics programs, but MMX did start the idea that CPUs should have special circuitry just for such programs. Over time, the graphics community began to work with Intel to improve MMX, eventually replacing it with better solutions.

Increased Clocks and Multipliers

Later Pentiums all have vastly increased multipliers, resulting in higher speeds. Most early Pentiums used 2.5× multipliers at best, but later Pentium-class processors had up to 4.5× multipliers.

Pentium II

Intel's next major CPU was the Pentium II. Although highly touted as the next generation of CPUs, the Pentium II was little more than a faster Pentium Pro with MMX and a refined instruction set. The Pentium II came in a distinctive **single-edge cartridge (SEC)** that gave more space for the L2 cache and made CPU cooling easier while freeing up more room on the motherboard (Figure 5.40). Aggressive advertising and pricing made the Pentium II extremely popular.

The Pentium II initially achieved the higher clock speeds by using high multiples of a 66-MHz external speed. During this time, however, AMD began to sell CPUs designed to run on 100-MHz motherboards. Although the final Pentium II models also ran on 100-MHz motherboards, Intel's slow adoption of 100-MHz external-speed CPUs lost market share for Intel.

The SEC cartridge also created another problem: it was not free to copy. This prevented other CPU manufacturers from making CPUs that fit in the SEC's special Slot 1 connection and forced AMD to create its own SEC packages that were incompatible with Intel's. From the Pentium II to today, AMD and Intel CPUs are no longer interchangeable. We live in a world where AMD CPUs have motherboards designed for AMD, while Intel CPUs must have motherboards designed for Intel.

• **Figure 5.40**   Pentium II

AMD K6 Series

From 1997 to 2000, AMD produced a series of processors called the K6 that matched—and in many people's view, surpassed—the Pentium II, propelling AMD into serious competition with Intel (Figure 5.41). Four models were included in the K6 series: the K6, K6-2, K6-2+, and K6-III, each incorporating more advanced features than the previous model. The K6 processors incorporated a number of improvements, including a 64-KB L1 cache, extremely advanced pipelining, and support for motherboard speeds of up to 100 MHz (on later models). The K6-2 added AMD's proprietary 3DNow! instruction set—a direct competitor to Intel's MMX and a significant advancement in graphics-handling capabilities—and increased clock speeds. The K6-III included even more advancements in pipelining and added a 256-KB L2 cache, all on a standard Socket 7 PGA package.

• **Figure 5.41**   AMD K6 (*photo courtesy of AMD*)

Pentium III

The Pentium III improved on the Pentium II by incorporating *Streaming SIMD Extensions (SSE)*, Intel's direct competitor to AMD's 3DNow!; a number of internal processing/pipelining improvements; full support for 100-MHz and 133-MHz motherboard speeds; and a high-speed L2 cache. The Pentium III was first produced by using an SEC package (Figure 5.42), but improvements in die technology enabled Intel to produce PGA versions later, ending the short reign of the SEC-package CPUs.

• **Figure 5.42**   Intel Pentium III

Practical Application

Processing and Wattage

To make smarter CPUs, Intel and AMD need to increase the number of microscopic transistor circuits in the CPU. The more circuits you add, the more power they need. CPUs measure their power use in units called watts, just like a common light bulb. Higher wattage also means higher heat, forcing modern CPUs to use powerful cooling methods. Good techs know how many watts a CPU needs, because this tells them how hot the CPU will get inside a PC. Known hot CPUs are often avoided for general-purpose PCs because these CPUs require more aggressive cooling.

CPU makers really hate heat, but they still want to add more circuits; they constantly try to reduce the size of the circuits, because smaller circuits use less power. CPUs are made from silicon wafers. The electrical circuitry is etched onto the wafers with a process called photo lithography. Photo lithography is an amazingly complex process but basically requires placing a thin layer of chemicals on the wafer. These chemicals are sensitive to ultraviolet light; if a part of this mask is exposed to UV light, it gets hard and resistant. If it isn't exposed, it's easy to remove. To make the circuitry, a mask of the circuits is placed over the wafer, and then the mask and wafer are exposed to UV light. The mask is removed and the wafer is washed in chemicals, leaving the circuits. If you want microscopic circuits, you need a mask with the pattern of the microscopic circuits. This is done though a photographic process. The old 8088 used a 3-micrometer (one millionth of a meter) process to make the mask. Most of today's CPUs are created with a 45-nanometer process, and a 32-nanometer process is appearing in some chips. The same CPU created with a smaller process is usually cooler.

 As you read the wattages for the various CPUs, imagine a light bulb with that wattage inside your system unit.

 A nanometer is one billionth of a meter.

CPU Codenames

Intel and AMD fight to bring out new CPUs with an almost alarming frequency, making the job of documenting all of these CPUs challenging.

Luckily for us, the CPU makers use special CPU codenames for new CPUs, such as Bloomfield and Deneb to describe the first version of the Core i7 and the Phenom II X4, respectively. These codenames are in common use, and a good tech should recognize these names—plus they make a dandy way to learn about what's taking place in the CPU business.

AMD Athlon

Athlon is the brand name for a series of CPUs released by AMD. A number of different CPUs have been launched under this brand to compete head to head against the latest Intel chips. The original Athlon, now referred to as *Athlon Classic*, was the first AMD CPU to drop any attempt at pin compatibility with Intel chips. Instead, AMD decided to make its own AMD-only slots and sockets. The first of these sockets used an SEC package and was called Slot A (Figure 5.43).

AMD then shifted back to a PGA package with the release of an Athlon CPU codenamed Thunderbird (Figure 5.44). This CPU, along with several Athlon CPUs to come, used a proprietary 462-pin socket called Socket A. Thunderbird (like its predecessor) had an interesting double-pumped frontside bus that doubled the data rate without increasing the clock speed. The Athlon Thunderbird CPUs have a smaller but far more powerful L2 cache, as well as a number of other minor improvements when compared to the Athlon Classic.

Next, AMD launched the Athlon XP, first under the codename Palomino. AMD incorporated a number of performance enhancements to the Athlon core, including support for Intel's SSE instructions. AMD released an update to Palomino, codenamed Thoroughbred, which featured increased external bus speeds and was manufactured by using a 130-nm process that reduced the required CPU wattage. The last 32-bit CPUs to wear the Athlon badge were codenamed Barton and Thorton. Barton featured double the L2 cache of Thoroughbred and had an even faster external bus. Thorton was a cheaper version that did not increase the size of the cache.

One interesting aspect of the Athlon XP was AMD's attempt to ignore clock speeds and instead market the CPUs by using a performance rating (PR) number that matched the equivalent power of an Intel Pentium 4 processor. For example, the Athlon XP 1800+ actually ran at 1.6 GHz, but AMD claimed it processed as fast as or faster than a Pentium 4 1.8 GHz—ergo "1800+."

AMD Duron

Duron is the generic name given to lower-end CPUs based on the Athlon processor. A Duron is basically an Athlon with a smaller cache. Because the Duron supported the same frontside bus as the Athlon, it had a slight performance edge over its low-end rival from Intel at the time. The Duron connected to the same 462-pin Socket A as the later Athlon CPUs (Figure 5.45). AMD discontinued the Duron brand in 2004 and replaced it with the Sempron brand, discussed later in this chapter.

• **Figure 5.43**   Early Athlon CPU

• **Figure 5.44**   Athlon Thunderbird (*photo courtesy of AMD*)

• **Figure 5.45**   AMD Duron (*photo courtesy of AMD*)

Intel Pentium 4

Although the Pentium II and III were little more than improvements on the Intel Pentium Pro, the Pentium 4 introduced a completely redesigned core, called NetBurst. NetBurst centered around a totally new 20-stage pipeline combined with features to support this huge pipeline. Each stage of the pipeline performed fewer operations than typical pipeline stages in earlier processors, allowing Intel to crank up the clock speed for the Pentium 4 CPUs. The first Pentium 4s, codenamed Willamette, included a new version of SSE called SSE2, and later versions introduced SSE3.

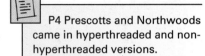

P4 Prescotts and Northwoods came in hyperthreaded and non-hyperthreaded versions.

The Pentium 4 featured a *quad-pumped frontside bus* where the external data bus was sampled four times per clock cycle. In the early going, there were two packages for the Pentium 4 CPUs. The first Pentium 4 CPUs came in a 423-pin PGA package. This was followed with a 478-pin PGA package (Figure 5.46). Even though the new package has more pins, it is considerably smaller than the earlier package.

• **Figure 5.46**   Pentium 4 (478- and 423-pin)

Intel switched to the Land Grid Array (LGA) 775 package with the release of a Pentium 4 CPU codenamed Prescott (Figure 5.47). Again, even though the LGA 775 package has more pins than a Socket 478 package, it is smaller. With the Pentium 4 CPUs codenamed Northwood and Prescott, Intel unveiled an interesting advancement in superscalar architecture called hyperthreading.

With *hyperthreading*, each individual pipeline can run more than one thread at a time—a tricky act to achieve. A single Intel P4 with hyperthreading looks like two CPUs to the operating system. Figure 5.48 shows the Task Manager in Windows XP on a system running a hyperthreaded Pentium 4. Note how the CPU box is broken into two groups—Windows thinks this one CPU is two CPUs.

Hyperthreading enhances a CPU's efficiency but with a couple of limitations. First, the operating system and the application have to be designed to take advantage of the feature. Second, although the CPU simulates the

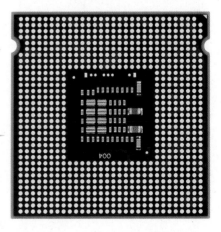

• **Figure 5.47**   Pentium 4 LGA

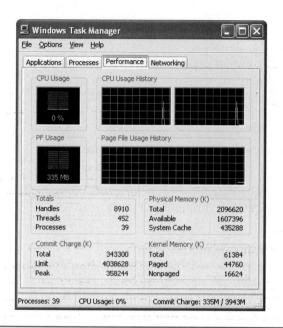

• **Figure 5.48**   Windows Task Manager with the Performance tab displayed for a system running a hyperthreaded Pentium 4

actions of a second processor, it doesn't double the processing power because the main execution resources are not duplicated.

Starting with the LGA 775 Prescotts, Intel dumped the convention of naming CPUs by their clock speed and adopted a cryptic three-digit model-numbering system. All Prescott Pentium 4s received a three-digit number starting with a 5 or a 6. One of the 2.8-GHz Pentium 4 CPUs is a 521, for example, and one of the 3-GHz processors is called the 630.

A late version of the Pentium 4 CPU was released, called the Pentium 4 Extreme Edition. The Extreme Edition CPUs incorporated a large L3 cache and other architectural details borrowed from Intel's Xeon line of server CPUs. The Pentium 4 Extreme Edition also had some of the highest wattages ever recorded on any Intel desktop CPU—over 110 watts! Extreme Edition CPUs ran incredibly fast, but their high price kept them from making any significant impact on the market.

These Pentiums reached the apex of clock speeds, approaching 4 GHz. After this, Intel (and AMD) stopped the CPU clock-speed race and instead began to concentrate on parallel and 64-bit processing (both to be discussed later in this chapter).

Mobile Processors

The inside of a laptop PC is a cramped, hot environment where no self-respecting CPU should ever need to operate. Since the mid-1980s, CPU manufacturers have endeavored to make specialized versions of their processors to function in the rugged world of laptops. Over the years, a number of CPU laptop solutions have appeared. Virtually every CPU made by Intel or AMD has come in a mobile version. You can usually tell a mobile version by the word "mobile" or the letter "M" in its name. Here are a few examples:

- Mobile Intel Pentium III

- Intel Pentium M

- Mobile AMD Athlon 64

- AMD Turion 64 (All Turions are mobile processors but don't have "mobile" or "M" in their name. AMD usually adds "mobile technology" as part of the Turion description.)

- Intel Core Duo (see the "Intel Core" section later in the chapter)

A mobile processor uses less power than an equivalent desktop model. This provides two advantages. First, the battery in the laptop lasts longer. Second, the CPU runs cooler, and the cooler the CPU, the fewer cooling devices you need.

Almost every mobile processor today runs at a lower voltage than the desktop version of the same CPU. As a result, most mobile CPUs also run at lower speeds—it takes juice if you want the speed! Mobile CPUs usually top out at about 75 percent of the speed of the same CPU's desktop version.

Reducing voltage is a good first step, but making a smart CPU that can use less power in low-demand situations reduces power usage even more. The first manifestation of this was the classic **System Management Mode (SMM)**. Introduced back in the times of the Intel 80386 processor, SMM provided the CPU with the capability to turn off devices that use a lot of power, such as the monitor or the hard drives. Although originally designed just for laptops, SMM has been replaced with more advanced power-management functions that are now built into all AMD and Intel CPUs.

CPU makers have taken power reduction one step further with **throttling**—the capability of modern CPUs to slow themselves down during low demand times or if the CPU detects that it is getting too hot. Intel's version of throttling is called *SpeedStep*, and AMD's version is known as *PowerNow!*

Tech Tip

Centrino

Intel uses the marketing term **Centrino** *in the laptop market to define complete mobile solutions, including a mobile processor, support chips, and wireless networking. There is no Centrino CPU, only Centrino solutions that include some type of Intel mobile CPU.*

Early 64-Bit CPUs

Both AMD and Intel now produce 64-bit CPUs. A 64-bit CPU has general-purpose, floating point, and address registers that are 64 bits wide, meaning they can handle 64-bit-wide code in one pass—twice as wide as a 32-bit processor. And they can address much, much more memory.

With the 32-bit address bus of the Pentium and later CPUs, the maximum amount of memory the CPU can address is 2^{32} or 4,294,967,296 bytes. With a 64-bit address bus, CPUs can address 2^{64} bytes of memory, or more precisely, 18,446,744,073,709,551,616 bytes of memory—that's a lot of RAM! This number is so big that gigabytes and terabytes are no longer convenient, so we now go to an exabyte (2^{60}). A 64-bit address bus can address 16 exabytes of RAM.

No 64-bit CPU uses an actual 64-bit address bus. Every 64-bit processor gets its address bus clipped down to something reasonable. The Intel Itanium, for example, only has a 44-bit address bus, for a maximum address space of 2^{44} or 17,592,186,044,416 bytes. AMD's Phenom II, on the other hand, can allow for a 48-bit physical address space for 2^{48} or 281,474,976,710,656 bytes of memory.

Initially, both AMD and Intel raced ahead with competing 64-bit processors. Interestingly, they took very different paths. Let's look at the two CPUs

that made the first wave of 64-bit processing: the Intel Itanium and the AMD Opteron.

Intel Itanium (Original and Itanium 2)

Intel made the first strike into the 64-bit world for PCs with the Itanium CPU. The Itanium was more of a proof-of-concept product than one that was going to make Intel any money, but it paved the way for subsequent 64-bit processors. The Itanium had a unique 418-pin **pin array cartridge (PAC)** to help house its 2- or 4-MB Level 3 cache (Figure 5.49).

The Intel Itanium 2 was Intel's first serious foray into the 64-bit world. To describe the Itanium 2 in terms of bus sizes and clock speeds is unfair. The power of this processor goes far deeper. Massive pipelines, high-speed caching, and literally hundreds of other improvements make the Itanium 2 a powerful CPU for high-end PCs. The Itanium 2 uses a unique form of PGA that Intel calls *organic land grid array* (*OLGA*) (see Figure 5.50).

• Figure 5.49   Intel Itanium (*photo courtesy of Intel*)

Intel made a bold move with the Itanium and the Itanium 2 by not making them backward-compatible to 32-bit programming. In other words, every OS, every application, and every driver of every device has to be rewritten to work on the Itanium and Itanium 2. In theory, developers would create excellent new applications and devices that dump all of the old stuff (and problems) and thus would be more efficient and streamlined. If a company has a lot invested in 32-bit applications and can't make the jump to 64-bit, Intel continues to offer the Pentium 4 or Pentium Xeon. If you need 64-bit, get an Itanium 2. AMD didn't agree with Intel and made 64-bit processors that also ran 32-bit when needed. Intel would eventually follow AMD in this decision.

AMD Opteron

• Figure 5.50   Intel Itanium 2 (*photo courtesy of Intel*)

Coming in after the Itanium, AMD's Opteron doesn't try to take on the Itanium head to head. Instead, AMD presents the Opteron as the lower-end 64-bit CPU. But don't let the moniker "lower-end" fool you. Although the Opteron borrowed heavily from the Athlon, it included an I/O data path known as HyperTransport. Think of HyperTransport as a very high speed link, providing direct connection to other parts of the PC—and to other CPUs for multiprocessing—at a blistering speed of over 6 GB per second! The Opteron comes in a micro-PGA package, looking remarkably like a Pentium 4 (Figure 5.51).

Unlike the Itanium, the Opteron runs both 32-bit and 64-bit code. AMD gives customers the choice to move slowly into 64-bit without purchasing

new equipment. This was the crucial difference between AMD and Intel in the early days of 64-bit processing.

Intel and AMD pitch the Itanium 2 and Opteron CPUs at the server market. This means that as a CompTIA A+ tech, you won't see them unless you go to work for a company that has massive computer needs. Newer CPUs from both companies fight for the desktop dollar.

Athlon 64

To place the Athlon 64 with the early generation CPUs is hardly fair. The Athlon 64 was the first for-the-desktop 64-bit processor, so in that aspect it is an early 64-bit CPU (Figure 5.52). AMD made two lines of Athlons: the "regular" Athlon 64 and the Athlon FX series. The FX series runs faster than the regular Athlon 64s, uses more wattage, and is marketed to power users who are willing to pay a premium. Underneath those two lines, AMD has almost twenty sub-lines of Athlon 64s in different codenames, making listing all of them here unwieldy.

The AMD 64s have a number of enhancements beyond simply moving into the 64-bit world. The most fascinating is the inclusion of a memory controller into the CPU, eliminating the need for an external MCC and for all intents also eliminating the idea of the frontside bus. The RAM directly connects to the Athlon 64. AMD 64s support Intel's SSE and SSE2 graphics extensions (later versions support SSE3).

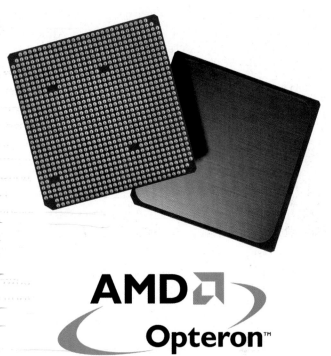

• **Figure 5.51** AMD Opteron (*photo courtesy of AMD*)

> ### Tech Tip
>
> **Athlon 64 Clock Speed**
>
> *Although the Athlon 64 may not have a true frontside bus anymore, it does have a system clock that runs at 200 MHz to talk to RAM. This is still multiplied to get the internal speed of the CPU.*

• **Figure 5.52** Athlon 64

While regular Athlon 64s use the same AMD PR numbers to describe CPUs, Athlon 64 FXs use a two-digit model number that's just as cryptic as Intel's current three-digit numbers.

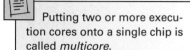
Putting two or more execution cores onto a single chip is called *multicore*.

AMD Sempron CPUs

AMD produces various Sempron CPUs for the low end of the market. Semprons come in two socket sizes and have less cache than the Athlon 64, but they offer a reasonable trade-off between price and performance.

Multicore CPUs

CPU clock speeds hit a practical limit of roughly 4 GHz around 2002–2003, motivating the CPU makers to find new ways to get more processing power for CPUs. Although Intel and AMD had different opinions about 64-bit CPUs, both decided at virtually the same time to combine two CPUs into a single chip, creating a **dual-core** architecture. Dual core isn't just two CPUs on the same chip. A dual-core CPU has two execution units—two sets of pipelines—but the two sets of pipelines share caches (how they share caches differs between Intel and AMD) and RAM.

A multicore CPU can process more than one thread at a time; this is called **parallel processing**. Through parallel processing, the CPU can more readily juggle the demands of both applications and Windows, making the overall computing experience better. With multithreaded applications (programs written to take advantage of multiple CPUs or CPUs with multiple cores), this parallel processing can dramatically improve the performance of those applications.

Pentium D

Intel won the race for first dual-core processor with the Pentium D line of processors (Figure 5.53). The Pentium D is simply two late-generation Pentium 4s molded onto the same chip, with each CPU using its own cache—although they do share the same frontside bus. One very interesting aspect to the Pentium D is the licensing of AMD's *AMD64* extensions—the "smarts" inside AMD CPUs that enable AMD CPUs to run either 64- or 32-bit code. Intel named their version *EM64T*. There are two codenames for Pentium D processors: the Smithfield (model numbers 8*xx*), using a 90-nm process, and the Presler (model numbers 9*xx*), using a 65-nm process. Pentium Ds use the same LGA 775 package seen on the later Pentium 4s.

• **Figure 5.53**   Pentium D (*photo courtesy of Intel*)

Athlon Dual Cores

AMD's introduction to dual core came with the Athlon 64 X2 CPUs. The X2s are truly two separate cores that share L1 caches, unlike the Intel Pentium D. Athlon 64 X2s initially came in both "regular" and FX versions packaged in the well-known AMD Socket 939. To upgrade from a regular Athlon 64 to an Athlon 64 X2, assuming you have a Socket 939 motherboard, is often as easy as simply doing a minor motherboard update, called *flashing the BIOS*. Chapter 7, "BIOS and CMOS," goes through this process in detail, or you can simply check your motherboard manufacturer's Web site for the

information on the process. In 2006, AMD announced the *Socket AM2*, designed to replace the Socket 939 across the Athlon line.

Intel Core

Intel introduced the *Intel Core* CPUs in 2006. Intel then followed up with the Core 2 processors, the first generation of CPUs to use the Intel Core architecture. Are you confused yet? Let's look a little closer at the Core and Core 2 CPUs.

Intel Core

Intel based the first generation of core processors, simply called Core, on the 32-bit-only Pentium M platform. Like the Pentium M, Core processors don't use the NetBurst architecture, instead falling back to a more Pentium Pro–style architecture (codenamed Yonah) with a 12-stage pipeline. Core CPUs come in single- (Solo) and dual-core (Duo) versions, but they all use the same 478-pin FCPGA package. Core also dispenses with the three-digit Pentium numbering system, using instead a letter followed by four numbers, such as T2300.

Intel Core 2

With the Core 2 line of processors (Figure 5.54), Intel released a radically revised processor architecture called Core. Redesigned to maximize efficiency, the Core 2 processors offer up to 40 percent in energy savings at the same performance level compared to the Pentium D processors. To achieve the efficiency, Intel cranked up the cache size (to 2 or 4 MB) and went with a wide, short pipeline. The CPU can perform multiple actions in a single clock cycle and, in the process, run circles around the competition.

Intel released three Core 2 versions for the desktop: the Core 2 Solo, Core 2 Duo, and Core 2 Quad. Intel has also released an enthusiast version named the Core 2 Extreme that comes in both Duo and Quad configurations. The Core 2 line also includes mobile versions. All versions incorporate AMD's 64-bit technology, rebranding it as Intel 64, so they can run 64-bit versions of Windows natively.

AMD Phenom

To achieve a quad-core processor, AMD took a different approach than Intel. Intel's Core 2 Quad series of processors combine two dual-core processors, each with their own caches, on the same physical die. These two on-die chips share a frontside bus to communicate with each other and memory.

For AMD's first quad-core desktop processor, called the Phenom, AMD decided to have each CPU core possess its own L1 and L2 caches but have all four cores share an L3 cache to facilitate communication between cores. This is why AMD refers to the Phenom as a native quad-core processor. The Phenom series of processors are all 64-bit CPUs that feature the AMD64 technology also found in the Athlon 64 CPUs.

Tech Tip

Core versus Core 2
Intel's naming conventions can leave a lot to be desired. Note that the Core Solo and Core Duo processors were based on the Pentium M architecture. The Core 2 processors are based on the Core architecture.

• **Figure 5.54**   Intel Core 2 CPU

The Phenom series processors have an integrated memory controller that supports two channels of DDR2 memory. With the inclusion of an integrated memory controller, the Phenom processors do not possess a traditional frontside bus. Instead, they use the same HyperTransport bus that the Athlon 64 / Opteron series of processors have. Phenom processors are supported by AMD's Socket AM2+ or Socket AM3. The CPU may also use Socket AM2, but this may incur a performance penalty.

AMD refers to a Phenom processor with four cores as a Phenom X4. A Phenom X3 also exists and, as the name suggests, it possesses only three cores. In reality, the Phenom X3 is a quad-core processor with one of the cores shut off due to a defect. As such, AMD sells the Phenom X3 processors at a discount compared to the Phenom X4.

Similar to Intel's Extreme Edition CPUs for enthusiasts, AMD offers versions of the Phenom dubbed Black Edition. Not only are the Black Edition CPUs in the higher-end of their CPU range, but they also feature an unlocked clock multiplier allowing for fine-tuned overclocking.

AMD Phenom II

The Phenom II is a revision of the Phenom with a few improvements (see Figure 5.55). It includes triple the amount of L3 cache as the original Phenom, support for Intel's SSE4a instructions, increased HyperTransport bus speeds, and an enhanced memory controller that can support two channels of DDR2 or DDR3 memory.

The Phenom II is built using a 45-nm process instead of the 65-nm process used with the original Phenom. The Phenom II is supported by Socket AM3 and AM2+; however, the CPU only supports DDR3 memory when using Socket AM3.

Like the Phenom before it, the Phenom II is available in both an X4 quad-core version and an X3 triple-core version. But unlike the Phenom, the Phenom II is also available in an X2 dual-core version. Enthusiast Black Editions of all Phenom II configurations are also available.

• **Figure 5.55** AMD Phenom II

• **Figure 5.56** Intel Core i7

Intel Core i7

Intel's Core i7 family of processors is based off of a new microarchitecture called Nehalem, which succeeds Intel's Core microarchitecture. Like AMD's Phenom series of processors, the Core i7 is a native quad-core processor and all four cores share an L3 cache. This processor is Intel's first to feature an integrated memory controller. The memory controller supports up to three channels of DDR3 memory.

The Core i7 also marks the return of hyperthreading to Intel's CPUs (see Figure 5.56). With hyperthreading, each individual core can support two simultaneous threads, which, in aggregate, allows a single Core i7 to support up to eight simultaneous threads.

The processor features a large 8-MB L3 cache and was first manufactured using a 45-nm process. Intel designed a new 1366-pin socket for the Core i7 family of processors, called LGA 1366. Like the Core 2 Quad before it, the Core i7 is a 64-bit CPU conforming to the Intel-64 standard, meaning that it can also run 32-bit code.

With Nehalem, Intel has done away with the traditional frontside bus and replaced it with a technology they named QuickPath Interconnect (QPI). QPI is very similar to the HyperTransport bus found on the Opteron and Phenom series of processors.

Intel Celeron

Intel uses the brand Celeron for its entire family of lower-end CPUs. There are Celerons based on the Pentium II, Pentium III, Pentium 4, Pentium-M, Core and Core 2 Duo. The first Celerons were SEC but lacked the protective covering of the Pentium II. Intel calls this the **single-edge processor (SEP)** package (Figure 5.57). The Pentium III–based Celerons were PGA and used Socket 370 (Figure 5.58).

Celeron processors based on the Pentium 4 appeared first using Socket 478, but LGA 775 versions were eventually released. Over time, these Pentium 4-based Celerons borrowed more and more advanced features from their desktop counterparts, including support for SSE3 extensions and Intel-64 addressing.

Processors designed to rival AMD's Sempron series chips were also released under the Celeron brand. At first, these chips were based on Intel's Yonah architecture, but Intel released Celerons based on the Core microarchitecture shortly thereafter. Many processors from the latest generation of Celerons are available in dual-core models.

An entire line of Celerons for mobile computers also exists. Traditionally these chips went by the names Mobile Celeron or Celeron-M. However, Intel dropped that nomenclature with the latest mobile releases, simply referring to them as Celeron.

• **Figure 5.57** Pentium II Celeron

• **Figure 5.58** Intel Celeron

Intel Pentium Dual-Core

Intel resurrected the Pentium brand in 2006 with the release of the Pentium Dual-Core. Although similar in name, the Pentium Dual-Core is not the same processor as the Pentium D. The Pentium Dual-Core was originally a 32-bit processor based on the Yonah core, but Intel quickly followed that processor up with a 64-bit Pentium Dual-Core based on the Core microarchitecture.

The Pentium Dual-Core line contains both mobile and desktop processors, and recently, just as with the Celeron brand, Intel has started referring to them simply as Pentium. These Pentiums constitute a middle-of-the-road series of processors for Intel, more powerful than the Celeron line but less powerful than the Core 2 line.

Intel Xeon Processors

Just as the term Celeron describes a series of lower-end processors, the term Xeon (pronounced "Zee-on") defines a series of high-end processors Intel built around the P6, NetBurst, Core, and Nehalem microarchitectures. Both

• **Figure 5.59**   Intel Pentium III Xeon

• **Figure 5.60**   Intel Pentium 4-based Xeon (*photo courtesy of Intel*)

the Pentium II Xeon and the Pentium III Xeon used a unique SEC package that snapped into a Xeon-only slot called Slot 2 (Figure 5.59). With the release of the Xeon based off of the Pentium 4, however, Intel moved to PGA packaging, such as the Xeon-only 603-pin package depicted in Figure 5.60.

Xeon processors add large L2 caches and, especially with more recent Xeons, L3 caches as well. Although a few Xeon processors can only work alone, most are carefully designed to work together in sets of two, four, or more. Today's Xeon processors themselves can contain 2, 4, and even 8 CPU

 Try This!

Comparing CPUs

AMD and Intel are in a constant battle to have the fastest and cleverest CPU on the market. One result is that computer system vendors have a range of CPUs for you to choose from when customizing a system. So how do you know what you can and should choose? Try this:

1. Surf over to one of the major computer vendor's Web sites: www.dell.com, www.gateway.com, and www.hp.com all have customization features on their sites.

2. Select a low-end desktop from the available offerings, and pretend you're considering purchasing it. Select the customization option and record the CPU choices you're given, as well as the price differentials involved. Note which CPU comes as the default choice. Is it the fastest one? The slowest?

3. Now start again, only this time select a high-end model. Again choose to customize it as if you're a potential purchaser. Record the CPU choices you get with this model, the price differentials, and which choice is the default.

4. Finally, do an Internet search for benchmarking results on the fastest, slowest, and at least one other of the CPU choices you found. What differences in performance do you find? How does that compare to the differences in price?

cores per package. Put those two elements together, and modern Xeon systems can contain 32 CPU cores, each with hyperthreading, to support 64 simultaneous threads.

Intel and their partners are working on delivering configurations that will allow for even more CPUs, facilitating even greater processing power. Although expensive, the Xeon's immense power lets them enjoy broad popularity in the high-horsepower world of server systems.

■ Installing CPUs

Installing or upgrading a CPU is a remarkably straightforward process. You take off the fan and heat-sink assembly, remove the CPU, put a new CPU in, and snap the fan and heat-sink assembly back on. The trick to installing or replacing a CPU begins with two important questions: Do you need to replace your CPU? What CPU can you put in the computer?

Why Replace a CPU?

The CPU is the brain of your system, so it seems a natural assumption that taking out an old, slow CPU and replacing it with some new, fast CPU will make your computer run faster. No doubt it will, but first you need to consider a few issues, such as cost, cooling, and performance.

Cost

If you have an older CPU, there's a better than average chance that a faster version of your CPU is no longer available for retail purchase. In that case, replacing your CPU with a new one would require you to replace the motherboard and probably the RAM too. This is doable, but does it make sense in terms of cost? How much would this upgrade compare to a whole new system?

Cooling

Faster CPUs run hotter than slower ones. If you get a new CPU, you will almost certainly need a new CPU cooler to dissipate the heat generated by the more powerful processor. In addition, you may discover that your case fans are not sufficient, causing the CPU to overheat and the system to lock up. You can add improved cooling, but it might require a new case.

Performance

A faster CPU will make your computer run faster, but by how much? The results are often disappointing. As you go through this book, you will discover many other areas where upgrading might make a much stronger impact on your system's performance.

Determining the Right CPU

So you go through all of the decision-making and decide to go for a new CPU. Perhaps you're building a brand new system or maybe you're ready to

• **Figure 5.61**   Sample motherboard books

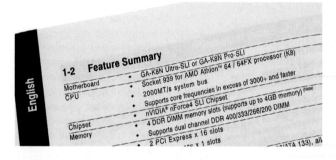

• **Figure 5.62**   Allowed CPUs

go for that CPU upgrade. The single most important bit of documentation is called the motherboard book (Figure 5.61). Every computer should come with this important book that contains all of the details about what CPUs you can use as well as any special considerations for installing a CPU. Usually in the first few pages, the motherboard book will tell you exactly which CPUs your system can handle (as shown in Figure 5.62).

If you don't have a motherboard book, call the place where you bought the PC and ask for it. If they don't have it, get online and find it—I'll show you where to look in later chapters.

Your first concern is the socket. You can't install an Athlon 64 X2 into a Pentium D's Socket 775—it won't fit! If your motherboard book lists the CPU you want to install, you're ready to start shopping.

Buying a CPU

Buying a CPU is a tricky game because most stores will not accept returns unless the CPU is bad. If you're not careful, you could get stuck with a useless CPU. Here are a few tricks.

CPUs come packaged two ways, as retail-boxed CPUs or OEM CPUs. Retail-boxed CPUs have two advantages. First, they are the genuine article. There are a surprising number of illegal CPUs on the market. Second, they come with a fan and heat sink that is rated to work with that CPU.

Most stores have an installation deal and will install a new CPU for very cheap. I take advantage of this sometimes, even though it may mean I don't have my PC for a few days. Why does your humble author, the Alpha Geek, have others do work he can do himself? Well, that way I'm not out of luck if there is a problem. Heck, I can change my own oil in my car, but I let others do that too.

If you buy an OEM CPU, you will need the right fan and heat-sink assembly. See "The Art of Cooling" section later in this chapter.

Preparing to Install

Once you're comfortable that your new CPU will work with your motherboard, get back to that motherboard book and see if you must adjust any tiny jumpers or switches for your CPU. These jumpers might adjust the motherboard speed, the multiplier, or the voltage. Take your time, read the motherboard book, and set those jumpers or switches properly. Locate the fan power connector, usually called the CPU fan, as shown in Figure 5.63.

Most CPUs use some form of mounting bracket for the CPU cooler. Some of these brackets require mounting underneath the motherboard, which means removing the motherboard from the system case.

If you're removing an old CPU, you'll need to take off the old CPU cooler. Removing CPU coolers scares me more than any other physical act I do on a PC. Many (not all) CPU fans use a metal clamp on both sides of the socket. These clamps usually require you to pry them off to remove them, using a flat-head screwdriver (Figure 5.64). You need a lot of force—usually far more than you think you should use, so take your time to pry that old fan off. Don't let the screwdriver slip; you could damage some fragile components on the motherboard, rendering the motherboard inoperable.

Fan power connector

• **Figure 5.63**   Fan connection

 Many motherboards have no jumpers or switches.

 Before attempting to do anything inside the system unit, make sure you have adequate ESD protection. Make sure the power is off and the system is unplugged.

 Using a new fan when you replace a CPU is a good idea—even if the old fan works with your new CPU. Fans get old and die too.

• **Figure 5.64**   Removing an old fan

● **Figure 5.65**   Orienting the CPU

Inserting a PGA-Type CPU

Inserting and removing PGA CPUs is a relatively simple process; just *don't touch the pins* or you might destroy the CPU. Figure 5.65 shows a technician installing a Sempron into a Socket 754. Note that the pins on the CPU only fit in one orientation. These *orientation markers* are designed to help you align the CPU correctly. Although the orientation markers make it difficult to install a CPU improperly, be careful: Incorrectly installing your CPU will almost certainly destroy the CPU or the motherboard, or both!

To install, first lift the arm or open the metal cover. Align the CPU, and it should drop right in (Figure 5.66). If it doesn't, verify your alignment and check for bent pins on the CPU. If you encounter a slightly bent pin, try a mechanical pencil that takes thick (0.9mm) lead. Take the lead out of the mechanical pencil, slide the pencil tip over the bent pin, and straighten it out. Be careful! A broken CPU pin ruins the CPU. Make sure the CPU is all the way in (no visible pins), and snap down the arm or drop over the metal cover.

● **Figure 5.66**   CPU inserted

Mike Meyers' CompTIA A+ Guide to Managing and Troubleshooting PCs

Now it's time for the CPU cooler. Before inserting the heat sink, you need to add a small amount of **thermal compound** (also called **heat dope**). Many coolers come with some heat-sink compound already on them; the heat-sink compound on these pre-doped coolers is covered by a small square of tape—take the tape off before you snap down the fan. If you need to put heat dope on from a tube, know that it only takes a tiny amount of this compound (see Figure 5.67). Spread it on as thinly, completely, and evenly as you can. Unlike so many other things in life, you *can* have too much heat dope!

Securing heat sinks makes even the most jaded PC technician a little nervous (Figure 5.68). In most cases, you must apply a fairly strong amount of force to snap the heat sink into place—far more than you might think. Also, make certain that the CPU cooler you install works with your CPU package.

● **Figure 5.67**   Applying thermal compound

● **Figure 5.68**   Installing the fan

Testing Your New CPU

The next step is to turn on the PC and see if the system boots up. If life were perfect, every CPU installation would end right here as you watch the system happily boot up. Unfortunately, the reality is that sometimes nothing happens when you press the power button. Here's what to do if this happens.

First, make sure the system has power—we'll be going through lots of power issues throughout the book. Second, make sure the CPU is firmly pressed down into the socket. Get your head down and look at the mounted CPU from the side—do you see any of the CPU's wires showing? Does the CPU look unlevel in its mount? If so, reinstall the CPU. If the system still does not boot, double-check any jumper settings—messing them up is very easy.

As the computer starts, make sure the CPU fan is spinning within a few seconds. If it doesn't spin up instantly, that's okay, but it must start within about 30 seconds at the least.

The Art of Cooling

There was a time, long ago, when CPUs didn't need any type of cooling device. You just snapped in the CPU and it worked. Well, those days are gone. Long gone. If you're installing a modern CPU, you will have to cool it. Fortunately, you have choices.

- **OEM CPU Coolers** OEM heat-sink and fan assemblies are included with a retail-boxed CPU. OEM CPUs, on the other hand, don't normally come bundled with CPU coolers. Crazy, isn't it? OEM CPU coolers have one big advantage: you know absolutely they will work with your CPU.

- **Specialized CPU Coolers** Lots of companies sell third-party heat sinks and fans for a variety of CPUs. These usually exceed the OEM heat sinks in the amount of heat they dissipate. These CPU coolers invariably come with eye-catching designs to look really cool inside your system—some are even lighted (see Figure 5.69).

The last choice is the most impressive of all: liquid cooling! That's right, you can put a little liquid-cooling system right inside your PC case. Liquid cooling works by running some liquid—usually water—through a metal block that sits on top of your CPU, absorbing heat. The liquid gets heated by the block, runs out of the block and into something that cools the liquid, and is then

• **Figure 5.69**   Cool retail heat sink

pumped through the block again. Any liquid-cooling system consists of three main parts:

- A hollow metal block that sits on the CPU
- A pump to move the liquid around
- Some device to cool the liquid

CPUs are *thermally sensitive devices*—keep those fans clean!

And of course, you need plenty of hosing to hook them all together. Figure 5.70 shows a typical liquid-cooled CPU.

A number of companies sell these liquid-cooling systems. Although they look impressive and certainly cool your CPU, unless you're overclocking or want a quiet system, a good fan will more than suffice.

Whether you have a silent or noisy cooling system for your CPU, always remember to keep everything clean. Once a month or so, take a can of compressed air and clean dust off the fan or radiator. CPUs are very susceptible to heat; a poorly working fan can create all sorts of problems, such as system lockups, spontaneous reboots, and more.

Know Your CPUs

In this chapter, you have seen the basic components and functions of a PC's CPU. A historical view has been provided to help you better understand the amazing evolution of CPUs in the more than 20-year life span of the personal computer.

The information in this chapter will be referred to again and again throughout the book. Take the time to memorize certain facts, such as the size of the various caches, CPU speeds, and clock-doubling features. Good technicians can spout off these facts without having to refer to a book.

• **Figure 5.70**   Liquid-cooled CPU

Beyond A+

Overclocking

For the CPU to work, the motherboard speed, multiplier, and voltage must be set properly. In most modern systems, the motherboard uses the CPUID functions to set these options automatically. Some motherboards enable you to adjust these settings manually by moving a jumper, changing a CMOS setting, or using software; many enthusiasts deliberately change these settings to enhance performance.

Starting way back in the days of the Intel 80486 CPU, people intentionally ran their systems at clock speeds higher than the CPU was rated, a process called **overclocking**, and it worked. Well, *sometimes* the systems worked, and sometimes they didn't. Intel and AMD have a reason for marking a CPU at a particular clock speed—that's the highest speed they guarantee will work.

Before I say anything else, I must warn you that intentional overclocking of a CPU immediately voids any warranty. Overclocking has been known to destroy CPUs. Overclocking might make your system unstable and prone to lockups and reboots. I neither applaud nor decry the practice of overclocking. My goal here is simply to inform you of the practice. You make your own decisions.

CPU makers dislike overclocking. Why would you pay more for a faster processor when you can take a cheaper, slower CPU and just make it run faster? To that end, CPU makers, especially Intel, have gone to great lengths to discourage the practice. For example, both AMD and Intel now make all of their CPUs with locked multipliers and special overspeed electronics to deter the practice.

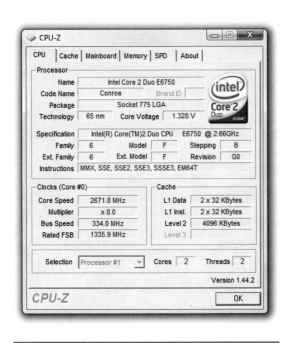

I don't think Intel or AMD really care too much what *end users* do with their CPUs. You own it; you take the risks. A number of criminals, however, learned to make a good business of re-marking CPUs with higher than rated speeds and selling them as legitimate CPUs. These counterfeit CPUs have created a nightmare where unsuspecting retailers and end users have been given overclocked CPUs. When they run into trouble, they innocently ask for warranty support, only to discover that their CPU is counterfeit and the warranty is void.

If you want to know exactly what type of CPU you're running, download a copy of the very popular and free CPU-Z utility from www.cpuid.com. CPU-Z gives you every piece of information you'll ever want to know about your CPU (Figure 5.71).

Most people make a couple of adjustments to overclock successfully. First, through jumpers, CMOS settings, or software configuration, you would increase the bus speed for the system. Second, you often have to increase the voltage going into the CPU by just a little to provide stability. You do that by changing a jumper or CMOS setting.

Overriding the defaults can completely lock up your system, to the point where even removing and reinstalling the CPU doesn't bring the motherboard back to life. (There's also a slight risk of toasting the processor, although all modern processors have circuitry that shuts them down quickly before they overheat.) Most motherboards have a jumper setting called *CMOS clear* (Figure 5.72) that makes the CMOS go back to default settings. Before you try overclocking on a modern system, find the CMOS-clear jumper and make sure you know how to use it! Hint: Look in the motherboard manual.

• **Figure 5.71** CPU-Z in action

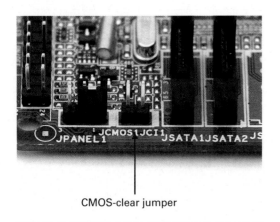

CMOS-clear jumper

• **Figure 5.72** CMOS-clear jumper

To clear the CMOS, turn off the PC. Then locate one of those tiny little plastic pieces (officially called a *shunt*) and place it over the two jumper wires for a moment. Next, restart the PC and immediately go into CMOS and restore the settings you need.

Intel Atom

Intel's Atom processors are very power-efficient processors designed for applications such as ultra mobile PCs, mobile Internet devices, netbooks, and low-power desktops. The Atom range of CPUs consists of both 32-bit and 64-bit models; however, only the models aimed at the low-power desktop segment support 64-bit so far. Many Atom processors also support hyperthreading, and there are now several dual-core models. Figure 5.73 shows an Atom processor.

Atom processors support Intel's SSE3 instructions, but they do not support SSE4. As of this writing, Intel Atom processors have only been released in a package that is soldered directly to the motherboard. Atom processors are manufactured using a 45nm-process, and many feature Intel's SpeedStep Technology to further reduce their power consumption. The Atom line of processors has become extremely popular for use in netbooks, where heat and power consumption are a primary concern.

● **Figure 5.73** Intel Atom processor

■ Chapter Summary

After reading this chapter and completing the exercises, you should understand the following facts about microprocessors.

Identify the core components of a CPU

■ The central processing unit performs calculations on binary numbers to make the magic of computers work. The CPU interfaces with the motherboard and other components through the external data bus or frontside bus.

■ CPUs contain several areas of internal memory, known as registers, in which data and addresses are stored while processing. The commands a CPU knows how to perform are dictated by its instruction set.

■ A quartz crystal soldered to the motherboard and known as the system crystal provides a constant pulse known as the clock. The frequency of this pulse, or clock speed, dictates the maximum speed at which a processor can run, measured in megahertz or gigahertz. The processor typically runs at some multiple of this clock pulse, known as the internal clock speed. You can set the internal clock speed by adjusting the multiplier (which multiplies the clock speed by some number) or by configuring motherboard jumpers or making a change to a CMOS setting, or it is set automatically via CPU circuitry. Setting the clock speed higher to force the CPU to run faster than its rating is known as overclocking.

Describe the relationship of CPUs and memory

■ A computer uses random access memory to take copies of programs from the hard drive and send them, one line at a time, to the CPU quickly enough to keep up with its demands. The CPU accesses any one row of RAM as easily and as quickly as any other row, which explains the "random access" part of RAM. RAM is not only randomly accessible but also fast. By storing programs on RAM, the CPU can access and run them very quickly. RAM also stores any data that the CPU actively uses.

■ The CPU communicates with RAM on the motherboard via the address bus. The number of wires comprising the address bus dictates the amount of memory the CPU can access.

Explain the varieties of modern CPUs

■ Most CPUs in modern PCs are manufactured by Intel or AMD.

■ CPUs come in two main form factors: pin grid array (PGA) and single-edge cartridge (SEC).

■ PGA CPUs connect to the motherboard by way of a zero insertion force (ZIF) socket that allows the CPU to be inserted with no force. ZIF sockets work by way of a mechanical arm that locks the CPU in place.

■ The original Intel Pentium was introduced in 1990 and discontinued in 1995. AMD's competing CPU was the AMD K5.

■ Pipelining enables a CPU to perform calculations as an assembly line. No longer does one calculation need to be completed before the next can begin. Modern CPUs have multiple pipelines.

■ Modern CPUs contain small amounts of high-speed SRAM called a cache. As CPUs advanced, the capacities of the cache increased, as did the number of cache areas. CPU caches are also known as L1, L2, or L3 caches. Data and instructions are stored in the cache while they await processing. This increases performance, because the CPU can access data in the cache more rapidly than data in motherboard RAM.

■ In 1995 Intel released the Pentium Pro. It improved on the original Pentium by offering quad pipelining, dynamic processing, and on-chip L2 cache. With four pipelines, it was guaranteed to run at least two processes at the same time. The capability to run more than one process in a single clock cycle is called superscalar execution. The Pentium Pro's advanced branch prediction allowed it to run processes out of order to increase performance in a procedure called speculative execution.

- In 1996 Intel released the Pentium II. It improved on the Pentium Pro by offering multimedia extensions (MMX) and a refined instruction set. The AMD K6 (and its varieties) was the main competitor.

- The Intel Celeron is a low-end processor. The generic name of Celeron, with no identifying letters or numbers to indicate which version, made purchasing one difficult unless you asked the right questions.

- Intel's Pentium III improved on the Pentium II by offering Streaming SIMD Extensions (SSE). AMD responded with the 3DNow! instruction set.

- The AMD Athlon was the first AMD CPU to use AMD-only slots and sockets. If you wanted an AMD Athlon, you had to purchase a motherboard with the special AMD slot/socket.

- The AMD Duron is similar to the Intel Celeron in that it was marketed toward the low-end PCs. The Duron is similar to the Athlon but contains a smaller cache.

- The Intel Pentium 4 came in several varieties identified by codenames Willamette, Northwood, and Prescott.

- The Athlon XP came in several varieties: Palomino, Thoroughbred, Thorton, and Barton.

- The Intel Pentium 4 Extreme Edition was the first non-server CPU to offer an L3 cache.

- Mobile processors, or CPUs for laptops, are usually identified by the word "mobile" or the letter "M" in their names. A mobile processor uses less power than a desktop CPU, allowing for longer battery life and cooler running. They run on a lower voltage than a desktop CPU, which usually translates to lower speeds. The term Centrino defines a complete mobile solution consisting of a mobile processor, support chips, and wireless networking. There is no Centrino CPU.

- Intel's SpeedStep and AMD's PowerNow! technologies enable CPUs to slow themselves down during times of low demand or if the CPU senses it is getting too hot. Generically, this is called throttling.

- The Intel Xeon is a high-end processor aimed at the server or power-user market. Xeons are intended to be used in PCs with multiple processors.

- The original Intel Itanium was Intel's first 64-bit processor. The Itanium and the follow-up Itanium 2 were not backwardly compatible with 32-bit systems, so users had to use a 64-bit operating system, 64-bit software, and 64-bit drivers.

- The AMD Opteron, AMD's first 64-bit processor, was backwardly compatible with 32-bit systems.

- The AMD Athlon 64 comes in two varieties, Athlon 64 and Athlon 64 FX, with the FX being faster and more expensive. The AMD Sempron is AMD's low-end 64-bit processor.

- Dual-core CPUs combine two CPUs into a single chip. The two CPUs have different sets of pipelines but share common caches. The Intel Pentium D (codenames Smithfield and Presler) is one such processor that can run both 32- and 64-bit code. AMD's Athlon 64 X2 CPUs are dual-core.

- The AMD Phenom X4, Phenom II X4, and Intel Core i7 are all native quad-core CPUs.

- The AMD Phenom X3 is a native triple-core CPU.

Install and upgrade CPUs

- Before upgrading your CPU, consider the implications on your whole system, because an upgraded CPU may require an updated motherboard and RAM.

- Consult your motherboard documentation to see what CPUs are compatible with your system. Not all CPUs are compatible with all motherboards.

- Cooling is critical. Make sure you have a fan rated to work with your CPU.

- Never touch the pins on the underside of a CPU; this can permanently damage the processor.

- A PGA CPU fits only one way in the ZIF socket. Don't force it. If you find the CPU will not seat properly, take a second look at the orientation markers and verify the CPU is in the correct direction. Check the pins on the underside to make sure none are bent.

- There should be a small amount of heat-sink compound between the CPU and heat-sink/fan assembly. If your fan came with the compound already applied, be sure to remove the protective tape covering the compound before attaching the fan to the CPU. If you are using your own heat dope from a tube, spread it thinly and evenly.

Key Terms

address bus *(133)*

arithmetic logic unit (ALU) *(136)*

backside bus *(146)*

binary *(126)*

bit *(132)*

byte *(132)*

cache *(142)*

central processing unit (CPU) *(124)*

Centrino *(153)*

clock cycle *(129)*

clock-multiplying CPU *(143)*

clock speed *(129)*

clock wire *(129)*

dual-core *(156)*

dynamic RAM (DRAM) *(133)*

external data bus (EDB) *(125)*

floating point unit (FPU) *(140)*

frontside bus *(146)*

heat dope *(165)*

instruction set *(127)*

machine language *(127)*

memory *(131)*

memory controller chip (MCC) *(133)*

microprocessor *(124)*

multimedia extensions (MMX) *(147)*

overclocking *(167)*

parallel processing *(156)*

pipeline *(140)*

program *(131)*

random access memory (RAM) *(132)*

registers *(127)*

single-edge cartridge (SEC) *(148)*

single-edge processor (SEP) *(159)*

static RAM (SRAM) *(142)*

system crystal *(129)*

System Management Mode (SMM) *(153)*

thermal compound *(165)*

throttling *(153)*

voltage regulator module (VRM) *(144)*

wait state *(142)*

zero insertion force (ZIF) socket *(138)*

Key Term Quiz

Use the Key Terms list to complete the sentences that follow. Not all terms will be used.

1. All of the machine language commands that the CPU understands make up the CPU's _____.

2. By lifting the arm on the _____, you can easily install a PGA CPU.

3. Computers use _____ for main system memory.

4. Computers use the _____ numbering system.

5. Areas inside the CPU where it temporarily stores internal commands and data while it is processing them are called _____.

6. Divided into L1 and L2, the _____ consists of a small amount of _____

that serves as a holding area. This provides data to the CPU faster than getting it from regular memory or when RAM is unavailable because of refreshes.

7. A _____ enables a motherboard to support CPUs that run at differing voltage requirements.

8. Laptops sporting the _____ logo indicate that they contain a mobile processor, support chips, and a wireless network interface.

9. In a process known as _____, a CPU can slow itself down in low demand times or if it gets too hot.

10. An Athlon 64 X2 is an example of a(n) _____ processor.

■ Multiple-Choice Quiz

1. What device enables a PC to retrieve a specific row of data from system memory and place it on the external data bus?

   A. Advanced micro device

   B. Arithmetic logic unit

   C. Floating-point processor

   D. Memory controller chip

2. Which of the following statements is true?

   A. The address bus enables the CPU to communicate with the MCC.

   B. The external data bus enables the CPU to communicate with the MCC.

   C. The address bus enables the CPU to communicate with the hard drive.

   D. The system bus enables the CPU to communicate with the memory.

3. Which of the following CPUs was the first microprocessor to include both an L1 and an L2 cache with the CPU?

   A. Pentium

   B. Pentium Pro

   C. Pentium II

   D. Pentium III

4. What do 64-bit processors expand beyond what 32-bit processors have?

   A. System bus

   B. Frontside bus

   C. Address bus

   D. Registers

5. What is the first stage in a typical four-stage CPU pipeline?

   A. Decode

   B. Execute

   C. Fetch

   D. Write

6. Which of the following terms are measures of CPU speed?

   A. Megahertz and gigahertz

   B. Megabytes and gigabytes

   C. Megahertz and gigabytes

   D. Frontside bus, backside bus

7. Which of the following CPUs features a QuickPath Interconnect interface?

   A. Pentium 4

   B. Phenom II X2

   C. Core i7

   D. Opteron

8. Which of the following statements is true?

   A. If you have an AMD-compatible motherboard, you can install a Celeron processor.

   B. Replacing the CPU may not be the upgrade that is most cost effective or that has the strongest impact on your system's performance.

   C. As the size of the address bus increases, the amount of RAM the CPU can use decreases.

   D. You can upgrade your CPU if you make sure that a new CPU will fit into the socket or slot on your motherboard.

9. Which processor comes in an SEC package that fits into Slot A?

   A. Pentium II

   B. Pentium III

   C. Athlon

   D. Celeron

10. What's the main difference between the Itanium and Opteron CPUs?

    A. The Itanium is a 32-bit processor; the Opteron is a 64-bit processor.

    B. The Itanium can run only 64-bit code; the Opteron can run both 32-bit and 64-bit code.

    C. The Itanium is made by AMD; the Opteron is made by Intel.

    D. The Itanium fits in Slot 1; the Opteron fits in Slot A.

11. What connects on the backside bus?

    A. CPU, MCC, RAM

    B. CPU, MCC, L1 cache

    C. CPU, L1 cache

    D. CPU, L2 cache

12. What improvement(s) have CPU manufacturers put into processors to deal with pipeline stalls?

   A. Added multiple pipelines

   B. Increased the speed of the SRAM

   C. Created new die sizes with more pins

   D. Bundled better fans with their retail CPUs

13. What steps do you need to take to install an Athlon 64 X2 CPU into an LGA 775 motherboard?

   A. Lift the ZIF socket arm; place the CPU according to the orientation markings; snap on the heat-sink and fan assembly.

   B. Lift the ZIF socket arm; place the CPU according to the orientation markings; add a dash of heat dope; snap on the heat-sink and fan assembly.

   C. Lift the ZIF socket arm; place the CPU according to the orientation markings; snap on the heat-sink and fan assembly; plug in the fan.

   D. Take all of the steps you want to take because it's not going to work.

14. Which of the following CPU manufacturing processes offers a final product that most likely uses the least amount of electricity for the same number of circuits?

   A. 3 micrometer

   B. 45 nanometer

   C. 65 nanometer

   D. 90 nanometer

15. What improvement does the Athlon 64 offer over the Athlon XP?

   A. Lower wattage

   B. Larger L1 cache

   C. Larger process size

   D. 64-bit processing

■ Essay Quiz

1. It is important for the CPU to stay cool. A number of technical advances have been made in the design of CPUs, along with various devices made to keep the CPU from overheating. Discuss at least two cooling features or cooling options.

2. Juan wants to buy a laptop computer, but he finds that laptops are more expensive than desktop computers. Moreover, he is complaining that he can't find a laptop that is as fast as the newest desktop PCs. Explain to Juan three special considerations that make a laptop more expensive and less powerful than desktop computers.

3. On the bulletin board outside your classroom, your friend Shelley notices two flyers advertising used computers. The first one is a 700-MHz Celeron with a 100-MHz system bus, 32 KB of L1 cache, 128 KB of L2 cache, and 128 MB of RAM. The other one is an 800-MHz Athlon with a 200-MHz system bus, 128 KB of L1 cache, 512 KB of L2 cache, and 256 MB of RAM. Shelley does not know much about computer hardware, so she asks you which one is the better computer and why. In simple terms that Shelley will understand, explain five differences that determine which computer is better.

4. You're forming a study group with a few of your friends to review microprocessors. Each one of you has decided to study a particular aspect of this chapter to explain to the group. Your responsibility is buses, including the system bus, address bus, backside bus, and frontside bus. Write a few sentences that will help you explain what each bus does and the differences between the buses.

5. This chapter makes the statement that "The secret to making clock multiplying work is caching." Write a paragraph in which you explain why that statement is true. Be sure to explain what caching does and the different kinds of caches found in today's computers.

Lab Projects

• Lab Project 5.1

Perhaps newer and faster CPUs have come out recently. Go to www.intel.com and www.amd.com and investigate the newest CPUs for desktop computers from each manufacturer. Write a paragraph comparing the newest Intel CPU with the newest AMD CPU. Try to include the following information:

- What is the size of the system bus?
- What is the size of the address bus?
- What is the speed of the CPU?
- What is the speed of the frontside bus?
- What are the sizes of the L1 and L2 caches?
- Does either CPU offer an L3 cache?
- What kind of chip package houses each CPU?
- What kind of slot or socket does each use?
- What other new features does each site advertise for its newest CPU?

• Lab Project 5.2

Imagine that you are going to buy components to build your own computer. What processor will you use? Typically, the latest and greatest CPU is a lot more expensive than less recent models. Intel processors usually cost more than comparable AMD processors. Check CPU features and prices in newspapers or magazines or on the Internet at a site such as www.newegg.com. Decide what CPU you want to use for your computer. Write a paragraph explaining why you selected it and how much you will spend for the CPU.

• Lab Project 5.3

If your school hardware lab has motherboards and processors for hands-on labs, practice removing and installing PGA processors on the motherboards. Take note of how the mechanical arm on a ZIF socket works. Answer the following about your experience:

- How do you know in which direction to place the CPU?
- How does the mechanical arm lift up? Does it lift straight up or must it clear a lip?
- What effect does lifting the arm have on the socket?
- How does the ZIF socket hold the CPU in place?

RAM

"The memory be green."

—William Shakespeare, *Hamlet*, Act I, Scene 2

In this chapter, you will learn how to

- Identify the different types of DRAM packaging
- Explain the varieties of RAM
- Select and install RAM
- Perform basic RAM troubleshooting

Whenever people come up to me and start professing their computer savvy, I ask them a few questions to see how much they really know. In case you and I ever meet and you decide you want to "talk tech" with me, I'll tell you my first two questions just so you'll be ready. Both involve *random access memory* (RAM), the working memory for the CPU.

1. "How much RAM is in your computer?"
2. "What is RAM and why is it so important that every PC has some?"

Can you answer either of these questions? Don't fret if you can't—you'll know how to answer both of them before you finish this chapter. Let's start by reviewing what you know about RAM thus far.

When not in use, programs and data are held in mass storage, which usually means a hard drive but could also mean a USB thumb drive, a CD-ROM, or some other device that can hold data when the computer is turned off. When you load a program by clicking an icon in Windows, the program is copied from the mass storage device to RAM and then run (Figure 6.1).

You saw in Chapter 5, "Microprocessors," that the CPU uses dynamic random access memory (DRAM) as RAM for all PCs. Just like CPUs, DRAM has gone through a number of evolutionary changes over the years, resulting in improved DRAM technologies with names such as SDRAM, RDRAM, and DDR RAM. This chapter starts by explaining how DRAM works, and then moves into the types of DRAM used over the past few years to see how they improve on the original DRAM. The third section, "Working with RAM," goes into the details of finding and installing RAM. The chapter finishes with troubleshooting RAM problems.

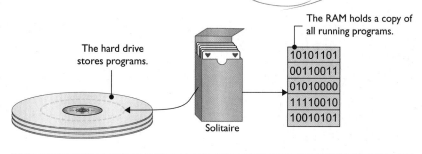

• **Figure 6.1**   Mass storage holds programs, but programs need to run in RAM.

Historical/Conceptual

Understanding DRAM

As discussed in Chapter 5, "Microprocessors," DRAM functions like an electronic spreadsheet, with numbered rows containing cells and each cell holding a one or a zero. Now let's look at what's physically happening. Each spreadsheet cell is a special type of semiconductor that can hold a single bit—one or zero—by using microscopic capacitors and transistors. DRAM makers put these semiconductors into chips that can hold a certain number of bits. The bits inside the chips are organized in a rectangular fashion, using rows and columns.

Each chip has a limit on the number of lines of code it can contain. Think of each line of code as one of the rows on the electronic spreadsheet; one chip might be able to store a million rows of code while another chip can store over a billion lines. Each chip also has a limit on the width of the lines of code it can handle, so one chip might handle 8-bit-wide data while another might handle 16-bit-wide data. Techs describe chips by bits rather than bytes, so ×8 and ×16, respectively. Just as you could describe a spreadsheet by the number of rows

and columns—John's accounting spreadsheet is huge, 48 rows × 12 columns—memory makers describe RAM chips the same way. An individual DRAM chip that holds 1,048,576 rows and 8 columns, for example, would be a *1 M × 8* chip, with "M" as shorthand for "mega," just like in megabytes (2^{20} bytes). It is difficult if not impossible to tell the size of a DRAM chip just by looking at it—only the DRAM makers know the meaning of the tiny numbers on the chips (see Figure 6.2), although sometimes you can make a good guess.

Organizing DRAM

Because of its low cost, high speed, and capability to contain a lot of data in a relatively small package, DRAM has been the standard RAM used in all computers—not just PCs—since the mid-1970s. DRAM can be found in just about everything, from automobiles to automatic bread makers.

The PC has very specific requirements for DRAM. The original 8088 processor had an 8-bit frontside bus. All the commands given to an 8088 processor were in discrete 8-bit chunks. You needed RAM that could store data in 8-bit (1-byte) chunks, so that each time the CPU asked for a line of code, the memory controller could put an 8-bit chunk on the data bus. This optimized the flow of data into (and out from) the CPU.

Although today's DRAM chips may have widths greater than 1 bit, back in the old days all DRAM chips were 1 bit wide. That means you only had such sizes as 64 K × 1 or 256 K × 1—always 1 bit wide. So how was 1-bit-wide DRAM turned into 8-bit-wide memory? The answer was quite simple: Just take eight 1-bit-wide chips and electronically organize them with the memory controller chip to be eight wide. First, put eight 1-bit-wide chips in a row on the motherboard and then wire up this row of DRAM chips to the memory controller chip (which has to be designed to handle this) to make byte-wide memory (Figure 6.3). You just made eight 1-bit-wide DRAM chips look like a single 8-bit-wide DRAM chip to the CPU.

> **✓ Cross Check**
>
> ### Riding the 8088 Bus
>
> You first saw the Intel 8088 CPU in Chapter 5, "Microprocessors," and now it pops up again. What components inside the 8088 handle the data once the CPU gets it from RAM? How does the CPU know when the data is complete and ready to take?

The CPU requires data in byte-sized pieces.

The MCC can produce byte-sized pieces out of eight bit-sized RAM chips.

● **Figure 6.3** The MCC accessing data on RAM soldered onto the motherboard

Practical DRAM

Okay, before you learn more about DRAM, I need to make a critical point extremely clear. When you first saw the 8088's machine language in Chapter 5,

"Microprocessors," all the examples in the "codebook" were exactly 1-byte commands. Figure 6.4 shows the codebook again—see how all the commands are 1 byte?

Well, the reality is slightly different. Most of the 8088 machine language commands are 1 byte, but a few more complex commands need 2 bytes. For example, the following command tells the CPU to move 163 bytes "up the RAM spreadsheet" and run whatever command is there. Cool, eh?

11101001/10100011

The problem here is that the command is 2 bytes wide, not 1 byte. So how did the 8088 handle this? Simple—it just took the command 1 byte at a time. It took twice as long to handle the command because the MCC had to go to RAM twice, but it worked.

Okay, so if some of the commands are more than 1 byte wide, why didn't Intel make the 8088 with a 16-bit frontside bus? Wouldn't that have been better? Well, Intel did. Intel invented a CPU called the 8086. The 8086 actually predates the 8088 and was absolutely identical to the 8088 except for one small detail: it had a 16-bit frontside bus. IBM could have used the 8086 instead of the 8088 and used 2-byte-wide RAM instead of 1-byte-wide RAM. Of course, they would have needed to invent a memory controller chip that handled that kind of RAM (Figure 6.5).

Why didn't Intel sell IBM the 8086 instead of the 8088? There were two reasons. First, nobody had invented an affordable MCC or RAM that handled 2 bytes at a time. Sure, chips were invented, but they were *expensive* and IBM didn't think anyone would want to pay $12,000 for a personal computer. So IBM bought the Intel 8088, not the Intel 8086, and all our RAM came in bytes. But as you might imagine, it didn't stay that way too long.

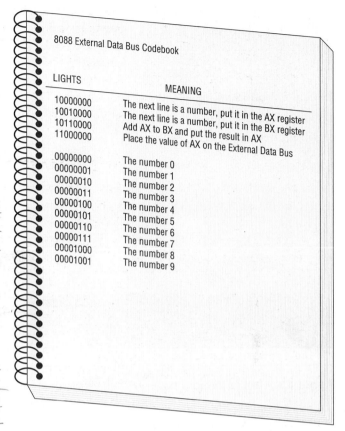

8088 External Data Bus Codebook

LIGHTS	MEANING
10000000	The next line is a number, put it in the AX register
10010000	The next line is a number, put it in the BX register
10110000	Add AX to BX and put the result in AX
11000000	Place the value of AX on the External Data Bus
00000000	The number 0
00000001	The number 1
00000010	The number 2
00000011	The number 3
00000100	The number 4
00000101	The number 5
00000110	The number 6
00000111	The number 7
00001000	The number 8
00001001	The number 9

• **Figure 6.4** Codebook again

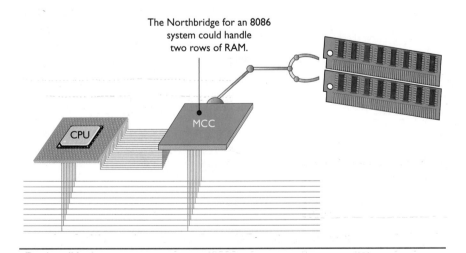

The Northbridge for an **8086** system could handle two rows of RAM.

MCC

CPU

• **Figure 6.5** Pumped-up 8086 MCC at work

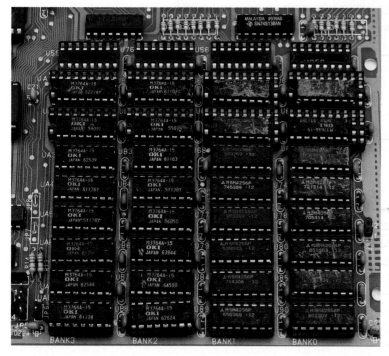

• **Figure 6.6** That's a lot of real estate used by RAM chips!

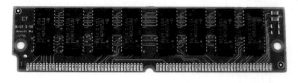

• **Figure 6.7** A 72-pin SIMM

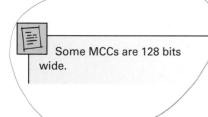

Some MCCs are 128 bits wide.

DRAM Sticks

As CPU data bus sizes increased, so too did the need for RAM wide enough to fill the bus. The Intel 80386 CPU, for example, had a 32-bit data bus and thus the need for 32-bit-wide DRAM. Imagine having to line up 32 one-bit-wide DRAM chips on a motherboard. Talk about a waste of space! Figure 6.6 shows motherboard RAM run amuck.

DRAM manufacturers responded by creating wider DRAM chips, such as ×4, ×8, and ×16, and putting multiples of them on a small circuit board called a **stick** or **module**. Figure 6.7 shows an early stick, called a **single inline memory module (SIMM)**, with eight DRAM chips. To add RAM to a modern machine means you need to get the right stick or sticks for the particular motherboard. Your motherboard manual tells you precisely what sort of module you need and how much RAM you can install.

Modern CPUs are a lot smarter than the old Intel 8088. Their machine languages have some commands that are up to 64 bits (8 bytes) wide. They also have at least a 64-bit frontside bus that can handle more than just 8 bits. They don't want RAM to give them a puny 8 bits at a time! To optimize the flow of data into and out of the CPU, the modern MCC provides at least 64 bits of data every time the CPU requests information from RAM.

Try This!

Dealing with Old RAM

Often in the PC world, old technology and ways of doing things are reimplemented with some newer technology. Learning how things worked back in the ancient days can stand a tech in good stead. Perhaps more importantly, many thousands of companies—including hospitals, auto repair places, and more—use very old, proprietary applications that keep track of medical records, inventory, and so on. If you're called to work on one of these ancient systems, you need to know how to work with old parts, so try this.

Obtain an old computer, such as a 386 or 486. Ask your uncle, cousin, or Great Aunt Edna if they have a PC collecting dust in a closet that you can use. Failing that, go to a secondhand store or market and buy one for a few dollars.

Open up the system and check out the RAM. Remove the RAM from the motherboard and then replace it to familiarize yourself with the internals. You never know when some critical system will go down and need repair immediately—and you're the one to do it!

Modern DRAM sticks come in 32-bit- and 64-bit-wide form factors with a varying number of chips. Many techs describe these memory modules by their width, so ×32 and ×64. Note that this number does *not* describe the width of the individual DRAM chips on the module. When you read or hear about *by whatever* memory, simply note that you need to know whether that person is talking about the DRAM width or the module width. When the CPU needs certain bytes of data, it requests those bytes via the address bus. The CPU does not know the physical location of the RAM that stores that data, nor the physical makeup of the RAM—such as how many DRAM chips work together to provide the 64-bit-wide memory rows. The MCC keeps track of this and just gives the CPU whichever bytes it requests (Figure 6.8).

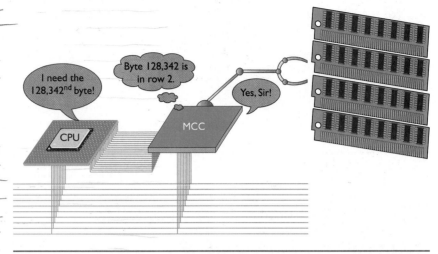

• **Figure 6.8**   The MCC knows the real location of the DRAM.

Consumer RAM

If modern DRAM modules come in sizes much wider than a byte, why do people still use the word "byte" to describe how much DRAM they have? Convention. Habit. Rather than using a label that describes the electronic structure of RAM, common usage describes the *total capacity of RAM on a stick in bytes*. John has a single 512-MB stick of RAM on his motherboard, for example, and Sally has two 256-MB sticks. Both systems have a total of 512 MB of system RAM. That's what your clients care about, after all, because having enough RAM makes their systems snappy and stable; not enough and the systems run poorly. As a tech, you need to know more, of course, to pick the right RAM for many different types of computers.

Essentials

■ Types of RAM

Development of newer, wider, and faster CPUs and MCCs motivate DRAM manufacturers to invent new DRAM technologies that deliver enough data at a single pop to optimize the flow of data into and out of the CPU.

SDRAM

Most modern systems use some form of **synchronous DRAM (SDRAM)**. SDRAM is still DRAM, but it is *synchronous*—tied to the system clock, just like the CPU and MCC, so the MCC knows when data is ready to be grabbed from SDRAM. This results in little wasted time.

 Old RAM—really old RAM—was called *fast page mode* (*FPM*) RAM. This ancient RAM used a totally different technology that was not tied to the system clock. If you ever hear of FPM RAM, it's going to be in a system that's over a decade old. Be careful! CompTIA likes to use older terms like this to throw you off!

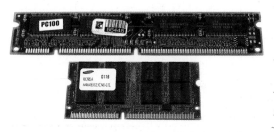

• **Figure 6.9** 144-pin micro-DIMM (*photo courtesy of Micron Technology, Inc.*)

• **Figure 6.10** A 168-pin DIMM above a 144-pin SO-DIMM

SDRAM made its debut in 1996 on a stick called a **dual inline memory module (DIMM)**. The early SDRAM DIMMs came in a wide variety of pin sizes. The most common pin sizes found on desktops were the 168-pin variety. Laptop DIMMs came in 68-pin, 144-pin (Figure 6.9), or 172-pin *micro-DIMM* packages; and the 72-pin, 144-pin, or 200-pin **small-outline DIMM (SO-DIMM)** form factors (Figure 6.10). With the exception of the 32-bit 72-pin SO-DIMM, all these DIMM varieties delivered 64-bit-wide data to match the 64-bit data bus of every CPU since the Pentium.

To take advantage of SDRAM, you needed a PC designed to use SDRAM. If you had a system with slots for 168-pin DIMMs, for example, your system used SDRAM. A DIMM in any one of the DIMM slots could fill the 64-bit bus, so each slot was called a **bank**. You could install one, two, or more sticks and the system would work. Note that on laptops that used the 72-pin SO-DIMM, you needed to install two sticks of RAM to make a full bank, because each stick only provided half the bus width.

SDRAM tied to the system clock, so its clock speed matched the frontside bus. Five clock speeds were commonly used on the early SDRAM systems: 66, 75, 83, 100, and 133 MHz. The RAM speed had to match or exceed the system speed or the computer would be unstable or wouldn't work at all. These speeds were prefixed with a "PC" in the front, based on a standard forwarded by Intel, so SDRAM speeds were PC66 through PC133. For a Pentium III computer with a 100-MHz frontside bus, you needed to buy SDRAM DIMMs rated to handle it, such as PC100 or PC133.

RDRAM

When Intel was developing the Pentium 4, they knew that regular SDRAM just wasn't going to be fast enough to handle the quad-pumped 400-MHz frontside bus. Intel announced plans to replace SDRAM with a very fast, new type of RAM developed by Rambus, Inc., called **Rambus DRAM**, or simply **RDRAM** (Figure 6.11). Hailed by Intel as the next great leap in DRAM technology, RDRAM could handle speeds up to 800 MHz, which gave Intel plenty of room to improve the Pentium 4.

RDRAM was greatly anticipated by the industry for years, but industry support for RDRAM proved less than enthusiastic due to significant delays in development and a price many times that of SDRAM. Despite this grudging support, almost

• **Figure 6.11**   RDRAM

The 400-MHz frontside bus speed wasn't achieved by making the system clock faster—it was done by making CPUs and MCCs capable of sending 64 bits of data two or four times for every clock cycle, effectively doubling or quadrupling the system bus speed.

Cross Check

Double-Pumped and Quad-Pumped

You've seen double-pumped and quad-pumped frontside buses in Chapter 5, "Microprocessors," so see if you can answer these questions. What CPU—by codename—started the double-pumped bus bandwagon? What socket did it use?

all major PC makers sold systems that used RDRAM—for a while. From a tech's standpoint, RDRAM shares almost all of the characteristics of SDRAM. A stick of RDRAM is called a **RIMM**. In this case, however, the letters don't actually stand for anything; they just rhyme: SIMMs, DIMMs, and now RIMMs, get it?

RDRAM RIMMs came in two sizes: a 184-pin for desktops and a 160-pin SO-RIMM for laptops. RIMMs were keyed differently from DIMMs to ensure that even though they are the same basic size, you couldn't accidentally install a RIMM in a DIMM slot or vice versa. RDRAM also had a speed rating: 600 MHz, 700 MHz, 800 MHz, or 1066 MHz. RDRAM employed an interesting **dual-channel architecture**. Each RIMM was 64 bits wide, but the Rambus MCC alternated between two sticks to increase the speed of data retrieval. You were required to install RIMMs in pairs to use this dual-channel architecture.

RDRAM motherboards also required that all RIMM slots be populated. Unused pairs of slots needed a passive device called a **continuity RIMM (CRIMM)** installed in each slot to enable the RDRAM system to terminate properly. Figure 6.12 shows a CRIMM.

RDRAM offered dramatic possibilities for high-speed PCs but ran into three roadblocks that Betamaxed it. First, the technology was owned wholly by Rambus; if you wanted to make it, you had to pay the licensing fees they charged. That led directly to the second problem, expense. RDRAM cost substantially more than SDRAM. Third, Rambus and Intel made a completely closed deal for the technology. RDRAM worked only on Pentium 4 systems using Intel-made MCCs. AMD was out of luck. Clearly, the rest of the industry had to look for another high-speed RAM solution.

 On the CompTIA A+ exams, you'll see RDRAM referred to as RAMBUS RAM. Don't get thrown by the odd usage.

• **Figure 6.12**   CRIMM

Betamaxed is slang for "made it obsolete because no one bought it, even though it was a superior technology to the winner in the marketplace." Refers to the VHS versus Betamax wars in the old days of video cassette recorders.

DDR SDRAM

AMD and many major system and memory makers threw their support behind **double data rate SDRAM (DDR SDRAM)**. DDR SDRAM basically copied Rambus, doubling the throughput of SDRAM by making two processes for every clock cycle. This synchronized (pardon the pun) nicely with the Athlon and later AMD processors' double-pumped frontside bus. DDR SDRAM could not run as fast as RDRAM—although relatively low frontside bus speeds made that a moot point—but cost only slightly more than regular SDRAM.

DDR SDRAM for desktops comes in 184-pin DIMMs. These DIMMs match 168-pin DIMMs in physical size but not in pin compatibility (Figure 6.13). The slots for the two types of RAM appear similar as well but have different guide notches, so you can't insert either type of RAM into the other's slot.

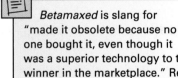

Tech Tip

RAM Slang

Most techs drop some or all of the SDRAM part of DDR SDRAM when engaged in normal geekspeak. You'll hear the memory referred to as DDR, DDR RAM, and the weird hybrid, DDRAM.

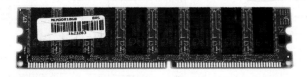

• **Figure 6.13**   DDR SDRAM

RAM makers use the term *single data rate SDRAM* (*SDR SDRAM*) for the original SDRAM to differentiate it from DDR SDRAM.

• Figure 6.14
172-pin DDR SDRAM micro-DIMM (*photo courtesy of Kingston/Joint Harvest*)

DDR SDRAM for laptops comes in either 200-pin SO-DIMMs or 172-pin micro-DIMMs (Figure 6.14).

DDR sticks use a rather interesting naming convention—actually started by the Rambus folks—based on the number of bytes per second of data throughput the RAM can handle. To determine the bytes per second, take the MHz speed and multiply by 8 bytes (the width of all DDR SDRAM sticks). So 400 MHz multiplied by 8 is 3200 megabytes per second. Put the abbreviation "PC" in the front to make the new term: PC3200. Many techs also use the naming convention used for the individual DDR chips; for example, *DDR400* refers to a 400-MHz DDR SDRAM chip running on a 200-MHz clock.

Even though the term DDR*xxx* is really just for individual DDR chips and the term PC*xxxx* is for DDR sticks, this tradition of two names for every speed of RAM is a bit of a challenge because you'll often hear both terms used interchangeably. Table 6.1 shows all the speeds for DDR—not all of these are commonly used.

Following the lead of AMD, VIA, and other manufacturers, the PC industry adopted DDR SDRAM as the standard system RAM. In the summer of 2003, Intel relented and stopped producing motherboards and memory controllers that required RDRAM.

One thing is sure about PC technologies: Any good idea that can be copied will be copied. One of Rambus' best concepts was the dual-channel architecture—using two sticks of RDRAM together to increase throughput. Manufacturers have released motherboards with MCCs that support dual-channel architecture using

Try This!

DRAM Availability

The DRAM market changes fairly rapidly at the higher end, but products tend to linger at the low end, seemingly well past their usefulness. What do your class systems need? What's available in your area today? Try this.

Check out the RAM requirements for the PCs available in your class (or home or office). You can open them up for physical examination or read the motherboard books. Then go to your friendly neighborhood computer store and see what's available. Does the store offer memory that your system cannot use, such as EDO DRAM on 72-pin SIMMs or registered DDR SDRAM? What does this tell you about the PCs available to you?

Table 6.1	DDR Speeds	
Clock Speed	**DDR Speed Rating**	**PC Speed Rating**
100 MHz	DDR200	PC1600
133 MHz	DDR266	PC2100
166 MHz	DDR333	PC2700
200 MHz	DDR400	PC3200
217 MHz	DDR433	PC3500
233 MHz	DDR466	PC3700
250 MHz	DDR500	PC4000
275 MHz	DDR550	PC4400
300 MHz	DDR600	PC4800

DDR SDRAM. Dual-channel DDR motherboards use regular DDR sticks, although manufacturers often sell RAM in matched pairs, branding them as dual-channel RAM.

Dual-channel DDR works like RDRAM in that you must have two identical sticks of DDR and they must snap into two paired slots. Unlike RDRAM, dual-channel DDR doesn't have anything like CRIMMs—you don't need to put anything into unused slot pairs. Dual-channel DDR technology is very flexible but also has a few quirks that vary with each system. Some motherboards have three DDR SDRAM slots, but the dual-channel DDR works only if you install DDR SDRAM in two of the slots. Other boards have four slots and you must install matching pairs in the same colored slots to run in dual-channel mode (Figure 6.15). If you populate a third slot, the system uses the full capacity of RAM installed but turns off the dual-channel feature.

• Figure 6.15 A motherboard showing the four RAM slots. By populating the same color slots with identical RAM, you can run in dual-channel mode.

DDR2

The fastest versions of DDR RAM run at a blistering PC4800. That's 4.8 gigabytes per second (GBps) of data throughput! You'd think that kind of speed would satisfy most users, and to be honest, DRAM running at approximately 5 GBps really is plenty fast—for yesterday. However, the ongoing speed increases ensure that even these speeds won't be good enough in the future. Knowing this, the RAM industry came out with DDR2, the successor to DDR. *DDR2* is DDR RAM with some improvements in its electrical characteristics, enabling it to run even faster than DDR while using less power. The big speed increase from DDR2 comes by clock-doubling the input/output circuits on the chips. This does not speed up the core RAM—the part that holds the data—but speeding up the input/output and adding special buffers (sort of like a cache) make DDR2 run much faster than regular DDR. DDR2 uses a 240-pin DIMM that's not compatible with DDR (Figure 6.16). Likewise, the DDR2 200-pin SO-DIMM is incompatible with the DDR SO-DIMM. You'll find motherboards running both single-channel and dual-channel DDR2.

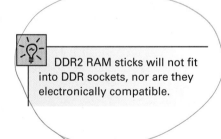

DDR2 RAM sticks will not fit into DDR sockets, nor are they electronically compatible.

• Figure 6.16 240-pin DDR2 DIMM

Table 6.2 shows some of the common DDR2 speeds.

Table 6.2	DDR2 Speeds		
Core RAM Clock Speed	DDR I/O Speed	DDR2 Speed Rating	PC Speed Rating
100 MHz	200 MHz	DDR2-400	PC2-3200
133 MHz	266 MHz	DDR2-533	PC2-4200
166 MHz	333 MHz	DDR2-667	PC2-5300
200 MHz	400 MHz	DDR2-800	PC2-6400
250 MHz	500 MHz	DDR2-1000	PC2-8000

DDR3

DDR2 has been the standard for several years, but now there's a new kid on the block. *DDR3* boasts higher speeds, more efficient architecture, and around 30 percent lower power consumption than DDR2 RAM, making it a compelling choice for system builders. Just like its predecessor, DDR3 uses a 240-pin DIMM, albeit one that is slotted differently to make it difficult for users to install the wrong RAM in their system without using a hammer (Figure 6.17). DDR3 SO-DIMMs for portable computers have 204 pins. Neither fits into a DDR2 socket.

DDR3 doubles the buffer of DDR2 from 4 bits to 8 bits, giving it a huge boost in bandwidth over older RAM. Not only that, but some DDR3 modules also include a feature called XMP, or extended memory profile, that enables power users to overclock their RAM easily, boosting their already fast memory to speeds that would make Chuck Yeager nervous. DDR3 modules also use higher-density memory chips, which means we may eventually see 16 GB DDR3 modules.

Some chipsets that support DDR3 also support a feature called *triple-channel memory*, which works a lot like dual-channel before it, but with three sticks of RAM instead of two. You'll need three of the same type of memory modules and a motherboard that supports it, but triple-channel memory can greatly increase performance for those who can afford it.

• **Figure 6.17**   DDR2 DIMM on top of a DDR3 DIMM

Do not confuse DDR3 with GDDR3; the latter is a type of memory used solely in video cards. See Chapter 19, "Video," for the scoop on video-specific types of memory.

In keeping with established tradition, Table 6.3 is a chart of common DDR3 speeds. Note how DDR3 I/O speeds are quadruple the clock speeds, whereas DDR2 I/O speeds are only double the clock. This speed increase is due to the increased buffer size, which enables DDR3 to grab twice as much data every clock cycle as DDR2 can.

Table 6.3	DDR3 Speeds		
Core RAM Clock Speed	DDR I/O Speed	DDR3 Speed Rating	PC Speed Rating
100 MHz	400 MHz	DDR3-800	PC3-6400
133 MHz	533 MHz	DDR3-1066	PC3-8500
166 MHz	667 MHz	DDR3-1333	PC3-10667
200 MHz	800 MHz	DDR3-1600	PC3-12800

RAM Variations

Within each class of RAM, you'll find variations in packaging, speed, quality, and the capability to handle data with more or fewer errors. Higher-end systems often need higher-end RAM, so knowing these variations is of crucial importance to techs.

Double-Sided DIMMs

Every type of RAM stick, starting with the old FPM SIMMs and continuing through to 240-pin DDR3 SDRAM, comes in one of two types: **single-sided** and **double-sided**. As their name implies, single-sided sticks have chips on only one side of the stick. Double-sided sticks have chips on both sides (Figure 6.18). The vast majority of RAM sticks are single-sided, but plenty of double-sided sticks are out there. Double-sided sticks are basically two sticks of RAM soldered onto one board. There's nothing wrong with double-sided RAM other than the fact that some motherboards either can't use them or can only use them in certain ways—for example, only if you use a single stick and it goes into a certain slot.

• **Figure 6.18**   Double-sided DDR SDRAM

Latency

If you've shopped for RAM lately, you may have noticed terms such as "CL2" or "low latency" as you tried to determine which RAM to purchase. You might find two otherwise identical RAM sticks with a 20 percent price difference and a salesperson pressuring you to buy the more expensive one because it's "faster" even though both sticks say DDR 3200 (Figure 6.19).

RAM responds to electrical signals at varying rates. When the memory controller starts to grab a line of memory, for example, a slight delay occurs; think of it as the RAM getting off the couch. After the RAM sends out the

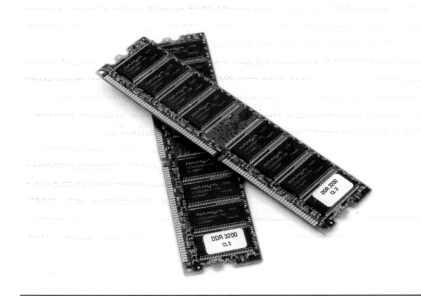

• **Figure 6.19**   Why is one more expensive than the other?

Tech Tip

Latency Is Relative
Latency numbers reflect how many clicks of the system clock it takes before the RAM responds. If you speed up the system clock, say from 166 MHz to 200 MHz, the same stick of RAM might take an extra click before it can respond. When you take RAM out of an older system and put it into a newer one, you might get a seemingly dead PC, even though the RAM fits in the DIMM slot. Many motherboards enable you to adjust the RAM timings manually. If so, try raising the latency to give the slower RAM time to respond. See Chapter 7, "BIOS and CMOS," to learn how to make these adjustments (and how to recover if you make a mistake.

requested line of memory, there's another slight delay before the memory controller can ask for another line—the RAM sat back down. The delay in RAM's response time is called its **latency**. RAM with a lower latency—such as CL2—is faster than RAM with a higher latency—such as CL3—because it responds more quickly. The CL refers to clock cycle delays. The 2 means that the memory delays two clock cycles before delivering the requested data; the 3 means a three-cycle delay.

From a tech's standpoint, you need to get the proper RAM for the system you're working on. If you put a high-latency stick in a motherboard set up for a low-latency stick, you'll get an unstable or completely dead PC. Check the motherboard manual and get the quickest RAM the motherboard can handle, and you should be fine.

CAS stands for *column array strobe*, one of the wires (along with the *row array strobe*) in the RAM that helps the memory controller find a particular bit of memory. Each of these wires requires electricity to charge up before it can do its job. This is one of the aspects of latency.

Parity and ECC

Given the high speeds and phenomenal amount of data moved by the typical DRAM chip, a RAM chip might occasionally give bad data to the memory controller. This doesn't necessarily mean that the RAM has gone bad. It could be a hiccup caused by some unknown event that makes a good DRAM chip say a bit is a zero when it's really a one. In most cases you won't even notice when such a rare event happens. In some environments, however, even these rare events are intolerable. A bank server handling thousands of online transactions per second, for example, can't risk even the smallest error. These important computers need a more robust, fault-resistant RAM.

The first type of error-detecting RAM was known as parity RAM (Figure 6.20). **Parity RAM** stored an extra bit of data (called the parity bit) that the MCC used to verify whether the data was correct. Parity wasn't perfect—it wouldn't always detect an error, and if the MCC did find an error, it couldn't correct the error. For years, parity was the only available way to tell if the RAM made a mistake.

• **Figure 6.20** Ancient parity RAM stick

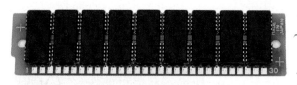

Today's PCs that need to watch for RAM errors use a special type of RAM called **error correction code RAM (ECC RAM)**. ECC is a major advance in error checking on DRAM. First, ECC detects any time a single bit is incorrect. Second, ECC fixes these errors on the fly. The checking and fixing come at a price, however, as ECC RAM is always slower than non-ECC RAM.

Some memory manufacturers call the technology *Error Checking and Correction* (*ECC*). Don't be thrown off if you see the phrase—it's the same thing, just a different marketing slant for error correction code.

ECC DRAM comes in every DIMM package type and can lead to some odd-sounding numbers. You can find DDR2 or DDR3 RAM sticks, for example, that come in 240-pin, 72-bit versions. Similarly, you'll see 200-pin, 72-bit SO-DIMM format. The extra 8 bits beyond the 64-bit data stream are for the ECC.

You might be tempted to say "Gee, maybe I want to try this ECC RAM." Well, don't! To take advantage of ECC RAM, you need a motherboard with an MCC designed to use ECC. Only expensive motherboards for high-end systems use ECC. The special-use-only nature of ECC makes it fairly rare. Plenty of techs with years of experience have never even seen ECC RAM.

Tech Tip

Counting Chips

To determine if a DRAM stick is parity or ECC, count the individual chips on the stick. If you have an odd number of chips on the stick, you have ECC or parity DRAM.

Buffered/Registered DRAM

Your average PC motherboard accepts no more than four sticks of DRAM, because more than four physical slots for sticks gives motherboard designers some serious electrical headaches. Yet some systems that use a lot of RAM need the capability to use more DRAM sticks on the motherboard, often six or eight. To get around the electrical hassles, special DRAM sticks add a buffering chip to the stick that acts as an intermediary between the DRAM and the MCC. These special DRAM sticks are called **buffered** or **registered DRAM** (Figure 6.21).

Like ECC, you must have a motherboard with an MCC designed to use this type of DRAM. Rest assured that such a motherboard has a large number of RAM slots. Buffered/registered RAM is rare (maybe not quite as rare as ECC RAM), and you'll never see it in the typical desktop system.

• **Figure 6.21** Buffered DRAM

■ Working with RAM

Whenever someone comes up to me and asks what single hardware upgrade they can do to improve their system performance, I always tell them the same thing—add more RAM. Adding more RAM can improve overall system performance, processing speed, and stability—if you get it right. Botching the job can cause dramatic system instability, such as frequent, random crashes and reboots. Every tech needs to know how to install and upgrade system RAM of all types.

To get the desired results from a RAM upgrade, you must first determine if insufficient RAM is the cause of system problems. Second, you need to pick the proper RAM for the system. Finally, you must use good installation practices. Always store RAM sticks in anti-static packaging whenever they're not in use, and use strict ESD handling procedures. Like many other pieces of the PC, RAM is *very* sensitive to ESD and other technician abuse (Figure 6.22)!

• **Figure 6.22** Don't do this! Grabbing the contacts is a

Do You Need RAM?

Two symptoms point to the need for more RAM in a PC: general system sluggishness and excessive hard drive accessing. If programs take forever to load and running programs seem to stall and move more slowly than you would like, the problem could stem from insufficient RAM. A friend with a new Windows Vista system complained that her PC seemed snappy when she first got it but takes a long time to do the things she wants to do with it, such as photograph retouching in Adobe Photoshop and document layout for a print zine she produces. Her system had only 1 GB of RAM, sufficient to run Windows Vista, but woefully insufficient for her tasks—she kept

maxing out the RAM and thus the system slowed to a crawl. I replaced her stick with a pair of 2-GB sticks and suddenly she had the powerhouse workstation she desired.

Excessive hard drive activity when you move between programs points to a need for more RAM. Every Windows PC has the capability to make a portion of your hard drive look like RAM in case you run out of real RAM. This is called the **page file** or **swap file**, as you'll recall from Chapter 4, "Understanding Windows." If you fill your RAM up with programs, your PC automatically starts loading some programs into the page file. You can't see this process taking place just by looking at the screen—these swaps are done in the background. But you will notice the hard drive access LED going crazy as Windows rushes to move programs between RAM and the page file in a process called **disk thrashing**. Windows uses the page file all the time, but excessive disk thrashing suggests that you need more RAM.

You can diagnose excessive disk thrashing through simply observing the hard drive access LED flashing or through various third-party tools. I like FreeMeter (www.tiler.com/freemeter/). It's been around for quite a while, runs on all versions of Windows, and is easy to use (Figure 6.23). Notice on the FreeMeter screenshot that some amount of the page file is being used. That's perfectly normal.

System RAM Recommendations

Microsoft sets very low the minimum RAM requirements listed for the various Windows operating systems to get the maximum number of users to upgrade or convert, and that's fine. A Windows XP Professional machine runs well enough on 128 MB of RAM. Just don't ask it to do any serious computing, such as running Doom III! Windows

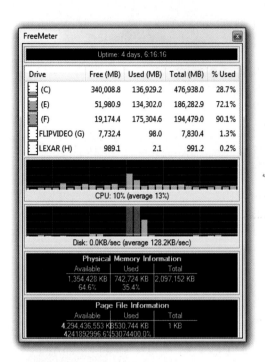

• **Figure 6.23**   FreeMeter

Try This!

Checking the Page File

How much of your hard drive does Windows use for a page file? Does the level change dramatically when you open typical applications, such as Microsoft Word, Solitaire, and Paint Shop Pro? The answers to these questions can give a tech a quick estimation about RAM usage and possibly RAM needs for a particular system, so try this.

In Windows 2000/XP you can easily glance at your page file usage through the Task Manager. To access the Task Manager, press CTRL-ALT-DEL simultaneously once. Click the Performance tab. The second box on the left, titled PF Usage, displays the amount of hard drive the page file is currently using. In Windows Vista, the process of viewing the page file is exactly the same, but Vista uses a less descriptive way of displaying its usage. In the bottom-right corner of the Performance tab, you'll see the title "Page File," which gives you a numeric representation.

1. How big is the page file when you have no applications open?

2. How much does it change when you open applications?

Mike Meyers' CompTIA A+ Guide to Managing and Troubleshooting PCs

Vista has raised the bar considerably, especially with the 64-bit version of the operating system. Here are my recommendations for system RAM.

Operating System	Reasonable Minimum	Solid Performance	Power User
Windows 2000	128 MB	256 MB	512 MB
Windows XP	256 MB	1 GB	2 GB
Windows Vista	2 GB	4 GB	8 GB

Determining Current RAM Capacity

Before you go get RAM, you obviously need to know how much RAM you currently have in your PC. Every version of Windows works the same way. Just select the Properties for My Computer or Computer to see how much RAM is in your system (Figure 6.24). If you have a newer keyboard, you can access the screen with the WINDOWS-PAUSE/BREAK keystroke combination. Windows 2000, XP, and Vista come with the handy Performance tab under the Task Manager (as shown in Figure 6.25).

Getting the Right RAM

To do the perfect RAM upgrade, determine the optimum capacity of RAM to install and then get the right RAM for the motherboard. Your first two stops toward these goals are the inside of the case and your motherboard manual. Open the case to see how many sticks of RAM you have installed currently and how many free slots you have open. Check the motherboard book to determine the total capacity of RAM the system can handle and what specific technology works with your system. You can't put DDR2 into a system that can only handle DDR SDRAM, after all, and it won't do you much good to install a pair of 2-GB DIMMs when your system tops out at 1.5 GB. Figure 6.26 shows the RAM limits for my ASUS Crosshair motherboard.

• **Figure 6.24**   Mike has a lot of RAM!

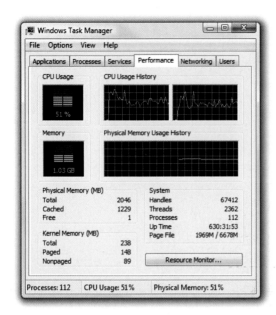

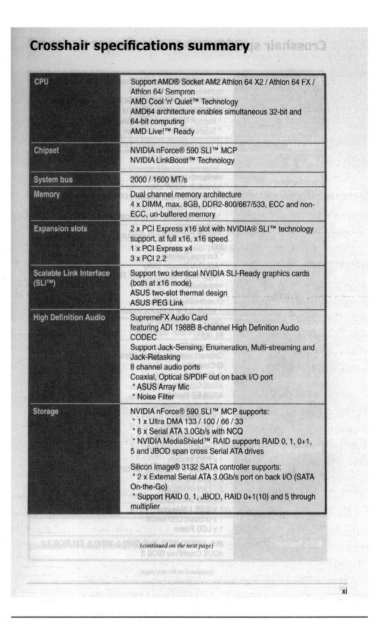

Crosshair specifications summary

CPU	Support AMD® Socket AM2 Athlon 64 X2 / Athlon 64 FX / Athlon 64/ Sempron AMD Cool 'n' Quiet™ Technology AMD64 architecture enables simultaneous 32-bit and 64-bit computing AMD Live!™ Ready
Chipset	NVIDIA nForce® 590 SLI™ MCP NVIDIA LinkBoost™ Technology
System bus	2000 / 1600 MT/s
Memory	Dual channel memory architecture 4 x DIMM, max. 8GB, DDR2-800/667/533, ECC and non-ECC, un-buffered memory
Expansion slots	2 x PCI Express x16 slot with NVIDIA® SLI™ technology support, at full x16, x16 speed 1 x PCI Express x4 3 x PCI 2.2
Scalable Link Interface (SLI™)	Support two identical NVIDIA SLI-Ready graphics cards (both at x16 mode) ASUS two-slot thermal design ASUS PEG Link
High Definition Audio	SupremeFX Audio Card featuring ADI 1988B 8-channel High Definition Audio CODEC Support Jack-Sensing, Enumeration, Multi-streaming and Jack-Retasking 8 channel audio ports Coaxial, Optical S/PDIF out on back I/O port * ASUS Array Mic * Noise Filter
Storage	NVIDIA nForce® 590 SLI™ MCP supports: * 1 x Ultra DMA 133 / 100 / 66 / 33 * 6 x Serial ATA 3.0Gb/s with NCQ * NVIDIA MediaShield™ RAID supports RAID 0, 1, 0+1, 5 and JBOD span cross Serial ATA drives Silicon Image® 3132 SATA controller supports: * 2 x External Serial ATA 3.0Gb/s port on back I/O (SATA On-the-Go) * Support RAID 0, 1, JBOD, RAID 0+1(10) and 5 through multiplier

(continued on the next page)

xi

● Figure 6.25 Performance tab in Windows XP Task Manager

Tech Tip

CPU-Z

The freeware CPU-Z program tells you the total number of slots on your motherboard, the number of slots used, and the exact type of RAM in each slot—very handy. CPU-Z not only determines the latency of your RAM, but also lists the latency at a variety of motherboard speeds. The CD accompanying this book has a copy of CPU-Z, so check it out.

● Figure 6.26 The motherboard book shows how much RAM the motherboard will handle.

Mix and Match at Your Peril

All motherboards can handle different capacities of RAM. If you have three slots, you may put a 512-MB stick in one and a 1-GB stick in the other with a high chance of success. To ensure maximum stability in a system, however, shoot for as close as you can get to uniformity of RAM. Choose RAM sticks that match in technology, capacity, and speed. Even on motherboards that offer slots for radically different RAM types, I recommend uniformity.

Mixing Speeds

With so many different DRAM speeds available, you may often find yourself tempted to mix speeds of DRAM in the same system. Although you may get away with mixing speeds on a system, the safest, easiest rule to follow is

to use the speed of DRAM specified in the motherboard book, and make sure that every piece of DRAM runs at that speed. In a worst-case scenario, mixing DRAM speeds can cause the system to lock up every few seconds or every few minutes. You might also get some data corruption. Mixing speeds sometimes works fine, but don't do your income tax on a machine with mixed DRAM speeds until the system has proven to be stable for a few days. The important thing to note here is that you won't break anything, other than possibly data, by experimenting.

Okay, I have mentioned enough disclaimers. Modern motherboards provide some flexibility regarding RAM speeds and mixing. First, you can use RAM that is faster than the motherboard specifies. For example, if the system needs PC3200 DDR2 SDRAM, you may put in PC4200 DDR2 SDRAM and it should work fine. Faster DRAM is not going to make the system run any faster, however, so don't look for any system improvement.

Second, you can sometimes get away with putting one speed of DRAM in one bank and another speed in another bank, as long as all the speeds are as fast as or faster than the speed specified by the motherboard. Don't bother trying to put different-speed DRAM sticks in the same bank with a motherboard that uses dual-channel DDR. Yes, it works once in a while, but it's too chancy. I avoid it.

Installing DIMMs and RIMMs

Installing DRAM is so easy that it's one of the very few jobs I recommend to non-techie folks. First, attach an anti-static wrist strap or touch some bare metal on the power supply to ground yourself and avoid ESD. Then swing the side tabs on the RAM slots down from the upright position. Pick up a stick of RAM—don't touch those contacts—and line up the notch or notches with the raised portion(s) of the DIMM socket (Figure 6.27). A good hard push down is usually all you need to ensure a solid connection. Make sure that the DIMM snaps into position to show it is completely seated. Also, notice that the two side tabs move in to reflect a tight connection.

• **Figure 6.27**   Inserting a DIMM

Serial Presence Detect (SPD)

Your motherboard should detect and automatically set up any DIMM or RIMM you install, assuming you have the right RAM for the system, using a technology called **serial presence detect (SPD)**. RAM makers add a handy chip to modern sticks called the SPD chip (Figure 6.28). The SPD chip stores all the information about your DRAM, including size, speed, ECC or non-ECC, registered or unregistered, and a number of other more technical bits of information.

When a PC boots, it queries the SPD chip so that the MCC knows how much RAM is on the stick, how fast it runs, and other information.

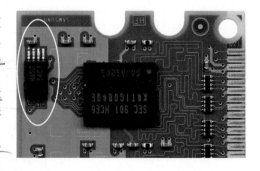

• **Figure 6.28**   SPD chip on a stick

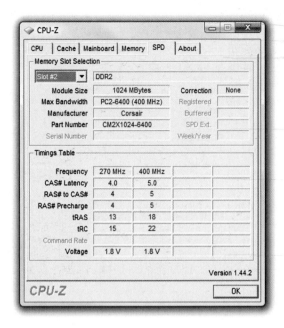

Any program can query the SPD chip. Take a look at Figure 6.29 with the results of the popular CPU-Z program showing RAM information from the SPD chip.

All new systems count on SPD to set the RAM timings properly for your system when it boots. If you add a RAM stick with a bad SPD chip, you'll get a POST error message and the system will not boot. You can't fix a broken SPD chip; you just buy a new stick of RAM.

The RAM Count

After installing the new RAM, turn on the PC and watch the boot process closely. If you installed the RAM correctly, the RAM count on the PC reflects the new value (compare Figures 6.30 and 6.31). If the RAM value stays the same, you probably have installed the RAM in a slot the motherboard doesn't want you to use (for example, you may need to use a particular slot first) or have not installed the RAM properly. If the computer does not boot and you've got a blank screen, you probably have not installed all the RAM sticks correctly. Usually, a good second look is all you need to determine the problem. Reseat or reinstall the RAM stick and try again.

RAM counts are confusing because RAM uses megabytes and gigabytes as opposed to millions and billions. Here are some examples of how different systems would show 256 MB of RAM:

268435456 (exactly 256 × 1 MB)

256M (some PCs try to make it easy for you)

262,144 (number of KB)

You should know how much RAM you're trying to install and use some common sense. If you have 512 MB and you add another 512-MB stick, you need a number that looks like one gigabyte. After you add the second stick, if you see a RAM count of 524582912—that sure looks like 512 MB, not the one gigabyte!

• **Figure 6.29** CPU-Z showing RAM information

```
Award Modular BIOS v6.00PG, An Energy Star Ally
Copyright (C) 1984-2005, Award Software, Inc.

GA-K8NP F13

Processor : AMD Athlon(tm) 64 Processor 3200+
<CPUID:0000F4A Patch ID:003A>
Memory Testing : 1048576K OK  ⬅
CPU clock frequency : 200 Mhz

Detecting IDE drives ...
```

• **Figure 6.30** Hey, where's the rest of my RAM?!

```
Award Modular BIOS v6.00PG, An Energy Star Ally
Copyright (C) 1984-2005, Award Software, Inc.

GA-K8NP F13

Processor : AMD Athlon(tm) 64 Processor 3200+
<CPUID:0000F4A Patch ID:003A>
Memory Testing : 3145728K OK
CPU clock frequency : 200 Mhz

Detecting IDE drives ...
```

• **Figure 6.31** RAM count after proper insertion of DIMMs

Installing SO-DIMMs in Laptops

It wasn't that long ago that adding RAM to a laptop was either impossible or required you to send the system back to the manufacturer. For years, every laptop maker had custom-made, proprietary RAM packages that were difficult to handle and staggeringly expensive. The wide acceptance of SO-DIMMs over the last few years has virtually erased these problems. All laptops now provide relatively convenient access to their SO-DIMMs, enabling easy replacement or addition of RAM.

Access to RAM usually requires removing a panel or lifting up the keyboard—the procedure varies among laptop manufacturers. Figure 6.32 shows a typical laptop RAM access panel. You can slide the panel off to reveal the SO-DIMMs. SO-DIMMs usually insert exactly like the old SIMMs; slide the pins into position and snap the SO-DIMM down into the retaining clips (Figure 6.33).

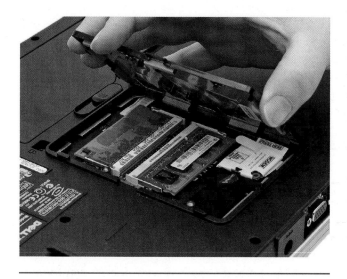

• **Figure 6.32**   A RAM access panel on a laptop

• **Figure 6.33**   Snapping in an SO-DIMM

Before doing any work on a laptop, turn the system off, disconnect it from the AC wall socket, and remove all batteries. Use an anti-static wrist strap because laptops are far more susceptible to ESD than desktop PCs.

Practical Application

■ Troubleshooting RAM

"Memory" errors show up in a variety of ways on modern systems, including parity errors, ECC error messages, system lockups, page faults, and other error screens in Windows. These errors can indicate bad RAM but often point to something completely unrelated to RAM. This is especially true with intermittent problems. The challenge for techs is to recognize these errors and then determine which part of the system caused the memory error.

You can get two radically different types of parity errors: real and phantom. Real parity errors are simply errors that the MCC detects from the parity or ECC chips (if you have them). The operating system then reports the problem in an error message, such as "Parity error at *xxxx:xxxxxxxx*," where *xxxx:xxxxxxxx* is a hexadecimal value (a string of numbers and letters, such as A5F2:004EEAB9). If you get an error like this, write down the value (Figure 6.34). A real parity/ECC error shows up at the same place in memory each time and almost always indicates that you have a bad RAM stick.

Phantom parity errors show up on systems that don't have parity or ECC memory. If Windows generates parity errors with different addresses, you most likely do *not* have a problem with RAM. These phantom errors can occur for a variety of reasons, including software problems, heat or dust, solar flares, fluctuations in the Force...you get the idea.

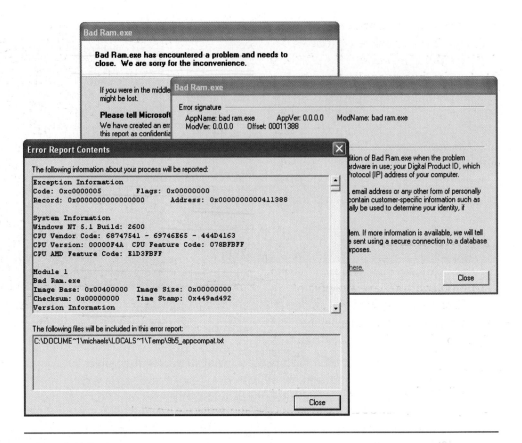

Bad Ram.exe

Bad Ram.exe has encountered a problem and needs to close. We are sorry for the inconvenience.

If you were in the middle might be lost.

Please tell Microsoft
We have created an err
this report as confidentia

Bad Ram.exe

Error signature
AppName: bad ram.exe   AppVer: 0.0.0.0   ModName: bad ram.exe
ModVer: 0.0.0.0   Offset: 00011388

Error Report Contents

The following information about your process will be reported:

```
Exception Information
Code: 0xc0000005        Flags: 0x00000000
Record: 0x0000000000000000        Address: 0x0000000000411388

System Information
Windows NT 5.1 Build: 2600
CPU Vendor Code: 68747541 - 69746E65 - 444D4163
CPU Version: 00000F4A  CPU Feature Code: 078BFBFF
CPU AMD Feature Code: E1D3FBFF

Module 1
Bad Ram.exe
Image Base: 0x00400000   Image Size: 0x00000000
Checksum: 0x00000000      Time Stamp: 0x449ad492
Version Information
```

The following files will be included in this error report:

C:\DOCUME~1\michaels\LOCALS~1\Temp\9b5_appcompat.txt

Close

• **Figure 6.34**   Windows error message

System lockups and page faults (they often go hand in hand) in Windows can indicate a problem with RAM. A system lockup is when the computer stops functioning. A **page fault** is a milder error that can be caused by memory issues but not necessarily system RAM problems. Certainly page faults *look* like RAM issues because Windows generates frightening error messages filled with long strings of hexadecimal digits, such as "KRNL386 caused a page fault at 03F2:25A003BC." Just because the error message contains a memory address, however, does not mean that you have a problem with your RAM. Write down the address. If it repeats in later error messages, you probably have a bad RAM stick. If Windows displays different memory locations, you need to look elsewhere for the culprit.

Every once in a while, something potentially catastrophic happens within the PC, some little electron hits the big red panic button, and the operating system has to shut down certain functions running before it can save data. This panic button inside the PC is called a **non-maskable interrupt (NMI)**, more simply defined as an interruption the CPU cannot ignore. An NMI manifests to the user as what techs lovingly call the **Blue Screen of Death (BSoD)**—a bright blue screen with a scary-sounding error message on it (Figure 6.35).

Bad RAM sometimes triggers an NMI, although often the culprit lies with buggy programming or clashing code. The BSoD varies according to the operating system, and it would require a much lengthier tome than this one to cover all the variations. Suffice it to say that RAM *could* be the problem when that delightful blue screen appears.

Finally, intermittent memory errors can come from a variety of sources, including a dying power supply, electrical interference, buggy applications, buggy hardware, and so on. These errors show up as lockups, general protection faults, page faults, and parity errors, but they never have the same address or happen with the same applications. Try the power supply first with non-application-specific intermittent errors of any sort.

Testing RAM

Once you discover that you may have a RAM problem, you have a couple of options. First, several companies manufacture hardware RAM-testing devices, but unless you have a lot of disposable income, they're probably priced way too high for the average tech ($1,500 and higher). Second, you can use the method I use—*replace and pray*. Open the system case and replace each stick, one at a time, with a known good replacement stick. (You have one of those lying around, don't you?) This method, although potentially time-consuming, certainly works. With PC prices as low as they are now, you could simply replace the whole system for less than the price of a dedicated RAM tester.

Third, you could run a software-based tester on the RAM. Because you have to load a software tester into the memory it's about to scan, there's always a small chance that simply starting the software RAM tester might cause an error. Still, you can find some pretty good free ones out there. My favorite is the venerable Memtest86 written by Mr. Chris Brady (www.memtest86.com). Memtest86 exhaustively checks your RAM and reports bad RAM when it finds it (Figure 6.36).

```
A problem has been detected and windows has been shut down to prevent damage
to your computer.

The problem seems to be caused by the following file: SPCMDCON.SYS

PAGE_FAULT_IN_NONPAGED_AREA

If this is the first time you've seen this Stop error screen,
restart your computer. If this screen appears again, follow
these steps:

Check to make sure any new hardware or software is properly installed.
If this is a new installation, ask your hardware or software manufacturer
for any windows updates you might need.

If problems continue, disable or remove any newly installed hardware
or software. Disable BIOS memory options such as caching or shadowing.
If you need to use Safe Mode to remove or disable components, restart
your computer, press F8 to select Advanced Startup Options, and then
select Safe Mode.

Technical information:

*** STOP: 0x00000050 (0xFD3094C2,0x00000001,0xFBFE7617,0x00000000)

*** SPCMDCON.SYS - Address FBFE7617 base at FBFE5000, DateStamp 3d6dd67c
```

• **Figure 6.35**   Blue Screen of Death

A **general protection fault (GPF)** is an error that can cause an application to crash. Often they're caused by programs stepping on each other's toes. Chapter 17, "Maintaining and Troubleshooting Windows," goes into more detail on GPFs and other Windows errors.

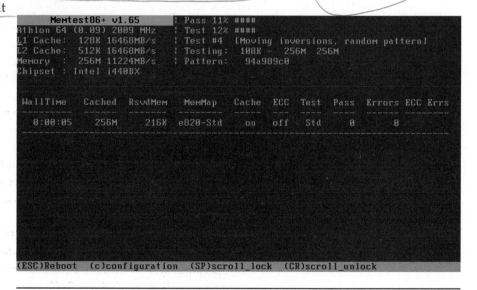

```
    MemTest86+ v1.65          | Pass 11% ####
Athlon 64 (0.09) 2009 MHz     | Test 12% ####
L1 Cache:   128K 16468MB/s    | Test #4  [Moving inversions, random pattern]
L2 Cache:   512K 16468MB/s    | Testing:   108K -  256M  256M
Memory  :   256M 11224MB/s    | Pattern:   94a989c0
Chipset : Intel i440BX

 WallTime   Cached   RsvdMem   MemMap   Cache   ECC   Test   Pass   Errors ECC Errs
 --------   ------   -------   ------   -----   ---   ----   ----   ------ --------
  0:00:05    256M     216K   e820-Std    on    off   Std     0       0

(ESC)Reboot  (c)configuration  (SP)scroll_lock  (CR)scroll_unlock
```

• **Figure 6.36**   Memtest86 in action

Chapter 6 Review

■ Chapter Summary

After reading this chapter and completing the exercises, you should understand the following about RAM.

Identify the different types of DRAM packaging

■ The sticks of RAM snapped into your motherboard are DRAM. Think of DRAM as a spreadsheet in which each cell holds a one or a zero. Each cell represents a single bit. The number of columns and rows are finite.

■ If a chip contains 1,048,576 rows and eight columns, it can be described as a 1 M x 8 chip. A chip containing 2,097,152 rows and 16 columns can be described as a 2 M x 16 chip.

■ DRAM needs to be able to fill the data bus. A 1 M x 8 DRAM chip is only 8 bits wide and would provide the CPU with only 8 bits of data. You would need eight of the 1 M x 8 chips to fill a 64-bit data bus.

■ DRAM chips are soldered to a circuit board called a stick or module, and when these chips are combined, a single stick can fill the data bus. Modern DRAM sticks come in 32-bit- and 64-bit-wide varieties.

Explain the varieties of RAM

■ Synchronous dynamic random access memory, or SDRAM, is tied to the system clock. The CPU, memory controller, and RAM all work in tandem with the clock pulse. This results in little wasted time when the CPU requests data from RAM.

■ SDRAM comes in sticks called dual inline memory modules (DIMMs). SDRAM DIMMs come in a variety of pin sizes, with 168 pins being the most common for desktop systems. DIMMs are 64 bits wide so that they match the 64-bit data bus of modern CPUs. DIMMs snap into slots on the motherboard. Each DIMM is 64 bits, so snapping in a single DIMM fills the data bus; therefore, each slot is called a bank.

■ SDRAM is advertised by capacity and speed. The speed is prefixed with "PC"; for example, PC66 runs at 66 MHz. A stick of SDRAM advertised as 256 MB PC133 has a capacity of 256 MB and runs at

133 MHz. Five clock speeds are commonly used: 66, 75, 83, 100, and 133 MHz.

■ RAM speed must match or exceed that of the system. For example, PC66 RAM can only be used on a motherboard running at (or below) 66 MHz. A motherboard with a frontside bus of 100 MHz needs at least PC100 RAM.

■ Rambus DRAM (RDRAM) was created by Rambus, Inc., and came in sticks called RIMMs. Due to cost, licensing issues, and compatibility, RDRAM is now obsolete.

■ RIMMs were 64 bits wide and came in speeds of 600 MHz, 700 MHz, 800 MHz, and 1066 MHz. Differences in the notches prevented you from snapping a RIMM into a motherboard DIMM slot or vice versa.

■ The RIMM memory controller uses a dual-channel architecture: it alternates between two banks to increase the speed of data retrieval. You need to install RIMMs in pairs to accommodate this feature.

■ All RIMM slots on the motherboard must be filled with either a RIMM or a CRIMM. A CRIMM, or continuity RIMM, is simply a stick with no memory chips on it.

■ Double data rate SDRAM (DDR RAM) is faster than regular SDRAM because it doubles the throughput. Desktop PCs use 184-pin DDR DIMMs, whereas laptops use either 200-pin or 172-pin small-outline DIMMs (SO-DIMM). DDR RAM modules have notches that differ from both regular SDRAM and RDRAM, so DDR RAM only snaps into DDR slots on a motherboard.

■ DDR RAM is advertised one of two ways. One way is with "DDR" followed by the speed; for example, DDR400 for a stick of RAM runs at 400 MHz. Because DDR RAM runs at twice the clock speed, DDR400 is meant for a 200-MHz frontside bus. DDR RAM is also advertised by "PC" followed by the throughput; for example, PC3200. The number is determined by multiplying the speed by eight (as all DDR sticks are 64 bits, or 8 bytes, wide). Thus, DDR400 has a throughput of 3200 bytes per second (400 MHz × 8 bytes). DDR400 and PC3200 are equivalent.

- Dual-channel DDR improves upon DDR by using the DIMMs in pairs, much like RDRAM. For systems to use dual-channel DDR, the motherboard and memory controller must support dual-channel DDR RAM, and the DDR DIMMs must be identical. Dual-channel DDR does not require dummy modules such as CRIMMs. Dual-channel slots are identified on a motherboard by their blue color. Some motherboards offer a third slot in black, but filling that third slot to increase your total system RAM also turns off the dual-channel feature.

- DDR2 is an improvement of DDR. DDR2 runs faster than DDR and uses a 240-pin form factor that is not compatible with DDR. You need a motherboard with DDR2 slots to use DDR2 RAM. DDR2 is rated by speed or throughput. Thus DDR2-400 is the same as PC2-3200 and is meant for a 200-MHz frontside bus.

- DDR3 boasts higher speeds, more efficient architecture, and around 30 percent lower power consumption than DDR2 RAM. DDR3 doubles the buffer of DDR2 from 4 bits to 8 bits, giving it a huge boost in bandwidth over older RAM. Some chipsets that support DDR3 also support triple-channel memory, which works a lot like dual-channel but with three sticks of RAM instead of two.

- RAM modules are either single-sided or double-sided. Single-sided sticks have chips on only one side, whereas double-sided sticks have chips on both sides. Most RAM is single-sided.

- Latency refers to the time lag between when the memory controller starts to fetch data from RAM and when RAM actually sends out the requested data. Another lag occurs when the memory controller asks for the next line from RAM. The shorter this lag time, the faster the system. CL2 indicates a shorter lag time, or lower latency, than CL3, so CL2 is faster. Check your motherboard documentation and get the lowest latency RAM your system will support.

- Error correction code (ECC) RAM improved upon parity RAM by being able to fix single-bit errors on the fly. ECC RAM is always slower than non-ECC RAM due to the overhead of the correcting code. Only high-end motherboards and memory controllers can use ECC RAM.

- Buffered or registered RAM adds a buffering chip to compensate for the electrical interference that can result from using more than four DIMMs on a single motherboard. The motherboard and memory controller must be designed specifically to support buffered or registered RAM. You are not likely to see it in a typical desktop system.

Select and install RAM

- Disk thrashing is constant hard drive activity symptomatic of insufficient RAM. It occurs when Windows repeatedly uses up all available RAM space and has to move data not immediately needed out of the RAM into a temporary file on the hard drive called a swap file or page file and then swap the data back into RAM when it is needed by the program. You can monitor the size of your swap file in the Task Manager.

- You must know what type of RAM (such as regular SDRAM, DDR, DDR2, or DDR3) your motherboard accepts before you purchase a RAM upgrade. You also need to know the maximum amount of RAM your motherboard supports and the maximum supported per slot.

- Though not required, it is good practice to make sure all sticks of RAM in any system are as close to identical as possible. Matching your RAM modules in technology, capacity, speed, and manufacturer lessens the chance of problems and incompatibility.

- The serial presence detect (SPD) chip on modern DIMMs automatically supplies all the information about the RAM to the system, such as the size, speed, ECC or non-ECC, registered or unregistered, and other details.

- To install SO-DIMMs in a laptop, you must remove a panel on the underside of the laptop or remove the keyboard to find the RAM slots. The SO-DIMM slides into the slot and snaps down into position. Unplug the laptop and remove the battery before attempting a RAM upgrade, and protect the RAM from ESD by wearing an anti-static wristband.

Perform basic RAM troubleshooting

- Symptoms of bad RAM include parity errors, system lockups, page faults, and other error screens in Windows. However, other failing components can cause similar problems. Bad RAM usually results in error screens displaying messages such as "Parity error at *xxxx:xxxxxxxx*"

where *xxxx:xxxxxxxx* is a hexadecimal value such as A5F2:004EEAB9. A real parity error shows up in the same place in memory each time—if that hexadecimal code is always the same, you probably have bad RAM.

■ Page faults result in error screens such as "KRNL386 caused a page fault at 03F2:25A003BC." The process that caused the page fault (in this case, KRNL386) may change, but if the hexadecimal address is the same across numerous error screens, you probably have bad RAM.

■ A non-maskable interrupt (NMI) results in a Blue Screen of Death (BSoD). Although BSoDs are often blamed on bad RAM, they are more often caused by buggy application program code.

■ If you suspect you have bad RAM and you don't have a hardware RAM-testing device, swap one of the sticks in your system with a known good stick. If the system works, you've found the bad stick. If the system still has errors, replace the stick you removed and swap a different stick for the known good stick. Another option is to use a software RAM tester such as Memtest86.

■ Key Terms

bank *(182)*
Blue Screen of Death (BSoD) *(196)*
buffered/registered DRAM *(189)*
continuity RIMM (CRIMM) *(183)*
disk thrashing *(190)*
double data rate SDRAM (DDR SDRAM) *(183)*
double-sided RAM *(187)*
dual-channel architecture *(183)*
dual inline memory module (DIMM) *(182)*
dynamic random access memory (DRAM) *(177)*
error correction code RAM (ECC RAM) *(188)*
general protection fault (GPF) *(197)*
latency *(188)*
module *(180)*

non-maskable interrupt (NMI) *(196)*
page fault *(196)*
page file *(190)*
parity RAM *(188)*
Rambus DRAM (RDRAM) *(182)*
RIMM *(183)*
serial presence detect (SPD) *(193)*
single inline memory module (SIMM) *(180)*
single-sided RAM *(187)*
small-outline DIMM (SO-DIMM) *(182)*
stick *(180)*
swap file *(190)*
synchronous DRAM (SDRAM) *(181)*

■ Key Term Quiz

Use the Key Terms list to complete the sentences that follow. Not all terms will be used.

1. If your motherboard uses RDRAM, you must fill each slot with either a(n) _____ or a(n) _____.

2. If the LED for your hard drive stays on most of the time, your computer is suffering from _____, a sure sign you need to add more memory.

3. A special kind of memory stick for laptops is called a(n) _____.

4. Memory that makes two data accesses during each clock tick is called _____.

5. Unlike regular DRAM, _____ is tied to the system clock.

6. Unlike regular DRAM, _____ enables error checking and correcting.

7. The time lag between when the memory controller starts to fetch a line of data from RAM and when the RAM actually starts to deliver the data is known as _____.

8. Systems automatically detect new RAM by polling the module's _____ chip.

9. Motherboards that support more than four sticks of RAM may require _____ to accommodate for the additional electrical hassles caused by the additional sticks.

10. Memory chips are soldered to a small circuit board called a(n) _____ or a(n) _____.

1. What is the correct throughput of DDR-SDRAM, and what is the speed of PC1600 RAM?

   A. 4 bytes per second, 133 MHz

   B. 8 bytes per second, 200 MHz

   C. 4 bits per second, 400 MHz

   D. 8 bits per second, 200 MHz

2. How many sticks of RAM do you need to fill a bank in a computer that can use 168-pin DIMMs?

   A. One

   B. Two

   C. Four

   D. Eight

3. If you upgrade your memory but notice that the RAM count does not reflect the additional memory, what should you do?

   A. Remove the RAM and try to reinstall it.

   B. Restart the computer.

   C. Return the memory because it's probably bad.

   D. Go to Setup and configure the memory to reflect the new amount.

4. What does a non-maskable interrupt cause the CPU to produce?

   A. The Blue Screen of Death

   B. A parity error

   C. Excessive heat

   D. An incorrect memory count

5. What does the CPU use to access the system's RAM?

   A. The system bus

   B. The MMC

   C. The address bus

   D. The expansion bus

6. Which of the following statements is true about RDRAM?

   A. It uses dual-channel architecture.

   B. It offers speeds ranging from 200 MHz to 600 MHz.

   C. It is less expensive than SDRAM.

   D. It is used by AMD but not Intel processors.

7. Which of the following SDRAM speeds would not work with a 100-MHz motherboard?

   A. 66 MHz

   B. 100 MHz

   C. 133 MHz

   D. 200 MHz

8. Which of the following is a valid package size for DDR3 DIMMs?

   A. 168-pin

   B. 172-pin

   C. 184-pin

   D. 240-pin

9. If you are running Windows 2000, Windows XP, or Windows Vista, you can use all of the following methods to find out how much RAM is installed in your computer except _____.

   A. From the Control Panel, select System and then the Hardware tab.

   B. Use the Performance tab under the Task Manager.

   C. Select Properties from My Computer/Computer.

   D. With a newer keyboard, press the WINDOWS-PAUSE/BREAK keystroke combination.

10. What package does DDR-SDRAM use for desktop PCs?

    A. 30-pin

    B. 72-pin

    C. 168-pin

    D. 184-pin

11. What happens if you mix RAM sticks of different speeds?

    A. Your computer will work fine as long as it uses dual-channel architecture.

    B. Your computer may slow down.

    C. Your computer will work fine if all the memory sticks are slower than the speed of the motherboard.

    D. Your computer may lock up every few seconds or provide corrupted data.

12. Why is SDRAM faster than regular DRAM?

    A. It makes two processes per clock cycle.

    B. It runs synchronously with the system clock.

    C. It uses dual-channel architecture.

    D. It has fewer pins, resulting in fewer corrupt bits.

13. What is true about a double-sided DIMM?

    A. It has memory chips on the front and back.

    B. It can be installed forward or backwards.

    C. It is twice as fast as a single-sided DIMM.

    D. It has half the capacity of a quad-sided DIMM.

14. What is the minimum requirement for RAM for Windows XP?

    A. 128 MB

    B. 256 MB

    C. 512 MB

    D. 1 GB

15. What happens if you add two RAM sticks to your PC, and one has a bad SPD?

    A. When your system boots, it will recognize both RAM sticks but will not register any special features (such as ECC) of the stick with the bad SPD.

    B. When your system boots, it will only register the presence of the RAM stick with the good SPD.

    C. When your system boots, it won't register the presence of the RAM stick with the bad SPD until you configure the RAM settings by using the Setup utility.

    D. When you try to boot the system, you will get a POST error message and the system will not boot.

■ Essay Quiz

1. Celia tells you she just received a new motherboard for the system she is building. She is confused about the RAM slots. The motherboard has three of them, but two are blue and one is black. What can you tell her about the RAM slots on her motherboard?

2. Your cousin James recently bought a new computer with 512 MB of RAM and a Windows Vista operating system. He's complaining about how slow his new computer is, especially when he's working with his graphics applications. How can you convince him that he needs more memory?

3. Now that you've convinced your cousin James that he needs more memory for his new PC, how will you explain what kind he should buy and how he should install it? You may assume that he has the motherboard book and that his computer has a 166-MHz system bus and can support DDR2 RAM.

4. Your computer is acting funny. Sometimes you get an error message on the screen. Other times data seems to be corrupted. Sometimes the computer just locks up. You suspect that it may be bad memory. How can you find out whether a memory problem or something else is causing your trouble?

Lab Project

• Lab Project 6.1

To learn more about memory, go to the Web site www.kingston.com, select Memory Tools from the buttons at the top of the screen, and examine the "Ultimate Memory Guide." This resource contains information about all aspects of computer memory. After using this guide, answer the following questions:

1 Why do memory prices vary so frequently?

2 What are the differences in tin- and gold-edged memory sticks, and how does one know which to choose when upgrading?

3 Describe the notches on a 30-pin SIMM, a 72-pin SIMM, a 168-pin DIMM, and a 184-pin DIMM. What function do the notches serve?

BIOS and CMOS

"Nearly right, Penfold, it's a 32 K ROM C-moss flip flop digital homing device."

—Danger Mouse, *Danger Mouse*

In this chapter, you will learn how to

- **Explain the function of BIOS**
- **Distinguish among various CMOS setup utility options**
- **Describe option ROM and device drivers**
- **Troubleshoot the power-on self test (POST)**
- **Maintain BIOS and CMOS properly**

In Chapter 5, "Microprocessors," you saw how the address bus and external data bus connect RAM to the CPU via the memory controller chip (MCC) to run programs and transfer data. Assuming you apply power in the right places, you don't need anything else to make a simple computer. The only problem with such a simple computer is that it would bore you to death—there's no way to do anything with it! A PC needs devices such as keyboards and mice to provide input, and output devices such as monitors and sound cards to communicate the current state of the running programs to you. A computer also needs permanent storage devices, such as hard drives and optical drives, to store programs and data when you turn off the computer.

Historical/Conceptual

■ We Need to Talk

Simply placing a number of components into a computer is useless if the CPU can't communicate with them. Getting the CPU to communicate with a device starts with some kind of interconnection—a communication bus that enables the CPU to send commands to and from devices. To make this connection, let's promote the MCC, giving it extra firepower to act as not only the interconnection between the CPU and RAM, but also the interconnection between the CPU and the other devices on the PC. The MCC isn't just the memory controller anymore, so let's now call it the **Northbridge** because it acts as the primary bridge between the CPU and the rest of the computer (Figure 7.1).

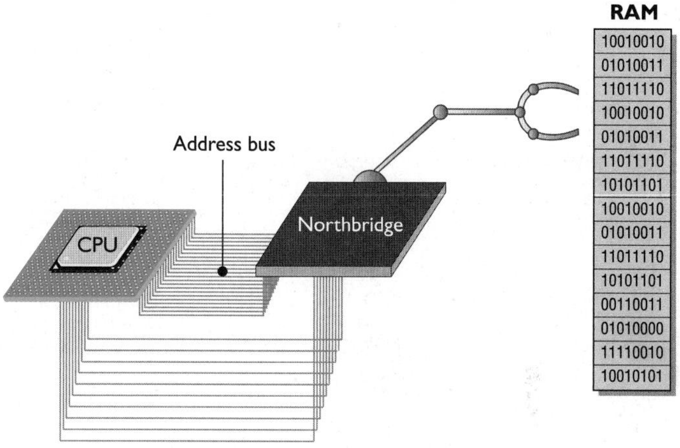

Your PC is full of devices, so the PC industry decided to delegate some of the interconnectivity work to a second chip called the **Southbridge**. The Northbridge only deals with high-speed interfaces such as the connection to your video card and RAM. The Southbridge works mainly with lower-speed devices such as the USB controller and hard drive controllers. Chip makers design matched sets of particular models of Northbridge and Southbridge to work together. You don't buy a Northbridge from one company and a Southbridge from another—they're sold as a set. We call this set of Northbridge and Southbridge the **chipset**.

The chipset extends the data bus to every device on the PC. The CPU uses the data bus to move data to and from all of the devices of the PC. Data constantly flows on the external data bus among the CPU, chipset, RAM, and other devices on the PC (Figure 7.2).

The first use for the address bus, as you know, is for the CPU to tell the chipset to send or store data in memory and to tell the chipset which section of memory to access or use. Just as with the external data bus, the chipset extends the address bus to all of the devices (Figure 7.3). That way the CPU can use the address bus to send commands to devices, just as it sends commands to the chipset. You'll see this in action a lot more in Chapter 8, "Expansion Bus," but for now just go with the concept.

It's not too hard to swallow the concept that the CPU uses the address bus to talk to the devices, but how does it know what to *say* to them? How does it know all of the patterns of ones and zeros to place on the address bus to tell the hard drive it needs to send a file? Let's look at the interaction between the keyboard and CPU for insight into this process.

● **Figure 7.1**   Meet the Northbridge

Chipset makers rarely use the terms "Northbridge" and "Southbridge" anymore, but because most modern chipsets consist of only two or three chips with basically the same functions, techs continue to use the terms.

Techs commonly talk about various functions of the chipset as if those functions were still handled by discrete chips. So you'll hear about memory controllers, keyboard controllers, mouse controllers, USB controllers, and so on, even though they're all just circuits on the Northbridge or Southbridge chips.

Talking to the Keyboard

The keyboard provides a great example of how the buses and support programming help the CPU get the job done. In early computers, the keyboard

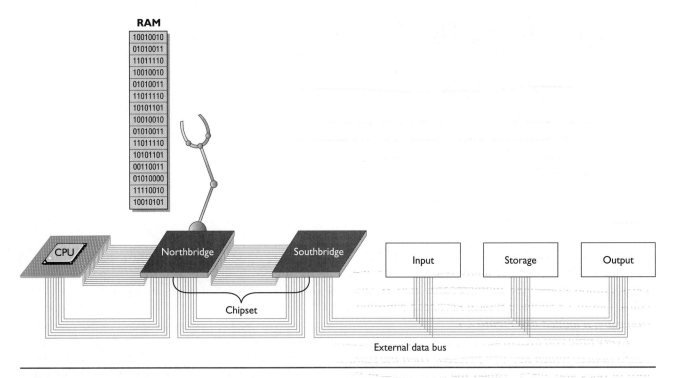

• **Figure 7.2** The chipset extending the data bus

connected to the external data bus via a special chip known as the *keyboard controller*. Don't bother looking for this chip on your motherboard—the Southbridge now handles keyboard controller functions. The way the keyboard controller—or technically, the keyboard controller *circuitry*—works with the CPU, however, has changed only a small amount in the past 20+ years, making it a perfect tool to illustrate how the CPU talks to a device.

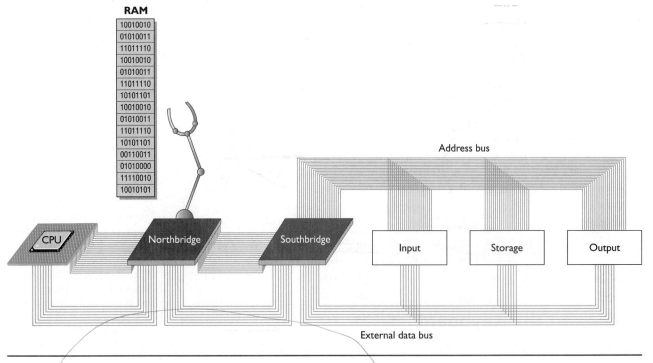

• **Figure 7.3**   Every device in your computer connects to the address bus.

• **Figure 7.4** A keyboard chip on a Pentium motherboard

The keyboard controller was one of the last single-function chips to be absorbed into the chipset. For many years—in fact, well into the Pentium III/ Early Athlon era—most motherboards had separate keyboard controller chips. Figure 7.4 shows a typical keyboard controller from those days. Electronically, it looked like Figure 7.5.

Every time you press a key on your keyboard, a scanning chip in the keyboard notices which key you pressed. Then the scanner sends a coded pattern of ones and zeros—called the **scan code**—to the keyboard controller. Every key on your keyboard has a unique scan code. The keyboard controller stores the scan code in its own register. Does it surprise you that the lowly keyboard controller has a register similar to a CPU? Lots of chips have registers—not just CPUs (Figure 7.6)!

How does the CPU get the scan code out of the keyboard controller (see Figure 7.7)? While we're at it, how does the CPU tell the keyboard to change

 Tech Tip

The 8042

Even though the model numbers changed over the years, you'll still hear techs refer to the keyboard controller as the 8042, after the original keyboard controller chip.

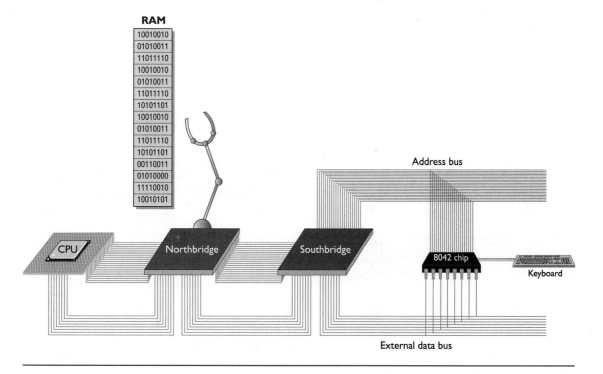

• **Figure 7.5** Electronic view of the keyboard controller

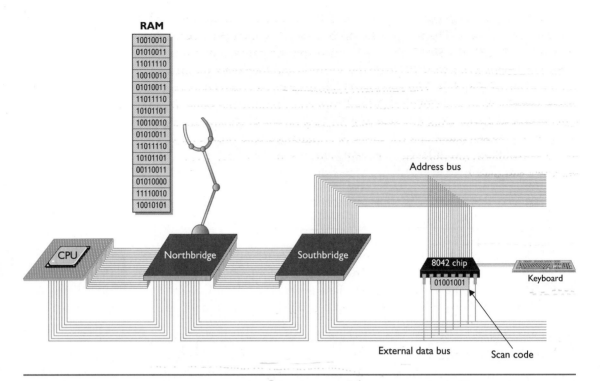

● **Figure 7.6**   Scan code stored in keyboard controller's register

the typematic buffer rate (when you hold down a key and the letter repeats) or to turn the number lock LED on and off, to mention just a few other jobs the keyboard needs to do for the system? The point is that the keyboard controller must be able to respond to multiple commands, not just one.

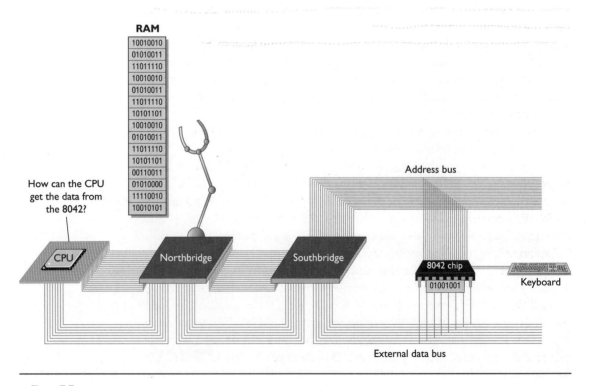

● **Figure 7.7**   The CPU ponders the age-old dilemma of how to get the 8042 to cough up its data.

The keyboard controller accepts commands exactly as you saw the CPU accept commands in Chapter 5 "Microprocessors." Remember when you added 2 to 3 with the 8088? You had to use specific commands from the 8088's codebook to tell the CPU to do the addition and then place the answer on the external data bus. The keyboard controller has its own codebook—much simpler than any CPU's codebook, but conceptually the same. If the CPU wants to know what key was last pressed on the keyboard, the CPU needs to know the command (or series of commands) that orders the keyboard controller to put the scan code of the letter on the external data bus so the CPU can read it.

Essentials

BIOS

The CPU can't magically or otherwise automatically know how to talk with any device; it needs some sort of support programming loaded into memory that teaches it about a particular device. This programming is called **basic input/output services (BIOS)**. The programs dedicated to enabling the CPU to communicate with devices are called services (or device drivers, as you'll see later in the chapter). This goes well beyond the keyboard, by the way. In fact, *every* device on the computer needs BIOS! But let's continue with the keyboard for now.

Bringing BIOS to the PC

A talented programmer could write BIOS for a keyboard if the programmer knew the keyboard's codebook; keyboards are pretty simple devices. This begs the question: where would this support programming be stored? Well, programming could be incorporated into the operating system. Storing programming to talk to the hardware of your PC in the operating system is great—all operating systems have built-in code that knows how to talk to your keyboard, your mouse, and just about every piece of hardware you may put into your PC.

That's fine once the operating system's up and running, but what about a brand new stack of parts you're about to assemble into a new PC? When a new system's being built, it has no operating system. The CPU must have access to BIOS for the most important hardware on your PC: not only the keyboard, but also the monitor, hard drives, optical drives, USB ports, and RAM. This code can't be stored on a hard drive or CD-ROM disc—these important devices need to be ready at any time the CPU calls them, even before installing a mass storage device or an operating system.

The perfect place to store the support programming is on the motherboard. That settles one issue, but another looms: What storage medium should the motherboard use? DRAM won't work, because all of the data would be erased every time the computer was turned off. You need some type of permanent program storage device that does not depend on other peripherals to work. And you need that storage device to sit on the motherboard.

ROM

Motherboards store the keyboard controller support programming, among other programs, on a special type of device called a **read-only memory (ROM)** chip. A ROM chip stores programs, called **services**, exactly like RAM: that is, like an 8-bit-wide spreadsheet. But ROM differs from RAM in two important ways. First, ROM chips are **nonvolatile**, meaning that the information stored on ROM isn't erased when the computer is turned off. Second, traditional ROM chips are read-only, meaning that once you store a program on one, you can't change it. Modern motherboards use a type of ROM called **flash ROM** that differs from traditional ROM in that you can update and change the contents through a very specific process called "flashing the ROM," covered later in this chapter. Figure 7.8 shows a typical flash ROM chip on a motherboard. When the CPU wants to talk to the keyboard controller, it goes to the flash ROM chip to access the proper programming.

Every motherboard has a flash ROM, called the **system ROM** chip because it contains code that enables your CPU to talk to the basic hardware of your PC (Figure 7.9). As alluded to earlier, the system ROM holds BIOS for more than just the keyboard controller. It also stores programs for communicating with the floppy drives, hard drives, CD and DVD drives, video, USB ports, and other basic devices on your motherboard.

• **Figure 7.8**   Typical flash ROM

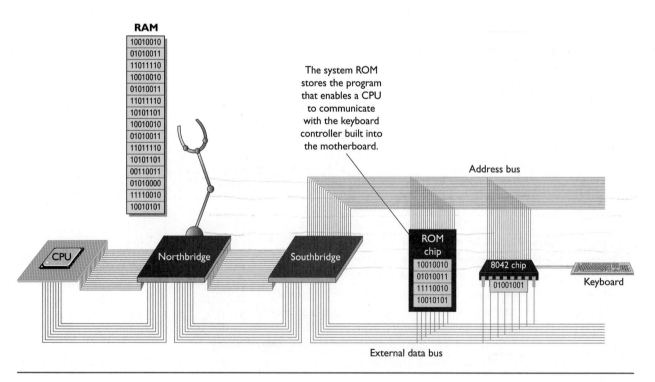

• **Figure 7.9**   Function of the flash ROM chip

To talk to all of that hardware requires hundreds of little services (2 to 30 lines of code each). These hundreds of little programs stored on the system ROM chip on the motherboard are called, collectively, the **system BIOS** (see Figure 7.10). Techs call programs stored on ROM chips of any sort **firmware**.

The system ROM chips used on modern PCs store as much as 2 MB of programs, although only 65,536 bytes are used to store the system BIOS. This allows for backward compatibility with earlier systems. The rest of the ROM space is put to good use doing other jobs.

Programs stored on ROM chips—flash or any other kind of ROM chip—are known collectively as *firmware*, as opposed to programs stored on erasable media that are collectively called *software*.

System BIOS Support

Every system BIOS has two types of hardware to support. First, the system BIOS supports all of the hardware that never changes, such as the keyboard. (You can change your keyboard, but you can't change the keyboard controller built into the Southbridge.) Another example of hardware that never changes is the PC speaker (the tiny one that beeps at you, not the ones that play music). The system ROM chip stores the BIOS for these and other devices that never change.

Second, the system BIOS supports all of the hardware that might change from time to time. This includes RAM (you can add RAM), hard drives (you can replace your hard drive with a larger drive or add a second hard drive), and floppy drives (you can add another floppy drive, although that's not common today). The system ROM chip stores the *BIOS* for these devices, but the system needs another place to store information about the specific *details* of a piece of hardware. This enables the system to differentiate between a Western Digital Caviar Black 1.5-TB hard drive and a Seagate Barracuda 60-GB drive, and yet still support both drives right out of the box.

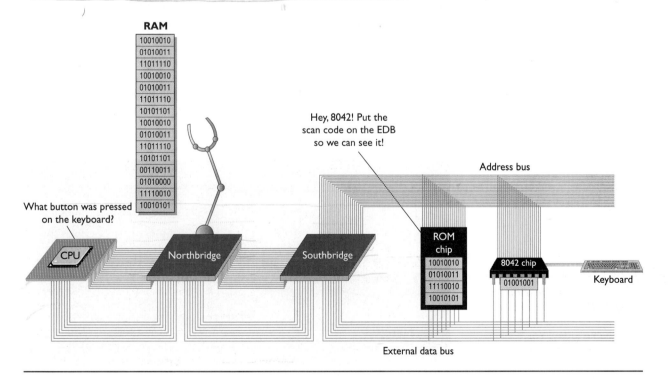

• **Figure 7.10** CPU running BIOS service

Try This!

Accessing CMOS Setup

The key or key combination required to access CMOS setup varies, depending on your particular BIOS. It's important to know how to access CMOS setup, and how to find the BIOS information once you're in, so try this:

1. Boot your system and turn on your monitor. Watch the information that scrolls by on the screen as your computer boots. Most BIOS makers include a line indicating what key(s) to press to access the CMOS setup program. Make a note of this useful information! You can also check your motherboard book to determine the process for accessing the CMOS setup program.

2. Reboot the system, and this time watch for information on the BIOS manufacturer. If you don't see it, and if it's okay to do so, open the system case and check the name printed on the system ROM chip. Make a note of this useful information.

3. Reboot one more time, and this time use the key or key combination you found to run the CMOS setup program. Locate and make a note of the manufacturer, date, and version number of your PC's current BIOS.

4. If you can, make a note of the exact model information for your system and visit the Web site of the company that manufactured your PC. Search their support files for the specs on your specific system and see if you can locate your BIOS information. Now take the detailed BIOS information and search the BIOS manufacturer's Web site for the same information.

A Quick Tour Through a Typical CMOS Setup Program

Accessing the CMOS setup utility for a system is perfectly fine, but do not make changes unless you fully understand that system!

Every BIOS maker's CMOS setup program looks a little different, but don't let that confuse you. They all contain basically the same settings; you just have to be comfortable poking around. To avoid doing something foolish, *do not save anything* unless you are sure you have it set correctly.

As an example, let's say your machine has Award BIOS. You boot the system and press DEL to enter CMOS setup. The screen in Figure 7.14 appears. You are now in the Main menu of the Award CMOS setup program. The setup program itself is stored on the ROM chip, but it edits only the data on the CMOS chip.

If you select the Standard CMOS Features option, the Standard CMOS Features screen appears (Figure 7.15). On this screen you can change floppy drive and hard drive settings, as well as the system's date and time. You will learn how to set up the CMOS for these devices in later chapters. At this point, your only goal is to understand CMOS and know how to access the CMOS setup on your PC, so don't try to change anything yet. If you have a system that you are allowed to reboot, try accessing the CMOS setup now.

Does it look anything like these examples? If not, can you find the screen that enables you to change the floppy and hard drives? Trust me, every CMOS setup has that screen somewhere! Figure 7.16 shows the same standard CMOS setup screen on a system with Phoenix BIOS. Note that this CMOS setup utility calls this screen "Main."

The first BIOS was nothing more than this standard CMOS setup. Today, all computers have many extra CMOS settings. They control items such as memory management, password and booting options, diagnostic and error handling, and power management. The following section takes a quick tour of an Award CMOS setup program. Remember that your CMOS setup almost certainly looks at least a little different from mine, unless you happen to have the *same* BIOS. The chances of that happening are quite slim.

Phoenix has virtually cornered the desktop PC BIOS market with its Award Modular BIOS. Motherboard makers buy a boilerplate BIOS, designed for a particular chipset, and add or remove options (Phoenix calls them *modules*) based on the needs of each motherboard. This means that

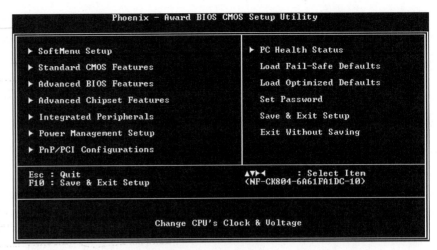

● **Figure 7.14**   Typical CMOS Main screen by Award

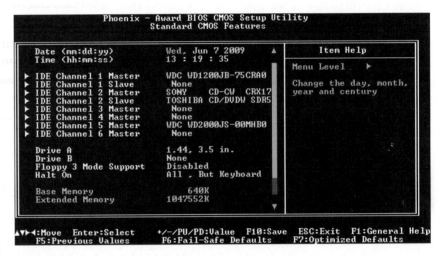

● **Figure 7.15**   Standard CMOS Features screen

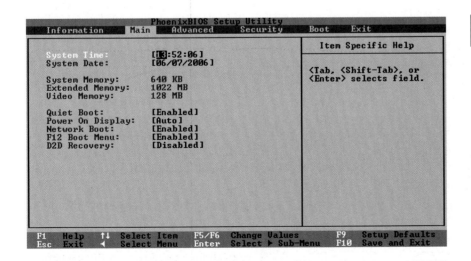

● **Figure 7.16**   Phoenix BIOS CMOS setup utility Main screen

All of these screens tend to overwhelm new techs. When they first encounter the many options, some techs feel they need to understand every option on every screen to configure CMOS properly. Relax—every new motherboard comes with settings that befuddle even the most experienced techs. If I don't talk about a particular CMOS setting somewhere in this book, it's probably not important, either to the CompTIA A+ certification exams or to a real tech.

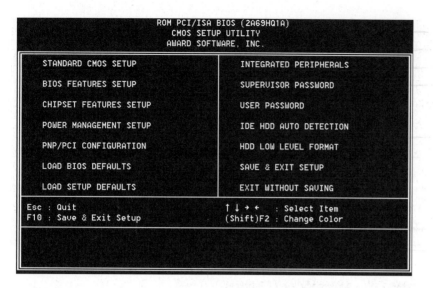

```
                ROM PCI/ISA BIOS (2A69HQ1A)
                   CMOS SETUP UTILITY
                  AWARD SOFTWARE, INC.

  STANDARD CMOS SETUP              INTEGRATED PERIPHERALS

  BIOS FEATURES SETUP             SUPERVISOR PASSWORD

  CHIPSET FEATURES SETUP          USER PASSWORD

  POWER MANAGEMENT SETUP          IDE HDD AUTO DETECTION

  PNP/PCI CONFIGURATION           HDD LOW LEVEL FORMAT

  LOAD BIOS DEFAULTS              SAVE & EXIT SETUP

  LOAD SETUP DEFAULTS            EXIT WITHOUT SAVING

Esc : Quit                    ↑ ↓ → ←   : Select Item
F10 : Save & Exit Setup       (Shift)F2 : Change Color
```

• **Figure 7.17** Older Award setup screen

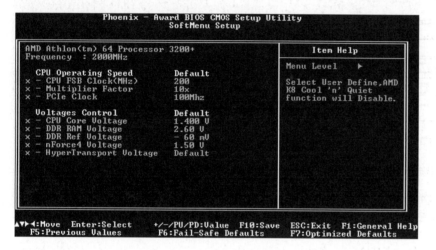

```
            Phoenix - Award BIOS CMOS Setup Utility
                       SoftMenu Setup

 AMD Athlon(tm) 64 Processor 3200+           Item Help
 Frequency  : 2000MHz
                                      Menu Level    ▶
   CPU Operating Speed        Default
 x - CPU FSB Clock(MHz)       200      Select User Define,AMD
 x - Multiplier Factor        10x      K8 Cool 'n' Quiet
 x - PCIe Clock               100Mhz   function will Disable.

   Voltages Control           Default
 x - CPU Core Voltage         1.400 V
 x - DDR RAM Voltage          2.60 V
 x - DDR Ref Voltage          - 60 mV
 x - nForce4 Voltage          1.50 V
 x - HyperTransport Voltage   Default

▲▼►◄:Move  Enter:Select   +/-/PU/PD:Value  F10:Save  ESC:Exit  F1:General Help
  F5:Previous Values           F6:Fail-Safe Defaults   F7:Optimized Defaults
```

• **Figure 7.18** SoftMenu

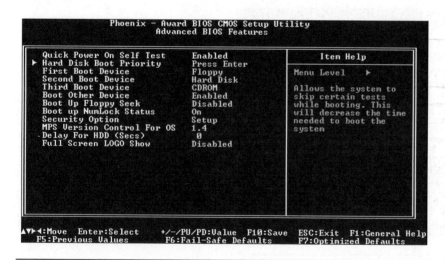

```
            Phoenix - Award BIOS CMOS Setup Utility
                    Advanced BIOS Features

  Quick Power On Self Test    Enabled          Item Help
▶ Hard Disk Boot Priority     Press Enter
  First Boot Device           Floppy      Menu Level    ▶
  Second Boot Device          Hard Disk
  Third Boot Device           CDROM       Allows the system to
  Boot Other Device           Enabled     skip certain tests
  Boot Up Floppy Seek         Disabled    while booting. This
  Boot up NumLock Status      On          will decrease the time
  Security Option             Setup       needed to boot the
  MPS Version Control For OS   1.4        system
  Delay For HDD (Secs)        0
  Full Screen LOGO Show       Disabled

▲▼►◄:Move  Enter:Select   +/-/PU/PD:Value  F10:Save  ESC:Exit  F1:General Help
  F5:Previous Values           F6:Fail-Safe Defaults   F7:Optimized Defaults
```

• **Figure 7.19** Advanced BIOS Features

seemingly identical CMOS setup utilities can be extremely different. Options that show up on one computer might be missing from another. Compare the older Award screen in Figure 7.17 with the more modern Award CMOS screen in Figure 7.14. Figure 7.17 looks different—and it should—as this much older system simply doesn't need the extra options available on the newer system.

The next section starts the walkthrough of a CMOS setup utility with the SoftMenu, followed by some of the Advanced screens. Then you'll go through other common screens, such as Integrated Peripherals, Power, and more.

SoftMenu

You can use the SoftMenu to change the voltage and multiplier settings on the motherboard for the CPU from the defaults. Motherboards that cater to overclockers tend to have this option. Usually you just set this to Auto or Default and stay away from this screen (Figure 7.18).

Advanced BIOS Features

Advanced BIOS Features is the dumping ground for all of the settings that aren't covered in the Standard menu and don't fit nicely under any other screen. This screen varies wildly from one system to the next. You most often use this screen to select the boot options (Figure 7.19).

Chassis Intrusion Detection Many motherboards support the **chassis intrusion detection** feature provided by the computer case, or chassis. Compatible cases contain a switch that trips when someone opens the case. With motherboard support and a proper connection between the motherboard and the case, the CMOS logs whether the case has been opened and, if it has, posts an

appropriate alert to the screen on the subsequent boot. How cool is that?

Advanced Chipset Features

The Advanced Chipset Features screen strikes fear into most everyone, because it deals with extremely low-level chipset functions. Avoid this screen unless a high-level tech (such as a motherboard maker's support tech) explicitly tells you to do something in here (Figure 7.20).

Integrated Peripherals

You will use the Integrated Peripherals screen quite often. Here you configure, enable, or disable the onboard devices, such as the integrated sound card (Figure 7.21).

Power Management Setup

As the name implies, you can use the Power Management Setup screen to set up the power management settings for the system. These settings work in concert (sometimes in conflict) with Windows' power management settings to control how and when devices turn off and back on to conserve power (Figure 7.22).

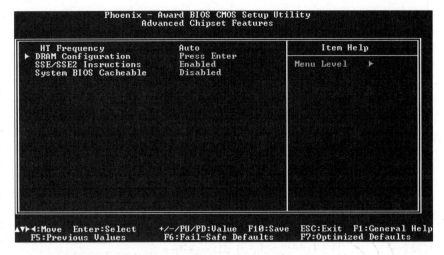

• **Figure 7.20** Advanced Chipset Features

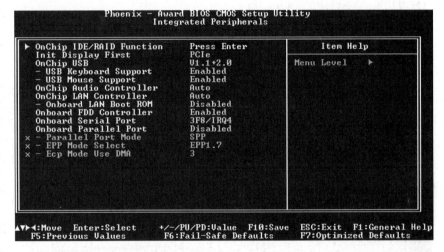

• **Figure 7.21** Integrated Peripherals

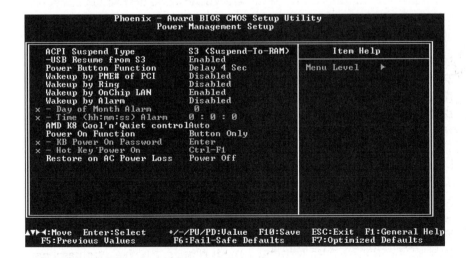

• **Figure 7.22** Power Management Setup

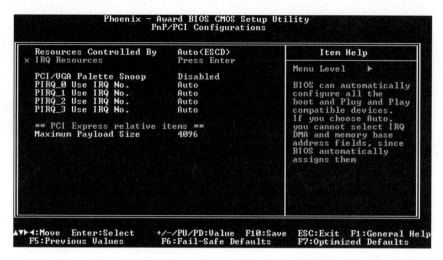

Resources Controlled By	Auto(ESCD)	Item Help
x IRQ Resources	Press Enter	
		Menu Level ▶
PCI/VGA Palette Snoop	Disabled	
PIRQ_0 Use IRQ No.	Auto	BIOS can automatically
PIRQ_1 Use IRQ No.	Auto	configure all the
PIRQ_2 Use IRQ No.	Auto	boot and Plug and Play
PIRQ_3 Use IRQ No.	Auto	compatible devices.
		If you choose Auto,
** PCI Express relative items **		you cannot select IRQ
Maximum Payload Size	4096	DMA and memory base
		address fields, since
		BIOS automatically
		assigns them

```
▲▼▶◀:Move  Enter:Select    +/-/PU/PD:Value  F10:Save  ESC:Exit  F1:General Help
 F5:Previous Values        F6:Fail-Safe Defaults    F7:Optimized Defaults
```

• **Figure 7.23** PnP/PCI Configurations

• **Figure 7.24** CMOS password prompt

PnP/PCI Configurations

All CMOS setup utilities come with menu items that are for the most part no longer needed, but no one wants to remove them. PnP/PCI Configurations is a perfect example. Plug and play (PnP) is how devices automatically work when you snap them into your PC. PCI is a type of slot used for cards. Odds are very good you'll never deal with this screen (Figure 7.23).

And the Rest of the CMOS Settings...

The other options on the main menu of an Award CMOS do not have their own screens. Rather, these simply have small dialog boxes that pop up, usually with "Are you sure?" messages. The Load Fail-Safe/Optimized default options keep you from having to memorize all of those weird settings you'll never touch. Fail-Safe sets everything to very simple settings—you might occasionally use this setting when very low-level problems such as freeze-ups occur and you've checked more obvious areas first. Optimized sets the CMOS to the best possible speed/stability for the system. You would use this option after you've tampered with the CMOS too much and you need to put it back like it was!

Many CMOS setup programs enable you to set a password in CMOS to force the user to enter a password every time the system boots. Don't confuse this with the Windows logon password. This CMOS password shows up at boot, long before Windows even starts to load. Figure 7.24 shows a typical CMOS password prompt.

Some CMOS setup utilities enable you to create two passwords: one for boot and another for accessing the CMOS setup program. This extra password just for entering CMOS setup is a godsend in, for example, schools, where non-techs tend to wreak havoc in areas (such as CMOS) that they should not access!

DriveLock Passwords   On some motherboards, the CMOS setup program enables you to control the ATA Security Mode Feature Set, also commonly referred to as drive lock or **DriveLock**. ATA Security Mode is the first line of defense for protecting hard disks from unwanted access when a system is lost or stolen. It has two passwords, a user password and a master password; and two modes, high security mode and max security mode. In high security mode, the drive can be accessed by both the master and user passwords. In addition, the master can reset the user password in CMOS setup.

In max security mode, the drive is accessible only with the user password. In this mode, the master can reset the user password, but all of the data on the drive is destroyed. Note that in either mode, if the master and user passwords are both lost, the drive is rendered unusable; these passwords are stored in the hard disk's control circuitry and cannot be reset by clearing CMOS.

Trusted Platform Module The *Trusted Platform Module* (TPM) acts as a secure cryptoprocessor, which is to say that it is a hardware platform for the acceleration of cryptographic functions and the secure storage of associated information. The specification for the TPM is published by the Trusted Computing Group, an organization whose corporate members include Intel, Microsoft, AMD, IBM, Lenovo, Dell, Hewlett-Packard, and many others.

The TPM can be a small circuit board plugged into the motherboard, or it can be built directly into the chipset. The CMOS setup program usually contains settings that can turn the TPM on or off and enable or disable it.

TPMs can be used in a wide array of cryptographic operations, but one of the most common uses of TPMs is hard disk encryption. For example, the BitLocker Drive Encryption feature of Microsoft's Windows Vista can be accelerated by a TPM, which is more secure because the encryption key is stored in the tamper-resistant TPM hardware rather than on an external flash drive. Other possible uses of TPMs include digital rights management (DRM), network access control, application execution control, and password protection.

Exiting and Saving Settings

Of course, all CMOS setups provide some method to Save and Exit or to Exit *Without* Saving. Use these as needed for your situation. Exit Without Saving is particularly nice for those folks who want to poke around the CMOS setup utility but don't want to mess anything up. Use it!

The CMOS setup utility would meet all of the needs of a modern system for BIOS if manufacturers would just stop creating new devices. That's not going to happen, of course, so let's turn now to devices that need to have BIOS loaded from elsewhere.

■ Option ROM and Device Drivers

Every piece of hardware in your computer needs some kind of programming that tells the CPU how to talk to that device. When IBM invented the PC more than a quarter century ago, they couldn't possibly have included all of the necessary BIOS routines for every conceivable piece of hardware on the system ROM chip. How could they? Most of the devices in use today didn't exist on the first PCs. When programmers wrote the first BIOS, for example, network cards, mice, and sound cards did not exist. Early PC designers at IBM understood that they could not anticipate every new type of hardware, so they gave us a few ways to add programming other than on the BIOS. I call this *BYOB*—Bring Your Own BIOS. You can BYOB in two ways: option ROM and device drivers. Let's look at both.

Option ROM

The first way to BYOB is to put the BIOS on the hardware device itself. Look at the card displayed in Figure 7.25. This is a serial ATA RAID hard drive controller—basically just a card that lets you add more hard drives to a PC. The chip in the center with the wires coming out the sides is a flash ROM storing BIOS for the card. The system BIOS does not have a clue about how

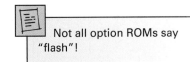

Not all option ROMs say "flash"!

• **Figure 7.25** Option ROM

• **Figure 7.26** Option ROM at boot

to talk to this card, but that's okay, because this card brings its own BIOS on what's called an **option ROM** chip.

Most BIOS that come on option ROMs tell you that they exist by displaying information when you boot the system. Figure 7.26 shows a typical example of an option ROM advertising itself.

In the early days of the PC, you could find all sorts of devices with BIOS on option ROMs. Today, option ROMs have mostly been replaced by more flexible software methods (more on device driver software in the next section), with one major exception: video cards. Every video card made today contains its own BIOS. Option ROMs work well but are hard to upgrade. For this reason, most hardware in PCs relies on software for BYOB.

Device Drivers

A **device driver** is a file stored on the PC's hard drive that contains all of the commands necessary to talk to whatever device it was written to support. All operating systems employ a method of loading these device drivers into RAM every time the system boots. They know which device drivers to install by reading a file (or files) that lists which device drivers the system needs to load at boot time. All operating systems are designed to look at this list early on in the boot process and copy the listed files into RAM, thereby giving the CPU the capability to communicate with the hardware supported by the device driver.

Device drivers come with the device when you buy it. When you buy a sound card, for example, it comes with a CD-ROM that holds all of the necessary device drivers (and usually a bunch of extra goodies). The generic name for this type of CD-ROM is **installation disc**. In most cases, you install a new device, start the computer, and wait for Windows to prompt you for the installation disc (Figure 7.27).

• **Figure 7.27** Windows asking for the installation disc

Mike Meyers' CompTIA A+ Guide to Managing and Troubleshooting PCs

You might want to add or remove device drivers manually at times. Windows uses a special database called the **Registry** that stores everything you want to know about your system, including the device drivers. You shouldn't access the Registry directly to access these drivers, but instead use the venerable Device Manager utility (Figure 7.28).

By using the **Device Manager**, you can manually change or remove the drivers for any particular device. You access the Device Manager by first opening the System applet in the Control Panel; then select the Hardware tab and click the Device Manager button. Make sure you know how to access the Device Manager. You'll see lots more of the Device Manager as you learn about different types of devices in the rest of the book.

BIOS, BIOS, Everywhere!

As you should now understand, every piece of hardware on a system must have an accompanying program that provides the CPU with the code necessary to communicate with that particular device. This code may reside on the system ROM on the motherboard, on ROM on a card, or in a device driver file on the hard drive loaded into RAM at boot. BIOS is everywhere on your system, and you need to deal with it occasionally.

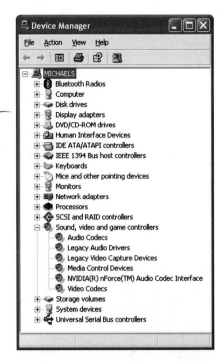

• Figure 7.28   Typical Device Manager

You can also access the Device Manager by right-clicking My Computer or Computer and selecting Manage. When the Computer Management dialog box comes up, click on Device Manager.

Practical Application

■ Power-On Self Test (POST)

BIOS isn't the only program on your system ROM. When the computer is turned on or reset, it initiates a special program, also stored on the system ROM chip, called the **power-on self test (POST)**. The POST program checks out the system every time the computer boots. To perform this check, the POST sends out a command that says to all of the devices, "Check yourselves out!" All of the standard devices in the computer then run their own internal diagnostic—the POST doesn't specify what they must check. The quality of the diagnostic is up to the people who made that particular device.

Let's consider the POST for a moment. Suppose some device—let's say it's the keyboard controller chip—runs its diagnostic and determines that it is not working properly. What can the POST do about it? Only one thing really: Tell the human in front of the PC! So how does the computer tell the human? PCs convey POST information to you in two ways: beep codes and text messages.

Before and During the Video Test: The Beep Codes

The computer tests the most basic parts of the computer first, up to and including the video card. In early PCs, you'd hear a series of beeps—called **beep codes**—if anything went wrong. By using beep codes before and during

You'll find lots of online documentation about beep codes, but it's usually badly outdated.

```
PhoenixBIOS 4.0 release 6.0
Copyright 1985-2000 Phoenix Technologies Ltd.
All Rights Reserved

CPU = Pentium III  500MHz
640K System RAM Passed
47M Extended RAM Passed
USB upper limit segment address:  EEFE
Mouse initialized

HDD Controller Failure
Press <F1> to resume
```

• **Figure 7.29**   POST text error messages

the video test, the computer could communicate with you. (If a POST error occurs before the video is available, obviously the error must manifest itself as beeps, because nothing can display on the screen.) The meaning of the beep code you'd hear varied among different BIOS manufacturers. You could find the beep codes for a specific motherboard in its motherboard manual.

Most modern PCs have only a single beep code, which is for bad or missing video—one long beep followed by two or three short beeps.

You'll hear three other beep sequences on most PCs (although they're not officially beep codes). At the end of a successful POST, the PC produces one or two short beeps, simply to inform you that all is well. Most systems make a rather strange noise when the RAM is missing or very seriously damaged. Unlike traditional beep codes, this code repeats until you shut off the system. Finally, your speaker might make beeps for reasons that aren't POST or boot related. One of the more common is a series of short beeps after the system's been running for a while. That's a CPU alarm telling you the CPU is approaching its high heat limit.

Text Errors

After the video has tested okay, any POST errors display on the screen as text errors. If you get a text error, the problem is usually, but not always, self-explanatory (Figure 7.29). Text errors are far more useful than beep codes, because you can simply read the screen to determine the bad device.

POST Cards

Beep codes, numeric codes, and text error codes, although helpful, can sometimes be misleading. Worse than that, an inoperative device can sometimes disrupt the POST, forcing the machine into an endless loop. This causes the PC to act dead—no beeps and nothing on the screen. In this case, you need a device, called a **POST card**, to monitor the POST and identify which piece of hardware is causing the trouble.

POST cards are simple cards that snap into expansion slots on your system. A small, two-character light-emitting diode (LED) readout on the card indicates what device the POST is currently testing (Figure 7.30). The documentation that comes with the POST card tells you what the codes mean. BIOS makers also provide this information on their Web sites. Manufacturers make POST cards for all types of desktop PCs. POST cards work with any BIOS, but you need to know the type of BIOS you have so you can interpret the readout properly.

I usually only pull out a POST card when the usual POST errors fail to appear. When a computer provides a beep or text error code that doesn't make sense, or your machine keeps locking up, some device has stalled the POST. Because the POST card tells you which device is being tested, the frozen system stays at that point in the POST, and the error stays on the POST card's readout.

Many companies sell POST cards today, with prices ranging from the affordable to the outrageous. Spend the absolute least amount of money you

• Figure 7.30   POST card in action

can. The more expensive cards add bells and whistles you do not need, such as diagnostic software and voltmeters.

Using a POST card is straightforward. Simply power down the PC, install the POST card in any unused slot, and turn the PC back on. As you watch the POST display, notice the hexadecimal readouts and refer to them as the POST progresses. Notice how quickly they change. If you get an "FF" or "00," that means the POST is over and everything passed—time to check the operating system. If a device stalls the POST, however, the POST card displays an error code. That's the problem device! Good technicians often memorize a dozen or more POST codes because it's much faster than looking them up in a book.

So you got a beep code, a text error code, or a POST error. Now what do you do with that knowledge? Remember that a POST error does not fix the computer; it only tells you where to look. You then have to know how to deal with that bad or improperly configured component. If you use a POST card, for example, and it hangs at the "Initializing Floppy Drive" test, you'd better know how to work on a floppy drive.

Sometimes the POST card returns a bizarre or confusing error code. What device do you point at when you get a "CMOS shutdown register read/write error" beep code from an older system? First of all, read the error carefully. Let's say that on that same system you got an "8042—gate A20 failure" beep code. What will you do? Assuming you know (and you should!) that the "8042" refers to the keyboard, a quick peek at the keyboard and its connection would be a good first step. Beyond that specific example, here is a good general rule: If you don't know what the error means or the bad part isn't replaceable, replace the motherboard. Clearly, you will stumble across exceptions to this rule, but more often than not, the rule stands.

The Boot Process

All PCs need a process to begin their operations. Once you feed power to the PC, the tight interrelation of hardware, firmware, and software enables the PC to start itself, to "pull itself up by the bootstraps" or boot itself.

When you first power on the PC, the power supply circuitry tests for proper voltage and then sends a signal down a special wire called the **power good** wire to awaken the CPU. The moment the power good wire wakes it up, every Intel and clone CPU immediately sends a built-in memory address via its address bus. This special address is the same on every Intel and clone CPU, from the oldest 8086 to the most recent microprocessor. This address is the first line of the POST program on the system ROM! That's how the system starts the POST. After the POST has finished, there must be a way for the computer to find the programs on the hard drive to start the operating system. The POST passes control to the last BIOS function: the bootstrap loader. The **bootstrap loader** is little more than a few dozen lines of BIOS code tacked to the end of the POST program. Its job is to find the operating system. The bootstrap loader reads CMOS information to tell it where to look first for an operating system. Your PC's CMOS setup utility has an option that you configure to tell the bootstrap loader which devices to check for an operating system and in which order (Figure 7.31).

Almost all storage devices—floppy disks, hard disks, CDs, DVDs, and even USB thumb drives—can be configured to boot an operating system by setting aside a specific location called the *boot sector*. (Later chapters show you how to do this.) If the device is bootable, its boot sector contains special programming designed to tell the system where to locate the operating system. Any device with a functional operating system is called a **bootable disk** or a **system disk**. If the bootstrap loader locates a good boot sector, it passes control to the operating system and removes itself from memory. If it doesn't, it goes to the next device in the boot order you set in the CMOS setup utility. Boot order is an important tool for techs because you can set it to load in special bootable devices so you can run utilities to maintain PCs without using the primary operating system.

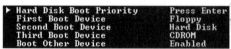

• **Figure 7.31**   CMOS boot order

■ Care and Feeding of BIOS and CMOS

BIOS and CMOS are areas in your PC that you don't go to very often. BIOS itself is invisible. The only real clue you have that it even exists is the POST. The CMOS setup utility, on the other hand, is very visible if you start it. Most CMOS setup utilities today work acceptably well without ever being touched. You're an aspiring tech, however, and all self-respecting techs start up the CMOS setup utility and make changes. That's when most CMOS setup utility problems take place.

If you mess with the CMOS setup utility, remember to make only as many changes at one time as you can remember. Document the original settings and the changes on a piece of paper so you can put things back if necessary. Don't make changes unless you know what they mean! It's easy to

screw up a computer fairly seriously by playing with CMOS settings you don't understand.

Losing CMOS Settings

Your CMOS needs a continuous trickle charge to retain its data. Motherboards use some type of battery, usually a coin battery like those in wrist watches, to give the CMOS the charge it needs when the computer is turned off (Figure 7.32). This battery also keeps track of the date and time when the PC is turned off.

If the battery runs out of charge, you lose all of your CMOS information. If some mishap suddenly erases the information on the CMOS chip, the computer might not boot up or you'll get nasty-looking errors at boot. Any PC made after 2002 will boot to factory defaults if the CMOS clears, so the chances of not booting are slim—but you'll still get errors at boot. Here are a few examples of errors that point to lost CMOS information:

- CMOS configuration mismatch
- CMOS date/time not set
- No boot device available
- CMOS battery state low

Here are some of the more common reasons for losing CMOS data:

- Pulling and inserting cards
- Touching the motherboard
- Dropping something on the motherboard
- Dirt on the motherboard

• **Figure 7.32**   A CMOS battery

Cross Check

Clearing CMOS

All techs invariably do things in CMOS they want to undo, but sometimes simply making a change in CMOS prevents you from getting back to the CMOS setup utility to undo the change. A great example is when someone sets a CMOS password and then forgets the password. If you ever run into a system with an unknown CMOS password, you'll need to erase the CMOS and then reset everything.

You'll recall from Chapter 5, "Microprocessors," that all motherboards have a clear CMOS jumper, so check your memory. How do you find out where the CMOS clear jumper is located? What steps do you take to clear the CMOS? What scenario would definitely require you to clear the CMOS jumper?

- Faulty power supplies
- Electrical surges
- Chip creep

Most of these items should be fairly self-explanatory, but chip creep might be a new term for some of you. As PCs run, the components inside get warm. When a PC is turned off, the components cool off. This cycling of hot and cold causes the chips to expand and contract in their mounts. Although the chip designers account for this, in some extreme cases this thermal expansion and contraction causes a chip to work out of its mount and causes a failure called *chip creep*. Chip creep was a common problem in the earlier days of PCs, but after more than a quarter century of experience, the PC industry has done a pretty good job of designing mounts that hold all of your chips in place dependably.

If you encounter any of these errors, or if the clock in Windows resets itself to January 1st every time you reboot the system, the battery on the motherboard is losing its charge and needs to be replaced. To replace the battery, use a screwdriver to pry the battery's catch gently back. The battery should pop up for easy removal. Before you install the new battery, double-check that it has the same voltage and amperage as the old battery. To retain your CMOS settings while replacing the battery, simply leave your PC plugged into an AC outlet. The 5-volt soft power on all modern motherboards provides enough electricity to keep the CMOS charged and the data secure. Of course, I know you're going to be *extremely* careful about ESD while prying up the battery from a live system!

Flashing ROM

Flash ROM chips can be reprogrammed to update their contents. With flash ROM, when you need to update your system BIOS to add support for a new technology, you can simply run a small command-line program, combined with an update file, and voilà, you have a new, updated BIOS! Different BIOS makers use slightly different processes for *flashing the BIOS*, but in general you must boot from a floppy diskette and then run the relevant

• **Figure 7.33**   ROM updating program for an ASUS motherboard

updating command from the A:\> prompt. This example shows how simple it can be:

```
A:\> aw athxpt2.bin
```

Some motherboard makers provide Windows-based flash ROM update utilities that check the Internet for updates and download them for you to install (Figure 7.33). Most of these utilities also enable you to back up your current BIOS so you can return to it if the updated version causes trouble. Without a good backup, you could end up throwing away your motherboard if a flash BIOS update goes wrong, so you should always make one. Other motherboards have drivers to read flash ROM-based USB drives and have a flashing utility built in to ROM. You can download an update, put it on a thumb drive, and boot to the CMOS setup utility to update the firmware. Nice!

Finally, don't update your BIOS unless you have some compelling reason to do so. As the old saying goes, "If it ain't broke, don't fix it!"

Beyond A+

UEFI

In modern systems, the classic roles of BIOS—start the PC, test the hardware, load drivers for essential hardware, and boot the operating system—have diminished considerably. Yes, the BIOS still starts the PC and runs the POST, but drivers? As soon as the operating system loads, most if not all of the BIOS drivers are replaced with drivers loaded by the operating system. Plus, the whole boot sequence of a PC has sort of grown organically over the

decades of the personal computer. Even with its full unlocked potential, the BIOS is still limited to a 16-bit environment with support for a mere 1 megabyte of RAM. That was fine in the early DOS days, but not so much today. At some point, it's time to throw the whole thing out and rewrite the startup sequence for the PC from scratch.

Realizing the limits traditional 16-bit BIOS imposes on modern systems, Intel, along with Hewlett-Packard, created a new firmware interface they titled **Extensible Firmware Interface (EFI)**. EFI, which is a BIOS replacement, was first seen in 2000 with the launch of the original Itanium systems. It ended the need for the firmware to execute in 16-bit mode, which eliminated the 1 MB pre-boot RAM address barrier. EFI also included a slew of new enhancements. Some of the more notable new features are the addition of a new hard disk addressing scheme called GUID Partition Table (GPT) that facilitates partitions of greater than 2 TB in size, the introduction of a pre-boot shell environment for executing EFI utility programs, the addition of an enhanced device driver model where firmware drivers can be loaded from the system partition, and the inclusion of its own boot manager that can load a variety of operating systems.

In 2005 a consortium of companies, including Microsoft, Intel, American Megatrends Incorporated (AMI), Phoenix Technologies, AMD, Hewlett-Packard, and Apple, came together to form the **Unified Extensible Firmware Interface (UEFI)** Forum. The UEFI Forum created the UEFI standard, which is based off of, and supersedes, Intel's original EFI specification. UEFI firmware is now being produced by such companies as AMI, Phoenix Technologies, and Insyde Software and is supported by the latest operating systems from both Microsoft and Apple. Most UEFI systems also have the capability to boot operating systems that require traditional BIOS by loading what is known as a Compatibility Support Module (CSM) before loading the legacy OS.

Chapter 7 Review

■ Chapter Summary

After reading this chapter and completing the exercises, you should understand the following about BIOS and CMOS.

Explain the function of BIOS

- The CPU must be able to communicate with all devices in a computer system. The Northbridge chip is the primary communication bridge between the CPU and the rest of the computer. The Northbridge deals with high-speed devices such as the video card, RAM, and PCI bus. A second chip, the Southbridge, works with the other devices. The Northbridge and Southbridge chips are manufactured as a set called the chipset. The chipset extends the data and address buses to every device in the PC.

- A ROM (read-only memory) chip is nonvolatile, meaning it retains the information stored on it even when the power is turned off. Usually attached to the Southbridge, the ROM chip stores hundreds of little programs that enable the CPU to communicate with basic devices such as the floppy drive, CD and DVD drives, hard drives, video card, and others. These programs, called services, are collectively referred to as the basic input/output services (BIOS). These programs are stored on a read-only medium and can't be changed by the user, so they are known as firmware, in contrast to software, which is programs stored on erasable media. The term "system ROM" refers to the ROM chip on the motherboard.

- Although the system ROM chip has room for as much as 2 MB of programs, only 65,536 bytes store the BIOS. Correspondingly, the last 65,536 addresses on the address bus are reserved for the BIOS on the ROM chip. When the CPU indicates one of these reserved addresses, the Northbridge sends the address directly to the ROM BIOS.

- The ROM BIOS includes programs that enable the CPU to talk to many basic hardware devices such as the keyboard, but other devices not supported by the ROM BIOS may have their own ROM chips.

- Each piece of hardware in the computer needs programs for everything that piece of hardware performs. The CPU must access these programs to get the hardware to do its job. IBM also devised other methods to get BIOS to the hardware of the computer. If the hardware is common, necessary, and does not change, such as the keyboard, the system ROM chip stores the BIOS. If the hardware is common and necessary but may change from time to time, such as when you install a larger hard drive or add more RAM, the BIOS for the general type of device (e.g., a hard drive) can be on the system ROM chip. The information describing specific features unique to that particular device (e.g., a Seagate Barracuda 60-GB drive), however, must be stored on a changeable storage medium such as a complementary metal-oxide semiconductor (CMOS) chip.

Distinguish among various CMOS setup utility options

- Your motherboard includes a changeable chip, capable of storing about 64 KB of data, called the complementary metal-oxide semiconductor (CMOS) chip. CMOS does not store programs. It stores the data that is read by BIOS, and that data is used by the programs residing in BIOS. Although CMOS used to be a separate chip on the motherboard, it is almost always built into the Southbridge on modern motherboards. The CMOS chip also keeps track of the date and time. To maintain its date, CMOS requires a constant trickle of electricity supplied by a small battery on the motherboard. If the data you have stored in CMOS continues to disappear or if the date/time resets itself, it may be time to change the motherboard battery.

- Within the system ROM is a CMOS setup program that lets you access and update the data on the CMOS chip. The terms CMOS setup program, CMOS, and system setup utility are functionally interchangeable today. Most techs just call it the CMOS. Two major manufacturers control 99 percent

of the BIOS business: American Megatrends (AMI) and Phoenix Technology (which includes Award Software). The CMOS setup program can be started in many different ways, depending on the brand of BIOS you have on your computer. Pressing DEL when the computer boots is the most common way to access the CMOS setup program. The screen itself usually tells you how to access setup. If it doesn't, you can check the motherboard book or the Web site of your PC or BIOS manufacturer.

- All CMOS setup programs have basically the same main options. On the Standard CMOS Features screen, you can change floppy drive, hard drive, and date/time settings. Today's setup programs have extra CMOS settings that control such items as memory management, password and booting options, diagnostic and error handling, and power management. The Award Modular BIOS enables motherboard manufacturers to add or remove options from the setup program.

- Among the other things you can configure in CMOS setup are the voltage and multiplier settings for the CPU (the CPU SoftMenu), boot options (check the Advanced BIOS Features menu), power management, password protection, and ports (the Integrated Peripherals menu). All setup programs include options to *Save and Exit* or *Exit Without Saving*. You should not change CMOS settings unless you know exactly what you're doing.

- On older systems, if the information on the CMOS chip was lost or erased, the computer would not boot. The most common cause was a dead onboard battery, but other factors such as electrical surges, chip creep, or a dirty motherboard could also erase CMOS data. Lost CMOS information produces errors such as *No boot device available* or *CMOS date/time not set*. Making a backup copy of the CMOS data enabled you to restore the information and recover from this catastrophe.

- Unlike earlier ROM chips that you had to replace when you wanted to upgrade the BIOS programs, today's computers use flash ROM chips that you can reprogram without removing. If you install a CPU or other new hardware that the flash ROM chip does not support, you can run a small command-line program combined with an update file to change your BIOS. The exact process varies

from one motherboard maker to another. If the flash ROM utility allows you to make a backup of your BIOS, you should always do so. Don't update your BIOS unless you have a good reason. As the old saying goes, "If it ain't broke, don't fix it!"

- Many CMOS setup programs enable you to set a boot password, a password to enter the CMOS setup program itself, or both. These passwords are stored in CMOS. If you forget your password, you simply need to clear the CMOS data. Unplug the AC power from the PC and remove the motherboard battery. This removes the trickle charge that enables CMOS to store information and clears all CMOS data, including the passwords. Reinstall the battery, plug in the power cord, boot up the computer, and re-enter your CMOS settings. Alternatively, many motherboards provide a clear CMOS jumper you can use to clear the CMOS data without removing the battery. Small padlocks on the system chassis can prevent unauthorized users from accessing the motherboard and clearing CMOS data.

Describe option ROM and device drivers

- Newer hardware devices that are not supported by the system BIOS have other ways to BYOB—bring your own BIOS. A hardware device, such as a SCSI host adapter, may contain its own BIOS chip or ROM chip known as option ROM. Every video card contains its own BIOS for internal functions. A more flexible way to BYOB is to use files called device drivers that contain instructions to support the hardware device. Device drivers load when the system boots.

- Many devices come with device driver files on installation discs. These drivers must be loaded for the PC to recognize and use the devices. In a database called the Registry, Windows keeps a list of what drivers should be loaded. Editing the Registry directly is dangerous (a mistake can prevent Windows from booting up), but you can safely install or remove drivers by using the Device Manager.

Troubleshoot the power-on self test (POST)

- In addition to the BIOS routines and the CMOS setup program, the system ROM also includes a special program called the power-on self test

(POST) that is executed every time the computer boots. POST first has basic devices, up to and including video, run self-diagnostics. If a device detects an error, the computer alerts you with a series of beeps. Different ROM manufacturers have used different beep codes, but your motherboard book should explain them (particularly in older systems). After the basic devices, POST tells the rest of the devices to run tests and displays a text error message on the screen if anything is wrong. Some manufacturers use numeric error codes or combine numeric and text messages.

- The computer may beep in two situations that are not related to POST beep codes. If the computer beeps constantly until you shut it off, it means RAM is missing or damaged. If the computer beeps after it is booted, it is probably warning you that the system is overheating.

- If the computer appears dead, with no beeps or screen response, you can place a POST card in an expansion slot to diagnose the problem by using the LED readout on the card. The documentation that comes with the POST card explains the LED codes for your particular BIOS.

- A beep code, text error message, or POST error may identify a problem, but it does not fix it. After you know which device is causing the problem, you should check the connection for the troublesome device and replace it if possible. If you cannot remove the bad part or if you cannot interpret the error message, you may need to replace the motherboard.

- When you first power on the PC, the power supply circuitry tests for proper voltage and then sends a signal down a special wire called the power good wire to awaken the CPU. The moment the power good wire wakes it up, the CPU sends a built-in memory address via its address bus. This address is the first line of the POST program on the system

ROM, which is how the system starts the POST. After the POST has finished, it passes control to the bootstrap loader function on the system BIOS. This program looks for an operating system, checking the floppy drive, hard drives, or other bootable devices to find the boot sector that identifies the location of the OS. When the BIOS finds a bootable or system disk or device that has a functional operating system, it passes control to that disk or device.

Maintain BIOS and CMOS properly

- When you make changes to the CMOS settings, make only as many changes at one time as you can remember. Document the original settings and the changes on a piece of paper so you can reverse any changes that had the wrong effect.

- If you have CMOS settings that keep reverting to defaults or if the clock in Windows resets itself to January 1st every time you reboot the system, the battery on the motherboard is losing its charge and needs to be replaced.

- You can update the firmware in ROM by flashing the BIOS. This process is often done by booting to a bootable floppy diskette after downloading a flashing program and the update BIOS from the manufacturer. Some motherboards enable you to update the BIOS through Windows programs; others come with drivers for USB devices and have a flashing utility built in.

- To overcome the limitations in the traditional BIOS, Intel and other companies created first the Extensible Firmware Interface (EFI) and then the Unified Extensible Firmware Interface (UEFI) to replace the BIOS. UEFI offers support for larger hard drives, better drivers, and more. Apple Computers have gone fully UEFI, as have some Windows PCs.

■ Key Terms

basic input/output services (BIOS) *(209)*
beep codes *(221)*
bootable disk *(224)*
bootstrap loader *(224)*
chassis intrusion detection *(216)*
chipset *(205)*

CMOS setup program *(212)*
complementary metal-oxide semiconductor (CMOS) *(212)*
device driver *(220)*
Device Manager *(221)*
DriveLock *(218)*

Extensible Firmware Interface (EFI) *(228)*
firmware *(211)*
flash ROM *(210)*
installation disc *(220)*
nonvolatile *(210)*
Northbridge *(205)*
option ROM *(220)*
POST card *(222)*
power good *(224)*
power-on self test (POST) *(221)*

Registry *(221)*
read-only memory (ROM) *(210)*
scan code *(207)*
services *(210)*
Southbridge *(205)*
system BIOS *(211)*
system disk *(224)*
system ROM *(210)*
Unified Extensible Firmware Interface (UEFI) *(228)*

■ Key Term Quiz

Use the Key Terms list to complete the sentences that follow. Not all terms will be used.

1. Loaded when the system boots, a(n) _____ is a file that contains instructions to support a hardware device.

2. If the computer appears dead, with no beeps or screen responses, you can insert a(n) _____ in an expansion slot to diagnose what is wrong.

3. The combination of a specific Northbridge and a specific _____ is collectively referred to as the _____.

4. If a disk contains the operating system files necessary to start the computer, it is called a(n) _____.

5. You can reprogram a(n) _____ chip without removing the chip.

6. Unlike RAM, which loses all data when the computer is shut down, a ROM chip is _____, retaining the information even when the power is off.

7. The hundreds of programs in the system ROM chip are collectively called the _____.

8. The _____ is a complex binary file used with Windows that combines the CONFIG.SYS, SYSTEM.INI, and other configuration files.

9. The low-energy chip that holds configuration information and keeps track of date and time is called the _____ chip.

10. When the computer starts, it runs a program on the system BIOS called _____ that checks the hardware.

■ Multiple-Choice Quiz

1. A user calls first thing Monday morning saying she has an error message at bootup that says her case was opened. She's looked at the computer, but it seems normal. What does this tell you about her computer?

   A. Her computer has TPM enabled in the CMOS.

   B. Her computer has fan monitoring enabled in CMOS and the fan stopped over the weekend.

   C. Her computer case has chassis intrusion detection and the feature is enabled in CMOS.

   D. It doesn't tell you anything about the computer, only that the user has a problem.

2. What is the correct boot sequence for a PC?

   A. CPU, POST, power good, boot loader, operating system

   B. POST, power good, CPU, boot loader, operating system

   C. Power good, boot loader, CPU, POST, operating system

   D. Power good, CPU, POST, boot loader, operating system

3. When you turn on your computer, what is accessed first?

   A. The CPU

   B. The setup program

C. The POST

D. The CMOS chip

4. Jack decided to go retro and added a second floppy disk drive to his computer. He thinks he has it physically installed correctly, but it doesn't show up in Windows. Which of the following options will most likely lead Jack where he needs to go to resolve the issue?

A. Reboot the computer and press the F key on the keyboard twice. This signals that the computer has two floppy disk drives.

B. Reboot the computer and watch for instructions to enter the CMOS setup utility (for example, a message may say to press the DELETE key). Do what it says to go into CMOS setup.

C. In Windows, press the DELETE key twice to enter the CMOS setup utility.

D. In Windows, go to Start | Run and type **floppy**. Click OK to open the Floppy Disk Drive Setup Wizard.

5. What does BIOS provide for the computer? (Choose the best answer.)

A. BIOS provides the physical interface for various devices such as USB and FireWire ports.

B. BIOS provides the programming that enables the CPU to communicate with other hardware.

C. BIOS provides memory space for applications to load into from the hard drive.

D. BIOS provides memory space for applications to load into from the main system RAM.

6. Which of the following will result in a POST beep code message?

A. The system is overheating.

B. The video card is not seated properly.

C. The keyboard is unplugged.

D. The hard drive has crashed.

7. Which of the following statements is true about CMOS?

A. CMOS is a configuration program that runs from the hard drive during booting.

B. CMOS is a low-energy chip that draws power from a battery while the computer is turned off.

C. CMOS includes the power-on self test (POST) routines.

D. CMOS is the Southbridge chip that controls input and output devices.

8. Which of the following most typically enables you to upgrade a flash ROM chip?

A. Remove the chip and replace it with a different one.

B. Reboot the computer.

C. Install a different operating system.

D. Run a small command-line program combined with a BIOS update file.

9. After a sudden power outage, Morgan's PC rebooted, but nothing appeared on the screen. The PC just beeps at him, over and over and over. What's most likely the problem?

A. The power outage toasted his RAM.

B. The power outage toasted his video card.

C. The power outage toasted his hard drive.

D. The power outage toasted his CPU.

10. Henry bought a new card for capturing television on his computer. When he finished going through the packaging, though, he found no driver disc, only an application disc for setting up the TV capture software. After installing the card and software, it all works flawlessly. What's the most likely explanation?

A. The device doesn't need BIOS, so there's no need for a driver disc.

B. The device has an option ROM that loads BIOS, so there's no need for a driver disc.

C. Windows supports TV capture cards out of the box, so there's no need for a driver disc.

D. The manufacturer made a mistake and didn't include everything needed to set up the device.

11. Mohinder finds that a disgruntled former employee decided to sabotage her computer when she left by putting a password in CMOS that stops the computer from booting. What can Mohinder do to solve this problem?

A. Mohinder should boot the computer while holding the left SHIFT key. This will clear the CMOS information.

B. Mohinder should try various combinations of the former employee's name. The vast majority of people use their name or initials for CMOS passwords.

C. Mohinder should find the CMOS clear jumper on the motherboard. Then he can boot the computer with a shunt on the jumper to clear the CMOS information.

D. Mohinder should find a replacement motherboard. Unless he knows the CMOS password, there's nothing he can do.

12. Which chip does the CPU use to communicate with high-speed devices such as video cards or RAM?

   A. Complementary metal-oxide semiconductor

   B. Northbridge

   C. Southbridge

   D. Scan code

13. When your computer boots up and you press the appropriate key to enter the CMOS setup utility, a small program loads, allowing you to specify settings for various hardware devices. Where is this small program permanently stored?

   A. In the ROM

   B. In CMOS

   C. On the hard drive

   D. In RAM

14. When you enter the CMOS setup utility (as in the previous question) and make changes, where are your settings stored?

   A. In the BIOS

   B. In CMOS

   C. On the hard drive

   D. In RAM

15. Jill boots up an older Pentium III system that has been the cause of several user complaints at the office. The system powers up and starts to run through POST but then stops. The screen displays a "CMOS configuration mismatch" error. Of the following list, what is the most likely cause of this error?

   A. Dying CMOS battery

   B. Bad CPU

   C. Bad RAM

   D. Corrupt system BIOS

■ Essay Quiz

1. From this chapter you learned that every piece of hardware in the computer needs BIOS to make it work. Explain three ways in which these essential programs may be provided to the CPU.

2. You've been hired as a tutor for Tom, a fellow student in your hardware class. He's having a difficult time understanding the role that the system BIOS plays in booting the computer. How will you explain this process to him? Be sure to explain in order the step-by-step process that the BIOS goes through from the time you turn on the computer until it relinquishes control to the operating system. Make sure Tom understands why you may get an error message if you leave a diskette in the floppy drive.

3. Why do some POST error messages manifest themselves as beep codes while others display as text messages? What should you do if you get a POST error message?

4. Your instructor has asked you to give a report on the Northbridge and Southbridge chips, their functions, and how they use the address bus. Write a short essay on the subject that you can use in class.

5. What symptoms will your computer show if the CMOS battery is dying or dead? What happens to the information stored in CMOS when you replace the battery? What must you do if a built-in battery goes dead?

Lab Projects

• Lab Project 7.1

Use the motherboard book (if you have one or can download one) or check the Web site of your BIOS manufacturer to identify what each of the following POST error messages means:

- A numeric message of 301

- One long beep followed by three short beeps
- A numeric message of 601
- HDD controller failure

• Lab Project 7.2

Watch closely as your computer boots to see if it displays a message about how to reach the setup program. If it does not, consult your motherboard book to try to locate this information. Then, using the method appropriate for your system BIOS chip, access the setup program and examine the various screens. Do not change anything! Usually, your motherboard book includes default settings for the various setup screens and perhaps includes explanations of the various choices. Compare what you see on the screen with what the book says. Do you see any differences? If so, how do you account for these differences? As you examine the setup program, answer the following questions:

1. How do you navigate from one screen to the next? Are there menus across the top or do you simply jump from one page of options to the next? Are there instructions on the screen for navigating the setup program?
2. What is the boot sequence for your computer? In other words, in what order does the BIOS look for a bootable device?
3. What is the core voltage of the CPU?
4. How many SATA drives does the BIOS list?

When you have finished, choose "Exit Without Saving."

Expansion Bus

"*So what makes AGP so mouth-watering that we bumped mega-gig storage? Intel's new port puts the pedal to the metal for 3D accelerators caught in bus traffic.*"

—BRAD DOSLAND, *BOOT* (AUGUST 1997)

In this chapter, you will learn how to

- **Identify the structure and function of the expansion bus**
- **Describe the modern expansion bus**
- **Explain classic system resources**
- **Install expansion cards properly**
- **Troubleshoot expansion card problems**

Expansion slots have been part of the PC from the very beginning. Way back then, IBM created the PC with an eye to the future; the original IBM PC had slots built into the motherboard—called **expansion slots**—for adding expansion cards and thus new functions to the PC. The slots and accompanying wires and support chips on the first PC and on the latest and greatest PC are called the **expansion bus**.

The expandability enabled by an expansion bus might seem obvious today, but think about the three big hurdles a would-be expansion card developer needed to cross to make a card that would work successfully in an expansion slot. First, any expansion card needed to be built specifically for the expansion slots—that would require the creation of industry standards. Second, the card needed some way to communicate with the CPU, both to receive instructions and to relay information. And third, the operating system would need some means of enabling the user to control the new device and thus take advantage of its functions. Here's the short form of those three hurdles:

- Physical connection
- Communication
- Drivers

This chapter covers the expansion bus in detail, starting almost at the very beginning of the PC—not because the history of the PC is inherently thrilling, but rather because the way the old PCs worked affects the latest systems. Installation today remains very similar to installation in 1987 in that you must have a physical connection, communication, and drivers for the operating system. Taking the time to learn the old ways first most definitely helps you understand and implement current technology, terminology, and practices.

Historical/Conceptual

■ Structure and Function of the Expansion Bus

As you've learned, every device in the computer—whether soldered to the motherboard or snapped into a socket—connects to the external data bus and the address bus. The expansion slots are no exception. They connect to the rest of the PC through the chipset. Exactly *where* on the chipset varies depending on the system. On some systems, the expansion slots connect to the Southbridge (Figure 8.1). On other systems, the expansion slots connect to the Northbridge (Figure 8.2). Finally, many systems have more than one type of expansion bus, with slots of one type connecting to the Northbridge and slots of another type connecting to the Southbridge (Figure 8.3).

The chipset provides an extension of the address bus and data bus to the expansion slots, and thus to any expansion cards in those slots. If you plug a hard drive controller card into an expansion slot, it functions just as if it were built into the motherboard, albeit with one big difference: speed. As you'll recall from Chapter 5, "Microprocessors," the system crystal—the clock—pushes the CPU. The system crystal provides a critical function for the entire PC, acting like a drill sergeant

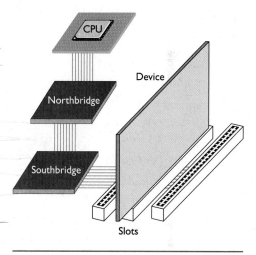

• **Figure 8.1** Expansion slots connecting to Southbridge

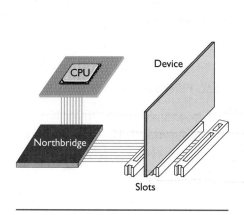

• **Figure 8.2** Expansion slots connecting to Northbridge

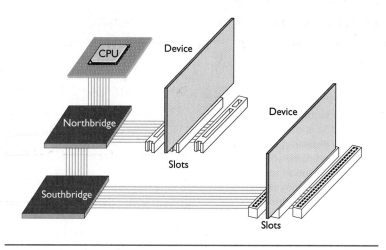

• **Figure 8.3** Expansion slots connecting to both Northbridge and Southbridge

calling a cadence, setting the pace of activity in the computer. Every device soldered to the motherboard is designed to run at the speed of the system crystal. A 133-MHz motherboard, for example, has at least a 133-MHz Northbridge chip and a 133-MHz Southbridge chip, all timed by a 133-MHz crystal (Figure 8.4).

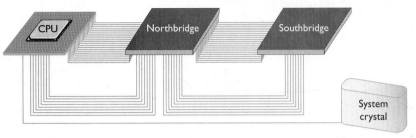

The system crystal sits on its own bus.

• **Figure 8.4**   The system crystal sets the speed.

Clock crystals aren't just for CPUs and chipsets. Pretty much every chip in your computer has a CLK wire and needs to be pushed by a clock chip, including the chips on your expansion cards. Suppose you buy a device that did not come with your computer— say, a sound card. The chips on the sound card need to be pushed by a CLK signal from a crystal. If PCs were designed to use the system crystal to push that sound card, sound card manufacturers would need to make sound cards for every possible motherboard speed. You would have to buy a 100-MHz sound card for a 100-MHz system or a 133-MHz sound card for a 133-MHz system.

That would be ridiculous, and IBM knew it when they designed the PC. They had to make an extension to the external data bus that *ran at its own standardized speed*. You would use this part of the external data bus to snap new devices into the PC. IBM achieved this goal by adding a different crystal, called the **expansion bus crystal**, which controlled the part of the external data bus connected to the expansion slots (Figure 8.5).

The expansion slots run at a much slower speed than the frontside bus. The chipset acts as the divider between the two buses, compensating for the speed difference with wait states and special buffering (storage) areas. No matter how fast the motherboard runs, the expansion slots run at a standard speed. In the original IBM PC, that speed was about 14.318 MHz ÷ 2, or about 7.16 MHz. The latest expansion buses run much faster, but remember that old speed of roughly 7 MHz; as you learn more about expansion slots, you'll see that it's still needed on even the most modern systems.

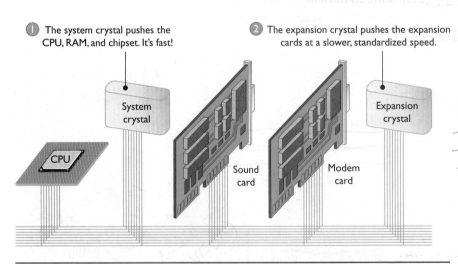

① The system crystal pushes the CPU, RAM, and chipset. It's fast!

② The expansion crystal pushes the expansion cards at a slower, standardized speed.

• **Figure 8.5**   Function of system and expansion bus crystals

PC Bus

On first-generation IBM PCs, the 8088 CPU had an 8-bit external data bus and ran at a top speed of 4.77 MHz. IBM made the expansion slots on the

first PCs with an 8-bit external bus connection. IBM wanted the bus to run as fast as the CPU, and even way back then, 4.77 MHz was an easy speed to achieve. IBM settled on a standard expansion bus speed of about 7 MHz—faster than the CPU! (This was the only occurrence in the history of PCs when the expansion bus was faster than the CPU.) This expansion bus was called the **PC bus** or **XT bus**. Figure 8.6 shows these ancient 8-bit expansion slots.

IBM certainly didn't invent the idea of the expansion bus—plenty of earlier computers, including many mainframes, had expansion slots—but IBM did something no one had ever done. They allowed competitors to copy the PC bus and make their own PCs without having to pay a licensing or royalty fee. They also allowed third parties to make cards that would snap into their PC bus. Remember that IBM invented the PC bus—it was (and still is) a patented product of IBM Corporation. By allowing everyone to copy the PC expansion bus technology, however, IBM established the industry standard and fostered the emergence of the clone market. If IBM had not allowed others to copy their patented technologies for free, companies such as Compaq, Dell, and Gateway never would have existed. Equally, component makers such as Logitech, Creative, and 3Com would never be the companies they are today without the help of IBM. Who knows? If IBM had not opened the PC bus to the world, this book and the A+ Certification exams might have been based on Apple computers.

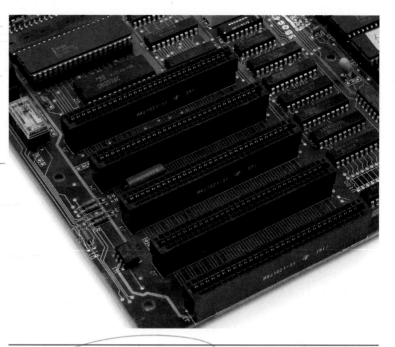

• **Figure 8.6** Eight-bit PC/XT slots

PC Bus

8 bits wide

7-MHz speed

Manual configuration

ISA

When Intel invented the 286 processor, IBM wanted to create a new expansion bus that took advantage of the 286's 16-bit external data bus, yet also supported 8-bit cards. IBM achieved this by simply adding a set of connections to the end of the PC bus, creating a new 16-bit bus (Figure 8.7). Many techs called this bus the *AT bus* after the first system to use these slots, the 286-based IBM Advanced Technology (AT) computer. The AT bus ran at the same speed (approximately 7 MHz) as the earlier PC bus.

• **Figure 8.7** Sixteen-bit ISA or AT slots

Even though IBM allowed third parties to copy the PC and AT expansion bus architecture, they never released the complete specifications for these two types of expansion buses. In the early 1980s, a number of clone makers pooled their combined knowledge of the PC/XT and AT buses to create the **Industry Standard Architecture (ISA)**.

The ISA bus enabled manufacturers to jump the first of the three hurdles for successful expansion cards, namely connectivity. If a company wanted to build a new kind of adapter card for the PC, they simply followed the specifications in the ISA standard.

ISA Bus

16 bits wide

7-MHz speed

Manual configuration

Essentials

■ Modern Expansion Buses

The ISA expansion bus was both excellent and cutting edge for its time, and was *the* expansion bus in every PC for the first ten years of the PC's existence. Yet ISA suffered from three tremendous limitations that began to cause serious bottlenecks by the late 1980s. First, ISA was slow, running at only about 7 MHz. Second, ISA was narrow—only 16 bits wide—and therefore unable to handle the 32-bit and 64-bit external data buses of more modern processors. Finally, techs had to configure ISA cards manually, making installation a time-consuming nightmare of running proprietary configuration programs and moving tiny jumpers just to get a single card to work.

Manufacturers clearly needed to come up with a better bus that addressed the many problems associated with ISA. They needed a bus that could take advantage of the 33-MHz motherboard speed and 32-bit-wide data bus found in 386 and 486 systems. They also wanted a bus that was self-configuring, freeing techs from the drudgery of manual configuration. Finally, they had to make the new bus backward compatible, so end users wouldn't have to throw out their oftentimes substantial investment in ISA expansion cards.

False Starts

In the late 1980s, several new expansion buses designed to address these shortcomings appeared on the market. Three in particular—IBM's Micro Channel Architecture (MCA), the open standard Extended ISA (EISA), and the Video Electronics Standards Association's VESA Local Bus (VL-Bus)—all had a few years of modest popularity from the late 1980s to the mid 1990s. Although all of these alternative buses worked well, they also had shortcomings that made them less than optimal replacements for ISA: IBM charged a heavy licensing fee for MCA, EISA was expensive to make, and

VL-Bus only worked in tandem with the ISA bus. By 1993, the PC world was eager for a big name to come forward with a fast, wide, easy-to-configure, and cheap new expansion bus. Intel saw the need and stepped up to the plate with the now famous PCI bus.

PCI

Intel introduced the **peripheral component interconnect (PCI)** bus architecture (Figure 8.8) in the early 1990s, and the PC expansion bus was never again the same. Intel made many smart moves with PCI, not the least of which was releasing PCI to the public domain to make PCI very attractive to manufacturers. PCI provided a wider, faster, more flexible alternative than any previous expansion bus. The exceptional technology of the new bus, combined with the lack of a price tag, made manufacturers quickly drop ISA and the other alternatives and adopt PCI.

PCI really shook up the PC world with its capabilities. The original PCI bus was 32 bits wide and ran at 33 MHz, which was superb, but these features were expected and not earth-shattering. The coolness of PCI came from its capability to coexist with other expansion buses. When PCI first came out, you could buy a motherboard with both PCI and ISA slots. This was important because users could keep their old ISA cards and slowly migrate to PCI. Equally impressive was that PCI devices were (and still are) self-configuring, a feature that led to the industry standard that became known as plug and play. Finally, PCI had a powerful burst-mode feature that enabled very efficient data transfers.

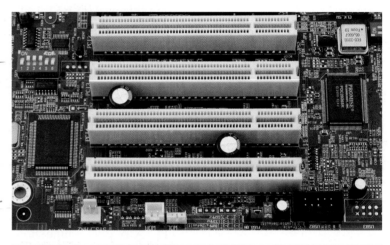

 Figure 8.8   PCI expansion bus slots

 Before PCI, it was rare to see more than one type of expansion slot on a motherboard. Today this is not only common— it's expected!

PCI Bus

32 bits wide

33-MHz speed

Self-configuring

There was a 64-bit version of the original PCI standard, but it was quite rare.

The original PCI expansion bus has soldiered on in PCs for over ten years. Recently, more advanced forms have begun to appear. Although these new PCI expansion buses are faster than the original PCI, they're only improvements to PCI, not entirely new expansion buses. The original PCI might be fading away, but PCI in its many new forms is still "King of the Motherboard."

AGP

One of the big reasons for ISA's demise was video cards. When video started going graphical with the introduction of Windows, ISA buses were too slow and graphics looked terrible. PCI certainly improved graphics when it came out, but Intel was thinking ahead. Shortly after Intel invented PCI, they

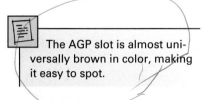

(The 4) ➤

• **Figure 8.9**   AGP slot

presented a specialized, video-only version of PCI called the **accelerated graphics port (AGP)**. An AGP slot is a PCI slot, but one with a direct connection to the Northbridge. AGP slots are only for video cards—don't try to snap a sound card or modem into one. You'll learn much more about this fascinating technology in Chapter 19, "Video." Figure 8.9 shows a typical AGP slot.

PCI-X

PCI Extended (PCI-X), available in such systems as the Macintosh G5, is a huge enhancement to current PCI that is also fully backward compatible in terms of both hardware and software. PCI-X is a 64-bit-wide bus (see Figure 8.10). Its slots will accept regular PCI cards. The real bonus of PCI-X is its much enhanced speed. The PCI-X 2.0 standard features four speed grades (measured in MHz): PCI-X 66, PCI-X 133, PCI-X 266, and PCI-X 533.

• **Figure 8.10**   PCI-X slot

The obvious candidates for PCI-X are businesses using workstations and servers, because they have the "need for speed" and also the need for backward compatibility. Large vendors, especially in the high-end market, are already on board. HP, Dell, and Intel server products, for example, support PCI-X. A quick online shopping trip reveals tons of PCI-X stuff for sale: gigabit NICs, Fibre Channel cards, video adapters, and more.

• **Figure 8.11**   Tiny card in Mini-PCI slot. See the contacts at the bottom of the picture?

Mini-PCI

PCI has even made it into laptops in the specialty **Mini-PCI** format (Figure 8.11). You'll find Mini-PCI in just about every laptop these days. Mini-PCI is designed to use low power and to lie flat—both good features for a laptop expansion slot. Mini-PCI returns in Chapter 21, "Portable Computing."

PCI Express

PCI Express (PCIe) is the latest, fastest, and most popular expansion bus in use today. As its name implies, PCI Express is still PCI, but it uses a point-to-point serial connection instead of PCI's shared parallel communication. Consider a single 32-bit chunk of data moving from a device to the CPU. In PCI parallel communication, 32 wires each carry one bit of that chunk of data. In serial communication, only one wire carries those 32 bits. You'd think that 32 are better than one, correct? Well, first of all, PCIe doesn't share the bus. A PCIe device has its own direct connection (a point-to-point connection) to the Northbridge, so it does not wait for other devices. Plus, when you start going really fast (think gigabits per second), getting all 32 bits of data to go from one device to another at the same time is difficult, because some bits get there slightly faster than others. That means you need some serious, high-speed checking of the data when it arrives to verify that it's all there and in good shape. Serial data doesn't have this problem, as all of the bits arrive one after the other in a

single stream. When data is really going fast, a single point-to-point serial connection is faster than a shared 32-wire parallel connection.

And boy howdy, is PCIe ever fast! A PCIe connection uses one wire for sending and one for receiving. Each of these pairs of wires between a PCIe controller and a device is called a *lane*. Each direction of a lane runs at 2.5 Gbps, or 5 Gbps with PCIe 2.0. Better yet, each point-to-point connection can use 1, 2, 4, 8, 12, 16, or 32 lanes to achieve a maximum theoretical bandwidth of 320 Gbps. The effective data rate drops a little bit because of the *encoding scheme*—the way the data is broken down and reassembled—but full duplex data throughput can go up to a whopping 16 Gbps on a ×16 connection.

The most common PCIe slot is the 16-lane (×16) version most commonly used for video cards, as shown in Figure 8.12. The first versions of PCIe motherboards used a combination of a single PCIe ×16 slot and a number of standard PCI slots. (Remember, PCI is designed to work with other expansion slots, even other types of PCI.) There is also a small form factor version of PCI Express for mobile computers called PCI Express Mini Card.

The bandwidth generated by a ×16 slot is far more than anything other than a video card would need, so most PCIe motherboards also contain slots with fewer lanes. Currently ×1 and ×4 are the most common general-purpose PCIe slots, but PCIe is still pretty new—so expect things to change as PCIe matures (see Figure 8.13).

• **Figure 8.12** PCIe ×16 slot (black) with PCI slots (white)

When you talk about the lanes, such as ×1 or ×8, use "by" rather than "ex" for the multiplication mark. So "by 1" and "by 8" is the correct pronunciation. You'll of course hear it spoken as both "by 8" and "8 ex" for the next few years until the technology has become a household term.

• **Figure 8.13** PCIe ×1 slots

Try This!

Shopping Trip

So, what's the latest PCIe motherboard out there? Get online or go to your local computer store and research higher-end motherboards. What combinations of PCIe slots can you find on a single motherboard? Jot them down and compare with your classmates.

■ System Resources

All devices on your computer, including your expansion cards, need to communicate with the CPU. Unfortunately, just using the word *communication* is too simplistic, because communication between the CPU and devices isn't like a human conversation. In the PC, only the CPU "talks" in the form of BIOS or driver commands—devices only react to the CPU's commands. You can divide communication into four aspects called **system resources**: I/O addresses, IRQs, DMA channels, and memory addresses.

Not all devices use all four system resources. All devices use I/O addressing and most use IRQs, but very few use DMA or memory. System resources are not new; they've been with PCs since the first IBM PC.

New devices must have their system resources configured. Configuration happens more or less automatically now through the plug and play process, but in the old days, configuration was handled through a painstaking manual process. (You kids don't know how good you have it. Oops! Sorry—Old Man Voice.) Even though system resources are now automated, you still might run into them in a few places on a modern PC. On those rare occasions, you'll need to understand I/O addresses, IRQs, DMAs, and memory to make changes as needed. Let's look at each system resource in detail to understand what they are and how they work.

I/O Addresses

The CPU gives a command to a device by using a pattern of ones and zeros called an **I/O address**. Every device responds to at least four I/O addresses, meaning the CPU can give at least four different commands to each device. The process of communicating through I/O addresses is called, quite logically, **I/O addressing**. Here's how it works.

The chipset extends the address bus to the expansion slots, which makes two interesting things happen. First, you can place RAM on a card, and the CPU can address it just as it can your regular RAM. Devices such as video cards come with their own RAM. The CPU draws the screen by writing directly to the RAM on the video card. Second, the CPU can use the address bus to talk to all of the devices on your computer through I/O addressing.

Normally the address bus on an expansion bus works exactly like the address bus on a frontside bus—different patterns of ones and zeros point to different memory locations. If the CPU wants to send an I/O address, however, it puts the expansion bus into what can be called I/O mode. When the bus goes into I/O mode, all devices on the bus look for patterns of ones and zeros to appear on the address bus.

Back in the old Intel 8088 days, the CPU used an extra wire, called the *input/output or memory (IO/MEM) wire*, to notify devices that it was using the address bus either to specify an address in memory or to communicate with a particular device (Figure 8.14). You won't find an IO/MEM wire on a modern CPU, as the process has changed and become more complex—but the concept hasn't changed one bit. The CPU sends commands to devices by placing patterns of ones and zeros—I/O addresses—on the address bus.

No two devices share the same I/O address because that would defeat the entire concept. To make sure no two devices share I/O addresses, all I/O addresses either are preset by standard (for example, all hard drive controllers use the same I/O addresses on every PC) or are set at boot by the operating system. You can see the I/O addresses for all of the devices on your computer by going into the Device Manager. Go to the View menu option and select *Resources by type.* Click on the plus sign directly to the left of the Input/output (IO) option to see a list of I/O addresses, as shown in Figure 8.15.

Whoa! What's with all the letters and numbers? The address bus is always 32 bits (even if you have a 64-bit processor, the Northbridge only allows the first 32 bits to pass to the expansion slots), so instead of showing you the raw ones and zeros, the Device Manager shows you the I/O address ranges in hexadecimal. Don't know hex? No worries—**hexadecimal** is just quick shorthand for representing the strings of ones and zeros—*binary*—that you *do* know. One hex character is used to represent four binary characters. Here's the key:

0000 = 0
0001 = 1
0010 = 2
0011 = 3
0100 = 4
0101 = 5
0110 = 6
0111 = 7
1000 = 8
1001 = 9
1010 = A
1011 = B
1100 = C
1101 = D

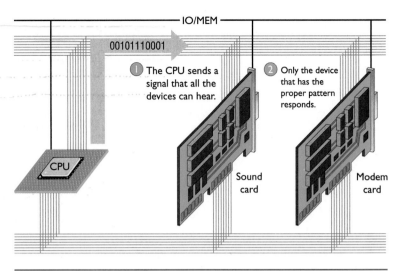

• **Figure 8.14**   Sending out an I/O address

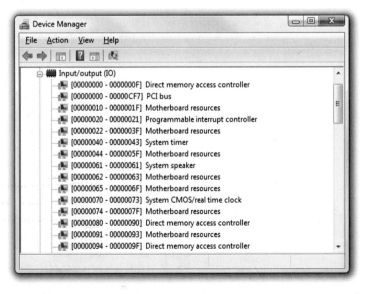

• **Figure 8.15**   Viewing resources by type, with I/O addresses expanded

1110 = E

1111 = F

Let's pick an arbitrary string of ones and zeros:

00000000000000000000000111110000

To convert to hex, just chop them into chunks of four:

0000 0000 0000 0000 0000 0001 1111 0000

Then use the key above to convert:

0 0 0 0 0 1 F 0

Then push the hex values together:

000001F0

You now understand what those values mean in the Device Manager. Scroll down until you find the "[000001F0 – 000001F7] Primary IDE Channel" setting. Notice that two I/O addresses are listed. These show the entire range of I/O addresses for this device; the more complex the device, the more I/O addresses it uses. Address ranges are generally referred to by the first value in the range, commonly known as the **I/O base address**.

Here are the most important items to remember about I/O addresses. First, every device on your PC has an I/O address. Without it, the CPU wouldn't have a way to send a device commands. Second, I/O addresses are configured automatically: you just plug in a device and it works. Third, no two devices should share I/O addresses. The system handles configuration, so this happens automatically.

All I/O addresses only use the last 16 bits (they all start with 0000). Sixteen bits makes 2^{16} = 65,536 I/O address ranges— plenty for even the most modern PCs. Should PCs begin to need more I/O addresses in the future, the current I/O addressing system is ready.

Interrupt Requests

Between the standardized expansion bus connections and BIOS using I/O addressing, the CPU can now communicate with all of the devices inside the computer, but a third and final hurdle remains. I/O addressing enables the CPU to talk to devices, but how does a device tell the CPU it needs attention? How does the mouse tell the CPU that it has moved, for example, or how does the keyboard tell the CPU that somebody just pressed the J key? The PC needs some kind of mechanism to tell the CPU to stop doing whatever it is doing and talk to a particular device (Figure 8.16). This mechanism is called **interruption**.

Every CPU in the PC world has an INT (interrupt) wire, shown in Figure 8.17. If a device puts voltage on this wire, the CPU stops what it's doing and deals with the interrupting device. Suppose you have a PC with only one peripheral, a keyboard that directly connects to the INT wire. If the user presses the J key, the keyboard charges the INT wire.

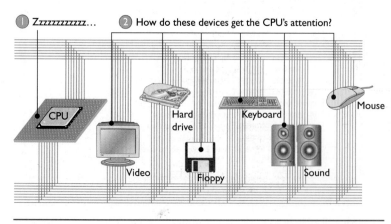

• **Figure 8.16** How do devices tell the CPU they need attention?

The CPU temporarily stops running the browser (or whatever program is active) and runs the necessary BIOS routine to query the keyboard.

This would be fine if the computer had only one device. As you know, however, PCs have many devices, and almost all of them need to interrupt the CPU at some point. So the PC needs some kind of traffic cop to act as an intermediary between all of the devices and the CPU's INT wire. This traffic-cop chip, called the **I/O advanced programmable interrupt controller (IOAPIC)**, uses special interrupt wires that run to all devices on the expansion bus (Figure 8.18).

If a device wants to get the CPU's attention, it lights the interrupt wires with a special pattern of ones and zeros just for that device. The IOAPIC then interrupts the CPU. The CPU queries the IOAPIC to see which device interrupted, and then it begins to communicate with the device over the address bus (Figure 8.19).

These unique patterns of ones and zeros manifest themselves as something called **interrupt requests (IRQs)**. Before IOAPICs, IRQs were actual wires leading to the previous generation of traffic cops, called PICs. It's easy to see if your system has a PIC or an IOAPIC. Go into the Device Manager and select Interrupt request (IRQ) with the resources set to show by type.

Figure 8.20 shows nearly a dozen IRQs, numbered 0 through 22, making this an IOAPIC system. IRQ 9 is special—this IRQ is assigned to the controller itself and is the IOAPIC's connection to the CPU. If you look closely, you'll also notice that some IRQs aren't listed. These are unused or "open" IRQs. If you add another device to the

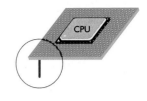

• **Figure 8.17**   The INT wire

IOAPIC functions are usually built into the Southbridge. Many developers drop the I/O part and simply call them *APICs*.

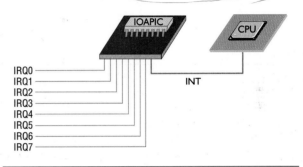

• **Figure 8.18**   Eight interrupt wires (IRQs) run from the expansion bus to the IOAPIC.

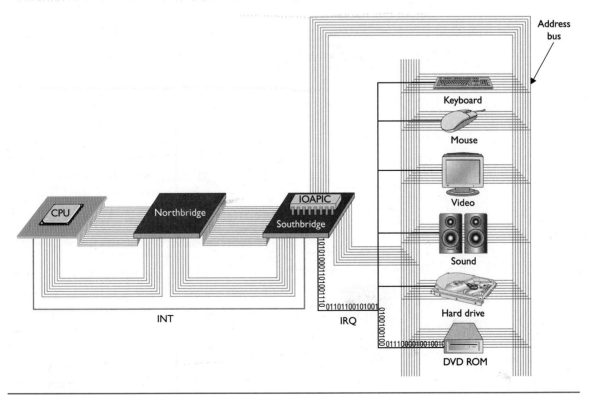

• **Figure 8.19**   IOAPIC at work

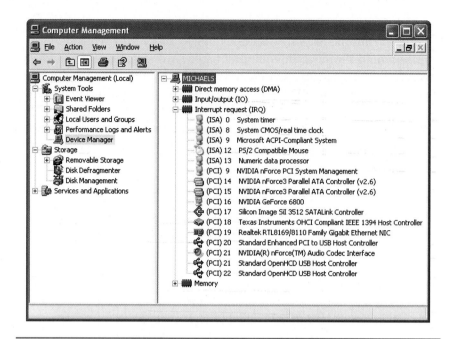

● **Figure 8.20**   IRQs in an IOAPIC system

system, the new device will take up one of these unused IRQs. Now look at the older PIC system in Figure 8.21—note that it only shows IRQs ranging from 0 through 15.

Modern systems running Windows Vista or Windows 7 can use virtual IRQs to support devices. A quick glance at the Device Manager IRQ list in Vista

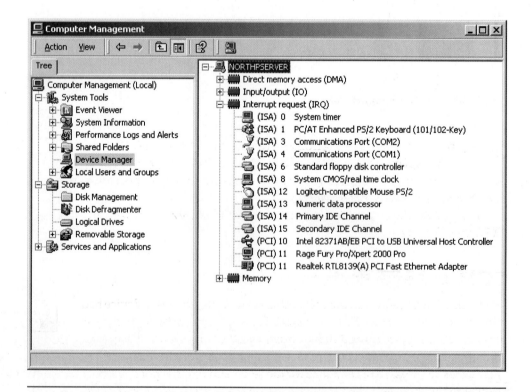

● **Figure 8.21**   IRQs in a PIC system

Mike Meyers' CompTIA A+ Guide to Managing and Troubleshooting PCs

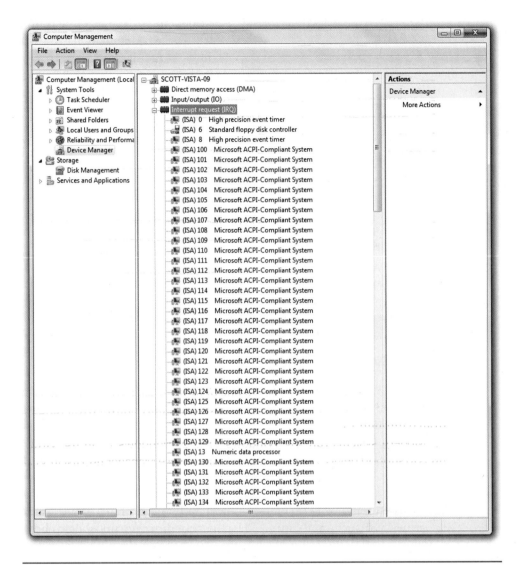

IRQs in Windows Vista

shows a giant list of IRQs, ranging from 0 to upwards of 190 (Figure 8.22). Some systems even display negative IRQs, such as –2 or –4. Once you get into a Windows Vista or Windows 7 machine, you can pretty much forget about IRQs. The OS handles it all automatically.

Let's look at the last serious vestige of the "bad old days" on your PC: COM and LPT ports.

COM and LPT Ports

When the PC first came out, the I/O addresses and IRQ for every device had to be manually configured. How you did this varied from device to device: you moved jumpers, turned dials, or ran weird configuration programs. It was never easy. IBM tried to make configuration easier by creating preset I/O address and IRQ combinations for the serial and parallel ports, because they were the most commonly used ports on the original PC. These preset combinations were called **COM ports** for serial connections and **LPT ports** for

 The term "COM" for serial ports came from "communication," and the term "LPT" for parallel ports came from "line printer."

Table 8.1	COM and LPT Assignments	
Port	I/O Base Address	IRQ
COM1	03F8	4
COM2	02F8	3
COM3	03E8	4
COM4	02E8	3
LPT1	0378	7
LPT2	0278	5

parallel ports. Table 8.1 lists the early preset combinations of I/O addresses and IRQs.

Notice that the four COM ports share two IRQs. In the old days, if two devices shared an IRQ, the system instantly locked up. The lack of available IRQs in early systems led IBM to double up the IRQs for the serial devices, creating one of the few exceptions to the rule that no two devices could share IRQs. You could share an IRQ between two devices, but only if one of the devices would never actually access the IRQ. You'd see this with a dedicated fax/modem card, for example, which has a single phone line connected to a single card that has two different functions. The CPU needed distinct sets of I/O addresses for fax commands and modem commands, but as there was only the one modem doing both jobs, it needed only a single IRQ.

Direct Memory Access

CPUs do a lot of work. They run the BIOS, operating system, and applications. CPUs handle interrupts and I/O addresses. CPUs also deal with one other item: data. CPUs constantly move data between devices and RAM. CPUs move files from the hard drive to RAM. They move print jobs from RAM to laser printers, and they move images from scanners to RAM, just to name a very few examples of this RAM-to-device-and-back process.

Moving all this data is obviously necessary, but it is a simple task—the CPU has better things to do with its power and time. Moreover, with all of the caches and such on today's CPUs, the system spends most of its time waiting around doing nothing while the CPU handles some internal calculation. Add these facts together and the question arises: Why not make devices that access memory directly, without involving the CPU (Figure 8.23)? The process of accessing memory without using the CPU is called **direct memory access (DMA)**.

DMA is very common and is excellent for creating background sounds in games and for moving data from floppy and hard drives into RAM (Figure 8.24).

Nice as it may sound, the concept of DMA as just described has a problem—there's only one expansion bus. What if more than one device wants to use DMA? What keeps these devices from stomping on the external data bus all at the same

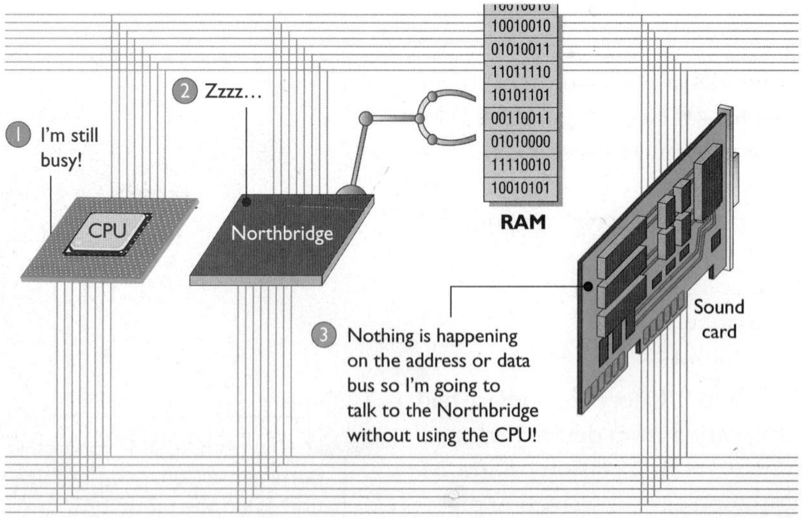

1 I'm still busy!

2 Zzzz...

3 Nothing is happening on the address or data bus so I'm going to talk to the Northbridge without using the CPU!

CPU

Northbridge

RAM

10010010
10010010
01010011
11011110
10101101
00110011
01010000
11110010
10010101

Sound card

● Figure 8.23 Why not talk to the chipset directly?

time? Plus, what if the CPU suddenly needs the data bus? How can you stop the device using DMA so the CPU, which should have priority, can access the bus? To deal with this, IBM added another traffic cop.

The **DMA controller**, which seasoned techs often call the *8237* after its old chip name, controls all DMA functions. DMA is similar to IRQ handling in that the DMA controller assigns numbers, called DMA channels, by which devices can request use of the DMA. The DMA also handles the data passing from peripherals to RAM and vice versa. This takes necessary but simple work away from the CPU so the CPU can spend time doing more productive work.

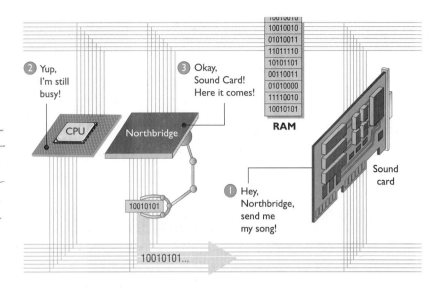

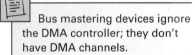

• **Figure 8.24**   DMA in action

The DMA chip sends data along the external data bus when the CPU is busy with internal calculations and not using the external data bus. This is perfectly acceptable, because the CPU accesses the external data bus only about five percent of the time on a modern CPU.

The DMA just described is called classic DMA; it was the first and for a long time the only way to do DMA. Classic DMA is dying out because it's very slow and only supports 16-bit data transfers, a silly waste in a world of much wider buses. On most systems, only floppy drives still use classic DMA.

All systems still support classic DMA, but most devices today that use DMA do so without going through the DMA controller. These devices are known as bus masters. **Bus mastering** devices have circuitry that enables them to watch for other devices accessing the external data bus; they can detect a potential conflict and get out of the way on their own. Bus mastering has become extremely popular in hard drives. All modern hard drives take advantage of bus mastering. Hard drive bus mastering is hidden under terms such as *Ultra DMA*, and for the most part is totally automatic and invisible. See Chapter 12, "Implementing Hard Drives," for more details on bus mastering hard drives.

> Bus mastering devices ignore the DMA controller; they don't have DMA channels.

If you want to see your DMA usage, head back to the Device Manager and change the view to *Resources by type*. Click on *Direct memory access* (*DMA*) and you'll see something like Figure 8.25. This system has only two DMA channels: one for the floppy drive and one for the connection to the CPU.

One interesting note to DMA is that neither PCI nor PCIe supports DMA, so you'll never find a DMA device that snaps into these expansion buses. A hard drive, floppy drive, or any other device that still wants to use DMA must do so through

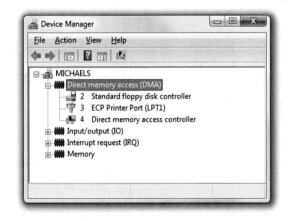

• **Figure 8.25**   DMA settings in the Device Manager

onboard connections. Sure, you can find hard drive and floppy drive cards, but they're not using DMA.

Memory Addresses

Some expansion cards need memory addresses, just like the system RAM. There are two reasons a card may need memory addresses. First, a card may have onboard RAM that the CPU needs to address. Second, a few cards come with an onboard ROM, the so-called adapter or option ROM you read about in Chapter 5, "Microprocessors." In either of these situations, the RAM or ROM must steal memory addresses away from the main system RAM to enable the CPU to access the RAM or ROM. This process is called **memory addressing**. You can see memory addresses assigned to expansion cards by clicking on Memory in the Device Manager when viewing resources by type.

Try This

What's in Your Machine?

If you haven't already, open up the Device Manager and check out the resources assigned to your devices. Does anything use an IRQ? How many devices use the same IRQ? What about memory addresses? Where are all those devices located?

The key fact for techs is that, just like I/O addresses, IRQs, and DMA channels, memory addressing is fully automatic and no longer an issue.

■ Installing Expansion Cards

Installing an expansion card successfully—another one of those bread-and-butter tasks for the PC tech—requires at least four steps. First, you need to know that the card works with your system and your operating system. Second, you have to insert the card in an expansion slot properly and without damaging that card or the motherboard. Third, you need to provide drivers for the operating system—that's *proper* drivers for the *specific* OS. Fourth, you should always verify that the card functions properly before you walk away from the PC.

Step 1: Knowledge

Learn about the device you plan to install—preferably before you purchase it! Does the device work with your system and operating system? Does it have drivers for your operating system? If you use Windows, the answer to these questions is almost always "yes." If you use an old operating system such as Windows 98 or a less common operating system such as Linux, these questions become critical. A lot of older, pre-XP hardware simply won't work with Windows XP or Vista at all. Check the device's documentation and check the device manufacturer's Web site to verify that you have the correct drivers. While you're checking, make sure you have the latest version of the driver; most devices get driver updates more often than the weather changes in Texas.

For Windows systems, your best resource for this knowledge is the Windows Logo'd Products List. This used to be called the Hardware

Tech Tip

Installation Order

Some manufacturers insist on a different order for device installation than the traditional one listed here. The most common variation requires you to install the drivers and support software for an expansion card before you insert the card. Failure to follow the manufacturer's directions with such a card can lead to hours of frustration while you uninstall the card and reinstall the drivers, sometimes manually removing some drivers and software from the system. The bottom line? Read the instructions that come with a particular card! I'll provide more specific examples of problem devices in later chapters.

Compatibility List (HCL), and you'll still hear lots of people refer to it as such. You can check out the Web site (http://winqual.microsoft.com/hcl/Default.aspx) to see if your product is listed, but most people just look on the box of the device in question (Figure 8.26)—all Windows-certified devices proudly display that they work with Windows.

Microsoft keeps the Logo'd Product List available for all supported operating systems, so you'll see Windows 7, Windows Vista, and most likely Windows XP (depending on when you're reading this book). Windows 2000 is already gone.

Step 2: Physical Installation

To install an expansion card successfully, you need to take steps to avoid damaging the card, the motherboard, or both. This means knowing how to handle a card and avoiding electrostatic discharge (ESD) or any other electrical issue. You also need to place the card firmly and completely into an available expansion slot.

Optimally, a card should always be in one of two places: in a computer or in an anti-static bag. When inserting or removing a card, be careful to hold the card only by its edges. Do not hold the card by the slot connectors or touch any components on the board (Figure 8.27).

Use an anti-static wrist strap if possible, properly attached to the PC, as noted in Chapter 2, "Operational Procedures." If you don't have a wrist strap, you can use the tech way of avoiding ESD by touching the power supply after you remove the expansion card from its anti-static bag. This puts you, the card, and the PC at the same electrical potential and thus minimizes the risk of ESD.

Modern systems have a trickle of voltage on the motherboard at all times when the computer is plugged into a power outlet. Chapter 10, "Power Supplies," covers power for the PC and how to deal with it in detail, but here's the short version: *Always unplug the PC before inserting an expansion card!* Failure to do so can destroy the card, the motherboard, or both. It's not worth the risk.

Never insert or remove a card at an extreme angle. This may damage the card. A slight angle is acceptable and even necessary when removing a card. Always screw the card to the case with a connection screw. This keeps the card from slipping out and potentially shorting against other cards. Also, many cards use the screw connection to ground the card to the case (Figure 8.28).

Many technicians have been told to clean the slot connectors if a particular card is not working. This is almost never necessary after a card is installed, and if done improperly, can cause damage. You should clean slot connectors only if you have a card that's been on the shelf for a while and the contacts are obviously dull.

• **Figure 8.26**   Works with Windows!

The Windows Vista Compatibility Center (www.microsoft.com/windows/compatibility/) is also a great resource to check whether a particular software program works with Windows Vista.

• **Figure 8.27**   Where to handle a card

• **Figure 8.28**   Always screw down all cards.

Never use a pencil eraser for this purpose. Pencil erasers can leave behind bits of residue that wedge between the card and slot, preventing contact and causing the card to fail. Grab a can of contact cleaning solution and use it instead. Contact cleaning solution is designed exactly for this purpose, cleans contacts nicely, and doesn't leave any residue. You can find contact cleaning solution at any electronics store.

A fully inserted expansion card sits flush against the back of the PC case—assuming the motherboard is mounted properly, of course—with no gap between the mounting bracket on the card and the screw hole on the case. If the card is properly seated, no contacts are exposed above the slot. Figure 8.29 shows a properly seated (meaning fitted snugly in the slot) expansion card.

Step 3: Device Drivers

You know from Chapter 7, "BIOS and CMOS," that all devices, whether built into the motherboard or added along the way, require BIOS. For almost all expansion cards, that BIOS comes in the form of **device drivers**—software support programs—loaded from a CD-ROM disc provided by the card manufacturer.

Installing device drivers is fairly straightforward. You should use the correct drivers—kind of obvious, but you'd be surprised how many techs mess this up—and, if you're upgrading, you might have to unload current drivers before loading new drivers. Finally, if you have a problem, you may need to uninstall the drivers you just loaded or, with Windows XP or Vista, roll back to earlier, more stable drivers.

 Cross Check

BIOS

Although most devices bring their own BIOS in the form of device drivers, that's not always the case, as you know from Chapter 7, "BIOS and CMOS." So turn there now and see if you can answer these questions. Aside from device drivers, how can a device bring BIOS to a system so the device will work properly? What about devices that are common and necessary, such as the keyboard? How do they bring their own BIOS to a system? Or do they?

● **Figure 8.29**   Properly seated expansion card; note the tight fit between case and mounting bracket and the evenness of the card in the slot.

Getting the Correct Drivers

To be sure you have the best possible driver you can get for your device, you should always check the manufacturer's Web site. The drivers that come with a device may work well, but odds are good that you'll find a newer and better driver on the Web site. How do you know that the drivers on the Web site are newer? First, take the easy route: look on the CD. Often the version is printed right on the CD itself. If it's not printed there, you're going to have to load the CD in your CD-ROM drive and poke around. Many driver discs have an AutoRun screen that advertises the version. If nothing is on the pop-up screen, look for a Readme file (Figure 8.30).

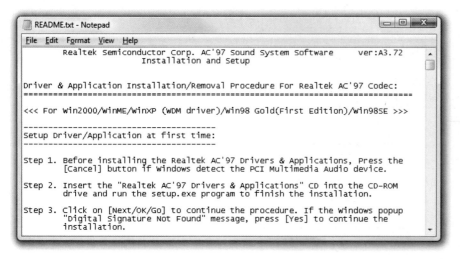

Driver or Device?

In almost all cases, you should install the device driver after you install the device. Without the device installed, the driver installation will not see the device and will give an error screen. The only exception to this rule is USB and FireWire devices—with these you should always install the driver first.

Removing the Old Drivers

Some cards—and this is especially true with video cards—require you to remove old drivers of the same type before you install the new device. To do this, you must first locate the driver in the Device Manager. Right-click the device driver you want to uninstall and select Uninstall (Figure 8.31). Many devices, especially ones that come with a lot of applications, will have an uninstall option in the Add/Remove Programs (Windows 2000), Add or Remove Programs (Windows XP), or Programs and Features (Windows Vista) applet in the Control Panel (Figure 8.32).

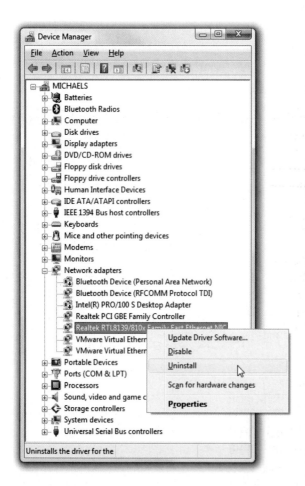

Figure 8.31   Uninstalling a device

Unsigned Drivers

Microsoft wants your computer to work, truly, and the company provides an excellent and rigorous testing program for hardware manufacturers called the **Microsoft Windows Logo Program**. Developers initially use software to test their devices and, when they're ready, submit the device to the **Windows Hardware Quality Labs (WHQL)** for further testing. Hardware and drivers that survive the WHQL and other processes get to wear the *Designed for Windows* logo. The drivers get a digital signature that says Microsoft tested them and found all was well.

Not all driver makers go through the rather involved process of the WHQL and other steps in the Windows Logo Program, so their software does not get a digital signature from Microsoft. When Windows runs into such a driver, it brings up a scary-looking screen (Figure 8.33) that says you're about to install an **unsigned driver**.

The fact that a company refuses to use the Windows Logo Program doesn't mean its drivers are bad—it simply means they haven't gone through Microsoft's exhaustive quality-assurance certification procedure. If I run into this, I usually check the driver's version to make sure I'm not installing

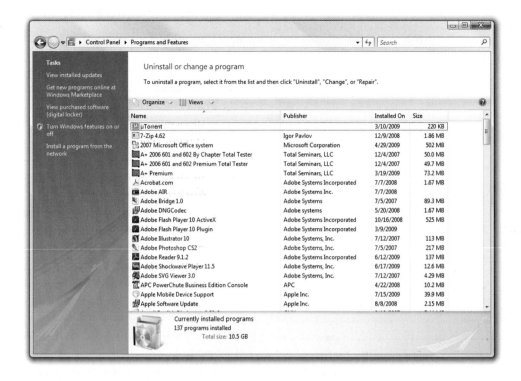

● **Figure 8.32**   The Change/Remove option in Programs and Features

something outdated, and then I just take my chances and install it. (I've yet to encounter a problem with an unsigned driver that I haven't also seen with Designed for Windows drivers.)

With Windows Vista 64-bit, Microsoft tightened the rules to try to provide the most stable platform possible. You simply cannot install unsigned drivers. Microsoft must approve each one.

Installing the New Driver

You have two ways to install a new driver: by using the installation CD directly or by using the Add Hardware Wizard in the Control Panel. Most experienced techs prefer to run from the installation CD. Most devices come with extra programs. My motherboard comes with a number of handy applications for monitoring temperature and overclocking. The Add Hardware Wizard does not install anything but the drivers. Granted, some techs find this a blessing because they don't want all of the extra junk that sometimes comes with a device, but most installation discs give clear options so you can pick and choose what you want to install (Figure 8.34).

The other reason to use installation CDs instead of the Add Hardware Wizard stems from the fact that many expansion cards are actually many devices in one, and each device needs its own drivers. Some sound cards come with joystick ports, for example, and some video cards have built-in TV tuners. The Add Hardware Wizard will install all of the devices, but the installation CD brings them to your attention. Go for the CD program first

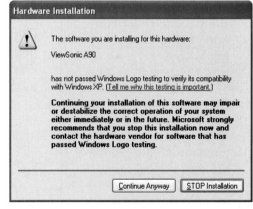

● **Figure 8.33**   Unsigned driver warning

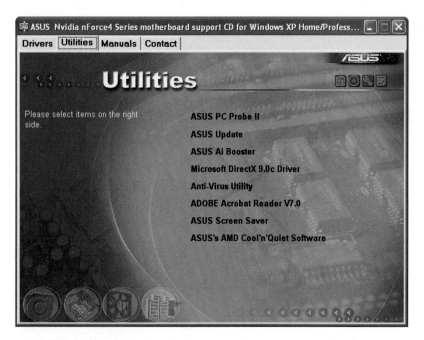

● **Figure 8.34** Installation menu

and save the Add Hardware Wizard for problems, as you'll see in the next section.

Driver Rollback

Windows XP and Windows Vista offer the nifty feature of rolling back to previous drivers after an installation or driver upgrade. If you decide to live on the edge and install beta drivers for your video card, for example, and your system becomes frightfully unstable, you can back up to the drivers that worked before. (Not that I've ever had to use that feature, of course.) To access the rollback feature, simply open the Device Manager and access the properties for the device you want to adjust. On the Driver tab (Figure 8.35), you'll find the Roll Back Driver button.

Step 4: Verify

As a last step in the installation process, inspect the results of the installation and verify that the device works properly. Immediately after installing, you should open the Device Manager and verify that Windows sees the device (Figure 8.36). Assuming that the Device Manager shows the device working properly, your next check is to put the device to work by making it do whatever it is supposed to do. If you installed a printer, print something; if you installed a scanner, scan something. If it works, you're finished!

Tech Tip

Permissions

To install drivers in a Windows computer, you need to have the proper permission. I'm not talking about asking somebody if you're allowed to install the device. Per-missions are granted in Windows to enable people to do certain things, such as add a printer to a computer or install software, or to stop people from being able to do such tasks. Specifically, you need administrative *permissions to install drivers. Chapter 16, "Securing Windows Resources," goes into a lot of detail about per-missions, so no need to worry about them here.*

● **Figure 8.35** Driver rollback feature

Tech Tip

Beta Drivers

Many PC enthusiasts try to squeeze every bit of performance out of their PC components, much as auto enthusiasts tinker with engine tunings to get a little extra horsepower out of their engines. Expansion card manufacturers love enthusiasts, who often act as free testers for their unpolished drivers, known as beta drivers. *Beta drivers are fine for the most part, but they can sometimes cause amazing system instability—never a good thing! If you use beta drivers, make sure you know how to uninstall or roll back to previous drivers.*

• **Figure 8.36**   Device Manager shows the device working properly.

Practical Application

■ Troubleshooting Expansion Cards

A properly installed expansion card rarely makes trouble; it's the botched installations that produce headaches. Chances are high that you'll have to troubleshoot an expansion card installation at some point, usually from an installation you botched personally.

The first sign of an improperly installed card usually shows up the moment you first try to get that card to do whatever it's supposed to do and it doesn't do it. When this happens, your primary troubleshooting process is a reinstallation—after checking in with the Device Manager.

Other chapters in this book cover specific hardware troubleshooting: sound cards in Chapter 20, "Multimedia," for example, and video cards in Chapter 19, "Video." Use this section to help you decide what to look for and how to deal with the problem.

The Device Manager provides the first diagnostic and troubleshooting tool in Windows. After you install a new device, the Device Manager gives you many clues if something has gone wrong.

Occasionally, the Device Manager may not even show the new device. If that happens, verify that you inserted the device properly and, if needed, that the device has power. Run the Add/Remove Hardware Wizard and see if Windows recognizes the device. If the Device Manager doesn't recognize the device at this point, you have one of two problems: either the device is physically damaged and you must replace it, or the device is an onboard device, not a card, and is turned off in CMOS.

The Device Manager rarely completely fails to see a device. More commonly, device problems manifest themselves in the Device Manager via error icons—a black "!" or a red "X" or a blue "i."

- A black "!" on a yellow circle indicates that a device is missing (Figure 8.37), that Windows does not recognize a device, or that there's a device driver problem. A device may still work even while producing this error.

- A red "X" indicates a disabled device. This usually points to a device that's been manually turned off, or a damaged device. A device producing this error will not work.

- A blue "i" on a white field indicates a device on which someone has configured the system resources manually. This only occurs on non-ACPI systems. This symbol merely provides information and does not indicate an error with the device.

• **Figure 8.37** An "!" in the Device Manager, indicating a problem with the selected device

The "!" symbol is the most common error symbol and usually the easiest to fix. First, double-check the device's connections. Second, try reinstalling the driver with the Update Driver button. To get to the Update Driver button, right-click the desired device in the Device Manager and select Properties. In the Properties dialog box, select the Driver tab. On the Driver tab, click the Update Driver button to open the updating wizard (Figure 8.38).

A red "X" error strikes fear into most technicians. If you get one, first check that the device isn't disabled. Right-click on the device and select Enable. If that doesn't work (it often does not), try rolling back the driver (if you updated the driver) or uninstalling (if it's a new install). Shut the system down and make triple-sure you have the card physically installed. Then redo the entire driver installation procedure, making sure you have the most current driver for that device. If none of these procedures works, return the card—it's almost certainly bad.

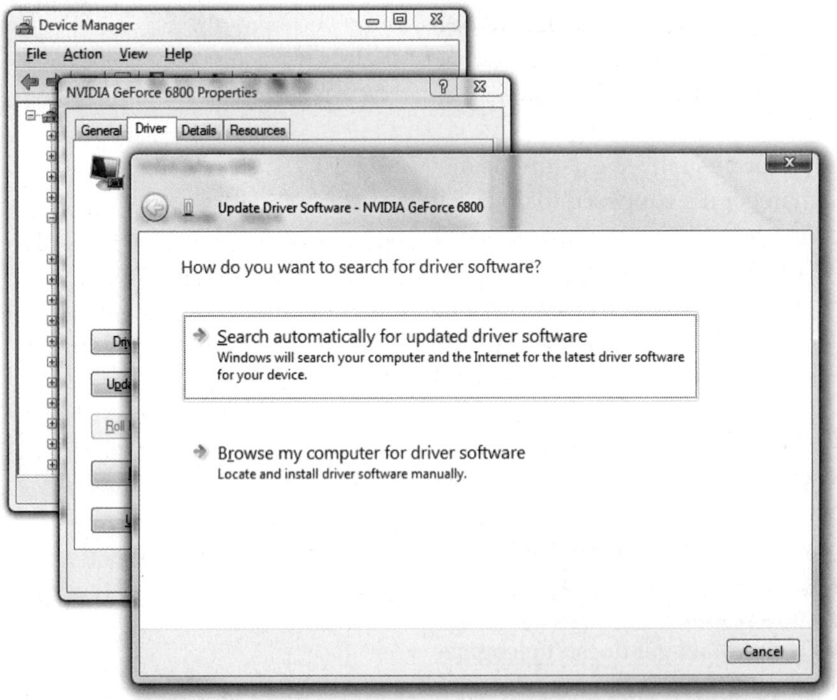

As you look at the errors in the Device Manager, you'll notice error codes for the device that does not work properly. Windows has about 20 error codes, but the fixes still boil down to the same methods just shown. If you really want to frustrate yourself, try the Troubleshooter. It starts most fixes the same way: by reinstalling the device driver.

• **Figure 8.38** Updating the driver

Mike Meyers' CompTIA A+ Guide to Managing and Troubleshooting PCs

Chapter 8 Review

■ Chapter Summary

After reading this chapter and completing the exercises, you should understand the following about the expansion bus.

Identify the structure and function of the expansion bus

■ IBM developed the first expansion bus, the PC bus (or XT bus), as a means for users to install after-market hardware. The standardized expansion bus design addressed three main hurdles faced by expansion card manufacturers: physically connecting expansion cards to the motherboard, facilitating communication between the expansion card and the rest of the system, and allowing the user to control the expansion card to take advantage of its features.

■ Every device in the computer connects to the external data bus and the address bus. Expansion slots enable expansion cards to connect to these same buses. Depending on the system, the expansion slots may connect to the Southbridge or the Northbridge. Many systems have more than one type of expansion bus, with slots connecting to both the Southbridge and the Northbridge. It is the chipset that extends the address bus and data bus to the expansion slots.

■ Expansion buses run at a standardized speed, depending on the type of expansion bus. This speed, which is much slower than the frontside bus, is dictated by the expansion bus crystal. The chipset uses wait states and buffers to compensate for the difference in speed between the expansion and frontside buses.

■ The original IBM PCs ran an 8088 CPU with an 8-bit external data bus at a speed of 4.77 MHz, which was actually slower than the 7-MHz expansion bus. With the introduction of the Intel 286 CPU and its 16-bit external data bus, IBM developed what was called the AT bus and is now known as the ISA bus. The ISA expansion bus was 16 bits and ran at about 7 MHz. ISA cards required tedious manual configuration.

■ The limitations of the ISA bus led to the development of other buses, including MCA, EISA, VL-Bus, and the PCI bus.

Describe the modern expansion bus

■ PCI improved upon ISA in several ways. It was 32 bits, ran at 33 MHz, and was self-configuring (no more manual configuration of expansion card jumpers). Additionally, it could coexist with other expansion buses.

■ As operating systems such as Windows became more graphically intense, the demand for sending video data quickly was too much for the ISA or standard PCI bus. The AGP slot is a special PCI slot for video cards, with a direct connection to the Northbridge. You can easily find the AGP slot on a motherboard: a lone slot that's brown in color.

■ Enhancements to the PCI bus paved the way for a few modern variations. PCI-X is 64 bits wide, backward compatible with PCI, and available in a variety of speeds up to 533 MHz. Mini-PCI is designed for laptops with an emphasis on low power consumption and a small, flat physical design. Finally, PCIe, with its point-to-point serial connection, touts speeds as high as 16 Gbps.

Explain classic system resources

■ Devices in a computer system communicate via the four system resources: I/O addresses, IRQs, DMAs, and memory addresses. Not all devices use all four system resources. Earlier systems required manual configuration of each device's system resources through jumpers, DIP switches, dials, or software. Modern systems feature plug and play, which automatically configures system resources for each device. The system resources assigned to each device can be seen in the Device Manager.

■ I/O addresses enable the CPU to send commands to devices. These addresses are configured automatically, and no two devices may share an I/O address. A single device may be assigned a range of I/O addresses; the first address in the range is called the I/O base address.

- IRQs enable devices to signal the CPU that they need attention. Before reaching the CPU, all interrupts pass through the I/O advanced programmable interrupt controller, which manages all of the incoming interrupts and forwards them to the CPU. In older systems, scarce IRQs and manual resource allocation meant that IRQ conflicts (and subsequent system lockups) were common. This is not a problem in modern systems, which have more IRQs and handle them automatically to avoid such conflicts.

- COM and LPT ports are simply presets of an IRQ–I/O address combination developed to make configuration of common devices easier. COM ports are for serial connections and LPT ports are for parallel connections.

- DMA enables devices to communicate with RAM without involving the CPU. The DMA controller sits between the devices and RAM and handles the DMA requests much as IRQ requests are handled. Newer systems use a type of DMA called bus mastering, which works without the need of a DMA controller.

- Memory addresses are used by devices that have either their own RAM (such as video cards) or their own ROM (such as the option ROM discussed in Chapter 7, "BIOS and CMOS"). When devices have their own RAM or ROM, they get memory addresses just like system RAM so the CPU can access their onboard memory.

Install expansion cards properly

- There are four basic steps to install an expansion card: determine that the card is compatible with your system, physically install the card, install the drivers, and verify that the card works.

- Determine that the card is compatible with your system. Many older cards do not work with Windows XP or Windows Vista, and not every card works with older versions of Windows or other operating systems (such as Linux or Macintosh). Read the box before you buy, consult the device manufacturer's Web site, and, if Windows is your operating system, consult the Windows Logo'd Products List (formerly the Hardware Compatibility List).

- Physically install the card without damaging it or other system components. Keep the card in its anti-static bag until you are ready to install it.

Power off and unplug the computer. Wear an anti-static wrist strap or use an alternative method of dissipating static electricity.

- Install the correct drivers, which should come on a CD with the device. If you don't have the CD, you may be able to download the drivers from the manufacturer's Web site.

- Some manufacturers use the Microsoft Windows Logo Program to verify and digitally sign their drivers. This means their drivers have been verified by Microsoft to work properly. Other manufacturers skip the certification process and produce unsigned drivers that in most cases work just fine.

- Sometimes driver updates go bad and you find that the new driver just doesn't work. With Windows XP and later, you can roll back to the previous version driver by double-clicking the device in the Device Manager, clicking the Driver tab, and then clicking the Roll Back Driver button.

- Always verify that your newly installed device works. Immediately after installation, open the Device Manager and verify that no error icons are displayed. Next, check the physical device. Finally, test the device's functionality.

Troubleshoot expansion card problems

- If you find a device is not working as expected, your first step is to check the Device Manager. If the device is not listed in the Device Manager, verify that you inserted it correctly and it has power. You can also try the Add Hardware Wizard to see if Windows recognizes the device.

- A good tech is familiar with the Device Manager's trouble icons. A black "!" on a yellow circle indicates that the device is missing, the device is not recognized, or there is a problem with the driver. A device may work even when displaying this icon. A red "X" indicates a disabled device and usually means the device has been turned off or is damaged. A device with a red "X" will not work. A blue "i" on a white circle indicates that system resources have been configured manually. This icon is informational and does not imply any error.

- If you encounter the "!" icon, verify the device's connections. Next, try to reinstall the driver by right-clicking the device in the Device Manager and selecting Properties. Click the Driver tab and then click the Update Driver button.

If a device displays the red "X" icon, right-click the device in the Device Manager and select Enable. If that doesn't work, try rolling back or uninstalling the driver. Shut down the system, verify the device's connections, and repeat the installation procedure. If the device still doesn't work, it is likely the device is either bad or not compatible with your operating system. Return the card to the place of purchase.

■ Key Terms

accelerated graphics port (AGP) *(242)*

bus mastering *(251)*

COM ports *(249)*

device driver *(254)*

direct memory access (DMA) *(250)*

DMA controller *(251)*

expansion bus *(236)*

expansion bus crystal *(238)*

expansion slots *(236)*

hexadecimal *(245)*

I/O address *(244)*

I/O addressing *(244)*

I/O advanced programmable interrupt controller (IOAPIC) *(247)*

I/O base address *(246)*

Industry Standard Architecture (ISA) *(240)*

interrupt request (IRQ) *(247)*

interruption *(246)*

LPT ports *(249)*

memory addressing *(252)*

Microsoft Windows Logo Program *(256)*

Mini-PCI *(242)*

PC bus *(239)*

PCI Express (PCIe) *(242)*

PCI Extended (PCI-X) *(242)*

peripheral component interconnect (PCI) *(241)*

system resources *(244)*

unsigned driver *(256)*

Windows Hardware Quality Labs (WHQL) *(256)*

XT bus *(239)*

■ Key Term Quiz

Use the Key Terms list to complete the sentences that follow. Not all terms will be used.

1. The _____ bus was designed for laptop computers.

2. A shorthand system for binary numbers is called _____.

3. The _____ is usually a brown slot used only by the video card.

4. The CPU uses the _____, a unique pattern of ones and zeros on the address bus, to communicate with a device.

5. The most common bus on today's computers, whether PC or Apple Macintosh, is the flexible _____.

6. A(n) _____ is a parallel port that has been assigned a particular IRQ and I/O address, traditionally for a printer.

7. A device uses its _____, controlled by an 8259 chip, to get the attention of the CPU.

8. Devices that can access RAM directly without passing through a DMA controller are called _____ devices.

9. Device drivers for devices manufactured by companies not participating in the Windows Certification program are reported as _____.

10. The newest and fastest expansion bus in use today, with speeds up to 16 Gbps, is _____.

■ Multiple-Choice Quiz

1. Which of the following enables you to add more devices to a computer? (Select the best answer.)

   A. Device bus

   B. Expansion bus

   C. Peripheral bus

   D. Yellow bus

2. John argues that expansion slot wires always connect to the Southbridge. Is he correct?

   A. Yes, expansion slots always connect to the Southbridge.

   B. No, expansion slots always connect to the Northbridge.

   C. No, expansion slots connect to both the Northbridge and the Southbridge.

   D. No, expansion slots connect to the Northbridge in some systems and the Southbridge in others.

3. Which of the following devices sets the speed for expansion slots?

   A. Component crystal

   B. Expansion bus crystal

   C. Expansion slot crystal

   D. Peripheral crystal

4. You could find 16-bit ISA slots on which of these buses?

   A. AT bus

   B. BT bus

   C. PC bus

   D. XT bus

5. What advantages did PCI have over ISA? (Select two.)

   A. Faster (33 MHz versus 7 MHz)

   B. Longer (2 m versus 1 m)

   C. Shorter (1 m versus 2 m)

   D. Wider (32 bit versus 16 bit)

6. Which of the following slots offer 64-bit-wide data transfers? (Select the two most common.)

   A. AGP

   B. PCI

   C. PCIe

   D. PCI-X

7. What's the minimum number of I/O addresses a device will have?

   A. One

   B. Two

   C. Four

   D. Eight

8. Which of the following slots features serial data transfers?

   A. AGP

   B. PCI

   C. PCIe

   D. PCI-X

9. How many IRQs does the typical device use?

   A. One

   B. Two

   C. Four

   D. Eight

10. Which of the following is the testing part of the Windows Logo Program?

    A. ACL

    B. HCL

    C. WHQL

    D. WKRP

11. What should you do *before* installing an expansion card? (Select two.)

    A. Attach an anti-static wrist strap

    B. Install the drivers

    C. Plug the PC into a grounded outlet

    D. Unplug the PC

12. In a Windows XP workstation, Steven updated the drivers for a NIC that worked, but he thought it could be faster. Almost immediately, he discovered that the new drivers not only didn't speed up the NIC but they made it start dropping data! What his best option?

    A. Download the driver pack from Microsoft

    B. Reinstall the networking software

    C. Remove the NIC

    D. Use the driver rollback feature to return to the previous drivers

13. What are the standard system resource assignments for COM1?

    A. I/O address 03F8 and IRQ3

    B. I/O address 03F8 and IRQ4

    C. I/O address 02F8 and IRQ3

    D. I/O address 02F8 and IRQ4

14. Which of these devices is likely to still use DMA?

    A. USB flash drive

    B. Floppy drive

    C. Hard drive

    D. CD-ROM drive

15. What does a red "X" next to a device in the Device Manager indicate?

    A. A compatible driver has been installed that may not provide all of the functions for the device.

    B. The device is missing or Windows cannot recognize it.

    C. The system resources have been assigned manually.

    D. The device has been disabled because it is damaged or has a system resource conflict.

■ Essay Quiz

1. Although today's computers use plug and play to assign system resources automatically, CompTIA still expects you to know about system resources. Why is this knowledge important? Briefly explain two scenarios where your knowledge of system resources may help solve computer problems.

2. Your friend Merrill just called. He bought a new sound card for his computer and tried to install it. It's not working. What should he do now? Using the methodology for card installation that you learned in this chapter, explain the steps he should follow to determine whether he installed the card incorrectly or the card itself is faulty.

3. The Device Manager is the main tool for determining if devices have been installed and configured correctly. Write a quick user manual to help a new technician determine how to use the Device Manager for the Windows operating system you use. Include how to access the Device Manager and which buttons/tabs to use to see if devices are installed correctly. Also include how to use the Device Manager to update and uninstall drivers.

Lab Projects

• Lab Project 8.1

Open your computer case and determine the kind of expansion slots available on your motherboard. How many of each kind are available? What cards are installed in the slots? Now examine the back and front of the computer case to see what ports are available. What devices do you have plugged into the ports?

• Lab Project 8.2

As technologies improve, manufacturers are continually upgrading their products. Use the Internet to find three prebuilt computer systems, each from a different manufacturer. (You may want to try www.dell.com, www.hp.com, www.gateway.com, www.alienware.com, or www.voodoopc.com to name a few.) Do your three systems offer the same expansion buses? Do any support ISA? PCI? PCI-X? PCIe? If one supports PCIe, what version or speeds does it support? Do any systems support AGP?

Motherboards

chapter
9

"Did anybody hear that?"

—Michael "Motherboard" Pampin,
Rainbow Six: Vegas

In this chapter, you will learn how to

■ **Explain how motherboards work**

■ **Identify the types of motherboards**

■ **Explain chipset varieties**

■ **Upgrade and install motherboards**

■ **Troubleshoot motherboard problems**

The **motherboard** provides the foundation for the personal computer. Every piece of hardware, from the CPU to the lowliest expansion card, directly or indirectly plugs into the motherboard. The motherboard contains the wires—called **traces**—that make up the buses of the system. It holds the vast majority of the ports used by the peripherals, and it distributes the power from the power supply (Figure 9.1). Without the motherboard, you literally have no PC.

● **Figure 9.1** Traces visible beneath the CPU socket on a motherboard

Historical/Conceptual

■ How Motherboards Work

Three variable and interrelated characteristics define modern mother-boards: form factor, chipset, and components. The **form factor** determines the physical size of the motherboard as well as the general location of components and ports. The **chipset** defines the type of processor and RAM the motherboard requires and determines to a degree the built-in devices the motherboard supports, including the expansion slots. Finally, the built-in components determine the core functionality of the system.

Any good tech should be able to make a recommendation to a client about a particular motherboard simply by perusing the specs. Because the motherboard determines function, expansion, and stability for the whole PC, it's essential that you know your motherboards!

Form Factors

Form factors are industry-standardized shapes and layouts that enable motherboards to work with cases and power supplies. A single form factor applies to all three components. All motherboards come in a basic rectangular or square shape but vary in overall size and in the layout of built-in

Tech Tip

Layers of the PCB

Modern motherboards are layered **printed circuit boards (PCBs)**, *copper etched onto a nonconductive material and then coated with some sort of epoxy for strength. The layers mask some of their complexity. You can see some of the traces on the board, but every motherboard is two or more layers thick. The layers contain a veritable highway of wires, carrying data and commands back and forth between CPU, Northbridge, RAM, and peripherals. The layered structure enables multiple wires to send data without their signals interfering with each other. The layered approach allows the manufacturer to add complexity and additional components to the board without extending the overall length and width of the board. Shorter traces also allow signals to travel faster than they would if the wires were longer, as would be necessary if motherboards did not use layers. The multiple layers also add strength to the board itself, so it doesn't bend easily.*

• **Figure 9.2**   Typical motherboard

components (Figure 9.2). You need to install a motherboard in a case designed to fit it, so the ports and slot openings on the back fit correctly.

The power supply and the motherboard need matching connectors, and different form factors define different connections. Given that the term "form factor" applies to the case, motherboard, and power supply—the three parts of the PC most responsible for moving air around inside the PC—the form factor also defines how the air moves around in the case.

To perform motherboard upgrades and provide knowledgeable recommendations to clients, techs need to know their form factors. The PC industry has adopted—and dropped—a number of form factors over the years with such names as AT, ATX, and BTX. Let's start with the granddaddy of all PC form factors, AT.

AT Form Factor

The **AT** form factor (Figure 9.3), invented by IBM in the early 1980s, was the predominant form factor for motherboards through the mid-1990s. AT is now obsolete.

The AT motherboard had a few size variations (see Figure 9.4), ranging from large to very large. The original AT motherboard was huge, around 12 inches wide by 13 inches deep. PC technology was new and needed lots of space for the various chips necessary to run the components of the PC.

The single greatest problem with AT motherboards was the lack of external ports. When PCs were first invented, the only devices plugged into the average PC were a monitor and a keyboard. That's what the AT was designed to handle—the only dedicated connector on an AT motherboard was the keyboard port (Figure 9.5).

> All AT motherboards had a split power socket called **P8/P9**. You can see the white P8/P9 socket near the keyboard port in Figures 9.3 and 9.4.

• **Figure 9.3**   AT-style motherboard

• **Figure 9.5**   Keyboard connector on the back of an AT motherboard

• **Figure 9.4**   AT motherboard (bottom) and Baby AT motherboard (top)

Over the years, the number of devices plugged into the back of the PC has grown tremendously. Your average PC today has a keyboard, a mouse, a printer, some speakers, a monitor, and—if your system's like mine—four to six USB devices connected to it at any given time. These added components created a demand for a new type of form factor, one with more dedicated connectors for more devices. Many attempts were made to create a new standard form factor. Invariably, these new form factors integrated dedicated connectors for at least the mouse and printer, and many even added connectors for video, sound, and phone lines.

One variation from the AT form factor that enjoyed a degree of success was the **slimline** form factor. The first slimline form factor was known as **LPX** (defined in some sources as *low profile extended,* although there's some disagreement). It was replaced by the **NLX** form factor. (NLX apparently stands for nothing, by the way. It's just a cool grouping of letters.) The LPX and NLX form factors met the demands of the slimline market by providing a central riser slot to enable the insertion of a special **riser card** (Figure 9.6) or, as it's sometimes called, a *daughterboard.* Expansion cards then fit into the riser card horizontally. Combining built-in connections with a riser card enabled manufacturers to produce PCs shorter than 4 inches.

• **Figure 9.6**   Riser card on an older motherboard

The main problem with form factors such as LPX and NLX was their inflexibility. Certainly, no problem occurred with dedicated connections for such devices as mice or printers, but the new form factors also added connectors for such devices as video and sound—devices that were prone to obsolescence, making the motherboard out of date the moment a new type of video or sound card came into popularity.

Essentials

ATX Form Factor

There continued to be a tremendous demand for a new form factor: a form factor that had more standard connectors and also was flexible enough for possible changes in technology. This demand led to the creation of the ATX form factor in 1995 (Figure 9.7). ATX got off to a slow start, but by around 1998, ATX overtook AT to become the most common form factor used today.

ATX is distinct from AT in the lack of an AT keyboard port, replaced with a rear panel that has all necessary ports built in. Note the mini-DIN (PS/2) keyboard and mouse ports at the left of Figure 9.8, standard features on almost all ATX boards. You recall those from Chapter 3, "The Visible PC," right?

The ATX form factor includes many improvements over AT. The position of the power supply allows better air movement. The CPU and RAM are placed to provide easier access, and the rearrangement of components prevents long expansion cards from colliding with the CPU or Northbridge. Other improvements, such as placing the RAM closer to the Northbridge and CPU than on AT boards, offer users enhanced performance as well. The shorter the wires, the easier to shield them and make them capable of

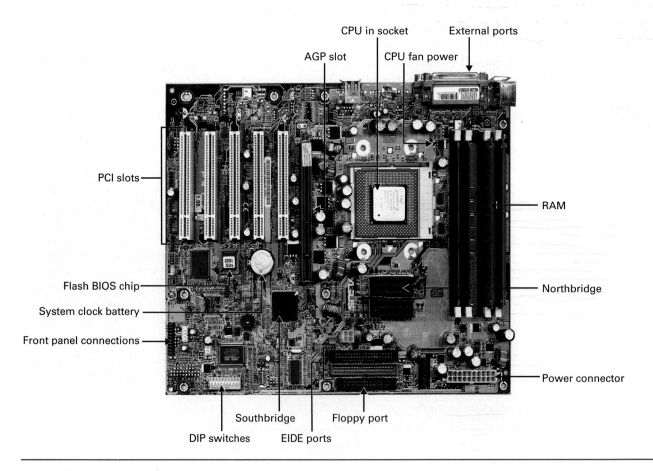

• **Figure 9.7**   Early ATX motherboard

Mike Meyers' CompTIA A+ Guide to Managing and Troubleshooting PCs

• **Figure 9.8** ATX ports

handling double or quadruple the clock speed of the motherboard. Figure 9.9 shows AT and ATX motherboards—note the radical differences in placement of internal connections.

The success of ATX has spawned two form factor subtypes for specialty uses. The **microATX** motherboard (Figure 9.10) floats in at a svelte 9.6 by 9.6 inches or about 30 percent smaller than standard ATX, yet uses the standard ATX connections. A microATX motherboard fits into a standard ATX case or in the much smaller microATX cases. Note that not all microATX motherboards have the same physical size. You'll sometimes see microATX motherboards referred to with the Greek symbol for micro, as in µATX.

In 1999, Intel created a variant of the microATX called the FlexATX. **FlexATX** motherboards have maximum dimensions of just 9 by 7.5 inches, which makes them the smallest motherboards in the ATX standard. Although FlexATX motherboards can use a standard ATX power supply, most

• **Figure 9.9** AT (left) and ATX (right) motherboards for quick visual comparison

Tech Tip

Soft Power

*ATX motherboards use a feature called **soft power**. This means they can use software to turn the PC on and off. The physical manifestation of soft power is the power switch. Instead of the thick power cord used in AT systems, an ATX power switch is little more than a pair of small wires leading to the motherboard. We delve into this in more detail in Chapter 10, "Power Supplies."*

• **Figure 9.10** A microATX motherboard

Many techs and Web sites use the term *mini-ATX* to refer to motherboards smaller than a full ATX board. This is technically incorrect. The specifications for these small boards use only the terms *microATX* and *FlexATX*.

Cross Check

High-Speed CPUs and RAM

Modern CPUs such as the Intel Core i7 and the AMD Phenom II incorporate the memory controller on the processor rather than locating it on the Northbridge. This move has facilitated even further increases in the speed at which the processor can fetch data from RAM. Refer to Chapters 5, "Microprocessors," and 6, "RAM," and see if you can answer these questions.

1. What different clock frequencies are supported by DDR2 and DDR3 types of memory?

2. What processors support DDR3 memory?

FlexATX systems use a special FlexATX-only power supply. This diminutive power supply fits into tight FlexATX cases.

Keep in mind that each main type of form factor requires its own case. AT motherboards go into AT cases, NLX motherboards go into NLX cases, and ATX motherboards go into ATX cases. You cannot replace one form factor with another without purchasing a new case (Figure 9.11). The exception to this rule is that larger form factor ATX cases can handle any smaller-sized form factor motherboards.

BTX Form Factor

Even though ATX addressed ventilation, faster CPUs and powerful graphics cards create phenomenal amounts of heat, motivating the PC industry to create the "coolest" new form factor used today—the **Balanced Technology eXtended (BTX)** form factor (Figure 9.12). BTX defines three subtypes: standard BTX, **microBTX**, and **picoBTX**, designed to replace ATX, microATX, and FlexATX, respectively.

At first glance, BTX looks like ATX, but notice that the I/O ports and the expansion slots have switched sides. You can't put a BTX motherboard in an ATX case. BTX does not change the power connection, so there's no such thing as a BTX power supply.

• **Figure 9.11**   That's not going to fit!

 Many manufacturers sell what they call BTX power supplies. These are actually marketing gimmicks. See Chapter 10, "Power Supplies," for details.

Everything in the BTX form factor is designed to improve cooling. BTX cases vent cool air in from the front and warm air out the back. CPUs are moved to the front of the motherboard so they get cool air coming in from the front of the case. BTX defines a special heat sink and fan assembly called the **thermal unit**. The thermal unit's fan blows the hot CPU air directly out the back of the case, as opposed to the ATX method of just blowing the air into the case.

• **Figure 9.12**   A microBTX motherboard

The BTX standard is clearly a much cooler option than ATX, but the PC industry tends to take its time when making big changes such as moving to a new form factor. As a result, BTX has not yet made much of an impact in the industry, and BTX motherboards, cases, and thermal units are still fairly rare. BTX could take off to become the next big thing or disappear in a cloud of disinterest—only time will tell.

Proprietary Form Factors

Several major PC makers, including Dell and Sony, make motherboards that work only with their cases. These *proprietary* motherboards enable these companies to create systems that stand out from the generic ones and, not coincidently, push you to get service and upgrades from their authorized dealers. Some of the features you'll see in proprietary systems are riser boards like you see with the NLX form factor—part of a motherboard separate from the main one but connected by a cable of some sort—and unique power connections. Proprietary motherboards drive techs crazy because replacement parts tend to cost more and are not readily available.

 Try This

Motherboard Varieties

Motherboards come in a wide variety of form factors. Go to your local computer store and check out what is on display. Note the different features offered by ATX, microATX, and FlexATX (if any) motherboards.

1. Does the store still stock any AT motherboards?
2. What about NLX, BTX, or proprietary motherboards?
3. Did the clerk use tech slang and call the motherboards "mobos"? (It's what most of us call them outside of formal textbooks, after all!)

Chipset

Every motherboard has a chipset. The chipset determines the type of processor the motherboard accepts, the type and capacity of RAM, and the sort of internal and external devices that the motherboard supports. As you

● **Figure 9.13** Northbridge (under the fan) and Southbridge (lower right, labeled VIA)

📄 Super I/O chips work with chipsets but are not part of the chipset. Motherboard makers purchase them separate from chipsets.

learned in earlier chapters, the chips in a PC's chipset serve as electronic interfaces through which the CPU, RAM, and input/output devices interact. Chipsets vary in features, performance, and stability, so they factor hugely in the purchase or recommendation of a particular motherboard. Good techs know their chipsets!

Because the chipset facilitates communication between the CPU and other devices in the system, its component chips are relatively centrally located on the motherboard (Figure 9.13). Most modern chipsets are composed of two primary chips: the Northbridge and the Southbridge.

The Northbridge chip on traditional Intel-based motherboards helps the CPU work with RAM, as mentioned in earlier chapters. On newer AMD and Intel-based motherboards, however, the Northbridge does not work directly with RAM, but instead provides the communication with the video card. The CPU has taken on the role of the memory controller. Current Northbridge chips do a lot and thus get pretty hot, so they get their own heat sink and fan assembly.

The Southbridge handles some expansion devices and mass storage drives, such as hard drives. Most Southbridge chips don't need extra cooling, leaving the chip exposed or passively cooled with only a heat sink. This makes the Southbridge a great place to see the manufacturer of the chipset, such as Intel.

Many motherboards support very old technologies such as floppy drives, infrared connections, parallel ports, and modems. Although supporting these old devices was once part of the Southbridge's job, hardly any modern chipsets still support these devices. Motherboard manufacturers add a third chip called the **Super I/O chip** to handle these chores. Figure 9.14 shows a typical Super I/O chip.

The system ROM chip provides part of the BIOS for the chipset, but only at a barebones, generic level. The chipset still needs support for the rest of the things it can do. So how do expansion devices get BIOS? From software drivers, of course, and the same holds true for modern chipsets. You have to load the proper drivers for the specific OS to support all of the features of today's chipsets. Without software drivers, you'll never create a stable, fully functional PC. All motherboards ship with a CD-ROM disc with drivers, support programs, and extra-special goodies such as antivirus software (Figure 9.15).

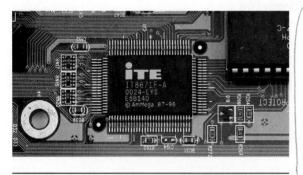

● **Figure 9.14** Super I/O chip on ASUS motherboard

There are a limited number of chipset makers. The dominant chipset vendors today are Intel and NVIDIA, although several other companies continue to produce chipsets, such as AMD through its ATI brand. Motherboard manufacturers incorporate the chipsets into motherboards that match the feature set of the chipset. Chipset companies rise and fall every few years, with one company seeming to hold the hot position for a while until another company comes along to unseat them.

Chipset makers don't always use the terms Northbridge and Southbridge. Chipsets for AMD-based motherboards tend to use the terms, but Intel-based motherboards prefer to say **Memory Controller Hub (MCH)** for the Northbridge and **I/O Controller Hub (ICH)** for the Southbridge. With the launch of the X58 Express Chipset, Intel has further refined their terminology, calling the Northbridge simply the *I/O Hub (IOH)* since the memory controller is located on the CPU. Sometimes Intel refers to the Southbridge as the *Legacy I/O Controller Hub*. Regardless of the official name, Northbridge and Southbridge are the commonly used terms. Figure 9.16 shows a schematic with typical chipset chores for a VIA K8T900 chipset.

It would be impossible to provide an inclusive chipset chart here that wouldn't be obsolete by the time you pick this book up off the shelf at your local tech pub (doesn't everybody have one of those?), but Table 9.1 gives you an idea of what to look for as you research motherboards for recommendations and purchases.

• **Figure 9.15** Driver disc for ASUS motherboard

In an average year, chipset makers collectively produce around one hundred new chipset models for the PC market.

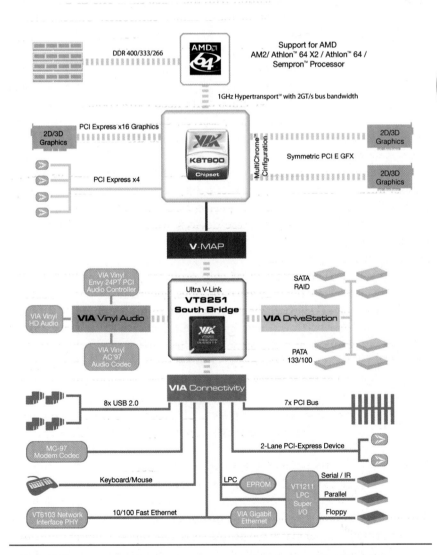

• **Figure 9.16** Schematic of a modern chipset (*image courtesy of VIA Technologies*)

Table 9.1   Chipset Comparison Chart

Chipset	Northbridge	Southbridge	CPU	CPU Interconnect	CPU RAM Interface	Northbridge RAM Interface	Northbridge PCIe	Southbridge PCIe	SATA	RAID	USB	Integrated Video
Intel X58 Express Chipset	Intel 82X58 Express Chipset I/O Hub (IOH)	Intel 82801JIB ICH10, Intel 82801JIR ICH10R, Intel 82801JD ICH10D, or Intel 82801JDO ICH10D	LGA1366: Core i7	QuickPath Interconnect (6.4 GT/s, 4.8 GT/s)	Yes, triple-channel DDR3 (24 GB max)	No	1x16, 2x16, or 4x8	6x1	6	Yes: 0,1,5,10	12 Hi-Speed	No
Intel Q45 Express Chipset	Intel 82Q45 Graphics and Memory Controller Hub (GMCH)	Intel 82801JIB ICH10, Intel 82801JIR ICH10R, Intel 82801JD ICH10D, or Intel 82801JDO ICH10D	LGA775: Core2 Duo, Core2 Quad	Frontside bus (1333 MHz, 1066 MHz, 800 MHz)	No	Yes, dual-channel, DDR2 (16 GB max) or DDR3 (8 GB max)	1x16	6x1	6	Yes: 0,1,5,10	12 Hi-Speed	Yes
Intel Q965 Express Chipset	Intel 82Q965 Graphics and Memory Controller Hub (GMCH)	Intel 82801HB ICH8 or Intel 82801HR ICH8R	LGA775: Core2 Duo, Pentium D, Pentium 4 supporting hyper-threading technology	Frontside bus (1066 MHz, 800 MHz, 533 MHz)	No	Yes, dual-channel DDR2 (8 GB max)	1x16	6x1	6	Yes: 0,1,5,10	10 Hi-Speed	Yes
NVIDIA nForce 980a SLI	NVIDIA nForce 980a SLI	N/A¹	AM3, AM2+, AM2: Phenom X4, Phenom X3, Phenom II X4, Phenom II X3, Athlon X2, Athlon	HyperTransport 3.0 (5.2 GT/s, 2 GT/s, 1.6 GT/s)	Yes, dual-channel DDR3 (16 GB max)	No	3x16, 2x16, 1x16, 2x8, or 4x8 + 4x1	N/A¹	6	Yes: 0, 1, 0+1, 5	12 Hi-Speed	No

Table 9.1   Chipset Comparison Chart (Continued)

Chipset	Northbridge	Southbridge	CPU	CPU Interconnect	CPU RAM Interface	Northbridge RAM Interface	Northbridge PCIe	Southbridge PCIe	SATA	RAID	USB	Integrated Video
NVIDIA GeForce 9400 mGPU	NVIDIA GeForce 9400 mGPU	N/A[1]	LGA775: Pentium D, Core 2 Quad, Core 2 Extreme, Core 2 Duo, Celeron D	Frontside bus (1333 MHz, 1066 MHz, 800 MHz)	No	Yes, dual channel, DDR2 (16 GB max) or DDR3 (8 GB max)	1x16 + 4x1	N/A[1]	6	Yes: 0, 1, 0+1, 5	12 Hi-Speed	Yes
AMD 770 Chipset	AMD 770	AMD SB600 or AMD SB700	AM2, AM2+: Phenom X4, Phenom X3, Athlon FX, Athlon X2, Athlon, Sempron	HyperTransport 3.0 (5.2 GT/s, 2 GT/s, 1.6 GT/s)	Yes, dual-channel DDR2 (8 GB max)	No	1x16	6x1	6	Yes: 0, 1, 10	12 Hi-Speed	No
AMD 790GX Chipset	AMD 790GX	AMD SB750	AM2+: Phenom X4, Phenom X3, Athlon FX, Athlon X2, Athlon, Sempron	HyperTransport 3.0 (5.2 GT/s, 2 GT/s)	Yes, dual-channel DDR2 (16 GB max)	No	1x16 or 2x16	6x1	6	Yes: 0, 1, 5, 10	12 Hi-Speed	Yes

1 NVIDIA does not make a Northbridge/Southbridge distinction with their chipsets.

So why do good techs need to know the hot chipsets in detail? The chipset defines almost every motherboard feature short of the CPU itself. Techs love to discuss chipsets and expect a fellow tech to know the differences between one chipset and another. You also need to be able to recommend a motherboard that suits a client's needs.

Motherboard Components

The connections and capabilities of a motherboard sometimes differ from those of the chipset the motherboard uses. This disparity happens for a couple of reasons. First, a particular chipset may support eight USB ports, but to keep costs down, the manufacturer might include only four ports. Second, a motherboard maker may choose to install extra features—ones not supported by the chipset—by adding additional chips. A common example is a motherboard that supports FireWire. Other technologies you might find are built-in sound, hard drive RAID controllers, and AMR or CNR slots for modems, network cards, and more.

USB/FireWire

Most chipsets support USB, and most motherboards come with FireWire as well, but it seems no two motherboards offer the same port arrangement. My motherboard supports eight USB ports and two FireWire ports, for example, but if you look on the back of the motherboard, you'll only see four USB ports and one FireWire port. So, where are the other ports? Well, this motherboard has special connectors for the other ports, and the motherboard comes with the dongles you need to connect them (Figure 9.17). These dongles typically use an extra slot on the back of the case.

These dongle connectors are standardized, so many cases have built-in front USB/FireWire ports that have dongles attached. This is very handy for USB or FireWire devices you might want to plug and unplug frequently, such as thumb drives or digital cameras. You can also buy add-on front USB and FireWire devices that go into a 3.5-inch drive bay (Figure 9.18).

• **Figure 9.17**   USB/FireWire dongle

• **Figure 9.18**   Front USB and FireWire drive bay device

Sound

Quite a few motherboards come with onboard sound chips. These sound chips are usually pretty low quality compared to even a lower-end sound card, but onboard sound is cheap and doesn't take up a slot. These connectors are identical to the ones used on sound cards, so we'll save more discussion for Chapter 20, "Multimedia."

RAID

RAID stands for *redundant array of independent (or inexpensive) disks* and is very common on motherboards. There are many types of RAID, but the RAID found on motherboards usually only supports *mirroring* (the process

of using two drives to hold the same data, which is good for safety, because if one drive dies, the other still has all of the data) or *striping* (making two drives act as one drive by spreading data across them, which is good for speed). RAID is a very cool but complex topic that's discussed in detail in Chapter 11, "Hard Drive Technologies."

AMR/CNR

The U.S. Federal Communications Commission (FCC) must certify any electronic device to ensure that it does not transmit unwanted electronic signals. This process is a bit expensive, so in the very late 1990s, Intel came up with a special slot called the **audio modem riser (AMR)**, shown in Figure 9.19. An AMR slot was designed to take specialized AMR devices (modems, sound cards, and network cards). An AMR device would get one FCC certification and then be used on as many motherboards as the manufacturer wanted without going through the FCC certification process again. AMR was quickly replaced with the more advanced **communications and networking riser (CNR)**. Many motherboard manufacturers used these slots in the early 2000s, but they've lost popularity because most motherboard makers simply use onboard networking and sound.

• **Figure 9.19**   AMR slot

Practical Application

■ Upgrading and Installing Motherboards

To most techs, the concept of adding or replacing a motherboard can be extremely intimidating. It really shouldn't be; motherboard installation is a common and necessary part of PC repair. It is inexpensive and easy, although it can sometimes be a little tedious and messy because of the large number of parts involved. This section covers the process of installation and replacement and shows you some of the tricks that make this necessary process easy to handle.

Choosing the Motherboard and Case

Choosing a motherboard and case can prove quite a challenge for any tech, whether newly minted or a seasoned veteran. You first have to figure out the type of motherboard you want, such as AMD- or Intel-based. Then you

> Being able to select and install a motherboard appropriate for a client or customer is something every CompTIA A+ technician should know.

Try This!

Building a Recommendation

Family, friends, and potential clients often solicit the advice of a tech when they're thinking about upgrading their PC. This solicitation puts you on the spot to make not just any old recommendation but one that works with the needs and budget of the potential upgrader. To do this successfully, you need to manage expectations and ask the right questions, so Try This!

1. What does the upgrader want to do that compels him or her to upgrade? Write it down! Some of the common motivations for upgrading are to play that hot new game or to take advantage of new technology. What's the minimum system needed to run tomorrow's action games? What do you need to make multimedia sing? Does the motherboard need to have FireWire and Hi-Speed USB built in to accommodate digital video and better printers?

2. How much of the current system does the upgrader want to save? Upgrading a motherboard can very quickly turn into a complete system rebuild. What form factor is the old case? If it's a microATX case, that constrains the motherboards you can use with it to microATX or the smaller FlexATX. If the desired motherboard is a full-sized ATX board, you'll need to get a new case. Does the new motherboard possess the same type of CPU socket as the old motherboard? If not, that's a sure sign you'll need to upgrade the CPU as well. What about RAM? If the old motherboard was using DDR SDRAM, and the new motherboard requires DDR2 SDRAM, you'll need to replace the RAM. If you need to upgrade the memory, it is best to know how many channels the new RAM interface supports, because performance is best when all channels are populated.

   What if the old motherboard was using an AGP graphics accelerator that the new motherboard does not support, but you don't want to splurge on a PCI Express graphics accelerator right now? In this situation you might want to consider moving to a motherboard with integrated graphics. What's great about integrated graphics is that if the motherboard also possesses a ×16 PCI Express slot, you can upgrade to a more powerful discrete graphics accelerator later.

3. Once you've gathered information on motivation and assessed the current PC of the upgrader, it's time to get down to business: field trip time! This is a great excuse to get to the computer store and check out the latest motherboards and gadgets. Don't forget to jot down notes and prices while you're there. By the end of the field trip, you should have the information to give the upgrader an honest assessment of what an upgrade will entail, at least in monetary terms. Be honest—in other words, don't just tell upgraders what you think they want to hear—and you won't get in trouble.

need to think about the form factor, which of course influences the type of case you'll need. Third, how rich in features is the motherboard and how tough is it to configure? You have to read the motherboard manual to find out. Finally, you need to select the case that matches your space needs, budget, and form factor. Now look at each step in a little more detail.

First, determine what motherboard you need. What CPU are you using? Will the motherboard work with that CPU? Because most of us buy the CPU and the motherboard at the same time, make the seller guarantee that the CPU will work with the motherboard. If you can, choose a motherboard that works with much higher speeds than the CPU you can afford; that way you can upgrade later. How much RAM do you intend to install? Are extra RAM sockets available for future upgrades?

A number of excellent motherboard manufacturers are available today. Some of the more popular brands are abit, ASUS, BIOSTAR, DFI, GIGABYTE, Intel, MSI, and Shuttle. Your supplier may also have some lesser-known but perfectly acceptable brands of motherboards. As long as the supplier has an easy return policy, it's perfectly fine to try one of these.

Second, make sure you're getting a form factor that works with your case. Don't try to put a regular ATX motherboard into a microATX case!

Third, all motherboards come with a technical manual, better known as the **motherboard book** (Figure 9.20). You must have this book! This book is your primary source for all of the critical information about the motherboard.

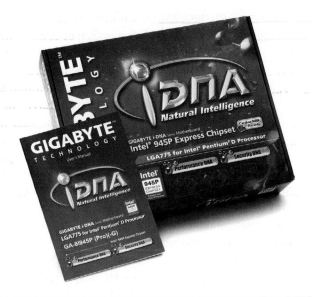

• **Figure 9.20**   Motherboard box and book

If you set up CPU or RAM timings incorrectly in CMOS, for example, and you have a dead PC, where would you find the CMOS clear jumper? Where do you plug in the speaker? Even if you let someone else install the mother-board, insist on the motherboard book; you will need it.

Fourth, pick your case carefully. Cases come in six basic sizes: slimline, desktop, mini-tower, mid-tower, tower, and cube. Slimline and desktop models generally sit on the desk, beneath the monitor. The various tower cases usually occupy a bit of floor space next to the desk. The mini-tower and mid-tower cases are the most popular choices. Make sure you get a case that fits your motherboard—many microATX and all FlexATX cases are too small for a regular ATX motherboard. Cube cases generally require a specific motherboard, so be prepared to buy both pieces at once. A quick test-fit before you buy saves a lot of return trips to the supplier.

Cases come with many options, but three more common options point to a better case. One option is a removable face (Figure 9.21)—many cheaper

• **Figure 9.21**   Removable face

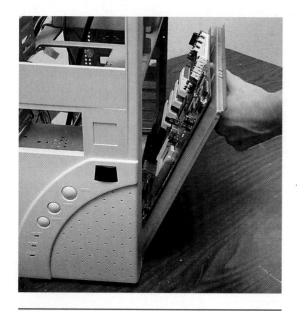

cases screw the face into the metal frame with wood screws. A removable face makes disassembly much easier.

Another option is a detachable motherboard mount. Clearly, the motherboard has to be attached to the case in some fashion. In better cases, this is handled by a removable tray or plate (Figure 9.22). This enables you to attach the motherboard to the case separately, saving you from sticking your arms into the case to turn screws.

The third option, front-mounted ports for USB, FireWire, and headphones, can make using a PC much easier. Better cases offer these ports, although you can also get add-on components that fit into the increasingly useless floppy drive bay to bring added front connectivity to the PC. Figure 9.23 shows a case with both types of front connectors.

Power supplies often come with the case. Watch out for "really good deal" cases because that invariably points to a cheap or missing power supply. You also need to verify that the power supply has sufficient wattage. This issue is handled in Chapter 10, "Power Supplies."

Installing the Motherboard

If you're replacing a motherboard, first remove the old motherboard. Begin by removing all of the cards. Also remove anything else that might impede removal or installation of the motherboard, such as hard or floppy drives.

The CompTIA A+ Essentials exam will test you on the basics of installing a motherboard, so you need to know this section for both exams.

Watch out for ESD here! Remember that it's very easy to damage or destroy a CPU and RAM with a little electrostatic discharge. It's also fairly easy to damage the motherboard with ESD. Always wear your antistatic wrist strap.

• Figure 9.23   Case with both front-mounted ports and an add-on flash memory card reader

Keep track of your screws—the best idea is to return the screws to their mounting holes temporarily, at least until you can reinstall the parts. Sometimes you even have to remove the power supply temporarily to enable access to the motherboard. Document the position of the little wires for the speaker, power switch, and reset button in case you need to reinstall them.

Unscrew the motherboard. *It will not simply lift out.* The motherboard mounts to the case via small connectors called **standouts** that slide into keyed slots or screw into the bottom of the case (Figure 9.24). Screws then go into the standouts to hold the motherboard in place. Be sure to place the standouts properly before installing the new motherboard.

When you insert the new motherboard, do not assume that you will put the screws and standouts in the same place as they were in your old motherboard. When it comes to the placement of screws and standouts, only one rule applies: anywhere it fits. Do not be afraid to be a little tough here! Installing motherboards can be a wiggling, twisting, knuckle-scraping process.

Once you get the motherboard mounted in the case, with the CPU and RAM properly installed, it's time to insert the power connections and test it. A POST card can be helpful with the system test because you won't have to add the speaker, a video card, monitor, and keyboard to verify that the system is booting. If you have a POST card, start the system, and watch to see if the POST takes place—you should see a number of POST codes before the POST stops. If you don't have a POST card, install a keyboard, speaker, video card, and monitor. Boot the system and see if the BIOS information shows up on the screen. If it does, you're probably okay. If it doesn't, it's time to refer to the motherboard book to see where you made a mistake.

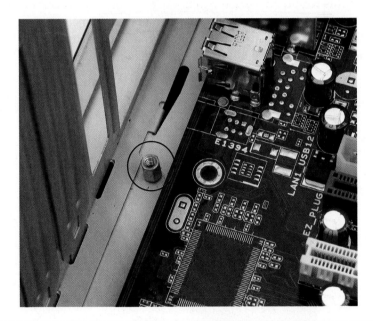

• **Figure 9.24**   Standout in a case, ready for the motherboard

Tech Tip

Before the Case

A lot of techs install the CPU, CPU fan, and RAM into the motherboard before installing the motherboard into the case. This helps in several ways, especially with a new system. First, you want to make certain that the CPU and RAM work well with the motherboard and with each other—without that, you have no hope of setting up a stable system. Second, installing these components first prevents the phenomenon of flexing the motherboard. Some cases don't provide quite enough support for the motherboard, and pushing in RAM can make the board bend. Third, attaching a CPU fan can be a bear of a task, one that's considerably easier to do on a table top than within the confines of a case. Finally, on motherboards that require you to set jumpers or switches, you can much more easily read the tiny information stenciled on the PCB before you add the shadows from the case. If necessary, set any jumpers and switches for the specific CPU according to information from the motherboard manual.

Pay attention to the location of the standouts if you're swapping a motherboard. If you leave a screw-type standout beneath a spot on the motherboard where you can't add a screw and then apply power to the motherboard, you run the risk of shorting the motherboard.

Wires, Wires, Wires

The last part of motherboard installation is connecting the LEDs, buttons, and front-mounted ports on the front of the box. These usually include the following:

- Soft power
- Reset button
- Speaker
- Hard drive activity LED
- Power LED
- USB
- FireWire
- Sound

These wires have specific pin connections to the motherboard. Although you can refer to the motherboard book for their location, usually a quick inspection of the motherboard will suffice for an experienced tech (Figure 9.25).

You need to follow a few rules when installing these wires. First, the lights are LEDs, not light bulbs; they have a positive and negative side. If they don't work one way, turn the connector around and try the other. Second, when in doubt, guess. Incorrect installation only results in the device not working; it won't damage the computer. Refer to the motherboard book for the correct installation. The third and last rule is that, with the exception of the soft power switch on an ATX system, you do not need any of these wires for the computer to run. Many techs often simply ignore these wires, although this would not be something I'd do to any system but my own.

No hard-and-fast rule exists for determining the function of each wire. Often the function of each wire is printed on the connector (Figure 9.26). If not, track each wire to the LED or switch to determine its function.

• **Figure 9.25**   Motherboard wire connections labeled on the motherboard

• **Figure 9.26**   Sample of case wires

■ Troubleshooting Motherboards

Motherboards fail. Not often, but motherboards and motherboard components can die from many causes: time, dust, cat hair, or simply slight manufacturing defects made worse by the millions of amps of current sluicing through the motherboard traces. Installing cards, electrostatic discharge, flexing the motherboard one time too many when swapping out RAM or drives—any of these factors can cause a motherboard to fail. The motherboard is a hard-working, often abused component of the PC. Unfortunately for the common tech, troubleshooting a motherboard problem can be difficult and time consuming. Let's wrap this chapter with a look at symptoms of a failing motherboard, techniques for troubleshooting, and the options you have when you discover a motherboard problem.

Symptoms

Motherboard failures commonly fall into three types: catastrophic, component, and ethereal. With a **catastrophic failure**, the PC just won't boot. This sort of problem happens to brand-new systems because of manufacturing defects—often called a **burn-in failure**—and to any system that gets a shock of electrostatic discharge. Burn-in failure is uncommon and usually happens in the first 30 days of use. Swap out the motherboard for a replacement and you should be fine. If you accidentally zap your motherboard when inserting a card or moving wires around, be chagrined. Change your daring ways and wear an anti-static wrist strap!

Component failure happens rarely and appears as flaky connections between a device and motherboard, or as intermittent problems. A hard drive plugged into a faulty controller on the motherboard, for example, might show up in CMOS autodetect but be inaccessible in Windows. Another example is a serial controller that worked fine for months until a big storm took out the external modem hooked to it, and doesn't work anymore, even with a replacement modem.

The most difficult of the three types of symptoms to diagnose are those I call *ethereal* symptoms. Stuff just doesn't work all of the time. The PC reboots itself. You get a Blue Screen of Death (BSoD) in the midst of heavy computing, such as right before you smack the villain and rescue the damsel. What can cause such symptoms? If you answered any of the following, you win the prize:

- Faulty component
- Buggy device driver
- Buggy application software
- Slight corruption of the operating system
- Power supply problems

Err…you get the picture.

What a nightmare scenario to troubleshoot! The Way of the Tech knows paths through such perils, though, so let's turn to troubleshooting techniques now.

Techniques

To troubleshoot a potential motherboard failure requires time, patience, and organization. Some problems will certainly be quicker to solve than others. If the hard drive doesn't work as expected, as in the previous example, check the settings on the drive. Try a different drive. Try the same drive with a different motherboard to verify that it's a good drive. Like every other troubleshooting technique, all you try to do with motherboard testing is to isolate the problem by eliminating potential factors.

This three-part system—check, replace, verify good component—works for the simpler and the more complicated motherboard problems. You can even apply the same technique to ethereal-type problems that might be anything, but you should add one more verb: *document*. Take notes on the individual components you test so you don't repeat efforts or waste time. Plus, taking notes can lead to the establishment of patterns. Being able to re-create a system crash by performing certain actions in a specific order can often lead you to the root of the problem. Document your actions. Motherboard testing is time-consuming enough without adding inefficiency.

If you've lost components because of ESD or a power surge, you would most likely be better off replacing the motherboard. The damage you *can't* see can definitely sneak up to bite you and create system instability.

Tech Tip

Limits of BIOS Upgrades

Flashing the BIOS for a motherboard can fix a lot of system stability problems and provide better implementation of built-in technology. What it cannot do for your system is improve the hardware. If AMD comes out with a new, improved, lower-voltage Athlon 64, for example, and your motherboard cannot scale down the voltage properly, you cannot use that CPU—even if it fits in your motherboard's Socket AM2. No amount of BIOS flashing can change the hardware built into your motherboard.

Options

Once you determine that the motherboard has problems, you have several options for fixing the three types of failures. If you have a catastrophic failure, you must replace the motherboard. Even if it works somewhat, don't mess around. The motherboard should provide bedrock stability for the system. If it's even remotely buggy or problematic, get rid of it!

If you have a component failure, you can often replace the component with an add-on card that will be as good as or better than the failed device. Adaptec, for example, makes fine cards that can replace the built-in SATA ports on the motherboard (Figure 9.27).

If your component failure is more a technology issue than physical damage, you can try upgrading the BIOS on the motherboard. As you'll recall from Chapter 7 on BIOS and CMOS, every motherboard comes with a small set of code that enables the CPU to communicate properly with the devices built into the motherboard. You can quite readily upgrade this programming by *flashing the BIOS*: running a small command-line program to write

• **Figure 9.27** Adaptec PCIe SATA card

new BIOS in the flash ROM chip. Refer to Chapter 7, "BIOS and CMOS," for the details on flashing.

Finally, if you have an ethereal, ghost-in-the-machine type of problem that you have finally determined to be motherboard related, you have only a couple of options for fixing the problem. You can flash the BIOS in a desperate attempt to correct whatever it is, which sometimes does work and is less expensive than the other option. Or you can replace the motherboard.

Beyond A+

Shuttle Form Factor

In the early 2000s, Shuttle started making a very interesting line of tiny cube-shaped PCs called XPCs that became an overnight sensation and continue to be popular today (Figure 9.28). These boxes use a tiny, proprietary form factor motherboard, called *Shuttle Form Factor*, installed in a proprietary case with a proprietary power supply. Originally, these systems were sold *barebones*, meaning they came with only a motherboard, case, and power supply. You had to supply a CPU, RAM, video card, keyboard, mouse, and monitor. Shuttle now produces a full line of computers.

● **Figure 9.28** Shuttle XPC (*photo courtesy of Shuttle Computer Group, Inc.*)

Mini-ITX

If you really want to get small, check out Mini-ITX (Figure 9.29). Developed by VIA Technologies in 2001, Mini-ITX has a maximum size of only 17 centimeters by 17 centimeters. Most Mini-ITX systems feature low-power processors such as the Intel Atom or the VIA C7. Many new enthusiast-grade Mini-ITX motherboards support more powerful processors such as the Intel Core2 Duo or the AMD Phenom.

● **Figure 9.29** Mini-ITX motherboard

> **Tech Tip**
>
> **Small Form Factor**
> *Many companies followed Shuttle's lead and started making cube or cube-like small cases. You'll hear these cases commonly referred to as* small form factor (SFF), *but there's no industry-wide standard. Some SFF cases accommodate microATX and FlexATX motherboards.*

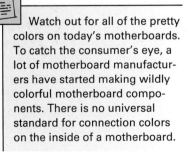

Watch out for all of the pretty colors on today's motherboards. To catch the consumer's eye, a lot of motherboard manufacturers have started making wildly colorful motherboard components. There is no universal standard for connection colors on the inside of a motherboard.

Chapter 9 Review

■ Chapter Summary

After reading this chapter and completing the exercises, you should understand the following about motherboards.

Explain how motherboards work

- Every piece of hardware connects either directly or indirectly to the motherboard. Wires called traces make up the buses on the system, enabling hardware to communicate. Motherboards are several layers thick, with traces running across each layer, creating a veritable highway of wires.

- Motherboards are defined by their form factor, chipset, and components. The form factor defines the physical size and airflow; the chipset defines the type of CPU, the type and amount of RAM, and the components a motherboard will support.

Identify the types of motherboards

- The Advanced Technology (AT) form factor, though now obsolete, was the predominant form factor for motherboards through the mid-1990s. Its identifying features included a large keyboard plug and a split power socket called P8/P9.

- LPX and NLX were slimline form factors, meaning they were ideal for low-profile cases. They offered a central riser slot to accept a special riser card into which expansion cards fit horizontally.

- The Advanced Technology Extended (ATX) form factor replaced AT as the form factor of choice by the late 1990s. It offered several improvements over AT, including repositioning the power supply for better airflow, easier access to CPU and RAM slots, and better performance by moving RAM closer to the Northbridge and CPU. The microATX (μATX) and FlexATX are subtypes of ATX and are considerably smaller.

- The Balanced Technology eXtended (BTX) form factor is newer than ATX and was designed to improve cooling. BTX cases take cool air in from the front and blow warm air out the back. As BTX motherboards place the CPU toward the front of the case, the CPU receives additional cooling from the improved airflow. Standard BTX, microBTX, and picoBTX are designed to replace ATX, microATX, and FlexATX, respectively.

- Several PC manufacturers make proprietary motherboards, meaning they do not adhere to a standard form factor such as ATX or BTX. Servicing a system like this can be frustrating, as parts may be difficult to find and are often available only from authorized dealers.

- Motherboards come with differing features or components such as USB/FireWire ports, audio, video, RAID, and AMR or CNR slots for modems and network cards. Sometimes a motherboard supports several USB/FireWire ports but does not have rear ports for all of them. In this case, the motherboard likely has connections for the additional ports to be used in conjunction with a dongle to create front-mounted ports.

- Popular motherboard manufacturers include abit, ASUS, BIOSTAR, DFI, GGIGABYTE, Intel, MSI, and Shuttle.

Explain chipset varieties

- Every motherboard has a chipset that determines the type of CPU the motherboard supports, the type and capacity of RAM, and the devices the motherboard supports without an expansion card. Most modern chipsets are composed of two primary chips: the Northbridge and the Southbridge. As the Northbridge works with the CPU and RAM, it gets very hot and therefore needs its own heat sink and fan. The Southbridge usually does not require any extra cooling and is thus exposed, making it a great place to find the stamp of the chipset manufacturer.

- Because almost no modern chipset supports old technologies such as floppy disk drives, infrared connections, and parallel ports, motherboards contain a third chip called the Super I/O chip to support these technologies. The Super I/O chip is not part of the chipset.

- The system ROM chip provides basic support for the chipset, but to benefit from all of the features of a chipset, you need to install the operating

system–specific drivers for the chipset once you've installed the operating system.

- Chipset manufacturers for AMD-based motherboards tend to use the terms Northbridge and Southbridge, whereas Intel-based boards tend to use different terminology. You might see the Northbridge referred to as the Memory Controller Hub (MCH) or I/O Hub (IOH) and the Southbridge referred to as the I/O Controller Hub (ICH) or Legacy I/O Controller Hub.

- Popular chipset manufacturers today include Intel, AMD, and NVIDIA.

Upgrade and install motherboards

- Not all motherboards fit in all cases. If you upgrade a motherboard, make sure the new motherboard fits in the existing case. If you purchase a new motherboard and a new case, make sure you purchase a case that supports the form factor of your motherboard.

- Determine the CPU you or your client wants before purchasing a motherboard. Not all CPUs are supported by, or even fit in, all motherboards. Make sure your motherboard supports your CPU and, if possible, purchase a motherboard that supports higher speeds than your CPU in case you want to upgrade the processor at a later time.

- To replace a motherboard, first remove all of the expansion cards from the old motherboard. Document the position of all of the little wires before removing them. Unscrew the motherboard and remove it from the case.

- Before installing a new motherboard in the case, attach the CPU, heat sink/fan, and RAM. Check the standouts in the case—you might have to add or remove a few to accommodate the new motherboard. Once installed, boot the system and make sure there are no POST errors and the BIOS information appears on the screen. Then install any expansion cards.

- Cases come with a series of little wires that connect to LEDs on the front of the case. You need to plug these wires in to the motherboard for the LEDs to

function. LEDs have a positive and a negative side, so the wires must be connected the right way or the LEDs will not work. If you find that the LEDs are not working, turn the connector around to reverse the positive/negative connection. Getting it wrong will not damage your system; it will only cause the LEDs not to light up.

Troubleshoot motherboard problems

- Motherboards and motherboard components can die for many reasons, including time, dust, pet hair, manufacturing defects, ESD, or physical damage. Motherboard failures usually fall into one of three main categories: catastrophic, component, or ethereal.

- Catastrophic failure is typically caused by manufacturing defects (burn-in failure) or ESD. Burn-in failures are uncommon and usually manifest within the first 30 days of use. In the case of a catastrophic failure, replace the motherboard.

- Component failure appears as a flaky connection between a device and the motherboard or as intermittent problems. In the case of a component failure, replace the failed component with an expansion card or peripheral device. Sometimes a BIOS upgrade can fix component failures.

- Ethereal failure is the most difficult to diagnose. Symptoms vary from the PC rebooting itself to Blue Screens of Death and can be caused by a faulty component, buggy device driver, buggy application software, operating system corruption, or power supply problems.

- Use three steps to troubleshoot problems: check, replace, and verify. For example, first check the settings of the problem device. If the device still fails, replace the device. If the device continues to malfunction, try the device with a different motherboard. Remember to document your troubleshooting steps. Not only will it help you to become an efficient troubleshooter, but it also can lead to the establishment of patterns. Being able to re-create a system crash by performing certain actions in a specific order can often lead you to the root of the problem.

■ Key Terms

AT *(268)*
ATX *(270)*

audio modem riser (AMR) *(279)*
Balanced Technology eXtended (BTX) *(272)*

burn-in failure *(285)*

catastrophic failure *(285)*

chipset *(267)*

communications and networking riser (CNR) *(279)*

component failure *(285)*

FlexATX *(271)*

form factor *(267)*

I/O Controller Hub (ICH) *(275)*

LPX *(269)*

Memory Controller Hub (MCH) *(275)*

microATX (μATX) *(271)*

microBTX *(272)*

motherboard *(266)*

motherboard book *(280)*

NLX *(269)*

P8/P9 *(268)*

picoBTX *(272)*

printed circuit board *(267)*

riser card *(269)*

slimline *(269)*

soft power *(271)*

standouts *(283)*

Super I/O chip *(274)*

thermal unit *(272)*

traces *(266)*

■ Key Term Quiz

Use the Key Terms list to complete the sentences that follow. Not all terms will be used.

1. The _____ defines the type of processor and RAM required for the motherboard and determines to a degree the built-in devices supported by a motherboard, including the expansion slots.

2. The AT type of motherboard had a unique, split power socket called _____.

3. The _____ form factor replaced the LPX slimline form factor.

4. Everything in the _____ form factor is designed to improve cooling.

5. The _____ determines the physical size of the motherboard as well as the general location of components and ports.

6. The smallest ATX motherboard form factor is the _____.

7. The smallest BTX motherboard form factor is the _____.

8. The fan of the BTX _____ blows the hot CPU air directly out the back of the case.

9. The _____ is your primary source for all of the critical information about the motherboard.

10. The motherboard mounts to the case via small connectors called _____ that slide into keyed slots or screw into the bottom of the case.

■ Multiple-Choice Quiz

1. Which of the following are part of the ATX form factor? (Select two.)

   A. FlexATX

   B. macroATX

   C. microATX

   D. picoATX

2. Which of the following form factors dominates the PC market?

   A. AT

   B. ATX

   C. BTX

   D. NLX

3. The nonprofit agency that Sid works for received a half dozen new motherboards as a donation, but when he tried to install one into a case, it didn't fit at all. The ports and expansion slots seemed to be switched. What's most likely the issue?

   A. Sid's trying to install a proprietary motherboard into an ATX case.

   B. Sid's trying to install an LPX motherboard into an ATX case.

C. Sid's trying to install a microATX motherboard into an ATX case.

D. Sid's trying to install a microBTX motherboard into an ATX case.

4. A client brought in an old computer that won't boot. He wants to see if any data can be recovered from the hard drive. When the tech opened the case, he noted that two expansion cards were plugged into some kind of circuit board that plugged into the motherboard. The expansion cards were parallel with the motherboard, in other words, rather than perpendicular. Into what kind of circuit board did the expansion cards most likely connect? (Select two.)

A. daughterboard

B. expansion board

C. riser card

D. Southbridge

5. In a routine check of a system newly built by her latest intern, Sarah discovers that everything works except the hard drive and power LEDs on the front of the case. What could be the problem? (Select two.)

A. The intern forgot to connect the LED leads to the motherboard.

B. The intern reversed the LED leads to the motherboard.

C. There is no power to the motherboard.

D. There is no activity on the hard drive.

6. Robert installed a new motherboard, CPU, and RAM into his old case. After he attached the power correctly and pressed the power button, not only did the system not boot up, he also could smell ozone and realized the motherboard had shorted out. What could have been the cause?

A. Robert installed an ATX motherboard into a BTX case.

B. Robert installed a BTX motherboard into an ATX case.

C. Robert used an AT power supply on an ATX motherboard.

D. Robert left a standout in the wrong place under the motherboard.

7. Which chip enables an Intel Core2 Duo processor to interact with RAM?

A. Memorybridge

B. Northbridge

C. Southbridge

D. Super I/O

8. Brian bought a new motherboard that advertised support for eight USB ports. When he pulled the motherboard out of the box, though, he found that it only had four USB ports. What's likely the issue here?

A. The extra four USB ports will connect to the front of the case or via a dongle to an expansion slot.

B. The extra four USB ports require an add-on expansion card.

C. The FireWire port will have a splitter that makes it four USB ports.

D. The motherboard chipset might support eight USB ports, but the manufacturer only included four ports.

9. Martin bought a new motherboard to replace his older ATX motherboard. As he left the shop, the tech on duty called after him, "Check your standouts!" What could the tech have meant?

A. Standouts are the connectors on the motherboard for the front panel buttons, such as the on/off switch and reset button.

B. Standouts are the metal edges on some cases that aren't rolled.

C. Standouts are the metal connectors that attach the motherboard to the case.

D. Standouts are the dongles that enable a motherboard to support more than four USB ports.

10. Amanda bought a new system that, right in the middle of an important presentation, gave her a Blue Screen of Death. Now her system won't boot at all, not even to CMOS. After extensive troubleshooting, she determined that the motherboard was at fault and replaced it. Now the system runs fine. What was the most likely cause of the problem?

A. Burn-in failure

B. Electrostatic discharge

C. Component failure

D. Power supply failure

11. Solon has a very buggy computer that keeps locking up at odd moments and rebooting spontaneously. He suspects the motherboard. How should he test it?

A. Check settings and verify good components.

B. Verify good components and document all testing.

C. Replace the motherboard first to see if the problems disappear.

D. Check settings, verify good components, replace components, and document all testing.

12. As tech support for a computer shop, you receive a call from an irate customer insisting that you sent him the wrong motherboard because it won't fit in his old case. Which of the following questions might enable you to determine the problem? Select the best answer.

A. Will you describe the location of the connectors on the back of the motherboard?

B. Will you describe the location of the standouts on the case?

C. What kind of CPU are you using?

D. What type of RAM are you using?

13. Which of the following companies makes chipsets?

A. AMI

B. GIGABYTE

C. MSI

D. NVIDIA

14. What purpose does the Super I/O chip serve?

A. The Super I/O chip handles the communication with RAM.

B. The Super I/O chip handles the communication with video.

C. The Super I/O chip handles the communication with legacy devices.

D. The Super I/O chip handles the communication between the Northbridge and Southbridge chips.

15. Which of the following case types would you most likely not use to build a home-made system?

A. Desktop

B. Mini-tower

C. Mid-tower

D. Nettop

■ Essay Quiz

1. This chapter talks about motherboards made in layers that contain the wires or traces. Find an Internet site that talks about the motherboard manufacturing process. Why do you think motherboards are made in layers? What advantages do the layers provide?

2. Some people believe that selecting a motherboard based on the motherboard chipset is even more important than basing the decision on the kind of processor. Do you agree or disagree, and why?

3. Prepare a PowerPoint presentation or write a paper that would help your classmates select and

replace a bad motherboard. Be sure to walk through all of the necessary steps.

4. Your neighbors Dora and Jim just learned that you're studying computer hardware. They feel that their computer is slightly out of date. They want to upgrade the processor, but not the motherboard. Prepare a list of at least five questions you should ask them before you know what CPU they can choose or whether it is feasible to upgrade their system.

Lab Projects

• Lab Project 9.1

Examine all of the ports and connectors on the back of your computer. With the computer turned off, you may disconnect the cables from the ports. (If necessary, document where and how the cables are connected so you can replace them correctly.) Determine the kinds of ports that are built in and those that are provided by expansion cards. From this information alone, ascertain whether your motherboard is a BTX or an ATX form factor. Draw a diagram of the back of your system and label every port and all connectors. State if their sources are from the motherboard or from an expansion card. Last, state the form factor of the motherboard.

• Lab Project 9.2

One of the most important skills a PC technician can possess is the ability to read and interpret documentation. No single piece of documentation is as important as the motherboard book. Let's see how well you can understand this documentation. Consult your motherboard book or use one that your instructor provides. (If you do not have the motherboard book, try to download it from the manufacturer's Web site.) Then write a paragraph about your motherboard that includes answers to the following questions:

- What make and model is the motherboard?
- What chipset does it use?
- What kinds of RAM slots does it contain?
- What kinds of expansion slots does your motherboard have and how many of each kind does it have?

- What kinds of onboard ports does it have?
- What kinds of CPUs does it support and what kind of processor slot does it have?
- Does your motherboard use jumpers or dip switches for configuration? If so, what do the jumpers or dip switches control?
- The motherboard book probably contains an illustration of the way the motherboard components are laid out. By examining this illustration, determine what form factor your motherboard uses.
- Does your motherboard have any unusual or proprietary features?

• Lab Project 9.3

You know now how important the motherboard chipset is in determining the kind of CPU and RAM that you can install in the computer. You also know that motherboards may look similar but have very different features and prices. Imagine that you are going to build a new computer by ordering the components. Price is not a problem, so you will want to select the best and most powerful components. On the Internet, search sites such as www.intel.com or www.amd.com along with sites such as www .newegg.com to select a motherboard and a particular chipset. Then select a compatible CPU and RAM. Explain where you found the information about the components, what brands/models you selected, and how much each will cost.

Now imagine that your budget will not allow you to buy these components at this time. In fact, you've decided that you can afford only 75 percent of the cost of these components. What will you do to save money? Will you change the motherboard and the chipset or will you use a less powerful CPU with a smaller amount of RAM? Consider what you can upgrade at a later time when you have more available cash. Again search the Internet and select components that would be satisfactory but are not the latest and the greatest. Be sure that the CPU and RAM you select are indeed compatible with your motherboard and chipset. What did you select and how much will it cost you?

Power Supplies

chapter

10

"This flipping circuit board, Jen. Some chump has run the data lines right through the power supply. Amateur hour! I've got tears in my eyes!"

—Moss, THE IT CROWD ("THE RED DOOR")

In this chapter, you will learn how to

- **Explain the basics of electricity**
- **Describe the details about powering the PC**
- **Install, maintain, and troubleshoot power supplies**

Powering the PC requires a single box—the power supply—that takes electricity from the wall socket and transforms it into electricity to run the motherboard and other internal components. Figure 10.1 shows a typical power supply inside a case. All of the wires dangling out of it connect to the motherboard and peripherals.

As simple as this appears on the surface, power supply issues are of critical importance for techs. Problems with power can create system instability, crashes, and data loss—all things most computer users would rather avoid! Good techs therefore know an awful lot about powering the PC, from understanding the basic principles of electricity to knowing the many variations of PC power supplies. Plus, you need to know how to recognize power problems and implement the proper solutions. Too many techs fall into the "just plug it in" camp and never learn how to deal with power, much to their clients' unhappiness.

Some questions on the CompTIA A+ certification exams could refer to a power supply as a *PSU*, for **power supply unit**. A power supply also falls into the category of **field replaceable unit (FRU)**, which refers to the typical parts a tech should carry, such as RAM and a hard drive.

• **Figure 10.1**   Typical power supply mounted inside the PC system unit

Historical/Conceptual

■ Understanding Electricity

Electricity is simply a flow of negatively charged particles, called electrons, through matter. All matter enables the flow of electrons to some extent. This flow of electrons is very similar to the flow of water through pipes; so similar that the best way to learn about electricity is by comparing it to how water flows though pipes. So let's talk about water for a moment.

Water comes from the ground, through wells, aquifers, rivers, and so forth. In a typical city, water comes to you through pipes from the water supply company that took it from the ground. What do you pay for when you pay your water bill each month? You pay for the water you use, certainly, but built into the price of the water you use is the surety that when you turn the spigot, water will flow at a more or less constant rate. The water sits in the pipes under pressure from the water company, waiting for you to turn the spigot.

Electricity works essentially the same way as water. Electric companies gather or generate electricity and then push it to your house under pressure through wires. Just like water, the electricity sits in the wires, waiting for you to plug something into the wall socket, at which time it'll flow at a more or less constant rate. You plug a lamp into an electrical outlet and flip the switch, electricity flows, and you have light. You pay for reliability, electrical pressure, and electricity used.

The pressure of the electrons in the wire is called *voltage* and is measured in units called **volts (V)**. The amount of electrons moving past a certain point on a wire is called the *current* or *amperage*, which is measured in units called **amperes (amps or A)**. The amount of amps and volts needed so that a particular device will function is expressed as how much **wattage (watts or W)** that device needs.

The correlation between the three is very simple math: V × A = W. You'll learn more about wattage a little later in this chapter.

Wires of all sorts—whether copper, tin, gold, or platinum—have a slight **resistance** to the flow of electrons, just as water pipes have a slight amount of friction that resists the flow of water. Resistance to the flow of electrons is measured in **ohms (Ω)**.

- Pressure = voltage (V)
- Volume flowing = amperes (A)
- Work = wattage (W)
- Resistance = ohms (Ω)

A particular thickness of wire only handles so much electricity at a time. If you push too much through, the wire will overheat and break, much as an overloaded water pipe will burst. To make sure you use the right wire for the right job, all electrical wires have an amperage rating, such as 20 amps. If you try to push 30 amps through a 20-amp wire, the wire will break and electrons will seek a way to return into the ground. Not a good thing, especially if the path back to the ground is through you!

Circuit breakers and ground wires provide the basic protection from accidental overflow. A circuit breaker is a heat-sensitive electrical switch rated at a certain amperage. If you push too much amperage through the circuit breaker, the wiring inside detects the increase in heat and automatically opens, stopping the flow of electricity before the wiring overheats and breaks. You reset the circuit breaker to reestablish the circuit and electricity flows once more through the wires. A ground wire provides a path of least resistance for electrons to flow back to ground in case of an accidental overflow.

Many years ago your electrical supply used fuses instead of circuit breakers. Fuses are small devices with a tiny filament designed to break if subjected to too much current. Unfortunately, fuses had to be replaced every time they blew, making circuit breakers much more preferable. Even though you no longer see fuses in a building's electrical circuits, many electrical devices—such as a PC's power supply—often still use fuses for their own internal protection.

Electricity comes in two flavors: **direct current (DC)**, in which the electrons flow in one direction around a continuous circuit, and **alternating current (AC)**, in which the flow of electrons alternates direction back and forth in a circuit (see Figure 10.2). Most electronic devices use DC power, but all

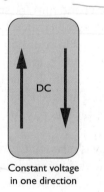

An electrical outlet must have a ground wire to be suitable for PC use.

DC
Constant voltage in one direction

AC
Voltage in both directions, constantly switching back and forth

• **Figure 10.2**   Diagrams showing DC and AC flow of electrons

power companies supply AC power because AC travels long distances much more efficiently than DC.

Essentials

■ Powering the PC

Your PC uses DC voltage, so some conversion process must take place before the PC can use AC power from the power company. The power supply in a computer converts high-voltage AC power from the wall socket to low-voltage DC. The first step in powering the PC, therefore, is to get and maintain a good supply of AC power. Second, you need a power supply to convert AC to the proper voltage and amperage of DC power for the motherboard and peripherals. Finally, you need to control the byproduct of electricity use, namely heat. Let's look at the specifics of powering the PC.

Supplying AC

Every PC power supply must have standard AC power from the power company, supplied steadily rather than in fits and spurts, and protection against accidental blurps in the supply. The power supply connects to the power cord (and thus to an electrical outlet) via a standard **IEC-320** connector. In the United States, standard AC comes in somewhere between 110 and 120 V, often written as ~115 VAC (volts of alternating current). The rest of the world uses 220–240 VAC, so most power supplies have a little switch in the back so you can use them anywhere. These power supplies with voltage-selection switches are referred to as fixed-input. Power supplies that you do not have to manually switch for different voltages are known as auto-switching. Figure 10.3 shows the back of a power supply. Note the

• **Figure 10.3**   Back of fixed-input power supply, showing typical switches and power connection

Flipping the AC switch on the back of a power supply can wreak all kinds of havoc on a PC. Moving the switch to ~230 V in the United States makes for a great practical joke (as long as the PC is off when you do it)— the PC might try to boot up but probably won't get far. You don't risk damaging anything by running at half the AC the power supply is expecting. In countries that run ~230 standard, on the other hand, firing up the PC with the AC switch set to ~115 can cause the power supply to die a horrid, smoking death. Watch that switch!

three components, from top to bottom: the hard on/off switch, the 115/230 switch, and the IEC-320 connector.

Before plugging anything into an AC outlet, take a moment to test the outlet first by using a multimeter or a device designed exclusively to test outlets. Failure to test AC outlets properly can result in inoperable or destroyed equipment, as well as possible electrocution. The IEC-320 plug has three holes, called hot, neutral, and ground. These names describe the function of the wires that connect to them behind the wall plate. The hot wire carries electrical voltage, much like a pipe that delivers water. The neutral wire carries no voltage, but instead acts like a water drain, completing the circuit by returning electricity to the local source, normally a breaker panel. The ground wire makes it possible for excess electricity to return safely to the ground. When testing AC power, you want to check for three things: that the hot outputs approximately 115 V (or whatever the proper voltage is for your part of the world), that the neutral connects to ground (0 V output), and that the ground connects to ground (again, 0 V). Figure 10.4 shows the voltages at an outlet.

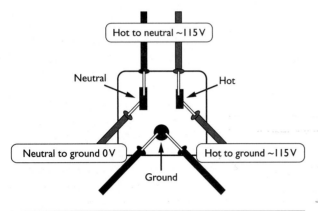

• **Figure 10.4**   Outlet voltages

You can use a **multimeter**—often also referred to as a *volt-ohm meter* (*VOM*) or *digital multimeter* (*DMM*)—to measure a number of aspects of electrical current. A multimeter consists of two probes, an analog or digital meter, and a dial to set the type of test you want to perform. Refer to Figure 10.5 to become familiar with the components of the multimeter.

Note that some multimeters use symbols rather than letters to describe AC and DC settings. The *V* with the solid line above a dashed line, for example, in Figure 10.6, refers to direct current. The *V~* stands for alternating current.

Every multimeter offers at least four types of electrical tests: continuity, resistance, AC voltage (VAC), and DC voltage (VDC). Continuity tests whether electrons can flow from one end of a wire to the other end. If so, you have continuity; if not, you don't. You can use this setting to determine if a fuse is good or to check for breaks in wires. If your multimeter doesn't

• **Figure 10.5**   Digital multimeter

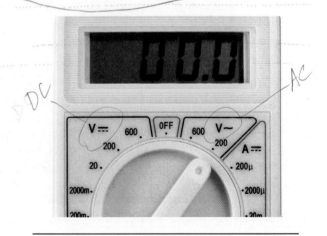

• **Figure 10.6**   Multimeter featuring DC and AC symbols

 **Try This!**

Using a Multimeter to Test AC Outlets

Every competent technician knows how to use a multimeter, so if you haven't used one in the past, get hold of one and Try This!

First you need to set up the meter for measuring AC. Follow these steps:

1. Move the selector switch to the AC V (usually red). If multiple settings are available, put it into the first scale higher than 120 V (usually 200 V). *Auto-range* meters set their own range; they don't need any selection except AC V.

2. Place the black lead in the common (–) hole. If the black lead is permanently attached, ignore this step.

3. Place the red lead in the V-Ohm-A (+) hole. If the red lead is permanently attached, ignore this step.

Once you have the meter set up for AC, go through the process of testing the various wires on an AC socket. Just don't put your fingers on the metal parts of the leads when you stick them into the socket! Follow these steps:

1. Put either lead in hot, the other in neutral. You should read 110 to 120 V AC.

2. Put either lead in hot, the other in ground. You should read 110 to 120 V AC.

3. Put either lead in neutral, the other in ground. You should read 0 V AC.

If any of these readings is different from what is described here, it's time to call an electrician.

 Tech Tip

AC Adapters

Many devices in the computing world use an AC adapter rather than an internal power supply. Even though it sits outside a device, an AC adapter converts AC current to DC, just like a power supply. Unlike power supplies, AC adapters are rarely interchangeable. Although manufacturers of different devices often use the same kind of plug on the end of the AC adapter cable, these adapters are not necessarily interchangeable. In other words, just because you can plug an AC adapter from your friend's laptop into your laptop does not mean it's going to work.

You need to make sure that three things match before you plug an AC adapter into a device: voltage, amperage, and polarity. If either the voltage or amperage output is too low, the device won't run. If the polarity is reversed, it won't work, just like putting a battery in a flashlight backwards. If either the voltage or amperage—especially the latter— is too high, on the other hand, you can very quickly toast your device. Don't do it! Always check the voltage, amperage, and polarity of a replacement AC adapter before you plug it into a device.

have a continuity tester (many cheaper multimeters do not), you can use the resistance tester. A broken wire or fuse will show infinite resistance, while a good wire or fuse will show no resistance. Testing AC and DC voltages is a matter of making sure the measured voltage is what it should be.

Using Special Equipment to Test AC Voltage

A number of good AC-only testing devices are available. With these devices, you can test all voltages for an AC outlet by simply inserting them into the outlet. Be sure to test all of the outlets the computer system uses: power supply, external devices, and monitor. Although convenient, these devices aren't as accurate as a multimeter. My favorite tester is made by Radio Shack, a simple-seeming tool (see Figure 10.7). This handy device provides three light-emitting diodes (LEDs) that describe everything that can go wrong with a plug.

Protecting the PC from Spikes and Sags in AC Power

If all power companies could supply electricity in smooth, continuous flows with no dips or spikes in pressure, the next two sections of this chapter would

be irrelevant. Unfortunately, no matter how clean the AC supply appears to a multimeter, the truth is that voltage from the power company tends to drop well below (sag) and shoot far above (surge or spike) the standard 115 V (in the United States). These sags and spikes usually don't affect lamps and refrigerators, but they can keep your PC from running or can even destroy a PC or peripheral device. Two essential devices handle spikes and sags in the supply of AC: surge suppressors and uninterruptible power supplies.

Surge Suppressors   Surges or spikes are far more dangerous than sags. Even a strong sag only shuts off or reboots your PC; any surge can harm your computer, and a strong surge destroys components. Given the seriousness of surges, every PC should use a **surge suppressor** device that absorbs the extra voltage from a surge to protect the PC. The power supply does a good job of surge suppression and can handle many of the smaller surges that take place fairly often. But the power supply takes a lot of damage from this and will eventually fail. To protect your power supply, a dedicated surge suppressor works between the power supply and the outlet to protect the system from power surges (see Figure 10.8).

Most people tend to spend a lot of money on their PC and for some reason suddenly get cheap on the surge suppressor. Don't do that! Make sure your surge suppressor has the Underwriters Laboratories UL 1449 for 330-V rating to ensure substantial protection for your system. Underwriters Laboratories (www.ul.com) is a U.S.-based, not-for-profit, widely recognized industry testing laboratory whose testing standards are very important to the consumer electronics industry. Additionally, check the joules rating before buying a new surge suppressor. A **joule** is a unit of electrical energy. How much energy a surge suppressor can handle before it fails is described in joules. Most authorities agree that your surge suppressor should rate at a minimum of 800 joules—and the more joules, the better the protection. My surge suppressor rates out at 1,750 joules.

While you're protecting your system, don't forget that surges also come from telephone and cable connections. If you use a modem, DSL, or cable modem, make sure to get a surge suppressor that includes support for these types of connections. Many manufacturers make surge suppressors with telephone line protection (see Figure 10.9).

No surge suppressor works forever. Make sure your surge suppressor has a test/reset button so you'll know when the device has—as we say in the

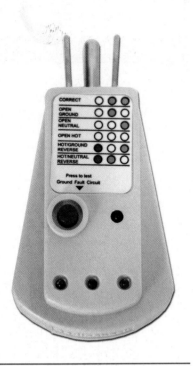

• **Figure 10.7**   Circuit tester

• **Figure 10.8**   Surge suppressor

No surge suppressor in the world can handle the ultimate surge, the ESD of a lightning strike. If your electrical system takes such a hit, you can kiss your PC goodbye if it was plugged in at the time. *Always* unplug electronics during electrical storms!

• **Figure 10.9**   Surge suppressor with telephone line protection

business—turned into an extension cord. If your system takes a hit and you have a surge suppressor, call the company! Many companies provide cash guarantees against system failure due to surges, but only if you follow their guidelines.

If you want really great surge suppression, you need to move up to **power conditioning**. Your power lines take in all kinds of strange signals that have no business being in there, such as electromagnetic interference (EMI) and radio frequency interference (RFI). Most of the time, this line noise is so minimal it's not worth addressing, but occasionally events (such as lightning) generate enough line noise to cause weird things to happen to your PC (keyboard lockups, messed-up data). All better surge suppressors add power conditioning to filter out EMI and RFI.

UPS An **uninterruptible power supply (UPS)** protects your computer (and, more importantly, your data) in the event of a power sag or power outage. Figure 10.10 shows a typical UPS. A UPS essentially contains a big battery that provides AC power to your computer regardless of the power coming from the AC outlet.

All uninterruptible power supplies are measured in both watts (the true amount of power they supply in the event of a power outage) and in *volt-amps* (*VA*). Volt-amps is the amount of power the UPS could supply if the devices took power from the UPS in a perfect way. Your UPS provides perfect AC power, moving current smoothly back and forth 60 times a second. Power supplies, monitors, and other devices, however, may not take all of the power the UPS has to offer at every point as the AC power moves back and forth, resulting in inefficiencies. If your devices took all of the power the UPS offered at every point as the power moved back and forth, VA would equal watts.

If the UPS makers knew ahead of time exactly what devices you planned to plug into their UPS, they could tell you the exact watts, but different devices have different efficiencies, forcing the UPS makers to go by what they can offer (VAs), not what your devices will take (watts). The watts value they give is a guess, and it's never as high as the VAs. The VA rating is always higher than the watt rating.

Because you have no way to calculate the exact efficiency of every device you'll plug into the UPS, go with the wattage rating. You add up the total wattage of every component in your PC and buy a UPS with a higher wattage. You'll spend a lot of time and mental energy figuring precisely how much wattage your computer, monitor, drives, and so on require to get the proper UPS for your system. But you're still not finished! Remember that the UPS is a battery with a limited amount of power, so you then need to figure out how long you want the UPS to run when you lose power.

The quicker and far better method to use for determining the UPS you need is to go to any of the major surge suppressor/UPS makers' Web sites and use their handy power calculators. My personal favorite is on the American Power Conversion Web site: www.apc.com. APC makes great surge suppressors and UPSs, and the company's online calculator will show you the true wattage you need—and teach you about whatever new thing is happening in power at the same time.

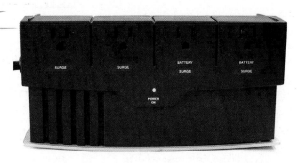

● **Figure 10.10** Uninterruptible power supply

Tech Tip

UPS Technologies
There are two main types of UPS: online, *where devices are constantly powered through the UPS's battery, and* standby, *where devices connected to the UPS only receive battery power when the AC sags below ~80–90 V. Another type of UPS is called* line-interactive, *which is similar to a standby UPS but has special circuitry to handle moderate AC sags and surges without the need to switch to battery power.*

Try This!

Shopping for a UPS

When it comes to getting a UPS for yourself or a client, nothing quite cuts through the hype and marketing terms like a trip to the local computer store to see for yourself. You need excuses to go to the computer store, so Try This!

1. Go to your local computer store—or visit an online computer site if no stores are nearby—and find out what's available.

2. Answer this question: How can you tell the difference between an online and a standby UPS?

Every UPS also has surge suppression and power conditioning, so look for the joule and UL 1449 ratings. Also look for replacement battery costs—some UPS replacement batteries are very expensive. Last, look for a UPS with a USB or serial port connection. These handy UPSs come with monitoring and maintenance software (Figure 10.11) that tells you the status of your system and the amount of battery power available, logs power events, and provides other handy options.

Table 10.1 gives you a quick look at the low end and the very high end of UPS products (as of late 2009).

• **Figure 10.11** APC PowerChute software

Supplying DC

After you've assured the supply of good AC electricity for the PC, the power supply unit (PSU) takes over, converting high-voltage AC into several DC voltages (notably, 5.0, 12.0, and 3.3 V) usable

Table 10.1		Typical UPS Devices			
Brand	**Model**	**Outlets Protected**	**Backup Time**	**Price**	**Type**
APC	BE350G	3 @ 120 V	3 min @ 200 W, 10 min @ 100 W	$49.99	Standby
APC	BP500UC	4 @ 120 V	4 min @ 315 W, 14 min @ 157 W	$129.99	Standby
CyberPower	CPS1500AVR	3 @ 120 V	18 min @ 950 W, 6 min @ 475 W	$299.99	Line-interactive
APC	SYA4K8RMP	6 @ 120,208 V	6 min @ 3200 W, 17 min @ 1600 W	$6,925.00	Double-conversion online

by the delicate interior components. Power supplies come in a large number of shapes and sizes, but the most common size by far is the standard 150 mm × 140 mm × 86 mm desktop PSU shown in Figure 10.12.

The PC uses the 12.0-V current to power motors on devices such as hard drives and CD-ROM drives, and it uses the 5.0-V and 3.3-V current for support of onboard electronics. Manufacturers may use these voltages any way they wish, however, and may deviate from these assumptions. Power supplies also come with standard connectors for the motherboard and interior devices.

Power to the Motherboard

Modern motherboards use a 20- or 24-pin **P1 power connector**. Some motherboards may require special 4-, 6-, or 8-pin connectors to supply extra power (Figure 10.13). We'll talk about each of these connectors in the form factor standards discussion later in this chapter.

• **Figure 10.12** Desktop PSU

Power to Peripherals: Molex, Mini, and SATA

Many devices inside the PC require power. These include hard drives, floppy drives, optical drives, Zip drives (for techs who enjoy retro computing), and fans. The typical PC power supply has up to three types of connectors that plug into peripherals: Molex, mini, and SATA.

Molex Connectors The most common type of power connection for devices that need 5 or 12 V of power is the **Molex connector** (Figure 10.14). The Molex connector has notches, called *chamfers*, that guide its installation. The tricky part is that Molex connectors require a firm push to plug in properly, and a strong person can defeat the chamfers, plugging a Molex in upside down. Not a good thing. *Always* check for proper orientation before you push it in!

• **Figure 10.13** Motherboard power connectors

Mini Connectors All power supplies have a second type of connector, called a **mini connector** (Figure 10.15), that supplies 5 and 12 V to peripherals, although only floppy disk drives in modern systems use this connector. Drive manufacturers adopted the mini as the standard connector on 3.5-inch floppy disk drives. Often these mini connectors are referred to as floppy power connectors.

• **Figure 10.14** Molex connector

• **Figure 10.15** Mini connector

Try This!

Testing DC

A common practice for techs troubleshooting a system is to test the DC voltages coming out of the power supply. Even with good AC, a bad power supply can fail to transform AC to DC at voltages needed by the motherboard and peripherals. So grab your trusty multimeter and Try This! on a powered-up PC with the side cover removed. Note that you must have P1 connected to the motherboard and the system must be running (you don't have to be in Windows, of course).

1. Switch your multimeter to DC, somewhere around 20 V DC if you need to make that choice. Make sure your leads are plugged into the multimeter properly: red to hot, black to ground. The key to testing DC is that which lead you touch to which wire matters. Red goes to hot wires of all colors; black *always* goes to ground.

2. Plug the red lead into the red wire socket of a free Molex connector and plug the black lead into one of the two black wire sockets. You should get a reading of ~5 V. What do you have?

3. Now move the red lead to the yellow socket. What voltage do you get?

4. Testing the P1 connector is a little more complicated. You push the red and black leads into the top of P1, sliding in alongside the wires until you bottom out. Leave the black lead in one of the black wire ground sockets. Move the red lead through all of the colored wire sockets. What voltages do you find?

⚠️ As with any power connector, plugging a mini connector into a device the wrong way will almost certainly destroy the device. Check twice before you plug one in!

Be extra careful when plugging in a mini connector! Whereas Molex connectors are difficult to plug in backward, you can insert a mini connector incorrectly with very little effort. As with a Molex connector, doing so will almost certainly destroy the floppy drive. Figure 10.16 depicts a correctly oriented mini connection, with the small ridge on the connector away from the body of the data socket.

• **Figure 10.16**   Correct orientation of a mini connector

SATA Power Connectors   Serial ATA (SATA) drives need a special 15-pin **SATA power connector** (Figure 10.17). The larger pin count supports the SATA hot-swappable feature and 3.3-, 5.0-, and 12.0-V devices. SATA power connectors are *L* shaped, making it almost impossible to insert one incorrectly into a SATA drive. No other device on your computer uses the SATA power connector. For more information about SATA drives, see Chapter 11, "Hard Drive Technologies."

Splitters and Adapters   You may occasionally find yourself without enough connectors to power all of the devices inside your PC. In this case, you can purchase splitters to create more connections (see Figure 10.18). You might also run into the phenomenon of needing a SATA connector but having only a spare Molex. Because the voltages on the wires are the same, a simple adapter will take care of the problem nicely.

• Figure 10.17   SATA power connector

   SATA also supports a slimline connector that has a 6-pin power segment and a micro connector that has a 9-pin power segment.

   It's normal and common to have unused power connectors inside your PC case.

ATX

The original ATX power supplies had two distinguishing physical features: the motherboard power connector and soft power. Motherboard power came from a single cable with a 20-pin P1 motherboard power connector. ATX power supplies also had at least two other cables, each populated with two or more Molex or mini connectors for peripheral power.

When plugged in, ATX systems have 5 V running to the motherboard. They're always "on" even when powered down. The power switch you press to power up the PC isn't a true power switch like the light switch on the wall in your bedroom. The power switch on an ATX system simply tells the computer whether it has been pressed. The BIOS or operating system takes over from there and handles the chore of turning the PC on or off. This is called **soft power**.

Using soft power instead of a physical switch has a number of important benefits. Soft power prevents a user from turning off a system before the operating system has been shut down. It enables the PC to use power-saving modes that put the system to sleep and then wake it up when you press a key, move a mouse, or receive an e-mail. (See Chapter 21, "Portable Computing," for more details on sleep mode.)

All of the most important settings for ATX soft power reside in CMOS setup. Boot into CMOS and look for a Power Management section. Take a look at the Power On Function option in Figure 10.19. This determines the function of the on/off switch. You may set this switch to turn off the computer, or you may set it to the more common *4-second delay*.

ATX did a great job supplying power for more than a decade, but over time more powerful CPUs, multiple CPUs, video cards, and other components began to need more current than the original ATX provided. This motivated the industry to introduce a number of updates to the ATX power standards: ATX12V 1.3, EPS12V, multiple rails, ATX12V 2.0, other form factors, and active PFC.

ATX12V 1.3   The first widespread update to the ATX standard, ATX12V 1.3, came out in 2003. This introduced a 4-pin motherboard power connector, unofficially but commonly called the P4, that provided more 12-V power to assist the 20-pin P1 motherboard power connector. Any power supply that provides a P4 connector is called an ATX12V power supply. The term "ATX" was dropped from the ATX power standard, so if you want to

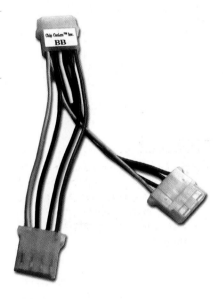

• Figure 10.18   Molex splitter

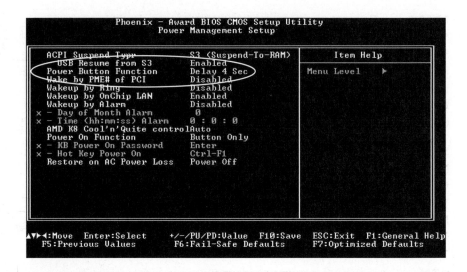

```
                    Phoenix - Award BIOS CMOS Setup Utility
                           Power Management Setup

   ACPI Suspend Type           S3 (Suspend-To-RAM)          Item Help
     USB Resume from S3         Enabled
   Power Button Function        Delay 4 Sec          Menu Level    ▶
   Wake by PME# of PCI          Disabled
   Wakeup by Ring               Disabled
   Wakeup by OnChip LAN         Enabled
   Wakeup by Alarm              Disabled
 x - Day of Month Alarm           0
 x - Time (hh:mm:ss) Alarm      0 : 0 : 0
   AMD K8 Cool'n'Quite controlAuto
   Power On Function            Button Only
 x - KB Power On Password       Enter
 x - Hot Key Power On           Ctrl-F1
   Restore on AC Power Loss     Power Off




 ▲▼►◄:Move  Enter:Select     +/-/PU/PD:Value  F10:Save    ESC:Exit  F1:General Help
    F5:Previous Values          F6:Fail-Safe Defaults      F7:Optimized Defaults
```

• **Figure 10.19**   Soft power setting in CMOS

Cross Check

ATX Form Factor

The power supply form factor alone does not define a system as ATX or one of the later varieties; you have to discuss the motherboard as well. Flip back to Chapter 9, "Motherboards," and see if you can put the full picture of the ATX standard together. What defines a system as ATX? What improvements did ATX incorporate over AT? What ATX form factors can you purchase?

get really nerdy you can say—accurately—that there's no such thing as an ATX power supply. All power supplies—assuming they have a P4 connector—are ATX12V or one of the later standards.

The ATX12V 1.3 standard also introduced a 6-pin auxiliary connector—commonly called an *AUX* connector—to supply increased 3.3- and 5.0-V current to the motherboard (see Figure 10.20). This connector was based on the motherboard power connector from the precursor of ATX, called *AT*.

• **Figure 10.20**   Auxiliary power connector

The introduction of these two extra power connectors caused the industry some teething problems. In particular, motherboards using AMD CPUs tended to need the AUX connector, while motherboards using Intel CPUs needed only the P4. As a result, many power supplies came with only a P4 or only an AUX connector to save money. A few motherboard makers skipped adding either connector and used a standard Molex connector so people with older power supplies wouldn't have to upgrade just because they bought a new motherboard (Figure 10.21).

The biggest problem with ATX12V was its lack of teeth—it made a lot of recommendations but few requirements, giving PSU makers too much choice (such as choosing or not choosing to add AUX and P4 connectors) that weren't fixed until later versions.

EPS12V   Server motherboards are thirsty for power, and sometimes ATX12V 1.3 just didn't cut it. An industry group called the Server System Infrastructure (SSI) developed a non-ATX standard motherboard and power supply called EPS12V. An EPS12V power supply came with a 24-pin main motherboard power connector that resembled a 20-pin ATX connector, but it offered more current and thus more stability for motherboards. It also came

Mike Meyers' CompTIA A+ Guide to Managing and Troubleshooting PCs

with an AUX connector, an ATX12V P4 connector, and a unique 8-pin connector. That's a lot of connectors! EPS12V power supplies were not interchangeable with ATX12V power supplies.

EPS12V may not have seen much life beyond servers, but it introduced a number of power features, some of which eventually became part of the ATX12V standard. The most important issue was something called **rails**.

Rails Generally, all of the PC's power comes from a single transformer that takes the AC current from a wall socket and converts it into DC current that is split into three primary DC voltage rails: 12.0 V, 5.0 V, and 3.3 V. Individual lines run from each of these voltage rails to the various connectors. That means the 12-V connector on a P4 draws from the same rail as the main 12-V connector feeding power to the motherboard. This works fine as long as the collective needs of the connectors sharing a rail don't exceed its capacity to feed them power. To avoid this, EPS12V divided the 12-V supply into two or three separate 12-V rails, each one providing a separate source of power.

• **Figure 10.21**   Molex power on motherboard

ATX12V 2.0 The ATX12V 2.0 standard incorporated many of the good ideas of EPS12V into the ATX world, starting with the 24-pin connector. This 24-pin motherboard power connector is backward compatible with the older 20-pin connector so users don't have to buy a new motherboard if they use an ATX12V 2.0 power supply. ATX12V 2.0 requires two 12-V rails for any power supply rated higher than 230 W. ATX12V 2.0 dropped the AUX connector and required SATA hard drive connectors.

In theory, a 20-pin motherboard power supply connector will work on a motherboard with a 24-pin socket, but doing this is risky in that the 20-pin connector may not provide enough power to your system. Try to use the right power supply for your motherboard to avoid problems. Many ATX12V 2.0 power supplies have a convertible 24-to-20-pin converter. These are handy if you want to make a nice "clean" connection, because many 20-pin connectors have capacitors that prevent plugging in a 24-pin connector. You'll also see the occasional 24-pin connector constructed in such a way that you can slide off the extra four pins. Figure 10.22 shows 20-pin and 24-pin connectors; Figure 10.23 shows a convertible connector. Although they look similar, those extra four pins won't replace the P4 connector. They are incompatible!

Many modern ATX motherboards feature an 8-pin CPU power connector like the one found in the EPS12V standard to help support high-end CPUs that demand a lot of power. This connector is referred to by several names, including EPS12V, EATX12V, and ATX12V 2x4. One half of this connector will be pin compatible with the P4 power connector and the other half may be under a protective cap. Be sure to check the motherboard installation manuals for recommendations on if and when you need to use the full 8 pins. For backward compatibility, some power supplies provide an 8-pin power connector that can split into two 4-pin sets, one of which is the P4 connector.

• **Figure 10.22**   20- and 24-pin connectors

• **Figure 10.23**   Convertible motherboard power connector

• **Figure 10.24** PCI Express 6-pin power connector

Another notable connector is the auxiliary PCI Express (PCIe) power connector. Figure 10.24 shows the 6-pin PCIe power connector. Some motherboards add a Molex socket for PCIe, and some cards come with a Molex socket as well. Higher-end cards have a dedicated 6-pin or 8-pin PCIe power connector. The 8-pin PCIe connector should not be confused with the EPS12V connector, as they are not compatible. Some PCIe devices with the 8-pin connector will accept a 6-pin PCIe power connection instead, but this may put limits on their performance. Often you'll find that 8-pin PCIe power cables have two pins at the end that you can detach for easy compatibility with 6-pin devices.

Practical Application

Niche-Market Power Supply Form Factors The demand for smaller and quieter PCs and, to a lesser extent, the emergence of the BTX form factor has led to the development of a number of niche-market power supply form factors. All use standard ATX connectors but differ in size and shape from standard ATX power supplies.

You'll commonly find niche-market power supplies bundled with computer cases (and often motherboards as well). These form factors are rarely sold alone.

Here are some of the more common specialty power supply types:

- **TFX12V**   A small power supply form factor optimized for low-profile ATX systems

- **SFX12V**   A small power supply form factor optimized for systems using FlexATX motherboards (see Figure 10.25)

- **CFX12V**   An L-shaped power supply optimized for microBTX systems

- **LFX12V**   A small power supply form factor optimized for low-profile BTX systems

The CompTIA A+ exams test you pretty heavily on power supplies. You need to know what power supply works with a particular system or with a particular computing goal in mind.

• **Figure 10.25**   SFX power supply

Active PFC Visualize the AC current coming from the power company as water in a pipe, smoothly moving back and forth, 60 times a second. A PC's power supply, simply due to the process of changing this AC current into DC current, is like a person sucking on a straw on the end of this pipe. It takes gulps only when the current is fully pushing or pulling at the top and bottom of each cycle and creating an electrical phenomena—sort of a back pressure—that's called *harmonics* in the power industry. These harmonics create the humming sound you hear from electrical components. Over time, harmonics damage electrical equipment, causing serious problems with the power supply and other electrical devices on the circuit. Once you put a few thousand PCs with power supplies in the same local area, harmonics can even damage the electrical power supplier's equipment!

Good PC power supplies come with **active power factor correction (active PFC)**, extra circuitry that smoothes out the way the power supply takes power from the power company and eliminates harmonics (Figure 10.26). Never buy a power supply that does not have active PFC—all power supplies with active PFC proudly show you on the box.

Wattage Requirements

Every device in a PC requires a certain amount of wattage to function. A typical hard drive draws 15 W of power when accessed, for example, whereas some Athlon 64 X2 CPUs draw a whopping 110 W at peak usage—with average usage around 70 W. The total wattage of all devices combined is the minimum you need the power supply to provide.

If the power supply cannot produce the wattage a system needs, that PC won't work properly. Because most devices in the PC require maximum wattage when first starting, the most common result of insufficient wattage is a paperweight that looks like a PC. This can lead to some embarrassing moments. You might plug in a new hard drive for a client, push the power button on the case, and nothing happens—a dead PC! Eek! You can quickly determine if insufficient wattage is the problem. Unplug the drive and power up the system. If the system boots up, the power supply is a likely suspect. The only fix for this problem is to replace the power supply with one that provides more wattage (or leave the new drive out—a less-than-ideal solution).

No power supply can turn 100 percent of the AC power coming from the power company into DC current, so all power supplies provide less power to the system than the wattage advertised on the box. ATX12V 2.0 standards require a power supply to be at least 70 percent efficient, but you can find power supplies with better than 80 percent efficiency. More efficiency can

[ENGLISH] Model: Neo HE 550

- ATX12V v2.2 and EPS12V compliant.
- Dual CPU and dual core ready.
- **Advanced cable management system** improves internal airflow and reduces system clutter by allowing you to use only the cables that you need.
- **Universal Input** automatically accepts line voltages from 100V to 240V AC.
- **Active PFC** (Power Factor Correction) delivers environmentally-friendlier power.
- **Up to 85% efficiency** reduces heat generation and saves power and money.
- **Dedicated voltage outputs** to deliver more stable power.
- **Voltage feedback** and tight ±3% regulation for improved system stability.
- **Three +12V output circuits** provide maximum stable power for the CPU independently and for other peripherals.
- **Dual PCI Express** graphics card power connectors.
- **Low-speed 80mm fan** delivers whisper-quiet cooling and ensures quiet operation by varying fan speed in response to load and conditions.
- **SATA connectors** for your Serial ATA drives.
- **Industrial grade protection circuitry** prevents damage resulting from short circuits (SCP), power overloads (OPP), excessive current (OCP), excessive voltages (OVP), and under voltage (UVP).
- **Approvals:** UL, CUL, CE, CB, FCC Class B, TÜV, CCC, C-tick.
- **MTBF:** 80,000 hrs.
- **Size:** 5.9" (D) x 5.9" (W) x 3.4" (H)
  15cm (D) x 15cm (W) x 8.6cm (H)
- **AQ3*** – Antec's unbeatable three-year parts and labor warranty.

• **Figure 10.26** Power supply advertising active PFC

> The CompTIA A+ certification exams do not require you to figure precise wattage needs for a particular system. When building a PC for a client, however, you do need to know this stuff!

tell you how many watts the system puts out to the PC in actual use. Plus, the added efficiency means the power supply uses less power, saving you money.

One common argument these days is that people buy power supplies that provide far more wattage than a system needs and therefore waste power. This is untrue. A power supply provides only the amount of power your system needs. If you put a 1000-W power supply (yes, they really exist) into a system that needs only 250 W, that big power supply will put out only 250 W to the system. So buying an efficient, higher-wattage power supply gives you two benefits. First, running a power supply at less than 100 percent load lets it live longer. Second, you'll have plenty of extra power when adding new components.

As a general recommendation for a new system, use at least a 500-W power supply. This is a common wattage and gives you plenty of extra power for booting as well as for whatever other components you might add to the system in the future.

■ Installing, Maintaining, and Troubleshooting Power Supplies

Although installing, maintaining, and troubleshooting power supplies take a little less math than selecting the proper power supply for a system, they remain essential skills for any tech. Installing takes but a moment, and maintaining is almost as simple, but troubleshooting can cause headaches. Let's take a look.

Installing

The typical power supply connects to the PC with four standard computer screws, mounted in the back of the case (Figure 10.27). Unscrew the four screws and the power supply lifts out easily (Figure 10.28). Insert a new power supply that fits the case and attach it by using the same four screws.

• **Figure 10.27** Mounting screws for power supply

• **Figure 10.28** Removing power supply from system unit

Handling ATX power supplies requires special consideration. Understand that an ATX power supply *never turns off*. As long as that power supply stays connected to a power outlet, the power supply will continue to supply 5 V to the motherboard. Always unplug an ATX system before you do any work! For years, techs bickered about the merits of leaving a PC plugged in or unplugged while you serviced it. ATX settled this issue forever. Many ATX power supplies provide a real on/off switch on the back of the PSU (see Figure 10.29). If you really need the system shut down with no power to the motherboard, use this switch.

When working on an ATX system, you may find using the power button inconvenient because you're not using a case or you haven't bothered to plug the power button's leads into the motherboard. That means there is no power button. One trick when in that situation is to use a set of car keys or a screwdriver to contact the two wires to start and stop the system (see Figure 10.30).

Your first task after acquiring a new power supply is simply making sure it works. Insert the motherboard power connectors before starting the system. If you have video cards with power connectors, plug them in too. Other connectors such as hard drives can wait until you have one successful boot—or if you're cocky, just plug everything in!

Cooling

Heat and computers are not the best of friends. Cooling is therefore a vital consideration when building a computer. Electricity equals heat. Computers, being electrical devices, generate heat as they operate, and too much can seriously damage a computer's internal components.

The **power supply fan** provides the basic cooling for the PC (Figure 10.31). It not only cools the voltage regulator circuits *within* the power supply, but it also provides a constant flow of outside air throughout the interior of the computer case. A dead power supply fan can rapidly cause tremendous problems, even equipment failure. If you ever turn on a computer and it boots just fine but you notice that it seems unusually quiet, check to see if the power supply fan has died. If it has, quickly turn off the PC and replace the power supply.

Some power supplies come with a built-in sensor to help regulate the airflow. If the system gets too hot, the power supply fan spins faster. The 3-pin, 3-wire fan sensor connector plugs into the motherboard directly (Figure 10.32).

Case fans are large, square fans that snap into special brackets on the case or screw directly to the case, providing extra cooling for key components (see Figure 10.33). Most cases come with a case fan, and no modern computer should really be without one or two.

● **Figure 10.29**   On/off switch for an ATX system

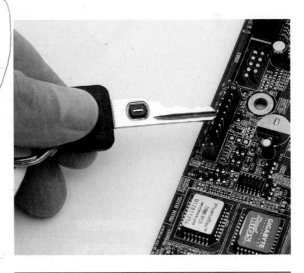

● **Figure 10.30**   Shorting the soft on/off jumpers

● **Figure 10.31**   Power supply fan

• **Figure 10.33**   Case fan

• **Figure 10.32**   3-wire fan sensor connector

The single biggest issue related to case fans is where to plug them in. Most case fans come with standard Molex connectors, which are easy to plug in, but other case fans come with special three-pronged power connectors that need to connect to the motherboard. You can get adapters to plug three-pronged connectors into Molex connectors or vice versa.

Maintaining Airflow

A computer is a closed system, and computer cases help the fans keep things cool: everything is inside a box. Although many tech types like to run their systems with the side panel of the case open for easy access to the components, in the end they are cheating themselves. Why? A closed case enables the fans to create airflow. This airflow substantially cools off interior components. When the side of the case is open, you ruin the airflow of the system, and you lose a lot of cooling efficiency.

An important point to remember when implementing good airflow inside your computer case is that hot air rises. Warm air always rises above cold air, and you can use this principle to your advantage in keeping your computer cool.

In the typical layout of case fans for a computer case, an intake fan is located near the bottom of the front bezel of the case. This fan draws cool air in from outside the case and blows it over the components inside the case. Near the top and rear of the case (usually near the power supply), you'll usually find an exhaust fan. This fan works the opposite of the intake fan: it takes the warm air from inside the case and sends it to the outside.

Another important part of maintaining proper airflow inside the case is ensuring that **slot covers** are covering all empty expansion bays (Figure 10.34). To maintain good airflow inside your case, you shouldn't provide too many opportunities for air to escape. Slot covers not only assist in maintaining a steady airflow; they also help keep dust and smoke out of your case.

Missing slot covers can cause the PC to overheat!

Reducing Fan Noise

Fans generate noise. In an effort to ensure proper cooling, many techs put several high-speed fans into a case, making the PC sound like a jet engine. You can reduce fan noise by using manually adjustable fans, larger fans, or specialty "quiet" fans. Many motherboards enable you to control fans through software.

Manually adjustable fans have a little knob you can turn to speed up or slow down the fan (Figure 10.35). This kind of fan can reduce some of the noise, but you run the risk of slowing down the fan too much and thus letting the interior of the case heat up. A better solution is to get quieter fans.

Larger fans that spin more slowly are another way to reduce noise while maintaining good airflow. Fans sizes are measured in millimeters (mm) or centimeters (cm). Traditionally, the industry used 80-mm power supply and cooling fans, but today you'll find 100-mm, 120-mm, and even larger fans in power supplies and cases.

Many companies manufacture and sell higher-end low-noise fans. The fans have better bearings than run-of-the-mill fans, so they cost a little more, but they're definitely worth it. They market these fans as "quiet" or "silencer" or other similar adjectives. If you run into a PC that sounds like a jet, try swapping out the case fans for a low-decibel fan from Papst, Panasonic, or Cooler Master. Just check the decibel rating to decide which one to get. Lower, of course, is better.

Because the temperature inside a PC changes depending on the load put on the PC, the best solution for noise reduction combines a good set of fans with temperature sensors to speed up or slow down the fans automatically. A PC at rest uses less than half of the power of a PC running a video-intensive computer game and therefore makes a lot less heat. Virtually all modern systems support three fans through three 3-pin fan connectors on the motherboard. The CPU fan uses one of these connectors, and the other two are for system fans or the power supply fan.

Most CMOS setup utilities provide a little control over fans plugged into the motherboard. Figure 10.36 shows a typical CMOS setting for the fans. Note that you can't tell the fans when to come on or off—only when to set off an alarm when they reach a certain temperature.

Software is the best way to control your fans. Some motherboards come with system-monitoring software that enables you to set the temperature at which you want the fans to come on and off. If no program came with your motherboard, and the manufacturer's

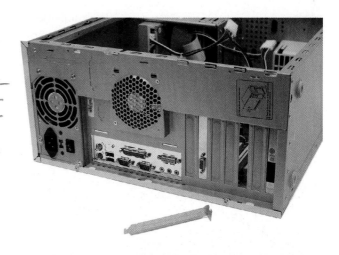

• **Figure 10.34** Slot covers

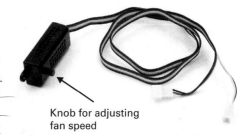

Knob for adjusting fan speed

• **Figure 10.35** Manual fan adjustment device

> When shopping for fans, remember your metric system: 80 mm = 8 cm; 120 mm = 12 cm. You'll find fans marketed both ways.

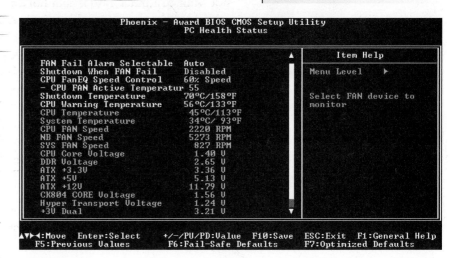

• **Figure 10.36** CMOS fan options

SpeedFan is a powerful tool that does far more than work with fans. Don't tweak any settings you don't understand!

Web site doesn't offer one for download, try the popular freeware SpeedFan utility (Figure 10.37). Written by Alfredo Milani Comparetti, SpeedFan monitors voltages, fan speeds, and temperatures in computers with hardware monitor chips. SpeedFan can even access S.M.A.R.T. information (see Chapter 11, "Hard Drive Technologies") for hard disks that support this feature and shows hard disk temperatures, too, if supported. You can find SpeedFan at www.almico.com/speedfan.php.

Even if you don't want to mess with your fans, always make a point to turn on your temperature alarms in CMOS. If the system gets too hot, an alarm will warn you. There's no way to know if a fan dies other than to have an alarm.

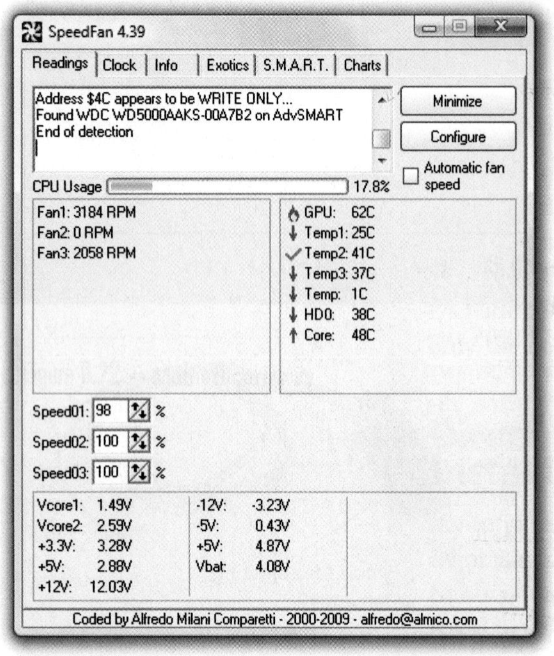

• **Figure 10.37** SpeedFan

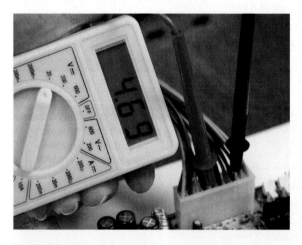

• **Figure 10.38** Testing one of the 5-V DC connections

Many CMOS utilities and software programs monitor voltage, saving you the hassle of using a multimeter.

When Power Supplies Die

Power supplies fail in two ways: sudden death and slowly over time. When they die suddenly, the computer will not start and the fan in the power supply will not turn. In this case, verify that electricity is getting to the power supply before you do anything. Avoid the embarrassment of trying to repair a power supply when the only problem is a bad outlet or an extension cord that is not plugged in. Assuming that the system has electricity, the best way to verify that a power supply is working or not working is to use a multimeter to check the voltages coming out of the power supply (see Figure 10.38).

Do not panic if your power supply puts out slightly more or less voltage than its nominal value. The voltages supplied by most PC power supplies can safely vary by as much as ±10 percent of their stated values. This means that the 12-V line can vary from roughly 10.5 to 12.9 V without exceeding the tolerance of the various systems in the PC. The 5.0- and 3.3-V lines offer similar tolerances.

Be sure to test every connection on the power supply—that means every connection on your main power as well as every Molex and mini. Because all voltages are between –20 and +20 VDC, simply set the voltmeter to the 20-V DC setting for everything. If the power supply fails to provide power, throw it into the recycling bin and get a new one—even if you're a component expert and a whiz with a soldering iron. Don't waste your or your company's time; the price of new power supplies makes replacement the obvious way to go.

No Motherboard

Power supplies will not start unless they're connected to a motherboard, so what do you do if you don't have a motherboard you trust to test? First, try an ATX tester. Many companies make these devices. Look for one that supports both 20- and 24-pin motherboard connectors as well as all of the other connectors on your motherboard. Figure 10.39 shows a power supply tester.

Switches

Broken power switches form an occasional source of problems for power supplies that fail to start. The power switch is behind the on/off button on every PC. It is usually secured to the front cover or inside front frame on your PC, making it a rather challenging part to access. To test, try shorting the soft power jumpers as described earlier. A key or screwdriver will do the trick.

When Power Supplies Die Slowly

If all power supplies died suddenly, this would be a much shorter chapter. Unfortunately, the majority of PC problems occur when power supplies die slowly over time. This means that one of the internal electronics of the power supply has begun to fail. The failures are *always* intermittent and tend to cause some of the most difficult to diagnose problems in PC repair. The secret to discovering that a power supply is dying lies in one word: intermittent. Whenever you experience intermittent problems, your first guess should be that the power supply is bad. Here are some other clues you may hear from users:

• **Figure 10.39**   ATX power supply tester

- "Whenever I start my computer in the morning, it starts to boot, and then locks up. If I press CTRL-ALT-DEL two or three times, it will boot up fine."

- "Sometimes when I start my PC, I get an error code. If I reboot, it goes away. Sometimes I get different errors."

- "My computer will run fine for an hour or so. Then it locks up, sometimes once or twice an hour."

Sometimes something bad happens and sometimes it does not. That's the clue for replacing the power supply. And don't bother with the voltmeter; the voltages will show up within tolerances, but only *once in a while* they will spike and sag (far more quickly than your voltmeter can measure) and cause these intermittent errors. When in doubt, change the power supply. Power supplies break in computers more often than any other part of the PC except the floppy disk drives. You might choose to keep power supplies on hand for swapping and testing.

Fuses and Fire

Inside every power supply resides a simple fuse. If your power supply simply pops and stops working, you might be tempted to go inside the power supply and check the fuse. This is not a good idea. First off, the capacitors in most power supplies carry high voltage charges that can hurt a lot if you touch them. Second, fuses blow for a reason. If a power supply is malfunctioning inside, you want that fuse to blow, because the alternative is much less desirable.

Failure to respect the power of electricity will eventually result in the most catastrophic of all situations: a fire. Don't think it won't happen to you! Keep a fire extinguisher handy. Every PC workbench needs a fire

extinguisher, but make sure you have the right one. The fire prevention industry has divided fire extinguishers into four fire classes:

- **Class A** Ordinary free-burning combustible, such as wood or paper
- **Class B** Flammable liquids, such as gasoline, solvents, or paint
- **Class C** Live electrical equipment
- **Class D** Combustible metals such as titanium or magnesium

As you might expect, you should only use a Class C fire extinguisher on your PC if it should catch fire. All fire extinguishers are required to have their type labeled prominently on them. Many fire extinguishers are multi-class in that they can handle more than one type of fire. The most common fire extinguisher is type ABC—it works on all common types of fires.

Beyond A+

Power supplies provide essential services for the PC, creating DC out of AC and cooling the system, but that utilitarian role does not stop the power supply from being an enthusiast's plaything. Plus, server and high-end workstations have somewhat different needs than more typical systems, so naturally they need a boost in power. Let's take a look Beyond A+ at these issues.

It Glows!

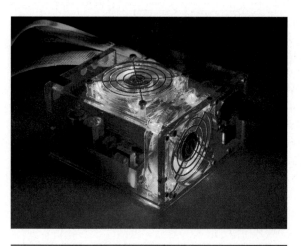

The enthusiast community has been modifying, or *modding*, their PCs for years, cutting holes in the cases, adding fans to make overclocking feasible, and slapping in glowing strips of neon and cold cathode tubes. The power supply escaped the scene for a while, but it's back. A quick visit to a good computer store off- or online, such as http://directron.com, reveals power supplies that light up, sport a fancy color, or have more fans than some rock stars. Figure 10.40 shows a see-through PSU.

On the other hand, you also find super-quiet stealth power supplies, with single or double high-end fans that react to the temperature inside your PC—speeding up when necessary but running slowly and silently when not. One of these would make a perfect power supply for a home entertainment PC because it would provide function without adding excessive decibels of noise.

● **Figure 10.40**   See-through power supply that glows blue

Modular Power Supplies

It's getting more and more popular to make PCs look good on both the inside and the outside. Unused power cables dangling around inside PCs creates a not-so-pretty picture. To help stylish people, manufacturers created power supplies with modular cables (Figure 10.41).

Modular cables are pretty cool, because you add only the lines you need for your system. On the other hand, some techs claim that modular cables hurt efficiency because the modular connectors add resistance to the lines. You make the choice; is a slight reduction in efficiency worth a pretty look?

Rail Power

When you start using more powerful CPUs and video cards, you can run into a problem I call "rail power." Every ATX12V power supply using multiple rails supplies only a certain amount of power, measured in amps (A), on each rail. The problem is with the 12-V rails. The ATX12V standard requires up to 18 A for each 12-V rail—more than enough for the majority of users, but not enough when you're using a powerful CPU and one or more PCIe video cards. If you have a powerful system, get online and read the detailed specs for your power supply. Figure 10.42 shows sample power supply specs. Many power supply makers do not release detailed specs—avoid them!

Look for power supplies that offer about 16 to 18 A per rail. These will be big power supplies—400 W and up. Nothing less will be able to support a big CPU and one or two PCIe video cards.

Watch out for power supplies that list their operating temperature at 25° C—about room temperature. A power supply that provides 500 W at 25° C will supply substantially less in warmer temperatures, and the inside of your PC is usually 15° C warmer than the outside air. Sadly, many power supply makers— even those who make good power supplies—fudge this fact.

● **Figure 10.41** Modular-cable power supply

NeoHE 550

FEATURES	
Switches	ATX Logic on-off Additional power rocker switch
Maximum Power	550W
Transient Response	+12V, +5Vand +3.3V independent output circuitry provides stable power and tighter cross regulation (+/- 3%)
P. G. Signal	100-500ms
Over Voltage Protection recycle AC to reset	+5V trip point < +6.5V +3.3V trip point < +4.1V +12V trip point < +14.3V
Special Connectors	ATX12V/EPS12V Compatible 4 + 4 pin +12V Molex Peripheral Floppy SATA PCI Express
Leakage Current	<3.5mA @ 115VAC

OUTPUT							
Output Voltage	+3.3V	+5V	+12V1	+12V2	+12V3	-12V	+5Vsb
Max. Load	24A	20A	18A	18A	18A	0.8A	2.5A
Min. Load	0.5A	0.3A	1A	1A	1A	0A	0A
Regulation	3%	3%	3%	3%	3%	6%	3%
Ripple & Noise(mV)	50	50	120	120	120	120	50
Available Power	79.2W	100W	504W			9.6W	12.5W
Total Power	550W continuous output @ 50C ambient temperature						

● **Figure 10.42** Sample specs

Chapter 10 Review

■ Chapter Summary

After reading this chapter and completing the exercises, you should understand the following about power supplies.

Explain the basics of electricity

■ The power supply takes electricity from the wall outlet and transforms it into the kind of electricity that the motherboard and other internal components use. To remove the power supply, unscrew the four screws in the back of the case and lift it out. Installing it is just as simple. Be careful never to open the power supply itself, as the capacitors inside can store a dangerous electrical charge.

■ Techs need to know basic principles of electricity and how to recognize power problems. Electricity is a flow of negatively charged particles or electrons through matter. Metallic wire is a good conductor, allowing electrons to move freely. The pressure of the electrons in the wire is called voltage and is measured in volts (V). Measured in units called amperes (amps or A), current or amperage is the amount of electrons flowing past a certain point on a wire. Wattage (watts or W) refers to the amount of amps and volts a particular device needs. The formula $VA = W$ expresses the correlation among the three. Resistance to the flow of electrons is measured in ohms. Fuses and ground wires set limits for the flow of electrons. A ground wire provides a path of least resistance to allow the electrons to flow to the ground.

■ Electricity may be either direct current (DC), with electrons flowing in one direction around a continuous circuit, or alternating current (AC), with electrons flowing back and forth in a circuit.

Describe the details about powering the PC

■ Because power companies supply high-voltage AC, the computer's power supply converts AC to low-voltage DC that is then portioned out to the internal devices. Heat is a byproduct of electricity and must be controlled in the computer.

■ The power supply connects to the electrical outlet via a standard IEC-320 connector. Although power in the U.S. ranges from 110 to 120 V, the rest of the world uses 200 to 240 VAC. Most power supplies can switch between 115 and 230 V. The IEC-320 plug has three holes, called hot, neutral, and ground. The hot carries electrical voltage and should output approximately 115 V in the U.S. The neutral returns electricity to the breaker panel and should have 0 V output. The ground wire returns excess electricity to the ground and should also have a 0 V output. You can use a multimeter to test voltages at the outlet.

■ A multimeter, also called a volt-ohm meter (VOM), uses two probes to provide at least four measurements: AC voltage (V~), DC voltage (V with a solid line above a dashed line), continuity (whether electrons flow from one end of a wire to the other end), and resistance (whether a fuse is good or blown or whether a wire has breaks). Some AC-only testing devices are available that simply plug into the AC outlet and may display results via three light-emitting diodes (LEDs).

■ A surge suppressor is an inexpensive device that protects your computer from voltage spikes. Inserted between the wall outlet and the power supply, a surge suppressor has a joule rating that measures how much electrical energy it can suppress. Be sure your surge suppressor has at least an 800 joules rating. Because telephone lines and cable connections also produce spikes, your surge suppressor should include connections for a modem, DSL, or cable modem. Make sure you purchase a surge suppressor that has the UL 1449 for 330-V rating, as this will ensure substantial protection for your system. Because surge suppressors work for only a limited time, you should check the manufacturer's recommended replacement schedules. If your surge suppressor comes with a cash guarantee, be aware that manufacturers honor it only if you follow their guidelines.

■ Because the AC supply lacks consistency and actually provides power with sags and spikes, it is important that you use two devices with a computer: an uninterruptible power supply and a surge suppressor. An uninterruptible power supply (UPS) continues to supply AC power to your computer during both brownouts and

blackouts via a battery that is charged from the AC current. All uninterruptible power supplies measure the amount of power or watts they supply, as well as listing the number of minutes the UPS will last with a certain voltage. It's difficult to estimate exactly how much wattage your computer and devices will require, so the better method to determine the UPS you need is to go to the UPS makers' Web sites and use their power calculators.

- The power supply converts AC into several DC voltages (5.0, 12.0, and 3.3 V). Devices such as hard drives and CD-ROM drives require 12.0 V, and onboard electronics use 3.3- and 5.0-V currents.

- The power supply has several standard connectors for the motherboard and interior devices. Today's motherboards have a P1 socket that uses the P1 connector from the power supply. A standard ATX power supply has a 20-pin P1 connector, while the newer ATX12V 2.0 power supplies come with a 24-pin P1 connector. Some motherboards also need a 4-, 6-, or 8-pin connector to provide an additional 12 V of power.

- Peripherals use two or possibly three different kinds of connectors: the larger Molex connector, the smaller mini connector, and the SATA connector. Used with hard drives and CD- and DVD-media drives, the Molex has chamfers to ensure that it is connected properly. Used today only for floppy drives, the mini connector can easily be inserted incorrectly, thus destroying the floppy drive. The SATA connector is used for SATA drives. If you do not have enough connectors for all of the devices inside your PC, you can create more connections with a splitter. Similarly, if your power supply does not have the connector a device needs, you can purchase adapters to convert one type to another.

- The ATX power supply includes full support for power-saving functions, with the modem or network interface card able to wake up the PC when there is incoming traffic. Using the soft power feature, the ATX power supply puts a 5-V charge on the motherboard as long as there is AC from the wall socket. You can configure the ATX soft power through the Power Management section of the CMOS setup. Always unplug an ATX system before you work on it. ATX power supplies use a single P1 connector for motherboard power.

- The ATX standard has undergone several updates. ATX12V 1.3 introduced additional 4-pin (P4) and 6-pin auxiliary (AUX) connectors. ATX12V 2.0 introduced the 24-pin connector (inspired by EPS12V), dropped the AUX connector, and required SATA connectors. Additionally, ATX12V 2.0 required two 12-V rails for any power supply larger than 230 W.

- The non-ATX standard EPS12V introduced a 24-pin motherboard connector and a unique 8-pin connector. It was not swappable with ATX power supplies, and while its popularity was short-lived, it introduced several features that became part of the ATX12V standard, including rails.

- The demand for smaller and quieter PCs and the introduction of the BTX motherboard form factors led to the development of niche-market power supply form factors. TFX12V, SFX12V, CFX12V, and LFX12V have the same connectors as standard ATX power supplies but differ in size or shape.

- Active power factor correction (active PFC) helps to eliminate harmonics, which can damage electrical components. Never buy a power supply that does not have active PFC.

- Power supplies are rated in watts. If you know the amount of wattage that every device in the PC needs, you can arrive at the total wattage required for all devices, and that is the minimum wattage your power supply should provide. If the power supply does not provide sufficient wattage, the computer will not work. For a new computer system, you should select at least a 500-W power supply to have extra power for adding components in the future.

- Because converting from AC to DC may result in a significant loss of wattage, purchase a power supply that offers a high percentage of efficiency. The ATX12V 2.0 standard requires a power supply to be at least 70 percent efficient, but you can find power supplies with better then 80 percent efficiency. Be aware that power supplies produce less wattage over time, so don't cut the wattage specification too tightly. While power supplies range from 200 to 600 W, you should know that the more AC the power supply draws, the more heat it produces.

Install, maintain, and troubleshoot power supplies

- Power supplies connect to the PC case via four screws mounted in the rear of the case. Unscrew the four screws and the power supply will lift out. Because an ATX power supply is always on, be sure to unplug it from the wall outlet before working on it.

- Adequate cooling is important to prevent damage to the computer's internal components. The fan inside the power supply itself cools the voltage regulator circuits within the power supply and provides a constant flow of outside air throughout the interior of the computer case. If the fan is not working, turn the computer off before you experience equipment failure. Some power supplies regulate airflow by using a sensor with a three-wire connector that plugs into the motherboard.

- To improve cooling, most cases come with a case fan. If the case does not have one, you should add one. Most case fans use standard Molex connectors, but some use a special three-pronged power connector that plugs directly into the motherboard. To enable the fans to create airflow, the case needs to be closed. If slot covers are left off of empty expansion bays, the computer can overheat. Slot covers also help keep dust and smoke out of the case. Beware of "great deals" on cases that come with power supplies, because the included power supply is often substandard.

- Electrical problems range from irregular AC to dying or faulty power supplies. Power supplies may fail suddenly or slowly over time. After you make sure that the wall outlet is providing electricity, checking voltages from the power supply with a voltmeter is the best way to verify that the power supply is working or has failed. A power supply is functioning properly if the output voltages are within 10 percent over or under the expected voltage. Be sure to check all of the connections on the power supply. If you determine that the power supply is bad, the most economical solution is to throw it away and replace it with a new one.

- Power supplies will not start unless they are connected to a motherboard. If you need to test a power supply but don't have a motherboard, use an ATX tester.

- If one of the internal electrical components in the power supply begins to fail, the result is usually intermittent problems, making diagnosis difficult. If you are experiencing intermittent problems, such as lockups or different error codes that disappear after rebooting, suspect the power supply. Unfortunately, the voltmeter is not good for diagnosing intermittent problems. Because power supply failures rank second behind floppy drive failures, it is a good idea to keep power supplies in stock for swapping and testing.

- Never open a power supply, even to check the fuse; the unit contains capacitors that carry high-voltage charges that can hurt you.

- Every PC workbench should have a Class C fire extinguisher handy in case of an electrical fire. Some fire extinguishers are multi-class and will work fine for a PC as well.

■ Key Terms

active power factor correction (active PFC) *(309)*

alternating current (AC) *(296)*

amperes (amps or A) *(295)*

direct current (DC) *(296)*

field replaceable unit (FRU) *(295)*

IEC-320 *(297)*

joule *(300)*

mini connector *(303)*

Molex connector *(303)*

multimeter *(298)*

ohms (Ω) *(296)*

P1 power connector *(303)*

power conditioning *(301)*

power supply fan *(311)*

power supply unit (PSU) *(295)*

rails *(307)*

resistance *(296)*

SATA power connector *(305)*

slot covers *(312)*

soft power *(305)*

surge suppressor *(300)*

uninterruptible power supply (UPS) *(301)*

volts (V) *(295)*

wattage (watts or W) *(295)*

Key Term Quiz

Use the Key Terms list to complete the sentences that follow. Not all terms will be used.

1. Supply power to the floppy drive by using the _____ from the power supply.

2. The electric company provides _____ power that the power supply converts to _____ for use by the computer components.

3. If the _____ are left off the expansion slots, the computer may overheat.

4. An ATX form factor power supply attaches to the motherboard with a _____ connector and supplies 5 V to the motherboard at all times.

5. Be sure your surge suppressor has a _____ rating of at least 800.

6. The measurement unit for the amount of electrons flowing past a certain point on a wire is _____.

7. The _____ provides the basic cooling for the PC.

8. Be sure the _____ rating for your power supply is greater than the minimum required by all devices in the computer.

9. The ability to split voltage supplies into separate _____ ensures that no device will hog all of the available power.

10. A spare part that a tech typically carries to replace a failed component in the field is called a(n) _____.

Multiple-Choice Quiz

1. Which of the following ATX12V features was introduced as part of the EPS12V standard?

    A. The P4 motherboard power connector

    B. Voltage rails

    C. The 6-pin AUX connector

    D. Soft power

2. Which kind of fire extinguisher should you use for computer equipment?

    A. Class A

    B. Class B

    C. Class C

    D. Class D

3. Under what conditions should a PC technician work inside the power supply?

    A. Only when it is unplugged.

    B. Only when the technician is wearing an anti-static wrist strap.

    C. Anytime, because the power supply only has low-energy DC electricity that will not hurt the technician.

    D. Never, because the power supply has capacitors that hold electrical charges that may harm the technician.

4. What should you check first if a computer will not start and the fan in the power supply will not turn?

    A. Check the voltages coming out of the power supply.

    B. Check the motherboard power connector.

    C. Check the power coming into the power supply.

    D. Check the power switch.

5. When you test voltage with a multimeter, you can assume the outlet or connector is functioning properly if the reading is within a certain percentage of the expected number. What is that maximum percentage by which the reading can vary?

    A. 5 percent

    B. 10 percent

    C. 20 percent

    D. 25 percent

6. What voltage does an ATX12V P4 connector provide for motherboards?

    A. 3.3 V

    B. 3.3 V, 5 V

    C. 5 V

    D. 12 V

7. When testing an AC outlet, what voltage should the multimeter show between the neutral and ground wires?

   A. 120 V

   B. 60 V

   C. 0 V

   D. –120 V

8. What sort of power connector does a hard drive typically use?

   A. Molex

   B. Mini

   C. Sub-mini

   D. Micro

9. Arthur installed a new motherboard in his case and connected the ATX power, but his system would not turn on. He sees an extra 4-wire port on the motherboard. What's he missing?

   A. He needs a power supply with a P2 connector for plugging in auxiliary components.

   B. He needs a power supply with a P3 connector for plugging in case fans.

   C. He needs a power supply with a P4 connector for plugging into more modern motherboards.

   D. He needs a power supply with an Aux connector for plugging into a secondary power supply.

10. What is the effect of exceeding the wattage capabilities of a power supply by inserting too many devices?

    A. The system will boot normally, but some of the devices will not function properly.

    B. The system will boot normally and all of the devices will work, but only for a limited time. After an hour or so, the system will spontaneously shut down.

    C. The system will not boot or turn on at all.

    D. The system will try to boot, but the overloaded power supply will fail, burning up delicate internal capacitors.

11. Where do you put the multimeter leads when you test a Molex connector?

    A. The red lead should always touch the red wire; the black lead should touch a black ground wire.

    B. The red lead should always touch the black ground wire; the black lead should always touch the red hot wire.

    C. The red lead should always touch the yellow hot wire; the black lead should touch the red hot wire.

    D. The red lead should touch either the red or yellow hot wire; the black lead should touch a black ground wire.

12. Which of the following problems points to a dying power supply?

    A. Intermittent lockups at bootup

    B. A power supply fan that does not turn

    C. A multimeter reading of 11 V for the 12-V power line

    D. A computer that won't start by shorting the soft power jumpers

13. What is the minimum PSU required for an ATX system that requires Molex, mini connectors, and SATA connectors?

    A. ATX

    B. ATX12V 1.3

    C. ATX12V 2.0

    D. EPS12V

14. Which of the following is not a PSU form factor?

    A. TFX12V

    B. SFX12V

    C. CFX12V

    D. LPX12V

15. Which statement is true?

    A. Removing the expansion slot covers on the back of your case will improve cooling by allowing hot air to escape.

    B. Shop around when purchasing a case as you will often find good deals that include a powerful PSU.

    C. Always keep the power supply plugged in to the wall outlet when working on the inside of a computer as this helps to ground it.

    D. An AC testing device is never as accurate as a multimeter.

■ Essay Quiz

1. Jack and Denise have joined your study group. Because neither has any previous experience with basic electricity and its jargon, they want you to explain voltage, amperage, and wattage. In plain language, define these terms and explain what VA = W means.

2. In the computer field, advances in one area often lead to advances in another area. Do you think improvements in the CPU and other computer devices and functions made the ATX form factor power supply necessary?

3. Because microprocessors have become more powerful and more devices have been invented for the computer, the wattage demands for the PC have gone up. So has the need for cooling. Discuss the cooling devices that come with today's PCs and what the user needs to know about keeping the PC cool.

4. Helene's computer worked fine last week. Although she has not changed anything since then, today her computer won't even boot. You suspect that the power supply died. You know she does not have a multimeter. What will you tell her to check to confirm this opinion? If she does need to replace the power supply, how can she be sure the new one will work with her PC?

Lab Projects

• Lab Project 10.1

This chapter recommends a 500-W power supply for a new computer. Is that the wattage that manufacturers usually offer with their computers? Check the following Web sites to see what wattage comes with a new PC:

- www.dell.com

- www.gateway.com
- www.hp.com

Do any of these companies mention a power supply upgrade with a higher wattage rating? If so, what are the wattages and what are the additional costs?

• Lab Project 10.2

Every technician needs a multimeter. Visit a local electronics store and look at its line of multimeters. (If a store is not nearby, you may use the Internet instead.) What features do the various multimeters offer? What kinds of measurements do they provide? Is the output from some in digital format and others in analog? Which output do you find easier to read? Is one kind more accurate than another? What price ranges are available for multimeters? Then, select the multimeter you would like to add to your toolkit. Why did you choose that model? Now start saving your pennies so you can buy it!

Hard Drive Technologies

In this chapter, you will learn how to

■ **Explain how hard drives work**

■ **Identify and explain the PATA and SATA hard drive interfaces**

■ **Identify and explain the SCSI hard drive interfaces**

■ **Describe how to protect data with RAID**

■ **Install hard drives**

■ **Configure CMOS and install drivers**

■ **Troubleshoot hard drive installation**

O f all the hardware on a PC, none gets more attention—or gives more anguish—than the hard drive. There's a good reason for this: if the hard drive breaks, you lose data. As you probably know, when the data goes, you have to redo work or restore from backup—or worse. It's good to worry about the data, because the data runs the office, maintains the payrolls, and stores the e-mail. This level of concern is so strong that even the most neophyte PC users are exposed to terms such as *IDE*, *PATA*, *SATA*, and *controller*—even if they don't put the terms into practice.

This chapter focuses on how hard drives work, beginning with the internal layout and organization of hard drives. You'll look at the different types of hard drives used today (PATA, SATA, SSD, and SCSI), how they interface with the PC, and how to install them properly into a system. The chapter covers how more than one drive may work with other drives to provide data safety and improve speed through a feature called RAID. Let's get started.

Historical/Conceptual

■ How Hard Drives Work

Hard drives sport one of two technologies today. The most common type has moving parts; the newer and more expensive technology has none. Let's look at both.

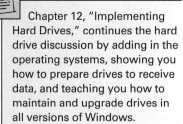
Chapter 12, "Implementing Hard Drives," continues the hard drive discussion by adding in the operating systems, showing you how to prepare drives to receive data, and teaching you how to maintain and upgrade drives in all versions of Windows.

Platter-Based Hard Drives

A traditional **hard disk drive (HDD)** is composed of individual disks, or *platters*, with read/write heads on actuator arms controlled by a servo motor—all contained in a sealed case that prevents contamination by outside air (see Figure 11.1).

The aluminum platters are coated with a magnetic medium. Two tiny read/write heads service each platter, one to read the top and the other to read the bottom of the platter (see Figure 11.2).

The coating on the platters is phenomenally smooth. It has to be, as the read/write heads actually float on a cushion of air above the platters, which spin at speeds between 3500 and 10,000 rpm. The distance (flying height) between the heads and the disk surface is less than the thickness of a fingerprint. The closer the read/write heads are to the platter, the more densely the data packs onto the drive. These infinitesimal tolerances demand that the platters never be exposed to outside air. Even a tiny dust particle on a platter would act like a mountain in the way of the read/write heads and would cause catastrophic damage to the drive. To keep the air clean inside the drive, all hard drives use a tiny, heavily filtered aperture to keep the air pressure equalized between the interior and the exterior of the drive.

• **Figure 11.1**   Inside the hard drive

• **Figure 11.2**   Read/write heads on actuator arms

Data Encoding

Although the hard drive stores data in binary form, visualizing a magnetized spot representing a one and a non-magnetized spot representing a zero grossly oversimplifies the process. Hard drives store data in tiny magnetic fields—think of them as tiny magnets that can be placed in either direction on the platter. Each tiny magnetic field, called a *flux*, can switch north/south polarity back and forth through a process called *flux reversal*. When a read/write head goes over an area where a flux reversal has occurred, the head reads a small electrical current.

Today's hard drives use a complex and efficient method to interpret flux reversals. Instead of reading individual flux reversals, a modern hard drive reads groups of them called *runs*. Starting around 1991, hard drives began using a data encoding system known as *run length limited (RLL)*. With RLL, any combination of ones and zeros can be stored in a preset combination of about 15 different runs. The hard drive looks for these runs and reads them as a group, resulting in much faster and much more densely-packed data.

Current drives use an extremely advanced method of RLL called **Partial Response Maximum Likelihood (PRML)** encoding. As hard drives pack more and more fluxes on the drive, the individual fluxes start to interact with each other, making it more and more difficult for the drive to verify where one flux stops and another starts. PRML uses powerful, intelligent circuitry to analyze each flux reversal and to make a "best guess" as to what type of flux reversal it just read. As a result, the maximum run length for PRML drives reaches up to 16 to 20 fluxes, far more than the 7 or so on RLL drives. Longer run lengths enable the hard drive to use more complicated run combinations so the hard drive can store a phenomenal amount of data. For example, a run of only 12 fluxes on a hard drive might equal a string of 30 or 40 ones and zeros when handed to the system from the hard drive.

The size required by each magnetic flux on a hard drive has reduced considerably over the years, resulting in higher capacities. As fluxes become smaller, they begin to interfere with each other in weird ways. I have to say *weird* because to make sense of what's going on at this subatomic level (I told you these fluxes were small!) would require you to take a semester of quantum mechanics. Let's just say that laying fluxes flat against the platter has reached its limit. To get around this problem, hard drive makers recently began to make hard drives that store their fluxes vertically (up and down) rather than longitudinally (forward and backward), enabling them to make hard drives in the 1 terabyte (1024 gigabyte) range. Manufacturers call this vertical storage method *perpendicular recording*.

For all this discussion and detail on data encoding, the day-to-day PC technician never deals with encoding. Sometimes, however, knowing what you don't need to know helps as much as knowing what you do need to know. Fortunately, data encoding is inherent to the hard drive and completely invisible to the system. You're never going to have to deal with data encoding, but you'll sure sound smart when talking to other PC techs if you know your RLL from your PRML!

Moving the Arms

The read/write heads move across the platter on the ends of *actuator arms* or **head actuators**. In the entire history of hard drives, manufacturers have used

only two technologies to move the arms: **stepper motor** and **voice coil**. Hard drives first used stepper motor technology, but today they've all moved to voice coil.

Stepper motor technology moved the arm in fixed increments or steps, but the technology had several limitations that doomed it. Because the interface between motor and actuator arm required minimal slippage to ensure precise and reproducible movements, the positioning of the arms became less precise over time. This physical deterioration caused data transfer errors. Additionally, heat deformation wreaked havoc with stepper motor drives. Just as valve clearances in automobile engines change with operating temperature, the positioning accuracy changed as the PC operated and various hard drive components got warmer. Although very small, these changes caused problems. Accessing the data written on a cold hard drive, for example, became difficult after the disk warmed. In addition, the read/write heads could damage the disk surface if not parked (set in a non-data area) when not in use, requiring techs to use special parking programs before transporting a stepper motor drive.

All magnetic hard drives made today employ a linear motor to move the actuator arms. The linear motor, more popularly called a voice coil motor, uses a permanent magnet surrounding a coil on the actuator arm. When an electrical current passes, the coil generates a magnetic field that moves the actuator arm. The direction of the actuator arm's movement depends on the polarity of the electrical current through the coil. Because the voice coil and the actuator arm never touch, no degradation in positional accuracy takes place over time. Voice coil drives automatically park the heads when the drive loses power, making the old stepper motor park programs obsolete.

Lacking the discrete steps of the stepper motor drive, a voice coil drive cannot accurately predict the movement of the heads across the disk. To make sure voice coil drives land exactly in the correct area, the drive reserves one side of one platter for navigational purposes. This area essentially maps the exact location of the data on the drive. The voice coil moves the read/write head to its best guess about the correct position on the hard drive. The read/write head then uses this map to fine-tune its true position and make any necessary adjustments.

Now that you have a basic understanding of how a drive physically stores data, let's turn to how the hard drive organizes that data so we can use that drive.

Geometry

Have you ever seen a cassette tape? If you look at the actual brown Mylar (a type of plastic) tape, nothing will tell you whether sound is recorded on that tape. Assuming the tape is not blank, however, you know *something* is on the tape. Cassettes store music in distinct magnetized lines. You could say that the physical placement of those lines of magnetism is the tape's "geometry."

Geometry also determines where a hard drive stores data. As with a cassette tape, if you opened up a hard drive, you would not see the geometry. But rest assured that the drive has geometry; in fact, every model of hard drive uses a different geometry. We describe the geometry for a particular hard drive with a set of numbers representing three values: heads, cylinders, and sectors per track.

Floppy disk drives still use stepper motors.

Tech Tip

Fluid Bearings

Currently, almost all hard drives (except solid state) use a motor located in the center spindle supporting the drive platters. Traditionally, tiny ball bearings support the spindle motor, and as disk technology has advanced, these ball bearings have become the limiting factor in the three critical design criteria for hard drives: rotational speed, storage capacity, and noise levels. The higher the rotational speed of a drive, the more the metal-on-metal contact creates heat and lubricant problems that impact the lifespan of the bearings. However precisely machined, ball bearings are not perfectly round. Runout, the measurement of how much the ball bearings wobble (and thus how much the drive platters wobble), is now the limiting factor on how densely you can pack information together on a disk drive.

The technological fix for this comes in the form of fluid bearings. A fluid bearing is basically a small amount of lubricant trapped in a carefully machined housing. The use of fluid in place of metal balls means that no contact occurs between metal surfaces to generate heat and wear. The fluid also creates no mechanical vibration, so fluid bearings can support higher rotational speeds. The runout of a fluid bearing is about one-tenth that of the best ball bearing, significantly increasing potential information density. The absence of a mechanical connection between moving parts also dramatically reduces noise levels, and the fluid itself acts to dampen the sound further. Finally, liquid bearings provide better shock resistance than ball bearings.

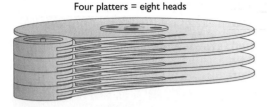

Four platters = eight heads

• **Figure 11.3**   Two heads per platter

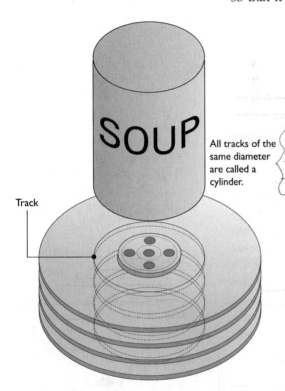

Track

All tracks of the same diameter are called a cylinder.

SOUP

• **Figure 11.4**   Cylinder

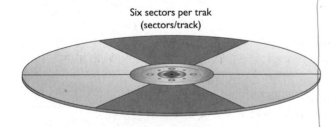

Six sectors per trak (sectors/track)

• **Figure 11.5**   Sectors per track

Heads   The number of **heads** for a specific hard drive describes, rather logically, the number of read/write heads used by the drive to store data. Every platter requires two heads. If a hard drive has four platters, for example, it needs eight heads (see Figure 11.3).

Based on this description of heads, you would think that hard drives would always have an even number of heads, right? Wrong! Most hard drives reserve a head or two for their own use. Therefore, a hard drive can have either an even or an odd number of heads.

Cylinders   To visualize cylinders, imagine taking an empty soup can and opening both ends. Look at the shape of the can; it is a geometric shape called a cylinder. Now imagine taking that cylinder and sharpening one end so that it easily cuts through the hardest metal. Visualize placing the ex-soup can over the hard drive and pushing it down through the drive. The can cuts into one side and out the other of each platter. Each circle transcribed by the can is where you store data on the drive, and is called a **track.**

Each side of each platter contains tens of thousands of tracks. Interestingly enough, the individual tracks themselves are not directly part of the drive geometry. Our interest lies only in the groups of tracks of the same diameter, going all of the way through the drive. Each group of tracks of the same diameter is a called a **cylinder** (see Figure 11.4). There's more than one cylinder. Go get yourself about a thousand more cans, each one a different diameter, and push them through the hard drive.

Sectors per Track   Now imagine cutting the hard drive like a birthday cake, slicing all of the tracks into tens of thousands of small slivers. Each sliver then has many thousands of small pieces of track. The term **sector** refers to a specific piece of track on a sliver, and each sector stores 512 bytes of data.

The sector is the universal atom of all hard drives. You can't divide data into anything smaller than a sector. Although sectors are important, the number of sectors is not a geometry value that describes a hard drive. The geometry value is called **sectors per track (sectors/track).** The sectors/track value describes the number of sectors in each track (see Figure 11.5).

The Big Three   Cylinders, heads, and sectors/track combine to define the hard drive's geometry. In most cases, these three critical values are referred to as *CHS*. The three values are important because the PC's BIOS needs to know the drive's geometry to know how to talk to the drive. Back in the old days, a technician needed to enter these values into the CMOS setup program manually. Today, every hard drive stores the CHS information in the drive itself, in an electronic format that enables the BIOS to query the drive automatically to determine these values. You'll see more on this later in the chapter, in the "Autodetection" section.

Two other values—write precompensation cylinder and landing zone—no longer have relevance in today's PCs; however, people still toss around these terms and a few CMOS setup utilities still support them—another classic example of a technology appendix. Let's look at these two holdouts from another era so when you access CMOS, you won't say, "What the heck are these?"

Write Precompensation Cylinder   Older hard drives had a real problem with the fact that sectors toward the inside of the drives were much smaller than sectors toward the outside. To handle this, an older drive would spread data a little farther apart once it got to a particular cylinder. This cylinder was called the write precompensation (write precomp) cylinder, and the PC had to know which cylinder began this wider data spacing. Hard drives no longer have this problem, making the write precomp setting obsolete.

Landing Zone   On older hard drives with stepper motors, the landing zone value designated an unused cylinder as a "parking place" for the read/write heads. As mentioned earlier, before moving old stepper motor hard drives, the read/write heads needed to be parked to avoid accidental damage. Today's voice coil drives park themselves whenever they're not accessing data, automatically placing the read/write heads on the landing zone. As a result, the BIOS no longer needs the landing zone geometry.

Essentials

Solid-State Drives

Booting up a computer takes time in part because of the time it takes for a traditional hard drive to spin up and for the read/write heads to retrieve the data off the drive to load the operating system and drivers into RAM. All of the moving metal parts of a platter-based drive use a lot of power, create a lot of heat, take up space, wear down over time, and take a lot of nanoseconds to get things done. A **solid-state drive (SSD)** addresses all of these issues nicely.

In technical terms, solid-state technology and devices are based on the combination of semiconductors, transistors, and bubble memory used to create electrical components with no moving parts. That's a mouthful! Here's the translation.

In simple terms, SSDs (see Figure 11.6) use memory chips to store data instead of all those pesky metal spinning parts used in platter-based hard drives. Solid-state technology has been around for many moons. It was originally developed to transition vacuum tube–based technologies to semiconductor technologies, such as the move from cathode ray tubes (CRTs) to liquid crystal displays (LCDs) in monitors. (You'll get the scoop on monitor technologies in Chapter 19, "Video.")

Solid-state devices use current flow and negative/positive electron charges to achieve their magic. Although Mr. Spock may find the physics of how this technology actually works "fascinating," it's more important for

• **Figure 11.6**   A solid-state drive (*photo courtesy of Corsair*)

With solid-state drives coming into more regular use, you see the initials *HDD* used more frequently than in previous years to refer to the traditional, platter-based hard drives. Thus we have two drive technologies: SSDs and HDDs.

you to know the following points regarding solid-state drives, devices, and technology.

- Solid-state technology is commonly used in desktop and laptop hard drives, memory cards, cameras, USB thumb drives, and other handheld devices.
- SSD form factors are typically 1.8-inch, 2.5-inch, or 3.5-inch.
- SSDs can be PATA, SATA, eSATA, SCSI, or USB for desktop systems. Some portable computers have mini-PCI Express versions.
- SSDs that use SDRAM cache are volatile and lose data when powered off. Others that use nonvolatile flash memory such as NAND retain data when power is turned off or disconnected. (See Chapter 13, "Removable Media," for the scoop on flash memory technology.)
- SSDs are more expensive than traditional HDDs. Less expensive SSDs typically implement less reliable multi-level cell (MLC) memory technology in place of the more efficient single-level cell (SLC) technology to cut costs.

■ Parallel and Serial ATA

Over the years, many interfaces existed for hard drives, with such names as ST-506 and ESDI. Don't worry about what these abbreviations stood for; neither the CompTIA A+ certification exams nor the computer world at large has an interest in these prehistoric interfaces. Starting around 1990, an interface called **advanced technology attachment (ATA)** appeared that now virtually monopolizes the hard drive market. ATA hard drives are often referred to as **integrated drive electronics (IDE)** drives. Only one other type of interface, the moderately popular small computer system interface (SCSI), has any relevance for hard drives.

ATA drives come in two basic flavors. The older **parallel ATA (PATA)** drives send data in parallel, on a 40- or 80-wire data cable. PATA drives dominated the industry for more than a decade but have been mostly replaced by **serial ATA (SATA)** drives that send data in serial, using only one wire for data transfers. The leap from PATA to SATA is only one of a large number of changes that have taken place with ATA. To appreciate these changes, we'll run through the many ATA standards that have appeared over the years.

ATA-1

When IBM unveiled the 80286-powered IBM PC AT in the early 1980s, it introduced the first PC to include BIOS support for hard drives. This BIOS supported up to two physical drives, and each drive could be up to 504 MB—far larger than the 5-MB and 10-MB drives of the time. Although having built-in support for hard drives certainly improved the power of the PC, installing, configuring, and troubleshooting hard drives could at best be called difficult at that time.

Tech Tip

IDE

The term IDE (integrated drive electronics) refers to any hard drive with a built-in controller. All hard drives are technically IDE drives, although we only use the term IDE when discussing ATA drives.

Tech Tip

External Hard Drives

A quick trip to any major computer store will reveal a thriving trade in external hard drives. You used to be able to find external drives that connected to the slow parallel port, but external drives today connect to a FireWire, Hi-Speed USB 2.0, or eSATA port. All three interfaces offer high data transfer rates and hot-swap capability, making them ideal for transporting huge files such as digital video clips. Regardless of the external interface, however, inside the casing you'll find an ordinary PATA or SATA drive, just like those described in this chapter.

To address these problems, Western Digital and Compaq developed a new hard drive interface and placed this specification before the *American National Standards Institute* (*ANSI*) committees, which in turn put out the AT Attachment (ATA) interface in March of 1989. The ATA interface specified a cable and a built-in controller on the drive itself. Most importantly, the ATA standard used the existing AT BIOS on a PC, which meant that you didn't have to replace the old system BIOS to make the drive work—a very important consideration for compatibility but one that would later haunt ATA drives. The official name for the standard, ATA, never made it into the common vernacular until recently, and then only as PATA to distinguish it from SATA drives.

The ANSI subcommittee directly responsible for the ATA standard is called Technical Committee T13. If you want to know what's happening with ATA, check out the T13 Web site: www.t13.org.

Early ATA Physical Connections

The first ATA drives connected to the computer with a **40-pin ribbon cable** that plugged into the drive and into a hard drive controller. The cable has a colored stripe down one side that denotes pin 1 and should connect to the drive's pin 1 and to the controller's pin 1. Figure 11.7 shows the business end of an early ATA drive, with the connectors for the ribbon cable and the power cable.

The controller is the support circuitry that acts as the intermediary between the hard drive and the external data bus. Electronically, the setup looks like Figure 11.8.

Wait a minute! If ATA drives are IDE (see the Tech Tip), they already have a built-in controller. Why do they then have to plug into a *controller* on the motherboard? Well, this is a great example of a term that's not used properly, but everyone (including the motherboard and hard drive makers) uses it this way. What we call the ATA controller is really no more than an interface providing a connection to the rest of the PC system. When your BIOS talks to the hard drive, it actually talks to the onboard circuitry on the drive, not the connection on the motherboard. But, even though the *real* controller resides on the hard drive, the 40-pin connection on the motherboard is called the controller. We have a lot of misnomers to live with in the ATA world.

The ATA-1 standard defined that no more than two drives attach to a single IDE connector on a single ribbon cable. Because up to two drives can attach to one connector via a single cable, you need to be able to identify each drive on the cable. The ATA standard identifies the two drives as "master" and "slave." You set one drive as master and one as slave by using tiny jumpers on the drives (Figure 11.9).

The controllers are on the motherboard and manifest themselves as two 40-pin male ports, as shown in Figure 11.10.

PIO and DMA Modes

If you're making a hard drive standard, you must define both the method and the speed at which the data's going to move.

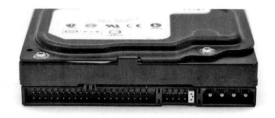

• **Figure 11.7** Back of IDE drive showing 40-pin connector (left), jumpers (center), and power connector (right)

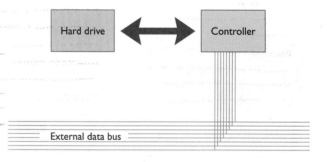

• **Figure 11.8** Relation of drive, controller, and bus

• **Figure 11.9** A typical hard drive with directions (top) for setting a jumper (bottom)

• **Figure 11.10** IDE interfaces on a motherboard

ATA-1 defined two methods, the first using programmed I/O (PIO) addressing and the second using direct memory access (DMA) mode.

PIO is nothing more than the traditional I/O addressing scheme, where the CPU talks directly to the hard drive via the BIOS to send and receive data. Three different PIO speeds called **PIO modes** were initially adopted:

- PIO mode 0: 3.3 MBps (megabytes per second)
- PIO mode 1: 5.2 MBps
- PIO mode 2: 8.3 MBps

DMA modes defined a method to enable the hard drives to talk to RAM directly, using old-style DMA commands. (The ATA folks called this *single-word DMA*.) This old-style DMA was slow, and the resulting three ATA single-word DMA modes were also slow:

- Single-word DMA mode 0: 2.1 MBps
- Single-word DMA mode 1: 4.2 MBps
- Single-word DMA mode 2: 8.3 MBps

When a computer booted up, the BIOS queried the hard drive to see what modes it could use and then automatically adjusted to the fastest possible mode.

ATA-2

The terms *ATA*, *IDE*, and *EIDE* are used interchangeably.

In 1990, the industry adopted a series of improvements to the ATA standard called ATA-2. Many people called these new features **Enhanced IDE (EIDE)**. EIDE was really no more than a marketing term invented by Western Digital, but it caught on in common vernacular and is still used today, although its use is fading. Regular IDE drives quickly disappeared, and by 1995, EIDE drives dominated the PC world. Figure 11.11 shows a typical EIDE drive.

ATA-2 was the most important ATA standard, as it included powerful new features such as higher capacities, support for non–hard drive storage devices, support for two more ATA devices for a maximum of four, and substantially improved throughput.

Higher Capacity with LBA

IBM created the AT BIOS to support hard drives many years before IDE drives were invented, and every system had that BIOS. The developers of IDE made certain that the new drives would run from the same AT BIOS command set. With this capability, you could use the same CMOS and BIOS routines to talk to a much more advanced drive. Your motherboard or hard drive controller wouldn't become instantly obsolete when you installed a new hard drive.

Unfortunately, the BIOS routines for the original AT command set allowed a hard drive size of only up to 528 million bytes (or 504 MB—remember that a mega = 1,048,576, not

• **Figure 11.11** EIDE drive

1,000,000). A drive could have no more than 1024 cylinders, 16 heads, and 63 sectors/track:

$$1024 \text{ cylinders} \times 16 \text{ heads} \times 63 \text{ sectors/track} \times 512 \text{ bytes/sector} = 504 \text{ MB}$$

For years, this was not a problem. But when hard drives began to approach the 504 MB barrier, it became clear that there needed to be a way of getting past 504 MB. The ATA-2 standard defined a way to get past this limit with **logical block addressing (LBA)**. With LBA, the hard drive lies to the computer about its geometry through an advanced type of sector translation. Let's take a moment to understand sector translation, and then come back to LBA.

Sector Translation   Long before hard drives approached the 504 MB limit, the limits of 1024 cylinders, 16 heads, and 63 sectors/track gave hard drive makers fits. The big problem was the heads. Remember that every two heads means another platter, another physical disk that you have to squeeze into a hard drive. If you wanted a hard drive with the maximum number of 16 heads, you would need a hard drive with eight physical platters inside the drive. Nobody wanted that many platters: it made the drives too tall, it took more power to spin up the drive, and that many parts cost too much money (see Figure 11.12).

Manufacturers could readily produce a hard drive that had fewer heads and more cylinders, but the stupid 1024/16/63 limit got in the way. Plus, the traditional sector arrangement wasted a lot of useful space. Sectors toward the inside of the drive, for example, are much shorter than the sectors on the outside. The sectors on the outside don't need to be that long, but with the traditional geometry setup, hard drive makers had no choice. They could make a hard drive store a lot more information, however, if they could make hard drives with more sectors/track on the outside tracks (see Figure 11.13).

The ATA specification was designed to have two geometries. The *physical geometry* defined the real layout of the CHS inside the drive. The *logical geometry* described what the drive told the CMOS. In other words, the IDE drive "lied" to the CMOS, thus side-stepping the artificial limits of the BIOS. When data was being transferred to and from the drive, the onboard circuitry of the drive translated the logical geometry into the physical geometry. This function was, and still is, called **sector translation**.

Let's look at a couple of hypothetical examples in action. First, pretend that Seagate came out with a new, cheap, fast hard drive called the ST108. To get the ST108 drive fast and cheap, however, Seagate had to use a rather strange geometry, shown in Table 11.1.

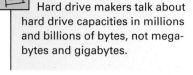

Hard drive makers talk about hard drive capacities in millions and billions of bytes, not megabytes and gigabytes.

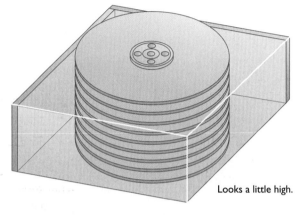

Looks a little high.

• **Figure 11.12**   Too many heads

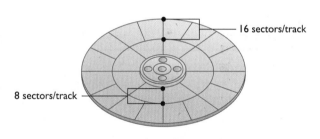

16 sectors/track

8 sectors/track

• **Figure 11.13**   Multiple sectors/track

Table 11.1		Seagate's ST108 Drive Geometry	
ST108 Physical		**BIOS Limits**	
Cylinders	2048	Cylinders	1024
Heads	2	Heads	16
Sectors/track	52	Sectors/track	63
Total capacity	108 MB		

Table 11.2	Physical and Logical Geometries of the ST108 Drive		
Physical		**Logical**	
Cylinders	2048	Cylinders	512
Heads	2	Heads	8
Sectors/track	52	Sectors/track	52
Total capacity	108 MB	Total capacity	108 MB

Notice that the cylinder number is greater than 1024. To overcome this problem, the IDE drive performs a sector translation that reports a geometry to the BIOS that is totally different from the true geometry of the drive. Table 11.2 shows the actual geometry and the "logical" geometry of our mythical ST108 drive. Notice that the logical geometry is now within the acceptable parameters of the BIOS limitations. Sector translation never changes the capacity of the drive; it changes only the geometry to stay within the BIOS limits.

Back to LBA Now let's watch how the advanced sector translation of LBA provides support for hard drives greater than 504 MB. Let's use an old drive, the Western Digital WD2160, a 2.1-GB hard drive, as an example. This drive is no longer in production but its smaller CHS values make understanding LBA easier. Table 11.3 lists its physical and logical geometries.

Table 11.3	Western Digital WD2160's Physical and Logical Geometries		
Physical		**Logical**	
Cylinders	16,384	Cylinders	1024
Heads	4	Heads	**64**
Sectors/track	63	Sectors/track	63
Total capacity	2.1 GB	Total capacity	2.1 GB

Note that, even with sector translation, the number of heads is greater than the allowed 16. So here's where the magic of LBA comes in. The WD2160 is capable of LBA. Now assuming that the BIOS is also capable of LBA, here's what happens. When the computer boots up, the BIOS asks the drives if they can perform LBA. If they say yes, the BIOS and the drive work together to change the way they talk to each other. They can do this without conflicting with the original AT BIOS commands by taking advantage of unused commands to use up to 256 heads. LBA enables support for a maximum of 1024 × 256 × 63 × 512 bytes = 8.4-GB hard drives. Back in 1990, 8.4 GB was hundreds of times larger than the drives used at the time. Don't worry, later ATA standards will get the BIOS up to today's huge drives.

Not Just Hard Drives Anymore: ATAPI

ATA-2 added an extension to the ATA specification, called **advanced technology attachment packet interface (ATAPI)**, that enabled non–hard drive devices such as CD-ROM drives and tape backups to connect to the PC via the ATA controllers. ATAPI drives have the same 40-pin interface and master/slave jumpers as ATA hard drives. Figure 11.14 shows an ATAPI CD-RW drive attached to a motherboard. The key difference

• **Figure 11.14** ATAPI CD-RW drive attached to a motherboard via a standard 40-pin ribbon cable

between hard drives and every other type of drive that attaches to the ATA controller is in how the drives get BIOS support. Hard drives get it through the system BIOS, whereas non–hard drives require the operating system to load a software driver.

More Drives with ATA-2

ATA-2 added support for a second controller, raising the total number of supported drives from two to four. Each of the two controllers is equal in power and capability. Figure 11.15 is a close-up of a typical motherboard, showing the primary controller marked as *IDE1* and the secondary marked as *IDE2*.

Increased Speed

ATA-2 defined two new PIO modes and a new type of DMA called *multi-word DMA* that was a substantial improvement over the old DMA. Technically, multi-word DMA was still the old-style DMA, but it worked in a much more efficient manner so it was much faster.

- PIO mode 3: 11.1 MBps
- PIO mode 4: 16.6 MBps
- Multi-word DMA mode 0: 4.2 MBps
- Multi-word DMA mode 1: 13.3 MBps
- Multi-word DMA mode 2: 16.6 MBps

With the introduction of ATAPI, the ATA standards are often referred to as ATA/ATAPI instead of just ATA.

• **Figure 11.15**   Primary and secondary controllers labeled on a motherboard

ATA-3

ATA-3 came on quickly after ATA-2 and added one new feature called **Self-Monitoring, Analysis, and Reporting Technology (S.M.A.R.T.)**, one of the few PC acronyms that requires the use of periods after each letter. S.M.A.R.T. helps predict when a hard drive is going to fail by monitoring the hard drive's mechanical components.

S.M.A.R.T. is a great idea and is popular in specialized server systems, but it's complex, imperfect, and hard to understand. As a result, only a few utilities can read the S.M.A.R.T. data on your hard drive. Your best sources are the hard drive manufacturers. Every hard drive maker has a free diagnostic tool (which usually works only for their drives) that will do a S.M.A.R.T. check along with other tests. Figure 11.16 shows Western Digital's Data Lifeguard Tools in action. Note that it says only whether the drive has passed or not. Figure 11.17 shows some S.M.A.R.T. information.

Although you can see the actual S.M.A.R.T. data, it's generally useless or indecipherable. Your best choice is to trust the manufacturer's opinion and run the software provided.

ATA-4

Anyone who has opened a big database file on a hard drive appreciates that a faster hard drive is better. ATA-4 introduced a new DMA mode called

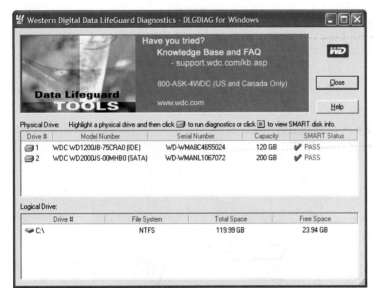

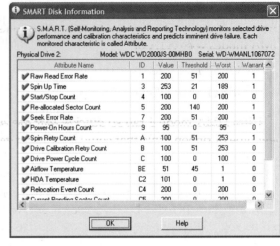

• **Figure 11.17** S.M.A.R.T. information

• **Figure 11.16** Data Lifeguard

> Ultra DMA mode 2, the most popular of the ATA-4 DMA modes, is also called ATA/33.

Ultra DMA that is now the primary way a hard drive communicates with a PC. **Ultra DMA** uses DMA bus mastering to achieve far faster speeds than were possible with PIO or old-style DMA. ATA-4 defined three Ultra DMA modes:

- Ultra DMA mode 0: 16.7 MBps
- Ultra DMA mode 1: 25.0 MBps
- Ultra DMA mode 2: 33.3 MBps

INT13 Extensions

Here's an interesting factoid for you: The original ATA-1 standard allowed for hard drives up to 137 GB. It wasn't the ATA standard that caused the 504-MB size limit; the standard used the old AT BIOS, and the BIOS, not the ATA standard, could support only 504 MB. LBA was a work-around that told the hard drive to lie to the BIOS to get it up to 8.4 GB. But eventually hard drives started edging close to the LBA limit and something had to be done. The T13 folks said, "This isn't *our* problem. It's the ancient BIOS problem. You BIOS makers need to fix the BIOS." And they did.

In 1994, Phoenix Technologies (the BIOS manufacturer) came up with a new set of BIOS commands called **Interrupt 13 (INT13) extensions**. INT13 extensions broke the 8.4-GB barrier by completely ignoring the CHS values and instead feeding the LBA a stream of addressable sectors. A system with INT13 extensions can handle drives up to 137 GB. The entire PC industry quickly adopted INT13 extensions, and every system made since 2000–2001 supports INT13 extensions.

ATA-5

Ultra DMA was such a huge hit that the ATA folks adopted two faster Ultra DMA modes with ATA-5:

- Ultra DMA mode 3: 44.4 MBps
- Ultra DMA mode 4: 66.6 MBps

Ultra DMA mode 4 ran so quickly that the ATA-5 standard defined a new type of ribbon cable that could handle the higher speeds. This **80-wire cable** still has 40 pins on the connectors, but it also includes another 40 wires in the cable that act as grounds to improve the cable's capability to handle high-speed signals. The 80-wire cable, just like the 40-pin ribbon cable, has a colored stripe down one side to give you proper orientation for pin 1 on the controller and the hard drive. Previous versions of ATA didn't define where the various drives were plugged into the ribbon cable, but ATA-5 defined exactly where the controller, master, and slave drives connected, even defining colors to identify them. Take a look at the ATA/66 cable in Figure 11.18. The connector on the left is colored blue—and you must use that connector to plug into the controller. The connector in the middle is grey—that's for the slave drive. The connector on the right is black—that's for the master drive. Any ATA/66 controller connections are colored blue to let you know it is an ATA/66 controller.

• **Figure 11.18**   ATA/66 cable

ATA/66 is backward compatible, so you may safely plug an earlier drive into an ATA/66 cable and controller. If you plug an ATA/66 drive into an older controller, it will work—just not in ATA/66 mode. The only risky action is to use an ATA/66 controller and hard drive with a non-ATA/66 cable. Doing so will almost certainly cause nasty data losses!

ATA-6

Hard drive size exploded in the early 21st century, and the seemingly impossible-to-fill 137-GB limit created by INT13 extensions became a barrier to fine computing more quickly than most people had anticipated. When drives started hitting the 120-GB mark, the T13 committee adopted an industry proposal pushed by Maxtor (a major hard drive maker) called *Big Drive* that increased the limit to more than 144 petabytes (approximately 144,000,000 GB). Thankfully, T13 also gave the new standard a less-silly name, calling it **ATA/ATAPI-6** or simply ATA-6. Big Drive was basically just a 48-bit LBA, supplanting the older 24-bit addressing of LBA and INT13 extensions. Plus, the standard defined an enhanced block mode, enabling drives to transfer up to 65,536 sectors in one chunk, up from the measly 256 sectors of lesser drive technologies.

ATA-6 also introduced Ultra DMA mode 5, kicking the data transfer rate up to 100 MBps. Ultra DMA mode 5 is more commonly referred to as ATA/100 and requires the same 80-wire cable as ATA/66.

Essentials/Practical Application

ATA-7

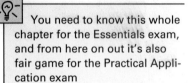
You need to know this whole chapter for the Essentials exam, and from here on out it's also fair game for the Practical Application exam

ATA-7 brought two new innovations to the ATA world: one evolutionary and the other revolutionary. The evolutionary innovation came with the last of the parallel ATA Ultra DMA modes; the revolutionary was a new form of ATA called serial ATA (SATA).

ATA/133

ATA-7 introduced the fastest and probably least adopted of all of the ATA speeds, Ultra DMA mode 6 (**ATA/133**). Even though it runs at a speed of 133 MBps, the fact that it came out with SATA kept many hard drive manufacturers away. ATA/133 uses the same cables as Ultra DMA 66 and 100.

While you won't find many ATA/133 hard drives, you will find plenty of ATA/133 controllers. There's a trend in the industry to color the controller connections on the hard drive red, although this is not part of the ATA-7 standard.

Serial ATA

The real story of ATA-7 is SATA. For all its longevity as the mass storage interface of choice for the PC, parallel ATA has problems. First, the flat ribbon cables impede airflow and can be a pain to insert properly. Second, the cables have a limited length, only 18 inches. Third, you can't hot-swap PATA drives. You have to shut down completely before installing or replacing a drive. Finally, the technology has simply reached the limits of what it can do in terms of throughput.

Serial ATA addresses these issues. SATA creates a point-to-point connection between the SATA device—hard disk, CD-ROM, CD-RW, DVD-ROM, DVD-RW, BD-R, BD-RE, and so on—and the SATA controller, the **host bus adapter (HBA)**. At a glance, SATA devices look identical to standard PATA devices. Take a closer look at the cable and power connectors, however, and you'll see significant differences (Figure 11.19).

Because SATA devices send data serially instead of in parallel, the SATA interface needs far fewer physical wires—seven instead of the eighty wires that is typical of PATA—resulting in much thinner cabling. This might not seem significant, but the benefit is that thinner cabling means better cable control and better airflow through the PC case, resulting in better cooling.

• **Figure 11.19**   SATA hard disk power (left) and data (right) cables

Further, the maximum SATA-device cable length is more than twice that of an IDE cable—about 40 inches (1 meter) instead of 18 inches. Again, this might not seem like a big deal unless you've struggled to connect a PATA hard disk installed into the top bay of a full-tower case to an IDE connector located all the way at the bottom of the motherboard.

SATA does away with the entire master/slave concept. Each drive connects to one port, so no more daisy-chaining drives. Further, there's no maximum number of drives—many motherboards are now available that

support up to eight SATA drives. Want more? Snap in a SATA HBA and load 'em up!

The big news, however, is in data throughput. As the name implies, SATA devices transfer data in serial bursts instead of parallel, as PATA devices do. Typically, you might not think of serial devices as being faster than parallel, but in this case, that's exactly the case. A SATA device's single stream of data moves much faster than the multiple streams of data coming from a parallel IDE device—theoretically up to 30 times faster. SATA drives come in two common varieties, the 1.5Gb and the 3Gb, that have a maximum throughput of 150 MBps and 300 MBps, respectively.

SATA is backward compatible with current PATA standards and enables you to install a parallel ATA device, including a hard drive, optical drive, and other devices, to a serial ATA controller by using a **SATA bridge**. A SATA bridge manifests as a tiny card that you plug directly into the 40-pin connector on a PATA drive. As you can see in Figure 11.20, the controller chip on the bridge requires separate power; you plug a Molex connector into the PATA drive as normal. When you boot the system, the PATA drive shows up to the system as a SATA drive.

SATA's ease of use has made it the choice for desktop system storage, and its success is already showing in the fact that more than 90 percent of all hard drives sold today are SATA drives.

AHCI   Windows Vista and later operating systems support the *Advanced Host Controller Interface (AHCI)*, a more efficient way to work with SATA HBAs. Using AHCI unlocks some of the advanced features of SATA, such as hot-swapping and native command queuing.

When you plug in a SATA drive to a Windows computer that does not have AHCI enabled, the drive doesn't appear automatically. You need to go to the Control Panel and run the Add New Hardware Wizard to make the drive appear. AHCI makes the drive appear in Computer, just what you'd expect from a hot-swappable device.

Native command queuing (NCQ) is a disk-optimization feature for SATA drives. It enables faster read and write speeds.

AHCI is implemented at the CMOS level (see "BIOS Support" later in this chapter) and generally needs to be enabled before you install the operating system. Enabling it after installation will cause Vista to Blue Screen. How nice.

• **Figure 11.20**   SATA bridge

Tech Tip

SATA Names

Number-savvy readers might have noticed a discrepancy between the names and throughput of the two SATA drives. After all, 1.5 Gb per second throughput translates to 192 MB per second, a lot higher than the advertised speed of a "mere" 150 MBps. The same is true of the 3Gb/300 MBps drives. The encoding scheme used on SATA drives takes about 20 percent of the overhead for the drive, leaving 80 percent for pure bandwidth. The 3Gb drive created all kinds of problems, because the committee working on the specifications was called the SATA II committee, and marketers picked up on the SATA II name. As a result, you'll find many brands called SATA II rather than 3Gb. The SATA committee now goes by the name SATA-IO.

As this book went to press, a few motherboards and hard drive controller cards appeared that support the SATA 3.0 standard, with data rates up to 6 GBps. Look for the SATA 3.0 drives on the store shelves after you read this, but don't expect the technology to be on the CompTIA A+ exams this time around.

Tech Tip

Enabling AHCI After the Fact

If you want to enable AHCI but you've already installed Windows Vista, don't worry! Microsoft has developed a procedure (http://support.microsoft.com/kb/922976) that will have you enjoying all that AHCI fun in no time. Before you jump in, note that this procedure requires you to edit your Registry, so remember to always make a backup before you start editing.

For the scoop on PC Cards and ExpressCards—both technologies designed to add expansion options for portable computers—see Chapter 21, "Portable Computing."

• Figure 11.21   eSATA connectors

eSATA   **External SATA (eSATA)** extends the SATA bus to external devices, as the name would imply. The eSATA drives use connectors similar to internal SATA, but they're keyed differently so you can't mistake one for the other. Figure 11.21 shows eSATA connectors on the back of a motherboard.

External SATA uses shielded cable lengths up to 2 meters outside the PC and is hot pluggable. The beauty of eSATA is that it extends the SATA bus at full speed, so you're not limited to the meager 50 or 60 MBps of FireWire or USB.

If a desktop system doesn't have an eSATA external connector, or if you need more external SATA devices, you can install an eSATA HBA PCIe card or eSATA internal-to-external slot plate. You can similarly upgrade laptop systems to support external SATA devices by inserting an eSATA ExpressCard (Figure 11.22). There are also USB to eSATA adapter plugs, although you'll be limited to the much slower USB data-transfer rates. Install eSATA PCIe, PC Card, or ExpressCard following the same rules and precautions for installing any expansion device.

• Figure 11.22   eSATA ExpressCard

■ SCSI: Still Around

Many specialized server machines and enthusiasts' systems use the **small computer system interface (SCSI)** technologies for various pieces of core hardware and peripherals, from hard drives to printers to high-end tape-backup machines. SCSI is different from ATA in that SCSI devices connect together in a string of devices called a *chain*. Each device in the chain gets a SCSI ID to distinguish it from other devices on the chain. Last, the ends of a SCSI chain must be terminated. Let's dive into SCSI now, and see how SCSI chains, SCSI IDs, and termination all work.

SCSI is an old technology dating from the late 1970s, but it has been updated continually. SCSI is faster than ATA (though the gap is closing fast), and until SATA arrived, SCSI was the only good choice for anyone using RAID (see the "RAID" section a little later). SCSI is arguably fading away, but it deserves some mention.

SCSI Chains

SCSI manifests itself through a **SCSI chain**, a series of SCSI devices working together through a host adapter. The host adapter provides the interface between the SCSI chain and the PC. Figure 11.23 shows a typical SCSI PCI host adapter. Many techs refer to the host adapter as the *SCSI controller*, so you should be comfortable with both terms.

All SCSI devices can be divided into two groups: internal and external. Internal SCSI devices are attached inside the PC and connect to the host adapter through the latter's internal connector. Figure 11.24 shows an internal SCSI device, in this case a CD-ROM drive. External devices hook to the external connector of the host adapter. Figure 11.25 is an example of an external SCSI device.

Internal SCSI devices connect to the host adapter with a 68-pin ribbon cable (Figure 11.26). This flat, flexible cable functions precisely like a PATA cable. Many external devices connect to the host adapter with a 50-pin high-density (HD) connector. Figure 11.27 shows a host adapter external port. Higher-end SCSI devices use a 68-pin HD connector.

Multiple internal devices can be connected simply by using a cable with enough connectors. Figure 11.28, for example, shows a cable that can take up to four SCSI devices, including the host adapter.

Assuming the SCSI host adapter has a standard external port (some controllers don't have external connections at all), plugging in an external SCSI device is as simple as running a cable from device to controller. The external SCSI connectors are D-shaped so you can't plug them in backward. As an added bonus, some external SCSI devices have two ports, one to connect to the host adapter and a second to connect to another SCSI device. The process of connecting a device directly to another device is called *daisy-chaining*. You can daisy-chain as many as 15 devices to one host adapter. SCSI chains can be internal, external, or both (see Figure 11.29).

• **Figure 11.23**   SCSI host adapter

• **Figure 11.24**   Internal SCSI CD-ROM

• **Figure 11.25**   Back of external SCSI device

• **Figure 11.26**   Typical 68-pin ribbon cable

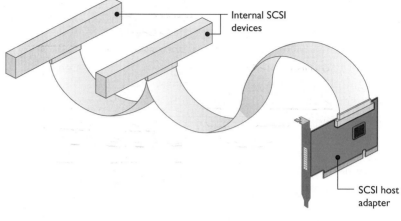

Internal SCSI devices

SCSI host adapter

• **Figure 11.27**   50-pin HD port on SCSI host adapter

• **Figure 11.28**   Internal SCSI chain with two devices

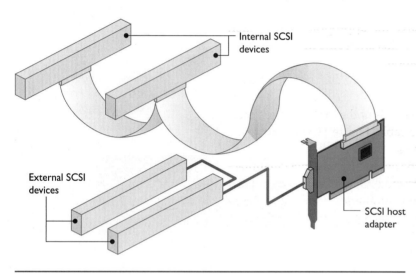

Internal SCSI devices

External SCSI devices

SCSI host adapter

• **Figure 11.29**   Internal and external devices on one SCSI chain

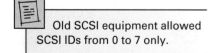
Old SCSI equipment allowed SCSI IDs from 0 to 7 only.

SCSI IDs

If you're going to connect a number of devices on the same SCSI chain, you must provide some way for the host adapter to tell one device from another. To differentiate devices, SCSI uses a unique identifier called the **SCSI ID**. The SCSI ID number can range from 0 to 15. SCSI IDs are similar to many other PC hardware settings in that a SCSI device can theoretically have any SCSI ID as long as that ID is not already taken by another device connected to the same host adapter.

Some conventions should be followed when setting SCSI IDs. Typically, most people set the host adapter to 7 or 15, but you can change this setting. Note that there is no order for the use of SCSI IDs. It does not matter which device gets which number, and you can skip numbers. Restrictions on IDs apply only within a single chain. Two devices can have the same ID, in other words, as long as they are on different chains (Figure 11.30).

Every SCSI device has some method of setting its SCSI ID. The trick is to figure out how as you're holding the device in your hand. A SCSI device may use jumpers, dip switches, or even tiny dials; every new SCSI device is a new adventure as you try to determine how to set its SCSI ID.

Termination

Whenever you send a signal down a wire, some of that signal reflects back up the wire, creating an echo and causing electronic chaos. SCSI chains use **termination** to prevent this problem. Termination simply means putting something on the ends of the wire to prevent this echo. Terminators are usually pull-down resistors and can manifest themselves in many different

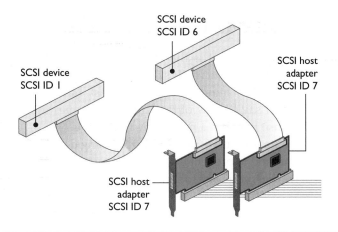

SCSI device
SCSI ID 6

SCSI device
SCSI ID 1

SCSI host adapter
SCSI ID 7

SCSI host adapter
SCSI ID 7

• **Figure 11.30** IDs don't conflict between separate SCSI chains.

ways. Most of the devices within a PC have the appropriate termination built in. On other devices, including SCSI chains and some network cables, you have to set termination during installation.

The rule with SCSI is that you *must* terminate *only* the ends of the SCSI chain. You have to terminate the ends of the cable, which usually means that you need to terminate the two devices at the ends of the cable. Do *not* terminate devices that are not on the ends of the cable. Figure 11.31 shows some examples of where to terminate SCSI devices.

Because any SCSI device might be on the end of a chain, most manufacturers build SCSI devices that can self-terminate. Some devices can detect that they are on the end of the SCSI chain and automatically terminate themselves. Most devices, however, require you to set a jumper or switch to enable termination (Figure 11.32).

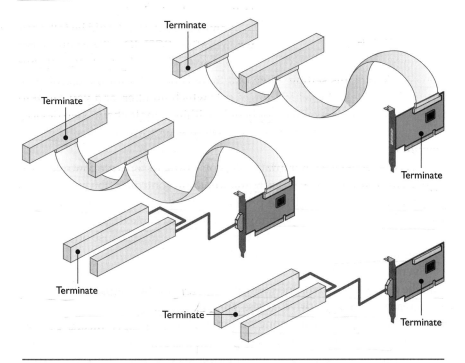

Terminate

Terminate

Terminate

Terminate

Terminate

Terminate

Terminate

• **Figure 11.31** Location of the terminated devices

• **Figure 11.32** Setting termination

The one and only advantage of disk striping is speed—it is a fast way to read and write to hard drives. But if either drive fails, *all* data is lost. You should not do disk striping—unless you're willing to increase the risk of losing data to increase the speed at which your hard drives save and restore data.

Disk striping with parity, in contrast, protects data by adding extra information, called *parity data*, that can be used to rebuild data if one of the drives fails. Disk striping with parity requires at least three drives, but it is common to use more than three. Disk striping with parity combines the best of disk mirroring and plain disk striping. It protects data and is quite fast. The majority of network servers use a type of disk striping with parity.

RAID

An *array* in the context of RAID refers to a collection of two or more hard drives.

A couple of sharp guys in Berkeley back in the 1980s organized the many techniques for using multiple drives for data protection and increasing speeds as the **redundant array of independent (or inexpensive) disks (RAID)**. They outlined seven levels of RAID, numbered 0 through 6.

- **RAID 0—Disk Striping**   Disk striping requires at least two drives. It does not provide redundancy to data. If any one drive fails, all data is lost.

- **RAID 1—Disk Mirroring/Duplexing**   RAID 1 arrays require at least two hard drives, although they also work with any even number of drives. RAID 1 is the ultimate in safety, but you lose storage space because the data is duplicated; you need two 100-GB drives to store 100 GB of data.

- **RAID 2—Disk Striping with Multiple Parity Drives**   RAID 2 was a weird RAID idea that never saw practical use. Unused, ignore it.

- **RAID 3 and 4—Disk Striping with Dedicated Parity**   RAID 3 and 4 combined dedicated data drives with dedicated parity drives. The differences between the two are trivial. Unlike RAID 2, these versions did see some use in the real world but were quickly replaced by RAID 5.

- **RAID 5—Disk Striping with Distributed Parity**   Instead of dedicated data and parity drives, RAID 5 distributes data and parity information evenly across all drives. This is the fastest way to provide data redundancy. RAID 5 is by far the most common RAID implementation and requires at least three drives. RAID 5 arrays effectively use one drive's worth of space for parity. If, for example, you have three 200-GB drives, your total storage capacity is 400 GB. If you have four 200-GB drives, your total capacity is 600 GB.

- **RAID 6—Disk Striping with Extra Parity**   If you lose a hard drive in a RAID 5 array, your data is at great risk until you replace the bad hard drive and rebuild the array. RAID 6 is RAID 5 with extra parity information. RAID 6 needs at least five drives, but in exchange you can lose up to two drives at the same time. RAID 6 is gaining in popularity for those willing to use larger arrays.

Tech Tip

RAID Lingo

No tech worth her salt says such things as "We're implementing disk striping with parity." Use the RAID level. Say, "We're implementing RAID 5." It's more accurate and very impressive to the folks in the accounting department!

After these first RAID levels were defined, some manufacturers came up with ways to combine different RAIDs. For example, what if you took two pairs of striped drives and mirrored the pairs? You would get what is called RAID 0+1. Or what if (read this carefully now) you took two pairs of mirrored drives and striped the pairs? You then get what we call RAID 1+0 or what is often called RAID 10. Combinations of different types of single RAID are called *multiple RAID* or *nested RAID* solutions.

 There is actually a term for a storage system composed of multiple independent disks rather than disks organized by using RAID: *JBOD*, which stands for *just a bunch of disks* (or *drives*).

Implementing RAID

RAID levels describe different methods of providing data redundancy or enhancing the speed of data throughput to and from groups of hard drives. They do not say *how* to implement these methods. Literally thousands of methods can be used to set up RAID. The method you use depends largely on the level of RAID you desire, the operating system you use, and the thickness of your wallet.

The obvious starting place for RAID is to connect at least two hard drives in some fashion to create a RAID array. For many years, if you wanted to do RAID beyond RAID 0 and RAID 1, the only technology you could use was good-old SCSI. SCSI's chaining of multiple devices to a single controller made it a natural for RAID. SCSI drives make superb RAID arrays, but the high cost of SCSI drives and RAID-capable host adapters kept RAID away from all but the most critical systems—usually big file servers.

In the past few years, substantial leaps in ATA technology have made ATA a viable alternative to SCSI drive technology for RAID arrays. Specialized ATA RAID controller cards support ATA RAID arrays of up to 15 drives—plenty to support even the most complex RAID needs. In addition, the inherent hot-swap capabilities of serial ATA have virtually guaranteed that serial ATA will quickly take over the lower end of the RAID business. Personally, I think the price and performance of serial ATA mean SCSI's days are numbered.

Once you have a number of hard drives, the next question is whether to use hardware or software to control the array. Let's look at both options.

 Try This!

Managing Heat with Multiple Drives

Adding three or more fast hard drives into a cramped PC case can be a recipe for disaster to the unwary tech. All those disks spinning constantly create a phenomenal amount of heat. Heat kills PCs! You have to manage the heat inside a RAID-enabled system or risk losing your data, drives, and basic system stability. The easiest way to do this is to add fans, so Try This!

Open up your PC case and look for built-in places to mount fans. How many case fans do you have installed now? What size are they? What sizes can you use? (Most cases use 80-mm fans, but 60- and 120-mm fans are common as well.) Jot down the particulars of your system and take a trip to the local PC store to check out the fans.

Before you get all fan-happy and grab the biggest and baddest fans to throw in your case, don't forget to think about the added noise level. Try to get a compromise between keeping your case cool enough and avoiding early deafness.

Hardware versus Software

All RAID implementations break down into either hardware or software methods. Software is often used when price takes priority over performance. Hardware is used when you need speed along with data redundancy. Software RAID does not require special controllers; you can use the

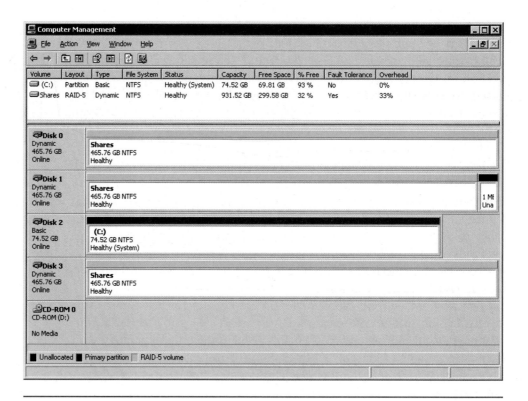

Figure 11.36 Disk Management tool of Computer Management in Windows 2003 Server

You can use Disk Management in Windows 2000, Windows XP Professional, and Windows Vista to create RAID 1 and RAID 5 arrays, but you can use Disk Management only remotely on a Windows 2000, 2003, or 2008 Server OS. In other words, the capability is there, but Microsoft has limited the OS. If you want to use software RAID in Windows 2000, XP (Home or Professional), or Vista, you need to use a third-party tool to set it up.

regular ATA, SATA controllers, or SCSI host adapters to make a software RAID array. But you do need "smart" software. The most common software implementation of RAID is the built-in RAID software that comes with Windows 2000, 2003, and 2008 Server. The Disk Management program in these Windows Server versions can configure drives for RAID 0, 1, or 5, and it works with PATA, SATA, and/or SCSI (Figure 11.36). Disk Management in Windows 2000 Professional, Windows XP, and Windows Vista, in contrast, can only do RAID 0.

Windows Disk Management is not the only software RAID game in town. A number of third-party software programs work with Windows or other operating systems.

Software RAID means the operating system is in charge of all RAID functions. It works for small RAID solutions but tends to overwork your operating system easily, creating slowdowns. When you *really* need to keep going, when you need RAID that doesn't even let the users know a problem has occurred, hardware RAID is the answer.

Hardware RAID centers around an *intelligent* controller—either a SCSI host adapter or a PATA/SATA controller that handles all of the RAID functions (Figure 11.37). Unlike a regular PATA/SATA controller or SCSI host adapter, these controllers have chips that have their own processor and memory. This allows the card, instead of the operating system, to handle all of the work of implementing RAID.

Most RAID setups in the real world are hardware-based. Almost all of the many hardware RAID solutions provide *hot-swapping*—the ability to replace a bad drive without disturbing the operating system. Hot-swapping is common in hardware RAID.

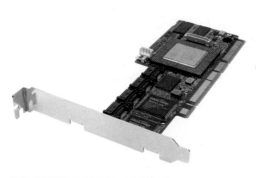

Figure 11.37 Serial ATA RAID controller

Mike Meyers' CompTIA A+ Guide to Managing and Troubleshooting PCs

Hardware-based RAID is invisible to the operating system and is configured in several ways, depending on the specific chips involved. Most RAID systems have a special configuration utility in Flash ROM that you access after CMOS but before the OS loads. Figure 11.38 shows a typical firmware program used to configure a hardware RAID solution.

Personal RAID

Due to drastic reductions in the cost of ATA RAID controller chips, in the past few years we've seen an explosion of ATA-based hardware RAID solutions built into mainstream motherboards. While this "ATA RAID on the motherboard" began with parallel ATA, the introduction of serial ATA made motherboards with built-in RAID extremely common.

These personal RAID motherboards might be common but they're not used too terribly often given that these RAID solutions usually provide only RAID 0 or RAID 1. If you want to use RAID, spend a few extra dollars and buy a RAID 5–capable controller.

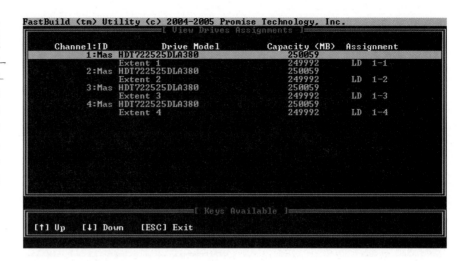

• **Figure 11.38**   RAID configuration utility

RAID controllers aren't just for internal drives; some models can handle multiple eSATA drives configured at any of the RAID levels. If you're feeling lucky, you can create a RAID array using both internal and external SATA drives.

The Future Is RAID

RAID has been with us for about 20 years, but until only recently it was the domain of big systems and deep pockets. During those 20 years, however, a number of factors have come together to make RAID a reality for both big servers and common desktop systems. Imagine a world where dirt-cheap RAID on every computer means no one ever again losing critical data. I get goose bumps just thinking about it!

■ Installing Drives

Installing a drive is a fairly simple process if you take the time to make sure you have the right drive for your system, configure the drive properly, and do a few quick tests to see if it's running properly. Since PATA, SATA, and SCSI have different cabling requirements, we'll look at each separately.

Choosing Your Drive

First, decide where you're going to put the drive. Look for an open ATA connection. Is it PATA or SATA? Is it a dedicated RAID controller? Many

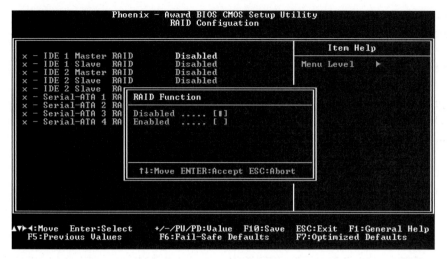

Phoenix - Award BIOS CMOS Setup Utility
RAID Configuration

```
                                              Item Help
x - IDE 1 Master RAID      Disabled
x - IDE 1 Slave  RAID      Disabled     Menu Level    ▶
x - IDE 2 Master RAID      Disabled
x - IDE 2 Slave  RAID      Disabled
x - IDE 2 Slave  RA ┌─────────────────────────────┐
x - Serial-ATA 1 RA │ RAID Function               │
x - Serial-ATA 2 RA │                             │
x - Serial-ATA 3 RA │ Disabled ..... [■]          │
x - Serial-ATA 4 RA │ Enabled  ..... [ ]          │
                    │                             │
                    │                             │
                    │                             │
                    │ ↑↓:Move ENTER:Accept ESC:Abort │
                    └─────────────────────────────┘

▲▼►◄:Move  Enter:Select    +/-/PU/PD:Value  F10:Save  ESC:Exit  F1:General Help
   F5:Previous Values       F6:Fail-Safe Defaults   F7:Optimized Defaults
```

• **Figure 11.39**   Settings for RAID in CMOS

motherboards with built-in RAID controllers have a CMOS setting that enables you to turn the RAID on or off (Figure 11.39).

Second, make sure you have room for the drive in the case. Where will place it? Do you have a spare power connector? Will the data and power cables reach the drive? A quick test fit is always a good idea.

Don't worry about PIO modes and DMA—a new drive will support anything your controller wants to do.

Jumpers and Cabling on PATA Drives

If you have only one hard drive, set the drive's jumpers to master or standalone. If you have two drives, set one to master and the other to slave. See Figure 11.40 for a close-up of a PATA hard drive, showing the jumpers.

At first glance, you might notice that the jumpers aren't actually labeled *master* and *slave*. So how do you know how to set them properly? The easiest way is to read the front of the drive; most drives have a diagram on housing that explains how to set the jumpers properly. Figure 11.41 shows the front of one of these drives, so you can see how to set the drive to master or slave.

Hard disk drives may have other jumpers that may or may not concern you during installation. One common set of jumpers is used for diagnostics at the manufacturing plant or for special settings in other kinds of devices that use hard drives. Ignore them; they have no bearing in the PC world. Second, many drives provide a third setting to be used if only one drive connects to a controller. Often, master and single drive are the same setting on the hard drive, although some hard drives require separate settings. Note

• **Figure 11.40**   Master/slave jumpers on a hard drive

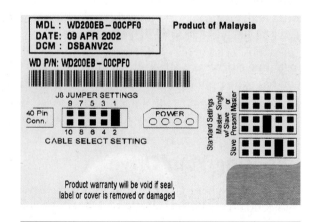

• **Figure 11.41**   Drive label showing master/slave settings

that the name for the single drive setting varies among manufacturers. Some use Single; others use 1 Drive or Standalone.

Many current PATA hard drives use a jumper setting called *cable select* rather than master or slave. As the name implies, the position on the cable determines which drive will be master or slave: master on the end, slave in the middle. For cable select to work properly with two drives, you must set both drives as cable select and the cable itself must be a special cable-select cable. If you see a ribbon cable with a pinhole through one wire, watch out! That's a cable-select cable.

If you don't see a label on the drive that tells you how to set the jumpers, you have several options. First, look for the drive maker's Web site. Every drive manufacturer lists its drive jumper settings on the Web, although finding the information you want can take a while. Second, try phoning the hard drive maker directly. Unlike many other PC parts manufacturers, hard drive producers tend to stay in business for a long time and offer great technical support.

Most of the high-speed ATA/66/100/133 cables support cable select—try one and see!

Hard drive cables have a colored stripe that corresponds to the number-one pin—called *pin 1*—on the connector. You need to make certain that pin 1 on the controller is on the same wire as pin 1 on the hard drive. Failing to plug in the drive properly will also prevent the PC from recognizing the drive. If you incorrectly set the master/slave jumpers or cable to the hard drives, you won't break anything; it just won't work.

Finally, you need to plug a Molex connector from the power supply into the drive. All modern PATA drives use a Molex connector.

> ### ✓ Cross Check
>
> **Molex Connectors**
>
> Hard drives and other internal devices use Molex connectors for power. Refer to Chapter 10, "Power Supplies," and check your memory. What voltages go through the four wires on a Molex connector? What should you note about the connector and inserting it into the corresponding socket on the drive?

Cabling SATA Drives

Installing SATA hard disk drives is even easier than installing PATA devices because there's no master, slave, or cable select configuration to mess with. In fact, there are no jumper settings to worry about at all, as SATA supports only a single device per controller channel. Simply connect the power and plug in the controller cable as shown in Figure 11.42—the OS automatically detects the drive and it's ready to go. The keying on SATA controller and power cables makes it impossible to install either incorrectly.

The biggest problem with SATA drives is that many motherboards come with four or more. Sure, the cabling is easy enough, but what do you do when it comes time to start the computer and the system is trying to find the right hard drive to boot up? That's where CMOS comes into play.

● **Figure 11.42**   Properly connected SATA cable

Connecting Solid-State Drives

You install a solid-state drive as you would any PATA or SATA drive. Just as with earlier hard drive types, you either connect SSDs correctly and they

Installing solid-state removable media such as USB thumb drives and flash memory cards (such as SD cards) is covered in Chapter 13, "Removable Media."

 SSDs are more dependable as well as more expensive than traditional hard drives. They use less energy overall, have smaller form factors, are noiseless, and use either NAND (nonvolatile flash memory) or SDRAM (volatile "RAM drive") technology to store and retrieve data. They can retrieve (read) data much faster than typical HDDs. Their write times, on the other hand, are often slower.

Tech Tip

Don't Defragment SSDs

Don't defragment an SSD! Because solid-state drives access data without having to find that data on the surface of a physical disk first, there's never any reason to defrag one. What's more, SSDs have a limited (albeit massive) number of read/write operations before they turn into expensive paperweights, and the defragmentation process uses those up greedily.

work, or you connect them incorrectly and they don't. If they fail, nine times out of ten they will need to be replaced.

You're most likely to run into solid-state drives today in portable computers. SSDs are expensive and offer a lot less storage capacity compared to traditional hard drives. Because they require a lot less electricity to run, on the other hand, they make a lot of sense in portable computers where battery life is the Holy Grail. You can often use solid-state drives to replace existing platter-based drives in laptops.

Keep in mind the following considerations before installing or replacing an existing HDD with an SSD:

- Does the system currently use a PATA or SATA interface? You need to make sure your solid-state drive can connect properly.

- Do you have the appropriate drivers and firmware for the SDD? This is especially important if you run Windows XP. Windows Vista, on the other hand, is likely to load most currently implemented SDD drivers. As always, check the manufacturer's specifications before you do anything.

- Do you have everything important backed up? Good! You are ready to turn the system off, unplug the battery, ground yourself, and join the wonderful world of solid state.

SSDs address the many shortcomings of traditional HDDs. With solid-state technology, there are no moving metal parts, less energy is used, they come in smaller form factors, and you can access that fancy PowerPoint presentation you created and saved almost instantaneously. In geek terms, little or no latency is involved in accessing fragmented data with solid-state devices.

Connecting SCSI Drives

Connecting SCSI drives requires three things. You must use a controller that works with your drive. You need to set unique SCSI IDs on the controller and the drive. You also need to connect the ribbon cable and power connections properly.

With SCSI, you need to attach the data cable correctly. You can reverse a PATA cable, for example, and nothing happens except the drive doesn't work. If you reverse a SCSI cable, however, you can seriously damage the drive. Just as with PATA cables, pin 1 on the SCSI data cable must go to pin 1 on both the drive and the host adapter.

■ BIOS Support: Configuring CMOS and Installing Drivers

Every device in your PC needs BIOS support, and the hard drive controllers are no exception. Motherboards provide support for the ATA hard drive controllers via the system BIOS, but they require configuration in CMOS for the specific hard drives attached. SCSI drives require software drivers or firmware on the host adapter.

In the old days, you had to fire up CMOS and manually enter CHS information whenever you installed a new ATA drive to ensure the system saw the drive. Today, this process takes place, but it's much more automated. Still, there's plenty to do in CMOS when you install a new hard drive.

CMOS settings for hard drives vary a lot among motherboards. The following information provides a generic look at the most common settings, but you'll need to look at your specific motherboard manual to understand all of the options available.

Configuring Controllers

As a first step in configuring controllers, make certain they're enabled. It's easy to turn off controllers in CMOS, and many motherboards turn off secondary ATA controllers by default. Scan through your CMOS settings to locate the controller on/off options (see Figure 11.43 for typical settings). This is also the time to check whether your onboard RAID controllers work in both RAID and non-RAID settings.

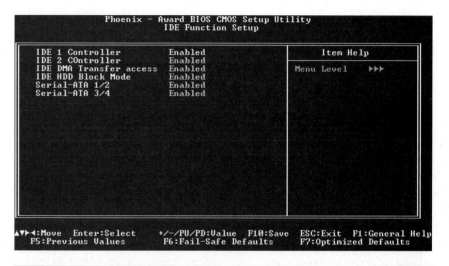

• **Figure 11.43**   Typical controller settings in CMOS

Autodetection

If the controllers are enabled and the drive is properly connected, the drive should appear in CMOS through a process called *autodetection*. Autodetection is a powerful and handy feature, but it seems that every CMOS has a different way to manifest it, and how it is manifested may affect how your computer decides which hard drive to try to boot when you start your PC.

One of your hard drives stores the operating system needed when you boot your computer, and your system needs a way to know where to look for this operating system. The traditional BIOS supported a maximum of only four ATA drives on two controllers, called the *primary controller* and the *secondary controller*. The BIOS looked for the master drive on the primary controller when the system booted up. If you used only one controller, you used the primary controller. The secondary controller was used for CD-ROMs, DVDs, or other nonbootable drives.

Older CMOS made this clear and easy, as shown in Figure 11.44. When

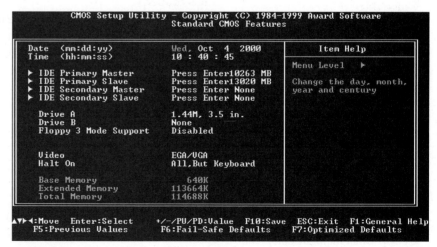

• **Figure 11.44**   Old standard CMOS settings

you booted up, the CMOS queried the drives through autodetection, and whatever drives the CMOS saw, showed up here. In some even older CMOS, you had to run a special menu option called Autodetect to see the drives in this screen. There are places for up to four devices; notice that not all of them actually have a device.

The autodetection screen indicated that you installed a PATA drive correctly. If you installed a hard drive on the primary controller as master but messed up the jumper and set it to slave, it showed up in the autodetection screen as the slave. If you had two drives and set them both to master, one drive or the other (or sometimes both) didn't appear, telling you that something was messed up in the physical installation. If you forgot to plug in the ribbon cable or the power, the drives wouldn't autodetect.

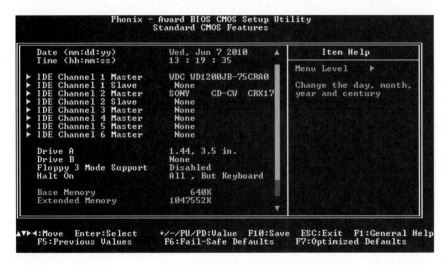

• **Figure 11.45** New standard CMOS features

SATA changed the autodetection happiness. The SATA world has no such thing as master, slave, or even primary and secondary controller. To get around this, motherboards with PATA and SATA today use a numbering system—and every motherboard uses its own numbering system! One common numbering method uses the term *channels* for each controller. The first boot device is channel 1, the second is channel 2, and so on. PATA channels may have a master and a slave, but a SATA channel has only a master, because SATA controllers support only one drive. So instead of names of drives, you see numbers. Take a look at Figure 11.45.

Whew! Lots of hard drives! This motherboard supports the traditional four PATA drives, and it also supports four SATA drives. Each controller is assigned a number; note that channel 1 and channel 2 have master/slave settings, and that's how you know channel 1 and 2 are the PATA drives. Channels 3 through 6 are SATA, even though the listing says *master*. (SATA is still somewhat new, and a CMOS using incorrect terms such as *master* is common.)

Boot Order

If you want your computer to run, it's going to need an operating system to boot. While the PCs of our forefathers (those of the 1980s and early 1990s) absolutely required you to put the operating system on the primary master, most BIOS makers by 1995 enabled you to put the OS on any of the four drives and then tell the system through CMOS which hard drive to boot. With the many SATA drives available on modern systems, you're not even limited to a mere four choices. Additionally, you may need to boot from an optical disc, a USB thumb drive, or even a floppy disk (if you're feeling retro). CMOS takes care of this by enabling you to set a *boot order*.

Boot order is the first place to look when you see this error at boot:

Invalid Boot Disk

The system is trying to boot to a non-bootable disk. Remove any devices that might be before the desired device in the boot order.

Mike Meyers' CompTIA A+ Guide to Managing and Troubleshooting PCs

Figure 11.46 shows a typical boot-order screen, with a first, second, and third boot option. Many users like to boot first from optical and then from a hard drive. This enables them to put in a bootable optical disc if they're having problems with the system. Of course, you can set it to boot first from your hard drive and then go into CMOS and change it when you need to—it's your choice.

Most modern CMOS setup utilities lump the hard drive boot order onto a second screen. This screen works like an autodetect in that it shows only actual hard drives attached. This beats the heck out of guessing.

```
► Hard Disk Boot Priority    Press Enter
  First Boot Device          Floppy
  Second Boot Device         Hard Disk
  Third Boot Device          CDROM
  Boot Other Device          Enabled
```

• **Figure 11.46**   Boot order

Enabling AHCI

On motherboards that support AHCI, you implement it in CMOS. You'll generally have up to three options: IDE or compatibility mode, AHCI, or RAID. Use compatibility mode to install older operating systems, such as Windows XP. Going to AHCI or RAID enables the ACHI option for the HBA.

Try This!

Working with CMOS

One of the best ways to get your mind around the different drive standards and capabilities is to run benchmarking software on the hard drive to get a baseline of its capabilities. Then, change CMOS settings to alter the performance of the drive and run the diagnostics again. Try This!

1. Get a reliable hard drive benchmarking program. I recommend HD Tach (www.simplisoftware.com) as reliable and rugged.

2. Run the software, and record the scores.

3. Change some or all of the following CMOS settings, and then run the benchmarking utility again: PIO mode, DMA mode, block mode.

4. What were the effects of changing settings?

Device Drivers

Devices that do not get BIOS via the system BIOS routines naturally require some other source for BIOS. For ATAPI devices and many SATA controllers, the source of choice is software device drivers, but both technologies have a couple of quirks you should know about.

ATAPI Devices and BIOS

ATAPI drives plug into an ATA controller on the motherboard and follow the same conventions on cabling and jumpers used by PATA hard drives. In fact, all current CMOS setup utilities *seem* to autodetect optical ATAPI drives. If you go into CMOS after installing a CD-ROM drive as master on the secondary IDE controller, for example, the drive will show up just fine, as in Figure 11.47.

The reporting of installed optical drives in CMOS serves two purposes. First, it tells the technician that the ATAPI drive has good connectivity. Second, it shows that you have the

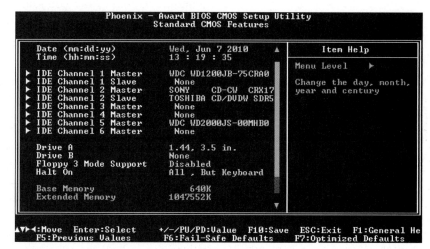

```
           Phoenix - Award BIOS CMOS Setup Utility
                  Standard CMOS Features

   Date (mm:dd:yy)      Wed, Jun 7 2010    ▲        Item Help
   Time (hh:mm:ss)      13 : 19 : 35
                                                Menu Level  ►
 ► IDE Channel 1 Master  WDC WD1200JB-75CRA0
 ► IDE Channel 1 Slave   None                   Change the day, month,
 ► IDE Channel 2 Master  SONY    CD-CW  CRX17    year and century
 ► IDE Channel 2 Slave   TOSHIBA CD/DVDW SDR5
 ► IDE Channel 3 Master  None
 ► IDE Channel 4 Master  None
 ► IDE Channel 5 Master  WDC WD2000JS-00MHB0
 ► IDE Channel 6 Master  None

   Drive A              1.44, 3.5 in.
   Drive B              None
   Floppy 3 Mode Support Disabled
   Halt On              All , But Keyboard

   Base Memory              640K
   Extended Memory       1047552K          ▼

 ▲▼►◄:Move  Enter:Select  +/-/PU/PD:Value  F10:Save  ESC:Exit  F1:General He
    F5:Previous Values     F6:Fail-Safe Defaults    F7:Optimized Defaults
```

• **Figure 11.47**   CMOS screen showing a CD-ROM drive detected

option to boot to an optical disc, such as a Windows XP disc. What it *doesn't* do, however, is provide true BIOS support for that drive. That has to come with a driver loaded at boot-up.

■ Troubleshooting Hard Drive Installation

The best friend a tech has when it comes to troubleshooting hard drive installation is the autodetection feature of the CMOS setup utility. When a drive doesn't work, the biggest question, especially during installation, is "Did I plug it in correctly?" With autodetection, the answer is simple; if the system doesn't see the drive, something is wrong with the hardware configuration. Either a device has physically failed or, more likely, you didn't give the hard drive power, plugged a cable in backward, or messed up some other connectivity issue.

Getting a drive installed and recognized by the system takes four things: jumpers (PATA only), data cable, power, and the CMOS setup recognizing the drive. If you miss or mess up any of these steps, you have a drive that doesn't exist according to the PC! To troubleshoot hard drives, simply work your way through each step to figure out what went wrong.

First, set the drive to master, slave, standalone, or cable select, depending on where you decide to install it. If a drive is alone on the cable, set it to master or standalone. With two drives, one must be master and the other slave. Alternatively, you can set both drives to cable select and use a cable-select cable.

Second, you must connect the data cable to both the drive and the controller, pin 1 to pin 1. Reversing the data cable at one end is remarkably easy to do, especially with the rounded cables. They obviously don't have a big red stripe down the side to indicate the location of pin 1! If you can't autodetect the drive, check the cabling.

Third, be sure to give the hard drive power. Most hard drives use a standard Molex connector. If you don't hear the whirring of the drive, make certain you plugged in a Molex from the power supply rather than from another source such as an otherwise disconnected fan. You'd be surprised how often I've seen that.

Fourth, you need to provide BIOS for the controller and the drive. This can get tricky because the typical CMOS setup program has a lot of hard drive options. Plus, you have an added level of confusion with RAID settings and nonintegrated controllers that require software drivers.

Once you've checked the physical connections, run through these issues in CMOS. Is the controller enabled? Is the storage technology—LBA, INT13, ATA/ATAPI-6—properly set up? Similarly, can the motherboard support the type of drive you're installing? If not, you have a couple of options. You can flash the BIOS with an upgraded BIOS from the manufacturer or you can get a hard drive controller that goes into an expansion slot.

Finally, with nonintegrated hard drive controllers such as those that come with many SATA drives, make certain that you've installed the proper drivers for the controller. Driver issues can crop up with new, very large drives and with changes in technology. Always check the manufacturer's Web site for new drivers.

Beyond A+

Spindle (or Rotational) Speed

Hard drives run at a set spindle speed, measured in *revolutions per minute* (*RPM*). Older drives run at the long-standard speed of 3600 RPM, but new drives are hitting 15,000 RPM. The faster the spindle speed, the faster the controller can store and retrieve data. Here are the common speeds: 4500, 5400, 7200, and 10,000 RPM.

Faster drives mean better system performance, but they can also cause the computer to overheat. This is especially true in tight cases, such as minitowers, and in cases containing many drives. Two 4500-RPM drives might run forever, snugly tucked together in your old case. But slap a hot new 10,000 RPM drive in that same case and watch your system start crashing right and left!

You can deal with these very fast drives by adding drive bay fans between the drives or migrating to a more spacious case. Most enthusiasts end up doing both. Drive bay fans sit at the front of a bay and blow air across the drive. They range in price from $10 to $100 (U.S.) and can lower the temperature of your drives dramatically. Some cases come with a bay fan built in (Figure 11.48).

• **Figure 11.48**   Bay fan

Airflow in a case can make or break your system stability, especially when you add new drives that increase the ambient temperature. Hot systems get flaky and lock up at odd moments. Many things can impede the airflow—jumbled-up ribbon cables, drives squished together in a tiny case, fans clogged by dust or animal hair, and so on.

Technicians need to be aware of the dangers when adding a new hard drive to an older system. Get into the habit of tying off ribbon cables, adding front fans to cases when systems lock up intermittently, and making sure any fans run well. Finally, if a client wants a new drive for a system in a tiny minitower with only the power supply fan to cool it off, be gentle, but definitely steer the client to one of the slower drives!

Hybrid Hard Drives

Windows Vista supports hybrid hard drives (HHDs), drives that combine flash memory and spinning platters to provide fast and reliable storage, and offers ReadyBoost and Superfetch for faster caching and booting. Samsung has drives with 128-MB and 256-MB flash cache, for example, that shave boot times in half and, because the platters don't have to spin all of the time, add 20–30 minutes more of battery life for portable computers. Adding that much more run time with only a tiny price premium and no extra weight is the Holy Grail of portable computing.

Chapter 11 Review

■ Chapter Summary

After reading this chapter and completing the exercises, you should understand the following about hard drive technologies.

Explain how hard drives work

■ Traditional hard drives contain aluminum platters coated with a magnetic medium and read/write heads that float on a cushion of air. Hard drives store data in a tiny magnetic field called a flux that defines a zero or a one. The switching back and forth of the field is called flux reversal. The incredible storage capacity of today's drives results from Partial Response Maximum Likelihood (PRML) encoding that includes intelligent circuitry to analyze each flux reversal.

■ Two technologies have been used to move read/write heads across the platters: stepper motors and voice coil. Very susceptible to physical deterioration and temperature changes, the now obsolete stepper motors moved the actuator arm in fixed increments or steps, often resulting in data-transfer errors or the inability to access data on a cold drive. The heads had to be parked to a non-data area when not in use to prevent possible damage to the disk surface. Today's drives use a linear or voice coil motor consisting of a permanent magnet surrounding a coil on the actuator arm. Electrical current causes the coil to generate a magnetic field that moves the actuator arm and thus the read/write heads. Containing no data, one side of one platter is used as a map to position the heads directly over the data. Voice coil technology automatically parks the heads when the drive loses power.

■ Disk geometry for a particular hard drive consists of three primary values: heads, cylinders, and sectors per track (sectors/track). There are two read/write heads per platter. A hard drive can have either an even or an odd number of heads. A cylinder defines a group of tracks of the same diameter. Each track is sliced into tiny slivers called sectors, each of which stores 512 bytes of data. Disk geometry uses the number of sectors per track. Combining cylinders, heads, and sectors/track is referred to as CHS. Write precompensation and landing zone, two other geometric values, have no relevance in today's PCs, but most CMOS utilities still support them.

■ Solid-state drives use memory chips to store data and don't have any metal spinning parts. They require less electricity than platter-based drives and offer faster reads and writes. At the time of this writing, they cost substantially more than traditional drives.

Identify and explain the PATA and SATA hard drive interfaces

■ Today's hard drives have either an ATA interface or a SCSI interface. ATA drives may be parallel ATA (PATA) or the newer serial ATA (SATA). A specification of the American National Standards Institute (ANSI), the AT Attachment (ATA) interface (commonly but incorrectly referred to as IDE) used a 40-pin ribbon cable, had a built-in controller, and did not require a low-level format. By 1995, EIDE was the dominant interface. Its features include higher capacities, support for non–hard drive storage devices, a four-device maximum, and improved throughput. The terms ATA, IDE, and EIDE are used interchangeably to describe all PATA devices.

■ PATA drives use a 40-pin plug and a controller that connects them to the external data bus. Although the real controller is built into the hard drive itself, the 40-pin connector on the motherboard is called the controller. Most modern motherboards contain two PATA controllers, each capable of supporting up to two PATA devices. By looking at the motherboard itself or at the motherboard book, you can determine which is the primary controller and which is the secondary. If you are using only one controller, it should be the primary one.

■ The advanced technology attachment packet interface (ATAPI) enables non–hard drive devices to use a PATA controller. ATAPI devices, such as CD-ROM drives, use the same 40-pin interface and follow the same rules of master, slave, and cable select jumper settings. Non–hard drives must get their BIOS from option RAM or a software driver.

- Originally, IDE drives used the same BIOS command set introduced years earlier. Maximum values of 1024 cylinders, 16 heads, and 63 sectors per track limited an IDE drive's capacity to 528 million bytes (504 MB). Western Digital developed the LBA sector translation method to accommodate larger EIDE drives. LBA supports drives with up to 256 heads, for a storage capacity limit of 8.4 GB.

- As drive capacity neared the 8.4-GB maximum, Phoenix Technologies broke the limit by coming up with a new set of BIOS commands called Interrupt 13 extensions (INT13). Completely ignoring the CHS values, INT13 supports drives up to 137 GB by reporting a stream of addressable sectors to LBA.

- As drive capacity neared the 137-GB limit, the ANSI ATA committee adopted ATA/ATAPI-6, a new standard that increased the limit to more than 144 petabytes (144,000,000 GB). It uses a 48-bit addressing scheme and an enhanced block mode that transfers up to 65,536 sectors at a time.

- Newer hard drives use direct memory access (DMA) mode to send data directly to RAM, bypassing the CPU. Instead of using the slow DMA controller chip, today's DMA transfers use bus mastering to transfer 32 bits of data. Hard drives typically use one of the following modes: Ultra DMA mode 4 (ATA/66), Ultra DMA mode 5 (ATA/100), and Ultra DMA mode 6 (ATA/133). To use Ultra DMA, you must have a controller and an 80-wire ribbon cable. Some motherboards combine different speeds of ATA controllers, with the higher-speed controller indicated with a bright color. The 80-wire ribbon cable indicates where to connect the master and slave drives. High-end PATA devices can use lower-end controllers, but they will operate at the slower speed.

- Serial ATA (SATA) devices look identical to standard PATA devices (except their data and power connectors), but their thinner seven-wire cables provide better airflow and may be up to a meter (39.4 inches) long. SATA does away with the entire master/slave concept. Each drive connects to one port, so no more daisy-chaining drives.

- SATA devices are hot-swappable, great for RAID technology. SATA transfers data in serial bursts for up to 30 times the throughput of PATA. SATA drives come in two common varieties, the 1.5Gb

and the 3Gb, that have a maximum throughput of 150 MBps and 300 MBps, respectively.

Identify and explain the SCSI hard drive interfaces

- All SCSI chains, which support either 8 or 16 devices including the controller, require proper termination to prevent signal echo. Additionally, each device on a chain requires a unique SCSI ID, which can be set by jumpers, switches, or dials.

- All SCSI devices can be divided into two groups: internal and external. Internal SCSI devices connect to the host adapter with a 68-pin ribbon cable. External devices connect to the host adapter with either a 50-pin HD connector or a 68-pin HD connector. SCSI enables you to daisy-chain devices together to form longer SCSI chains.

- Improper termination or incorrect SCSI ID settings are the two most common causes of SCSI devices not working. The key factor here is that you must terminate only the ends of the SCSI chain.

Describe how to protect data with RAID

- Drive mirroring writes data simultaneously to two hard drives, enabling the system to continue to work if one hard drive dies. A faster and even more effective technique is drive duplexing, which performs mirroring by using separate controllers for each drive. A third way to create redundant data is disk striping with parity. This technique, requiring at least three drives, combines the redundancy of disk mirroring with the speed of disk striping. Although disk striping without parity works very fast, splitting the data across two drives means you'll lose *all* data if either drive fails.

- Numbered 0 through 6, there are seven official levels of RAID, but the most commonly used ones are RAID 0 (disk striping), RAID 1 (disk mirroring or duplexing), and RAID 5 (disk striping with distributed parity).

- RAID may be implemented through hardware or software methods. Although software implementation is cheaper, hardware techniques provide better performance. Windows 2000 Server, Windows Server 2003, and Windows Server 2008 include built-in RAID software for RAID 0, RAID 1, and RAID 5 for either ATA or SCSI. Windows 2000, Windows XP, and Windows Vista include Disk Management for RAID 0. RAID software solutions tend to overwork your operating system,

resulting in slowdowns. Hardware RAID is invisible to the OS and is usually hot-swappable. A hardware ATA RAID controller usually requires CMOS configuration. Many motherboards include built-in ATA-based hardware RAID 0 and RAID 1 capabilities.

- SCSI drives were a natural for the multiple-disk RAID. Specialized ATA RAID controller cards support ATA RAID arrays of up to 15 drives. With its hot-swap capabilities, SATA may soon take over lower-end RAID from SCSI.

Install hard drives

- Older PATA drives use a 40-wire cable, while the newer Ultra DMA drives use an 80-wire cable. Either round or flat and containing no twists, each ribbon cable supports two drives. A diagram on the hard drive's housing shows how to set its jumpers to identify it as master, slave, standalone (on some drives), or cable select (cable position determines whether the drive will be master or slave). Two devices on one cable must both be set to cable select, and the cable itself must also be cable select, as indicated with a pinhole through one wire. Align the colored stripe on the cable with pin 1 on the controller and the drive. Use a Molex connector to provide power to the drive.

- SATA supports only a single device per controller channel, so there are no master, slave, or cable select jumpers. SATA controller and power cables are keyed to prevent incorrect insertion. You can connect a PATA device to a SATA motherboard controller by way of a SATA bridge.

- Solid-state drives are PATA, SATA, eSATA, SCSI, or USB. Before upgrading or installing an SDD, you should verify that the new drive uses the same interface as the old drive or that you have the proper connection type available. As for any hardware device, it is also important to ensure you have the appropriate SDD drivers and firmware before installation.

Configure CMOS and install drivers

- While system BIOS supports built-in PATA controllers, hard drives require configuration in CMOS. ATAPI devices require software drivers to provide BIOS support. Built-in SATA controllers on a motherboard also require software drivers, as does a SATA controller on a separate expansion card. All SATA devices get BIOS support from the SATA controller, but some drives require additional configuration. In particular, with RAID systems, you may also have to configure controller Flash ROM settings for the specific drives you install.

- When the hard drive type is set to Auto, PATA devices can be queried directly by BIOS routines, resulting in the correct CMOS settings for up to four ATA devices. Autodetection made hard drive types obsolete. Because PATA drives have CHS values stored inside them, the BIOS routine, when set to Auto, updates the CMOS each time the computer boots. An alternative is to run the autodetection option from the CMOS screen.

- Even if the autodetect feature indicates that an optical ATAPI drive has been installed, this merely shows that the drive is connected properly and has the option to function as a boot device. This autodetection does *not* provide true BIOS support. You must still install drivers to provide the BIOS.

- If the autodetection feature of the CMOS utility does not detect a drive, it is installed incorrectly or the drive itself is bad. Check the master/slave jumper settings. Make sure that the ribbon cable aligns pin 1 with pin 1, and that the Molex connector is supplying power to the drive.

- Once you've checked the physical connections, run through these issues in CMOS. Is the controller enabled? Is the storage technology—LBA, Large, INT13, ATA/ATAPI-6—properly set up? What about the data-transfer settings for PIO and DMA modes? Similarly, can the motherboard support the type of drive you're installing? If not, you can flash the BIOS or get a hard drive controller that goes into an expansion slot. With nonintegrated hard drive controllers, such as those that come with many SATA drives, make sure that you've installed the proper drivers for the controller. Always check the manufacturer's Web site for new drivers.

Troubleshoot hard drive installation

- Getting a drive installed and recognized by the system takes four things: jumpers (PATA only), data cable, power, and CMOS setup recognizing the drive. If you miss or mess up any of these steps, you have a drive that doesn't exist according to

the PC! To troubleshoot hard drives, simply work your way through each step to figure out what went wrong.

- Once you've checked the physical connections, run through these issues in CMOS. Is the controller enabled? Is the storage technology—LBA, INT13, ATA/ATAPI-6—properly set up? Similarly, can the motherboard support the type of drive you're installing? If not, you have a couple of options. You can flash the BIOS with an upgraded BIOS from the manufacturer or you can get a hard drive controller that goes into an expansion slot.

■ Key Terms

40-pin ribbon cable *(331)*
80-wire cable *(337)*
advanced technology attachment (ATA) *(330)*
advanced technology attachment packet interface (ATAPI) *(334)*
ATA/133 *(338)*
ATA/ATAPI-6 *(337)*
cylinder *(328)*
disk duplexing *(344)*
disk mirroring *(344)*
disk striping *(344)*
disk striping with parity *(346)*
DMA modes *(332)*
Enhanced IDE (EIDE) *(332)*
external SATA (eSATA) *(340)*
geometry *(327)*
hard disk drive (HDD) *(325)*
head actuator *(326)*
heads *(328)*
host bus adapter (HBA) *(338)*
integrated drive electronics (IDE) *(330)*
Interrupt 13 (INT13) extensions *(336)*

logical block addressing (LBA) *(333)*
parallel ATA (PATA) *(330)*
Partial Response Maximum Likelihood (PRML) *(326)*
PIO modes *(332)*
redundant array of independent (or inexpensive) disks (RAID) *(346)*
SATA bridge *(339)*
SCSI chain *(341)*
SCSI ID *(342)*
sector *(328)*
sectors per track (sectors/track) *(328)*
sector translation *(333)*
serial ATA (SATA) *(330)*
Self-Monitoring, Analysis, and Reporting Technology (S.M.A.R.T.) *()*
small computer system interface (SCSI) *(340)*
solid-state drive (SSD) *(329)*
stepper motor *(327)*
termination *(342)*
track *(328)*
Ultra DMA *(336)*
voice coil *(327)*

■ Key Term Quiz

Use the Key Terms list to complete the sentences that follow. Not all terms will be used.

1. An ATA hard drive connects to the controller with a(n) _____, while an Ultra DMA mode 4 drive uses a(n) _____.

2. A(n) _____ is composed of a group of tracks of the same diameter that the read/write heads can access without moving.

3. To install a parallel ATA device to a serial ATA controller, use a tiny card called a(n) _____.

4. LBA, developed by Western Digital, uses _____ to get around the limits of 1024 cylinders, 16 heads, and 63 sectors/track.

5. Seen in RAID 5, _____ uses at least three drives and combines the best features of disk mirroring and disk striping.

6. A CD-ROM drive that is _____-compliant installs and cables just like an EIDE drive.

7. The ANSI ATA committee adopted the _____ standard, called "Big Drives" by Maxtor, that allows drives with more than 144 petabytes.

8. Drives known as _____ transfer data at 133 MBps.

9. Drives that use _____ bypass the CPU and send data directly to memory.

10. Devices known as _____ devices require termination at both ends of a chain.

■ Multiple-Choice Quiz

1. Which of the following is *not* used to compute storage capacity in CHS disk geometry?

   A. Sectors per track

   B. Tracks

   C. Heads

   D. Cylinders

2. Which level of RAID is disk striping with distributed parity?

   A. RAID 0

   B. RAID 1

   C. RAID 5

   D. RAID 6

3. Counting both channels, what is the maximum number of drives/devices that EIDE can support?

   A. One

   B. Two

   C. Seven

   D. Four

4. Which of the following is *not* true about cable select?

   A. Both drives/devices should be set for cable select.

   B. Cable select requires a special cable with a pinhole through one wire.

   C. The colored stripe on the ribbon cable should align with pin 1 on the controller and drive.

   D. Position of the drives on the cable does not matter.

5. If you install two IDE drives on the same cable, how will the computer differentiate them?

   A. The CMOS setup allows you to configure them.

   B. You must set jumpers to determine which drive functions as master and which functions as slave.

   C. You will set jumpers so each drive has a unique ID number.

   D. The drives will be differentiated by whether you place them before or after the twist in the ribbon cable.

6. What was the maximum hard drive size allowed by BIOS routines for the original AT command set?

   A. 528 MB

   B. 1024 MB

   C. 504 MB

   D. 1028 MB

7. Which of the following terms does *not* describe parallel ATA devices?

   A. IDE

   B. EIDE

   C. SCSI

   D. ATA

8. Shelby wants to add a 100-GB hard drive to her computer. Which of the following will allow her to do so?

   A. CHS

   B. LBA

   C. ECHS

   D. INT13

9. Which of the following techniques provides redundancy by using two disks and two controllers?

   A. Drive mirroring

   B. Drive duplexing

C. Disk striping

D. Disk striping with parity

10. How many wires does an Ultra DMA ATA cable have?

   A. 24

   B. 34

   C. 40

   D. 80

11. Billy just installed a second hard drive, but the autodetection utility in CMOS does not detect it. Sara told him he probably had the jumpers set incorrectly or had forgotten to connect the Molex power connector. John told him his new hard drive is probably bad and he should return it. Is Sara or John probably correct?

   A. Sara is correct.

   B. John is correct.

   C. Neither is correct.

   D. Either John or Sara may be correct.

12. Which of the following is *not* an advantage of serial ATA (SATA)?

   A. It is hot-swappable.

   B. Thinner cables provide better airflow inside the case.

C. SATA provides faster data throughput than PATA.

D. SATA cables must be shorter than PATA cables.

13. What standard did the ANSI ATA committee adopt that increased disk storage capacity to more than 144 petabytes?

   A. ATA/ATAPI-6

   B. LBA

   C. INT13

   D. ECHS

14. Which of the following can SSDs use to retain data integrity when a system loses power or is turned off?

   A. DRAM

   B. RAM drive

   C. NAND

   D. SDRAM

15. Which of the following represent common solid-state drive form factors?

   A. AT, ATX, and BTX

   B. 8-inch, 2.5-inch, and 5.25-inch

   C. 1.8-inch, 2.5-inch, and 3.5-inch

   D. IEEE 1394, USB and SCSI

■ Essay Quiz

1. Discuss at least three advantages of serial ATA over parallel ATA.

2. Compare and contrast hardware and software RAID implementation.

3. Your friend Blaine has a Pentium 4 computer with a 100-MHz bus. Currently, it has only an 80-GB ATA/100 hard drive and a CD-RW drive. Because he's interested in video, he knows he needs more storage capacity and wants to add a second hard drive. What advice will you give him about selecting a new hard drive?

4. Hard drives include other features and characteristics not included in this chapter.

Choose one of the following topics and use the Internet to define and explain it to the class.

   ■ Zone bit recording

   ■ "Pixie dust" hard drives

5. Your office is about to purchase 10 new portable computers for the sales force and needs a recommendation. Prepare a short essay that compares and contrasts platter-based and solid-state drives so your boss can pick what's best for the staff.

Lab Projects

• Lab Project 11.1

Access the CMOS setup for your computer and examine the settings that apply to your hard drive(s) and EIDE interface. In particular, look at the initial screen to see if it is set to autodetect the kind of hard drive. Is the mode set to LBA or something else? Now find the screen that includes the autodetect utility and run it. Does it offer different modes with different drive capacities? Try to find a screen that includes PIO modes and examine this setting. What other screens apply to the hard drive? When you finish, be sure to choose Quit without saving.

• Lab Project 11.2

Visit your local computer store or use the Internet to discover what kinds of hard drives and hard drive interfaces are commonly offered with new computers. Try to determine whether the motherboards offer only parallel ATA interfaces or if they offer serial ATA interfaces, either onboard or through an expansion card. If you were purchasing a new computer, would you select PATA or SATA? Why?

• Lab Project 11.3

Your supervisor has decided to implement RAID on the old company server machine, where everyone stores their work-related data. Come up with two competing RAID setups, one that maximizes security of data at the lowest cost possible and another that maximizes speed but retains some security. Cost is not a factor for the second RAID plan.

• Lab Project 11.4

If your lab has the equipment, install a second hard drive in your system. Install it on the same cable as the existing drive and jumper it as the slave. (You may need to jumper the existing drive as master.) Reboot, enter CMOS, and verify that both drives are detected. Boot into your operating system and verify that both drives are accessible. (You may need to partition and format the second drive before it is actually usable.)

Implementing Hard Drives

"Wisely and slow; they stumble that run fast."

—Shakespeare, *Romeo and Juliet*, Act II, Scene 3

In this chapter, you will learn how to

■ **Explain the partitions available in Windows**

■ **Discuss hard drive formatting options**

■ **Partition and format hard drives**

■ **Maintain and troubleshoot hard drives**

From the standpoint of your PC, a new hard drive successfully installed is nothing more than a huge pile of sectors. CMOS sees the drive; it shows up in your **autodetect** screen (listed as the Standard Features screen in many CMOS versions, this screen lets you know which drives CMOS can see) and BIOS knows how to talk to the drive, but as far as an operating system is concerned, that drive is unreadable. Your operating system must organize that big pile of sectors so you can create two things: folders and files. This chapter covers that process.

No cluster questions.

Historical/Conceptual

After you've successfully installed a hard drive, you must perform two more steps to translate a drive's geometry and circuits into something the system can use: partitioning and formatting. **Partitioning** is the process of electronically subdividing the physical hard drive into groups of cylinders called **partitions** (or **volumes**). A hard drive must have at least one partition, and you can create multiple partitions on a single hard drive if you wish. In Windows, each of these partitions typically is assigned a drive letter such as C: or D:. After partitioning, you must *format* the drive. **Formatting** installs a **file system** onto the drive that organizes each partition in such a way that the operating system can store files and folders on the drive. Several types of file systems are used in the Windows world. This chapter will go through them after covering partitioning.

Partitioning and formatting a drive is one of the few areas remaining on the software side of PC assembly that requires you to perform a series of fairly complex manual steps. The CompTIA A+ certification exams test your knowledge of *what* these processes do to make the drive work, as well as the steps needed to partition and format hard drives in Windows 2000, XP, and Vista.

This chapter continues the exploration of hard drive installation by explaining partitioning and formatting and then going through the process of partitioning and formatting hard drives. The chapter wraps with a discussion on hard drive maintenance and troubleshooting issues.

▪ Hard Drive Partitions

Partitions provide tremendous flexibility in hard drive organization. With partitions, you can organize a drive to suit your personal taste. For example, I partitioned my 1.5 TB hard drive into a 250-GB partition where I store Windows Vista and all my programs, a second 250-GB partition for Windows 7, and a 1-TB partition where I store all my personal data. This is a matter of personal choice; in my case, backups are simpler because the data is stored in one partition, and I can back up that partition without including the applications.

You can partition a hard drive to store more than one **operating system (OS)**. Store one OS in one partition and create a second partition for another OS. Granted, most people use only one OS, but if you want the option to boot to Windows or Linux, partitions are the key.

Essentials

Windows 2000/XP and Windows Vista/7 support two different partitioning methods: the older but more universal master boot record (MBR) partitioning scheme and the newer (but proprietary to Microsoft) dynamic storage partitioning scheme. Microsoft calls a hard drive that uses the MBR partitioning scheme a **basic disk** and a drive using the dynamic storage

partitioning scheme a dynamic disk. A single Windows system with two hard drives may have one of the drives partitioned as a basic disk and the other as a dynamic disk, and the system will run perfectly well. The bottom line? You get to learn about two totally different types of partitioning. Yay! Given that basic disks are much older, we'll start there.

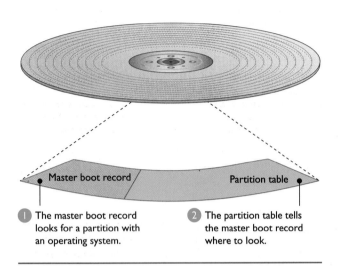

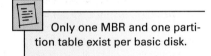

The master boot record looks for a partition with an operating system.

The partition table tells the master boot record where to look.

• **Figure 12.1**   Functions of the MBR and partition table

Only one MBR and one partition table exist per basic disk.

Basic Disks

Basic disk partitioning creates two very small data structures on a drive, the **master boot record (MBR)** and a **partition table**, and stores them on the first sector of the hard drive—called the **boot sector**. The MBR is nothing more than a tiny bit of code that takes control of the boot process from the system BIOS. When the computer boots to a hard drive, the BIOS automatically looks for MBR code on the boot sector. The MBR has only one job: to look in the partition table for a partition with a valid operating system (Figure 12.1).

All basic disk partition tables support up to four partitions. The partition table supports two types of partitions: primary partitions and extended partitions. **Primary partitions** are designed to support bootable operating systems. **Extended partitions** are not bootable. A single basic disk may have up to three primary partitions and one extended partition. If you do not have an extended partition, you may have up to four primary partitions.

Each partition must have some unique identifier so users can recognize it as an individual partition. Microsoft operating systems (DOS and Windows) traditionally assign primary partitions a drive letter from C: to Z:. Extended partitions do not get drive letters.

After you create an extended partition, you must create **logical drives** within that extended partition. A logical drive traditionally gets a drive letter from D: to Z:. (The drive letter C: is always reserved for the first primary partition in a Windows PC.)

Windows 2000/XP and Windows Vista/7 partitions are not limited to drive letters. With the exception of the partition that stores the boot files for Windows (which will always be C:), any other primary partitions or logical drives may get either a drive letter or a folder on a primary partition. You'll see how all of this works later in this chapter.

If a primary partition is a bootable partition, why does a basic drive's partition table support up to four primary partitions? Remember when I said that partitioning allows multiple operating systems? This is how it works. You can install up to four different operating systems, each OS installed on its own primary partition, and boot to your choice each time you fire up the computer.

Every primary partition on a single drive has a special setting called *active* stored in the partition table. This setting is either on or off on each primary partition, determining which is the **active partition**. At boot, the MBR uses the active setting in the partition table to determine which primary partition to choose to try to load an OS. Only one partition at a time can be the active partition, because you can run only one OS at a time (see Figure 12.2).

This restriction refers to a single drive, by the way. You can have active partitions on more than one physical drive; the settings in CMOS will dictate which drive is the current bootable or system drive.

The boot sector at the beginning of the hard drive isn't the only special sector on a hard drive. The first sector of the first cylinder of each partition also has a special sector called the **volume boot sector**. Although the "main" boot sector defines the partitions, the volume boot sector stores information important to its partition, such as the location of the OS boot files. Figure 12.3 shows a hard drive with two partitions. The first partition's volume boot sector contains information about the size of the partition and the code pointing to the boot files on this partition. The second volume boot sector contains information about the size of the partition.

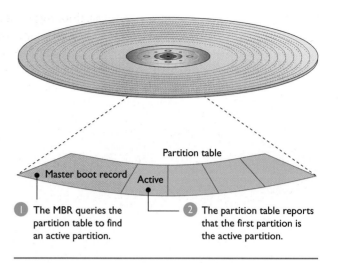

Partition table

Master boot record / Active

1 The MBR queries the partition table to find an active partition.

2 The partition table reports that the first partition is the active partition.

● **Figure 12.2**   The MBR checks the partition table to find the active partition.

Primary Partitions

If you want to boot an operating system from a hard drive, that hard drive must have a primary partition. The MBR checks the partition table for the active primary partition (see Figure 12.4). In Windows, the primary partition is C:, and that cannot be changed.

Even though hard drives support up to four primary partitions, you almost never see four partitions in the Windows world. Windows support up to four primary partitions on one drive, but how many people (other than nerdy CompTIA A+ people like you and me) really want to boot up more than one OS? We use a number of terms for this function, but **dual-boot** and **multiboot** are the most common. The system in my house, for example, uses four primary partitions, each holding one OS: Ubuntu Linux, Windows 2000, Windows XP, and Windows Vista. In other words, I chopped my drive up into four chunks and installed a different OS in each.

To do multiboot, most people use a free, Linux-based boot manager called GRUB (Grand Unified Boot Manager), although some people prefer a

Every partition on a hard drive has a volume boot sector.

Don't confuse primary partition with primary controller. The latter, as you'll recall from Chapter 11, "Hard Drive Technologies," refers to the first PATA drive controller on a motherboard.

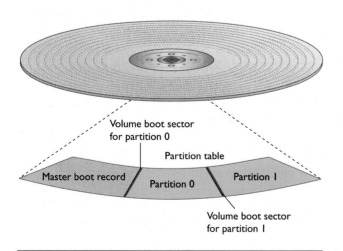

Volume boot sector for partition 0

Partition table

Master boot record   Partition 1

Partition 0

Volume boot sector for partition 1

● **Figure 12.3**   Volume boot sector

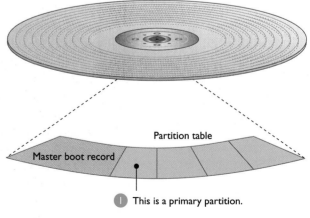

Partition table

Master boot record

1 This is a primary partition.

● **Figure 12.4**   The MBR checks the partition table to find a primary partition.

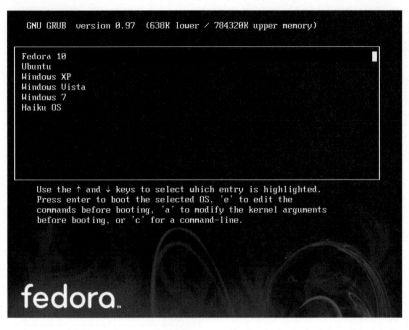

```
GNU GRUB  version 0.97  (638K lower / 784320K upper memory)

 ┌──────────────────────────────────────────────────────────────────────┐
 │ Fedora 10                                                            ▐ │
 │ Ubuntu                                                                 │
 │ Windows XP                                                             │
 │ Windows Vista                                                          │
 │ Windows 7                                                              │
 │ Haiku OS                                                               │
 │                                                                        │
 │                                                                        │
 │                                                                        │
 │                                                                        │
 └──────────────────────────────────────────────────────────────────────┘
      Use the ↑ and ↓ keys to select which entry is highlighted.
      Press enter to boot the selected OS, 'e' to edit the
      commands before booting, 'a' to modify the kernel arguments
      before booting, or 'c' for a command-line.

 fedora.
```

• **Figure 12.5**   GRUB's OS selection menu

third-party tool such as System Commander 9 by VCOM to set up the partitions. Windows 2000 and up come with similar tools that can do this, but they can be messy to use, and GRUB helps simplify the process. When the computer boots, GRUB yanks control from the MBR and asks which OS you wish to boot (see Figure 12.5). You select an OS and it appears.

Again, few systems use more than one primary partition. You may work on PCs for years and never see a system with more than one primary partition. The CompTIA A+ certification exams certainly don't expect you to demonstrate how to create a system with multiple primary partitions, but they assume that you know you *can* add more than one primary partition to a hard drive if you so desire. The rest of this book assumes that you want only one primary partition.

Active Partition

When you create a primary partition and decide to place an OS on that partition, you must set that partition as active. You must do this even if you use only a single primary partition. Luckily, this step is automated in the Windows installation process. Consider this: When would you want to go though the steps to define a partition as active? That would be when you install an OS on that partition. So when you install Windows on a new system, the installation program automatically sets up your first primary partition as the active partition. It never actually says this in the installation, it just does it for you.

So if you raise your right hand and promise to use only Microsoft Windows and make only single primary partitions on your hard drives, odds are good you'll never have to mess with manually adjusting your active partitions. Of course, because you're crazy enough to want to get into PCs, that means within a year of reading this text you're going to want to install other operating systems such as Linux on your PC (and that's okay—all techs want to try this at some point). The moment you do, you'll enter the world of boot manager programs of which the just-described System Commander is only one of many, many choices. You also might use tools to change the active partition manually—exactly when and how this is done varies tremendously for each situation and is way outside the scope of the CompTIA A+ exams, but make sure you know why you might need to set a partition as active.

When my System Commander boot screen comes up, it essentially asks me, "What primary partition do you want me to make active?"

Extended Partition

Understanding the purpose of extended partitions requires a brief look at the historical PC. The first versions of the old DOS operating system to

support hard drives only supported primary partitions up to 32 MB. As hard drives went past 32 MB, Microsoft needed a way to support them. Instead of rewriting DOS to handle larger drives, Microsoft developers created the idea of the extended partition. That way, if you had a hard drive larger than 32 MB, you could make a 32-MB primary partition and the rest of the drive an extended partition. Over the years, DOS and then Windows were rewritten to support large hard drives, but the extended partition is still fully supported.

The beauty of an extended partition is in the way it handles drive letters. When you create a primary partition, it gets a drive letter and that's it. But when you create an extended partition, it does not automatically get a drive letter. Instead, you go through a second step where you divide the extended partition into one or more logical drives. An extended partition may have as many logical drives as you wish. By default, Windows gives each logical drive in an extended partition a drive letter, and most Windows users use drive letters. However, if you'd like, you may even mount the drive letter as a folder on any lettered drive. You can set the size of each logical drive to any size you want. You'll learn how to mount drives later in this chapter—for now, just get the idea that a partition may be mounted with a drive letter or as a folder.

 Primary partitions and logical drives on basic disks are also called *basic volumes*.

Extended partitions are completely optional; you do not have to create an extended partition on a hard drive. So, if you can't boot to an extended partition and your hard drive doesn't need an extended partition, why would you want to create one? First of all, the majority of systems do not use extended partitions. Most systems use only one hard drive, and that single drive is partitioned as one big primary partition—nothing wrong with that! Some users like having an extended partition with one or more logical drives, and they use the extended partitions as a way to separate data. For example, I might store all of my movie files on my G: logical drive.

Instead of assigning drive letters, you can mount logical drives as folders on an existing drive. It's easy to make a logical drive and call it C:\ STORAGE. If the C:\STORAGE folder fills up, you could add an extra hard drive, make the entire extra drive an extended partition with one logical drive, unmount the old C:\ STORAGE drive, and then mount the new huge logical drive as C:\ STORAGE. It's as though you made your C: drive bigger without replacing it.

 **Try This!**

Folder Swapping

What steps would you have to go through to add a new drive to a system and remount it as the C:\STORAGE folder without losing any data in the existing C:\STORAGE folder? Don't bother telling me the tools you need, just think about the logical steps you'd need to do this.

Dynamic Disks

With the introduction of Windows 2000, Microsoft defined an entirely new type of partitioning called *dynamic storage partitioning*, better known as **dynamic disks**. Dynamic disks drop the word *partition* and instead use the term *volume*. There is no dynamic disk equivalent to primary versus extended partitions. A volume is still technically a partition, but it can do things a regular partition cannot do, such as spanning. A **spanned volume** goes across more than one drive. Windows allows you to span up to 32 drives under a single volume. Dynamic disks also support RAID 0 in Windows 2000 Professional,

Cross Check

RAID 5

You read about RAID 5 in Chapter 11, "Hard Drive Technologies," so turn there now and see if you can answer these questions. What type of hard drives can do RAID 5? What common phrase designates RAID 5 in the real world? How many drives do you need?

Windows XP Professional, and Windows Vista Business and Ultimate. Windows 2000, 2003, and 2008 Server editions support RAID 0, 1, and 5.

Dynamic disks use an MBR and a partition table, but these older structures are there only for backward compatibility. All of the information about a dynamic disk is stored in a hidden partition that takes up the last 1 MB of the hard drive. Every partition in a partition table holds a 2-byte value that describes the partition. For example, an extended partition gets the number 05. Windows adds a new number, 42, to the first partition on a dynamic disk. When Windows 2000 or XP reads the partition table for a dynamic disk, it sees the number 42 and immediately jumps to the 1-MB hidden partition, ignoring the old-style partition table. By supporting an MBR and partition table, Windows also prevents other disk partitioning programs from messing with a dynamic disk. If you use a third-party partitioning program, it simply sees the entire hard drive as either an unformatted primary partition or a non-readable partition.

Windows XP Home and Windows Media Center do not support dynamic disks, nor do any Vista editions besides Business and Ultimate.

A key thing to understand about dynamic drives is that the technology is *proprietary*. Microsoft has no intention of telling anyone exactly how dynamic disks work. Only fairly recent Microsoft operating systems (Windows 2000 and up) can read a drive configured as a dynamic disk.

You can use five volume types with dynamic disks: simple, spanned, striped, mirrored, and RAID 5. Most folks stick with simple volumes.

Simple volumes work much like primary partitions. If you have a hard drive and you want to make half of it C: and the other half D:, you create two volumes on a dynamic disk. That's it: no choosing between primary and extended partitions. Remember that you were limited to four primary partitions when using basic disks. To make more than four volumes with a basic disk, you first had to create an extended partition and then make logical drives within the extended partition. Dynamic disks simplify the process by treating all partitions as volumes, so you can make as many as you need.

Spanned volumes use unallocated space on multiple drives to create a single volume. Spanned volumes are a bit risky: if any of the spanned drives fails, the entire volume is permanently lost.

Striped volumes are RAID 0 volumes. You may take any two unallocated spaces on two separate hard drives and stripe them. But again, if either drive fails, you lose all of your data.

Mirrored volumes are RAID 1 volumes. You may take any two unallocated spaces on two separate hard drives and mirror them. If one of the two mirrored drives fails, the other keeps running.

RAID 5 volumes, as the name implies, are for RAID 5 arrays. A RAID 5 volume requires three or more dynamic disks with equal-sized unallocated spaces.

Other Partitions

The partition types supported by Windows are not the only partition types you may encounter; other types exist. One of the most common is called the *hidden partition*. A hidden partition is just a primary partition that is hidden from your operating system. Only special BIOS tools may access a hidden partition. Hidden partitions are used by some PC makers to hide a backup copy of an installed OS that you can use to restore your system if

you accidentally trash it—by, for example, learning about partitions and using a partitioning program incorrectly.

A *swap partition* is another special type of partition, but swap partitions are only found on Linux and BSD systems. A swap partition's only job is to act like RAM when your system needs more RAM than you have installed. Windows has a similar function called a *page file* that uses a special file instead of a partition. Most OS experts believe a swap partition is a little bit faster than a page file. You'll learn all about page files and swap partitions in Chapter 17, "Maintaining and Troubleshooting Windows."

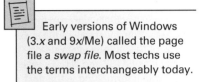

Early versions of Windows (3.*x* and 9*x*/Me) called the page file a *swap file*. Most techs use the terms interchangeably today.

When to Partition

Partitioning is not a common task. The two most common situations likely to require partitioning are when you're installing an OS on a new system, and when you are adding a second drive to an existing system. When you install a new OS, the installation CD at some point asks you how you would like to partition the drive. When you're adding a new hard drive to an existing system, every OS has a built-in tool to help you partition it.

Each version of Windows offers a different tool for partitioning hard drives. For more than 20 years, through the days of DOS and early Windows (up to Windows Me), you used a command-line program called **FDISK** to partition drives. Figure 12.6 shows the FDISK program. Windows 2000, Windows XP, and Windows Vista use a graphical partitioning program called **Disk Management** (Figure 12.7).

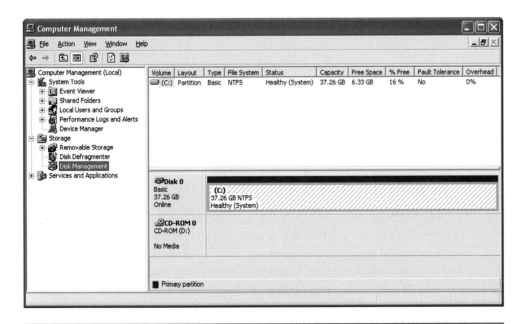

• **Figure 12.6**   FDISK

• **Figure 12.7**   Windows XP Disk Management tool in Computer Management

This chapter explains how to partition a hard drive *before* it explains formatting because that is the order in which you as a PC tech will actually perform those tasks. You'll learn all of the specifics of the various file systems—such as FAT32 and NTFS—when I explain formatting in the next section, but until then, just accept that there are several systems for organizing the files on a hard drive, and that part of setting up a hard drive involves choosing among them.

Linux uses a number of different tools for partitioning. The oldest is called FDISK—yup, the exact same name as the DOS/Windows version. However, that's where the similarities end, as Linux FDISK has a totally different command set. Even though every copy of Linux comes with the Linux FDISK, it's rarely used because so many better partitioning tools are available. One of the newer Linux partitioning tools is called GParted. GParted is graphical like Disk Management and is fairly easy to use (Figure 12.8). GParted is also a powerful partition management tool—so powerful that it also works with Windows partitions.

Traditionally, once you make a partition, you cannot change its size or type other than by erasing it. You might, however, want to take a hard drive partitioned as a single primary partition and change it to half primary and half extended. Before Windows 2000, there was no way to do this nondestructively. As a result, a few third-party tools, led by Symantec's now famous Norton PartitionMagic, gave techs the tools to resize partitions without losing the data they held. Windows 2000 and XP can nondestructively resize a partition to be larger but not smaller.

In Vista, you can nondestructively resize partitions by shrinking or expanding existing partitions with available free space. Although undoubtedly handy, this is sometimes hampered by the presence of unmovable system files, such as the MBR. You can sometimes circumvent this problem by disabling such things as Hibernation mode and System Restore, but that doesn't always work, and third-party tools remain necessary in many cases.

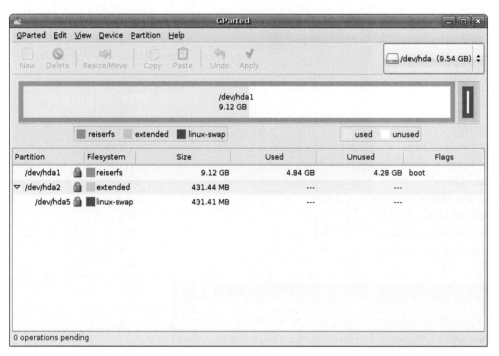

• **Figure 12.8** GParted in action

■ Hard Drive Formatting

Once you've partitioned a hard drive, you must perform one more step before your OS can use that drive: formatting. *Formatting* does two things: it creates a file system—like a library's card catalog—and makes the root directory in that file system. You must format every partition and volume you create so it can hold data that you can easily retrieve. The various versions of Windows you're likely to encounter today can use several different file systems, so we'll look at those in detail next. The *root directory* provides the foundation upon which the OS builds files and folders.

File Systems in Windows

Every version of Windows comes with a built-in formatting utility with which to create one or more file systems on a partition or volume. The versions of Windows in current use support three separate Microsoft file systems: FAT16, FAT32, and NTFS.

The simplest hard drive file system, called FAT or FAT16, provides a good introduction to how file systems work. More complex file systems fix many of the problems inherent in FAT and add extra features as well.

FAT

The base storage area for hard drives is a sector; each sector stores up to 512 bytes of data. If an OS stores a file smaller than 512 bytes in a sector, the rest of the sector goes to waste. We accept this waste because most files are far larger than 512 bytes. So what happens when an OS stores a file larger than 512 bytes? The OS needs a method to fill one sector, find another that's unused, and fill it, continuing to fill sectors until the file is completely stored. Once the OS stores a file, it must remember which sectors hold the file, so it can be retrieved later.

MS-DOS version 2.1 first supported hard drives using a special data structure to keep track of stored data on the hard drive, and Microsoft called this structure the **file allocation table (FAT)**. Think of the FAT as nothing more than a card catalog that keeps track of which sectors store the various parts of a file. The official jargon term for a FAT is **data structure**, but it is more like a two-column spreadsheet.

The left column (see Figure 12.9) gives each sector a number from 0000 to FFFF (in hex, of course). This means there are 65,536 (64 K) sectors.

Notice that each value in the left column contains 16 bits. (Four hex characters make 16 bits, remember?) We call this type of FAT a *16-bit FAT* or *FAT16*. Not just hard drives have FATs. Some USB thumb drives also use FAT16. Floppy disks use FATs, but their FATs are only 12 bits because they store much less data.

The right column of the FAT contains information on the status of sectors. All hard drives, even brand-new drives fresh from the factory, contain faulty sectors that cannot store data because of imperfections in the construction of the drives. The OS must locate these bad sectors, mark them as unusable, and then prevent any files from being written to them. This mapping of bad sectors is one of the functions of **high-level formatting**. After the format program creates the FAT, it proceeds through the entire partition, writing and attempting to read from each sector sequentially. If it finds a bad sector, it places a special status code (FFF7) in the sector's FAT location, indicating that the sector is unavailable for use. Formatting also marks the good sectors as 0000.

Using the FAT to track sectors, however, creates a problem. The 16-bit FAT addresses a maximum of 64 K (2^{16}) locations. Therefore, the size of a hard drive partition should be limited to 64 K × 512 bytes per sector, or 32 MB. When Microsoft first unveiled FAT16, this 32-MB limit presented no problem because most hard drives were only 5 to 10 MB. As hard drives grew in size, you could use FDISK to break them up into multiple partitions. You could divide a 40-MB hard drive into two partitions, for example,

0000	
0001	
0002	
0003	
0004	
0005	
0006	
FFF9	
FFFA	
FFFB	
FFFC	
FFFD	
FFFF	
FFFF	

• **Figure 12.9**   16-bit FAT

 There is such a thing as "low-level formatting," but that's generally done at the factory and doesn't concern techs. This is especially true if you're working with modern hard drives (post-2001).

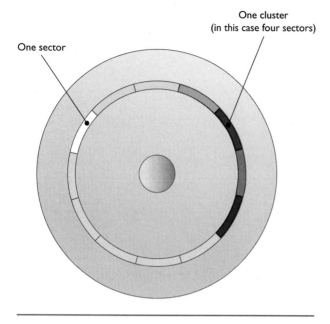

One sector

One cluster
(in this case four sectors)

• **Figure 12.10**   Cluster versus sector

making each partition smaller than 32 MB. But as hard drives started to become much larger, Microsoft realized that the 32-MB limit for drives was unacceptable. We needed an improvement to the 16-bit FAT, a new and improved FAT16 that would support larger drives while still maintaining backward compatibility with the old style 16-bit FAT. This need led to the development of a dramatic improvement in FAT16, called *clustering*, that enabled you to format partitions larger than 32 MB (see Figure 12.10). This new FAT16 appeared way back in the DOS-4 days.

Clustering simply refers to combining a set of contiguous sectors and treating them as a single unit in the FAT. These units are called **file allocation units** or **clusters**. Each row of the FAT addressed a cluster instead of a sector. Unlike sectors, the size of a cluster is not fixed. Clusters improved FAT16, but it still only supported a maximum of 64 K storage units, so the formatting program set the number of sectors in each cluster according to the size of the partition. The larger the partition, the more sectors per cluster. This method kept clustering completely compatible with the 64-K locations in the old 16-bit FAT. The new FAT16 could support partitions up to 2 GB. (The old 16-bit FAT is so old it doesn't really even have a name—if someone says "FAT16," they mean the newer FAT16 that supports clustering.) Table 12.1 shows the number of sectors per cluster for FAT16.

Table 12.1	FAT16 Cluster Sizes
If FDISK makes a partition this big:	**You'll get this many sectors/cluster:**
16 to 127.9 MB	4
128 to 255.9 MB	8
256 to 511.9 MB	16
512 to 1023.9 MB	32
1024 to 2048 MB	64

FAT16 in Action

Assume you have a copy of Windows using FAT16. When an application such as Microsoft Word tells the OS to save a file, Windows starts at the beginning of the FAT, looking for the first space marked "open for use" (0000), and begins to write to that cluster. If the entire file fits within that one cluster, Windows places the code *FFFF* (last cluster) into the cluster's status area in the FAT. That's called the *end-of-file marker*. Windows then goes to the folder storing the file and adds the filename and the cluster's number to the folder list. If the file requires more than one cluster, Windows searches for the next open cluster and places the number of the next cluster in the status area, filling and adding clusters until the entire file is saved. The last cluster then receives the end-of-file marker (FFFF).

Let's run through an example of this process, and start by selecting an arbitrary part of the FAT: from 3ABB to 3AC7. Assume you want to save a file called MOM.TXT. Before saving the file, the FAT looks like Figure 12.11.

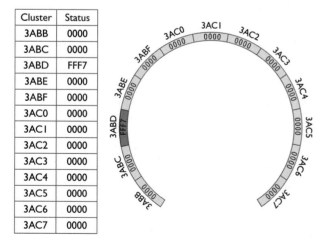

Cluster	Status
3ABB	0000
3ABC	0000
3ABD	FFF7
3ABE	0000
3ABF	0000
3AC0	0000
3AC1	0000
3AC2	0000
3AC3	0000
3AC4	0000
3AC5	0000
3AC6	0000
3AC7	0000

• **Figure 12.11**   The initial FAT

376

Windows finds the first open cluster, 3ABB, and fills it. But not all of the MOM.TXT file fits into that cluster. Needing more space, the OS goes through the FAT to find the next open cluster. It finds cluster 3ABC. Before filling 3ABC, the value *3ABC* is placed in 3ABB's status (see Figure 12.12).

Even after filling two clusters, more of the MOM.TXT file remains, so Windows must find one more cluster. The 3ABD has been marked FFF7 (bad cluster or *bad-sector marker*), so Windows skips over 3ABD, finding 3ABE (see Figure 12.13).

Before filling 3ABE, Windows enters the value *3ABE* in 3ABC's status. Windows does not completely fill 3ABE, signifying that the entire MOM.TXT file has been stored. Windows enters the value *FFFF* in 3ABE's status, indicating the end of file (see Figure 12.14).

After saving all of the clusters, Windows locates the file's folder (yes, folders also are stored on clusters, but they get a different set of clusters, somewhere else on the disk) and records the filename, size, date/time, and starting cluster, like this:

MOM.TXT 19234 05-19-09 2:04p 3ABB

If a program requests that file, the process is reversed. Windows locates the folder containing the file to determine the starting cluster and then pulls a piece of the file from each cluster until it sees the end-of-file cluster. Windows then hands the reassembled file to the requesting application.

Clearly, without the FAT, Windows cannot locate files. FAT16 automatically makes two copies of the FAT. One FAT backs up the other to provide special utilities a way to recover a FAT that gets corrupted—a painfully common occurrence.

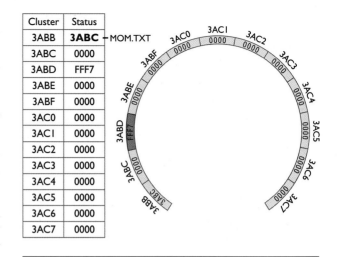

● **Figure 12.12** The first cluster used

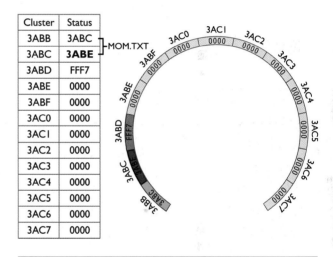

● **Figure 12.13** The second cluster used

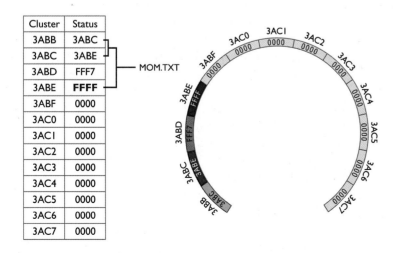

● **Figure 12.14** End of file reached

Even when FAT works perfectly, over time the files begin to separate in a process called **fragmentation**.

Fragmentation

Continuing with the example, let's use Microsoft Word to save two more files: a letter to the IRS (IRSROB.DOC) and a letter to IBM (IBMHELP.DOC). IRSROB.DOC takes the next three clusters—3ABF, 3AC0, and 3AC1—and IBMHELP.DOC takes two clusters—3AC2 and 3AC3 (see Figure 12.15).

Now suppose you erase MOM.TXT. Windows does not delete the cluster entries for MOM.TXT when it erases a file. Windows only alters the information in the folder, simply changing the first letter of MOM.TXT to the Greek letter σ (sigma). This causes the file to "disappear" as far as the OS knows. It won't show up, for example, in Windows Explorer, even though the data still resides on the hard drive for the moment (see Figure 12.16).

Note that under normal circumstances, Windows does not actually delete files when you press the DELETE key. Instead, Windows moves the files to a special hidden directory that you can access via the Recycle Bin. The files themselves are not actually deleted until you empty the Recycle Bin. (You can skip the Recycle Bin entirely if you wish, by highlighting a file and then holding down the SHIFT key when you press DELETE).

Because all of the data for MOM.TXT is intact, you could use some program to change the σ back into another letter and thus get the document back. A number of third-party undelete tools are available. Figure 12.17 shows one such program at work. Just remember that if you want to use an undelete tool, you must use it quickly. The space allocated to your deleted file may soon be overwritten by a new file.

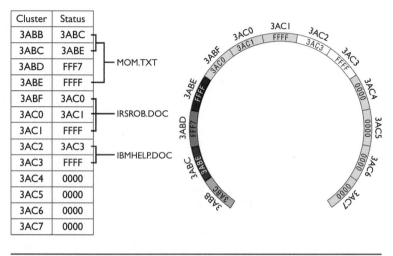

• **Figure 12.15** Three files saved

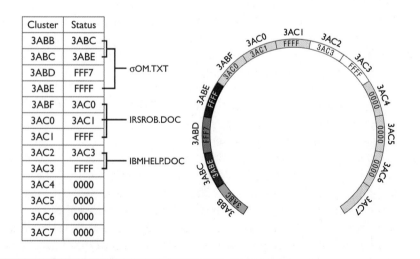

• **Figure 12.16** MOM.TXT erased

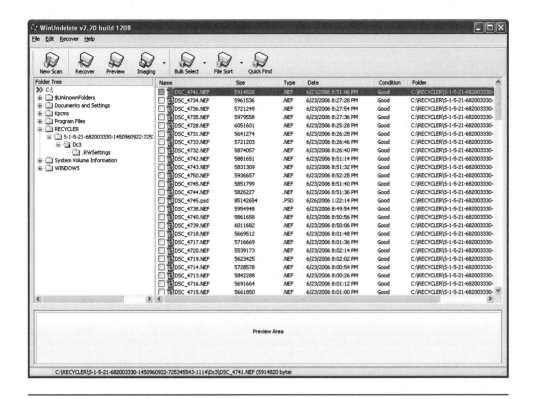

● **Figure 12.17**   WinUndelete in action

Let's say you just emptied your Recycle Bin. You now save one more file, TAXREC.XLS, a big spreadsheet that will take six clusters, into the same folder that once held MOM.TXT. As Windows writes the file to the drive, it overwrites the space that MOM.TXT used, but it needs three more clusters. The next three available clusters are 3AC4, 3AC5, and 3AC6 (see Figure 12.18).

Notice that TAXREC.XLS is in two pieces, thus *fragmented*. Fragmentation takes place all of the time on FAT16 systems. Although the system easily negotiates a tiny fragmented file split into only two parts, excess fragmentation slows down the system during hard drive reads and writes. This example is fragmented into two pieces; in the real world, a file might fragment into hundreds of pieces, forcing the read/write heads to travel all over the hard drive to retrieve a single file. You can dramatically improve the speed at which the hard drive reads and writes files by eliminating this fragmentation.

Every version of Windows comes with a program called Disk Defragmenter, which can rearrange the files into neat contiguous chunks (see Figure 12.19). Defragmentation is crucial for ensuring the top performance of a hard drive. The "Maintaining and Troubleshooting Hard Drives"

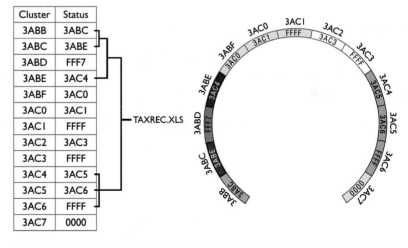

● **Figure 12.18**   TAXREC.XLS fragmented

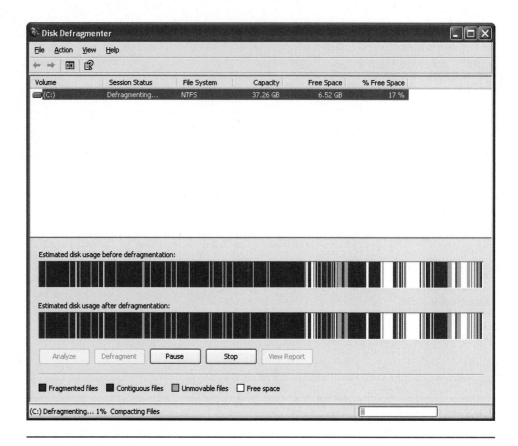

• **Figure 12.19**   Windows Disk Defragmenter

section of this chapter gives the details on working with the various Disk Defragmenters in Windows.

FAT32

When Microsoft introduced Windows 95 OSR2 (OEM Service Release 2), it also unveiled a totally new file format called **FAT32** that brought a couple of dramatic improvements. First, FAT32 supports partitions up to 2 terabytes (more than 2 trillion bytes). Second, as its name implies, FAT32 uses 32 bits to describe each cluster, which means clusters can drop to more reasonable sizes. FAT32's use of so many FAT entries gives it the power to use small clusters, making the old "keep your partitions small" rule obsolete. A 2-GB volume using FAT16 would use 32-KB clusters, while the same 2-GB volume using FAT32 would use 4-KB clusters. You get far more efficient use of disk space with FAT32, without the need to make multiple small partitions. FAT32 partitions still need defragmentation, however, just as often as FAT16 partitions.

Table 12.2 shows cluster sizes for FAT32 partitions.

Table 12.2	FAT32 Cluster Sizes
Drive Size	**Cluster Size**
512 MB or 1023 MB	4 KB
1024 MB to 2 GB	4 KB
2 GB to 8 GB	4 KB
8 GB to 16 GB	8 KB
16 GB to 32 GB	16 KB
>32 GB	32 KB

Essentials/Practical Application

NTFS

The Windows format of choice these days is the **New Technology File System (NTFS)**. NTFS came out a long time ago with the first version of Windows NT, thus the name. Over the years, NTFS has undergone a number of improvements. The version used in Windows 2000 is NTFS 3.0; the version used in Windows XP and Vista is called NTFS 3.1, although you'll see it referred to as NTFS 5.0/5.1 (Windows 2000 was unofficially Windows NT version 5). NTFS uses clusters and file allocation tables but in a much more complex and powerful way compared to FAT or FAT32. NTFS offers six major improvements and refinements: redundancy, security, compression, encryption, disk quotas, and cluster sizing.

NTFS Structure

NTFS utilizes an enhanced file allocation table called the **master file table (MFT)**. An NTFS partition keeps a backup copy of the most critical parts of the MFT in the middle of the disk, reducing the chance that a serious drive error can wipe out both the MFT and the MFT copy. Whenever you defragment an NTFS partition, you'll see a small, immovable chunk in the middle of the drive; that's the backup MFT (Figure 12.20). Notice the bright green in both the key at the bottom of the screen and in the estimated disk usage bars.

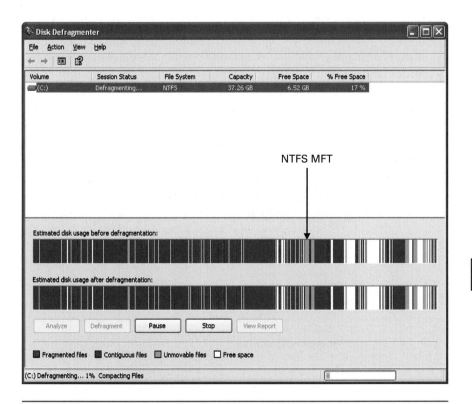

Both of the CompTIA A+ exams test you on NTFS, such as when to use it, what advantages it has over FAT32, and how to lock down information. You'll also be quizzed on the tools, such as Disk Management, in both exams. Don't skip anything in this chapter!

Tech Tip

NTFS Naming Nightmare
Most computer writers, including those at Microsoft (until recently), label the version of NTFS that shipped with a particular version of Windows by the version number of Windows. So the NTFS that shipped with Windows NT 4.0 is frequently called NTFS 4, although that's not technically correct. Similarly, because the NTFS that shipped with Windows 2000 offered great improvements over the earlier versions, it became NTFS 5 in the minds of most techs.

Current Microsoft Knowledge Base articles refer to the NTFS that ships with Windows XP specifically as NTFS 3.1. Windows Vista still technically uses NTFS 3.1, even though it adds a few minor features such as transactional NTFS, which reduces the incidence of data corruption, and self-healing, which is basically a CHKDSK command that runs all of the time.

If you have a geeky interest in what version of NTFS you are running, open up a prompt and type this command: **fsutil fsinfo ntfsinfo c:**

• **Figure 12.20**   An NTFS MFT appears in a defragmenter program as an immovable file.

Security

NTFS views individual files and folders as objects and provides security for those objects through a feature called the *access control list (ACL)*. Future chapters go into this in much more detail, but a quick example here should make the basic concept clear.

Suppose Bill the IT Guy sets up a Windows XP PC as a workstation for three users: John, Wilma, and Felipe. John logs into the PC with his user name and password (johns and f3f2f1f0, respectively, in case you're curious) and begins to work on his project. The project folder is stored on the C: drive as C:\Projects\JohnSuperSecret. When John saves his work and gets ready to leave, he alters the permissions on his folder to deny access to anyone but him. When curious Wilma logs into the PC after John leaves, she cannot access the C:\Programs\JohnSuperSecret folder contents at all, although she can see the entry in Explorer. Without the ACL provided by NTFS, John would have no security over his files or folders at all.

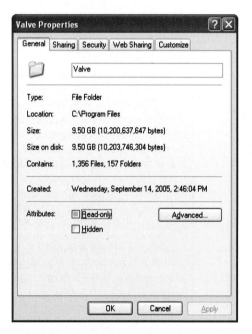

Microsoft has never released the exact workings of NTFS to the public.

Compression

NTFS enables you to compress individual files and folders to save space on a hard drive. Compression makes access time to the data slower because the OS has to uncompress files every time you use them, but in a space-limited environment, sometimes that's what you have to do.

Encryption

One of the big draws with NTFS is file encryption, the black art of making files unreadable to anybody who doesn't have the right key. You can encrypt a single file, a folder, or a folder full of files. Microsoft calls the encryption utility in NTFS the **encrypting file system (EFS)**, but it's simply an aspect of NTFS, not a standalone file system. To encrypt a file or folder, right-click it in My Computer or Computer and select Properties to open the Properties dialog box (Figure 12.21). Click the Advanced button to open the Advanced Attributes dialog box. As you can see in Figure 12.22, encryption (and compression) is simply a selectable checkbox. Click the box next to *Encrypt contents to secure data* and then click the OK button—instantly your file is safe from prying eyes!

• Figure 12.21   Folder Properties

Windows XP Home and Media Center editions do not support EFS.

• Figure 12.22   Options for compression and encryption

Encryption does not hide files; it simply makes them unreadable to other users. Figure 12.23 shows a couple of image files encrypted by another user. Note that in addition to the pale green color of the filenames, the files seem readily accessible. Windows XP can't provide a thumbnail, however, even though it can read the type of image file (JPEG) easily. Further, double-clicking the files opens the Windows Picture and Fax Viewer, but you still can't see the image (Figure 12.24). Better still, you can try to access the files across your network and the encryption does precisely what it's supposed to do: blocks unwanted access to sensitive data.

Remember that encryption is separate from the NTFS file security provided by the ACL—to access encrypted files, you need both permission to access the files based on the ACL and the keys used to encrypt the files. We discuss key management in much more detail in Chapter 16, "Securing Windows Resources."

• **Figure 12.23**   Encrypted files

Disk Quotas

NTFS supports **disk quotas**, enabling administrators to set limits on drive space usage for users. To set quotas, you must log in as an Administrator, right-click the hard drive name, and select Properties. In the Drive Properties dialog box, select the Quota tab and make changes. Figure 12.25 shows configured quotas for a hard drive. Although rarely used on single-user systems, setting disk quotas on multi-user systems prevents any individual user from monopolizing your hard disk space.

Encryption protects against other users, but only if you log out. It might seem obvious, but I've had lots of users get confused by encryption, thinking that the PC *knows* who's clicking the keyboard. All protections and security are based on user accounts. If someone logs into your computer with a different account, the encrypted files will be unreadable. We'll get to user accounts, permissions, and such in later chapters in detail.

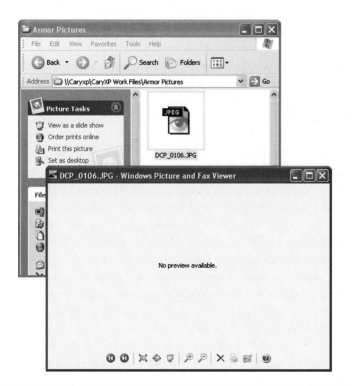

• **Figure 12.24**   Windows Picture and Fax Viewer blocked by file encryption

• **Figure 12.25**   Hard drive quotas in Windows XP

Table 12.3	NTFS Cluster Sizes	
Drive Size	**Cluster Size**	**Number of Sectors**
512 MB or less	512 bytes	1
513 MB to 1024 MB (1 GB)	1024 bytes (1 KB)	2
1,025 MB to 2048 MB (2 GB)	2048 bytes (2 KB)	4
2,049 MB and larger	4096 bytes (4 KB)	8

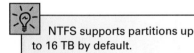
NTFS supports partitions up to 16 TB by default.

Cluster Sizes

Unlike FAT16 or FAT32, you can adjust the cluster sizes in NTFS, although you'll probably rarely do so. Table 12.4 shows the default cluster sizes for NTFS.

By default, NTFS supports partitions up to ~16 terabytes on a dynamic disk, (though only up to 2 TB on a basic disk). By tweaking the cluster sizes, you can get NTFS to support partitions up to 16 exabytes, or 18,446,744,073,709,551,616 bytes! That might support any and all upcoming hard drive capacities for the next 100 years or so.

With so many file systems, how do you know which one to use? In the case of internal hard drives, you should use the most feature-rich system your OS supports. If you have Windows 2000 or greater, use NTFS. External hard drives still often use FAT32 because NTFS features such as the ACL and encryption can make access difficult when you move the drive between systems, but with that exception, NTFS is your best choice on a Windows-based system.

The Partitioning and Formatting Process

Now that you understand the concepts of formatting and partitioning, let's go through the process of setting up an installed hard drive by using different partitioning and formatting tools. If you have access to a system, try following along with these descriptions. Remember, don't make any changes to a drive you want to keep, because both partitioning and formatting are destructive processes.

Bootable Disks

Imagine you've built a brand-new PC. The hard drive has no OS so you need to boot up something to set up that hard drive. Any software that can boot up a system is by definition an operating system. You need a floppy disk, optical disk, or USB thumb drive with a bootable OS installed. Any removable media that has a bootable OS is generically called a *boot device* or *boot disk*. Your system boots off of the boot device, which then loads some kind of OS that enables you to partition, format, and install an OS on your new hard drive. Boot devices come from many sources. All Windows OS installation discs are boot devices, as are Linux installation discs. You can make your own bootable devices, and most techs do, because a boot device often has a number of handy tools included to do certain jobs.

In Chapter 13, "Removable Media," I go through the steps to make a number of different boot devices for different jobs. If you want to follow along with some of the steps in this chapter, you may want to jump ahead to the next chapter to make a boot device or two and then return here.

Partitioning and Formatting with the Windows XP Installation CD

When you boot up a Windows XP installation CD and the installation program detects a hard drive that is not yet partitioned, it prompts you through a sequence of steps to partition (and format) the hard drive. Chapter 14, "Installing and Configuring Windows," covers the entire installation process, but we'll jump ahead and dive into the partitioning part of the installation here to see how this is done, working through two examples by using one and then two partitions. Even though this example uses the Windows XP installation CD, don't worry, because this part of the Windows 2000 installation is almost identical and the next section discusses Vista in detail.

Single Partition

The most common partitioning scenario involves turning a new blank drive into a single bootable C: drive. To accomplish this goal, you need to make the entire drive a primary partition and then make it active. Let's go through the process of partitioning and formatting a single, brand-new, 200-GB hard drive.

The Windows installation begins by booting from a Windows installation CD-ROM like the one shown in Figure 12.26. The installation program starts automatically from the CD. The installation first loads some needed files but eventually prompts you with the screen shown in Figure 12.27. This is your clue that partitioning is about to start.

Press the ENTER key to start a new Windows installation and accept the license agreement to see the main partitioning screen (Figure 12.28). The bar that says Unpartitioned space is the drive.

• **Figure 12.26**   Windows installation CD

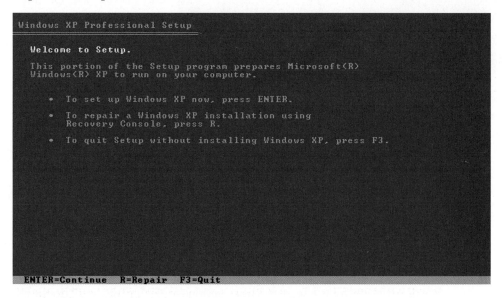

• **Figure 12.27**   Welcome to Setup

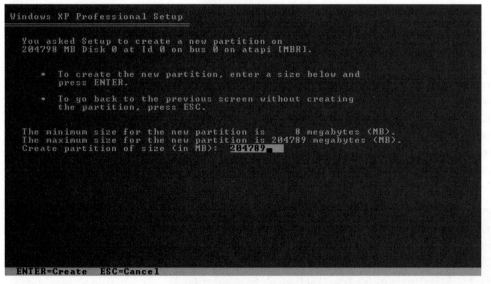

```
Windows XP Professional Setup

   The following list shows the existing partitions and
   unpartitioned space on this computer.

   Use the UP and DOWN ARROW keys to select an item in the list.

      •  To set up Windows XP on the selected item, press ENTER.

      •  To create a partition in the unpartitioned space, press C.

      •  To delete the selected partition, press D.

   ┌─────────────────────────────────────────────────────────────┐
   │ 204798 MB Disk 0 at Id 0 on bus 0 on atapi [MBR]             │
   │        Unpartitioned space                    204797 MB      │
   │                                                               │
   │                                                               │
   └─────────────────────────────────────────────────────────────┘

   ENTER=Install   C=Create Partition   F3=Quit
```

• **Figure 12.28**   Partitioning screen

```
Windows XP Professional Setup

   You asked Setup to create a new partition on
   204798 MB Disk 0 at Id 0 on bus 0 on atapi [MBR].

      •  To create the new partition, enter a size below and
         press ENTER.

      •  To go back to the previous screen without creating
         the partition, press ESC.

   The minimum size for the new partition is       8 megabytes (MB).
   The maximum size for the new partition is 204789 megabytes (MB).
   Create partition of size (in MB):  204789_

   ENTER=Create   ESC=Cancel
```

• **Figure 12.29**   Setting partition size

The Windows installer is pretty smart. If you press ENTER at this point, it partitions the hard drive as a single primary partition, makes it active, and installs Windows for you—but what fun is that? Instead, press C to create a partition. The installer then asks you how large a partition to make (Figure 12.29). You may make the partition any size you want by typing in a number, from a minimum of 8 MB up to the size of the entire drive (in this case, 204789 MB). Let's just make the entire drive a single C: drive by pressing ENTER.

Ta-da! You just partitioned the drive! Now Windows asks you how you want to format that drive (Figure 12.30). So you might be asking, where's the basic versus dynamic? Where do you tell Windows to make the partition primary instead of extended? Where do you set it as active?

The Windows installer makes a number of assumptions for you, such as always making the first partition primary and setting it as active. The installer also makes all hard drives basic disks. You'll have to convert it to dynamic later (if you even want to convert it at all).

Select NTFS for the format. Either option—quick or full—will do the job here. (Quick format is quicker, as the name would suggest, but the full

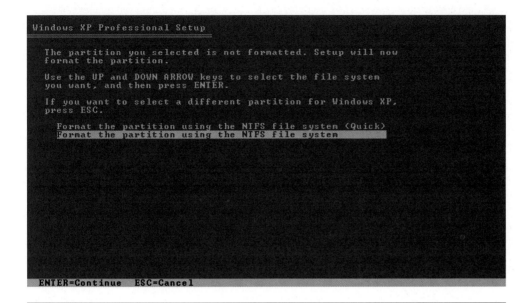

Windows XP Professional Setup

The partition you selected is not formatted. Setup will now
format the partition.

Use the UP and DOWN ARROW keys to select the file system
you want, and then press ENTER.

If you want to select a different partition for Windows XP,
press ESC.

    Format the partition using the NTFS file system (Quick)
    Format the partition using the NTFS file system

ENTER=Continue   ESC=Cancel

● **Figure 12.30**   Format screen

option is more thorough and thus safer.) After Windows formats the drive, the installation continues, copying the new Windows installation to the C: drive.

Two Partitions

Well, that was fun! So much fun that I'd like to do another new Windows installation, with a bit more complex partitioning. This time, you again have the 200-GB hard drive, but you want to split the drive into three drive letters of roughly 66 GB each. That means you need to make a single 66-GB primary partition, then a 133-GB extended partition, and then split that extended partition into two logical drives of 66 GB each.

> Windows almost always adjusts the number you type in for a partition size. In this case, it changed 66666 to 66668, a number that makes more sense when translated to binary. Don't worry about it!

Back at the Windows installation main partitioning screen, first press C to make a new partition, but this time change the 204789 to 66666, which will give you a partition of about 66 GB. When you press ENTER, the partitioning screen should look like Figure 12.31. Even though the installation program doesn't tell you, the partition is primary.

Notice that two-thirds of the drive is still unpartitioned space. Move the selection down to this option and press C to create the next partition.

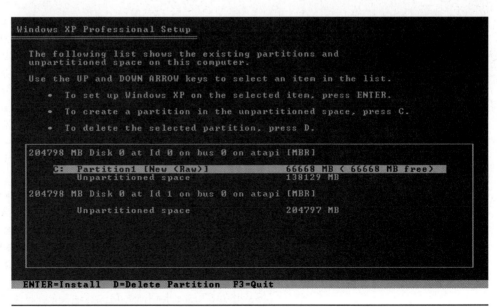

Windows XP Professional Setup

    The following list shows the existing partitions and
    unpartitioned space on this computer.

Use the UP and DOWN ARROW keys to select an item in the list.

    ●   To set up Windows XP on the selected item, press ENTER.
    ●   To create a partition in the unpartitioned space, press C.
    ●   To delete the selected partition, press D.

    204798 MB Disk 0 at Id 0 on bus 0 on atapi [MBR]
        C: Partition1 [New (Raw)]   66668 MB (66668 MB free)
             Unpartitioned space   138129 MB
    204798 MB Disk 0 at Id 1 on bus 0 on atapi [MBR]
             Unpartitioned space   204797 MB

ENTER=Install   D=Delete Partition   F3=Quit

● **Figure 12.31**   You've created a 66-GB partition.

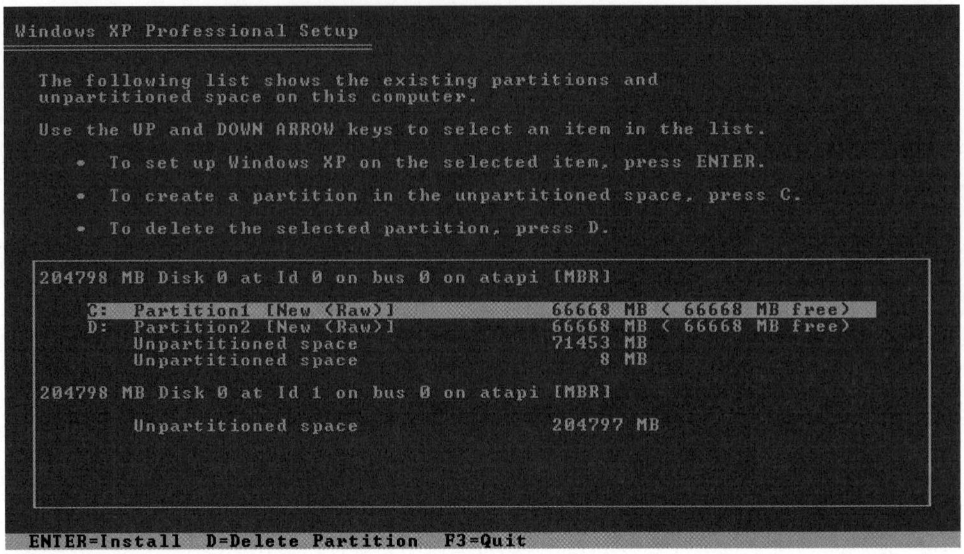

```
Windows XP Professional Setup

    The following list shows the existing partitions and
    unpartitioned space on this computer.

    Use the UP and DOWN ARROW keys to select an item in the list.

      •  To set up Windows XP on the selected item, press ENTER.
      •  To create a partition in the unpartitioned space, press C.
      •  To delete the selected partition, press D.

    204798 MB Disk 0 at Id 0 on bus 0 on atapi [MBR]

        C:  Partition1 [New (Raw)]            66668 MB ( 66668 MB free)
        D:  Partition2 [New (Raw)]            66668 MB ( 66668 MB free)
            Unpartitioned space               71453 MB
            Unpartitioned space                   8 MB

    204798 MB Disk 0 at Id 1 on bus 0 on atapi [MBR]

            Unpartitioned space              204797 MB


    ENTER=Install  D=Delete Partition   F3=Quit
```

● **Figure 12.32** Second partition created

Once again, type **66666** in the partition size screen and press ENTER, and you'll see something similar to Figure 12.32.

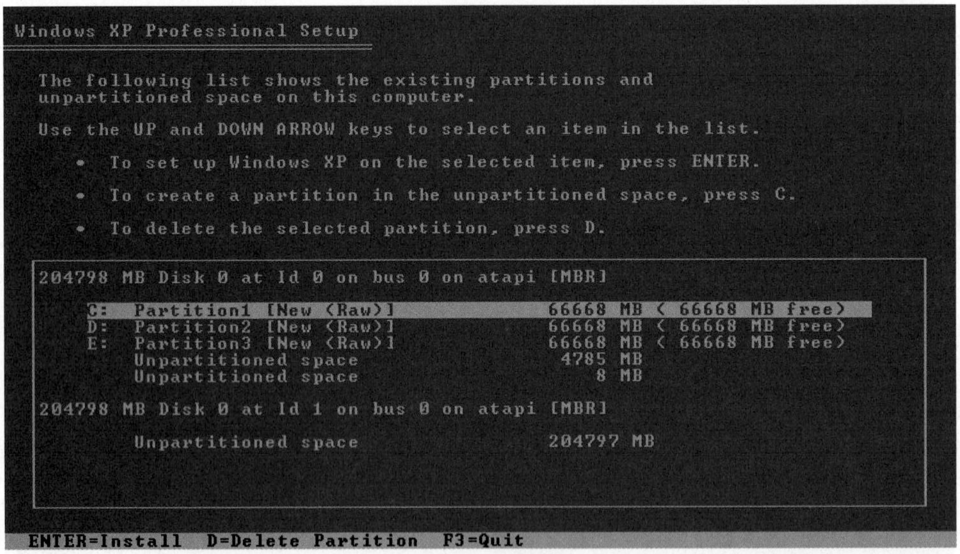

```
Windows XP Professional Setup

    The following list shows the existing partitions and
    unpartitioned space on this computer.

    Use the UP and DOWN ARROW keys to select an item in the list.

      •  To set up Windows XP on the selected item, press ENTER.
      •  To create a partition in the unpartitioned space, press C.
      •  To delete the selected partition, press D.

    204798 MB Disk 0 at Id 0 on bus 0 on atapi [MBR]

        C:  Partition1 [New (Raw)]            66668 MB ( 66668 MB free)
        D:  Partition2 [New (Raw)]            66668 MB ( 66668 MB free)
        E:  Partition3 [New (Raw)]            66668 MB ( 66668 MB free)
            Unpartitioned space                4785 MB
            Unpartitioned space                   8 MB

    204798 MB Disk 0 at Id 1 on bus 0 on atapi [MBR]

            Unpartitioned space              204797 MB


    ENTER=Install  D=Delete Partition   F3=Quit
```

● **Figure 12.33** Fully partitioned drive

Create your last partition exactly as you made the other two to see your almost-completely partitioned drive (Figure 12.33). (Note that the example is not realistic in one respect: you would never leave any unpartitioned space on a drive in a typical PC.)

Even though the Windows installation shows that you've made three partitions, you've really made only two: the primary partition, which is C:, and then two logical drives (D: and E:) in an extended partition. Once again, the next step, formatting, is saved for a later section in this chapter.

You've just created three drive letters. Keep in mind that the only drive you must partition during installation is the drive on which you install Windows.

The installation program can delete partitions just as easily as it makes them. If you use a hard drive that already has partitions, for example, you just select the partition you wish to delete and press the letter D. This brings up a dialog box where Windows gives you one last chance to change your mind (Figure 12.34). Press L to kill the partition.

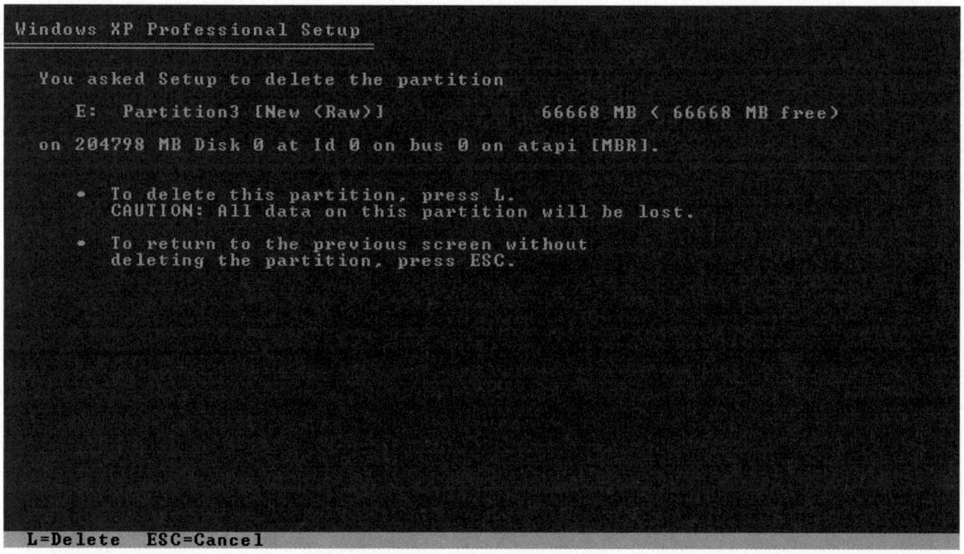

```
Windows XP Professional Setup

You asked Setup to delete the partition

    E:  Partition3 [New (Raw)]                 66668 MB ( 66668 MB free)

on 204798 MB Disk 0 at Id 0 on bus 0 on atapi [MBR].

    •  To delete this partition, press L.
       CAUTION: All data on this partition will be lost.

    •  To return to the previous screen without
       deleting the partition, press ESC.


 L=Delete    ESC=Cancel
```

• **Figure 12.34**   Option to delete partition

Partitioning and Formatting with the Windows Vista Installation DVD

Among the many changes in Microsoft's newest operating system is a completely revamped installation process, complete with a fancy looking and, more importantly, easy-to-use graphical user interface. Again, the entire installation process will be covered in Chapter 14, "Installing and Configuring Windows," but because you've already looked at partitioning in Windows XP, you should at least be familiar with what's changed in Vista.

Single Partition

One thing that definitely hasn't changed with Vista is that the most common installation is on a single active partition, so let's start there. Again, you're going to partition and format a single 200-GB drive.

The Vista installation GUI has a few more steps than XP before you get to the actual formatting page, so let's get through those as quickly as possible to get to the fun stuff. When you boot from the installation DVD, you'll be greeted with a screen asking you for language and regional information (Figure 12.35). Unless you're having this book read to you by a translator, I expect you'll want to keep the language set to English, but set the other entries as needed.

The next page has a large Install Now button, so click that and move on. After that, the installer asks for a product key (Figure 12.36). Don't bother entering one yet—just leave the field blank and click Next to move on to the next page.

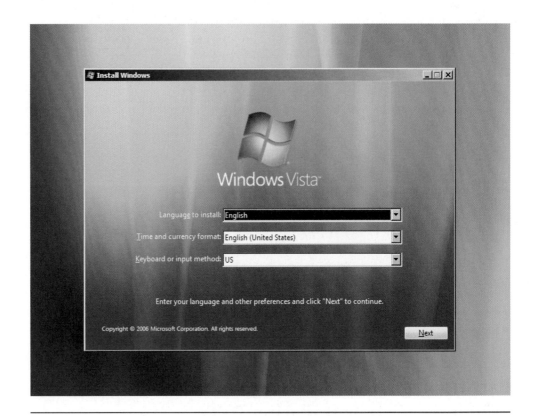

• **Figure 12.35**   The Windows Vista language preferences screen

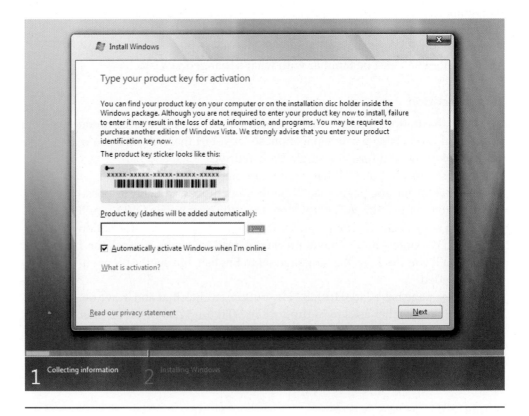

• **Figure 12.36**   The product key page

The next page asks which version of Vista you want to install (Figure 12.37). Every Vista installation DVD contains all editions of the operating system—your product key ultimately determines which edition you can install, so you wouldn't get this page if you entered a product key when first prompted. Select Windows Vista ULTIMATE (in this example) and move on to the next page.

The next page is just a license agreement that you'll need to, ahem, agree with before moving on. Getting impatient to do some formatting? Don't worry—I know this process is a tad longer than on XP, but you're almost there. Click the Custom install button on the next page and you'll be greeted with the partitioning page (Figure 12.38). Whew!

Your hard drive is the bar that says Disk 0 Unallocated Space, which is currently the only thing there. If you just click Next, Windows automatically partitions and formats the drive for you, but I still fail to see any fun in that, so let's once again manually create a partition on the drive. Click *Drive options (advanced)* to see the advanced drive features. To create a new partition, click the New button. You could simply click Apply to make a 200-GB partition, but, to demonstrate one of Vista's handy new features, type **100000** and then click Apply (Figure 12.39).

Once you have created your 100-GB partition, click the Format button. Notice that the installer never asks you what file system to use. Vista can read FAT drives, but it will not install itself to one by default. There are, of course, some people on the Internet who have figured out how to install Vista to a FAT32 drive, but why anyone would want to lose all of NTFS's functionality is beyond me.

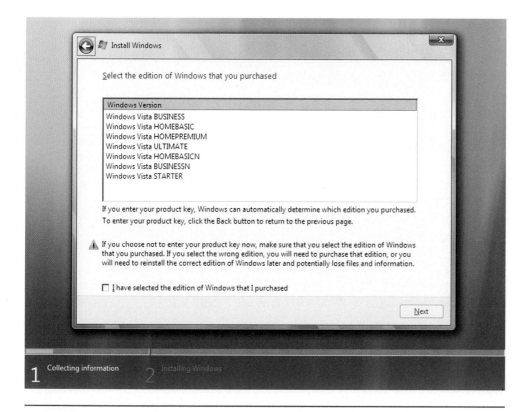

• **Figure 12.37**   Choosing your edition

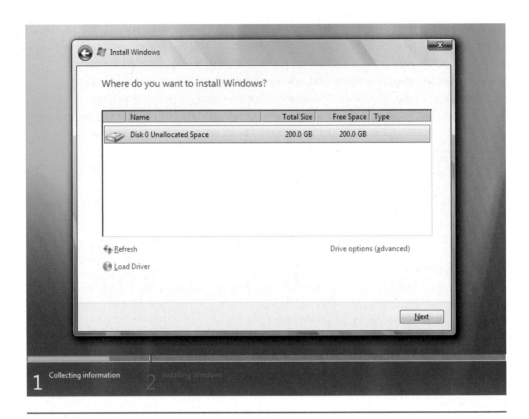

• **Figure 12.38** The Vista partitioning page

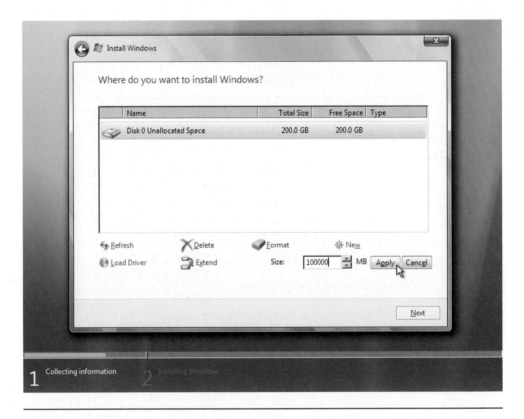

• **Figure 12.39** Setting partition size

So now you have set up a 100-GB partition, but what if you want to make it a 200-GB partition? In XP, you would have to delete the partition and start over, but not so in Vista. You can simply click the Extend button and then apply the rest of the unallocated space to your currently formatted partition. The extend function allows you to easily tack unpartitioned space onto an already partitioned drive.

Multiple Partitions

You can format a drive to contain two partitions just as easily as formatting a single drive. Just as in the XP example, you'll be creating three 66-GB partitions. Unlike in Windows XP, this process actually leaves you with three primary partitions, not a primary partition and an extended partition with two logical drives. Vista will not create extended partitions if a user has fewer than four partitions on a drive, so if you're making three partitions, you're actually creating three primary partitions. If you made a fourth, it would manifest itself as a logical drive on an extended partition.

However, you're not going to create four partitions for this exercise, so you don't need to worry about that. You'll start out, again, with a 200-GB drive, but this time, after clicking the New button, type **66666** into the Size box and click Apply. That will give you a 66-GB (more or less) primary partition (Figure 12.40).

Do the same thing to create the next two drives and you're finished. That was pretty easy, wasn't it?

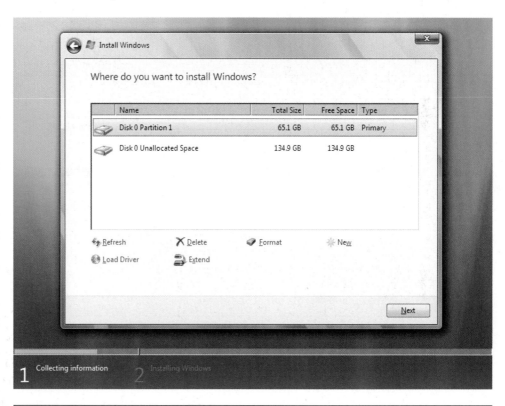

• **Figure 12.40**   The first 66-GB partition

Partitions and Drive Letters

So you have a hard drive, maybe several hard drives, all partitioned up, and you've installed Windows on one of them, but where do those drive letters come from? Older systems assigned drive letters based on some fairly complicated rules having to do with master and slave drives, but things are much simpler on modern systems.

The primary active partition will always be C: and you can't change that, but the rest of the drives are assigned the next available letter, with hard drives taking priority over optical drives. If you have two hard drives and an optical drive in your computer, the hard drives will be C: and D:, and the

optical drive will be E:. If, however, you later install another hard drive in the computer, it will become your F: drive. Newly installed drives do not take drive letters from previously installed drives.

You can change the lettering on every drive but your system partition, which you'll find out how to do in the next section.

Disk Management

The real tool for partitioning and formatting is the Disk Management utility. You can use Disk Management to do everything you want to do to a hard drive in one handy tool. You can access Disk Management by going to the Control Panel and opening the Computer Management applet. If you're cool, you can click Start | Run, type in **diskmgmt.msc**, and press ENTER. Windows 2000/XP and Windows Vista/7 come with Disk Management (Figure 12.41).

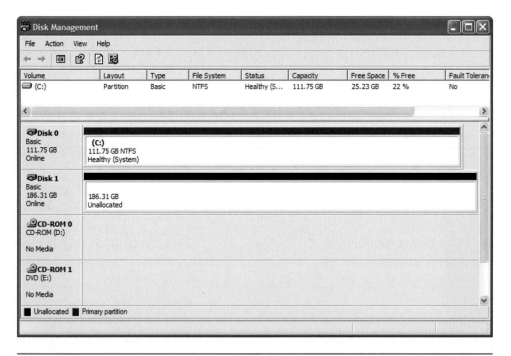

Disk Management works only within Windows, so you can't use Disk Management from a boot device. If you install Windows from an installation disc, in other words, you must use the special partitioning/formatting software built into the installation program you just saw in action.

One of the most interesting parts of Disk Management is disk initialization. Every hard drive in a Windows system has special informa-

• **Figure 12.41** Disk Management

tion placed onto the drive. This initialization information includes identifiers that say "this drive belongs in this system" and other information that defines what this hard drive does in the system. If the hard drive is part of a RAID array, its RAID information is stored in the initialization. If it's part of a spanned volume, this is also stored there. All new drives must be initialized before you can use them. When you install an extra hard drive into a Windows system and start Disk Management, it notices the new drive and starts the Hard Drive Initialization Wizard. If you don't let the wizard run, the drive will be listed as unknown (Figure 12.42).

To initialize a disk, right-click the disk icon and select Initialize. Once a disk is initialized, you can see the status of the drive—a handy tool for troubleshooting.

Disk Management enables you to view the status of every drive in your system. Hopefully, you'll mostly see the drive listed as Healthy, meaning that nothing is happening to it and things are going along swimmingly.

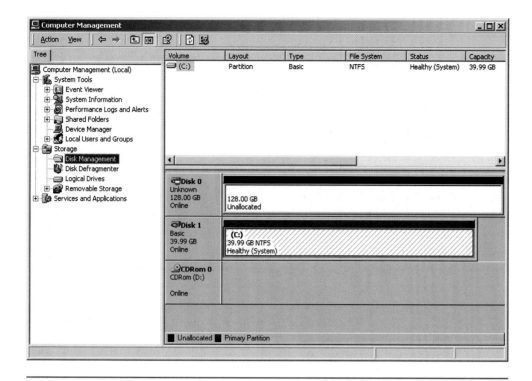

• Figure 12.42 Unknown drive in Disk Management

You're also already familiar with the Unallocated and Active status, but here are a few more to be familiar with for the test:

- **Foreign drive**   You see this when you move a dynamic disk from one computer to another.

- **Formatting**   As you might have guessed, you see this when you're formatting a drive.

- **Failed**   Pray you never see this status, because it means that the disk is damaged or corrupt and you've probably lost some data.

- **Online**   This is what you see if a disk is healthy and communicating properly with the computer.

- **Offline**   The disk is either corrupted or having communication problems.

A newly installed drive is always set as a basic disk. There's nothing wrong with using basic disks, other than that you miss out on some handy features. To create partitions, right-click the unallocated part of the drive and select New Partition. Disk Management runs the New Partition Wizard, with which you can select a primary or extended partition (Figure 12.43). Afterward, you see a screen where you specify the size partition you prefer (Figure 12.44).

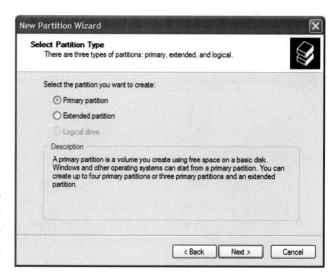

• Figure 12.43   The New Partition Wizard

If you choose to make a primary partition, the wizard asks if you want to assign a drive letter to the partition, mount it as a folder to an existing partition, or do neither (Figure 12.45). (If you choose to make an extended

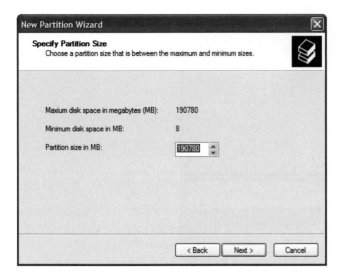

• **Figure 12.44** Specifying the partition size

• **Figure 12.45** Assigning a drive letter to a primary partition

Tech Tip

Big FAT Partitions
Windows 2000/XP and Windows Vista/7 read and write to FAT32 partitions larger than 32 GB; they just don't allow Disk Management to make them. If you ever stumble across a drive from a system that ran the old Windows 9x/Me that has a FAT32 partition larger than 32 GB, it will work just fine in a modern Windows system.

partition, you just get a confirmation screen and you are returned to Disk Management.) In almost all cases, you'll want to give primary partitions a drive letter.

The last screen of the New Partition Wizard asks for the type of format you want to use for this partition (Figure 12.46). If your partition is 4 GB or less, you may format it as FAT, FAT32, or NTFS. If your partition is greater than 4 GB but less than 32 GB, you can make the drive FAT32 or NTFS. Windows requires NTFS on any partition greater than 32 GB. Although FAT32 supports partitions up to 2 TB, Microsoft wants you to use NTFS on larger partitions and creates this limit. In today's world of big hard drives, there's no good reason to use anything other than NTFS.

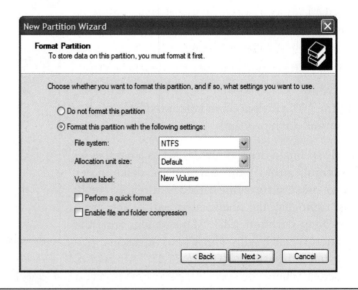

• **Figure 12.46** Choosing a file system type

You have a few more tasks to complete at this screen. You can add a volume label if you want. You can also choose the size of your clusters (Allocation unit size). There's no reason to change the default cluster size, so leave that alone—but you can sure speed up the format if you select the *Perform a quick format* checkbox. This will format your drive without checking every cluster. It's fast and a bit risky, but new hard drives almost always come from the factory in perfect shape—so you must decide whether to use it or not.

Last, if you chose NTFS, you may enable file and folder compression. If you select this option, you'll be able to right-click any file or folder on this partition and compress it. To compress a file or folder, choose the one you want to compress, right-click, and select Properties. Then click the Advanced button to turn compression on or off (Figure 12.47). Compression is handy for opening up space on a hard drive that's filling up, but it also slows down disk access, so use it only when you need it.

After the drive finishes formatting, you'll go back to Disk Management and see a changed hard drive landscape. If you made a primary partition, you will see your new drive letter. If you made an extended partition, things will look a bit different. Figure 12.48 shows the extended partition as free space because it has no logical drive yet. As you can easily guess from Figure 12.49, to create a logical drive, simply right-click in that extended partition and choose New Logical Drive. Disk Management fires up the New Partition Wizard again, this time with the option to create a logical drive.

• **Figure 12.47**   Turning on compression

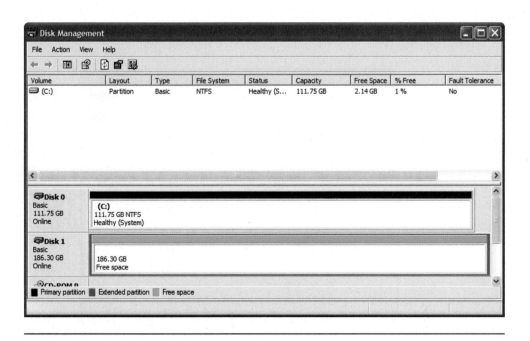

• **Figure 12.48**   Extended partition with no logical drives

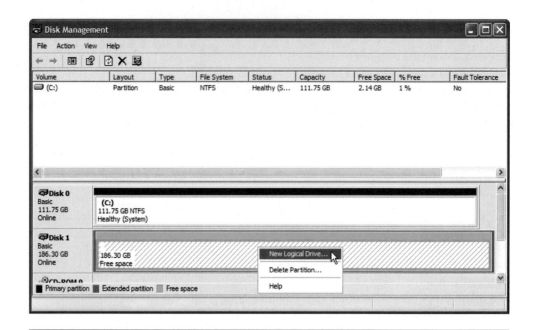

• **Figure 12.49**   Selecting to create a logical drive in the extended (free space) partition

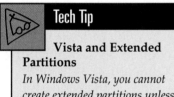

Tech Tip

Vista and Extended Partitions

In Windows Vista, you cannot create extended partitions unless you already have three primary partitions on a drive and are creating a fourth. Microsoft has tried to simplify drive implementation as much as possible.

When you create a logical drive, the New Partition Wizard automatically gives you the same options to format the partition by using one of the three file systems you saw earlier with primary partitions (Figure 12.50). You get another confirmation screen, and then the Disk Management console shows you the newly created drive.

One interesting aspect of Windows is the tiny (approximately 8 MB) mysterious unallocated partition that shows up on the C: drive. The Windows installation program does this when you first install Windows on a new system, to reserve a space Windows needs for converting the C: drive to a dynamic disk. It doesn't hurt anything and it's tiny, so just leave it alone. If you want to make a volume and format it, feel free to do so.

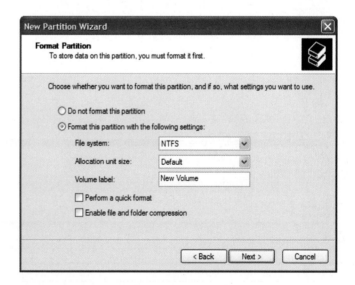

• **Figure 12.50**   The New Partition Wizard offering formatting options

Mike Meyers' CompTIA A+ Guide to Managing and Troubleshooting PCs

Dynamic Disks

You create dynamic disks from basic disks in Disk Management. Once you convert a drive from a basic to a dynamic disk, primary and extended partitions no longer exist; dynamic disks are divided into volumes instead of partitions.

To convert a basic disk to dynamic, just right-click the drive icon and select Convert to Dynamic Disk (Figure 12.51). The process is very quick and safe, although the reverse is not true. The conversion from dynamic disk to basic disk first requires you to delete all partitions off of the hard drive.

Once you've converted, no partitions exist, only volumes. You can make five types of volumes on a dynamic disk: simple, spanned, striped, mirrored, and RAID 5, although you'll commonly see only the first three in a Windows 2000/XP Professional or Windows Vista Business environment. You'll next learn how to implement the three most common volume types. The final step involves assigning a drive letter or mounting the volume as a folder.

Simple Volumes

A simple volume acts just like a primary partition. If you have only one dynamic disk in a system, it can have only a simple volume. It's important to note here that a simple volume may act like a traditional primary partition, but it is very different. If you install a hard drive partitioned as a simple volume dynamic disk into any version of Windows prior to Windows 2000, you would see no usable partition.

In Disk Management, right-click any unallocated space on the dynamic disk and choose New Volume (Figure 12.52) to run the New Volume Wizard. You'll see a series of screens that prompt you on size and file system, and then you're finished. Figure 12.53 shows Disk Management with three simple volumes.

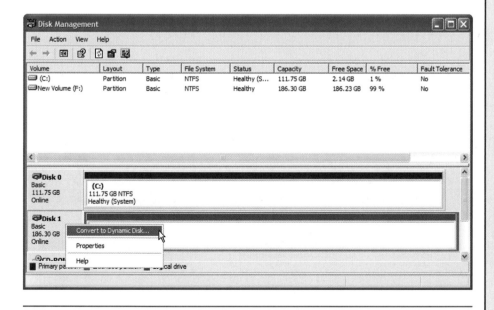

● **Figure 12.51**   Converting to a dynamic disk

 When you move a dynamic disk from one computer to another, it shows up in Disk Management as a foreign drive. You can import a foreign drive into the new system by right-clicking the disk icon and selecting Import Foreign Disks.

The home editions of Windows XP and Windows Vista do not support dynamic disks.

Tech Tip

Mirrored and Striped with Parity Volumes

Disk Management enables you to create mirrored and striped with parity volumes, but only on Windows Server machines, a fact you might recall from the brief note in Chapter 11, "Hard Drive Technologies." The cool thing is that you can do this remotely across a network. You can sit at your Windows XP Professional workstation, in other words, and open Disk Management, surf to a Windows Server that you want to work with, and poof!

You have two new options for configuring volumes. By limiting the implementation of mirroring and RAID 5 to server machines, Microsoft clearly meant to encourage small businesses to pony up for a copy of Server rather than using the less-expensive Professional or Business OS for the company server. Both mirrored and striped-with-parity volumes are included here for completeness and because they show up in the Windows Help Files when you search for dynamic disks. Both are cool, but definitely way beyond CompTIA A+!

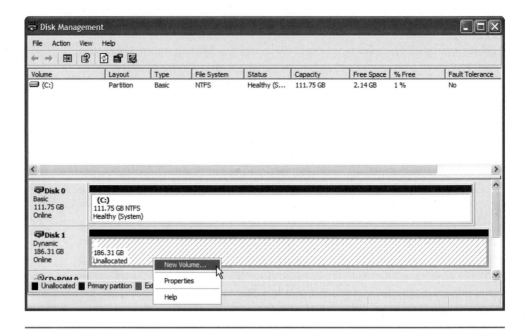

● **Figure 12.52**   Selecting to open the New Volume Wizard

Spanning Volumes

You can extend the size of a simple volume to any unallocated space on a dynamic disk. You can also extend the volume to grab extra space on completely different dynamic disks, creating a spanned volume. To extend or span, simply right-click the volume you want to make bigger, and choose Extend Volume from the options (Figure 12.54). This opens the Extend Volume Wizard, which prompts you for the location of free space on a dynamic

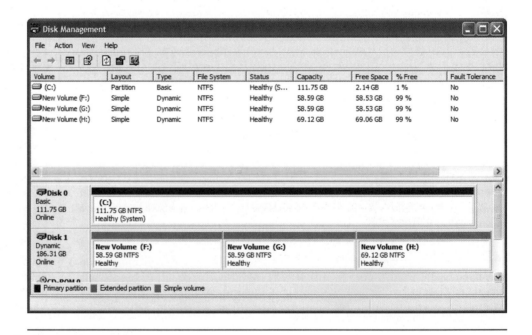

● **Figure 12.53**   Simple volumes

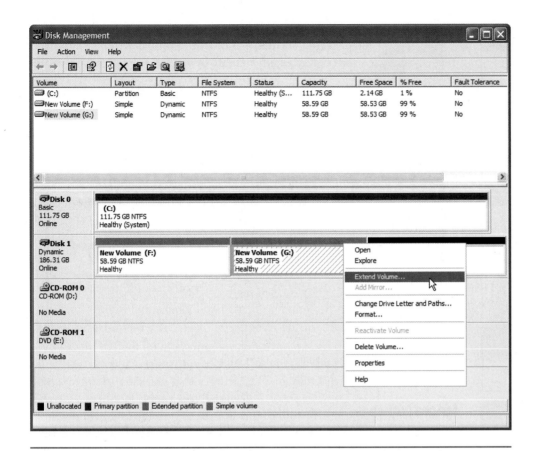

● **Figure 12.54**   Selecting the Extend Volume option

disk and the increased volume size you want to assign (Figure 12.55). If you have multiple drives, you can span the volume just as easily to one of those drives.

The capability to extend and span volumes makes dynamic disks worth their weight in gold. If you start running out of space on a volume, you can simply add another physical hard drive to the system and span the volume to the new drive. This keeps your drive letters consistent and unchanging so your programs don't get confused, yet enables you to expand drive space when needed.

You can extend or span any simple volume on a dynamic disk, not just the "one on the end" in the Disk Management console. You simply select the volume to expand and the total volume increase you want. Figure 12.56 shows a simple 4-GB volume named Extended that has been enlarged an extra 7.91 GB in a portion of the hard drive, skipping the 2-GB section of unallocated space contiguous to it. This created an 11.91-GB volume. Windows has no problem skipping areas on a drive.

Once you convert a drive to dynamic, you cannot revert it to a basic disk without losing all of the data on that drive. Be prepared to back up all data before you convert.

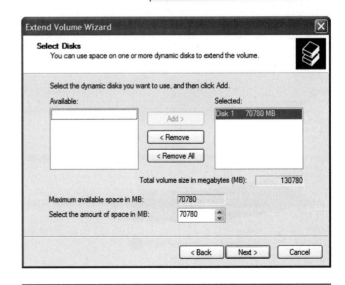

● **Figure 12.55**   The Extend Volume Wizard

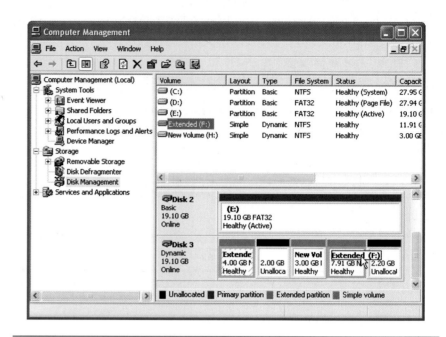

● **Figure 12.56**   Extended volume

Striped Volumes

If you have two or more dynamic disks in a PC, Disk Management enables you to combine them into a *striped* volume. A striped volume spreads out blocks of each file across multiple disks. Using two or more drives in a group called a **stripe set**, striping writes data first to a certain number of clusters on one drive, then on the next, and so on. It speeds up data throughput because the system has to wait a much shorter time for a drive to read or write data. The drawback of striping is that if any single drive in the stripe set fails, all the data in the stripe set is lost.

To create a striped volume, right-click any unused space on a drive, choose New Volume, and then choose Striped. The wizard asks for the other drives you want to add to the stripe, and you need to select two unallocated spaces on other dynamic disks. Select the other unallocated spaces and go through the remaining screens on sizing and formatting until you've created a new striped volume (Figure 12.57). The two stripes in Figure 12.57 appear to have different sizes,

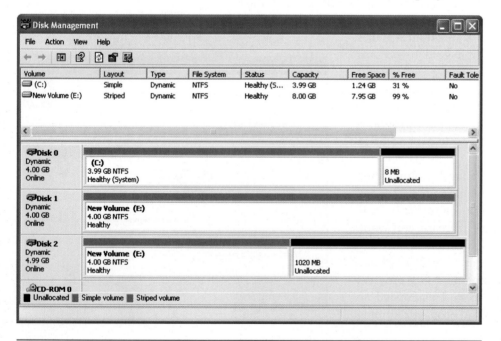

● **Figure 12.57**   Two striped drives

but if you look closely you'll see they are both 4 GB. All stripes must be the same size on each drive.

Mount Points

The one drive that can't take full advantage of being dynamic is the drive containing the operating system, your primary master C: drive. You can make it dynamic, but you still can't do all of the cool dynamic things such as extending and spanning. So what good is being able to allocate more space to a volume if you can't use it when you start to fill up your C: drive? If you can't add to that drive, your only option is to replace it with a new, bigger drive, right?

Not at all! Earlier we discussed the idea of mounting a drive as a folder instead of a drive letter, and here's where you get to do it. A *volume mount point* (or simply **mount point**) is a place in the directory structure of an existing volume that you can point to a volume or partition. The mounted volume then functions just like a folder, but all files stored in that segment of the directory structure will go to the mounted volume. After partitioning and formatting the drive, you don't give it a drive letter; instead, you *mount* the volume to a folder on the C: drive and make it nothing more than just another folder (Figure 12.58). You can load programs to that folder, just as you

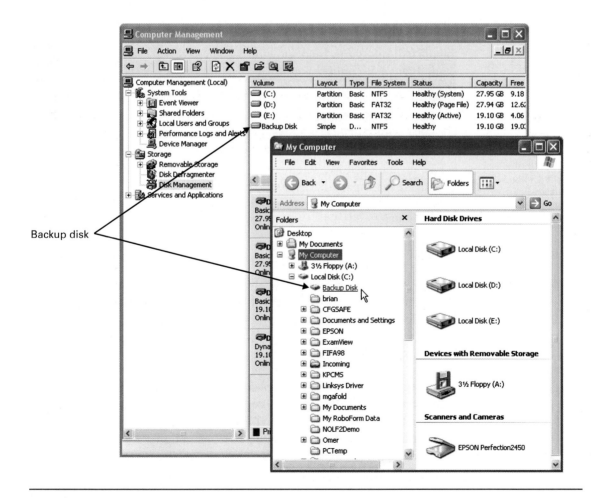

Backup disk

• **Figure 12.58**   A drive volume mounted as a folder of drive C:

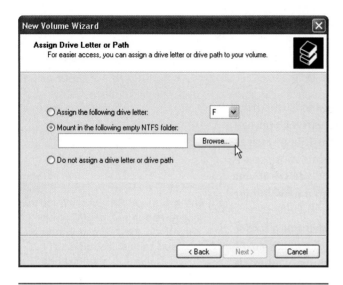

New Volume Wizard

Assign Drive Letter or Path
For easier access, you can assign a drive letter or drive path to your volume.

○ Assign the following drive letter: F

● Mount in the following empty NTFS folder:

[   ] Browse...

○ Do not assign a drive letter or drive path

< Back   Next >   Cancel

• **Figure 12.59**   Choosing to create a mounted volume

would to your Program Files folder. You can use it to store data files or backed-up system files. In *function*, therefore, the new hard drive simply extends the capacity of the C: drive, so neither you nor your client need ever trouble yourselves with dealing with multiple drive letters.

To create a mount point, right-click an unallocated section of a dynamic disk and choose New Volume. This opens the New Volume Wizard. In the second screen, you can select a mount point rather than a drive letter (Figure 12.59). Browse to a blank folder on an NTFS-formatted drive or create a new folder and you're in business.

With mount points, Microsoft dramatically changed the way you can work with hard drives. You're no longer stuck in the rut of adding drive letters that mess up Windows' mapping of the optical drive. You don't have to confuse clients with multiple drive letters when they just want a little more space. You can resurrect smaller hard drives, making them a functional part of today's computer. With the Disk Management console in Windows 2000/XP and Windows Vista/7, Microsoft got it right.

Try This!

Working with Dynamic Drives and Mount Points

You can't begin to appreciate the ease and elegant simplicity of dynamic drives until you play with them, so Try This! Get a couple of spare drives and install them into a PC running Windows 2000, XP, or Vista. Fire up the Disk Management console and try the following setups. Convert both spare drives to dynamic drives.

1. Make a mirror set.

2. Make a stripe set.

3. Make them into a single volume spanned between both drives.

4. Make a single volume that takes up a portion of one drive, and then extend that volume onto another portion of that drive. Finally, span that volume to the other hard drive as well.

5. Create a volume of some sort—you decide—and then mount that volume to a folder on the C: drive.

You'll need to format the volumes after you create them so you can see how they manifest in My Computer/Computer. (See the next section of this chapter for details on formatting.) Also, you'll need to delete volumes to create a new setup. To delete a volume, simply right-click the volume and choose Delete Volume. It's almost too easy.

Formatting a Partition

You can format any Windows partition/volume in My Computer/Computer. Just right-click the drive name and choose Format (Figure 12.60). You'll see a dialog box that asks for the type of file system you want to use, the cluster size, a place to put a volume label, and two other options. The Quick Format option tells Windows not to test the clusters and is a handy option when you're in a hurry—and feeling lucky. The Enable Compression option tells Windows to give users the capability to compress folders or files. It works well but slows down your hard drive.

Disk Management is today's preferred formatting tool for Windows 2000, XP, and Vista. When you create a new volume on a dynamic disk or a new partition on a basic disk, the New Volume Wizard also asks you what type of format you want to use. Always use NTFS unless you're that rare and strange person who wants to dual-boot Windows XP or Windows Vista with some ancient version of Windows.

All OS installation discs partition and format as part of the OS installation. Windows simply prompts you to partition and then format the drive. Read the screens and you'll do great.

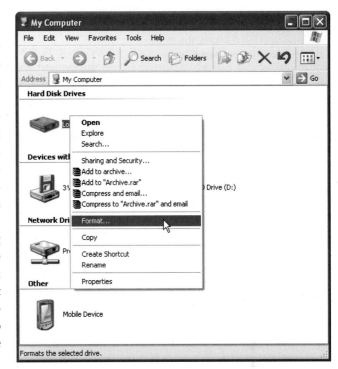

• **Figure 12.60**   Choosing Format in My Computer

Maintaining and Troubleshooting Hard Drives

Hard drives are complex mechanical and electrical devices. With platters spinning at thousands of rotations per minute, they also generate heat and vibration. All of these factors make hard drives susceptible to failure. In this section, you will learn some basic maintenance tasks that will keep your hard drives healthy, and for those inevitable instances when a hard drive fails, you will also learn what you can do to repair them.

Maintenance

Hard drive maintenance can be broken down into two distinct functions: checking the disk occasionally for failed clusters, and keeping data organized on the drive so it can be accessed quickly.

Error-Checking

Individual clusters on hard drives sometimes go bad. There's nothing you can do to prevent this from happening, so it's important that you check occasionally for bad clusters on drives. The tools used to perform this checking are generically called error-checking utilities, although the terms for two older Microsoft tools—ScanDisk and **CHKDSK** (pronounced "Checkdisk")—are

often used. Microsoft calls the tool **Error-checking** in Windows XP/Vista/7. Whatever the name of the utility, each does the same job: when the tool finds bad clusters, it puts the electronic equivalent of orange cones around them so the system won't try to place data in those bad clusters.

Most error-checking tools do far more than just check for bad clusters. They go through all of the drive's filenames, looking for invalid names and attempting to fix them. They look for clusters that have no filenames associated with them (we call these *lost chains*) and erase them. From time to time, the underlying links between parent and child folders are lost, so a good error-checking tool checks every parent and child folder. With a folder such as C:\TEST\DATA, for example, they make sure that the folder DATA is properly associated with its parent folder, C:\TEST, and that C:\TEST is properly associated with its child folder, C:\TEST\DATA.

To access Error-checking on a Windows 2000/XP or Windows Vista/7 system, open My Computer/Computer, right-click the drive you want to check, and choose Properties to open the drive's Properties dialog box. Select the Tools tab and click the Check Now button (Figure 12.61) to display the Check Disk dialog box, which has two options (Figure 12.62). Check the box next to *Automatically fix file system errors*, but save the option to *Scan for and attempt recovery of bad sectors* for times when you actually suspect a problem, because it takes a while on bigger hard drives.

Now that you know how to run Error-checking, your next question should be, "How often do I run it?" A reasonable maintenance plan would include running it about once a week. Error-checking is fast (unless you use the *Scan for and attempt recovery* option), and it's a great tool for keeping your system in top shape.

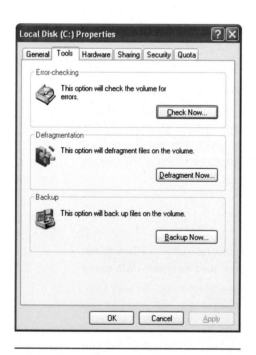

• **Figure 12.61**   The Tools tab in the Properties dialog box in Windows XP

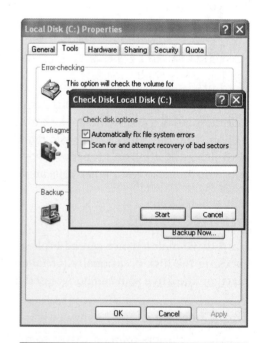

• **Figure 12.62**   Options

Defragmentation

Fragmentation of clusters can increase your drive access times dramatically. It's a good idea to **defragment**—or *defrag*—your drives as part of monthly maintenance. You access the defrag tool that runs with Windows 2000, XP, Vista, and 7, called Disk Defragmenter, the same way you access Error-checking—right-click a drive in My Computer/Computer and choose Properties—except you click the Defragment Now button on the Tools tab to open the Defragmenter (Figure 12.63).

Defragmentation is interesting to watch—once. From then on, schedule it to run late at night. You should defragment your drives about once a month, although you could run it every week, and if you run it every night, it takes only a few minutes. The longer you go between defrags, the longer it takes. If you don't run Disk Defragmenter, your system will run slower. If you don't run Error-checking, you may lose data.

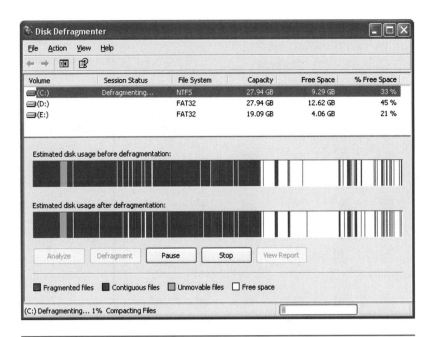

• **Figure 12.63**   Disk Defragmenter in Windows XP

Disk Cleanup

Did you know that the average hard drive is full of trash? Not the junk you intentionally put in your hard drive such as the 23,000 e-mail messages that you refuse to delete from your e-mail program. This kind of trash is all of the files that you never see that Windows keeps for you. Here are a few examples:

■ **Files in the Recycle Bin**   When you delete a file, it isn't really deleted. It's placed in the Recycle Bin in case you decide you need the file later. I just checked my Recycle Bin and found 3 GB worth of files (Figure 12.64). That's a lot of trash!

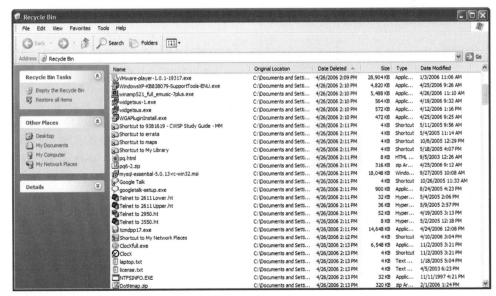

• **Figure 12.64**   Mike's Recycle Bin

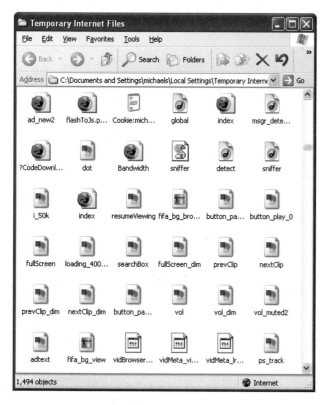

• **Figure 12.65**   Lots of temporary Internet files

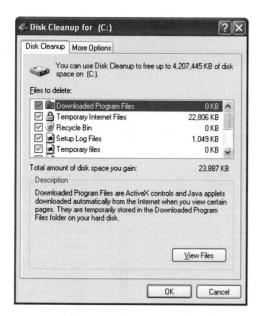

• **Figure 12.66**   Disk Cleanup

■ **Temporary Internet files**   When you go to a Web site, Windows keeps copies of the graphics and other items so the page will load more quickly the next time you access it. You can see these files by opening the Internet Options applet on the Control Panel. Figure 12.65 shows my temporary Internet files.

■ **Downloaded program files**   Your system always keeps a copy of any Java or ActiveX applets it downloads. You can see these in the Internet Options applet. You'll generally find only a few tiny files here.

■ **Temporary files**   Many applications create temporary files that are supposed to be deleted when the application is closed. For one reason or another, these temporary files sometimes aren't deleted. The location of these files varies with the version of Windows, but they always reside in a folder called TEMP.

Every hard drive eventually becomes filled with lots of unnecessary trash. All versions of Windows tend to act erratically when the drives run out of unused space. Fortunately, all versions of Windows have a powerful tool called **Disk Cleanup** (Figure 12.66). You can access Disk Cleanup in all versions of Windows by choosing Start | All Programs | Accessories | System Tools | Disk Cleanup. Disk Cleanup gets rid of the four types of files just described (and a few others). Run Disk Cleanup once a month or so to keep plenty of space available on your hard drive.

Troubleshooting Hard Drive Implementation

There's no scarier computer problem than an error that points to trouble with a hard drive. This section looks at some of the more common problems that occur with hard drives and how to fix them. These issues fall into three broad categories: installation, data corruption, and dying hard drives.

Installation Errors

Installing a drive and getting to the point where it can hold data requires four distinct steps: connectivity, CMOS, partitioning, and formatting. If you make a mistake at any point on any of these steps, the drive won't work. The beauty of this is that if you make an error, you can walk back through each step and check for problems. The troubleshooting section in Chapter 11 covered physical connections and CMOS, so this section concentrates on the latter two issues.

Partitioning   Partitioning errors generally fall into two groups: failing to partition at all and making the wrong size or type of partition. You'll recognize the former type of error the first time you open My Computer/Computer after installing a drive. If you forgot to partition it, the drive won't even show up in My Computer, only in Disk Management. If you made the partition too small, that'll become painfully obvious when you start filling it up with files.

The fix for partitioning errors is simply to open Disk Management and do the partitioning correctly. If you've added files to the wrongly sized drive, don't forget to back them up before you repartition.

Formatting   Failing to format a drive makes the drive unable to hold data. Accessing the drive in Windows results in a drive "is not accessible" error, and from a C:\ prompt, you'll get the famous "Invalid media" type error. Format the drive unless you're certain that the drive has a format already. Corrupted files can create the invalid media error. Check one of the sections on corrupted data later in this chapter for the fix.

Most of the time, formatting is a slow, boring process. But sometimes the drive makes "bad sounds" and you start seeing errors like the one shown in Figure 12.67 at the top of the screen.

An *allocation unit* is format's term for a cluster. The drive has run across a bad cluster

```
A:\>format C:/s
WARNING:  ALL DATA ON NON-REMOVABLE DISK
DRIVE C:  WILL BE LOST!
Proceed with Format  (Y/N)?y

Formatting  30709.65M

Trying to recover lost allocation unit 37,925
```

• **Figure 12.67**   The "Trying to recover lost allocation unit" error

and is trying to fix it. For years, I've told techs that seeing this error a few (610) times doesn't mean anything; every drive comes with a few bad spots. This is no longer true. Modern drives actually hide a significant number of extra sectors that they use to replace bad sectors automatically. If a new drive gets a lot of "Trying to recover lost allocation unit" errors, you can bet that the drive is dying and needs to be replaced. Get the hard drive maker's diagnostic to be sure. Bad clusters are reported by S.M.A.R.T.

Mental Reinstallation   Focus on the fact that all of these errors share a common thread—you just installed a drive! Installation errors don't show up on a system that has been running correctly for three weeks; they show up the moment you try to do something with the drive you just installed. If a newly installed drive fails to work, do a "mental reinstallation." Does the drive show up in the CMOS autodetect? No? Then recheck the cables, master/slave settings, and power. If it does show up, did you remember to partition and format the drive? Did it need to be set to active? These are common-sense questions that come to mind as you march through your mental reinstallation. Even if you've installed thousands of drives over the years, you'll be amazed at how often you do things such as forget to plug in power to a drive, forget CMOS, or install a cable backward. Do the mental reinstallation—it really works!

● **Figure 12.68**   A corrupted data error

Data Corruption

All hard drives occasionally get corrupted data in individual sectors. Power surges, accidental shutdowns, corrupted installation media, and viruses, along with hundreds of other problems, can cause this corruption. In most cases, this type of error shows up while Windows is running. Figure 12.68 shows a classic example.

You may also see Windows error messages saying one of the following:

- "The following file is missing or corrupt"
- "The download location information is damaged"
- "Unable to load file"

If core boot files become corrupted, you may see text errors at boot, such as the following:

- "Cannot find COMMAND.COM"
- "Error loading operating system"
- "Invalid BOOT.INI"
- "NTLDR is missing or corrupt"

On older programs, you may see a command prompt open with errors such as this one:

```
Sector not found reading drive C: Abort, Retry, Fail?
```

The first fix for any of these problems is to run the Error-checking utility. Error-checking will go through and mark bad clusters and hopefully move your data to a good cluster.

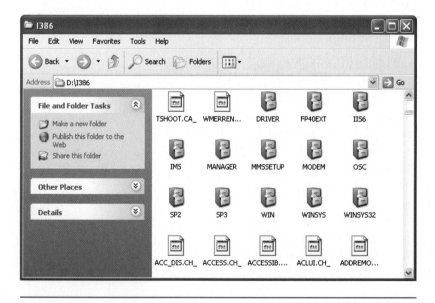

● **Figure 12.69**   CAB files

Windows 2000/XP Extract/Expand   If Error-checking fails to move a critically important file—such as a file Windows needs so it can load—on pre-Vista systems you can always resort to the command line and try to extract the file from the Windows cabinet files. Most Windows programs store all files in a compressed format called CAB (which is short for cabinet file). One CAB file contains many files, and most installation discs have lots of CAB files (see Figure 12.69).

To replace a single corrupt file this way, you need to know two things: the location of the CAB file that contains the file you need, and how to get the file out so you can copy it back to its original spot. Microsoft supplies the

EXPAND program to enable you to get a new copy of the missing file from the CAB files on the installation CD-ROM. Also notice how they are numbered—that's the secret to understanding these programs.

In most cases, all of the CAB files for a program are piled into some folder, as shown in Figure 12.69. Let's say you need a file called OLEPRO32.DLL. (I have no idea what this file does. I only know that Windows can't find it and you need to put it back.) Get to a command prompt within Windows and tell EXPAND to check *all* of the CAB files on your installation CD (drive E: in this example) with this command:

```
EXPAND e:\I386\*.CAB -F:OLEPRO32.DLL
```

EXPAND goes through all of the CAB files and finds the file. If you want to see details on the EXPAND command, use Windows Help or type **EXPAND /?** at a command prompt.

Corrupted Data on Bad Sectors   If the same errors continue to appear after you run the disk-checking utility, there's a chance that the drive has bad sectors.

Almost all drives today take advantage of built-in **error correction code (ECC)** that constantly checks the drive for bad sectors. If the ECC detects a bad sector, it marks the sector as bad in the drive's internal error map. Don't confuse this error map with a FAT. The partitioning program creates the FAT. The drive's internal error map was created at the factory on reserved drive heads and is invisible to the system. If the ECC finds a bad sector, you will get a corrupted data error as the computer attempts to read the bad sector. Disk-checking utilities fix this problem most of the time.

Many times, the ECC thinks a bad sector is good, however, and fails to update the internal error map. In this case, you need a program that goes back into the drive and marks the sectors as bad. That's where the powerful SpinRite utility from Gibson Research comes into play. SpinRite marks sectors as bad or good more accurately than ECC and does not disturb the data, enabling you to run SpinRite without fear of losing anything. And if it finds a bad sector with data in it, SpinRite has powerful algorithms that usually recover the data on all but the most badly damaged sectors (see Figure 12.70).

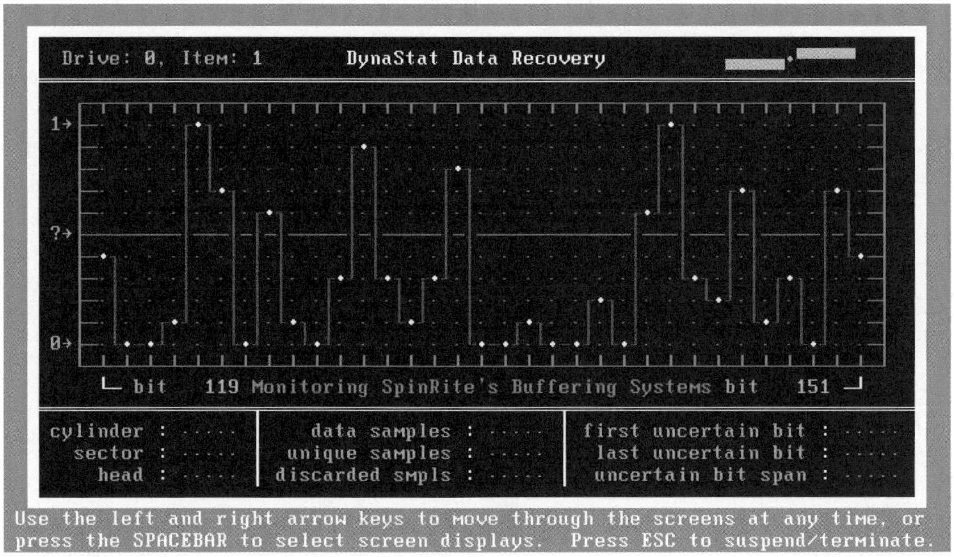

Without SpinRite, you must use a low-level format program supplied by the hard drive maker, assuming you can get one (not all are willing to distribute these). These programs work like

> Chapter 15, "Working with the Command-Line Interface," goes into a lot of detail on using the command line.

• **Figure 12.70**   SpinRite at work

SpinRite in that they aggressively check the hard drive's sectors and update the internal error map. Unfortunately, all of them wipe out all data on the drive. At least you can use the drive, even if it means repartitioning, formatting, and reinstalling everything.

Dying Hard Drive

Physical problems are rare but devastating when they happen. If a hard drive is truly damaged physically, there is nothing that you or any service technician can do to fix it. Fortunately, hard drives are designed to take a phenomenal amount of punishment without failing. Physical problems manifest themselves in two ways: either the drive works properly but makes a lot of noise, or the drive seems to disappear.

All hard drives make noise—the hum as the platters spin and the occasional slight scratching noise as the read/write heads access sectors are normal. However, if your drive begins to make any of the following sounds, it is about to die:

- Continuous high-pitched squeal
- Series of clacks, a short pause, and then another series of clacks
- Continuous grinding or rumbling

Back up your critical data and replace the drive. Windows comes with great tools for backing up data.

You'll know when a drive simply disappears. If it's the drive that contains your operating system, the system will lock up. When you try to restart the computer, you'll see this error message or something similar to it:

```
No Boot Device Present
```

If it's a second drive, it will simply stop showing up in My Computer/Computer. The first thing to do in this case is to fire up the System Setup program and see if autodetect sees the drive. If it does, you do not have a physical problem with the drive. If autodetect fails, shut off the system and remove the ribbon cable, but leave the power cable attached. Restart the system and listen to the drive. If the drive spins up, you know it is getting good power. This is usually a clue that the drive is probably good. In that case, you need to look for more mundane problems such as an unplugged data cord or jumpers incorrectly set. If the drive doesn't spin up, try another power connector. If it still doesn't spin up and you've triple-checked the jumpers and ribbon cable, you have a problem with the onboard electronics, and the drive is dead.

Beyond A+

Modern hard drives have many other features that are worth knowing about but that rarely impact beginning techs. A couple of the more interesting ones are spindle speed and third-party hard drive tools. If you have a burning desire to dive into hard drives in all their glory, you need not go any farther than the Storage Review, an excellent site dedicated solely to hard drives. Here's the link: www.storagereview.com.

Tech Tip

Long Warranties

Most hard drives have three-year warranties. Before you throw away a dead drive, check the hard drive maker's Web site or call them to see if the drive is still under warranty. Ask for a return material authorization (RMA). You'll be amazed how many times you get a newer, usually larger, hard drive for free. It never hurts to check!

Tech Tip

Data Rescue Specialists

If you ever lose a hard drive that contains absolutely critical information, you can turn to a company that specializes in hard drive data recovery. The job will be expensive—prices usually start around $1000 (U.S.)—but when you have to have the data, such companies are your only hope. Do a Web search for "data recovery" or check the Yellow Pages for companies in this line of business.

Third-Party Partition Tools

Disk Management is a good tool, but it's limited for some situations. Some really great third-party tools on the market can give you incredible flexibility and power to structure and restructure your hard drive storage to meet your changing needs. They each have interesting unique features, but in general they enable you to create, change, and delete partitions on a hard drive *without* destroying any of the programs or data stored there. Slick! These programs aren't on the CompTIA A+ exams, but all PC techs use at least one of them, so let's explore three of the most well-known examples: Symantec's Norton PartitionMagic, Avanquest Partition Commander Professional, and the open source Linux tool, GParted.

Probably the most well-known third-party partition tool is PartitionMagic, although it's quite dated at this point. It supports older versions of Windows but has problems with Windows Vista/7. With it, you can create, resize, split, merge, delete, undelete, and convert partitions without destroying your data. Among the additional features it advertises are the capability to browse, copy, or move files and folders between supported partitions; to expand an NTFS partition—even if it's a system partition—without rebooting; to change NTFS cluster sizes; and to add new partitions for multiple OSs by using a simple wizard.

Avanquest offers a variety of related products, one of which is the very useful Partition Commander Professional. It supports all versions of Windows (unlike PartitionMagic) and enables you to play with your partitions without destroying your data. Among its niftier features are the capability to convert a dynamic disk to a basic disk nondestructively (which you can't do with the Microsoft-supplied Windows tools); to defrag the master file table on an NTFS partition; and to move unused space from one partition to another on the same physical drive, automatically resizing the partitions based on the amount of space you tell it to move. Figure 12.71 shows

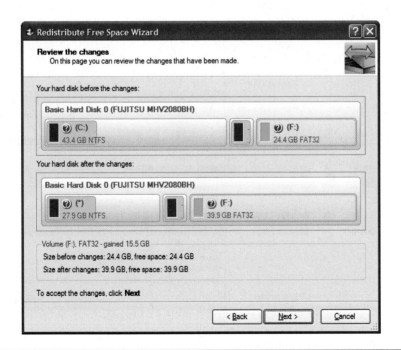

• **Figure 12.71**　Partition Commander

the Partition Commander dialog box for moving unused space between partitions.

The only problem with PartitionMagic and Partition Commander is that they cost money. There's nothing wrong with spending money on a good product, but if you can find something that does the job for free, why not try it? If you think like I do, check out the Gnome Partition Editor, better known as GParted. You can find it at http://sourceforge.net/.

GParted is an incredibly powerful partition editor and does almost everything the for-pay partition editors do, but it's free. It's still in beta—which means it's constantly changing and it has a few bugs (that are constantly being fixed)—but I use it all of the time and love it. If you look closely at Figure 12.72, you'll notice that it uses strange names for the partitions, such as HDA1 or HDB3. These are Linux conventions and are well documented in GParted's Help screens. Take a little time and you'll love GParted too.

The one downside to GParted is that it is a Linux program—because no Windows version exists, you need Linux to run it. So how do you run Linux on a Windows system without actually installing Linux on your hard drive? The answer is easy—the folks at GParted will give you the tools to burn a live CD that boots Linux so you can run GParted!

A live CD is a complete OS on a CD. Understand this is not an installation CD like your Windows installation disc. The OS is already installed on the CD. You boot from the live CD and the OS loads into RAM, just like the

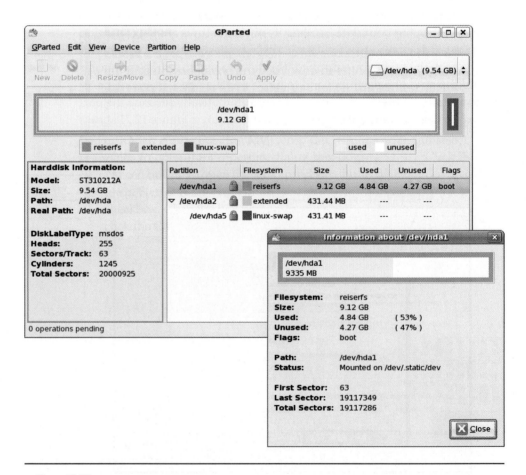

• **Figure 12.72**   GParted in action

OS on your hard drive loads into RAM at boot. As the live CD boots, it recognizes your hardware and loads the proper drivers into RAM so everything works. You get everything you'd expect from an OS with one big exception: a live CD does not touch your hard drive. Of course you may run programs (such as GParted) that work on your hard drive, which makes live CDs popular with PC techs, because you can toss them into a cranky system and run utilities.

The truly intrepid might want to consider using The Ultimate Boot CD (UBCD), basically a huge pile of useful freeware utilities compiled by frustrated technician Ben Burrows, who couldn't find a boot disk when he needed one. His Web site is www.ultimatebootcd.com. The UBCD has more than 100 different tools, all placed on a single live CD. It has all of the low-level diagnostic tools for all of the hard drive makers, four or five different partitioning tools, S.M.A.R.T. viewers, hard drive wiping utilities, and hard drive cloning tools (nice for when you want to replace a hard drive with a larger one). Little documentation is provided, however, and many of the tools require experience way beyond the scope of the CompTIA A+ exams. I will tell you that I have a copy and I use it.

space per user by enforcing disk quotas. Finally, you can adjust cluster sizes to allow support of partitions up to 16 exabytes.

Partition and format hard drives

- Any software that can boot up a system is called an operating system, and any removable media that contains a bootable operating system is generically called a boot device or boot disk. All Windows and Linux operating system installation CD/DVDs are boot devices. You can also make your own boot device, complete with handy tech tools.

- Windows 2000/XP installation discs walk you through the process of partitioning and formatting your hard drive. After accepting the license agreement, you can simply press ENTER and Windows partitions and formats your drive as one large primary partition. If you prefer to partition only a portion of the hard drive, you can do so manually by pressing the letter C to create a partition, entering the desired size in MB, and pressing ENTER. Finally, you are offered several options for formatting before the installation continues. It is recommended that you choose NTFS. Note that the disk is partitioned and formatted as a basic disk. Once Windows is installed, you can convert basic disks to dynamic disks with the Disk Management tool.

- Windows Vista installation discs also walk you through the partitioning and formatting process but use a graphical user interface, thus greatly simplifying the process. When you click the Custom install button, you're taken to the partitioning screen, where you can create, delete, edit, and format partitions. You can only format partitions as NTFS off of the Vista installation disc, and you can't create extended partitions unless you create more than three partitions on a single disk.

- You can change or remove drive letters with the Disk Management tool. Only the C: drive cannot be changed. Drive letters are assigned by going down the list of drives and assigning the next available drive letter, with hard drives taking precedence over optical drives.

- All new disk drives must be initialized by Disk Management before you can use them. The initialization process places information on the drive identifying it as part of a particular system. New drives are always initialized as basic disks but

can be converted to dynamic disks by right-clicking and choosing Convert to Dynamic Disk. Creating a partition or volume is just as simple. Right-click the drive and choose Create Partition or New Volume. Remember that you must create logical drives inside an extended partition before you can format and use it to store files.

- Once a disk has been initialized and partitioned, you can format it. Microsoft requires using NTFS for any partition larger than 32 GB. Performing a Quick Format skips the checking of clusters, which results in a faster format but is risky.

- The Windows installation program creates a tiny partition on the C: drive, which is used to later convert the disk to a dynamic disk. Although you can format and use that space for file storage, it is recommended that you leave it as is.

- A mount point is a folder on an NTFS drive that provides access to another drive that may or may not have a drive letter. The new drive extends the capacity of the drive providing the folder mount point. Although the files in the mount point folder appear to be stored on the first drive, they are actually stored on the additional drive. Create a mount point by first creating a folder on an NTFS drive. Then launch Disk Management, select the additional partition/volume, right-click, and choose Change Drive Letter and Paths. From there, choose Add and browse to the mount point folder you created earlier.

- You can format any partition/volume in My Computer/Computer by right-clicking and choosing Format. Alternatively, you can format partitions/volumes from the Disk Management tool. Both methods offer you options to perform a Quick Format and enable compression.

Maintain and troubleshoot hard drives

- Hard drive maintenance can be broken down into two distinct functions: checking the disk occasionally for failed clusters and keeping data organized on the drive so it can be accessed quickly.

- Microsoft offers Error-checking for scanning hard drives. It checks for bad clusters and, if found, marks them as bad so no data gets written to those areas of the hard drive. Additionally, it looks for invalid filenames and attempts to fix them, and it searches for and erases lost cluster chains.

- To run Error-checking in Windows, right-click a drive to view its Properties window, choose the Tools tab, and click the Check Now button. Check the box next to *Automatically fix file system errors*, but save the option to *Scan for and attempt recovery of bad sectors* for times when you actually suspect a problem.

- Run Error-checking and Disk Defragmenter once a month as preventive maintenance to keep your system running smoothly. Both are available on the Tools tab of the drive's Properties window.

- The Disk Cleanup utility deletes files from the Recycle Bin, temporary Internet files, copies of downloaded Java or ActiveX applets, and other temporary files on your hard drive. You can access Disk Cleanup in all versions of Windows by choosing Start | All Programs | Accessories | System Tools | Disk Cleanup. Run Disk Cleanup once a month.

- Hard drive problems fall into three broad categories: installation, data corruption, and dying hard drives. Installation errors can happen at any of the four steps: connectivity, CMOS, partitioning, or formatting. When troubleshooting, you should always walk back through each step and check for problems.

- Usually showing up at boot time, a connectivity error indicates that something isn't plugged in correctly or something has become unplugged. Some connectivity errors are harmless, such as plugging in the data cable backward for a PATA drive, while others, such as installing the power cable backward, will destroy your drive. The autodetect function of your BIOS will not detect a drive unless it is installed correctly, making it a great connectivity verifier. Some PATA drives simply will not work on the same controller.

- If autodetect fails to see the drive in question, it's probably a connectivity problem.

- Partitioning errors generally fall into two groups: failing to partition at all and making the wrong size/type of partition. If you try to access a nonpartitioned drive, you'll get an "Invalid Drive Specifications" error and you won't be able to see the drive in anything but CMOS, FDISK, and Disk Management.

- If you try to access a drive that's not formatted, Windows displays a drive "is not accessible" error, while you'll get an "Invalid media" error from a C:\ prompt. Format the drive unless you're certain that the drive has already been formatted. Corrupted files can also create the "Invalid media" error.

- The "Trying to recover lost allocation unit" error means the drive has bad sectors. Time to replace the drive.

- If a newly installed drive fails to work, do a "mental reinstall." If the drive does not show in CMOS autodetect, recheck the cables, master/slave jumper settings, and power. If it shows up, make sure you remembered to partition and format it. Remember the drive must be marked as Active to be bootable.

- Power surges, accidental shutdowns, corrupted installation media, and viruses are among the causes of corrupted data in individual sectors. These errors usually show while Windows is running. If core boot files become corrupted, you may see text errors such as "NTLDR is missing or corrupt," "Error loading operating system," or "Invalid BOOT.INI." Older systems may generate a "sector not found" error. The first fix for any of these problems is to run an error-checking utility.

- To replace a single corrupt file on a Windows XP or earlier, you must know the location of the numbered Windows CAB (cabinet) file that contains the file you need and how to extract the file from the CAB file. Use the EXPAND program with Windows 2000/XP to get a new copy of the desired file from the CAB file on the installation disc. EXPAND searches all CAB files to find the file you specify, and then expands it and places it in the C:\ folder.

- Almost all drives today have built-in error correction code (ECC) that constantly checks the drive for bad sectors. If it detects a bad sector, it marks the sector as bad in the drive's internal error map so it's invisible to the system. If the ECC finds a bad sector, however, you will get a corrupted data error when the computer attempts to read the bad sector.

- The powerful SpinRite utility from Gibson Research marks sectors as bad or good more accurately than ECC and does not disturb the data. When it finds a bad sector with data in it, SpinRite

uses powerful algorithms that usually recover the data on all but the most badly damaged sectors. Without SpinRite, you must use a low-level formatting program supplied by the hard drive manufacturer, which will wipe out all data on the drive.

- If a hard drive is truly physically damaged, it cannot be fixed. Physical problems manifest themselves in two ways: either the drive works properly but makes a lot of noise, or the drive seems to disappear. If you hear a continuous high-pitched squeal; a series of clacks, a short pause, and then another series of clacks; or a continuous grinding or rumbling, your hard drive is about to die. Back up your critical data and replace the drive. If the drive that contains your operating system disappears, the system locks up or you get the error message "No Boot Device Present"

when you try to reboot. If the problem is with a second drive, it simply stops showing up in My Computer/Computer.

- If your drive makes noise or disappears, first run the System Setup program to see if autodetect sees the drive. If it does, the drive doesn't have a physical problem. If autodetect fails, shut down the system and remove the ribbon cable, but leave the power cable attached. Restart the system and listen to the drive. If the drive spins up, the drive is getting good power, which usually means the drive is good. Next, check for an unplugged power cord or incorrectly set jumpers. If the drive doesn't spin up, try another power connector. If it still doesn't spin up and you've triple-checked the jumpers and ribbon cable, you have a problem with the onboard electronics and the drive is dead.

■ Key Terms

active partition *(368)*
autodetect *(366)*
basic disk *(367)*
boot sector *(368)*
CHKDSK *(405)*
cluster *(376)*
data structure *(375)*
defragment *(407)*
Disk Cleanup *(408)*
Disk Management *(373)*
disk quotas *(383)*
dual-boot *(369)*
dynamic disk *(371)*
encrypting file system (EFS) *(382)*
Error-checking *(406)*
error correction code (ECC) *(411)*
extended partition *(368)*
EXPAND *(411)*
FAT32 *(380)*
FDISK *(373)*
file allocation table (FAT) *(375)*
file allocation unit *(376)*

file system *(367)*
formatting *(367)*
fragmentation *(378)*
high-level formatting *(375)*
logical drive *(368)*
master boot record (MBR) *(368)*
master file table (MFT) *(381)*
mirrored volume *(372)*
mount point *(403)*
multiboot *(369)*
New Technology File System (NTFS) *(381)*
operating system (OS) *(367)*
partition *(367)*
partition table *(368)*
partitioning *(367)*
primary partition *(368)*
RAID 5 volume *(372)*
simple volume *(372)*
spanned volume *(371)*
stripe set *(402)*
volume *(367)*
volume boot sector *(369)*

Key Term Quiz

Use the Key Terms list to complete the sentences that follow. Not all terms will be used.

1. The MBR checks the partition table to find the _____ or bootable partition.

2. If a file is not stored in contiguous clusters, you can improve hard drive performance by using the _____ tool.

3. Instead of using a FAT, NTFS uses a(n) _____ with a backup copy placed in the middle of the disk for better security.

4. If you are installing Windows 2000/XP or Windows Vista/7, the best file system to choose is _____.

5. The Windows tool that attempts to fix invalid filenames, erases lost clusters, and seals off bad clusters is called _____ (or *CHKDSK*).

6. A great way to verify that a drive is installed correctly is to use _____.

7. If an XP or earlier operating system file has become corrupted or is missing, you can replace it by using _____ to extract a specific file from a CAB file.

8. Only a single _____ may be set to active on one drive.

9. The _____ utility is useful for purging your system of unnecessary temporary files.

10. A(n) _____ requires exactly two volumes and is extremely fault tolerant.

Multiple-Choice Quiz

1. Which is the most complete list of file systems Windows 2000/XP and Vista/7 can use?

    A. FAT16, FAT32, NTFS

    B. FAT16, FAT32, FAT64, NTFS

    C. FAT16, FAT32

    D. FAT16, NTFS

2. The Disk Cleanup utility removes which types of unneeded files?

    A. Temporary Internet files

    B. Temporary files that remain when an application is closed

    C. Programs no longer in use

    D. Both A and B

3. Which of the following correctly identifies the four possible entries in a file allocation table?

    A. Filename, date, time, size

    B. Number of the starting cluster, number of the ending cluster, number of used clusters, number of available clusters

    C. An end-of-file marker, a bad-sector marker, code indicating the cluster is available, the number of the cluster where the next part of the file is stored

    D. Filename, folder location, starting cluster number, ending cluster number

4. You receive an "Invalid media" error when trying to access a hard drive. What is the most likely cause of the error?

    A. The drive has not been partitioned.

    B. The drive has not been set to active.

    C. The drive has not been formatted.

    D. The drive has died.

5. Which of the following is an advantage of partitioning a hard drive into more than one partition?

    A. It enables a single hard drive to store more than one operating system.

    B. It protects against boot sector viruses.

    C. It uses less power.

    D. It allows for dynamic disk RAID 5.

6. What graphical program does Microsoft include with Windows 2000/XP and Windows Vista/7 to partition and format a drive?

   A. Format

   B. Disk Management console

   C. Disk Administrator console

   D. System Commander

7. What does NTFS use to provide security for individual files and folders?

   A. Dynamic disks

   B. ECC

   C. Access control list

   D. MFT

8. Which of the following statements is true about extended partitions?

   A. They are optional.

   B. They are assigned drive letters when they are created.

   C. They may be set to active.

   D. Each drive must have at least one extended partition.

9. Adam wants to create a new simple volume in some unallocated space on his hard drive, but when he right-clicks the space in Disk Management he sees only an option to create a new partition. What is the problem?

   A. The drive has developed bad sectors.

   B. The drive is a basic disk and not a dynamic disk.

   C. The drive has less than 32 GB of unallocated space.

   D. The drive is jumpered as a slave.

10. Jaime wishes to check her hard drive for errors. What tool should she use?

   A. FDISK

   B. Format

   C. Disk Management

   D. Error-checking

11. To make your files unreadable by others, what should you use?

   A. Clustering

   B. Compression

   C. Disk quotas

   D. Encryption

12. Which of the following utilities should you run once a month to maintain the speed of your PC?

   A. Disk Defragmenter

   B. FDISK

   C. Disk Management

   D. System Commander

13. Which two terms identify a bootable partition?

   A. Master, FAT

   B. Slave, FAT

   C. Primary, Active

   D. Primary, NTFS

14. For what purpose can you use disk quotas?

   A. Limit users to a specific drive.

   B. Extend the capacity of a volume.

   C. Manage dual-boot environments.

   D. Limit users' space on a drive.

15. What is the capacity of a single sector?

   A. 256 bytes

   B. 512 bits

   C. 512 bytes

   D. 4 kilobytes

■ Essay Quiz

1. Your new boss is pretty old-school, having cut his teeth on Windows 3.11 and Windows 95. Accordingly, you discover that all of the Windows XP computers in the office use only FAT32 for their hard drives. Write a two- to three-paragraph memo that (gently) extols the virtues and benefits of NTFS over FAT32.

2. You've been tasked by your supervisor to teach basic hard drive partitioning to a couple of new hires. Write a short essay describing the difference between simple volumes, spanned volumes, and striped volumes. What's better? When would you use one and not the other?

3. One of your employees doesn't quite get it when it comes to computers and keeps complaining that his hard drive is stopped up, by which he most likely means "full." He installed a second hard drive by using some steps he found on the Internet, but he claims it doesn't work. On closer examination, you determine that the drive shows up in CMOS but not in Windows—he didn't partition or format the drive! Write a short essay describing partitioning and formatting, including the tools used to accomplish this task on a second hard drive.

4. Your office has a PC shared by four people to do intensive graphics work. The hard drive has about 400 GB of free space. Write a memo on how you could use disk quotas to make certain that each user takes no more than 25 percent of the free space.

5. Your office has several computers with three 20-GB drives in them in addition to the C: drive. Write a short essay that describes how you could use spanning and mount points to make the extra drives more easily usable for your users.

Lab Projects

• Lab Project 12.1

Grab a test system with multiple drives and experiment with the partitioning tools in Windows Disk Management. Create various partition combinations, such as all primary or all extended with logical drives. Change basic disks into dynamic disks and create volumes that span multiple drives. Add to them. You get the idea—experiment and have fun!

• Lab Project 12.2

Partitioning gets all the glory and exposure in tech classes because, frankly, it's cool to be able to do some of the things possible with the Disk Management console. But the experienced tech does not forget about the other half of drive preparation: formatting. Windows offers you at least two different file systems. In this lab, you'll put them through their paces.

In at least one OS, partition a drive with two equal partitions and format one as FAT32 and the other as NTFS. Then get a couple of monster files (larger than 50 MB) and move them to those partitions. Did you notice any difference in transfer speed? Examine the drives in My Computer. Do they show the same amount of used space?

Removable Media

In this chapter, you will learn how to

- **Explain and install floppy disk drives**
- **Demonstrate the variations among flash drives and other tiny drives**
- **Identify and install optical-media technology**
- **Troubleshoot removable media**

Removable media refers to any type of mass storage device that you may use in one system and then physically remove from that system and use in another. Removable media has been a part of the personal PC since its first introduction back in 1980. Granted, back then the only removable media available were floppy disks, but being able to move programs and data easily from one machine to another was quickly established as one of the strongest points of the personal computer. Over time, higher-capacity removable media technologies were introduced. Some technologies—CDs, DVDs, Blu-ray Discs, and thumb drives, for example—have become very common. Other technologies (which you may or may not have heard of), such as Iomega Zip drives or HD DVDs, were popular for a time but faded away or were discontinued. The history of PCs has also left a trash heap of removable media technologies that were trumpeted in with fanfare and a lot of money but never really saw any adoption.

Today's highly internetworked computers have reduced the need for removable media as a method of sharing programs and data, but removable media have so many other uses that this hasn't slowed things down a bit. Removable media is the perfect tool for software distribution, data archiving, and system backup. Figure 13.1 shows my software toolbox. As a PC technician, you'll not only need to install, maintain, and troubleshoot removable media on systems for users, but also find yourself turning to removable media as a way to store and run software tools to perform all types of PC support (remember the live CDs in Chapter 12?).

This chapter covers the most common types of removable media used today. For the sake of organization, all removable media are broken down into these groups:

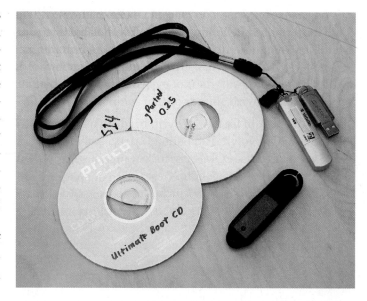

• **Figure 13.1**   Author's toolbox

- **Floppy drives**   The traditional floppy drive

- **Flash memory**   From USB thumb drives to flash memory cards

- **Optical discs**   Any shiny disc technology from CD-ROMs and DVDs to Blu-ray Discs

- **External drives**   Any hard drive or optical drive that connects to a PC via an external cable

If you go by the earlier description of removable memory, two other technologies, PC Cards and tape backups, also fit as removable media. PC Cards are a laptop-centric technology and are covered in Chapter 21, "Portable Computing," whereas tape backups are part of the big world of backups and are covered in Chapter 17, "Maintaining and Troubleshooting Windows."

Historical/Conceptual

Floppy Drives

Good old floppies! These little disks, storing a whopping 1.44 MB of data per disk, have been part of PCs from the beginning. For decades, the PC industry made one attempt after another to replace the floppy with some higher-capacity removable media, only to keep falling back to the floppy disk. Floppy drive technology was well entrenched: motherboard makers found floppies easy to add, all BIOS supported them, and they were almost always the first boot device, so techs loved floppies when they helped boot a system.

Only in the past few years have we finally seen systems without floppy drives due to an industry push called *legacy-free computing*: an initiative forwarded by Microsoft and Intel back in 2001 to rid computers of old

technologies such as PS/2 ports, serial ports, parallel ports—and floppy drives (interesting how long it took to start being adopted by PC makers). Thus, the venerable floppy drive will probably soon disappear from PCs. Until then, the floppy drive, that artifact from the Dark Ages of the PC world, will continue to be a viable technology you must know.

Floppy Drive Basics

When you insert a **floppy disk** into a **floppy drive**, the protective slide on the disk opens, revealing the magnetic media inside the plastic casing. A motor-driven spindle snaps into the center of the drive to make it spin. A set of read/write heads then moves back and forth across the disk, reading or writing tracks on the disk as needed. The current floppy disks are 3½ inches wide and store 1.44 MB (Figure 13.2). You use a **3½-inch floppy drive** to access the contents of the disk.

Whenever your system accesses a floppy disk in its floppy drive, a read/write LED on the outside front of the drive flashes on. You should not try to remove the floppy disk from the drive when this light is lit! That light means that the read/write heads are accessing the floppy drive, so pulling the disk out while the light is on can damage the floppy disk. When the light is off, you can push in the small release button on the front of the drive to eject the floppy disk.

• **Figure 13.2**   Floppy drive and floppy disk

The term "floppy" comes from the fact that early floppy disks were actually floppy. You could easily bend one. Newer floppy disks came in much more robust, rigid plastic casings, but the term has stuck—we still call them floppies.

The first PC floppy drives used a 5¼-inch floppy drive format (Figure 13.3). The 5¼-inch measurement actually described the drive, but most users also called the disks for those drives 5¼-inch disks. In the 1970s and early 1980s, before PCs became predominant, you would occasionally see an 8-inch format floppy drive in computers. Fortunately, these never saw any noticeable use in PCs. If you happen to run into an 8-inch drive or disk, keep it! Collectors of old computers pay big money for these old drives.

Around 1986, the 3½-inch drives appeared and, within a few years, came to dominate the floppy world completely. Today, both 3½-inch and 5¼-inch floppy drives have mostly been replaced by CD and DVD burners and USB

• **Figure 13.3**   A 5¼-inch floppy drive and disk

flash drives. If you are really interested, however, you can still purchase these drives on the Internet or special-order a custom-built system complete with floppy drives pre-installed.

Essentials

Installing Floppy Drives

All Windows systems reserve the drive letters A: and B: for floppy drives. You cannot name them anything other than A: or B:, but you can configure a floppy to get either drive letter. However, convention dictates that if you have only one floppy drive, you should call it A:. The second floppy drive is then called B:.

Floppy drives connect to the computer via a **34-pin ribbon cable**. If the cable supports two floppy drives, it has a seven-wire twist in the middle to differentiate electronically between the A: and B: drives. Given that the majority of users do not want two floppy drives, many system makers have dropped the twist and saved a couple of pennies on a simpler cable (Figure 13.4).

By default, almost all PCs (well, the ones that still support floppy drives) first try to boot to a floppy before any other boot device, looking for an operating system. This process enables technicians to insert a floppy disk into a sick computer to run programs when the hard drives fail. It also means hackers can insert bootable floppy disks into servers and do bad things. You do have a choice, however, because most systems have special CMOS settings with which you can change this default boot order to something other than the default drive A: and then C:; I'll show you how in a minute.

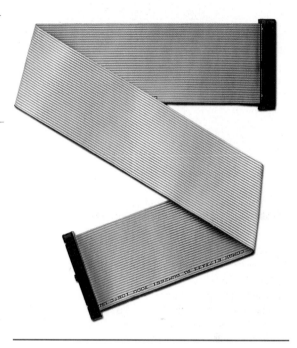

• **Figure 13.4**   Floppy cable for only one drive

Inserting Ribbon Cables

Look at the floppy cable in Figure 13.4. Notice the connector on the left side. This connector, identical to the other connector on the same cable, plugs into the floppy controller on the motherboard, as shown in Figure 13.5. Notice how clearly the motherboard has **pin 1** marked in Figure 13.5. Not all motherboards are so clear. Make sure to orient the cable so that the colored stripe on the side of the cable is aligned with pin 1.

Here are a few tips on cable orientation. (By the way, these rules work for all ribbon cables, not just floppy cables.) Ribbon cable connectors usually have a distinct orientation notch in the middle. If your cable connector has an orientation notch and the controller socket has a slot in which the orientation notch fits, your job is easy (Figure 13.6).

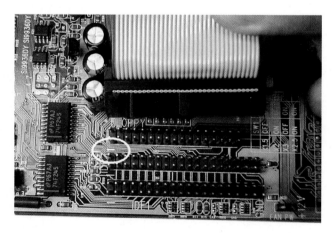

• **Figure 13.5**   Plugging a floppy cable into a controller, pin 1 labeled at left

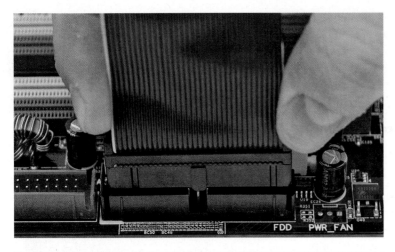

• **Figure 13.6** Floppy controller with notch

Unfortunately, not all connectors use the orientation notch. Try looking in the motherboard book. All motherboard books provide a graphic of the motherboard showing the proper orientation position. Look at other ribbon cables on the motherboard. In almost all motherboards, all plugs orient the same way. Last of all, just guess! You will not destroy anything by inserting the cable backward. When you boot up, the floppy drive will not work. This is not a big deal; turn off the system and try again.

After you insert the floppy ribbon cable into the floppy controller, you need to insert the ribbon cable into the floppy drive. Watch out here! You still need to orient the cable by pin 1—all the rules of ribbon cable insertion apply here, too. Before you plug in the floppy ribbon cable to the floppy drive, you need to know which connector on the cable to use; it makes a big difference. The specific connector that you insert into the floppy drive determines its drive letter.

If the floppy drive is installed on the end connector, it becomes the A: drive; if the drive is installed on the middle connector, it is the B: drive (Figure 13.7). If you're installing only one floppy, make sure you install it in the A: drive position.

In the past, the CompTIA A+ certification exams have been very focused on the pins on cables! Know the number (34) and orientation (pin 1 to pin 1) for the pins on the floppy drive ribbon cable.

Drive A   Drive B   To Controller

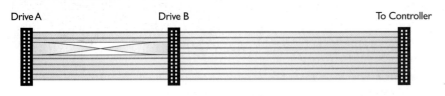

• **Figure 13.7** Cable placement determines the drive letter.

Power

Floppy drives need electricity to work, just like every other device in the PC. Modern 3½-inch floppy drives use the small **mini power connector**. Be careful! Inserting a mini connector incorrectly is easy, and if you install it incorrectly, you'll destroy the floppy drive and make what we call "The Nasty Smell." Look at Figure 13.8, a bottom view of a properly installed mini connector—note the chamfers (beveled edges) that show correct orientation. The problem lies in the plastic used to make the

• **Figure 13.8** Properly installed mini connector

connector. The plastic connector bends easily, so even the least brawny techs can put the plug in a mini backward or hit only three of the four pins.

Great! You have installed a floppy drive! Once you have physically installed the floppy drive, it's time to go into CMOS.

CMOS

After the floppy drive is installed, you need to configure the CMOS settings, which must correspond to the capacities of the drives. Look in your CMOS for a menu called "Standard CMOS Features" (or something similar to that) to see your floppy settings. Most CMOS setups configure the A: drive by default as a 3½-inch, 1.44 MB drive, so in most cases the floppy is already configured. Simply double-check the setting in CMOS; if it's okay, exit without changing anything. Figure 13.9 shows a typical CMOS setting for a single floppy drive. On the rare occasion that you require a setting other than the typical 3½-inch, 1.44-MB A: drive, simply select the drive (A: or B:) and enter the correct capacity.

Disabling the Boot Up Floppy Seek option tells the PC not to check the floppy disk during the POST, which isn't very handy except for slightly speeding up the boot process (Figure 13.10).

Many CMOS setup utilities have an option called Floppy 3 Mode Support. Refer to Figure 13.9 to see an example of a CMOS with this option. A Mode 3 floppy is a special 1.2-MB format used outside the United States, primarily in Japan. Unless you live in Japan and use Mode 3 floppy disks, ignore this option.

 Installing *any* power connector incorrectly will destroy whatever device is unfortunate enough to be so abused. However, with the exception of minis, most power connectors are constructed so that it's almost impossible to do so unintentionally.

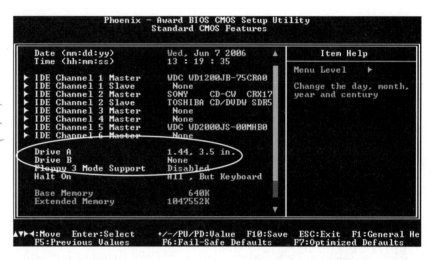

• **Figure 13.9**   CMOS setting for one standard floppy drive

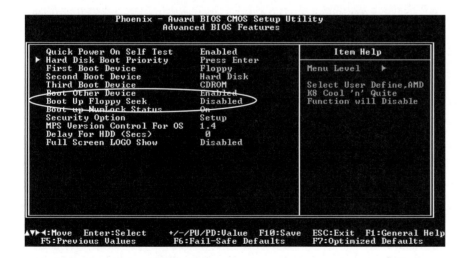

• **Figure 13.10**   CMOS Boot Up Floppy Seek option

■ Flash Memory

Flash memory, the same flash memory that replaced CMOS technology for your system BIOS, found another home in PCs in the form of removable mass storage devices. Flash memory comes in two families: USB thumb drives and memory cards. USB thumb drives are flash devices that contain a standard USB connection. "Memory card" is a generic term for a number of tiny cards that are used in cameras, PDAs, and other devices. Both of these families can manifest themselves as drives in Windows, but they usually perform different jobs. USB thumb drives have replaced virtually all other rewritable removable media as the way people transfer files or keep copies of important programs. My thumb drives (yes, I have two on me at all times) keep backups of my current work, important photos, and a stack of utilities I need to fix computers. Memory cards are very small and make a great way to store data on small devices and then transfer that data to your PC.

USB Thumb Drives

Moving data between computers is always a pain, and even more so since digital photography and multimedia storage have littered hard drives with huge files that won't fit on a single floppy disk. The latest entry into the floppy disk replacement sweepstakes is a winner: the USB flash memory drive, also known as the **USB thumb drive**, jump drive, or flash drive. These tiny new drives are incredibly popular (Figure 13.11). For a low price in US$, you can get an 8-GB thumb drive that holds as much data as 5600 standard 3½-inch floppy disks.

The smallest thumb drives are slightly larger than an adult thumbnail; others are larger and more rounded. The drives are hot-swappable in Windows 2000/XP/Vista. You simply plug one into any USB port and it appears as a removable storage device in My Computer or Computer. After you plug the drive into a USB port, you can copy or move data to or from your hard disk and then unplug the unit and take it with you. You can read, write, and delete files directly from the drive.

• **Figure 13.11**   USB thumb drives

Because these are USB devices, they don't need an external power source. The nonvolatile flash memory is solid-state, so it's shock resistant and is supposed to retain data safely for a decade. One big improvement over floppies is cross-platform compatibility—you can transfer files among Macintosh, Windows, and Linux operating systems.

The latest systems enable you to boot to a thumb drive. With a bootable thumb drive you can replace bootable floppies, CDs, and DVDs with fast flash drives. Making a thumb drive bootable is a bit of a challenge, so most of the classic bootable-utility CD makers have created USB versions that seek out your thumb drive and add an operating system with the utilities you wish to use. Most of these are simply versions of Linux-based live CDs. At this point there's no single magic USB thumb drive to recommend because bootable USB drives are still quite new, and updated versions come out almost daily. If you just have to try this new technology now, check out

the GParted LiveUSB at http://gparted.sourceforge.net and click on the Live CD/USB/PXE link.

Flash Cards

Flash cards are the way people store data on small appliances. Every digital camera, virtually every PDA, and many cell phones come with slots for some type of memory card. Memory cards come in a number of incompatible formats, so let's start by making sure you know the more common ones.

CompactFlash

CompactFlash (CF) is the oldest, most complex, and physically largest of all removable flash media cards (Figure 13.12). Roughly one inch wide, CF cards use a simplified PCMCIA bus (see Chapter 21, "Portable Computing," for details) for interconnection. CF cards come in two sizes: CF I (3.3 mm thick) and CF II (5 mm thick). CF II cards are too thick to fit into CF I slots.

Clever manufacturers have repurposed the CF form factor to create the microdrive (Figure 13.13). **Microdrives** are true hard drives, using platters and read/write heads that fit into the tiny CF form factor. Microdrives are slower and use more power than flash drives and, when they were first introduced, cost much less than an equivalent CF flash card. From the user's standpoint, CF flash cards and microdrives look and act exactly the same way, although the greater power consumption of microdrives makes them incompatible with some devices. These days, microdrives have been surpassed in size, speed, and cost by their flash cousins and have become more difficult to find.

SmartMedia

SmartMedia came out as a competitor to CF cards and for a few years was quite popular in digital cameras (Figure 13.14). The introduction of SD media reduced SmartMedia's popularity, and no new devices use this media.

Secure Digital

Secure Digital (SD) cards are arguably the most common flash media format today. About the size of a small postage stamp, you'll see SD cards in just about any type of device that uses flash media. SD comes in two types: the original SD and SDIO. SD cards store only data. The more advanced SDIO (the "IO" denoting input/output rather than storage) cards also support devices such as GPSs and cameras. If you want to use an SDIO device, you must have an SDIO slot. There is no way to tell an SD slot from an SDIO slot, so read the technical specs for your device!

SD cards also come in three tiny forms called *SD*, *Mini Secure Digital (MiniSD)*, and *Micro Secure Digital (MicroSD)* cards. They're extremely popular in cellular phones that use flash memory, but see little use in other devices. Figure 13.15 shows the three forms of SD cards.

SD cards come in three storage capacities. *Standard SD* cards store from 4 MB to 4 GB, *Secure Digital High Capacity (SDHC)* cards store 4 GB to 32 GB, and *Secure Digital Extended Capacity (SDXC)* cards have a storage capacity of 32 GB to 2 TB. Early SD card readers and devices cannot read the SDHC or SDXC cards, though the latter standards provide backward compatibility.

• **Figure 13.12**   CF card

• **Figure 13.13**   Microdrive

• **Figure 13.14**   SmartMedia

SD cards developed out of an older, slower flash memory technology called *MultiMediaCard* (*MMC*). If you happen to have an MMC card lying around, you can use it in almost any SD card slot. SD cards are a little thicker than MMC cards, though, so the reverse is not true.

• **Figure 13.15**   SD, MiniSD, and MicroSD cards

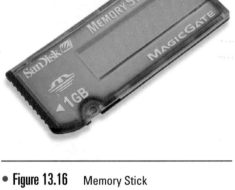

• **Figure 13.16**   Memory Stick

• **Figure 13.17**   xD card

Memory Stick

Sony always likes to use proprietary formats, and their **Memory Stick** flash memory is no exception. If you own something from Sony and it uses flash memory, you'll need a Memory Stick (Figure 13.16). There are several Memory Stick formats, including Standard, Pro, Duo, Pro Duo, and Micro.

xD Picture Card

The proprietary **Extreme Digital (xD) Picture Cards** (Figure 13.17) are about half the size of an SD card. They're almost exclusively used in Olympus and Fujifilm digital cameras, although Olympus (the developer of the xD technology) produces a USB housing so you can use an xD Picture Card like any other USB flash memory drive. The xD Picture Cards come in three flavors: original, Standard (Type M), and Hi-Speed (Type H). The Standard cards are slower than the original cards but offer greater storage capacity. The Hi-Speed cards are two to three times faster than the others and enable you to capture full-motion video—assuming the camera has that capability, naturally!

Card Readers

Whatever type of flash memory you use, your PC must have a **card reader** to access the data on the card directly. A number of inexpensive USB card readers are available today (Figure 13.18), and some PCs, especially those

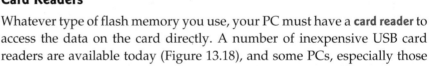

• **Figure 13.18**   USB card reader

tuned to home theater use, often come with built-in readers—handy to have when someone pulls out an SD card and says "Let's look at the pictures I just took!" Of course, if the person just happened to bring her camera and the usually proprietary USB cable along, you could connect the camera to the PC and pull pictures in that way. Just make sure you have spare batteries, too! Wouldn't a card reader be a more elegant solution?

Whichever type of flash memory you have, understand that it acts exactly like a hard drive. If you wish, you can format a memory card as well as copy, paste, and rename files.

■ Optical Drives

CD, DVD, and Blu-ray Disc drives and discs come in a variety of flavors and formats, enabling you to back up data, record music, master home videos, and much, much more. **Optical disc** is the generic term for all those different types of shiny, 12-centimeter-wide discs that, if you're a slob like me, collect around your computer like pizza boxes. The drives that support them are called **optical drives**. This section examines optical discs, finishing with the details about installing optical drives.

CD stands for **compact disc**, a medium that was originally designed more than 20 years ago as a replacement for vinyl records. The CD now reigns as the primary method of long-term storage for sound and data. The **digital versatile disc (DVD)** first eliminated VHS cassette tapes from the commercial home movie market, and has also grown into a contender for backups and high-capacity storage. **Blu-ray Disc (BD)** eliminated the High-Definition DVD (HD DVD) format and may very well supersede DVD in the future as the high-definition video and data storage war wages on.

Going beyond those big three household names, the term optical disc refers to technologies such as CD-ROM, CD-R, CD-RW, DVD, DVD+RW, HD DVD, BD-R, BD-RE, and so on. Each of these technologies will be discussed in detail in this chapter—for now, understand that although optical disc describes a variety of exciting formats, they all basically boil down to the same physical object: that little shiny disc.

CD-Media

The best way to understand the world of optical discs is to sort out the many types of technologies available, starting with the first: the compact disc. All you're about to read is relevant and fair game for the CompTIA A+ certification exams. Begin by looking at how CDs work.

How CDs Work

CDs—the discs that you buy in music stores or may find in software boxes—store data via microscopic pits. CD producers use a power laser to burn these pits into a glass master CD. Once the CD producer creates a master, expensive machines create plastic copies, using a very high-tolerance injection molding process. The copies are coated with a reflective metallic covering and then finished with lacquer for protection. CDs store data on only one side of the disc—we don't flip a CD as we used to flip vinyl records. Did I

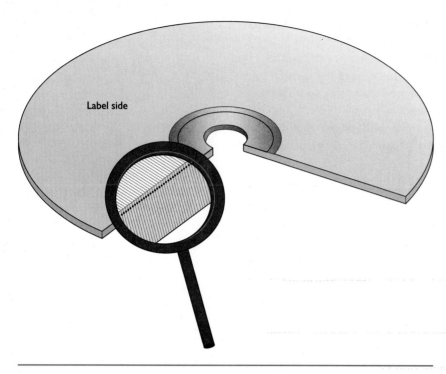

Label side

• **Figure 13.19**   Location of the data

just sound really old? The data on a CD is near the top of the CD, where the label is located (see Figure 13.19).

Many people believe that scratching a CD on the bottom makes it unreadable. This is untrue. If you scratch a CD on the bottom (the shiny side), just polish out the scratches—assuming that they aren't too deep—and reread the CD. A number of companies sell inexpensive CD-polishing kits. It's the scratches on the *top* of the disc that wreak havoc on CDs. Avoid writing on the top with anything other than a soft-tipped pen, and certainly don't scratch the top!

CD readers (such as the one in your car or the one in your PC) use a laser and mirrors to read the data from the CD. The metallic covering of the CD makes a highly reflective surface; the pits create interruptions in that surface, while the non-pitted spots, called *lands*, leave it intact. The laser picks up on the reflected pattern that the pits and lands create, and the CD drive converts this pattern into binary ones and zeros. Because the pits are so densely packed on the CD, a vast amount of data can be stored: a standard CD holds up to 5.2 billion bits, or 650 million bytes, of data.

CD Formats

The first CDs were designed for playing music and organized the music in a special format called **CD-Digital Audio (CDDA)**, which we usually just call CD-audio. CD-audio divides the CD's data into variable-length tracks; on

 Try This!

Repairing a CD-ROM

To revive scratched CD-ROMs and other CD-media in the comfort of your home or office, get a CD polishing kit and familiarize yourself with its operation. Try this:

1. Obtain a CD-polishing kit from your local computer store, or find one online.

2. Take a CD-ROM *that you don't mind potentially ruining* and make light scratches on the bottom of the disc. Be sure not to scratch too heavily! Just try to replicate the everyday wear and tear that you've probably seen on CD-ROMs before. If you have a disc that's already lightly scratched, that's even better.

3. Use the CD-polishing kit, following the provided instructions exactly.

music CDs, each song gets one track. CD-audio is an excellent way to store music, but it lacks any error checking, file support, or directory structure, making it a terrible way to store data. For this reason, The Powers That Be created a special method for storing data on a CD, called—are you ready—**CD-ROM**. The CD-ROM format divides the CD into fixed sectors, each holding 2353 bytes.

Most CD-ROM drives also support a number of older, less well-known formats. You may never come across these formats—CD Text, CD+G, and so forth—although you may see them listed among compatible formats on the packaging for a new drive or with a program like Nero InfoTool (Figure 13.20). Don't let these oddball formats throw you—with few exceptions, they've pretty much fallen by the wayside. All CD-ROM drives read all of these formats, assuming that the system is loaded with the proper software.

The CD-ROM format is something like a partition in the hard drive world. CD-ROM may define the sectors (and some other information), but it doesn't enable a CD-ROM disc to act like a hard drive, with a file structure, directories, and such. To make a CD-ROM act like a hard drive, there's another layer of formatting that defines the file system used on the drive.

At first glance you might think "Why don't CD-ROMs just use a FAT or an NTFS format like hard drives?" Well, first of all, they could. There's no law of physics that prevented the CD-ROM world from adopting any file system. The problem is that the CD makers did not want CD-ROM to be tied to Microsoft's or Apple's or anyone else's file format. In addition, they wanted non-PC devices to read CDs, so they invented their own file system just for CD-ROMs called **ISO-9660**. This format is sometimes referred by the more generic term, CD File System (CDFS). The vast majority of data CD-ROMs today use this format.

Over the years, extensions of the ISO-9660 have addressed certain limitations, such as the characters used in file and directory names, filename length, and directory depth. It's important to know these ISO-9660 extensions:

- **Joliet**   Microsoft's extension of the ISO-9660. Macintosh and Linux also support Joliet-formatted discs.

- **Rock Ridge**   An open standard to provide UNIX file system support for discs; rarely used outside of UNIX systems.

- **El Torito**   Added support to enable bootable CD-media. All bootable CDs use the El Torito standard, which is supported by the BIOS on all modern PCs.

- **Apple Extensions**   Apple's added support for their HFS file system. Windows systems cannot read these CDs without third-party tools.

It is important to appreciate that all of these file systems are extensions, not replacements for ISO-9660. That means a single CD/DVD can have both regular ISO-9660 information and an extension. For example, it's very common to have a CD-media that is ISO-9660 and Joliet. If you place the CD into a device that cannot read Joliet, it will still be able to read the ISO-9660 information.

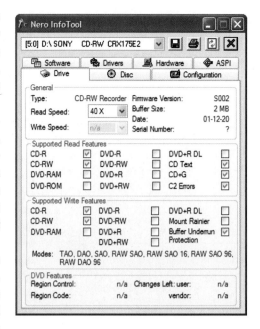

• **Figure 13.20**   Crazy CD formats

CD-ROM Speeds

The first CD-ROM drives processed data at roughly 150,000 bytes per second (150 KBps), copying the speed from the original CD-audio format. Although this speed is excellent for listening to music, the CD-ROM industry quickly recognized that installing programs or transferring files from a CD-ROM at 150 KBps was the electronic equivalent of watching paint dry. Since the day the first CD-ROM drives for PCs hit the market, there has been a desire to speed them up to increase their data throughput. Each increase in speed is measured in multiples of the original 150 KBps drives and given an × to show speed relative to the first (1×) drives. Here's a list of the common CD-ROM speeds, including most of the early speeds that are no longer produced:

1× 150 KBps	10× 1500 KBps	40× 6000 KBps
2× 300 KBps	12× 1800 KBps	48× 7200 KBps
3× 450 KBps	16× 2400 KBps	52× 7800 KBps
4× 600 KBps	24× 3600 KBps	60× 9000 KBps
6× 900 KBps	32× 4800 KBps	72× 10800 KBps
8× 1200 KBps	36× 5400 KBps	

Keep in mind that these are maximum speeds that are rarely met in real-life operation. You can, however, count on a 32× drive to read data faster than an 8× drive. As multipliers continue to increase, so many other factors come into play that telling the difference between a 48× and a 52× drive, for example, becomes difficult. High-speed CD-ROM drives are so inexpensive, however, that most folks buy the fastest drive possible—at least installations go faster!

CD-R

Making CD-ROMs requires specialized, expensive equipment and substantial expertise, so a relatively small number of CD-ROM production companies do it. Yet, since the day the first CD-ROMs came to market, demand has been terrific for a way that ordinary PC users could make their own CDs. The CD industry made a number of attempts to create a technology that would let users record, or *burn*, their own CDs.

In the mid-1990s, the CD industry introduced the **CD-recordable (CD-R)** standard, which enables affordable CD-R drives, often referred to as *CD burners*, to add data to special CD-R discs. Any CD-ROM drive can then read the data stored on the CD-R, and all CD-R drives can read regular CD-ROMs. CD-R discs come in two varieties: a 74-minute disc that holds approximately 650 MB, and an 80-minute variety that holds approximately 700 MB (see Figure 13.21). A CD-R burner must be specifically designed to support the longer 80-minute CD-R format, but most drives you'll encounter can do this.

CD-R discs function similarly to regular CD-ROMs, although the chemicals used to make them produce a brightly colored recording side on almost all CD-R discs. CD-ROM discs, in contrast, have a silver recording side. CD-R technology records data by using special organic dyes embedded into the disc. This dye is what gives the CD-R its distinctive bottom color. CD-R burners have a second burn laser,

• **Figure 13.21**   A CD-R disc, with its capacity clearly labeled

roughly ten times as powerful as the read laser, that heats the organic dye. This causes a change in the reflectivity of the surface, creating the functional equivalent of a CD-ROM's pits.

Once the CD-R drive burns data onto a CD-R, the data cannot be erased or changed short of destroying the disc itself. Early CD-R drives required that the entire disc be burned in one burn session, wasting any unused part of the CD-R disc. These were called single-session drives. All modern CD-R drives are **multisession drives** so you can go back and burn additional data onto the CD-R disc until the disc is full. Multisession drives also have the capability to "close" a partially filled CD-R so that no more data can be burned onto that disc.

CD-R drives have two speeds that matter: the record speed and the read speed, both expressed as multiples of the 150-KBps speed of the original CD-ROM drives. The record speed, which is listed first, is always equal to or slower than the read speed. For example, a CD-R drive with a specification of 8×24× would burn at 8× and read at 24×.

CD-RW

For all their usefulness, CD-R drives have disappeared from the market. Notice that I didn't say CD-R *discs* have disappeared; more CD-R discs are burned now than ever before. Just as CD-R drives could both burn CD-R discs and read CD-ROMs, a newer type of drive called **CD-rewritable (CD-RW)** took over the burning market from CD-R drives. Although this drive has its own type of CD-RW discs, it also can burn to CD-R discs, which are much cheaper.

CD-RW technology enables you not only to burn a disc, but to *burn over* existing data on a CD-RW disc. This is not something you need for every disc—for example, I create CD-R archives of my completed books to store the text and graphics for posterity—this is data I want to access later but do not need to modify. While I'm working on content for the CD that accompanies this book, however, I may decide to delete an item; I couldn't do that with a CD-R. The CD-RW format, on the other hand, essentially takes CD-media to the functional equivalent of a 650-MB floppy disk. Once again, CD-RW discs look exactly like CD-ROM discs with the exception of a colored bottom side. Figure 13.22 shows all three formats.

A CD-RW drive works by using a laser to heat an amorphous (noncrystalline) substance that, when cooled, slowly becomes crystalline. The crystalline areas are reflective, whereas the amorphous areas are not. Because both CD-R and CD-RW drives require a powerful laser, making a drive that could burn CD-Rs and CD-RWs was a simple process, and plain CD-R drives disappeared almost overnight. Why buy a CD-R drive when a comparably priced CD-RW drive could burn both CD-R and CD-RW discs?

CD-RW drive specs have three multiplier values. The first shows the CD-R write speed, the second shows the CD-RW rewrite speed, and the third shows the read speed. Write, rewrite, and read speeds vary tremendously among

> Some music CD players can't handle CD-R discs.

> You can rewrite CD-RW discs a limited number of times. The number varies according to the source, but expect a maximum life of about 1000 rewrites, although in real life you'll get considerably fewer.

• **Figure 13.22**   CD-ROM, CD-R, and CD-RW discs

the various brands of CD-RW drives; here are just a few representative samples: 8×4×32×, 12×10×32×, and 48×24×48×.

One of the goals with the introduction of CD-RWs was the idea of making a CD-RW act like a hard drive so you could simply drag a file onto the CD-RW (or CD-R) and just as easily drag it off again. This goal was difficult for two reasons: first, the different file formats made on-the-fly conversion risky; second, CD-RWs don't store data exactly the same way as hard drives and would quickly wear out if data were copied in the same manner.

Two developments, UDF and packet writing, enable you to treat a CD-RW just like a hard drive—with a few gotchas. The not-so-new kid in town with CD-media file formats is the **universal data format (UDF)**. UDF is a replacement for ISO-9660 and all of its various extensions, resulting in a single file format that any drive and operating system can read. UDF has taken over the DVD world (all movie DVDs use this format) and is poised to also become the CD-media file format in the near future. UDF handles very large files and is excellent for all rewritable CD-media. UDF has been available for quite a while, but until Windows Vista came out, no version of Windows could write to UDF-formatted discs. They could *read* the discs, but if you wanted to *write* to them in Windows you had to use one of a number of third-party UDF tools such as Roxio's DirectCD and Nero's InCD. UDF also supports a feature called Mount Rainier—better known as packet writing—that works with UDF so you can copy individual files back and forth like a hard drive. With UDF and packet writing, rewritable CD-media is as easy to use as a hard drive.

Try This!

Deleting Files from a CD-RW

Windows XP comes with built-in support for CD-Rs and CD-RWs. If you have a CD-RW drive with Windows XP, copy a couple of files onto a CD-RW and burn them to the disc. Now try to delete only one file—you can't! That's because no version of Windows before Vista supports packet writing. Try installing a copy of Roxio's Creator 9 or Nero 2009 and try again on a fresh CD-RW—it works! All third-party UDF tools support packet writing.

I cover more on installation and ATAPI compliance later in this chapter.

Windows and CD-Media

Virtually all optical drives are **ATAPI-compliant**, meaning they plug into the ATA controllers on the motherboard, just like a hard drive, so you don't need to install drivers. You just plug in the drive and, assuming you didn't make any physical installation mistakes, the drive appears in Windows (Figure 13.23).

Windows displays an optical drive in My Computer or Computer with the typical optical drive icon and assigns it a drive letter. If you want to put data on a CD-R disc, however, you need special *burner software* to get that data onto the disc. Windows XP comes with burning support—you just drop a CD-R disc into your CD-RW drive, open the drive in My Computer, drag the files you wish to copy, and click Write to Disc. Also, Windows Media Player versions such as 9, 10, and 11 enable you to create music and data CDs within Windows XP. With Windows Vista, you can burn music and data directly to disc. Just put your CD-R into your CD-RW drive and, if AutoPlay is set to detect blank CDs, the OS presents you with the options to burn an audio CD by using Windows Media Player or to burn files to disc by using Windows. Almost every new CD-RW drive comes with some type of

● **Figure 13.23**   CD-media drive in Windows

burner software as well, so you rarely need to go out and buy your own unless you have a preference for a particular brand. Figure 13.24 shows the opening menu of one that I like, the popular Nero optical disc burning program.

When I buy a new program on CD, the first thing I do is make a backup copy; then I stash the original under lock and key. If I break, melt, or otherwise destroy the backup, I quickly create a new one from the original. I can easily copy the disc, because my system, like many, has both a regular CD-ROM and a CD-RW drive (even though CD-RW drives read CD-ROM discs). I can place a CD in the CD-ROM drive and a CD-R or CD-RW disc in the CD-RW drive. Then I use a disk-copy application to create an exact replica of the CD quickly. CD-RW drives work great for another, bigger type of backup: not the archival "put it on the disc and stash

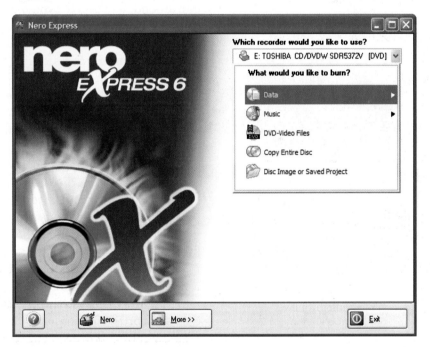

● **Figure 13.24**   Nero optical disc burning program

it in the closet" type of backup but rather the daily/weekly backups that most of us do (or should do!) on our systems. Using CD-R discs for these backups is wasteful; once a disc fills up, you throw it away at the next backup. But with CD-RW, you can use the same set of CD-RW discs time and again to perform backups.

Music CDs

Computers do not hold a monopoly on CD burning. Many companies offer consumer CD burners that work with your stereo system. These come in a wide variety of formats, but they're usually dual-deck player/recorder combinations. These recorders do not use regular CD-R or CD-RW discs. Instead, under U.S. law, these home recorders must use a slightly different disc called a **music CD-R**. Makers of music CDs pay a small royalty for each CD (and add it to your price). You can record *to* a music CD-R or CD-RW, but you cannot record *from* one—the idea being to restrict duplication. If you decide to buy one of these burners, make sure to buy the special music CD-Rs. Music CD-Rs are designed specifically for these types of devices and may not work well in a PC.

DVD-Media

For years, the video industry tried to create an optical-media replacement for videotape. The 12-inch diameter *laserdisc* format originally introduced by Philips gained some ground in the 1980s and 1990s. But the high cost of both the discs and the players, plus various marketing factors, meant there was never a very large laserdisc market. You may still find one of them sitting around, however, or you may know someone who invested in a small collection during the laserdisc's heyday.

The DVD was developed by a large consortium of electronics and entertainment firms during the early 1990s and released as digital *video* discs in 1995. The transformation of DVD to a data storage medium quickly required a name change to digital *versatile* discs. You'll still hear both terms used. The industry also uses the term **DVD-video** to distinguish the movie format from the data formats.

With the exception of the DVD logo stamped on all commercial DVDs (see Figure 13.25), DVDs look exactly like CD-media discs; but that's pretty much where the similarities end. DVD has become the fastest growing media format in history and has completely overtaken VHS as the preferred media for video. Additionally, one variant of DVD called DVD-RAM has enjoyed some success as a mass storage medium.

• **Figure 13.25** Typical DVD-video

The single best word to describe DVD is *capacity*. All previous optical discs stored a maximum of 700 MB of data or 80 minutes of video. The lowest capacity DVD holds 4.37 GB of data, or two hours of standard-definition video. The highest capacity version DVDs store roughly 16 GB of data, or more than eight hours of video! DVD achieves these amazing capacities by using a number of technologies, but three are most important. First, DVD uses smaller pits than CD-media, and packs them much more densely. Second, DVD comes in both *single-sided* (*SS*) and *double-sided* (*DS*) formats. As the name implies, a DS disc holds twice the data of an SS disc, but it also requires you to flip the disc to read the other side. Third, DVDs come in *single-layer* (*SL*) and *dual-layer* (*DL*) formats. DL formats use two pitted layers on each side, each with a slightly different reflectivity index. Table 13.1 shows the common DVD capacities.

Table 13.1	DVD Versions/Capacities	
DVD Version	**Capacity**
DVD-5 (12 cm, SS/SL)	4.37 GB, more than two hours of video
DVD-9 (12 cm, SS/DL)	7.95 GB, about four hours of video
DVD-10 (12 cm, DS/SL)	8.74 GB, about four and a half hours of video
DVD-18 (12 cm, DS/DL)	15.90 GB, more than eight hours of video

DVD-Video

The most beautiful trait of DVD-video lies in its capability to store two hours of video on one side. You drop in a DVD-video and get to watch an entire movie without flipping it over. DVD-video supports TV-style 4:3 aspect-ratio screens as well as 16:9 theater screens, but it is up to the producer to decide which to use. Many DVD-video producers distribute DVD movies on DS media with a 4:3 ratio on one side and 16:9 ratio on the other. DVD-video relies on the **MPEG-2** standard of video and audio compression to reach the magic of two hours of video per side. *Moving Picture Experts Group (MPEG)* is a group of compression standards for both audio and video. The MPEG-2 standard offers resolutions of up to 1280 × 720 at 60 frames per second (fps), with full CD-quality audio (standard DVDs only offer 480 vertical resolution, the same as regular television).

DVD-ROM

DVD-ROM is the DVD equivalent of the standard CD-ROM data format except that it's capable of storing up to almost 16 GB of data. Almost all DVD-ROM drives also fully support DVD-video, as well as most CD-ROM formats. Most DVD drives sold with PCs are DVD-ROM drives.

 Tech Tip

MPEG Standards

Reproducing video and sound on the PC provides interesting challenges for developers. How do you take a motion picture from film, translate it into ones and zeros that the CPU understands, process those bits, and then send high-quality video and sound to the monitor and speakers for the pleasure of the computer user? How much data do you think is required to display even a two-minute clip of a car racing through a city street, in all the minute detail of the shops, people, screeching tires, road debris, and so on? For that matter, how do you store the obviously huge amount of data required to do this?

To handle these chores, the Moving Picture Experts Group (MPEG) has released coding standards such as MPEG-1, MPEG-2, and MPEG-4. Each standard provides a different compression algorithm, which makes the files manageable. The standards also implement various technologies to handle movement, called motion compensation. The details of the standards matter a lot to the folks producing the movies and other video and audio content, but here's the short answer that should suffice for the purposes of a PC tech.

MPEG-1 is the standard on which video and MP3, among other technologies, are based. The most common implementations of this standard provide a resolution of 352 × 240 at 30 fps. This video quality falls just below that of a conventional VHS video.

One very well-known subset of MPEG-1 is better known for audio than video. MPEG-1 Layer 3, better known as MP3 format, dominates the world of audio. MP3 takes an uncompressed audio file and compresses it dramatically, but the algorithm is so tight that the music that comes out of the speakers remains almost completely faithful to the original audio file. To paraphrase a catchphrase from the 1980s—I want my MP3s!

MPEG-2 provides resolutions of 720 × 480 and 1280 × 720 at 60 fps (as well as others), plus CD-quality audio, making it adequate for all major TV standards, even HDTV. MPEG-2 is the standard that covers DVD-ROM technology—it can compress two hours of video into a file no larger than a few gigabytes. Although encoding video into MPEG-2 format requires a computer with some serious firepower, even a modest PC can decompress and play such a video.

The MPEG-4 standard is based on MPEG-1, MPEG-2, and Apple's QuickTime technology. MPEG-4 graphics and video files use what's known as wavelet compression to create files that are more compact than either JPEG or QuickTime files. This superior compression makes MPEG-4 popular for delivering video and images over the Web. MPEG-4 higher-efficiency standards such as advanced video coding are included with MPEG-4 and used for Blu-ray Discs. And notably, MPEG-4 provides Intellectual Property Management and Protection (IPMP), which supports digital rights management.

MPEG-7 is designed to complement the previous standards as a fast and efficient multimedia content searching tool.

MPEG-21 is concerned with and focuses on coding and digital rights. MPEG-21 uses a Rights Expression Language (REL) and a Rights Data Dictionary to protect digital material from illicit file sharing.

• Figure 13.26 DVD-RAM disc

Recordable DVD

The IT industry has no fewer than *six* distinct standards of recordable DVD-media: DVD-ROM for general use, DVD-R for authoring, **DVD-RW**, DVD+R, **DVD+RW**, and DVD-RAM. Both DVD-R standard discs and DVD+R discs work like CD-Rs. You can write to them but not erase or alter what's written. DVD-RW, DVD+RW, and DVD-RAM discs can be written and rewritten, just like CD-RW discs. Most DVD drives can read all formats with the exception of DVD-RAM. DVD-RAM is the only DVD format that uses a cartridge, so it requires a special drive (Figure 13.26). DVD-RAM is still around but fading away.

Although there is little if any difference in quality among the standards, the competition between corporations pushing their preferred standards has raged for years. Sony and Phillips, for example, pushed the + series, whereas other manufacturers pushed the – series. Worse, no recordable DVD drive manufactured before 2003 could write any format except its own. You could plop down US$250 on a brand-new DVD+RW drive and still find yourself unable to edit a disc from your friend who used the DVD-RW format! Half of the time, the drive couldn't even *read* the competing format disc.

The situation is much better today, as DVD±RW combo drives in PCs play just about anyone else's DVDs. The challenge is DVD players. If you want to make a DVD of your family picnic and then play it on the DVD player hooked to your television, take the time to read the documentation for your player to make sure it reads that particular DVD format—not all players read all formats.

Blu-ray Disc-Media

Blu-ray Disc is considered the next generation in optical disc formatting and storage technology after CD and DVD. Because of its near-perfect audio and video quality; mass acceptance by industry-leading computer, electronics, game, music, retail, and motion picture companies; and huge storage capacities of up to 25 GB (single-layer disc) and 50 GB (dual-layer disc), Blu-ray Disc technology is expected to eventually make CD- and DVD-media and devices obsolete.

Blu-ray Discs come in two sizes, standard and mini. The standard size matches that of earlier optical discs, such as CD-R and DVD-RW, and is what you'll see used in computers and for movies (Figure 13.27). The mini-size discs are a lot smaller and, naturally, offer less storage. You'll find mini Blu-ray Discs in very high-end camcorders. Table 13.2 shows the details of the two formats.

Unlike with DVD discs, Blu-ray Disc offers no option at this time of a double-sided disc. I wouldn't be surprised to see this option in the coming years.

• Figure 13.27   Standard Blu-ray Disc

Table 13.2	Standard and Mini Blu-ray Disc Comparison Chart			
Type	**Size**	**Capacity (single layer)**	**Capacity (dual layer)**	
Standard disc	12 cm	25 GB	50 GB	
Mini disc	8 cm	7.8 GB	15.6 GB	

 There was a brief battle for supremacy in the high-definition digital war between Blu-ray Disc and a competing high-definition optical disc standard called HD DVD. Major content manufacturers and developers leaned toward Blu-ray Disc, and in early 2008, Toshiba—the primary company behind HD DVD—threw in the towel. HD DVD is no longer being developed or supported.

Blu-ray Disc technology offers several advantages over DVD aside from raw capacity. First, Blu-ray Disc uses a blue-violet laser (hence the Blu in the name) with a wavelength of 405 nm. (DVD uses a red laser technology with a wavelength of 650nm.) The 405-nm wavelength is smaller and much more precise, enabling better use of space during the creation process and ultimately resulting in a sharper image. Second, Blu-ray Disc can handle high-definition (HD) video in resolutions far higher than DVD. Finally, Blu-ray Disc supports many more video compression schemes, giving producers more options for putting content on discs.

BD-ROM

BD-ROM (read only) is the Blu-ray Disc equivalent of the standard DVD-ROM data format except, as noted earlier, it can store much more data and produces superior audio and video results. Almost all BD-ROM drives are fully backward compatible and support DVD-video as well as most CD-ROM formats. If you want to display the best possible movie picture quality on your HDTV, you should get a Blu-ray Disc player and use Blu-ray Discs in place of DVDs. Most new computer systems don't come standard with Blu-ray Disc drives installed. You can often custom-order a system with a Blu-ray Disc drive or you can simply install one yourself. Figure 13.28 shows a Blu-ray Disc drive.

 If you own a PlayStation 3, you already have a Blu-ray Disc player. That's the optical format the game system uses.

BD-R and BD-RE

Blu-ray Discs come in two writable formats, BD-R (for recordable) and BD-RE (for rewritable). You can write to a **BD-R** disc one time. You can write to and erase a **BD-RE** (rewritable) several times. There are also BD-R and BD-RE versions of mini Blu-ray Discs.

Blu-ray Burners

Most Blu-ray Disc burners cost a lot (at the time of this writing) and are out of the price range for the average consumer, but they will eventually be as common as the average CD-RW or DVD-RW. Blu-ray Disc burners and other Blu-ray Disc drives can be connected internally or externally to a system. It is common for them to be connected externally via Hi-Speed USB 2.0, FireWire, or eSATA or internally through PATA, SATA, SCSI, or USB connections. Operating systems such as Windows 2000, XP, Vista, and Windows 7 all support Blu-ray Disc burners and software. The software you use for burning is totally up to you; however, as always, you should follow the manufacturer's

• Figure 13.28 A combination CD/DVD/Blu-ray Disc drive

specifications for the best results. Most multidrive Blu-ray Disc burners offer the following support features.

- **Media Support** BD-R, BD-RE, DVD-ROM, DVD-RAM, DVD-Video, DVD+/-R DL, DVD+/-R, DVD+/-RW, CD-DA, CD-ROM, CD-R, and CD-RW

- **Write speed (max)** 2× BD-R, 4× DVD+/-R DL, 8× DVD+/-R(8×), and 24× CD-R

- **Rewrite speed (max)** 2× BD-RE, 8× DVD+RW, 6× DVD-RW, 5× DVD-RAM, and 16× CD-RW

- **Read speed (max)** 2× BD-ROM, 8× DVD-ROM, and 32× CD-ROM

- **Compatibility** Most Blu-ray Disc drives are backward compatible, meaning they can read and play CDs and DVDs. CD and DVD drives and players cannot read or play Blu-ray Discs.

Installing Optical Drives

From ten feet away, optical drives of all flavors look absolutely identical. Figure 13.29 shows a CD-RW, DVD, and BD-R drive. Can you tell them apart just by a glance? In case you were wondering, the CD-RW is on the bottom, the DVD is next, and finally the BD-R is on the top. If you look closely at an optical drive, you will normally see its function either stamped on the front of the case or printed on a label somewhere less obvious (see Figure 13.30).

Connections

Most internal optical drives use PATA or SATA connections and support the ATAPI standard. (Other connections, such as SCSI and USB, are possible but less common.) External optical drives often use USB, FireWire, or eSATA connections. ATAPI treats an optical drive exactly as though it were an ATA drive. PATA optical drives have regular 40-pin IDE connectors and master/slave jumpers. SATA optical drives use standard SATA or eSATA cables. You install them the same way you

• **Figure 13.29**   CD-RW, DVD, and BD-R drives

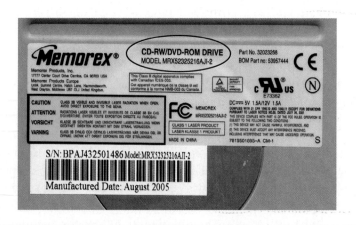

• **Figure 13.30**   Label on optical drive indicating its type and speeds

● **Figure 13.31**   Typical DVD installation

would install any ATA hard drive. Figure 13.31 shows a typical DVD installation using PATA. The DVD is configured as slave with a master hard drive on a system's primary IDE controller.

ATAPI drives require no CMOS changes as part of the installation process. When the industry first introduced ATAPI drives, techs familiar with hard-drive installations swamped the CD-ROM makers' service departments asking how to set up the drives in CMOS. To reduce these calls, BIOS makers added a CD-ROM option in many CMOS setup utilities, just to give the techs something to do! You can find this option in many older CMOS setup utilities. This setting actually didn't do anything at all; it just kept users from bothering the CD-ROM makers with silly support calls. Modern motherboards report the actual model numbers of optical drives, giving techs a degree of assurance that they configured and installed the drive correctly (Figure 13.32).

Cross Check

Master/Slave Settings

You normally set up an ATAPI optical drive as a slave to a hard drive master. You learned about master and slave settings for PATA drives in Chapter 11, "Hard Drive Technologies," so cross-check your memory!

1. What are the various ways you can determine which drive on an IDE controller acts as slave and which acts as master?

2. What factors should you consider when deciding where to install an optical drive, either as a master or as a slave? Any difference in your answer for a system with one hard drive versus one with two hard drives?

Device Manager

When you install a new optical drive, such as a DVD drive, into an existing system, the first question to ask is "Does Windows recognize my DVD drive?" You can determine this by opening the My Computer icon and verifying that a DVD drive is present (see Figure 13.33). When you want to know more, go to Device Manager.

The Device Manager contains most of the information about the DVD drive. The General tab tells you about the current status of the DVD drive, basically saying whether the device is

● **Figure 13.32**   Autodetect settings for two optical drives

External Optical Drives

Almost all new PCs have one, two, or three external expansion buses—USB, FireWire, or eSATA—and the makers of optical drives have quickly taken this fact to heart. Many manufacturers have released external versions of CD, DVD, and Blu-ray Disc drives, both readers and burners. Of the two most common expansion options, I prefer FireWire simply because it's the standard for most digital video cameras, and its 400-Mbps sustained data transfer rate easily trumps the Hi-Speed USB 480-Mbps burst rate for transferring huge files.

The only benefit to the USB versions is that USB is still more common than FireWire, particularly on portable computers. In fact, quite a few super-light laptops don't have an optical drive built in; the only way to load an OS on them is through an external drive. If you can't decide which expansion type to use, several manufacturers have taken pity on you.

You won't find any CD or DVD drives with eSATA—they just can't take advantage of the blazing speed offered by the best of the external ports. Blu-ray Disc drive manufacturers, on the other hand, have released several drives with both eSATA and Hi-Speed USB connections. If you have the choice, there is no choice. Choose eSATA every time.

● **Figure 13.33**   DVD drive letter in My Computer

working properly or not—rather less useful than actually trying the device. Other tabs, such as the Driver tab, provide other pertinent information about the drive.

Auto Insert Notification

Another setting of note is the Auto Insert Notification option, often referred to as **AutoPlay** in Windows 2000/XP/Vista. This setting enables Windows to detect automatically the presence of audio or data optical discs when they are placed in the drive.

Windows 2000, Windows XP, and Windows Vista all have very different ways of dealing with AutoPlay. In Windows 2000, if the CD is an audio disc, track 1 plays automatically. If the CD-ROM is a data disc, Windows searches the disc's root directory for a special text file called **AUTORUN.INF**.

Although handy, the AutoPlay option can sometimes be annoying and unproductive. Windows 2000 does not provide a simple method to turn off AutoPlay. The only way to turn it off is to edit the Registry. You can use the REGEDT32 version of the Registry Editor and do it directly. In REGEDT32, access this subkey:

HKEY_LOCAL_MACHINE\SYSTEM\CurrentControlSet\Services\Cdrom

Change Autorun 0 x 1 to 0 x 0.

Most techs use Group Policy to make the change because it gives you much more control in multiple optical drive situations. With Group Policy, you can turn off AutoPlay on your CD-RW drive, for example, but leave it enabled for your DVD drive. Group Policy is a powerful tool that goes well beyond CompTIA A+, so be careful with what you're about to do. To run Group Policy, go to Start | Run and type **gpedit.msc** in the Run dialog box; or in Vista, just go to Start and type **gpedit.msc** in the Start Search text box. Click OK to open the MMC. To turn off AutoPlay, navigate down in the

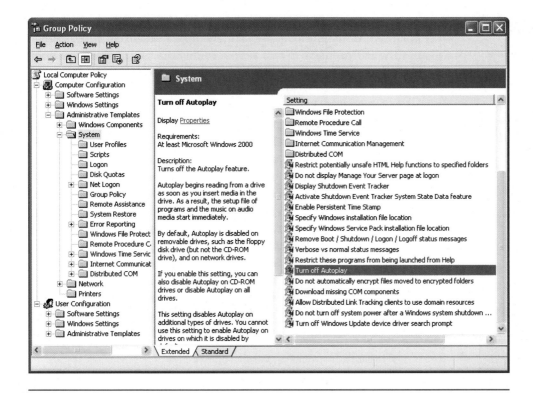

• **Figure 13.34** Group Policy MMC with *Turn off Autoplay* selected

menu to the left as follows: Local Computer Policy | Computer Configuration | Administrative Templates. Select the System option and you'll see the *Turn off Autoplay* option in the Setting section on the right pane of the MMC (Figure 13.34).

Double-click or right-click *Turn off Autoplay* to open the Properties. Note in Figure 13.35 that the default option is Not Configured, but you can enable or disable it here. The words are messy here, so make sure you know what you're doing. *Enabling* Turn off Autoplay gives you the option to stop an optical device from automatically playing a disc. *Disabling* Turn off Autoplay prevents you or any other user from stopping any optical device from automatically playing a disc. Got the distinction?

Windows XP provides a much more sophisticated and simpler approach to AutoPlay. By default, when you insert a CD- or DVD-media disc that doesn't have an AUTORUN.INF file, XP asks you what you want to do (Figure 13.36). You can change the default behavior simply by accessing the properties for a particular drive in My Computer and making your selection on the AutoPlay tab. Figure 13.37 shows some of the options for a typical Windows XP machine.

AutoPlay in Windows Vista is much more robust and offers many more options than in Windows 2000 or Windows XP. For example, you can choose to enable or disable AutoPlay for all media and devices. (Using AutoPlay for all media and devices is the default.) But what's more interesting is that you can enable very specific actions for Windows to take when digital media or devices are inserted or detected. For an audio CD, for example, you can specify that Windows should use Windows Media

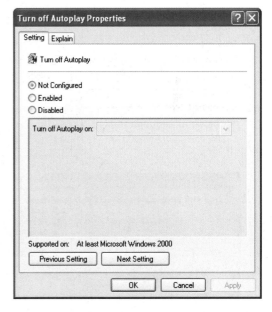

• **Figure 13.35** Turn off Autoplay Properties dialog box

● **Figure 13.36**   XP prompting user for action

● **Figure 13.37**   AutoPlay tab for a CD-RW drive

Player. If a DVD movie is detected, you can tell AutoPlay to play the DVD by using PowerDVD 8 or some other program. You can adjust AutoPlay options in Windows Vista through Control Panel | Hardware and Sound | AutoPlay.

As a final note, in Windows 2000, XP, and Vista, you can change the drive letter for an optical drive, just as you can change the letter of a hard drive. You'll find that option in Disk Management (Figure 13.38).

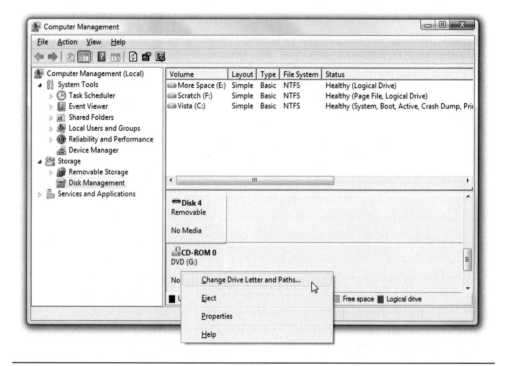

● **Figure 13.38**   Change CD drive letter option in Disk Management

Applications

A regular CD-ROM drive installation involves no applications. You install it, Windows sees it, and you're finished. CD-R and CD-RW drives, in contrast, require applications to enable their burning features. DVD and Blu-ray Disc drives need software to enable you to watch movies, burn DVDs and Blu-ray Discs, and so on. As of this writing, Nero (www.nero.com) and Roxio Creator (www.roxio .com) share the reigns as the most popular CD-burning software programs. CyberLink PowerDVD and Corel WinDVD fight for Blu-ray Disc burning supremacy rights. If you're looking for a free burner, try CDBurnerXP Pro, pictured in Figure 13.39 (www.cdburnerxp .se). Windows XP contains basic CD-burning capabilities built into the operating system. With XP, you can readily drag and drop files to your CD-R or CD-RW drive and move those files from PC to PC. Almost all optical drives will read the discs burned in an XP system.

Windows Media Player makes an excellent DVD-watching application, but for DVD burning you need to turn to a third-party tool. Nero and Roxio make great software that handles every DVD recordable standard your drive can use (as well as CD-R and CD-RW).

Ever wanted to make a perfect copy of a CD so you can keep your original in a safe place? You can do so by using a special file type called an ISO file. An **ISO file** is a complete copy—an ISO image as we say—of a CD or DVD. As you might imagine, they are huge files, but they are also very important to techs. Techs use ISO images to send each other copies of bootable utility CDs. For example, if you want a copy of the Ultimate Boot CD, you go

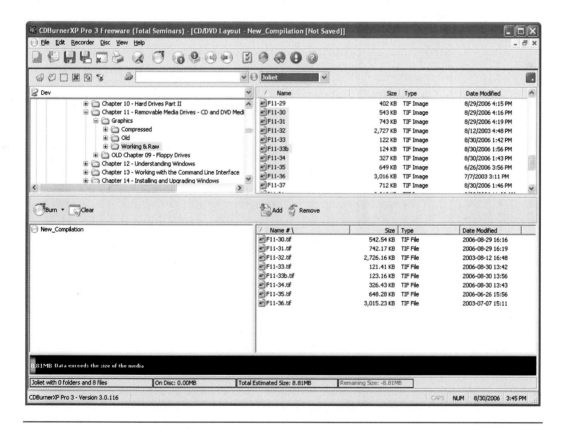

• **Figure 13.39**   Typical third-party CD-burning program

Burning Digital Music Files to a CD

Almost all computers and many portable CD players now can play recordable CDs loaded with MP3 files. This enables you to mix songs from your music collection and fit a lot of songs on a disc (MP3s are smaller than CD-audio files). That's a great feature—but where do digital audio files come from and how do you put them on a CD?

You can create MP3s from your favorite CDs by using a *ripper*. A ripper is a piece of software that takes standard CD-audio files and compresses them, using specialized algorithms, into much smaller files while maintaining most of the audio qualities of the original file. One legal note, however: you should only make MP3s from CDs that you have purchased. Borrowing a CD from a friend and ripping MP3s from it is illegal! Likewise, downloading MP3s from unauthorized sources on the Internet is also illegal. You don't want to go to jail because you just had to listen to the latest, greatest single from your favorite artist, right?

Now that I've taken care of the legal disclaimer, get ready to burn your MP3s. You need three things: a recordable/rewritable optical drive, some CD authoring software, and of course, a blank disc. I recommend a CD-R. (Audio-only devices stand a much better chance of playing a CD-R successfully rather than a CD-RW.)

1. Confirm that you have a CD-R/RW drive installed in your computer. You don't have to have a drive like this to rip audio files *from* a CD, but you must have one to burn digital audio to a CD-R.

2. Launch your favorite CD authoring software. Popular titles in this category include Nero Burning ROM and Roxio Creator.

3. Most CD authoring programs use a simple drag-and-drop interface, similar to the Windows Explorer interface. Browse to the location of the audio files and select them. Then drag them into the appropriate area—this is often called the *queue*.

4. After you've selected all the files you want to have on your CD, it's time to burn. The procedure for initiating the CD-burning sequence is different for each program. You should always make sure to *close* the CD after you've burned it. Most standalone CD players (even ones that play MP3s) won't play CD-Rs that haven't been closed.

Once you've keyed in all of the configuration information, just sit back and watch the fireworks. Always be sure to use CD-media that is rated appropriately for your drive, for both speed and media type. In no time at all, you'll be listening to MP3s while jogging around the park.

to their Web site and download an ISO image. You then take your third-party burning program (Windows XP/Vista built-in burning software can't do this) and go through a special process called burning an ISO image. Learn how to burn ISO images with your burning program; you'll use it all the time.

Blu-ray Disc Drive Considerations

Physically installing, attaching, and maintaining optical drives is pretty straightforward, but a Blu-ray Disc drive installation requires some special considerations. If you plan to use your Blu-ray Disc drive primarily for storage purposes, for example, system requirements are minimal. If you plan on watching Blu-ray Disc movies in HD resolution (720p, 1080i, or 1080p), on the other hand, the requirements are quite hefty. Here's a list of recommended minimum specs.

- **Processor**   At the very least, a Pentium 4, Pentium D, or dual or multicore processor; or an AMD Athlon 64 X2 or Phenom multicore processor.

- **System Memory**   At least 1 GB RAM for Windows XP; 2 GB RAM for Windows Vista.

- **Video**   You need an HDCP-compliant (either DVI or HDMI) video card and drivers. That's a lot of initials in one sentence! Here's the scoop. The High-Bandwidth Digital Content Protection (HDCP) is a standard developed by Intel to ensure copyright protection on behalf of the Motion Picture Association of America. The Digital Video Interface (DVI) and High-Definition Multimedia Interface (HDMI) standards enable fast uncompressed connections between an HDTV, PC, and any other DVI/HDMI component. HDMI, which transmits both video and audio signals, has all but replaced the older DVI standard that only supports video. ATI and NVIDIA both offer Blu-ray Disc–compliant PCIe video cards with enough horsepower to get the job done.

CyberLink provides an awesome tool called BD Advisor that will tell you if your system meets the requirements to play Blu-ray Discs. You can get it at http://www.cyberlink.com/prog/bd-support/diagnosis.do.

Region Codes

Production movies on DVD and Blu-ray Disc can feature a **region code**, encoding that enables you to play those movies only on a player that shares the same region code. This was instituted to try to stop piracy of movies, though it didn't manage to accomplish that goal.

Can you play a DVD or Blu-ray Disc encoded to play in the geographical region location of Somalia on your system manufactured in the U.S.A.? Why sure you can. To do so, however, you have to change the region code on your DVD or Blu-ray Disc player to match Somalia (5 or B, respectively, in case you're curious). You can only change the region code on your player four times. After that, you get stuck with whatever was the last-used region code. Today, most optical discs are sold *region free*, meaning you can play them anywhere. Many optical devices are set to play only discs encoded for the region in which they were sold or manufactured. You can easily check and set your device's current region code under the hardware properties of your optical device in any version of Windows. As either a technician or home enthusiast, you should be familiar with the following optical device and media region codes.

 Be sure you are familiar with the Blu-ray Disc requirements discussed in this section, especially the stringent requirements for supporting high-definition video and audio. Also, be aware that CompTIA expects you to be somewhat knowledgeable of DVD/BD region codes, so pay attention to those as well.

DVD Region Codes:

- **REGION 0** All regions
- **REGION 1** USA, Canada
- **REGION 2** Europe, Japan, Middle East, South Africa, Greenland
- **REGION 3** South Korea, Taiwan, Hong Kong, Areas of Southeast Asia
- **REGION 4** Australia, New Zealand, Central and South America
- **REGION 5** Eastern Europe, Russia, India, Africa
- **REGION 6** China
- **REGION 7** Reserved for special and future use
- **REGION 8** Reserved for cruise ships and airlines

Blu-ray Disc Region Codes:

- **A** East Asia (China and Mongolia excluded), Southeast Asia, Americas, and their dependencies
- **B** Africa, Southwest Asia, Europe (except Russia), Oceania, and their dependencies
- **C** Central Asia, East Asia (China and Mongolia only), South Asia, central Eurasia (including Russia), and their dependencies

Practical Application

■ Troubleshooting Removable Media

Floppy disk drives, flash memory, and optical drives are fairly robust devices that rarely require troubleshooting due to an actual hardware failure. Most problems with removable media stem from lack of knowledge, improper installation, abuse, and incorrect use of associated applications. There's no way to repair a truly broken flash memory—once a flash card dies you replace it—so let's concentrate on troubleshooting floppy drives and optical drives.

Floppy Drive Maintenance and Troubleshooting

No single component fails more often than the floppy drive. This is not really that surprising because floppy drives have more exposure to the outside environment than anything but the keyboard. Only a small door (or in the case of 5¼-inch drives, not even a door) divides the read/write heads from dust and grime. Floppy drives are also exposed to the threat of mechanical damage. Many folks destroy floppy drives by accidentally inserting inverted disks, paper clips, and other foreign objects. Life is tough for floppy drives.

In the face of this abuse, the key preventative maintenance performed on floppy drives is cleaning. You can find floppy drive **cleaning kits** at some electronics stores, or you can use a cotton swab and some denatured alcohol to scour gently inside the drive for dust and other particles.

If cleaning the drive doesn't help, try replacing the suspect disk with another one to see if the floppy drive itself is bad. If it turns out that your floppy drive won't read any disks, it's time to replace the drive.

Troubleshooting Optical Drives and Discs

Optical drives are extremely reliable and durable PC components. At times, however, a reliable and durable device decides to turn into an unreliable, nondurable pile of plastic and metal frustration. This section covers a few of the more common problems with optical drives and discs—installation issues, burning issues, and firmware updates—and how to fix them.

Installation Issues

The single biggest problem with optical drives, especially in a new installation, is the connection. Your first guess should be that the drive has not been properly installed in some way. A few of the common culprits are forgetting to plug in a power connector, inserting a cable backward, and misconfiguring jumpers/switches. Although you need to know the type of drive, the test for an improper physical connection is always the same: using BIOS to see whether the system can see the optical drive.

How BIOS detects an optical drive depends on the system. Most BIOS makers have created intelligent BIOS software that can see an installed CD-media drive. Figure 13.40 shows a modern Award Software, Inc. BIOS recognizing a CD-RW during startup.

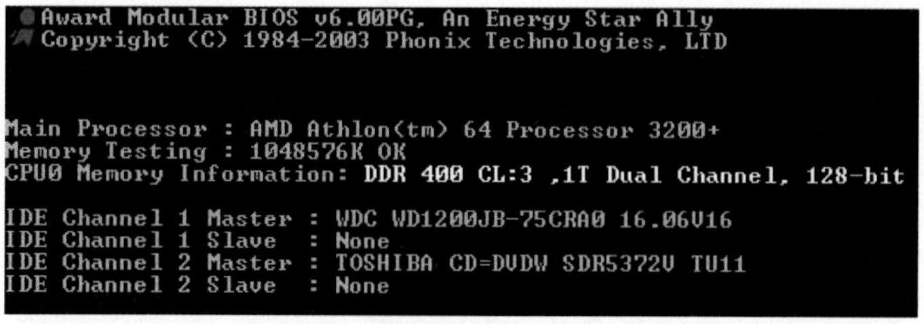

If BIOS detects the device, Windows recognizes the drive and you'll see it in My Computer or Computer and Device Manager.

If the drive won't read a CD-R or CD-RW disc, first try a commercial CD-ROM disc that is in good condition. CD-R and CD-RW discs sometimes have compatibility issues with CD-ROM drives. The same goes for DVD-RWs or any other writable DVD discs in your DVD drive or writable Blu-ray Discs in your Blu-ray Disc drive. Also, no optical drive will read badly scratched discs.

```
Award Modular BIOS v6.00PG, An Energy Star Ally
Copyright (C) 1984-2003 Phonix Technologies, LTD


Main Processor : AMD Athlon(tm) 64 Processor 3200+
Memory Testing : 1048576K OK
CPU0 Memory Information: DDR 400 CL:3 ,1T Dual Channel, 128-bit

IDE Channel 1 Master : WDC WD1200JB-75CRA0 16.06V16
IDE Channel 1 Slave  : None
IDE Channel 2 Master : TOSHIBA CD-DVDW SDR5372U TU11
IDE Channel 2 Slave  : None
```

• **Figure 13.40**   BIOS recognizing an optical drive at boot

If the drive still does not see a disc, try cleaning the drive. Most modern optical drives have built-in cleaning mechanisms, but from time to time, you need to use a commercial optical-drive cleaning kit (see Figure 13.41).

Optical drives are not cleaned too often, but the discs are. Although a number of fine optical disc cleaning kits are available, you can clean most discs quite well with nothing more than a damp soft cloth. Occasionally, you can add a mild detergent. Always wipe from the center of the optical disc to the edge—never use a circular motion when cleaning a CD, DVD, or Blu-ray Disc! A common old tech's tale about cleaning optical discs is that you can wash them in a dishwasher. Although this may seem laughable,

• **Figure 13.41** Optical-drive cleaning kit

the tale has become so common that it requires a serious response. This is *not true* for two reasons: First, the water in most dishwashers is too hot and can cause the discs to warp. Second, the water pushes the discs around, causing them to hit other objects and get scratched. Don't do it!

The final problem with optical drives—stuck discs—comes from *technician* error and is not actually the fault of the drives. I can't tell you the number of times I've pulled an optical drive out of a system to replace it, only to discover that I or my customer left an essential disc inside the now-powerless drive. Luckily, most optical drives have a small hole in the front, usually just below the drive opening, into which you can insert a wire—an unbent paper clip is the standard tool for this purpose—and push on an internal release lever that ejects the disc. Try it!

Burning Issues

The tremendous growth of the CD-R and CD-RW industry—and to a lesser extent, the recordable DVD industry—has led to a substantial number of incompatibility issues between discs and drives. Some of these incompatibilities trace back to serious IO (Ignorant Operator) problems; people try to make these discs do jobs they aren't designed to do. Even when people read the manuals and jump through the proper hoops, real problems do arise, many of which you can easily solve with a few checks.

Know What It Can Do   Most mistakes take place at the point of purchase, when someone buys a drive without completely understanding its capabilities. Don't just assume that the device will do everything. Before I purchase a CD-RW or DVD-RW drive, for example, I make it a point to get my hands on every technical document the maker provides to verify exactly what capabilities the drive possesses. I make sure the drive has a good reputation; just use any search engine and type in **review** and the model number of the drive to get several people's opinions.

Media Issues   The optical disc standards committees refused to mandate the types of materials used in the construction of discs. As a result, you see substantial quality differences among CD-R and CD-RW discs of different brands and sources (they are made in several different countries). As mentioned earlier, CD-R discs use organic inks as part of the burning process. Fellow techs love to talk about which color to use or which color gives the best results. Ignore them; the color itself means nothing. Instead, try several brands of CD-R discs when you first get your drive to determine what works best for you. If you have a particular reason for burning CDs, such as music recording, you may want to ask for opinions and recommendations among folks in online communities with the same focus. They're usually happy to share their hard-won knowledge about what works.

In general, two items can affect media quality: speed and inks. Most CD-R and CD-RW media makers certify their CDs to work up to a certain speed multiplier. A media maker often has two product lines: a quality line guaranteed to work at a certain speed, and a generic line where you take your chances. As a rule, I buy both. I primarily use cheap discs, but I always stash

five to ten good-quality discs in case I run into a problem. Again, this in large part depends on what you want them for: you may want to pull out the cheapies for temporary backups but stick with the high-end discs for archiving musical performances.

All of this discussion about CD-Rs and CD-RWs definitely holds true for recordable DVD and BD discs and drives as well. Factor in the incompatibility of standards and you're looking at a fine mess. Do your homework before you buy or advise a client to buy a DVD/BD-writable or -rewritable drive.

Buffer Underrun   Every CD, DVD, and Blu-ray Disc burner comes with onboard RAM, called *buffer RAM*—usually just called the buffer—that stores the incoming data from the recording source. **Buffer underrun**, the inability of the source device to keep the burner loaded with data, creates more *coasters*—that is, improperly burned and therefore useless CDs, DVDs, and Blu-ray Discs—than any other single problem. Buffer underrun most often occurs when copying from CD-ROM to CD-R/RW or from DVD-ROM to DVD-writable of all stripes. Many factors contribute to buffer underrun, but two stand out as the most important. The first factor is buffer size. Make sure you purchase drives with large buffers, a minimum of 2 MB. Unlike with system RAM, you can't get a buffer upgrade. Second is multitasking. Most systems won't enable you to run any other programs while the burner is running.

One trick to reduce underrun is using an ISO. Unlike some optical drives, *any* hard drive can keep up with an optical burner. Doing a bit-by-bit copy from disc to disc dramatically reduces the chances that a buffer underrun will add to your coaster collection.

All current optical disc burners include the BURN-Proof technology developed by Sanyo, which has eliminated the underrun issue. These drives can literally turn off the burning process if the buffer runs out of information and automatically restart as soon as the buffer refills. I love this feature, as I can now burn CDs in the background and run other programs without fear of underrun. If you're buying a new burner, make sure you get one that uses the BURN-Proof technology.

The majority of problems that occur with CD, DVD, and Blu-ray Disc drives are usually a direct result of incorrectly installed or updated device drivers, disconnected cables, or incompatible or just plain bad media. Also, keep in mind DVD and Blu-ray Disc drives use specific region codes that are often misconfigured. Blu-ray Disc drives have very specific hardware and driver specifications that must be met for trouble-free end-user experiences. CompTIA is likely to target these areas specifically on the 220-702 exam, so make sure you understand this information.

Firmware Updates

Almost all optical drives come with an upgradeable flash ROM chip. If your drive doesn't read a particular type of media, or if any other nonintermittent reading/writing problems develop, check the manufacturer's Web site to see if it offers a firmware upgrade. Almost every optical drive seems to get one or two firmware updates during its production cycle.

Beyond A+

Color Books

The term *color books* is often used in the world of CD-media. Books are—well, books! In this case, they're the standards developed in the industry to describe various media. For example, the Red book describes the original

audio CD format. If you have a lot of money—say, US$3000—you may purchase copies of these books, and yes, their covers really match the colors of the standards. You might hear a fellow computer support person using these terms. Instead of saying, "Does your CD-ROM read CD-RWs?" they will say, "Is that CD-ROM of yours Orange book?" Technical specifications also use these terms. I personally don't like the way many people refer to these book colors, but the terms are used enough that you should memorize the meanings of at least three book colors: Red, Yellow, and Orange. Table 13.3 shows a complete list of CD-media book colors.

Table 13.3	CD-Media Book Colors
Application	**Book**
Audio CDs	Red book
Data CDs	Yellow book
CD-I	Green book
Recordable CDs	Orange book
Video CD	White book
CD Extra	Blue book

Blu-ray Disc Java

Blu-ray Disc Java (BD-J) is a program application environment based on Java ME (Java Platform, Micro Edition) that enables content providers to develop and deliver highly interactive Blu-ray Disc movies, games, and content to you. Most state-of-the-art (or state-of-the-business) mobile devices, smart cards, and other gadgets use Java APIs (application programmming interfaces) to support requests made by the device, program, or operating system. BD-J APIs are used for similar purposes with Blu-ray Disc devices. They enable and detail the interaction of such things as fancy menus, downloaded games and content, and certain playback capabilities. If you play online games through your PlayStation 3 and HDTV, for example, you use BD-J in more ways than you probably know.

Chapter 13 Review

■ Chapter Summary

After reading this chapter and completing the exercises, you should understand the following about floppy disk drives, flash memory, and optical media technology.

Explain and install floppy disk drives

- Floppy disk drives are becoming a thing of the past as Microsoft and Intel push for legacy-free computing. The small, 1.44-MB capacity floppy disks are being replaced by higher-capacity removable media.

- Floppy disks are constructed of a flexible magnetic disc housed inside a square plastic case. The case has a sliding protective cover that opens to reveal a portion of the magnetic media when inside a floppy drive. Read/write heads inside the floppy disk drive move back and forth across the media, reading or writing data as necessary.

- During disk access, an LED on the front of the drive lights up. Never eject a floppy disk when this light is on.

- Floppy disks have gone through several stages of improvement, becoming smaller with each phase. Pre-PC computers used an 8-inch floppy. Early PCs used a 5¼-inch floppy. Modern floppy disks, which appeared around 1986, are 3½ inches.

- You may have a maximum of two floppy disk drives in a system, and they must use either the drive letter A: or B:; however, a single floppy disk drive can be configured to use either drive letter. By convention, if your system has only one floppy disk drive, you should configure it as drive A:. A 34-pin ribbon data cable is used to connect the floppy disk drive to the motherboard; a 4-pin mini connector supplies power. Attaching the data cable backward won't damage anything, but the drive won't work. If you attach the power connector incorrectly, you risk damaging the drive.

- Most floppy ribbon cables have three connectors and a twist. The end without the twist connects to the motherboard, matching the red stripe on the cable with pin 1 of the motherboard connector. The drive attached to the middle connector on the cable receives the drive letter B:. The drive attached to the other end of the cable (after the twist) is assigned the drive letter A:.

- After connecting a floppy disk drive, configure the CMOS settings. Make sure the CMOS settings match your floppy disk drive size/capacity; for example, 3½ inches and 1.44 MB.

Demonstrate the variations among flash drives and other tiny drives

- Flash memory includes USB thumb drives and memory cards. USB thumb drives contain a standard USB connection and have replaced many other forms of removable media as the way to transfer files. Memory cards, a generic term, are used in digital cameras, PDAs, and other devices.

- Thumb drives store much more data than floppies—sometimes up to the equivalent of thousands of floppy disks. They are hot-swappable in Windows 2000/XP/Vista and don't require an external power source, as they are powered directly from the USB bus. Most new PCs enable you to boot from a USB thumb drive.

- Flash cards, which are used in portable devices such as digital cameras, PDAs, and phones, come in many varieties. The most common types are CompactFlash, SmartMedia, Secure Digital, Memory Stick, and Extreme Digital (xD) Picture Card. CompactFlash cards are the oldest of these. At about 1 inch wide, they use the PCMCIA bus and come in two thicknesses: CF I at 3.3 mm thick and CF II at 5 mm thick. SmartMedia competed directly with CompactFlash and was used mainly in digital cameras. The introduction of Secure Digital has made SmartMedia all but obsolete. Secure Digital is perhaps the most popular flash card today and comes in two types: original SD and SDIO. Smaller versions of Secure Digital cards, MiniSD and MicroSD, are also available. Memory Stick, a proprietary format from Sony, comes in several formats, including Standard, Pro, Duo, Pro Duo, and Micro. xD Picture Cards, developed by Olympus, are about half the size of Secure Digital cards and are used almost exclusively in digital cameras.

- No matter what type of flash card you have, you need a card reader to access it. Some PCs have built-in card readers. External USB card readers are also available. Sometimes a device such as a digital camera or PDA can double as a card reader.

Identify and install optical-media technology

- CDs store data by using microscopic pits burned into a glass master CD with a powerful laser. Expensive machines create plastic copies of the glass master that are then coated with a reflective metallic coating. CDs store data on one side of the disc only. The CD drive reads the pits and the non-pitted areas (lands) and converts the pattern into ones and zeros.

- CDs come in many varieties. CD-Digital Audio is for playing music, but it lacks error checking, file support, and directory structure. CD-ROM discs are for storing data. They use the ISO-9660 file system, also known as CDFS. Extensions of ISO-9660 have offered improvements to file and directory naming, filename length, and directory depth and include Joliet, Rock Ridge, El Torito, and Apple Extensions.

- CD-ROM speeds have increased substantially from the original 150 KBps. Increased speeds are measured in multiples of 150 KBps, so a 10× CD-ROM has a maximum speed of 1500 KBps.

- CD-recordable (CD-R) discs hold either 650 MB or 700 MB and can store either audio or data. Special organic dyes that give the CD-Rs their distinctive bottom color aid in the burning process. A strong laser in the CD drive heats the dye and changes the reflectivity of the CD-R's surface, resulting in a reflective/less-reflective pattern that is converted to ones and zeros. Once data is burned to a CD-R, the data cannot be erased. With multisession drives, you can burn data to a portion of a disc and then go back later and burn more data to the disc. CD-R discs are rated with two speeds: a write speed followed by a read speed.

- CD-rewritable (CD-RW) discs, unlike CD-Rs, enable you to erase data and burn new data. CD-RWs are rated with three speeds: write speed followed by rewrite speed followed by read speed. The UDF file format (the replacement for ISO-9660) handles large files better than CDFS. Packet writing, a feature used by UDF, allows you to copy files back and forth to a CD-RW like a hard drive.

- Most CD drives are ATAPI-compliant and do not need drivers installed for them to work. Windows XP can burn CD-Rs and CD-RWs with no additional software but cannot burn bootable CDs. If you need to create a bootable CD, you need a third-party application such as Ahead's Nero Express. Many companies offer standalone CD burners that attach to your stereo system instead of your PC; however, these machines use a different type of CD called a music CD-R and are not compatible with standard CD-R or CD-RW discs.

- DVDs were released as digital video discs in 1995, but as usage evolved to include data storage, the name was changed to digital versatile disc. The lowest capacity DVD holds 4.37 GB of data. DVDs offer much higher capacities than CDs, because DVDs use smaller and more densely packed pits, can be burned on both sides of the disc, and can burn two layers of pits per side for a total of four layers. DVD video uses the MPEG-2 video standard and can store two hours of video on a single side.

- DVD-ROM, the DVD equivalent of CD-ROM, can store up to 16 GB of data. Recordable DVD-media comes in many varieties: DVD-R for general purpose, DVD-R for authoring, DVD+R, DVD-RW, DVD+RW, and DVD-RAM. You can write to DVD-R and DVD+R but not erase them. You can both burn and erase DVD-RW, DVD+RW, and DVD-RAM.

- Standard Blu-ray Discs have storage capacities of up to 25 GB (single-layer disc) and 50 GB (dual-layer disc) and provide near-perfect picture quality.

- You can write to a BD-R (recordable) disc one time. You can erase and write to a BD-RE (rewritable) several times.

- Blu-ray Disc external devices are connected via USB, FireWire, or eSATA and internally via PATA, SATA, SCSI, or USB connections.

- Most Blu-ray Disc burners support BD-R, BD-RE, DVD-ROM, DVD-RAM, DVD-Video, DVD+/-R DL, DVD+/-R, DVD+/-RW, CD-DA, CD-ROM, CD-R, and CD-RW formats. CD and DVD drives do not support Blu-ray Disc technologies. Most optical drives use PATA or SATA connections and support the ATAPI standard. PATA drives use a regular 40-pin IDE connector; SATA drives use a standard SATA or eSATA (for external use) connector. You install them just as you would any ATA hard drive. After installing a new optical

drive, check My Computer or Device Manager to confirm that Windows sees the drive.

- The Windows feature Auto Insert Notification (or AutoPlay) causes Windows to automatically begin an action when an optical disc is inserted in the drive. In Windows 2000, if an audio CD is inserted, track 1 plays automatically. If a data CD or DVD is inserted, AutoPlay scans the root of the disc for the AUTORUN.INF file and executes the commands in that file. In Windows 2000, the only way to disable AutoPlay is to manually edit the Registry. Windows XP can be configured by accessing the AutoPlay tab in the drive's Properties window. AutoPlay options in Windows Vista can be adjusted through Control Panel | Hardware and Sound | AutoPlay.

- An ISO file is a complete copy of an entire CD, DVD, or BD disc. Windows 2000/XP/Vista can't burn an ISO back to disc, but third-party programs such as Nero or Roxio Creator can.

Troubleshoot removable media

- The key preventative maintenance for floppy drives is cleaning. If your floppy drive won't read a disk, try another. If your floppy drive won't read any disks, replace the drive.

- If your optical drive doesn't work, first check the installation. Specifically, look at the master/slave jumper settings, data cable, and power cable. If the drive is seen by Windows but can't read a particular disc, try a commercial disc. It's also possible that your drive doesn't support your media type; for example, your DVD-R drive may not be able to read your DVD+RW disc. Clean the disc with a soft damp cloth, wiping from the center toward the edge. Never clean an optical disc in the dishwasher!

- If an optical disc becomes stuck in a drive, or if the drive has no power and you need to eject the disc, straighten a paper clip and look for the small hole on the front of the drive. Insert the paper clip in the hole and push the internal release lever to eject the disc.

- Not all media brands are created equally, and not all drives play nicely with all brands of media. Experiment and try several brands of media until you find one that works reliably with your drive.

- DVD and Blu-ray Disc drives have very specific hardware and driver specifications that must be met and use specific region codes that are often misconfigured. If a user is experiencing problems with a Blu-ray Disc device, it is likely to be associated with a video adapter, driver, or noncompliant media issue.

- A buffer underrun is caused when the source device fails to keep the recording device loaded with data. Buffer underruns are the leading cause of improperly burned, and therefore useless, CDs and DVDs. Purchase a drive with a large buffer—at least 2 MB. Some drives protect against buffer underrun with a technology called BURN-Proof. Purchase a BURN-Proof drive and your buffer underruns will be eliminated.

- Most optical drives come with an upgradeable flash ROM chip. If your drive is suffering read/write problems, check the manufacturer's Web site for a firmware upgrade.

■ Key Terms

34-pin ribbon cable *(427)*

3½-inch floppy drive *(426)*

ATAPI-compliant *(438)*

AutoPlay *(446)*

AUTORUN.INF *(446)*

BD-ROM *(443)*

Blu-ray Disc (BD) *(433)*

Blu-ray Disc recordable (BD-R) *(443)*

Blu-ray Disc rewritable (BD-RE) *(443)*

buffer underrun *(455)*

card reader *(432)*

CD-Digital Audio (CDDA) *(434)*

CD-recordable (CD-R) *(436)*

CD-rewritable (CD-RW) *(437)*

CD-ROM *(435)*

cleaning kit *(453)*

compact disc (CD) *(433)*

CompactFlash (CF) *(431)*

digital versatile disc (DVD) *(433)*

DVD-ROM *(441)*

DVD-RW *(442)*

DVD+RW *(442)*

DVD-video *(440)*
Extreme Digital (xD) Picture Card *(432)*
floppy disk *(426)*
floppy drive *(426)*
ISO file *(449)*
ISO-9660 *(435)*
Memory Stick *(432)*
microdrives *(431)*
mini power connector *(428)*
MPEG-2 *(441)*
MPEG-4 *(441)*

multisession drive *(437)*
music CD-R *(440)*
optical disc *(433)*
optical drive *(433)*
pin I *(427)*
region code *(451)*
removable media *(424)*
Secure Digital (SD) *(431)*
SmartMedia *(431)*
universal data format (UDF) *(438)*
USB thumb drive *(430)*

■ Key Term Quiz

Use the Key Terms list to complete the sentences that follow. Not all terms will be used.

1. If you want to burn part of a disc and finish burning it at a later time, you need to select a(n) _____.

2. Drives with BURN-Proof technology were designed to eliminate the problem of _____.

3. The first kind of CD disc was the _____ that is still used for music but is inappropriate for data because it lacks any error correction techniques.

4. While a CD-ROM disc holds about 650 MB of data, a(n) _____ stores from 4.37 GB

to 15.9 GB, depending on the number of sides and layers used.

5. Floppy drives use a(n) _____ to connect the floppy drive to the motherboard.

6. The red stripe on a floppy drive cable must be oriented to _____ on the controller.

7. Currently, the most popular flash memory cards are _____.

8. The floppy disk is quickly being replaced by the _____ because of its large capacity and portability.

9. DVD video uses the _____ standard of video.

10. DVDs use the _____ file structure.

■ Multiple-Choice Quiz

1. You just installed a floppy drive and you notice that the floppy drive LED stays on. What is most likely the problem?

   A. You attached the floppy drive to the wrong connector on the ribbon cable.

   B. You forgot to configure the floppy drive through the CMOS setup.

   C. You did not attach the colored stripe on the ribbon cable to pin 1 at the drive or at the controller.

   D. You forgot to attach the power cable to the floppy drive.

2. If the floppy disk you used last week will not work today in your floppy drive, what should you do first to determine if the problem is the drive or the disk?

   A. Try another disk in the drive or try the disk in another drive.

   B. Open the computer and check the ribbon cable.

   C. Replace the floppy drive.

   D. Check the CMOS settings.

3. What kind of disc must you use in a non-PC CD burner that works with your stereo system?

   A. CDDA

   B. CD-RW

   C. CD-UDF

   D. Music CD-R

4. What is the minimum capacity of a DVD?

   A. 650 MB

   B. 3.47 GB

   C. 4.37 GB

   D. 7.34 GB

5. If you have two floppy disc drives in your system, which one receives the drive letter A:?

   A. The drive jumpered for master

   B. The drive connected to the primary floppy drive controller

   C. The drive in the middle of the floppy cable

   D. The drive at the end of the floppy cable

6. Which type of flash memory card is currently the oldest?

   A. CompactFlash

   B. Memory Stick

   C. Secure Digital

   D. SmartMedia

7. Which device allows your computer to read flash memory cards?

   A. Scanner

   B. Card reader

   C. Floppy drive

   D. ZIP drive

8. AutoPlay reads which of the following files when an optical disc is inserted?

   A. AUTOPLAY.INF

   B. AUTORUN.INF

   C. AUTORUN.INI

   D. AUTORUN.EXE

9. The contents of an optical disc can be saved as what kind of file?

   A. ISO

   B. ISO-9660

   C. INF

   D. CDDA

10. Both CD and DVD drive speeds are based on multiples of the original CD-ROM drive speed. What is that speed?

    A. 100 KBps

    B. 150 KBps

    C. 100 MBps

    D. 150 MBps

11. You are looking for a CD-RW drive that can write CD-Rs at 48×, read CDs at 52×, and write CD-RWs at 32×. Which of the following answers meets your specifications?

    A. 52×48×32

    B. 32×48×52

    C. 48×32×52

    D. 48×52×32

12. What settings in the CMOS setup must you change to install an optical drive?

    A. Number of heads and cylinders the drive has

    B. Whether the drive is installed on the primary or secondary IDE channel

    C. Whether the jumpers on the drive are set to master or slave

    D. None, because an optical drive is not configured through the CMOS setup

13. What type of DVD can store 15.9 GB of data or more than eight hours of video?

    A. Double-sided, single-layered

    B. Single-sided, single-layered

    C. Single-sided, dual-layered

    D. Double-sided, dual-layered

14. Which of the following kinds of discs is the best choice for performing regular backups?

    A. CD-ROM/XA

    B. CD-Interactive (CD-I)

    C. CD-R

    D. CD-RW

15. While studying abroad, you purchased brand-new Blu-ray Discs produced in China. After returning to the United States, you find they will not work in your Blu-ray Disc player. What is most likely the problem?

A. The Blu-ray Discs have a C region code.

B. The Blu-ray Discs have a 6 region code.

C. The Blu-ray Discs have a B region code.

D. The Blu-Ray Discs have an A region code.

■ Essay Quiz

1. Why do many manufacturers build computers without floppy drives? If you bought a new computer, would you still want a floppy disk on it? Write a short essay defending or attacking the floppy drive.

2. You have been tasked to provide removable media for each of the technicians in your department. One tech wants a card reader and SD cards, and another wants a USB thumb drive. Write a memo outlining the advantages of each technology and make a recommendation.

3. Your friend Jack's hard drive died last week, so he bought a new hard drive and installed it. Now he's trying to install Windows 2000, but his computer will not boot to the CD-ROM drive. He's called you for help. What does he need to do to get his computer to recognize and boot to the CD-ROM drive so he can install the OS?

4. Your department is getting ready to replace the old computers, and your boss Mrs. Turner has asked you to investigate what kind of optical drives the new computers should have. Write a memo to your boss listing the device(s) you have selected and justifying your choice(s).

5. Your friend Dudley wants to burn high-definition movies on his desktop system, which currently only has a CD-RW drive. He eventually wants to play back the movies with the highest possible picture quality on his brand-new HDTV. What kind of technology and other considerations would you suggest to Dudley to achieve his goal?

Lab Projects

• Lab Project 13.1

If your lab PC has a floppy disk drive, install a second floppy disk drive. How does your system determine which is drive A: and which is drive B:? Reverse the ribbon cable on the A: drive so the red stripe no longer aligns with pin 1. What happens when you boot the system back up? Can the drive read disks in this condition?

• Lab Project 13.2

Flash media comes in a bunch of different forms. Take a trip to your local computer store—or even to a drugstore that has digital picture processing—and see what sort of media or flash devices they have available. What are some of the advantages or disadvantages of one form factor over another?

• Lab Project 13.3

Use the Internet to check these sites: www.compaq.com, www.dell.com, and www.gateway.com. What kinds of optical drives do these companies offer with their new computers? Do any of the companies offer multiple optical drives? If so, which ones and what devices? What upgrades for optical drives do the companies offer and how expensive are the upgrades? If you were buying a new PC, which optical drive(s) would you want on your computer? Why?

• Lab Project 13.4

Adding a second optical drive to a PC enables you to do some fun things, from making your own music CDs to watching movies. Assuming you want to install an ATAPI drive, you then need to face some issues. Which controller should you use, primary or secondary? Should both optical drives be on the same controller or on different controllers? Why?

Most techs would install a burner as secondary master and put a read-only drive on the primary as slave, but different drives require different considerations. If you don't plan to copy CD to CD, there's no reason the read-only CD shouldn't be secondary slave. The key is you have to experiment.

Install a second optical drive—preferably a burner—and run it through its paces. Copy files and burn discs to and from the optical and hard drives. Then change the configuration of your drives (such as having both optical drives on the same controller) and run through the testing process again. Do you notice any differences?

• Lab Project 13.5

Use a map of the world, atlas, or globe. See if you can identify the three assigned Blu-ray region code areas. (Hint: The codes are A, B and C.) Next, see if you can identify the specifically assigned DVD region code areas. (Hint: The codes are 1, 2, 3, 4, 5, 6.) Next, using Windows 2000, XP, or Vista, look under the hardware properties of your DVD or Blu-ray Disc player to identify your region code.

Installing and Upgrading Windows

"Microsoft has a new version out…which according to everybody is the 'most reliable Windows ever.' To me, this is like saying that asparagus is 'the most articulate vegetable ever.'"

—DAVE BARRY

In this chapter, you will learn how to

- **Identify and implement pre-installation tasks**
- **Install and upgrade Windows 2000, Windows XP, and Windows Vista**
- **Troubleshoot installation problems**
- **Identify and implement post-installation tasks**
- **Explain the structures created during the installation process**

An operating system (OS) provides the fundamental link between the user and the hardware that makes up the PC. Without an operating system, all of the greatest, slickest PC hardware in the world is but so much copper, silicon, and gold wrapped up as a big, beige paperweight (or, if you're a teenaged boy, a big, gleaming, black paperweight with a window and glowing fluorescent lights, possibly shaped like a robot). The operating system creates the interface between human and machine, enabling you to unleash the astonishing power locked up in the sophisticated electronics of the PC to create amazing pictures, games, documents, business tools, medical miracles, and much more.

This chapter takes you through the processes for installing and upgrading Windows. It starts by analyzing the preinstallation tasks, steps not to be skipped by the wise tech. The bulk of the chapter comes in the second section, where you'll learn about installing and upgrading Windows 2000, XP, and Vista. Not all installations go smoothly, so section three looks at troubleshooting installation issues. Section four walks you through the typical post-installation tasks. The chapter finishes by examining what you've created in the installation process, such as where the various operating system (OS) files reside and how they interact to create a seamlessly booting new installation of Windows.

Essentials/Practical Application

■ Preparing for Installation or Upgrade

Installing or upgrading an OS is like any good story: it has a beginning, a middle, and an end. In this case, the beginning is the several tasks you need to do before you actually do the installation or upgrade. If you do your homework here, the installation process is a breeze, and the post-installation tasks are minimal.

Don't get discouraged at all of the preparation tasks. They usually go pretty fast, and skipping them can cause you gobs of grief later when you're in the middle of installing and things blow up. Well, maybe there isn't a real explosion, but the computer might lock up and refuse to boot into anything usable. With that in mind, look at the nine tasks you need to complete *before* you insert that CD or DVD. Here's the list; discussion follows:

1. Identify hardware requirements.
2. Verify hardware and software compatibility.
3. Decide what type of installation to perform.
4. Determine how to back up and restore existing data, if necessary.
5. Select an installation method.
6. Determine how to partition the hard drive and what file system to use.
7. Determine your computer's network role.
8. Decide on your computer's language and locale settings.
9. Plan for post-installation tasks.

The CompTIA A+ exams don't test you directly on the basics of installation, but you need to understand installation and installation troubleshooting to understand the types of questions you'll be asked on both exams.

Identify Hardware Requirements

Hardware requirements help you decide whether a computer system is a reasonable host for a particular operating system. Requirements include the CPU model, the amount of RAM, the amount of free hard disk space, and the video adapter, display, and storage devices that may be required to install and run the operating system. They are stated as minimums or, more recently, as recommended minimums. Although you could install an operating system on a computer with the old minimums that Microsoft published, they were not realistic if you wanted to actually accomplish work. With the last few versions of Windows, Microsoft has published recommended minimums that are much more realistic. You will find the published minimums on the packaging and at Microsoft's Web site (www.microsoft.com). Later in this chapter, I'll also tell you what I recommend as minimums for Windows 2000, Windows XP, and Windows Vista.

Verify Hardware and Software Compatibility

Assuming your system meets the requirements, you next need to find out how well Windows supports the brand and model of hardware and application software you intend to use under Windows. You have two basic sources for this information: Microsoft and the manufacturer of the device or software. How do you actually access this information? Use the Web!

If you're installing Windows XP or Vista, the Setup Wizard automatically checks your hardware and software and reports any potential conflicts. But please don't wait until you are all ready to install to check this out. With any flavor of Windows, *first do your homework*.

Microsoft goes to great lengths to test any piece of hardware that might be used in a system running Windows through their **Windows Logo'd Product List** (Figure 14.1). This list, formerly known as the *Hardware Compatibility List (HCL)*, is the definitive authority as to whether your component is compatible with the OS. Every component listed on the Windows Logo'd Product List Web site has been extensively tested to verify that it works with Windows XP, Windows Vista, or Windows 7 and is guaranteed by Microsoft to work with your installation. The URL for the Windows Logo'd Product List is www.microsoft.com/whdc/hcl/default.mspx. Sadly, Microsoft no longer maintains a compatibility list specifically for Windows 2000, but in general, products compatible with XP will also be compatible with 2000.

When you install a device that's not been tested by Microsoft, a rather scary screen appears (Figure 14.2). This doesn't mean the component won't

> You'll occasionally hear the HCL or Windows Logo'd Product List referred to as the Windows Catalog. The Windows Catalog was a list of supported hardware Microsoft would add to the Windows installation CD. The Windows Logo'd Product List Web site is the modern tech's best source, so use that rather than any printed resources.

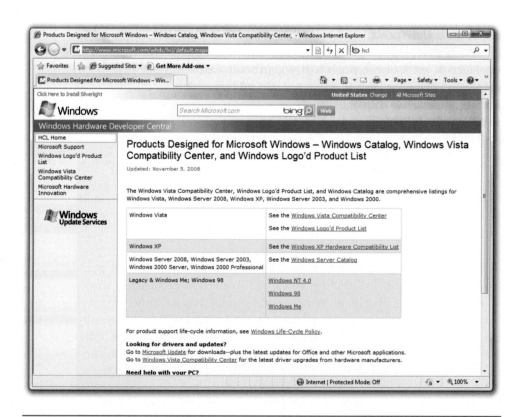

• **Figure 14.1**   Windows Logo'd Product List

work, only that it's not been tested. Not all component makers go through the rather painful process of getting the Microsoft approval so they can list their component in the Windows Logo'd Product List. As a general rule, unless the device is more than five years old, go ahead and install it. If it still doesn't work, you can simply uninstall it later.

Don't panic if you don't see your device on the list; many supported devices aren't on it. Check the optical discs that came with your hardware for proper drivers. Better yet, check the manufacturer's Web site for compatible drivers. Even when the Windows Logo'd Product List lists a piece of hardware, I still make a point of checking the manufacturer's Web site for newer drivers.

When preparing to upgrade, check with the manufacturers of the applications already installed in the previous OS. If there are software compatibility problems with the versions you have, the manufacturer should provide upgrade packs that you can install during the Windows setup process.

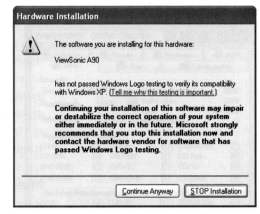

• **Figure 14.2**   Untested device in Windows XP

Decide What Type of Installation to Perform

You can install Windows in several ways. A **clean installation** of an OS involves installing it onto an empty hard drive with no previous OS installed. An **upgrade installation** means installing an OS on top of an earlier installed version, thus inheriting all previous hardware and software settings. You can combine versions of Windows by creating a **multiboot installation**. Installing usually involves some sort of optical disc, but other methods also exist. Let's look at all the options.

Clean Installation

A clean installation usually begins with a completely empty hard disk. The advantage to doing a clean installation is that you don't carry problems from the old OS over to the new one, but the disadvantage is that you have to reinstall all applications and reconfigure the desktop and each application to the user's preferences. You perform a clean installation by resetting your CMOS to tell the system to boot from the optical drive before your hard drive. You then boot off of a Windows installation disc, and Windows gives you the opportunity to partition and format the hard drive and then install Windows.

Upgrade Installation

In an upgrade installation, the new OS installs into the same folders as the old OS, or in tech speak, the new installs *on top of* the old. The new OS replaces the old OS but retains all saved data and inherits all of the previous settings (such as font styles, desktop colors and background, and so on), hardware, and applications. You don't have to reinstall your favorite programs!

To begin the upgrade of Windows, you must run the appropriate program from the optical disc. This usually means inserting a Windows installation disc into your system while your old OS is running, which starts the installation program. Then, to do an upgrade, you indicate that the new

CompTIA tests you on knowing how to upgrade a Windows 9x or Windows NT system to Windows 2000 or Windows XP and how to upgrade from Windows XP to Windows Vista. You do not need to know about Windows 9x or NT for the tests, but you do need to know how to upgrade them.

Before starting an OS upgrade, make sure you have shut down all other open applications!

version of Windows should install into a directory that already contains an installation of Windows (it will do this by default). You will be asked whether it is an upgrade or a new installation; if you select new installation, it will remove the existing OS before installing.

If for some reason the Windows 2000 or Windows XP installation program doesn't start automatically, go to My Computer, open the installation disc, and locate WINNT32.EXE. This program starts an upgrade to Windows 2000 or XP. In Windows Vista, open the disc in Windows Explorer and run Setup.exe in the disc's root directory, which starts the Vista upgrade.

Multiboot Installation

A third option that you need to be aware of is the dual boot or multiboot installation. Both Windows 2000 and Windows XP can install in a separate folder from your existing copy of Windows so you can put both operating systems on the same partition. Then every time your computer boots, you'll get a menu asking you which version of Windows you wish to boot. Multiboot requires that you format your active partition with a file system that every operating system you install can use. This hasn't been much of a problem since the Windows 9x family stopped being relevant, because there's really no reason to use anything other than NTFS. Windows Vista doesn't let you define its install folder, so to multiboot Vista and XP, for example, you'd need to install each OS on a different partition.

Other Installation Methods

In medium to large organizations, more advanced installation methods are often employed, especially when many computers need to be configured identically. A common method is to place the source files in a shared directory on a network server. Then, whenever a tech needs to install a new OS, it is a simple task of booting up the computer, connecting to the source location on the network, and starting the installation from there. This method alone has many variations and can be automated with special scripts that automatically select the options and components needed. The scripts can even install the necessary applications at the end of the OS installation—all without user intervention once the installation has been started.

Another type of installation that is very popular for re-creating standard configurations is an **image installation**. An image is a complete copy of a hard disk volume on which an operating system and, usually, all required application software programs have been preinstalled. Images can be stored on optical discs, in which case the tech runs special software on the computer that copies the image onto the local hard drive. Images can also be stored on special network servers, in which case the tech connects to the image server by using special software and copies the image from the server to the local hard drive. A leader in this technology has been Norton Ghost, which is available from Symantec. Other similar programs are Clonezilla and Acronis's True Image.

Beginning with Windows 2000 Server, Microsoft added *Remote Installation Services (RIS)*, which can be used to initiate either a scripted installation or an installation of an image.

Determine How to Back Up and Restore Existing Data, If Necessary

Whether you are installing or upgrading, you may need to back up existing user data first, because things can go very wrong either way, and the data on the hard drive might be damaged. You'll need to find out where the user is currently saving data files. If they are saving onto the local hard drive, it must be backed up before the installation or replacement takes place, to preserve the data. However, if all data has been saved to a network location, you are in luck, because the data is safe from damage during installation.

If the user saves data locally, and the computer is connected to a network, save the data, at least temporarily, to a network location until after the upgrade or installation has taken place. If the computer is not connected to a network but the computer has a burnable optical drive, copy the data to DVDs. You can also use an external hard drive, which is a handy thing for any tech to have. Wherever you save the data, you will need to copy or restore any lost or damaged data back to the local hard disk after the installation.

If you plan to migrate a user from one system to another, here's where you might start the process by running the Files and Settings Transfer Wizard (Windows XP) or Windows Easy Transfer (Windows Vista). You'll complete that process during the post-installation tasks. Rather than discuss the process twice, I leave the full discussion on migration for the "Post-Installation Tasks" section later in this chapter.

Select an Installation Method

Once you've backed up everything important, you need to select an installation method. You have two basic choices: insert the installation disc into the drive and go, or install over a network. The latter method falls into the realm of CompTIA Network+ technicians or even network administrators, so this book assumes you'll install from disc.

Determine How to Partition the Hard Drive and What File System to Use

If you are performing a clean installation, you need to decide ahead of time how to partition the disk space on your hard disk drive, including the number and size of partitions and the file system (or systems) you will use. Actually, in the decision process, the file system comes first, and then the space issue follows, as you will see.

This was a much bigger issue back in the days when older operating systems couldn't use newer file systems, but now that every Windows OS that you could reasonably want to install supports NTFS, there's really no reason to use anything else. You still might have a reason to partition your drive, but as for choosing a file system, your work is done for you.

Determine Your Computer's Network Role

The question of your computer's network role comes up in one form or another during a Windows installation. A Windows computer can have one of several roles relative to a network (in Microsoft terms). One role, called *standalone*, is actually a non-network role, and it simply means that the computer does not participate on a network. You can install any version of Windows on a standalone computer, and this is the only role that a Windows XP Home computer can play on a network. Every other modern version of Windows can be a member of either a workgroup or a domain (or, if you're using Windows 7, a HomeGroup). You will learn more about the workgroup and domain member roles in Chapter 23, "Local Area Networking."

Decide on Your Computer's Language and Locale Settings

These settings are especially important for Windows operating systems because they determine how date and time information is displayed and which math separators and currency symbols are used for various locations.

Plan for Post-Installation Tasks

After installing Windows, you may need to install the latest service pack or updates. You may also need to install updated drivers and reconfigure any settings, such as network settings, that were found not to work. You will also need to install and configure any applications (word processor, spreadsheet, database, e-mail, games, etc.) required by the user of the computer. Finally, don't forget to restore any data backed up before the installation or upgrade.

■ Installing and Upgrading Windows

At the most basic level, installing any operating system follows a fairly standard set of steps. You turn on the computer, insert an operating system disc into the optical drive, and follow the installation wizard until you have everything completed. Along the way, you'll accept the **End User License Agreement (EULA)** and enter the product key that says you're not a pirate; the product key is invariably located on the installation disc's case. At the same time, there are nuances between installing Windows 2000 or upgrading to Windows Vista that every CompTIA A+ certified tech must know, so this section goes through many installation processes in some detail.

Installing or Upgrading to Windows 2000 Professional

On the face of it, installing Windows 2000 Professional seems fairly simple. You insert the installation disc, access the setup routine, and go! But that conceptualization does not hold up in practice.

Hardware Requirements

The minimum specs represent what Microsoft says you need so you can install the Windows 2000 Professional OS. However, you need to take these specifications and at least double them if you want to be happy with your system's performance.

Here is a more realistic recommendation for a useful Windows 2000 Professional computer system:

Component	Minimum for a Windows 2000 Professional Computer	Recommended for a Windows 2000 Professional Computer
CPU	Intel Pentium 133 MHz	Intel Pentium II 350 MHz
Memory	64 MB	128 MB
Hard disk	2 GB with 650 MB of free space	6.4 GB with 2 GB of free space
Network	None	Modern network card
Display	Video adapter and monitor with VGA resolution	Video adapter and monitor with SVGA resolution, capable of high-color (16-bit) display
Optical drive	If you don't have an optical drive, you must use a floppy disk drive or install over a network.	If you don't have an optical drive, you must use a floppy disk drive or install over a network.

If your test system(s) exceeds the recommended configuration, all the better. You can never have too fast a processor or too much hard disk space.

Installing or Upgrading to Windows XP Professional

You prepare for installing Windows XP just as you do for installing Windows 2000. Windows XP has a few different aspects to it that are worth considering as a separate issue.

Upgrade Paths

You can upgrade to Windows XP Professional from all of the following versions of Windows:

- Windows 98 (all versions)
- Windows Me
- Windows NT 4.0 Workstation (Service Pack 5 and later)
- Windows 2000 Professional (including service packs)
- Windows XP Home Edition

XP Hardware Requirements

Hardware requirements for Windows XP Professional are higher than for previous versions of Windows, but are still very low by modern hardware standards.

Microsoft XP runs on a wide range of computers, but you need to be sure that your computer meets the minimum hardware requirements as shown here.

Also shown is my recommended minimum for a system running a typical selection of business productivity software.

Component	Minimum for a Windows XP Computer	Recommended for a Windows XP Computer
CPU	Any Intel or AMD 233 MHz or higher processor	Any Intel or AMD 300 MHz or higher processor
Memory	64 MB of RAM (though Microsoft admits XP will be somewhat crippled with only this amount)	512 MB of RAM or higher
Hard disk	1.5 GB of available hard drive space	4 GB of available hard drive space
Network	None	Modern network card
Display	Video card that supports SVGA with at least 800 × 600 resolution	Video card that supports DirectX with at least 1024 × 768 resolution
Optical drive	Any CD- or DVD-media drive	Any CD- or DVD-media drive

Hardware and Software Compatibility

You'll need to check hardware and software compatibility before installing Windows XP Professional—as either an upgrade or a new installation. Of course, if you purchase a computer with Windows XP preinstalled, you're spared this task, but you'll still need to verify that the application software you plan to add to the computer will be compatible. Luckily, Microsoft includes the Upgrade Advisor on the Windows XP disc.

Upgrade Advisor   You would be hard-pressed these days to find a computer incapable of running Windows XP, but if you are ever uncertain about whether a computer you excavated at an archeological dig can run XP, fear not! The **Upgrade Advisor** is the first process that runs on the XP installation disc. It examines your hardware and installed software (in the case of an upgrade) and provides a list of devices and software that are known to have issues with XP. Be sure to follow the suggestions on this list.

You can also run the Upgrade Advisor separately from the Windows XP installation. You can run it from the Windows XP disc. Microsoft used to offer the XP Upgrade Advisor on its Web site, but searching for it now will just redirect you to the Vista Upgrade Advisor (more on that later), so running it from the disc is the way to go nowadays.

Booting into Windows XP Setup

The Windows XP discs are bootable, and Microsoft no longer includes a program to create a set of setup boot disks. This should not be an issue, because PCs manufactured in the past several years can boot from the optical drive. This system BIOS setting, usually described as boot order, is controlled through a PC's BIOS-based Setup program.

In the unlikely event that your lab computer can't be made to boot from its optical drive, you can create a set of six (yes, six!) Windows XP setup boot floppy disks by using a special program you can download from Microsoft's Web site. Note that Microsoft provides separate boot disk programs for XP Home and XP Pro.

Running the Upgrade Advisor

If you have a PC with Windows XP or an older version of Windows, you should know how to run the Upgrade Advisor on your system, so try this:

1. Insert the Windows XP installation disc. If Autorun is enabled, the Welcome to Microsoft Windows XP screen appears. If this does not appear, select Start | Run, enter the following, and then click OK:

   `d:\SETUP.EXE`

   (Where *d* is the drive letter for the optical drive.)

2. At the Welcome to Microsoft Windows XP screen, select Check System Compatibility to start the Upgrade Advisor. On the following page, select Check My System Automatically.

3. In the Upgrade Advisor dialog box, select the first choice if you have an Internet connection. If you don't have an Internet connection, select No, Skip This Step and Continue Installing Windows. (Don't worry, you aren't really going to install yet.)

4. Click Next. The Upgrade Advisor shows the tasks that Dynamic Update is performing, and then it restarts Setup.

5. After Setup restarts, you'll be back at the same page in the Upgrade Advisor. This time, select No, Skip This Step and Continue Installing Windows, and click Next. The Upgrade Report page appears next. You can save the information in a file by clicking Save As and selecting a location.

6. Read the findings that the Upgrade Advisor presents. If a problem was found, click the Full Details button for instructions, and be sure to follow them. When you have recorded any necessary instructions, click Finish.

Registration Versus Activation

During setup, you will be prompted to register your product and activate it. Many people confuse activation with registration, but these are separate operations. **Registration** tells Microsoft who the official owner or user of the product is, providing contact information such as name, address, company, phone number, and e-mail address. Registration is still entirely optional. Activation is a way to combat software piracy, meaning that Microsoft wishes to ensure that each license for Windows XP is used solely on a single computer. It's more formally called **Microsoft Product Activation (MPA)**.

Mandatory Activation Within 30 Days of Installation   Activation is mandatory, but you can skip this step during installation. You have 30 days in which to activate the product, during which time it works normally. If you don't activate it within that time frame, it will be disabled. Don't worry about forgetting, though, because once it's installed, Windows XP frequently reminds you

to activate it with a balloon message over the tray area of the taskbar. The messages even tell you how many days you have left.

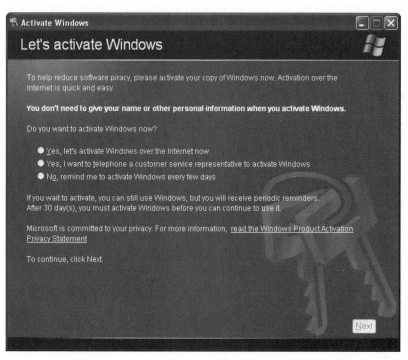

• **Figure 14.3**   Activation takes just seconds with an Internet connection.

Activation Mechanics   Here's how product activation works. When you choose to activate, either during setup or later when XP reminds you to do it, an installation ID code is created from the product ID code that you entered during installation and a 50-digit value that identifies your key hardware components. You must send this code to Microsoft, either automatically if you have an Internet connection or verbally via a phone call to Microsoft. Microsoft then returns a 42-digit product activation code. If you are activating online, you don't have to enter the activation code; it happens automatically. If you are activating over the phone, you must read the installation ID to a representative and enter the resulting 42-digit activation code into the Activate Windows by Phone dialog box.

No personal information about you is sent as part of the activation process. Figure 14.3 shows the dialog box that opens when you start activation by clicking on the reminder message balloon.

Installing or Upgrading to Windows Vista

Preparing for a Windows Vista installation is not really different from preparing for a Windows 2000 or XP install. There are, of course, a few things to consider before installing or upgrading your system to Vista.

Upgrade Paths

Windows Vista is persnickety about doing Upgrade installs with different editions; although you can upgrade to any edition of Vista from any version of Windows XP, many upgrade paths will require you to do a clean installation of the Vista operating system. Note that you cannot upgrade from Windows 2000 to Vista, but must do a clean installation. Vista's upgrade paths are so complicated that the only way to really explain them is using a grid showing the OS you're trying to upgrade from and the edition of Vista you're upgrading to. Fortunately for you, Microsoft provides such a grid, which I've re-created in Table 14.1.

Hardware Requirements

Windows Vista requires a substantially more powerful computer to run than Windows 2000 or XP. Make sure your computer meets at least the

Table 14.1	Vista's Labyrinthine Upgrade Paths			
	Vista Home Basic	**Vista Home Premium**	**Vista Business**	**Vista Ultimate**
XP Professional	Clean Install	Clean Install	Upgrade Install	Upgrade Install
XP Home	Upgrade Install	Upgrade Install	Upgrade Install	Upgrade Install
XP Media Center	Clean Install	Upgrade Install	Clean Install	Upgrade Install
XP Tablet PC	Clean Install	Clean Install	Upgrade Install	Upgrade Install
XP Professional x64	Clean Install	Clean Install	Clean Install	Clean Install
Windows 2000	Clean Install	Clean Install	Clean Install	Clean Install

following minimum hardware requirements suggested by Microsoft, though it would be far better to meet my recommended requirements:

Component	Minimum for a Windows Vista Computer	Recommended for a Windows Vista Computer
CPU	1 GHz 32-bit (x86) or 64-bit (x64) processor	Any dual-core Intel or AMD processor or better
Memory	512 MB of RAM for Vista Basic (for all other editions, 1 GB of RAM)	2 GB of RAM or higher
Hard disk	20 GB hard drive with 15 GB of available hard drive space for Vista Basic (for all other editions, 40 GB hard drive with 15 GB of free space)	100 GB hard drive or greater
Network	Modern network card with Internet access	Modern network card with Internet access
Display	Support for DirectX 9 graphics and 32 MB of graphics memory for Vista Basic (for all other editions, 128 MB of graphics memory, plus pixel shader 2.0 support, the WDDM driver, and 32 bits per pixel)	DirectX 10 capable graphics card with at least 512 MB of graphics memory
Optical drive	Any DVD-media drive	Any DVD-media drive

If you're uncertain about whether your computer will run Vista, you can download and run the Windows Vista Upgrade Advisor from www.microsoft.com/windows/windows-vista/get/upgrade-advisor.aspx, which will tell you if your computer meets Microsoft's minimum requirements.

 The CompTIA exams are likely to test your knowledge regarding the minimum installation requirements for Windows Vista Home Basic, Home Premium, Business, or Ultimate. Know them well!

Hardware and Software Compatibility

Windows Vista is markedly different from Windows XP in many very basic, fundamental ways, and this causes all sorts of difficulty with programs and device drivers designed for Windows XP. When Vista came out, you probably heard a lot of people grumbling about it, and likely they were grumbling about hardware and software incompatibility. Simply put, a lot of old programs and devices don't work in Windows Vista, which is bad news for people who are still running Microsoft Word 97.

Software incompatibility in Vista was such a problem for many corporate customers and end users that Microsoft is including a Windows XP Mode in the higher-end editions of Windows 7, enabling most Windows XP programs to be run despite the different OS.

Fortunately, Microsoft offers a Windows Vista Compatibility Center where you can check whether a piece of software or hardware will work with Vista. Most programs developed since Vista's release in 2007 should work, but checking the compatibility of any programs you absolutely cannot do without is always a good idea.

Upgrading Issues

A few extra steps before you pop in that installation disc are worth your time. If you plan to upgrade rather than perform a clean installation, follow these steps first:

1. Check out the Windows Logo'd Product List site or the Windows Vista Compatibility Center site, or run a compatibility report by using the Check Upgrade utility provided with Windows 2000 Professional or the Upgrade Advisor for Windows XP or Vista, depending on which OS you're planning on installing. These utilities generate a detailed list of potentially problematic devices and applications. You can run the utility in both 2000 and XP as follows: Insert the Windows Installation disc and, from your current OS, open a command prompt or use the Start Run dialog box to run the WINNT32.EXE program with the CHECKUPGRADEONLY switch turned on. The command line will look like this:

```
d:\i386\winnt32 /checkupgradeonly
```

(where d: is the optical drive).

2. Have an up-to-date backup of your data and configuration files handy.

3. Perform a "spring cleaning" on your system by uninstalling unused or unnecessary applications and deleting old files.

4. Perform a disk scan and a disk defragmentation.

5. Uncompress all files, folders, and partitions.

6. Perform a virus scan, and then remove or disable all virus-checking software.

7. Disable virus checking in your system CMOS.

8. Keep in mind that if worse comes to worst, you may have to start over and do a clean installation anyway. This makes step 2 exceedingly important. Back up your data!

The Windows 2000/XP Clean Installation Process

The steps involved in a clean installation of Windows 2000 Professional and Windows XP are virtually identical. The only differences are the order of two steps and some of the art on the screens that appear, so we can comfortably discuss both installations at the same time.

A clean installation begins with your system set to boot to your optical drive and the Windows installation disc in the drive. You start your PC, and assuming you have the boot order right, the installation program starts

Not all screens in the installation process are shown!

booting (Figure 14.4). Note at the bottom that it says to press F6 for a third-party SCSI or RAID driver. You only do this if you want to install Windows onto a strange drive and Windows does not already have the driver for that drive. Don't worry about this; Windows has a huge assortment of drivers for just about every hard drive ever made, and in the rare situation where you need a third-party driver, the folks who sell you the SCSI or RAID array will tell you ahead of time.

After the system copies a number of files, you'll see the Welcome screen (Figure 14.5). This is an important screen! As you'll see in later chapters, techs often use the Windows installation disc as a repair tool, and this is the screen that lets you choose between installing Windows or repairing an existing installation. Because you're making a new install, just press ENTER.

You're now prompted to read and accept the EULA. Nobody ever reads this—it gives you a stomachache when you see what you're really agreeing to—so just press F8 and move to the next screen to start partitioning the drive (Figure 14.6).

• **Figure 14.4** Windows Setup text screen

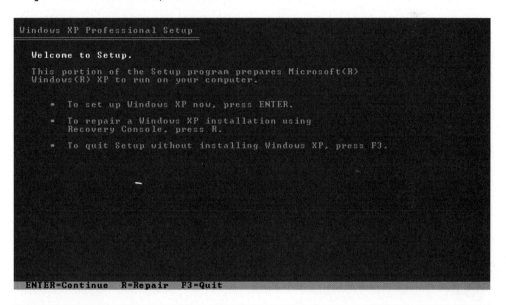

• **Figure 14.5** Welcome text screen

If your hard disk is unpartitioned, you need to create a new partition when prompted. Follow the instructions. In most cases, you can make a single partition, although you can easily make as many partitions as you wish. You can also delete partitions if you're using a hard drive that was partitioned in the past (or if you mess up your partitioning). Note that there is no option to make a primary or extended partition; this tool makes the first partition primary and the rest extended.

After you've made the partition(s), you must select the partition on which to install XP (sort of trivial if you only have one partition), and then you need to decide which file system format to use for the new partition.

Tech Tip

Save Some Space
Many techie types, at least those with big (> 500 GB) hard drives, only partition half of their hard drive for Windows. This makes it easy for them to install an alternative OS (usually Linux) at a later date.

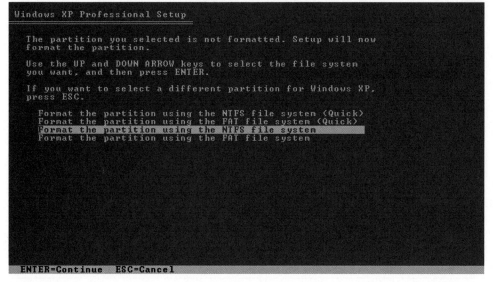

```
Windows XP Professional Setup

   The following list shows the existing partitions and
   unpartitioned space on this computer.

   Use the UP and DOWN ARROW keys to select an item in the list.

      •  To set up Windows XP on the selected item, press ENTER.
      •  To create a partition in the unpartitioned space, press C.
      •  To delete the selected partition, press D.

   ┌─────────────────────────────────────────────────────────────┐
   │  8190 MB Disk 0 at Id 0 on bus 0 on atapi [MBR]               │
   │                                                               │
   │      Unpartitioned space                        8189 MB       │
   │                                                               │
   │                                                               │
   │                                                               │
   │                                                               │
   │                                                               │
   │                                                               │
   └─────────────────────────────────────────────────────────────┘

   ENTER=Install   C=Create Partition   F3=Quit
```

• **Figure 14.6**   Partitioning text screen

```
Windows XP Professional Setup

   The partition you selected is not formatted. Setup will now
   format the partition.

   Use the UP and DOWN ARROW keys to select the file system
   you want, and then press ENTER.

   If you want to select a different partition for Windows XP,
   press ESC.

      Format the partition using the NTFS file system (Quick)
      Format the partition using the FAT file system (Quick)
      Format the partition using the NTFS file system
      Format the partition using the FAT file system

   ENTER=Continue   ESC=Cancel
```

• **Figure 14.7**   Choosing NTFS

Unless you have some weird need to support FAT or FAT32, format the partition by using NTFS (Figure 14.7).

Setup now formats the drive and copies some basic installation files to the newly formatted partition, displaying another progress bar. Go get a book to read while you wait.

After it completes copying the base set of files to the hard drive, your computer reboots, and the graphical mode of Windows setup begins. This is where 2000 and XP begin to vary in appearance, even though they are performing the same steps. The rest of this section shows Windows XP. If you're running a Windows 2000 install, compare it to the screens you see here; it's interesting to see the different presentation doing the same job.

You will see a generic screen during the installation that looks like Figure 14.8. On the left of the screen, uncompleted tasks have a white button, completed tasks have a green button, and the current task has a red button. You'll get plenty of advertising to read as you install.

The following screens ask questions about a number of things the computer needs to know. They include the desired region and language the computer will operate in, your name and organization for personalizing

Mike Meyers' CompTIA A+ Guide to Managing and Troubleshooting PCs

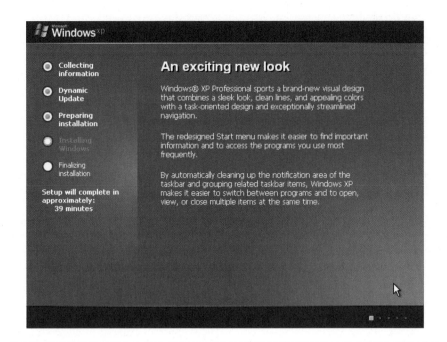

• **Figure 14.8** Beginning of graphical mode

your computer, and a valid **product key** for Windows XP (Figure 14.9). Be sure to enter the product key exactly, or you will be unable to continue.

Next, you need to give your computer a name that will identify it on a network. Check with your system administrator for an appropriate name. If you don't have a system administrator, just enter a simple name such as MYPC for now—you can change this at any time—and read up on networking later in this book. You also need to create a password for the Administrator user account (Figure 14.10). Every Windows system has an Administrator user

Losing your product key is a bad idea! Document it—at least write it on the installation CD-ROM.

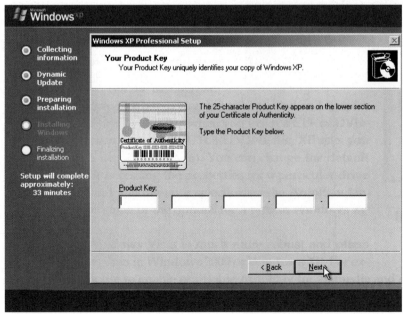

• **Figure 14.9** Product key

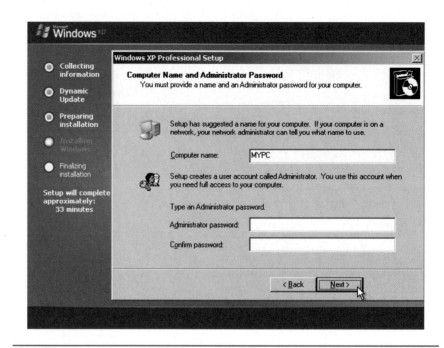

● **Figure 14.10**   Computer name and Administrator password

account that can do anything on the computer. Techs will need this account to modify and fix the computer in the future.

Last, you're asked for the correct date, time, and time zone. Then Windows tries to detect a network card. If a network card is detected, the network components will be installed and you'll have an opportunity to configure the network settings. Unless you know you need special settings for your network, just select the Typical Settings option (Figure 14.11).

Relax; XP will do most of the work for you. Plus you can easily change network settings after the installation.

The big copy of files now begins from the CD-ROM to your hard drive. This is a good time to pick your book up again, because watching the ads is boring (Figure 14.12).

After the files required for the final configuration are copied, XP reboots again. During this reboot, XP determines your screen size and applies the appropriate resolution. This reboot can take several minutes to complete, so be patient.

Once the reboot is complete, you can log on as the Administrator. Balloon messages may appear over the tray area of the taskbar—a common message concerns the display resolution. Click the balloon and allow Windows XP to automatically adjust the display settings.

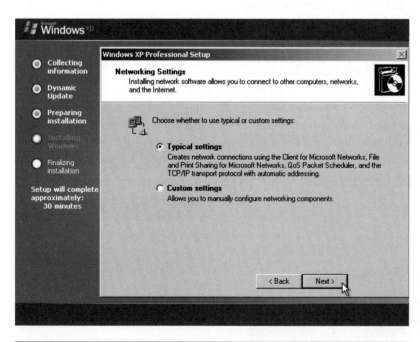

● **Figure 14.11**   Selecting typical network settings

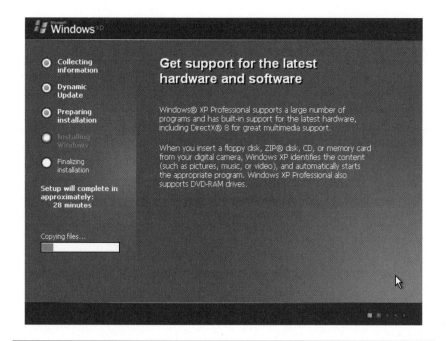

• **Figure 14.12**   The Big Copy

The final message in the installation process reminds you that you have 30 days left for activation. Go ahead and activate now over the Internet or by telephone. It's painless and quick. If you choose not to activate, simply click the Close button on the message balloon. That's it! You have successfully installed Windows XP and should have a desktop with the default Bliss background, as shown in Figure 14.13.

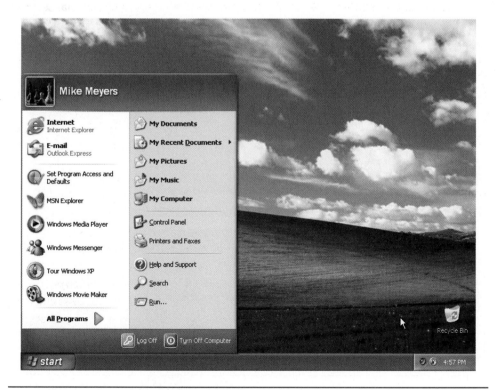

• **Figure 14.13**   Windows XP desktop with Bliss background

The Windows Vista Clean Installation Process

With Windows Vista, Microsoft has dramatically changed the installation process. No longer will you spend your time looking at a boring blue ASCII screen and entering commands by keyboard—the Vista installer has a full graphical interface, making it easy to partition drives and install your operating system. You already saw some of this process back in Chapter 12, "Implementing Hard Drives," but this chapter will go into a bit more detail.

Just as when installing Windows 2000 or XP, you need to boot your computer from some sort of Windows installation media. Usually, you'll use a DVD disc, though you can also install Vista from a USB drive, over a network, or even off of several CD-ROMs that you have to specially order from Microsoft. When you've booted into the installer, the first screen you see asks you to set your language, time/currency, and keyboard settings, as in Figure 14.14.

The next screen in the installation process is somewhat akin to the 2000 and XP Welcome screen, in that it enables techs to start the installation disc's repair tools (Figure 14.15). Just like the completely revamped installer, the Vista repair tools are markedly different from the ones for Microsoft's previous operating systems. You'll learn more about those tools in Chapter 17, "Maintaining and Troubleshooting Windows," but for now all you need to know is that you click where it says *Repair your computer* to use the repair tools. Because you're just installing Windows in this chapter, click *Install now*.

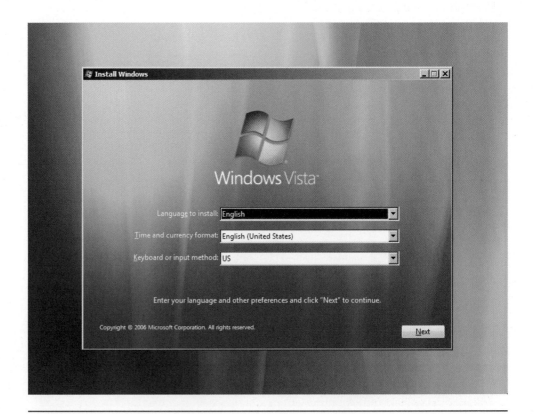

• **Figure 14.14**   Windows Vista language settings screen

The next screen shows just how wildly different the Vista installation order is. When installing Vista, you enter your product key before you do anything else, as you can see in Figure 14.16. With Windows 2000 and XP, this didn't come until much, much later in the process, and there's a very interesting reason for this change.

Microsoft has dramatically altered the method they use to distribute different editions of their operating system; instead of having different discs for each edition of Windows Vista, every Vista installation disc contains all of the available editions. In Windows 2000 and XP, your product key did very little besides let the installation disc know that you had legitimately purchased the OS. In Vista, your product key not only verifies the legitimacy of your purchase; it also tells the installer which edition you purchased, which, when you think about it, is a lot to ask of a randomly generated string of numbers and letters.

If you leave the product key blank and click the Next button, you will be taken to a screen asking you which version of Vista you would like to install (Figure 14.17). Lest you start to think that you've discovered a way to install Vista without paying for it, you should know that doing this

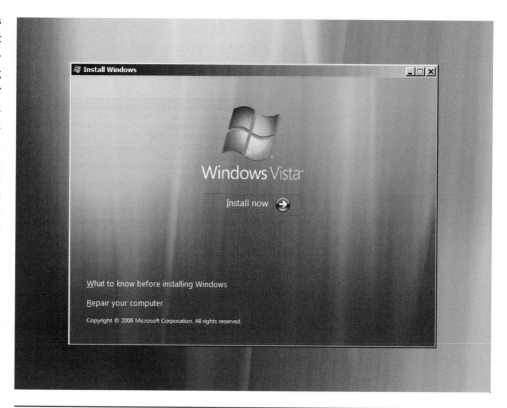

● **Figure 14.15**   The Windows Vista setup Welcome screen

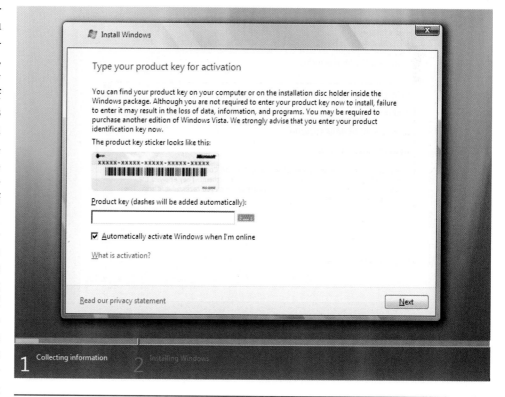

● **Figure 14.16**   The Windows Vista product key screen

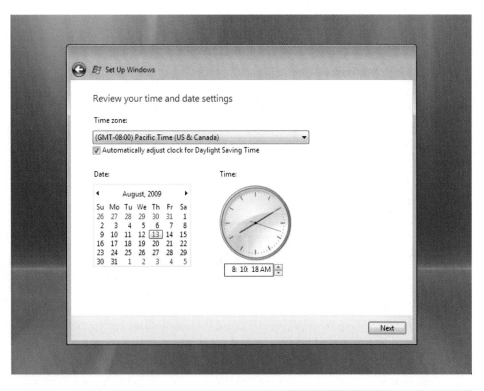

installs only the most critical security fixes and updates and leaves the rest of the updates up to you. This is useful when setting up computers for businesses, as many companies' IT departments like to test out any updates before rolling them out to the employees. You should only select the last option, *Ask me later*, if you can dedicate yourself to checking weekly for updates, as it will not install any automatically.

Next up is the time and date screen, where you can make sure your operating system knows what time it is, as in Figure 14.25. This screen should be pretty self-explanatory, so set the correct time zone, the correct date, and the correct time, and move to the next screen.

• **Figure 14.25** Vista pities the fool who doesn't know what time it is.

If you have your computer connected to a network while running the installer, the next screen will ask you about your current location (Figure 14.26). If you're on a trusted network, such as your home or office network, make the appropriate selection and your computer will be discoverable on the network. If you're on, say, a Starbucks' network, choose *Public location* so the caffeine addicts around you can't see your computer and potentially do malicious things to it.

Once you're past that screen, Windows thanks you for installing it, which is awfully polite for a piece of software, don't you think (Figure 14.27)?

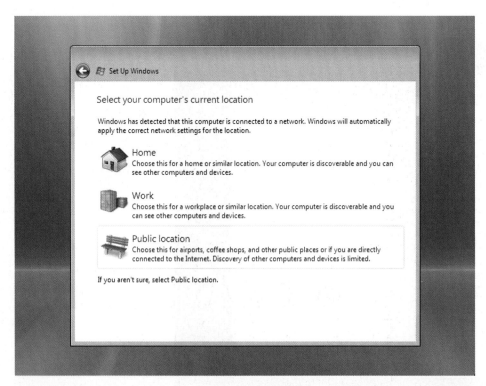

• **Figure 14.26** Tell Windows what kind of network you're on.

● **Figure 14.27**   Aw, shucks, Microsoft Windows Vista. Don't mention it.

Lest you think you're completely through the woods, Windows will run some tests on your computer to give it a performance rating, which, in theory, will tell you how well programs will run on your computer. You'll sometimes see minimum performance ratings on the sides of game boxes, but even then, you're more likely to need plain, old-fashioned minimum system requirements. This process can take anywhere from 5 to 20 minutes, so this is another one of those coffee-break moments in the installation process.

Once the performance test finishes, Vista boots up and you have 30 days to activate your new operating system.

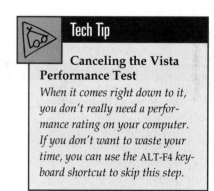

Tech Tip

Canceling the Vista Performance Test
When it comes right down to it, you don't really need a performance rating on your computer. If you don't want to waste your time, you can use the ALT-F4 keyboard shortcut to skip this step.

Automating the Installation

As you can see, you may have to sit around for quite a while when installing Windows. Instead of having to sit there answering questions and typing in CD keys, wouldn't it be nice just to boot up the machine and have the installation process finish without any intervention on your part—especially if you have 30 PCs that need to be ready to go tomorrow morning? Fortunately, Windows offers two good options for automating the installation process: scripted installations and disk cloning.

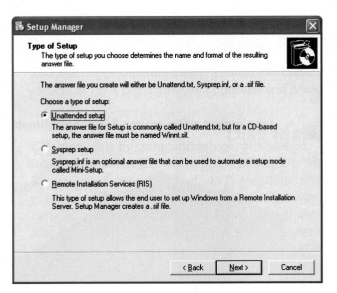

• **Figure 14.28** Setup Manager can create answer files for three types of setups.

Scripting Windows 2000 and XP Installations with Setup Manager

For automating a Windows 2000 or XP install, Microsoft provides *Setup Manager* to help you create a text file—called an *answer file*—containing all of your answers to the installation questions. Windows doesn't come with Setup Manager, but you can download it from the Microsoft Download Center (www.microsoft.com/downloads) as part of the Windows XP Service Pack 2 Deployment Tools. Setup Manager supports creating answer files for three types of setups: Unattended, Sysprep, and Remote Installation Services (Figure 14.28). The current version of the tool can create answer files for Windows XP Home Edition, Windows XP Professional, and Windows Server 2003 (Standard, Enterprise, or Web Edition); see Figure 14.29.

Setup Manager can create an answer file to completely automate the process, or you can use it to set default options. You'll almost always want to create an answer file that automates the entire process (Figure 14.30).

When running a scripted installation, you have to decide how to make the installation files themselves available to the PC. Although you can boot your new machine from an installation CD, you can save yourself a lot of CD swapping if you just put the installation files on a network share and install your OS over the network (Figure 14.31).

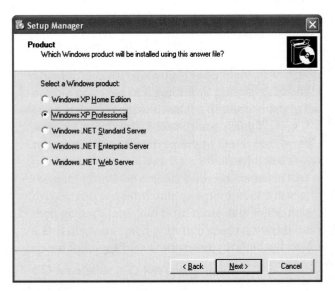

• **Figure 14.29** Setup Manager can create answer files for five versions of Windows.

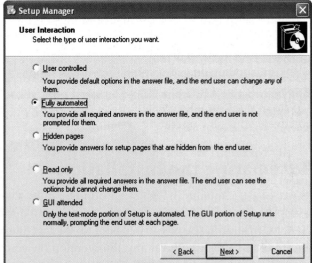

• **Figure 14.30** Setup Manager can create several kinds of answer files.

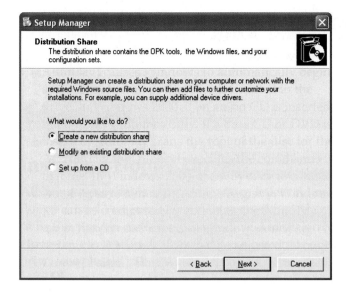

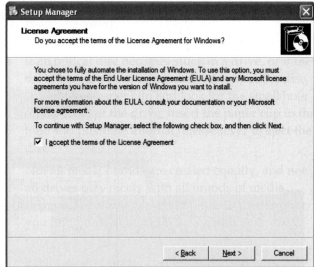

• **Figure 14.31**   Choose where to store the installation files.

• **Figure 14.32**   Don't forget to accept the license agreement.

When you run Setup Manager, you get to answer all those pesky questions. As always, you will also have to "accept the terms of the License Agreement" (Figure 14.32) and specify the product key (Figure 14.33), but at least by scripting these steps you can do it once and get it over with.

Now it's time to get to the good stuff, customizing your installation. Using the graphical interface, decide what configuration options you want to use: screen resolutions, network options, browser settings, regional settings, and so on. You can even add finishing touches to the installation, installing additional programs such as Microsoft Office and Adobe Reader by

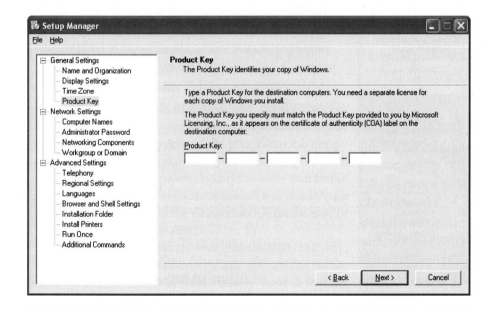

• **Figure 14.33**   Enter the product key.

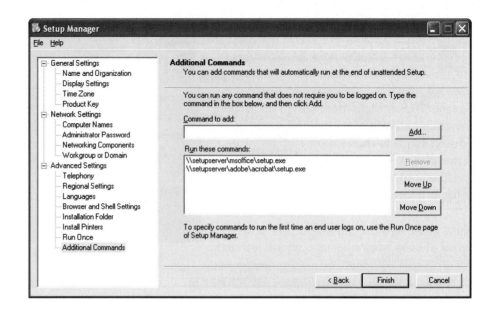

• **Figure 14.34**   Running additional commands

automatically running additional commands after the Windows installation finishes (Figure 14.34). You can also set programs to run once (Figure 14.35).

Remember that computer names must be unique on the network. If you're going to use the same answer files for multiple machines on the same network, you need to make sure that each machine gets its own unique name. You can either provide a list of names to use, or you can have the Setup program randomly generate names (Figure 14.36).

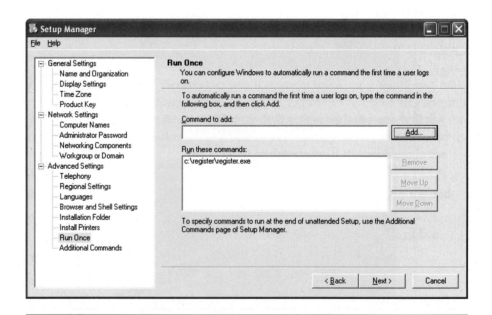

• **Figure 14.35**   Running a program once

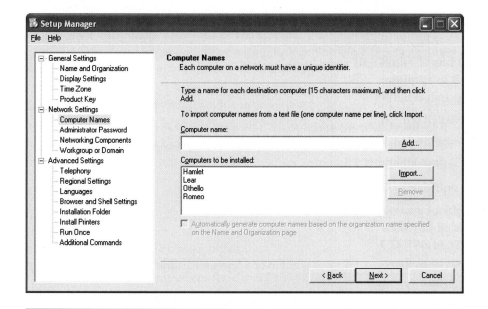

● **Figure 14.36** Pick your computer names.

When you're finished, Setup Manager prompts you to save your answers as a text file. The contents of the file will look something like this:

```
;SetupMgrTag
[Data]
    AutoPartition=1
    MsDosInitiated="0"
    UnattendedInstall="Yes"

[Unattended]
    UnattendMode=FullUnattended
    OemSkipEula=Yes
    OemPreinstall=No
    TargetPath=\WINDOWS

[GuiUnattended]
    AdminPassword=414c11f760b0064 ... [out to 64 characters]
    EncryptedAdminPassword=Yes
    OEMSkipRegional=1
    TimeZone=85
    OemSkipWelcome=1
    AutoLogon=Yes
    AutoLogonCount=1

[UserData]
    ProductKey=FFFFF-FFFFF-FFFFF-FFFFF-FFFFF
    FullName="Scott"
    OrgName="Total Seminars"
    ComputerName=*
```

```
[Identification]
    JoinDomain=TOTAL
    DomainAdmin=admin09
    DomainAdminPassword=my-password
```

The list goes on for another hundred lines or so, and this is a fairly simple answer file. One thing to note is that if you provide a domain administrator's user name and password for the purpose of automatically adding new PCs to your domain, that user name and password will be in the text file in clear text:

```
[Identification]
    JoinDomain=TOTAL
    DomainAdmin=admin09
    DomainAdminPassword=my-password
```

In that case, you will want to be very careful about protecting your setup files.

Once you have your answer file created, you can start your installation with this command, and go enjoy a nice cup of coffee while the installation runs:

```
D:\i386\winnt32 /s:%SetupFiles% /unattend:%AnswerFile%
```

For %SetupFiles%, substitute the location of your setup files—either a local path (D:\i386 if you are installing from a CD) or a network path. If you use a network path, don't forget to create a network boot disk so that the installation program can access the files. For %AnswerFile%, substitute the name of the text file you created with Setup Manager (usually unattend.txt).

Of course, you don't have to use Setup Manager to create your answer file. Feel free to pull out your favorite text editor and write one from scratch. Most techs, however, find it much easier to use the provided tool than to wrestle with the answer file's sometimes arcane syntax.

Tech Tip

Creating a Network-Aware Bootable Disc
If you need help creating a network boot floppy or CD, check out www.netbootdisk.com/bootcd.htm.

Automating a Vista Installation with the Automated Installation Kit

As of Windows Vista, Setup Manager is history—as is any method of automating an installation that isn't extremely complicated and intimidating. Microsoft has replaced Setup Manager with the Windows Vista Automated Installation Kit (AIK), a set of tools which, although quite powerful, seem to have made something of a Faustian deal to obtain that power at the expense of usability (Figure 14.37).

Writing a step-by-step guide to creating an answer file in the AIK would almost warrant its own chapter, and as the CompTIA A+ exams don't cover it at all, I'm not going to go into too much gory detail. I will, however, give a brief account of the process involved.

The basic idea behind the AIK is that a tech can create an answer file by using a tool called the Windows System Image Monitor, and then use that answer file to build a Master Installation file that can be burned to DVD. Vista's answer files are no longer simple text documents but .XML files, and

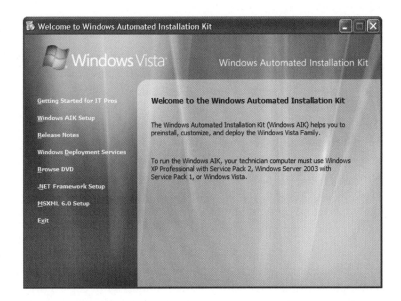

• **Figure 14.37**   The Automated Installation Kit

the process of creating one is much, much more complicated than it used to be. Gone are the days of simply running a wizard and modifying options as you see fit, replaced instead with a method of choosing components (which represent the things you want your automated installation to do, such as create a partition, enter a certain product key, and much, much more) out of a huge, often baffling list and then modifying their settings (Figure 14.38).

Once you've selected and modified all of the components you're interested in, you have to save your answer file, copy it to either a floppy disk or a USB thumb drive, and plug that into a new computer that you're going to install Vista on. When you boot a computer off of the Vista installation disc, it automatically searches all removable media for an answer file, and, finding one, uses it to automatically install itself. If you're only installing Vista to this one computer, you're finished, but if you want to install it to multiple computers, you'll probably want to create a disc image based off of your Master Installation file.

To create such an image, you must use a couple more tools in the AIK—Windows PE and ImageX—to "capture" the installation and create a disc image from it. If the rest of the process seemed a bit complicated, this part is like solving a Rubik's cube with your teeth while balancing on top of a flag pole and juggling. Suffice it to say that

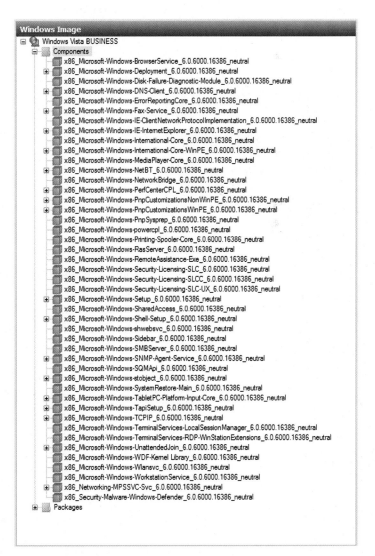

• **Figure 14.38**   The list of components in the Image Monitor

Tech Tip

Slipstreaming

You can save time by "slip-streaming" your installation files to include the latest patches. See the following site for instructions on how to merge (slipstream) Service Pack 3 into your Windows XP installation files:

www.helpwithwindows.com/ WindowsXP/Slipstreaming_ Windows_XP_Service_Pack_ 3.html

You can also slipstream Windows Vista Service Pack 1 (though not, as of this writing, Service Pack 2) into a Vista installation disc. Check out the following article for instructions:

www.helpwithwindows.com/ WindowsVista/Slipstream_ Windows_Vista_SP1.html

Tech Tip

Ghosting

Norton Ghost is not the only disk imaging software out there, but it is so widely used that techs often refer to disk cloning as "ghosting the drive."

the AIK comes with documentation that tells you how to do this, so with a bit of patience, you can get through it.

After you've created an image from your Master Installation file, you can burn it to discs or share it on a network to set up new computers. All in all, this is an extremely complicated process that will, when you're finished with it, make installing Windows Vista a snap.

Scripted installations are a fine option, but they don't work well in all scenarios. Creating a fully scripted installation, including the installation of all additional drivers, software updates, and applications, can be a time-consuming process involving lots of trial-and-error adjustments. Wouldn't it be easier, at least some of the time, to manually set up one PC exactly the way you want it, and then automatically create exact copies of that installation on other machines? That's where disk cloning comes into play.

Disk Cloning

Disk cloning simply takes an existing PC and makes a full copy of the drive, including all data, software, and configuration files. You can then transfer that copy to as many machines as you like, essentially creating clones of the original machine. In the old days, making a clone was pretty simple. You just hooked up two hard drives and copied the files from the original to the clone by using something like the venerable XCOPY program (as long as the hard drive was formatted with FAT or FAT32). Today, you'll want to use a more sophisticated program, such as Norton Ghost, to make an image file that contains a copy of an entire hard drive and then lets you copy that image either locally or over the network.

Sysprep

Cloning a Windows PC works great for some situations, but what if you need to send the same image out to machines that have slightly different hardware? What if you need the customer to go through the final steps of the Windows installation (creating a user account, accepting the license agreement, etc.)? That's when you need to combine a scripted setup with cloning by using the System Preparation Tool, **Sysprep**, which can undo portions of the Windows installation process.

After installing Windows and adding any additional software (Microsoft Office, Adobe Acrobat, Yahoo Instant Messenger, etc.), run Sysprep (Figure 14.39) and then create your disk image by using the cloning

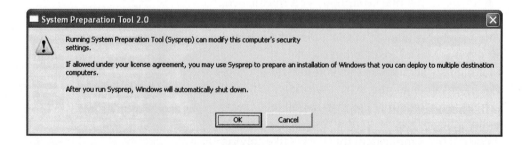

• **Figure 14.39**   Sysprep, the System Preparation Tool

Mike Meyers' CompTIA A+ Guide to Managing and Troubleshooting PCs

application of your choice. The first time a new system cloned from the image boots, an abbreviated version of setup, Mini-Setup, runs and completes the last few steps of the installation process: installing drivers for hardware, prompting the user to accept the license agreement and create user accounts, and so on. Optionally, you can use Setup Manager to create an answer file to customize Mini-Setup, just as you would with a standard scripted installation.

Tech Tip

RIS
Microsoft offers an even more advanced way of rolling out new systems: Remote Installation Services (RIS). *RIS requires at least Windows Server 2003 and is well beyond the scope of the CompTIA A+ exams.*

■ Troubleshooting Installation Problems

The term "installation problem" is rather deceptive. The installation process itself almost never fails. Usually, something else fails during the process that is generally interpreted as an "install failure." Let's look at some typical installation problems and how to correct them.

Text Mode Errors

If you're going to have a problem with a Windows installation, this is the place to get one. It's always better to have the error right off the bat as opposed to when the installation is nearly complete. Text mode errors most often take place during clean installations and usually point to one of the following problems:

No Boot Device Present When Booting Off the Startup Disk

Either the startup disk is bad or the CMOS is not set to look at that disk drive first.

Windows Setup Requires XXXX Amount of Available Drive Space

You forgot to format the C: drive, or there's a bunch of stuff on the drive already.

Not Ready Error on Optical Drive

You probably just need to give the optical drive a moment to catch up. Press R for retry a few times. You may also have a damaged installation disc, or the optical drive may be too slow for the system.

A Stop Error (Blue Screen of Death) After the Reboot at the End of Text Mode

This may mean you didn't do your homework in checking hardware compatibility, especially the BIOS. I'll tell you more about stop errors in Chapter 17, "Maintaining and Troubleshooting Windows," but if you encounter one of these errors during installation, check out the Microsoft Knowledge Base.

Graphical Mode Errors

Once the installation passes the text mode and moves into graphical mode, a whole new crop of problems may arise.

Hardware Detection Errors

Failure to detect hardware properly by any version of Windows Setup can be avoided by simply researching compatibility beforehand. Or, if you decided to skip that step, you might be lucky and only have a hardware detection error involving a noncritical hardware device. You can troubleshoot this problem at your leisure. In a sense, you are handing in your homework late, checking out compatibility and finding a proper driver after Windows is installed.

Every Windows installation depends on Windows Setup properly detecting the computer type (motherboard and BIOS stuff, in particular) and installing the correct hardware support. Microsoft designed Windows to run on several hardware platforms using a layer of software tailored specifically for the hardware, called the **hardware abstraction layer (HAL)**.

Can't Read CAB Files   *If you can't read a .cab file CD is scratched.*

This is probably the most common of all installation errors. **CAB files** (as in cabinet) are special compressed files, recognizable by their .CAB file extension, that Microsoft uses to distribute copies of Windows. If your system can't read them, first check the installation disc for scratches. Then try copying all of the files from the source directory on the disc (\i386) into a directory on your local hard drive. Then run Windows Setup from there, remembering to use the correct program (WINNT32.EXE). If you can't read any of the files on the installation disc, you may have a defective drive.

Lockups During Installation

Lockups are one of the most challenging problems that can take place during installation, because they don't give you a clue as to what's causing the problem. Here are a few things to check if you get a lockup during installation.

Smart Recovery, Repair Installation

Most system lockups occur when Windows Setup queries the hardware. If a system locks up once during setup, turn off the computer—literally. Unplug the system! Do *not* press CTRL-ALT-DEL. Do *not* click Reset. Unplug it! Then turn the system back on, boot into Setup, and rerun the Setup program. Windows will see the partial installation and either restart the installation process automatically (Smart Recovery) or prompt you to repair the installation. Both of these look at the installation progress and complete the installation.

Optical Drive, Hard Drive

Bad optical discs, optical drives, or hard drives may cause lockups. Check the optical disc for scratches or dirt, and clean it up or replace it. Try a known good disc in the drive. If you get the same error, you may need to replace the drive.

Log Files

Windows generates a number of special text files called **log files** that track the progress of certain processes. Although Windows creates different log files for different purposes, two files most interest us:

- **SETUPLOG.TXT** tracks the complete installation process, logging the success or failure of file copying, Registry updates, reboots, and so on.

- **SETUPAPI.LOG** tracks each piece of hardware as it is installed. This is not an easy log file to read, as it uses Plug and Play code, but it will show you the last device installed before Windows locked up.

Windows stores these log files in the WINNT or Windows directory (the location in which the OS is installed). These operating systems have powerful recovery options, so, honestly, the chances of your ever actually having to read a log file, understand it, and then get something fixed as a result of that understanding are pretty small. What makes log files handy is when you call Microsoft or a hardware manufacturer. They *love* to read these files, and they actually have people who understand them. Don't worry about trying to understand log files for the CompTIA A+ exams; just make sure you know the names of the log files and their location. Leave the details to the übergeeks.

▪ Post-Installation Tasks

You might think that's enough work for one day, but your task list has a few more things. They include updating the OS with patches and service packs, upgrading drivers, restoring user data files, and migrating and retiring.

Patches, Service Packs, and Updates

Someone once described an airliner as consisting of millions of parts flying in close formation. I think that's also a good description for an operating system. And we can even carry that analogy further by thinking about all of the maintenance required to keep an airliner safely flying. Like an airliner, the parts (programming code) of your OS were created by different people, and some parts may even have been contracted out. Although each component is tested as much as possible, and the assembled OS is also tested, it's not possible to test for every possible combination of events. Sometimes a piece is simply found to be defective. The fix for such a problem is a corrective program called a **patch**.

In the past, Microsoft provided patches for individual problems. They also accumulated patches until they reached some sort of critical mass and then bundled them together as a **service pack**. They still do this. But they also make it easier for you to find and install the appropriate patches and service packs, which, when combined, are called *updates*. They make these updates available at their Web site or on optical disc. Many organizations make the updates available for distribution from network servers. Immediately after installing Windows, install the latest updates on the computer. Chapter 17, "Maintaining and Troubleshooting Windows," covers this process more fully.

Upgrading Drivers

Even if you did all your preinstallation tasks, you may decide to go with the default drivers that come with Windows and then upgrade them to the latest drivers after the fact. This is a good strategy, because installation is a complicated task and you can simplify it by installing old but adequate drivers. Maybe those newest drivers are just a week old—waiting until after the Windows installation to install new drivers gives you a usable driver to go back to if the new driver turns out to be a lemon. In Chapters 17, "Maintaining and Troubleshooting Windows," and 18, "Input/Output," you'll learn more about working with drivers, including a little driver magic called "Roll Back Driver."

Restoring User Data Files (If Applicable)

Remember when you backed up the user data files before installation? You don't? Well, check again, because now is the time to restore that data. Your method of restoring depends on how you backed up the files in the first place. If you used a third-party backup program, you need to install it before you can restore those files, but if you used the Windows Backup utility (Windows 2000 or XP) or the Backup and Restore Center (Windows Vista), you are in luck, because they are installed by default (with the exception of Windows XP Home edition). If you did something simpler, such as copying to optical discs or a network location, all you have to do is copy the files back to the local hard disk. Good luck!

Migrating and Retiring   *for Domain*

Seasons change and so does the state of the art in computing. At a certain point in a computer's life, you'll need to retire an old system. This means you must move the data and users to a new system or at least a new hard drive—a process called **migration**—and then safely dispose of the old system. Microsoft offers a few tools to accomplish this task, and because it's important to know about them for the A+ exam (not to mention for your next new computer purchase), I'm going to go over them.

Files and Settings Transfer Wizard

You've already heard a bit about the **Files and Settings Transfer Wizard (FSTW)** back in Chapter 4, "Understanding Windows," but the CompTIA A+ exams expect you to have more than just a passing knowledge of it. When migrating to a new system, you would run the Files and Settings Transfer Wizard on the newer computer (assuming the newer computer is running Windows XP, but more on Vista's migration options later), which would then use the wizard to pull files off of the older one. You start the wizard by going to Accessories | System Tools in Windows XP's All Programs menu. Once you've fired it up, you're presented with the screen in Figure 14.40.

Files and Settings Transfer Wizard

Welcome to the Files and Settings Transfer Wizard

This wizard helps you transfer files and settings from your old computer to your new one.

You can transfer settings for Internet Explorer and Outlook Express, as well as desktop and display settings, dial-up connections, and other types of settings.

The best way to use this wizard for transferring files and settings is to use either a direct cable connection or a network. Learn more about connecting your computers.

Please close any other programs before you continue.

To continue, click Next.

[< Back] [Next >] [Cancel]

• **Figure 14.40**   The Files and Settings Transfer Wizard's initial screen

When you click the Next button on the wizard's first screen, you're asked whether the computer you're using is the new or old computer, as in Figure 14.41.

Note that the old computer can be running any version of Windows all the way back to Windows 95. Older Windows operating systems didn't come with the Files and Settings Transfer Wizard installed, so if you're migrating from an older version of Windows, you'll have to either install the wizard onto the older computer with the XP disc or create a Wizard Disk that will enable you to do the same thing. You're given the option to create such a disk by clicking Next with New computer selected, as in Figure 14.42.

Once you've either created a Wizard Disk (or told the wizard that you're going to install the wizard from the XP CD), you're taken to a screen that asks where to look for the files and settings that you've collected (Figure 14.43). The first two options are slightly outdated, because the first refers to a direct serial connection, now a rarity in the personal computing world, and the second asks for a floppy disc, though you can use it with USB thumb drives as well. The third option is the most likely candidate for a migration, because it enables you to look for your older computer on your home network.

Meanwhile, to actually determine which files and settings are going to be transferred, you need to run the wizard on your old computer. If you're migrating from another Windows XP machine, you need to tell the wizard where it's being run; otherwise, you skip to the next step, which asks how you want to transfer the files (Figure 14.44). The best option is to transfer them over a home network, but you can also save the files on a USB thumb drive or simply on a folder on your computer, though, obviously, that doesn't do a lot for transferring the files.

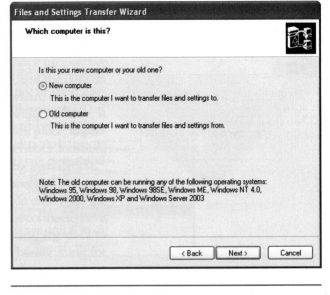

• **Figure 14.41**   Is this the new computer or your old one?

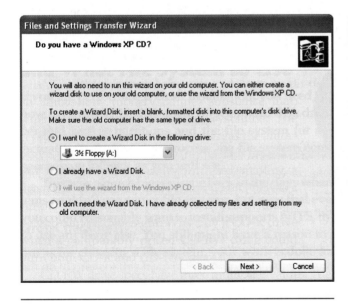

• **Figure 14.42**   Creating a Wizard Disk

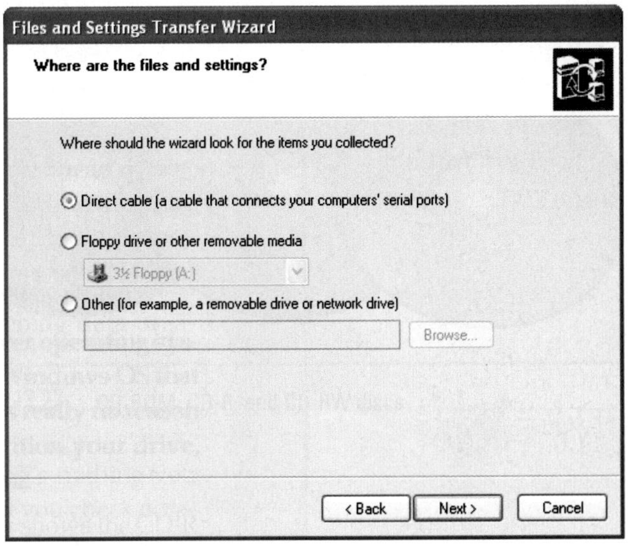

• **Figure 14.43**   Where are the files and settings?

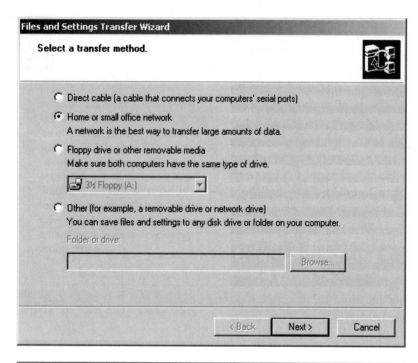

• Figure 14.44   How will you transfer the files?

When you click Next, the wizard shows its default list of folders and settings to save, but being the savvy PC tech you are, you'll probably want to customize which folders are migrated. You can do that by checking the box that says *Let me select a custom list of files and settings when I click Next* (Figure 14.45).

If you've checked that box, the next page enables you to add additional settings and browse for additional folders, files, or even file types to back up, making it pretty easy to simply back up every .MP3 on your computer (Figure 14.46). Neat, huh?

Once you click Next on that screen, the wizard begins the actual transfer process, which can take quite a lot of time depending on how much stuff you're transferring. This is an excellent time to, for example, read the complete works of Pliny the Elder, or, even more usefully, to memorize all of the previous chapters of this book word-for-word, because you'll probably have plenty of time.

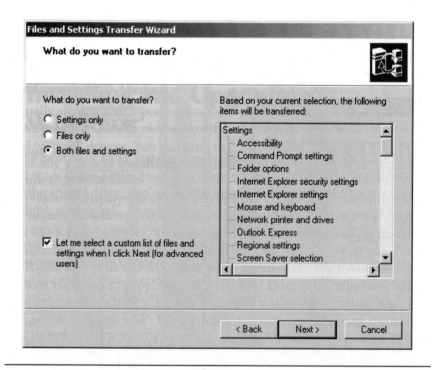

• Figure 14.45   The files and settings you're going to transfer

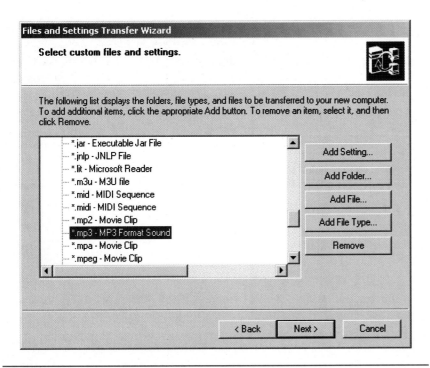

• **Figure 14.46**   Customizing the transfer

User State Migration Tool

If you're the sort of computer user who demands maximum functionality and power from your operating system, you'll probably want to use the **User State Migration Tool (USMT)**. The USMT has all of the same features as the Files and Settings Transfer Wizard, but with much more control over advanced configurations for the new computer. Its primary use is in businesses, because it has to be run in a Windows Server domain. In practice, if you're migrating a single user, use the FSTW. If you need to migrate multiple users, the USMT is the tool.

Windows Easy Transfer

With Windows Vista and 7, Microsoft has upgraded the Files and Settings Transfer Wizard, calling it **Windows Easy Transfer**. Windows Easy Transfer comes native in Vista/7 and can be downloaded and installed on Windows XP or 2000 as well, though you won't be able to transfer settings from a 2000 computer, only files. Windows Easy Transfer is located in the System Tools subfolder of the Accessories folder in your Programs menu. The first screen of the Windows Easy Transfer simply gives you a bit of information about the process, so there's not really much to do there.

When you click Next, you're taken to a screen that asks if you want to start a new transfer or continue an old one (Figure 14.47). If you've already set up your old computer to transfer the files, select the latter option; if you haven't, select the former.

If you choose to start a new transfer, the process is very similar to the Files and Settings Transfer Wizard: you select whether you're using your new or old computer and then follow the same basic steps as before.

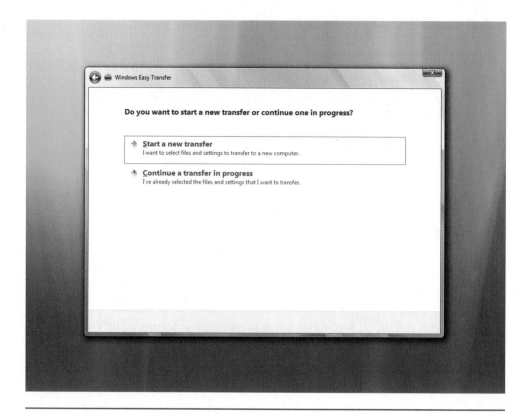

● Figure 14.47   Start a new transfer or continue one?

There are some differences, of course—network security is improved by using Transfer Keys to protect your files from others on the network, there's an option to use a special Easy Transfer cable to transfer your files between USB ports, and the order of some screens is changed around a bit—but if you understand the Files and Settings Transfer Wizard transfer process, Windows Easy Transfer shouldn't be too difficult.

Migration Practices

When talking about migration or retirement in terms of security, you need to answer one question: What do you do with the old system or drive?

All but the most vanilla new installations have sensitive data on them, even if it's simply e-mail messages or notes-to-self that would cause embarrassment if discovered. Most PCs, especially in a work environment, contain a lot of sensitive data. You can't just format C: and hand over the drive.

Follow three principles when migrating or retiring a computer. First, migrate your users and data information in a secure environment. Until you get passwords properly in place and test the security of the new system, you can't consider that system secure. Second, remove data remnants from hard drives that you store or give to charity. Third, recycle the older equipment; don't throw it in the trash. PC recyclers go through a process of deconstructing hardware, breaking system units, keyboards, printers, and even monitors into their basic plastics, metals, and glass for reuse.

The easiest way for someone to compromise or access sensitive data is to simply walk up and take it when you're not looking. This is especially true when you are in the process of copying information to a new, unprotected system. Don't set a copy to run while you go out to lunch, but rather be there

to supervise and remove any remnant data that might still reside on any mass storage devices, especially hard drives.

You might think that, as easy as it seems to be to lose data, you could readily get rid of data if you tried. That's not the case with magnetic media, though, such as hard drives and flash memory. Cleaning a drive completely is very difficult. Repeated formatting won't do the trick. Partitioning and formatting won't work. Data doesn't necessarily get written over in the same place every time, which means that a solid wipe of a hard drive by writing zeros to all of the clusters still potentially leaves a lot of sensitive and recoverable data, typically called **remnants**, on the drive.

Although you can't make data 100 percent unrecoverable short of physically shredding or pulverizing a drive, you can do well enough for donation purposes by using one of the better drive-wiping utilities, such as Webroot's Window Washer (Figure 14.48). With Window Washer, you can erase your Web browsing history, your recent activity in Windows (such as what programs you ran), and even your e-mail messages permanently. As an added bonus, you can create a bootable disk that enables you to wipe a drive completely.

Recycle

An important and relatively easy way to be an environmentally conscious computer user is to *recycle*. Recycling products such as paper and printer cartridges not only keeps them out of overcrowded landfills but also ensures that the more toxic products are disposed of in the right way. Safely disposing of hardware containing hazardous materials, such as computer monitors, protects both people and the environment.

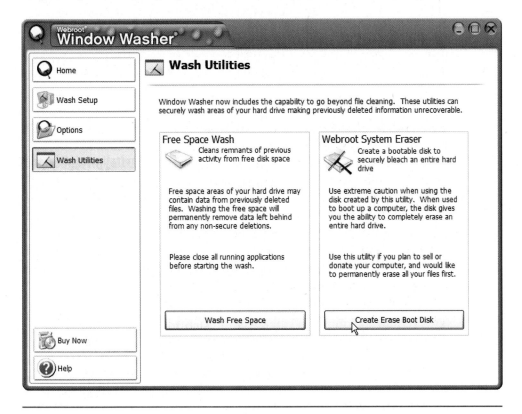

• **Figure 14.48**   Webroot Window Washer security software

Anyone who's ever tried to sell a computer more than three or four years old learns a hard lesson: they're not worth much if anything at all. It's a real temptation to take that old computer and just toss it in the garbage, but never do that!

First of all, many parts of your computer—such as your computer monitor—contain hazardous materials that pollute the environment. Luckily, thousands of companies now specialize in computer recycling and will gladly accept your old computer. If you have enough computers, they might even pick them up. If you can't find a recycler, call your local municipality's waste authority to see where to drop off your system.

An even better alternative for your old computer is donation. Many organizations actively look for old computers to refurbish and to donate to schools and other organizations. Just keep in mind that the computer can be too old—not even a school wants a computer more than five or six years old.

▪ Post-Installation: How All the Pieces Fit Together

You know from previous chapters the locations of many of the user-focused folders that are installed automatically. The Windows desktop, for example, is simply a folder, most commonly found in the user folders section of the C: drive. Similarly, My Documents/Documents is just another folder.

Installation creates a set of Windows-specific files and folders that the OS needs to run a PC. Some of these files and folders are directly on the root of the C: drive; others can be elsewhere. The best way to remember the locations of these files and folders and to know their importance to the OS is by looking at how they interact to boot the PC. Windows 2000 and Windows XP have pretty much the same files and boot process; Windows Vista differs a bit, so we'll look at the latter OS separately.

The 2000/XP Boot Process

Windows 2000 and XP distinguish between the files that start the operating system (called the *system files*) and the rest of the operating system files (usually in the \WINDOWS or \WINNT folders). The system files (memorize these!) consist of three required files: NTLDR, BOOT.INI, and NTDETECT.COM. If you're using a SCSI hard drive, there's a fourth file called NTBOOTDD.SYS. The NTLDR (pronounced *NT loader*) file begins the boot process.

You know from earlier chapters that to make a drive bootable requires an active, primary partition, right? Let's look at the process in a PC with a hard drive partitioned as C: and D:.

The CPU wakes up and runs the system BIOS, and then the BIOS sends out a routine looking for a valid operating system in the boot sector of the primary master hard drive. The master file table (MFT) lives in the boot sector of the C: partition. It points to the location of the Windows 2000/XP system files, also on the C: drive, because that's the bootable drive. Windows calls the primary active partition the *system partition* or the *system volume* (if it's a dynamic disk).

The Windows 2000/XP *boot files* consist of NTOSKRNL.EXE (the Windows kernel), the \WINNT\SYSTEM32\CONFIG\SYSTEM file (which controls the loading of device drivers), and the device drivers. Although these files are the core of the Windows 2000/XP OS, they are not capable of booting, or starting, the system. For that feat, they require NTLDR, NTDETECT.COM, and BOOT.INI—the system files.

The system files start the PC and then, at the end of that process, point the CPU to the location of the boot files. The CPU goes over and chats with NTOSKRNL, and the GUI starts to load. The operating system is then up and running, and you're able to do work.

The odd part about all this is that Microsoft decided to make the OS files mobile. *The Windows operating system files can reside on any partition or volume in the PC.* The \WINDOWS folder, for example, could very well be on drive D:, not drive C:. Whichever drive holds the core OS files is called the *boot partition*. This can lead to a little confusion when you say the system files are on the C: drive and Windows is on the D: drive, but that's just the way it is. The vast majority of Windows 2000/XP systems have the system partition and the boot partition both on the same big C: partition.

You have the process now in general, so let's look more specifically at the makeup and function of the individual files involved in the boot process.

2000/XP System Partition Files

Windows 2000 and XP require the three system files in the root directory of the system partition:

- NTLDR
- BOOT.INI
- NTDETECT.COM

To see these files, go into My Computer and open the C: drive. Go to Tools | Folder Options. Click *Show hidden files and folders*, uncheck the *Hide protected operating system files (Recommended)* option, and click OK. Now when you return to viewing the folder in My Computer, you will see certain critical files that Windows otherwise hides from you to prevent you from accidentally moving, deleting, or changing them in some unintended way (Figure 14.49).

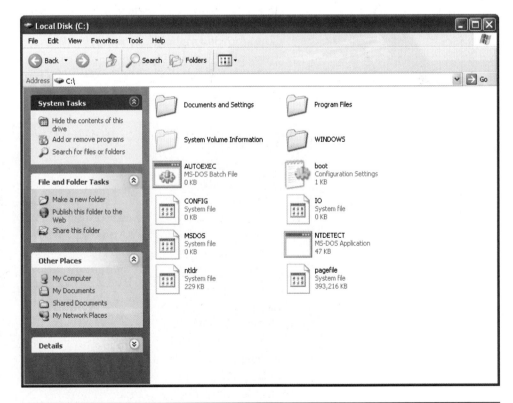

• **Figure 14.49**   My Computer showing the system files

NTLDR

When the system boots up, the master boot record (MBR) or MFT on the hard drive starts the NTLDR program. The **NTLDR** program then launches Windows 2000/XP or another OS. To find the available OSs, the NTLDR program must read the BOOT.INI configuration file. To do so, it loads its own minimal file system, which enables it to read the BOOT.INI file off of the system partition.

BOOT.INI File

The **BOOT.INI** file is a text file that lists the OSs available to NTLDR and tells NTLDR where to find the boot partition (where the OS is stored) for each of them. The BOOT.INI file has sections defined by headings enclosed in brackets. A basic BOOT.INI in Windows XP looks like this:

```
[boot loader]
timeout=30
default=multi(0)disk(0)rdisk(0)partition(1)\WINDOWS
[operating systems]
multi(0)disk(0)rdisk(0)partition(1)\WINDOWS="Microsoft Windows XP
Professional" /fastdetect
```

A more complex BOOT.INI may look like this:

```
[boot loader]
timeout=30
default=multi(0)disk(0)rdisk(0)partition(1)\WINDOWS
[operating systems]
multi(0)disk(0)rdisk(0)partition(1)\WINDOWS="Microsoft Windows XP
Professional" /fastdetect
multi(0)disk(0)rdisk(0)partition(1)\WINNT="Microsoft Windows 2000
Professional" /fastdetect
```

Such a BOOT.INI would result in the boot menu that appears in Figure 14.50.

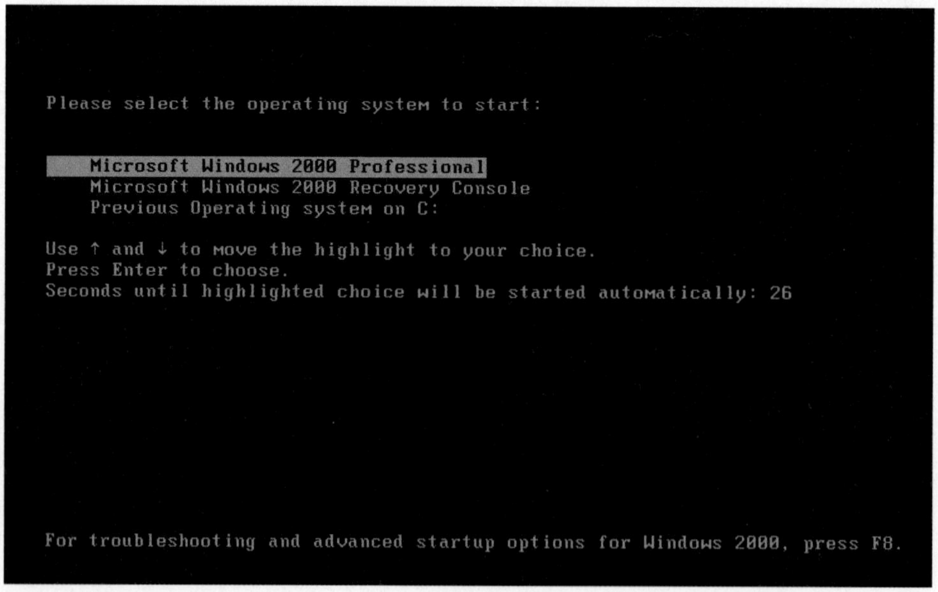

Please select the operating system to start:

    Microsoft Windows 2000 Professional
    Microsoft Windows 2000 Recovery Console
    Previous Operating system on C:

Use ↑ and ↓ to move the highlight to your choice.
Press Enter to choose.
Seconds until highlighted choice will be started automatically: 26

For troubleshooting and advanced startup options for Windows 2000, press F8.

• **Figure 14.50**   Boot loader in Windows 2000 with System Recovery Console

This crazy `multi(0)disk(0)rdisk(0)partition(1)` is an example of the Advanced RISC Computing (ARC) naming system. It's a system that's designed to enable your PC to boot Windows from any hard drive, including removable devices. Let's take a quick peek at each ARC setting to see how it works.

`Multi(x)` is the number of the adapter and always starts with 0. The adapter is determined by the boot order you set in your CMOS setting. For example, if you have a single PATA controller and a SATA controller, and you set the system to boot first from the PATA, any drive on that controller will get the value `multi(0)` placed in its ARC format. Any SATA drive will get `multi(1)`.

`Disk(x)` is only used for SCSI drives, but the value is required in the ARC format, so with ATA systems it's always set to `disk(0)`.

`Rdisk(x)` specifies the number of the disk on the adapter. On a PATA drive, the master is `rdisk(0)` and the slave is `rdisk(1)`. On SATA drives, the order is usually based on the number of the SATA connection printed on the motherboard, though some systems allow you to change this in CMOS.

`Partition(x)` is the number of the partition or logical drive in an extended partition. The numbering starts at 1, so the first partition is `partition(1)`, the second is `partition(2)`, and so on.

The `\WINDOWS` is the name of the folder that holds the boot files. This is important to appreciate! The ARC format looks at the folder, so there's no problem running different versions of Windows on a single partition. You can simply install them in different folders. Of course, you have other limitations, such as file system type, but in general, multibooting in Windows is pretty trivial. Better yet, this is all handled during the installation process.

ARC format can get far more complicated. SCSI drives get a slightly different ARC format. For example, if you installed Windows on a SCSI drive, you might see this ARC setting in your BOOT.INI:

```
scsi(0)disk(1)rdisk(0)partition(1)
```

If you want to boot to a SCSI drive, Windows adds a fourth file to your system files called NTBOOTDD.SYS. This file only exists if you want to boot to a SCSI drive. Most people don't boot to a SCSI, so don't worry if you don't see this file with the other three system files.

On rare occasions, you might find yourself needing to edit the BOOT.INI file. Any text editor handily edits this file, but most of us prefer to edit BOOT.INI via the System Setup dialog box. In Windows 2000/XP, open the System applet from the Control Panel. Click the Advanced tab and then click the Startup and Recovery button. The BOOT.INI options show up at the top (Figure 14.51).

BOOT.INI has some interesting switches at the end of the ARC formats that give special instructions on how the operating system should boot. Sometimes Windows puts these in automatically, and sometimes you will add them manually for troubleshooting. Here are a few of the more common ones:

- **/BOOTLOG** Tells Windows to create a log of the boot process and write it to a file called Ntbtlog.txt.

- **/CMDCONS** Tells Windows to start the Recovery Console (see Chapter 15, "Working with the Command-Line Interface").

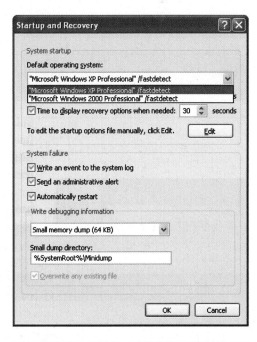

• **Figure 14.51**   BOOT.INI

- **/LASTKNOWNGOOD** Tells Windows to boot the Last Known Good set of files (see Chapter 15, "Working with the Command-Line Interface").
- **/NOEXECUTE** Newer CPUs come with Data Execute Protection (DEP) to prevent unruly programs from causing system lockups. The setting for this, /NOEXECUTE=OPTIN, is the default on Windows systems.

NTDETECT.COM

If the NTLDR determines that you have chosen to start Windows 2000/XP, it boots the system into protected mode and then calls on **NTDETECT.COM** to detect the installed hardware on the system. NTLDR then refers to the BOOT.INI file to locate the Windows boot files.

Critical Boot Files

Naming all the critical boot files for Windows 2000/XP is akin to naming every muscle in the human body—completely possible, but time-consuming and without any real benefit. However, a few of the *most* important files certainly deserve a short mention.

Once NTLDR finishes detections, it loads NTOSKRNL.EXE, HAL.DLL, some of the Registry, and some basic device drivers; then it passes control to the NTOSKRNL.EXE file. NTOSKRNL.EXE completes the Registry loading, initializes all device drivers, and starts the WINLOGON .EXE program, which displays the Windows 2000/XP logon screen (Figure 14.52).

Take the time to memorize the primary boot files and the boot process for Windows 2000/XP. Most boot errors are easily repaired if you know which files are used for booting and in which order they load.

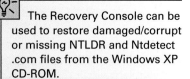

The Recovery Console can be used to restore damaged/corrupt or missing NTLDR and Ntdetect .com files from the Windows XP CD-ROM.

● **Figure 14.52** Where do you want to go today?

The Vista/7 Boot Process

Windows Vista has a very different boot process than previous versions of Windows. For one thing, Vista supports both BIOS and UEFI, whereas older versions of Windows did not, so things are a bit more complex right off the bat. Instead of having a unified Windows Vista boot process, there are actually two slightly different boot processes: one for systems using BIOS and one for systems with UEFI.

The very first thing that happens when you power on a system with Windows Vista is that either the BIOS or the UEFI starts up. The difference between BIOS and UEFI systems is in what happens next. In a BIOS-based system, the BIOS uses its boot order to scan partitions, one by one, for a Master Boot Record (MBR). The MBR holds a small bit of file system boot code that scans the system's partition table for the system partition and then loads its boot sector. The boot sector in turn contains code that does nothing but point the boot process toward a file called BOOTMGR (pronounced "boot manager," or

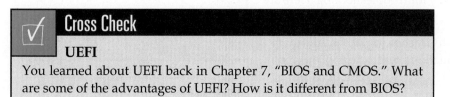

Cross Check

UEFI

You learned about UEFI back in Chapter 7, "BIOS and CMOS." What are some of the advantages of UEFI? How is it different from BIOS?

"boot mugger" if you're trying to make nerds laugh). On an UEFI system, on the other hand, neither the MBR nor the file system boot code is run, and UEFI simply loads up BOOTMGR directly.

If you've ever run a dual-boot system with Vista on it, you're probably already somewhat familiar with the BOOTMGR; one of its jobs is displaying that "Which operating system do you want to load?" screen and then loading the appropriate operating system. When the BOOTMGR starts, it reads data from a Boot Configuration Data (BCD) file that contains information about the various operating systems installed on the system as well as instructions for how to actually load (bootstrap) them. Once an operating system is selected (or immediately if only one is present), BOOTMGR loads a program called WINLOAD.EXE, which readies your system to load the operating system kernel itself rather like the way you clean up your house before Aunt Edna comes to visit. It does this by loading into memory the hardware abstraction layer, the system Registry, and the drivers for any boot devices before the operating system itself takes over.

Once the operating system process (called NTOSKRNL.EXE) takes over, it loads up all of the various processes and systems that comprise Windows, the Windows Vista logo comes up, and you're happily computing, completely oblivious to all of the complex electronic communication that just took place inside your computer.

No Installation Is Perfect

Even when the installation seems smooth, issues may slowly surface, especially in the case of upgrades. Be prepared to reinstall applications or deal with new functions that were absent in the previous OS. If things really fall apart, you can go back to the previous OS or, if you have an OEM computer (one built by, for example, Dell or HP instead of by you), your computer likely came with either a special recovery partition on its hard drive or a set of recovery discs that you can utilize to restore your operating system to its factory settings. You usually invoke a system recovery by hitting a certain key during boot-up—usually F10 or F11—and then following a set of prompts.

The procedures I've laid out in this chapter may seem like a lot of work—how bad could it be to grab an installation CD/DVD-ROM, fling a copy of Windows onto a system, and, as the saying goes, let the chips fall where they may? Plenty bad, is how bad. Not only is understanding these procedures important for the CompTIA A+ certification exams; they can also save your, ah, hide, once you're a working PC tech and you're tasked to install the latest version of Windows on the boss's new computer!

Tech Tip

BOOTMGR Is Missing!
If you use Vista long enough, you may encounter an error message saying that Windows cannot boot because the BOOTMGR is missing. This message is generated when the boot sector code is unable to locate the BOOTMGR, which can be caused by file system corruption, a botched installation, or viruses.

 BOOTMGR is also responsible for bringing Windows out of hibernation, so if your computer refuses to wake up, blame BOOTMGR!

 Unlike with Windows 2000 and XP, the boot files and the system files must all reside on the same partition in Vista and Windows 7.

 Boot Configuration Data (BCD) replaces the boot.ini used in previous operating systems and can be altered by using the command-line tool bcdedit.exe.

■ Chapter Summary

After reading this chapter and completing the exercises, you should understand the following about Windows.

Identify and implement preinstallation tasks

■ Identify hardware requirements, making sure your computer meets the recommended minimums for CPU, RAM, free hard disk space, video adapter, display, and other components. Check the Windows Logo'd Product List or the Windows Compatibility Center at the Microsoft Web site to verify that the Windows version you're installing supports the hardware and application software you will run.

■ A clean OS installation takes place on a new hard drive or one that has been reformatted and repartitioned. You must reinstall all applications and reconfigure user preferences. In an upgrade installation, the new OS is installed in the directory where the old OS was located. The new OS retains the hardware and software settings of the old OS, including user preferences. Before you upgrade, back up any data that the user has saved on the local hard drive.

■ Use the most advanced file system your version of Windows supports unless you are planning a multiboot configuration. Windows Vista will not multiboot with another OS on the same partition.

Install and upgrade Windows 2000, Windows XP, and Windows Vista

■ You can install Windows 2000 with floppy diskettes or a CD-ROM. Windows XP does not create a set of setup boot disks and does not use a floppy disk by default. If you install from the CD, you must add an optical drive to your PC's boot sequence and boot directly to the Windows 2000 or Windows XP CD-ROM. If this isn't possible in Windows XP, you can download a set of six setup boot floppy disks from the Microsoft Web site.

■ You can install Windows Vista/7 from a DVD-ROM, a USB drive, or specially ordered CD-ROMs, from over a network, or by using a disc image.

■ During installation, you will be prompted for registration information, including your name, address, and other details. Registration is optional. Designed to prevent a Windows license from being used for more than one PC, Microsoft Product Activation (MPA) is *mandatory* within 30 days of installing Windows XP, Vista, or 7, or the operating system will be disabled. You can activate the OS by using an Internet connection or by calling Microsoft. You give Microsoft an installation code—a 50-digit value that identifies your key hardware components—and Microsoft gives you a 42-digit product activation code.

■ To do a clean installation of Windows 2000/XP, boot the computer to the Windows installation disc, which will copy files to your hard drive. You then remove the disc, the system reboots, and Windows loads system devices and displays the Welcome to Setup screen. When prompted, accept the End User License Agreement (EULA). If necessary, create a new partition (default size or smaller). After you select the partition where Windows should be installed and the file system to use (NTFS is recommended), Setup copies files to the Windows folder and appropriate subfolders. Several reboots later and you're good to go.

■ Installing Windows Vista/7 is very different from installing 2000 or XP, but most of the concepts are the same. You still boot the computer from the installation disc, accept a EULA, partition your system drive, and enter a product key. You just do all those things in a different order and by using a graphical user interface instead of a primitive text mode.

■ The system requirements for Windows Vista are slightly different, depending on whether you're installing the Home Basic edition or any other edition. The non-Basic editions all require a 1-GHz processor, 1 GB of RAM, and 40 GB of hard drive space (with at least 15 MB of free space); a DirectX 9 capable graphics card with at least 128 MB of memory, pixel shader 2.0 support, the WDDM driver, and 32 bits per pixel; a network card with

Internet access; and a DVD drive. Home Basic is similar but only requires 512 MB of RAM, a 20-GB hard drive (again, with 15 GB free), and a basic 32-MB graphics card without any fancy features.

- You can automate the installation process through scripted installations and disk cloning. Windows 2000 and Windows XP can use Setup Manager to help you create an answer file that contains all of the answers to the installation questions, such as computer name, locale, screen resolution, and so on. Windows Vista comes with the Automated Installation Kit (AIK) that you can use to create an answer file. It's a substantially more complex tool than the older Setup Manager.

- With disc cloning, you simply take an existing PC and make a full copy of the drive, including all data, software, and configuration files. You can then transfer that copy to as many machines as you like, essentially creating clones of the original machine.

Troubleshoot installation problems

- Although the installation process itself rarely fails, you may encounter an installation failure caused by something else. Text mode errors during a clean installation may range from "No Boot Device Present" (the startup disk is bad or CMOS is not set to look at the appropriate drive first), to "Drive C: does not contain a Valid FAT Partition" (there is no partition or a partition Windows cannot use), to insufficient space on the drive. If you get a "Not Ready Error on CD-ROM," you could have a damaged installation disc or a slow optical drive that needs to catch up. A stop error (Blue Screen of Death) after the reboot at the end of the text mode points to a hardware incompatibility problem.

- Graphical mode errors indicate a different set of problems than text mode errors. Windows Setup must be able to detect the computer type (especially the motherboard and BIOS) and install the correct hardware abstraction layer (HAL). You may get a hardware detection error if Windows Setup fails to detect a device. If it is a noncritical piece of hardware, you can work on this problem later. This error may be solved by finding the proper driver.

- Probably the most common installation problem is failure to read the compressed Windows OS

distribution files called CAB files. Try copying these files to your local hard drive and running the Setup program from there.

- If the system locks up during installation, do *not* press CTRL-ALT-DEL or the Reset button to restart the installation. Instead, unplug the system and then turn it back on so Windows will recognize a partial installation and go to the Safe Recovery mode, where it can often complete the installation. A bad CD-ROM, optical drive, or hard drive can cause an installation lockup.

- During installation, Windows creates several log files. The two files of interest are SETUPLOG.TXT, which tracks the installation process (logging success and failures), and SETUPAPI.LOG, which tracks each piece of hardware as it is installed and shows you the last device installed before Windows locked up. Windows 2000 and XP store these log files in the OS installation directory (usually WINNT or Windows).

Identify and implement post-installation tasks

- The first essential tasks post installation include updating Windows by applying patches you download from Microsoft and updating drivers for hardware to the latest and hopefully most stable versions.

- After updating, you can go through the process of restoring a user's files through the various backup utilities available or by using the Files and Settings Transfer Wizard (FSTW) or Windows Easy Transfer.

- When migrating data to a new computer, it's important to follow three principles: migrate in a secure environment, remove data remnants when disposing of hard drives, and recycle old equipment.

- Completely removing data from a hard drive is difficult, short of physically destroying the drive. Tools such as Webroot's Window Washer are necessary to permanently erase files.

- When getting rid of old computer parts, it's important to recycle or donate them. This is not only helpful to the environment but also to the community.

Explain the structures created during the installation process

- Windows 2000 and XP use three primary system files (NTLDR, BOOT.INI, and NTDETECT.COM) to boot the system. These three files find and boot the operating system (NTOSKRNL.EXE) as well as any files necessary to run the OS.

- NTLDR is responsible for starting the operating system process in Windows 2000 and XP, and it does so by reading the BOOT.INI file, using its own tiny file system.

- The BOOT.INI file stores information about the location of all operating systems installed on the system.

- NTDETECT.COM detects the hardware on a Windows 2000/XP system before the actual OS is loaded.

- The Windows Vista/7 boot process first loads up some code in the MBR, which in turn calls the BOOTMGR. The BOOTMGR uses Boot Configuration Data (BCD) files to present the user with a list of all of the system's installed operating systems. Once an OS has been selected, the BOOTMGR loads a program called WINLOAD.EXE, which prepares the system environment for the operating system before loading the NTOSKRNL.

■ Key Terms

BOOT.INI *(508)*

CAB files *(498)*

clean installation *(467)*

disk cloning *(496)*

End User License Agreement (EULA) *(470)*

Files and Settings Transfer Wizard *(500)*

hardware abstraction layer (HAL) *(498)*

image installation *(468)*

log files *(499)*

Microsoft Product Activation (MPA) *(473)*

migration *(500)*

multiboot installation *(467)*

NTDETECT.COM *(510)*

NTLDR *(508)*

operating system (OS) *(464)*

patch *(499)*

product key *(479)*

registration *(473)*

remnants *(505)*

service pack *(499)*

SETUPAPI.LOG *(499)*

SETUPLOG.TXT *(499)*

Sysprep *(496)*

Upgrade Advisor *(472)*

upgrade installation *(467)*

User State Migration Tool (USMT) *(503)*

Windows Easy Transfer *(503)*

Windows Logo'd Product List *(466)*

■ Key Term Quiz

Use the Key Terms list to complete the sentences that follow. Not all terms will be used.

1. If you do not complete the _____ within 30 days, Windows stops working.

2. If you have a new hard drive with nothing on it, you will likely choose to do a(n)_____.

3. A(n) _____ is a fix for a single problem with the OS, while a(n) _____ is a combination of fixes.

4. If you wish to have only one OS and keep the applications and configuration of the current system, you should choose to do a(n) _____ of the new OS.

5. Microsoft uses compressed _____ to distribute installation files.

6. The _____ is a list of hardware devices and services that are guaranteed to work on Windows.

7. The Windows XP boot process accesses a list of installed operating systems stored in the _____ file.

8. If you're not sure your system can support Windows Vista, run the _____.

9. Windows creates _____ during the installation, which contains information about all installed hardware.

10. Windows XP and Vista have tools for migrating user files and settings. The tool in Vista is called _____.

■ Multiple-Choice Quiz

1. Which of the following is an advantage of running Windows 2000 on NTFS as opposed to FAT32?

   A. Security

   B. Support for DOS applications

   C. Long filenames

   D. Network support

2. Ricardo's Windows XP installation has failed. What file should he check to see what files failed to copy?

   A. INSTALL.LOG

   B. SETUP.LOG

   C. SETUP.TXT

   D. SETUPLOG.TXT

3. If you do not complete the activation process for Windows XP, Vista, or 7, what will happen to your computer?

   A. Nothing. Activation is optional.

   B. The computer will work fine for 30 days and then Windows will be disabled.

   C. Microsoft will not know how to contact you to provide upgrade information.

   D. You will have to use a floppy disk set to boot to Windows.

4. After you have completed a Windows installation and verified that the system starts and runs okay, what should you do next?

   A. Do nothing. You're through.

   B. Install World of Warcraft and enjoy.

   C. Install productivity applications and restore data.

   D. Install the latest service pack or updates along with any updated drivers.

5. If Windows locks up during the installation, what should you do?

   A. Press CTRL-ALT-DEL to restart the installation process.

   B. Push the Reset button to restart the installation process.

   C. Press the ESC key to cancel the installation process.

   D. Unplug the computer and restart the installation process.

6. You can upgrade directly to Windows Vista from which of these operating systems?

   A. Windows 3.11

   B. Windows XP

   C. Windows 2000

   D. All of the above

7. If you get an error message saying that the Setup program cannot read the CAB files, what should you do?

   A. Copy the CAB files from the Windows installation disc to your local hard drive and run the Setup program from there.

   B. Skip this step because the CAB files are not necessary to install Windows successfully.

   C. Go to the Microsoft Web site and download the latest version of the CAB File Wizard.

   D. Cancel the installation process and keep your old operating system because your hardware does not meet the minimum requirements.

8. If you receive a graphical mode error in a Windows 2000 or XP installation saying that Windows failed to detect a noncritical piece of hardware, what should you do?

   A. You need to remove the hardware device or replace it with one that is compatible with the OS.

B. You can probably solve the problem after the installation is complete by finding the proper driver.

C. You will get a stop error and be unable to complete the installation process.

D. You should reboot the computer and restart the installation.

9. If you are not sure your Windows XP system can support Windows Vista, what should you do?

A. Consult the Windows Catalog.

B. Consult the Windows Logo'd Product List.

C. Run the Vista Upgrade Advisor.

D. Install Vista and hope for the best, because it will probably work.

10. If you are experiencing problems with Windows 2000 and wish to install Windows XP, what type of installation is preferred?

A. Clean installation

B. Upgrade installation

C. Network installation

D. Image installation

11. What does the BOOT.INI file do in the Windows 2000/XP boot process?

A. It takes control of the system from the BIOS.

B. It loads all of the necessary device drivers and hardware devices.

C. It lists the locations of all Windows operating systems on the system.

D. It loads the BOOTMGR.

12. What does the BOOTMGR do in the normal Windows Vista/7 boot process?

A. It loads device drivers and files from the system Registry to prepare for the loading of the operating system.

B. It gathers information about a system's installed operating systems, enables a user to select between them, and then loads WINLOADER.EXE.

C. It manages a system's boot order.

D. It's the name of the operating system process.

13. When the text mode of Windows Setup completes and the computer reboots to continue in graphical mode, what must you enter to continue the installation?

A. Activation key

B. CPU ID

C. Registration information

D. Product key

14. The Norton Ghost software is most helpful with which method of installation?

A. Clean installation

B. Upgrade installation

C. Network installation

D. Image installation

15. Which setting affects the way currency and math separators display?

A. Currency

B. Language

C. Locale

D. Date/Time

■ Essay Quiz

1. You've been tasked to teach some new hires how to do a rollout of the latest version of Windows. Write a short essay that outlines what the newbies need to know to upgrade 10 machines. You can assume that the network roles, language, and local settings will stay the same. Make an argument for a clean, upgrade, or multiboot installation. You can use Windows XP or, if you're feeling adventurous, Windows Vista. If you go for the latter, do a Web search for any special steps or procedures not included in the book. Check my Web site Tech Files for one on Windows Vista installation: www.totalsem.com.

2. The same group of newbies will need help with post-installation tasks, so write a second memo that tells them what to do after installing.

3. Your boss has decided to go higher tech on you and wants the next rollout of 10 Windows machines to be automatic, rather than have techs sit through the whole process. Select one of the three methods outlined in the chapter for automating the installation process and make a case for one over the other two.

4. Your boss decided to upgrade her computer from Windows 2000 to Windows XP Professional, but Windows keeps crashing in the middle. Write a short note discussing what could be happening so you can walk her through the installation troubleshooting over the phone.

5. Take the analysis of the functions of a computer operating system and apply it to a device you might encounter in everyday life. For example, describe the automobile or a washing machine in terms of operating system functions. Be creative!

Lab Projects

• Lab Project 14.1

The chapter mentions a couple of alternative operating systems, including Mac OS X and Linux. Do an Internet search or a tour of your local PC superstore and compare the operating systems available. Are Mac OS X, Linux, and Windows the only operating systems out there?

• Lab Project 14.2

Search the Microsoft Knowledge Base for articles about "Stop Error 0x0A" during a Windows 2000 installation. (Hint: Use the Advanced Search feature!) Based on one of the articles you locate, prepare a five-minute report for the class about the cause of this error and the steps Microsoft recommends to solve it.

• Lab Project 14.3

You know that some printers may work in Windows 2000 but not with Windows XP. Check the Windows Logo'd Product List to determine whether the following printers are compatible with Windows XP:

- HP LaserJet 4100
- HP Photosmart 2000
- HP DeskJet 722C
- Epson Stylus Color 1160
- Canon LBP 660

If you have a different printer, check it also while you're looking at the Windows Logo'd Product List.

Working with the Command-Line Interface

"You wanted to know who I am, Zero Cool? Well, let me explain the New World Order. Governments and corporations need people like you and me. We are Samurai...the Keyboard Cowboys...and all those other people who have no idea what's going on are the cattle.... Moooo."

—THE PLAGUE, *HACKERS*

In this chapter, you will learn how to

■ **Explain the operation of the command-line interface**

■ **Execute fundamental commands from the command line**

■ **Manipulate files from the command line**

Whenever I teach a class of new techs and we get to the section on working with the command line, I'm invariably met with a chorus of moans and a barrage of questions and statements. "Why do we need to learn this old stuff?" "We're running Windows Vista, not Windows 3.1!" "Is this ritualistic hazing appropriate in an IT class?"

For techs who master the interface, the command line provides a powerful, quick, and elegant tool for working on a PC. Learning that interface and understanding how to make it work is not only useful, but also necessary for all techs who want to go beyond baby-tech status. You simply cannot work on all PCs without knowing the command line! I'm not the only one who thinks this way. The CompTIA A+ certification exams test you on a variety of command-line commands for doing everything from renaming a file to rebuilding a system file.

If you're interested in moving beyond Windows and into other operating systems such as Linux, you'll find that pretty much all of the serious work is done at a command prompt. Even the Apple Macintosh operating system (OS), for years a purely graphical operating system, now supports a command prompt. Why is the command prompt so popular? Well, for three reasons: First, if you know what you're doing, you can do most jobs more quickly by typing a text command than by clicking through a graphical user interface (GUI). Second, a command-line interface doesn't take much operating system firepower, so it's the natural choice for jobs where you don't need or don't want (or can't get to, in the case of Linux) a full-blown GUI for your OS. Third, text commands take very little bandwidth when sent across the network to another system.

So, are you sold on the idea of the command prompt? Good! This chapter gives you a tour of the Windows command-line interface, explaining how it works and what's happening behind the scenes. You'll learn the concepts and master essential commands, and then you'll work with files and folders throughout your drives. The chapter wraps up with a brief section on encryption and file compression in the "Beyond A+" section. A good tactic for absorbing the material in this chapter is to try out each command or bit of information as it is presented. If you have some experience working with a command prompt, many of these commands should be familiar to you. If the command line is completely new to you, please take the red pill and join me as we step into the matrix.

Historical/Conceptual

Operating systems existed long before PCs were invented. Ancient, massive computers called *mainframes* and *minicomputers* employed sophisticated operating systems. It wasn't until the late 1970s that IBM went looking for an OS for a new *microcomputer*—the official name for the PC—the company was developing, called the IBM Personal Computer, better known as the PC. After being rebuffed by a company called Digital Research, IBM went to a tiny company that had written a popular new version of the programming language called BASIC. They asked the company president if he could create an OS for the IBM PC. Although his company had never actually written an OS, he brazenly said "Sure!" That man was Bill Gates, and the tiny company was Microsoft.

After shaking hands with IBM representatives, Bill Gates hurriedly began to search for an OS based on the Intel 8086 processor. He found a primitive OS called *Quick-and-Dirty Operating System* (*QDOS*), which was written by a one-man shop, and he purchased it for a few thousand dollars. After several minor changes, Microsoft released it as MS-DOS (Microsoft Disk Operating System) version 1.1. Although primitive by today's standards, MS-DOS 1.1 could provide all of the functions an OS needed. Over the years, MS-DOS went through version after version until the last Microsoft version, MS-DOS 6.22, was released in 1994. Microsoft licensed MS-DOS to PC makers so they could add their own changes and then rename the program. IBM called its version PC-DOS.

DOS used a command-line interface. You typed a command at a prompt, and DOS responded to that command. When Microsoft introduced Windows 95 and Windows NT, many computer users and techs thought that the

command-line interface would go away, but techs not only continued to use the command line, they also *needed it* to troubleshoot and fix problems. With Windows 2000, it seemed once again that the command line would die, but again, that just didn't turn out to be the case.

Finally recognizing the importance of the command-line interface, Microsoft beefed it up in Windows XP and then again in Windows Vista. The command line in Windows XP and in Vista offers commands and options for those commands that go well beyond anything seen in previous Microsoft operating systems. This chapter starts with some essential concepts of the command line and then turns to more specific commands.

Practical Application

▉ Deciphering the Command-line Interface

So how does a command-line interface work? It's a little like having an Instant Message conversation with your computer. The computer tells you it's ready to receive commands by displaying a specific set of characters called a **prompt**.

```
Computer: Want to play a game?
Mike: _
```

You type a command and press ENTER to send it.

```
Mike: What kind of game?
Computer: _
```

The PC goes off and executes the command, and when it's finished, it displays a new prompt, often along with some information about what it did.

```
Computer: A very fun game...
Mike: _
```

Once you get a new prompt, it means the computer is ready for your next instruction. You can give the computer commands in the graphical user interface (GUI) of Windows as well, just in a different way, by clicking buttons and menu options with your mouse instead of typing on the keyboard. The results are basically the same: you tell the computer to do something and it responds.

When you type in a command from the command line, you cause the computer to respond. As an example, suppose you want to find out the contents of a particular folder. From the command line, you'd type a command (in this case **DIR**, but more on that in a minute), and the computer would respond by displaying a screen like the one in Figure 15.1.

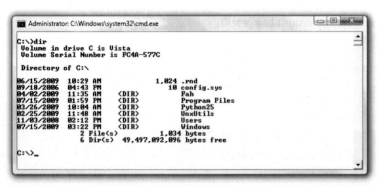

• **Figure 15.1**   Contents of C: directory from the command line

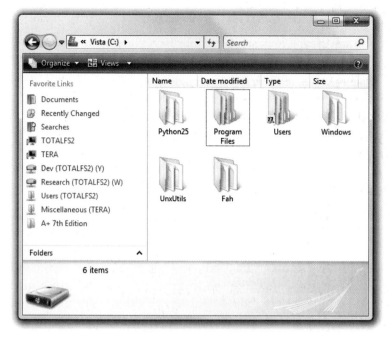

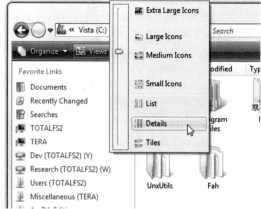

● **Figure 15.2** Contents of C: in Computer—Icon view

● **Figure 15.3** Selecting Details view in Computer

In the Windows GUI, you would open My Computer or Computer and click the C: drive icon to see the contents of that directory. The results might look like Figure 15.2, which at first glance isn't much like the command-line screen; however, simply by choosing a different view (Figure 15.3), you can make the results look quite a bit like the command-line version, albeit much prettier (Figure 15.4). The point here is that whichever interface you use, the information available to you is essentially the same.

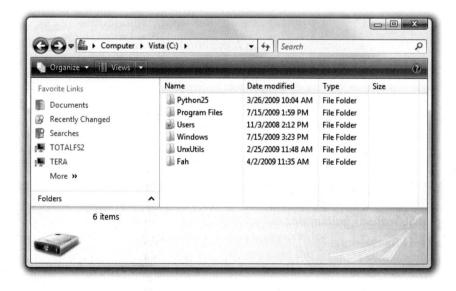

● **Figure 15.4** Contents of C: in Computer—Details view

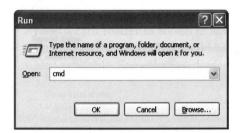

• **Figure 15.5**
Type **CMD** in the Run dialog box to open a command-line window.

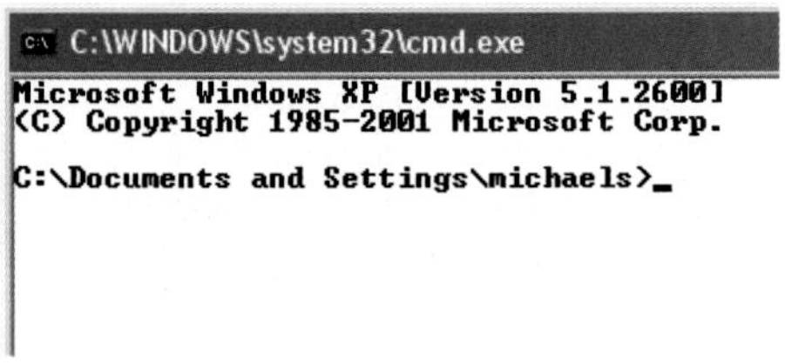

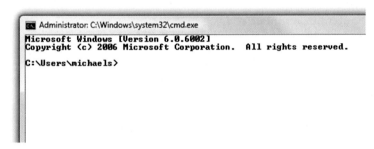

• **Figure 15.6**
The command-line-interface window with a C:\prompt

Microsoft Windows [Version 6.0.6002]
Copyright (c) 2006 Microsoft Corporation. All rights reserved.

C:\Users\michaels>

• **Figure 15.7**
The Windows Vista command-line-interface window

You can also create an administrator shortcut to the Windows Vista command prompt by right-clicking on the desktop and selecting New | Shortcut. Then for the location of the item, type **CMD** and click Next. Type **CMD** to name the shortcut and click Finish. Your shortcut appears on the desktop. Next, right-click the shortcut and select the Advanced button. In the Advanced Properties dialog box, check the *Run as administrator* box and click OK. You have now created a Windows Vista command-prompt shortcut that will always run with administrative privileges.

Accessing the Command Line

Before you can use the command-line interface, you have to open it. You can use various methods to do this, depending on the flavor of Windows you are using. Some methods are simpler than others; just make sure that you know at least one, or you'll never get off the starting line!

One easy way to access the command-line interface in Windows 2000 or XP is by using the **Run dialog box**. Click the Start button, and then select Run. If you're using Windows 2000 or Windows XP, type **CMD** or **COMMAND** and press the ENTER key (Figure 15.5). If you are using Vista, you access the command-line interface through the Start menu Search box with the same two commands. A window pops up on your screen with a black background and white text—this is the command-line interface. Alternatively, buried in the Start menu of *most* computers, under Programs | Accessories, is a link to the command-line interface. In Windows 2000, XP, and Vista, it's called command prompt. These links, just like the Run dialog box, pull up a nice command-line-interface window (Figure 15.6). If you are displaying the command-line-interface in Windows Vista, notice that it uses a newer version number and copyright date. Also notice that the default user profile directory is C:\Users*User name* rather than C:\Documents and Settings*User name* as in previous operating systems (shown in Figure 15.7). To close the command-line-interface window, you can either click the Close box, as on any other window, or simply type **EXIT** at any command prompt and press ENTER.

If you attempt to enter a command at the Windows Vista command prompt that requires elevated or administrative privileges, you receive a UAC "Windows needs your permission to continue" dialog box (you'll learn more about UAC in the next chapter, "Securing Windows Resources"). You can also "manually" run a command with elevated privileges by right-clicking a command-prompt shortcut and then selecting *Run as administrator*. If you are prompted for administrator password or credentials, enter them as needed.

Try This!

Accessing the Command Line

This chapter will be much more fun if you follow along with your own command line, so Try This! Using one of the methods outlined in this section, access a command prompt in Windows. Just remember that everything you do at the prompt can affect the functioning of your PC. So don't delete stuff if you don't know what it's for.

The Command Prompt

The command prompt is always *focused* on a specific folder. This is important because any commands you issue are performed *on the files in the folder* on which the prompt is focused. For example, if you see a prompt that looks like the following line, you know that the focus is on the root directory of the C: drive:

`C:\>`

If you see a prompt that looks like Figure 15.8, you know that the focus is on the C:\Diploma\APLUS\ folder of the C: drive. The trick to using a command line is first to focus the prompt on the drive and folder where you want to work.

Filenames and File Formats

Windows manifests each program and piece of data as an individual file. Each file has a name, which is stored with the file on the drive. Windows inherits the idea of files from older operating systems—namely DOS—so a quick review of the old-style DOS filenames helps in understanding how Windows filenames work. Names are broken down into two parts: the filename and the extension. In true DOS, the filename could be no longer than eight characters, so you'll often see oddly named files on older systems. The extension, which is optional, could be up to three characters long in true DOS, and most computer programs and users continue to honor that old limit, even though it does not apply to modern PCs. No spaces or other illegal characters (/ \ [ ] | ÷ + = ; , * ?) could be used in the filename or extension. The filename and extension are separated by a period, or *dot*. This naming system was known as the **8.3 (eight-dot-three) naming system**.

Here are some examples of acceptable true DOS filenames:

FRED.EXE   SYSTEM.INI   FILE1.DOC
DRIVER3.SYS   JANET   CODE33.H

Here are some unacceptable true DOS filenames:

4CHAREXT.EXEC   WAYTOOLONG.FIL   BAD÷CHAR.BAT   .NO

I mention the true DOS limitations for a simple reason: *backward compatibility*. Starting with 9x, Windows versions did not suffer from the 8.3 filename limitation. Instead they supported filenames of up to 255 characters (but still with the three-character extension) by using a trick called long filenames (LFN). Windows systems using LFN retained complete backward compatibility by automatically creating two names for every file, an 8.3 filename and a long filename. Modern Windows using NTFS works almost exactly the same way as LFNs.

Tech Tip

Booting Directly to a Prompt

Early versions of Windows (3.x, 9x—though not Me) enabled you to boot directly to the command-line interface, not loading the GUI at all. Windows 2000 and Windows XP do not have that option, as the graphical portion of the OS is the OS. You can simulate the old user interface, if you're feeling brave, by altering the way the shortcut to a command prompt works.

In Windows 2000 or Windows XP (this won't work for Vista), go to Start | All Programs | Accessories (or Start | Programs | Accessories, depending on the configuration of your Start menu). Right-click the Command Prompt icon and select Properties to open the Command Prompt Properties dialog box. Select the Options tab, where you'll find four option boxes. The one you want is Display Options. By default, the command prompt displays in a window. Click the radio button for Full Screen, click OK, and you're good to go. The next time you open the command-line interface—from the shortcut only—it'll be full screen.

At about this time, a lot of users who have been following along are staring at a screen with no buttons to click, and ESC doesn't do anything! No worries; remember that you can type EXIT and press ENTER to get out of the command-line interface.

• Figure 15.8 Command prompt indicating focus on the C:\Diploma\APLUS\ folder

You can hold down the F5 or F8 key during boot-up to access the Windows 2000, Windows XP, or Windows Vista Advanced Boot Options menu. This has an option to boot to Safe Mode with Command Prompt, which loads the GUI into Safe Mode and then overlays that with a command-line interface for rapid access to a prompt. This saves you the step of going to Start | Run and typing CMD. This is not the old-style command prompt–only interface!

• **Figure 15.9**   What kind of file is the one on the lower right?

Whether you're running an ancient DOS system or the latest version of Windows Vista, the extension is very important, because the extension part of the filename tells the computer the type or function of the file. Program files use the extension .EXE (for executable) or .COM (for command). Anything that is not a program is some form of data to support a program. Different programs use different types of data files. The extension usually indicates which program uses that particular data file. For example, Microsoft Word uses the extension .DOC (.DOCX for Microsoft Office Word 2007), while WordPerfect uses .WPD and PowerPoint uses .PPT (.PPTX for Microsoft Office PowerPoint 2007). Graphics file extensions, in contrast, often reflect the graphics standard used to render the image, such as .GIF for CompuServe's Graphics Interchange Format or .JPG for the JPEG (Joint Photographic Experts Group) format.

Changing the extension of a data file does not affect its contents, but without the proper extension, Windows won't know which program uses it. You can see this clearly in My Computer. Figure 15.9 shows a folder with two identical image files. The one on top shows the Photoshop icon, which is the program Windows will use to open that file; the one on the bottom shows a generic icon because I deleted the extension. Windows GUI doesn't show file extensions by default. Figure 15.10 shows the contents of that same folder from the command line.

All files are stored on the hard drive in binary format, but every program has its own way of reading and writing this binary data. Each unique method of binary organization is called a file *format*. One program cannot read another program's files unless it can convert the other program's format into its format. In the early days of DOS, no programs were capable of performing this type of conversion, yet people wanted to exchange files. They wanted some type of common format that any program could read. The answer was a special format called **American Standard Code for Information Interchange (ASCII)**.

The ASCII standard defines 256 eight-bit characters. These characters include all of the letters of the alphabet (uppercase and lowercase), numbers, punctuation, many foreign characters (such as accented letters for French and Spanish—é, ñ, ô—and other typical non-English characters), box-drawing characters, and a series of special characters for commands such as a carriage return, bell, and end of file (Figure 15.11). ASCII files, more commonly

• **Figure 15.10**   One file has no extension.

```
Administrator: C:\Windows\system32\cmd.exe

C:\Photos>dir
 Volume in drive C is Vista
 Volume Serial Number is FC4A-577C

 Directory of C:\Photos

07/23/2009  10:44 AM    <DIR>          .
07/23/2009  10:44 AM    <DIR>          ..
07/23/2009  10:43 AM         6,903,739 Squirrel
07/23/2009  10:43 AM         6,903,739 Squirrel.psd
               2 File(s)     13,807,478 bytes
               2 Dir(s)  49,308,864,512 bytes free

C:\Photos>
```

• **Figure 15.11**   ASCII characters

Mike Meyers' CompTIA A+ Guide to Managing and Troubleshooting PCs

known as *text files*, store all data in ASCII format. The ASCII standard, however, is for more than just files. For example, when you press a key, the keyboard sends the letter of that key to the PC in ASCII code. Even the monitor outputs in ASCII when you are running DOS.

ASCII was the first universal file format. Virtually every type of program—word processors, spreadsheets, databases, presentation programs—can read and write text files. However, text files have severe limitations. A text file can't store important information such as shapes, colors, margins, or text attributes (bold, underline, font, and so on). Therefore, even though text files are fairly universal, they are also limited to the 256 ASCII characters.

Try This!

Make Some Unicode!

A lot of e-mail programs can use Unicode characters, as can Internet message boards such as my Tech Forums. You can use Unicode characters to accent your writing or simply to spell a person's name correctly—Martin *Acuña*—when you address him. Working with Unicode is fun, so Try This!

1. Open a text editing program such as Notepad in the Windows GUI.

2. Hold down the ALT key on your keyboard and, referring to Figure 15.11, press numbers on your keyboard's number pad to enter special characters. For example, pressing ALT-164 should display an *ñ*, whereas ALT-168 shows a *¿*.

3. If you have access to the Internet, surf over to the Tech Forums (www.totalsem.com/techforum/index.php) and say howdy. Include some Unicode in your post, of course!

Even in the most basic text, you need to perform a number of actions beyond just printing simple characters. For example, how does the program reading the text file know when to start a new line? This is where the first 32 ASCII characters come into play. These first 32 characters are special commands (actually, some of them are both commands and characters). For example, the ASCII value 7 can be either a large dot or a command to play a note (bell) on the PC speaker. ASCII value 9 is a Tab. ASCII value 27 is an Escape.

ASCII worked well for years, but as computers became used worldwide, the industry began to run into a problem: there are a lot more than 256 characters used all over the world! Nobody could use Arabic, Greek, Hebrew, or even Braille! In 1991, the Unicode Consortium, an international standards group, introduced Unicode. Basic **Unicode** is a 16-bit code that covers every character for the most common languages, plus a few thousand symbols. With Unicode you can make just about any character or symbol you might imagine—plus a few thousand more you'd never even think of. The first 256 Unicode characters are exactly the same as ASCII characters, making for easy backward compatibility.

Drives and Folders

When working from the command line, you need to be able to focus the prompt at the specific drive and folder that contains the files or programs with which you want to work. This can be a little more complicated than it seems, especially in Windows 2000, Windows XP, and Windows Vista.

At boot, Windows assigns a drive letter (or name) to each hard drive partition and to each floppy or other disk drive. The first floppy drive is called A:, and the second, if installed, is called B:. Hard drives usually start with the letter C: and can continue to Z: if necessary. Optical drives by

default get the next available drive letter after the last hard drive. Windows 2000, XP, and Vista enable you to change the default lettering for drives, so you're likely to see all sorts of lettering schemes. On top of that, Windows 2000, XP, and Vista let you mount a hard drive as a volume in another drive.

Whatever the names of the drives, Windows uses a hierarchical directory tree to organize the contents of these drives. All files are put into groups Windows calls *folders*, although you'll often hear techs use the term *directory* rather than *folder*, a holdover from the true DOS days. Any file not in a folder *within* the tree—that is, any file in the folder at the root of the directory tree—is said to be in the **root directory**. A folder inside another folder is called a *subfolder*. Any folder can have multiple subfolders. Two or more files with the same name can exist in different folders on a PC, but two files in the same folder cannot have the same name. In the same way, no two subfolders under the same folder can have the same name, but two subfolders under different folders can have the same name.

When describing a drive, you use its letter and a colon. For example, the hard drive would be represented by C:. To describe the root directory, put a backslash (\) after the C:, as in C:\. To describe a particular directory, add the name of the directory. For example, if a PC has a directory in the root directory called TEST, it is C:\TEST. Subdirectories in a directory are displayed by adding backslashes and names. If the TEST directory has a subdirectory called SYSTEM, it is shown like this: C:\TEST\SYSTEM. This naming convention provides for a complete description of the location and name of any file. If the C:\TEST\SYSTEM directory includes a file called TEST2.TXT, it is C:\TEST\SYSTEM\TEST2.TXT.

The exact location of a file is called its **path**. The path for the TEST2.TXT file is C:\TEST\SYSTEM. Here are some examples of possible paths:

```
C:\PROGRAM FILES
C:\WINNT\system32\1025
F:\FRUSCH3\CLEAR
A:\REPORTS
D:\
```

Here are a few items to remember about folder names and filenames:

- Folders and files may have spaces in their names.
- The only disallowed characters are the following eleven: * " / \ [ ] : ; | = ,
- Files aren't required to have extensions, but Windows won't know the file type without an extension.
- Folder names may have extensions—but they are not commonly used.

Mastering Fundamental Commands

It's time to try using the command line, but before you begin, a note of warning is in order: the command-line interface is picky and unforgiving. It will do what you *say*, not what you *mean*, so it always pays to double-check that

those are one and the same before you press ENTER and commit the command. One careless keystroke can result in the loss of crucial data, with no warning and no going back. In this section, you'll explore the structure of commands and then play with four commands built into all versions of Microsoft's command-line interface: DIR, CD, MD, and RD.

Structure: Syntax and Switches

All commands in the Windows command-line interface use a similar structure and execute in the same way. You type the name of the command, followed by the target of that command and any modifications of that command that you want to apply. You can call up a modification by using an extra letter or number, called a **switch** or *option*, which may follow either the command or the target, depending on the command. The proper way to write a command is called its **syntax**. The key with commands is that you can't spell anything incorrectly or use a \ when the syntax calls for a /. The command line is completely inflexible, so you have to learn the correct syntax for each command.

```
command] [target (if any)] [switches]
```

or

```
command] [switches] [target (if any)]
```

How do you know what switches are allowed? How do you know whether the switches come before or after the target? If you want to find out the syntax and switches used by a particular command, always type the command followed by a **/?** to get help.

DIR Command

The **DIR command** shows you the contents of the directory where the prompt is focused. DIR is used more often than any other command at the command prompt. When you open a command-line window in Windows, it opens focused on your user folder. You will know this because the prompt in 2000/ XP will look like this: C:\Documents and Settings\username>. By typing in **DIR** and then pressing the ENTER key (remember that you must always press ENTER to execute a command from the command line), you will see something like Figure 15.12.

If you are following along on a PC, remember that different computers contain different files and programs, so you will absolutely see something different from what's shown in Figure 15.12! If a lot of text scrolls quickly down the screen, try typing **DIR /P** (pause). Don't forget to press ENTER.

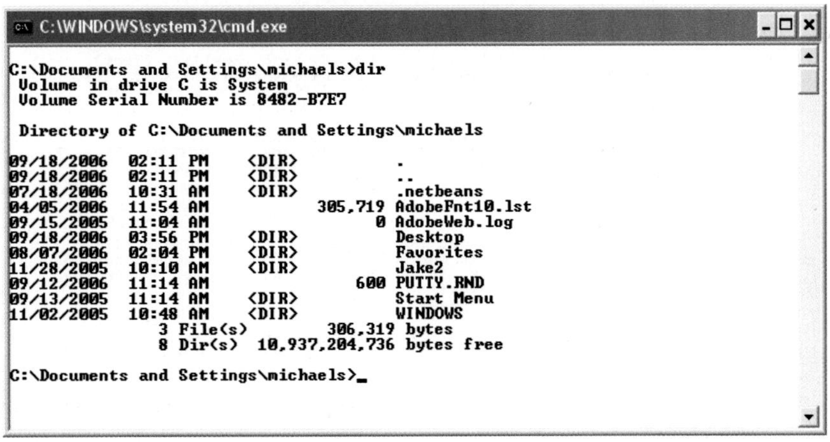

• **Figure 15.12**   DIR in a user's folder

Extra text typed after a command to modify its operation, such as the /W or /P after DIR, is called a *switch*. Almost all switches can be used simultaneously to modify a command. For example, try typing **DIR /W /P**.

The DIR /P command is a lifesaver when you're looking for something in a large directory.

When you type a simple DIR command, you will see that some of the entries look like this:

```
09/04/2008   05:51 PM            63,664 bambi.jpg
```

All of these entries are files. The DIR command lists the creation date, creation time, file size in bytes, filename, and extension. Any entries that look like this are folders:

```
12/31/2009   10:18 AM    <DIR>         WINDOWS
```

The DIR command lists the creation date, creation time, *<DIR>* to tell you it is a folder, and the folder name. If you ever see a listing with *<JUNCTION>* instead of *<DIR>*, you're looking at a hard drive partition that's been mounted as a folder instead of a drive letter:

```
08/06/2008   02:28 PM    <JUNCTION>    Other Drive
```

Now type the **DIR /W** command. Note that the DIR /W command shows only the filenames, but they are arranged in five columns across your screen. Finally, type **DIR /?** to see the screen shown in Figure 15.13, which lists all possible switches for the command.

Typing any command followed by a **/?** brings up a help screen for that particular command. Although these help screens can sometimes seem a little cryptic, they're useful when you're not too familiar with a command or you can't figure out how to get a command to do what you need. Even though I have almost every command memorized, I still refer to these help screens; you should use them as well. If you're really lost, type **HELP** at the command prompt for a list of commands you may type. Once you find one, type **HELP** and then the name of the command. For example, if you type **HELP DIR**, you'll see the screen shown in Figure 15.13.

Directories: The CD Command

You can use the **CD (or CHDIR) command** to change the focus of the command prompt to a different directory. To use the CD command, type **CD** followed by the name of the directory on which you want the prompt to focus. For example, to go to the C:\ OBIWAN directory, you type

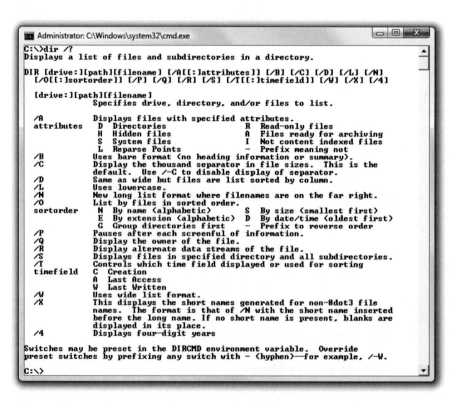

• **Figure 15.13**   Typing **DIR /?** lists all possible switches for DIR command.

CD\OBIWAN and then press ENTER. If the system has an OBIWAN directory, the prompt changes focus to that directory and appears as `C:\`
`OBIWAN>`. If no OBIWAN directory exists or if you accidentally type something like **OBIWAM**, you get the error "The system cannot find the path specified." If only I had a dollar for every time I've seen those errors! I usually get them because I've typed too fast. If you get this error, check what you typed and try again.

To return to the root directory, type **CD** and press ENTER. You can use the CD command to point DOS to any directory. For example, you could type **CD\FRED\BACKUP\TEST** from a C:\ prompt, and the prompt would change to C:\FRED\BACKUP\TEST\>—assuming, of course, that your system *has* a directory called C:\FRED\BACKUP\TEST.

Once the prompt has changed, type **DIR** again. You should see a different list of files and directories. Every directory holds different files and subdirectories, so when you point DOS to different directories, the DIR command shows you different contents.

The CD command allows you to use a space instead of a backslash, a convenient shortcut. For example, you could go to the C:\WINDOWS directory from the root directory simply by typing **CD WINDOWS** at the C:\ prompt. You can use the CD [space] command to move one level at a time, like this:

```
C:\>CD FRED
C:\FRED\>CD BACKUP
C:\FRED\BACKUP>CD TEST
```

Or, you can jump multiple directory levels in one step, like this:

```
C:\>CD FRED\BACKUP\TEST
C:\FRED\BACKUP\TEST>
```

A final trick: If you want to go *up* a single directory level, you can type **CD** followed immediately by two periods. So, for example, if you're in the C:\FRED\BACKUP directory and you want to move up to the C:\FRED directory, you can simply type **CD..** and you'll be there:

```
C:\FRED\BACKUP>CD..
C:\FRED>
```

Take some time to move the DOS focus around the directories of your PC, using the CD and DIR commands. Use DIR to find a directory, and then use CD to move the focus to that directory. Remember, CD\ always gets you back to the root directory.

Moving Between Drives

The CD command is *not* used to move between drives. To get the prompt to point to another drive ("point" is command-line geekspeak for "switch its focus"), just type the drive letter and a colon. If the prompt points at the C:\ Sierra directory and you want to see what is on the USB thumb drive (E:), just type **E:** and DOS will point to the USB drive. You'll see the following on the screen:

```
C:\Sierra>E:
E:\>
```

Tech Tip

Errors Are Good!

Consider errors in general for a moment—not just command-prompt errors such as "Invalid directory," but any error, including Windows errors. Many new computer users freeze in horror when they see an error message. Do not fear error messages. Error messages are good! Love them. Worship them. They will save you.

Seriously, think how confusing it would be if the computer didn't tell you when you messed up. Error messages tell you what you did wrong so you can fix it. You absolutely cannot hurt your PC in any way by typing the DIR or CD command incorrectly. Take advantage of this knowledge and experiment. Intentionally make mistakes to familiarize yourself with the error messages. Have fun and learn from errors!

To return to the C: drive, just type **C:** and you'll see the following:

```
E:\>C:
C:\Sierra>
```

Note that you return to the same directory you left. Just for fun, try typing in a drive letter that you know doesn't exist. For example, I know that my system doesn't have a W: drive. If I type in a nonexistent drive on a Windows system, I get the following error:

```
The system cannot find the drive specified.
```

Try inserting a floppy disk and using the CD command to point to its drive. Do the same with an optical disc. Type **DIR** to see the contents of the floppy or optical disc. Type **CD** to move the focus to any folders on the floppy or optical disc. Now return focus to the C: drive.

Using the DIR, CD, and drive letter commands, you can access any folder on any storage device on your system. Make sure you can use these commands comfortably to navigate inside your computer.

Making Directories

Now that you have learned how to navigate in a command-prompt world, it's time to start making stuff, beginning with a new directory.

To make a directory, use the **MD (or MKDIR) command**. To create a directory called STEAM under the root directory C:, for example, first type **CD** to ensure that you are in the root directory. You should see the prompt

```
C:\>
```

Now that the prompt points to the root directory, type **MD STEAM** to create the directory:

```
C:\>MD STEAM
```

Once you press ENTER, Windows executes the command, but it won't volunteer any information about what it did. You must use the DIR command to see that you have, in fact, created a new directory. Note that the STEAM directory in this example is not listed last, as you might expect.

```
C:\>DIR
 Volume in Drive C is
 Volume Serial Number is 1734-3234
 Directory of C:\

07/12/2009  04:46 AM    <DIR>          Documents and Settings
06/04/2008  10:22 PM    <DIR>          STEAM
09/11/2009  11:32 AM    <DIR>          NVIDIA
08/06/2007  02:28 PM    <JUNCTION>     Other Drive
09/14/2008  11:11 AM    <DIR>          Program Files
09/12/2009  08:32 PM                21 statusclient.log
07/31/2008  10:40 PM               153 systemscandata.txt
03/13/2008  09:54 AM         1,111,040 t3h0
04/21/2008  04:19 PM    <DIR>          temp
07/12/2008  10:18 AM    <DIR>          WINDOWS
               3 file(s)      1,111,214 bytes
                        294,182,881,834   bytes free
```

What about uppercase and lowercase? Windows supports both, but it interprets all commands as uppercase. Use the MD command to make a folder called steam (note the lowercase) and see what happens. This also happens in the graphical Windows. Go to your desktop and try to make two folders, one called STEAM and the other called steam, and see what Windows tells you.

To create a FILES subdirectory in the STEAM directory, first use the CD\ command to point the prompt to the STEAM directory:

```
CD\STEAM
```

Then run the MD command to make the FILES directory:

```
MD FILES
```

Make sure that the prompt points to the directory in which you want to make the new subdirectory before you execute the MD command. When you're finished, type **DIR** to see the new FILES subdirectory. Just for fun, try the process again and add a GAMES directory under the STEAM directory. Type **DIR** to verify success.

Removing Directories

Removing subdirectories works exactly like making them. First, get to the directory that contains the subdirectory you want to delete, and then execute the **RD (or RMDIR) command**. In this example, let's delete the FILES subdirectory in the C:\STEAM directory. First, get to where the FILES directory is located—C:\STEAM—by typing **CD\STEAM**. Then type **RD FILES**. If you received no response from Windows, you probably did it right! Type **DIR** to check that the FILES subdirectory is gone.

The plain RD command will not delete a directory in Windows if the directory contains files or subdirectories. If you want to delete a directory that contains files or subdirectories, you must first empty that directory by using the DEL (for files) or RD (for subdirectories) command. You can use the RD command followed by the /S switch to delete a directory as well as all files and subdirectories. RD followed by the /S switch is handy but dangerous, because it's easy to delete more than you want. When deleting, always follow the maxim "Check twice and delete once."

Let's delete the STEAM and GAMES directories with RD followed by the /S switch. Because the STEAM directory is in the root directory, point to the root directory with CD\. Now execute the command **RD C:\STEAM /S**. In a rare display of mercy, Windows responds with the following:

```
C:\>rd steam /s
steam, Are you sure (Y/N)?
```

Press the Y key and both C:\STEAM and C:\STEAM\GAMES are eliminated.

Working with Directories

PC techs should be comfortable creating and deleting directories. To get some practice, try this:

1. Create a new directory in the root directory by using the make directory command (MD). Type **CD** to return to the root directory. At the command prompt, make a directory called JEDI:

   `C:\>MD JEDI`

2. As usual, the prompt tells you nothing; it just presents a fresh prompt. Do a DIR (that is, type the **DIR** command) to see your new directory. Windows creates the new directory wherever it is pointing when you issue the command, whether or not that's where you meant to put it. To demonstrate, point the prompt to your new directory by using the CD command:

   `C:\>CD JEDI`

3. Now use the make directory command again to create a directory called YODA:

   `C:\JEDI>MD YODA`

   Do a DIR again, and you should see that your JEDI directory now contains a YODA directory.

4. Type **CD** to return to the root directory so you can delete your new directories by using the remove directory command (RD):

   `C:\>`**RD /S JEDI**

   In another rare display of mercy, Windows responds with the following:

   `jedi, Are you sure <Y/N>?`

5. Press Y to eliminate both C:\JEDI and C:\JEDI\YODA.

Windows includes a lot of command-line tools for specific jobs such as starting and stopping services, viewing computers on a network, converting hard drive file systems, and more. The book discusses these task-specific tools in the chapters that reflect their task. Chapter 23, "Local Area Networking," goes into detail on the versatile and powerful NET command, for example. You'll read about the CONVERT command in Chapter 26, "Securing Computers." I couldn't resist throwing in two of the more interesting tools, COMPACT and CIPHER, in the Beyond A+ section of this chapter.

Running a Program

To run a program from the command line, simply change the prompt focus to the folder where the program is located, type the name of the program, and then press the ENTER key on your keyboard. Try this safe example. Go to the C:\WINNT\System32 or C:\WINDOWS\System32 folder—the exact name of this folder varies by system. Type **DIR /P** to see the files one page at a time. You should see a file called MEM.EXE (Figure 15.14).

As mentioned earlier, all files with extensions .EXE and .COM are programs, so MEM.EXE is a program. To run the MEM.EXE program, just type the filename, in this case **MEM**, and press ENTER (Figure 15.15). Note that you do not have to type the .EXE extension, although you can. Congratulations! You have just run your first program from the command line.

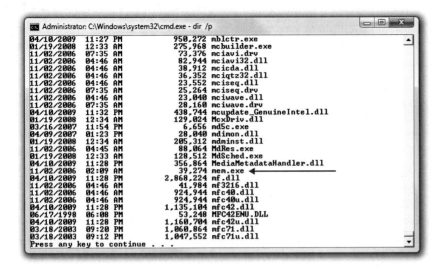

• **Figure 15.14** MEM.EXE displayed in the System32 folder

■ Working with Files

This section deals with basic file manipulation. You will learn how to look at, copy, move, rename, and delete files. You'll look at the ins and outs of batch files. The examples in this section are based on a C: root directory with the following files and directories:

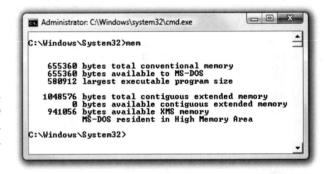

• **Figure 15.15** Running MEM in Windows Vista

```
C:\>dir
 Volume in drive C has no label.
 Volume Serial Number is 4C62-1572

 Directory of C:\

05/26/2009  11:37 PM                 0 AILog.txt
05/29/2009  05:33 PM             5,776 aoedoppl.txt
05/29/2009  05:33 PM             2,238 aoeWVlog.txt
07/12/2009  10:38 AM    <DIR>          books
07/15/2009  02:45 PM             1,708 CtDrvStp.log
07/12/2008  04:46 AM    <DIR>          Documents and Settings
06/04/2009  10:22 PM    <DIR>          Impressions Games
09/11/2008  11:32 AM    <DIR>          NVIDIA
08/06/2009  02:28 PM    <JUNCTION>     Other Drive
01/03/2009  01:12 PM    <DIR>          pers-drv
09/14/2008  11:11 AM    <DIR>          Program Files
09/12/2009  08:32 PM                21 statusclient.log
07/31/2009  10:40 PM               153 systemscandata.txt
03/13/2009  09:54 AM         1,111,040 t3h0
04/21/2009  04:19 PM    <DIR>          temp
01/10/2008  07:07 PM    <DIR>          WebCam
12/31/2007  10:18 AM    <DIR>          WINDOWS
09/14/2008  12:48 PM    <DIR>          WINNT
01/03/2008  09:06 AM    <DIR>          WUTemp
               7 File(s)      1,120,936 bytes
              12 Dir(s)  94,630,002,688 bytes free
```

Because you probably don't have a PC with these files and directories, follow the examples but use what's on your drive. In other words, create your own folders and copy files to them from various folders currently on your system.

Attributes

Remember way back in Chapter 4, "Understanding Windows," when you had to make changes to the folder options in My Computer to see NTLDR, NTDETECT.COM, and other files? You were actually seeing files with special attributes.

All files have four special values, or **attributes**, that determine how programs (such as My Computer in Windows XP or Computer in Windows Vista) treat the file in special situations. The first attribute is the hidden attribute. If a file is hidden, it is not displayed when you issue the DIR command. Next is the read-only attribute. A file with a **read-only attribute** cannot be modified or deleted. Third is the system attribute, which is used only for system files such as NTLDR and BOOT.INI. In reality, it does nothing more than provide an easy identifier for these files. Fourth is the archive attribute, which is used by backup software to identify files that have been changed since their last backup.

ATTRIB.EXE is an external command-line program you can use to inspect and change file attributes. To inspect a file's attributes, type the **ATTRIB** command followed by the name of the file. To see the attributes of the file AILog.txt, type **ATTRIB AILOG.TXT**. The result is

```
A       AILog.txt
```

The letter A stands for archive, the only attribute of AILog.txt.

Go to the C:\ directory and type **ATTRIB** by itself. You'll see a result similar to the following:

```
C:\>attrib
A               C:\AILog.txt
A               C:\aoedoppl.txt
A               C:\aoeWVlog.txt
A       H       C:\AUTOEXEC.BAT
A       SH      C:\boot.ini
A       H       C:\CONFIG.SYS
A               C:\CtDrvStp.log
A       SH      C:\hiberfil.sys
A       SHR     C:\IO.SYS
A       SHR     C:\MSDOS.SYS
A       SHR     C:\NTDETECT.COM
A       SHR     C:\ntldr
A       SH      C:\pagefile.sys
A               C:\statusclient.log
A               C:\systemscandata.txt
A               C:\t3h0
```

The letter R means read-only, H is hidden, and S is system. Hey! There are some new files there. That's right, some were hidden. Don't panic if you see a number of files different from those just listed. No two C:\ directories are ever the same. In most cases, you'll see many more files than just these.

Notice that important files such as NTLDR and NTDETECT.COM have the system, hidden, and read-only attributes set. Microsoft does this to protect them from accidental deletion.

You also use the ATTRIB command to change a file's attributes. To add an attribute to a file, type the attribute letter preceded by a plus sign (+) as an option, and then type the filename. To delete an attribute, use a minus sign (–). For example, to add the read-only attribute to the file AILog.txt, type this:

```
ATTRIB +R AILOG.TXT
```

To remove the archive attribute, type this:

```
ATTRIB -A AILOG.TXT
```

You can add or remove multiple attributes in one command. Here's an example of removing three attributes from the NTDETECT.COM file:

```
ATTRIB -R -S -H NTDETECT.COM
```

You can also automatically apply ATTRIB to matching files in subdirectories by using the /s switch at the end of the statement. For example, if you have lots of files in your My Music folder that you want to hide, but they are neatly organized in many subdirectories, you could readily use ATTRIB to change all of them with a simple command. Change directories from the prompt until you're at the My Music folder and then type the following:

```
ATTRIB +H *.MP3 /S
```

When you press the ENTER key, all your music files in My Music and any My Music subdirectories will become hidden files.

Wildcards

Visualize having 273 files in one directory. A few of these files have the extension .DOC, but most do not. You are looking only for files with the .DOC extension. Wouldn't it be nice to type the DIR command so that only the .DOC files come up? You can do this by using wildcards.

A **wildcard** is one of two special characters—asterisk (*) and question mark (?)—that you can use in place of all or part of a filename, often so that a command-line command will act on more than one file at a time. Wildcards work with all command-line commands that take filenames. A great example is the DIR command. When you execute a plain DIR command, it finds and displays all of the files and folders in the specified directory; however, you can also narrow its search by adding a filename. For example, if you

Try This!

Working with Attributes

It's important for you to know that everything you do at the command line affects the same files at the GUI level, so Try This!

1. In Windows XP, go to My Computer and create a folder in the root directory of your C: drive called TEST.

2. Copy a couple of files into that folder and then right-click one to see its properties.

3. Open a command-line window and navigate to the C:\TEST folder. Type **DIR** to see that the contents match what you see in My Computer.

4. From the command line, change the attributes of one or both files. Make one a hidden file, for example, and the other read-only.

5. Now go back to My Computer and access the properties of each file. Any changes?

type the command **DIR AILOG.TXT** while in your root (C:\) directory, you get the following result:

```
C:\>dir AILOG.TXT
 Volume in drive C has no label.
 Volume Serial Number is 4C62-1572
 Directory of C:\
05/26/2009  11:37 PM                    0 AILog.txt
               1 File(s)               0 bytes
               0 Dir(s)   94,630,195,200 bytes free
```

If you just want to confirm the presence of a particular file in a particular place, this is very convenient. But suppose you want to see all files with the extension .TXT. In that case, you use the * wildcard, like this: **DIR *.TXT**. A good way to think of the * wildcard is *"I don't care."* Replace the part of the filename that you don't care about with an asterisk (*). The result of DIR *.TXT would look like this:

```
 Volume in drive C has no label.
 Volume Serial Number is 4C62-1572

 Directory of C:\

05/26/2009  11:37 PM                    0 AILog.txt
05/29/2009  05:33 PM                5,776 aoedoppl.txt
05/29/2009  05:33 PM                2,238 aoeWVlog.txt
07/31/2008  10:40 PM                  153 systemscandata.txt
               4 File(s)           8,167 bytes
               0 Dir(s)   94,630,002,688 bytes free
```

Wildcards also substitute for parts of filenames. This DIR command will find every file that starts with the letter *a:*

```
C:\>dir a*.*
 Volume in drive C has no label.
 Volume Serial Number is 4C62-1572

 Directory of C:\

05/26/2009  11:37 PM                    0 AILog.txt
05/29/2009  05:33 PM                5,776 aoedoppl.txt
05/29/2009  05:33 PM                2,238 aoeWVlog.txt
               3 File(s)           8,014 bytes
               0 Dir(s)   94,629,675,008 bytes free
```

We've used wildcards only with the DIR command, but virtually every command that deals with files will take wildcards. Let's examine the REN and DEL commands and see how they use wildcards.

Renaming Files

To rename files, you use the **REN (or RENAME) command**, which seems pretty straightforward. To rename the file IMG033.jpg to park.jpg, type the following followed by the ENTER key:

```
ren img033.jpg park.jpg
```

"That's great," you might be thinking, "but what about using a more complex and descriptive filename, such as Sunny day in the park.jpg?" Type what should work, like this:

```
ren img033.jpg Sunny day in the park.jpg
```

But you'll get an error message (Figure 15.16). Even the tried-and-true method of seeking help by typing the command followed by /? doesn't give you the answer.

You can use more complicated names by putting them in quotation marks. Figure 15.17 shows the same command that failed but now succeeds because of the quotation marks.

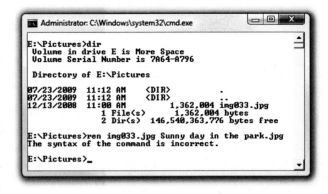

• **Figure 15.16**   Rename failed me.

Deleting Files

To delete files, you use the **DEL (or ERASE) command**. DEL and ERASE are identical commands that you can use interchangeably. Deleting files is simple—maybe too simple. Windows users enjoy the luxury of retrieving deleted files from the Recycle Bin on those "Oops, I didn't mean to delete that" occasions everyone encounters at one time or another. The command line, however, shows no such mercy to the careless user. It has no function equivalent to the Windows Recycle Bin. Once you have erased a file, you can recover it only by using a special recovery utility such as Norton's UNERASE. Again, the rule here is to *check twice and delete once*.

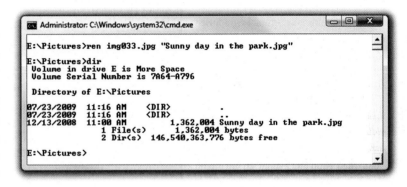

• **Figure 15.17**   Success at last.

To delete a single file, type the **DEL** command followed by the name of the file to delete. To delete the file AILOG.TXT, for example, type this:

```
DEL AILOG.TXT
```

Although nothing appears on the screen to confirm it, the file is now gone. To confirm that the AILOG.TXT file is no longer listed, use the DIR command.

As with the DIR command, you can use wildcards with the DEL and ERASE commands to delete multiple files. For example, to delete all files with the extension .TXT in a directory, you would type this:

```
DEL *.TXT
```

To delete all files with the filename CONFIG in a directory, type **DEL CONFIG.***. To delete all of the files in a directory, you can use the popular *.* wildcard (often pronounced "star-dot-star"), like this:

```
DEL *.*
```

This is one of the few command-line commands that elicits a response. Upon receiving the DEL *.* command, Windows responds with "Are you

sure? (Y/N)," to which you respond with a *Y* or *N*. Pressing Y erases every file in the directory, so use *.* with care!

Don't confuse deleting *files* with deleting *directories*. DEL deletes files, but it will not remove directories. Use RD to delete directories.

Copying and Moving Files

Being able to copy and move files in a command line is crucial to all technicians. Because of its finicky nature and many options, the COPY command is also rather painful to learn, especially if you're used to dragging icons in Windows. The following tried-and-true, five-step process makes it easier, but the real secret is to get in front of a C:\ prompt and just copy and move files around until you're comfortable. Keep in mind that the only difference between copying and moving is whether the original is left behind (COPY) or not (MOVE). Once you've learned the **COPY command**, you've also learned the **MOVE command**!

Mike's Five-Step COPY/MOVE Process

I've been teaching folks how to copy and move files for years by using this handy process. Keep in mind that hundreds of variations on this process exist. As you become more confident with these commands, try doing a COPY /? or MOVE /? at any handy prompt to see the real power of the commands. But first, follow this process step by step:

1. Point the command prompt to the directory containing the files you want to copy or move.

2. Type **COPY** or **MOVE** and a space.

3. Type the *name*(s) of the file(s) to be copied/moved (with or without wildcards) and a space.

4. Type the *path* of the new location for the files.

5. Press ENTER.

Let's try an example. The directory C:\STEAM contains the file README.TXT. Copy this file to a USB thumb drive (E:).

1. Type **CD\STEAM** to point the command prompt to the STEAM directory.

   ```
   C:\>CD\STEAM
   ```

2. Type **COPY** and a space.

   ```
   C:\STEAM>COPY
   ```

3. Type **README.TXT** and a space.

   ```
   C:\STEAM>COPY README.TXT
   ```

4. Type **E:**.

   ```
   C:\STEAM>COPY README.TXT E:\
   ```

5. Press ENTER.

The entire command and response would look like this:

```
C:\STEAM>COPY README.TXT E:\
1 file(s) copied
```

If you point the command prompt to the E: drive and type **DIR**, the README.TXT file will be visible. Let's try another example. Suppose 100 files are in the C:\DOCS directory, 30 of which have the .DOC extension, and suppose you want to move those files to the C:\STEAM directory. Follow these steps:

1. Type **CD\DOCS** to point the command prompt to the DOCS directory.

   ```
   C:\>CD\DOCS
   ```

2. Type **MOVE** and a space.

   ```
   C:\DOCS>MOVE
   ```

3. Type ***.DOC** and a space.

   ```
   C:\DOCS>MOVE *.DOC
   ```

4. Type **C:\STEAM**.

   ```
   C:\DOCS>MOVE *.DOC C:\STEAM
   ```

5. Press ENTER.

   ```
   C:\DOCS>MOVE *.DOC C:\STEAM
   30 file(s) copied
   ```

The power of the COPY/MOVE command makes it rather dangerous. The COPY/MOVE command not only lets you put a file in a new location; it also lets you change the name of the file at the same time. Suppose you want to copy a file called AUTOEXEC.BAT from your C:\ folder to a thumb drive, for example, but you want the name of the copy on the thumb drive to be AUTO1.BAT. You can do both things with one COPY command, like this:

```
COPY C:\AUTOEXEC.BAT E:\AUTO1.BAT
```

Not only does the AUTOEXEC.BAT file get copied to the thumb drive, but the copy also gets the new name AUTO1.BAT.

As another example, move all of the files with the extension .DOC from the C:\DOCS directory to the C:\BACK directory and simultaneously change the .DOC extension to .SAV. Here is the command:

```
MOVE C:\DOCS\*.DOC C:\BACK\*.SAV
```

This says, "Move all files that have the extension .DOC from the directory C:\DOCS into the directory C:\BACK, and while you're at it, change their file extensions to .SAV." This is very handy, but very dangerous!

Let's say, for example, that I made one tiny typo. Here I typed a semicolon instead of a colon after the second *C:*

```
MOVE C:\DOCS\*.DOC C;\BACK\*.SAV
```

The command line understands the semicolon to mean "end of command" and therefore ignores both the semicolon and anything I type after it. As far as the command line is concerned, I typed this:

```
MOVE C:\DOCS\*.DOC C
```

This, unfortunately for me, means "take all of the files with the extension .DOC in the directory C:\DOCS and copy them back into that same directory, but squish them all together into a single file called C." If I run this command, Windows gives me only one clue that something went wrong:

```
MOVE C:\DOCS\*.DOC C
1 file(s) copied
```

See "1 file(s) copied"? Feeling the chilly hand of fate slide down my spine, I do a DIR of the directory, and I now see a single file called C, where there used to be 30 files with the extension .DOC. All of my DOC files are gone, completely unrecoverable.

XCOPY

The standard COPY and MOVE commands can work only in one directory at a time, making them a poor choice for copying or moving files in multiple directories. To help with these multi-directory jobs, Microsoft added the **XCOPY command**. (Note that there is no XMOVE, only XCOPY.)

XCOPY works similar to COPY, but XCOPY has extra switches that give it the power to work with multiple directories. Here's how it works. Let's say I have a directory on my C: drive called \DATA. The \DATA directory has three subdirectories: \JAN, \FEB, and \MAR. All of these directories, including the \DATA directory, contain about 50 files. If I wanted to copy all of these files to my D: drive in one command, I would use XCOPY in the following manner:

```
XCOPY C:\DATA D:\DATA /S
```

Because XCOPY works on directories, you don't have to use filenames as you would in COPY, although XCOPY certainly accepts filenames and wildcards. The /S switch, the most commonly used of all of the many switches that come with XCOPY, tells XCOPY to copy all subdirectories except for empty ones. The /E switch tells XCOPY to copy empty subdirectories. When you have a lot of copying to do over many directories, XCOPY is the tool to use.

Their power and utility make the DEL, COPY/MOVE, and XCOPY commands indispensable for a PC technician, but that same power and utility can cause disaster. Only a trained Jedi, with The Force as his ally…well, wrong book, but the principle remains: Beware of the quick and easy keystroke, for it may spell your doom. Think twice and execute the command once. The data you save may be yours!

Working with Batch Files

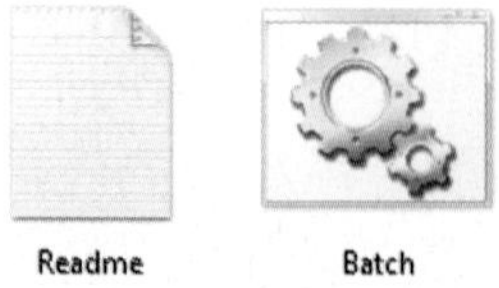

Batch files are nothing more than text files that store a series of commands, one command per line. The only thing that differentiates a batch file from any other text file is the .BAT extension. Take a look at Figure 15.18, and note

Readme   Batch

• **Figure 15.18**   Text and batch file icons

the unique icon used for a batch file compared to the icon for a regular text file.

You can create and edit batch files by using any text editor program—good old Notepad is often the tool of choice. This is the command-line chapter, though, so let's dust off the ancient but still important Edit program—it comes with every version of Windows—and use it to create and edit batch files.

Get to a command prompt on any Windows system and use the CD\ command to get to the root directory (use C: to get to the C: drive if you're not on the C: drive by default). From there, type **EDIT** at the command prompt to see the Edit program's interface (Figure 15.19).

Now that you've started Edit, type in the two commands as shown in Figure 15.20. Make sure they look exactly the same as the lines in Figure 15.20.

Great! You have just made your first batch file. All you need to do now is save it with some name—the name doesn't matter, but this example uses FIRST as the filename. It is imperative, however, that you use the extension .BAT. Even though you could probably figure this out on your own later, do it now. Hold down the ALT key to activate the menu. Press the F (File) key. Then press S (Save). Type in the name **first.bat** as shown in Figure 15.21. Press ENTER and the file is now saved.

Now that you've saved the file, exit the Edit program by pressing ALT-F and then pressing X (Exit). You're back at the command prompt. Go ahead and run the program by typing **FIRST** and pressing ENTER. Your results should look something like Figure 15.22.

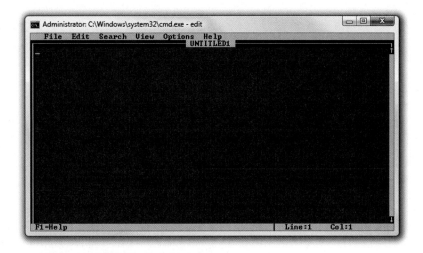

• **Figure 15.19**   Edit interface

• **Figure 15.20**   Edit with two commands

• **Figure 15.21**   Saving the batch file

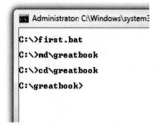

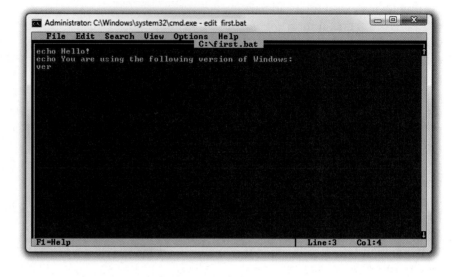

• Figure 15.22   Running the batch file

• Figure 15.23   New version of FIRST.BAT

Super! The batch file created a folder and moved the prompt to focus on that folder. Don't run the First batch file again or you'll create another folder inside the first one.

Let's now get back to the root directory of C: and edit the FIRST.BAT file again. This time type **EDIT FIRST.BAT** and press ENTER. The batch file will come up, ready to edit. Now change the batch file to look like Figure 15.23. Use the ARROW keys to move your cursor and the DELETE key to delete.

The VER command shows the current version of Windows. The ECHO command tells the batch file to put text on the screen. Run the batch file, and it should look like Figure 15.24.

Gee, that's kind of ugly. Try editing the FIRST.BAT file one more time and add the following line as the first line of the batch file:

```
@echo off
```

Run FIRST.BAT again. It should look quite a bit nicer. The @echo off command tells the system not to show the command, just the result.

Most of the keyboard short-cuts used in WordPad, Word, and so on, were first used in the Edit program. If you know keyboard shortcuts for WordPad or Word, many will work in Edit.

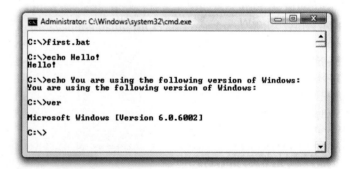

• Figure 15.24   Running first.bat

Sometimes you just want to look at a batch file. The TYPE command displays the contents of a text file on the screen, as shown in Figure 15.25.

One of the more irritating aspects to batch files is that sometimes they don't work unless you run them in the folder in which they are stored. This is because of the path setting. Every time you open a command prompt, Windows loads a number of settings by default. You can see all of these settings by running the SET command. Figure 15.26 shows the results of running the SET command.

Don't worry about understanding everything the SET command shows you, but do notice a line that starts with `Path=`. This line tells Windows where to look for a program (or batch file) if you run a program that's not in your current folder. For example, let's say I make a folder called C:\batch to store all of my batch files. I can run the PATH command from the command prompt to see my current path (Figure 15.27).

I can then run the PATH command again, this time adding **%PATH%;C:\batch** (Figure 15.28). The %PATH% bit is a variable that represents what is currently in the path. By placing it before my batch folder, I am telling the path command to keep what is there and just add c:\batch. I can now place all of my batch files in this folder, and they will always work, no matter where I am in the system.

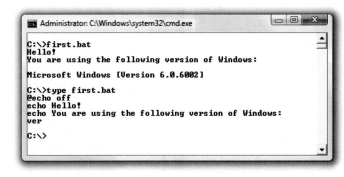

• **Figure 15.25**   Using the TYPE command to see file contents

 Don't try using the TYPE command on anything other than a text file—the results will be unpredictable.

• **Figure 15.26**   Using the SET command to see settings

In Windows 2000 and XP, you can edit the BOOT.INI file by using the Edit program. Just make sure you use ATTRIB first to turn off the System and Hidden attributes! In Windows Vista, the boot configuration data (BCD) store contains boot configuration parameters and objects that control how the operating system starts. You use the bcdedit.exe command-line tool to add, delete, and edit the objects and entries stored in the BCD store.

• **Figure 15.27** Using the PATH command to see the current path

• **Figure 15.28** Using PATH to add a folder

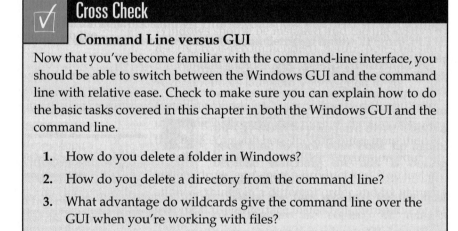

Cross Check

Command Line versus GUI

Now that you've become familiar with the command-line interface, you should be able to switch between the Windows GUI and the command line with relative ease. Check to make sure you can explain how to do the basic tasks covered in this chapter in both the Windows GUI and the command line.

1. How do you delete a folder in Windows?
2. How do you delete a directory from the command line?
3. What advantage do wildcards give the command line over the GUI when you're working with files?

And Even More Tools, Utilities, and Commands

As a proficient IT technician in the field, you need to be familiar with a whole slew of command-line tools and other important utilities. The CompTIA 220-702 exam focuses in on several of them, and although many have been discussed in detail in previous chapters, it is extremely important that you understand and practice with CHKDSK, FORMAT, and SFC.

CHKDSK (/f /r)

The **CHKDSK (Checkdisk) command** scans, detects, and repairs hard drive– and volume-related issues and errors. You can run the CHKDSK utility from a command prompt with the switches /f and /r. The /f switch attempts to fix volume-related errors, while the /r switch attempts to locate and repair bad sectors. To run successfully, CHKDSK needs direct access to a drive. In other words, the drive needs to be "unlocked." For example, if you run CHKDSK /f /r and CHKDSK does not consider your drive unlocked, you will receive a "cannot lock current drive" message, meaning that another process has the drive locked and is preventing CHKDSK from locking the drive itself. After this, CHKDSK presents you with the option to run it the next time the system restarts (Figure 15.29).

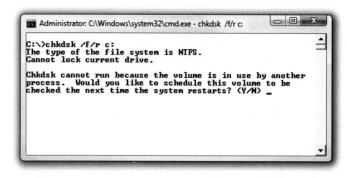

• **Figure 15.29**   The CHKDSK /f /r utility and switches on a locked drive

FORMAT

After the previous chapters, you should have an expert-level knowledge of (or, at the very least, a passing familiarity with) formatting and partitioning hard drives. Formatting, you may remember, is the process of wiping or preparing a disk to be partitioned so it can hold an operating system or data. We have already discussed the various built-in Windows utilities available to provide the formatting of drives, and you no doubt know that a myriad of third-party formatting tools are out there. In this chapter, you just need to become familiar with the FORMAT command and its switches.

The **FORMAT command**, you may have guessed, enables you to format disks from the command line. The very best way to familiarize yourself with FORMAT and its available switches is simply to enter **FORMAT /?** from the command prompt. Your results should be similar to those displayed in Figure 15.30.

Although the new CompTIA A+ exams focus primarily on operating system formatting utilities and options, you should familiarize yourself with the FORMAT command and its switches by practicing them on a test system you are literally not afraid to wipe out. Besides, you never know what skeletons CompTIA may pull out of the closet.

Cross Check

Error-checking

You've seen the graphical version of CHKDSK way back in Chapter 12, "Implementing Hard Drives," but how about refreshing your memory? How do you get to the Error-checking utility in Windows' graphical user interface? Does it have the same functionality as the command-line version's switches?

SFC (System File Checker)

The Windows **SFC (System File Checker),** or simply SFC.exe, scans, detects, and restores important Windows system files, folders, and paths. Techs often use the SFC utility from within a working version of Windows or from a Windows installation disc to restore a corrupt Windows environment. If you run SFC and it finds issues, it attempts to replace corrupted or missing files from cached DLLs located in the %WinDir%\System32\Dllcache\ directory. Without getting very deep into the mad science involved, just

• **Figure 15.30** Using Format /? at the command prompt

know that you can use SFC to correct corruption. To run SFC from a command prompt, enter **SFC /SCANNOW**. To familiarize yourself with SFC's switches, enter **SFC /?** (Figure 15.31).

• **Figure 15.31** Checking SFC options with SFC /? at a command prompt

Beyond A+

Using Special Keys

You might find yourself repeatedly typing the same commands, or at least very similar commands, when working at a prompt. Microsoft has provided a number of ways to access previously typed commands. Type the **DIR** command at a command prompt. When you get back to a prompt, press F1, and the letter *D* appears. Press F1 again. Now the letter *I* appears after the *D*. Do you see what is happening? The F1 key brings back the previous command one letter at a time. Pressing F3 brings back the entire command at once. Now try running these three commands:

DIR /W

ATTRIB

MD FRED

Now press the UP ARROW key. Keep pressing it till you see your original DIR command—it's a history of all your old commands. Now use the RIGHT ARROW key to add /P to the end of your DIR command. Windows command history is very handy.

Compact and Cipher

Windows XP and Vista offer two cool commands at the command-line interface: COMPACT and CIPHER. COMPACT displays or alters the compression of files on NTFS partitions. CIPHER displays or alters the encryption of folders and files on NTFS partitions. If you type just the command with no added parameters, COMPACT and CIPHER display the compression state and the encryption state, respectively, of the current directory and any files it contains. You may specify multiple directory names, and you may use wildcards, as you learned earlier in the chapter. You must add parameters to make the commands change things. For example, you add /C to compress and /U to uncompress directories and/or files with the COMPACT command, and you add /E to encrypt and /D to decrypt directories and/or files with the CIPHER command. When you do these operations, you also mark the directories involved so that any files you add to them in the future will take on their encryption or compression characteristics. In other words, if you encrypt a directory and all its files, any files you add later will also be encrypted. Same thing if you compress a directory. I'll run through a quick example of each.

COMPACT

First let's try the COMPACT command. Figure 15.32 shows the result of entering the COMPACT command with no switches. It displays the compression status of the contents of a directory called compact on a system's C: drive. Notice that after the file listing, COMPACT helpfully tells you that 0 files are compressed and 6 files (all of them) are not compressed, with a total compression ratio of 1.0 to 1.

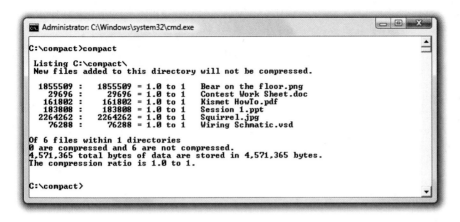

• **Figure 15.32**   The COMPACT command with no switches

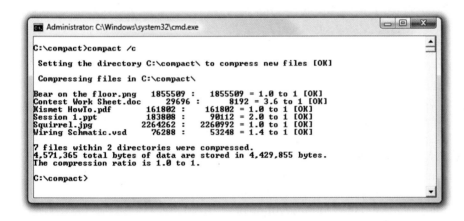

• **Figure 15.33**   Typing **COMPACT /C** compresses the contents of the directory.

If you enter the COMPACT command with the /C switch, it compresses all of the files in the directory, as shown in Figure 15.33. Look closely at the listing. Notice that it includes the original and compressed file sizes and calculates the compression ratio for you. Notice also that the JPG and PNG files (both compressed graphics files) didn't compress at all, while the Word file and the PowerPoint file compressed down to around a third of their original sizes. Also, can you spot what's different in the text at the bottom of the screen? COMPACT claims to have compressed *seven* files in *two* directories! How can this be? The secret is that when it compresses all of the files in a directory, it must also compress the directory file itself, which is "in" the C: directory above it. Thus it correctly reports that it compressed seven files: six in the compact directory, and one in the C: directory.

Typing **COMPACT** again shows you the directory listing, and now there's a C next to each filename, indicating that the file is compressed (Figure 15.34).

Okay, now suppose you want to uncompress a file—say a PowerPoint file, Session 1.ppt. To do this, you must specify the decompression operation, using the /U switch and the name of the file you want decompressed,

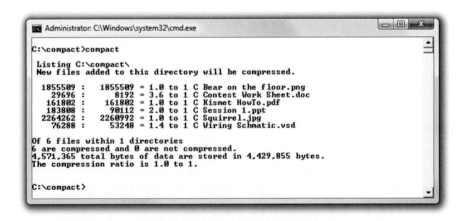

• **Figure 15.34**   The contents of C:\COMPACT have been compressed.

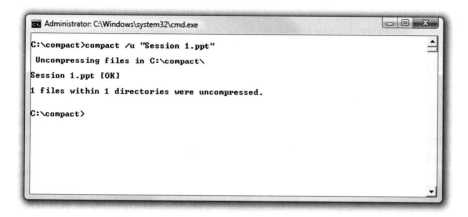

• **Figure 15.35**   Typing **COMPACT /U "Session 1.ppt"** decompresses only that file.

as shown in Figure 15.35. Note that COMPACT reports the successful de-compression of one file only: Session 1.ppt. You could do the same thing in reverse, using the /C switch and a filename to compress an individual file.

CIPHER

The CIPHER command is a bit complex, but in its most basic implementation, it's pretty straightforward. Figure 15.36 shows two steps in the process. Like the COMPACT command, the CIPHER command simply displays the current state of affairs when entered with no switches. In this case, it

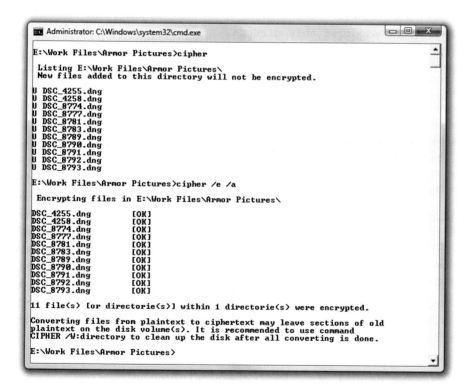

• **Figure 15.36**   Typing **CIPHER /E /A** encrypts the contents of the directory.

Securing Windows Resources

"Only the insecure strive for security."

—WAYNE DYER

In this chapter, you will learn how to

- **Create and administer Windows users and groups**
- **Define and utilize NTFS permissions for authorization**
- **Describe how to share a Windows computer securely**

You might ask me, "What's the single greatest aspect that keeps Microsoft Windows the number one operating system in the world?" My answer is "Windows is the easiest operating system for securing resources, individual computers, and entire networks." Windows really gets it right when it comes to protection. Windows uses a combination of user accounts and groups that tie into the NTFS file system to provide incredibly powerful file and folder protection. This user/group/NTFS combo scales down to just a single computer and scales up to a network of computers that can span the world. Windows doesn't just stop at files and folders, either.

The only serious challenge to all this great security is that Windows blurs the line between protecting just a single computer versus protecting a single computer over a network. In this chapter you will see Windows security from the aspect of a single, or *standalone*, machine. In Chapter 26, "Securing Computers," we will revisit most of these security issues and see how the same tools scale up to help you protect a computer in a networked environment.

Essentials/Practical Application

▪ Authentication with Users and Groups

The key to protecting your data is based on two related processes: authentication and authorization. **Authentication** is the process by which you determine a person at your computer is who he says he is. The most common way to authenticate is by using a user name and password. Once a user is authenticated, he needs **authorization**, the process that states what a user can and cannot do on that system. Authorization, at least for files and folders, is controlled by the NTFS file system, so we'll tackle that in the second section of this chapter.

Microsoft's answer to the authentication/authorization process is amazing. Inside every Windows computer is a list of names of users who are allowed access to the system. When Windows starts, it presents some form of logon screen where you enter (or select) your user name and then enter something secret (usually a password) that confirms you are the person assigned to that user name. Each of these individual records is called a **local user account**. If you don't have a local user account created on a particular system, you won't be able to log on to that computer (Figure 16.1).

Each version of Windows has a similar application for creating user accounts. But each one differs enough that it's useful to view them individually. Then we'll look at using passwords and groups to manage users, tasks that all Windows versions share.

 The competencies on Essentials and Practical Application overlap a lot on the subjects in this chapter. You should know the information here for either exam.

 Tech Tip

Principle of Least Privilege
A good security practice to determine what type of user account to give to a specific person is the principle of least privilege. In essence, you want to give users just enough—but no more— permissions to accomplish their tasks. Giving more than needed begs for problems or accidents and should be avoided.

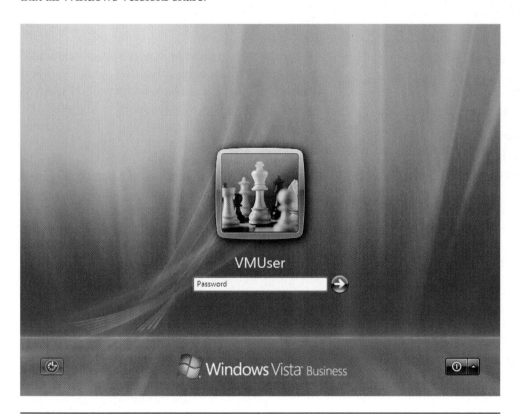

• **Figure 16.1**   Windows Logon screen

Managing Users in Windows 2000

One handy tool for managing users in Windows 2000 is called the **Users and Passwords applet** (Figure 16.2). You access this tool from the Control Panel.

When you install Windows 2000, by default you add two user accounts to the computer: administrator and guest. You can also choose to let the operating system assume that you are the sole user of the computer and not prompt you for a password for logging into Windows. As you might imagine, this severely limits any security on that Windows machine.

You can check this setting after installation by opening the Users and Passwords applet in Control Panel to see the setting for *Users must enter a user name and password to use this computer*. Figure 16.3 shows this choice selected, which means you will see a logon box every time you restart your computer. Also notice that the only user is administrator. That's the account used to log on when no other user is assumed.

Using the administrator account is just fine when you're doing administrative tasks such as installing updates, adding printers, adding and removing programs and Windows components, updating device drivers, and creating users and groups. Best practice for the workplace is to create one or more user accounts and only log in with the user accounts, not the administrator account. This gives you a lot more control over who or what happens to the computer.

For the sake of security, a wise administrator also enables the setting on the Advanced tab of Users and Passwords under Secure Boot Settings. If checked, as shown in Figure 16.4, it requires users to press CTRL-ALT-DELETE before logging on. This setting is a defense against certain viruses that try to capture your user name and password, sometimes by presenting a fake logon prompt. Pressing CTRL-ALT-DELETE removes such programs from memory and allows the actual logon dialog box to appear.

Creating a new user account enables that user to log on with a user name and password. The administrator can set the rights and permissions for the user and audit the user's access to certain network resources. For that reason, it is good practice to create users on a desktop computer. You are working with the same concepts on a small scale that an administrator must work with in a domain. Let's review the steps in this procedure for Windows 2000.

If you're logged on in Windows 2000 as the administrator or a member of the local Administrators group, open the Users and Passwords applet

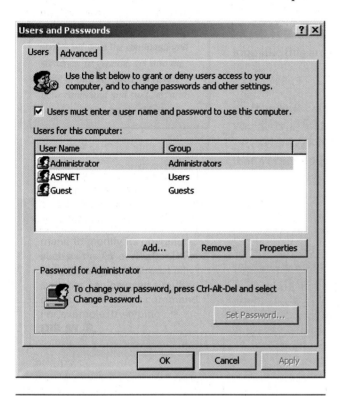

● **Figure 16.2**   Users and Passwords

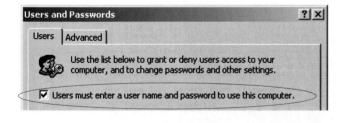

● **Figure 16.3**   Security begins with turning on *Users must enter a user name and password to use this computer.*

When you install Windows, assuming your computer is not made a member of a domain, you may choose to let the OS assume that you are the only user of the computer and do not want to see the logon dialog box.

Try This!

Turning On Logon Requirements and Secure Boot Settings

Security is all the rage in today's world, so having a computer with wonderful built-in security features sitting there with those features disabled makes little sense. Try This! Turn on the option to require a logon.

To complete this, you need a computer running Windows 2000 Professional.

1. Go to Control Panel and open Users and Passwords.

2. Make sure the box by *Users must enter a user name and password to use this computer* is checked.

3. Click the Advanced tab and make sure the box under Secure Boot Settings is checked.

4. Click OK to close the dialog box.

The next time anyone logs on to this computer, they will first have to press CTRL-ALT-DELETE to open a logon dialog box. Then they will be required to provide a user name and password.

If the password requirement is turned off and you have user accounts that aren't password protected in Windows 2000 (or other versions of Windows, for that matter), anyone with physical access to your computer can turn it on and use it by pressing the power button. This is potentially a very bad thing!

To create and manage users, you must be logged on as the administrator, be a member of the Administrators group, or have an administrator account. Assign a password to the administrator account so that only authorized users can access this all-powerful account.

Blank passwords or those that are easily visible on a sticky note provide *no security*. Always insist on non-blank passwords, and do not let anyone leave a password sitting out in the open. See the section on passwords later in the chapter.

---

from Control Panel and click the Add button. This opens the Add New User Wizard (Figure 16.5). Enter the user name that the user will use to log on. Enter the user's first and last names in the Full name field, and if you wish, enter some text that describes this person in the Description field. If this is at work, enter a job description in this field. The Full name and Description fields are optional.

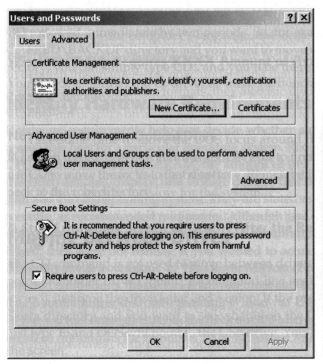

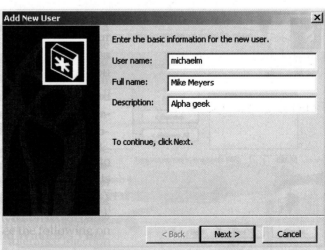

● **Figure 16.4** Make your computer more secure by enabling Secure Boot Settings.

● **Figure 16.5** Adding a new user

• **Figure 16.6**   Create user password

After entering the user information, click the Next button to continue. This opens a password dialog box where you can enter and confirm the initial password for this new user (Figure 16.6). Click the Next button to continue.

Now you get to decide what groups the new user should belong to. Select one of the two suggested options—standard user or restricted user—or select the Other option button and choose a group from the drop-down list. Select **Standard User**, which on a Windows 2000 Professional desktop makes this person a member of the local Power Users group as well as the Local Users group. Click the Finish button to close the dialog box. You should see your new user listed in the Users and Passwords dialog box. While you're there, note how easy it is for an administrator to change a user's password. Simply select a user from the list and then click on the Set Password button. Enter and confirm the new password in the Set Password dialog box. Figure 16.7 shows the Set Password dialog box with the Users and Passwords dialog box in the background.

Now let's say you want to change a password. Select the new user in the *Users for this computer* list on the Users page. Then click the Set Password button on the Users page. Enter and confirm the new password and then click the OK button to apply the changes.

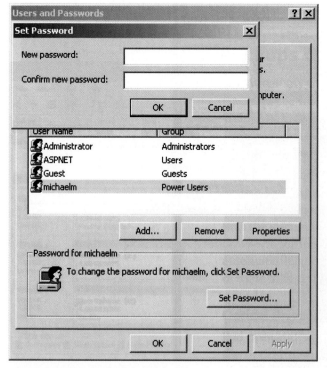

• **Figure 16.7**   Set Password dialog box

Managing Users in Windows XP

Although Windows XP has essentially the same type of accounts database as Windows 2000, the **User Accounts applet** in the Control Panel replaces the Users and Passwords applet and further simplifies user management tasks.

Windows XP has two very different ways to deal with user accounts and how you log on to a system: the blank user name and password text boxes, reminiscent of Windows 2000, and the Windows XP **Welcome screen** (Figure 16.8). If your Windows XP computer is a member of a Windows domain, your system automatically uses the Windows Classic style, including the requirement to press CTRL-ALT-DEL to get to the user name and password text boxes, just as in Windows 2000. If your Windows XP computer is not a member of a domain, you may use either method, although the Welcome screen is the default. Windows XP Home and Windows XP Media Center cannot join a domain, so these versions of Windows only use the Welcome screen. Windows Tablet PC Edition functions just as Windows XP Professional.

To begin, click your user name

VMUser

Turn off computer

After you log on, you can add or change accounts.
Just go to Control Panel and click User Accounts.

• **Figure 16.8**   Windows XP Welcome screen

Assuming that your Windows XP system is *not* a member of a domain, I'll concentrate on the XP Welcome screen and some of the options you'll see in the User Accounts Control Panel applet.

The User Accounts applet is very different from the old Users and Passwords applet in Windows 2000. User Accounts hides the complete list of users, using a simplistic reference to account types that is actually a reference to its group membership. An account that is a member of the local administrators group is said to be a **computer administrator**; an account that only belongs to the Local Users group is said to be a **limited user** account. Which users the applet displays depends on which type of user is currently logged on (see Figure 16.9). When an administrator is logged on, the administrator sees both types of accounts and the guest account. Limited users see only their own account in User Accounts.

Windows XP requires you to create a second account that is a member of the administrators group during the initial Windows installation. This is for simple redundancy—if one administrator is not available or is not able to log on to the computer, another one can.

Creating users is a straightforward process. You need to provide a user name (a password can be added later), and you need to know which type of account to create: computer administrator or limited. To create a new user in Windows XP, open the User Accounts applet from the Control Panel and

Chapter 16: Securing Windows Resources

• **Figure 16.9** User Accounts dialog box showing a computer administrator, a couple of limited accounts, and the guest account (disabled)

click *Create a new account*. On the *Pick an account type* page, you can create either type of account (Figure 16.10). Simply follow the prompts on the screen. After you create your local accounts, you'll see them listed when you open the User Accounts applet.

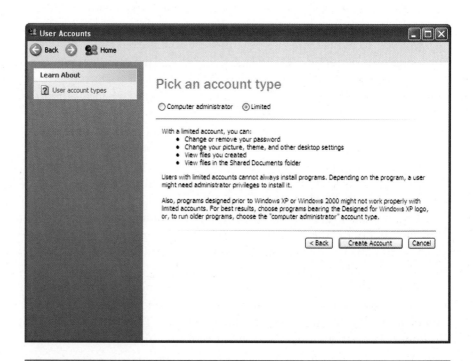

• **Figure 16.10** The *Pick an account type* page showing both options available

Mike Meyers' CompTIA A+ Guide to Managing and Troubleshooting PCs

Head back to the User Accounts applet and look at the *Change the way users log on and off* option. Select it to see two checkboxes (Figure 16.11). If you select the *Use the Welcome screen* checkbox, Windows brings up the friendly Welcome screen shown in Figure 16.12 each time users log in. If this box is unchecked, you'll get the classic login screen (Figure 16.13).

Tech Tip

Going Retro

The old Users and Passwords Control Panel applet is still in every version of Windows XP. If you're on a Windows XP Professional or Windows XP Tablet PC Edition system and your system is part of a domain, the old program comes up automatically when you click the User Accounts applet. If you're running Window XP Professional or Windows XP Tablet PC Edition but not on a domain, or if you're running XP Home or Media Center, go to Start | Run and type the following:

```
control userpasswords2
```

This brings up the old applet, which is the best way to change the administrator password on a system.

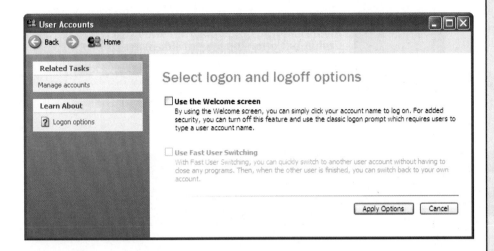

• **Figure 16.11**   Select logon and logoff options

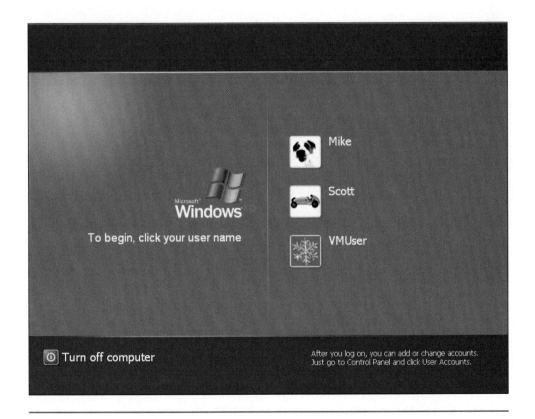

• **Figure 16.12**   Welcome screen with three accounts

The second option, Use Fast User Switching, enables you to switch to another user without logging off of the currently running user, a feature appropriately called **Fast User Switching**. This option is handy when two people actively share a system, or when someone wants to borrow your system for a moment but you don't want to close all of your programs. This option is only active if you have the *Use the Welcome screen* checkbox enabled. If Fast User Switching is enabled, when you click the Log Off button on the Start menu, you get the option to switch users, as shown in Figure 16.14.

• **Figure 16.13**   Classic Logon screen, XP style

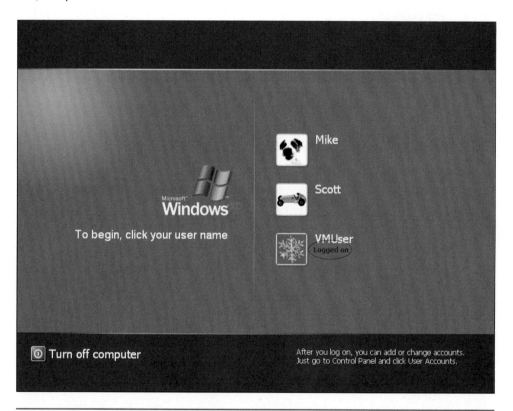

• **Figure 16.14**   Switching users on the Welcome screen

Managing Users in Windows Vista

Microsoft made some major changes in the transition to Windows Vista, including to the user accounts and the applet used to create and modify them. Just as with Windows XP, you create three accounts when you set up a computer: guest, administrator, and a local account that's a member of the Administrators group. That's about where the similarities end.

To add or modify a user account, you have numerous options depending on which Control Panel view you select and which version and update of Vista you have installed. Windows Vista Business and Ultimate, for example, in the default Control Panel Home view, offer the User Accounts

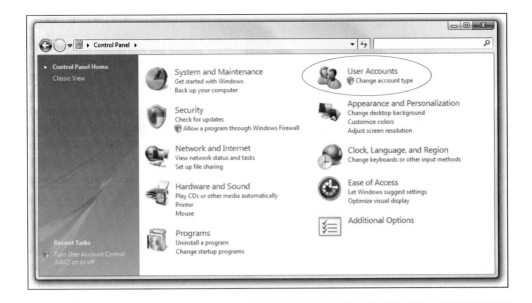

• **Figure 16.15**   User Accounts applet in the Control Panel Home in Windows Vista Ultimate

applet (Figure 16.15). Windows Home Premium, in contrast, gives you the User Accounts and Family Safety applet (Figure 16.16). The options under each applet differ as well, as you can see in the screenshots.

Most techs almost immediately change the Control Panel view to Classic, but even there the different versions of Windows—and whether you're logged into a workgroup or a domain—give you different versions of the User Accounts applet. Figure 16.17 shows the User Accounts applet in

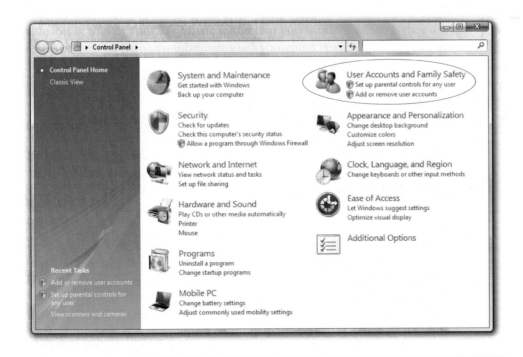

• **Figure 16.16**   User Accounts and Family Safety applet in the Control Panel Home in Windows Vista Home Premium

• **Figure 16.17**   User Accounts applet in Windows Vista Business

Windows Vista Business in a domain environment. Figure 16.18 shows the applet in Windows Vista Home Premium.

The Tasks options on the left are similar, with the addition of Parental Controls in the Home Premium edition, but the main options differ a lot. This chapter assumes a standalone machine, so we'll look more closely at the options with Vista Home Premium.

Windows Vista Home Premium uses Vista's version of the Welcome screen for logging in, so each user account has a picture associated with it. You can change the picture from the User Accounts applet. You can also change the name of the user account here and alter the account type, demoting an account from administrator to standard user, for example.

You must have one account as an administrator. If you try to demote the sole administrator account, you'll find the option dimmed.

• **Figure 16.18**   User Accounts applet in Windows Vista Home Premium

User Account Control

Windows XP made it too easy—and, in fact, almost necessary—to make your primary account on a computer an administrator account. Because limited users can't do common tasks, such as running certain programs, installing applications, updating applications, updating Windows, and so on, most users simply created an administrator-level account and logged in. Because such accounts have full control over the computer, malware that slipped in with that account could do a lot more harm.

Microsoft addressed this problem with the **User Account Control (UAC)**, a feature that enables standard users to do common tasks and provides a permissions dialog (Figure 16.19) when standard users *and* administrators do certain things that could potentially harm the computer (such as attempt to install a program). Vista user accounts now function much more like user accounts in Linux and Macintosh OS X, with programs asking for administrative permission before making changes to the computer.

Parental Controls

With **Parental Controls**, you can monitor and limit the activities of any Standard User in Windows Vista, a feature that gives parents and managers an excellent level of control over the content their children and employees can access (Figure 16.20). Activity Reporting logs applications run or attempted to run, Web sites visited or attempted to visit, any kind of files downloaded, and more. You can block various Web sites by type or specific URL, or you can allow only certain Web sites, a far more powerful option.

Parental Controls enable you to limit the time that standard users can spend logged in. You can specify acceptable and unacceptable times of day when standard users can log in. You can restrict access both to types of games and to specific applications. If you like playing rather gruesome games filled with monsters and blood that you don't want your kids to play, for example, you can simply block any games with

Tech Tip

Turning User Account Control Off

When Windows Vista debuted, most users and techs hated the User Account Control. The dialog box came up seemingly whenever you tried to do anything, prompting for a password if you were logged in as a Standard User or for confirmation if logged in as an administrator. Turning off the UAC prompt—though definitely not recommended by Microsoft—is readily accomplished in the User Accounts applet in the Control Panel. Click the link to Turn User Account Control on or off *and deselect the checkbox next to* Use User Account Control (UAC) to help protect your computer.

● **Figure 16.19**   Prompting for permission

• Figure 16.20   Parental Controls

certain ESRB (Entertainment Software Rating Board) ratings, such as E for Everyone, T for Teen, or M for Mature or Mature 17+.

Managing Users in General

Aside from the specific aspects of managing users in each particular version of Windows, there are a few security considerations that apply to every version of Windows, such as using appropriate passwords and creating user groups.

Passwords

Passwords are the ultimate key to protecting your computers. A user account with a valid password gets you into any system. Even if the user account only has limited permissions, you still have a security breach. Remember: for a hacker, just getting into the network is half the battle.

Protect your passwords. Never give out passwords over the phone. If a user forgets a password, an administrator should reset the password to a complex combination of letters and numbers, and then allow the user to change the password to something the user wants, according to the parameters set by the administrator.

Make your users choose good passwords. I once attended a security seminar, and the speaker had everyone stand up. She then began to ask questions about our passwords—if we responded yes to the question, we were to sit down. She began to ask questions such as

"Do you use the name of your spouse as a password?" and

"Do you use your pet's name?"

Using non-alphanumeric characters makes any password much more difficult to crack, for two reasons. First, adding non-alphanumeric characters forces the hacker to consider many more possible characters than just letters and numbers. Second, most password crackers use combinations of common words and numbers to try to hack a password.

Because non-alphanumeric characters don't fit into common words or numbers, including a character such as an exclamation point defeats these common-word hacks. Not all serving systems allow you to use characters such as @, $, %, or \, however, so you need to experiment to see if a particular server will accept them.

By the time she had asked about 15 questions, only 6 people out of some 300 were still standing! The reality is that most of us choose passwords that are amazingly easy to hack. Make sure you use a **strong password**: at least eight characters in length, including letters, numbers, and punctuation symbols.

Once you've forced your users to choose strong passwords, you should make them change passwords at regular intervals. Although this concept sounds good on paper, in the real world it is a hard policy to maintain. For starters, users tend to forget passwords when they change a lot. This can lead to an even bigger security problem because users start writing passwords down!

If your organization forces you to change passwords often, one way to remember the password is to use a numbering system. I worked at a company that required me to change my password at the beginning of each month, so I did something very simple. I took a root password—let's say it was "m3y3rs5"—and simply added a number to the end representing the current month. So when June rolled around, for example, I would change my password to "m3y3rs56." It worked pretty well!

Windows XP and Windows Vista enable currently logged-on users to create a **password reset disk** they can use if they forget a password. This is very important to have. If an administrator resets the password by using User Accounts or Local Users and Groups, and you then log on with the new password, you will discover that you cannot access some items, including files you encrypted when logged on with the forgotten password. When you reset a password with a password reset disk, you can log on with the new password and still have access to previously encrypted files.

Best of all, with the password reset disk, users have the power to fix their own passwords. Encourage your users to create this disk; they only have this power if they create a password reset disk *before* they forget the password! If you need to create a password reset disk for a computer on a network (domain), search the Help system for "password reset disk" and follow the instructions for password reset disks for a computer on a domain.

Windows Vista has an obvious option in the Tasks list to *Create a password reset disk*. You'll need to have a floppy disk inserted or a USB flash drive to create the disk.

Groups

A **group** is simply a collection of accounts that share the same access capabilities. A single account can be a member of multiple groups. Groups are essential for managing a network of computers but also can come in handy on a single computer with multiple users.

Groups make Windows administration much easier in two ways. First, you can assign a certain level of access for a file or folder to a group instead of to just a single user account. For example, you can make a group called Accounting and put all of the accounting user accounts in that group. If a person quits, you don't need to worry about assigning all of the proper access levels when you create a new account for his or her replacement. After you make an account for the new person, you just add the new account to the appropriate access group! Second, Windows provides numerous built-in groups with various access levels already predetermined. As you might imagine, there are differences among the versions.

 Every secure organization sets up various security policies and procedures to ensure that security is maintained. Windows has various mechanisms to implement such things as requiring a strong password, for example. Chapter 26, "Securing Computers," goes into detail about setting up Local Policies and Group Policy.

 See the last section of this chapter, "Protecting Data with Encryption," for the scoop on the ultimate in security.

Groups in Windows 2000 Windows 2000 provides seven built-in groups: Administrators, Power Users, Users, Backup Operators, Replicator, Everyone, and Guests. These built-in groups have a number of preset capabilities. You cannot delete these groups.

- **Administrators** Any account that is a member of the **Administrators group** has complete administrator privileges. It is common for the primary user of a Windows system to have her account in the Administrators group.

- **Power Users** Members of the **Power Users group** are almost as powerful as Administrators, but they cannot install new devices or access other users' files or folders unless the files or folders specifically provide them access.

- **Users** Members of the **Users group** cannot edit the Registry or access critical system files. They can create groups but can manage only those they create.

- **Backup Operators** Backup operators have the same rights as users, except that they can run backup programs that access any file or folder—for backup purposes only.

- **Replicator** Members of the Replicator group can replicate files and folders in a domain.

- **Everyone** This group applies to any user who can log on to the system. You cannot edit this group.

- **Guests** Enabling the **Guests group** allows someone who does not have an account on the system to log on by using a guest account. You might use this feature at a party, for example, to provide casual Internet access to guests, or at a library terminal. Most often, the guest account remains disabled for every version of Windows.

Groups in Windows XP Windows XP diverges a lot from Windows 2000 on user accounts. If you're running XP Professional and you are on a Windows domain, XP offers all of the accounts listed previously, but it adds other specialized groups, including HelpServicesGroup and Remote Desktop Users. Windows XP Home and XP Professional, when installed on standalone PCs or PCs that are connected to a workgroup but not a domain, run in a specialized networking mode called *simple file sharing*. A Windows XP system running simple file sharing has only three account types: computer administrator, limited user, and guest. Computer administrators can do anything, as you might suspect. Limited users can access only certain things and have limits on where they can save files on the PC. The guest account is disabled by default but works the same way as in Windows 2000.

Groups in Windows Vista The professional editions of Windows Vista (Business, Ultimate, and Enterprise) offer the same groups found in Windows XP Professional and throw in a lot more. Some of the default groups, such as Distributed COM Users, target specific roles in certain industries and mean little for the average user or tech. Other specific group types enable people to check on the performance and reliability of a computer, but without gaining access to any of the documents on the computer. These groups include Event Log Readers, Performance Log Users, and Performance

Monitor Users. These groups provide excellent levels of access for technicians to help keep busy Vista machines healthy.

Like Windows XP, the home editions of Windows Vista (Home Basic and Home Premium) offer only three groups: administrators, users, and guests. Administrators and guests function as they do in all of the other versions of Windows. Members of the Users group, on the other hand, are called standard users and differ significantly from the limited users of Windows XP infamy. Standard users are prevented from harming the computer or uninstalling applications but can run most applications. Technicians don't have to run over to standard user accounts to enable access to common tasks such as printing or doing e-mail.

• **Figure 16.21**   Local Users and Groups in Windows Vista

Adding Groups and Changing Group

Membership   The professional versions of Windows—including Windows 2000, XP, and Vista—enable you to add new groups to your computer by using the **Local Users and Groups** tool, found in the Computer Management applet of the Administrative Tools. This tool also enables you to create user accounts and change group membership for users. Figure 16.21 shows the Local Users and Groups in Windows Vista with the Groups selected.

To add a group, simply right-click on a blank spot in the Groups folder and select New Group. This opens the New Group dialog box, where you can type in a group name and description in their respective fields (Figure 16.22).

To add users to this group, click the Add button. The dialog box that opens varies a little in name among the three operating systems. In Vista it's called the Se-

• **Figure 16.22**   New Group dialog box in Windows Vista

lect Users, Computers, or Groups dialog box (Figure 16.23). The Windows 2000 dialog box presents a list of user accounts. Windows XP and Vista add some complexity to the tool.

A user account, a group, a computer; these are all object types in Microsoft lingo. To give you a lot of control over what you do or how you select various objects, Microsoft beefed up this dialog box. The short story of how to select a user account is to click the Advanced button to expand the dialog box and then click the Find Now button (Figure 16.24).

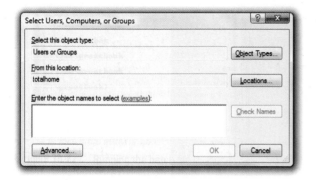

● **Figure 16.23** Select Users, Computers, or Groups dialog box

● **Figure 16.24** Select Users, Computers, or Groups dialog box with Advanced options expanded to show user accounts

● **Figure 16.25** Properties dialog box of a user account, where you can change group memberships for that account

You can add or remove user accounts from groups with the Local Users and Groups tool. You select the Users folder, right-click a user account you want to change, and select Properties from the context menu. Then select the Member Of tab on the user account's Properties dialog box (Figure 16.25). Click Add to add group membership. Select a group and click Remove to take away a group membership. It's a clean, well-designed tool.

■ Authorization Through NTFS

User accounts and passwords provide the foundation for securing a Windows computer, enabling users to authenticate onto that PC. The essential next step in security is authorization, determining what a legitimate user can do with the resources—files, folders, applications, and so on—on that computer. Windows uses the NT file system and permissions to protect its resources.

NTFS Permissions

In Windows 2000, XP, Vista, and 7, every folder and file on an NTFS partition has a list that contains two sets of data. First, the list details every user

and group that has access to that file or folder. Second, the list specifies the level of access that each user or group has to that file or folder. The level of access is defined by a set of restrictions called NTFS permissions.

NTFS permissions define exactly what a particular account can or cannot do to the file or folder and are thus quite detailed and powerful. You can make it possible, for example, for a person to edit a file but not delete it. You can let someone create a folder and not allow other people to make subfolders. NTFS file and folder permissions are so complicated that entire books have been written on them! Fortunately, the CompTIA A+ certification exams test your understanding of only a few basic concepts of NTFS permissions: Ownership, Take Ownership permission, Change permission, Folder permissions, and File permissions.

- **Ownership** When you create a new file or folder on an NTFS partition, you become the *owner* of that file or folder. A newly created file or folder by default gives everyone full permission to access, delete, and otherwise manipulate that file or folder. Owners can do anything they want to the files or folders they own, including changing the permissions to prevent anybody, even administrators, from accessing them.

- **Take Ownership permission** With the **Take Ownership** special permission, anyone with the permission can seize control of a file or folder. Administrator accounts have Take Ownership permission for everything. Note the difference here between owning a file and accessing a file. If you own a file, you can prevent anyone from accessing that file. An administrator whom you have blocked, however, can take that ownership away from you and *then* access that file!

- **Change permission** Another important permission for all NTFS files and folders is the Change permission. An account with this permission can give or take away permissions for other accounts.

- **Folder permissions** Let's look at a typical folder in my Windows XP system to see how this one works. My E: drive is formatted as NTFS, and on it I created a folder called E:\MIKE. I set the permissions for the E:\MIKE folder by right-clicking on the folder, selecting Properties, and clicking the Security tab (see Figure 16.26).

- **File permissions** File permissions are similar to Folder permissions. We'll talk about File permissions right after we cover Folder permissions.

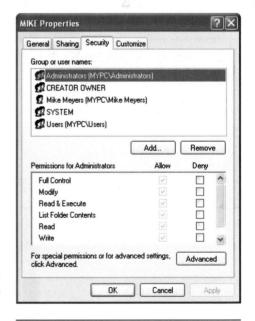

• **Figure 16.26** The Security tab lets you set permissions.

In Windows, just about everything in the computer has a Security tab in its properties, and every Security tab contains two main areas. The top area shows the list of accounts that have permissions for that resource. The lower area shows exactly what permissions have been assigned to the selected account.

Here are the standard permissions for a folder:

- **Full Control** Enables you to do anything you want.
- **Modify** Enables you to do anything except delete files or subfolders.
- **Read & Execute** Enables you to see the contents of the folder and any subfolders.
- **List Folder Contents** Enables you to see the contents of the folder and any subfolders. (This permission seems the same as the Read & Execute permission, but it is only inherited by folders.)
- **Read** Enables you to read any file in the folder.
- **Write** Enables you to write to files and create new files and folders.

File permissions are quite similar to folder permissions, with the main difference being the Special Permissions option, which I'll talk about a bit later in the chapter.

- **Full Control** Enables you to do anything you want.
- **Modify** Enables you to do anything except take ownership or change permissions on the file.
- **Read & Execute** If the file is a program, you can run it.
- **Read** If the file is data, you can read it.
- **Write** Enables you to write to the file.

Windows versions for home use have only a limited set of permissions you can assign. As far as folder permissions go, you can assign only one: Make This Folder Private. To see this in action, right-click a file or folder and select Sharing and Security from the options. Note that you can't just select the properties and see a Security tab as you can in the professional-oriented versions of Windows. Windows Home versions do not have file-level permissions.

Take some time to think about these permissions. Why would Microsoft create them? Think of situations where you might want to give a group Modify permission. Also, you can assign more than one permission. In many situations, we like to give users both the Read as well as the Write permission.

Permissions are cumulative. If you have Full Control on a folder and only Read permission on a file in the folder, you get Full Control permission on the file.

Permission Propagation

Permissions present an interesting challenge when you're moving and copying files. Techs need to understand what happens to permissions in several circumstances:

- Copying data within one NTFS-based partition
- Moving data within one NTFS-based partition
- Copying data between two NTFS-based partitions
- Moving data between two NTFS-based partitions

- Copying data from an NTFS-based partition to a FAT- or FAT32-based partition

- Moving data from an NTFS-based partition to a FAT- or FAT32-based partition

Do the permissions stay as they were on the original resource? Do they change to something else? Microsoft would describe the questions as such: Do inheritable permissions propagate? Ugh. CompTIA describes the process with the term **permission propagation**, which I take to mean "what happens to permissions on an object when you move or copy that object."

If you look at the bottom of the Security tab in Windows 2000, you'll see a little checkbox that says *Allow Inheritable Permissions from Parent to Propagate to This Object*. In other words, any files or subfolders created in this folder get the same permissions for the same users/groups that the folder has, a feature called **inheritance**. Deselecting this option enables you to stop users from getting a specific permission via inheritance. Windows XP and Windows Vista have the same feature, only it's accessed through the Advanced button in the Security tab. Windows also provides explicit Deny functions for each option (Figure 16.27). Deny overrules inheritance.

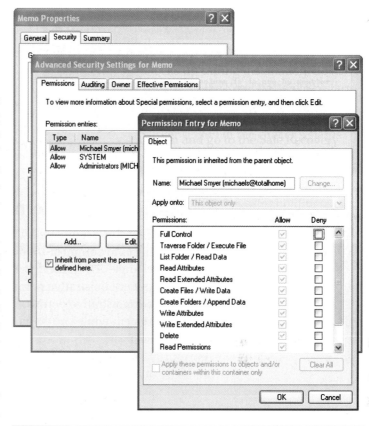

• **Figure 16.27** Special permissions

Let's look at our list of six things techs need to know to see what happens when you copy or move an object, such as a file or folder.

1. Copying within a partition creates two copies of the object. The object in the original location *retains* its permissions, unchanged. The copy of the object in the new location *inherits* the permissions from that new location. So the new copy can have different permissions than the original.

2. Moving within a partition creates one copy of the object. That object *retains* its permissions, unchanged.

3. Copying from one NTFS partition to another creates two copies of the object. The object in the original location *retains* its permissions, unchanged. The copy of the object in the new location *inherits* the permissions from that new location. So the new copy can have different permissions than the original.

4. Moving from one NTFS partition to another creates one copy of the object. The object in the new location *inherits* the permissions from that new location. So the newly moved file can have different permissions than the original.

5. Copying from an NTFS-based partition to a FAT- or FAT32-based partition creates two copies of the object. The object in the original location *retains* its permissions, unchanged. The copy of the object in the new location has no permissions at all.

> Don't panic about memorizing special permissions; just appreciate that they exist and that the permissions you see in the Security tab cover the vast majority of our needs.

6. Moving from an NTFS-based partition to a FAT- or FAT32-based partition creates one copy of the object. That object has no permissions at all.

From a tech's standpoint, you simply need to be aware of how permissions can change when you move or copy files and, if in doubt about a sensitive file, check it before you sign off to a client. Having a top secret document totally locked down on a hard drive doesn't do you a lot of good if you put that document on a thumb drive to transport it and the thumb drive is FAT32!

Techs and Permissions

Techs, as a rule, hate NTFS permissions. You must have administrative privileges to do almost anything on a Windows machine, such as install updates, change drivers, and install applications; most administrators hate giving out administrative permissions (for obvious reasons). If one does give you administrative permission for a PC, and something goes wrong with that system while you're working on it, you immediately become the primary suspect!

If you're working on a Windows system administered by someone else, make sure he understands what you are doing and how long you think it will take. Have the administrator create a new account for you that's a member of the Administrators group. Never ask for the password for a permanent administrator account! That way, you won't be blamed if anything goes wrong on that system: "Well, I told Janet the password when she installed the new hard drive…maybe she did it!" When you have fixed the system, *make sure the administrator deletes the account you used.*

This "protect yourself from passwords" attitude applies to areas other than just doing tech support on Windows. PC support folks get lots of passwords, scan cards, keys, and ID tags. New techs tend to get an "I can go anywhere and access anything" attitude, and this is dangerous. I've seen many jobs lost and friendships ruined when a tape backup suddenly disappears or a critical file gets erased. Everybody points to the support tech in these situations. In physical security situations, make other people unlock doors for you. In some cases, I've literally asked the administrator or system owner to sit behind me, read a magazine, and be ready to punch in passwords as needed. What you don't have access to can't hurt you.

■ Sharing a Windows PC Securely

User accounts, groups, and NTFS work together to enable you to share a Windows PC securely with multiple user accounts. You can readily share files, folders, programs, and more. More to the point, you can share only what should be shared, locking access to files and folders that you want to make private. Each version of Windows handles multiple user accounts and sharing among those accounts differently, so let's look at Windows 2000, Windows XP, and Windows Vista separately and then finish with a look at a few other sharing and security issues involving sharing.

Sharing in Windows 2000

Every user account on a Windows 2000 computer gets a My Documents folder, the default storage area for personal documents. That sounds great, but every account that's a member of the Administrators group can view the contents of everybody's My Documents folder, by default.

A typical way to create a secure shared Windows 2000 computer is to change the permissions on your My Documents folder to give yourself full control, but take away the permissions that allow other accounts access. You also should not create user accounts that go beyond Power Users or even Standard Users.

Finally, make a folder for people to share so that moving files to and from accounts is easy. A typical example would be to create a folder on the C: drive called Shared and then alter the permissions, giving full control to everyone.

To make changes to the permissions on folders, right-click and select Sharing to open the Properties dialog box with the Sharing tab already selected (Figure 16.28). Select *Share this folder* and change the options to what you want.

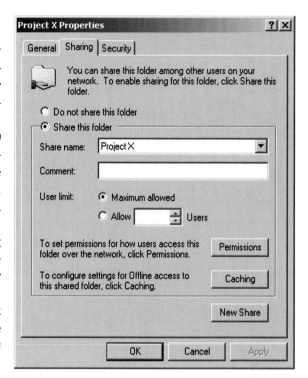

Sharing in Windows XP

Microsoft tried to make Windows XP secure sharing easier than previous versions of Windows. To this end, they included several features. First, just as with Windows 2000, each user account gets a series of folders in My Documents that the user can share and administrators can access. But Windows XP also comes with a set of pre-made folders called **Shared Documents** accessible by all of the users on the computer. Also, Windows XP comes with simple file sharing enabled by default, which makes the option to share or not pretty easy. Finally, Windows XP Professional provides the option to use the full NTFS permissions and make customized shares possible.

Making Personal Documents Secure

The fact that most users of Windows XP computers will be computer administrators rather than limited users creates a bit of an issue with computers shared by many users. By default, administrators can see all of the contents of Documents and Settings, where the My Documents folder for each user account resides. You can override this option in the My Documents Properties dialog box. Selecting the option to *Make this folder private* blocks the contents from anyone accessing them (Figure 16.29).

Note that an administrator can take ownership of anything, so the only true way to lock down your data is to encrypt it. In the My Documents Properties dialog box, select the General tab and then click the Advanced button to open the Advanced Attributes dialog box. Click the checkbox next to *Encrypt contents to secure data* and that'll handle the encryption. Just make sure you have a password reset disk if you're going to use encryption to secure your files.

• **Figure 16.28** Sharing tab on Properties for the Shared folder

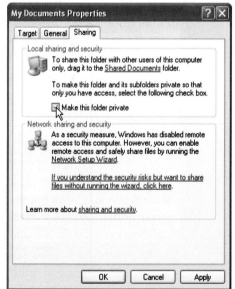

• **Figure 16.29** Making personal documents secure from prying eyes

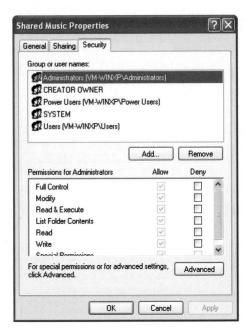

• **Figure 16.30** Shared Music Properties dialog box

When you join Windows XP Professional to a domain, simple file sharing is disabled. You must use the full power of NTFS.

Shared Documents

You can use the Shared Documents folders to move files and folders among many users of a single machine. Every account can access the Shared Documents and the sub-folders within, such as Shared Music and Shared Pictures (Figure 16.30). Because new folders inherit the permissions of parent folders, by default any new subfolder you create in Shared Folders can be accessed by any account.

Simple File Sharing

With **simple file sharing**, you essentially have one local sharing option, and that's to put anything you want to share into the Shared Documents. To share a folder over a network, you only have a couple of options as well, such as to share or not and, if so, to give full control to everybody. Note that the sharing option is enabled in Figure 16.31. It's pretty much all or nothing.

Windows XP Home and Media Center only give you the simple file sharing, so the sharing of files and folders is straightforward. Windows XP Professional, on the other hand, enables you to turn off simple file sharing and unlock the true power of NTFS and permissions. To turn off simple file sharing, in some form of Windows Explorer, such as My Documents, go to Tools | Folder Options and select the View tab. The very last option on the View tab is *Use simple file sharing (Recommended)*. Deselect that option, as in Figure 16.32, and then click OK.

When you access sharing and security now, you'll see a more fully formed security dialog box reminiscent of the one you saw with Windows 2000 (Figure 16.33).

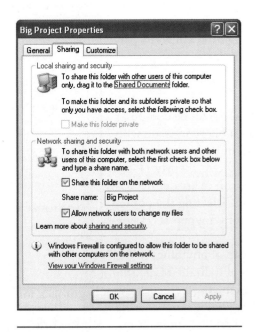

• **Figure 16.31** Folder shared, but seriously not secure

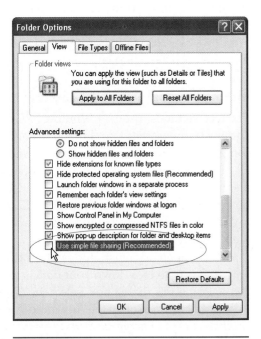

• **Figure 16.32** Turning off simple file sharing

Sharing in Windows Vista

Microsoft tweaked the settings for sharing a single PC with multiple users in Windows Vista to fix the all-or-nothing approach offered by simple file sharing; for example, enabling you to target shared files and folders to specific user accounts. They beefed up the Standard User account (as you read about earlier in the chapter) so users could access what they needed to get meaningful work done. Plus they expanded the concept of the Shared Documents into the Public folder.

Targeted Sharing

To share a folder or file with specific users—or to everyone, for that matter—you simply right-click on it and select Share. This opens the File Sharing dialog box where you can select specific user accounts from a drop-down list (Figure 16.34).

Once you select a user account, you can then choose what permission level to give that user. You have three choices: Reader, Contributor, or Co-owner (Figure 16.35). *Reader* simply means the user has read-only permissions. *Contributor* gives the user read and write permissions and the permission to delete any file the user contributed to the folder. (Contributor only works at the folder level.) A *co-owner* can do anything.

Public Folder

The **Public folder** offers another way to share files and folders. Anything you want to share with all other users on the local machine—or if on a network, throughout the network—simply place in the Public folder or one of the

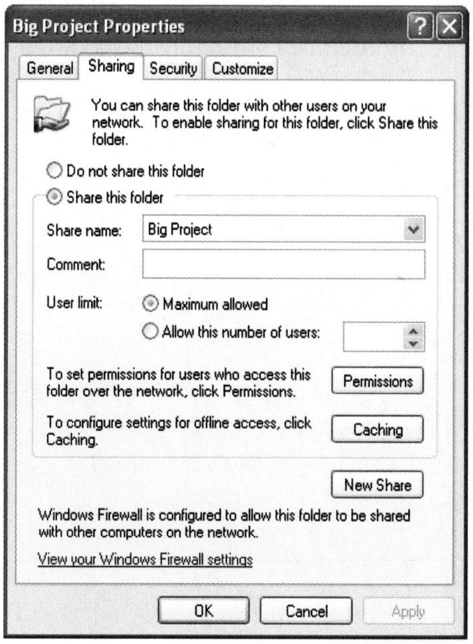

• **Figure 16.33** Full sharing and security options in Windows XP

If the computer in question is on a Windows domain, the File Sharing dialog box differs such that you can search the network for user accounts in the domain. This makes it easy to share throughout the network.

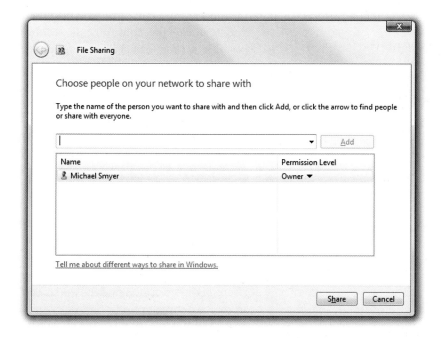

• **Figure 16.34** File Sharing dialog box on a standalone machine

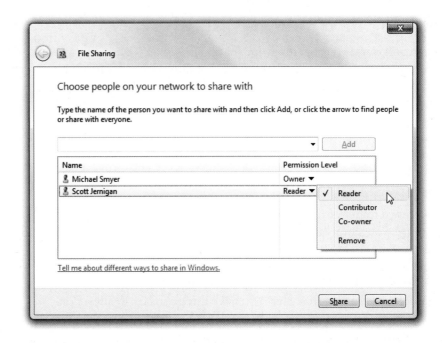

• **Figure 16.35**   Permissions options

many subfolders, such as Public Documents or Public Pictures (Figure 16.36). Note that the Public folder does not give you any control over what someone accessing the files contained within can do with those files.

Locating Shared Folders

Before you walk away from a computer, you should check for any unnecessary or unknown (to you) shared folders on the hard drives. This enables you to make the computer as secure as possible for the user. When you open My Computer or Computer, shared folders don't just jump out at you, especially if they're buried deep within the file system. A shared C: drive is obvious, but a shared folder all the way down in D:\temp\ backup\Simon\secret share would not be obvious, especially if none of the parent folders were shared.

Windows comes with a handy tool for locating all of the shared folders on a computer, regardless of where they reside on the drives. The Computer Management console in the Administrative Tools has a Shared Folders option under System Tools. In that are three options: Shares, Sessions, and Open Files. Select Shares to reveal all of the shared folders (Figure 16.37).

• **Figure 16.36**   Shared folders in the Public folder

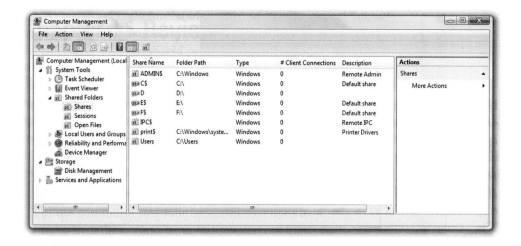

● **Figure 16.37**   Shared Folders tool in Computer Management

You can double-click on any share to open the Properties dialog box for that folder. At that point, you can make changes to the share—such as users and permissions—just as you would from any other sharing dialog.

Administrative Shares

A close glance at the screenshot in Figure 16.37 might have left some of you with raised eyebrows and quizzical looks. What kind of share is ADMIN$ or F$?

Every version of Windows since Windows NT comes with several default shares, notably all hard drives—not optical drives or removable devices, such as thumb drives—plus the %systemroot% folder—usually C:\Windows or C:\WINNT—and a couple of others, depending on the system. These **administrative shares** give local administrators administrative access to these resources, whether they log in locally or remotely. (In contrast, shares added manually are called *local shares*.)

Administrative shares are odd ducks. You cannot change the default permissions on them. You can delete them, but Windows will re-create them automatically every time you reboot. They're hidden, so they don't appear when you browse a machine over the network, though you can map them by name. Keep the administrator password safe, and these default shares won't affect the overall security of the computer.

Administrative shares have been exploited by malware programs, especially because many users who set up their computers never give the administrator account a password. Starting with Windows XP Home, Microsoft changed the remote access permissions for such machines. If you log into a computer remotely as administrator with no password, you get guest access rather than administrator access. That neatly nips potential exploits in the bud.

Protecting Data with Encryption

The scrambling of data through **encryption** techniques provides the only true way to secure your data from access by any other user. Administrators can use the Take Ownership permission to seize any file or folder on a computer, even those you don't actively share. Thus you need to implement other security measures for that data that needs to be ultra secure. Depending on the version of Windows, you have between zero and three encryptions tools: Windows Home versions have basically no security features; Windows XP Professional uses the Encrypting File System to, well,

● **Figure 16.38**   Click the Advanced button on the
Properties, General tab

● **Figure 16.39**   Selecting encryption

encrypt files; and Windows Vista Ultimate and Enterprise add an encryption system that can encrypt entire hard drives.

Encrypting File System

The professional versions of Windows offer a feature called the **Encrypting File System (EFS)**, an encryption scheme that any user can use to encrypt individual files or folders on a computer. The home versions of Windows do not enable encryption through the built-in tools, though you have the option to use third-party encryption methods, such as TrueCrypt, to lock down data.

To encrypt a file or folder takes but a moment. You right-click the file or folder you want to encrypt and select Properties. In the Properties for that object, General tab, click the Advanced button (Figure 16.38) to open the Advanced Attributes dialog box. Click the checkbox next to *Encrypt contents to secure data* (Figure 16.39). Click OK to close the Advanced Attributes dialog box and then click OK again on the Properties dialog box, and you've locked that file or folder from any user account aside from your own.

As long as you maintain the integrity of your password, any data you encrypt by using EFS is secure from prying. That security comes at a potential price, though, and your password is the key. The Windows security database stores the password (securely, not plain text, so no worries there), but that means access to your encrypted files is based on that specific installation of Windows. If you lose your password or an administrator resets your password, you're locked out of your encrypted files permanently. There's no recovery. Also, if the computer dies and you try to retrieve your data by installing the hard drive in another system, you're likewise out of luck. Even if you have an identical user name on the new system, the security ID that defines that user account will differ from what you had on the old system. You're out of luck.

Remember the password reset disk we discussed earlier in the chapter? If you use EFS, you simply must have a valid password reset disk in the event of some horrible catastrophe.

And one last caveat. If you copy an encrypted file to a disk formatted as anything but NTFS, you'll get a prompt saying that the copied file will not be encrypted. If you copy to a disk with NTFS, the encryption stays. The encrypted file—even if on a removable disk—will only be readable on your system with your login.

BitLocker Drive Encryption

Windows Vista Ultimate and Enterprise editions offer full drive encryption through **BitLocker Drive Encryption**. BitLocker does the whole drive, including every user's files, so it's not dependent on any one account. The beauty of BitLocker is that if your hard drive is stolen, such as in the case of a stolen portable computer, all of the data on the hard drive is safe. The thief can't get

access, even if you have a user on that laptop that failed to secure his or her data through EFS.

BitLocker requires a special Trusted Platform Module (TPM) chip on the motherboard to function. The TPM chip validates on boot that the Vista computer has not changed, that you still have the same operating system installed, for example, and that the computer wasn't hacked by some malevolent program. The TPM also works in cases where you move the BitLocker drive from one system to another.

If you have a legitimate BitLocker failure (rather than a theft) because of tampering or moving the drive to another system, you need to have a properly created and accessible recovery key or recovery password. The key or password is generally created at the time you enable BitLocker and should be kept somewhere secure, such as a printed copy in a safe or a file on a network server accessible only to administrators.

To enable BitLocker, double-click the BitLocker Drive Encryption icon in the Classic Control Panel, or select Security in Control Panel Home view and then click *Protect your computer by encrypting data on your disk* (Figure 16.40).

Tech Tip

TrueCrypt

TrueCrypt is an open-source disk encryption application with versions available for just about every operating system. You can use TrueCrypt to encrypt an entire partition or you can create an encrypted volume into which you can securely store data. The beauty of the encrypted volume is that it acts like a folder that you can move around or toss on a USB flash drive. You can take the volume to another system and, as long as you have the password and TrueCrypt installed on the other system, you can read the contents of the encrypted volume. If the thumb drive is big enough, you can even put a copy of TrueCrypt on it and run the program directly from the thumb drive, enabling you to read the contents of the encrypted volume—as long as you know the proper password.

TrueCrypt has some limitations, such as a lack of support for dynamic disks and some problems with multi-boot systems, but considering the price—free, though donations are cheerfully accepted—and the amazing power, it's hard not to love the program. This discussion of TrueCrypt barely scratches the surface of what the application can do, so check it out at www.truecrypt.org. If you're running Windows XP Home or Windows Vista Home Premium, you can't get a better tool for securing your data.

• **Figure 16.40**   Enabling BitLocker Drive Encryption

■ Chapter Summary

After reading this chapter and completing the exercises, you should understand the following about securing Windows resources.

Create and administer Windows users and groups

■ The key to protecting your data is based on two related processes: authentication and authorization. Authentication is the process by which you determine a person at your computer is who he says he is. The most common way to authenticate is by using a user name and password. Once a user is authenticated, he needs authorization, the process that states what a user can and cannot do on that system. Authorization, at least for files and folders, is controlled by the NTFS file system.

■ The tool for managing users in Windows 2000 is the Users and Passwords Control Panel applet. You can use the applet to create accounts and control password use, such as require a user to type in a password at logon. You can also require users to press CTRL-ALT-DELETE to make logon even more secure.

■ Administrators can create new users and then assign the users to a specific group. Selecting Standard User makes that user a member of both the Power Users group and the Local Users group.

■ Windows XP uses the User Accounts applet in Control Panel to create and manage user accounts. Windows XP has two very different ways to deal with user accounts and how you log on to a system: the blank user name and password text boxes, reminiscent of Windows 2000, and the Windows XP Welcome screen.

■ User Accounts hides the complete list of users, using a simplistic reference to account types that is actually a reference to its group membership. An account that is a member of the local Administrators group is said to be a computer administrator; an account that only belongs to the Local Users group is said to be a limited account.

■ Creating users is a straightforward process. You need to provide a user name (a password can be added later), and you need to know which type of account to create: computer administrator or limited.

■ You can option out of the Welcome screen and thus require a user to type both a user name and a password. You can also enable or disable Fast User Switching—a feature that enables you to switch to another user account without logging out and thus having to close open programs.

■ To add or modify a user account in Windows Vista, you have numerous options depending on which Control Panel view you select and which edition and update of Vista you have installed. Windows Vista Business and Ultimate, for example, in the default Control Panel Home view, offer the User Accounts applet. Windows Home Premium, in contrast, gives you the User Accounts and Family Safety applet. The Tasks options on the left are similar, with the addition of Parental Controls in the Home Premium edition, but the main options differ a lot.

■ Windows Vista Home Premium uses Vista's version of the Welcome screen for logging in, so each user account has a picture associated with it. You can change the picture from the User Accounts applet. You can also change the name of the user account here and alter the account type.

■ Passwords are the ultimate key to protecting your computers. A user account with a valid password will get you into any system. Protect your passwords. Never give out passwords over the phone. If a user forgets or loses a password, an administrator should reset the password to a complex combination of letters and numbers, and then allow the user to change the password to something they want.

■ Make sure you use strong passwords: at least eight characters in length, including letters, numbers, and punctuation symbols.

■ Windows XP and Windows Vista enable currently logged-on users to create a password reset disk they can use if they forget a password. This is very important to have. If an administrator resets the password by using User Accounts or Local Users and Groups, and you then log on with the new

password, you will discover that you cannot access some items, including files that you encrypted when logged on with the forgotten password. When you reset a password with a password reset disk, you can log on with the new password and still have access to previously encrypted files.

- A group is simply a collection of accounts that share the same access capabilities. A single account can be a member of multiple groups. Groups are essential for managing a network of computers but also can come in handy on a single computer with multiple users.

- Windows 2000 provides seven built-in groups: Administrators, Power Users, Users, Backup Operators, Replicator, Everyone, and Guests. These built-in groups have a number of preset capabilities. You cannot delete these groups.

- If you're running XP Professional and you are on a Windows domain, XP offers all of the accounts Windows 2000 has, but it adds other specialized types, such as HelpServicesGroup and Remote Desktop Users. Windows XP Home and XP Professional, when installed on standalone PCs or PCs that are connected to a workgroup but not a domain, run in a specialized networking mode called simple file sharing. A Windows XP system running simple file sharing has only three account types: computer administrator, limited user, and guest.

- The professional editions of Windows Vista (Business, Ultimate, and Enterprise) offer the groups found in Windows XP Professional and throw in a lot more. Some group types enable people to check on the performance and reliability of a computer but without gaining access to any of the documents on the computer. These groups include Event Log Readers, Performance Log Users, and Performance Monitor Users and provide excellent levels of access for technicians to help keep busy Vista machines healthy.

- The professional versions of Windows—including Windows 2000, XP, and Vista—enable you to add new groups to your computer by using the Local Users and Groups tool, found in the Computer Management applet of the Administrative Tools. This tool also enables you to create user accounts and change group membership for users.

- Windows XP made it almost necessary to make your primary account on a computer an administrator account, because limited users can't do common tasks such as installing applications or updating Windows. In Vista, Microsoft rolled out User Account Control, a feature where a standard user account is prompted for the login information for an administrator account when trying to do something potentially nefarious, such as uninstall an application.

- With Parental Controls, you can monitor and limit the activities of any standard user in Windows Vista, a feature that gives parents and managers an excellent level of control over the content their children and employees can access. Parental Controls enable you to limit the time that standard users can spend logged in, for example. You can specify acceptable and unacceptable times of day when standard users can log in. Parental Controls offer a lot of control.

Define and utilize NTFS permissions for authorization

- In Windows, every folder and file on an NTFS partition has a list that contains two sets of data: every user and group that has access to that file or folder, and the level of access each user or group has to that file or folder. A set of detailed and powerful restrictions called permissions define exactly what a particular account can or cannot do to the file or folder.

- When you create a new file or folder on an NTFS partition, you become the owner of that file or folder, which means you can do anything you want to it, including changing the permissions to prevent anybody, even administrators, from accessing it. The special Take Ownership permission enables an account to seize control of a file or folder. Administrator accounts have Take Ownership permission for everything. Change permission-equipped accounts can give or take away permissions for other accounts.

- In Windows, just about everything in the computer has a Security tab in its properties (provided the hard drive is NTFS). Every Security tab contains a list of accounts that have permissions for that resource, and the permissions assigned to those accounts. The standard permissions for a folder are Full Control, Modify, Read & Execute, List Folder Contents, Read, and Write. The standard file permissions are Full Control, Modify, Read & Execute, Read, and Write. Permissions are cumulative.

- Moving or copying objects such as files and folders can have an effect on the permissions of those objects, something that techs need to understand. If you copy or move an object from one NTFS partition to another, the new object inherits the permissions associated with the new location. If you copy an object within a partition, the newly created copy inherits the permissions associated with the new location, but the original copy retains its permissions. Any object that you put on a FAT or FAT32 partition loses any permissions because FAT and FAT32 don't support NTFS permissions.

Describe how to share a Windows computer securely

- User accounts, groups, and NTFS work together to enable you to share a Windows PC securely with multiple user accounts. You can readily share files, folders, programs, and more. You can share only what should be shared, locking access to files and folders that you want to make private.

- Every user account on a Windows 2000 computer gets a My Documents folder, the default storage area for personal documents. Every account that's a member of the Administrators group can view the contents of everybody's My Documents folder, by default. A typical way to create a secure shared Windows 2000 computer is to change the permissions on your My Documents folder to give yourself Full Control but take away the permissions that allow other accounts access.

- Make a folder for people to share so that moving files to and from accounts is easy. A typical example would be to create a folder on the C: drive called Shared and then alter the permissions, giving full control to everyone.

- The fact that most users of Windows XP computers will be computer administrators rather than limited users creates a bit of an issue with a computer shared by many users. By default, administrators can see all of the contents of Documents and Settings, where the My Documents folders for each user account reside. Selecting the option to *Make this folder private* in the My Documents Properties dialog box blocks anyone from accessing the contents.

- Use the Shared Documents folders to move files and folders among many users of a single machine. Every account can access the Shared Documents and the sub-folders within.

- With simple file sharing, you essentially have one local sharing option, and that's to put anything you want to share into the Shared Documents. To share a folder over a network, you only have a couple of options as well, such as to share or not and, if so, to give full control to everybody. Windows XP Professional enables you to disable simple file sharing and have full control over sharing and permissions.

- Windows Vista enables you to permit specific user accounts to access shared resources and to set the level of access permitted, such as reader, contributor, or co-owner. Vista also has an expanded default shares, called the Public folder, which contains multiple shared folders. Any user account can access the Public folder.

- The scrambling of data through encryption techniques provides the only true way to secure your data from access by any other user. The professional versions of Windows enable a feature called the Encrypting File System (EFS), an encryption scheme that any user can use to encrypt individual files or folders on a computer. The home versions of Windows do not enable encryption.

- Windows Vista Ultimate and Enterprise editions offer full drive encryption through BitLocker Drive Encryption. BitLocker encrypts the whole drive, including every user's files, so it's not dependent on any one account. BitLocker requires a special Trusted Platform Module (TPM) chip on the motherboard to function. The TPM chip validates on boot that the Vista computer hasn't changed and that you still have the same operating system installed.

■ Key Terms

administrative shares (583)
Administrators group (572)
authentication (559)
authorization (559)
BitLocker Drive Encryption (584)
computer administrator (563)

Encrypting File System (EFS) (584)
encryption (583)
Fast User Switching (566)
group (571)
Guests group (572)
inheritance (577)

limited user *(563)*
local user account *(559)*
Local Users and Groups *(573)*
NTFS permissions *(575)*
Parental Controls *(569)*
password reset disk *(571)*
permission propagation *(577)*
Power Users group *(572)*
Public folder *(581)*
Shared Documents *(579)*

simple file sharing *(580)*
standard user *(562)*
strong password *(571)*
Take Ownership *(575)*
User Account Control (UAC) *(569)*
User Accounts applet *(562)*
Users and Passwords applet *(560)*
Users group *(572)*
Welcome screen *(562)*

■ Key Term Quiz

Use the Key Terms list to complete the sentences that follow. Not all terms will be used.

1. The _____ enables you to manage user accounts in Windows 2000.

2. To log on to a standalone Windows PC, you need a(n) _____.

3. An account that belongs only to the Local Users group in Windows XP is called a(n) _____.

4. On the _____ in Windows XP and Vista, you can click on an icon and type a password to log into the computer.

5. A(n) _____ is a collection of user accounts that share the same access capabilities.

6. The _____ enables standard users to perform common tasks and provides a permissions dialog when standard users and administrators do certain things that could potentially harm the computer.

7. By default, any file you drop into a folder on an NTFS drive gets the same permissions as those assigned to the folder, a feature called _____.

8. The _____ feature of Windows XP Home means you can share or not share a folder. You don't have any finer control than that.

9. Windows Vista has the _____ available for sharing files and folders with other users of a particular computer.

10. The _____ enables you to scramble a file or folder and thus hide the contents from anyone, even an administrator.

■ Multiple-Choice Quiz

1. What process determines the identity of a user?
   A. Authentication
   B. Authorization
   C. Identification
   D. Indemnification

2. Which of the following user account types can create other user accounts?
   A. Administrator
   B. Limited User
   C. Restricted User
   D. Standard User

3. To which of the following groups does a standard user in Windows 2000 belong by default? (Select two.)
   A. Limited Users
   B. Power Users
   C. Restricted Users
   D. Users

4. Which utility enables you to add a user account in Windows XP?
   A. User Account Control
   B. User Accounts applet
   C. Users and Groups applet
   D. Users and Passwords applet

5. Which of the following is the strongest password?

   A. 5551212

   B. Spot01

   C. 43*xv

   D. 479love*

6. Which tool would enable a user to recover his encrypted files if he forgets his password?

   A. BitLocker

   B. Encrypting File System

   C. Password reset disk

   D. Password restore disk

7. Which of the following groups can you assign a user to in Windows Vista Home Premium? (Select two.)

   A. Administrators

   B. Power Users

   C. Replicators

   D. Users

8. Which tool in Windows Vista enables an administrator to create a log that shows all of the applications a user runs or attempts to run?

   A. Create Log

   B. NTFS

   C. Parental Controls

   D. User Account Control

9. Which of the following is *not* a standard NTFS permission?

   A. Copy

   B. Full Control

   C. Modify

   D. Read & Execute

10. As a member of the accounting group, John has Write permission to the Database folder; as a member of the technicians group, John has Read permission to the Database folder. What permission or permissions does John have to the Database folder?

    A. Read only

    B. Write only

C. Read and Write

D. Full Control

11. When you copy a file from one folder on the C: drive to another folder on the C: drive, by default what permissions will the copy of that file have if the C: drive is formatted with NTFS?

    A. The copy will retain the permissions the original file has.

    B. The copy will inherit the permissions of the new location.

    C. The copy will lose all permissions.

    D. You can't do that.

12. In a Windows XP Professional computer, where can you place files that other users can access easily?

    A. Public Documents

    B. Public folder

    C. Shared Documents

    D. Shared folder

13. John wants to share a folder in Windows Vista with Liz but wants to make sure she can only delete files she creates in that folder, not the ones he creates. What permission level should he use?

    A. Contributor

    B. Co-owner

    C. Full Control

    D. Reader

14. Which tool in Windows Vista enables you to encrypt the contents of a drive, including folders of users other than you?

    A. BitLocker

    B. Drive Encryptor

    C. Encrypting File System

    D. TrueCrypt

15. Which of the following is a safe way to deal with your new password?

    A. Memorize it

    B. Put a note in your wallet

    C. Tape it under your keyboard

    D. E-mail it to yourself

Essay Quiz

1. Your boss has tasked you with setting up five Windows Vista workstations, each to be used by three different users. Write a short essay on procedures or policies that should be implemented at each workstation to ensure that each user can share files that need to be shared but can also keep private files that need to be private.

2. Your company has a shared database in Windows Vista. Management must have full access to the database. The salespeople need to be able to access the database and make changes, but can't delete the database. All other employees should be able to read the contents of the database, but not make any changes. Write a short essay describing what groups and permissions you would need to set to make this work.

3. You have a computer with three users, plus an administrator. The three users need to be able to add documents to a folder, but only the administrator should be allowed to see the contents of those documents. Write a short essay describing how you would set up the folder, user accounts, groups, and permissions to make this work.

Lab Projects

• Lab Project 16.1

Take a single computer and create multiple user accounts and groups. Create some shared folders and change permissions on those folders to vary what different user accounts can do. Then experiment. Try to make as many different access types as you can make.

• Lab Project 16.2

Experiment with permission propagation. On a computer with two hard drives, both formatted as NTFS, go through the process of copying and moving files and folders—with differing permissions—between folders on a single drive and between the two drives. Note carefully how permissions change or do not change with each step.

• Lab Project 16.3

On a computer with multiple user accounts, experiment with encryption. Encrypt files with one user account and then place those files into shared folders. What happens? Can other accounts access those files? Can they see the filenames? What about the administrator account? Go through the process of taking ownership to see if you can recover the contents of the encrypted files.

• Lab Project 16.4

On a Windows Vista Ultimate computer, experiment with BitLocker on a second hard drive. Make note of what happens when you remove the drive and put it into another computer. How can you access the data that's been encrypted?

Maintaining and Troubleshooting Windows

chapter 17

"Chaos is inherent in all compounded things. Strive on with diligence."

—Buddha

In this chapter, you will learn how to

- **Maintain Windows**
- **Optimize Windows**
- **Troubleshoot Windows**

Every computer running a Windows operating system requires occasional optimization to keep the system running snappily, ongoing maintenance to make sure nothing goes wrong, and troubleshooting when the system doesn't work correctly. Not that long ago, Windows had a bad rap as being difficult to maintain and challenging when troubleshooting problems. That's no longer true. Microsoft used its decades of experience with operating systems to search for ways to make the tasks of maintaining and troubleshooting less onerous. They've done such a good job with the latest versions of Windows that, out of the box, they are easy to optimize and maintain, although troubleshooting—and all operating systems share this—is still a bit of a challenge.

The chapter starts with maintenance and optimization, so let's make sure you know what these two terms mean. *Maintenance* means jobs you do from time to time to keep Windows running well, such as running hard drive utilities. CompTIA sees *optimization* as jobs you do to your Windows system to make it better—a good example is adding RAM. This chapter covers the standard maintenance and optimization activities performed on Windows and the tools techs use to perform them.

The last part of this chapter dives into *troubleshooting* Windows, examining steps you can take to bring a system back from the brink of disaster. You'll learn techniques for recovering a PC that won't boot and a PC that almost boots into Windows but fails.

Essentials

▪ Maintaining Windows

Maintaining Windows can be compared to maintaining a new automobile. Of course, a new automobile comes with a warranty, so most of us just take it to the dealer to get work done. In this case, *you* are the mechanic, so you need to think as an auto mechanic would think. First, an auto mechanic needs to apply recalls when the automaker finds a serious problem. For a PC tech, that means keeping the system patches announced by Microsoft up to date. You also need to check on the parts that wear down over time. On a car that might mean changing the oil or rotating the tires. In a Windows system that includes keeping the hard drive and the Registry organized and uncluttered.

Patches, Updates, and Service Packs

Updating Windows has been an important, but often neglected, task for computer users. Typically, Microsoft finds and corrects problems with its software and releases patches on the second Tuesday of every month. Sadly, because earlier versions of Windows let users decide when, if ever, to update their computers, the net result could be disastrous. The Blaster worm hammered computers all over the world in the summer of 2003, causing thousands of computers to start rebooting spontaneously—no small feat for a tiny piece of programming! Blaster exploited a flaw in Windows 2000/XP and spread like wildfire, but Microsoft had *already corrected* the flaw with a security update weeks earlier. If users had simply updated their computers, the virus would not have caused such widespread damage.

The Internet has enabled Microsoft to make updates available, and **Windows Update** can grab those updates and patch user systems easily and automatically. Even if you don't want to allow Windows Update to patch your computer automatically, it'll nag you about updates until you patch your system. Microsoft provides the Windows Update service for all versions of Windows.

Once Microsoft released Service Pack 2 for Windows XP, it began pushing for wholesale acceptance of automatic updates from Windows Update. You can also start Windows Update manually. When your computer is connected to the Internet, start the utility in Windows 2000 by selecting Start | Windows Update. In Windows XP/Vista/7 you will find it at Start | All Programs | Windows Update. When you run Windows Update manually, the software connects to the Microsoft Web site and scans your computer to determine what updates you may need. Within a few seconds or minutes,

> You might be asked about installing service packs and patches on the CompTIA A+ 220-701 and 220-702 exams. Pay attention to the steps listed here.

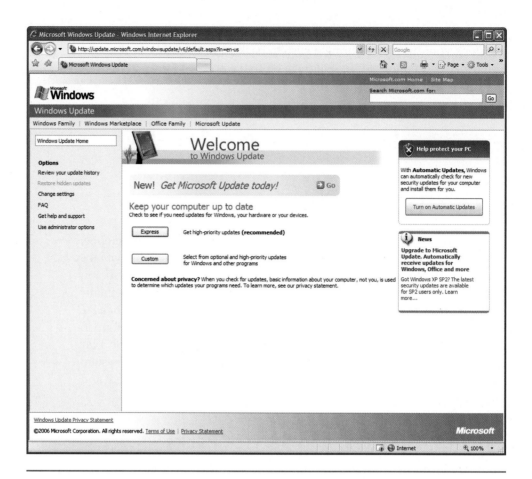

• Figure 17.1   Microsoft Windows Update page

depending on your connection speed, you'll get a straightforward screen like the one shown in Figure 17.1.

You have several choices here, although two are most obvious. If you click the Express button, Windows Update will grab any high-priority updates—these are security patches—and install them on your computer. If you click the Custom button, you can select from a list of optional updates.

Figure 17.2 shows the updater with a list of patches and security updates. You can scroll through the list and review the description of each update. You can deselect the checkbox next to a patch or update, and Windows Update will not download or install it. If you click the Clear All button, as you might suspect, all the updates will be removed from the list. When you click Install Updates, all the updates remaining in the list will be installed.

Automatic Updates

Updates are so important that Microsoft gives you the option to update Windows automatically through the **Automatic Updates** feature. Actually, it nags you about it! Soon after installing Windows (a day or two, in my experience), a message balloon will pop up from the taskbar suggesting that you automate updates. If you click this balloon, the Automatic Updates Setup Wizard runs, with which you can configure the update program. You say you've never seen this message balloon but would like to automate the update process? No problem. In Windows 2000 and XP, simply right-click My

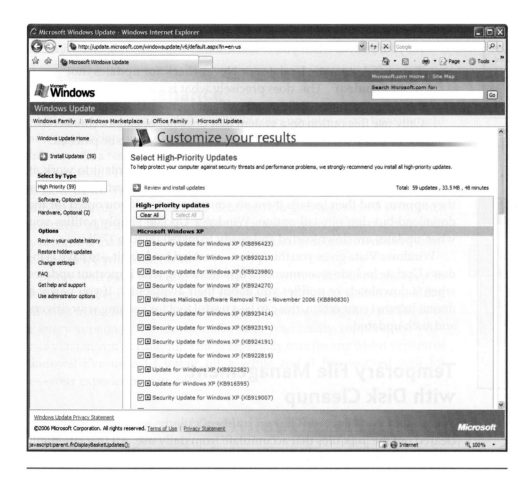

● **Figure 17.2** Choose updates to be installed.

Computer (on the Start menu), select Properties, click the Automatic Updates tab, and select Automatic Update options. Or, open the Control Panel and double-click the Automatic Updates icon. In Windows Vista, go to Start | Windows Update to open the Windows Update dialog box. Click the Change settings menu item on the left for options. Whenever your computer connects to the Web, it checks the Windows Update page. What happens next depends on the setting you choose. You have four choices:

- **Automatic (recommended)** or **Install updates automatically (recommended)** Windows Update will simply keep your computer patched up and ready to go. This is the best option for most users, although not necessarily good for users of portable computers. Nobody wants to log into a slow hotel dial-up connection and have most of your bandwidth sucked away by Automatic Update downloading hot fixes!

- **Download updates…** Windows Update downloads all patches in the background and then, when complete, tells you about them. You have the option at that point to install or not install.

- **Notify me…** or **Check for updates…** Windows Update simply flashes a dialog box that tells you updates are available but does not download anything until you say go. This is the best option for users

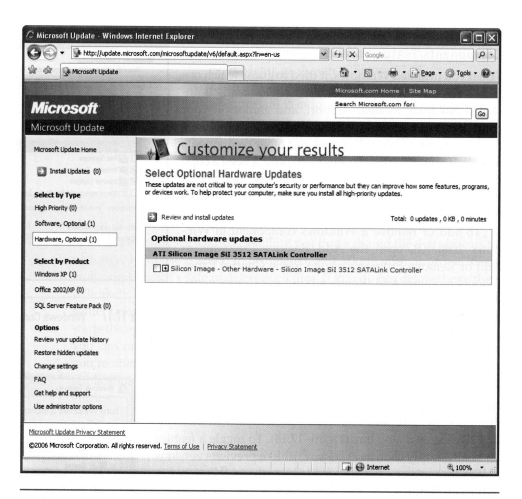

● **Figure 17.19** Optional hardware updates

If you are using Vista/7, you will need to click *View available updates* to see if any drivers are available for your system. No matter what version of Windows you have, take some time to read what these updates do—sometimes you may choose not to install a driver update because it's not necessary or useful to your system.

If Windows does not put a driver update in the Windows Update tool, how do you know a device needs updating? The trick is to know your devices. Video card manufacturers update drivers quite often. Get in the habit of registering your video card with the manufacturer to stay up to date. Any very new device is also a good candidate for an update. When you buy that new cool toy for your system, make a point to head over to the manufacturer's Web site and see if any updates have come out since it was packaged for sale. That happens more often than you might think!

Driver Signing

Device drivers become part of the operating system and thus have the potential to cause lots of problems if they're written poorly. To protect Windows systems from

Cross Check

Driver Signing

You learned about signed and unsigned drivers way back in Chapter 8, "Expansion Bus," so turn there now and see if you can answer these questions. What does the WHQL do for devices? Are all unsigned drivers dangerous? What does a manufacturer get for participating successfully in the Microsoft Windows Logo Program?

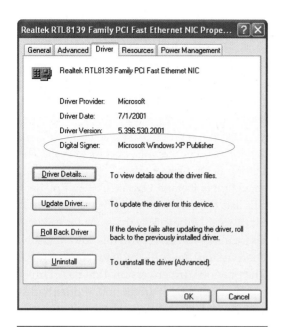

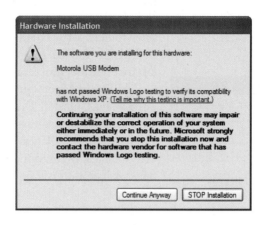

• **Figure 17.20** A digitally signed driver

• **Figure 17.21** Stop or continue installation of an unsigned driver

bad device drivers, Microsoft uses **driver signing**, which means that each driver has a digital signature. Any drivers included on the Windows installation media or at the Windows Update Web site are digitally signed. Once you have installed a driver, you can look at its Properties to confirm that it was digitally signed. Figure 17.20 shows a digitally signed network card driver.

When an unsigned driver is detected during hardware installation, you'll see the message in Figure 17.21 offering you the choice to stop or continue the installation. Signed drivers are more or less a sure thing, but that doesn't mean unsigned ones are a problem—just consider the source of the driver and ensure that your device works properly after installation.

You can control how Windows behaves when drivers are being installed. Click the Driver Signing button on the Hardware tab of the System Properties dialog box to display the Driver Signing Options dialog box shown in Figure 17.22. If you select Ignore, Windows will install an unsigned driver without warning you. If you select Warn, you will be prompted when Windows detects an unsigned driver during driver installation, and you will be given the opportunity to either stop or continue the installation. Choosing Block will prevent the installation of unsigned drivers.

The default Driver Signing setting is Warn. This also is the default setting during installation, so you will always be warned when Windows detects an unsigned driver during Windows installation. This is no problem for a standard installation, when you are sitting at the computer, responding to all prompts—but it is a problem for automated, unattended installations. This is a good reason to check out all your device drivers before installing Windows. In 64-bit versions of Windows, all drivers must be signed. No exceptions. Microsoft wants to keep tight controls on the drivers to improve stability.

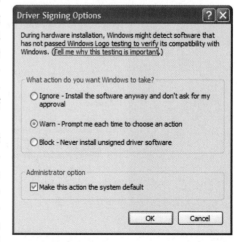

• **Figure 17.22** Driver Signing Options dialog box

Device Manager

You've worked with **Device Manager** in other chapters when installing and troubleshooting devices; it's also the tool to use when optimizing device drivers. Right-click on a device in Device Manager to display the context menu. From here you can update or uninstall the driver, disable the device, scan for hardware changes, or display the Properties dialog box. When you open the Properties dialog box, you'll see several tabs that vary according to the specific device. Most have General, Driver, Details, and Resources. The tab that matters most for optimization is the Driver tab.

The Driver tab has buttons labeled Driver Details, Update Driver, Roll Back Driver, and Uninstall. Driver Details lists the driver files and their locations on disk. Update Driver opens the Hardware Update Wizard—not very useful given that the installation programs for almost all drivers do this automatically. The Roll Back Driver option is a different story. It enables you to remove an updated driver, thus rolling back to the previous driver version. Roll Back Driver (Figure 17.23) is a lifesaver when you install a new driver and suddenly discover it's worse than the driver it replaced! Uninstall removes the driver.

Lucent Win Modem
Are you sure you would like to roll back to the previous driver?
Yes
No

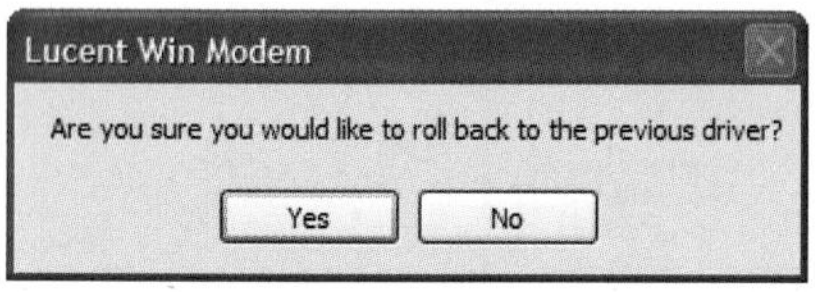

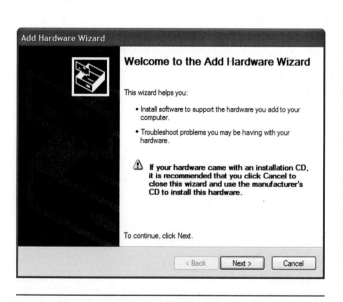

• **Figure 17.23** Rolling back to the previous driver

Adding a New Device

Windows should automatically detect any new device you install in your system. If Windows does not detect a newly connected device, use the Add Hardware Wizard or Add Hardware to get the device recognized and drivers installed (Figure 17.24). You'll find it on the Hardware tab of the System Properties dialog box.

Click Next on the Welcome screen, and the wizard searches for hardware that has been connected but does not yet have a driver installed. If it detects the device, select it, and the wizard installs the driver. You may have to point to the source location for the driver files. If it does not detect the device, which is very likely, it will ask you if the hardware is connected. When you answer yes and click Next, it gives you a list of installed hardware, similar to Figure 17.25.

Add Hardware Wizard
Welcome to the Add Hardware Wizard
This wizard helps you:
• Install software to support the hardware you add to your computer.
• Troubleshoot problems you may be having with your hardware.
If your hardware came with an installation CD, it is recommended that you click Cancel to close this wizard and use the manufacturer's CD to install this hardware.
To continue, click Next.
< Back
Next >
Cancel

• **Figure 17.24** Add Hardware Wizard

Add Hardware Wizard
The following hardware is already installed on your computer
From the list below, select an installed hardware device, then click Next to check properties or troubleshoot a problem you might be having.
To add hardware not shown in the list, click "Add a new hardware device."
Installed hardware:
NVIDIA RIVA TNT2 Model 64/Model 64 Pro
SoundMAX Integrated Digital Audio
Audio Codecs
Legacy Audio Drivers
Media Control Devices
Legacy Video Capture Devices
< Back
Next >
Cancel

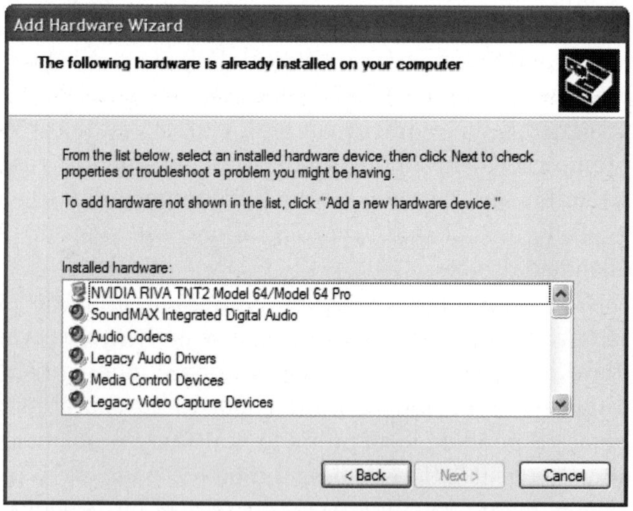

• **Figure 17.25** List of installed hardware

If the device is in the list, select it and click Next. If not, scroll to the bottom and select *Add a new hardware device,* and then click Next. If the device is a printer, network card, or modem, select *Search for and install the hardware automatically* and click Next. In that case, once the wizard detects the device and installs the driver, you're finished. If you do see your device on the list, your best hope is to select *Install the hardware that I manually select from a list.* In the subsequent screens, select the appropriate device category, select the device manufacturer and the correct model, and respond to the prompts from the Add Hardware Wizard to complete the installation.

Performance Options

One optimization you can perform on all Windows versions is setting Performance Options. **Performance Options** are used to configure CPU, RAM, and virtual memory (page file) settings. To access these options in Windows 2000/XP, right-click My Computer and select Properties, click the Advanced tab, and click the Options button (Windows 2000) or Settings button (Windows XP) in the Performance section of that tab. In Windows Vista/7, right-click Computer and select Properties; then click the Advanced system settings option in the Tasks list. If you are prompted for an administrator password or confirmation, type the password or confirmation. Click on the Advanced tab and click the Settings button in the Performance section of that tab. Once you get to the Performance Options dialog box, its behavior differs between Windows 2000 and Windows XP/Vista (one of the few places where Vista acts the same as XP!).

In Windows 2000, the Performance Options dialog box shows a pair of radio buttons called Applications and Background Services. These radio buttons set how processor time is divided between the foreground application and all other background tasks. Set this to Applications if you run applications that need more processor time. Set it to Background Services to give all running programs the same processor usage. You can also adjust the size of the page file in this dialog box, but in most cases I don't mess with these settings and instead leave control of the page file to Windows.

The Windows XP/Vista Performance Options dialog box has three tabs: Visual Effects, Advanced, and Data Execution Prevention (Figure 17.26). The Visual Effects tab enables you to adjust visual effects that impact performance. Try clicking the top three choices in turn and watch the list of settings. Notice the tiny difference between the first two choices. The third choice, *Adjust for best performance,* turns off all visual effects, and the fourth option is an invitation to make your own adjustments. If you're on a computer that barely supports Windows XP, turning off visual effects can make a huge difference in the responsiveness of the computer. For the most part, though, just leave these settings alone.

The Advanced tab in Windows XP, shown in Figure 17.27, has three sections: Processor scheduling, Memory usage, and Virtual memory. Under the Processor scheduling section, you can choose to adjust for best performance of either Programs or Background services. The Memory usage settings enable you to allocate a greater share of memory to programs or to the system cache. The Virtual memory section of this tab enables you to modify the size and location of the page file. Microsoft dropped the Memory usage settings option in Windows Vista.

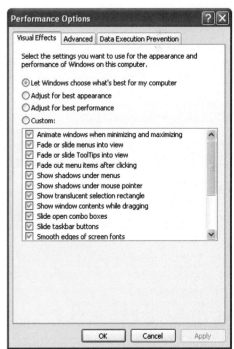

• **Figure 17.26** Windows XP Performance Options dialog box

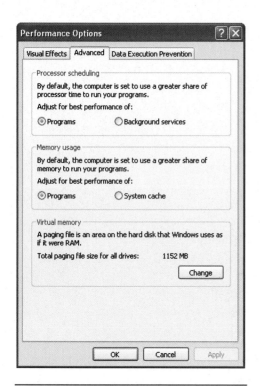

● **Figure 17.27** Advanced tab of Performance Options dialog box

Every program that runs on your system is composed of one or more processes.

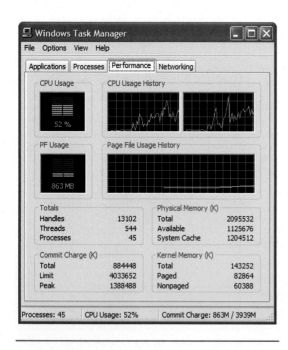

● **Figure 17.28** Task Manager

Microsoft introduced *Data Execution Prevention* (*DEP*) with Windows XP Service Pack 2. DEP works in the background to stop viruses and other malware from taking over programs loaded in system memory. It doesn't prevent viruses from being installed on your computer, but makes them less effective. By default, DEP monitors only critical operating system files in RAM, but the Data Execution Prevention tab enables you to have DEP monitor all running programs. It works, but you'll take a performance hit. Like other options in the Performance Options dialog box, leaving the DEP settings as default is the best option most of the time.

Resource Tracking

One big issue with optimization is knowing when something needs optimization. Let's say your Windows computer seems to be running more slowly. Resource tracking is very important for identifying the performance problem. Task Manager and the Performance console are tools you can use to figure out what (if anything) has become a bottleneck.

Task Manager

The **Task Manager** has many uses. Most users are only aware of the Applications tab, used to shut down a troublesome program. For optimization purposes, Task Manager is a great tool for investigating how hard your RAM and CPU are working at any given moment and why. The quick way to open the Task Manager is to press CTRL-SHIFT-ESC. Click the Performance tab to reveal a handy screen with the most commonly used information: CPU usage, available physical memory, size of the disk cache, commit charge (memory for programs), and kernel memory (memory used by Windows). Figure 17.28 shows a system with a dual-core processor, which is why you see two screens under CPU Usage History. A system with a single-core processor would have a single screen.

Not only does Task Manager tell you how much CPU and RAM usage is taking place, it also tells you what program is using those resources. Let's say your system is running slowly. You open up Task Manager and see that your CPU usage is at 100 percent. You then click on the Processes tab to see all the processes running on your system. Click on the CPU column heading to sort all processes by CPU usage to see who's hogging the CPU (Figure 17.29)! To shut off a process, just right-click the process and select End Process. Many times a single process opens many other processes. If you want to be thorough, click End Process Tree to turn off not only the one process but also any other processes it started.

Task Manager is also a great tool for turning off processes that are hogging memory. Let's say you're experiencing a slowdown, but this time you also notice your hard drive light is flickering nonstop—a clear sign that you've run out of memory and the page file is now in use. You go into Task

Manager and see no available system memory—now you *know* the page file is in use! To make the PC run faster, you have to start unloading programs—but which ones? By going into the Processes tab in Task Manager, you can see exactly which processes are using the most memory. Just be careful not to shut down processes you don't recognize; they might be something the computer needs.

Performance Console

Task Manager is good for identifying current problems, but what about problems that happen when you're not around? What if your system is always running at a CPU utilization of 20 percent—is that good or bad? Windows 2000 and XP provide a tool called the **Performance console** that logs resource usage so you can track items such as CPU and RAM usage over time. Performance is an MMC console file, PERFMON.MSC, so you call it from Start | Run or through the Performance icon in Administrative Tools. Use either method to open the Performance console (Figure 17.30). As you can see, there are two nodes, System Monitor and Performance Logs and Alerts.

Objects and Counters To begin working with the Performance console, you need to understand two terms: object and counter. An **object** is a system component that is given a set of characteristics and can be managed by the operating system as a single entity. A **counter** tracks specific information about an object. For example, the Processor object has a counter, %Processor Time, that tracks the percentage of elapsed time the processor uses to execute a non-idle thread. Many counters can be associated with an object.

System Monitor **System Monitor** gathers real-time data on objects such as memory, physical disk, processor, and network, and displays this data as a

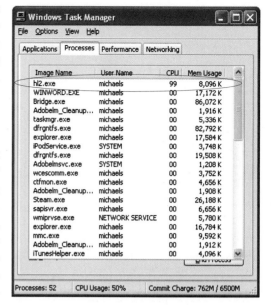

● **Figure 17.29**   CPU usage

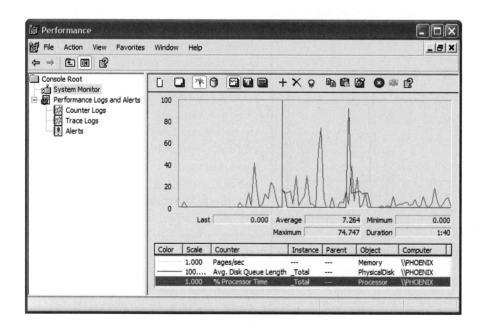

● **Figure 17.30**   Performance console

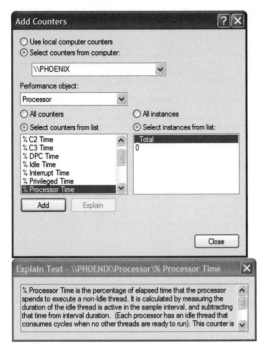

● **Figure 17.31**   Add Counters dialog box

graph (line graph), histogram (bar graph), or simple report. Think of System Monitor as a more detailed, customizable Task Manager. When you first open the Performance console, the System Monitor shows data in graph form. The data displayed is from the set of three counters listed below the chart. If you want to add counters, click the Add button (the one that looks like a plus sign) or press CTRL-I to open the Add Counters dialog box. Click the Performance object drop-down list and select one of the many different objects you can monitor. The Add Counters dialog box includes a helpful feature: you can select a counter and click the Explain button to learn about the counter, as in Figure 17.31.

Even with just three counters selected, the graph can get a little busy. That's where one of my favorite System Monitor features shines. If you want the line of charted data from just one counter to stand out, select the counter in the list below the graph and then press CTRL-H. See how this trick makes the %Processor Time line stand out in Figure 17.32? Imagine how useful that is when you are monitoring a dozen counters.

Performance Logs and Alerts   The **Performance Logs and Alerts** snap-in enables Windows to create a written record of just about anything that happens on your system. Do you want to know if someone is trying to log on to your system when you're not around? The following procedure is specific to Windows XP, but the steps are nearly identical in Windows 2000.

To create the new event log, right-click Counter Logs and select New Log Settings. Give the new log a name—in this example, "Unauthorized Accesses." Click OK, and a properties box for the new log appears, similar to that in Figure 17.33.

To select counters for the log, click Add Counters and then select the *Use local computer counters* radio button. Select Server from the Performance object pull-down menu and then select Errors Logon from the list of counters; click Add and then click Close.

Back in the Properties box for your new log, click the Schedule tab and set up when you want this thing to start running—probably at the end of the workday today. Then select when it should stop logging—probably tomorrow morning when you start work. Click the Log Files tab to see where the log file will be saved—probably C:\PerfLogs—and make a note of the filename. The filename will consist of the name you gave the log and a number. In this example I named the new performance log "Unauthorized Accesses," so the filename is Unauthorized Accesses_000001.blg.

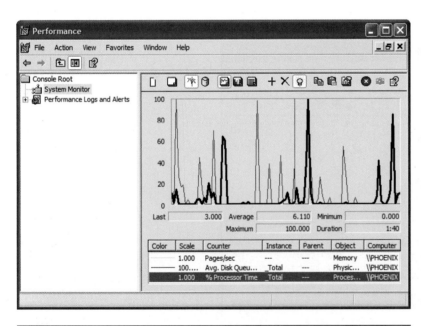

● **Figure 17.32**   CTRL-H makes one set of data stand out.

When you come back in the morning, open the Performance console, select Performance Logs and Alerts, and then select Counter Logs. Your log should be listed on the right. The icon by the log name will be green if the log is still running or red if it has stopped. If it has not stopped, select it and click the Stop button (the one with the black square, circled in Figure 17.34).

To view the log, open the Performance console, select System Monitor, change to Report view, and load the file as a new source by using the Properties box.

Reliability and Performance Monitor   Windows Vista improves on the old Performance console dramatically with the Reliability and Performance Monitor. The Reliability and Performance Monitor still has a complete Performance console with all the objects and counters you see in Windows 2000 and XP, but it adds an excellent Resource Overview, a Reliability Monitor, and a much more flexible way to use counters with Data Collector Set and Reports.

You can open Reliability and Performance Monitor in Windows Vista by starting the Performance Information and Tools in the Administrative Tools Control Panel applet to get the Resource Overview dialog box (Figure 17.35). You can also open the tool by going to Start | Start Searching, typing **perfmon.msc**, and pressing ENTER.

Think of the Resource Overview as an advanced Task Manager, giving details on CPU, hard drive, network, and memory usage. When you click on one of the four bars, you get details on exactly which processes are using those resources—a powerful tool when you suspect a program might be hogging something! Figure 17.36 shows the Network bar opened to reveal the processes using the network and how much data each is sending.

• **Figure 17.33**   Creating a new performance log

• **Figure 17.34**   Stopping the performance log

The Reliability and Performance Monitor option you can select under the Monitoring Tools is simply a re-creation of the Performance console and works as described earlier for Windows 2000 and XP (Figure 17.37). This is a great tool for quick checks on specific counters.

Microsoft included Data Collector Sets in the Reliability and Performance Monitor, groupings of counters you can use to make reports. You can make you own Data Collector Sets (User Defined) or you can just grab one of the predefined system sets. Once you start a Data Collector Set, you can use the Reports option to see the results (Figure 17.38). Data Collector Sets not only enable you to choose counter objects to track, but they also enable you to schedule when you want them to run.

A complete discussion of the Reliability and Performance Monitor is outside the scope of the CompTIA A+ objectives, but it's an amazing tool!

The CompTIA A+ exams aren't going to ask too many detailed questions on either Performance Monitor or Reliability and Performance Monitor. That doesn't mean you can ignore these amazing tools! Make sure you understand that these tools give you the power to inspect anything happening on your system to help you diagnose problems.

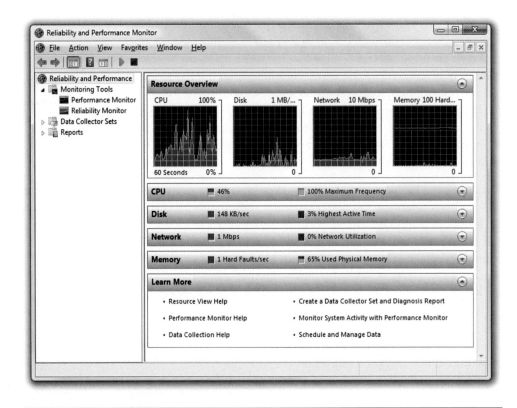

● **Figure 17.35**   Resource Overview in Vista

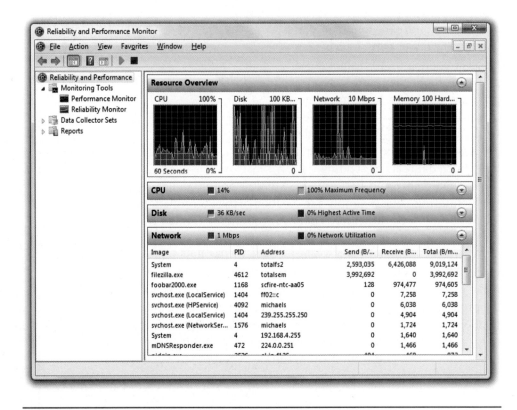

● **Figure 17.36**   Network Bar in Reliability and Performance Monitor

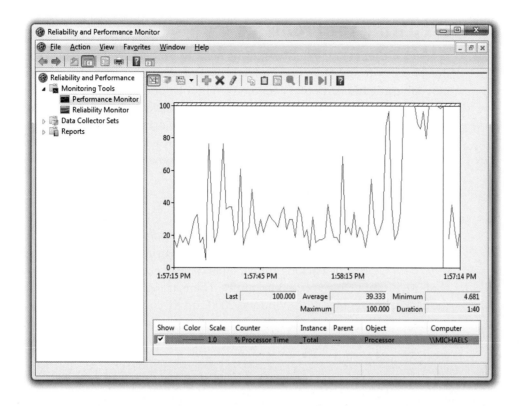

• Figure 17.37   Reliability and Performance Monitor

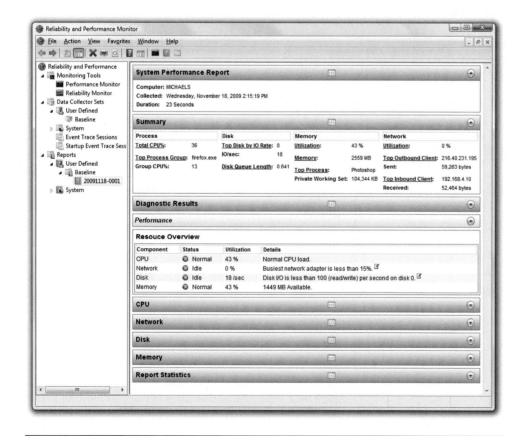

• Figure 17.38   Sample Performance Report

Preparing for Problems

As part of optimizing Windows, techs need to prepare for problems. You must have critical system files and data backed up and tools in place for the inevitable glitches. Different versions of Windows enable you to prepare for problems differently. Microsoft seems to break backups into certain areas: backing up personal data, backing up local copies of critical system state information, backing up a small amount of very critical system information on some form of removable media, and providing some way to use backups if your system won't boot. Let's see all of these.

Back Up Personal Data

The most important data on your computer is the personal data: your documents, e-mail messages and contacts, Web favorites, photographs, and other files. To handle backing up personal data, every version of Windows comes with some form of backup utility. There are big differences between the backup that comes with Windows 2000 and XP compared to the one that comes with Vista (and the one that comes with Windows 7 is different still), so let's break up the idea of backing up personal data between Windows 2000/XP and Vista.

Backup Utility for Windows 2000 and XP (NTBackup)

Windows 2000 Backup/Windows XP **Backup Utility** (different names, but the same program under the hood, **NTBackup**) provides almost all the tools you need to back up files and folders. It has come a long way from its origins in Windows NT. NTBackup supports a greater variety of devices, enabling you to back up to network drives, logical drives, tape, and removable disks (but not optical discs). Most folks, however, still turn to third-party utilities to create system, e-mail, browser, and personal data backups.

You can start NTBackup by navigating the Start menu to Accessories | System Tools, or by clicking the Backup Now button on the Tools page of the local disk properties box. I prefer to start it from Start | Run with the command **ntbackup**. Click the Backup Wizard button to run the Backup Wizard. This technique works in both Windows 2000 and Windows XP. To use the Windows XP version in Advanced Mode, click Advanced Mode on the opening screen (Figure 17.39). To have it always open in Advanced Mode, deselect the *Always start in wizard mode* checkbox. If the program is in Advanced Mode and you want to run it as a wizard, click the Wizard Mode link to open the Backup or Restore Wizard.

To create a backup, start the Backup Utility, click Advanced Mode, and choose the Backup tab. Check the boxes next to the drives and files you want to include in the backup. To include your system state information, such as Registry and boot files (which you should do), click the System State checkbox. To specify where to put the backup file you're creating, either type the path and file name in the *Backup media or file name* box or click

> The Backup Utility is not included in the default installation of Windows XP Home. You must install it manually from the Windows CD-ROM.

• **Figure 17.39**   Choosing to run the Backup Wizard in Advanced Mode

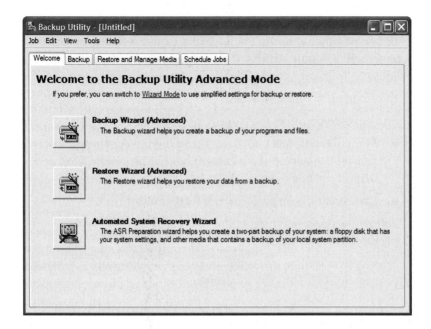

• **Figure 17.40**   Windows XP Backup Utility options

Browse, select a location, type the file name, and click Save. Click Start Backup. Choose whether you want to append this backup to a previous one or overwrite it. Click Advanced to open the Advanced Backup Options dialog box, select *Verify data after backup*, and click OK. Click Start Backup again. A dialog box shows you the utility's progress. When it finishes, click Close and then close the Backup Utility.

Both versions of NTBackup give you three choices after you click Advanced Mode: Backup Wizard (Advanced), Restore Wizard (Advanced), and a third choice that is very important. The third option in Windows 2000 is the Emergency Repair Disk. As you can see in Figure 17.40, the third option in Windows XP is the Automated System Recovery Wizard.

Windows 2000 Emergency Repair Disk (ERD)   The Windows 2000 **Emergency Repair Disk (ERD)** saves critical boot files and partition information and is your main tool for fixing boot problems in Windows 2000. It is not a bootable disk, nor does it store very much information; the ERD does not replace a good system backup! It works with a special folder called \WINNT\ REPAIR to store a copy of your Registry. It's not perfect, but it gets you out of most startup problems. Making a new ERD before you install a new device or program is good practice. Then the ERD is ready if you need it.

So you have this great Emergency Repair Disk that'll take care of all of your system repair problems. You just pop it in the floppy drive and go, right?

Not just yet. As I mentioned, the ERD itself is not a bootable disk. To use the ERD, you must first boot the system by using the Windows installation CD-ROM. Follow these steps to repair a system by using the ERD:

1. Boot the system, using either your set of boot diskettes or the installation CD-ROM.

2. In the Welcome to Setup dialog box, press the R key to select the option to repair a Windows 2000 installation.

3. The Windows 2000 Repair Options menu appears. You have the option of either entering the Recovery Console or using the Emergency Repair Disk.

4. Press the R key to select the option to repair Windows 2000 by using the emergency repair process.

5. The next screen offers the choice of Manual or Fast repair.

   ■ Manual repair lets you select the following repair options: inspect the startup environment, verify the system files, and inspect the boot sector.

   ■ Fast repair doesn't ask for any further input.

6. Follow the onscreen instructions and insert the ERD when prompted.

7. Your system will be inspected and, if possible, restored. When the process finishes, the system restarts.

Windows XP Automated System Recovery (ASR) The Windows XP **Automated System Recovery (ASR)** looks and acts very similar to the Windows 2000 ERD. The ASR Preparation Wizard lets you create a backup of your system. This backup includes a floppy disk and backup media (tape or CD-R) containing the system partition and disks containing operating system components (Figure 17.41).

The restore side of ASR involves a complete reinstallation of the operating system, preferably on a new partition. This is something you do when all is lost. Run Setup and press F2 when prompted during the text-mode portion of Setup. Follow the prompts on the screen, which will first ask for the floppy disk and then for the backup media.

• **Figure 17.41** Creating an ASR backup

Backup Wizard Data files are not backed up by the ERD or by the ASR. Therefore, you have to back up data files. If you run the Backup Wizard and click the Next button on the Welcome screen, you'll open the dialog box in Figure 17.42. You have three options here. The first two are fairly self-explanatory: You can back up everything or just selected drives and files.

The third option needs some explanation. The *Only back up the System State data* radio button enables you to save "other" system-critical files, but with Windows 2000/XP, it's not much more than making an ERD with the Registry backup. This option really makes sense for Windows 2000 Server and Windows Server 2003 systems because it saves Active Directory information (which your Windows 2000/XP systems do not store) as well as other critical, server-specific functions. (I cover more on these topics in

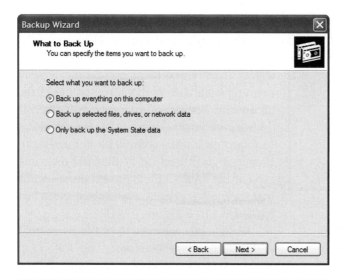

• **Figure 17.42** Backup Wizard options

• **Figure 17.43** Backup tapes

Chapter 23, "Local Area Networking.") But the CompTIA A+ certification exams may still expect you to know about it!

Tape Backup The odd fact that Microsoft has not updated the Backup or Restore Wizard to enable you to back up to optical discs of any sort has kept alive the practice of tape backups. Tape drives connect to the ATA or SCSI bus, just like optical drives, but rather than using a shiny CD-R or DVD+R disc, you have to back up to magnetic tape (Figure 17.43).

Tape drive manufacturers have done pretty much everything they can do to make tape backups as fast as possible, but the technology suffers from two huge drawbacks. First, it's tape, which means all data must be stored and restored in sequential access. In other words, the drive has to go through files 1 and 2 before reaching file 3. Second, tape is painfully slow in comparison to hard drives, optical drives, or Flash-media drives.

The only great benefit to tape is that it's relatively cheap to buy multiple tapes with a lot of storage capacity. With hard drive and recordable DVD prices at rock bottom today, though, tape's days are numbered.

Backup Options The goal of backing up data is to ensure that when a system dies, there will be an available, recent copy you can use to restore the system. You could simply back up the complete system at the end of each day—or whatever interval you feel is prudent to keep the backups fresh—but complete backups can be a tremendous waste of time and materials. Instead of backing up the entire system, take advantage of the fact that all the files won't be changed in any given period; much of the time you only need to back up what's changed since your last backup. Recognizing this, most backup software solutions have a series of options available beyond the complete backup.

The key to understanding backups other than the full backup is *attributes*, 1-bit storage areas that all files have. The most common attributes are Hidden (don't show the file in Computer or when `dir` is typed at the command line), System (it's a critical file for the system), Read-Only (can't erase it), and Archive. These attributes were first used in FAT-formatted drives in

> Windows Explorer (My Computer in Windows XP, Computer in Vista) by default does not show much about files in any view, even when you select Details from the View menu. The Details view is highly customizable, however, and can reveal a phenomenal amount and variety of information about files.
>
> To customize your view, right-click the column bar (the gray bar that says Name, Size, Type, Date Modified, and so forth) to look at the default choices. You'll see everything from Attributes, Owner, Author, and Title to file-type specific information such as Genre, Duration, and Bit Rate (for music files). If the default extra view options don't get your motor revving, selecting the More option brings up a menu offering many more view options! For the purposes of this section, click the Attribute box to display file and folder attributes.

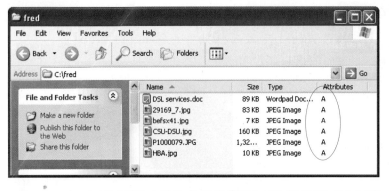

● **Figure 17.44** The archive bit on these files is on.

Be sure you know the types of backups, including which ones change the archive bits and which ones do not.

the DOS era, but they are still completely supported by all file formats. The *archive bit* works basically like this: Whenever a file is saved, the archive bit is turned on. Simply opening a file affects the current state of the archive bit. Backup programs usually turn off a file's archive bit when the file is backed up. In theory, if a file's archive bit is turned off, there's a good backup of that file on some tape. If the archive bit is turned on, it means that the file has been changed since it was last backed up (see Figure 17.44).

Archive bits are used to perform backups that are not full backups. The following backup types are most often supported:

- A *normal backup* is a full backup. Every file selected is backed up, and the archive bit is turned off for every file backed up. This is the standard "back it all up" option.

- A *copy backup* is identical to a normal backup, with the important distinction being that the archive bits are *not* changed. This is used (although not often) for making extra copies of a previously completed backup.

- An *incremental backup* includes only files with the archive bit turned on. In other words, it copies only the files that have been changed since the last backup. This backup turns off the archive bits.

- A *differential backup* is identical to an incremental backup, except that it doesn't turn off the archive bits.

- A *daily backup*, also known as a *daily copy backup*, makes copies of all the files that have been changed that day. It does not change the archive bits.

The motivation for having both the incremental and differential backups may not be clear at first glance—they seem so similar as to be basically the same. Incremental seems the better option at first. If a file is backed up, you would want to turn off the archive bit, right? Well, maybe. But there is one scenario where that might not be too attractive. Most backups do a big weekly normal backup, followed by daily incremental or differential backups at the end of every business day. Figure 17.45 shows the difference between incremental and differential backups.

Notice that a differential backup is a cumulative backup. Because the archive bits are not set, it keeps backing up all changes since the last normal backup. This means the backup files will get progressively larger throughout the week (assuming a standard weekly normal backup). The incremental backup, by contrast, only backs up files changed since the last backup. Each incremental backup file will be relatively small and also totally different from the previous backup file.

Incremental

MON	TUE	WED	THU	FRI
Full backup	All Tuesday changes	All Wednesday changes	All Thursday changes	All Friday changes

Differential

MON	TUE	WED	THU	FRI
Full backup	All changes through Tuesday	All changes through Wednesday	All changes through Thursday	All changes through Friday

● **Figure 17.45** Incremental versus differential

Mike Meyers' CompTIA A+ Guide to Managing and Troubleshooting PCs

Let's assume that the system is wiped out on a Thursday morning. How can you restore the system to a useful state?

If you're using an incremental backup, you will first have to restore the last weekly backup you ran on Monday, then the Tuesday backup, and then the Wednesday backup before the system is restored to its Thursday morning state. The longer the time between normal backups, the more incremental backups you must restore.

Using the same scenario but assuming you're doing differential instead of incremental backups, you only need the weekly backup and then the Wednesday backup to restore your system. A differential backup always requires only two backups to restore a system. Suddenly, the differential backup looks better than the incremental! On the other hand, one big benefit of incremental over differential is backup file size. Differential backup files are massive compared to incremental ones.

Backup and Restore Center for Vista

One of the many changes between XP and Vista was the elimination of NTBackup, replaced with the Windows Backup and Restore Center. If you open this program, you'll notice that you only have two options: back up everything or restore from a backup (Figure 17.46).

If you choose to back up your computer, you have another two choices: back up files or back up the entire computer. *Back up files* gives you a choice of the file

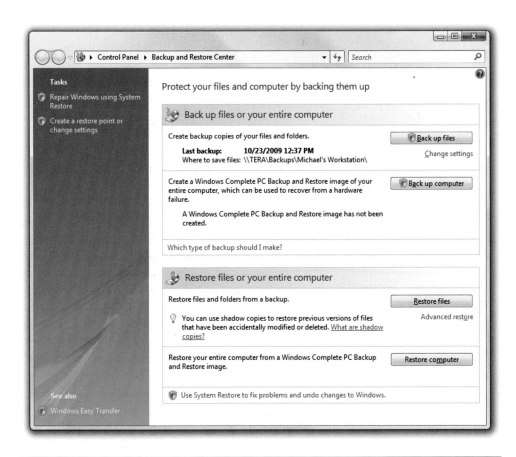

• **Figure 17.46**   Backup and Restore Center

• **Figure 17.47** Back Up Files option

types you wish to back up (Figure 17.47). *Back up computer* backs up the entire computer: every single file and folder. Vista no longer supports tape backups nor can you choose between differential or incremental backups. If you want these options, you need to buy a third-party backup tool.

The Vista tool comes with a handy wizard that automatically configures when you want to back up. So although you lose some of the options from NTBackup, you'll find this to be a powerful tool that works for most of your backup needs.

System Restore

Every technician has war stories about the user who likes to add the latest gadget and cool software to his computer. Then he's amazed when things go very, very wrong: the system locks up, refuses to boot, or simply acts weird. This guy also can't remember what he added or when. All he knows is that you should be able to fix it—fast.

This is not news to the folks at Microsoft, and they have a solution to this problem. It's called **System Restore**, and they first introduced it in Windows Me, with further refinements in Windows XP. The System Restore tool enables you to create a **restore point**, a copy of your computer's configuration at a specific point in time. If you later crash or have a corrupted OS, you can restore the system to its previous state.

To create a restore point, go to Start | All Programs | Accessories | System Tools | System Restore. When the tool opens, select *Create a restore point* and then click Next (Figure 17.48). Type in a description on the next screen. There's no need to include the date and time because the System Restore adds them automatically. Click Create and you're finished.

System Restore in Windows Vista is much more automatic, with the operating system making a number of restore points automatically. To make your own restore point, go to System Properties, select System Protection, and then click the Create button as shown in Figure 17.49.

If you click the System Restore button, you might be surprised at how many system restore points are already made for you (Figure 17.50). In most cases, one of these is all you'll need to return your system to an earlier point.

The System Restore tool creates some of the restore points in time automatically. For instance, by default, every time you install new software, XP creates a restore point. Thus, if installation of a program causes your computer to malfunction, simply restore the system to a time point prior to that installation, and the computer should work again.

During the restore process, only settings and programs are changed. No data is lost. Your computer includes all programs and settings as of the restore

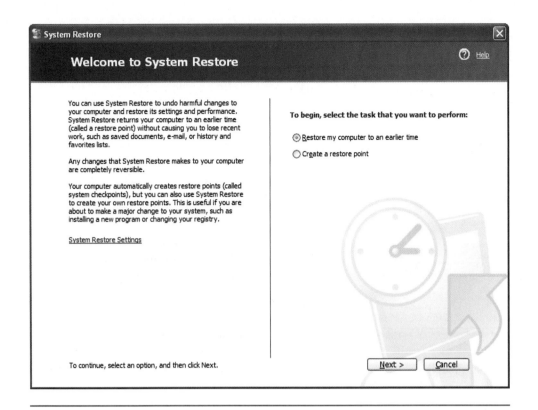

● **Figure 17.48**   Create a restore point

date. This feature is absolutely invaluable for overworked techs. A simple restore fixes many user-generated problems.

To restore to a previous time point, start the System Restore Wizard by choosing Start | All Programs | Accessories | System Tools | System Restore. Then select the first radio button, *Restore my computer to an earlier time,* and click Next. Figure 17.51 shows a calendar with restore points. Any day with a boldface date has at least one restore point. These points are created after you add or remove software or install Windows updates and during the normal shutdown of your computer. Select a date on the calendar; then select a restore point from the list on the right and click Next.

The last screen before the system is restored shows a warning. It advises you to close all open programs and reminds you that Windows will shut down during the restore process. It also states that the restore operation is completely reversible. Thus, if you go too far back in time, you can restore to a more recent date.

You don't have to count on the automatic creation of restore points. You can open System Restore at any time and simply select *Create a restore point.* Consider doing this before making changes that might not trigger an automatic restore point, such as directly editing the Registry.

System Restore is turned on by default and uses some of your disk space to save information on restore points. To turn

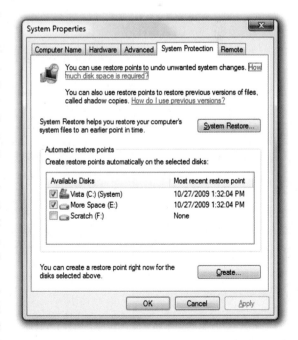

● **Figure 17.49**   Creating a manual System Restore in Vista

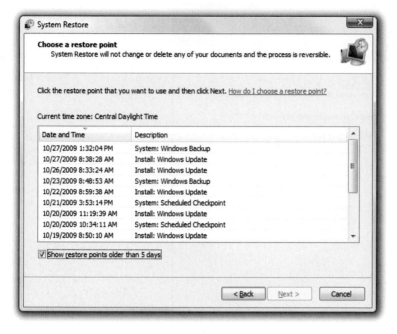

• **Figure 17.50**   Restore points in Vista

System Restore off or change the disk space usage, open the System Properties applet in Control Panel and select the System Restore tab (Figure 17.52).

Installing Recovery Console

When things get really bad on a Windows system, you need to turn to the Recovery Console. The **Recovery Console** is a text-based startup of Windows that gets you to a command prompt similar to the Windows command prompt.

If you have the Windows 2000/XP CD-ROM, you can start the Recovery Console by running Setup, selecting Repair, and then selecting Recovery Console. If you like to be proactive, however, you can install the Recovery Console on your hard drive so that it is one of your startup options and does not require the Windows 2000 or XP CD-ROM to run. The steps to do this in Windows 2000 and Windows XP are very nearly identical.

First, you need to log into the system with the Administrator account. Grab your Windows 2000 or XP installation CD-ROM and drop it in your system. If the Autorun function kicks in, just click the No button. To install

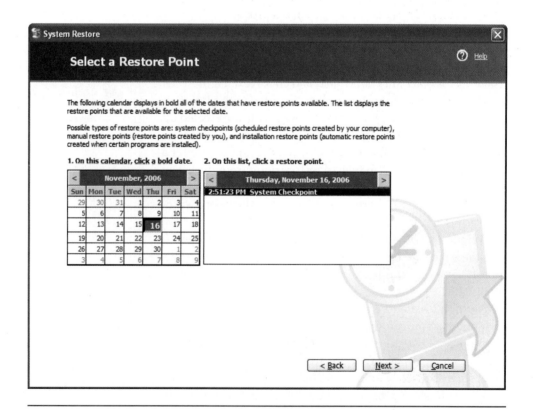

• **Figure 17.51**   Calendar of restore points

the Recovery Console and make it a part of your startup options, click the Start button, select Run, and type the following:

```
d:\i386\winnt32 /cmdcons
```

If your CD-ROM drive uses a different drive letter, substitute it for the D: drive. Then just follow the instructions on the screen. If you are connected to the Internet, allow the Setup program to download updated files. From now on, every time the system boots, the OS selection menu will show your Windows OS (Windows 2000 Professional or Windows XP) and the Microsoft Windows Recovery Console. It may also show other choices if yours is a multi-boot computer.

System Recovery Options

Windows Vista and Windows 7 have dropped the Recovery Console, replacing it with the graphical System Recovery Options. System Recovery Options is on the Vista/7 installation media, and you run it by booting to the media as though you were installing Windows. When you boot from the installation media, choose your language settings, click Next, select *Repair your computer*, and then click Next a second time to see the System Recovery Options menu, as shown in Figure 17.53. The System Recover Options menu has a number of items, each designed to help in a particular situation.

Startup Repair Startup Repair should be your first choice when running System Recovery. This option tells Windows to attempt to repair your system automatically. Startup Repair rebuilds all of your most important system files, which in most

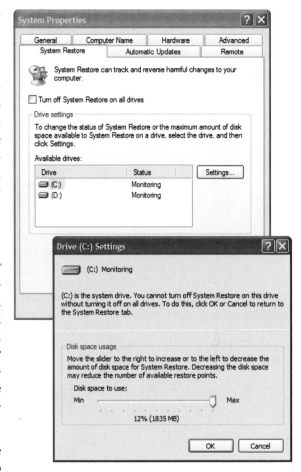

• **Figure 17.52** System Restore tab in System Properties applet

• **Figure 17.53** System Recovery Options in Windows Vista

cases will at least enable you to get Windows to boot. If Startup Repair doesn't work, hope you made some system restore points!

System Restore   The System Restore option searches your computer for restore points, enabling you to choose one. This will hopefully fix whatever is preventing your system from booting. If not, you may want to consider the Complete PC Backup option.

Windows Complete PC Backup   Assuming you made a backup while the system was running properly, you can select this option to restore your PC.

Windows Memory Diagnostic Tool   Bad RAM is an all-too-common problem for any computer and often shows itself during startup. Recognizing this, Microsoft added this tool to test your RAM for errors. This is an incredibly powerful tool for the job. If your RAM is bad, the Memory Diagnostic Tool will locate and report the error to you. You replace your RAM and the problem is solved.

Command Prompt   The Command Prompt is just as it is named: a full-blown command prompt, not to be confused with the Windows 2000/XP Recovery Console. You can run any command-prompt program from here.

Practical Application

■ Troubleshooting Windows

Chapters 4, 12, 14, 15, and 16 introduced you to the essential tools for troubleshooting and repairing Windows. You know about Disk Management, Device Manager, Event Viewer, and more. You've spent countless hours preparing systems for disaster with Windows Backup and System Restore. While learning about the tools, you also learned how to use them. This section puts it all together and shows you a plan to deal with potential disasters for a Windows computer.

   This section looks at Windows problems from the ground up. It starts with catastrophic failure—a PC that won't boot—and then discusses ways to get past that problem. The next section covers the causes and work-arounds when the Windows GUI fails to load. Once you can access the GUI, the world of Windows diagnostic and troubleshooting tools that you've spent so much time learning about comes to your fingertips. First, though, you have to get there.

Failure to Boot

Windows boot errors take place in those short moments between the time the POST ends and the Loading Windows screen begins. For Windows 2000/XP to start loading the main operating system, the critical system files NTLDR, NTDETECT.COM, and BOOT.INI must reside in the root directory of the C: drive, and BOOT.INI must point to the Windows boot files. If any

of these requirements isn't in place, the system won't get past this step. Here are some of the common errors you see at this point:

No Boot Device Present/Inaccessible Boot Device

NTLDR Bad or Missing

Invalid BOOT.INI

Windows Vista or 7 no longer use these files, so you need to look for an entirely new set of errors to tell you that there's a boot failure. Luckily, the only truly critical file that has any hope of corruption is the BOOTMGR file, and Windows Vista will normally restore this on the fly if it detects an error. In all but the rarest cases, the Windows Boot Manager detects a problem and brings up a Windows Boot Manager error like the one shown in Figure 17.54.

Note that these text errors take place very early in the startup process. That's your big clue that you have a boot issue. If you get to the Windows splash screen and then lock up, that's a whole different game, so know the difference.

If you get one of the catastrophic error messages and you're running Windows 2000 or XP, you have a three-level process to get back up and running. You first should attempt to repair. If that fails, attempt to restore from a backup copy of Windows. If restore is either not available or fails, your only recourse is to rebuild. You will lose data at the restore and rebuild phases, so you definitely want to spend a lot of energy on the repair effort first! If you're running Vista, the repair process for boot failures is exactly the same as a failure to load the GUI. Read about the System Recovery Options in the next section to see what you need to do.

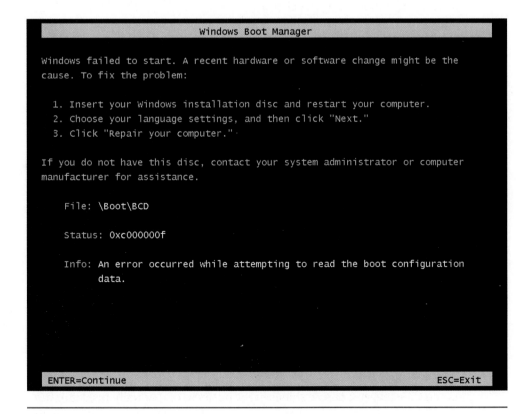

```
                        Windows Boot Manager

Windows failed to start. A recent hardware or software change might be the
cause. To fix the problem:

   1. Insert your Windows installation disc and restart your computer.
   2. Choose your language settings, and then click "Next."
   3. Click "Repair your computer."

If you do not have this disc, contact your system administrator or computer
manufacturer for assistance.

   File: \Boot\BCD

   Status: 0xc000000f

   Info: An error occurred while attempting to read the boot configuration
         data.




ENTER=Continue                                          ESC=Exit
```

• **Figure 17.54**   Boot Manager error

Attempt to Repair by Using Recovery Console (2000/XP)

To begin troubleshooting one of these errors, boot from the installation CD-ROM and have Windows do a repair of an existing installation. Windows prompts you if you want to use the Recovery Console or the emergency repair process (ASR/ERD). Start with the Recovery Console.

If you followed the instructions earlier in the lesson, you've installed the Recovery Console onto your system and have it as an option when you boot the system. If not, start it as described earlier, using the Windows 2000 or XP installation CD-ROM. When you select the Recovery Console, you will see a message about NTDETECT, another one that the Recovery Console is starting up, and then you are greeted with the following message and command prompt:

```
Microsoft Windows XP<TM> Recovery Console.
The Recovery Console provides system repair and recovery functionality.
Type Exit to quit the Recovery Console and restart the computer.

1: C:\WINDOWS
Which Windows XP installation would you like to log onto
<To cancel, press ENTER>?
```

The cursor is a small, white rectangle sitting to the right of the question mark on the last line. If you are not accustomed to working at the command prompt, this may be disorienting. If there is only one installation of Windows XP on your computer, type the number **1** at the prompt and press the ENTER key. If you press ENTER before typing in a valid selection, the Recovery Console will cancel and the computer will reboot. The only choice you can make in this example is 1. Having made that choice, the screen displays a new line, followed by the cursor:

```
Type the Administrator password:
```

Enter the Administrator password for that computer and press ENTER. The password does not display on the screen; you see asterisks in place of the password. The screen still shows everything that has happened so far, unless something has happened to cause an error message. It now looks like this:

```
Microsoft Windows XP<TM> Recovery Console.
The Recovery Console provides system repair and recovery functionality.
Type Exit to quit the Recovery Console and restart the computer.

1: C:\WINDOWS
Which Windows XP installation would you like to log onto
<To cancel, press ENTER>? 1
Type the Administrator password: ********
C:\Windows>
```

By now, you've caught on and know that there is a rectangular prompt immediately after the last line. Now what do you do? Use the Recovery Console commands, of course. Recovery Console uses many of the commands that worked in the Windows command-line interface that you explored in Chapter 15, "Working with the Command-Line Interface," as well as some uniquely its own. Table 17.1 lists the common Recovery Console commands.

The Recovery Console shines in the business of manually restoring Registries, stopping problem services, rebuilding partitions (other than the

Table 17.1	Common Recovery Console Commands
Command	**Description**
attrib	Changes attributes of selected file or folder
cd (or chdir)	Displays current directory or changes directories
chkdsk	Runs CheckDisk utility
cls	Clears screen
copy	Copies from removable media to system folders on hard disk. No wildcards
del (or delete)	Deletes service or folder
dir	Lists contents of selected directory on system partition only
disable	Disables service or driver
diskpart	Replaces FDISK—creates/deletes partitions
enable	Enables service or driver
extract	Extracts components from .CAB files
fixboot	Writes new partition boot sector on system partition
fixmbr	Writes new Master Boot Record for partition boot sector
format	Formats selected disk
listsvc	Lists all services on system
logon	Lets you choose which Windows installation to log onto if you have more than one
map	Displays current drive letter mappings
md (or mkdir)	Creates a directory
more (or type)	Displays contents of text file
rd (or rmdir)	Removes a directory
ren (or rename)	Renames a single file
systemroot	Makes current directory system root of drive you're logged into
type	Displays a text file

system partition), and using the EXPAND program to extract copies of corrupted files from a CD-ROM or floppy disk.

Using the Recovery Console, you can reconfigure a service so that it starts with different settings, format drives on the hard disk, read and write on local FAT or NTFS volumes, and copy replacement files from a floppy or CD-ROM. The Recovery Console enables you to access the file system and is still constrained by the file and folder security of NTFS, which makes it a more secure tool to use than some third-party solutions.

The Recovery Console is best at fixing three items: repairing the MBR, reinstalling the boot files, and rebuilding BOOT.INI. Let's look at each of these.

A bad boot sector usually shows up as a No Boot Device error. If it turns out that this isn't the problem, the Recovery Console command to fix it won't hurt anything. At the Recovery Console prompt, just type:

```
fixmbr
```

This fixes the master boot record.

The second problem the Recovery Console is best at fixing is missing system files, usually indicated by the error *NTLDR bad or missing*. Odds are

good that if NTDLR is missing, so are the rest of the system files. To fix this, get to the root directory (CD\—remember that from Chapter 15, "Working with the Command-Line Interface"?) and type the following line:

```
copy d:\i386\ntldr
```

Then type this line:

```
copy d:\i386\ntdetect.com
```

This takes care of two of the big three and leads us to the last issue, rebuilding BOOT.INI. If the BOOT.INI file is gone or corrupted, run this command from the Recovery Console:

```
bootcfg /rebuild
```

The Recovery Console will then try to locate all installed copies of Windows and ask you if you want to add them to the new BOOT.INI file it's about to create. Say yes to the ones you want.

If all goes well with the Recovery Console, do a thorough backup as soon as possible (just in case something else goes wrong). If the Recovery Console does not do the trick, the next step is to restore Windows XP.

Attempt to Restore

If you've been diligent about backing up, you can attempt to restore to an earlier, working copy of Windows. You have two basic choices, depending on your OS. In Windows 2000, you can try the ERD. Windows XP limits you to the ASR.

If you elected to create an ERD in Windows 2000, you can attempt to restore your system with it. Boot your system to the Windows 2000 installation CD-ROM and select repair installation, but in this case opt for the ERD. Follow the steps outlined earlier in the chapter and you might have some success.

ASR can restore your system to a previously installed state, but you should use it as a last resort. You lose everything on the system that was installed or added after you created the ASR disk. If that's the best option, though, follow the steps outlined earlier in the chapter.

Rebuild

If faced with a full system rebuild, you have several options, depending on the particular system. You could simply reboot to the Windows CD-ROM and install right on top of the existing system, but that's usually not the optimal solution. To avoid losing anything important, you'd be better off swapping the C: drive for a blank hard drive and installing a clean version of Windows.

Most OEM systems come with a misleadingly named *Recover CD* or *recovery partition*. The Recover CD is a CD-ROM that you boot to and run. The recovery partition is a hidden partition on the hard drive that you activate at boot by holding down a key combination specific to the manufacturer of that system. (See the motherboard manual or users' guide for the key combination and other details.) Both "recover" options do the same thing—restore your computer to the factory-installed state. If you run one of these tools,

To use the Windows XP System Restore, you need to be able to get into Windows. "Restore" in the context used here means to give you an option to get into Windows.

you will wipe everything off your system—all personal files, folders, and programs will go away! Before running either tool, make sure all important files and folders are backed up on an optical disc or spare hard drive.

Failure to Load the GUI

Assuming that Windows gets past the boot part of the startup, it then begins to load the real Windows OS. You will see the Windows startup image on the screen, hiding everything until Windows loads the desktop (Figure 17.55).

Several issues can cause Windows to hang during the GUI-loading phase, such as buggy device drivers or Registry problems. Even autoloading programs can cause the GUI to hang on load. The first step in troubleshooting these issues is to use one of the Advanced Startup options (covered later in the chapter) to try to get past the hang spot and into Windows.

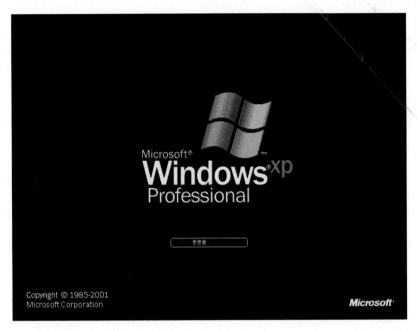

• **Figure 17.55**   GUI time!

Device Drivers

Device driver problems that stop Windows GUI from loading look pretty scary. Figure 17.56 shows the infamous Windows *Stop error*, better known as the **Blue Screen of Death (BSoD)**. The BSoD only appears when something causes an error from which Windows cannot recover. The BSoD is not limited to device driver problems, but device drivers are one of the reasons you'll see the BSoD.

Whenever you get a BSoD, take a moment and read what it says. Windows BSoDs tell you the name of the file that caused the problem and usually suggests a recommended action. Once in a while these are helpful—but not often.

BSoD problems due to device drivers almost always take place immediately after you've installed a new device and rebooted. Take out the device and reboot. If Windows loads properly, head over to the manufacturer's Web site. A new device producing this type of problem

```
A problem has been detected and windows has been shut down to prevent damage
to your computer.

NO_MORE_IRP_STACK_LOCATIONS

If this is the first time you've seen this stop error screen,
restart your computer. If this screen appears again, follow
these steps:

Check to make sure that any new hardware or software is properly installed.
If this is a new installation, ask your hardware or software manufacturer
for any windows updates you might need.

If problems continue, disable or remove any newly installed hardware
or software. Disable BIOS memory options such as caching or shadowing.
If you need to use Safe Mode to remove or disable components, restart
your computer, press F8 to select Advanced Startup Options, and then
select Safe Mode.

Technical information:

*** STOP: 0x00000035 (0x00000000,0xF7E562B2,0x00000008,0xC0000000)

***      wdmaud.sys - Address F7E562B2 base at F7E56000, DateStamp 36B047A5
```

• **Figure 17.56**   BSoD

is a serious issue that should have been caught before the device was released. In many cases, the manufacturer will have updated drivers available for download or will recommend a replacement device.

The second indication of a device problem that shows up during the GUI part of startup is a freeze-up: the Windows startup screen just stays there and you never get a chance to log on. If this happens, try one of the Advanced Startup Options, covered below.

Registry

Your Registry files load every time the computer boots. Windows does a pretty good job of protecting your Registry files from corruption, but from time to time something may slip by Windows and it will attempt to load a bad Registry. These errors may show up as BSoDs that say "Registry File Failure" or text errors that say "Windows could not start." Whatever the case, you need to restore a good Registry copy. The best way to do this is the Last Known Good Configuration boot option (see the upcoming section). If that fails, you can restore an earlier version of the Registry through the Recovery Console.

Boot to the Windows installation CD-ROM, select the repair installation to get to the Recovery Console, and type these commands to restore a Registry. Notice I didn't say "your" Registry in the previous sentence. Your Registry is corrupted and gone, so you need to rebuild.

```
delete c:\windows\system32\config\system
delete c:\windows\system32\config\software
delete c:\windows\system32\config\sam
delete c:\windows\system32\config\security
delete c:\windows\system32\config\default

copy c:\windows\repair\system c:\windows\system32\config\system
copy c:\windows\repair\software c:\windows\system32\config\software
copy c:\windows\repair\sam c:\windows\system32\config\sam
copy c:\windows\repair\security c:\windows\system32\config\security
copy c:\windows\repair\default c:\windows\system32\config\default
```

Advanced Startup Options

Windows 9x had an option for step-by-step confirmation, but that is not a choice in Windows 2000/XP/Vista. Look for it as a wrong answer on the exams!

If Windows fails to start up, use the Windows **Advanced Startup Options** menu to discover the cause. To get to this menu, restart the computer and press F8 after the POST messages but before the Windows logo screen appears. Windows 2000 and Windows XP have similar menus. Vista's is just a tad different. Central to these advanced options are Safe Mode and Last Known Good Configuration. Here's a rundown of the menu options.

Safe Mode (All Versions)   **Safe Mode** starts up Windows but loads only very basic, non–vendor-specific drivers for mouse, VGA monitor (not in Vista), keyboard, mass storage, and system services (see Figure 17.57).

Once in Safe Mode, you can use tools such as Device Manager to locate and correct the source of the problem. When you use Device Manager in Safe Mode, you can access the properties for all the devices, even those that are not working in Safe Mode. The status displayed for the device is the status for a normal startup. Even the network card will show as enabled. You can disable any suspect device or perform other tasks, such as removing or updating drivers. If a problem with a device driver is preventing the

operating system from starting normally, check the Device Manager for warning icons that indicate an unknown device.

Safe Mode with Networking (All Versions)

This mode is identical to plain Safe Mode except that you get network support. I use this mode to test for a problem with network drivers. If Windows won't start up normally but does start up in Safe Mode, I reboot into Safe Mode with Networking. If it fails to start up with Networking, the problem is a network driver. I reboot back to Safe Mode, open Device Manager, and start disabling network components, beginning with the network adapter.

Safe Mode with Command Prompt (All Versions)

When you start Windows in this mode, rather than loading the GUI desktop, it loads the command prompt (CMD.EXE) as the shell to the operating system after you log on, as shown in Figure 17.58. This is a handy option to remember if the desktop does not display at all, which, after you have eliminated video drivers, can be caused by corruption of the EXPLORER.EXE program. From the command prompt, you can delete the corrupted version of EXPLORER.EXE and copy in an undamaged version. This requires knowing the command-line commands for navigating the directory structure, as well as knowing the location of the file you are replacing. Although Explorer is not loaded, you can load other GUI tools that don't depend on Explorer. All you have to do is enter the correct command. For instance, to load Event Viewer, type **eventvwr.msc** at the command line and press ENTER.

Enable Boot Logging (All Versions)

This option starts Windows normally and creates a log file of the drivers as they load into memory. The file is named Ntbtlog.txt and is saved in the %SystemRoot% folder. If the startup failed because of a bad driver, the last entry in this file may be the driver the OS was initializing when it failed.

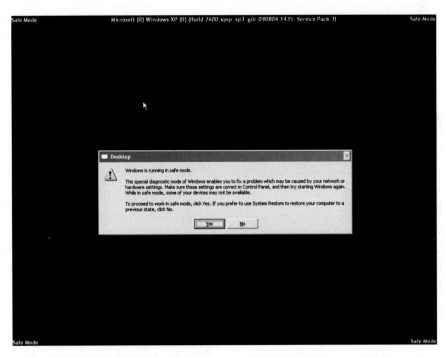

• **Figure 17.57**   Safe Mode

• **Figure 17.58**   Safe Mode with command prompt

Reboot and go into the Recovery Console. Use the Recovery Console tools to read the boot log (type **ntbtlog.txt**) and disable or enable problematic devices or services.

Enable VGA Mode (2000/XP)/Enable Low-Resolution Mode (Vista)   Enable VGA Mode/Enable Low-resolution Mode starts Windows normally but only loads a default VGA driver. If this mode works, it may mean you have a bad driver, or it may mean you are using the correct video driver but it is configured incorrectly (perhaps with the wrong refresh rate and/or resolution). Whereas Safe Mode loads a generic VGA driver, this mode loads the driver Windows is configured to use but starts it up in standard VGA mode rather than using the settings for which it is configured. After successfully starting in this mode, open the Display Properties and change the settings.

Last Known Good Configuration (All Versions)   When Windows' startup fails immediately after installing a new driver but before you have logged on again, you may want to try the **Last Known Good Configuration** option. This can be a rather fickle and limited tool, but it never hurts to try it.

Directory Services Restore Mode (All Versions)   The title says it all here; this option only applies to Active Directory domain controllers, and only Windows Server versions can be domain controllers. I have no idea why Microsoft includes this option. If you choose it, you simply boot into Safe Mode.

Debugging Mode (All Versions)   If you select this choice, Windows starts in kernel debug mode. It's a super-techie thing to do, and I doubt that even über techs do debug mode anymore. To do this, you have to connect the computer you are debugging to another computer via a serial connection, and as Windows starts up, a debug of the kernel is sent to the second computer, which must also be running a debugger program. I remember running debug for an early version of Windows 2000. My coworkers and I did it back then simply because we were studying for the MCSE exams and expected to be tested on it! We all decided it was an experience that we didn't need to repeat.

Disable Automatic Restart on System Failure (All Versions)   There are times that a BSoD will appear at startup, causing your computer to spontaneously reboot. That's all well and good, but if it happens too quickly, you might not be able to read the BSoD to see what caused the problem. Selecting *Disable automatic restart on system failure* from the Advanced Startup Options menu stops the computer from rebooting on Stop errors. This gives you the opportunity to write down the error and hopefully find a fix.

Disable Driver Signature Enforcement (Vista)   Windows Vista (and 7) requires that all very low-level drivers (kernel drivers) must have a Microsoft driver signature. If you are using an older driver to connect to your hard drive controller or some other low-level feature, you must use this option to get Windows to load the driver. Hopefully you will always check your motherboard and hard drives for Vista compatibility and never have to use this option.

Start Windows Normally (All Versions)   This choice will simply start Windows normally, without rebooting. You already rebooted to get to this menu. Select this if you changed your mind about using any of the other exotic choices.

Reboot (All Versions) This choice will actually do a soft reboot of the computer.

Return to OS Choices Menu (All Versions) On computers with multiple operating systems, you get an OS Choices menu to select which OS to load. If you load Windows and press F8 to get the Advanced Startup Options menu, you'll see this option. Choosing it returns you to the OS Choices menu, from which you can select the operating system to load.

Troubleshooting Tools in the GUI

Once you're able to load into Windows, whether through Safe Mode or one of the other options, the whole gamut of Windows tools is available for you. If a bad device driver caused the startup problems, for example, you can open Device Manager and begin troubleshooting just as you've learned in previous chapters. If you suspect some service or Registry issue caused the problem, head on over to Event Viewer and see what sort of logon events have happened recently.

Event Viewer might reveal problems with applications failing to load, a big cause of Windows loading problems (Figure 17.59). It might also reveal problems with services failing to start. Finally, Windows might run into problems loading DLLs. You can troubleshoot these issues individually or you can use System Restore in Windows XP to load a restore point that predates the bugginess.

> Chapter 26, "Securing Computers," goes into a lot more detail on using Event Viewer, especially *auditing*, a way to troubleshoot a buggy system.

Autoloading Programs

Windows loves to autoload programs so they start at boot. Most of the time this is an incredibly handy option, used by every Windows PC in existence. The problem with autoloading programs is that when one of them starts behaving badly, you need to shut off that program! Use the System Configuration utility to stop programs from autoloading.

Services

Windows loads a number of services as it starts. If any critical service fails to start, Windows tells you at this point with an error message. The important word here is *critical*. Windows will not report *all* service failures at this point. If a service that is less than critical in Windows' eyes doesn't start, Windows usually waits until you actually try to use a program that needs that service before it prompts you with an error message (Figure 17.60).

To work with your system's services, go to the Control Panel | Administrative Tools | Services and verify that the service you need is running. If not, turn it on. Also notice that each service

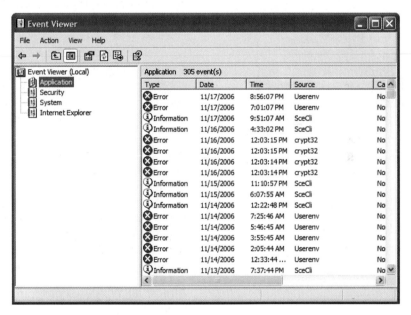

• **Figure 17.59**   Event Viewer showing some serious application errors!

• **Figure 17.60**   Service error

● **Figure 17.61** Autostarting a service

Many services require other services, called dependency services, to start before they can start. If your target service needs a dependency service, you'll get an error when you try to start your target service, telling you which dependency service needs to start first.

Remember that you need local administrator privileges to install applications in all versions of Windows.

has a Startup Type—Automatic, Manual, or Disabled—that defines when it starts. It's very common to find that a service has been set to Manual when it needs to be set to Automatic so that it starts when Windows boots (Figure 17.61).

System Files

Windows lives on dynamic link library (DLL) files. Almost every program used by Windows—and certainly all of the important ones—call to DLL files to do most of the heavy lifting that makes Windows work. Windows protects all of the critical DLL files very carefully, but once in a while you may get an error saying Windows can't load a particular DLL. Although rare, the core system files that make up Windows itself may become corrupted, preventing Windows from starting properly. You usually see something like "Error loading XXXX.DLL," or sometimes a program you need simply won't start when you double-click its icon. In these cases, the tool you need is the System File Checker. The System File Checker is a command-prompt program (SFC.EXE) you can use to check a number of critical files, including the ever-important DLL cache. SFC takes a number of switches, but by far the most important is /scannow. Go to a command prompt and type the following to start the program:

```
SFC /scannow
```

SFC automatically checks all critical files and replaces any it sees as corrupted. During this process, it may ask for the Windows installation CD-ROM, so keep it handy!

System Restore

With Windows XP and Vista systems, you can recover from a bad device or application installation by using System Restore to load a restore point. Follow the process explained earlier in the chapter. System Restore is the final step in recovering from a major Windows meltdown.

Application Problems

Almost all Windows programs come with some form of handy installer. You run the installer and the program runs. It almost couldn't be simpler.

A well-behaved program should always make itself easy to uninstall as well. In most cases, you should see an uninstallation option in the program's Start menu area; and in all cases (unless you have an application with a badly configured installer), the application should appear in either the Add/Remove Programs or Programs and Features Control Panel applet (Figure 17.62).

Despite Microsoft's best efforts, you can run into trouble with applications. Although these errors come in hundreds of varieties, the overwhelming majority of problems can be broken down into three categories: installation problems, compatibility problems, or uninstallation problems.

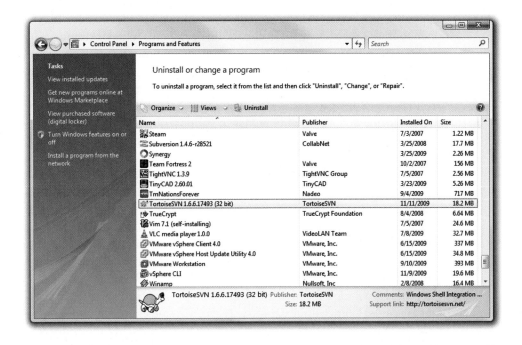

● **Figure 17.62** Programs and Features Control Panel applet

Installation Problems

Programs that fail to install usually aren't to blame in and of themselves. In most cases, a problem with Windows prevents them from installing, most notably the lack of some other program that the application needs so it can operate. One of the best examples of this is the popular .Net Framework. .Net is an extension to the Windows operating system that includes support for a number of powerful features, particularly more powerful interface tools and much more flexible database access. If a program is written to take advantage of .Net, .Net must itself be installed. In most cases if .Net is missing, the application should try to install it at the same time it is installed, but you can't count on this. If .Net is missing or if the version of .Net you are using is too old (there have been a number of .Net versions since it came out in 2002) you can get some of the most indecipherable errors in the history of Windows applications.

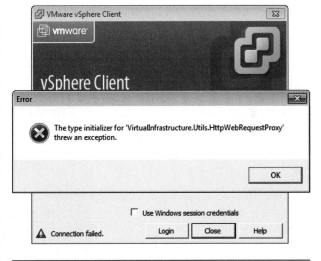

● **Figure 17.63** .Net error

Figure 17.63 shows one such example in Windows 7 where the popular VMware vSphere Client fails due to the wrong .Net version. Too bad the error doesn't give you any clues!

These types of errors invariably require you to go online and do Web searches, using the application name and the error. No matter how bad the error, someone else has already suffered from the same problem. The trick is to find out what they did to get around it.

Compatibility

Most applications are written with the most recent version of Windows in mind, but as you know, Windows versions change over time. In some cases,

> Although it's sometimes a challenge to get an older application to run on a newer version of Windows, the opposite is no problem at all: Installers know to check Windows versions and pop up an error if your version of Windows is too old.

such as the jump from Windows 2000 to Windows XP, the changes are minor enough to cause few if any compatibility problems when running an application designed for an earlier version of Windows. In other cases, especially the jump from Windows XP to Vista (and beyond), the underpinnings of the OS differ so much that you have to perform certain steps to ensure that the older programs run. Windows 2000, XP, and Vista provide different forms of **compatibility modes** to support older applications.

Windows 2000 only provides compatibility support for ancient DOS programs. DOS programs know nothing of Windows, so you normally just copy the EXE file to your computer. In Windows 2000, right-clicking on a DOS program shows two tabs: Memory and Program. The memory tab enables you to adjust the amount of memory used by the DOS program. Back in the year 2000, RAM was still precious and you could save a few kilobytes by some careful adjustments. More interesting was the Advanced button under the Program tab (Figure 17.64). This enabled you to let the DOS program load a custom AUTOEXEC.BAT or CONFIG.SYS file.

Windows XP took the idea of compatibility a step further by adding another tab called Compatibility (Figure 17.65). This tab enabled you to configure older Windows programs to work in XP by introducing the concept of compatibility modes. You can also set specific video settings on the Compatibility tab.

Windows Vista takes the Compatibility tab one step further by adding two important features: Windows XP mode and *Run this program as an administrator* (Figure 17.66).

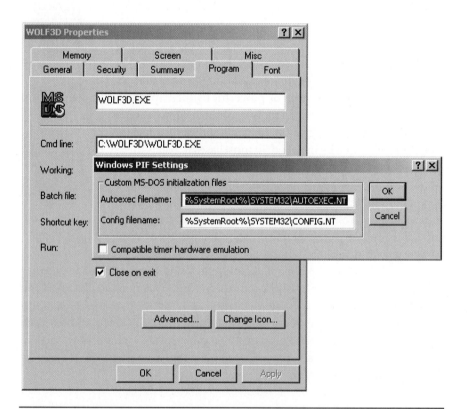

• **Figure 17.64**   Windows 2000 Program tab for DOS program

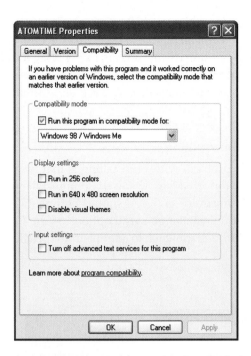

• **Figure 17.65**   XP compatibility mode

The secret to using compatibility mode isn't much of a secret at all: if the program doesn't run, try a compatibly mode! If you want to be really careful, do a Web search on your application before you try to run it. Compatibility mode is a handy tool to get older applications running.

• **Figure 17.66**   Vista compatibility mode

Chapter 17: Maintaining and Troubleshooting Windows

One error common on older systems, but largely absent or invisible on modern systems, is a *general protection fault* (*GPF*). A GPF occurs when a program tries to do something not permitted, like writing to protected memory or something else Windows doesn't like. This can cause an error message to appear or even crash the computer. You are very unlikely to encounter a GPF today.

Problems with Uninstalling

The single biggest problem with uninstalling is that people try to uninstall without administrator privileges. If you try to uninstall and get an error, log back in as an administrator and you should be fine. Don't forget you can right-click on most uninstallation menu options on the Programs menu and select *Run as administrator* to switch to administrator privileges (Figure 17.67).

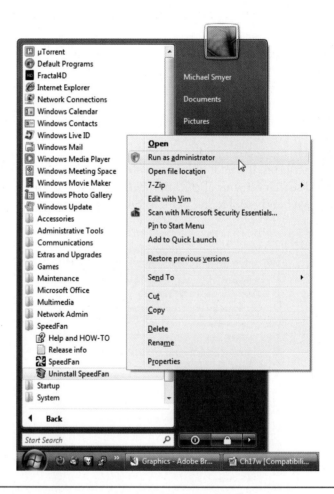

• **Figure 17.67**   Selecting *Run as administrator* from the context menu

Beyond A+

The majority of the tools and utilities discussed in this chapter are in direct correlation with the 2009 CompTIA A+ exams. There are also many others you should check out for your personal use. With that said, these commands available at the Windows Vista command prompt deserve mention:

- **CHOICE** A batch file command that allows users to select from a set of options.
- **CLIP** Redirects the output of another command to the Windows Clipboard.
- **CMDKEY** Creates, lists, and deletes stored user names, passwords, and other credentials.
- **FORFILES** Selects files in a particular folder for batch processing.
- **ICACLS** Displays, modifies, backs up, or restores ACLs for files and directories.
- **FSUTIL** Increases the file system memory cache.
- **MKLINK** Creates symbolic links and hard links.
- **TAKEOWN** Allows an administrator to take ownership of a file.
- **TIMEOUT** Pauses the command processor for the specified number of seconds.
- **VSP1CLN** Cleans up after a Windows Vista SP1 installation.
- **VSSADMIN** Volume Shadow Copy Service administration tool.
- **WHERE** Displays the location of files that match a search pattern.

Chapter 17 Review

■ Chapter Summary

After reading this chapter and completing the exercises, you should understand the following about maintaining, optimizing, and troubleshooting Windows.

Maintain Windows

■ The Internet has enabled Microsoft to make updates available, and Windows Update can grab those updates and patch user systems easily and automatically. Keeping your system updated prevents viruses and malicious software from exploiting vulnerabilities in your operating system. With the release of Windows XP Service Pack 2, Microsoft began pushing for wholesale acceptance of automatic updates from Windows Update. However, you can customize automatic updates to allow various levels of automation.

■ You have two choices when updating your system with Windows Update: Express installation or Custom installation. An Express installation installs only the essential security fixes and patches; a Custom installation enables you to select from a wide range of software and driver updates.

■ Disk Cleanup clears out the junk files that accumulate from daily use. You can reach this tool through the Start menu (Start | All Programs | Accessories | System Tools), or you can open My Computer or Computer, right-click the drive you want to clean up, select Properties, and click the Disk Cleanup button.

■ Keeping your Registry clean ensures that your system continues to run efficiently and without errors. Unfortunately, Microsoft doesn't offer any built-in Registry cleaner tools, so you have to use third-party tools such as CCleaner to perform this task.

■ If your computer is going to be connected to the Internet, it's critical that you run some sort of antispyware or antivirus software on your system.

■ When you can't find a software reason for a problem such as a system freezing on shutdown, the problem might be the actual physical hard drive. The tool to investigate that is Error-checking. You can perform Error-checking from a command line or the Start | Run dialog box, using the CHKDSK command.

■ Run the Disk Defragmenter on a regular basis to keep your system from slowing down because of files scattered in pieces on your hard drive.

■ Maintenance only works properly when it's done at regular intervals. You can use Task Scheduler to schedule regular maintenance on your computer.

■ The System Configuration utility enables techs to edit and troubleshoot operating system and program startup processes and services. Prior to Windows Vista, the System Configuration utility also offered quick access to troubleshoot and edit the boot.ini file.

Optimize Windows

■ Windows comes with the System Information tool, which collects information about hardware resources, components, and the software environment. When it finishes doing that, it provides a nice and tidy little report, allowing you to troubleshoot and diagnose any issues and conflicts. You can also use System Information to gather information about remote computers by simply selecting View | Remote Computer and then entering the remote computer's network machine name.

■ Windows supports Autorun, a feature that enables it to look for and read a special file called Autorun immediately after a CD-ROM is inserted and then run whatever program is listed in AUTORUN.INF. If you need to install a program manually, however, you can use the Add or Remove Programs applet in the Control Panel. With Windows Vista/7, you most likely will be prompted by UAC when installing an application. This is to give you time to review what is happening to your system in case you did not approve of the program being installed.

■ Each installed application program takes up space on your computer's hard drive, and programs that you no longer need simply waste space that could be used for other purposes. Removing unnecessary programs can be an important piece of optimization. You remove programs by using the Add or Remove Programs applet in the Control Panel by selecting

the desired program from the list of installed programs and then clicking Uninstall.

- The third function of the Add or Remove Programs applet is to add or remove Windows components and features. This is done by selecting Add/Remove Windows Components, which opens the Windows Components Wizard. In Windows Vista/7, Windows Components have been renamed to Windows Features.

- Windows/Microsoft Update provides an easy method to update drivers from manufacturers that take advantage of the service. If you are using 2000/XP, the only trick to this is that you usually need to select the Custom option to see these updates because Windows only installs high-priority updates when using the Express option. When you click on the Custom option, look under Hardware, Optional (on the left) to see if Windows has any driver updates. If you are using Vista/7, you will need to click "View available updates" to see if any drivers are available for your system.

- Device drivers become part of the operating system and thus have the potential to cause lots of problems if they're written poorly. To protect Windows systems from bad device drivers, Microsoft uses driver signing, which means that each driver has a digital signature. When an unsigned driver is detected during hardware installation, you'll see a message offering you the choice to stop or continue the installation. Signed drivers are more or less a sure thing, but that doesn't mean unsigned ones are a problem—just consider the source of the driver when installing it. You can control how Windows behaves when drivers are being installed by clicking the Driver Signing button on the Hardware tab of the System Properties dialog box. This displays the Driver Signing Options dialog box. If you select Ignore, Windows will install an unsigned driver without warning you.

- Right-clicking on a device in Device Manager displays the context menu. From here you can update or uninstall the driver, disable the device, scan for hardware changes, or display the Properties dialog box. The Driver tab has buttons labeled Driver Details, Update Driver, Roll Back Driver, and Uninstall. The Roll Back Driver option enables you to remove an updated driver, thus rolling back to the previous driver version.

- Windows should automatically detect any new device you install in your system. If not, use the Add Hardware Wizard (or simply Add Hardware if using Vista) to get the device recognized and drivers installed. You'll find it on the Hardware tab of the System Properties dialog box.

- One optimization you can perform on all Windows versions is setting Performance Options. Performance Options are used to configure CPU, RAM, and virtual memory (page file) settings. In Windows 2000, the Performance Options dialog box shows a pair of radio buttons called Applications and Background Services that set how processor time is divided between the foreground application and all other background tasks. In Windows XP, Vista, and 7, the Performance Options dialog box has three tabs: Visual Effects, Advanced, and Data Execution Prevention. The Visual Effects tab enables you to adjust visual effects that impact performance. The Advanced tab has three sections: Processor scheduling, Memory usage, and Virtual memory.

- Microsoft introduced Data Execution Prevention (DEP) with Windows XP Service Pack 2. DEP works in the background to stop viruses and other malware from taking over programs loaded in system memory. It doesn't prevent viruses from being installed on your computer, but makes them less effective.

- Task Manager is a great tool for investigating how hard your RAM and CPU are working at any given moment and why. The Performance tab reveals a handy screen with the most commonly used information: CPU usage, available physical memory, the size of the disk cache, commit charge (memory for programs), and kernel memory (memory used by Windows). Task Manager also tells you which program is using your system resources.

- The Performance console is used to log resource usage so you can track items such as CPU and RAM usage over time.

- System Monitor gathers real-time data on objects such as memory, physical disk, processor, and network, and displays this data as a graph (line graph), histogram (bar graph), or simple report.

- The Performance Logs and Alerts snap-in enables Windows to create a written record of just about anything that happens on your system.

- The most important data on your computer is the personal data: your documents, e-mail messages and contacts, Web favorites, photographs, and other files. To handle backing up personal data, every version of Windows comes with some form of backup utility.

- Windows 2000 Backup and Windows XP Backup Utility (NTBackup) provides almost all the tools you need to back up files and folders. It has come a long way from its origins in Windows NT. NTBackup supports a greater variety of devices, enabling you to back up to network drives, logical drives, tape, and removable disks (but not optical discs).

- The Windows 2000 Emergency Repair Disk (ERD) saves critical boot files and partition information and is your main tool for fixing boot problems in Windows 2000.

- The Windows XP Automated System Recovery (ASR) enables you to create a backup of your system. This backup includes a floppy disk and backup media (tape or CD-R) containing the system partition and disks containing operating system components.

- The archive bit works basically like this: Whenever a file is saved, the archive bit is turned on. Simply opening a file affects the current state of the archive bit. Backup programs usually turn off a file's archive bit when the file is backed up. If the archive bit is turned on, it means that the file has been changed since it was last backed up.

- A normal backup is a full backup. Every file selected is backed up, and the archive bit is turned off for every file backed up.

- A copy backup is identical to a normal backup, except that the archive bits are *not* changed. This is used (although not often) for making extra copies of a previously completed backup.

- An incremental backup includes only files with the archive bit turned on. In other words, it copies only the files that have been changed since the last backup. This backup turns off the archive bits.

- A differential backup is identical to an incremental backup, except that it doesn't turn off the archive bits.

- A daily backup, also known as a daily copy backup, makes copies of all the files that have been changed that day. It does not change the archive bits.

- In Windows Vista/7, NTBackup has been replaced with the Windows Backup and Restore Center, which has only two options: back up everything or restore from a previous backup. Vista no longer supports tape backups, nor does it let you choose between differential and incremental backups.

- You can use the System Restore tool to create a restore point, a copy of your computer's configuration at a specific point in time. If you later crash or have a corrupted OS, you can restore the system to its previous state. During the restore process, only settings and programs are changed. No data is lost. Your computer will include all programs and settings as of the restore date. System Restore is turned on by default and uses some of your disk space to save information on restore points. To turn System Restore off or change the disk space usage, open the System Properties applet in Control Panel and select the System Restore tab.

- The Recovery Console is a text-based startup of Windows that gets you to a command prompt similar to the Windows command prompt. If you have the Windows 2000/XP CD-ROM, you can start the Recovery Console by running Setup, selecting Repair, and then selecting Recovery Console.

- Windows Vista and Windows 7 have dropped the Recovery Console, replacing it with the graphical System Recovery Options. Startup Repair tells Windows to automatically attempt to repair your system. You can also perform a system restore from the System Recovery Options. The Memory Diagnostic Tool locates and reports RAM errors to you. The command prompt is also accessible from the System Recovery Options.

Troubleshoot Windows

- If you see a "No Boot Device Present," "Inaccessible Boot Device," "NTLDR Bad or Missing," or "Invalid BOOT.INI" error on startup, you first should attempt to repair. If that fails, attempt to restore from a backup copy of Windows. If restore is either not available or fails, your only recourse is to rebuild. Note that Vista has different error messages but almost always just automatically fixes the problem.

- The Recovery Console works as a command-line utility. Many of its commands are those familiar to DOS users, but some new commands have also been added. Because the file for the Recovery

Console is on the system partition in a folder called CMDCONS, this program is useless for system partition crashes, but it is excellent for restoring Registries, stopping problem services, or using EXPAND to extract copies of files from the CD-ROM. You can also use it to format hard drives and read and write on local FAT or NTFS volumes.

- The Recovery Console is best at fixing three items: repairing the MBR, reinstalling the boot files, and rebuilding BOOT.INI.

- A bad boot sector usually shows up as a No Boot Device error. If it turns out that this isn't the problem, the Recovery Console command to fix it won't hurt anything. At the Recovery Console prompt, just type **fixmbr**, which fixes the master boot record.

- The second problem the Recovery Console is best at fixing is missing system files, usually indicated by the error NTLDR bad or missing. To fix this, get to the root directory (CD\) and type the following line: **copy d:\i386\ntldr**. Then type **copy d:\i386\ntdetect.com**.

- Automated System Recovery can restore your system to a previously installed state, but you should use it as a last resort. You lose everything on the system that was installed or added after you created the ASR disk.

- When rebuilding your Windows installation, you're best off swapping the C: drive for a blank hard drive and installing a clean version of Windows.

- Several issues can cause Windows to hang during the GUI-loading phase, such as buggy device drivers, Registry problems, and even autoloading programs. The first step in troubleshooting these issues is to use one of the Advanced Startup options to try to get past the hang spot and into Windows.

- The Blue Screen of Death is not limited to device driver problems, but device drivers are one of the reasons you'll see the BSoD. BSoD problems due to device drivers almost always take place immediately after you've installed a new device and rebooted. Take out the device and reboot. In many cases the manufacturer will have updated drivers available for download or will recommend a replacement device.

- If the Windows startup screen just stays there and you never get a chance to log on, try starting up with the Last Known Good Configuration boot option. If that fails, you can restore an earlier version of the Registry through the Recovery Console.

- To get to the Advanced Startup Options menu, restart the computer and press F8 after the POST messages but before the Windows logo screen appears. From here, you can start your computer into Safe Mode or into the Last Known Good Configuration.

- Safe Mode starts up Windows but loads only very basic, non–vendor-specific drivers for mouse, VGA monitor (not in Vista), keyboard, mass storage, and system services.

- Safe Mode with Networking is identical to plain Safe Mode except that you get network support.

- When you start Windows in Safe Mode with Command Prompt, rather than loading the GUI desktop, it loads the command prompt (CMD.EXE) as the shell to the operating system after you log on. Use this if the desktop does not display at all, which can be caused by the corruption of the EXPLORER.EXE program. From the command prompt you can delete the corrupted version of EXPLORER.EXE and copy in an undamaged version.

- The Enable Boot Logging option starts Windows normally and creates a log file of the drivers as they load into memory. The file is named Ntbtlog.txt and is saved in the %SystemRoot% folder. If the startup failed because of a bad driver, the last entry in this file may be the driver the OS was initializing when it failed.

- Enable VGA Mode/Enable Low-resolution Mode starts Windows normally but only loads a default VGA driver. If this mode works, it may mean that you have a bad driver, or it may mean that you are using the correct video driver but it is configured incorrectly. This mode loads the graphics driver Windows is configured to use but starts it up in standard VGA mode rather than using the settings for which it is configured.

- Selecting *Disable automatic restart on system failure* from the Advanced Startup Options menu stops the computer from rebooting on Stop errors. This gives you the opportunity to write down the error and hopefully find a fix.

- Windows Vista (and 7) requires that all very low-level drivers (kernel drivers) must have a Microsoft driver signature. You can disable this by using the Disable Driver Signature Enforcement mode.

- The System Configuration utility enables you to keep individual programs and services from autoloading, but it does not actually remove the programs/services.

- Windows loads a number of services as it starts. If any critical service fails to load, Windows will tell you at this point with an error message.

- Windows protects all of its critical DLL files very carefully, but once in a while you may get an error saying Windows can't load a particular DLL. In these cases, the tool you need is the System File Checker, a command-prompt program (SFC.EXE) that is used to check a number of critical files, including the ever-important DLL cache. SFC automatically checks all critical files and replaces any it sees as corrupted.

- Programs that fail to install usually aren't to blame in and of themselves. In most cases a problem with Windows prevents them from installing, most notably the lack of some other program that the application needs so it can operate.

- Trying to run older programs in newer operating systems can cause compatibility errors that prevent the programs from running. Every Windows OS since 2000 has a compatibility mode that can often help older programs run.

■ Key Terms

Add or Remove Programs (602)
Advanced Startup Options (632)
Automated System Recovery (ASR) (618)
Automatic Updates (594)
Autorun (602)
Backup Utility (616)
Blue Screen of Death (BSoD) (631)
compatibility mode (638)
counter (611)
Device Manager (608)
Disk Cleanup (596)
driver signing (607)
Emergency Repair Disk (ERD) (617)
Last Known Good Configuration (634)
NT Backup (616)

object (611)
Performance console (611)
Performance Logs and Alerts (612)
Performance Options (609)
Programs and Features (603)
Recovery Console (624)
restore point (622)
Safe Mode (632)
System Configuration utility (MSCONFIG.EXE) (600)
System Information tool (MSINFO32.EXE) (601)
System Monitor (611)
System Restore (622)
Task Manager (610)
Windows Update (593)

■ Key Term Quiz

Use the Key Terms list to complete the sentences that follow. Not all terms will be used.

1. A(n) _____ is a system component with a set of characteristics that is managed by the OS as a single entity.

2. If Windows fails but you have *not* logged on, you can select _____ to restore the computer to the way it was the last time a user logged on.

3. In Windows Vista and 7, you use the _____ applet to add and remove programs.

4. Windows XP uses the _____ to create a backup of the system, using both a floppy diskette and a backup medium such as tape, but the restore side involves completely reinstalling the operating system.

5. Although not bootable, the _____ works with the \WINNT\REPAIR folder to store a copy of the Windows 2000 Registry.

6. System Monitor gathers real-time data about objects and places them in a(n) _____ that may be a graph, histogram, or report.

7. To start Windows using only the most basic and essential drivers and services, use _____.

8. Although not an MMC, the _____, accessed by pressing CTRL-ALT-DEL once, allows you to see all applications or programs currently running or to close an application that has stopped working.

9. To change what programs and services start with Windows, you would use the _____.

10. If installing a new driver causes problems in your system, the _____ enables you to roll back the driver to a previously installed version.

■ Multiple-Choice Quiz

1. Which of the following commands would you use to install the Recovery Console?

   A. Start | Run, then type d:\i386\winnt32 /cmdcons

   B. Start | Run, then type d:\i386\winnt32 /rc

   C. Start | Run, then type d:\i386\winnt32 /cmd:command_line

   D. Start | Run, then type d:\i386\winnt32 /copydir:recovery_console

2. Which tool in Windows XP Home loaded by default can you use to back up essential system files?

   A. Emergency Repair Disk

   B. Backup and Recovery Wizard

   C. System Restore

   D. Recovery Console

3. Mark loaded a new video card on his system, but now everything looks very bad. What should he do first?

   A. Go to Event Viewer and check the log

   B. Go to Device Manager

   C. Go to the printed manual

   D. Call tech support

4. Anthony sets up a new Windows XP Professional PC for his client in an insecure, networked environment. What's his first step for making the data safe?

   A. Make sure the user shuts the machine off every night

   B. Require the user to log in with a password

   C. Require the user to log in with a password composed of alphanumeric characters

   D. Nothing; anybody with a floppy disk can access the data on the PC

5. Which of the following should be your first choice to remove an application that you no longer need?

   A. Delete the program files

   B. Use the uninstall program that came with the application

   C. Use the Add or Remove Programs applet

   D. Use the Registry Editor to remove references to the application

6. Which utility is useful in identifying a program that is hogging the processor?

   A. Task Manager

   B. Device Manager

   C. System Monitor

   D. System Information

7. You've just installed a software update, rebooted, and now your system experiences random crashes. Which utility should you use first to try to fix the problem?

   A. Automated System Restore

   B. Device Manager

   C. System Restore

   D. Recovery Console

8. You suspect your system is failing to boot because of a corrupt master boot record. Which utility is the best to fix this?

   A. Automated System Restore

   B. Device Manager

   C. System Restore

   D. Recovery Console

9. What command should you run to check and fix corrupt system files, DLLs, and other critical files?

   A. CMDCONS /FIXBOOT

   B. SFC /SCANNOW

C. CHKDSK /R

D. DEFRAG –A

10. What program can you use to keep your systems patched and up-to-date?

   A. Windows Dispatcher

   B. Windows Patcher

   C. Windows Update

   D. Windows Upgrade

11. Pam needs to connect a hard drive controller to her new Windows Vista/7 computer but is unable to because of the older, unsigned driver. What can she do to make Windows load her driver?

   A. Start the computer in Disable Driver Signature Enforcement mode.

   B. Install the driver in Windows XP compatibility mode.

   C. She's plain out of luck.

   D. Use the Legacy Driver option in Device Manager.

12. Diane complains that her system seems sluggish and she keeps running out of disk space. What tool can you use to get rid of unnecessary files and compress older files? Select the best answer.

   A. Disk Cleanup

   B. Disk Doctor

   C. File Manager

   D. Registry Cleaner

13. Alberto installs a video card into a Windows XP computer and it seems to work just fine until he tries to run a game. Then he gets low-end graphics and it just doesn't look right. What might he try to fix the problem? Select the best answer.

   A. Check the video card manufacturer's Web site and download updated drivers

   B. Check the video card manufacturer's Web site and download the FAQ

   C. Run the Driver Update utility

   D. Reinstall Windows

14. Janet thinks that someone is logging into her computer after she leaves work. What tool could you use to track who logs on and off the computer?

   A. Log Monitor snap-in

   B. Performance Logs and Alerts snap-in

   C. System Monitor

   D. Task Manager

15. You get a tech call from a distraught Windows XP user who can't get into Windows. He says he has a Recover CD from the manufacturer and plans to run it. What would you suggest?

   A. Run the Recover CD to restore the system

   B. Run the Recover CD to return the system to the factory-installed state

   C. Try to get the computer to boot into Safe Mode

   D. Reinstall Windows by using a Windows XP disc

■ Essay Quiz

1. Your company's CEO is concerned about the backup policy in place for your file servers—namely, that there isn't one. He has asked you for advice, so write him a report about the types of backups available, how they work, and the storage requirements for each.

2. Your boss wants you to write a brief essay on how your users should back up their data for protection against accidental loss. Half the users have Windows 2000 PCs; the other half are running Windows XP Professional. Keep in mind that your target audience is users, not trained technicians, so you should go for the user-level tools.

3. You've been tasked with organizing the standard maintenance routines for the Boston office of 16 Windows XP Professional PCs. Write a couple of paragraphs describing the tools available and how often each should be run.

4. A fellow tech sends a message crying for help. He has a Windows 2000 system that has crashed hard and he's never worked with 2000 before. He's afraid to try to boot the machine up until he hears back from you. He found a copy of the OS

disc and a hand-labeled diskette called Emergency Repair Disk. What advice do you give him to try to get the system back up and running quickly?

5. Your friend Steve got a new Windows XP Home computer, but it's so loaded with trial-version software from the manufacturer that it confuses him. He wants to unload some of these useless programs, but he doesn't want to trash his new PC. Write a brief essay describing the tool(s) he needs to use to uninstall the programs and clean up afterward.

Lab Projects

• Lab Project 17.1

You learned that restore points are copies of your system's configuration at a specific point in time. You know that Windows automatically creates some restore points. But there may be situations when you would like to have a copy of the current system configuration. That's why Microsoft also allows users to create a restore point at any time. Review the process, decide on a description, and then create a restore point. Note that it automatically includes the date and time when you created it. If you are using Windows 2000, another prevention tool is the Emergency Repair Disk. Review the process for creating an ERD. Then create one and store it in a safe place in case of an emergency. (Note that Windows XP does not include the ERD option.)

• Lab Project 17.2

After reading this chapter you know how critical it is to keep patches, updates, and service packs current to help the computer stay healthy and to protect it from viruses that may exploit flaws in the operating system. Now's a good time to make sure your operating system is current. Run the Windows Update utility and decide which updates to install. (Now, don't you feel better about your system?)

chapter 18

Input/Output

"The Macintosh uses an experimental pointing device called a 'mouse.' There is no evidence that people want to use these things. I don't want one of these new fangled devices."
—JOHN C. DVORAK, 1984

In this chapter, you will learn how to

- **Explain how to support common input/output ports**
- **Identify certain common input/ output devices on a PC**
- **Describe how certain specialty input/output devices work on a PC**

In Chapter 3, "The Visible PC," you learned how to recognize and connect a number of common devices and the ports they use. Because these devices and their ports sometimes fail, it is important that you learn how they work and how to troubleshoot them when problems arise. This chapter reviews some of the major types of input ports, discusses a number of common and not-so-common input/output (I/O) devices, and deals with some of the troubleshooting issues you may encounter with I/O devices and their ports.

The CompTIA A+ certification exam domains split computer I/O devices into three groups: common, multimedia, and specialty. Common I/O devices, such as keyboards and mice, are found on virtually every PC. Multimedia I/O devices support video and sound functions. Specialty I/O devices run the gamut from common (touch screens) to rare (biometric devices). In fact, the exams deal with an entire set of I/O devices—networking devices—as completely distinct technologies. This book dedicates entire chapters to sound, printing, video, and networking, providing details about dealing with these types of devices and the ports they use. This chapter concentrates on two of the I/O device groups: the common devices and the specialty devices. You'll learn how to identify and support both the most common and some of the most unusual I/O devices used in today's PCs.

Essentials/Practical Application

■ Supporting Common I/O Ports

Whenever you're dealing with an I/O device that isn't playing nice, you need to remember that you're never dealing with just a device—you're dealing with a device and the port to which it is connected. Before you start looking at I/O devices, you need to take a look into the issues and technologies of some of the more common I/O ports and see what needs to be done to keep them running well.

Serial Ports

Finding a new PC with a real serial port is difficult, because devices that traditionally used serial ports have for the most part moved on to better interfaces, in particular, USB. Physical serial ports may be hard to find on new PC cases, but many devices—in particular, the modems many people still use to access the Internet—continue to use built-in serial ports.

In Chapter 8, "Expansion Bus," you learned that COM ports are nothing more than preset I/O addresses and interrupt request lines (IRQs) for serial ports. Want to see a built-in serial port? Open Device Manager on a system and see if you have an icon for Ports (COM and LPT). If you do, click the plus (+) sign to the left of the icon to open it and see the ports on your system—don't be surprised if you have COM ports on your PC. Even if you don't see any physical serial ports on your PC, the serial ports are there; they're simply built into some other device, probably a modem.

Your PC's expansion bus uses parallel communication: multiple data wires, each one sending one bit of data at a time between your devices. Many I/O devices use serial communication: one wire to send data and another wire to receive data. The job of a **serial port** is to convert data moving between parallel and serial devices. A traditional serial port consists of two pieces: the physical, 9-pin DB connector (Figure 18.1) and a chip that actually does the conversion between the serial data and parallel data, called the **universal asynchronous receiver/transmitter (UART)** chip. If you want to be completely accurate, the UART *is* the serial port. The port on the back of your PC is nothing more than a standardized connector that enables different serial devices to use the serial port. The UART holds all of the smarts that make the true serial port.

RS-232 is a very old standard that defines everything about serial ports: how fast they communicate, the language they use, even how the connectors should look. The RS-232 standard specifies that two serial devices must talk to each other in 8-bit chunks of data, but it also allows flexibility in other areas, such as speed and error-checking. Serial came out back in the days when devices were configured manually, and the RS-232 standard has never been updated for automatic configuration. Serial ports are a throwback to the old days of computer maintenance (though

This entire chapter shows up in both of the CompTIA A+ certification exams. Both exams test you on certain aspects of I/O devices, ports, configuration, and so on, so don't skip this chapter.

Having trouble finding a PC with serial ports? Try a laptop—almost all laptops come with built-in modems.

Tech Tip

Serial Ports Are RS-232 Ports
Speaking of standardization, all serial ports on PCs use the RS-232 standard. Many old techs will look at a serial port and say "That's an RS-232 port!" Because all physical serial ports are standardized on RS-232, they're right.

● **Figure 18.1**   Serial port

they're still very prevalent in some hardware, such as high-end routers) and are the last manually configured port you'll find on a PC.

So what type of settings do you need to configure on a serial port? Find a PC with a real serial port (a real 9-pin connector on the back of the PC). Right-click the COM port and choose Properties to see the properties of that port in Device Manager. Open the Port Settings tab and click the Advanced button to see a dialog box that looks like Figure 18.2.

Devices such as modems that have built-in serial ports don't have COM port icons in Device Manager, because there's nothing to change. Can you see why? Even though these devices are using a COM port, that port is never going to connect to anything other than the device it's soldered onto, so all of the settings are fixed and unchangeable—thank goodness!

When you are configuring a serial port, you will have a lot of different settings to configure, many which may or may not make sense. The convenient part about all this is that when you get a new serial device to plug into your serial port, the instructions will tell you what settings to use. Figure 18.3 shows an instruction sheet for a Cisco switch.

• **Figure 18.2** Serial port settings

USB Ports

You should be familiar with the concept of USB, USB connectors, and USB hubs from the discussion of those concepts in Chapter 3, "The Visible PC." Here's a more in-depth look at USB and some of the issues involved with using USB devices.

Understanding USB

The cornerstone of a USB connection is the **USB host controller**, an integrated circuit that is usually built into the chipset and controls every USB device that connects to it. Inside the host controller is a **USB root hub**: the part of the host controller that makes the physical connection to the USB ports. Every USB root hub is really just a bus—similar in many ways to an expansion bus. Figure 18.4 shows a diagram of the relationship between the host controller, root hub, and USB ports.

No rule says how many USB ports a single host adapter may use. Early USB host adapters had two USB ports. The most recent ones support up to ten. Even if a host adapter supports a certain number of ports, there's no guarantee that the motherboard maker will supply that many ports. To give

Connecting a PC or Terminal to the Console Port

To connect a PC to the console port, use the supplied RJ-45-to-DB-9 adapter cable. To connect the switch console port to a terminal, you need to provide a RJ-45-to-DB-25 female DTE adapter. You can order a kit (part number ACS-DSBUASYN=) containing that adapter from Cisco. For console port and adapter pinout information, see the "Cable and Adapter Specifications" section.

The PC or terminal must support VT100 terminal emulation. The terminal-emulation software—frequently a PC application such as Hyperterminal or Procomm Plus—makes communication between the switch and your PC or terminal possible during the setup program.

Follow these steps to connect the PC or terminal to the switch:

Step 1 Configure the baud rate and character format of the PC or terminal to match these console port default characteristics:

- 9600 baud

- 8 data bits

- 1 stop bit

- No parity

After you have gained access to the switch, you can change the console baud rate through the **Administration > Console Baud Rate** window in the Cluster Management Suite (CMS).

Step 2 Using the supplied RJ-45-to-DB-9 adapter cable, insert the RJ-45 connector into the console port, as shown in Figure 2-1.

Step 3 Attach the DB-9 female DTE adapter of the RJ-45-to-DB-9 adapter cable to a PC, or attach an appropriate adapter to the terminal.

Step 4 Start the terminal-emulation program if you are using a PC or terminal.

Figure 2-1: Connecting to the Console Port

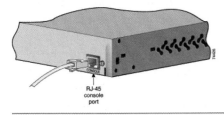

RJ-45
console
port

• Figure 18.3   Serial port instructions

a common example, a host adapter might support eight ports while the motherboard maker only supplies four adapters.

The most important point to remember about this is that every USB device connected to a single host adapter/root hub *shares* that USB bus with every other device connected to it. The more devices you place on a single host adapter, the more the total USB bus slows down and the more power they use. These issues are two of the biggest headaches that take place with USB devices in the real world.

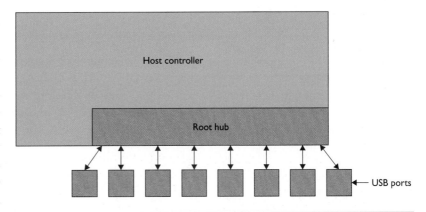

• Figure 18.4   Host controller, root hub, and USB ports

USB devices, like any electrical device, need power to run, but not all take care of their own power needs. A powered USB device comes with its own electrical cord that is usually connected in turn to an AC adapter. *Bus-powered* USB devices take power from the USB bus itself; they don't bring

any AC or DC power with them. When too many bus-powered devices take too much power from the USB bus, bad things happen—devices that work only some of the time and devices that lock up. You'll also often get a simple message from Windows saying that the hub power has been exceeded and it just won't work.

Every USB device is designed to run at one of three speeds. The first USB standard, version 1.1, defined two speeds: **Low-Speed USB**, running at a maximum of 1.5 Mbps (plenty for keyboards and mice), and **Full-Speed USB**, running up to 12 Mbps. Later, the USB 2.0 standard introduced **Hi-Speed USB** running at a whopping 480 Mbps. The industry sometimes refers to Low-Speed and Full-Speed USB as USB 1.1 and Hi-Speed as USB 2.0.

In addition to a much faster transfer rate, Hi-Speed USB is fully backward compatible with devices that operate under the slower USB standards. Those old devices won't run any faster than they used to, however. To take advantage of the fastest USB speed, you must connect Hi-Speed USB devices to Hi-Speed USB ports by using Hi-Speed USB cables. Hi-Speed USB devices function when plugged into Full-Speed USB ports, but at only 12 Mbps. Although backward compatibility at least allows you to use the newer USB device with an older port, a quick bit of math tells you how much time you're sacrificing when you're transferring a 240-MB file at 12 Mbps instead of 480 Mbps!

When USB 2.0 came out in 2001, folks scrambled to buy USB 2.0 controllers so their new hi-speed devices would work at their designed speeds. Of the variety of solutions people came up with, the most popular early on was to add a USB 2.0 adapter card like the one shown in Figure 18.5.

Motherboard makers quickly added a second USB 2.0 host controller—and they did it in a clever way. Instead of making the USB 2.0 host controller separate from the USB 1.1 host controller, they designed things so that both controllers share all of the connected USB ports (Figure 18.6). That way, no matter which USB port you choose, if you plug in a Low-Speed or Full-Speed device, the 1.1 host controller takes over, and if you plug in a Hi-Speed device, the USB 2.0 host controller takes over. Clever, and convenient!

USB 2.0 has remained the standard for quite a while, but, as of this writing, the future of USB is nigh! USB 3.0 (also called SuperSpeed) devices are set to appear on the market sometime in 2010, with massively increased speed (up to 4.8 Gbps), increased power to peripherals, and full backward compatibility with older devices. USB 3.0 probably won't show up on the CompTIA A+ exams until it becomes widely adopted, but you should definitely be aware of it, because if it retains the popularity USB has enjoyed up to this point, it's going to be huge.

• **Figure 18.5**   USB adapter card

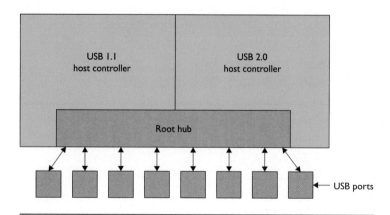

• **Figure 18.6**   Shared USB ports

USB Hubs and Cables

Each USB host controller supports up to 127 USB devices, but as mentioned earlier, most motherboard makers provide only six to eight

Mike Meyers' CompTIA A+ Guide to Managing and Troubleshooting PCs

Try This!

What Speed Is Your USB?

Using a PC running Windows 2000 or later, open the Device Manager and locate two controllers under the Universal Serial Bus icon. The one named Standard Enhanced Host Controller is the hi-speed controller. The Standard OpenHCD Host Controller is the Low- and Full-Speed controller.

real USB ports. So what do you do when you need to add more USB devices than the motherboard provides ports? You can add more host controllers (in the form of internal cards), or you can use a USB hub. A **USB hub** is a device that extends a single USB connection to two or more USB ports, almost always directly from one of the USB ports connected to the root hub. Figure 18.7 shows a typical USB hub. USB hubs are sometimes embedded into peripherals. The keyboard in Figure 18.8 comes with a built-in USB hub—very handy!

USB hubs are one of those parts of a PC that tend not to work nearly as well in the real world as they do on paper. (Sorry, USB folks, but it's true!) USB hubs have a speed just like any other USB device; for example, the hub in the keyboard in Figure 18.8 runs at Full-Speed. This becomes a problem when someone decides to insert a Hi-Speed USB device into one of those ports, as it forces the Hi-Speed device to crawl along at only 12 Mbps. Windows XP and Windows Vista are nice enough to warn you of this problem with a bubble over the system tray like the one shown in Figure 18.9.

Hubs also come in powered and bus-powered versions. If you choose to use a general purpose USB hub like the one shown in Figure 18.7, try to find a powered one, as too many devices on a single USB root hub will draw too much power and create problems.

Cable length is an important limitation to keep in mind with USB. USB specifications allow for a maximum cable length of 5 meters, although you may add a powered USB hub every 5 meters to extend this distance. Although most USB devices never get near this maximum, some devices, such as digital cameras, can come with cables at or near the maximum

• **Figure 18.7** USB hub

• **Figure 18.8** USB keyboard with built-in hub

• **Figure 18.9** Windows XP speed warning

Cross Check

USB Cable Connectors

You read about USB cables and connectors way back in Chapter 3, "The Visible PC," so turn there now and see if you can answer these questions. What are the three types of connectors found on USB cables? Which connector plugs into the PC or hub and not the device? What does downstream and upstream mean in terms of connectivity for USB?

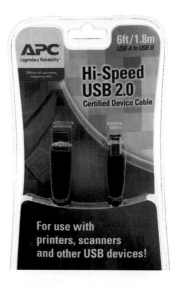

• **Figure 18.10** USB 2.0 cable

There are exceptions to the "install the driver first" rule. USB thumb drives, for example, as you will recall from Chapter 13, "Removable Media," don't need extra drivers at all. Just plug them in and Windows picks them up. (Technically speaking, though, that means the drivers came *preinstalled* with the operating system!)

• **Figure 18.11** USB hub Power tab

5-meter cable length. Because USB is a two-way (bi-directional) connection, as the cable grows longer, even a standard, well-shielded, 20-gauge, twisted-pair USB cable begins to suffer from electrical interference. To avoid these problems, I stick to cables that are no more than about 2 meters long.

If you really want to play it safe, spend a few extra dollars and get a high-quality USB 2.0 cable like the one shown in Figure 18.10. These cables come with extra shielding and improved electrical performance to make sure your USB data gets from the device to your computer safely.

USB Configuration

The biggest troubleshooting challenge you encounter with USB is a direct result of its widespread adoption and ease of use. Pretty much every modern PC comes with multiple USB ports, and anyone can easily pick up a cool new USB device at the local computer store. The problems arise when all of this USB installation activity gets out of control, with too many devices using the wrong types of ports or pulling too much power. Happily, by following a few easy steps, you can avoid or eliminate these issues.

The first and often-ignored rule of USB installation is this: Always install the device driver for a new USB device *before* you plug it into the USB port. Once you've installed the device and you know the ports are active (running properly in Device Manager), feel free to plug in the new device and hot-swap to your heart's content. USB device installation really is a breeze as long as you follow this rule!

Windows 2000, XP, and Vista have a large number of built-in drivers for USB devices. You can count on Windows 2000, Windows XP, and Windows Vista to recognize keyboards, mice, and other basic devices with their built-in drivers. Just be aware that if your new mouse or keyboard has some extras, the default USB drivers will probably not support them. To be sure I'm not missing any added functionality, I always install the driver that comes with the device or an updated one downloaded from the manufacturer's Web site.

When looking to add a new USB device to a system, first make sure your machine has a USB port that supports the speed you need for the USB device. On more modern PCs, this is likely to be a nonissue. Even then, if you start adding hubs and such, you can end up with devices that either won't run at all or, worse yet, exhibit strange behaviors.

The last and toughest issue is power. A mismatch between available and required power for USB devices can result in nonfunctioning or malfunctioning USB devices. If you're pulling too much power, you must take devices off that root hub until the error goes away. Buy an add-in USB hub card if you need to use more devices than your current USB hub supports.

To check the USB power usage in Windows, open Device Manager and locate any USB hub under the Universal Serial Bus Controller icon. Right-click the hub and select Properties, and then select the Power tab. This shows you the current use for each of the devices connected to that root hub (Figure 18.11).

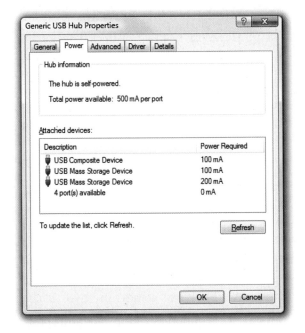

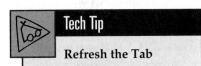

● **Figure 18.12**   General purpose bus-powered hub

● **Figure 18.13**   Power Management tab

Most root hubs provide 500 mA per port—more than enough for any USB device. Most power problems take place when you start adding hubs, especially bus-powered hubs, and then you add too many devices to them. Figure 18.12 shows the Power tab for a bus-powered hub; note that it provides a maximum of 200 mA per port.

There's one more problem with USB power: sometimes USB devices go to sleep and don't wake up. Actually, the system is telling them to sleep, to save power. You can suspect this problem if you try to access a USB device that was working earlier but that suddenly no longer appears in Device Manager. To fix this, head back in to Device Manager to inspect the hub's Properties, but this time open the Power Management tab and uncheck the *Allow the computer to turn off this device to save power* checkbox, as shown in Figure 18.13.

> **Tech Tip**
>
> **Refresh the Tab**
> *The USB Hub Power Properties tab shows you the power usage only for a given moment, so to ensure you keep getting an accurate readings, you must click the Refresh button to update its display. Make sure your USB device works, and then refresh to see the maximum power used.*

FireWire Ports

At first glance, **FireWire**, also known as IEEE 1394, looks and acts much like USB. FireWire has all of the features of USB, but it uses different connectors and is actually the older of the two technologies. For years, FireWire had the upper hand when it came to moving data quickly to and from external devices. The onset of Hi-Speed USB changed that, and FireWire has lost ground to USB in many areas. One area where FireWire still dominates is editing digital video. Most modern digital video cameras use the IEEE 1394 interface for transferring video from camera to PC for editing. The high transfer speed of FireWire makes transferring large video files quick and easy.

> Even Apple, the inventors of FireWire, dropped FireWire for USB in its iPod.

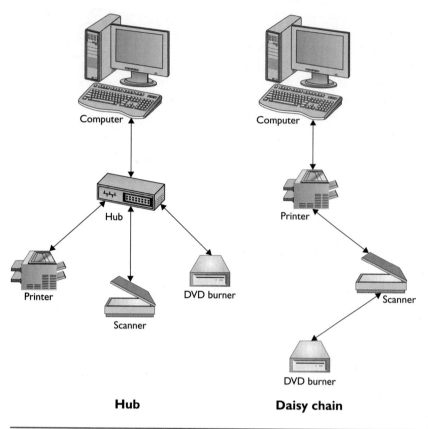

Computer

Hub

Printer

Scanner

DVD burner

Hub

Computer

Printer

Scanner

DVD burner

Daisy chain

• **Figure 18.14**   Hubbed versus daisy chain connections

Understanding FireWire

FireWire has two distinct types of connectors, both of which are commonly found on PCs. The first is a 6-pin *powered* connector, the type you see on many desktop PCs. Like USB, a FireWire port is capable of providing power to a device, and it carries the same cautions about powering high-power devices through the port. The other type of connector is a 4-pin *bus-powered* connector, which you see on portable computers and such FireWire devices as cameras. This type of connector does not provide power to a device, so you need to find another method of powering the external device.

FireWire comes in two blazing speeds: **IEEE 1394a**, which runs at 400 Mbps, and **IEEE 1394b**, which runs at 800 Mbps. FireWire devices can also take advantage of bus mastering, enabling two FireWire devices—such as a digital video camera and an external FireWire hard drive—to communicate directly with each other. When it comes to raw speed, FireWire 800—that would be 1394b, naturally—is much faster than Hi-Speed USB.

FireWire does have differences from USB other than just speed and a different-looking connector. First, a USB device must connect directly to a hub, but a FireWire device may use either a hub or daisy chaining. Figure 18.14 shows the difference between hubbed connections and daisy chaining. Second, FireWire supports a maximum of 63 devices, compared to USB's 127. Third, each cable in a FireWire daisy chain has a maximum length of 4.5 meters, as opposed to USB's 5 meters.

Configuring FireWire

FireWire was invented by and still controlled to a degree by Apple Computer. This single source of control makes FireWire more stable and more interchangeable than USB—in plain language, FireWire is ridiculously easy to use. In a Windows environment, FireWire is subject to many of the same issues as USB, such as the need to preinstall drivers, verify that onboard devices are active, and so on. But none of these issues is nearly as crucial with a FireWire connection. For example, as with USB, you really should install a FireWire device driver before attaching the device, but given that 95 percent of the FireWire devices used in PCs are either external hard drives or digital video connections, the preinstalled Windows drivers almost always work perfectly. FireWire devices do use much more power than USB devices, but the FireWire controllers are designed to handle higher voltages, and they'll warn you on the rare chance that your FireWire devices pull too much power.

General Port Issues

No matter what type of port you use, if it's not working, you should always check out a few issues. First of all, make sure you can tell a port problem from a device problem. Your best bet here is to try a second "known good" device in the same port to see if that device works. If it does *not*, you can assume the port is the problem. It's not a bad idea to reverse this and plug the device into a known good port.

If you're pretty sure the port's not working, you can check three things: First, make sure the port is turned on. Almost any I/O port on a motherboard can be turned off in CMOS. Reboot the system and find the device and see if the port's been turned off. You can also use Windows Device Manager to disable most ports. Figure 18.15 shows a disabled parallel port in Device Manager—you'll see a small down-pointing arrow in Windows Vista/7 or a red *X* over the device icon if you are using Windows 2000/XP. To turn the port back on, right-click the device's icon and choose Enable.

Being able to turn off a port in Device Manager points to another not-so-obvious fact: ports need drivers just as devices need drivers. Windows has excellent built-in drivers for all common ports, so if you fail to see a port in Device Manager (and you know the port is turned on in CMOS), you can bet the port itself has a physical problem.

Because ports have connectors inserted and removed from them repeatedly, eventually they can physically break. Figure 18.16 shows the back of a

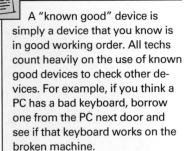

A "known good" device is simply a device that you know is in good working order. All techs count heavily on the use of known good devices to check other devices. For example, if you think a PC has a bad keyboard, borrow one from the PC next door and see if that keyboard works on the broken machine.

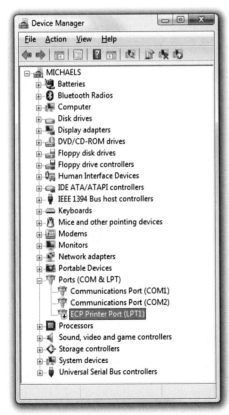

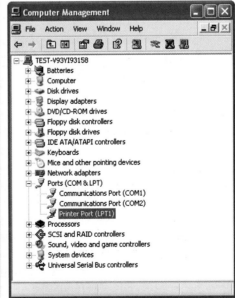

• **Figure 18.15**   Disabled parallel port in Device Manager in both Vista and XP

• Figure 18.16   Broken USB port

• Figure 18.17   Badly bent PS/2 plug

USB port that's been pushed on too hard for too long and has physically separated from the motherboard. Unless you're an expert solderer, you either must stop using those ports or replace the entire motherboard.

Many ports (or the plugs that fit into those ports) use tiny pins or relatively delicate metal casings that are susceptible to damage. PS/2 plugs are some of the worst for bent pins or misshaped casings. Figure 18.17 shows what happened to a PS/2 plug when I was in a hurry and thought that force was an alternative to lining up the plug properly. Replacement plugs are available—but again, unless you're excellent at soldering, they're not a viable alternative. Still, if you're patient, you might be able to save the plug. Using needle-nose pliers and a pair of scissors, I was able to reshape the plug so that it once again fit in the PS/2 port.

■ Common I/O Devices

So what is a "common" I/O device? I'm hoping you immediately thought of the mouse and the keyboard, two of the most basic, necessary, and abused I/O devices on a computer. Another fairly common input device that's been around a long time is the scanner. To these oldsters, you can add relative newcomers to the world of common devices: digital cameras and Web cameras.

> If you want to get picky, these five common I/O devices enable a user only to *input* data; they don't provide any output at all.

• Figure 18.18   CMOS USB Keyboard Support option

Tech Tip

Wireless Keyboards and Batteries

Wireless keyboards are a wonderful convenience because they remove the cable between you and the PC, but make sure you keep a complete set of spare batteries around.

Keyboards

Keyboards are both the oldest and still the primary way you input data into a PC. Windows comes with perfectly good drivers for any keyboard, although some fancier keyboards may come with specialized keys that require a special driver be installed to operate properly. About the only issue that might affect keyboard installation is if you're using a USB keyboard: make sure that the USB Keyboard Support option is enabled in your CMOS (Figure 18.18). Other than that, any keyboard installation issue you're likely to encounter is covered in the general port issues sections at the beginning of this chapter.

There's not much to do to configure a standard keyboard. The only configuration tool you might need is the Keyboard Control Panel applet. This tool enables you to change the repeat delay (the amount of time you must hold down a key before the keyboard starts repeating the character), the repeat rate (how quickly the character is repeated after the repeat delay), and the default cursor blink rate. Figure 18.19 shows the default Windows Keyboard Properties window—some keyboard makers provide drivers that add extra tabs.

Keyboards might be easy to install, but they do fail occasionally. Given their location—right in front of you—the three issues that cause the most keyboard problems stem from spills, physical damage, and dirt.

Spilling a soda onto your keyboard can make for a really bad day. If you're quick and unplug the keyboard from the PC before the liquid hits the electrical components, you might be able to save the keyboard. It'll take some cleaning, though (keep reading for cleaning tips). More often than not, you'll get a sticky, ill-performing keyboard that is not worth the hassle—just replace it!

Other common physical damage comes from dropping objects onto the keyboard, such as a heavy book (like the one in your hands). This can have bad results! Most keyboards are pretty resilient, though, and can bounce back from the hit.

Clean dirt and grime off the keys by using a cloth dampened with a little water, or if the water alone doesn't do the job, use a bit of isopropyl alcohol on a cloth (Figure 18.20).

Dirty keys might be unsightly, but dirt under the keys might cause the keyboard to stop working completely. When your keys start to stick, grab a bottle of compressed air and shoot some air under the keys. Do this outside or over a trash can—you'll be amazed how much junk gets caught under the keys! If you really mess up a keyboard by dumping a chocolate milkshake on the keys, you're probably going to need to dismantle the keyboard to clean it. This is pretty easy as long as you keep track of where all of the parts go. Keyboards are made of layers of plastic that create the electrical connections when you press a key. Unscrew the keyboard (keep track of the screws!) and gently peel away the plastic layers, using a damp cloth to clean each layer (Figure 18.21). Allow the sheets to dry and then reassemble the keyboard.

• **Figure 18.19**   Keyboard Control Panel applet

• **Figure 18.20**   Cleaning keys

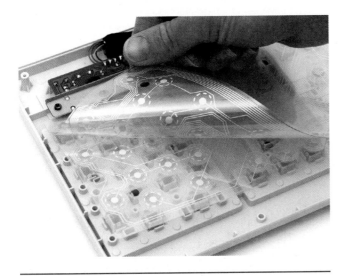

• **Figure 18.21**   Serious keyboard surgery

Sometimes dirt or foreign objects get under individual keys, requiring you to remove the key to get to the dirt or object. Removing individual keys from a keyboard is risky business, because keyboards are set up in many different ways. Most manufacturers use a process in which keys are placed on a single plastic post. In that case, you may use a screwdriver or other flat tool to safely pop off the key (Figure 18.22). Be careful! You'll need to use a good amount of force and the key will fly across the room. Other keyboard makers (mainly on laptops) use tiny plastic pins shaped like scissors. In that case, beware—if you try prying one of these off, you'll permanently break the key!

The bottom line when it comes to stuck keys is that the keyboard's probably useless with the stuck key, so you might as well try to clean it. Worse comes to worst, you can always buy another keyboard.

• **Figure 18.22** Prying off a key

Everything in this section works equally well for trackballs.

Mice

Have you ever tried to use Windows without a mouse? It's not fun, but it can be done. All techs eventually learn the Windows navigation hot keys for those times when mice fail, but all in all we do love our mice. Like keyboards, Windows comes with excellent drivers for all standard mice; the exception you're likely to encounter is the more advanced mice that come with extra buttons. Conveniently, the built-in Windows drivers consider a mouse's scroll wheel to be standard equipment and will support it.

You can adjust your mouse settings through the Mouse Control Panel applet. Figure 18.23 shows the Windows 2000 version. Be aware that the Mouse Properties window in Windows 2000 uses a different layout than that of Windows Vista (Figure 18.24) or Windows XP (which are almost identical).

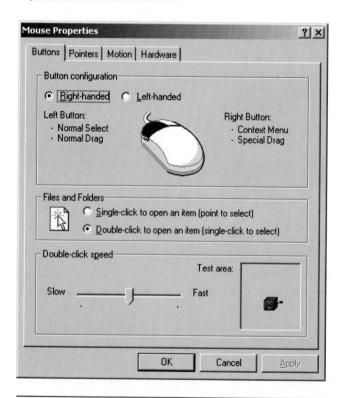

• **Figure 18.23** Windows 2000 Mouse Control Panel applet

• **Figure 18.24** Windows Vista Mouse Control Panel applet

Mike Meyers' CompTIA A+ Guide to Managing and Troubleshooting PCs

All of the settings you need for adjusting your mouse can be found in the Mouse Properties window. In particular, make sure to adjust the mouse speed, double-click speed, and acceleration to fit your preferences. Mouse speed and double-click speed are obvious, but mouse acceleration needs a bit of explaining as it has changed from Windows 2000 to Windows XP and Windows Vista. Originally, mouse *acceleration* referred to a feature that caused the mouse speed to increase when the mouse moved a relatively large distance across the screen. The Windows 2000 Mouse Properties window included a Motion tab where you could set the mouse speed and acceleration. Windows XP and Vista dropped the Motion tab in favor of an *Enhance pointer precision* checkbox on the Pointer Options tab (Figure 18.25). Enhance pointer precision is a much more advanced form of automatic acceleration. Although it works well, it can cause erratic mouse movements in some applications.

Currently, two types of mouse technologies dominate the market: ball mice and optical mice. **Ball mice** use a small round ball, while **optical mice** use LEDs or lasers and a camera to track their movements and thus move the mouse pointer across the screen. The problem with ball mice is that the ball inside the mouse picks up dirt over time and deposits the dirt on internal rollers that contact the ball. Dirt builds up to the point that the mouse stops responding smoothly. If you are struggling with your mouse to point at objects on your screen, you need to clean the mouse. Few mice manufacturers still make ball mice, as they tend to require far more maintenance than optical mice.

To access the internals of a ball mouse, turn it over and remove the protective cover over the mouse ball. The process of removing the cover varies, but it usually involves rotating the collar that surrounds the ball until the collar pops out (Figure 18.26). Be careful—without the collar, the mouse ball will drop out the instant you turn the mouse upright.

Use any nonmetallic tool to scrape the dirt from the roller without scratching or gouging the device. Although you could use a commercial "mouse cleaning kit," I find that a fingernail or a pencil eraser cleans the rollers quite nicely and at much less expense (Figure 18.27). Clean a ball mouse in this way at least every two or three months.

Optical mice require little maintenance and almost never need cleaning, as the optics that make them work are never in contact with the grimy outside world. On the rare occasion where an optical mouse begins to act erratically, try using a cloth or damp cotton swab to clean out any bits of dirt that may be blocking the optics (Figure 18.28).

• **Figure 18.25**   Enhance pointer precision checkbox on the Pointer Options tab

• **Figure 18.26**   Removing the collar on a ball mouse

• **Figure 18.27**   Cleaning the rollers on a ball mouse

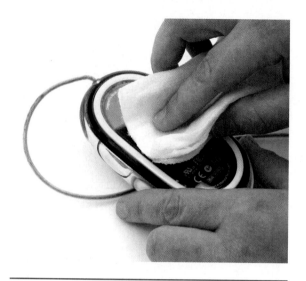

Scanners

You can use a scanner to make digital copies of existing paper photos, documents, drawings, and more. Better scanners give you the option of copying directly from a photographic negative or slide, providing images of stunning visual quality—assuming the original photo was halfway decent, of course! In this section, you'll look at how scanners work and then turn to what you need to know to select the correct scanner for you or your clients.

How Scanners Work

All consumer-level scanners—called **flatbed scanners**—work the same way. You place a photo or other object facedown on the glass, close the lid, and then use software to initiate the scan. The scanner runs a bright light along the length of the glass tray once or more to capture the image. Figure 18.29 shows an open scanner.

The scanning software that controls the hardware can be manifested in a variety of ways. Nearly every manufacturer has some sort of drivers and other software to create an interface between your computer and the scanner. When you push the front button on the Epson Perfection scanner in Figure 18.30, for example, the Epson software opens the Photoshop program as well as its own interface.

• **Figure 18.28**   Cleaning an optical mouse

• **Figure 18.29**   Scanner open with photograph face down

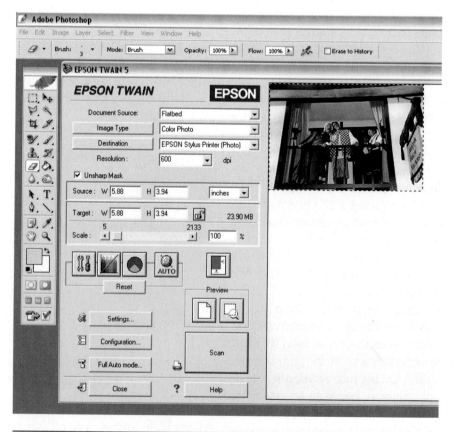

• **Figure 18.30**   Epson software with Photoshop open in the background

You can also open your favorite image-editing software first and choose to acquire a file from a scanner. Figure 18.31 shows the process of acquiring an image from a scanner in the popular shareware image-editing software, Paint Shop Pro. As in most such software, you choose File | Import and then select a source. In this case, the scanner uses the traditional TWAIN drivers. **TWAIN** stands for *Technology Without an Interesting Name*—I'm not making this up!—and has been the default driver type for scanners for a long time.

At this point, the drivers and other software controlling the scanner pop up, providing an interface with the scanner (as shown in Figure 18.31). Here you can set the resolution of the image as well as many other options.

How to Choose a Scanner

You must consider five primary variables when choosing a scanner: resolution, color depth, grayscale depth, connection, and scan speed. You can and will adjust the first three during the scanning process, although probably only down from their maximum. You need to decide on the connection before you buy. The scan speed relates to all four of the other variables, and the maximum speed is hard-coded into the scanner.

Configurable Variables   Scanners convert the scanned image into a grid of dots. The maximum number of dots determines how well you can capture an image and how the image will look when scaled up in size. Most folks use the term *resolution* to define the grid size. As you might imagine, the higher the resolution, the better the scanned image will look and scale.

Older scanners can create images of only 600 × 600 dots per inch (dpi), while newer models commonly achieve four times that density and high-end machines do much more. Manufacturers cite *two* sets of numbers for a scanner's resolution: the resolution it achieves mechanically—called the **optical resolution**—and the enhanced resolution it can achieve with assistance from some onboard software.

The enhanced resolution numbers are useless. I recommend at least 2400 × 2400 dpi optical resolution or better, although you can get by with a lower resolution for purely Web-destined images.

The **color depth** of a scan defines the number of bits of information the scanner can use to describe each individual dot. This number determines color, shade, hue, and so forth, so a higher number makes a dramatic difference in your picture quality. With binary numbers, each extra bit of information *doubles* the quality. An 8-bit scan, for example, can save up to 256 color variations per dot. A 16-bit scan, in contrast, can save up to 65,536 variations, not the 512 that you might expect!

Modern scanners come in 24-bit, 36-bit, and 48-bit variations. These days, 48-bit scanners are common enough that you shouldn't have to settle for less, even on a budget. Figures 18.32, 18.33, and 18.34 show pretty clearly the difference resolution makes when scanning.

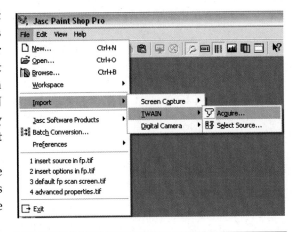

• **Figure 18.31**   Acquiring an image in Paint Shop Pro

• **Figure 18.32**   Earring scanned at 72 dpi and 24-bit color

---

• **Figure 18.33**   Same earring, scanned at 300 dpi and 24-bit color

• **Figure 18.34**   Same earring, scanned at 1200 dpi and 24-bit color

Scanners differ a lot in **grayscale depth**, a number that defines how many shades of gray the scanner can save per dot. This matters if you work with black-and-white images in any significant way, because grayscale depth is usually a much lower number than color depth. Current consumer-level scanners come in 8-bit, 12-bit, and 16-bit grayscale varieties. I recommend 16-bit or better.

Connection   Almost all modern scanners plug into the USB port on your PC, although some high-end models offer FireWire as well. Older scanners come in SCSI and parallel varieties.

Scanning Speed   Scanners have a maximum scanning speed defined by the manufacturer. The time required to complete a scan is also affected by the parameters you set; the time increases as you increase the amount of detail captured. A typical low-end scanner, for example, takes upwards of 30 seconds to scan a 4 × 6 photo at 300 dpi. A faster scanner, in contrast, can crank out the same scan in 10 seconds.

Raise the resolution of the scan to 600 dpi at 48-bit resolution, and that faster scanner can take a full minute to complete the scan. Adjust your scanning settings to optimize for your project. Don't always go for the highest possible scan if you don't need the resolution.

Connections matter as well. A good Hi-Speed USB scanner can scan an 8 × 10 image in about 12 seconds at 300 dpi. I made the mistake of taking the scanner to a friend's house to scan some of her jewelry, but she had only a Full-Speed USB port. I plugged the scanner into her PC and it took about 45 seconds to scan each 8 × 10 image. We were up all night finishing the project!

Installation and Scanning Tips

Most USB and FireWire devices require you to install the software drivers before you plug in the device for the first time. I have run into exceptions, though, so I strongly suggest you read the scanner's documentation before you install.

As a general rule, you should obtain the highest quality scan you can manage, and then play with the size and image quality when it's time to include it in a Web site or an e-mail. The amount of RAM in your system—and to a lesser extent, the processor speed—dictates how big a file you can handle.

For example, don't do 8 × 10 scans at 600 dpi if you have only 128 MB of RAM, because the image file alone weighs in at over 93 MB. Because your operating system, scanner software, image-editing program, and a lot of other things are taking up plenty of that RAM already, your system will likely crash.

If you travel a lot, you'll want to make sure to use the locking mechanism for the scanner light assembly. Just be sure to unlock before you try to use it or you'll get a light that's stuck in one position. That won't make for very good scans!

Digital Cameras

Another option available for those not-yet-taken pictures is to put away your point-and-shoot film camera and use a digital camera. **Digital cameras** electronically simulate older film-technology and provide a wonderful tool for capturing a moment and then sending it to friends and relatives.

The CompTIA A+ certification Practical Application exam tests you more thoroughly on troubleshooting scanner problems and preventive maintenance issues than does the Essentials exam. Look for questions on using the locking mechanism, keeping the scanner surface clean, and avoiding scanning sharp objects that could damage the scanner.

In a short period of time, digital camera prices have gone from levels that made them the province of a few wealthy technogeeks to being competitive with a wide range of electronic consumer goods. Because digital cameras interface with computers, CompTIA A+ certified techs need to know the basics.

Storage Media—Digital Film for Your Camera

Every consumer-grade camera saves the pictures it takes onto some type of *removable storage media*. Think of it as your digital film. Probably the most common removable storage media used in modern digital cameras (and probably your best choice) is the Secure Digital (SD) card (Figure 18.35). About the size of a Wheat Thin (roughly an inch square), you can find these tiny cards with capacities ranging from 64 MB to more than 1 GB. They are among the fastest of the various media types at transferring data to and from a PC, and they're quite sturdy.

• **Figure 18.35**   Secure Digital card

Connection

These days, almost all digital cameras plug directly into a USB port (Figure 18.36). Another common option, though, is to connect only the camera's storage media to the computer, using one of the many digital media readers available.

You can find readers designed specifically for SD cards, as well as other types. Plenty of readers can handle multiple media formats. Many computers come with a decent built-in digital media reader (Figure 18.37).

• **Figure 18.36**   Camera connecting to USB port

Quality

As with scanners, you should consider the amount of information a particular model of camera can capture, which in the digital camera world is expressed as some number of **megapixels**. Instead of light-sensitive film, digital cameras have one CCD (charged coupled device) or CMOS (complementary metal-oxide semiconductor) sensor covered with photosensitive pixels (called *photosites*) to capture the image; the more pixels on the sensor, the higher the resolution of the images it captures.

Not so long ago, a 1-megapixel digital camera was the bleeding edge of digital photographic technology, but now you can find cameras with 10 times that resolution for a few hundred dollars. As a basis of reference, a 2-megapixel camera produces snapshot-sized (4 × 6 inch) pictures with print photograph quality, whereas a 5-megapixel unit can produce a high-quality 8 × 10 inch print.

Another feature of most digital cameras is the capability to zoom in on your subject. The way you ideally want to do this is the way film cameras do it, by using the camera's optics—that's the lens. Most cameras above the

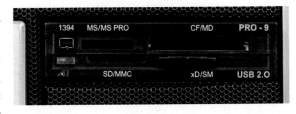

• **Figure 18.37**   Digital media reader built into computer

basic level have some **optical zoom**—meaning the zoom is built into the lens of the camera—but almost all models include multiple levels of **digital zoom**, accomplished by some very clever software in the camera. Choose your camera based on optical zoom: 3× at a minimum or better if you can afford it. Digital zoom is useless.

Form Factor

As was the case with film cameras, size matters on digital cameras. Digital cameras come in several form factors. They range from tiny, ultra-compact models that readily fit in a shirt pocket to monster cameras with huge lenses. Although it's not universally true, the bigger the camera, the more features and sensors it can have. Thus bigger is usually better in terms of quality. In shape, they come in a rectangular package, in which the lens retracts into the body, or as an SLR-type, with a lens that sticks out of the body. Figure 18.38 shows both styles.

- **Figure 18.38**   Typical digital cameras

- **Figure 18.39**   Video chatting by webcam with Skype

Read more about pixels and frame rates in Chapter 19, "Video."

Web Cameras

PC cameras, often called **webcams** because their most common use is for Internet video communication, are fairly new to the world of common I/O devices. Too many people run out and buy the cheapest one, not appreciating the vast difference between a discount webcam and more expensive models; nor do they take the time to configure the webcam properly. Let's consider some of the features you should look for when buying webcams and some of the problems you can run into when using them.

The biggest issue with webcams is the image quality. Webcams measure their resolution in pixels. You can find webcams with resolutions of as few as 100,000 pixels and webcams with millions of pixels. Most people who use webcams agree that 1.3 million pixels (megapixels) is pretty much the highest resolution quality you can use before your video becomes so large it will bog down even a broadband connection.

The next issue with webcams is the frame rate, that is, the number of times the camera "takes your picture" each second. Higher frame rates make for smoother video; 30 frames per second is considered the best. A good camera with a high megapixel resolution and fast frame rate will provide you with excellent video conferencing capabilities. Figure 18.39 shows the author using his headset to chat via webcam using Skype software.

Most people who use online video also want a microphone. Many cameras come with microphones, or you can use your own. Those who do a lot of video chatting may prefer to get a camera without a microphone and then buy a good quality headset with which to speak and listen.

Many cameras now can track you when you move, to keep your face in the picture—a handy feature for fidgety folks using video conferencing! This interesting technology recognizes a human face with little or no "training"

and rotates its position to keep your face in the picture. Some companies even add funny extras, which, although not very productive, are good for a laugh (Figure 18.40).

Almost all webcams use USB connections. Windows comes with a limited set of webcam drivers, so always make sure to install the drivers supplied with the camera before you plug it in. Most webcams use Hi-Speed USB, so make sure you're plugging your webcam into a Hi-Speed USB port.

Once the camera's plugged in, you'll need to test it. All cameras come with some type of program, but finding the program can be a challenge. Some brands put the program in the system tray, some place it in My Computer, others put it in the Control Panel—and some do all three! Figure 18.41 shows the Control Panel applet that appeared when I installed the webcam driver.

The biggest challenge to using webcams is getting your webcam applications to recognize that your webcam is available and configured for use. Every program does this differently, but conceptually the steps are basically the same (with plenty of exceptions):

1. Tell the program you want to use a camera.

2. Tell the program whether you want the camera to turn on automatically when you chat.

3. Configure the image quality.

4. Test the camera.

If you're having problems with a camera, always go through the general I/O problems first, as this will clear up most problems. If you're still having trouble getting the camera to work in a program, be sure to turn off all other programs that may be using the camera. Windows allows only one program at a time to use a webcam.

• **Figure 18.40** This webcam program's animated character mirrors your movements as you conference with friends or coworkers.

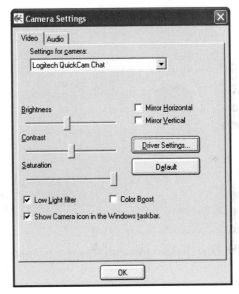

• **Figure 18.41** Camera Settings applet

■ Specialty I/O Devices

The CompTIA A+ certification exams want to make sure you're aware of four other types of I/O devices: biometric scanners, bar code readers, touch screens, and KVM switches. Let's look at these fairly specialized devices.

Biometric Devices

If you look up *biometrics* on the popular Wikipedia Web site, you'll get the following definition: "Biometrics (ancient Greek: *bios* ='life,' *metron* ='measure') is the study of automated methods for uniquely recognizing humans based upon one or more intrinsic physical or behavioral traits." (The quote might differ from what you find because Wikipedia changes pretty frequently, but the gist should be the same.)

The field of biometrics also encompasses a number of security devices, such as door locks and security cameras, that don't really fit into the world of PCs. This section concentrates on the types of biometrics that you can actually buy and use on your PC. Within the realm of computers, biometrics

includes a huge number of technologies, from thumb drives that read fingerprints to software that does voice recognition.

PCs use biometrics for security. **Biometric devices** scan and remember unique aspects of various body parts such as your retina, iris, head image, or fingerprint, using some form of sensing device such as a retinal scanner. This information is used as a key to prevent unauthorized people from accessing whatever the biometric device is securing. Most biometric devices currently used in PCs secure only themselves. The USB thumb drive in Figure 18.42 has a tiny fingerprint scanner. You slide your finger (any finger you choose) over the drive to unlock the contents of the thumb drive.

• **Figure 18.42** USB thumb drive with fingerprint scanner (*photo courtesy of Lexar Media, Inc.*)

Less common are biometric security devices that secure entire computers. The Microsoft fingerprint scanner is a USB device that replaces standard user name and password security. Figure 18.43 shows the scanner built into a keyboard. When a program or Web site asks for a user name and password, you simply press your finger against the fingerprint scanner. It confirms your identity (assuming your fingerprint matches), and then special software that comes with the scanner supplies the program or Web site with your stored user name and password.

Biometric devices are also used for recognition. Recognition is different from security in that the biometric device doesn't care who you are, it just wants to know what you're doing. The best example of this is voice recognition. Voice recognition programs convert human voice input into commands or text. Voice recognition for PCs has been around for some time. Although it has never achieved enough accuracy to replace a keyboard completely, voice recognition is common in devices that have a limited number of commands to interpret, such as cell phones and PDAs. If you speak the words "Call Mike Meyers" into your smartphone, your phone knows what to do—at least, *my* phone does!

• **Figure 18.43** Microsoft fingerprint scanner on a keyboard

No matter what biometric device you use, you use the same steps to make it work:

1. Install the device.

2. Register your identity with the device by sticking your eye, finger, or other unique body part (Why are you snickering?) into the device so it can scan you.

3. Configure its software to tell the device what to do when it recognizes your scanned identity.

• **Figure 18.44** Typical UPC code

Bar Code Readers

Bar code readers are designed to read standard **Universal Product Code (UPC)** bar codes (Figure 18.44). We read bar codes for only one reason—to track inventory. Bar code readers enable easy updating of inventory databases stored on PCs. Bar code readers are just about the oldest "specialty" I/O device used with PCs.

Two types of bar code readers are commonly found with PCs: pen scanners and hand scanners. Pen scanners look like an ink pen and must be swiped across the bar code (Figure 18.45). Hand scanners are held in front of the UPC code while a button is pressed to scan. All bar code readers emit a tone to let you know the scan was successful.

Older bar code readers used serial ports, but all of the newer readers use either PS/2 or USB ports. No configuration is usually necessary, other than making sure that the particular bar code reader works with whatever database/point of sale software you use. When in doubt, most people find the PS/2-style bar code readers work best, as they simply act like a keyboard. You plug the reader into your keyboard port and then plug your keyboard into the reader. Then all you need is software that accepts keyboard input (and what one doesn't!), and it will work.

• **Figure 18.45**   Pen scanner (*photo courtesy of Wasp Barcode Technologies*)

Touch Screens

A **touch screen** is a monitor with some type of sensing device across its face that detects the location and duration of contact, usually by a finger or stylus. All touch screens then supply this contact information to the PC as though it were a click event from a mouse. Touch screens are used in situations for which conventional mouse/keyboard input is either impossible or impractical. Here are a few places you'll see touch screens at work:

- Information kiosks
- PDAs
- Point of sale systems
- Tablet PCs

Touch screens can be separated into two groups: built-in screens like the ones in PDAs, and standalone touch screen monitors like those used in many point of sale systems. From a technician's standpoint, you can think of a standalone touch screen as a monitor with a built-in mouse. All touch screens have a separate USB or PS/2 port for the "mouse" part of the device, along with drivers you install just as you would for any USB mouse.

KVM Switches

A **keyboard, video, mouse (KVM) switch** is a hardware device that most commonly enables multiple computers to be viewed and controlled by a single mouse, keyboard, and screen. Some KVMs reverse that capability, enabling a single computer to be controlled by multiple keyboards, mice, or other devices. KVMs are especially useful in data centers where multiple servers are rack mounted, space is limited, and power is a concern. An administrator can use a single KVM to control multiple server systems from a single keyboard, mouse, and monitor.

There are many brands and types of KVM switches. Some enable you to connect to only two systems, and some support hundreds. Some even come with audio output jacks to support speakers. Typical KVMs come with two

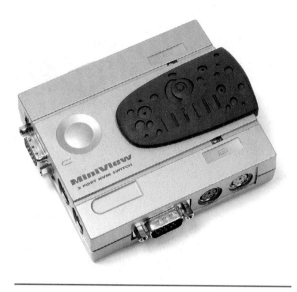

● **Figure 18.46**   A typical KVM switch

Older KVMs are said to be passive, meaning they don't continuously communicate with all connected systems. This can cause problems if the connected systems automatically reboot after a power surge or loss. Modern-day active KVMs resolve this issue through *peripheral emulation*, meaning they communicate with and monitor all systems connected to the KVM.

or more sets of wires that are used for input devices such as PS/2 and/or USB mice and video output (Figure 18.46).

To use a KVM, you simply connect a keyboard, mouse, and monitor to the KVM and then connect the KVM to the desired computers. Once connected and properly configured, assigned keyboard hotkeys—a combination of keys typically assigned by the KVM manufacturer—enable you to toggle between the computers connected to the KVM. In most cases, you simply tap the Scroll Lock key twice to switch between sessions.

Installing a KVM is not difficult; the most important point to remember is to connect the individual sets of cables between the KVM ports and each computer one at a time, keeping track of which keyboard, mouse, and video cable go to which computers. (I highly recommend labeling and using twist ties or zip ties.)

If you get the connections wrong, the KVM won't function as desired. If you connect a mouse and keyboard wires to the correct KVM port, for example, but attach the same computer's video cable to a different port on the KVM, you won't get the correct video when you try to switch to that computer. The same holds true for the mouse and keyboard cables. Don't cross the cables!

Chapter 18 Review

■ Chapter Summary

After reading this chapter and completing the exercises, you should understand the following about input/output.

Explain how to support common input/output ports

- Many new computers do not come with serial ports as other high-speed ports such as USB have replaced them. You can tell if you have serial ports by checking for the Ports (COM and LPT) icon in Device Manager.

- The UART chip that comprises the serial port converts data moving between the parallel expansion bus on a PC and the serial bus used by many I/O devices. Most serial port connectors consist of a 9-pin DB style connector. The connector on the PC or device itself (not the cable) is male. Serial ports are also known as RS-232, which is the standard that describes how serial ports work.

- The USB host controller (sometimes called a host adapter) controls every USB device connected to it. The host controller includes a root hub that provides the physical connection for devices. Host controllers support many ports, but the number of USB ports a system has is usually dependent on what the motherboard manufacturer decided to supply. The host controller is shared by every device plugged into it, so speed and power are reduced with each new device.

- Powered USB devices require their own power cord, in which case they do not pull power from the USB bus itself. Bus-powered devices draw their power directly from the USB bus and do not require a separate power cord. Too many bus-powered devices may result in system lockups, device lockups, or devices that just don't work. To solve the power problem, unplugging a device or two will lower the demand for bus power. Alternatively, you can purchase and install a USB expansion card, which will provide another USB host controller with its own set of connection ports.

- Three flavors of USB are in use today, and one is just around the bend: Low-Speed USB that runs at 1.5 Mbps, Full-Speed USB that runs at 12 Mbps, Hi-Speed USB that runs at 480 Mbps, and SuperSpeed USB that will run at up to 4.8 Gbps when it comes out in 2010. Many people refer to the low-speed

and full-speed devices as USB 1.1, although that's not correct; all three speeds are part of the USB 2.0 specification. You can plug a hi-speed device into a low-speed host—or *vice versa*—and the device will work just fine, but at the lower speed.

- In theory, the USB interface can support up to 127 devices on a single USB port; in reality, too many devices on a single USB chain will overtax its power capabilities. USB specifications allow for a maximum cable length of 5 meters, although you may add a powered USB hub every 5 meters to extend this distance.

- USB hubs extend the number of USB devices you can connect to a single port. Make sure you get a powered Hi-Speed USB hub so it will support the fastest speed and not draw power away from other devices.

- Normally, you will install the device driver before connecting the USB device to the system. Although this is the norm, it is not carved in stone. Be sure to read the manual that came with your device for instructions on installation. For example, many USB devices, such as flash drives, do not need a separate driver installed and work fine if simply plugged in (they can use the generic driver provided by Windows 2000/XP/Vista).

- The high transfer speed of FireWire makes transferring large video files quick and easy. Most modern digital video cameras use the IEEE 1394 interface for transferring video from camera to PC for editing. FireWire has two distinct types of connectors: a 6-pin powered connector and a 4-pin bus-powered connector. IEEE 1394a runs at 400 Mbps and IEEE 1394b runs at 800 Mbps.

- FireWire devices must connect directly to a root hub but may be daisy chained to support up to 63 devices. Similar to USB devices, you should install the drivers before connecting the FireWire device, but most devices can use the generic Windows driver and thus can be plugged in immediately.

- When troubleshooting problems, first determine if the issue is a port problem or a device problem. Swap out the troubled device for a known good device (one that works in another computer). If a known good device fails, you can safely assume you have a port

problem. If a known good device functions properly, you most likely have a device problem. For device problems, replace the device. For port problems, verify that the port is enabled, make sure you have the drive installed for the port itself, and check the condition of the cables and physical connectors.

Identify certain common input/output devices on a PC

- Keyboards are the oldest type of input device and still the primary way users input data. Although a keyboard works without the installation of additional drivers, you need to install drivers for specialty keyboards, such as keyboards with fancy buttons or other programmable features. If you're using a USB keyboard, make sure to enable USB keyboard support in CMOS Setup.

- Configure basic keyboard settings in the Keyboard Control Panel applet. You can change the repeat delay, repeat rate, and cursor blink rate. Clean dirty keys with a damp cloth or isopropyl alcohol. Compressed air works well to dislodge hair, dust, and other small objects from the keys. With most keyboards you can pop off individual keys to do some deep cleaning. Some keyboards (such as those on laptops) are not meant to have keys removed and doing so might permanently damage the keyboard.

- Mice work with the generic Windows drivers. You only need to install mouse drivers if your mouse has special programmable features, such as additional buttons. Various mouse settings can be configured via the Mouse control panel applet. Configurable settings include mouse speed, double-click speed, and acceleration.

- The internal rubber ball on a ball mouse should be cleaned every few months. Rotate the collar on the underside of the mouse to release the rubber ball. Optical mice, which use LEDs or lasers to track movement, may occasionally need their lenses wiped free of grime, but overall outperform and outlive ball mice.

- Flatbed scanners have a hinged lid and flat glass surface on which you can place material to be scanned. Most scanners come with software to control the hardware and to control the scanning process itself. The scan software allows you to select the color mode and resolution of the scanned document. Scanners use a traditional TWAIN driver to transfer digital images to the PC. Some scanners offer additional features, such as OCR capabilities.

- When choosing a scanner, consider the scanner's optical resolution (ignore the enhanced resolution), color depth, grayscale depth, connection type, and scan speed. The higher these numbers, the better quality the scanned images will be. Shoot for a minimum 2400 x 2400 dpi optical resolution, 48-bit color depth, 16-bit grayscale depth, and a Hi-Speed USB or FireWire connection.

- Most digital cameras store images on removable media, such as SD cards. Photos can be transferred to a PC by connecting the camera directly to a USB or FireWire port. Alternatively, if the PC is equipped with a media card reader, the flash memory card can be removed from the camera and inserted directly to the PC's card reader.

- A 2-megapixel camera will produce 4 × 6 pictures with print photograph quality, while a 5-megapixel camera will produce 8 × 10 pictures with print photograph quality. The more sensors a camera has, the better the image quality, so you'll find that physically larger cameras take better pictures than the tiny ones. Look for a camera with at least 3× optical zoom and ignore the digital zoom that is advertised.

- Webcams are often used for Internet video communication. A 1.3-megapixel webcam delivers a decent resolution video without bogging down a broadband connection. Look for a webcam that has a frame rate of about 30 frames per second. Some webcams come with built-in microphones, but if you want high-quality audio without feedback or echo, invest in a microphone headset. After installing the driver and connecting a webcam, be sure to configure it properly so your Internet chat software knows to use the webcam.

Describe how certain specialty input/output devices work on a PC

- Biometric devices scan various body parts, such as fingerprints or retinas, for authentication, security, and recognition. Some biometric devices control access to an entire PC, while some small devices, such as USB thumb drives, have biometric fingerprint scanners built in to control access to the single device. Voice recognition allows users to speak commands to the computer, such as "Call Mike Meyers" to dial the phone via a modem.

- Bar code readers read the standard Universal Product Code (UPC) bar code. The two types of bar code readers are pen scanners and hand scanners.

Pen scanners look like ink pens and must be swiped across the bar code. Hand scanners are aimed at the bar code and when a button or trigger is pressed, the reader scans the bar code. All bar code scanners produce an audible tone to verify that the bar code has been read. Old bar code readers used serial ports, but newer ones use either USB or PS/2 connections.

- Tablet PCs feature touch screens, as do information kiosks, PDAs, and point of sale systems. Touch screens can be operated with either a finger or a stylus. Some devices, such as PDAs, have built-in touch screens, while a point of sale system may use a standalone touch screen monitor.

- KVM switches are hardware devices with which multiple systems can be monitored and controlled by a single mouse, keyboard, and monitor. KVMs are most commonly used in datacenters, enabling administrators to control multiple rack-mounted servers from a single keyboard, mouse, and monitor station.

■ Key Terms

ball mouse (663)	megapixel (667)
bar code reader (670)	optical mouse (663)
biometric device (670)	optical resolution (665)
color depth (665)	optical zoom (668)
digital camera (666)	RS-232 (651)
digital zoom (668)	serial port (651)
FireWire (657)	touch screen (671)
flatbed scanner (664)	TWAIN (665)
Full-Speed USB (654)	universal asynchronous
grayscale depth (666)	receiver/transmitter (UART) (651)
Hi-Speed USB (654)	Universal Product Code (UPC) (670)
IEEE 1394a (658)	USB host controller (652)
IEEE 1394b (658)	USB hub (655)
keyboard, video, mouse (KVM) switch (671)	USB root hub (652)
Low-Speed USB (654)	webcam (668)

■ Key Term Quiz

Use the Key Terms list to complete the sentences that follow. Not all terms will be used.

1. Serial ports are defined by the _____ standard.

2. A(n) _____ is useful when scanning a page from a book; a(n) _____ is useful when scanning the price of retail items at a store.

3. A(n) _____ device transfers data at up to 12 Mbps on the universal serial bus.

4. A(n) _____ FireWire device transfers data at up to 800 Mbps.

5. A(n) _____ captures digital images on removable media; a(n) _____ transmits digital images across the Internet for video communication.

6. The amount of information a digital camera can capture is measured in _____.

7. A scanner's ability to produce color, hue, and shade is defined by its _____.

8. The _____ contains the logic to convert data moving between parallel and serial devices.

9. When comparing digital cameras and their zoom capabilities, pay attention to the _____ and ignore the _____.

10. For moving the mouse pointer, most people prefer a(n) _____ over a(n) _____ because the former is much easier to keep clean.

■ Multiple-Choice Quiz

1. How many devices can a single USB host controller support?

   A. 2

   B. 4

   C. 63

   D. 127

2. What is the maximum USB cable length as defined by the USB specifications?

   A. 4.5 feet

   B. 4.5 meters

   C. 5 feet

   D. 5 meters

3. Malfunctioning USB devices may be caused by which of the following?

   A. Too many USB devices attached to the host controller

   B. Improper IRQ settings for the device

   C. Device plugged in upside-down

   D. USB 1.1 device plugged into USB 2.0 port

4. FireWire dominates USB in which area?

   A. Keyboards and mice

   B. Digital video editing

   C. MP3 players

   D. Biometric devices

5. Which FireWire standard is properly matched with its speed?

   A. IEEE 1394a, 400 Mbps

   B. IEEE 1394a, 480 Mbps

   C. IEEE 1394b, 400 Mbps

   D. IEEE 1394b, 480 Mbps

6. FireWire supports a maximum of how many devices?

   A. 2

   B. 4

   C. 63

   D. 127

7. What icon does Device Manager display over disabled devices?

   A. Yellow triangle

   B. Red X

   C. Blue I

   D. Green D

8. A user reports that his mouse is jittery. What is the most likely cause?

   A. His optical mouse has the wrong driver installed.

   B. His wireless mouse has a dead battery.

   C. His ball mouse has acquired dirt in the rollers.

   D. He had one too many cups of coffee that morning.

9. Which specifications describe a high-quality webcam that won't bog down an Internet connection?

   A. 5 megapixels at 15 frames per second

   B. 1.3 megapixels at 15 frames per second

   C. 5 megapixels at 40 frames per second

   D. 1.3 megapixels at 30 frames per second

10. Which device is a biometric device?

    A. Bar code reader

    B. Optical mouse

    C. Retinal scanner

    D. Flatbed scanner

11. The number that defines how many shades of gray per dot a scanner can save is referred to as what?

    A. Resolution

    B. DPI

    C. Color depth

    D. Grayscale depth

12. A color depth of 16 bits can store how many color variations per dot?

    A. 16

    B. 32

    C. 512

    D. 65,536

13. Which of the following lists the technologies in order from slowest to fastest?

    A. serial, Full-Speed USB, Hi-Speed USB, IEEE 1394a, IEEE 1394b

    B. serial, Full-Speed USB, IEEE 1394a, Hi-Speed USB, IEEE 1394b

C. Full-Speed USB, serial, Hi-Speed USB, IEEE 1394a, IEEE 1394b

D. Low-Speed USB, serial, IEEE 1394a, Hi-Speed USB, IEEE 1394b

14. What do serial ports use to ensure that the sending device doesn't overload the receiving device with data?

A. Flow control

B. Parity

C. Stop bits

D. 7-bit chunking

15. While testing a newly installed KVM switch, you can't display the second connected system while tapping the SCROLL LOCK key. What is most likely the problem?

A. Incorrect KVM UPC code

B. Crossed video cable

C. Locked SCROLL LOCK key

D. Active KVM

■ Essay Quiz

1. A friend at the local film school needs a new keyboard and external hard drive. What advice can you give her about the connection style for each of these devices?

2. Dylan is excited because he just got a new USB digital camera. He tried to install it on his laptop, but the computer doesn't recognize it. He's called you for help. What will you tell him?

3. Ken asks for your help because he is always forgetting his Windows password. What can you recommend to make logons easier for him?

4. Sandra is having trouble with her modem and suspects her port settings may be off. She vaguely remembers reading in the manual that the stop bit should be set to 1. Explain to Sandra where she can verify this setting.

5. The new head of sales is frustrated because when she tries to use her keyboard, letters continue to print across the screen even if she quickly taps a key, resulting in messages that lllloooooooookkkk llllliiiiikkkkeeee tttthhhhiiiissss. How can you walk her through fixing this problem over the phone?

Lab Projects

• Lab Project 18.1

Many personal computers do not normally include FireWire ports. Check the following three Web sites: www.dell.com, www.hp.com, and www.apple.com. Is a FireWire port standard built-in equipment on their new computers? If so, how many FireWire ports are included? If not, do the sites offer FireWire as an optional add-on?

• Lab Project 18.2

Explore the Keyboard and Mouse Control Panel applets. Change the settings and try to use the devices. Which settings caused the most frustration?

Were there any changes you made that you preferred over the original settings?

• Lab Project 18.3

Grab a lab partner and a stop watch. How many input devices can you two name in 30 seconds? Reset the timer. How many output devices can you two name in 30 seconds? Are any devices considered both input and output?

Video

In this chapter, you will learn how to

- **Explain how video displays work**
- **Select the proper video card**
- **Install and configure video**
- **Troubleshoot basic video problems**

The term *video* encompasses a complex interaction among numerous parts of the PC, all designed to put a picture on the screen. The **monitor** or **video display** shows you what's going on with your programs and operating system. It's the primary output device for the PC. The video card or **display adapter** handles all of the communication between the CPU and the monitor (see Figure 19.1). The operating system needs to know how to handle communication between the CPU and the display adapter, which requires drivers specific for each card and proper setup within Windows. Finally, each application needs to be able to interact with the rest of the video system.

Let's look at monitors and video cards individually. I'll bring them back together as a team later in the chapter so you can understand the many nuances that make video so challenging. Let's begin with the video display and then move to the video card.

• Figure 19.1   Typical monitor and video card

Video Displays

To understand displays, you need a good grasp of each component and how they work together to make a beautiful (or not so beautiful) picture on the screen. Different types of displays use different methods and technologies to accomplish this task. Video displays for PCs come in three varieties: CRT, LCD, and projectors. The first two you'll see on the desktop or laptop; the last you'll find in boardrooms and classrooms, splashing a picture onto a screen.

Historical/Conceptual

CRT Monitors

Cathode ray tube (CRT) monitors were the original computer monitors—those heavy, boxy monitors that take up half your desk. Although for the most part they've been replaced by LCD technology on new systems, plenty of CRT monitors are still chugging away in the field. As the name implies, this type of display contains a large cathode ray tube, a type of airtight vacuum tube. One end of this tube is a slender cylinder that contains three electron guns. The other end of the tube, which is fatter and wider, is the display screen.

Before we begin in earnest, I want to give you a note of warning about the inside of a traditional monitor. I will discuss what can be repaired and what requires more specialized expertise. Make no mistake—the interior of a monitor might appear similar to the interior of a PC because of the printed circuit boards and related components, but the similarity ends there. No PC has voltages exceeding 15,000 to 30,000 V, but most monitors do. So let's get one thing perfectly clear: Opening up a monitor can kill you! Even when the power is disconnected, certain components retain a substantial voltage for an extended period of time. You can inadvertently short one of the components and fry yourself—to death. Given this risk, certain aspects of monitor repair lie outside the necessary skill set for a normal PC support person, and definitely outside the CompTIA A+ certification exam domains! I will show you how to address the problems you can fix safely and make sure you understand the ones you need to hand over to a monitor shop.

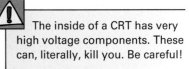
The inside of a CRT has very high voltage components. These can, literally, kill you. Be careful!

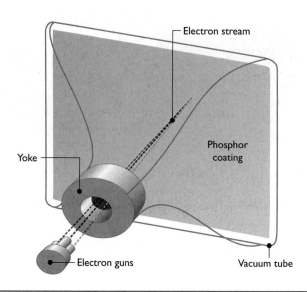

• **Figure 19.2** Electron stream in the CRT

Tech Tip

Perfect Flat

All CRT tubes can be categorized into two types: traditional curved-screen CRTs and CRTs that are often referred to as perfect flat—using a kind of vacuum tube that has a completely flat screen and no bending around the edges. The perfect flat screens offer a wider viewing angle than standard CRT screens. About the only negative to the perfect flat screens is that they tend to lack true black, so pictures seem just shy of a natural richness of color and contrast.

The inside of the display screen has a phosphor coating. When power is applied to one or more of the electron guns, a stream of electrons shoots towards the display end of the CRT (see Figure 19.2). Along the way, this stream is subjected to magnetic fields generated by a ring of electromagnets called a *yoke* that controls the electron beam's point of impact. When the phosphor coating is struck by the electron beam, it releases its energy as visible light.

When struck by a stream of electrons, a phosphor quickly releases a burst of energy. This happens far too quickly for the human eye and brain connection to register. Fortunately, the phosphors on the display screen have a quality called **persistence**, which means the phosphors continue to glow after being struck by the electron beam. Too much persistence and the image is smeary; too little and the image appears to flicker. The perfect combination of beam and persistence creates the illusion of a solid picture.

Essentials

Refresh Rate

The monitor displays video data as the electron guns make a series of horizontal sweeps across the screen, energizing the appropriate areas of the phosphorous coating. The sweeps start at the upper-left corner of the monitor and move across and down to the lower-right corner. The screen is "painted" only in one direction; then the electron guns turn and retrace their path across the screen, to be ready for the next sweep. These sweeps are called **raster lines** (see Figure 19.3).

The speed at which the electron beam moves across the screen is known as the **horizontal refresh rate (HRR)**, as shown in Figure 19.4. The monitor draws a number of lines across the screen, eventually covering the screen with glowing phosphors. The number of lines is not fixed, unlike television

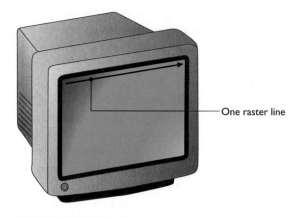

One raster line

The time it takes to draw one line across the screen and be ready for the next is called the horizontal refresh rate (HRR). This is measured in KHz (thousands of lines per second).

● **Figure 19.3** Electron guns sweep from left to right.

● **Figure 19.4** Horizontal refresh rate

screens, which have a set number of lines. After the guns reach the lower-right corner of the screen, they turn off and point back to the upper-left corner. The amount of time it takes to draw the entire screen and get the electron guns back to the upper-left corner is called the **vertical refresh rate (VRR)**, shown in Figure 19.5.

The monitor does not determine the HRR or VRR; the video card "pushes" the monitor at a certain VRR and then the monitor sets the corresponding HRR. If the video card is set to push at too low a VRR, the monitor produces a noticeable flicker, causing eyestrain and headaches for users. Pushing the monitor at too high a VRR, however, causes a definite distortion of the screen image and will damage the circuitry of the monitor and eventually destroy it. The number one killer of monitors is improper VRR settings, and the number one reason your office is filled with crabby workers is that the VRR is set too low. All

The number of times per second the electron guns can draw the entire screen and then return to the upper left-hand corner is called the vertical refresh rate (VRR). This is measured in Hz (screens per second).

● **Figure 19.5** Vertical refresh rate

good PC support techs understand this and take substantial time tweaking the VRR to ensure that the video card pushes the monitor at the highest VRR without damaging the monitor—this is the Holy Grail of monitor support!

Phosphors and Shadow Mask

All CRT monitors contain dots of phosphorous or some other light-sensitive compound that glows *red*, *green*, or *blue* (RGB) when an electron gun sweeps over it. These **phosphors** are evenly distributed across the front of the monitor (see Figure 19.6).

Try This!

Discovering Your Refresh Rate

You should know the refresh rate for all CRTs you service. Setting up monitors incorrectly can cause havoc in the workplace, so Try This!

1. Most PCs have two places where you can discover the current refresh rate of the monitor. Many monitors offer a menu button for adjusting the display. Often it shows the refresh rate when you push it once.

2. If that doesn't work, go to the Control Panel and open the Display applet (Windows 2000/XP) or Personalization applet (Windows Vista/7). Select the Settings tab (2000/XP) or Display Settings option (Vista/7) and then click the Advanced or Advanced Settings button. Select the Monitor tab in the Monitor Properties dialog box.

3. Write down your refresh rate. How does it compare with that of your classmates?

• **Figure 19.6** A monitor is a grid of red, green, and blue phosphors.

• **Figure 19.7** Shadow mask

A normal CRT has three electron guns: one for the red phosphors, one for the blue phosphors, and one for the green phosphors. It is important to understand that the electron guns do not fire colored light; they simply fire electrons at different intensities, which then make the phosphors glow. The higher the intensity of the electron stream, the brighter the color produced by the glowing phosphor.

Directly behind the phosphors in a CRT is the **shadow mask**, a screen that allows only the proper electron gun to light the proper phosphors (see Figure 19.7). This prevents, for example, the red electron beam from "bleeding over" and lighting neighboring blue and green dots.

The electron guns sweep across the phosphors as a group, turning rapidly on and off as they move across the screen. When the group reaches the end of the screen, it moves to the next line. It is crucial to understand that turning the guns on and off, combined with moving the guns to new lines, creates a mosaic that is the image you see on the screen. The number of times the guns turn on and off, combined with the number of lines drawn on the screen, determines the number of mosaic pieces used to create the image. These individual pieces are called **pixels**, from the term *picture elements*. You can't hold a pixel in your hand; it's just the area of phosphors lit at one instant when the group of guns is turned on. The size of pixels can change, depending on the number of times the group of guns is turned on and off and the number of lines drawn.

Resolution

Monitor **resolution** is always shown as the number of horizontal pixels times the number of vertical pixels. A resolution of 640 × 480, therefore, indicates a horizontal resolution of 640 pixels and a vertical resolution of 480 pixels. If you multiply the values together, you can see how many pixels are on each screen: 640 × 480 = 307,200 pixels per screen. An example of resolution affecting the pixel size is shown in Figure 19.8.

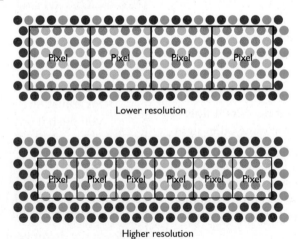

• **Figure 19.8** Resolution versus pixel size

Some common resolutions are 640 × 480, 800 × 600, 1024 × 768, 1280 × 960, 1280 × 1024, and 1600 × 1200. Notice that most of these resolutions match a 4:3 ratio. This is called the **aspect ratio**. Many monitors are shaped like television screens, with a 4:3 aspect ratio, so most resolutions are designed to match—or at least be close to—that shape. Other monitors, generically called *wide-screen monitors*, have a 16:9 or 16:10 ratio. Two of the common resolutions you'll see with these monitors are 1366 × 768 and 1920 × 1200.

See the "Modes" section later in this chapter for the names of each resolution.

The last important issue is to determine the maximum possible resolution for a monitor. In other words, how small can one pixel be? Well, the answer lies in the phosphors. A pixel must be made up of at least one red, one green, and one blue phosphor to make any color, so the smallest theoretical pixel would consist of one group of red, green, and blue phosphors: a **triad** (see Figure 19.9). Various limitations in screens, controlling electronics, and electron gun technology make the maximum resolution much bigger than one triad.

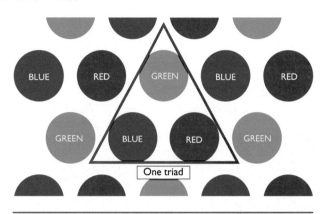

● **Figure 19.9**   One triad

Dot Pitch

The resolution of a monitor is defined by the maximum amount of detail the monitor can render. The dot pitch of the monitor ultimately limits this resolution. The **dot pitch** defines the diagonal distance between phosphorous dots of the same color, and is measured in *millimeters* (*mm*). Because a lower dot pitch means more dots on the screen, it usually produces a sharper, more defined image (see Figure 19.10). Dot pitch works in tandem with the maximum number of lines the monitor can support to determine the greatest working resolution of the monitor. It might be possible to place an image at 1600 × 1200 on a 15-inch monitor with a dot pitch of 0.31 mm, but it would not be very readable.

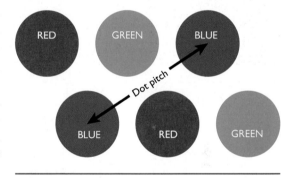

● **Figure 19.10**   Measuring dot pitch

The dot pitch can range from as high as 0.39 mm to as low as 0.18 mm. For most Windows-based applications on a 17-inch monitor, many people find that 0.28 mm is the maximum usable dot pitch that still produces a clear picture.

Bandwidth

Bandwidth defines the maximum number of times the electron gun can be turned on and off per second. Bandwidth is measured in *megahertz* (*MHz*). In essence, bandwidth tells us how fast the monitor can put an image on the screen. A typical value for a better-quality 17-inch color monitor would be around 150 MHz, which means that the electron beam can be turned on and off 150 million times per second. The value for a monitor's bandwidth determines the maximum VRR the video card should push the monitor for any given resolution. It reads as follows:

maximum VRR = bandwidth ÷ pixels per page

For example, what is the maximum VRR that a 17-inch monitor with a bandwidth of 100 MHz and a resolution of 1024 × 768 can support? The answer is

maximum VRR = 100,000,000 ÷ (1024 × 768) = 127 Hz

That's a pretty good monitor, as most video cards do not push beyond 120 Hz! At a resolution of 1200 × 1024, the vertical refresh would be

100,000,000 ÷ (1200 × 1024) = 81 Hz

So, we would make sure to set the video card's VRR to 80 Hz or less. If you had a monitor with a bandwidth of only 75 MHz, the maximum VRR at a 1200 × 1024 resolution would be only 61 Hz.

Most monitor makers know that people aren't going to take the time to do these calculations. Instead, they do the calculations for you and create tables of refresh rates at certain resolutions to show what a monitor can do.

Great! Now that you have the basics of CRT monitors, let's turn to LCD monitors. Although the technology differs dramatically between the monitor types, most of the terms used for CRTs also apply to LCD functions.

LCD Monitors

Liquid crystal displays (LCDs) are the most common type of display technology for PCs. LCD monitors have many advantages over CRTs. They are thinner and lighter, use much less power, are virtually flicker free, and don't emit potentially harmful radiation. LCDs still have resolution, refresh rates, and bandwidth, but LCDs also come with their own family of abbreviations, jargon, and terms you need to understand so you can install, maintain, and support LCDs.

How LCDs Work

The secret to understanding LCD panels is to understand the concept of the polarity of light. Anyone who played with a prism in sixth grade or has looked at a rainbow knows that light travels in waves (no quantum

mechanics here, please!), and the wavelength of the light determines the color. What you might not appreciate is the fact that light waves emanate from a light source in three dimensions. It's impossible to draw a clear diagram of three-dimensional waves, so instead, let's use an analogy. To visualize this, think of light emanating from a flashlight. Now think of the light emanating from that flashlight as though someone was shaking a jump rope. This is not a rhythmic shaking, back and forth or up and down; it's more as if a person went crazy and was shaking the jump rope all over the place—up, down, left, right—constantly changing the speed.

That's how light really acts. Well, I guess we could take the analogy one step further by saying the person has an infinite number of arms, each holding a jump rope shooting out in every direction to show the three-dimensionality of light waves, but (a) I can't draw that and (b) one jump rope will suffice to explain LCD panels. The varying speeds create wavelengths, from very short to very long. When light comes into your eyes at many different wavelengths, you see white light. If the light came in only one wavelength, you would see only that color. Light flowing through a polarized filter (like sunglasses) is like putting a picket fence between you and the people shaking the ropes. You see all of the wavelengths, but only the waves of similar orientation. You would still see all of the colors, just fewer of them because you only see the waves of the same orientation, making the image darker. That's why many sunglasses use polarizing filters.

Now, what would happen if you added another picket fence but put the slats in a horizontal direction? This would effectively cancel out all of the waves. This is what happens when two polarizing filters are combined at a 90-degree angle—no light passes through.

Now, what would happen if you added a third fence between the two fences with the slats at a 45-degree angle? Well, it would sort of "twist" some of the shakes in the rope so that the waves could then get through. The same thing is true with the polarizing filters. The third filter twists some of the light so that it gets through. If you're really feeling scientific, go to any teacher's supply store and pick up three polarizing filters for about (US)$3 each and try it. It works.

Liquid crystals take advantage of the property of polarization. Liquid crystals are composed of a specially formulated liquid full of long, thin crystals that always want to orient themselves in the same direction, as shown in Figure 19.11. This substance acts exactly like a liquid polarized filter. If you poured a thin film of this stuff between two sheets of glass, you'd get a darn good pair of sunglasses.

Imagine cutting extremely fine grooves on one side of one of those sheets of glass. When you place this liquid in contact with a finely grooved surface, the molecules naturally line up with the grooves in the surface (see Figure 19.12).

If you place another finely grooved surface, with the grooves at a 90- degree orientation to the other

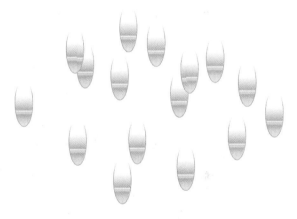

• **Figure 19.11**   Waves of similar orientation

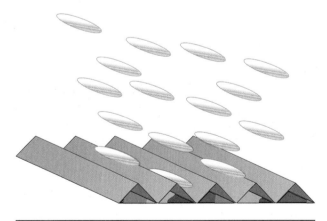

• **Figure 19.12**   Liquid crystal molecules tend to line up together.

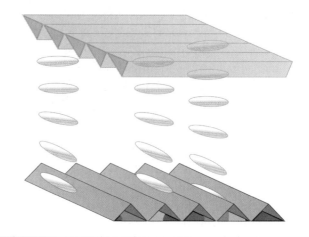

• Figure 19.13 Liquid crystal molecules twisting

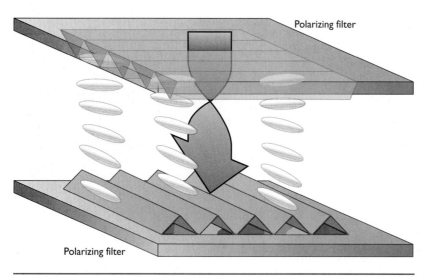

Polarizing filter

Polarizing filter

• Figure 19.14 No charge, enabling light to pass

surface, opposite of the first one, the molecules in contact with that side will attempt to line up with it. The molecules in between, in trying to line up with both sides, will immediately line up in a nice twist (see Figure 19.13). If two perpendicular polarizing filters are then placed on either side of the liquid crystal, the liquid crystal will twist the light and enable it to pass (see Figure 19.14).

If you expose the liquid crystal to an electrical potential, however, the crystals will change their orientation to match the direction of the electrical field. The twist goes away and no light passes through (see Figure 19.15).

LCD pixels are very different from the pixels in a CRT. A CRT pixel's size changes depending on the resolution. The pixels in an LCD panel are fixed and cannot be changed. See the section called "LCD Resolution" later in the chapter for the scoop.

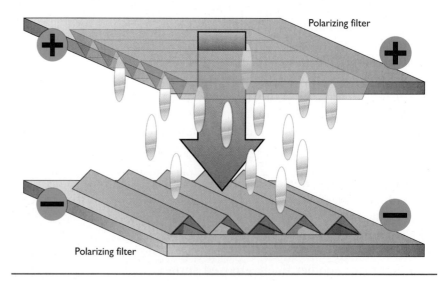

Polarizing filter

Polarizing filter

• Figure 19.15 Electrical charge, no light is able to pass

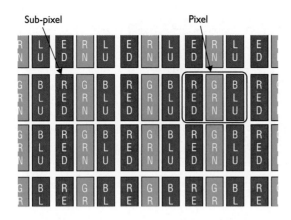

• Figure 19.16 LCD pixels

A color LCD screen is composed of a large number of tiny liquid crystal molecules (called **sub-pixels**) arranged in rows and columns between polarizing filters. A translucent sheet above the sub-pixels is colored red, green, or blue. Each tiny distinct group of three sub-pixels—one red, one green, and one blue—form a physical pixel, as shown in Figure 19.16.

Once all of the pixels are laid out, how do you charge the right spots to make an image? Early LCDs didn't use rectangular pixels. Instead, images were composed of different-shaped elements, each electrically separate from the others. To create an image, each area was charged at the same time. Figure 19.17 shows the number zero, a display made possible by charging six areas to make an ellipse of sorts. This process, called *static charging*, is still quite popular in more basic numeric displays such as calculators.

The static method would not work in PCs due to its inherent inflexibility. Instead, LCD screens use a matrix of wires (see Figure 19.18). The vertical wires, the Y wires, run to every sub-pixel in the column. The horizontal wires, the X wires, run along an entire row of sub-pixels. There must be a charge on both the X and the Y wires to make enough voltage to light a single sub-pixel.

If you want color, you have three matrices. The three matrices intersect very close together. Above the intersections, the glass is covered with tiny red, green, and blue dots. Varying the amount of voltage on the wires makes different levels of red, green, and blue, creating colors (see Figure 19.19).

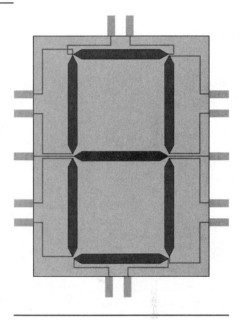

• Figure 19.17 Single character for static LCD numeric display

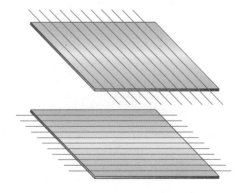

• Figure 19.18 An LCD matrix of wires

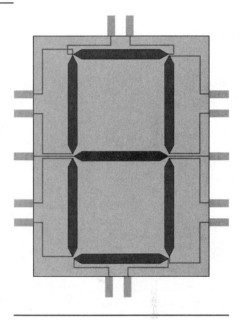

• Figure 19.19 Passive matrix display

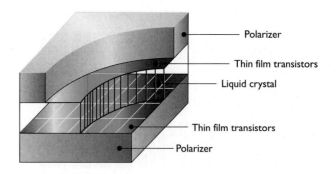

● **Figure 19.20**   Active matrix display

We call this usage of LCD technology **passive matrix**. All LCD displays on PCs used only passive matrix for many years. Unfortunately, passive matrix is slow and tends to create a little overlap between individual pixels. This gives a slightly blurred effect to the image displayed. Manufacturers eventually came up with a speedier method of display, called **dual-scan passive matrix**, in which the screen refreshed two lines at a time. Although other LCD technologies have since appeared, dual-scan continues to show up on some lower-end LCD panels.

Thin Film Transistor

A vast improvement over dual scan is called **thin film transistor (TFT)** or **active matrix** (Figure 19.20). Instead of using X and Y wires, one or more tiny transistors control each color dot, providing faster picture display, crisp definition, and much tighter color control. TFT is the LCD of choice today, even though it is much more expensive than passive matrix.

LCD Components

The typical LCD projector is composed of three main components: the LCD panel, the backlight(s), and the inverters. The LCD panel creates the image, the **backlights** illuminate the image so you can see it, and the **inverters** send power to the backlights. Figure 19.21 shows a typical layout for the internal components of an LCD monitor.

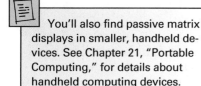

You'll also find passive matrix displays in smaller, handheld devices. See Chapter 21, "Portable Computing," for details about handheld computing devices.

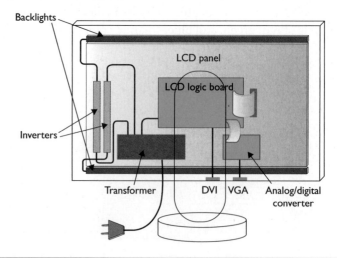

Backlights

LCD panel

LCD logic board

Inverters

Transformer   DVI VGA   Analog/digital converter

● **Figure 19.21**   LCD internals

One of the great challenges to LCD power stems from the fact that the backlights need AC power while the electronics need DC power. The figure shows one of the many ways that LCD monitor makers handle this issue. The AC power from your wall socket goes into an AC/DC transformer that changes the power to DC. The LCD panel uses this DC power.

Note in Figure 19.21 that this monitor has two backlights: one at the top and one at the bottom. Most LCDs have two backlights, although many only have one. All LCD backlights use **cold cathode fluorescent lamp (CCFL)** technology, popular for its low power use, even brightness, and long life. Figure 19.22 shows a CCFL from an LCD panel.

CCFLs need AC power to operate, but given that the transformer converts the incoming AC power to DC, each CCFL backlight needs a device called an inverter to convert the DC power back into AC. Figure 19.23 shows a typical inverter used in an LCD.

Looking once again at Figure 19.21, note the DVI and VGA inputs. DVI is a digital signal, so it connects directly to the LCD's logic circuitry. The VGA goes to an analog to digital converter before reaching the LCD logic board.

Keep in mind that Figure 19.21 is a generic illustration. The actual location and interconnections of the components are as variable as the number of LCD panels available today!

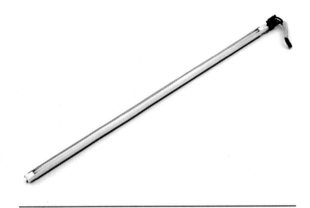

● **Figure 19.22** CCFL backlight

● **Figure 19.23** Inverter

 Try This!

Test the Viewing Angle of LCDs

Take a trip to your local computer store to look at LCD displays. Don't be distracted looking at all of the latest graphics cards, sound cards, CPUs, motherboards, and RAM—well, actually, it's okay to look at those things. Just don't forget to look at LCDs!

Stand about two feet in front of an LCD display. Look directly at the image on the screen and consider the image quality, screen brightness, and color. Take a small step to your right. Compare the image you see now to the image you saw previously. Continue taking small steps to the right until you are no longer able to discern the image on the display. You've reached the edge of the viewing angle for that LCD.

Do this test with a few different monitors. Do smaller LCDs, such as 15-inch displays, have smaller viewing angles? Do larger displays have better viewing angles? You might also want to test the vertical viewing angles of some monitors. Try to find an LCD that is on your eye level; then look at it from above and below—does it have a large viewing range vertically?

Two LCD panels that have the same physical size may have different native resolutions.

Tech Tip

Dealing with High-Resolution LCDs

The hard-wired nature of LCD resolution creates a problem for techs and consumers when dealing with bigger, better-quality monitors. A typical 15-inch LCD has a 1024 × 768 resolution, but a 17-inch usually has 1280 × 1024 or higher. These high resolutions make the menus and fonts on a monitor super tiny, a problem for people with less-than-stellar vision. Many folks throw in the towel and run these high-end LCDs at lower resolution and just live with the lower-quality picture, but that's not the best way to resolve this problem.

With Windows XP (and to a lesser extent with the earlier versions of Windows), Microsoft allows incredible customizing of the interface. You can change the font size, shape, and color. You can resize the icons, toolbars, and more. You can even change the number of dots per inch (DPI) for the full screen, making everything bigger or smaller!

For basic customizing, start at the Control Panel | Display applet | Appearance tab or Control Panel | Personalization applet. To change the DPI for the display, go to the Settings tab and click the Advanced button in Windows XP; in Windows Vista, just click the Adjust font size (DPI) *option in the Tasks list. Your clients will thank you!*

One nit equals one candela/ m². One candela is roughly equal to the amount of light created by a candle.

LCD Resolution

All LCD monitors have a **native resolution**, such as 1680 × 1050, that enables them to display the sharpest picture possible. As mentioned earlier, the pixels are fixed. You simply cannot run an LCD monitor at a resolution higher than the native one. Worse, because LCDs have no equivalent to a shadow mask, they can't run at a *lower* than native resolution without severely degrading image quality. A CRT can simply use more dots and the filtering and smoothing of the shadow mask to make a picture at a lower resolution look as good and crisp as the same picture at a higher resolution, but an LCD cannot. The LCD has to use an edge-blurring technique called **anti-aliasing** to soften the jagged corners of the pixels when running at lower than native resolution, which simply does not look as good. The bottom line? Always set the LCD at native resolution!

Brightness

The strength of an LCD monitor's backlights determines the brightness of the monitor. The brightness is measured in **nits**. LCD panels vary from 100 nits on the low end to over 1000 nits or more on the high end. Average LCD panels are around 300 nits, which most monitor authorities consider excellent brightness.

Response Rate

An LCD panel's **response rate** is the amount of time it takes for all of the sub-pixels on the panel to go from pure black to pure white and back again. This is roughly the same concept as the CRT refresh rate, but with one important difference. Once the electron gun on a CRT lights a phosphor, that phosphor begins to fade until it is lit again. Individual LCD sub-pixels hold their intensity until the LCD circuitry changes that sub-pixel, making the problem of flicker nonexistent on LCDs.

Manufacturers measure LCD response rates in milliseconds, with lower being better. A typical lower-end or older LCD has a response rate of 20–25 ms. The screens look fine, but you'll get some ghosting if you try to watch a movie or play a fast-paced video game. In recent years, manufacturers have figured out how to overcome this issue, and you can find many LCD monitors with a response rate of 6–8 ms.

Refresh Rate

The refresh rate for an LCD monitor uses numbers similar to that for a CRT monitor, such as 60 Hz, but the terms mean slightly different things between the two technologies. With CRTs, as you'll recall, the phosphors on the screen start to lose their glow and need to be hit again by the electron guns many times per second to achieve an unwavering or flicker-free image. Each dot on an active matrix LCD, in contrast, has its own transistor to light it up. There's no need to freshen up the dot; it's on or off. Regardless of the refresh rate for the LCD, therefore, there's never any flicker at all.

The refresh rate for an LCD monitor refers to how often a screen can change or update completely. Think of the refresh rate as a metronome or timer and you'll be closer to how it works in an LCD. For most computing issues, 60 Hz is fine and that's been the standard for the industry. Humans see

things that change as infrequently as 24 times per second—the standard for motion pictures at the cinema, for example, and the best high-definition (HD) signal—as a full motion video. To be able to change almost three times faster is perfectly acceptable, even in higher-end applications such as fast-moving games.

Monitor manufacturers have released 120-Hz LCD monitors in a response to the convergence of LCDs, televisions, and computers to enable you to see HD movies or standard-definition (SD) content without any problems or visual artifacts on an LCD monitor. The easiest number that provides a whole-number division for both 24 frames per second and 30 frames per second was 120 Hz. The latter is the standard for SD content.

> A video card needs to be able to support Dual-Link DVI to run a 120-Hz monitor or television. See the discussion on DVI later in this chapter for details.

Contrast Ratio

A big drawback of LCD monitors is that they don't have nearly the color saturation or richness of contrast of a good CRT monitor—although LCD technology continues to improve every year. A good contrast ratio—the difference between the darkest and lightest spots that the monitor can display—is 450:1, although a quick trip to a computer store will reveal LCDs with lower levels (250:1) and higher levels (1000:1).

LCD monitor manufacturers market a *dynamic contrast ratio* number for their monitors, which measures the difference between a full-on, all-white screen versus a full-off, all-black screen. This yields a much higher number than the standard contrast ratio. My Samsung panels have a 1000:1 contrast ratio, for example, but a 20,000:1 dynamic contrast ratio. Sounds awesome, right? In general, the dynamic contrast ratio doesn't affect viewing on computer monitors. Focus on the standard contrast ratio when making decisions on LCD screens.

Projectors

Projectors are a third option for displaying your computer images and the best choice when displaying to an audience or in a classroom. There are two ways to project an image on a screen: rear-view and front-view. As the name would suggest, a **rear-view projector** (Figure 19.24) shoots an image onto a screen from the rear. Rear-view projectors are always self-enclosed and very popular for televisions, but are virtually unheard of in the PC world.

A **front-view projector** shoots the image out the front and counts on you to put a screen in front at the proper distance. Front-view projectors connected to PCs running Microsoft PowerPoint have been the cornerstone of every meeting almost everywhere for at least the past ten years (Figure 19.25). This section deals exclusively with front-view projectors that connect to PCs.

• Figure 19.24   Rear-view projector (*photo courtesy of Samsung*)

• Figure 19.25   Front-view projector (*photo courtesy of Dell Inc.*)

• Figure 19.26   CRT projector

Another type of technology that's seen in projectors but is outside the scope of the CompTIA A+ exams is called digital light processing (DLP). Check out the "Beyond A+" section of this chapter for details.

Projector Technologies

Projectors that connect to PCs have been in existence for almost as long as PCs themselves. Given all that time, a number of technologies have been used in projectors. The first generation of projectors used CRTs. Each color used a separate CRT that projected the image onto a screen (Figure 19.26). CRT projectors create beautiful images but are expensive, large, and very heavy, and have for the most part been abandoned for more recent technologies.

Given that light shines through an LCD panel, LCD projectors are a natural fit for front projection. LCD projectors are light and very inexpensive compared to CRTs but lack the image quality. LCD projectors are so light that almost all portable projectors use LCD (Figure 19.27).

All projectors share the same issues as their equivalent technology monitors. LCD projectors have a specific native resolution, for example. In addition, you need to understand three concepts specific to projectors: lumens, throw, and lamps.

Lumens

The brightness of a projector is measured in lumens. A **lumen** is the amount of light given off by a light source from a certain angle that is perceived by the human eye. The greater the lumen rating of a projector, the brighter the projector will be. The best lumen rating depends on the size of the room and the amount of light in the room. There's no single answer for "the right lumen rating" for a projector, but use this as a rough guide. If you use a projector in a small, darkened room, 1000 to 1500 lumens will work well. If you use a projector in a mid-sized room with typical lighting, you'll need at least 2000 lumens. Projectors for large rooms have ratings over 10,000 lumens and are very expensive.

Throw

A projector's **throw** is the size of the image at a certain distance from the screen. All projectors have a recommended minimum and maximum throw distance that you need to take into consideration. A typical throw would be expressed as follows. A projector with a 16:9 image-aspect ratio needs to be 11 to 12 feet away from the projection surface to create a 100-inch diagonal screen. A *long throw lens* has about a 1:2 ratio of screen size to distance, so to display a 4-foot screen, you'd have to put the projector 8 feet away. Some *short throw lenses* drop that ratio down as low as 1:1!

• Figure 19.27   LCD projector (*photo courtesy of ViewSonic*)

Lamps

The bane of every projector is the lamp. Lamps work hard in your projector, as they must generate a tremendous amount of light. As a result, they generate quite a bit of heat, and all projectors come with a fan to keep the lamp from overheating. When you turn off a projector, the fan continues to run until the lamp is fully cooled. Lamps are also expensive, usually in the range of a few hundred dollars (U.S.), which comes as a nasty shock to someone who's not prepared for that price when the lamp dies!

Common Features

CRT or LCD, all monitors share a number of characteristics that you need to know for purchase, installation, maintenance, and troubleshooting.

Size

You need to take care when buying CRT monitors. CRT monitors come in a large number of sizes, all measured in inches (although most metric countries provide the metric equivalent value). All monitors provide two numbers: the monitor size and the actual size of the screen. The monitor size measures from two opposite diagonal corners. The actual screen is measured from one edge of the screen to the opposite diagonal side. This latter measurement is often referred to as the **viewable image size (VIS)**. You will commonly see a size difference of one to two inches between the two measurements (see Figure 19.28). A 17-inch CRT monitor, for example, might have a 15.5-inch VIS.

LCD monitors dispense with the two values and simply express the VIS value. You must consider this issue when comparing LCDs to CRTs. A 15-inch LCD monitor will have about the same viewing area as a 17-inch CRT.

Monitor size   Viewable image size

• **Figure 19.28**   Viewable image size of a CRT

Connections

CRT monitors for PCs all use the famous 15-pin, three-row, DB-type connector (see Figure 19.29) and a power plug. The DB connector is also called a *D-shell* or

You'll often hear the terms *flat-panel display* or *LCD panel* to describe LCD monitors. I prefer the term *LCD monitor*, but you should be prepared to hear it a few different ways.

• **Figure 19.29**   A traditional CRT connector

D-subminiature connector. Larger or multipurpose monitors may have a few other connectors, but as far as the CRT is concerned, these are the only two you need for video.

Unlike the analog CRTs, LCD monitors need a digital signal. This creates somewhat of an issue. The video information stored on a video card's RAM is clearly digital. All VGA and better video cards include a special chip (or function embedded into a chip that does several other jobs) called the **random access memory digital-to-analog converter (RAMDAC)**. As the name implies, RAMDAC takes the digital signal from the video card and turns it into an analog signal for the analog CRT (see Figure 19.30). The RAMDAC can also convert digital to analog.

Well, RAMDACs certainly make sense for analog CRT monitors. However, if you want to plug your LCD monitor into a regular video card, you need a RAMDAC on the LCD monitor to convert the signal from analog to digital (see Figure 19.31).

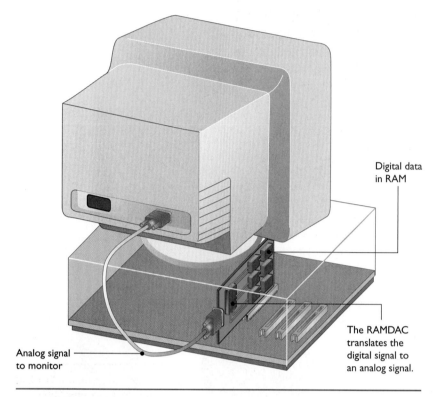

Digital data in RAM

The RAMDAC translates the digital signal to an analog signal.

Analog signal to monitor

• **Figure 19.30**   An analog signal sent to a CRT monitor

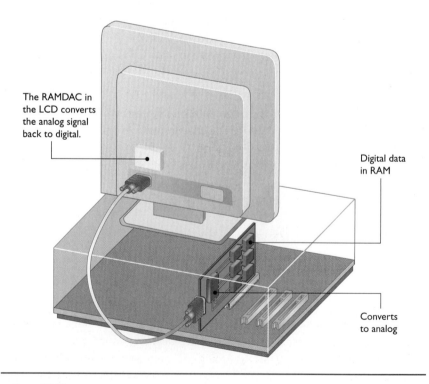

The RAMDAC in the LCD converts the analog signal back to digital.

Digital data in RAM

Converts to analog

• **Figure 19.31**   Converting analog back to digital on the LCD

Many LCD monitors use exactly this process. These are called *analog LCD monitors*. The monitor really isn't analog; it's digital, but it takes a standard VGA input. These monitors have one advantage: You may use any standard VGA video card. But these monitors require adjustment of the analog timing signal to the digital clock inside the monitor. This used to be a fairly painful process, but most analog LCD monitors now include intelligent circuitry to make this process either automatic or very easy.

Why convert the signal from digital to analog and then back to digital? Well, many monitor and video card people agree that it just doesn't make much sense. We now see quite a few digital LCD monitors and digital video cards. They use a completely different connector than the old 15-pin DB connector used on analog video cards and monitors. After a few false starts with connection standards, under names such as P&D and DFP, the digital LCD world, with a few holdouts, moved to the **digital visual interface (DVI)** standard. DVI is actually three different connectors that look very much alike: DVI-D is for digital, DVI-A is for analog (for backward compatibility if the monitor maker so desires), and the DVI-A/D or DVI-I (interchangeable) accepts either a DVI-D or DVI-A. DVI-D and DVI-A are keyed so that they will not connect.

DVI-D and DVI-I connectors come in two varieties, single-link and dual-link. *Single-link DVI* has a maximum bandwidth of 165 MHz, which, translated into practical terms, limits the maximum resolution of a monitor to 1920 × 1080 at 60 Hz or 1280 × 1024 at 85 Hz. *Dual-link DVI* uses more pins to double throughput and thus grant higher resolutions (Figure 19.32). With dual link, you can have displays up to a whopping 2048 × 1536 at 60 Hz!

Digital connectors are quickly replacing analog in the monitor world. Digital makes both the monitor and the video card cheaper, provides a clearer signal because no conversion is necessary, and makes installation easy. Many monitors and video cards these days only support digital signals, but there are still quite a few of each that provide both digital and analog connections.

The video card people have it easy. They either include both a VGA and a DVI-D connector or they use a DVI-I connector. The advantage to DVI-I is that you can add a cheap DVI-I to VGA adapter (one usually comes with the video card) like the one shown in Figure 19.33 and connect an analog monitor just fine.

Monitor makers have it tougher. Most LCD monitor makers have made the jump to DVI, but many include a VGA connector for those machines that still need it.

Unless you're buying a complete new system, you'll rarely buy a video card at the same time you buy a monitor. When you're buying a monitor or a video card, make sure that the new device will connect to the other!

Adjustments

Most adjustments to the monitor take place at installation, but for now, let's just make sure you know what they are and where they are located. Clearly, all monitors have an On/Off button or switch. Also, see if you can locate the Brightness and Contrast buttons. Beyond that, most monitors (at least the only ones you should buy) have an onboard menu system, enabling a number of adjustments. Every monitor maker provides a different way to access these menus, but they all provide two main functions: physical screen

● **Figure 19.32** Dual-link DVI-I connector

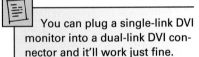

You can plug a single-link DVI monitor into a dual-link DVI connector and it'll work just fine.

● **Figure 19.33** DVI to VGA adapter

Video cards with two video connectors support dual monitors. See the "Dual Monitors" section later in this chapter.

• **Figure 19.34**   Typical menu controls

adjustment (bigger, smaller, move to the left, right, up, down, and others) and color adjustment. The color adjustment lets you adjust the red, green, and blue guns to give you the best color tones. All of these settings are a matter of personal taste. Make sure the person who will use the computer understands how to adjust these settings (see Figure 19.34).

Power Conservation

CRT and LCD monitors differ greatly in the amount of electricity they require. The bottom line is that CRTs use a lot and LCDs use a lot less. Here's the scoop.

Approximately half the power required to run a desktop PC is consumed by the CRT monitor. Monitors that meet the Video Electronics Standards Association (VESA) specification for **display power management signaling (DPMS)** can reduce monitor power consumption by roughly 75 percent. This is accomplished by reducing or eliminating the signals sent by the video card to the monitor during idle periods. By eliminating these pulses, the monitor essentially takes catnaps. The advantage over simply shutting the monitor off is in the time it takes to restore the display.

A typical CRT monitor consumes approximately 120 watts. During a catnap or power-down mode, the energy consumption is reduced to below 25 watts, while enabling the screen to return to use in less than ten seconds. Full shutoff is accomplished by eliminating all clocking pulses to the monitor. Although this reduces power consumption to below 15 watts, it also requires anywhere from 15 to 30 seconds to restore a usable display.

A typical LCD monitor, in contrast, uses less than half the electricity that a CRT uses. A 19-inch, 4:3 aspect-ratio flat panel, for example, uses around 33 watts at peak usage and less than 2 watts in DPMS mode. Larger LCDs use more power at peak usage than smaller ones. A 21-inch wide-screen model, for example, might draw ~75 watts at peak but drop down to less than 2 watts in DPMS mode. Swapping out CRTs with LCDs is a great way to save on your electric bill!

Tech Tip

Power Switch versus DPMS

Turning off the monitor with the power switch is the most basic form of power management. The downside to this is the wear and tear on the CRT. The CRT is the most expensive component of a monitor, and frequently turning it on and off can damage the CRT. When using a non-DPMS monitor or video card, it is best to turn the monitor on once during the day and then turn it off only when you are finished for the day. This on-off cycle must be balanced against the life of the CRT display phosphors. The typical monitor loses about half its original brightness after roughly 10,000 to 15,000 hours of display time. Leaving the monitor on all of the time brings a noticeable decrease in brightness in just over a year (8766 hours). The only way around this is enabling the DPMS features of the monitor or taking care to turn the monitor off.

■ Video Cards

The video card, or display adapter, handles the video chores within the PC, processing information from the CPU and sending it out to the monitor. The video card is composed of two major pieces: the video RAM and the video processor circuitry. The video RAM stores the video image. On the first video cards, this RAM was good old dynamic RAM (DRAM), just like the RAM on the motherboard. Today's video cards often have better RAM than your system has! The video processing circuitry takes the information on the video RAM and shoots it out to the monitor. Although early video processing circuitry was little more than an intermediary between the CPU and the video RAM, modern video processors are more powerful than all but the latest CPUs! It's not at all uncommon to see video cards that need fans to cool their onboard processors (see Figure 19.35).

This section looks at five aspects that define a video card: display modes, motherboard connection, graphics processor circuitry, video memory, and connections.

● **Figure 19.35**   Video card with a cooling fan

Modes

The trick to understanding video cards is to appreciate the beginnings and evolution of video. Video output to computers was around long before PCs were created. At the time PCs became popular, video was almost exclusively text-based, meaning that the only image the video card could place on the monitor was one of the 256 ASCII characters. These characters were made up of patterns of pixels that were stored in the system BIOS. When a program wanted to make a character, it talked to DOS or to the BIOS, which stored the image of that character in the video memory. The character then appeared on the screen.

The beauty of text video cards was that they were simple to use and cheap to make. The simplicity was based on the fact that only 256 characters existed, and no color choices were available—just monochrome text.

You could, however, choose to make the character bright, dim, normal, underlined, or blinking. Positioning the characters was easy, as space on the screen allowed for only 80 characters per row and 24 rows of characters.

Long ago, RAM was very expensive, so video card makers were interested in using the absolute least amount of RAM possible. Making a monochrome text video card was a great way to keep down RAM costs. Let's consider this for a minute. First, the video RAM is where the contents of the screen are located. You need enough video RAM to hold all of the necessary information for a completely full screen. Each ASCII character needs eight bits (by definition), so a monitor with 80 characters/row and 24 rows will need

80 characters × 24 rows = 1920 characters = 15,360 bits or 1920 bytes

The video card would need less than 2000 bytes of memory, which isn't much, not even in 1981 when the PC first came out. Now, be warned that I'm glossing over a few things—where you store the information about

underlines, blinking, and so on. The bottom line is that the tiny amount of necessary RAM kept monochrome text video cards cheap.

Very early on in the life of PCs, a new type of video, called a *graphics video card*, was invented. It was quite similar to a text card. The text card, however, was limited to the 256 ASCII characters, whereas a graphics video card enabled programs to turn any pixel on the screen on or off. It was still monochrome, but programs could access any individual pixel, enabling much more creative control of the screen. Of course, it took more video RAM. The first graphics cards ran at 320×200 pixels. One bit was needed for each pixel (on or off), so

$320 \times 200 = 64,000$ bits or 8000 bytes

That's a lot more RAM than was needed for text, but it was still a pretty low amount of RAM—even in the old days. As resolutions increased, however, the amount of video RAM needed to store this information also increased.

After monochrome video was invented, moving into color for both text and graphics video cards was a relatively easy step. The only question was how to store color information for each character (text cards) or pixel (graphics cards). This was easy—just set aside a few more bits for each pixel or character. So now the question becomes, "How many bits do you set aside?" Well, that depends on how many colors you want. Basically, the number of colors determines the number of bits. For example, if you want four colors, you need 2 bits (2 bits per pixel). Then, you could do something like this

00 = black	01 = cyan (blue)
10 = magenta (reddish pink)	11 = white

So if you set aside 2 bits, you could get four colors. If you want 16 colors, set aside 4 bits, which would make 16 different combinations. Nobody ever invented a text mode that used more than 16 colors, so let's start thinking in terms of only graphics mode and bits per pixels. To get 256 colors, each pixel would have to be represented with 8 bits. In PCs, the number of colors—called the **color depth**—is always a power of 2: 4, 16, 256, 64 K, and so on. Note that as more colors are added, more video RAM is needed to store the information. Here are the most common color depths and the number of bits necessary to store the color information per pixel:

2 colors = 1 bit (mono)

4 colors = 2 bits

16 colors = 4 bits

256 colors = 8 bits

64 K colors = 16 bits

16.7 million colors = 24 bits

Most technicians won't say, for example, "I set my video card to show over 16 million colors." Instead, they'll say, "I set my color depth to 24 bits." Talk in terms of bits, not colors. It is assumed that you know the number of colors for any color depth.

You can set the color depth for a Windows 2000 or Windows XP computer in the Display Properties applet on the Settings tab (Figure 19.36). If you set up a typical Windows XP computer, you'll notice that Windows offers you 32-bit color quality, which might make you assume you're about to crank out more than 4 billion colors, but that's simply not the case. The 32-bit color setting offers 24-bit color plus an 8-bit alpha channel. An alpha channel controls the opacity of a particular color. By using an alpha channel, Windows can more effectively blend colors to create the effect of semi-transparent images. In Windows XP, you see this in the drop shadow under a menu; in Windows Vista, almost every screen element can be semi-transparent (Figure 19.37).

Your video card and monitor are capable of showing Windows in a fixed number of different resolutions and color depths. The choices depend on the resolutions and color depths the video card can push to the monitor and the amount of bandwidth your monitor can support. Any single combination of resolution and color depth you set for your system is called a **mode**. For standardization, VESA defines a certain number of resolutions, all derived from the granddaddy of video modes: VGA.

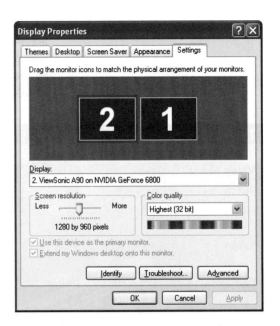

• **Figure 19.36** Adjusting color settings in Windows XP

VGA

With the introduction of the PS/2, IBM introduced the **video graphics array (VGA)** standard. This standard offered 16 colors at a resolution of 640 × 480 pixels. VGA supported such an amazing variety of colors by using an analog video signal instead of a digital one, as was the case prior to the VGA standard. A digital signal is either all on or all off. By using an analog signal, the VGA standard can provide 64 distinct levels for the three colors (RGB)—that is, 64^3 or 262,144 possible colors—although only 16 or 256 can be seen at

To accommodate rotated LCD monitors in portrait view, the video resolution numbers might be reversed. Rather than 1280 × 1024, for example, you might see 1024 × 1280. The amount of RAM needed remains the same regardless.

• **Figure 19.37** Semi-transparency in Windows Vista

Proprietary

S-video

• **Figure 19.47**   S-video and proprietary round connectors

• **Figure 19.48**   Composite and component connection options

• **Figure 19.49**   HDMI port on Lenovo laptop

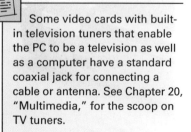

Some video cards with built-in television tuners that enable the PC to be a television as well as a computer have a standard coaxial jack for connecting a cable or antenna. See Chapter 20, "Multimedia," for the scoop on TV tuners.

DVD player, or video camera. The earliest type of connector commonly found is the S-video connector. This provides decent-quality video output or, in some cases, input. More commonly now you see both a proprietary round connector that supports S-video and a proprietary dongle that adds support for video through either component connection or composite connections. Figure 19.47 shows the similar round ports.

A composite connector provides a video signal through a single cable, whereas a component adapter provides a split signal, red, green, and blue. Figure 19.48 shows the two connector dongles.

The best connections for outputting to television are the High Definition Multimedia Interface (HDMI) connectors. Although a few devices offer HDMI output directly (such as the portable pictured in Figure 19.49), most video cards support HDMI through a special cable that connects to a dual-link DVI port. Figure 19.50 shows an example of such a cable.

• **Figure 19.50**   DVI to HDMI cable

■ Installing and Configuring Video

Once you've decided on the features and price for your new video card or monitor, you need to install them into your system. As long as you have the right connection to your video card, installing a monitor is straightforward. The challenge comes when installing the video card.

During the physical installation of a video card, watch out for two possible issues: long cards and proximity of the nearest PCI card. Some high-end video cards simply won't fit in certain cases or block access to needed motherboard connectors such as the IDE sockets. There's no clean fix for such a problem—you simply have to change at least one of the components (video card, motherboard, or case). Because high-end video cards run very hot, you don't want them sitting right next to another card; make sure the fan on the video card has plenty of ventilation space. A good practice is to leave the slot next to the video card empty to allow better airflow (Figure 19.51).

Once you've properly installed the video card and connected it to the monitor, you've conquered half the territory for making the video process work properly. You're ready to tackle the drivers and tweak the operating system, so let's go!

● **Figure 19.51**   Installing a video card

Try This!

Install a Video Card

You know how to install an expansion card from your reading in earlier chapters. Installing a video card is pretty much the same, so Try This!

1. Refer to Chapter 8, "Expansion Bus," for steps on installing a new card.

2. Plug the monitor cable into the video card port on the back of the PC and power up the system. If your PC seems dead after you install a video card, or if the screen is blank but you hear fans whirring and the internal speaker sounding off *long-short-short-short*, your video card likely did not get properly seated. Unplug the PC and try again.

Software

Configuring your video software is usually a two-step process. First you need to load drivers for the video card. Then you need to open the Control Panel and go to the Display applet (Windows 2000/ XP) or Personalization applet (Windows Vista/7) to make your adjustments. Let's explore how to make the video card and monitor work in Windows.

Drivers

Just like any other piece of hardware, your video card needs a driver to function. Video card drivers install pretty much the same way as all of the other drivers we've discussed thus far: either the driver is already built into Windows or you must use the installation CD that comes with the video card.

Video card makers are constantly updating their drivers. Odds are good that any video card more than a few months old has at least one driver update. If possible, check the manufacturer's Web site and use the driver

located there if there is one. If the Web site doesn't offer a driver, it's usually best to use the installation CD. Always avoid using the built-in Windows driver as it tends to be the most dated.

We'll explore driver issues in more detail after we discuss the Display applet. Like so many things about video, you can't fully understand one topic without understanding at least one other!

Using the Display/Personalization Applet

With the driver installed, you're ready to configure your display settings. The Display applet or Personalization applet on the Control Panel is your next stop. The **Display applet** and **Personalization applet** provide convenient, central locations for all of your display settings, including resolution, refresh rate, driver information, and color depth.

The default Display applet window in Windows XP, called the Display Properties dialog box (Figure 19.52), has five tabs: Themes, Desktop, Screen Saver, Appearance, and Settings. Earlier versions of Windows have a subset of these tabs. The first four tabs have options you can choose to change the look and feel of Windows and set up a screensaver; the fifth tab is where you make adjustments that relate directly to your monitor and video card.

The Personalization applet in Windows Vista offers functions similar to the Display applet, but each function manifests as a clickable option rather than as a separate tab (Figure 19.53). Four of the seven options mirror the look and feel options of earlier

• **Figure 19.52**   Display Properties dialog box in Windows XP

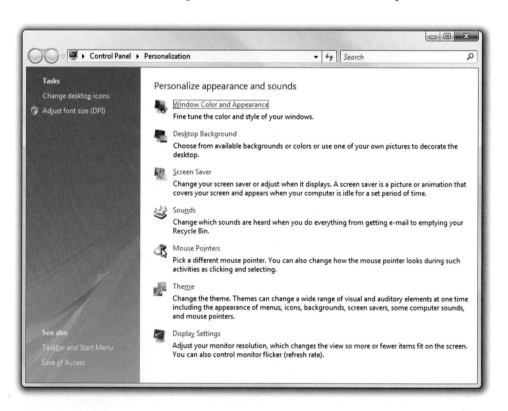

• **Figure 19.53**   Personalization applet in Windows Vista

versions of Windows, such as Window Color and Appearance, Desktop Background, Screen Saver, and Theme. The last option, Display Settings, is where you make adjustments to your monitor and video card. Two options, Sounds and Mouse Pointers, don't concern us at all at this time.

Whether discussing tabs or options, the functions on both applets are pretty much the same, so let's do this in one discussion. I'll point out any serious differences among the versions.

Making the Screen Pretty

Three tabs/options in the Display/Personalization applet have the job of adjusting the appearance of the screen: Themes/Theme, Desktop/Desktop Background, and Appearance/ Windows Color and Appearance. Windows themes are preset configurations of the look and feel of the entire Windows environment (Figure 19.54).

The Desktop tab/option (Figure 19.55) defines the background color or image. In Windows XP, it also includes the handy Customize Desktop button that enables you to define the icons as well as any Web pages you want to appear on the desktop. Windows Vista/7 give you the option to position the image on the screen (Figure 19.56), and the *Change desktop icons* option on the Tasks list in the Personalization applet enables you to choose which system icons (such as Computer, Recycle Bin, and Network) show up on your desktop, as well as which graphical icons they use.

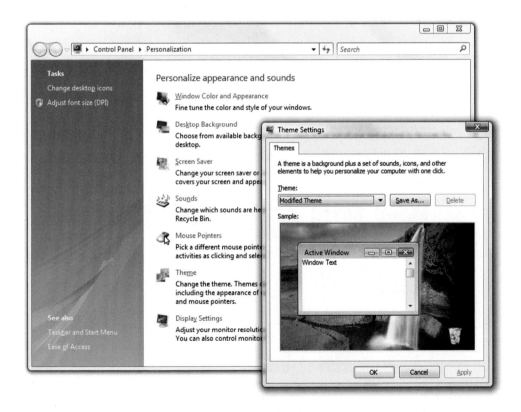

• **Figure 19.54** Theme option in the Personalization applet

• **Figure 19.55** Desktop tab on Display Properties dialog box

The last of the tabs for the look and feel of the desktop in Windows 2000/XP is the Appearance tab. Think of the Appearance tab as the way to fine-tune the theme to your liking. The main screen gives only a few options—the real power is when you click the Advanced button (Figure 19.57). Using

• **Figure 19.56** Desktop Background options in Windows Vista

this dialog box, you may adjust almost everything about the desktop, including the types of fonts and colors of every part of a window.

The Window Color and Appearance option in Windows Vista/7 is a little simpler on the surface, enabling you to change the color scheme, intensity, and transparency (Figure 19.58). You can unlock the full gamut of options, though, by clicking the *Open classic appearance properties for more color options* link.

Screen Saver

At first glance, the Screen Saver tab/option seems to do nothing but set the Windows screensaver—no big deal, just about everyone has set a screensaver. But another option on the Screen Saver tab gets you to one of the most important settings of your system: power management. Click on the Power button or *Change power settings* option to get to the Power Options Properties dialog box or Power Options applet (Figure 19.59).

The tabs and options define all of the power management of the system. Power management is a relatively involved process, so we'll save the big

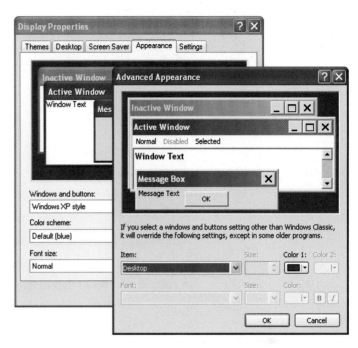

• **Figure 19.57** Advanced Appearance dialog box

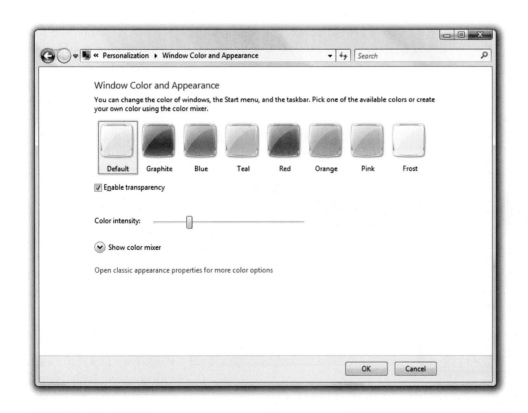

• **Figure 19.58** Window Color and Appearance option

• **Figure 19.59**   Power Options Properties dialog box

discussion for where we need to save power the most: Chapter 21, "Portable Computing."

Settings Tab/Display Settings Applet

The Settings tab or Display Settings applet (Figure 19.60) is the centralized location for configuring all of your video settings. From the main screen you can adjust both the resolution and the color depth. Windows only displays resolutions and color depths that your video card/monitor combination can accept and that are suitable for most situations. Everyone has a favorite resolution, and higher isn't always better. Especially for those with trouble seeing small screen elements, higher resolutions can present a difficulty—already small icons are *much* smaller at 1280 × 1024 than at 800 × 600. Try all of the resolutions to see which you like—just remember that LCD monitors look sharpest at their native resolution (usually the highest listed).

The color quality is the number of colors displayed on the screen. You can change the screen resolution with a simple slider, adjusting the color depth from 4-bit all of the way up to 32-bit color. Unless you have an older video card or a significant video speed issue, you'll probably set your system for 32-bit color and never touch this setting again.

• **Figure 19.60**   Settings tab

Another option you may see in the Settings tab is dual monitors. Windows supports the use of two (or more) monitors. These monitors may work together like two halves of one large monitor, or the second monitor might simply show a duplicate of what's happening on the first monitor. Dual monitors are handy if you need lots of screen space but don't want to buy a really large, expensive monitor (Figure 19.61). Microsoft calls this feature **DualView**.

There are two ways to set up dual monitors: plug in two video cards or use a single video card that supports two monitors (a "dual-head" video card). Both methods are quite common and work well. Dual monitors are easy to configure: just plug in the monitors and Windows should detect them. Windows will show both monitors in the Settings tab, as shown in Figure 19.62. By default, the second monitor is not enabled. To use the second monitor, just select the *Extend the desktop onto this monitor* checkbox.

If you need to see more advanced settings, click on…that's right, the Advanced or Advanced Settings button (Figure 19.63). The title of this dialog box reflects the monitor and video card. As you can see in the screen shot, this particular monitor is a Samsung SyncMaster T220 running off of an ATI Radeon 3800 series video card.

The two tabs you're most likely to use are the Adapter and Monitor tabs. The Adapter tab gives detailed information about the video card, including the amount of video memory, the graphics processor, and the BIOS

• **Figure 19.61**   My editor hard at work with dual monitors

Windows supports *DualView* technology, enabling you to use multiple monitors.

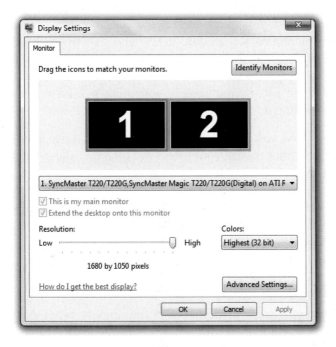

• **Figure 19.62**   Enabling dual monitors

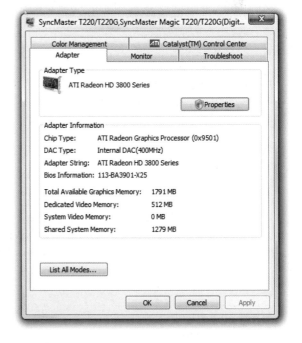

• **Figure 19.63**   Advanced video settings

• Figure 19.64   Monitor tab

All LCD monitors have a fixed refresh rate.

• Figure 19.65   Third-party video tab

information (yup, your video card has a BIOS, too!). You can also click on the *List All Modes* button to change the current mode of the video card, although any mode you may set here, you can also set in the sliders on the main screen.

If you're still using a CRT, you'll find the Monitor tab a handy place. This is where you can set the refresh rate (Figure 19.64). Windows only shows refresh rates that the monitor says it can handle, but many monitors can take a faster—and therefore easier on the eyes—refresh rate. To see all of the modes the video card can support, uncheck the *Hide modes that this monitor cannot display* option.

If you try this, always increase the refresh rate in small increments. If the screen looks better, use it. If the screen seems distorted or disappears, wait a moment and Windows will reset to the original refresh rate. Be careful when using modes that Windows says the monitor cannot display. Pushing a CRT past its fastest refresh rate for more than a minute or two can damage it.

Most video cards add their own tab to the Advanced dialog box, such as the one shown in Figure 19.65. This tab adjusts all of the specialized settings for that video card. What you see here varies by model of card and version of driver, but here's a list of some of the more interesting settings you might see.

Color Correction   Sometimes the colors on your monitor are not close enough for your tastes to the actual color you're trying to create. In this case you use color correction to fine-tune the colors on the screen to get the look you want.

Rotation   All monitors are by default wider than they are tall. This is called *landscape mode*. Some LCD monitors can be physically rotated to facilitate users who like to see their desktops taller than they are wide (*portrait mode*). Figure 19.66 shows the author's LCD monitors rotated in portrait mode. If you want to rotate your screen, you must tell the system you're rotating it.

Modes   Most video cards add very advanced settings to enable you to finely tweak your monitor. These very dangerous settings have names such as "sync polarity" or "front porch" and are outside the scope of both CompTIA A+ certification and the needs of all but the most geeky techs. These settings are mostly used to display a non-standard resolution. Stay out of those settings!

Working with Drivers

Now that you know the locations of the primary video tools within the operating system, it's time to learn about fine-tuning your video. You need to know how to work with video drivers

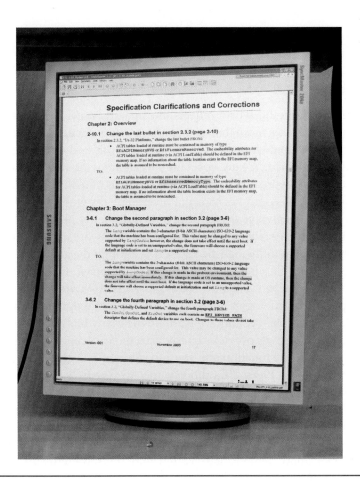

• **Figure 19.66** Portrait mode

from within the Display/Personalization applet, including how to update them, roll back updates, and uninstall them.

Windows is very persnickety when it comes to video card drivers. You can crash Windows and force a reinstallation simply by installing a new video card and not uninstalling the old card's drivers. This doesn't happen every time but certainly can happen. As a basic rule, always uninstall the old card's drivers before you install drivers for a new card.

When you update the drivers for a card, you have a choice of uninstalling the outdated drivers and then installing new drivers—which makes the process the same as for installing a new card—or you can let Windows flex some digital muscle and install the new ones right over the older drivers.

To update your drivers, go to the Control Panel and double-click the Display applet or Personalization applet. In the Display Properties/Display Settings dialog box, select the Settings tab/Monitor tab and click the Advanced or Advanced Settings button. In the Advanced button dialog box, click the Adapter tab and then click the Properties button. In the Properties dialog box for your adapter (Figure 19.67), select the Driver tab and then click the Update Driver button to run the Hardware Update wizard.

• **Figure 19.67** Adapter Properties dialog box

Practical Application

3-D Graphics

No other area of the PC world reflects the amazing acceleration of technological improvements more than **3-D graphics**—in particular, 3-D gaming—that attempts to create images with the same depth and texture as objects seen in the real world. We are spectators to an amazing new world where software and hardware race to produce new levels of realism and complexity displayed on the computer screen. Powered by the wallets of tens of millions of PC gamers always demanding more and better, the video industry constantly introduces new video cards and new software titles that make today's games so incredibly realistic and fun. Although the gaming world certainly leads the PC industry in 3-D technologies, many other PC applications—such as *Computer Aided Design* (*CAD*) programs—quickly snatch up these technologies, making 3-D more useful in many ways other than just games. In this section, we'll add to the many bits and pieces of 3-D video encountered over previous chapters in the book and put together an understanding of the function and configuration of 3-D graphics.

Before the early 1990s, PCs did not mix well with 3-D graphics. Certainly, many 3-D applications existed, primarily 3-D design programs such as AutoCAD and Intergraph, but these applications would often run only on expensive, specialized hardware—not so great for casual users.

The big change took place in 1992 when a small company called id Software created a new game called Wolfenstein 3D (see Figure 19.68). They launched an entirely new genre of games, now called *first-person shooters* (*FPSs*), in which the player looks out into a 3-D world, interacting with walls, doors, and other items, and shoots whatever bad guys the game provides.

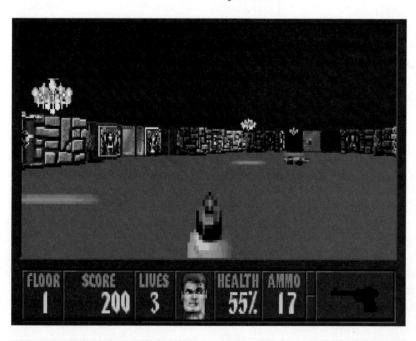

Wolfenstein 3D shook the PC gaming world to its foundations. That this innovative format came from an upstart little company made Wolfenstein 3D and id Software into overnight sensations. Even though their game was demanding on hardware, they gambled that enough people could run it to make it a success. The gamble paid off for John Carmack and John Romero, the creators of id Software, making them the fathers of 3-D gaming.

Early 3-D games used fixed 3-D images called **sprites** to create the 3-D world. A sprite is nothing more than a bitmapped graphic such as a BMP file. These early first-person shooters would calculate the position of an object from the player's perspective and place a sprite to represent the object. Any single object had only a fixed number of

• **Figure 19.68**   Wolfenstein 3D

sprites—if you walked around an object, you noticed an obvious jerk as the game replaced the current sprite with a new one to represent the new position. Figure 19.69 shows different sprites for the same bad guy in Wolfenstein 3D. Sprites weren't pretty, but they worked without seriously taxing the 486s and early Pentiums of the time.

The second generation of 3-D began to replace sprites with true 3-D objects, which are drastically more complex than sprites. A true 3-D object is composed of a group of points called **vertices**. Each vertex has a defined X, Y, and Z position in a 3-D world. Figure 19.70 shows the vertices for an airplane in a 3-D world.

The computer must track all of the vertices of all of the objects in the 3-D world, including the ones you cannot currently see. Keep in mind that objects may be motionless in the 3-D world (a wall, for example), may have animation (such as a door opening and closing), or may be moving (like bad monsters trying to spray you with evil alien goo). This calculation process is called *transformation* and, as you might imagine, is extremely taxing to most CPUs. Intel's SIMD and AMD's 3DNow! processor extensions were expressly designed to perform transformations.

Once the CPU has determined the positions of all vertices, the system begins to fill in the 3-D object. The process begins by drawing lines (the 3-D term is *edges*) between vertices to build the 3-D object into many triangles. Why triangles? Well, mainly by consensus of game developers. Any shape works, but triangles make the most sense from a mathematical standpoint. I could go into more depth here, but that would require talking about trigonometry, and I'm gambling you'd rather not read that detailed a description! All 3-D games use triangles to connect vertices. The 3-D process then groups triangles into various shapes called **polygons**. Figure 19.71 shows the same model as Figure 19.70, now displaying all of the connected vertices to create a large number of polygons.

Originally, the CPU handled these calculations to create triangles, but now special 3-D video cards do the job, greatly speeding up the process.

The last step in second-generation games was texturing. Every 3-D game stores a number of image files called **textures**. The program wraps textures around an object to give it a surface. Textures work well to provide dramatic detail without using a lot of triangles. A single object may take one texture or many textures, applied to single triangles or groups of triangles (polygons). Figure 19.72 shows the finished airplane.

True 3-D objects, more often referred to as *rendered*, immediately created the need for massively powerful video cards and much wider data buses. Intel's primary motivation for creating AGP was to provide a big enough pipe for massive data pumping between the video card and the CPU. Intel gave AGP the ability to read system RAM to support textures. If it weren't for 3-D games, AGP (and probably even PCIe) would almost certainly not exist.

3-D Video Cards

No CPU of the mid-1990s could ever hope to handle the massive processes required to render 3-D worlds. Keep in mind that to create realistic movement, the 3-D world must refresh at least 24 times per second. That means that this entire process, from transformation to texturing, must repeat once every 1/24th of a second! Furthermore, although the game re-creates each

• **Figure 19.69**   Each figure had a limited number of sprites.

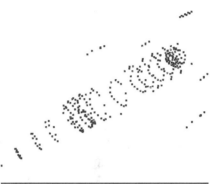

• **Figure 19.70**   Vertices for a 3-D airplane

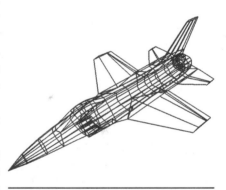

• **Figure 19.71**   Connected vertices forming polygons on a 3-D airplane

• **Figure 19.72**   3-D airplane with textures added

screen, it must also keep score, track the positions of all of the objects in the game, provide some type of intelligence to the bad guys, and so on. Something had to happen to take the workload off the CPU. The answer came from video cards.

Video cards were developed with smart onboard **graphics processing units (GPUs)**. The GPU helped the CPU by taking over some, and eventually all, of the 3-D rendering duties. These video cards not only have GPUs but also have massive amounts of RAM to store textures.

But a problem exists with this setup: How do we talk to these cards? This is done by means of a device driver, of course, but wouldn't it be great if we could create standard commands to speed up the process? The best thing to do would be to create a standardized set of instructions that any 3-D program could send to a video card to do all of the basic work, such as "make a cone" or "lay texture 237 on the cone you just made."

The video card instructions standards manifested themselves into a series of **application programming interfaces (APIs)**. In essence, an API is a library of commands that people who make 3-D games must use in their programs. The program currently using the video card sends API commands directly to the device driver. Device drivers must know how to understand the API commands. If you were to picture the graphics system of your computer as a layer cake, the top layer would be the program making a call to the video card driver that then directs the graphics hardware.

Several APIs have been developed over the years, with two clear winners among all of them: OpenGL and DirectX. The **OpenGL** standard was developed for UNIX systems but has since been *ported*, or made compatible with, a wide variety of computer systems, including Windows and Apple computers. As the demand for 3-D video became increasingly strong, Microsoft decided to throw its hat into the 3-D graphics ring with its own API, called DirectX. We look at DirectX in depth in the next section.

Although they might accomplish the same task (for instance, translating instructions and passing them on to the video driver), every API handles things just a little bit differently. In some 3-D games, the OpenGL standard might produce more precise images with less CPU overhead than the DirectX standard. In general, however, you won't notice a large difference between the images produced by using OpenGL and DirectX.

DirectX and Video Cards

In the old days, many applications communicated directly with much of the PC hardware and, as a result, could crash your computer if not written well enough. Microsoft tried to fix this problem by placing all hardware under the control of Windows, but programmers balked because Windows added too much work for the video process and slowed down everything. For the most demanding programs, such as games, only direct access of hardware would work.

This need to "get around Windows" motivated Microsoft to unveil a new set of protocols called **DirectX**. Programmers use DirectX to take control of certain pieces of hardware and to talk directly to that hardware; it provides the speed necessary to play the advanced games so popular today. The primary impetus for DirectX was to build a series of products to enable Windows to run 3-D games. That's not to say that you couldn't run 3-D games in Windows *before* DirectX; rather, it's just that Microsoft wasn't involved in the

API rat race at the time and wanted to be. Microsoft's goal in developing DirectX was to create a 100-percent stable environment, with direct hardware access, for running 3-D applications and games within Windows.

DirectX is not only for video; it also supports sound, network connections, input devices, and other parts of your PC. Each of these subsets of DirectX has a name, such as DirectDraw, Direct3D, or DirectSound.

- **DirectDraw** Supports direct access to the hardware for 2-D graphics.

- **Direct3D** Supports direct access to the hardware for 3-D graphics—the most important part of DirectX.

- **DirectInput** Supports direct access to the hardware for joysticks and other game controllers.

- **DirectSound** Supports direct access to the hardware for waveforms.

- **DirectMusic** Supports direct access to the hardware for MIDI devices.

- **DirectPlay** Supports direct access to network devices for multiplayer games.

- **DirectShow** Supports direct access to video and presentation devices.

Microsoft constantly adds to and tweaks this list. As almost all games need DirectX and all video cards have drivers to support DirectX, you need to verify that DirectX is installed and working properly on your system. To do this, use the DirectX Diagnostic Tool. In Windows 2000/XP, you can find it in the System Information program. After you open System Information (it usually lives in the Accessories | System Tools area of the Start menu), click the Tools menu and select DirectX Diagnostic Tool.

For Windows Vista/7, go to Start and type **dxdiag** in the Start search box. Press ENTER to run the program, shown in Figure 19.73.

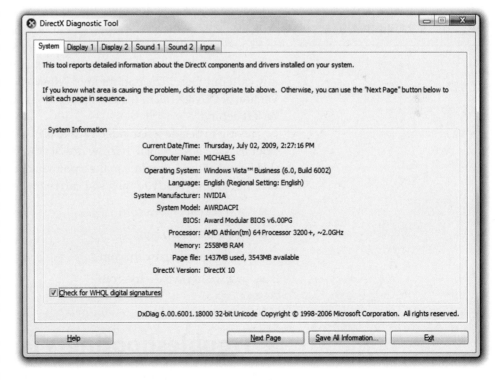

• **Figure 19.73** The DirectX Diagnostic Tool

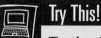

The System tab gives the version of DirectX. The system pictured in Figure 19.73 runs DirectX 10. You may then test the separate DirectX functions by running through the other tabs and running the tests.

So, what does DirectX do for video cards? Back in the bad old days before DirectX became popular with the game makers, many GPU makers created their own chip-specific APIs. 3dfx had Glide, for example, and S3 had ViRGE. This made buying 3-D games a mess. There would often be multiple versions of the same game for each card. Even worse, many games never used 3-D acceleration because it was just too much work to support all of the different cards.

That all changed when Microsoft beefed up DirectX and got more GPU makers to support it. That in turn enabled the game companies to write games by using DirectX and have them run on any card out there. The bottom line: When Microsoft comes out with a new version of DirectX, all of the GPU companies hurry to support it or they will be left behind.

Trying to decide what video card to buy gives me the shakes—too many options! One good way to narrow down your buying decision is to see what GPU is hot at the moment. I make a point to check out these Web sites whenever I'm getting ready to buy, so I can see what everyone says is the best.

- www.arstechnica.com
- www.hardocp.com
- www.tomshardware.com
- www.sharkyextreme.com

■ Troubleshooting Video

People tend to notice when their monitors stop showing the Windows desktop, making video problems a big issue for technicians. Users might temporarily ignore a bad sound card or other device, but will holler like crazy when the screen doesn't look the way they expect. To fix video problems quickly, the best place to start is to divide your video problems into two groups: video cards/drivers and monitors.

Troubleshooting Video Cards/Drivers

Video cards rarely go bad, so the vast majority of video card/driver problems are bad or incompatible drivers or incorrect settings. Always make sure you have the correct driver installed. If you're using an incompatible driver, Windows defaults to good old 640 × 480, 16-color VGA. A driver that is suddenly corrupted usually doesn't show the problem until the next reboot. If you reboot a system with a corrupted driver, Windows will do one of the following: go into VGA mode, blank the monitor, lock up, or display a garbled screen. Whatever the output, reboot into Safe mode and roll back or delete the driver. Keep in mind that more advanced video cards tend to show their drivers as installed programs under Add or Remove Programs, so always check there first before you try deleting a driver by using Device Manager. Download the latest driver and reinstall.

Video cards are pretty durable but they have two components that do go bad: the fan and the RAM. Lucky for you, if either of these goes out, it tends to show the same error—bizarre screen outputs followed shortly by a screen lockup. Usually Windows keeps running; you may see your mouse pointer moving around and windows refreshing, but the screen turns into a huge mess (Figure 19.74).

Bad drivers sometimes also make this error, so always first try going into Safe mode to see if the problem suddenly clears up. If it does, you do not have a problem with the video card!

The last and probably most common problem is nothing more than improperly configured video settings. Identifying the problem is just common sense—if your monitor is showing everything sideways, someone messed

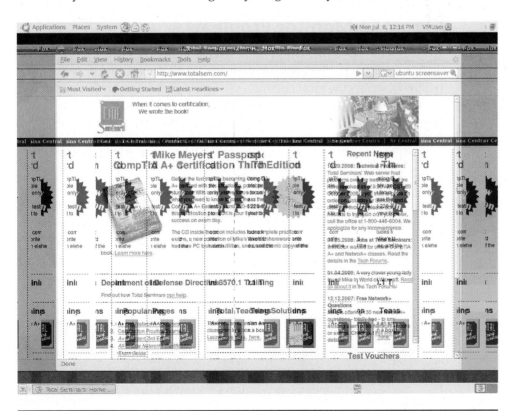

• **Figure 19.74**   Serious video problem

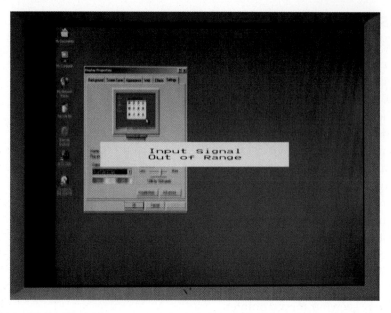

• **Figure 19.75**   Pushing a monitor too hard

with your rotation settings; if your gorgeous wallpaper of a mountain pass looks like an ugly four-color cartoon, someone lowered the color depth. Go into your Display Properties and reset them to a setting that works! The one serious configuration issue is pushing the resolution too high. If you adjust your resolution and then your monitor displays an error message such as "Input Signal Out of Range" (Figure 19.75), you need to set your resolution back to something that works for your video card/monitor combination!

Troubleshooting Monitors

Because of the inherent dangers of the high-frequency and high-voltage power required by monitors, and because proper adjustment requires specialized training, this section concentrates on giving a support person the information necessary to decide whether a trouble call is warranted. Virtually no monitor manufacturers make schematics of their monitors available to the public, because of liability issues regarding possible electrocution. To simplify troubleshooting, look at the process as three separate parts: common monitor problems, external adjustments, and internal adjustments.

Common Monitor Problems

Although I'm not super comfortable diving into the guts of a monitor, you can fix a substantial percentage of monitor problems yourself. The following list describes the most common monitor problems and tells you what to do—even when that means sending it to someone else.

- Almost all CRT and LCD monitors have replaceable controls. If the Brightness knob or Menu button stops working or seems loose, check with the manufacturer for replacement controls. They usually come as a complete package.

- For problems with ghosting, streaking, and/or fuzzy vertical edges, check the cable connections and the cable itself. These problems rarely apply to monitors; more commonly, they point to the video card.

- If one color is missing, check cables for breaks or bent pins. Check the front controls for that color. If the color adjustment is already maxed out, the monitor will require internal service.

- As monitors age, they lose brightness. If the brightness control is turned all of the way up and the picture seems dim, the monitor will require internal adjustment. This is a good argument for power-management functions. Use the power switch or the power-management options in Windows to turn off the monitor after a certain amount of time.

Common Problems Specific to CRTs

The complexity of CRTs compared to LCDs requires us to look at a number of monitor problems unique to CRTs. Most of these problems require opening the monitor, so be careful! When in doubt, take it to a repair shop.

- Most out-of-focus monitors can be fixed. Focus adjustments are usually on the inside, somewhere close to the flyback transformer. This is the transformer that provides power to the high-voltage anode.

- Hissing or sparking sounds are often indicative of an insulation rupture on the flyback transformer. This sound is usually accompanied by the smell of ozone. If your monitor has these symptoms, it definitely needs a qualified technician. Having replaced a flyback transformer once myself, I can say it is not worth the hassle and potential loss of life and limb.

- Big color blotches on the display are an easy and cheap repair. Find the Degauss button and use it. If your monitor doesn't have a Degauss button, you can purchase a special tool called a degaussing coil at any electronics store.

- Bird-like chirping sounds occurring at regular intervals usually indicate a problem with the monitor power supply.

- Suppose you got a good deal on a used 19-inch monitor, but the display is kind of dark, even though you have the brightness turned up all the way. This points to a dying CRT. So, how about replacing the CRT? Forget it. Even if the monitor was free, it just isn't worth it; a replacement tube runs into the hundreds of dollars. Nobody ever sold a monitor because it was too bright and too sharp. Save your money and buy a new monitor.

- If the monitor displays only a single horizontal or vertical line, the problem is probably between the main circuit board and the yoke, or a blown yoke coil. This definitely requires a service call.

- A single white dot on an otherwise black screen means the high-voltage flyback transformer is most likely shot. Take it into the repair shop.

External Adjustments

Monitor adjustments range from the simplest—brightness and contrast—to the more sophisticated—pincushioning and trapezoidal adjustments. The external controls provide users with the opportunity to fine-tune the monitor's image. Many monitors have controls for changing the tint and saturation of color, although plenty of monitors put those controls inside the monitor. Better monitors enable you to square up the visible portion of the screen with the monitor housing.

Finally, most monitors have the ability to **degauss** themselves with the push of a button. Over time, the shadow mask picks up a weak magnetic charge that interferes with the focus of the electron beams. This magnetic field makes the image look slightly fuzzy and streaked. Most monitors have a special built-in circuit called a *degaussing coil* to eliminate this magnetic buildup. When the degaussing circuit is used, an alternating current is sent through a coil of wire surrounding the CRT, and this current generates an alternating magnetic field that demagnetizes the shadow mask. You activate the

degaussing coil by using the Degauss button or menu selection on the monitor. Degaussing usually makes a rather nasty thunk sound and the screen goes crazy for a moment—don't worry, that's normal. Whenever a user calls me with a fuzzy monitor problem, I always have them degauss first.

Troubleshooting CRTs

As shipped, most monitors do not produce an image out to the limits of the screen, because of poor convergence at the outer display edges. **Convergence** defines how closely the three colors can meet at a single point on the display. At the point of convergence, the three colors combine to form a single white dot. With misconvergence, a noticeable halo of one or more colors appears around the outside of the white point. The farther away the colors are from the center of the screen, the more likely the chance for misconvergence. Low-end monitors are especially susceptible to this problem. Even though adjusting the convergence of a monitor is not difficult, it does require getting inside the monitor case and having a copy of the schematic, which shows the location of the variable resistors. For this reason, it is a good idea to leave this adjustment to a trained specialist.

I don't like opening a CRT monitor. I avoid doing this for two reasons: (1) I know very little about electronic circuits, and (2) I once almost electrocuted myself. At any rate, the CompTIA A+ exams expect you to have a passing understanding of adjustments you might need to perform inside a monitor. Before we go any further, let me remind you about a little issue with CRT monitors (see Figure 19.76).

The CRT monitor contains a wire called a **high-voltage anode**, covered with a suction cup. If you lift that suction cup, you will almost certainly be seriously electrocuted. The anode wire leads to the flyback transformer and produces up to 25,000 volts. Don't worry about what they do; just worry about what they can do to *you*! That charge is stored in a capacitor, which holds that charge even if the monitor is turned off. It will hold the charge even if the monitor is unplugged. That capacitor (depending on the system) can hold a charge for days, weeks, months, or even years. Knowing this, you should learn how to discharge a CRT.

• **Figure 19.76** Hey! That's 25,000 volts! *Be careful!*

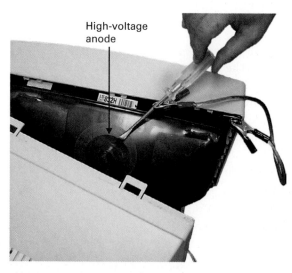

• **Figure 19.77** Discharging a CRT

High-voltage anode

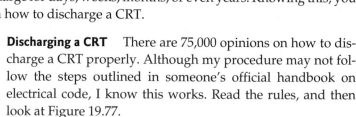

Discharging a CRT There are 75,000 opinions on how to discharge a CRT properly. Although my procedure may not follow the steps outlined in someone's official handbook on electrical code, I know this works. Read the rules, and then look at Figure 19.77.

1. Make sure everything is unplugged.

2. If possible, let the monitor sit for a couple of hours. Most good monitors discharge themselves in two to three hours, and many new monitors discharge in just a few moments.

3. Get a heavy, well-insulated, flat-head screwdriver.

4. Get a heavy-gauge wire with alligator clips on each end.

5. Do not let yourself be grounded in any way. Wear rubber-soled shoes, and no rings or watches.

6. Wear safety goggles to protect yourself in the very rare case that the CRT implodes.

7. Remove the monitor's case. Remember where the screw went in.

8. Attach one alligator clip to an unpainted part of the metal frame of the monitor.

9. Clip the other clip to the metal shaft of the screwdriver.

10. Slide the screwdriver blade under the suction cup. Make triple-sure that neither you nor the screwdriver is in any incidental contact with anything metal.

11. Slide the blade under until you hear a loud pop—you'll also see a nice blue flash.

12. If anyone is in the building, they will hear the pop and come running. Tell them everything's okay.

13. Wait about 15 minutes and repeat.

The main controls that require you to remove the monitor case to make adjustments include those for convergence, gain for each of the color guns, and sometimes the focus control. A technician with either informal or formal training in component-level repair can usually figure out which controls do what. In some cases, you can also readily spot and repair bad solder connections inside the monitor case, and thus fix a dead or dying CRT. Still, balance the cost of repairing the monitor against the cost of death or serious injury—is it worth it? Finally, before making adjustments to the display image, especially with the internal controls, give the monitor at least 15 to 30 minutes of warm-up time. This is necessary both for the components on the printed circuit boards and for the CRT itself.

Troubleshooting LCDs

With the proliferation of LCD panels in the computing world, PC techs need to have some understanding of what to do when they break. Some of the components you can fix, including replacing some of the internal components. I tend to use monitor repair shops for most LCD issues, but let's take a look.

An LCD monitor may have bad pixels. A bad pixel is any single pixel that does not react the way it should. A pixel that never lights up is a dead pixel, a pixel that is stuck on pure white is a lit pixel, and a pixel on a certain color is a stuck pixel. You cannot repair bad pixels; the panel must be replaced. All LCD panel makers allow a certain number of bad pixels, even on a brand-new LCD monitor! You need to check the warranty for your monitor and see how many they allow before you may return the monitor.

- If your LCD monitor cracks, it is not repairable and must be replaced.

- If the LCD goes dark but you can still barely see the image under bright lights, you lost either the lamp or the inverter. In many cases, especially with super-thin panels, you'll replace the entire panel and lamp as a unit. On the other hand, an inverter can be on a separate circuit board that you can replace, such as the one pictured in Figure 19.78.

- If your LCD makes a distinct hissing noise, an inverter is about to fail. Again, you can replace the inverter if need be.

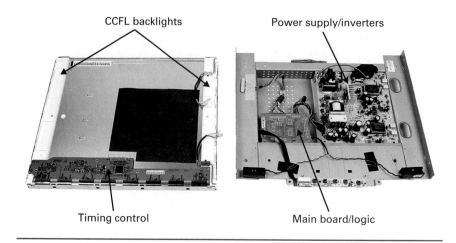

CCFL backlights   Power supply/inverters

Timing control   Main board/logic

• **Figure 19.78**   LCD components labeled

Be careful if you open an LCD to work on the inside. The inverter can bite you in several ways. First, it's powered by a high-voltage electrical circuit that can give you a nasty shock. Worse, the inverter will retain a charge for a few minutes after you unplug it, so unplug and wait for a bit. Second, inverters get very hot and present a very real danger of burning you at a touch. Again, wait for a while after you unplug it to try to replace. Finally, if you shock an inverter, you might irreparably damage it. So use proper ESD-avoidance techniques.

Bottom line on fixing LCD monitors? You can find companies that sell replacement parts for LCDs, but repairing an LCD is difficult, and there are folks who will do it for you faster and cheaper than you can. Search for a specialty LCD repair company. Hundreds of these companies exist all over the world.

Cleaning Monitors

Cleaning monitors is easy. Always use anti-static monitor wipes or at least a general anti-static cloth. Some LCD monitors may require special cleaning equipment. Never use window cleaners that contain ammonia or any liquid because getting liquid into the monitor may create a shocking experience! Many commercial cleaning solutions will also melt older LCD screens, which is never a good thing.

Beyond A+

Video and CMOS

I'm always impressed by the number of video options provided in CMOS, especially in some of the more advanced CMOS options. I'm equally impressed by the amount of disinformation provided on these settings. In this section, I'll touch on some of the most common CMOS settings that deal with video. You may notice that no power-management video options have been included.

Video

Every standard CMOS setup shows an option for video support. The default setting is invariably EGA/VGA. Many years ago, this setting told the BIOS what type of card was installed on the system, enabling it to know how to talk to that card. Today, this setting has no meaning. No matter what you put there, the system will ignore it and boot normally.

Init Display First

This CMOS setting usually resides in an advanced options or BIOS options screen. In multi-monitor systems, Init Display First enables you to decide between PCIe and PCI as to which monitor initializes at boot. This also determines the initial primary monitor for Windows.

Assign IRQ for VGA

Many video cards do not need an *interrupt request* (*IRQ*). This option gives you the ability to choose whether your video card gets an IRQ. In general, lower-end cards that do not provide input to the system do not need an IRQ. Most advanced cards will need one; try it both ways. If you need it, your system will freeze up without an IRQ assigned. If you don't need it, you get an extra IRQ.

VGA Palette Snoop

True-VGA devices only show 16 out of a possible 262,000 colors at a time. The 16 current colors are called the *palette*. VGA Palette Snoop opens a video card's palette to other devices that may need to read or temporarily change the palette. I am unaware of any device made today that still needs this option.

Video Shadowing Enabled

As mentioned in previous chapters, this setting enables you to shadow the Video ROM. In most cases, this option is ignored as today's video cards perform their own automatic shadowing. A few cards require this setting to be off, so I generally leave it off now, after years of leaving it on.

Other Display Technologies

A few other screen technologies exist, but not so much for computer monitors. Plasma and DLP screens grace many a household's media room as the primary television display.

Plasma

Plasma display panels (*PDP*) are a very popular technology for displaying movies. Unfortunately, plasma TVs have two issues that make them a bad choice for PC use. First, they have strange native resolutions (such as 1366 × 768) that are hard to get your video card to accept. Second is *burn-in*—the tendency for a screen to "ghost" an image even after the image is off the screen. Plasma TV makers have virtually eliminated burn-in, but even the latest plasma displays are subject to burn-in when used with PC displays.

• **Figure 19.79**   DLP chip (*photo courtesy of Texas Instruments*)

DLP

Digital Light Processing (DLP) displays use a chip covered in microscopically small mirrors (Figure 19.79).

These individual mirrors move thousands of times per second toward and away from a light source. The more times per second they move toward a light source, the whiter the image; the fewer times they move, the grayer the image. See Figure 19.80 for a diagram of how the mirrors would appear in a microscopic close-up of the chip.

Figure 19.81 shows a diagram of a typical DLP system. The lamp projects through a color wheel onto the DLP chip. The DLP chip creates the image by moving the tiny mirrors, which in turn reflect onto the screen.

DLP was very popular for a time in home theater systems, as it makes an amazingly rich image. DLP has had very little impact on PC monitors, but has had great success as projectors. DLP projectors are much more expensive than LCD projectors, but many customers feel the extra expense is worth the image quality.

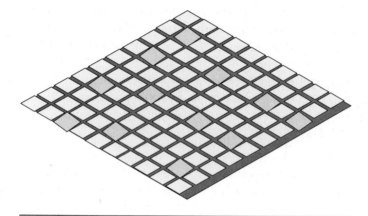

• **Figure 19.80**   Microscopic close-up of DLP showing tiny mirrors—note that some are tilted.

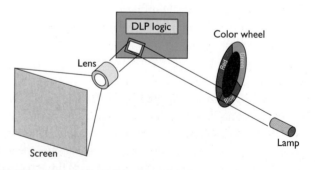

• **Figure 19.81**   DLP in action

Chapter 19 Review

■ Chapter Summary

After reading this chapter and completing the exercises, you should understand the following about video.

Explain how video displays work

- The term *video* encompasses a complex interaction among numerous parts of the PC, all designed to put a picture on the screen. The monitor is the primary output device for the PC and shows you what's going on with your programs and operating system. The video card or display adapter handles all of the communication between the CPU and the monitor. Video displays come in three varieties: CRT, LCD, and projectors.

- CRT monitors have a tube that contains three electron guns at the slender end and a display screen coated with phosphor at the wide end. The speed of the electron beam across the screen is the horizontal refresh rate (HRR), more commonly referred to as the refresh rate. The vertical refresh rate (VRR) is the time it takes to draw the entire screen and return the electron guns to the upper-left corner.

- Monitors do not determine the HRR or VRR. The video card "pushes" the monitor at a certain VRR that, in turn, determines the HRR. Setting the VRR too low results in screen flicker, which causes headaches and eyestrain. Setting the VRR too high results in image distortion and damage to the monitor's circuitry. The monitor's bandwidth dictates the maximum VRR.

- A monitor is a grid of red, green, and blue light-sensitive dots called phosphors. Normal CRT monitors have three electron guns that fire electrons of different intensities (not colors) at the colored phosphors. A shadow mask prevents electron bleed-over so electrons from any of the three guns hit only their own colored phosphors. The area of phosphors lit at one instant is a pixel and must consist of at least one red, one green, and one blue phosphor; therefore, the smallest pixel, a triad, would consist of three phosphors.

- Resolution is the number of horizontal pixels times the number of vertical pixels. A resolution of 640 × 480 means 640 pixels across and 480 pixels down, for a total of 307,200 pixels total. Many monitors have a resolution that matches a 4:3 aspect ratio. Widescreen monitors have an aspect ratio of 16:9 or 16:10.

- Dot pitch, measured in millimeters (mm), defines the diagonal distance between phosphorous dots of the same color.

- Liquid crystal displays are the most common type of display for PCs. They offer many advantages over CRTs. An LCD monitor is thinner, lighter, uses less power, is virtually flicker-free, and does not emit potentially harmful radiation.

- An LCD screen is composed of tiny liquid crystal molecules called sub-pixels. Although you may find a dual-scan passive matrix on some low-end LCD panels, most of today's LCD panels use active matrix or thin film transistor (TFT) technology.

- The typical LCD monitor is composed of the LCD panel, backlights, and inverters. The backlights require AC power and the electronics require DC. The AC/DC transformer changes the AC wall current into DC that the LCD panel can use. All LCD backlights use cold cathode fluorescent lamp (CCFL) technology. CCFLs require AC power, so inverters convert the DC back to AC.

- LCD monitors, unlike CRTs, have a native resolution and a fixed pixel size. LCDs cannot run at a resolution higher than their native resolution, and running a lower resolution results in degraded image quality. Anti-aliasing softens the edges of jagged pixel corners when running at lower resolutions, but as the image quality degrades, you should use the native resolution.

- LCD monitor brightness is determined by its backlights and is measured in nits. An average LCD measures around 300 nits, with higher numbers being brighter and better.

- The time it takes for sub-pixels to go from pure black to pure white and back again is the LCD's response rate. Response rate is measured in milliseconds, with lower numbers being faster and better. An excellent LCD monitor has a response rate somewhere between 6 and 8 ms.

Multimedia

Emmett Bradley: "Sir, are you telling me that your only real flight time is at the controls of a video game?"

Troy: "No, see, it's not—it's not a video game, all right? It's a flight simulator."

—Emmett Bradley and Troy, *Snakes on a Plane*

In this chapter, you will learn how to

- **Describe how to implement sound in a PC**
- **Install and configure video capture hardware and software**
- **Set up a PC to view television signals**

The PC long ago went well beyond a simple device used to create office documents and crunch numbers efficiently. With modern PCs, you can experience content on many levels, from realistic video to scintillating three-dimensional sound. Plus, you can add the hardware and software to turn the computer into a multimedia creation machine, making movies and more.

This chapter looks at the many aspects of multimedia available in a modern PC. First, the chapter discusses how sound works in a PC, both to record and play it back. Second, you'll dive into video capture concepts, hardware, and software. Finally, the chapter rolls through the essentials of setting up the computer to bridge the gap into the entertainment world fully by installing and configuring TV tuner hardware and software. Rolling...and...action!

■ Sound

Whether racing down the virtual track, pixels flying across the screen, hearing the engine roar as you take another turn and press down the accelerator—or surfing the Web for lovely scenic nature photos with the sweet, mellifluous music of Mozart filling the room—sound has become an integral component of the computing experience. Setting up and optimizing sound for the PC has become an integral skill for all computer techs.

Correctly setting up sound for a PC requires that you know about quite a few things, because the sound process has many components. You need a properly installed sound card with the correct drivers loaded, reasonably high-quality speakers, support software such as the API for a particular game correctly configured in Windows, and a properly set-up application that can use the features of the sound card. And every great tech needs to know troubleshooting to handle both routine and uncommon problems with sound.

Historical/Conceptual

How Sound Works in a PC

Like the ripples that roll across a pond when you drop a rock in the center, sound flows from a source in invisible but measurable waves that cause the membranes in your ears to vibrate and create noise. The sophistication of the human ear enables most people to differentiate the melodious from the raucous, the loud from the soft. Computers aren't nearly as sophisticated as the human ear and brain, so clear standards are a must for converting music into a format that a PC can use to record and play sound. Computer folks use the terms *capture* and *output* instead of record and play.

Sound-Capture Basics

Virtually every PC today comes with four critical components for capturing and outputting sound: a sound card, speakers, microphone, and recording/playback software. Computers capture (record) sound waves in electronic format through a process called **sampling**. In its simplest sense, sampling means capturing the state or quality of a particular sound wave a set number of times each second. The sampling rate is measured in units of thousands of cycles per second, or kilohertz (KHz). The more often a sound is sampled, the better the reproduction of that sound. Most sounds in the PC world are recorded with a sampling rate of from 11 KHz (very low quality, like a telephone) to 192 KHz (ultra-high quality, better than the human ear).

Sounds vary according to their loudness (**amplitude**), how high or low their tone (**frequency**), and the qualities that differentiate the same note played on different instruments (**timbre**). All the characteristics of a particular sound wave—amplitude, frequency, timbre—need to be recorded and translated into ones and zeros to reproduce that sound accurately within the computer and out to your speakers.

Tech Tip

Sound Terminology
Every modern motherboard comes with sound processing capabilities built in. By default, techs talk about built-in sound as either built-in sound or as a sound card, even when there's no expansion card for sound.

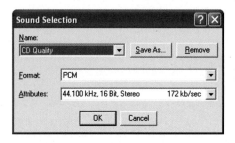

• **Figure 20.1**   Sound Recorder settings

WAV and MP3 are only two among a large number of file formats for sound. Not all sound players can play all of these formats; however, many sound formats are nothing more than some type of compressed WAV file, so with the right codec loaded, you can play most sound formats.

Tech Tip

Compressing WAV Files to MP3 Format

Using MP3 compression, you can shrink a WAV file by a factor of 12 without losing much sound quality. When you compress a WAV file into an MP3 file, the key decision is the bit rate. The bit rate is the amount of information (number of bits) transferred from the compressed file to the MP3 decoder in 1 second. The higher the bit rate of an MP3 file, the higher the sound quality. The bit rate of MP3 audio files is commonly measured in thousands of bits per second, abbreviated Kbps. *Most MP3 encoders support a range of bit rates from 24 Kbps up to 320 Kbps (or 320,000 bits per second). A CD-quality MP3 bit rate is 128 Kbps.*

The number of characteristics of a particular sound captured during sampling is measured by the **bit depth** of the sample, the number of bits used to describe the characteristics of a sound. The greater the bit depth used to capture a sample, the more characteristics of that sound can be stored and thus re-created. An 8-bit sample of a Jimi Hendrix guitar solo, for example, captures 2^8 (256) characteristics of that sound per sample. It would sound like a cheap recording of a recording, perhaps a little flat and thin. A 16-bit sample, in contrast, captures 2^{16} (65,536) different characteristics of his solo and reproduces all the fuzzy overtones and feedback that gave Hendrix his unique sound.

The last aspect of sound capture is the number of tracks of sound you capture. Most commonly, you can capture either a single track (**monaural**) or two tracks (**stereo**). More advanced captures record many more sound tracks, but that's a topic for a more advanced sound capture discussion.

The combination of sampling frequency and bit depth determines how faithfully a digital version of a sound captures what your ear would hear. A sound capture is considered **CD quality** when recorded at 44.1 KHz, with 16-bit depth and in stereo. Most recording programs let you set these values before you begin recording. Figure 20.1 shows the configuration settings for the Windows Sound Recorder.

Hey, wait a minute! Did you notice the Format setting in Figure 20.1? What's that? You can save those sampled sounds in lots of different ways—and that's where the term *format* comes into play.

Recorded Sound Formats

The granddaddy of all sound formats is **pulse code modulation (PCM)**. PCM was developed in the 1960s to carry telephone calls over the first digital lines. With just a few minor changes to allow for use in PCs, the PCM format is still alive and well, although it's better known as the *WAV* format so common in the PC world. WAV files are great for storing faithfully recorded sounds and music, but they do so at a price. WAV files can be huge, especially when sampled at high frequency and depth. A 4-minute song at 44.1 KHz and 16-bit stereo, for example, weighs in at a whopping 40-plus MB!

What's interesting about sound quality is that the human ear cannot perceive anywhere near the subtle variations of sound recorded at 44.1 KHz and 16-bit stereo. Clever programmers have written algorithms to store full-quality WAV files as compressed files, discarding unnecessary audio qualities of that file. These algorithms—really nothing more than a series of instructions in code—are called compressor/decompressor programs or, more simply, **codecs**. The most famous of the codecs is the Fraunhoffer MPEG-1 Layer 3 codec, more often called by its file extension, **MP3**.

MIDI

Every sound card can produce sounds in addition to playing prerecorded sound files. Every sound card comes with a second processor designed to interpret standardized **musical instrument digital interface (MIDI)** files. It's important to note that a MIDI file is not an independent music file, unlike a WAV file that sounds more or less the same on many different PCs. A MIDI file is a text file that takes advantage of the sound processing hardware to enable the PC to produce sound. Programmers use these small files to tell

the sound card what notes to play, how long, how loud, on which instruments, and so forth. Think of a MIDI file as a piece of electronic sheet music, with the instruments built into your sound card.

The beauty of MIDI files is that they're tiny in comparison to equivalent WAV files. The first movement of Beethoven's Fifth Symphony, for example, weighs in at a whopping 78 MB as a high-quality WAV file. The same seven-minute song as a MIDI file, in contrast, slips in at a svelte 60 KB.

MIDI is hardware dependent, meaning the capabilities and quality of the individual sound card make all the difference in the world on the sound produced. Sound cards play MIDI files by using one of two technologies: FM synthesis or wave table synthesis.

FM Synthesis Early processors used electronic emulation of various instruments—a technique often called **FM synthesis**—to produce music and other sound effects. Software developers could tell the sound processor to reproduce a piano playing certain notes, for example, and a sound resembling a piano would pour forth from the speakers. The problem with FM synthesis is that although the modulation sounds okay for a single note, such as middle C, it sounds increasingly electronic the farther up or down the scale you go from that prime note.

Wave Table Synthesis To address the odd techno-sound of early sound processors, manufacturers began embedding recordings of actual instruments or other sounds in the sound card. Modern sound cards use these recorded sounds to reproduce an instrument much more faithfully than with FM synthesis. When asked to play a C note on a piano or on a viola, for example, the sound processor grabs a prerecorded WAV file from its memory and adjusts it to match the specific sound and timing requested. This technique is called **wave table synthesis**. The number of instruments a sound card can play at once is called the **polyphony** of that card—typically 64 sounds on better cards. Most modern sound cards have samples of 128 instruments—a veritable symphony orchestra on a chip!

Other File Formats

The WAV, MP3, and MIDI formats may account for the majority of sound files, but plenty of other less common formats are out there. Here are the extensions of some other sound file formats you may run into in the PC world:

- **AAC** Advanced Audio Coding is the native format for songs downloaded into the Apple iTunes music library. The AAC format is part of the MPEG-4 standard, offers better compression algorithms than MP3, and is freely distributed. Apple wraps downloaded songs in a Digital Rights Management (DRM) encapsulation called FairPlay that gives them control over distribution of those songs.

- **AIFF** Audio Interchange File Format files are a popular sound format used on Macintosh computers. These files are often seen at Web sites, and you can use the well-known QuickTime Player to play them.

- **ASM** Assembly Language Source files are compressed sound files often seen on the Internet and used in streaming sound (streaming media is discussed later in this chapter).

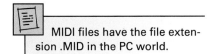 MIDI files have the file extension .MID in the PC world.

MIDI files are much less popular than other recorded formats on computers, but every Windows computer and every sound card still fully supports MIDI.

- **ASX**   Microsoft created the ASX format to facilitate streaming audio over the Internet through Windows Media Player. It's more than just a format, though; it acts like a super playlist and enables you to play other sound file types as well. The full name of the format is Microsoft Advanced Streaming Redirector.

- **AU**   This popular format is often seen in the Windows world. Many players can play these files, including players on non-Windows systems, such as Sun, Next, UNIX, and Macintosh.

- **OGG**   The Vorbis format is an open-source compression codec that competes well with the proprietary AAC and WMA codecs, as well as MP3. Vorbis files are saved with the .OGG filename extension, so you'll hear them (incorrectly) referred to as "Ogg" files.

- **RM**   RealMedia files play either just audio or audio and video. They are proprietary to RealMedia, a popular player often used on the Internet. You must have RealMedia Player installed on your computer to play these files.

- **WMA**   Windows Media Audio is Microsoft's proprietary compression format.

This list scratches the surface of the 100-plus sound file formats available, but it represents those you're most likely to encounter.

Playing Sounds

A large number of programs can play sounds on a typical Windows computer. First, virtually every Windows computer comes with Windows Media Player, possibly the most popular of all sound players. Figure 20.2 shows the default Media Player for Windows Vista. You can download many other players, of course, including iTunes, Apple's media program for Windows and OS X. This is good, because not all sound players can play all sounds.

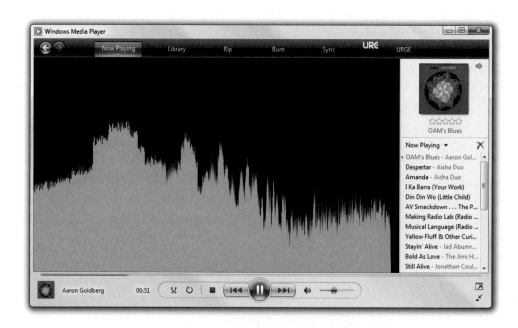

• **Figure 20.2**   Windows Media Player

Many applications, especially games, play sounds too. In the not-too-distant past, a game or an application sometimes had its own sound format, but most applications and games today use standard WAV, MP3, or MIDI files.

Streaming media is a broadcast of data that is played on your computer and immediately discarded. Streaming media is incredibly popular on the Internet. Streaming media has spawned an entire industry of Internet radio stations. The three most popular streaming media players are Windows Media Player, Winamp, and Apple's iTunes. With the spread of broadband Internet, the quality of streaming radio has improved dramatically. In fact, it is common to see Internet stations streaming 128 Kbps and better MP3 files. Some sites even have surround sound music for those who have the speakers to appreciate it.

 Try This!

Play Sounds in Windows

The typical Windows PC comes with a number of applications for playing sound files. Take a tour of a typical Windows system to see these applications. This exercise uses Windows XP, but almost any version of Windows (95 or later) will also work. For this exercise, you need a Windows XP or Vista system with a functioning sound card, microphone, and speakers.

1. Using the file search feature in Windows, locate all of the files on your computer that have the extension *.wav*—all versions of Windows come with a number of WAV files. Double-click one of the files to play it. What program is associated with WAV files?

2. Repeat step 1, but this time look for files with the extension *.mid*. Not all versions of Windows have MIDI files. Double-click one of the files to play it. What program is associated with MIDI files?

3. From the Start button, search for any sound programs that may be on your system. You'll almost certainly run into Windows Media Player and Sound Recorder, but check to see whether any third-party programs are installed.

4. If possible, install a popular sound player such as Winamp or iTunes on your system. Both programs are free. You can get Winamp at www.winamp.com and iTunes at www.apple.com/itunes. Check Winamp's help files to see what types of file formats Winamp supports—a lot of formats!

5. If you have an Internet connection, try running some streaming audio. If you have Windows Media Player versions 7 through 10, go to the Radio Tuner. If you are running Windows Media Player 11 or later, go to the Media Guide. If you have Winamp, try going to www.shoutcast.com. With iTunes, just click the Radio link in the Library.

Getting the Right Sound Hardware

Modern motherboards come with built-in sound processing, plus you can buy a sound card that plugs into a PCI or PCIe expansion slot or into a USB port. Sound cards come with many features, including two separate sound processors (one for all of the recorded formats such as WAV and another for MIDI), recording capabilities, support for MIDI instruments, and more. All sound cards, from the cheapest to the most expensive, can play music and drive a pair of speakers, so techs need to delve a little deeper to understand the crucial differences among low-, mid-, and high-end sound cards. Sound cards differ in six basic areas: sound standard, processor capabilities, speaker support, recording quality, jacks, and extra features.

But the sound card itself is only one part of the equation. You also need good-quality speakers if you have any intention of listening to music or enjoying some of the more advanced features such as surround sound.

Sound Card Standards

Most sound cards follow one of two standards, AC'97 or Intel High Definition Audio, although no rule says manufacturers must follow these standards. This applies both to the sound processing hardware built into motherboards and to add-on sound cards.

The **AC'97** standard applies to lower-end audio devices, having been created when most folks listened to stereo sound at best. Both playback and recording capabilities of such sound cards offer adequate quality, certainly enough for the typical office PC. When you want to go beyond average, though, turn to a motherboard or add-on sound card that offers a newer standard.

Intel designed the **Intel High Definition Audio (HDA)** standard to support features such as true surround sound with many discrete speakers. Technically speaking, whereas AC'97 offers support for up to six channels at 48 KHz/20-bit quality, HDA cranks that up to eight channels at 192 KHz/32-bit quality, a substantial improvement. HDA also supports sending multiple streams of audio from one computer to different output devices, so you can enjoy Internet radio in one room, for example, and listen to a CD in another room, both played on the same computer.

Processor Capabilities

Sound processor capabilities differ dramatically from the low end to the high end, even though the prices don't reflect the great divide. The sound processor handles the communication among the application, operating system, and CPU and translates commands into sounds coming out of the speakers. Low-end sound processors do little more than translate, which means that the CPU has to do the heavy lifting on the processing front.

Better sound processors, in contrast, shoulder much of the processing burden and bring a series of extra features to the table. By handling a lot of the processing onboard, these better sound processors free up the CPU for other duties and—in effect and in name—*accelerate* the sound process.

Tech Tip

Sound Cards

The hardware portion of sound-processing equipment in the PC comes either as a chip built into the motherboard or as an expansion card. Techs call both forms sound cards, though technically the first type is not a card at all. Still, the generic term has stuck for the time being.

As they do with new microprocessor models, Intel gave the HDA standard a codename as well. Look for motherboards offering the *Azalia* sound option. That's Intel High Definition Audio.

Tech Tip

Azalia's Not Just for Intel Boards

Most chipset makers have adopted Intel High Definition Audio for their better motherboard offerings. That includes direct Intel competitors, such as NVIDIA. Everybody plays Azalia these days!

These decent sound processors also provide excellent sound reproduction, so your MP3s sound as awesome on your PC as they do on your stereo.

Most mid-range and all high-end sound processors offer support for various surround sound standards, enabling equally equipped games and other applications to provide positional audio effects and detailed sound modeling—features that make PC gaming take on a whole new dimension. You'll learn about the various standards in detail in the "Speakers" section of this chapter, but for now let an example suffice. With properly implemented positional audio, when you're sneaking down the hall, ready to steal the Pasha's treasure, you will hear behind you the sounds of the guards marching up to capture you. Such added realism has many potential benefits beyond games, but games are currently the primary beneficiary of this technology.

Speaker Support

Every sound card supports two speakers or a pair of headphones, but many better sound cards support five or more speakers in discrete channels. These multiple speakers provide surround sound—popular not only for games but also for those who enjoy playing DVDs on their PCs. The card shown in Figure 20.3, for example, has outputs for many speakers.

• **Figure 20.3**   A sound card with multiple speaker connections

Another popular speaker addition is a subwoofer. A **subwoofer** provides the amazing low-frequency sounds that give an extra dimension to all of your sounds, from the surround sound of a game to the music of a simple stereo MP3 file. Almost all modern sound cards support both surround sound and a subwoofer and advertise this with a nomenclature such as Dolby Digital or DTS. Figure 20.4 shows one type of surround speaker system. (You'll learn more about surround sound in the upcoming "Speakers" section.)

Recording Quality

Almost every sound card has an input for a powered microphone, but the high-end cards record with substantially lower amounts of noise or other audible artifacts. The measure that describes the relative quality of an input port is **signal-to-noise ratio** and is expressed in **decibels.** The smaller the number, the worse the card is for recording, because you're more likely to get noise. Most sound cards at the low end and in the mid range have a signal-to-noise ratio of 30 to 50 decibels, which makes them unacceptable for recording. High-end cards offer a 96 to 100+ signal-to-noise ratio, a level near what professional musicians use. Check the documentation before you buy or recommend a sound card for recording purposes (see Figure 20.5).

• **Figure 20.4**   Surround speakers (*photo courtesy of Klipsch Group, Inc.*)

Jacks

Virtually every sound card comes with at least three connections: one for a stereo speaker system, one for a microphone, and one for a secondary input called line in. If you look at the back of a motherboard with a built-in sound card, you'll invariably see these three connections. On most systems, the main stereo speaker connector is green, the line in connector is blue, and the

Figure 20.5 The EMU 1820 advertises its excellent 112-decibel signal-to-noise ratio for recording.

Mini-audio connectors

Figure 20.6 Typical audio connections on a motherboard sound card

microphone connector is pink. You'll often find plenty of other connectors as well (Figure 20.6).

Here's a list of several of the standard connectors:

- **Main speaker out** Just what it sounds like, the main speaker output is where you plug in the standard speaker connector.

- **Line out** Some cards will have a separate line out connector that is often used to connect to an external device such as a cassette or CD player. This enables you to output sounds from your computer.

- **Line in** The line in port connects to an external device such as a cassette or CD player to allow you to import sounds into your computer.

- **Rear out** The rear out connector connects to the rear speakers for surround sound audio output.

- **Analog/digital out** The multifunction analog/digital out connection acts as a special digital connection to external digital devices or digital speaker systems, and it also acts as the analog connection to center and subwoofer channels. (See the "Speakers" section later in this chapter for a discussion of surround sound.)

- **Microphone** The microphone port connects to an external microphone for voice input.

- **Joystick** The now-obsolete joystick port connects a joystick or a MIDI device to the sound card. The joystick port is a two-row, DB15 female connection, but few motherboards or sound cards include the port these days.

Extra Features

With all motherboards including built-in sound these days, expansion sound card makers have responded by adding a host of extra goodies and capabilities to their cards that, for some folks, prove irresistibly tempting. These include a digital output to integrate the PC with a home entertainment unit, DVD receiver, and surround sound speaker connection capabilities; a breakout box that adds recording and output ports in a 5.25-inch bay; and a FireWire connection for direct gaming, file sharing, and immediate MP3 playing from a portable MP3 device. Figure 20.7 shows a version of the Creative Labs SoundBlaster breakout box. These features aren't for everyone, but they are compelling to many consumers.

Speakers

It always blows me away when I walk into someone's study and hear tinny music whining from a $10 pair of speakers connected to a $2000 computer. If you listen to music or play games on your computer, a decent set of speakers can significantly improve the experience. Speakers come in a wide variety of sizes, shapes, technologies, and quality and can stump the uninformed tech who can't easily tell that the $50 set on the right sounds 100 times better than the $25 pair on the left (Figure 20.8).

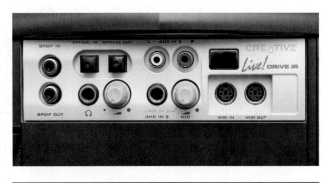

• **Figure 20.7** Breakout box for a SoundBlaster Live! Platinum sound card

Speaker Standards The advent of surround sound in the computing world has created a number of speaker standards. You should know these standards so you can choose the speakers that work best for you and your clients.

Stereo is the oldest speaker technology you'll see in the PC world. Stereo speakers are just what you might imagine: two speakers, a left and a right (Figure 20.9). The two speakers share a single jack that connects to the sound card. Most cheap speakers are stereo speakers.

A **2.1** speaker system consists of a pair of standard stereo speakers—called **satellites**—combined with a subwoofer (Figure 20.10). The average 2.1 speaker system has a single jack that connects to the sound card and runs into the subwoofer. Another wire runs from the subwoofer to the two stereo speakers. If you want to enjoy great music but don't really need surround sound, this is your speaker standard of choice.

Going beyond standard two-channel (stereo) sound has been a goal in the sound world since the 1970s. However, it wasn't until the advent of Dolby Laboratory's **Dolby Digital** sound standard in the early 1990s that surround sound began to take off. The Dolby Digital sound standard is designed to support five channels of sound: front-left, front-right, front-center, rear-left, and rear-right. Dolby Digital also supports a subwoofer—thus, the term **5.1**. Another company, **Digital Theatre Systems (DTS)**, created a competing standard that also supported a 5.1 speaker system. When DVDs were introduced, they included both Dolby Digital and DTS 5.1 standards, making 5.1 speakers an overnight requirement for home theater. If you want to enjoy your DVDs in full surround sound on your PC, you must purchase a full 5.1 speaker system. A number of 5.1 speaker systems are available for PCs. The choice you make is usually determined by what sounds best to you.

Many sound cards also come with a special **Sony/Philips digital interface (S/PDIF)** connector that enables you to connect your sound card directly to a 5.1 speaker system or receiver (Figure 20.11). Using a single S/PDIF instead of a tangle of separate wires for each speaker greatly simplifies your sound setup. S/PIDF connections come in two types, optical and coaxial. The optical variety looks like a square with a small door (at right in Figure 20.11). The coaxial is a standard RCA connector (at left), the same type used to

• **Figure 20.8** High-quality speaker set (right) versus another manufacturer's low-end speaker set (left)

• **Figure 20.9** Stereo speakers

• Figure 20.10   Typical 2.1 speakers

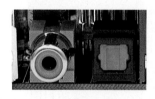

• Figure 20.11   S/PDIF connectors

📝 Only a few 5.1 PC speaker sets come with S/PDIF. In most cases, you'll have to use the regular audio outputs on the sound card. You'll find the connector more common on 6.1 and 7.1 sets.

connect a CD player to your stereo. It doesn't matter which one you use; just make sure you have an open spot on your receiver or speakers.

Games can also take advantage of 5.1, 6.1, and 7.1 speakers, but they use the DirectX standard. **DirectX** offers numerous commands, also known as APIs, that issue instructions such as "make a sound on the right speaker" or "play music in both the right and left channels." DirectX simplifies the programming needed to create sound and video: rather than having to program sounds in different ways for each sound card option, games can talk DirectX. The hardware manufacturers simply have to ensure that their sound cards are DirectX compatible.

DirectX version 3 introduced **DirectSound3D (DS3D)**, which offered a range of commands to place a sound anywhere in 3-D space. Known as **positional audio**, it fundamentally changed the way most PC games were played. DS3D could not handle all sound information, but it supported extensions to its instructions for more advanced sound features. This challenged the sound card designers to develop more fully the concept of positional audio. Creative Labs responded by rolling out **environmental audio extensions (EAX)**, a set of audio presets that gave developers the capability to create a convincing sense of environment in entertainment titles and a realistic sense of distance between the player and audio events. Figure 20.12 shows an EAX setup screen.

• Figure 20.12   EAX setup screen

In late 2000, a number of EAX effects were incorporated into the DirectX audio component of DirectX 8.0. This signaled the acceptance of EAX as the standard for audio effects in gaming. Shortly afterward, Creative Labs started releasing audio cards that were Dolby 5.1 compatible out of the box. This let you plug a 5.1 speaker system directly into your sound card. The sound card automatically decoded the Dolby/DTS sound track when you played a DVD and the EAX effects when you played a game that supports it. All current sound cards support DirectX and EAX.

Microsoft changed the way audio works in Windows Vista from the way it works in previous versions of Windows. Most notably, Vista doesn't support direct hardware access to sound, so DirectSound does not work. Third-party developers have created various workarounds for this lack of support to enable some older games and hardware to function in Windows Vista. Other developers have gotten behind the OpenAL API to provide environmental audio effects in Vista. Specific OpenAL drivers for games have to be included to provide that support.

Not all cards support Dolby Digital/DTS. Most software DVD players and some sound cards support Dolby Digital. DTS support is a little harder to come by. Check the manufacturer's Web site to determine whether your card will work with DTS.

Speaker Features   Speakers also come with a few other features that you should consider when choosing a set for yourself or your clients. Speakers offer a variety of power sources, controls accessibility, and headphone jacks.

Most speakers have volume controls as well as an on/off switch. Get a system that provides easy access to those controls by placing them on an easy-to-reach speaker or on a special control box.

The problem with headphones is that you need to plug them into the back of the sound card and then tell Windows to output to them from the Sound applet on the Control Panel. Save yourself a lot of hassle and get a speaker system that has a handy microphone jack on one of the speakers or on a control box.

Installing Sound in a Windows System

You've got two choices for sound hardware on today's PCs: a separate sound card or onboard sound built into the motherboard. The installation process for a sound card is basically the same as the process for any other card. You snap the card into a slot, plug some speakers into the card, load a driver—and for the most part, you're finished. With onboard sound, you need to make sure the sound is enabled in your CMOS and then load the driver. As with most of the devices discussed in this book, sound card installation consists of three major parts: physical installation, device driver installation, and configuration.

Physical Installation

Physical installation is easy. Onboard sound is already physically installed and most sound cards are run-of-the-mill PCI cards (Figure 20.13), although you can find PCIe and USB versions too. The real trick to physical installation is deciding where to plug in the speakers, microphone, and so on. The surround sound devices so common today feature a variety of

• **Figure 20.13**   Typical sound card

jacks, so you will probably want to refer to your sound card documentation for details, but here are a few guidelines:

- The typical stereo or 2.1 speaker system will use only a single jack. Look for the jack labeled Speaker or Speaker 1.

- Surround speakers either use a single digital (S/PDIF) connection, which in most cases runs from the sound card to the subwoofer, or they need three separate cables: one for the front two speakers that runs to the Speaker 1 connector, a second cable for the back two speakers that runs to the Speaker 2 connector, and a third cable for the center channel and subwoofer that runs to the digital/audio out or Speaker 3 connector.

Here's a quick look at sound card installation. As with any expansion card, you'll need a Phillips-head screwdriver to install a sound card, as well as your electrostatic discharge (ESD) prevention equipment. Of course, you'll also need the sound card itself, a set of speakers, an audio cable if it's an older system, and a microphone if you want to be able to record sounds.

1. Shut down your computer, unplug it, and open the case.

2. Find an open PCI or PCIe slot and snap in the sound card. Remember to handle the card with tender loving care—especially if you're installing an expensive, high-end card! Make sure the card is securely seated, and secure it to the chassis with a hex screw.

Installing Drivers

Sound card drivers are updated occasionally. Take a moment to check the manufacturer's Web site to see whether your sound card has any driver updates.

Once the sound card is installed, start the system and let Windows install the card's drivers. This applies to expansion cards and onboard sound. As you might expect by now, you'll probably have a choice between the built-in Windows drivers and the driver that comes on a CD-ROM with your sound card. Just as with other cards, it's always best to install the driver that comes with the card. All sound devices have easy-to-use autorun-enabled installation CD-ROMs that step you through the process (Figure 20.14).

You might run into one of the USB sound cards out on the market (Figure 20.15), in which case the installation process is reversed. The only secret to these devices is to follow the important rule of all USB devices: *Install the drivers before you plug in the device.* Windows, especially Windows XP and Vista, probably have basic drivers for these USB sound cards, but don't take a chance—always install the drivers first.

After your sound card and driver are installed, make a quick trip to the Device Manager to ensure that the driver was installed correctly, and you're two-thirds of the way there. Installing the driver is never the last step for a sound card. Your final step is to configure the sound card by using configuration programs and test it by using an application. Most sound cards come with both special configuration programs and a few sound applications on the same

- **Figure 20.14**   Typical autorun screen for a sound card

CD-ROM that supplies the drivers. Take a look at these extra bits of software that I call *sound programs*.

Installing Sound Programs

You've already seen that you need a program to play sounds on your PC: Windows Media Player, Winamp, or something similar. But several other classes of sound programs also reside on your computer: programs for the configuration of your sound card—tools built in to Windows as well as proprietary tools—and special applications that may or may not come with your sound card.

Windows Configuration Applications   Every Windows computer comes with at least one important sound configuration program built right into the operating system: the Control Panel applet called Sound in Windows Vista, Sounds and Audio Devices in Windows XP, or Sounds and Multimedia in Windows 2000. Whatever the name, this applet (or applets) performs the same job: it provides a location for performing most or all of the configuration you need for your sound card. Consider the Sounds and Audio Devices applet in Windows XP, for example; the Sounds and Multimedia applet in Windows 2000 works roughly the same, although it may have one control or another in a different place.

The Sounds and Audio Devices applet has five tabs: Volume, Sounds, Audio, Voice, and Hardware. The Volume tab is the most interesting. This tab adjusts the volume for the speakers, and it allows you to set up the type of speaker system you have, as shown in Figure 20.16.

The Sounds tab allows you to add customized sounds to Windows events, such as the startup of a program or Windows shutdown. The Audio tab (Figure 20.17) and Voice tab do roughly the same thing: they allow you to specify the device used for input and output of general sounds (Audio tab) and voice (Voice tab). These settings are handy for folks like me who have a regular microphone and speakers but also use a headset with microphone for voice recognition or Internet telephone software. By telling Windows to use the microphone for normal sounds and to use the headset for voice recognition, I don't have to make any manual changes when I switch from listening to an MP3 to listening to my brother when he calls me over the Internet.

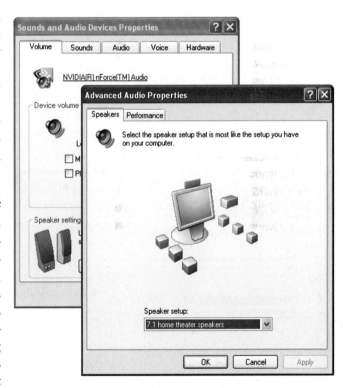

• **Figure 20.16**   Advanced Audio Properties dialog box

The Hardware tab isn't used very often, but it does have one interesting feature: it shows you all of the audio and video codecs installed in your system. (See the section on "Missing Codecs" later in this chapter for more details on codecs.)

Microsoft changed a few things between Windows XP and Windows Vista when it comes to configuring sound. The Sound applet offers better support for multiple speaker setup, for example, and integration with television via HDMI configuration options.

● **Figure 20.17**   Audio tab

● **Figure 20.18**   Sound applet in Windows Vista

To configure speakers, go to Control Panel and click Hardware and Sound; then click Sound if in Category View or double-click the Sound applet if in Classic View. Either route opens the Sound applet (Figure 20.18).

Select the Speakers option and click the Configure button to open the Speaker Setup dialog box (Figure 20.19). Select the audio channel option that's appropriate for your setup, such as the stereo system selected for my setup at the office and shown in Figure 20.19. You can click on individual speaker icons to test if the speakers are set up properly, or click the Test button to cycle through the whole range of speakers.

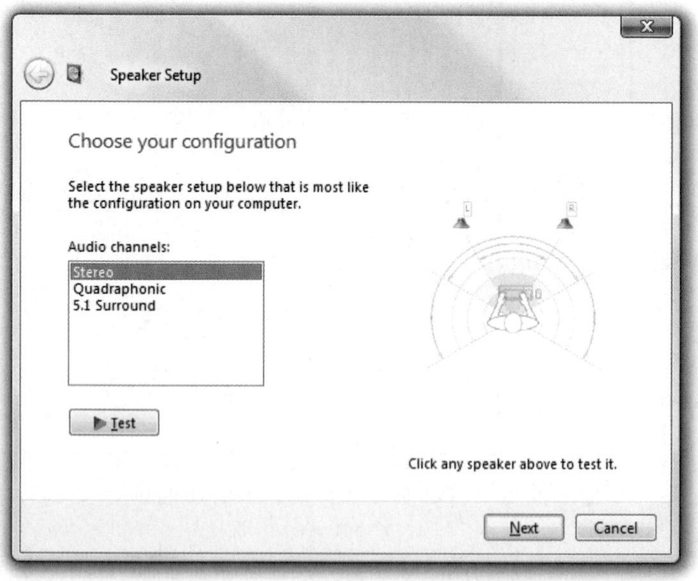

Proprietary Configuration Applications   Many sound cards install proprietary software to support configuration features not provided by Windows. Figure 20.20 shows one such application. This special configuration application comes with Creative Labs sound cards to add a few tweaks to the speaker setup that the Sounds and Audio Devices applet doesn't support.

Most sound cards come with some form of configuration program that works with the Control Panel applet to tweak the sound the way

● **Figure 20.19**   Speaker Setup dialog box in Windows Vista

● **Figure 20.20**   Creative Labs Speakers and Headphone panel

you want it. Figure 20.21 shows the applet that came with my motherboard. One of its many interesting features is to detect what types of devices are installed into the sound ports and adjust the system to use them. In other words, I don't even have to look where I'm plugging in anything! If I plug a microphone into the front speaker port, the system just adjusts the outputs—very cool. Software and sound cards that can do this are called **autosensing**.

Take some time to experiment with the program that comes with your sound card—this is a great way to learn about some of the card's features that you might otherwise not even know are there!

Specialized Applications Some sound cards—Creative Labs sound cards are by far the most infamous for this—install one or more applications, ostensibly to improve your sound experience. These are not the configuration programs just described. These applications enable you to do anything from composing music to organizing your sound files. Personally, I don't have much use for an application such as the 3DMIDI Player (Figure 20.22)—but you might be just the type of person who loves it. Be sure at least to install the applications that come with your card. If you don't like them, you can easily uninstall them.

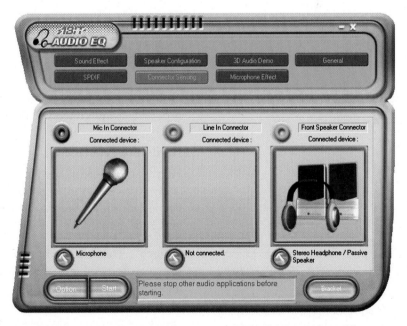

● **Figure 20.21**   Autosensing software detecting connected devices

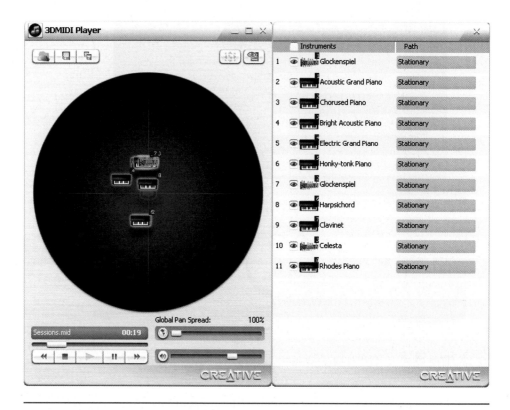

● **Figure 20.22** Creative Labs 3DMIDI Player program

Practical Application

Troubleshooting Sound

The problems you'll run into with sound seem to fall into one of two camps: those that are embarrassingly simple to repair and those that defy any possible logic and are seemingly impossible to fix. This section divides sound problems into three groups—hardware, configuration, and application problems—and gives you some ideas on how to fix these problems.

Hardware Problems

Hardware problems are by far the most common sound problems, especially if your sound card has worked for some amount of time already. Properly installed and configured sound cards almost never suddenly stop making sounds.

Volume   The absolute first item to check when a sound dies is the volume controls. Remember that you can set the volume in two places: in software and on the speakers. I can't tell you the number of times I've lost sound only to discover that my wife turned down the volume on the speakers. If the speaker volume is okay, open the volume controls in Windows by clicking the little speaker icon on the system tray, and make sure that both the master volume and the volume of the other controls are turned up (Figure 20.23).

Technically speaking, turning down the volume in the volume control program isn't a configuration problem; it's just something I always check at the same time I check the volume on the speakers.

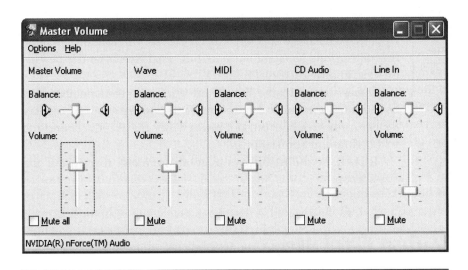

 If your system tray (i.e., the *notification area*) is cluttered and the little speaker icon hard to find, you can access the Play Control dialog box by opening the Sounds and Audio Devices applet in the Control Panel. On the Volume tab—the one that's on top by default—click the Advanced button under Device volume.

If you don't have a little speaker in your system tray at all in Windows XP, you can add it. Just check the box next to the Place volume icon in the taskbar option in the Sound and Audio Devices Properties dialog box, Volume tab. Presto!

• **Figure 20.23** Volume controls in Windows XP

Speakers The second place to look for sound problems is the speakers. Make sure the speakers are turned on and are getting good power. Then make sure the speakers are plugged into the proper connection on the back of the sound card. If this all checks out, try playing a sound, using any sound program. If the sound program *looks* like it is playing—maybe the application has an equalizer that is moving or a status marker that shows that the application is playing the sound—you may have blown speakers. Try another pair and see if the sound returns.

Configuration Problems

Configuration errors occur when the sound card is physically good but some setting hasn't been properly configured. I also include drive problems in this category. These errors happen almost exclusively at installation, but they can appear on a working system, too.

The first place to check is the Device Manager. If the driver has a problem, you'll see it right there. Try reinstalling the driver. If the driver doesn't show any problems, again try playing a sound and see if the player acts as though the sound is playing. If that's the case, you need to start touring the Sound applet or Sounds and Audio Devices applet to see if you've made a configuration error—perhaps you have the system configured for 5.1 when you have a stereo setup, or maybe you set the default sound output device to some other device. Take your time and look—configuration errors always show themselves.

Application Problems

Application problems are always the hardest to fix and tend to occur on a system that was previously playing sounds without trouble.

First, look for an error message (Figure 20.24). If an error code appears, write it down *exactly* as you see it and head to the program's support site.

Tech Tip

Sound Quality

Most of the time, speakers come in a matched set—whether it's a 2.1, 4.1, 5.1, or other system—and the manufacturer includes adequate connecting wires for the whole set. On occasion, you might run into a system in which the user has connected pairs of speakers from different sets or rigged a surround sound system by replacing the stock wires with much longer wires. Either option can create a perfectly functional surround sound system that works for a specific room, but you should make sure that all the speakers require the same wattage and that high-quality wire is used to connect them.

If you troubleshoot a system in which two of the speakers are very quiet and two are very loud, the wattages are probably different between the two pairs. A simple check of the labels should suffice to troubleshoot, or you can swap out one pair for a different pair and see if that affects the volume issues. Cheap wire, on the other hand, simply degrades the sound quality. If the speakers sounded good before being strung on long wires but they now have a lot of low-grade noise, blame the wires.

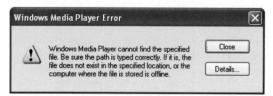

Windows Media Player Error

⚠ Windows Media Player cannot find the specified file. Be sure the path is typed correctly. If it is, the file does not exist in the specified location, or the computer where the file is stored is offline.

Close

Details...

• **Figure 20.24**   Sample error message

Odds are very good that if you have the error text, you'll get the fix right away from the support site. Of course, you can always hope the built-in help has some support, but help systems tend to be a little light in providing real fixes.

Don't always blame the sound application—remember that any sound file might be corrupted. Most sound players will display a clear error message, but not always. Try playing the sound file with a different application.

Last, it is almost always a good approach to reinstall the application.

Video Capture

A microphone, sound card, and software enable you to capture audio, but with a camera capable of capturing full motion video as well as sound, you can turn the PC into your very own movie studio. This is called **video capture**. To capture video from a source requires you to have the proper hardware installed to provide an interface with the camcorder or video player and, if the source is analog, provide translation of the signal as well; plus you need a properly configured application to do the capturing. Once captured, you can use an application to edit the video file. Then save it in some form for upload a la YouTube or save it to DVD or other removable media.

• **Figure 20.25**   A video capture device

📄 The FireWire connection seems redundant—just go straight to FireWire on the PC, right? But it's there to accomplish two goals. First, many PCs don't have a FireWire port, so you would either need to add a FireWire expansion card or use a different type of port. Second, Sony produced a series of Hi-8 camcorders some years ago that had FireWire connectors. Some translation has to happen to turn the analog signal digital.

Hardware

You need the proper hardware installed to capture video. From a digital signal, such as a modern camcorder that records directly to its own internal solid state hard drive, you simply run a cable from the FireWire out port on the camcorder to the FireWire port on your computer. If the camcorder doesn't offer FireWire, it'll most likely use Hi-Speed USB. When capturing from an analog source, such as a VHS cassette player or a Hi-8 tape, you'll need some kind of connection and translation hardware.

The Pinnacle blueBox pictured in Figure 20.25, for example, offers two different dedicated video connections (S-Video on the left and the yellow RCA jack next to it), stereo RCA audio jacks, plus a FireWire port (on the expansion card for it) for direct connection to FireWire onboard the camcorder. The breakout box uses a proprietary connection to plug into the PC.

You need a decent-grade computer with lots of free hard drive space and a substantial amount of RAM to import the video and audio streams from an external source. And you'll certainly need a serious processor when it comes time to edit and compile a new video from the source material. There's no simple rule for how much of any resource you'll need. Different projects have different demands on the hardware. If you're setting up a new computer for video capture, the simple rule is to get as powerful a system as possible with as much hard drive and RAM capacity as you can afford.

Once you have the hardware in place, the true heavy lifting in video capture falls on the software.

Software

With video editing applications, such as Pinnacle Studio or Apple Final Cut, you can import video and then work with it directly. Figure 20.26 shows the former software capturing video and audio translated through the Pinnacle blueBox from a Hi-8 camcorder. Most webcams—even those built into portable computers—are analog, rather than digital devices. Thus some software automatically creates break points in the import to make the editing process easier.

● **Figure 20.26**   Importing video in Adobe Premier Elements

The video editing software enables you to take video and audio from one or many sources and arrange clips into a time line. You can add and edit various transitions between clips, shorten clips, and so on. Figure 20.27 shows the storyboard from Final Cut Pro and a how-to video my team produced in-house.

Once you've finished the editing process, you can export to a file for archiving, sending out on optical disc, or posting to a video sharing site. With an audio file, as discussed earlier, this is a simple process. You pick a format such as MP3 and save the file. Video is far more complicated.

A video is two or more separate tracks—moving picture and audio—that each go through a compression algorithm. Otherwise, the resulting files would be huge, even for short videos. The compressed tracks then get wrapped up into a **container file**, what's often called a **wrapper**. When you receive a file saved in a standard wrapper, such as .MOV for a QuickTime Movie file, you have no way to know for certain which codecs were used to compress the video or audio tracks inside that container file (Figure 20.28).

• **Figure 20.27**　Editing in Final Cut Pro

• **Figure 20.28**　A standard container file holds multiple tracks, each encoded separately.

Codecs

Video files use standard audio codecs for the audio tracks, such as WAV or MP3, but vary wildly in the type of video codecs used. Just as with audio codecs, video codecs take a video stream and compress it by using various algorithms. Here are some of the standard video codecs.

- MPEG-2 Part 2, used for DVDs

- MPEG-4 Part 2, a codec often used for Internet broadcasts; you'll find implementations of it with other names, such as DivX

- H.264, used for high-definition movies for Blu-ray Discs, among others

- Windows Media Video (WMV), the family of Microsoft-developed codecs

- Theora, an open-source codec developed to go with the Vorbis audio codec as part of the Ogg project

- TrueMotion VP6, used in Adobe Flash; and VP7, used for Skype video conferencing, among others

- VC-1 is a Microsoft-designed codec that competes with H.264 and other higher-end codecs for the hearts and minds of Blu-ray Disc developers. You'll usually find it wrapped in a WMV container file (see the following section).

Wrappers

When both the video and audio streams of your video file are compressed, the file is placed into some sort of container file or wrapper. The key thing to note here is that the wrapper file doesn't necessarily specify how the video or audio tracks were encoded. You can look at two seemingly identical movie files, for example, both saved with the .MOV file extension, and find that one will play audio and video just fine in Windows Media Player, but the other one might play only the audio and not the video because Media Player lacks the specific codec needed to decode the video stream. (More on this in the "Troubleshooting" section.) Here are some of the standard video wrappers.

- ASF, a container used mainly for WMA and WMV streams; note that you can also have a WMV wrapper for a WMV-format file.

- AVI, the standard container file for Windows

- Flash Video (.FLV) contains streams encoded with various codecs, such as H.263 or VP6; can also handle H.264 codec. Flash Video has become the dominant standard for displaying video content on the Web through places such as YouTube and Hulu.

- MOV, the standard container file for Apple QuickTime for both Macintosh OS X and Windows

- MPEG-2 Transport Stream (MPEG-TS), a container for broadcasting that can handle many streams

- Ogg, a container file made for the open source Vorbis and Theora codecs

Troubleshooting

Video capture and playback suffer from several quirks. On the capture side, you'll find dropped frames, problems synchronizing video and audio when capturing content from an analog device, and generally poor quality captures. On the playback side, the only real issue is missing codecs.

Dropped Frames

Many things cause an initial capture to drop frames, the end result of which is loss of video information and choppy playback. This happens with both analog and digital sources, so it's not necessarily a conversion issue, and it's maddeningly common.

The most common fix for dropped frames is to *turn stuff off*. Some of this is obvious. If you're surfing the Web or doing instant messaging while trying to capture video, you'll drop frames with wild abandon. Don't do it. In fact, disconnect the computer completely from the Internet so no traffic happens in the background. Only do video capture on that machine and use another computer if you need to multitask.

Often the viewing of content you're capturing—while in the capture process—causes dropped frames. Best practice is to know what you're importing, turn off the playback or preview feature, and then start the capture. But the obvious programs aren't necessarily the primary cause of dropped frames.

Windows is a wildly extensible operating system, and programmers love to dump helper applications to run in the background to optimize their specific application. Install Apple's iTunes, for example, and you'll get more than you bargained for in programs installed. To go along with the iTunes player, the installation puts in automatic update-checking tools, iPod helpers, a quick-launch for QuickTime, and more.

The best solution is to have a machine dedicated to video capture. If you have a machine with multiple functions, however, you can turn off some of the automatically loading helper applications before you start the video capture process. You do this by stopping processes and services through the Task Manager.

In Windows Vista, get to the Task Manager by pressing CTRL-SHIFT-ESC or by pressing CTRL-ALT-DELETE and clicking the Start Task Manager option. The Processes tab shows your running processes. You can right-click any unnecessary process and close it by selecting *End process* or *End process tree* from the context menu (Figure 20.29). I generally go for the latter option, just in case some other process is running only because of the unnecessary process. That gets them all.

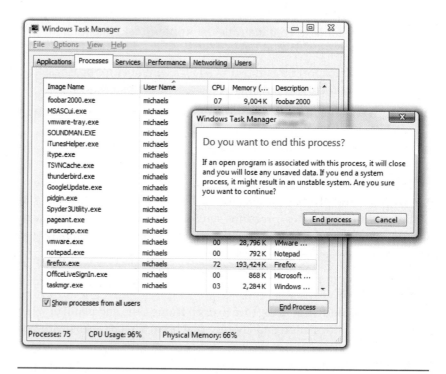

• **Figure 20.29**   Ending a process

You can disable services in the Services applet in Administrative Tools, but it's usually better to stop a service first through Task Manager, just to see if it's truly unnecessary for system stability or function.

Once you've stopped processes, click over to the Services tab. You can quickly see what's running, by sorting services by status. Just click the Status column heading to sort. Right-click any unnecessary service and select Stop Service from the context menu (Figure 20.30). Couldn't be easier!

If you find you've stopped a necessary service, you can simply right-click it again and select Start Service from the context menu. Or, if the system has become unstable, a simple reboot will reload everything.

• **Figure 20.30**   Stopping a service

Sync Problems

Capturing a video and audio stream simultaneously can be tough, because it takes the computer a lot longer to encode the video than the audio stream. This can lead to significant disconnection between the video and audio streams, so they become desynchronized. It's surprisingly easy to create a movie that's very badly lip-synced! The process of synchronizing audio and video is called **A/V sync**.

You can fix this problem sometimes by changing software or even versions of software. Alternatively, if you're having problems with an analog capture, you can record the analog signal into a digital video camcorder and then try to capture from the digital device. A bit clunky, perhaps, but it can work. Finally, you do the last solution in processing, where you manually separate the audio and video streams and then put the whole thing together synced properly.

Dealing with video capture can be difficult and time consuming, especially in the analog to digital process. A good resource to start learning the detailed ins and outs is with the folks at the Digital FAQ: www.digitalfaq.com.

Poor Capture Quality

Numerous factors can degrade the quality of a video capture, including background programs, marginal hardware for the job, and poor quality source materials. For the background program issue, follow the same procedures as you did above with the dropped frames. If the computer or the capture components can't do the job, the only fix is to upgrade. The best things to upgrade are the capture hardware and the CPU. It goes almost without saying that you'll need gobs of RAM too.

There's very little you can do if your source material, such as an old video cassette, has degraded. You're simply not going to get a pristine capture from a damaged source. You can sometimes get better quality by having the heads on the camcorder or player cleaned or by using the camcorder on which the tape was initially recorded.

There's also a common problem of video and audio going out of sync in the process of burning from a hard drive to a DVD, but that's a distinctly different problem than a lack of A/V sync in the capture process.

A dedicated A/V computer should have a fast processor and a lot of RAM. You'll want plenty of hard drive storage space too.

Missing Codecs

All versions of Windows come with some audio and video codecs installed. The default audio codecs will handle most common music formats, though you'll need to download the Vorbis codec if you want to use that format. Video codecs are a different animal.

The first clue you might have that your computer doesn't have the codec to process a video file properly is that the sound will play but no picture will appear. Occasionally, whatever media player you use will tell you that it's missing a video codec and attempt to go out onto the Internet to download a codec automatically. You can also download a codec or set of codecs manually.

Windows XP makes it easy to see the installed codecs. In Control Panel, open the Sounds and Audio Devices applet. Select the Hardware tab | Audio Codecs and click the Properties button. In the Audio Codec Properties dialog box, select the Properties tab and you'll see all the installed audio codecs (Figure 20.31).

Similarly, you can see the video codecs by choosing the Video Codecs option on the Hardware tab. Click through to the Properties tab. Figure 20.32 shows the default video codecs in Windows XP.

Microsoft made the codecs a bit more difficult to find in Windows Vista. In Vista, open Windows Media Player. Press CTRL-M to show the classic menus. Select Help | About Windows Media Player to open the About Windows Media Player dialog box (Figure 20.33).

Click the link for Technical Support Information and Windows will open your default Web browser with a long page showing various multimedia settings. Scroll down the page and you'll find the audio and video codecs installed (Figure 20.34).

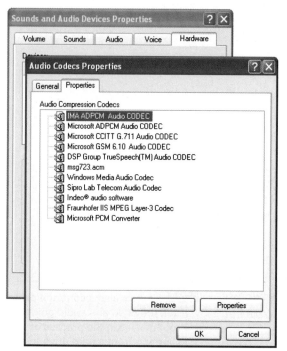

• **Figure 20.31**   Default audio codecs in Windows XP SP2

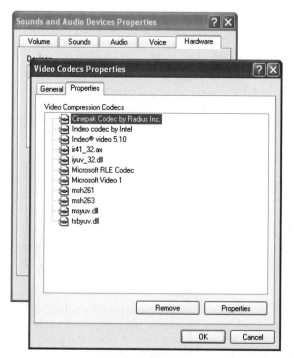

• **Figure 20.32**   Default video codecs in Windows XP SP2

• **Figure 20.33**   About Windows Media Player dialog box in Windows Vista

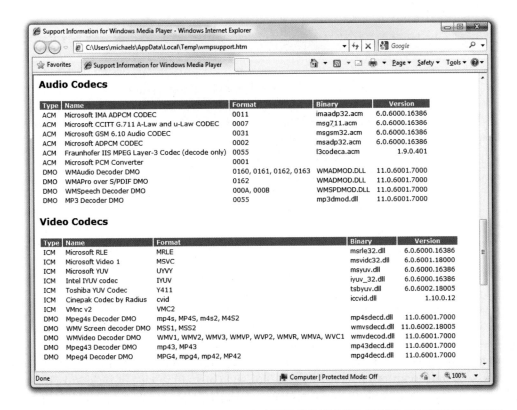

Audio Codecs

Type	Name	Format	Binary	Version
ACM	Microsoft IMA ADPCM CODEC	0011	imaadp32.acm	6.0.6000.16386
ACM	Microsoft CCITT G.711 A-Law and u-Law CODEC	0007	msg711.acm	6.0.6000.16386
ACM	Microsoft GSM 6.10 Audio CODEC	0031	msgsm32.acm	6.0.6000.16386
ACM	Microsoft ADPCM CODEC	0002	msadp32.acm	6.0.6000.16386
ACM	Fraunhofer IIS MPEG Layer-3 Codec (decode only)	0055	l3codeca.acm	1.9.0.401
ACM	Microsoft PCM Converter	0001		
DMO	WMAudio Decoder DMO	0160, 0161, 0162, 0163	WMADMOD.DLL	11.0.6001.7000
DMO	WMAPro over S/PDIF DMO	0162	WMADMOD.DLL	11.0.6001.7000
DMO	WMSpeech Decoder DMO	000A, 000B	WMSPDMOD.DLL	11.0.6001.7000
DMO	MP3 Decoder DMO	0055	mp3dmod.dll	11.0.6001.7000

Video Codecs

Type	Name	Format	Binary	Version
ICM	Microsoft RLE	MRLE	msrle32.dll	6.0.6000.16386
ICM	Microsoft Video 1	MSVC	msvidc32.dll	6.0.6001.18000
ICM	Microsoft YUV	UYVY	msyuv.dll	6.0.6000.16386
ICM	Intel IYUV codec	IYUV	iyuv_32.dll	6.0.6000.16386
ICM	Toshiba YUV Codec	Y411	tsbyuv.dll	6.0.6002.18005
ICM	Cinepak Codec by Radius	cvid	iccvid.dll	1.10.0.12
ICM	VMnc v2	VMC2		
DMO	Mpeg4s Decoder DMO	mp4s, MP4S, m4s2, M4S2	mp4sdecd.dll	11.0.6001.7000
DMO	WMV Screen decoder DMO	MSS1, MSS2	wmvsdecd.dll	11.0.6002.18005
DMO	WMVideo Decoder DMO	WMV1, WMV2, WMV3, WMVP, WVP2, WMVR, WMVA, WVC1	wmvdecod.dll	11.0.6001.7000
DMO	Mpeg43 Decoder DMO	mp43, MP43	mp43decd.dll	11.0.6001.7000
DMO	Mpeg4 Decoder DMO	MPG4, mpg4, mp42, MP42	mpg4decd.dll	11.0.6001.7000

• **Figure 20.34**   Viewing audio and video codecs installed in Windows Vista

If you don't have a codec that you need, you can download that specific codec. A great site for codec information is www.fourcc.org.

You can also download codec packs, such as the Vista Codec Package available at www.afreecodec.com. The packs contain just about everything you need to view and hear content found on the Internet.

TV Tuners

With a **TV tuner**, you can have it all in one package: a computer and the latest TV show as well. Most local stations (in the United States, at least) broadcast high-definition signals, so with the proper TV tuner, you can watch your HDTV without any of the artifacting you see with both cable and satellite feeds. Plus you can make use of typical cable or satellite feeds to watch television as you would with a regular TV. Making it all happen requires four components: a tuner device, an antenna or cable connection, a tuning application, and some sort of program guide. We'll look at troubleshooting at the end.

Tuner Hardware

TV tuners come in just about every expansion option available for computers: expansion cards that plug into PCI or PCIe slots on the motherboard; PC Card or ExpressCard for portable computers; or Hi-Speed USB for desktop and laptop computers. Figure 20.35 shows a PCIe version of an ATI tuner card.

Chapter 20: Multimedia

• Figure 20.35   ATI TV tuner card

To install a TV tuner, follow standard installation procedures.

To pick up a signal on the TV tuner, just as with a standalone television, you need some source. Most can handle a cable TV connection, for example, or an over-the-air antenna. Figure 20.36 shows a USB Hauppauge HDTV tuner card with retractable antenna. For such a small device, it picks up HDTV signals quite well. You'll get the best results for uncompressed HD signals by using a serious, mounted-on-the-rooftop metal antenna with lots of tines.

Tuner hardware comes with a standard coaxial connection. You can plug in a cable or satellite source just as you would any regular television.

Tuner Software

Once you've installed the hardware, you need to load the specific application or applications that make the tuner work as a tuner. If you have a copy

> TV tuners often include components for video capture, so you can get both devices on one card or expansion device.

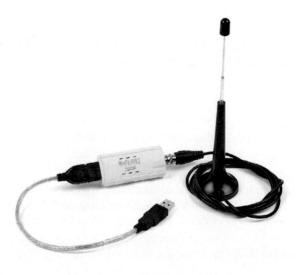

• Figure 20.36   Hauppauge TV tuner with retractable antenna

● **Figure 20.37**   EyeTV tuner application

of Windows Media Center (through either that version of Windows XP or Windows Vista Ultimate), that will often be the tool of choice. Tuner card distributors bundle third-party applications with their cards. Figure 20.37 shows the EyeTV software enabling the computer to show television shows.

Tuner Troubleshooting

The two biggest issues with TV tuner devices are operating system compatibility and poor reception. Some cards simply don't work with Windows Vista, due to driver incompatibility or some other issue. The only fix for this problem is to use one that does work.

The antenna that comes with your tuner should enable you to pick up TV broadcasts in most places, certainly around cities. But a small sliver of metal can only do so well, so you'll experience stuttering, essentially lost frames that may or may not make the program you're viewing unviewable. So an antenna used primarily for portable computing, such as the telescoping model pictured in Figure 20.36, is great, but if you install a tuner in a static computer, consider investing in a proper outdoor antenna.

Beyond A+

Sound Card Benchmarking

Sound cards can demand a huge share of system resources—particularly CPU time—during intense work (such as gaming). Most techs who find an otherwise serviceable PC stuttering during games will immediately blame the video card or the video card drivers. What they don't realize is that sound cards can be the cause of the problem. A test of a client's built-in audio, for example, revealed that at peak usage the sound card took more than 30 percent of the CPU cycles. Thirty percent? Holy smokes! And he wondered

why his system bogged down on yesterday's games! He could just forget about playing Crysis.

The folks at http://audio.rightmark.org make an excellent suite of sound card benchmarking utilities that helps you analyze the particulars of any sound card: RightMark 3DSound (Figure 20.38). It will run a system through fairly serious tests, from regular sound to 3-D positional audio, and reveal whether or not the sound processor—built-in or expansion card—is causing a problem with resource use. You can find the utility at http://audio.rightmark.org.

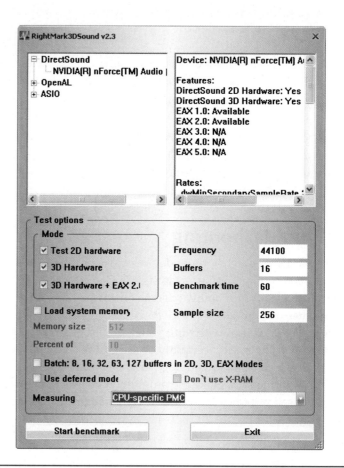

• **Figure 20.38**   RightMark 3DSound

■ Chapter Summary

After reading this chapter and completing the exercises, you should understand the following aspects of multimedia.

Describe how to implement sound in a PC

■ The process by which sounds are stored in electronic format on your PC is called sampling. Sampling means capturing the state or quality of a particular sound wave a set number of times each second. All the characteristics of a particular sound wave—amplitude, frequency, timbre—need to be recorded and translated into ones and zeros to reproduce that sound accurately within the computer and out to your speakers. Sounds are sampled thousands of times per second. The amount of information stored at each sampling is called the bit depth, and the higher the bit depth, the better the recording.

■ The popular WAV file format (as well as most other recorded sound formats) is based on PCM. WAV files can be huge, especially when sampled at high frequency and depth, so compression is a popular way to reduce the file size of recorded sounds. The most popular compressed file type is MP3.

■ To play sounds, you must have some form of player software, such as Windows Media Player. Not all players can play all types of sound files. Some file formats, such as RealMedia, require their own proprietary players.

■ MIDI files are not recordings like WAV files. A MIDI file is a text file that takes advantage of the sound processing hardware to enable the PC to produce sound. Programmers use these small files to tell the sound card what notes to play, how long, how loud, on which instruments, and so forth.

■ Sound cards use either FM synthesis or wave table synthesis to store notes for MIDI. FM synthesis electronically simulates various instruments, whereas wave table synthesis uses pre-recorded instruments.

■ A large number of other sound file formats are available, such as AAC and WMA. Sounds can also be found in video formats, applications, and streaming media, such as the Flash videos on YouTube.

■ Low-end sound processors do little more than translate, which means that the CPU has to do the heavy lifting on the processing front. Better sound processors, in contrast, shoulder much of the processing burden and bring a series of extra features to the table. Most mid-range and all high-end sound processors offer support for various surround sound standards, enabling equally equipped games and other applications to provide positional audio effects and detailed sound modeling.

■ Every sound card supports two speakers or a pair of headphones, but many better sound cards support five or more speakers in discrete channels. These multiple speakers provide surround sound and thumping bass through a subwoofer.

■ Better sound cards have a lower signal-to-noise ratio and support for multiple audio connections, such as a microphone, line in, and S/PDIF. The latter is for high-end audio.

■ Speaker standards include stereo (which uses a left speaker and a right speaker), 2.1 (stereo with an additional subwoofer), and surround sound. Do yourself or your client a favor and spend the extra money for good speakers. They don't cost that much more than cheap speakers and they make an enormous difference for the user experience.

■ Surround sound is popular for games and DVD/Blu-ray movies. A number of surround sound standards exist, but the most common are Dolby Digital and DTS. The Dolby Digital and DTS standards both require at least five speakers and a subwoofer.

■ Sound card installation can be divided into three major steps: physical installation, device driver installation, and configuration.

■ Although the physical installation of a sound card is straightforward, knowing where to plug in multiple speakers can be a bit of a challenge.

■ It is preferable to use the driver that comes with the sound card as opposed to the Windows built-in drivers.

Using such a laptop at an outdoor café, for example, is almost hopeless during daylight.

Manufacturers released high-gloss laptop screens in 2006, and they've rapidly taken over many store shelves. The high-gloss finish offers sharper contrast, richer colors, and wider viewing angles when compared to the matte screens. Each manufacturer has a different name for high-gloss coatings. Dell calls theirs TrueLife, Acer calls theirs CrystalBrite, and HP calls theirs BrightView. The drawback to the high-gloss screens is that, contrary to what the manufacturers claim, they pick up lots of reflection from nearby objects, including the user! So although they're usable outside during the day, you'll need to contend with increased reflection as well.

● **Figure 21.1** A notebook PC

Desktop Replacements

When asked about portable computing devices, most folks describe the traditional clamshell **laptop** computer, such as the one in Figure 21.1, with built-in LCD monitor, keyboard, and input device (a *touchpad*, in this case). A typical laptop computer functions as a fully standalone PC, potentially even replacing the desktop. The one in Figure 21.1, for example, has all of the features you expect the modern PC to have, such as a fast CPU, lots of RAM, a high-capacity hard drive, CD-RW and DVD drives, an excellent sound system, and a functioning copy of Windows. Attach it to a network and you can browse the Internet and send e-mail. Considering that it weighs almost as much as a mini-tower PC (or at least it feels like it does when I'm lugging it through the airport!), such a portable can be considered a **desktop replacement**, because it does everything most people want to do with a desktop PC and doesn't compromise performance just to make the laptop a few pounds lighter or the battery last an extra hour.

For input devices, desktop replacements (and other portables) used trackballs in the early days, often plugged in like a mouse and clipped to the side of the case. Other models with trackballs placed them in front of the keyboard at the edge of the case nearest the user, or behind the keyboard at the edge nearest the screen.

The next wave to hit the laptop market was IBM's **TrackPoint** device, a joystick the size of a pencil eraser, situated in the center of the keyboard. With the TrackPoint, you can move the pointer around without taking your fingers away from the "home" typing position. You use a forefinger to push the joystick around, and then click or right-click, using two buttons below the spacebar. This type of pointing device has since been licensed for use by other manufacturers, and it continues to appear on laptops today.

But by far the most common laptop pointing device found today is the **touchpad** (Figure 21.2)—a flat, touch-sensitive pad just in front of the keyboard. To operate a touchpad, you simply glide your finger across its surface to move the pointer, and tap the surface once or twice to single- or double-click. You can also click by using buttons just below the pad. Most people get the hang of this technique after just a few minutes of practice. The main advantage of the touchpad over previous laptop pointing devices is that it uses no moving parts—a fact that can really extend the life of a hard-working laptop. Some modern laptops actually provide both a TrackPoint-type device and a touchpad, to give the user a choice.

Desktop Extenders

Manufacturers offer **desktop extender** portable devices that don't replace the desktop but rather extend it by giving you a subset of features of the typical desktop that you can take away from the desk. Figure 21.3 shows a portable with a good but small 13.3-inch wide screen. The system has 2 GB of RAM, a 2-GHz processor, a 60-GB hard drive, and a battery that enables you to do work on it for more than five hours while disconnected from the wall socket. Even though it plays music and has a couple of decent tiny speakers, you can't game on this computer (Solitaire, perhaps, but definitely not Crysis!). But it weighs only five pounds, nearly half the weight of the typical desktop replacement portable.

Desktop extenders enable you to go mobile. When I'm on a roll writing, for example, I don't want to stop. But sometimes I do want to take a break from the office and stroll over to my favorite café for a latté or a pint of fine ale. At moments like these, I don't need a fully featured laptop with a monster 15-inch or 17-inch screen, but just a good word processing system—and perhaps the ability to surf the Internet on the café's wireless network so I can ~~goof off~~ research other important topics once I finish my project for the day. A lightweight laptop with a 12-inch or 13-inch screen, a reasonably fast processor, and gobs of RAM does nicely.

● **Figure 21.2**   Touchpad on a laptop

● **Figure 21.3**   Excellent mid-sized portable computer

Netbooks

Netbooks are computers that fill the gap between PDAs and the smaller laptops. These machines usually have displays in the 6- to 10-inch range, modest-sized hard drives, and CPUs geared more for minimal power usage than raw speed. With netbooks, the focus is on small and low priced compared to their more full-featured cousins. This segment of the market is ever evolving, though, and there is quite a bit a blurring between the various classes of laptops.

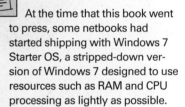 At the time that this book went to press, some netbooks had started shipping with Windows 7 Starter OS, a stripped-down version of Windows 7 designed to use resources such as RAM and CPU processing as lightly as possible.

 Tech Tip

Spin the Weight

Manufacturers advertise the weight of portable PCs, for the most part, without the weight of the battery or the removable drives. Although this deception is deplorable, it's pretty much universal in the industry because no manufacturer wants to be the first to say that their desktop-replacement portable, including battery and DVD-RW drive, weighs 15 pounds, when their competitor advertises the same kind of machine at 7.5 pounds! They'd lose market share quickly.

So when you shop or recommend portable PCs, take the real weight into consideration. By the time you fill your laptop bag with a power adapter, external mouse, spare battery, and all the extra accessories, you'll definitely be carrying more than the advertised 5–6 pounds.

● **Figure 21.4** Asus Eee PC sitting on a normal laptop

A prime example of the netbook is the Asus Eee PC, shown in Figure 21.4 sitting on a full-sized laptop. This netbook has a 9-inch screen, a 1.6-GHz Intel Atom CPU, a small solid-state drive, and runs a customized Linux distribution. A key distinguishing feature of these netbooks is the use of Intel's Atom processor. The Atom CPU is very useful for keeping power usage down but has much less computing power than its more power-hungry siblings. Therefore, most netbooks run either Windows XP or some form of Linux that is better suited for their limited resources.

PDAs and Smartphones

Having a few computing essentials on hand at all times eases the day and makes planning and scheduling much more likely to succeed. Several companies, such as Palm, Apple, HTC, RIM, and Hewlett-Packard, manufacture tiny handheld portable computing devices that hold such data as your address book, appointment schedules, music, movies, and more. Such machines are called **personal digital assistants (PDAs)**, or smartphones if they have calling capabilities. All modern PDAs have many applications, such as Web browsers for surfing the Web on the go, some sort of note-taking application for jotting down quick notes, and many more. Figure 21.5 shows an Apple iPhone smartphone.

> Sadly, the heavy Windows-only attitude of the CompTIA A+ exams means you won't get any questions about the Apple iPhone. All the same, the iPhone is a *great* example of what a smartphone should be; I own one.

PDAs don't run Windows XP or Vista but rather require specialized OSs such as Windows Mobile, Google Android, Apple iPhone OS, Palm WebOS, and various forms of Linux. All of these OSs provide a GUI that enables you to interact with the device by touching the screen directly. Many of today's PDAs use handwriting recognition combined with modified mouse functions, usually in the form of a pen-like **stylus** to make a type of input called **pen-based computing**. To make an application load, for example, you would slide the stylus out of its holder in the PDA case and touch the appropriate icon with the stylus tip.

Sync

PDAs make excellent pocket companions because you can quickly add a client's address or telephone number, verify the day's schedule before going to your next meeting, and check your e-mail. Best of all, you can then update all the equivalent features on your desktop PC automatically! PDAs synchronize with your primary PC so you have the same essential data on both machines. Many PDAs come with a cradle, a place to rest your PDA and recharge its battery. The cradle connects to the PC most often through a USB port. You can run software to synchronize the data between the PDA and the main PC (Figure 21.6). Setting up for a PDA running Windows Mobile, for example, requires you to install a program called Activesync if you're using Windows XP. Vista and Windows 7 drop Activesync and use the built-in **Windows Mobile Device Center (WMDC)**. This software handles all the synchronization chores. You simply place the PDA in the properly connected cradle to synchronize.

● **Figure 21.5** Apple iPhone

● **Figure 21.6** A sync operation

PDA to PDA Communication

Just about every PDA comes with a way to move data from one PDA to another. The original technology for this is called IrDA and the process is called *beaming*. IrDA uses infrared light just like a TV remote to transmit the data between devices. You can use beaming to quickly transfer contact info or small pictures, but larger files take much longer because of IrDA's slow speed.

Today, the primary way to move data between PDAs is with radio waves, be it Bluetooth, Wi-Fi, or what CompTIA calls *Cellular WAN*. Bluetooth can be thought of as the most direct replacement for the old IrDA tech. When you wish to transfer files between two Bluetooth devices, you first make each device *discoverable*, which allows other devices in the area to see that it exists. On the sending device, you then select the PDA you wish to send to. The receiving device asks you if you wish to accept the file, and once that's granted, you simply stand there and wait for a moment while the PDAs transfer data. Slick!

With Wi-Fi and Cellular WAN, your PDA acts just like any other computer on a network. You will have an IP address and—depending on the OS your PDA is running—the capability to share files and data. Most PDAs today use a touch screen for entering data and use IrDA, Wi-Fi, and/or Bluetooth connections to communicate with other devices.

PDA Storage

Almost every PDA has both internal flash ROM memory of 1 MB or more and some sort of removable and upgradeable storage medium. Secure Digital (SD) technology has the strongest market share among the many competing standards, but you'll find a bunch of different memory card types out there. SD is by far the most popular, with the cards coming in a variety of physical sizes (SD, Mini SD, and Micro SD) and fitting in a special SD slot. You'll find capacities ranging from 4 MB up to 32 GB—on a card the size of a postage stamp! Figure 21.7 shows some typical memory cards.

Chapter 24, "Wireless Networking," goes into more detail on all these technologies.

• **Figure 21.7**   SD and Micro SD cards

Tech Tip

Memory Cards
Memory cards made the leap in 2003 from the exclusive realm of tiny devices such as PDAs and digital photographic cameras to full-featured portable PCs and even desktop models. Many laptop PCs sport SD card slots, for example, and you can expect nearly every Sony PC—portable or otherwise—made in 2003 and later to offer a Memory Stick port.

Tablet PCs

Tablet PCs combine the handwriting benefits of PDAs with the full-fledged power of traditional portable PCs to create a machine that perfectly meets the needs of many professions. Unlike PDAs and smartphones, tablet PCs use a full-featured PC operating system such as Microsoft Vista Home Premium and up.

Instead of (or in addition to) a keyboard and mouse, tablet PCs provide a screen that doubles as an input device. With a special pen, called a *stylus*, you can actually write on the screen (see Figure 21.8). Just make sure you don't grab your fancy Cross ballpoint pen accidentally and start writing on the screen! Unlike many PDA screens, most tablet PC screens are not pressure sensitive—you have to use the stylus to write on the screen. Tablet PCs come in two main form factors: *convertibles*, which include a keyboard that you can fold out of the way, and *slates*, which do away with the keyboard entirely. The convertible tablet PC in Figure 21.8, for example, looks and functions just like

• **Figure 21.8**   A tablet PC

the typical clamshell laptop shown back in Figure 21.1. But here it's shown with the screen rotated 180 degrees and snapped flat so it functions as a slate. Pretty slick!

In applications that aren't "tablet-aware," the stylus acts just like a mouse, enabling you to select items, double-click, right-click, and so on. To input text with the stylus, you can either tap keys on a virtual keyboard (shown in Figure 21.9), write in the writing utility (shown in Figure 21.10), or use speech recognition software. With a little practice, most

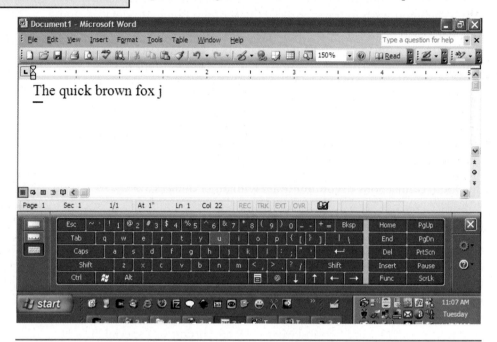

• **Figure 21.9** The virtual keyboard

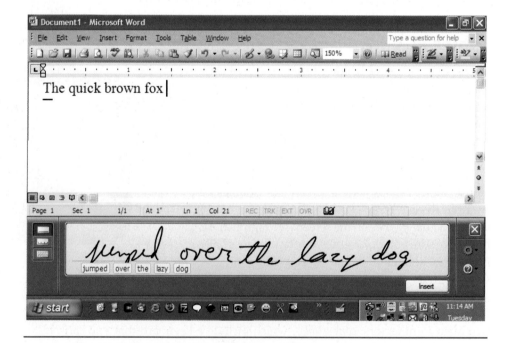

• **Figure 21.10** The writing pad

Mike Meyers' CompTIA A+ Guide to Managing and Troubleshooting PCs

users find the computer's accuracy in recognizing their handwriting to be sufficient for most text input, although speedy touch-typists will probably still want to use a keyboard when typing longer documents.

Tablet PCs work well when you have limited space or have to walk around and use a laptop. Anyone who has ever tried to type with one hand while walking around the factory floor and holding the laptop with the other hand will immediately appreciate the beauty of a tablet PC. In this scenario, tablet PCs are most effective when combined with applications designed to be used with a stylus instead of a keyboard. An inventory control program, for example, might present drop-down lists and radio buttons to the user, making a stylus the perfect input tool. With the right custom application, tablet PCs become indispensable tools.

Microsoft encourages software developers to take advantage of a feature they call *digital ink*, which allows applications to accept pen strokes as input without first converting the pen strokes into text or mouse-clicks. In Microsoft Journal, which comes with Windows-based tablet PCs, you can write on the screen just as though you were writing on a paper legal pad (see Figure 21.11). Many other applications, including Microsoft Office, allow you to add ink annotations. Imagine sitting on an airplane reviewing a Microsoft Word document and simply scribbling your comments on the screen (Figure 21.12). No more printing out hard copy and breaking out the red pen for me! Imagine running a PowerPoint presentation and being able to annotate your presentation as you go. In the future, look for more applications to support Microsoft's digital ink.

Many useful third-party applications are designed specifically to take advantage of the tablet PC form factor. In fields such as law and medicine, where tablet PCs have been especially

● **Figure 21.11**   Microsoft Journal preserves pen strokes as digital ink.

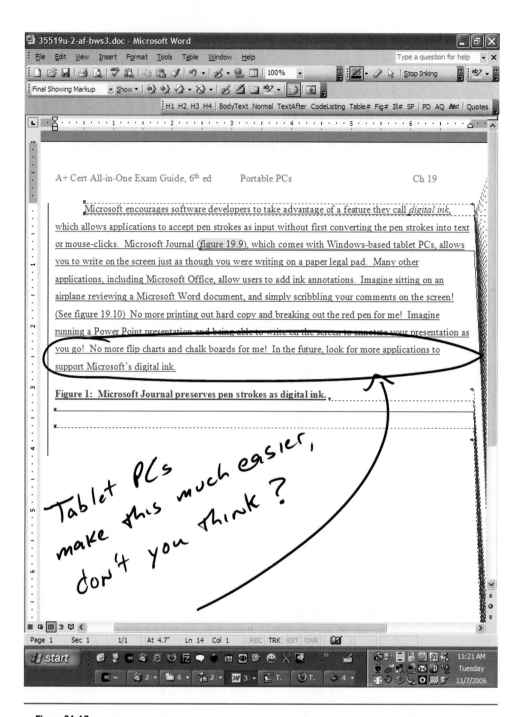

● **Figure 21.12**   Microsoft Office supports digital ink.

popular, the choices are endless. One handy free utility that anyone who spends time in front of an audience (teachers, salespeople, cult leaders, and so on) will appreciate is InkyBoard (www.cfcassidy.com/Inkyboard). InkyBoard provides a virtual dry-erase board, eliminating the need to find a flip chart or dry-erase board when holding meetings. Ever wished you could have a record of everything that was written on the chalkboard in a class (or business meeting)? If the professor had used InkyBoard, creating and distributing a copy would be a snap.

Portable Computer Device Types

Sorting through all the variations of portable computing devices out there would take entirely too much ink (and go well beyond CompTIA A+). Table 21.2 lists the seven most common styles of portable computing devices, some of their key features, and the intended use or audience for the product. This table is in no way comprehensive, but lists the highlights.

Table 21.2	Portable Computing Devices			
	Screen Size	**Weight**	**Features**	**Uses**
Desktop replacements	14–20 inch+	8–12+ lbs	Everything on a desktop.	Mobile multimedia editing, presentations, mobile gaming.
Desktop extenders	10–14 inch	4–7 lbs	Almost everything you'll find on a desktop. Better battery life than desktop replacements.	Presentations, note-taking in class or meetings, traveling companion for business folks.
Netbooks	6–10 inch	2–3 lbs	Ultimate mobility without sacrificing full PC status. Excellent battery life. No optical drives, limited SSD storage or modest HDD storage.	Long-term traveling companion and small enough to fit in a purse or backpack. Perfect for Web browsing or doing e-mail on the road.
Tablet PCs	10–12 inch	4 lbs	Pen-based interface so you can use them like a paper notepad; no optical drives but integrated wireless networking.	Niche market for people who need handwritten notes that have to be transcribed to the PC.
Ultra mobile PCs	4–7 inch	1–2 lbs	A variation of tablet PCs, UMPCs have Windows XP (Tablet or Home edition), pen-based or touch pad interface, and no optical drives.	More of a niche market than tablet PCs, UMPCs have been overshadowed by netbooks.
PDAs	Up to 4 inches	1 lb	Light, multifunctional devices that carry address book, scheduler, and such features as MP3 and video playback.	Helps busy people stay organized. Classic PDAs (without telephone functions) are rare today except for specialized uses (hospitals, point-of-sale).
Smartphones	Up to 4 inches	< 1 lbs	Tiny PDAs built into a cell phone; offer Web browsing, SMS, and other Internet connectivity features.	Reduces the number of gadgets some folks carry. Have all but replaced standard PDAs.

Try This!

Variations

Portables come in such a dizzying variety of sizes, styles, features, and shapes that a simple table in a book cannot do justice to the ingenuity and engineering of the manufacturers of these devices. Only a hands-on field trip can bring home the point for you, so Try This!

1. Visit your local computer or electronics store and tour the portable computing devices.

2. How many variations of laptops are there? Do any offer funky features, such as a swivel screen, portrait-to-landscape mode, or touch screen capabilities?

3. How many variations of PDA do you see? What operating systems do they run?

4. What other devices do you find? What about tablet PCs?

5. If you want to wander into the realm of extremes, check out www.dynamism.com. This company specializes in bringing Japanese-only products to the English-speaking market. You'll find the hottest desktop replacement laptops and the sleekest subnotebooks at the site, with all the details beautifully converted from native Japanese to English.

Practical Application

■ Enhancing and Upgrading Portable Computers

With fully 1 in 5 questions covering laptops and portables, pay attention to this chapter when studying for the CompTIA A+ certification!

In the dark ages of mobile computing, you had to shell out top dollar for any device that would unplug, and what you purchased was what you got. Upgrade a laptop? Add functions to your desktop replacement? You had few if any options, so you simply paid for a device that would be way behind the technology curve within a year and functionally obsolete within two.

Portable PCs today offer many ways to enhance their capabilities. Internal and external expansion buses enable you to add completely new functions to portables, such as attaching a scanner or mobile printer or both. You can take advantage of the latest wireless technology breakthrough simply by slipping a card into the appropriate slot on the laptop. Further, modern portables offer a modular interior. You can add or change RAM, for example—the first upgrade that almost every laptop owner wants to make. You can increase the hard drive storage space and, at least with some models, swap out the CPU, video card, sound card, and more. Gone forever are the days of buying guaranteed obsolescence! Let's look at four specific areas of technology that laptops use to enhance functions and upgrade components: PC Cards, single- and multiple-function expansion ports, and modular components.

PC Cards

The *Personal Computer Memory Card International Association (PCMCIA)* establishes standards involving portable computers, especially when it comes to expansion cards, which are generically called PC Cards. **PC Cards** are roughly credit card–sized devices that enhance and extend the functions of a portable PC. PC Cards are as standard on today's mobile computers as the hard drive. PC Cards are easy to use, inexpensive, and convenient. Figure 21.13 shows a typical PC Card.

Almost every portable PC has one or two PC Card slots, into which you insert a PC Card. Each card has at least one function, but many have two, three, or more! You can buy a PC Card that offers connections for removable media, for example, such as combination SD and CF card readers. You can also find PC Cards that enable you to plug into multiple types of networks. All PC Cards are hot-swappable, meaning you can plug them in without powering down the PC.

The PCMCIA has established two versions of PC Cards, one using a parallel bus and the other using a serial bus. Each version, in turn, offers two technology variations as well as several physical varieties. This might sound complicated at first, but here's the map to sort it all out.

> CompTIA uses the older term **PCMCIA cards** to describe PC Cards. Don't be shocked if you get that as an option on your exams! You'll hear many techs use the phrase as well, though the PCMCIA trade group has not used it for many years.

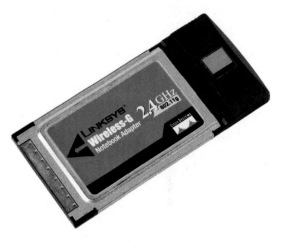

• **Figure 21.13** PC Card

Parallel PC Cards

Parallel PC Cards come in two flavors, **16-bit** and **CardBus**, and each flavor comes in three physical sizes, called Type I, Type II, and Type III. The 16-bit PC Cards, as the name suggests, are 16-bit, 5-V cards that can have up to two distinct functions or devices, such as a modem/network card combination. CardBus PC Cards are 32-bit, 3.3-V cards that can have up to eight (!) functions on a single card. Regular PC Cards fit into and work in CardBus slots, but the reverse is not true. CardBus totally dominates the current PC Card landscape, but you might still run into older 16-bit PC Cards.

> Many manufacturers use the term *hot-pluggable* rather than hot-swappable to describe the ability to plug in and replace PC Cards on the fly. Look for either term on the exams.

Type I, II, and III cards differ only in the thickness of the card (Type I being the thinnest, and Type III the thickest). All PC Cards share the same 68-pin interface, so any PC Card will work in any slot that accepts that card type. Type II cards are by far the most common of PC Cards. Therefore, most laptops have two Type II slots, one above the other, so the computer can accept two Type I or II cards or one Type III card (Figure 21.14).

Although PCMCIA doesn't require that certain sizes perform certain functions, most PC Cards follow their recommendations. Table 21.3 lists the sizes and typical uses of each type of PC Card.

ExpressCard

ExpressCard, the high-performance serial version of the PC Card, has begun to replace PC Card slots

• **Figure 21.14** PC Card slots

Tech Tip

Keeping Your PC Cards Healthy

PC Cards typically come with a hard plastic storage case. Always be sure to use this case to store the cards when you're not using them. If dust, dirt, or grime gets into the array of contacts at the end of the card, the card won't work when you try to use it next. Also, be careful when using PC Cards that extend out of the PC Card slot past the edge of your laptop. One dark night I set my laptop on the floor with a PC Card NIC sticking out of it while I went to get a drink of water. On my way back, I accidentally stepped on the card sticking out of my laptop and nearly snapped it in half. Luckily, my laptop wasn't damaged, but the card was toast!

ExpressCards don't require either socket or card services, at least not in the way PC Cards do. The ExpressCard modules automatically configure the software on your computer, which makes them truly plug and play.

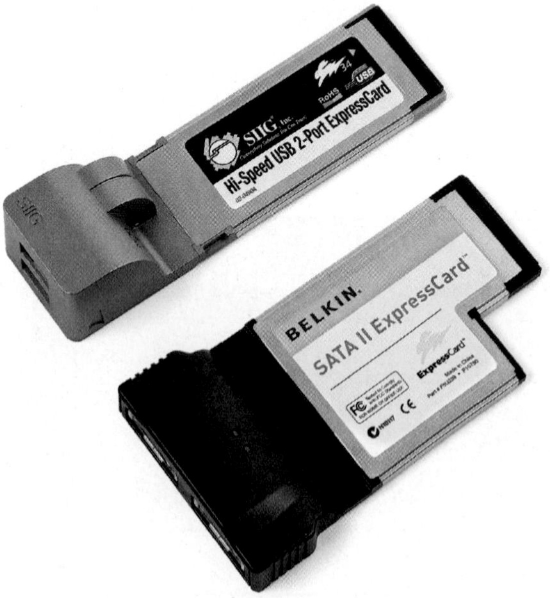

• **Figure 21.15** 34-mm and 54-mm ExpressCards

Table 21.3 PC Card Types and Their Typical Uses

Type	Length	Width	Thickness	Typical Use
Type I	85.6 mm	54.0 mm	3.3 mm	Flash memory
Type II	85.6 mm	54.0 mm	5.0 mm	I/O (Modem, NIC, and so on)
Type III	85.6 mm	54.0 mm	10.5 mm	Hard drives

on newer laptop PCs. Although ExpressCard offers significant performance benefits, keep in mind that ExpressCard and PC Cards are incompatible. You cannot use your PC Card in your new laptop's ExpressCard socket. The PC Card has had a remarkably long life in portable PCs, and you can still find it on some new laptops, but get ready to replace all of your PC Card devices. ExpressCard comes in two widths: 54 mm and 34 mm. Figure 21.15 shows a 34-mm ExpressCard. Both cards are 75 mm long and 5 mm thick, which makes them shorter than all previous PC Cards and the same thickness as a Type II PC Card.

ExpressCards connect to either the Hi-Speed USB 2.0 bus or a PCI Express bus. These differ phenomenally in speed. The amazingly slow-in-comparison USB version has a maximum throughput of 480 Mbps. The PCIe version, in contrast, roars in at 2.5 Gbps in unidirectional communication. Very nice!

Table 21.4 shows the throughput and variations for the parallel and serial PC Cards currently or soon to be on the market.

Software Support for PC Cards

The PCMCIA standard defines two levels of software drivers to support PC Cards. The first and lower level is known as **socket services**. Socket services are device drivers that support the PC Card socket, enabling the system to detect when a PC Card has been inserted or removed, and providing the necessary I/O to the device. The second and higher level is known as **card services**. The card services level recognizes the function of a particular PC Card and provides the specialized drivers necessary to make the card work.

In today's laptops, the socket services are standardized and are handled by the system BIOS. Windows itself handles all card services and has a large preinstalled base of PC Card device drivers, although most PC Cards come with their own drivers.

Table 21.4 PC Card Speeds

Standard	Maximum Theoretical Throughput
PC Card using 16-bit bus	160 Mbps
CardBus PC Card using PCI bus	1056 Mbps
ExpressCard using USB 2.0 bus	480 Mbps
ExpressCard using PCIe bus	2.5 Gbps

Single-Function Ports

All portable PCs and many PDAs come with one or more ports. You'd have a hard time finding a portable computing device that doesn't have a speaker port, and this includes modern PDAs. My Apple iPhone functions as an excellent MP3 player, by the way, a feature now included with most PDAs and smartphones. Some portables have line in and microphone jacks as well. Laptops invariably provide a video port such as a VGA or DVI connection for hooking up an external monitor and a PS/2 port for a keyboard or mouse. Finally, most current portable PCs come with built-in NICs or modems for networking support. (See "The Modular Laptop" section later in this chapter for more on networking capabilities.)

Ports work the same way on portable PCs as they do on desktop models. You plug in a device to a particular port and, as long as Windows has the proper drivers, you will have a functioning device when you boot. The only port that requires any extra effort is the video port.

Most laptops support a second monitor via an analog VGA port or a digital DVI, HDMI, or DisplayPort port in the back of the box. With a second monitor attached, you can display Windows on only the laptop LCD, only the external monitor, or both simultaneously. Not all portables can do all variations, but they're more common than not. Most portables have a special Function (FN) key on the keyboard that, when pressed, adds an additional option to certain keys on the keyboard. Figure 21.16 shows a close-up of a typical keyboard with the Function key; note the other options you can access with the Function key, such as indicated on the F2 key. To engage the second monitor or to cycle through the modes, hold the Function key and press F2.

> Although many laptops use the Function key method to cycle the monitor selections, that's not always the case. You might have to pop into the Display applet in the Control Panel to click a checkbox. Just be assured that if the laptop has a VGA or DVI or HDMI port, you can cycle through monitor choices!

• **Figure 21.16** Laptop keyboard showing Function (FN) key that enables you to access additional key options, as on the F2 key

General-Purpose Ports

Laptops rarely come with all of the hardware you want. PC Cards/Express cards certainly help, but today's laptops usually include at least USB ports to give you the option to add more hardware. Some laptops still provide legacy general-purpose expansion ports (PS/2, RS-232 serial ports, and so on) for installing peripheral hardware. If you're lucky, you might even get a FireWire port so you can plug in your fancy new digital video camera. If you're really lucky, you will have a docking station or port replicator so you don't have to plug in all of your peripheral devices one at a time.

USB, FireWire, and eSATA

Universal serial bus (USB), FireWire (or more properly, IEEE 1394), and eSATA feature easy-to-use connectors and give users the ability to connect or insert a device into a system while the PC is running—you won't have to reboot a system to install a new peripheral. With USB, FireWire, and eSATA,

Cross Check

How Much RAM Is Enough?

The amount of RAM needed to run a PC—portable or otherwise—smoothly and stably depends on both the type of applications that it will run and the needs of the OS. When making a recommendation to a client about upgrading a laptop's memory, you should ask the basic questions, such as what the client plans to do on the laptop. If the laptop will be used for e-mail, word processing, and Web surfing, a medium level of RAM, such as 1 GB, might be adequate. If the user travels, uses a high-end digital camera, and wants to use Photoshop to edit huge images, you'll need to augment the RAM accordingly. Then add the needs of the OS to give a good recommendation. Turn to Chapter 14, "Installing and Upgrading Windows," and cross check your knowledge about specific OS RAM needs. What's a good minimum for Windows XP? What about Vista?

Refer to the manufacturer's Web site or to the manual (if any) that came with the portable for the specific RAM needed.

Second, every portable PC offers a unique challenge to the tech who wants to upgrade the RAM, because there's no standard for RAM placement in portables. More often than not, you need to unscrew or pop open a panel on the underside of the portable (Figure 21.21). Then you press out on the restraining clips and the RAM stick pops up (Figure 21.22). Gently remove the old stick of RAM and insert the new one by reversing the steps.

Shared Memory   Some laptops (and desktops) support **shared memory**. Shared memory reduces the cost of video cards by reducing the amount of memory on the video card itself. Instead of having 256 MB of RAM, the video card might have only 64 MB of RAM but be able to borrow 192 MB of RAM from the system. This equates to a 256 MB video card. The video card uses regular system RAM to make up for the loss.

The obvious benefit of shared memory is a less expensive video card (and a less expensive laptop!) with performance comparable to its mega-memory alternative. The downside is that your overall system performance will suffer because a portion of the system RAM is no longer available to programs. (The term *shared* is a bit misleading because the video card takes control of a portion of RAM. The video portion of system RAM is *not* shared back and forth between the video card processor and the CPU.) Shared

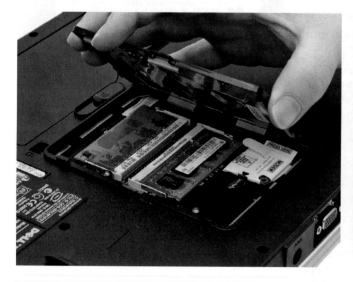

● **Figure 21.21**   Removing a RAM panel

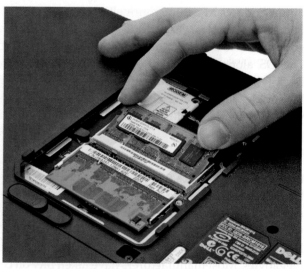

● **Figure 21.22**   Releasing the RAM

memory technologies include TurboCache (developed by NVIDIA) and HyperMemory (developed by ATI).

Some systems give you control over the amount of shared memory, while others simply allow you to turn shared memory on or off. The settings are found in CMOS setup and only on systems that support shared memory. Shared memory is not reported to Windows, so don't panic if you have 1 GB of RAM in your laptop but Windows only sees 924 MB—the missing memory is used for video.

Adding more system RAM to a laptop with shared memory will improve laptop performance. Although it might appear to improve video performance, that doesn't tell the true story. It'll improve overall performance because the OS and CPU get more usable RAM. On some laptops, you can improve video performance as well, but that depends on the CMOS setup. If the shared memory is not set to maximum by default, increasing the overall memory and upping the portion reserved for video will improve video performance specifically.

Tech Tip

Determining Shared Memory
You cannot tell if a laptop is using shared memory in Windows. You have to go to CMOS to be sure.

Hard Drives

SATA drives in the 2.5-inch drive format now rule in all laptops. Although much smaller than regular, 3.5-inch hard drives, they use all the same features and configurations. These smaller hard drives have suffered, however, from diminished storage capacity as compared to their 3.5-inch brothers. Currently, large 2.5-inch hard drives hold up to 1 TB, while the 3.5-inch hard drives can hold more than 2 TB of data! Some PATA drive manufacturers may require you to set the drive to use a cable-select setting as opposed to master or slave, so check with the laptop maker for any special issues. Otherwise, no difference exists between 2.5-inch drives and their larger 3.5-inch brethren (Figure 21.23).

Modular CPUs

You know from Chapter 5, "Microprocessors," that both AMD and Intel make specialized laptop CPUs that produce less heat and consume less power, yet only now are folks realizing that they can sometimes upgrade their laptops by removing the old CPU and replacing it with a new one. Be very careful to follow manufacturer's specifications! You should keep in mind, however, that replacing the CPU in a laptop often requires you to disassemble the entire machine. This can be a daunting task, even for professionals. If you want to upgrade the CPU in your laptop, it's often best to let the professionals take care of it.

• **Figure 21.23** The 2.5-inch and 3.5-inch drives are mostly the same.

Video Cards

Some video card makers make modular video cards for laptops. Although no single standard works in all systems, a quick phone call to the tech support department of the laptop maker often reveals upgrade options (if any). Modular video cards are the least standardized of all modular components, but as manufacturers adopt more industry-wide standards, we'll be able to replace video cards in laptops more readily.

Going Inside

To reach most modular components on a laptop, you need to do more than remove an exterior panel. You need to go inside to get access to devices directly connected to the motherboard. Many laptops have an easily removable keyboard that, once removed, gives you access to a metal heat spreader (just a plate that sits over the motherboard) and a half-dozen or more tiny screws. You'll need a special screwdriver to avoid stripping the screws—check a watch or eyeglass shop if your local hardware store doesn't carry anything appropriate.

You need to take major precautions when you remove the keyboard and heat spreader. The keyboard will be attached to a small cable that can easily disconnect if you pull hard. Don't forget to check this connection before you reinsert the keyboard at the end of the procedure! Avoid ESD as you would with any other PC, and definitely unplug the laptop from the wall and remove the battery before you do any work inside!

• **Figure 21.24**   Hardware Removal Tool in system tray

See Chapter 23, "Local Area Networking," for the scoop on dial-up networking and Ethernet.

• **Figure 21.25**   Safely Remove Hardware dialog box

Modular Drives

To add functionality to laptops, many manufacturers include "modular drives" with their portable machines. CD, DVD, and Blu-ray Disc drives are most common. The beauty of modular drives is that you can swap back and forth easily between different types of drives. Need more storage space? Pull out the DVD drive and put in another hard drive. Many laptops enable you to replace a drive with a second battery, which obviously can extend the time you can go before you have to plug the laptop into an AC outlet.

I have a laptop that allows me to swap out my CD/DVD drive for a second battery. If I don't need to access any CDs and don't need super-extended battery life, I just take out the component that's currently installed and put a blank faceplate into the empty slot. Traveling with an empty bay makes my hefty laptop weigh a little bit less, and every little bit helps!

Most modular drives are truly hot-swappable, enabling you to remove and insert devices without any special software. Many still require you to use the Hardware Removal Tool (also known as Safely Remove Hardware) located in the system tray or notification area (Figure 21.24). When in doubt, always remove modular devices by using this tool. Figure 21.25 shows the Safely Remove Hardware dialog box. To remove a device, highlight it and click the Stop button. Windows will shut down the device and tell you when it's safe to remove the device.

Mobile NICs and Mini PCI

Every laptop made in the last few years comes with networking capabilities built in. They have Ethernet ports for plugging into a wired network and Wi-Fi for wireless networking, and some have Cellular WAN radios so you can access the Internet over a cell phone network. Laptops run Windows just like a desktop system, so they have all the networking software ready to go.

Many of these integrated network cards are installed in a Mini PCI slot on the laptop motherboard. The **Mini PCI** bus is an adaptation of the standard PCI bus and was developed specifically for integrated communications peripherals such as modems and network adapters. Built-in networking support means you don't need an additional PC Card to provide a network adapter. The Mini PCI bus also provides support for other integrated devices, such as Bluetooth, modems, audio, or hard drive controllers. One great aspect of Mini PCI is that if some new technology eclipses the current wireless technology or some other technology that uses the bus, you can upgrade by swapping a card.

Officially released in 1999, Mini PCI is a 32-bit 33-MHz bus and is basically PCI v2.2 with a different form factor. Like PCI, it

supports bus mastering and DMA. Mini PCI cards are about a quarter the size of regular PCI cards and can be as small as 2.75 inches by 1.81 inches by .22 inches. They can be found in small products such as laptops, printers, and set-top boxes.

To extend battery life, you can toggle built-in communication devices such as Wi-Fi and Bluetooth adapters on and off without powering down the computer. Many laptops come with a physical switch along the front or side edge allowing you to power the communications adapter on or off. Similarly, you can often use a keyboard shortcut for this, generally by pressing the Function (FN) key along with some other key. The FN key, when pressed, allows other keys to accomplish specific tasks. For example, on my laptop, pressing FN-F2 toggles my Wi-Fi adapter on and off; pressing FN-F10 ejects my CD-ROM drive.

 A typical reason to upgrade a Mini PCI Wi-Fi NIC is to gain access to improved security options such as better encryption.

 Chapter 24 covers wireless networking in great detail.

■ Managing and Maintaining Portable Computers

Most portable PCs come from the factory solidly built and configured. Manufacturers know that few techs outside their factories know enough to work on them, so they don't cut corners. From a tech's standpoint, your most common work on managing and maintaining portables involves taking care of the batteries and extending the battery life through proper power management, keeping the machine clean, and avoiding excessive heat.

Everything you normally do to maintain a PC applies to portable PCs. You need to keep current on Windows patches and service packs and use stable, recent drivers. Run Check Disk with some frequency, and definitely defragment the hard drive. Disk Cleanup is a must if the laptop runs Windows XP or Windows Vista. That said, let's look at issues specifically involving portables.

Batteries

Manufacturers use three types of batteries for portable PCs and each battery type has its own special needs and quirks. Once you have a clear understanding of the quirks, you can *usually* spot and fix battery problems. The three types of batteries commonly used in mobile PCs are **Nickel-Cadmium (Ni-Cd)**, **Nickel-Metal Hydride (Ni-MH)**, and **Lithium-Ion (Li-Ion)** batteries. Manufacturers have also started working with **fuel cell** batteries, although most of that work is experimental at this writing.

Nickel-Cadmium

Ni-Cds were the first batteries commonly used in mobile PCs, which means the technology was full of little problems. Probably most irritating was a little thing called **battery memory,** or the tendency of a Ni-Cd battery to lose a significant amount of its rechargeability if it was charged repeatedly without being totally discharged. A battery that originally kept a laptop running for two hours would eventually only keep that same laptop going for 30 minutes or less. Figure 21.26 shows a typical Ni-Cd battery.

• Figure 21.26   Ni-Cd battery

To prevent memory problems, a Ni-Cd battery had to be discharged completely before each recharging. Recharging was tricky as well, because Ni-Cd batteries disliked being overcharged. Unfortunately, there was no way to verify when a battery was fully charged without an expensive charging machine, which none of us had. As a result, most Ni-Cd batteries lasted an extremely short time before having to be replaced. A quick fix was to purchase a **conditioning charger**. These chargers would first totally discharge the Ni-Cd battery and then generate a special "reverse" current that, in a way, cleaned internal parts of the battery so it could be recharged more often and would run longer on each recharge. Ni-Cd batteries would, at best, last for 1,000 charges, and far fewer with poor treatment. Ni-Cds were extremely susceptible to heat and would self-discharge over time if not used. Leaving a Ni-Cd in the car in the summer was guaranteed to result in a fully discharged battery in next to no time!

But Ni-Cd batteries didn't stop causing trouble after they died. The highly toxic metals inside the batteries made it unacceptable simply to throw them in the trash. Ni-Cd batteries should be disposed of via specialized disposal companies. This is very important! Even though Ni-Cd batteries aren't used in PCs very often anymore, many devices, such as cellular and cordless phones, still use Ni-Cd batteries. Don't trash the environment by tossing Ni-Cds in a landfill. Turn them in at the closest special disposal site; most recycling centers are glad to take them. Also, many battery manufacturers/distributors will take them. The environment you help preserve just might be yours—or your kids'!

> You *must* use disposal companies or battery recycling services to dispose of the highly toxic Ni-Cd batteries.

Nickel-Metal Hydride

Ni-MH batteries were the next generation of mobile PC batteries and are still quite common today. Basically, Ni-MH batteries are Ni-Cd batteries without most of the headaches. Ni-MH batteries are much less susceptible to memory problems, can tolerate overcharging better, can take more recharging, and can last longer between rechargings. Like Ni-Cds, Ni-MH batteries are susceptible to heat, but at least they are considered less toxic to the environment. A special disposal is still a good idea. Unlike Ni-Cds, it's usually better to recharge an Ni-MH with shallow recharges as opposed to a complete discharge/recharge. Ni-MH is a popular replacement battery for Ni-Cd systems (Figure 21.27).

Lithium-Ion

The most common battery used today is Li-Ion. Li-Ion batteries are powerful, completely immune to memory problems, and last at least twice as long as comparable Ni-MH batteries on one charge. Sadly, they can't handle as many charges as Ni-MH types, but today's users are usually more than glad to give up total battery lifespan in return for longer periods between charges. Li-Ion batteries will explode if they are overcharged, so all Li-Ion batteries sold with PCs have built-in circuitry to prevent accidental overcharging. Lithium batteries can only

• Figure 21.27   Ni-MH battery

be used on systems designed to use them. They can't be used as replacement batteries (Figure 21.28).

Other Portable Power Sources

In an attempt to provide better maintenance for laptop batteries, manufacturers have developed a new type of battery called the **smart battery**. Smart batteries tell the computer when they need to be charged, conditioned, or replaced.

The Care and Feeding of Batteries

In general, keep in mind the following basics. First, always store batteries in a cool place. Although a freezer is in concept an excellent storage place, the moisture, metal racks, and food make it a bad idea. Second, use a charger for your Ni-Cd and Ni-MH batteries that also conditions the batteries; they'll last longer. Third, keep battery contacts clean with a little alcohol or just a dry cloth. Fourth, *never* handle a battery that has ruptured or broken; battery chemicals are very dangerous. Finally, always recycle old batteries.

● **Figure 21.28** Li-Ion battery

Power Management

Many different parts are included in the typical laptop, and each part uses power. The problem with early laptops was that every one of these parts used power continuously, whether or not the system needed that device at that time. For example, the hard drive continued to spin even when it was not being accessed, and the LCD panel continued to display, even when the user walked away from the machine.

The optimal situation would be a system where the user could instruct the PC to shut down unused devices selectively, preferably by defining a maximum period of inactivity that, when reached, would trigger the PC to shut down the inactive device. Longer periods of inactivity would eventually enable the entire system to shut itself down, leaving critical information loaded in RAM, ready to restart if a wake-up event (such as moving the mouse or pressing a key) told the system to restart. The system would have to be sensitive to potential hazards, such as shutting down in the middle of writing to a drive, and so on. Also, this feature could not add significantly to the cost of the PC. Clearly, a machine that could perform these functions would need specialized hardware, BIOS, and operating system to operate properly. This process of cooperation among the hardware, the BIOS, and the OS to reduce power use is known generically as *power management*.

 Try This!

Recycling Old Portable PC Batteries

Got an old portable PC battery lying around? Well, you need to get rid of it, and there are some pretty nasty chemicals in that battery, so you can't just throw it in the trash. Sooner or later, you'll probably need to deal with such a battery, so Try This!

1. Do an online search to find the battery recycling center nearest to you.

2. Sometimes, you can take old laptop batteries to an auto parts store that disposes of old car batteries—I know it sounds odd, but it's true! See if you can find one in your area that will do this.

3. Many cities offer a hazardous materials disposal or recycling service. Check to see if and how your local government will help you dispose of your old batteries.

System Management Mode

Intel began the process of power management with a series of new features built into the 386SX CPU. These new features enabled the CPU to slow down or stop its clock without erasing the register information, as well as enabling power saving in peripherals. These features were collectively called **System Management Mode (SMM)**. All modern CPUs have SMM. Although a power-saving CPU was okay, power management was relegated to special "sleep" or "doze" buttons that would stop the CPU and all of the peripherals on the laptop. To take real advantage of SMM, the system needed a specialized BIOS and OS to go with the SMM CPU. To this end, Intel put forward the **Advanced Power Management (APM)** specification in 1992 and the **Advanced Configuration and Power Interface (ACPI)** standard in 1996.

Requirements for APM/ACPI

To function fully, APM and ACPI require a number of items. First is an SMM-capable CPU. As virtually all CPUs are SMM-capable, this is easy. Second is an APM-compliant BIOS that enables the CPU to shut off the peripherals when desired. The third requirement is devices that will accept being shut off. These devices are usually called Energy Star devices, which signals their compliance with the EPA's Energy Star standard. To be an Energy Star device, a peripheral must be able to shut down without actually turning off and show that they use much less power than the non–Energy Star equivalent. Last, the system's OS must know how to request that a particular device be shut down, and the CPU's clock must be slowed down or stopped.

ACPI goes beyond the APM standard by supplying support for hot-swappable devices—always a huge problem with APM. This feature aside, it is a challenge to tell the difference between an APM system and an ACPI system at first glance.

Don't limit your perception of APM, ACPI, and Energy Star just to laptops. Virtually all desktop systems and many appliances also use the power management functions.

APM/ACPI Levels

APM defined four power-usage operating levels for a system. These levels are intentionally fuzzy to give manufacturers considerable leeway in their use; the only real difference among them is the amount of time each takes to return to normal usage. These levels are as follows:

- **Full On** Everything in the system is running at full power. There is no power management.

- **APM Enabled** CPU and RAM are running at full power. Power management is enabled. An unused device may or may not be shut down.

- **APM Standby** CPU is stopped. RAM still stores all programs. All peripherals are shut down, although configuration options are still stored. (In other words, to get back to APM Enabled, you won't have to reinitialize the devices.)

- **APM Suspend** Everything in the PC is shut down or at its lowest power-consumption setting. Many systems use a special type of Suspend called **hibernation**, where critical configuration information

is written to the hard drive. Upon a wake-up event, the system is reinitialized, and the data is read from the drive to return the system to the APM Enabled mode. Clearly, the recovery time between Suspend and Enabled will be much longer than the time between Standby and Enabled.

ACPI, the successor to APM, handles all these levels plus a few more, such as "soft power on/off," that enables you to define the function of the power button. You should familiarize yourself with the following ACPI global (G) and sleeping (S) system power state specifications for both the A+ exams and your own practical application:

- **G0 (S0)** Working state
- **G1** Sleeping state mode. Further subdivided into four *S* states.
  - **S1** CPU stops processing. Power to CPU and memory (RAM) is maintained.
  - **S2** CPU is powered down.
  - **S3** Sleep or Standby mode. Power to RAM is still on.
  - **S4** Hibernation mode. Information in RAM is stored to nonvolatile memory or drive and powered off.
- **G2 (S5)** Soft power off mode. Certain devices used to wake a system—such as keyboard, LAN, USB, and other devices—remain on, while most other components are powered to a mechanical off state (G3).
- **G3** Mechanical off mode. The system and all components, with the exception of the real-time clock (RTC), are completely powered down.

Configuration of APM/ACPI

You configure APM/ACPI via CMOS settings or through Windows. Windows settings override CMOS settings. Although the APM/ACPI standards permit a great deal of flexibility, which can create some confusion among different implementations, certain settings apply generally to CMOS configuration. First is the ability to initialize power management; this enables the system to enter the APM Enabled mode. Often CMOS then presents time frames for entering Standby and Suspend modes, as well as settings to determine which events take place in each of these modes.

Many CMOS versions present settings to determine wake-up events, such as directing the system to monitor a modem or a NIC (Figure 21.29). You'll see

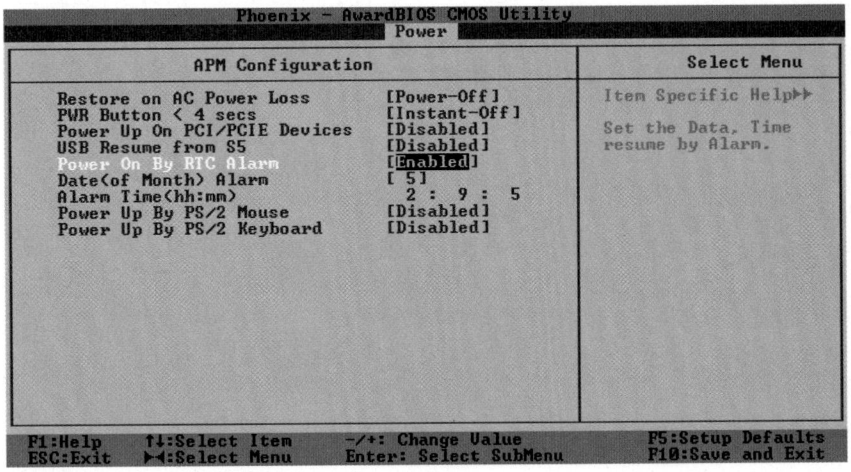

• **Figure 21.29** Setting a wake-up event in CMOS

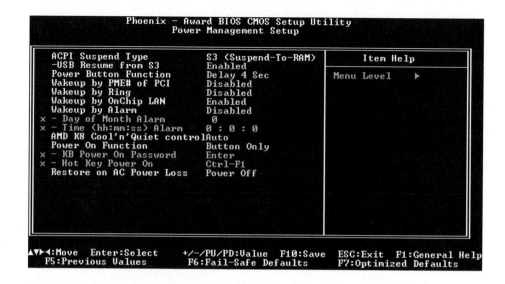

Phoenix — Award BIOS CMOS Setup Utility
Power Management Setup

```
ACPI Suspend Type          S3 (Suspend-To-RAM)        Item Help
-USB Resume from S3        Enabled
Power Button Function      Delay 4 Sec          Menu Level    ►
Wakeup by PME# of PCI      Disabled
Wakeup by Ring             Disabled
Wakeup by OnChip LAN       Enabled
Wakeup by Alarm            Disabled
x - Day of Month Alarm     0
x - Time (hh:mm:ss) Alarm  0 : 0 : 0
AMD K8 Cool'n'Quiet controlAuto
Power On Function          Button Only
x - KB Power On Password   Enter
x - Hot Key Power On       Ctrl-F1
Restore on AC Power Loss   Power Off
```

```
▲▼►◄:Move  Enter:Select      +/-/PU/PD:Value  F10:Save   ESC:Exit  F1:General Help
       F5:Previous Values          F6:Fail-Safe Defaults      F7:Optimized Defaults
```

• **Figure 21.30**   CMOS with ACPI setup option

In Windows XP you can also access your power options by right-clicking on the desktop, selecting Properties, and then clicking the Power button in the Monitor power section of the Screen Saver tab. In Windows Vista, right-click the desktop, select Personalize, select Screen Saver, and then click on the *Change power settings* link.

this feature as *Wake on LAN* or something similar. A true ACPI-compliant CMOS provides an ACPI setup option. Figure 21.30 shows a typical modern BIOS that provides this setting.

APM/ACPI settings can be found in the Windows 2000/XP/Vista Control Panel applet Power Options. In Windows XP, the Power Options applet has several built-in *power schemes* such as Home/Office and Max Battery that put the system into Standby or Suspend after a certain interval (Figure 21.31). You can also require the system to go into Standby after a set period of time or to turn off the monitor or hard drive after a time, thus creating your own custom power scheme. This is technically called adjusting the **sleep timers**.

Windows Vista's built-in power schemes are similar to Windows XP, though you can better control power utilization by customizing a Balanced, Power saver, or High performance power plan (Figure 21.32). You can customize a power saver plan for your laptop, for example, and configure it to turn off the display at a certain time interval while on battery or plugged in and configure it to put the computer to sleep as desired (Figure 21.33).

Another feature, Hibernate mode, takes everything in active memory and stores it on the hard drive just before the system powers down. When the PC comes out of hibernation, Windows reloads all the files and applications into RAM. Figure 21.34 shows the Power Options Properties applet in Windows XP.

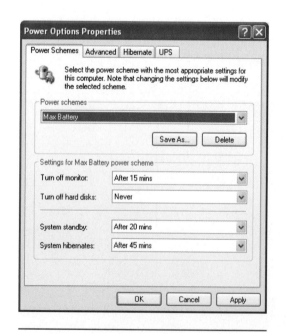

• **Figure 21.31**   The Windows XP Power Options applet's Power Schemes tab

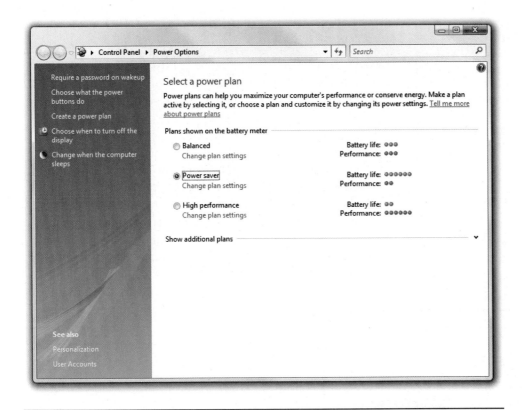

● **Figure 21.32**   Windows Vista Balanced, Power saver, or High performance power plans

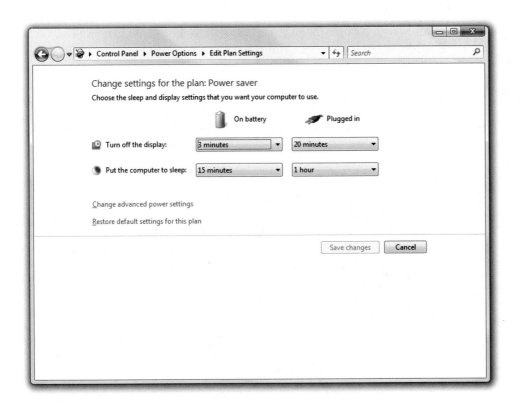

● **Figure 21.33**   Customizing a laptop power plan in Windows Vista

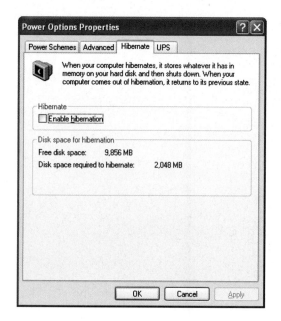

Try This!

Adjusting Your System's Power Management

Go into the Power Options applet and take a look at the various settings. What is the current power scheme for your computer? If you're using a laptop with Windows XP, is your system still using the Home/Office Desktop power scheme? If this is the case, change the power scheme to Portable/Laptop. If you're using a laptop with Windows Vista, check to see if you are running a Balanced or High performance power plan. If you are, change the power plan to Power saver and familiarize yourself with some of the advanced power settings (click on the *Change advanced power settings* link).

Try changing the individual settings for each power scheme. For instance, set a new value for the System Standby setting—try making your computer go into standby after five minutes. Don't worry; you aren't going to hurt anything if you fiddle with these settings.

• **Figure 21.34**   Windows XP hibernation settings in the Power Options applet

Cleaning

Laptop cooling fans tend to get dirty over time. Clean them occasionally using an anti-static vacuum. Never used canned air!

Most portable PCs take substantially more abuse than a corresponding desktop model. Constant handling, travel, airport food on the run, and so on can radically shorten the life of a portable if you don't take action. One of the most important things you should do is clean the laptop regularly. Use an appropriate screen cleaner (not a glass cleaner!) to remove fingerprints and dust from the fragile LCD panel. (Refer to Chapter 19, "Video," for specifics.)

If you've had the laptop in a smoky or dusty environment, try compressed air for cleaning. Compressed air works great for blowing out the dust and crumbs from the keyboard and for keeping PC Card sockets clear. Don't use water on your keyboard! Even a minor amount of moisture inside the portable can toast a component.

Heat

To manage and maintain a healthy portable PC, you need to deal with issues of heat. Every portable has a stack of electronic components crammed into a very small space. Unlike their desktop brethren, portables don't have lots of freely moving air space that enables fans to cool everything down. Even with lots of low-power-consumption devices inside, portable PCs crank out a good deal of heat. Excessive heat can cause system lockups and hardware failures, so you should handle the issue wisely. Try this as a starter guide.

- Use power management, even if you're plugged into the AC outlet. This is especially important if you're working in a warm (more than 80 degrees Fahrenheit) room.

- Keep air space between the bottom of the laptop and the surface on which it rests. Putting a laptop on a soft surface, such as a pillow on your lap, creates a great heat-retention system—not a good thing! Always use a hard, flat surface.

- Don't use a keyboard protector for extended amounts of time.

- Listen to your fan, assuming the laptop has one. If it's often running very fast—you can tell by the high-pitched whirring sound— examine your power management settings and your environment, and change whatever is causing heat retention.

- Speaking of fans, be alert to a fan that suddenly goes silent. Fans do fail on laptops, causing overheating and failure. All laptop fans can be replaced easily.

Protect the Machine

Although prices continue to drop for basic laptops, a fully loaded system is still pricey. To protect your investment, you'll want to adhere to certain best practices. You've already read tips in this chapter to deal with cleaning and heat, so let's look at the "portable" part of portable computers.

Tripping

Pay attention to where you run the power cord when you plug in a laptop. One of the primary causes of laptop destruction is people tripping over the power cord and knocking the laptop off of a desk. This is especially true if you plug in at a public place such as a café or airport. Remember, the life you save could be your portable PC's!

Storage

If you aren't going to use your laptop or PDA for a while, storing it safely will go a long way toward keeping it operable when you do power it up again. Investing in a quality case is worth the extra few dollars—preferably one with ample padding. Smaller devices such as PDAs are well protected inside small shock-resistant aluminum cases that clip onto your belt, while laptops do fine in well-padded cases or backpacks. Not only will this protect your system on a daily basis when transporting it from home to office, but it will keep dust and pet hair away as well. Lastly, protect from battery leakage by removing the battery if you'll be storing your device for an extended time.

Travel

If traveling with a laptop, take care to protect yourself from theft. If possible, use a case that doesn't look like a computer case. A well-padded backpack makes a great travel bag for a laptop and appears less tempting to would-be thieves. Don't forget to pack any accessories you might need, like modular devices, spare batteries, and AC adapters. Make sure to remove any disks, such as CD/DVD or floppies, from their drives. Most importantly—back up any important data before you leave!

Make sure to have at least a little battery power available. Heightened security at airports means you might have to power on your system to prove it's really a computer and not a transport case for questionable materials. And never let your laptop out of your sight. If going through an x-ray machine, request a manual search. The x-ray won't harm your computer like a metal detector would, but if the laptop gets through the line at security

before you do, someone else might walk away with it. If flying, stow your laptop under the seat in front of you where you can keep an eye on it.

If you travel to a foreign country, be very careful about the electricity. North America uses ~115 V power outlets, but the most of the rest of the world uses ~230 V outlets. Many portable computers have **auto-switching power supplies**, meaning they detect the voltage at the outlet and adjust accordingly. For these portables, a simple plug converter will do the trick. Other portable computers, however, have *fixed-input power supplies*, which means they run only on ~115 V or on ~230 V power. For these portables, you need a full-blown electricity converting device, either a step-down or step-up *transformer*. You can find converters and transformers at electrical parts stores, such as Radio Shack in the United States.

Shipping

Much of the storage and travel advice can be applied to shipping. Remove batteries and optical discs from their drives. Pack the laptop well and disguise the container as best you can. Back up any data and verify the warranty coverage. Ship with a reputable carrier and always request a tracking number and, if possible, delivery signature. It's also worth the extra couple of bucks to pay for the shipping insurance. And when the clerk asks what's in the box, it's safer to say "electronics" rather than "a new 20-inch laptop computer."

Security

The fact is, if someone really wants to steal your laptop, they'll find a way. There are, however, some things you can do to make yourself, and your equipment, less desirable targets. As you've already learned, disguise is a good idea. Although you don't need to camouflage your laptop or carry it in a brown grocery bag on a daily basis, an inconspicuous carrying case will draw less attention.

Another physical deterrent is a laptop lock. Similar to a steel bicycle cable, there is a loop on one end and a lock on the other. The idea is to loop the cable around a solid object, such as a bed frame, and secure the lock to the small security hole on the side of the laptop. Again, if someone really wants to steal your computer, they'll find a way. They'll dismantle the bed frame if they're desperate. The best protection is to be vigilant and not let the computer out of your sight.

An alternative to physically securing a laptop with a lock is to use a software tracking system. Software makers, such as Computer Security Products, Inc., at www.computersecurity.com, offer tracking software that transmits a signal to a central office if the computer is stolen and connected to a phone line or the Internet. The location of the stolen PC can be tracked, and sensitive files can even be deleted automatically with the aid of the stealth signal.

> Be sure to remove all thumb drives and PC Cards before shipping a laptop.

■ Troubleshooting Portable Computers

Many of the troubleshooting techniques you learned about for desktop systems can be applied to laptops. For example, take the proper precautions before and during disassembly. Use the proper hand tools, and document,

label, and organize each plastic part and screw location for reassembly. Additionally, here are some laptop-specific procedures to try.

Laptop Won't Power On

- Verify AC power by plugging another electronic device into the wall outlet. If the other device receives power, the outlet is good.

- If the outlet is good, connect the laptop to the wall outlet and try to power on. If no LEDs light up, you may have a bad AC adapter. Swap it out with a known good power adapter.

- A faulty peripheral device might keep the laptop from powering up. Remove any peripherals such as USB or FireWire devices.

Screen Doesn't Come On Properly

- If the laptop is booting (you hear the beeps and the drives), first make sure the display is turned on. Press the FN key and the key to activate the screen a number of times until the laptop display comes on. If that doesn't work, check the LCD cutoff switch—on many laptops, this is the small nub somewhere near the screen hinge that shuts the monitor off when you close the laptop—and make sure it isn't stuck in the down position.

- If the laptop display is very dim, you may have lost an inverter. The clue here is that inverters never go quietly. They can make a nasty hum as they are about to die and an equally nasty popping noise when they actually fail. Failure often occurs when you plug in the laptop's AC adapter, as the inverters take power directly from the AC adapter. It's also possible that the backlights in the LCD panel have died, though this is much less common than a bad inverter.

- If the screen won't come on or is cracked, most laptops have a port for plugging in an external monitor, which you can use to log into your laptop.

Wireless Networking Doesn't Work

- Check along the front, rear, or side edges of the laptop for a physical switch that toggles the internal wireless adapter on and off.

- Try the special key combination for your laptop to toggle the wireless adapter. You usually press the FN key in combination with another key.

- You might simply be out of range. Physically walk the laptop over to the wireless router or access point to ensure there are no out-of-range issues.

Handwriting Is Not Recognized

- If your PDA or tablet PC no longer recognizes your handwriting or stylus, you may need to retrain the digitizer. Look for an option in your PDA OS settings to align the screen. On Windows-based tablet PCs, you will find a similar option under Start | Settings | Control Panel.

Tech Tip

Battery Won't Charge
If you have a laptop with a battery that won't charge up, it could be one of two things: the battery might be cooked or the AC adapter isn't doing its job. To troubleshoot, replace the battery with a known good battery. If the new battery works, you've found the problem. Just replace the battery. Alternatively, remove the battery and run the laptop on AC only. If that works, you know the AC adapter is good. If it doesn't, replace the AC adapter.

Keypad Doesn't Work

■ If none of the keys work on your laptop, there's a good chance you've unseated the keypad connector. These connectors are quite fragile and are prone to unseating from any physical stress on the laptop. Check the manufacturer's disassembly procedures to locate and reseat the keypad.

■ If you're getting numbers when you're expecting to get letters, the number lock (NUMLOCK) function key is turned on. Turn it off.

Touchpad Doesn't Work

■ A shot of compressed air does wonders for cleaning pet hair out of the touchpad sensors. You'll get a cleaner shot if you remove the keyboard before using the compressed air. Remember to be gentle when lifting off the keyboard and make sure to follow the manufacturer's instructions.

■ The touchpad driver might need to be reconfigured. Try the various options in the Control Panel | Mouse applet.

Sprayed ink
forms chara

• Figure 22.

four cartri
black (Fig
effective f
quality pr
printers w
In additio
tridges pr
dark cyan
tridges a p
printed i
printer.

The tv
the **print**
which aff
Resolutio
higher nu
page are
ments wil
tant wher
full-color
plication
good. Pri
tion is no

■ Chapter Summary

After reading this chapter and completing the exercises, you should understand the following about portable computers.

Describe the many types of portable computing devices available

- All portable devices share certain features: video output using LCD screens, some kind of PC sound, and DC battery power. There's no industry standard for naming the vast majority of styles of portable computing devices.

- A laptop refers in general to the clamshell, keyboard-on-the-bottom and LCD-screen-at-the-top design that is considered the shape of mobile PCs. Most notebooks are laptops in the 8½ × 11–inch range. The traditional clamshell laptop computer features a built-in LCD monitor, keyboard, and input device and functions as a fully standalone PC. A portable PC can be considered a desktop replacement if it does everything most people want to do with a desktop PC.

- Desktop extender portable devices don't replace the desktop but rather extend it by giving you a subset of features that you can take away from the desk. They are usually smaller and lighter than desktop replacement portables. Netbook portables (sometimes called mini-books or subnotebooks, though the terms aren't necessarily synonymous) normally weigh less than three pounds and are less than an inch in thickness. These machines usually have smaller displays, lower-capacity hard drives, and CPUs that operate at lower speeds than their more full-sized brethren.

- Personal digital assistants (PDAs) are tiny handheld portable computing devices that hold such data as your address book and appointment schedules. Small enough to fit into a pocket, today's PDAs are pen-based computers, using a pen-like stylus and handwriting recognition. PDAs require specialized OSs such as Windows Mobile, PocketPC, PalmOS, or Linux. All of these OSs provide a GUI that enables you to interact with the device by touching the screen directly. PDAs synchronize with your PC, most often by using a

cradle and USB port, so you have the same essential data on both machines.

- Over the years, input devices for portables have ranged from trackballs that clipped to the case or were built in near the keyboard, to IBM's TrackPoint pencil-eraser-sized joystick embedded in the keyboard. The most common laptop pointing device found today, the touchpad, is a flat, touch-sensitive pad that you slide your finger across to move the cursor or pointer around the screen, and tap on to perform "mouse clicks."

Enhance and upgrade portable computers

- PC Cards are roughly credit-card-sized devices that enhance and extend the functions of a portable PC. Still commonly known by their older name, PCMCIA cards, PC Cards are as standard on today's mobile computers as the hard drive. Almost every portable PC has one or two PC Card slots. All PC Cards are hot-swappable.

- Parallel PC Cards come in two flavors, 16-bit and CardBus; and each flavor comes in three different physical sizes, called Type I, Type II, and Type III. Type I, II, and III cards differ only in the thickness of the card (Type I being the thinnest and Type III the thickest). Type II cards are by far the most common. All parallel PC Cards share the same 68-pin interface. The 16-bit PC Cards are 16-bit, 5-V cards that can have up to two distinct functions or devices, such as a modem/network card combination. CardBus PC Cards are 32-bit, 3.3-V cards that can have up to eight different functions on a single card. The 16-bit PC Cards will fit into and work in CardBus slots, but the reverse is not true.

- The serial ExpressCard comes in two widths: 54 mm and 34 mm. Both cards are 75 mm long and 5 mm thick, which makes them shorter than all previous PC Cards and the same thickness as a Type II PC Card. ExpressCards connect to either the Hi-Speed USB 2.0 bus (480 Mbps) or a PCI Express bus (2.5 Gbps).

- The PCMCIA standard defines two levels of software drivers to support PC Cards. The first and lower level is known as socket services. Socket

supply makes it one of the most dangerous devices in the world of PCs! Before opening a printer to insert a new toner cartridge, it is imperative that you *always turn off* a laser printer!

Turning Gears   A laser printer has many mechanical functions. First, the paper must be picked up. Next, the photosensitive roller must be turned and the laser, or a mirror, must be moved from left to right. The toner must be evenly distributed, and the fuser assembly must squish the toner into the paper. Finally, the paper must be kicked out of the printer and the assembly cleaned to prepare for the next page.

All of these functions are served by complex gear systems. In most laser printers, these gear systems are packed together in discrete units generically called *gear packs* or *gearboxes*. Most laser printers have two or three gearboxes that you can remove relatively easily in the rare case when one of them fails. Most gearboxes also have their own motor or solenoid to move the gears.

System Board   Every laser printer contains at least one electronic board. On this board is the main processor, the printer's ROM, and the RAM used to store the image before it is printed. Many printers divide these functions among two or three boards dispersed around the printer. An older printer may also have an extra ROM chip and/or a special slot where you can install an extra ROM chip, usually for special functions such as PostScript.

On some printer models you can upgrade the contents of these ROM chips (the *firmware*) by performing a process called *flashing* the ROM. Flashing is a lot like upgrading the system BIOS, which you learned about in Chapter 7, "BIOS and CMOS." Upgrading the firmware can help fix bugs, add new features, or update the fonts in the printer.

Of particular importance is the printer's RAM. When the printer doesn't have enough RAM to store the image before it prints, you get a memory overflow problem. Also, some printers store other information in the RAM, including fonts or special commands. Adding RAM is usually a simple job—just snapping in a SIMM or DIMM stick or two—but getting the *right* RAM is important. Call or check the printer manufacturer's Web site to see what type of RAM you need. Although most printer companies will happily sell you their expensive RAM, most printers can use generic DRAM like the kind you use in a PC.

Ozone Filter   The coronas inside laser printers generate ozone (O_3). Although not harmful to humans in small amounts, even tiny concentrations of ozone will cause damage to printer components. To counter this problem, most laser printers have a special ozone filter that needs to be vacuumed or replaced periodically.

Sensors and Switches   Every laser printer has a large number of sensors and switches spread throughout the machine. The sensors are used to detect a broad range of conditions such as paper jams, empty paper trays, or low toner levels. Many of these sensors are really tiny switches that detect open doors and so on. Most of the time these sensors/switches work reliably, yet occasionally they become dirty or broken, sending a false signal to the printer. Simple inspection is usually sufficient to determine if a problem is real or just the result of a faulty sensor/switch.

• Figu

Solid Ink

Solid ink printers use just what you'd expect—solid inks. The technology was originally developed by Tektronix, whose printer division was acquired by Xerox. Solid ink printers use solid sticks of nontoxic "ink" that produce more vibrant color than other print methods. The solid ink is melted and absorbed into the paper fibers; it then solidifies, producing a continuous-tone output. Unlike dye-sublimation printers, all colors are applied to the media in a single pass, reducing the chances of misalignment. Solid ink sticks do not rely on containers like ink for inkjet printers and can be "topped off" midway through a print job by inserting additional color sticks without taking the printer offline.

These printers are fast, too! A full-color print job outputs the first page in about six seconds. Of course, all that speed and quality comes at a price. Xerox's base model starts at about twice the cost of a laser printer, with the expensive model selling for about six times the cost! Solid ink printers become a bit more affordable when you factor in the cost of consumables. A single stick of ink costs about as much as an inkjet cartridge, for example, but with a print capacity of 1000 pages, that completely beats the cost of inkjet cartridges over time.

Printer Languages

Now that you've learned about the different types of print devices and techniques, it's time to take a look at how they communicate with the PC. How do you tell a printer to make a letter *A* or to print a picture of your pet iguana? Printers are designed to accept predefined printer languages that handle both characters and graphics. Your software must use the proper language when communicating with your printer, so that your printer can output your documents onto a piece of paper. Following are the more common printer languages.

ASCII

You might think of the **American Standard Code for Information Interchange (ASCII)** language as nothing more than a standard set of characters, the basic alphabet in upper and lowercase with a few strange symbols thrown in. ASCII actually contains a variety of control codes for transferring data, some of which can be used to control printers. For example, ASCII code 10 (or 0A in hex) means "Line Feed," and ASCII code 12 (0C) means "Form Feed." These commands have been standard since before the creation of IBM PCs, and all printers respond to them. If they did not, the PRT SCR (print screen) key would not work with every printer. Being highly standardized has advantages, but the control codes are extremely limited. Printing high-end graphics and a wide variety of fonts requires more advanced languages.

PostScript

Adobe Systems developed the **PostScript** page description language in the early 1980s as a device-independent printer language capable of high-resolution graphics and scalable fonts. PostScript interpreters are embedded in the printing device. Because PostScript is understood by printers at a

hardware level, the majority of the image processing is done by the printer and not the PC's CPU, so PostScript printers print faster. PostScript defines the page as a single raster image; this makes PostScript files extremely portable—they can be created on one machine or platform and reliably printed out on another machine or platform (including, for example, high-end typesetters).

Hewlett-Packard Printer Control Language (PCL)

Hewlett-Packard developed its **printer control language (PCL)** as a more advanced printer language to supersede simple ASCII codes. PCL features a set of printer commands greatly expanded from ASCII. Hewlett-Packard designed PCL with text-based output in mind; it does not support advanced graphical functions. The most recent version of PCL, PCL6 features scalable fonts and additional line drawing commands. Unlike PostScript, however, PCL is not a true page description language; it uses a series of commands to define the characters on the page. Those commands must be supported by each individual printer model, making PCL files less portable than Post-Script files.

Windows GDI and XPS

Windows 2000/XP use the **graphical device interface (GDI)** component of the operating system to handle print functions. Although you *can* use an external printer language such as PostScript, most users simply install printer drivers and let Windows do all the work. The GDI uses the CPU rather than the printer to process a print job and then sends the completed job to the printer. When you print a letter with a TrueType font in Windows, for example, the GDI processes the print job and then sends bitmapped images of each page to the printer. The printer sees a page of TrueType text, therefore, as a picture, not as text. As long as the printer has a capable enough raster image processor (explained later in this chapter) and plenty of RAM, you don't need to worry about the printer language in most situations. We'll revisit printing in Windows in more detail later in this chapter.

Windows Vista supports GDI printing, but it also includes a new printing subsystem called the **XML Paper Specification (XPS) print path**. XPS provides several improvements over GDI, including enhanced color management (which works with Windows Color System) and better print layout fidelity. The XPS print path requires a driver that supports XPS. Additionally, some printers natively support XPS, eliminating the requirement that the output be converted to a device-specific printer control language before printing.

Printer Connectivity

Most printers connect to one of two ports on the PC: a DB-25 parallel port or a USB port. The parallel connection is the classic way to plug in a printer, but most printers today use USB. You'll need to know how to support the more obscure parallel ports, cables, and connections as well as the plug-and-play USB connections.

Parallel Communication and Ports

The **parallel port** was included in the original IBM PC as a faster alternative to serial communication. The IBM engineers considered serial communication, limited to 1 bit at a time, to be too slow for the "high-speed" devices of the day (for example, dot-matrix printers). The standard parallel port has been kept around for backward compatibility despite several obvious weaknesses.

Parallel ports may be far faster than serial ports, but they are slow by modern standards. The maximum data transfer rate of a standard parallel port is still only approximately 150 kilobytes per second (KBps). Standard parallel communication on the PC also relies heavily on software, eating up a considerable amount of CPU time that could be used better.

Parallel ports are hindered by their lack of true bidirectional capability. Although one-way communication was acceptable for simple line printers and dot-matrix printers, parallel communication also became popular for a wide range of external devices that required two-way communication. Although it is possible to get two-way communication out of a standard parallel port, the performance is not impressive.

IEEE 1284 Standard

In 1991, a group of printer manufacturers proposed to the *Institute of Electrical and Electronics Engineers* (*IEEE*) that a committee be formed to propose a standard for a backward-compatible, high-speed, bidirectional parallel port for the PC. The committee was the IEEE 1284 committee (hence the name of the standard).

The **IEEE 1284 standard** requires the following:

- Support for five distinct modes of operation: *compatibility mode, nibble mode, byte mode, EPP,* and *ECP*

- A standard method of negotiation for determining which modes are supported both by the host PC and by the peripheral device

- A standard physical interface (that is, the cables and connectors)

- A standard electrical interface (that is, termination, impedance, and so on)

Because only one set of data wires exists, all data transfer modes included in the IEEE 1284 standard are half-duplex: Data is transferred in only one direction at a time.

Parallel Connections, Cabling, and Electricity

Although no true standard exists, *standard parallel cable* usually refers to a printer cable with the previously mentioned male **DB-25 connector** on one end and a 36-pin **Centronics connector** on the other (Figure 22.11). The shielding (or lack thereof) of the internal wiring and other electrical characteristics of a standard parallel printer cable are largely undefined except by custom. In practice, these standard cables are acceptable for transferring data at 150 KBps, and for distances of less than 6 feet, but they would be dangerously unreliable for some transfer modes.

For more reliability at distances up to 32 feet (10 meters), use proper IEEE 1284–compliant cabling. The transfer speed drops with the longer

 Although the phrase "Centronics standard" was common in the heyday of parallel ports, no such animal actually existed. Prior to the development of IEEE 1284, a very loose set of standards were adopted by manufacturers in an attempt to reduce incompatibility issues somewhat.

 Many techs confuse the concept of duplex printing—a process that requires special printers capable of printing on both sides of a sheet of paper—with bidirectional printing. They are two different things!

Tech Tip

IEEE 1284 Transfer Modes
The five modes of operation for parallel printing specified in the IEEE 1284 standard (compatibility, nibble, byte, EPP, ECP) are inching closer to obsolescence as USB printers take over the market. If you find yourself needing to optimize the performance of a legacy parallel printer, you can look up these modes by name, using various Web search tools.

● **Figure 22.11**   Standard parallel cable with 36-pin Centronics connector on one end and DB-25 connector on the other

cables, but it does work, and sometimes the trade-off between speed and distance is worth it.

Installing a parallel cable is a snap. Just insert the DB-25 connector into the parallel port on the back of the PC and insert the Centronics connector into the printer's Centronics port, and you're ready to go to press!

USB Printers

New printers now use USB connections that you can plug into any USB port on your computer. USB printers don't usually come with a USB cable, so you need to purchase one when you purchase a printer. (It's quite a disappointment to come home with your new printer only to find you can't connect it because it didn't come with a USB cable.) Most printers use the standard USB type A connector on one end and the smaller USB type B connector on the other end, although some use two type A connectors. Whichever configuration your USB printer has, just plug in the USB cable—it's literally that easy!

FireWire Printers

Some printers offer FireWire connections in addition to or instead of USB connections. A FireWire printer is just as easy to connect as a USB printer, because FireWire is also hot-swappable and hot-pluggable. Again, make sure you have the proper cable, as most printers don't come with one. If your printer has both connections, which one should you use? The answer is easy if your PC has only USB and not FireWire. If you have a choice, either connection is just as good as the other, and the speeds are comparable. If you already have many USB devices, you may want to use the FireWire printer connection, to leave a USB port free for another device.

Network Printers

Connecting a printer to a network isn't just for offices anymore. More and more homes and home offices are enjoying the benefits of network printing. It used to be that to share a printer on a network—that is, to make it available to all network users—you would physically connect the printer to a single computer and then share the printer on the network. The downside to this was that the computer to which the printer was connected had to be left on for others to use the printer.

Some printers come with both USB and parallel connections, but this has become very rare. If you need a parallel printer for a system, be sure to confirm that the particular model you want will work with your system!

In almost all cases, you must install drivers before you plug a USB printer into your computer. You'll learn about installing printer drivers later in this chapter.

Today, the typical **network printer** comes with its own onboard network adapter that uses a standard RJ-45 Ethernet cable to connect the printer directly to the network by way of a router. The printer can typically be assigned a static IP address, or it can acquire one dynamically from a DHCP server. (Don't know what a router, IP address, or DHCP server is? Take a look at Chapter 23, "Local Area Networking.") Once connected to the network, the printer acts independent of any single PC. Some of the more costly network printers come with a built-in Wi-Fi adapter to connect to the network wirelessly. Alternatively, some printers offer Bluetooth interfaces for networking.

Even if a printer does not come with built-in Ethernet, Wi-Fi, or Bluetooth, you can purchase a stand-alone network device known as a *print server* to connect your printer to the network. These print servers, which can be Ethernet or Wi-Fi, enable one or several printers to attach via parallel port or USB. So take that ancient ImageWriter dot-matrix printer and network it—I dare you!

Other Printers

Plenty of other connection types are available for printers. We've focused mainly on parallel, USB, FireWire, and networked connections. Be aware that you may run into an old serial port printer or a SCSI printer. Although this is unlikely, know that it's a possibility.

Practical Application

■ The Laser Printing Process

The laser printing process can be broken down into six steps, and the CompTIA A+ exams expect you to know them all. As a tech, you should be familiar with these phases, as this can help you troubleshoot printing problems. For example, if an odd line is printed down the middle of every page, you know there's a problem with the photosensitive drum or cleaning mechanism and the toner cartridge needs to be replaced.

You'll look into the physical steps that occur each time a laser printer revs up and prints a page; then you'll see what happens electronically to ensure that the data is processed properly into flawless, smooth text and graphics.

The Physical Side of the Process

Most laser printers perform the printing process in a series of six steps. Keep in mind that some brands of laser printers may depart somewhat from this process, although most work in exactly this order:

1. Clean
2. Charge
3. Write

4. Develop
5. Transfer
6. Fuse

Clean the Drum

The printing process begins with the physical and electrical cleaning of the photosensitive drum (Figure 22.12). Before printing each new page, the drum must be returned to a clean, fresh condition. All residual toner left over from printing the previous page must be removed, usually by scraping the surface of the drum with a rubber cleaning blade. If residual particles remain on the drum, they will appear as random black spots and streaks on the next page. The physical cleaning mechanism either deposits the residual toner in a debris cavity or recycles it by returning it to the toner supply in the toner cartridge. The physical cleaning must be done carefully. Damage to the drum will cause a permanent mark to be printed on every single page.

The printer must also be electrically cleaned. One or more erase lamps bombard the surface of the drum with the appropriate wavelengths of light, causing the surface particles to discharge into the grounded drum. After the cleaning process, the drum should be completely free of toner and have a neutral charge.

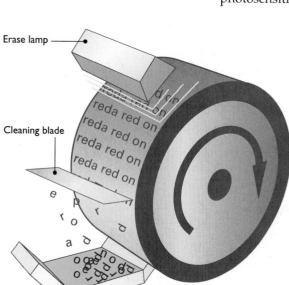

Erase lamp

Cleaning blade

• **Figure 22.12**   Cleaning and erasing the drum

Charge the Drum

To make the drum receptive to new images, it must be charged (Figure 22.13). Using the primary corona wire, a uniform negative charge is applied to the entire surface of the drum (usually between ~600 and ~1000 volts).

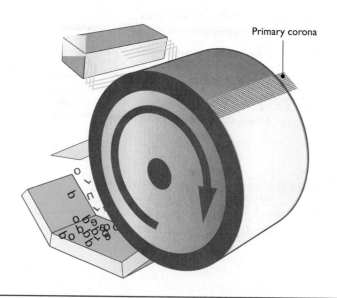

Primary corona

• **Figure 22.13**   Charging the drum with a uniform negative charge

Write and Develop the Image

A laser is used to write a positive image on the surface of the drum. Every particle on the drum hit by the laser releases most of its negative charge into the drum. Those particles with a lesser negative charge are positively charged relative to the toner particles and attract them, creating a developed image (Figure 22.14).

Transfer the Image

The printer must transfer the image from the drum onto the paper. The transfer corona gives the paper a positive charge; then the negatively charged toner particles leap from the drum to the paper. At this point, the particles are merely resting on the paper and must still be permanently fused to the paper.

Fuse the Image

The particles have been attracted to the paper because of the paper's positive charge, but if the process stopped here, the toner particles would fall off the page as soon as you lift it. Because the toner particles are mostly composed of plastic, they can be melted to the page. Two rollers—a heated roller coated in a nonstick material and a pressure roller—melt the toner to the paper, permanently affixing it. Finally, a static charge eliminator removes the paper's positive charge (Figure 22.15). Once the page is complete, the printer ejects the printed copy and the process begins again with the physical and electrical cleaning of the printer.

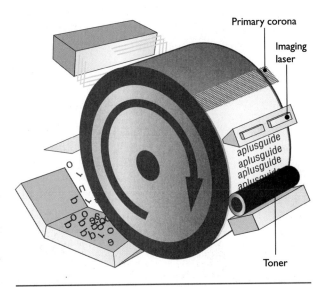

• **Figure 22.14**　Writing the image and applying the toner

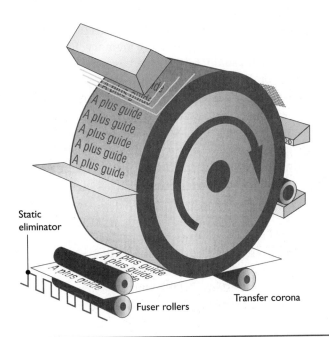

• **Figure 22.15**　Transferring the image to the paper and fusing the final image

Tech Tip

Color Laser Printers
Color laser printers use four different colors of toner (cyan, magenta, yellow, and black) to create their printouts. Most models put each page through four different passes, adding one color at each pass to create the needed results, while others place all the colors onto a special belt and then transfer them to the page in one pass. In some cases, the printer uses four separate toner cartridges and four lasers for the four toner colors, and in others the printer simply lays down one color after the other on the same drum, cleaning after each of four passes per page.

The heated roller produces enough heat to melt some types of plastic media, particularly overhead transparency materials. This could damage your laser printer (and void your warranty), so make sure you're printing on transparencies designed for laser printers!

The Electronic Side of the Process

When you click the Print button in an application, several things happen. First, the CPU processes your request and sends a print job to an area of memory called the print spooler. The **print spooler** enables you to queue up multiple print jobs that the printer will handle sequentially. Next, Windows sends the first print job to the printer. That's your first potential bottleneck—if it's a big job, the OS has to dole out a piece at a time and you'll see the little printer icon in the notification area at the bottom right of your screen. Once the printer icon goes away, you know the print queue is empty—all jobs have gone to the printer.

Once the printer receives some or all of a print job, the hardware of the printer takes over and processes the image. That's your second potential bottleneck and has multiple components.

Raster Images

Impact printers transfer data to the printer one character or one line at a time, whereas laser printers transfer entire pages at a time to the printer. A laser printer generates a **raster image** (a pattern of dots) of the page, representing what the final product should look like. It uses a device (the laser) to "paint" a raster image on the photosensitive drum. Because a laser printer has to paint the entire surface of the photosensitive drum before it can begin to transfer the image to paper, it processes the image one page at a time.

A laser printer uses a chip called the **raster image processor (RIP)** to translate the raster image into commands to the laser. The RIP takes the digital information about fonts and graphics and converts it to a rasterized image made up of dots that can then be printed. An inkjet printer also has a RIP, but it's part of the software driver instead of onboard hardware circuitry. The RIP needs memory (RAM) to store the data that it must process. A laser printer must have enough memory to process an entire page. Some images that require high resolutions require more memory. Insufficient memory to process the image will usually be indicated by a memory overflow ("MEM OVERFLOW") error. If you get a memory overflow error, try reducing the resolution, printing smaller graphics, or turning off RET (see the following section for the last option). Of course, the best solution to a memory overflow error is simply to add more RAM to the laser printer.

Do not assume that every error with the word *memory* in it can be fixed simply by adding more RAM to the printer. Just as adding more RAM chips will not solve every conventional PC memory problem, adding more RAM will not solve every laser printer memory problem. The message "21 ERROR" on an HP LaserJet, for example, indicates that "the printer is unable to process very complex data fast enough for the print engine." This means that the data is simply too complex for the RIP to handle. Adding more memory would *not* solve this problem; it would only make your wallet lighter. The only answer in this case is to reduce the complexity of the page image (that is, fewer fonts, less formatting, reduced graphics resolution, and so on).

Resolution

Laser printers can print at different resolutions, just as monitors can display different resolutions. The maximum resolution that a laser printer can

Tech Tip

Inkjet RIPs

Inkjet printers use RIPs as well, but they're written into the device drivers instead of the onboard programming. You can also buy third-party RIPs that can improve the image quality of your printouts; for an example, see www.colorbytesoftware.com.

handle is determined by its physical characteristics. Laser printer resolution is expressed in dots per inch (dpi). Common resolutions are 600 × 600 dpi or 1200 × 1200 dpi. The first number, the horizontal resolution, is determined by how fine a focus can be achieved by the laser. The second number is determined by the smallest increment by which the drum can be turned. Higher resolutions produce higher quality output, but keep in mind that higher resolutions also require more memory. In some instances, complex images can be printed only at lower resolutions because of their high-memory demands. Even printing at 300 dpi, laser printers produce far better quality than dot-matrix printers because of **resolution enhancement technology (RET)**.

RET enables the printer to insert smaller dots among the characters, smoothing out the jagged curves that are typical of printers that do not use RET (Figure 22.16). Using RET enables laser printers to output high-quality print jobs, but it also requires a portion of the printer's RAM. If you get a MEM OVERFLOW error, sometimes disabling RET will free up enough memory to complete the print job.

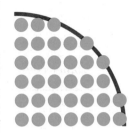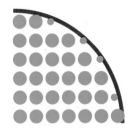

• **Figure 22.16**   RET fills in gaps with smaller dots to smooth out jagged characters.

■ Installing a Printer in Windows

You need to take a moment to understand how Windows handles printing, and then you'll see how to install, configure, and troubleshoot printers in these operating systems.

To Windows 2000, XP, and Vista/7, a printer is not a physical device; it is a *program* that controls one or more physical printers. The *physical* printer is called a print device to Windows (although I continue to use the term "printer" for most purposes, just like almost every tech on the planet). Printer drivers and a spooler are still present, but in Windows 2000/XP and Vista/7, they are integrated into the printer itself (Figure 22.17). This arrangement gives Windows amazing flexibility. For example, one printer can support multiple print devices, enabling a system to act as a print server. If one print device goes down, the printer automatically redirects the output to a working print device.

The general installation, configuration, and troubleshooting issues are basically identical in all modern versions of Windows. Here's a review of a typical Windows printer installation. I'll mention the trivial differences among Windows 2000, XP, and Vista as I go along.

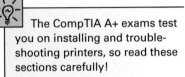

The CompTIA A+ exams test you on installing and troubleshooting printers, so read these sections carefully!

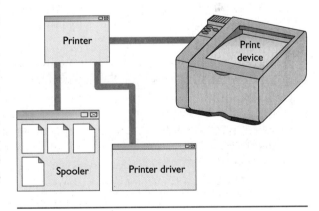

• **Figure 22.17**   Printer driver and spooler in Windows

Setting Up Printers

Setting up a printer is so easy that it's almost scary. Most printers are plug and play, so installing a printer is reduced to simply plugging it in and loading the driver if needed. If the system does not detect the printer or if the printer is not plug and play, click Start | Printers and Faxes in Windows XP to open the Printers applet; in Windows 2000, click Start | Settings | Printers. For Windows Vista, you need to open up the Control Panel and

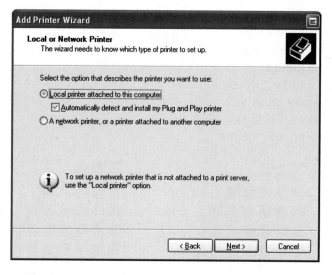

• Figure 22.18   Choosing local or network printer in Windows XP

find the Printer menu item—it is either by itself or, in the categorized view, under Hardware. You can also find the icon for this applet in the Control Panel of Windows 2000/XP.

As you might guess, you install a new printer by clicking the Add a Printer icon (somehow Microsoft has managed to leave the name of this applet unchanged through all Windows versions since 9*x*). This starts the Add Printer Wizard. After a pleasant intro screen, you must choose to install either a printer plugged directly into your system or a network printer (Figure 22.18). You also have the *Automatically detect and install my Plug and Play printer* option, which you can use in many cases when installing a USB printer.

If you choose a local printer (see Chapter 23, "Local Area Networking," for a discussion of networked printers), the applet next asks you to select a port; select the one where you installed the new printer (Figure 22.19). Once you select the port, Windows asks you to specify the type of printer, either by selecting the type from the list or by using the Have Disk option, just as you would for any other device (Figure 22.20). Note the handy Windows Update button, which you can use to get the latest printer driver from the Internet. When you click Next on this screen, Windows installs the printer.

Figure 22.21 shows a typical Windows XP Printers and Faxes screen on a system with one printer installed. Note the small checkmark in the icon's corner; this shows that the device is the default printer. If you have multiple printers, you can change the default printer by selecting the printer's properties and checking Make Default Printer.

In addition to the regular driver installation outlined previously, some installations use printer emulation. *Printer emulation* simply means using a substitute printer driver for a printer, as opposed to using one made

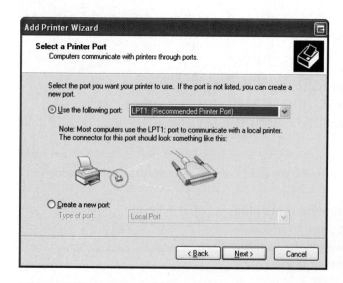

• Figure 22.19   Selecting a port in Windows XP

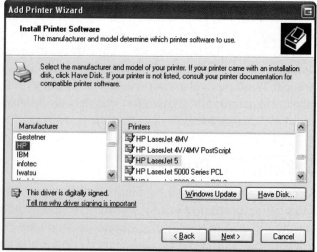

• Figure 22.20   Selecting a printer model/driver in Windows XP

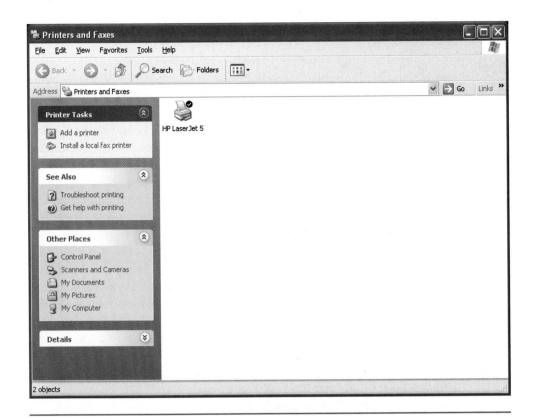

• **Figure 22.21** Installed default printer in the Printers and Faxes applet

exclusively for that printer. You'll run into printer emulation in two circumstances. First, some new printers do not come with their own drivers. They instead emulate a well-known printer (such as an HP LaserJet 4) and run perfectly well on that printer driver. Second, you may see emulation in the "I don't have the right driver!" scenario. I keep about three different HP LaserJet and Epson ink jet printers installed on my PC because I know that with these printer drivers, I can print to almost any printer. Some printers may require you to set them into an *emulation mode* to handle a driver other than their native one.

Optimizing Print Performance

Although a quality printer is the first step toward quality output, your output relies on factors other than the printer itself. What you see on the screen may not match what comes out of the printer, so calibration is important. Using the wrong type of paper can result in less than acceptable printed documents. Configuring the printer driver and spool settings can also affect your print jobs.

Calibration

If you've ever tweaked that digital photograph so it looks perfect on screen, only to discover that the final printout was darker than you had hoped, consider calibrating your monitor. **Calibration** matches the print output of your printer to the visual output on your monitor and governs that through

Tech Tip

Readme Files

You've seen how to get your system to recognize a printer, but what do you do when you add a brand-new printer? Like most peripherals, the printer will include an installation CD-ROM that contains various useful files. One of the most important but least used tools on this CD-ROM is the Readme file. This file, generally in TXT format, contains the absolute latest information on any idiosyncrasies, problems, or incompatibilities related to your printer or printer driver. Usually, you can find it in the root folder of the installation CD-ROM, although many printer drivers install the Readme file on your hard drive so you can access it from the Start menu. The rule here is read first to avoid a headache later!

software. All three parts need to be set up properly for you to print what you see consistently.

Computer monitors output in RGB—that is, they compose colors using red, green, and blue pixels, as discussed in Chapter 19, "Video"—while printers mix their colors differently to arrive at their output. As mentioned earlier, the CMYK method composes colors from cyan (blue), magenta (red), yellow, and black.

The upshot of all this is that the printer tries to output—by using CMYK (or another technique)—what you see on the screen using RGB. Because the two color modes do not create color the same way, you see color shifts and not-so-subtle differences between the onscreen image and the printed image. By calibrating your monitor, you can adjust the setting to match the output of your printer. You can do this manually through "eyeballing" it or automatically by using calibration hardware.

To calibrate your monitor manually, obtain a test image from the Web (try sites such as www.DigitalDog.net) and print it out. If you have a good eye, you can compare this printout to what you see on the screen and make the adjustments manually through your monitor's controls or display settings.

Another option is to calibrate your printer by using an International Color Consortium (ICC) color profile, a preference file that instructs your printer to print colors a certain way—for example, to match what is on your screen. Loading a different color profile results in a different color output. Color profiles are sometimes included on the installation CD-ROM with a printer, but you can create or purchase custom profiles as well. The use of ICC profiles is not limited to printers; you can also use them to control the output of monitors, scanners, or even digital cameras. Windows Vista includes *Windows Color System* (*WCS*) to help build color profiles for use across devices. WCS is based on a new standard Microsoft calls *color infrastructure and translation engine* (*CITE*).

■ Troubleshooting Printers

As easy as printers are to set up, they are equally robust at running, assuming that you install the proper drivers and keep the printer well maintained. But printer errors do occasionally develop. Take a look at the most common print problems with Windows, as well as problems that crop up with specific printer types.

General Troubleshooting Issues

Printers of all stripes share some common problems, such as print jobs that don't go, strangely sized prints, and misalignment. Other issues include consumables, sharing multiple printers, and crashing on power-up. Let's take a look at these general troubleshooting issues, but start with a recap of the tools of the trade.

Tools of the Trade

Before you jump in and start to work on a printer that's giving you fits, you'll need some tools. You can use the standard computer tech tools in your toolkit, plus a couple of printer-specific devices. Here are some that will come in handy:

- A multimeter for troubleshooting electrical problems such as faulty wall outlets

- Various cleaning solutions, such as denatured alcohol

- An extension magnet for grabbing loose screws in tight spaces and cleaning up iron-based toner

- An optical disc or USB thumb drive with test patterns for checking print quality

- Your trusty screwdriver—both a Phillips-head and flat-head, because if you bring just one kind, it's a sure bet that you'll need the other

Print Job Never Prints

If you click Print but nothing comes out of the printer, first check all the obvious things. Is the printer on? Is it connected? Is it online? Does it have paper? Assuming the printer is in good order, it's time to look at the spooler. You can see the spooler status either by double-clicking the printer's icon in the Printers applet or by double-clicking the tiny printer icon in the notification area if it's present. If you're having a problem, the printer icon will almost always be there. Figure 22.22 shows the print spooler open.

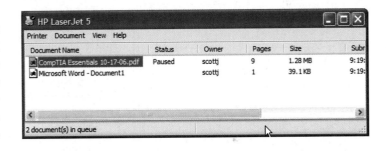

• **Figure 22.22** Print spooler

Print spoolers can easily overflow or become corrupt due to a lack of disk space, too many print jobs, or one of a thousand other factors. The status window shows all of the pending print jobs and enables you to delete, start, or pause jobs. I usually just delete the affected print job(s) and try again.

Print spoolers are handy. If the printer goes down, you can just leave the print jobs in the spooler until the printer comes back online. Some versions of Windows require you to select Resume Printing manually, but others automatically continue the print job(s). If you have a printer that isn't coming on anytime soon, you can simply delete the print job in the spooler window and try another printer.

If you have problems with the print spooler, you can get around them by changing your print spool settings. Go into the Printers and Faxes applet, right-click the icon of the printer in question, and choose Properties. In the resulting Properties window (see Figure 22.23), choose the *Print directly to the printer* radio button and click OK; then try sending your print job again. Note that this window also offers you the choice of printing immediately—that is, starting to print pages as soon as the spooler

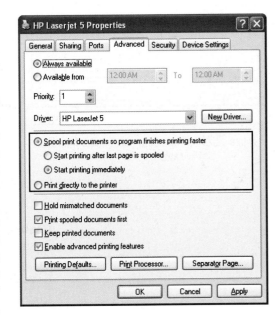

• **Figure 22.23** Print spool settings

has enough information to feed to the printer—or holding off on printing until the entire job is spooled.

Another possible cause for a stalled print job is that the printer is simply waiting for the correct paper! Laser printers in particular have settings that tell them what size paper is in their standard paper tray or trays. If the application sending a print job specifies a different paper size—for example, it wants to print a standard No. 10 envelope, or perhaps a legal sheet, but the standard paper tray holds only 8.5 × 11 letter paper—the printer usually pauses and holds up the queue until someone switches out the tray or manually feeds the type of paper that this print job requires. You can usually override this pause, even without having the specified paper, by pressing the OK or GO button on the printer.

The printer's default paper tray and paper size options will differ greatly depending on the printer type and model. To find these settings, go into the printer's Properties window from the Printers and Faxes applet, and then select the Device Settings tab. This list of settings includes Form To Tray Assignment, where you can specify which tray (in the case of a printer with multiple paper trays) holds which size paper.

> If you try all this and you still can't print, double-check your connections and make sure the printer is still plugged in. If it's plugged in, try turning the printer off and then back on. CompTIA calls this *power cycling*.

Strange Sizes

A print job that comes out a strange size usually points to a user mistake in setting up the print job. All applications have a Print command and a Page Setup interface. The Page Setup interface enables you to define a number of print options, which vary from application to application. Figure 22.24 shows the Page Setup options for Microsoft Word. Make sure the page is set up properly before you blame the printer for a problem.

If you know the page is set up correctly, recheck the printer drivers. If necessary, uninstall and reinstall the printer drivers. If the problem persists, you may have a serious problem with the printer's print engine, but that comes up as a likely answer only when you continually get the same strangely sized printouts using a variety of applications.

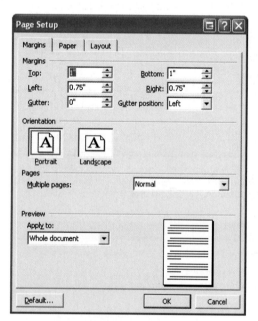

• **Figure 22.24**   Page Setup options for Microsoft Word

Misaligned or Garbage Prints

Misaligned or garbage printouts invariably point to a corrupted or incorrect driver. Make sure you're using the right driver (it's hard to mess this up, but not impossible) and then uninstall and reinstall the printer driver. If the problem persists, you may be asking the printer to do something it cannot do. For example, you may be printing to a PostScript printer with a PCL driver. Check the printer type to verify that you haven't installed the wrong type of driver for that printer!

Dealing with Consumables

All printers tend to generate a lot of trash in the form of **consumables**. Impact printers use paper and ribbons, inkjet printers use paper and ink cartridges, and laser printers use paper and toner cartridges. In today's environmentally sensitive world, many laws regulate the proper disposal of most printer components. Be sure to check with the local sanitation department or disposal services company before throwing away any component.

Of course, you should never throw away toner cartridges—certain companies will *pay* for used cartridges!

Problems Sharing Multiple Printers

If you want to use multiple printers attached to the same parallel port, you have to use a switch box. Laser printers should never be used with mechanical switch boxes. Mechanical switch boxes create power surges that can damage your printer. If you must use a switch box, use a box that switches between printers electronically and has built-in surge protection.

Crashes on Power-up

Both laser printers and PCs require more power during their initial power-up (the POST on a PC and the warm-up on a laser printer) than once they are running. Hewlett-Packard recommends a *reverse power-up*. Turn on the laser printer first and allow it to finish its warm-up before turning on the PC. This avoids having two devices drawing their peak loads simultaneously.

Troubleshooting Dot-Matrix Printers

Impact printers require regular maintenance but will run forever as long as you're diligent. Keep the platen (the roller or plate on which the pins impact) clean and the printhead clean with denatured alcohol. Be sure to lubricate gears and pulleys according to the manufacturer's specifications. Never lubricate the printhead, however, because the lubricant will smear and stain the paper.

Bad-looking Text

White bars going through the text point to a dirty or damaged printhead. Try cleaning the printhead with a little denatured alcohol. If the problem persists, replace the printhead. Printheads for most printers are readily available from the manufacturer or from companies that rebuild them. If the characters look chopped off at the top or bottom, the printhead probably needs to be adjusted. Refer to the manufacturer's instructions for proper adjustment.

Bad-looking Page

If the page is covered with dots and small smudges—the "pepper look"—the platen is dirty. Clean the platen with denatured alcohol. If the image is faded, and you know the ribbon is good, try adjusting the printhead closer to the platen. If the image is okay on one side of the paper but fades as you move to the other, the platen is out of adjustment. Platens are generally difficult to adjust, so your best plan is to take it to the manufacturer's local warranty/repair center.

Troubleshooting Inkjet Printers

Inkjet printers are reliable devices that require little maintenance as long as they are used within their design parameters (high-use machines will require more intensive maintenance). Because of the low price of these

Tech Tip

Check the MSDS

*When in doubt about what to do with a component, check with the manufacturer for a **material safety data sheet (MSDS)**. These standardized forms provide detailed information about the potential environmental hazards associated with different components and proper disposal methods. For example, surf to www .hp.com/hpinfo/globalcitizenship/ environment/productdata/index .html to find the latest MSDS for all Hewlett-Packard products. This isn't just a printer issue— you can find an MSDS for most PC components. When in doubt about how to get rid of any PC component, check with the manufacturer for an MSDS.*

MSDSs contain important information regarding hazardous materials such as safe use procedures and emergency response instructions. An MSDS is typically posted anywhere a hazardous chemical is used.

printers, manufacturers know that people don't want to spend a lot of money keeping them running. If you perform even the most basic maintenance tasks, they will soldier on for years without a whimper. Inkjets generally have built-in maintenance programs that you should run from time to time to keep your inkjet in good operating order.

Inkjet Printer Maintenance

Inkjet printers don't get nearly as dirty as laser printers, and most manufacturers do not recommend periodic cleaning. Unless your manufacturer explicitly tells you to do so, don't vacuum an inkjet. Inkjets generally do not have maintenance kits, but most inkjet printers come with extensive maintenance software (Figure 22.25). Usually, the hardest part of using this software is finding it in the first place. Look for an option in Printing Preferences, a selection on the Start menu, or an icon on your desktop. Don't worry—it's there!

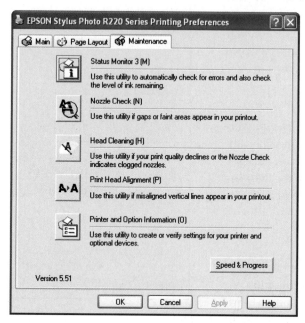

When you first set up an inkjet printer, it normally instructs you to perform a routine to align the printheads properly, wherein you print out a page and select from sets of numbered lines. If this isn't done, the print quality will show it, but the good news is that you can perform this procedure at any time. If a printer is moved or dropped or it's just been working away untended for a while, it's often worth running the alignment routine.

- **Figure 22.25** Inkjet printer maintenance screen

Inkjet Problems

Did I say that you never should clean an inkjet? Well, that may be true for the printer itself, but there is one part of your printer that will benefit from an occasional cleaning: the inkjet's printer head nozzles. The nozzles are the tiny pipes that squirt the ink onto the paper. A common problem with inkjet printers is the tendency for the ink inside the nozzles to dry out when not used even for a relatively short time, blocking any ink from exiting. If your printer is telling Windows that it's printing and it's feeding paper through, but either nothing is coming out (usually the case if you're just printing black text), or only certain colors are printing, the culprit is almost certainly dried ink clogging the nozzles.

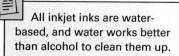
All inkjet inks are water-based, and water works better than alcohol to clean them up.

Cleaning the heads on an inkjet printer is sometimes necessary, but I don't recommend that you do it on a regular basis as preventive maintenance. The head-cleaning process uses up a lot of that very expensive inkjet ink—so do this only when a printing problem seems to indicate clogged or dirty print heads!

Every inkjet has a different procedure for cleaning the printhead nozzles. On older inkjets, you usually have to press buttons on the printer to start a maintenance program. On more modern inkjets, you can access the head-cleaning maintenance program from Windows.

Another problem that sometimes arises is the dreaded multi-sheet paper grab. This is often not actually your printer's fault—humidity can cause sheets of paper to cling to each other—but sometimes the culprit is an overheated printer, so if you've been cranking out a lot of documents without stopping, try giving the printer a bit of a coffee break. Also, fan the sheets of the paper stack before inserting it into the paper tray.

Finally, check to see if excess ink overflow is a problem. In the area where the printheads park, look for a small tank or tray that catches excess ink from the cleaning process. If the printer has one, check to see how full it is.

If this tray overflows onto the main board or even the power supply, it will kill your printer. If you discover that the tray is about to overflow, you can remove excess ink by inserting a twisted paper towel into the tank to soak up some of the ink. It is advisable to wear latex or vinyl gloves while doing this. Clean up any spilled ink with a paper towel dampened with distilled water.

Troubleshooting Laser Printers

Quite a few problems can arise with laser printers, but before getting into those details, you need to review some recommended procedures for *avoiding* those problems.

Laser Printer Maintenance

Unlike PC maintenance, laser printer maintenance follows a fairly well established procedure. Follow these steps to ensure a long, healthy life for your system.

Keep It Clean   Laser printers are quite robust as a rule. A good cleaning every time you replace the toner cartridge will help that printer last for many years. I know of many examples of original HP LaserJet I printers continuing to run perfectly after a dozen or more years of operation. The secret is that they were kept immaculately clean.

Your laser printer gets dirty in two ways: Excess toner, over time, will slowly coat the entire printer. Paper dust, sometimes called *paper dander*, tends to build up where the paper is bent around rollers or where pickup rollers grab paper. Unlike (black) toner, paper dust is easy to see and is usually a good indicator that a printer needs to be cleaned. Usually, a thorough cleaning using a can of pressurized air to blow out the printer is the best cleaning you can do. It's best to do this outdoors, or you may end up looking like one of those chimney sweeps from *Mary Poppins*! If you must clean a printer indoors, use a special low-static vacuum designed especially for electronic components (Figure 22.26).

Every laser printer has its own unique cleaning method, but the cleaning instructions tend to skip one little area. Every laser printer has a number of rubber guide rollers through which the paper is run during the print process. These little rollers tend to pick up dirt and paper dust over time, making them slip and jam paper. They are easily cleaned with a small amount of 90 percent or better alcohol on a fibrous cleaning towel. The alcohol will remove the debris and any dead rubber. You can also give the rollers and separator pads a textured surface that will restore their feeding properties by rubbing them with a little alcohol on a nonmetallic scouring pad.

If you're ready to get specific, get the printer's service manual. Almost every printer manufacturer sells these; they are a key source for information on how to keep a printer clean and running. Sadly, not all printer manufacturers provide these, but most do. While you're at it, see if the manufacturer has a Quick Reference Guide; these can be very handy for most printer problems!

Finally, be aware that Hewlett-Packard sells maintenance kits for most of its laser printers. These are sets of replacement parts for the parts most

• **Figure 22.26**   Low-static vacuum

likely to wear out on each particular type of HP LaserJet. Although their use is not required to maintain warranty coverage, using these kits when prescribed by HP helps assure the continuing reliability of your LaserJet.

Periodic Maintenance   Although keeping the printer clean is critical to its health and well-being, every laser printer has certain components that you need to replace periodically. Your ultimate source for determining the parts that need to be replaced (and when to replace them) is the printer manufacturer. Following the manufacturer's maintenance guidelines will help to ensure years of trouble-free, dependable printing from your laser printer.

Many manufacturers provide kits that contain components that you should replace on a regular schedule. These **maintenance kits** often include a fuser as well as one or more rollers or pads. Typically, you need to reset the page counter after installing a maintenance kit so the printer can remind you to perform maintenance again after a certain number of pages have been printed.

Some ozone filters can be cleaned with a vacuum and some can only be replaced—follow the manufacturer's recommendation. You can clean the fuser assembly with 90 percent or better denatured alcohol. Check the heat roller (the Teflon coated one with the light bulb inside) for pits and scratches. If you see surface damage on the rollers, replace the fuser unit.

Most printers will give you an error code when the fuser is damaged or overheating and needs to be replaced; others will produce the error code at a preset copy count as a preventive maintenance measure. Again, follow the manufacturer's recommendations.

The transfer corona can be cleaned with a 90 percent denatured alcohol solution on a cotton swab. If the wire is broken, you can replace it; many just snap in or are held in by a couple of screws. Paper guides can also be cleaned with alcohol on a fibrous towel.

Laser Printer Problems

Laser printers usually manifest problems by creating poor output. One of the most important tests you can do on any printer, not just a laser printer, is called a *diagnostic print page* or an *engine test page*. You do this by either holding down the On Line button as the printer is started or using the printer's maintenance software.

Blank Paper   Blank sheets of paper usually mean the printer is out of toner. If the printer does have toner and nothing prints, print a diagnostic print page. If that is also blank, remove the toner cartridge and look at the imaging drum inside. If the image is still there, you know the transfer corona or the high-voltage power supply has failed. Check the printer's maintenance guide to see how to focus on the bad part and replace it.

Dirty Printouts   If the fusing mechanism gets dirty in a laser printer, it will leave a light dusting of toner all over the paper, particularly on the back of the page. When you see toner speckles on your printouts, you should get the printer cleaned.

Ghosting   Ghost images sometimes appear at regular intervals on the printed page. This happens when the imaging drum has not fully discharged and is picking up toner from a previous image or when a previous

Failure of the thermal fuse (used to keep the fuser from overheating) can necessitate replacing the fuser assembly. Some machines contain more than one thermal fuse. As always, follow the manufacturer's recommendations. Many manufacturers have kits that alert you with an alarm code to replace the fuser unit and key rollers and guides at predetermined page counts.

The fuser assembly operates at 200 to 300 degrees Fahrenheit, so always allow time for this component to cool down before you attempt to clean it.

image has used up so much toner that either the supply of charged toner is insufficient or the toner has not been adequately charged. Sometimes it can also be caused by a worn-out cleaning blade that isn't removing the toner from the drum.

Light Ghosting versus Dark Ghosting   A variety of problems can cause both light and dark ghosting, but the most common source of light ghosting is "developer starvation." If you ask a laser printer to print an extremely dark or complex image, it can use up so much toner that the toner cartridge will not be able to charge enough toner to print the next image. The proper solution is to use less toner. You can fix ghosting problems in the following ways:

- Lower the resolution of the page (print at 300 dpi instead of 600 dpi).
- Use a different pattern.
- Avoid 50 percent grayscale and "dot-on/dot-off patterns."
- Change the layout so that grayscale patterns do not follow black areas.
- Make dark patterns lighter and light patterns darker.
- Print in landscape orientation.
- Adjust print density and RET settings.
- Print a completely blank page immediately prior to the page with the ghosting image, as part of the same print job.

In addition to these possibilities, low temperature and low humidity can aggravate ghosting problems. Check your users' manual for environmental recommendations. Dark ghosting can sometimes be caused by a damaged drum. It may be fixed by replacing the toner cartridge. Light ghosting would *not* be solved in this way. Switching other components will not usually affect ghosting problems because they are a side effect of the entire printing process.

Vertical White Lines   Vertical white lines usually happen when the toner is clogged, preventing the proper dispersion of toner on the drum. Try shaking the toner cartridge to dislodge the clog. If that doesn't work, replace the toner cartridge.

Blotchy Print   Blotches are commonly a result of uneven dispersion of toner, especially if the toner is low. Shake the toner from side to side and then try to print. Also be sure that the printer is sitting level. Finally, make sure the paper is not wet in spots. If the blotches are in a regular order, check the fusing rollers and the photosensitive drum for any foreign objects.

Spotty Print   If the spots appear at regular intervals, the drum may be damaged or some toner may be stuck to the fuser rollers. Try wiping off the fuser rollers. Check the drum for damage. If the drum is damaged, get a new toner cartridge.

Embossed Effect   If your prints are getting an embossed effect (like putting a penny under a piece of paper and rubbing it with a lead pencil), there is almost certainly a foreign object on a roller. Use 90 percent denatured alcohol or regular water with a soft cloth to try to remove it. If the foreign object is on

the photosensitive drum, you're going to have to use a new toner cartridge. An embossed effect can also be caused by the contrast control being set too high. The contrast control is actually a knob on the inside of the unit (sometimes accessible from the outside on older models). Check your manual for the specific location.

Incomplete Characters   You can sometimes correct incompletely printed characters on laser-printed transparencies by adjusting the print density. Be extremely careful to use only materials approved for laser printers.

Creased Pages   Laser printers have up to four rollers. In addition to the heat and pressure rollers of the fuser assembly, other rollers move the paper from the source tray to the output tray. These rollers crease the paper to avoid curling that would cause paper jams in the printer. If the creases are noticeable, try using a different paper type. Cotton bond paper is usually more susceptible to noticeable creasing than other bonds. You might also try sending the output to the face-up tray, which avoids one roller. There is no hardware solution to this problem; it is simply a side-effect of the process.

Paper Jams   Every printer jams now and then. If you get a jam, always refer first to the manufacturer's jam removal procedure. It is simply too easy to damage a printer by pulling on the jammed paper! If the printer reports a jam but there's no paper inside, you've almost certainly got a problem with one of the many jam sensors or paper feed sensors inside the printer, and you'll need to take it to a repair center.

Pulling Multiple Sheets   If the printer grabs multiple sheets at a time, first try opening a new ream of paper and loading that in the printer. If that works, you have a humidity problem. If the new paper angle doesn't work, check the separation pad on the printer. The separation pad is a small piece of cork or rubber that separates the sheets as they are pulled from the paper feed tray. A worn separation pad looks shiny and, well, *worn*! Most separation pads are easy to replace. Check out www.printerworks.com to see if you can replace yours.

Warped, Overprinted, or Poorly Formed Characters   Poorly formed characters can indicate either a problem with the paper (or other media) or a problem with the hardware.

Incorrect media cause a number of these types of problems. Avoid paper that is too rough or too smooth. Paper that is too rough interferes with the fusing of characters and their initial definition. If the paper is too smooth (like some coated papers, for example), it may feed improperly, causing distorted or overwritten characters. Even though you can purchase laser printer–specific paper, all laser printers print acceptably on standard photocopy paper. Try to keep the paper from becoming too wet. Don't open a ream of paper until it is time to load it into the printer. Always fan the paper before loading it into the printer, especially if the paper has been left out of the package for more than just a few days.

The durability of a well-maintained laser printer makes hardware a much rarer source of character printing problems, but you should be aware of the possibility. Fortunately, it is fairly easy to check the hardware. Most laser printers have a self-test function—often combined with a diagnostic printout but sometimes as a separate process. This self-test shows whether

the laser printer can properly develop an image without actually having to send print commands from the PC. The self-test is quite handy to verify the question "Is it the printer or is it the computer?" Run the self-test to check for connectivity and configuration problems.

Possible solutions include replacing the toner cartridge, especially if you hear popping noises; checking the cabling; and replacing the data cable, especially if it has bends or crimps or if objects are resting on the cable. If you have a front menu panel, turn off advanced functions and high-speed settings to determine whether the advanced functions are either not working properly or not supported by your current software configuration (check your manuals for configuration information). If these solutions do not work, the problem may not be user serviceable. Try contacting an authorized service center.

Beyond A+

DOT4

The IEEE 1284.4 standard, commonly known as DOT4, was created for multifunction peripherals (MFPs)—those nifty gadgets that combine the functions of printer, fax, and scanner in one big piece of equipment (Figure 22.27). The DOT4 protocol enables the individual devices within the MFP to send and receive multiple data packets simultaneously across a single physical channel. All data exchanges are independent of one another, so you can cancel one—for example, a print job—without affecting the others. DOT4 is an enhancement of the IEEE 1284 protocol for parallel printing; look for products that use it the next time you find yourself in a computer superstore.

• **Figure 22.27**   All-in-one printer/scanner/fax machine/copier/coffee maker/iPod dock

Chapter 22 Review

■ Chapter Summary

After reading this chapter and completing the exercises, you should understand the following aspects of printers.

Describe current printer technologies

- Impact printers create an image on paper by physically striking an ink ribbon against the paper's surface. The most commonly used impact printer technology is dot matrix. Dot-matrix printers have a large installed base in businesses, and they can be used for multipart forms because they actually strike the paper. Dot-matrix printers use a grid, or matrix, of tiny pins, also known as printwires, to strike an inked printer ribbon and produce images on paper. The case that holds the printwires is called a printhead. Dot-matrix printers come in two varieties: 9-pin (draft quality) and 24-pin (letter quality).

- Inkjet printers include a printhead mechanism, support electronics, a transfer mechanism to move the printhead back and forth, and a paper feed component to drag, move, and eject paper. They eject ink through tiny tubes. The heat or pressure used to move the ink is created by tiny resistors or electroconductive plates at the end of each tube.

- Ink is stored in ink cartridges. Older color printers used two cartridges: one for black and one for cyan, magenta, and yellow. Newer printers come with four, six, eight, or more cartridges.

- The quality of a print image is called the print resolution. The resolution is measured in dots per inch (dpi), which has two values: horizontal and vertical. An example of a resolution is 600 × 600 dpi. Printing speed is measured in pages per minute (ppm). Modern inkjet printers can print on a variety of media, including glossy photo paper, optical discs, or fabric.

- Dye-sublimation printers are used to achieve excellent print quality, especially in color, but they're expensive. Documents printed through the dye-sublimation process display continuous-tone images, meaning that each pixel dot is a blend of the dye colors. This is in contrast to other print technologies' dithered images, which use closely packed, single-color dots to simulate blended colors.

- Two kinds of thermal printers create either quick one-color printouts such as faxes or store receipts (direct thermal) or higher-quality color prints (thermal wax transfer).

- Using a process called electro-photographic imaging, laser printers produce high-quality and high-speed output. Laser printers usually use lasers as a light source because of their precision, but some lower-cost printers may use LED arrays instead. The toner cartridge in a laser printer supplies the toner that creates the image on the page; many other laser printer parts, especially those that suffer the most wear and tear, have been incorporated into the toner cartridge. Although the majority of laser printers are monochrome, you can find color laser printers capable of printing photographs.

- Be aware of the cost of consumables when purchasing a printer. Some less expensive printers may seem like a good deal, but ink or toner cartridge replacements can cost as much as the entire printer.

- The photosensitive drum in a laser printer is an aluminum cylinder coated with particles of photosensitive compounds. The erase lamp exposes the entire surface of the photosensitive drum to light, making the photosensitive coating conductive and leaving the surface particles electrically neutral. When the primary corona is charged with an extremely high voltage, an electric field (or corona) forms, enabling voltage to pass to the drum and charge the photosensitive particles on its surface; the surface of the drum receives a uniform negative voltage of between ~600 and ~1,000 volts.

- The laser acts as the writing mechanism of the printer. When particles are struck by the laser, they are discharged and left with a ~100 volt negative charge. The toner in a laser printer is a fine powder made up of plastic particles bonded to iron particles. The toner cylinder charges the toner with a negative charge of between ~200 and ~500 volts.

Because that charge falls between the original uniform negative charge of the photosensitive drum (~600 to ~1,000 volts) and the charge of the particles on the drum's surface hit by the laser (~100 volts), particles of toner are attracted to the areas of the photosensitive drum that have been hit by the laser. The transfer corona applies a positive charge to the paper, drawing the negatively charged toner particles on the drum to the paper. The toner is merely resting on top of the paper after the static charge eliminator has removed the paper's static charge. Two rollers, a pressure roller and a heated roller, are used to fuse the toner to the paper.

- All laser printers have at least two separate power supplies. The primary power supply, which may actually be more than one power supply, provides power to the motors that move the paper, the system electronics, the laser, and the transfer corona. The high-voltage power supply usually only provides power to the primary corona; it is one of the most dangerous devices in the world of PCs. Always turn off a laser printer before opening it up.

- A laser printer's mechanical functions are served by complex gear systems packed together in discrete units generically called gear packs or gearboxes. Most laser printers have two or three. Every laser printer has sensors that detect a broad range of conditions, such as paper jams, empty paper trays, or low toner levels.

- Every laser printer contains at least one electronic system board (many have two or three) that contains the main processor, the printer's ROM, and the RAM used to store the image before it is printed. When the printer doesn't have enough RAM to store the image before it prints, you get a memory overflow problem. Most printers can use generic DRAM like the kind you use in your PC, but check with the manufacturer to be sure.

- Because even tiny concentrations of ozone (O_3) will cause damage to printer components, most laser printers have a special ozone filter that needs to be vacuumed or replaced periodically.

- Solid ink printers use sticks of solid ink to produce extremely vibrant color. The inks are melted, absorbed into the paper fibers, and then solidify, producing continuous-tone output in a single pass. The solid ink sticks may be inserted midway

through a print job if a certain color needs to be topped off.

- ASCII contains a variety of control codes for transferring data, some of which can be used to control printers; ASCII code 10 (or 0A in hex) means "Line Feed," and ASCII code 12 (0C) means "Form Feed." These commands have been standard since before the creation of IBM PCs, and all printers respond to them; however, the control codes are extremely limited. Utilizing high-end graphics and a wide variety of fonts requires more advanced languages.

- Adobe Systems' PostScript page description language is a device-independent printer language capable of high-resolution graphics and scalable fonts. Because PostScript is understood by printers at a hardware level, the majority of the image processing is done by the printer and not the PC's CPU, so PostScript printers print faster. PostScript defines the page as a single raster image; this makes PostScript files extremely portable.

- Hewlett-Packard's printer control language (PCL) features a set of printer commands greatly expanded from ASCII, but it does not support advanced graphical functions. PCL6 features scalable fonts and additional line drawing commands. PCL uses a series of commands to define the characters on the page, rather than defining the page as a single raster image like PostScript.

- Windows 2000/XP use the graphical device interface (GDI) component of the operating system to handle print functions. The GDI uses the CPU rather than the printer to process a print job and then sends the completed job to the printer. As long as the printer has a capable-enough raster image processor (RIP) and plenty of RAM, you don't need to worry about the printer language at all in most situations. Windows Vista/7 includes support for the XML Paper Specification (XPS) print path, which requires an XPS compatible driver. Some devices support XPS natively.

- Most printers connect to one of two ports on the PC: a DB-25 parallel port or a USB port. The parallel connection is the classic way to plug in a printer, but most new printers use USB. The parallel port was included in the original IBM PC as a faster alternative to serial communication and has been kept around for backward compatibility.

9. The output from Diane's laser printer is fading evenly. What should she suspect first?

   A. A laser is blocked.

   B. The printer is out of toner.

   C. A nozzle is clogged.

   D. Her printer is dirty.

10. The dye-sublimation printing technique is an example of what method of color printing?

    A. CMYK

    B. Thermal wax transfer

    C. RGB

    D. Direct thermal

11. The output from your inkjet printer appears much darker than what you see on your screen. What is the problem?

    A. You are using a paper weight that is not supported in the MSDS.

    B. The printer and monitor need to be calibrated.

    C. The color ink cartridges are almost empty.

    D. The black ink cartridge is almost empty.

12. What is the best way to make a printer available to everyone on your network and maintain the highest level of availability?

    A. Use a FireWire printer connected to a user's PC and share that printer on the network.

    B. Use a USB printer connected to a user's PC and share that printer on the network.

    C. Use a network printer connected directly to the network.

    D. Use a mechanical switch box with the printer.

13. Sheila in accounting needs to print receipts in duplicate. The white copy stays with accounting and the pink copy goes to the customer. What type of printer should you install?

    A. Inkjet

    B. Impact

    C. Laser Jet

    D. Thermal wax transfer

14. Your laser printer fails to print your print jobs and instead displays a MEM OVERFLOW error. What can you do to rectify the problem? (Select two.)

    A. Install more printer RAM

    B. Install more PC RAM

    C. Upgrade the RIP

    D. Disable RET

15. What is the proper order of the laser printing process?

    A. Clean, charge, write, develop, transfer, and fuse

    B. Charge, write, transfer, fuse, develop, and clean

    C. Clean, write, develop, transfer, fuse, and charge

    D. Clean, charge, write, develop, fuse, and transfer

■ Essay Quiz

1. Your department needs a number of color inkjet printers. At your organization, though, all purchases are handled through professional buyers. Sadly, they know nothing about color inkjet printers. You need to submit a Criteria for Purchase form to your buyers. This is the standard form that your organization gives to buyers so they know what to look for in the products they buy. What are the top three purchasing criteria that you think they need to consider? Write the criteria as simply and clearly as possible.

2. Interview a person who uses a computer for work. Ask what the person does and then write a short description of the type of printer that would most suit that person's needs. Explain why this printer would be the best choice.

3. You have been tasked to make a recommendation for a printer purchase for a busy office of 10 people. Make a case for purchasing either an inkjet or laser printer, providing enough information to compare the two technologies. You can choose the type of business, so recommend the appropriate printer, such as a laser printer to an office that primarily

produces text documents. Make your recommendation opposite to the one you made for essay question #2.

4. Write a short essay comparing and contrasting inkjet printers with the three less-common print technologies: dye-sublimation, thermal, and solid ink.

5. Your boss is fascinated by the laser printing process. Write a short memo that outlines how it works, in the proper order.

Lab Projects

• Lab Project 22.1

Laser printers often have rather complex maintenance procedures and schedules. Select a laser printer—preferably one that you actually have on hand—and answer the following questions.

1 Using the user's guide or online sources, determine the exact cleaning procedures for your laser printer. How often should it be vacuumed? Do any parts need to be removed for cleaning? Does the manufacturer recommend any specialized cleaning steps? Does your printer come with any specialized cleaning tools? Does the manufacturer have any recommended cleaning tools you should purchase?

2 Based on the information you gathered, create a cleaning toolkit for your laser printer. Be sure to include a vacuum. Locate sources for these products and determine the cost of the toolkit.

3 Determine the model number of the toner cartridge. Locate an online company that sells name-brand (such as Hewlett-Packard) toner cartridges. Locate an equivalent third-party toner cartridge. Assuming that the printer uses a toner cartridge every three months, what is your per system annual cost savings using third-party toner cartridges?

4 All toner cartridges have a material safety data sheet (MSDS). Locate the MSDS for your model of toner cartridge and read it. Note any potential hazards of the toner cartridges.

5 Print out the description of the cleaning kit you created as well as the manufacturer's cleaning instructions.

• Lab Project 22.2

Using the same laser printer you used in the first project, locate and compile, on paper, all of the following information about your printer:

- User's guide
- List of error codes

- Troubleshooting guides
- Location of the latest drivers for Windows

Local Area Networking

In this chapter, you will learn how to

- **Explain networking technologies**
- **Explain network operating systems**
- **Install and configure wired networks**
- **Troubleshoot networks**

Networks dominate the modern computing environment. A vast percentage of businesses have PCs connected in a small local area network (LAN), and big businesses simply can't survive without connecting their many offices into a single wide area network (WAN). Even the operating systems of today demand networks. Windows XP, Vista, and 7, for example, come out of the box *assuming* you'll attach them to a network of some sort just to make them work past 30 days (product activation), and they get all indignant if you don't.

Because networks are so common today, every good tech needs to know the basics of networking technology, operating systems, implementation, and troubleshooting. Accordingly, this chapter teaches you how to build and troubleshoot a basic network.

Networking Technologies

When the first network designers sat down at a café to figure out how to get two or more PCs to share data and peripherals, they had to write a lot of details on little white napkins to answer even the most basic questions. The first big question was: *How*? It's easy to say, "Well, just run a wire between them!" Although most networks do manifest themselves via some type of cable, this barely touches the thousands of questions that come into play here. Here are a few of the *big* questions:

- How will each computer be identified? If two or more computers want to talk at the same time, how do you ensure that all conversations are understood?

- What kind of wire? What gauge? How many wires in the cable? Which wires do which things? How long can the cable be? What type of connectors?

- If more than one PC accesses the same file, how can they be prevented from destroying each other's changes to that file?

- How can access to data and peripherals be controlled?

Clearly, making a modern PC network entails a lot more than just stringing up some cable! Most commonly, you have a **client** machine, a PC that requests information or services. It needs a **network interface card (NIC)** that defines or labels the client on the network. A NIC also helps break files into smaller data units, called **packets**, to send across the network, and it helps reassemble the packets it receives into whole files. Second, you need some medium for delivering the packets between two or more PCs—most often this is a wire that can carry electrical pulses; sometimes it's radio waves or other wireless methods. Third, your PC's operating system has to be able to communicate with its own networking hardware and with other machines on the network. Finally, modern PC networks often employ a **server** machine that provides information or services. Figure 23.1 shows a typical network layout.

This section of the chapter looks at the inventive ways network engineers found to handle the first two of the four issues. After a brief look at core technology, the chapter dives into four specific types of networks. You'll dig into the software side of things later in the chapter.

Topology

If a bunch of computers connect together to make a network, some logic or order must influence the way they connect. Perhaps each computer connects to a single main line that snakes around the office. Each computer might have its own cable, with all of the cables coming together to a central point. Or maybe all of the cables from all of the computers connect to a main

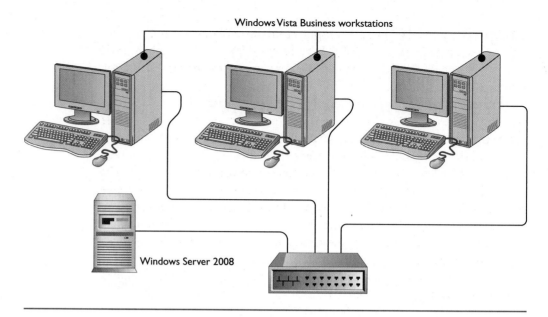

Windows Vista Business workstations

Windows Server 2008

• **Figure 23.1**   A typical network

loop that moves data along a track, picking up and dropping off data like a circular subway line.

A network's *topology* describes the way that computers connect to each other in that network. The most common network topologies are called *bus, ring, star,* and *mesh*. Figure 23.2 shows the four types: a **bus topology**, where all computers connect to the network via a main line called a *bus cable*; a **ring topology**, where all computers on the network attach to a central ring of

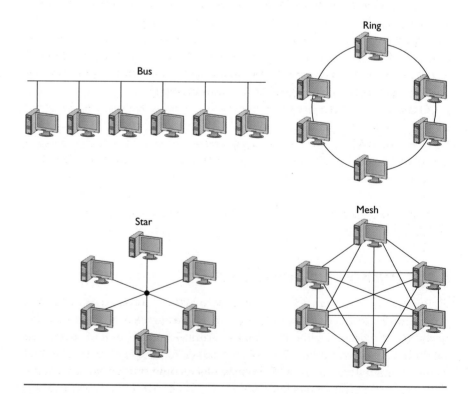

Bus

Ring

Star

Mesh

• **Figure 23.2**   Clockwise from top left: bus, ring, mesh, and star topologies

cable; a **star topology**, where the computers on the network connect to a central wiring point (usually called a *hub*); and a **mesh topology**, where each computer has a dedicated line to every other computer—the mesh topology is mostly used in wireless networks. There are also **hybrid topologies**, such as star bus or star ring, that combine aspects of the other topologies to capitalize on their strengths and minimize their weaknesses. You'll look at the most important hybrid topology, star bus, in a moment, but for now, make sure you know the four main topologies!

If you're looking at Figure 23.2 and thinking that a mesh topology looks amazingly resilient and robust, it is—at least on paper. Because every computer physically connects to every other computer on the network, even if half of the PCs crash, the network functions as well as ever (for the survivors). In a practical sense, however, implementing a true mesh topology network would be an expensive mess. For example, even for a tiny network with only 10 PCs, you would need *45* separate and distinct pieces of cable to connect every PC to every other PC. What a mesh mess! Because of this, mesh topologies have never been practical in a cabled network.

Although a topology describes the method by which systems in a network connect, the topology alone doesn't describe all of the features necessary to make a cabling system work. The term *bus topology*, for example, describes a network that consists of some number of machines connected to the network via the same piece of cable. Notice that this definition leaves a lot of questions unanswered. What is the cable made of? How long can it be? How do the machines decide which machine should send data at a specific moment? A network based on a bus topology can answer these questions in a number of different ways.

Most techs make a clear distinction between the *logical topology* of a network—how the network is laid out on paper, with nice straight lines and boxes—and the physical topology. The *physical topology* describes the typically messy computer network, with cables running diagonally through the ceiling space or snaking their way through walls. If someone describes the topology of a particular network, make sure you understand whether they're talking about the logical or physical topology.

Over the years, manufacturers and standards bodies created several specific network technologies based on different topologies. A *network technology* is a practical application of a topology and other critical technologies to provide a method to get data from one computer to another on a network.

Essentials

Packets/Frames and NICs

Data is moved from one PC to another in discrete chunks called *packets* or *frames*. The terms *packet* and *frame* are interchangeable. Every NIC in the world has a built-in identifier, a binary address unique to that single network card, called a **media access control (MAC) address**. You read that right—every network card in the world has its own unique MAC address! The MAC address is 48 bits long, providing more than 281 *trillion* MAC addresses, so there are plenty of MAC addresses to go around. MAC addresses

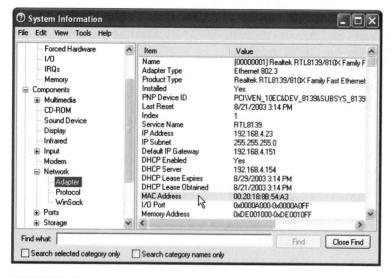

Item	Value
Name	[00000001] Realtek RTL8139/810X Family F
Adapter Type	Ethernet 802.3
Product Type	Realtek RTL8139/810X Family Fast Ethernet
Installed	Yes
PNP Device ID	PCI\VEN_10EC&DEV_8139&SUBSYS_8139
Last Reset	8/21/2003 3:14 PM
Index	1
Service Name	RTL8139
IP Address	192.168.4.23
IP Subnet	255.255.255.0
Default IP Gateway	192.168.4.151
DHCP Enabled	Yes
DHCP Server	192.168.4.154
DHCP Lease Expires	8/29/2003 3:14 PM
DHCP Lease Obtained	8/21/2003 3:14 PM
MAC Address	00:20:18:8B:54:A3
I/O Port	0x0000A000-0x0000A0FF
Memory Address	0xDE001000-0xDE0010FF

Find what: Find   Close Find

☐ Search selected category only   ☐ Search category names only

• **Figure 23.3**   MAC address

> Even though MAC addresses are embedded into the NIC, some NICs allow you to change the MAC address on the NIC. This is rarely done.

may be binary, but we represent them by using 12 hexadecimal characters. These MAC addresses are burned into every NIC, and some NIC makers print the MAC address on the card. Figure 23.3 shows the System Information utility description of a NIC, with the MAC address highlighted.

Hey! I thought we were talking about packets? Well, we are, but you need to understand MAC addresses to understand packets. The many varieties of packets share certain common features (Figure 23.4). First, packets contain the MAC address of the network card to which the data is being sent. Second, they have the MAC address of the network card that sent the data. Third is the data itself (at this point, we have no idea what the data is—certain software handles that question), which can vary in size depending on the type of frame. Finally, some type of data check—such as a **cyclic redundancy check (CRC)**—is performed and information is stored in the packet to enable the receiving network card to verify if the data was received in good order.

This discussion of packets raises the question, how big is the packet? Or more specifically, how much data do you put into each packet? How do you ensure that the receiving PC understands the *way* the data was broken down by the sending machine and can thus put the pieces back together? The problem in answering these questions is that they encompass so many items. When the first networks were created, *everything* from the frames to the connectors to the type of cable had to be invented from scratch.

To make a successful network, you need the sending and receiving PCs to use the same hardware protocol. A **hardware protocol** defines many aspects of a network, from the topology, to the packet type, to the cabling and connectors used. A hardware protocol defines everything necessary to get data from one computer to another. Over the years, many hardware protocols have been implemented, with such names as Token Ring, FDDI, and ARCnet, but one hardware protocol dominates the modern PC computing landscape: Ethernet.

Packet

CRC

Data

Sender MAC

Recipient MAC

• **Figure 23.4**   Generic packet/frame

Introducing Ethernet

A consortium of companies including Digital Equipment, Intel, and Xerox invented the first network in the mid 1970s. More than just creating a

network, they wrote a series of standards that defined everything necessary to get data from one computer to another. This series of standards was called **Ethernet**, and it is the dominant standard for today's networks. Ethernet comes in two main flavors defined by cabling type: unshielded twisted pair and fiber optic. Because all flavors of Ethernet use the same packet type, you can have any combination of hardware devices and cabling systems on an Ethernet network and all of the PCs will be able to communicate just fine.

Most modern Ethernet networks employ one of three technologies (and sometimes all three), **10BaseT**, **100BaseT**, or **1000BaseT**. As the numbers in the names suggest, 10BaseT networks run at 10 Mbps, 100BaseT networks run at 100 Mbps, and 1000BaseT networks—called Gigabit Ethernet—run at 1000 Mbps, or 1 Gbps. All three technologies—sometimes referred to collectively as *10/100/1000BaseT* or just plain Ethernet—use a *star bus* topology and connect via a type of cable called **unshielded twisted pair (UTP)**.

Earlier forms of Ethernet used coaxial cable: 10Base5 used RG-8 coaxial cables with DB-15 connectors (called AUI connectors) and could run up to 500 meters. 10Base2 used RG-62 cable with BNC connectors and could run up to 185 meters.

Star Bus

Imagine taking a bus network and shrinking the bus down so it will fit inside a box. Then, instead of attaching each PC directly to the wire, you attach them via cables to special ports on the box (Figure 23.5). The box with the bus takes care of all of the tedious details required by a bus network. The bus topology would look a lot like a star topology, wouldn't it?

The central box with the bus is called a hub or switch. The **hub** provides a common point for connection for network devices. Hubs can have a wide variety of ports. Most consumer-level hubs have four or eight, but business-level hubs can have 32 or more ports. A hub is the old-style device, rarely used in today's networks. A **switch** is a far superior and far more common version of a hub. Figure 23.6 shows a typical consumer-level switch.

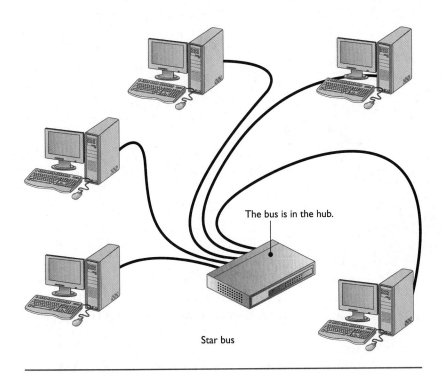

The bus is in the hub.

Star bus

• **Figure 23.5** Star bus

Different networks come in different speeds. One common speed is 100 Megabits per second (Mbps). We call this speed a **bandwidth**. If you put 32 PCs on a 32-port 100 Mbps hub, you have 32 PCs sharing the 100 Mbps bandwidth. A switch addresses that problem by making each port its own separate network. Each PC gets to use the full bandwidth available. The bottom line? Swap out your old hubs for newer switches and you'll dramatically improve your network performance.

Cheap and centralized, a star bus network does not go down if a cable breaks. True, the network would go down if the hub itself failed, but that is rare. Even if a hub fails, replacing a hub in a closet is much easier than tracing a bus running through walls and ceilings and trying to find a break!

• **Figure 23.6**   A switch

> Although Token Ring is very rarely seen today, CompTIA wants you to know a little of its terminology. Just as in Ethernet, the creators of Token Ring decided to move to a star topology and put the ring (as opposed to Ethernet's bus) in a box that looks like a hub/switch. They call the box the *media access* (or sometimes *attachment*) *unit* (*MAU*). Some techs call it a Multistation Access Unit (MSAU), but CompTIA uses MAU, so remember that for the exam!

Unshielded Twisted Pair

Unshielded twisted pair (UTP) cabling is the specified cabling for 10/100/1000BaseT and is the predominant cabling system used today. Many types of twisted pair cabling are available, and the type used depends on the needs of the network. Twisted pair cabling consists of AWG 22–26 gauge wire twisted together into color-coded pairs. Each wire is individually insulated and encased as a group in a common jacket.

CAT Levels   UTP cables come in categories that define the maximum speed at which data can be transferred (also called *bandwidth*). The major categories (CATs) are as follows:

CAT 1	Standard phone line	**CAT 2**	Data speeds up to 4 Mbps (ISDN and T1 lines)
CAT 3	Data speeds up to 16 Mbps	**CAT 4**	Data speeds up to 20 Mbps
CAT 5	Data speeds up to 100 Mbps	**CAT 5e**	Data speeds up to 1 Gbps
CAT 6	Data speeds up to 10 Gbps		

The CAT level should be clearly marked on the cable, as Figure 23.7 shows.

The *Telecommunication Industry Association/Electronics Industries Alliance (TIA/EIA)* establishes the UTP categories, which fall under the TIA/EIA 568 specification. Currently, most installers use CAT 5e or CAT 6 cable. Although many networks run at 10 Mbps, the industry standard has shifted to networks designed to run at 100 Mbps and faster. Because only CAT 5 or better handles these speeds, just about everyone is installing the higher rated cabling, even if they are running at speeds that CAT 3 or CAT 4 would do. Consequently, it is becoming more difficult to get anything but CAT 5, CAT 5e, or CAT 6 cables.

• **Figure 23.7**   Cable markings for CAT level

Shielded Twisted Pair

Shielded twisted pair (STP), as its name implies, consists of twisted pairs of wires surrounded by shielding to protect them from EMI, or electromagnetic interference. STP is pretty rare, primarily because there's so little need for STP's shielding; it only really matters in locations with excessive electronic noise, such as a shop floor area with lots of lights, electric motors, or other machinery that could cause problems for other cables.

Implementing 10/100/1000BaseT

The 10BaseT, 100BaseT, and 1000BaseT cabling standards require two pairs of wires: a pair for sending and a pair for receiving. 10BaseT runs on CAT 3, CAT 4, or CAT 5 cable. 100BaseT requires at least CAT 5 to run. 1000BaseT is a special case because it needs all four pairs of wires in a CAT 5e or CAT 6 cable. These cables use a connector called an **RJ-45** connector. The *RJ* (*registered jack*) designation was invented by Ma Bell (the phone company, for you youngsters) years ago and is still used today. Currently only two types of RJ connectors are used for networking: RJ-11 and RJ-45 (Figure 23.8). **RJ-11** is the connector that hooks your telephone to the telephone jack. It supports up to two pairs of wires, though most phone lines use only one pair. The other pair is used to support a second phone line. RJ-11 connectors are primarily used for dial-up networking (see Chapter 25, "The Internet") and are not used in any common LAN installation, although a few weird (and out of business) "network in a box" companies used them. RJ-45 is the standard for UTP connectors. RJ-45 has connections for up to four pairs and is visibly much wider than RJ-11. Figure 23.9 shows the position of the #1 and #8 pins on an RJ-45 jack.

The TIA/EIA has two standards for connecting the RJ-45 connector to the UTP cable: the TIA/EIA 568A and the TIA/EIA 568B. Both are acceptable. You do not have to follow any standard as long as you use the same pairings on each end of the cable; however, you will make your life simpler if you choose a standard. Make sure that all of your cabling uses the same standard and you will save a great deal of work in the end. Most importantly, *keep records*!

Like all wires, the wires in UTP are numbered. However, a number does not appear on each wire. Instead, each wire has a standardized color. Table 23.1 shows the official TIA/EIA Standard Color Chart for UTP.

• **Figure 23.8** RJ-11 and RJ-45

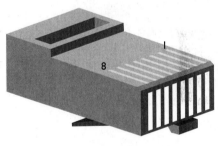

• **Figure 23.9** RJ-45 pin numbers

Table 23.1	UTP Cabling Color Chart				
Pin	568A	568B	Pin	568A	568B
1	White/Green	White/Orange	5	White/Blue	White/Blue
2	Green	Orange	6	Orange	Green
3	White/Orange	White/Green	7	White/Brown	White/Brown
4	Blue	Blue	8	Brown	Brown

Multispeed Cards   All Ethernet networks share the same language, so you can easily have mixed or combined networks. All it takes is a network card capable of running at multiple speeds or even over multiple cables. Most NICs built into motherboards today, for example, are Gigabit autosensing cards (Figure 23.10). If you plug into a 100BaseT network, they automatically run at 100 Mbps. If you plug into a 1000 Mbps network, they quickly ramp up and run at 1000 Mbps.

Duplex and Half-Duplex   All modern NICs can run in **full-duplex** mode, meaning they can send and receive data at the same time. The vast majority of NICs and switches use a feature called *autosensing* to accommodate very old devices that might attach to the network and need to run in half-duplex mode. Half-duplex means that the device can send and receive, but not at the same time. An obvious example of a half-duplex device is the walkie-talkies you played with as a kid that required you to press and hold the orange button to transmit—at which time you couldn't hear anything. Half-duplex devices are exceedingly rare in modern computers, but you need to understand this option. Some NICs just can't handle full-duplex communication when you plug them directly to another NIC by using a crossover cable—that is, no switch. Dropping both NICs down from full-duplex or auto-sensing can sometimes enable these odd NICs to communicate.

Link Lights   All NICs made today have some type of light-emitting diode (LED) *status indicator* that gives information about the state of the NIC's link to whatever's on the other end of the connection. Even though you know the lights are actually LEDs, get used to calling them **link lights**, as that's the term all network techs use. NICs can have between one and four different link lights, and the LEDs can be any color. These lights give you clues about what's happening with the link and are one of the first items to check whenever you think a system is disconnected from the network (Figure 23.11).

● **Figure 23.10**   NIC built into motherboard

● **Figure 23.11**   Mmmm, pretty lights!

Hubs and switches also have link lights, enabling you to check the connectivity at both ends of the cable. If a PC can't access a network, always first check the link lights. Multispeed devices usually have a link light that tells you the speed of the connection. In Figure 23.12, the light for port 2 on the top photo is orange, for example, signifying that the other end of the cable is plugged into either a 10BaseT or 100BaseT NIC. The same port connected to a Gigabit NIC—that's the lower picture—displays a green LED.

A properly functioning link light is steady on when the NIC is connected to another device. No flickering, no on and off, just on. A link light that is off or flickering shows a connection problem.

• **Figure 23.12**   Multispeed lights

Another light is the **activity light**. This little guy turns on when the card detects network traffic, so it makes an intermittent flickering when operating properly. The activity light is a lifesaver for detecting problems, because in the real world, the connection light sometimes lies to you. If the connection light says the connection is good, the next step is to try to copy a file or do something else to create network traffic. If the activity light does not flicker, you have a problem.

No standard governs how NIC manufacturers use their lights; as a result, they come in an amazing array of colors and layouts. When you encounter a NIC with a number of LEDs, take a moment to try to figure out what each one means. Although different NICs have different ways of arranging and using their LEDs, the functions are always the same: link, activity, and speed.

Fiber Optic Ethernet

Fiber optic cable is a very attractive way to transmit Ethernet network packets. First, because it uses light instead of electricity, fiber optic cable is immune to electrical problems such as lightning, short circuits, and static. Second, fiber optic signals travel much farther, up to 2000 meters (compared with 100 meters on UTP) with some standards. Most fiber Ethernet networks use *62.5/125 multimode* fiber optic cable. All fiber Ethernet networks that use these cables require two cables. Figure 23.13 shows three of the more common connectors used in fiber optic networks. Square *SC* connectors are shown in the middle and on the right, and the round *ST* connector is on the left.

Like many other fiber optic connectors, the SC and ST connectors are half-duplex, meaning data flows only one way—hence the need for two cables in a fiber installation. Other half-duplex connectors you might run into are FC/PC, SMA, D4, MU, and LC. They look similar to SC and ST connectors but offer variations in size and connection. Newer and higher-end fiber installations use full-duplex connectors, such as the MT-RJ connectors.

The two most common fiber optic standards are called 1000BaseSX and 10GBaseSR. The major difference is the speed of the network (there are also some important differences in the way systems interconnect, and so on). Fiber optic cabling is delicate, expensive, and

> Though no real standard exists for NIC LEDs, CompTIA will test you on some more-or-less de facto LED meanings. You should know that a solid green light means connectivity, a flashing green light means intermittent connectivity, no green light means no connectivity, and a flashing amber light means there are collisions on the network (which is sometimes okay). Also, know that the first things you should check when having connectivity issues are your NIC's LEDs.

> ST, SC, LC and MT-RJ fiber connectors will likely be questioned on both exams.

• **Figure 23.13**   Typical fiber optic cables with connectors

Tech Tip

Multimode and Single-Mode

Light can be sent down a fiber optic cable as regular light or as laser light. Each type of light requires totally different fiber optic cables. Most network technologies that use fiber optics use light-emitting diodes (LEDs) to send light signals. These use multimode *fiber optic cabling. Multimode fiber transmits multiple light signals at the same time, each using a different reflection angle within the core of the cable. The multiple reflection angles tend to disperse over long distances, so multimode fiber optic cables are used for relatively short distances.*

Network technologies that use laser light use single-mode *fiber optic cabling. Using laser light and single-mode fiber optic cables allows for phenomenally high transfer rates over long distances. Except for long-distance links, single-mode is currently quite rare; if you see fiber optic cabling, you can be relatively sure it is multimode.*

difficult to use, so it is usually reserved for use in data centers and is rarely used to connect desktop PCs.

Coax/BNC

Early versions of Ethernet ran on **coaxial cable** instead of UTP. Coax consists of a center cable (core) surrounded by insulation. This in turn is covered with a *shield* of braided cable. The inner core actually carries the signal. The shield effectively eliminates outside interference. The entire cable is then surrounded by a protective insulating cover. This type of coax looks like a skinny version of the RG-59 or RG-6 coax used by your cable television, but it is quite different. The RG rating is clearly marked on the cable. If it isn't, the cable should say something like "Thinnet" or "802.3" to let you know you had the right cable. To connect the cable to individual machines, a twist-on *BNC connector* is used.

Parallel/Serial

It would be unfair not to give at least a token nod to using the parallel or serial ports on a pair of PCs to make a direct cable connection. All versions of Windows have complete support for allowing two, and no more than two, systems to network together, using either parallel or serial cables. You need crossover versions of IEEE 1284 cables for parallel and RS-232 cables for serial. These should be considered only as a last resort option, given the incredibly slow speeds of parallel and especially serial cable transmission compared to that of Ethernet. You should never use direct cable connections unless no other viable alternative exists.

FireWire

You can connect two computers by using FireWire cables. Apple designed FireWire to be network aware, so the two machines will simply recognize each other and, assuming they're configured to share files and folders, you're up and running. See the section "Sharing and Security" later in this chapter for more details.

USB

You can also connect two computers by using USB, but it's not quite as elegant as FireWire. The most common way is to plug a USB NIC into each PC and then run a UTP crossover cable between the Ethernet ports. You also can buy a special USB crossover cable to connect the two machines. Finally, at least one company makes a product that enables you to connect with a normal USB cable, called USB Duet.

Essentials/Practical Application

■ Network Operating Systems

At this point in the discussion of networking, you've covered two of the four main requirements for making a network work. Through Ethernet, you have a NIC for the PC that handles splitting data into packets and putting the packets back together at the destination PC. You've got a cabling standard to connect the NIC to a hub or switch, thus making that data transfer possible. Now it's time to dive into the third and fourth requirements for a network. You need an operating system that can communicate with the hardware and with other networked PCs, and you need some sort of server machine to give out data or services. The third and fourth requirements are handled by a network operating system.

Both CompTIA A+ exams assume you have a working knowledge of network operating systems.

In a classic sense, a **network operating system (NOS)** is a portion of your operating system that communicates with the PC hardware and makes the connections among multiple machines on a network. The NOS enables one or more PCs to act as server machines and share data and services over a network—to share **resources**, in other words. You then need to run software on client computers so those computers can access the shared resources on the server machine.

Before you can share resources across a network, you must answer a number of questions. How do you make a resource available to share? Can everyone share his or her hard drives with everyone else? Should you place limits on sharing? If everyone needs access to a particular file, where will it be stored? What about security? Can anyone access the file? What if someone erases it accidentally? How are backups to be handled? Different versions of Windows answer these questions differently. Let's look at network organization and then turn to protocols, client software, and server software.

Network Organization

All NOSs can be broken into three basic organizational groups: client/server, peer-to-peer, and domain-based. Let's take a look at traditional network organization.

Client/Server

In a **client/server network**, one machine is dedicated as a resource to be shared over the network. This machine will have a dedicated NOS, optimized for sharing files. This special OS includes powerful caching software that enables high-speed file access. It will have extremely high levels of protection and an organization that permits extensive control of the data. This machine is called a *dedicated server*. All of the other machines that use the data are called *clients* (because it's what they usually are) or *workstations*.

The client/server system dedicates one machine to act as a server, whose purpose is to serve up resources to the other machines on the network. These servers do not run Windows XP or Vista. They use highly sophisticated

and expensive NOSs that are optimized for the sharing and administration of network resources. Dedicated server operating systems include Windows Server 2008, big UNIX systems such as IBM AIX and HP-UX, and some versions of Linux.

Peer-to-Peer

Some networks do not require dedicated servers—every computer can perform both server and client functions. A **peer-to-peer network** enables any or all of the machines on the network to act as a server. Peer-to-peer networks are much cheaper than client/server networks because the software costs less and does not require that you purchase a high-end machine to act as the dedicated server. The most popular peer-to-peer NOSs today are the various versions of Windows and Macintosh OS X.

The biggest limiting factor to peer-to-peer networking is that it's simply not designed for a large number of computers. Windows has a built-in limit (10) to the number of users who can concurrently access a shared file or folder. Microsoft recommends that peer-to-peer workgroups not exceed 15 PCs. Beyond that, creating a domain-based network makes more sense (see the following section).

Security is the other big weakness of peer-to-peer networks. Each system on a peer-to-peer network maintains its own security.

With the Windows Professional/Business versions, you can tighten security by setting NTFS permissions locally, but you are still required to place a local account on every system for any user who's going to access resources. So even though you get better security in a Windows Professional/Business peer-to-peer network, system administration entails a lot of running around to individual systems to create and delete local users every time someone joins or leaves the workgroup. In a word: bleh.

Peer-to-peer workgroups are little more than a pretty way to organize systems to make navigating through Windows networks a little easier (Figure 23.14). In reality, workgroups have no security value. Still, if your networking needs are limited—such as a small home network—peer-to-peer networking is an easy and cheap solution.

Cross Check

NTFS Permissions

NTFS permissions enable strong data security, even when sharing files and folders across a network, so now is a good time to revisit Chapter 16, "Securing Windows Resources," and refresh your memory on NTFS.

1. How do you access the permissions for a file or folder?

2. Which permission would stop someone from modifying a file on your server but still enable the person to read the contents of that file?

3. What's up with Windows XP Home and permissions, anyway?

• **Figure 23.14** Multiple workgroups in a network

Domain-Based

One of the similarities between the client/server network model and peer-to-peer networks is that each PC in the network maintains its own list of user accounts. If you want to access a server, you must log on. When only one server exists, the logon process takes only a second and works very well. The trouble comes when your network contains multiple servers. In that case, every time you access a different server, you must repeat the logon process (Figure 23.15). In larger networks containing many servers, this becomes a time-consuming nightmare not only for the user, but also for the network administrator.

• **Figure 23.15**   Multiple logins in a peer-to-peer network

A **domain-based network** provides an excellent solution for the problem of multiple logins. In a domain-based environment, one or more dedicated servers called *domain controllers* hold the security database for all systems. This database holds a list of all users and passwords in the domain. When you log on to your computer or to any computer, the logon request goes to an available domain controller to verify the account and password (Figure 23.16).

Modern domain-based networks use what is called a **directory service** to store user and computer account information. Large Microsoft-based networks use the *Active Directory* (*AD*) directory service. Think of a directory service as a big, centralized index, similar to a telephone book, that each PC accesses to locate resources in the domain.

Server versions of Microsoft Windows look and act similar to the workstation versions, but they come with extra networking capabilities, services, and tools so they can take on the role of domain controller, file server, *remote access services* (*RAS*) server, ap-

• **Figure 23.16**   A domain controller eliminates the need for multiple logins.

plication server, Web server, and so on. A quick glance at the options you have in Administrative Tools shows how much more full-featured the server versions are compared to the workstation versions of Windows. Figure 23.17 shows the Administrative Tools options on a typical Windows Vista workstation. These should be familiar to you. Figure 23.18 shows the many extra tools you need to work with Windows Server 2008.

Every Windows system contains a special account called the **administrator account**. This one account has complete and absolute power over the entire system. When you install Windows, you must create a password for the

• Figure 23.17   Administrative Tools in Windows Vista Business

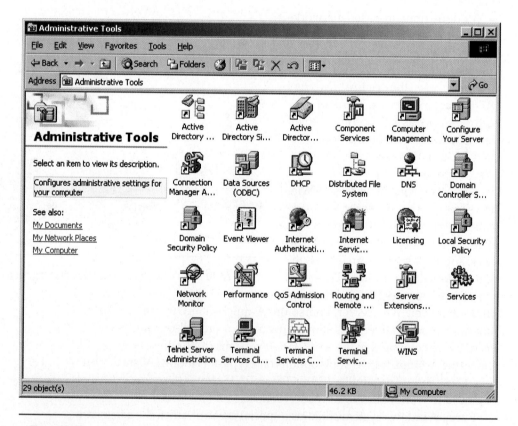

• Figure 23.18   Administrative Tools in Windows Server 2008

Mike Meyers' CompTIA A+ Guide to Managing and Troubleshooting PCs

administrator account. Anyone who knows the administrator password can install/delete any program, read/change/delete any file, run any program, and change any system setting. As you might imagine, you should protect the administrator password carefully. Without it, you cannot create additional accounts (including additional accounts with administrative privileges) or change system settings. If you lose the administrator password (and no other account with administrative privileges exists), you have to reinstall Windows completely to create a new administrator account—so don't lose it!

Cross Check

Administrative Tools

Windows comes with a set of utilities called Administrative Tools, as you know from previous chapters. Refer to Chapter 4, "Understanding Windows," and answer these questions.

1. How do you access Administrative Tools?

2. Which tool or tools might be useful for working with networks?

3. More specifically, which tool would help you analyze network performance?

In Windows XP, open the Properties window for My Computer, and select the Computer Name tab, as shown in Figure 23.19. This shows your current selection. Windows Vista and 7 show the computer name right on the System Properties dialog box and give you a link to the 2000/XP-style dialog box (Figure 23.20). Clicking the Network ID button opens the Network Identification Wizard, but most techs just use the Change button, which brings up the Computer Name/Domain Changes dialog box (Figure 23.21). Clicking the Change button does the same thing as clicking the Network ID button except that the wizard does a lot of explaining that you don't need if you know what you want to do. Make sure you have a valid domain account or you won't be able to log into a domain.

At this point, you've prepared the OS to network in general, but now you need to talk to the specific hardware. For that, you need to load protocols.

Protocols

Simply moving data from one machine to another is hardly sufficient to make a complete network; many other functions need to be handled. For example, if a file is being copied from one machine to another, something must keep track of all of the packets so the file can be properly reassembled. If many machines are talking to the same machine at once, that machine must somehow keep track of which packets it sends to or receives from each of the other PCs.

Another issue arises if one of the machines in the network has its network card replaced. Up to this point, the only way to distinguish one machine from another was by the MAC address on the network card. To solve this, each machine must have a name, an identifier for the network, which is "above" the MAC address. Each machine, or at least one of them, needs to keep a list of all of the MAC addresses on the network and the names of the machines, so that packets and names can be correlated. That way, if a PC's network card is replaced, the network, after some special

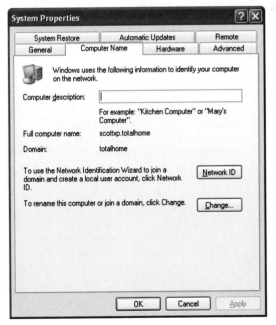

• **Figure 23.19** Computer Name tab in Windows XP

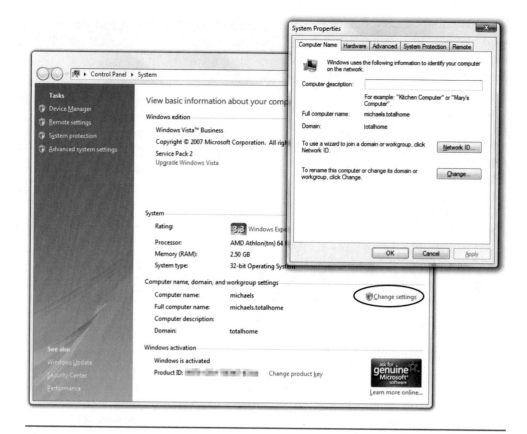

● **Figure 23.20**   Computer Name location in Vista

queries, can update the list to associate the name of the PC with its new network card's MAC address.

Network protocol software takes the incoming data received by the network card, keeps it organized, sends it to the application that needs it, and then takes outgoing data from the application and hands it to the NIC to be

● **Figure 23.21**   Using the Change button

Mike Meyers' CompTIA A+ Guide to Managing and Troubleshooting PCs

sent out over the network. All networks use some protocol. Although many protocols exist, one dominates the world of PCs—TCP/IP.

NetBEUI/NetBIOS

Before we talk about TCP/IP, we need to discuss a little history. During the 1980s, IBM developed **NetBIOS Extended User Interface (NetBEUI)**, the default protocol for Windows for Workgroups, LANtastic, and Windows 95. NetBEUI offers small size, easy configuration, and a relatively high speed, but it can't be used for routing. Its inability to handle routing limits NetBEUI to networks smaller than about 200 nodes.

You can connect multiple smaller networks into a bigger network, turning a group of LANs into one big WAN, but this raises a couple of issues with network traffic. A computer needs to be able to address a packet so that it goes to a computer within its own LAN or to a computer in another LAN in the WAN. If every computer saw every packet, the network traffic would quickly spin out of control! Plus, the machines that connect the LANs—called **routers**—need to be able to sort those packets and send them along to the proper LAN. This process, called *routing*, requires routers and a routing-capable protocol to function correctly.

NetBEUI was great for a LAN, but it lacked the extra addressing capabilities needed for a WAN. A new protocol was needed, one that could handle routing.

Novell developed the *Internetwork Packet Exchange/Sequenced Packet Exchange* **(IPX/SPX)** protocol exclusively for its NetWare products. The IPX/SPX protocol is speedy, works well with routers, and takes up relatively little RAM when loaded. Although once popular, it has all but disappeared in favor of TCP/IP. Microsoft implements a version of IPX/SPX called *NWLink*.

TCP/IP

Transmission Control Protocol/Internet Protocol (**TCP/IP**) was originally developed for the Internet's progenitor, the *Advanced Research Projects Agency Network* (*ARPANET*) of the U.S. Department of Defense. In 1983, TCP/IP became the built-in protocol for the popular BSD (Berkeley Software Distribution) UNIX, and other flavors of UNIX quickly adopted it as well. TCP/IP is the best protocol for larger networks with more than 200 nodes. The biggest network of all, the Internet, uses TCP/IP as its protocol. Windows also uses TCP/IP as its default protocol.

Client Software

To access data or resources across a network, Windows needs to have client software installed for every kind of server you want to access. When you install a network card and drivers, Windows installs at least one set of client software, called Client for Microsoft Networks (Figure 23.22). This client enables your machine to do the obvious: connect to a Microsoft network! Internet-based services work the same way. You need a Web client (such as Mozilla Firefox) to access a Web server. Windows PCs don't just access shared data magically but require that client software be installed.

Server Software

You can turn any Windows PC into a server simply by enabling the sharing of files, folders, and printers. Windows has file and printer

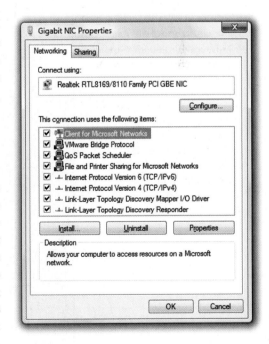

• **Figure 23.22**   LAN Properties window showing Client for Microsoft Networks installed (along with other network software)

Vista's Network and Sharing Center

If you right-click on the Network button in Windows Vista/7, you're taken to the Network and Sharing Center. In the Network and Sharing Center, you can view the status of your network connection and easily enable or disable various network settings, such as file sharing, network discovery, and printer sharing. You can also see what type of network you're on: Public, Private, or Domain. Windows Vista lets you select which type of network you're on, either Public or Private, the first time you join a particular network and modifies your network settings based on the type of network you select. Public networks are assumed not to be secure; as such, Windows automatically turns off all of the network sharing options so that do-bads can't access your computer. Private networks are assumed safe, so all of the file sharing options are turned on. If your computer is on a domain, your network administrator will control your network options.

Discovering Protocols and Clients

If you have a network card installed in your PC, chances are extremely high that you already have one or more protocols or clients installed. Try This!

1. Right-click My Network Places and select Properties. Then right-click on the Local Area Connection icon and select Properties once more. If you're using Vista, you'll do this by right-clicking Network and selecting Properties. After that, select *Manage network connections*, right-click on the Local Area Connection icon, and select Properties.

2. Which protocols or clients are loaded? If you have a classmate running through the same exercise, compare protocols. Can your two machines connect and swap data?

sharing installed but not activated by default (though a simpler form of file sharing, creatively named Simple File Sharing, is enabled by default in Windows XP Home to make sharing media over a home network easier). Activating file and printer sharing requires nothing more than a one-click selection, as you can see in Figure 23.23.

• **Figure 23.23**   Enabling file and printer sharing in Windows Vista

Installing and Configuring a Wired Network

Almost halfway through the chapter and we're finally getting to the good stuff: installing and configuring a network! To have network connectivity, you need to have three things in place:

- **NIC** The physical hardware that connects the computer system to the network media.

- **Protocol** The language that the computer systems use to communicate.

- **Network client** The interface that allows the computer system to speak to the protocol.

If you want to share resources on your PC with other network users, you also need to enable Microsoft's File and Printer Sharing. Plus, of course, you need to connect the PC to the network hub or switch via some sort of cable (preferably CAT 6 with Gigabit Ethernet cranking through the wires, but that's just me!). When you install a NIC, by default Windows installs the TCP/IP protocol, the Client for Microsoft Networks, and File and Printer Sharing for Microsoft Networks upon setup.

Installing a NIC

The NIC is your computer system's link to the network, and installing one is the first step required to connect to a network. NICs are manufactured to operate on specific media and network types, such as 1000BaseT Ethernet. Follow the manufacturer's instructions for installation. If your NIC is of recent vintage, it will be detected, installed, and configured automatically by Windows. You might need a driver disc or a driver download from the manufacturer's Web site if you install that funky PC Card or gamer NIC.

The Add Hardware Wizard automates installation of non–plug-and-play devices or plug-and-play devices that were not detected correctly. Start the wizard by clicking Start | Settings | Control Panel (2000 or classic start menu) or Start | Control Panel (XP/Vista/7) and then double-clicking the icon for the Add Hardware applet. (Note that Windows 2000 calls this the Add/Remove Hardware applet.) Click the Next button to select the hardware task you wish to perform, and follow the prompts to complete the wizard.

Configuring a Network Client

To establish network connectivity, you need a network client installed and configured properly. You need a client for every type of server NOS to which you plan to connect on the network. Let's look at Microsoft's client.

Installed as part of the OS installation, the Client for Microsoft Networks rarely needs configuration, and, in fact, few configuration options are available. To start it in Windows Vista/7, click Start; then right-click Network and select Properties. Then click *Manage network connections* on the left. In Windows XP, click Start, and then right-click My Network Places and select Properties. In Windows 2000, click Start | Settings | Network and Dial-up Connections.

Tech Tip

Windows Firewall
Every version of Windows since Windows XP SP 2 has included a built-in firewall that blocks out harmful Internet traffic. Windows Firewall functions slightly differently in each version of Windows, but you should be aware of one quirk in Windows XP: namely that the Firewall will block file and printer sharing by default. So if you find that you can't access shared folders or printers, you can check to make sure Windows Firewall isn't blocking them. You can do this by going into Control Panel and opening the Windows Firewall applet. Once that's open, click the Exceptions tab and make sure that the checkbox next to File and Printer Sharing is checked. If it isn't, that's your problem!

If you have the option, you should save yourself potential headaches and troubleshooting woes by acquiring new, name-brand NICs for your Windows installation.

In all versions of Windows, your next step is to double-click the Local Area Connection icon, click the Properties button, highlight Client for Microsoft Networks, and click the Properties button. Note that there's not much to do here. Unless told to do something by a network administrator, just leave this alone.

Configuring TCP/IP

This final section on protocols covers TCP/IP, the primary protocol of most modern networks, including the Internet. For a PC to access the Internet, it must have TCP/IP loaded and configured properly. TCP/IP has become so predominant that most network folks use it even on networks that do not connect to the Internet. Although TCP/IP is powerful, it is also a bit of a challenge to set up. So whether you are installing a modem for a dial-up connection to the Internet or setting up 500 computers on their own private *intranet*, you must understand some TCP/IP basics. You'll go through the following basic sections of the protocol and then you'll look at specific steps to install and configure TCP/IP.

Network Addressing

Any network address must provide two pieces of information: it must uniquely identify the machine and it must locate that machine within the larger network. In a TCP/IP network, the IP address identifies the PC and the network on which it resides.

IP Addresses   In a TCP/IP network, the systems don't have names but rather use IP addresses. The **IP address** is the unique identification number for your system on the network. Part of the address identifies the network, and part identifies the local computer (host) address on the network. IP addresses consist of four sets of eight binary numbers (octets), each set separated by a period. This is called *dotted-decimal notation*. So, instead of a computer being called SERVER1, it gets an address like so:

202.34.16.11

Written in binary form, the address would look like this:

11001010.00100010.00010000.00001011

To make the addresses more comprehensible to users, the TCP/IP folks decided to write the decimal equivalents:

00000000 = 0
00000001 = 1
00000010 = 2
. . .
11111111 = 255

IP addresses are divided into class licenses that correspond with the potential size of the network: Class A, Class B, and Class C. Class A licenses were intended for huge companies and organizations, such as major multinational corporations, universities, and governmental agencies. Class B licenses were assigned to medium-size companies, and Class C licenses were designated for smaller LANs. Class A networks use the first octet to identify

the network address and the remaining three octets to identify the host. Class B networks use the first two octets to identify the network address and the remaining two octets to identify the host. Class C networks use the first three octets to identify the network address and the last octet to identify the host. Table 23.2 lists range (class) assignments.

You'll note that the IP address ranges listed in the table skip from 126.x.x.x to 128.x.x.x. That's because the 127 address range (i.e., 127.0.0.1–127.255.255.255) is reserved for network testing (loopback) operations. (We usually just use the address 127.0.0.1 for loopback purposes and call it the *localhost* address, but any address that starts off with *127* will work just as well.) That's not the only reserved range, either! Each network class has a specific IP address range reserved for *private* networks—traffic from these networks doesn't get routed to the Internet at large. Class A's private range goes from 10.0.0.1 to 10.255.255.255. Class B has two private address ranges: 172.16.0.1 up to 172.16.255.255 for manually configured addresses and 169.254.0.1 to 169.254.255.254 (link-local addresses) to accommodate the **Automatic Private IP Addressing (APIPA)** function discussed later. Class C's private addresses range from 192.168.0.0 to 192.168.255.255.

Subnet Mask The **subnet mask** is a value that distinguishes which part of the IP address is the network address and which part of the address is the host address. The subnet mask blocks out (or masks) the network portions (octets) of an IP address. Certain subnet masks are applied by default. The default subnet mask for Class A addresses is 255.0.0.0; for Class B, it's 255.255.0.0; and for Class C, 255.255.255.0. For example, in the Class B IP address 131.190.4.121 with a subnet mask of 255.255.0.0, the first two octets (131.190) make up the network address, and the last two (4.121) make up the host address.

A New Kind of Port

The term "port" has several meanings in the computer world. Commonly, port defines the connector socket on an Ethernet NIC, where you insert an

Tech Tip

IPv6

The IP addresses I'm showing you here are technically IP version 4, or IPv4 addresses, but this type of addressing has a bit of a problem—namely, that we're running out of possible IP addresses, and there won't be any left in a few years. No big deal. Now, before you go running out into the streets shouting about the impending demise of the Internet or start hoarding canned food in your basement, let me tell you about the solution. IP version 6, the newest version of the Internet protocol, which will save us all from an Internetless world, uses a 128-bit address instead of IPv4's 32-bit address. What this means is that there are more possible addresses than with IPv4. A lot more. My favorite illustration is to think of all of the molecules that make up the Earth, and divide them by 7. That's how many possible IPv6 addresses there are. The drawback is that IPv6 addresses are not quite as svelte and easy to remember as in IPv4. For example, an IPv6 address looks like this: 2001:0db8:85a3:0000:0000:8a2e:0370:7334. Not quite as easy to work with as 192.168.1.1, eh? IPv6 also handles routing and various other things differently than IPv4, but the main things to know are that the IP addresses look remarkably different and there are enough of them to last for a while. There's no solid plan yet for when everyone is going to switch to IPv6, but it'll be a big change when it happens.

Pinging the loopback is the best way to test whether a NIC is working properly. To test a NIC's loopback, the other end of the cable must be in a working switch or you must use a loopback device such as a loopback adapter/plug.

Tech Tip

Link-local Addresses

If APIPA is enabled and the DHCP configured client can't reach a DHCP server, the client will automatically be configured with an APIPA link-local IP address in the range between 169.254.0.1 to 169.254.255.254 and get a Class B subnet mask of 255.255.0.0 until the DHCP server can be reached.

Table 23.2	Class A, B, and C Addresses		
Network Class	Address Range	No. of Network Addresses Available	No. of Host Nodes (Computers) Supported
A	1–126	129	16,777,214
B	128–191	16,384	65,534
C	192–223	2,097,152	254

RJ-45 jack. That's how I've used the term for the most part in this book. It's now time to see another use of the word ports.

In TCP/IP, **ports** are 16-bit numbers between 0 and 65,535, assigned to a particular TCP/IP session. All TCP/IP packets (except for some really low-level maintenance packets) contain port numbers that the two communicating computers use to determine not only the kind of session—and thus what software protocol—to use to handle the data in the packet, but also how to get the packet or response back to the sending computer.

Each packet has two ports assigned, a destination port and an ephemeral port. The **destination port** is a fixed, predetermined number that defines the function or session type. Common TCP/IP session types use destination port numbers in the range 0–1023. The **ephemeral port** is an arbitrary number generated by the sending computer; the receiving computer uses the ephemeral port as a destination address so that the sending computer knows which application to use for the returning packet. Ephemeral ports usually fall in the 1024–5000 range, but this varies slightly among the different operating systems.

Ports enable one computer to serve many different services, such as a Web server and e-mail server, at the same time. We will discuss the most common ports and the associated services in the next chapter.

TCP/IP Services

TCP/IP is a different type of protocol. Although it supports File and Printer Sharing, it adds a number of special sharing functions unique only to it, lumped together under the umbrella term *TCP/IP services*. The most famous TCP/IP service is called *Hypertext Transfer Protocol* (*HTTP*), the language of the World Wide Web. If you want to surf the Web, you must have TCP/IP. But TCP/IP supplies many other services beyond just HTTP. By using a service called Telnet, for example, you can access a remote system as though you were actually in front of that machine.

Another example is a handy utility called PING. **PING** enables one machine to check whether it can communicate with another machine. Figure 23.24 shows an example of PING running on a Windows Vista system. Isn't it interesting that many TCP/IP services run from a command prompt? Good thing you know how to access one! I'll show you other services in a moment.

The goal of TCP/IP is to link any two hosts (remember, a host is just a computer in TCP/IP lingo), whether the two computers are on the same LAN or on some other network within the WAN. The LANs within the WAN are linked together with a variety of connections, ranging

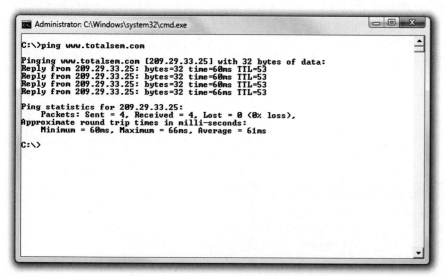

• **Figure 23.24**   PING in action

from basic dial-ups to dedicated high-speed (and expensive) data lines (Figure 23.25). To move traffic between networks, you use routers (Figure 23.26). Each host sends traffic to the router only when that data is destined for a remote network, cutting down on traffic across the more expensive WAN links. The host makes these decisions based on the destination IP address of each packet.

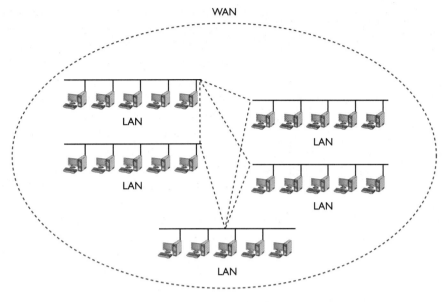

TCP/IP Settings

TCP/IP has a number of unique settings that you must set up correctly to ensure proper network functioning. Unfortunately, these settings can be quite confusing, and there are quite a few of them. Not all settings are used for every type of TCP/IP network, and it's not always obvious where you go to set them.

• **Figure 23.25**   WAN concept

Windows makes this fairly easy by letting you configure both dial-up and network connections by using the Network Connections dialog box (Figure 23.27). To get there, right-click on My Network Places (Windows 2000/ XP) or Network (Windows Vista/7) and select Properties. In Vista/7, you have to click the *Manage network connections* button, but in 2000 and XP, you simply select the connection you wish to configure and then set its TCP/IP properties.

• **Figure 23.26**   Typical router

The CompTIA A+ certification exams have a rather strange view of what you should know about networking. Take a lot of time practicing how to get to certain network configuration screens. Be ready for questions that ask, "Which of the following steps will enable you to change a particular value?"

• **Figure 23.27**   Network Connections dialog box showing dial-up and LAN connections

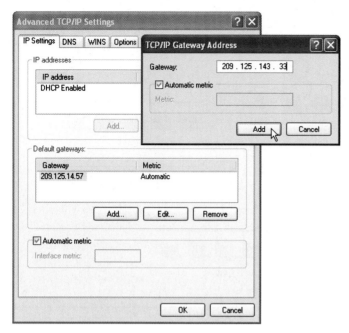

• **Figure 23.28** Setting a default gateway

• **Figure 23.29** Adding two DNS servers in Windows Vista

The CompTIA A+ certification exams assume that someone else, such as a tech support person or some network guru, will tell you the correct TCP/IP settings for the network. Your only job is to understand roughly what they do and to know where to enter them so the system works. Following are some of the most common TCP/IP settings.

Default Gateway   A computer that wants to send data to another machine outside its LAN is not expected to know exactly how to reach every other computer on the Internet. Instead, all IP hosts know the address of at least one router to which they pass all of the data packets they need to send outside the LAN. This router is called the **default gateway**, which is just another way of saying "the local router" (Figure 23.28).

Domain Name Service (DNS)   Knowing that users could not remember lots of IP addresses, early Internet pioneers came up with a way to correlate those numbers with more human-friendly computer designations. Special computers, called **domain name service (DNS)** servers, keep databases of IP addresses and their corresponding names. For example, a machine called TOTALSEMINAR1 will be listed in a DNS directory with a corresponding IP address, such as 209.34.45.163. So instead of accessing the \\209.34.45.163\FREDC share to copy a file, you can ask to see \\TOTALSEMINAR1\FREDC. Your system will then query the DNS server to get TOTALSEMINAR1's IP address and use that to find the right machine. Unless you want to type in IP addresses all of the time, a TCP/IP network will need at least one DNS server (Figure 23.29).

The Internet has regulated domain names. If you want a domain name that others can access on the Internet, you must register your domain name and pay a small yearly fee. In most cases, your ISP can handle this for you. Originally, DNS names all ended with one of the following seven domain name qualifiers, called *top level domains* (*TLDs*):

.com General business   **.org** Nonprofit organizations
.edu Educational organizations   **.gov** Government organizations
.mil Military organizations   **.net** Internet organizations
.int International

As more and more countries joined the Internet, an entire new level of domains was added to the original seven to indicate a DNS name in a particular country, such as .uk for the United Kingdom. It's common to see DNS names such as www.bbc.co.uk or www.louvre.fr. The *Internet Corporation for Assigned Names and Numbers* (*ICANN*) announced the creation of several more new domains, including .name, .biz, .info, and others. Given the

explosive growth of the Internet, these are unlikely to be the last ones! For the latest developments, check ICANN's Web site at www.icann.org.

WINS   Before Microsoft came fully on board with Internet standards such as TCP/IP, the company implemented its own type of name server: *Windows Internet Name Service* (WINS). WINS enables NetBIOS network names such as SERVER1 to be correlated to IP addresses, just as DNS does, except these names are *Windows* network names such as SERVER1, not fully qualified domain Internet names (FQDNs) such as server1.example.com. NetBIOS names must be unique and contain 15 or fewer characters, but other than that there isn't much to it. Assuming that a WINS server exists on your network, all you have to do to set up WINS on your PC is type in the IP address for the WINS server (Figure 23.30). Networks based on Windows 2000/XP/Vista/7 don't use WINS; they use an improved "dynamic" DNS (DDNS) that supports both Internet names and Windows names. On older networks that still need to support the occasional legacy Windows NT 4.0 server, you may need to configure WINS, but on most TCP/IP networks you can leave the WINS setting blank.

DHCP   The last feature that most TCP/IP networks support is **dynamic host configuration protocol (DHCP)**. To understand DHCP, you must first remember that every machine must be assigned an IP address, a subnet mask, a default gateway, and at least one DNS server (and maybe a WINS server). These settings can be added manually by using the TCP/IP Properties window. When you set the IP address manually, the IP address will not change and is called a **static IP address** (Figure 23.31).

DHCP enables you to create a pool of IP addresses that are given temporarily to machines. DHCP is especially handy for networks of a lot of laptops that join and leave the network on a regular basis. Why give a machine that is on the network for only a few hours a day a static IP address? For that reason, DHCP is quite popular. If you add a NIC to a Windows system, the default TCP/IP settings are set to use DHCP. When you accept those automatic settings, you're really telling the machine to use DHCP (Figure 23.32).

TCP/IP Tools

All versions of Windows come with handy tools to test TCP/IP. Those you're most likely to use in the field are PING, IPCONFIG, NSLOOKUP, and TRACERT. These programs are all command-prompt utilities. Open a command prompt to run them; if you just place these commands in the Run command, you'll see

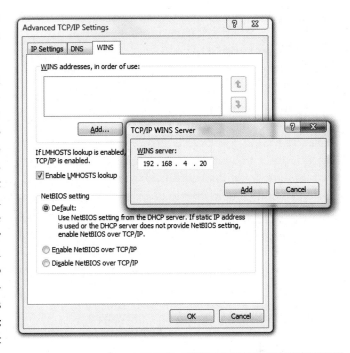

● **Figure 23.30**   Setting up WINS to use DHCP

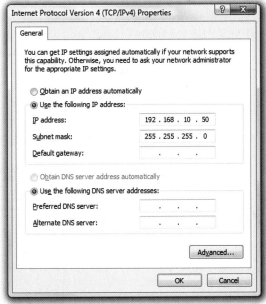

● **Figure 23.31**   Setting a static IP address

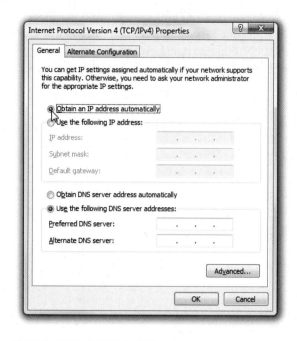

• **Figure 23.32** Automatically obtain an IP address

You can do some cool stuff with NSLOOKUP, and consequently some techs absolutely love the tool. It's way outside the scope of CompTIA A+ certification, but if you want to play with it, type **HELP** at the NSLOOKUP prompt and press ENTER to see a list of common commands and syntax.

the command-prompt window open for a moment and then quickly close!

PING You've already seen PING, a really great way to see if you can talk to another system. Here's how it works. Get to a command prompt and type **ping** followed by an IP address or by a DNS name, such as **ping www.chivalry.com**. Press the ENTER key on your keyboard and away it goes! Figure 23.33 shows the common syntax for PING.

PING has a few options beyond the basics that CompTIA wants you to know about. The first option is –*t*. By using the –*t* switch, PING continuously sends PING packets until you stop it with the break command (CTRL-C). The second option is the –*l* switch that enables you to specify how big a PING packet to send. This helps in diagnosing specific problems with the routers between your computer and the computer you PING.

IPCONFIG Windows offers the command-line tool **IPCONFIG** for a quick glance at your network settings. Click Start | Run and type **CMD** to get a command prompt. From the prompt, type **IPCONFIG /ALL** to see all of your TCP/IP settings (Figure 23.34). When you have a static IP address, IPCONFIG does little beyond reporting your current IP settings, including your IP address, subnet mask, default gateway, DNS servers, and WINS servers. When using DHCP, however, IPCONFIG is also the primary tool for releasing and renewing your IP address. Just type **ipconfig /renew** to get a new IP address or **ipconfig /release** to give up the IP address you currently have.

NSLOOKUP **NSLOOKUP** is a powerful command-line program that enables you to determine exactly what information the DNS server is giving you about a specific host name. Every version of Windows makes NSLOOKUP available when you install TCP/IP. To run the program, type **NSLOOKUP**

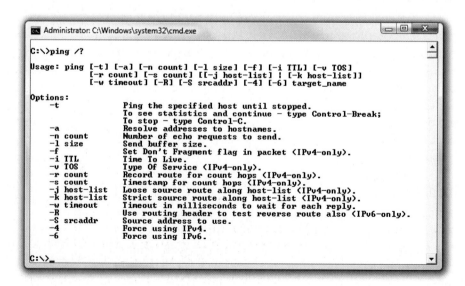

• **Figure 23.33** PING syntax

from the command line and press the ENTER key (Figure 23.35). Note that this gives you a little information but the prompt has changed? That's because you're running the application. Type exit and press the ENTER key to return to the command prompt.

TRACERT The **TRACERT** utility shows the route that a packet takes to get to its destination. From a command line, type **TRACERT** followed by a space and an IP address. The output describes the route from your machine to the destination machine, including all devices the packet passes through and how long each hop takes (Figure 23.36). TRACERT can come in handy when you have to troubleshoot bottlenecks. When users complain of difficulty reaching a particular destination by using TCP/IP, you can run this utility to determine whether the problem exists on a machine or connection over which you have control, or if it is a problem on another machine or router. Similarly, if a destination is completely unreachable, TRACERT can again determine whether the problem is on a machine or router over which you have control.

```
Administrator: C:\Windows\system32\cmd.exe

C:\>ipconfig /all

Windows IP Configuration

   Host Name . . . . . . . . . . . . : michaels
   Primary Dns Suffix  . . . . . . . : totalhome
   Node Type . . . . . . . . . . . . : Hybrid
   IP Routing Enabled. . . . . . . . : No
   WINS Proxy Enabled. . . . . . . . : No
   DNS Suffix Search List. . . . . . : totalhome

Ethernet adapter Intel Nic:

   Media State . . . . . . . . . . . : Media disconnected
   Connection-specific DNS Suffix  . :
   Description . . . . . . . . . . . : Intel(R) PRO/100 S Desktop Adapter
   Physical Address. . . . . . . . . : 00-02-B3-41-6F-07
   DHCP Enabled. . . . . . . . . . . : Yes
   Autoconfiguration Enabled . . . . : Yes

Ethernet adapter Gigabit NIC:

   Connection-specific DNS Suffix  . :
   Description . . . . . . . . . . . : Realtek RTL8169/8110 Family PCI Gigabit E
thernet NIC (NDIS 6.0)
   Physical Address. . . . . . . . . : 00-0D-61-52-4D-8F
   DHCP Enabled. . . . . . . . . . . : Yes
   Autoconfiguration Enabled . . . . : Yes
   Link-local IPv6 Address . . . . . : fe80::c547:4dd3:86a3:739d%8(Preferred)
   IPv4 Address. . . . . . . . . . . : 192.168.4.49(Preferred)
   Subnet Mask . . . . . . . . . . . : 255.255.255.0
   Lease Obtained. . . . . . . . . . : Thursday, September 25, 2008 8:27:19 AM
   Lease Expires . . . . . . . . . . : Friday, October 03, 2008 8:27:19 AM
   Default Gateway . . . . . . . . . : fe80::213:10ff:fee8:263d%8
                                       192.168.4.1
   DHCP Server . . . . . . . . . . . : 192.168.4.11
   DNS Servers . . . . . . . . . . . : 192.168.4.11
   NetBIOS over Tcpip. . . . . . . . : Enabled
```

• **Figure 23.34**   IPCONFIG /ALL on Windows Vista

Configuring TCP/IP

By default, TCP/IP is configured to receive an IP address automatically from a DHCP server on the network (and automatically assign a corresponding

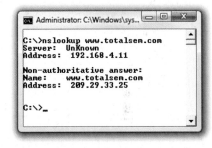

```
Administrator: C:\Windows\sys...

C:\>nslookup www.totalsem.com
Server:  UnKnown
Address:  192.168.4.11

Non-authoritative answer:
Name:    www.totalsem.com
Address:  209.29.33.25

C:\>_
```

• **Figure 23.35**   NSLOOKUP in action

```
Administrator: C:\Windows\system32\cmd.exe

C:\>tracert www.chivalry.com

Tracing route to www.chivalry.com [69.94.71.175]
over a maximum of 30 hops:

  1     1 ms     1 ms     1 ms  Router.totalhome [192.168.4.1]
  2     8 ms     8 ms    16 ms  adsl-208-190-121-38.dsl.hstntx.swbell.net [208.1
90.121.38]
  3     8 ms     8 ms     8 ms  dist2-vlan50.hstntx.sbcglobal.net [151.164.11.12
5]
  4     8 ms     8 ms     8 ms  bb2-g14-0.hstntx.sbcglobal.net [151.164.92.206]

  5    75 ms    61 ms    61 ms  12.83.63.165
  6    61 ms    61 ms    61 ms  dedi-g2-3-0.mrdnct.sbcglobal.net [151.164.42.55]

  7    90 ms    67 ms    62 ms  orm-llc-1123020.cust.snet.net [69.183.190.38]
  8    70 ms    66 ms   102 ms  69.94.1.69
  9    61 ms    61 ms    62 ms  chivalry.com [69.94.71.175]

Trace complete.

C:\>_
```

• **Figure 23.36**   TRACERT in action

Running TRACERT

Ever wonder why your e-mail takes *years* to get to some people but arrives instantly for others? Or why some Web sites are slower to load than others? Part of the blame could lie with how many hops away your connection is to the target server. You can use TRACERT to run a quick check of how many hops it takes to get to somewhere on a network, so Try This!

1. Run TRACERT on some known source, such as www.microsoft.com or www.totalsem.com.

2. How many hops did it take? Did your TRACERT time out or make it all of the way to the server? Try a TRACERT to a local address. If you're in a university town, run a TRACERT on the campus Web site, such as www.rice.edu for folks in Houston, or www.ucla.edu for those of you in Los Angeles. Did you get fewer hops with a local site?

subnet mask). As far as the CompTIA A+ certification exams are concerned, Network+ techs and administrators give you the IP address, subnet mask, and default gateway information and you plug them into the PC. That's about it, so here's how to do it manually:

1. In Windows XP, open the Control Panel and double-click the Network Connections applet. Double-click the Local Area Connection icon. In Windows 2000, click Start | Settings | Network and Dial-up Connections, and double-click the Local Area Connection icon. In Windows Vista/7, right-click on Network and then click *Manage network connections*. After that, double-click the Local Area Network icon.

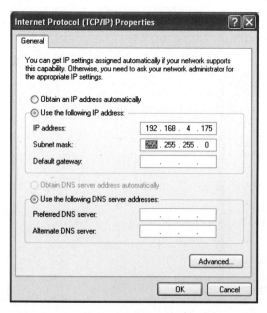

2. Click the Properties button, highlight Internet Protocol (TCP/IP), and click the Properties button. In Windows Vista/7, you should highlight Internet Protocol Version 4 (TCP/IPv4) because Vista and 7 both have IPv4 and IPv6 installed by default.

3. In the dialog box, click the radio button next to *Use the following IP address*.

4. Enter the IP address in the appropriate fields.

5. Press the TAB key to skip down to the Subnet mask field. Note that the subnet mask is entered automatically, although you can type over this if you want to enter a different subnet mask (see Figure 23.37).

6. Optionally, enter the IP address for a default gateway (a router or another computer system that will forward transmissions beyond your network).

7. Optionally, enter the IP addresses of a primary and a secondary DNS server.

• **Figure 23.37** Setting up IP

8. Click the OK button to close the dialog box.

9. Click the Close button to exit the Local Area Connection Status dialog box.

10. Windows will alert you that you must restart the system for the changes to take effect.

Automatic Private IP Addressing

Windows supports a feature called Automatic Private IP Addressing (APIPA) that automatically assigns an IP address to the system when the client cannot obtain an IP address automatically. The Internet Assigned Numbers Authority, the nonprofit corporation responsible for assigning IP addresses and managing root servers, has set aside the range of addresses from 169.254.0.1 to 169.254.255.254 for this purpose.

If the computer system cannot contact a DHCP server, the computer randomly chooses an address in the form of 169.254.*x.y* (where *x.y* is the computer's identifier) and a 16-bit subnet mask (255.255.0.0) and broadcasts it on the network segment (subnet). If no other computer responds to the address, the system assigns this address to itself. When using APIPA, the system can communicate only with other computers on the same subnet that also use the 169.254.*x.y* range with a 16-bit mask. APIPA is enabled by default if your system is configured to obtain an IP address automatically.

> A computer system on a network with an active DHCP server that has an IP address in this range usually indicates a problem connecting to the DHCP server.

Sharing and Security

Windows systems can share all kinds of resources: files, folders, entire drives, printers, faxes, Internet connections, and much more. Conveniently for you, the CompTIA A+ certification exams limit their interests to folders, printers, and Internet connections. You'll see how to share folders and printers now; Internet connection sharing is discussed in Chapter 25, "The Internet."

Sharing Drives and Folders

All versions of Windows share drives and folders in basically the same manner. Simply right-click any drive or folder and choose Properties. Select the Sharing tab (Figure 23.38). Select *Share this folder*, add something in the Comment or User Limit fields if you wish (they're not required), and click Permissions (Figure 23.39).

Hey! Doesn't NTFS have all those wild permissions such as Read, Execute, Take Ownership, and all that? Yes, it does, but NTFS permissions and network permissions are totally separate beasties. Microsoft wanted Windows to support many different file systems (NTFS, FAT16, FAT32), old and new. Network permissions are Microsoft's way of enabling you to administer file sharing on any type of partition supported by Windows, no matter how ancient. Sure, your options will be pretty limited if you are working with an older file system, but you *can* do it.

The beauty of Windows is that it provides another tool—NTFS permissions—that can do much more. NTFS is where the power lies, but power always comes with a price: You have to configure two separate sets of permissions. If you are sharing a folder on an NTFS drive, as

• **Figure 23.38**   Windows XP Sharing tab on NTFS volume

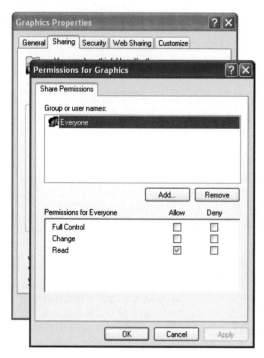

• **Figure 23.39**   Network permissions

Windows offers two types of sharing: share-level and NTFS permissions.

---

you normally are these days, you must set *both* the network permissions and the NTFS permissions to let others access your shared resources. Some good news: This is actually no big deal! Just set the network permissions to give everyone full control, and then use the NTFS permissions to exercise more precise control over *who* accesses the shared resources and *how* they access them. Open the Security tab to set the NTFS permissions.

Accessing Shared Drives/Directories

Once you have set up a drive or directory to be shared, the final step is to access that shared drive or directory from another machine. Windows 2000 and XP use My Network Places and Windows Vista and Windows 7 use Network, although you'll need to do a little clicking to get to the shared resources (Figure 23.40).

You can also map network resources to a local resource name. For example, the FREDC share can be mapped to be a local hard drive such as E: or F:. From within any Explorer window (such as My Documents or Documents), choose Tools | Map Network Drive to open the Map Network Drive dialog box (Figure 23.41). In Windows Vista/7, you'll need to press the ALT key once to see the menu bar. Click the Browse button to check out the neighborhood and find a shared drive (Figure 23.42).

In Windows 2000, you can also use the handy Add Network Place icon in My Network Places to add network locations you frequently access without using up drive letters. Windows XP removed the icon but added the menu option in its context bar on the left; Windows Vista and

• **Figure 23.40**   Shared resources in Network

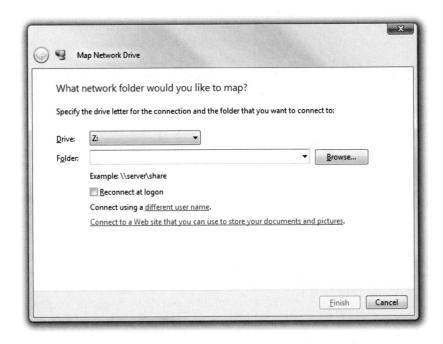

● **Figure 23.41**   Map Network Drive dialog box in Vista

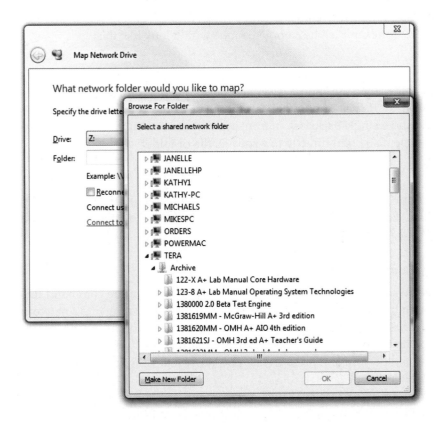

● **Figure 23.42**   Browsing for shared folders

Chapter 23: Local Area Networking

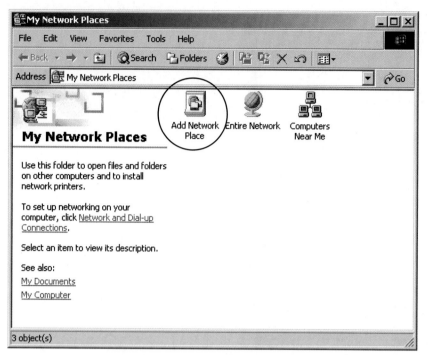

• **Figure 23.43**   Add Network Place icon in Windows 2000

All shared resources should show up in My Network Places (or Network in Vista/7). If a shared resource fails to show up, make sure you check the basics first: Is File and Printer Sharing activated? Is the device shared? Don't let silly errors fool you!

Windows 7 have removed it altogether. Here's how it looks on a Windows 2000 system (Figure 23.43).

Mapping shared network drives is a common practice, as it makes a remote network share look like just another drive on the local system. The only downside to drive mapping stems from the fact that users tend to forget they are on a network. A classic example is the user who always accesses a particular folder or file on the network and then suddenly gets a "file not found" error when the workstation is disconnected from the network. Instead of recognizing this as a network error, the user often imagines the problem is a missing or corrupted file.

UNC

All computers that share must have a network name, and all of the resources they share must also have network names. Any resource on a network can be described by combining the names of the resource being shared and the system sharing. If a machine called SERVER1 is sharing its C: drive as FREDC, for example, the complete name would look like this:

```
\\SERVER1\FREDC
```

This is called the **universal naming convention (UNC)**. The UNC is distinguished by its use of double backslashes in front of the sharing system's name and a single backslash in front of the shared resource's name. A UNC name can also point directly to a specific file or folder:

```
\\SERVER1\FREDC\INSTALL-FILES\SETUP.EXE
```

In this example, INSTALL-FILES is a subdirectory in the shared folder FREDC (which may or may not be called FREDC on the server), and SETUP.EXE is a specific file.

NET Command

Windows enables you to view a network quickly from the command line through the **NET command**. This works great when you plug into a network for the first time and, naturally, don't know the names of the other computers on that network. To see the many options that NET offers, type **net** at a command prompt and press ENTER. The VIEW and USE options offer excellent network tools.

You can think of NET VIEW as the command-line version of My Network Places. When run, NET VIEW returns a list of Windows computers on the network. Once you know the names of the computers, you type **NET**

VIEW followed by the computer name. NET VIEW will show any shares on that machine and whether they are mapped drives.

```
C:\>NET VIEW SERVER1
Shared resources at SERVER1
Share name   Type  Used as  Comment
_____

FREDC        Disk
Research     Disk  W:
The command completed successfully.
```

NET USE is a command-line method for mapping network shares. For example, if you wanted to map the Research share shown in the previous example to the X drive, you simply type:

```
C:\>NET USE X: \\SERVER1\Research
```

This will map drive X to the Research share on the SERVER1 computer.

Sharing Printers

Sharing printers in Windows is just as easy as sharing drives and directories. Assuming that the system has printer sharing services loaded, just go to the Printers folder in the Control Panel or Start Menu and right-click the printer you wish to share. Select Sharing; then click *Shared as* (Windows 2000) or *Share the printer* (Windows XP/Vista/7) and give it a name (see Figure 23.44).

To access a shared printer in any version of Windows, simply click the Add Printer icon in the Printers folder. When asked if the printer is Local or Network, select Network; browse the network for the printer you wish to access, and Windows takes care of the rest! In almost all cases, Windows will copy the printer driver from the sharing machine. In the rare case where it doesn't, it will prompt you for drivers.

One of the most pleasant aspects of configuring a system for networking under all versions of Microsoft Windows is the amazing amount of the process that is automated. For example, if Windows detects a NIC in a system, it automatically installs the NIC driver, a network protocol (TCP/IP), and Client for Microsoft Networks (the NetBIOS part of the Microsoft networking software). So if you want to share a resource, everything you need is automatically installed. Note that although File and Printer Sharing is also automatically installed, you still must activate it by clicking the appropriate checkbox in the Local Area Connection Properties dialog box, as explained earlier in the chapter.

● **Figure 23.44**   Giving a name to a shared printer on Windows XP

■ Troubleshooting Networks

Once you go beyond a single PC and enter the realm of networked computers, your troubleshooting skills need to take a giant leap up in quality. Think of the complexity added with networks. Suddenly you have multiple PCs with multiple users who could, at the drop of a hat, do all kinds of inadvertent damage to a fully functional PC. Networked PCs have a layer of networked hardware and resource sharing that adds a completely new dimension to a user's cry for help, "I can't print!"

Where can the problem lie in a *non-networked situation* if a person cannot print? Here are the obvious ones:

- Printer is not connected to the PC.

- Printer is out of ink.

- PC doesn't have the proper driver loaded.

- PC points by default to a printer other than the one that the user thinks should print.

That's about it. Maybe the parallel port configuration is wrong in CMOS or the USB drivers aren't correct, but still.... Now do the same thing with a *networked situation* where a user can't print. Here are the obvious *extra* issues, because all of the local machine issues apply as well:

- Print server is down.

- Printer is locked by another user.

- The client PC doesn't have network connectivity.

- The NIC driver is bad or incorrect.

- The client PC doesn't have the proper printer drivers installed for the networked printer.

- The cable between the client PC's NIC and the nearest switch is bad.

- The port to which the cable connects is bad.

- The switch failed.

- Somebody in an office down the hall spilled coffee on the printer, inside the mechanism, and then didn't fess up to the accident.

That's a lot of variables, and they just scratch the surface of possibilities. You live in a networked world—it's time to elevate your troubleshooting skills and methodologies to the next level. This section offers a series of steps you can use when performing any type of PC or network troubleshooting. You'll look at ways to apply your tech skills and general communication skills to get to the bottom of a problem and get that problem fixed.

Verify the Symptom

The one thing that all PC problems have in common is a symptom. If something odd wasn't happening (or not happening) to users as they tried to do

> The "Troubleshooting Networks" section covers a range of questions you're likely to see on the "Operational Procedure" exam domain. See also Chapter 27, "The Complete PC Technician," for more on the topic.

whatever they need to do on their computers, you wouldn't have a problem at all, would you? Unfortunately, the vast majority of users out there aren't CompTIA A+ certified technicians. As a tech, you need to overcome a rather nasty communication gap before you can begin to consider a fix. Let's bridge that gap right now.

Look for lots of questions on communication with users on the Essentials exam.

It usually starts with a phone call:

You: "Tech Support, this is Mike. How can I help you?"

User: "Uh, hi, Mike. This is Tom over in Accounting. I can't get into the network. Can you help me?"

Tom just started over in the Accounting department this week and has been a pain in the rear end so far. Ah, the things you might want to say to this person: "No. I only help non-pain-in-the-rear accountants." Or how about this? "Let me check my appointment schedule.... Ah, yes. I can check on your problem in two weeks. Monday at 4:00 P.M. okay for you?"

But, of course, you had the audacity to choose the beloved profession of IT tech support, so you don't get to ask the questions you want to ask. Rather, you need to take a position of leadership and get to the bottom of the problem, and that means understanding the symptom. Take a deep breath, smile, and get to work. You have two issues to deal with at this point. First, if you're working with a user, you must try to get the user to describe the symptom. Second, whether you're working on a system alone or you're talking to a user on the telephone, you must verify that the symptom is legitimate.

Getting a user to describe a symptom is often a challenge. Users are not techs and as a result their perception of the PC is very different than yours. But on the same token, most users know a bit about PCs and you want to take advantage of a user's skill and experience whenever you can. A personal example of verifying the symptom: Once I got a call from a user telling me that his "screen was blank." I told him to restart his system. To which he responded, "Shouldn't I shut down the PC first?" I said: "I thought you just told me the screen was blank!" He replied: "That's right. There's nothing on the screen but my desktop."

When Did It Happen?

Once you know the symptom, you need to try to inspect the problem yourself. This doesn't mean you need to go to the system; many real problems are easily fixed by the user, under your supervision. But you must understand when the problem occurs so that you can zero in on where to look for the solution. Does it happen at boot? It might be a CMOS/BIOS issue. Is it taking place as the OS loads? Then you need to start checking initialization files. Does it take place when the system runs untouched for a certain amount of time? Then maybe the power management could come into play.

What Has Changed?

Systems that run properly tend to continue to run properly. Systems that have undergone a hardware or software change have a much higher chance of not running properly than a system that has not been changed. If

something has gone wrong, talk to the user to determine whether anything in particular has occurred since the system last worked properly. Has new software been installed? Did the user add some new RAM? Change the Windows Domain? Run a Windows Update? Drop the monitor on the floor? Not only do you need to consider those types of changes, but you must also make sure that any unrelated changes don't send you down the wrong path. The fact that someone installed a new floppy drive yesterday probably doesn't have anything to do with the printer that isn't working today.

Last, consider side effects of changes that don't seem to have anything to do with the problem. For example, I once had a customer whose system kept freezing up in Windows. I knew he had just added a second hard drive, but the system booted up just fine and ran normally—except it would freeze up after a few minutes. The hard drive wasn't the problem. The problem was that he unplugged the CPU fan in the process of installing it. When I discover a change has been made, I like to visualize the process of the change to consider how that change may have directly or indirectly contributed to a problem. In other words, if you run into a situation where a person added a NIC to a functioning PC that now won't boot, you need to think about what part of the installation process could be fouled up to cause a PC to stop working.

Check the Environment

I use the term *environment* in two totally different fashions in this book. The first way is the most classic definition: the heat, humidity, dirt, and other outside factors that can affect the operation of the system. The other definition is more technical and addresses the computing environment of the system and other surrounding systems: What type of system do they run? What OS? What is their network connection? What are the primary applications they use? What antivirus program do they run? Do other people use the system?

Answering these questions gives you an overview of what is affecting this system both internally and externally. A quick rundown of these issues can reveal possible problems that might not be otherwise recognized. For example, I once got a call from a user complaining she had no network connection. I first checked the NIC to ensure it had link lights (always the first thing to check to ensure a good physical connection!) only to discover that she had no link lights—someone had decided to turn on a space heater, which destroyed the cable!

Reproducing the Problem

My official rule on problems with a PC is this: "If a problem happens only once, it is not a problem." PCs are notorious for occasionally locking up, popping errors, and displaying all types of little quirks that a quick reboot fixes, and they don't happen again. Why do these things happen? I don't know, although I'm sure if someone wanted me to guess I could come up with a clever explanation. But the majority of PCs simply don't have redundancy built in, and it's okay for them to occasionally hiccup.

A problem becomes interesting to me if it happens more than once. If it happens twice, the chances are much higher that it will happen a third time. I want to see it happen that third time—under my supervision. I will direct

the user to try to reproduce the problem while I am watching to see what triggers the failure. This is a huge clue to helping you localize the real problem. Intermittent failures are the single most frustrating events that take place in a technician's life. But do remember that many seemingly intermittent problems really aren't intermittent—you have simply failed to reproduce the events exactly enough to see the consistency of the problem. Always take the time to match every step that leads to a problem to try to recreate the same error.

Isolating the Symptom

With so many bits and pieces to a PC, you must take the time to try to isolate the symptom to ensure your fix is going to the software or hardware that really needs it. In hardware, that usually means removing suspect parts until only one possible part remains. In software, that usually means removing background programs, booting into Safe mode, or trying to create a situation where only the suspected program is running.

Isolation takes on a whole new meaning with networks. One of the greatest tools in networking is isolation—does this problem happen on other systems, on other workgroups, on other PCs running DHCP? Whenever a problem takes place in networking, isolation is the key to determining the problem.

Separating Hardware from Software

Many problems that occur on a PC are difficult to isolate given that it is difficult to determine whether the problem lies in the software or the hardware. If you find yourself in this situation, you can take a few steps to help you zero in on which side of the PC to suspect.

Known Good Hardware

The absolute best way to know whether a problem is hardware or software related is to replace the suspected piece of hardware with a known good part. If you can't tell whether a Windows page fault comes from bad RAM or a software incompatibility, quickly replacing the RAM with known good RAM should help you determine whether the RAM or the software is to blame.

Cable and Loopback Test

A bad NIC can also generate a "can't see the network" problem. Use whatever utility was provided with your OS to verify that the NIC works. If you have a NIC with diagnostic software, run it—this software will check the NIC's circuitry. The NIC's female connector is a common failure point, so NICs that come with diagnostic software often include a special test called a loopback test. A loopback test sends data out of the NIC and checks to see if it comes back. Some NICs perform only an internal loopback that tests the circuitry that sends and receives, but not the actual connecting pins. A true external loopback requires a **loopback plug** inserted into the NIC's port (Figure 23.45). If a NIC is bad, replace it—preferably with an identical NIC so you don't have to reinstall drivers.

● **Figure 23.45**   Loopback plug

The network cable is a common source of network troubles. You can use a cable tester if you suspect a cable problem. With the right equipment, diagnosing a bad cabling run is easy. Anyone with a network should own a midrange cable tester such as the Fluke Microscanner. With a little practice, you can easily determine not only whether a cable is disconnected, but also where the disconnection takes place. Sometimes patience is required, especially if the cable runs aren't labeled, but you will find the problem.

Uninstall/Reinstall

If you can do so easily, try uninstalling the suspected software and reinstalling. Many hardware/software problems magically disappear with a simple uninstall/reinstall.

Patching/Upgrading

Many hardware or software problems take place due to incompatibilities between the two suspect sides. Try upgrading drivers. Download patches or upgrades to software, especially if the hardware and the software are more than two years apart in age.

Virus Check

Last (maybe I should have put this first), always check for viruses. Today's viruses manifest so many different symptoms that failure to check for them is a study in time wasting. I recently got a new hard drive that started to make a nasty clicking noise—a sure sign of a failing hard drive. However, I ran an extensive virus check and guess what—it was a virus! Who would have thought? I checked with the hard drive maker's Web site, and my fears were confirmed. It just goes to show you—even the best of techs can be caught by the simplest problems.

Research

Once you have your mind wrapped around the problem, it's time to fix it. Unless the problem is either simple (network cable unplugged) or something you've seen before and know exactly how to fix, you'll almost certainly need to research it. The Internet makes this easy. I use one of my favorite tricks when I get some bizarre error text: I type the error message into my search engine—that would be Google, of course—and most times find a quick fix!

Make the Fix and Test

Once you have a good idea as to the problem and how to fix it, it's time to do the fix. Always make backups—or at least warn the user of the risk to the system. If possible, try to remember how the system was configured before the fix so you can go back to square one if the fix fails to work. After you perform the fix, do whatever you need to do to make sure the system is again working properly. Make sure the user sees that the system is working properly and can sign off on your work.

OSI Seven-Layer Model

A lot of people think about networks and trouble-shoot networking issues by using the OSI seven-layer model. Using this model (or my four-layer model, described in the next section of this chapter) helps you isolate problems and then implement solutions. Here are the seven layers of the OSI model:

- **Layer 1** Physical
- **Layer 2** Data Link
- **Layer 3** Network
- **Layer 4** Transport
- **Layer 5** Session
- **Layer 6** Presentation
- **Layer 7** Application

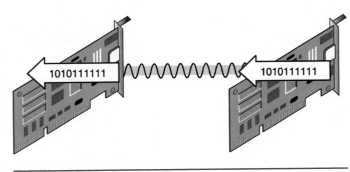

• **Figure 23.46** The Physical layer turns binary code into a physical signal and back into ones and zeros.

Basic switches reside at Layer 2 (Data Link) of the OSI model. They provide filtering based on MAC. More advanced switches that can perform InterVLAN and protocol support operate at Layer 3 (Layer 3 switch). Routers are often called Layer 3 switches.

The *Physical layer* defines the physical form taken by data when it travels across a cable. Devices that work at the physical layer include NICs and hubs. Figure 23.46 shows a sending NIC turning a string of ones and zeros into an electrical signal, and a receiving NIC turning it back into the same ones and zeros.

The *Data Link layer* defines the rules for accessing and using the Physical layer. MAC addresses and Ethernet's CSMA/CD operate at the Data Link layer.

The *Network layer* defines the rules for adding information to the data packet that controls how routers move it from its source on one network to its destination on a different network. The IP protocol that handles IP addressing works on Layer 3.

The *Transport layer*, Layer 4, breaks up data it receives from the upper layers (that is, Layers 5–7) into smaller pieces for transport within the data packets created at the lower layers. In TCP/IP networks, the protocols that typically handle this transition between upper and lower layers are TCP and UDP.

The *Session layer* manages the connections between machines on the network. Protocols such as NetBIOS and sockets enable a computer to connect to a server, for example, and send and receive e-mail or download a file. Each different task you can perform on a server would require a different kind of session.

The *Presentation layer* presents data from the sending system in a form that a receiving system can understand. Most Layer 6 functions are handled by the same software that handles Layer 7 functions.

The *Application layer* is where you (or a user) get to interact with the computers. These are programs that make networking happen, such as Web browsers and e-mail applications. Chapter 25, "The Internet," covers these applications in a lot more detail.

The key to using the OSI seven-layer model is to ask the traditional troubleshooting question: What can the problem be? If Jill can't browse a Web site, for example, could this be a Layer 7 issue? Sure: If her browser software was messed up, this could stop her from browsing. It could also be a lower-level problem, though, and you need to run through the questions. Can she

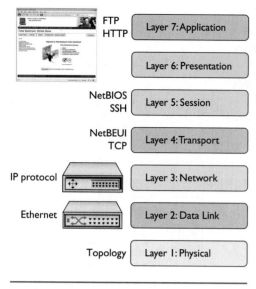

FTP
HTTP
Layer 7: Application

Layer 6: Presentation

NetBIOS
SSH
Layer 5: Session

NetBEUI
TCP
Layer 4: Transport

IP protocol
Layer 3: Network

Ethernet
Layer 2: Data Link

Topology
Layer 1: Physical

• **Figure 23.47**   OSI

do anything over the network? If her NIC doesn't show flashing link lights, that could point all the way down to the Physical layer and a bad NIC, cable, or hub.

If she has good connectivity to the overall network but can't ping the Web server, that could point to a different problem altogether. Figure 23.47 shows the OSI seven-layer model graphically.

The only drawback to the OSI seven-layer model, in my view, is that it's too complex. I like to conceptualize network issues into fewer layers—four to be precise. Let's take a look.

Mike's Four-Layer Model

Network problems, by the very nature of the complexity of a network, usually make for more complex problems. Given that, I have created a four-step process that I modestly call "Mike's Four-Layer Model." These four things go through my mind every time I have a problem. I think about four distinct categories to help me isolate the symptoms and make the right fix.

Hardware

Hardware is probably the most self-explanatory of the four categories. This covers the many ways data can be moved from one PC to another. Does the system have a good connection? How's the cabling? This also covers network cards: Are they installed properly and tested? Plus, the Hardware category hits on all of those interesting boxes, such as hubs, switches, and repeaters, among which all of the wires in the network run. If you can see it, it's under this category.

Protocols

This category covers the protocols, such as TCP/IP or NetBEUI. Is the protocol installed? Is it configured properly? Does any particular system's configuration prevent it from working with another system?

Network

The network category has two parts: servers and clients. Network operating systems must differentiate systems that act as server from those that do not. If a system is a server, some process must take place to tell it to share resources. Additionally, if a system is intended to share, it must be given a name. This category also includes defining and verifying users and groups; does your system need them? Do the right accounts exist, and are they working properly?

Shared Resources

Once all of the systems, users, and groups are working properly, you need to identify the resources they will share. If a drive or folder is to be shared, the OS must provide a way to identify that drive or folder as available for sharing. The rules for naming shared resources are called *naming conventions*. A great example would be a system that offers its D:\FRED directory

for sharing. This D:\FRED directory needs a network name, such as FRED_
FILES. This network name is displayed to all of the devices on the network.

Sharing a resource is only half the battle. Individual systems need to be able to access the shared resources. The network needs a process whereby a PC can look out on the network and see what is available. Having found those available resources, the PC then needs to make them look and act as though they were local resources. A network also needs to control access to resources. A laser printer, for example, might be available for sharing, but only for the accounting department, excluding other departments.

enhancements, WPA was intended only as an interim security solution until the IEEE 802.11i security standard was finalized and implemented.

WPA2

Today, Macintosh OS X and Microsoft Windows support the full IEEE **802.11i** standard, more commonly known as **Wi-Fi Protected Access 2 (WPA2)**, to lock down wireless networks. WPA2 uses the Advanced Encryption Standard (AES), among other improvements, to provide a secure wireless environment. If you haven't upgraded to WPA2, you should.

Speed and Range Issues

Wireless networking data throughput speeds depend on several factors. Foremost is the standard that the wireless devices use. Depending on the standard used, wireless throughput speeds range from a measly 2 Mbps to a snappy 100+ Mbps. One of the other factors affecting speed is the distance between wireless nodes (or between wireless nodes and centralized access points). Wireless devices dynamically negotiate the top speed at which they can communicate without dropping too many data packets. Speed decreases as distance increases, so the maximum throughput speed is achieved only at extremely close range (less than 25 feet or so). At the outer reaches of a device's effective range, speed may decrease to around 1 Mbps before it drops out altogether.

Speed is also affected by interference from other wireless devices operating in the same frequency range—such as cordless phones or baby monitors— and by solid objects. So-called *dead spots* occur when something capable of blocking the radio signal comes between the wireless network nodes. Large electrical appliances such as refrigerators are *very* effective at blocking a wireless network signal. Other culprits include electrical fuse boxes, metal plumbing, air conditioning units, and similar objects.

Wireless networking range is difficult to define, and you'll see most descriptions listed with qualifiers, such as "*around* 150 feet" and "*about* 300 feet." This is simply because, like throughput speed, range is greatly affected by outside factors. Interference from other wireless devices affects range, as does interference from solid objects. The maximum ranges listed in the next section are those presented by wireless manufacturers as the theoretical maximum ranges. In the real world, you'll experience these ranges only under the most ideal circumstances. True effective range is probably about half what you see listed.

■ Wireless Networking Standards

To help you gain a better understanding of wireless network technology, here is a brief look at the standards they use.

IEEE 802.11-Based Wireless Networking

The **IEEE 802.11** wireless Ethernet standard, more commonly known as **Wi-Fi**, defines methods by which devices may communicate by using

You can see the speed and signal strength on your wireless network by looking at the wireless NIC's properties.

Tech Tip

Increasing Wireless Range
You can increase range in a couple of ways. You can install multiple WAPs to permit "roaming" between one WAP's coverage area and another's—an EBSS, described earlier in this chapter. Or you can install a replacement that increases a single WAP's signal strength, thus increasing its range. If that is still not enough, signal boosters are available that can give you even more power.

Look for basic troubleshooting questions on the CompTIA A+ certification exams dealing with factors that affect wireless connectivity, range, and speed.

spread-spectrum radio waves. Spread-spectrum broadcasts data in small, discrete chunks over the frequencies available within a certain frequency range.

The 802.11-based wireless technologies broadcast and receive on one of two license-free industrial, scientific and industrial radio bands: 2.4 GHz and 5.8 GHz. Even though the ISM band is 5.8 GHz, we just say "5 GHz" for reasons I can't answer. Over the years, the original 802.11 standard has been extended to 802.11*a*, 802.11*b*, 802.11*g*, and 802.11*n* variations used in Wi-Fi wireless networks. Each of these versions of 802.11 uses one of the two ISM bands, with the exception of 802.11n, which uses one but may use both. Don't worry; I'll break this down for you in a moment.

Newer wireless devices can communicate with older wireless devices, so if you are using an 802.11n WAP, all of your 802.11g devices can use it. The exception to this is 802.11a, which requires that all of the equipment directly support it. The following paragraphs describe the important specifications of each of the popular 802.11-based wireless networking standards.

802.11a Despite the "a" designation for this extension to the 802.11 standard, **802.11a** was actually on the market *after* 802.11b. The 802.11a standard differs from the other 802.11-based standards in significant ways. Foremost is that it operates in the 5-ghz frequency range. This means that devices that use this standard are less prone to interference from other devices that use the same frequency range. 802.11a also offers considerably greater throughput than 802.11 and 802.11b at speeds up to 54 Mbps, though its actual throughput is no more than 25 Mbps in normal traffic conditions. Although its theoretical range tops out at about 150 feet, its maximum range will be lower in a typical office environment. Despite the superior speed of 802.11a, it isn't as widely adopted in the PC world as some of the following 802.11 versions.

> In the early days of wireless networking, many techs and marketing people assumed Wi-Fi stood for *Wireless Fidelity*, a sort of play on the common sound signal of high fidelity. It might have at one time, but the Wi-Fi Alliance, the governing standards body for 802.11-based networking, just uses the term Wi-Fi today.

Tech Tip

Spread-Spectrum Broadcasting

The 802.11 standard defines three spread-spectrum broadcasting methods: direct-sequence spread-spectrum (DSSS), frequency-hopping spread-spectrum (FHSS), and orthogonal frequency-division multiplexing (OFDM). DSSS sends data out on multiple frequencies at the same time, while FHSS sends data on one frequency at a time, constantly shifting (or hopping) frequencies. OFDM, the most common broadcast method, uses multiple data streams, each of which is constantly shifting (or hopping) frequencies. DSSS uses considerably more bandwidth than FHSS or OFDM, around 22 MHz as opposed to 1 MHz, respectively. DSSS is capable of greater data throughput, but DSSS is more prone to interference than FHSS. HomeRF wireless networks were the only types that used FHSS; all the other 802.11-based wireless networking standards use DSSS or OFDM.

> Wi-Fi is by far the most widely adopted wireless networking type today. Not only do millions of private businesses and homes have wireless networks, but many public places such as coffee shops and libraries also offer Internet access through wireless networks.

Tech Tip

Wi-Fi Certification

Technically, only wireless devices that conform to the extended versions of the 802.11 standard (802.11a, 802.11b, 802.11g, and 802.11n) are Wi-Fi certified. Wi-Fi certification comes from the Wi-Fi Alliance (formerly the Wireless Ethernet Compatibility Alliance, or WECA), a nonprofit industry group made up of more than 175 member companies who design and manufacture wireless networking products. Wi-Fi certification ensures compatibility among wireless networking devices made by different vendors. First-generation devices that use the older 802.11 standard are not Wi-Fi certified and may or may not work well with devices made by different vendors.

Table 24.2	Infrared Specs
Standard	Infrared (IrDA)
Max. throughput	Up to 4 Mbps
Max. range	1 meter (39 inches)
Security	None
Compatibility	IrDA
Communication mode	Point-to-point ad hoc

Bluetooth

Bluetooth wireless technology (named for ninth-century Danish king Harald Bluetooth) is designed to create small wireless networks preconfigured to do very specific jobs. Some great examples are audio devices such as headsets that connect to your smartphones, **personal area networks (PANs)** that link two PCs for a quick-and-dirty wireless network, and input devices such as keyboards and mice. Bluetooth is *not* designed to be a full-function networking solution, nor is it meant to compete with Wi-Fi. If anything, Bluetooth has replaced infrared as a means to connect PCs to peripherals.

Bluetooth, like any technology, has been upgraded over the years to make it faster and more secure. Two major versions of Bluetooth are widespread today. The first generation (versions 1.1 and 1.2) supports speeds around 1 Mbps. The second generation (2.0 and 2.1) is backward compatible with its first-generation cousins and adds support for more speed by introducing Enhanced Data Rate (EDR), which pushes top speeds to around 3 Mbps.

The IEEE organization has made first-generation Bluetooth the basis for its 802.15 standard for wireless PANs. Bluetooth uses the FHSS broadcasting method, switching between any of the 79 frequencies available in the 2.45-GHz range. Bluetooth hops frequencies some 1600 times per second, making it highly resistant to interference.

Generally, the faster and further a device sends data, the more power it needs to do so, and the Bluetooth designers understood a long time ago that some devices (such as a Bluetooth headset) could save power by not sending data as quickly or as far as other Bluetooth devices may need. To address this, all Bluetooth devices are configured for one of three classes that define maximum power usage in milliwatts (mW) and maximum distance:

Class 1	100 mW	100 meters
Class 2	2.5 mW	10 meters
Class 3	1 mW	1 meter

Bluetooth is *not* designed to be a full-fledged wireless networking solution. Bluetooth is made to replace the snake's nest of cables that currently connects most PCs to their various peripheral devices—keyboard, mouse, printer, speakers, scanner, and the like—but you won't be swapping out your 802.11-based networking devices with Bluetooth-based replacements anytime soon.

Having said that, Bluetooth-enabled wireless networking is comparable to other wireless technologies in a few ways:

- Like infrared, Bluetooth is acceptable for quick file transfers where a wired connection (or a faster wireless connection) is unavailable.

- Almost all wireless headsets are now Bluetooth.

- Bluetooth's speed and range make it a good match for wireless print server solutions.

Bluetooth hardware comes either integrated into many newer portable electronic gadgets such as PDAs and cell phones or as an adapter added to an internal or external expansion bus. Bluetooth networking is enabled through ad hoc–styled PC-to-PC (or PDA-, handheld computer–, or cell phone–to-PC) connections, or in an infrastructure-like mode through Bluetooth access points. Bluetooth access points are very similar to 802.11-based access points, bridging wireless Bluetooth PAN segments to wired LAN segments.

Cellular

A **cellular wireless network** enables you to connect to the Internet through a network-aware PDA, cell phone, or smartphone. Using an add-on PC Card or USB dongle, you can connect any laptop to a cellular network as well. Figure 24.10 shows an AT&T USBConnect Mercury 3G device for just that purpose.

In areas with broad cell phone coverage, such as big cities, cellular wireless networks offer high-speed access (around 1.5 Mbps download speeds) anywhere you go. Carriers use many protocols to provide the higher speeds, and collectively they are known as 3G. Just fire up your smartphone or portable computer and start surfing the Web! In remote areas where the 3G networks have not been built out, the speed drops down to something closer to modem connection speeds. (See Chapter 25, "The Internet," for the scoop on modems.)

Cellular networks use various protocols to connect, such as Global System for Mobile Communications (GSM), General Packet Radio Service (GPRS), and Code Division Multiple Access (CDMA). The 3G networks make use of protocols such as UMTS/HSPA (AT&T), EV-DO (Verizon), and UMTS (T-Mobile). These protocols are handled seamlessly by the software and hardware. What end users see is TCP/IP, just as if they connected through a wired network.

• **Figure 24.10**   AT&T USBConnect Mercury 3G

Practical Application

■ Installing and Configuring Wireless Networking

The mechanics of setting up a wireless network don't differ much from a wired network. Physically installing a wireless network adapter is the same as installing a wired NIC, whether it's an internal PCI card, a PC Card, or an

external USB device. Simply install the device and let plug and play handle detection and resource allocation. Install the device's supplied driver when prompted, and you're practically finished. Unless you're using Windows XP and later, you also need to install the wireless network configuration utility supplied with your wireless network adapter so you can set your communication mode, SSID, and so on.

As mentioned earlier, wireless devices want to talk to each other, so communicating with an available wireless network is usually a no-brainer. The trick is in configuring the wireless network so that only specific wireless nodes are able to use it and securing the data that's being sent through the air.

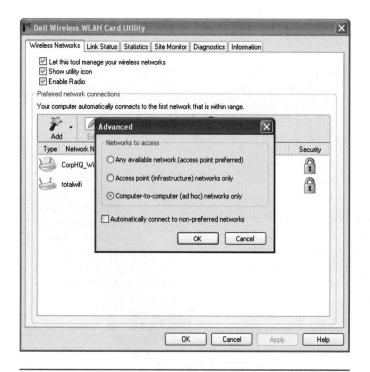

● **Figure 24.11** Selecting ad hoc mode in wireless configuration utility

● **Figure 24.12** Selecting infrastructure mode in wireless configuration utility

Wi-Fi

Wi-Fi networks support ad hoc and infrastructure operation modes. Which mode you choose depends on the number of wireless nodes you need to support, the type of data sharing they'll perform, and your management requirements.

Ad hoc Mode

Ad hoc wireless networks don't need a WAP. The only requirements in an ad hoc mode wireless network are that each wireless node be configured with the same network name (SSID) and that no two nodes use the same IP address. Figure 24.11 shows a wireless network configuration utility with ad hoc mode selected.

The only other configuration steps to take is to make sure that no two nodes are using the same IP address (this step is usually unnecessary if all PCs are using DHCP) and ensuring that the File and Printer Sharing service is running on all nodes.

Infrastructure Mode

Typically, infrastructure mode wireless networks employ one or more WAPs connected to a wired network segment, a corporate intranet or the Internet, or both. As with ad hoc mode wireless networks, infrastructure mode networks require that the same SSID be configured on all nodes and WAPs. Figure 24.12 shows a NETGEAR Wi-Fi configuration screen set to infrastructure mode and using WPA security.

WAPs have an integrated Web server and are configured through a browser-based setup utility. Typically, you fire up your Web browser on one of your network client workstations and enter the WAP's default IP address, such as 192.168.1.1, to bring up the configuration page. You will need to

• **Figure 24.13**   Security login for Linksys WAP

supply an administrative password, included with your WAP's documentation, to log in (see Figure 24.13). Setup screens vary from vendor to vendor and from model to model. Figure 24.14 shows the initial setup screen for a popular Linksys WAP/router.

Configure the SSID option where indicated. Channel selection is usually automatic, but you can reconfigure this option if you have particular needs in your organization (for example, if you have multiple wireless networks operating in the same area). Remember that it's always more secure to configure a unique SSID than it is to accept the well-known default one. You should also make sure that the option to allow broadcasting of the SSID is disabled. This ensures that only wireless nodes specifically configured with the correct SSID can join the wireless network.

To increase security even more, use MAC filtering. Figure 24.15 shows the MAC filtering configuration screen on a Linksys WAP. Simply enter the MAC address of a wireless node that you wish to allow (or deny) access to your wireless network. Set up encryption by turning encryption on at the WAP and then generating a unique security key. Then configure all connected wireless nodes on the network with the same key information. Figure 24.16 shows the WEP key configuration dialog for a Linksys WAP.

> As noted earlier in the chapter, the WEP protocol provides security, but it's easily cracked. Use WPA2 or, if you have older equipment, settle for WPA until you can upgrade.

• **Figure 24.14**   Linksys WAP setup screen

• **Figure 24.15**   MAC filtering configuration screen for a Linksys WAP

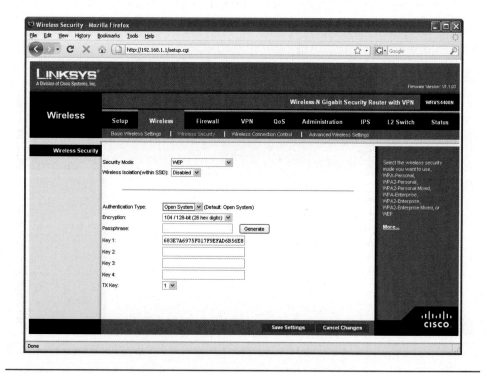

• **Figure 24.16**   WEP Encryption key configuration screen on Linksys WAP

When setting up WEP you have the option of automatically generating a set of encryption keys or doing it manually; save yourself a headache and use the automatic method. Select an encryption level—the usual choices are either 64-bit or 128-bit—and then enter a unique passphrase and click the Generate button (or whatever the equivalent button is called on your WAP). Then select a default key and save the settings. The encryption level, key, and passphrase must match on the wireless client node or communication will fail. Many WAPs have the capability to export the WEP encryption key data onto a media storage device for easy importing onto a client workstation, or you can manually configure encryption by using the vendor-supplied configuration utility, as shown in Figure 24.17.

WPA and WPA2 encryption is configured in much the same way as WEP. There are two ways to set up WPA/WPA2: Pre-shared Key (PSK) or Enterprise. WPA/WPA2-PSK is the most common for small and home networks. Enterprise is much more complex, requires extra equipment (a RADIUS server), and is only used in the most serious and secure wireless networks.

If you have the option, choose WPA2 encryption for the WAP as well as the NICs in your network. You configure WPA2 the same way you would WPA. Note that the settings such as WPA2 for the Enterprise assume you'll enable authentication by using a device called a RADIUS server (Figure 24.18). This way, businesses can allow only people with the proper credentials to connect to their Wi-Fi networks. For home use, select the PSK version of WPA/WPA2. Use the best encryption you can. If you have WPA2, use it. If not, use WPA. WEP is always a last choice.

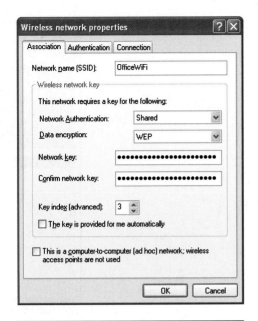

• **Figure 24.17**   WEP Encryption screen on client wireless network adapter configuration utility

Always try WPA2-PSK first. If you then have wireless computers that can't connect to your WAP, fall back to WPA-PSK.

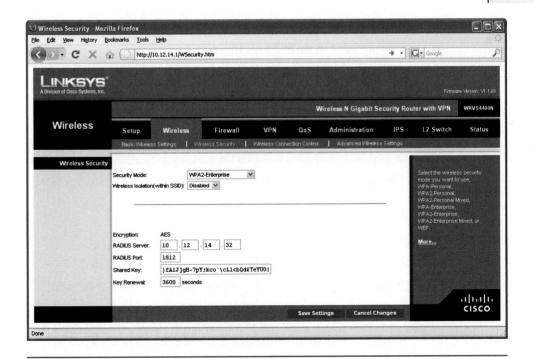

• **Figure 24.18**   Encryption screen with RADIUS option

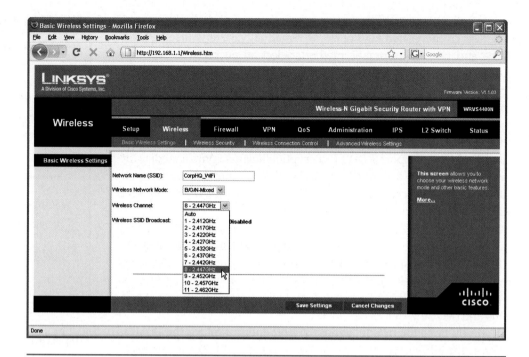

• Figure 24.19   Changing the channel

With most home networks, you can simply leave the channel and frequency of the WAP at the factory defaults, but in an environment with overlapping Wi-Fi signals, you'll want to adjust one or both features. To adjust the channel, find the option in the WAP configuration screens and simply change it. Figure 24.19 shows the channel option in a Linksys WAP.

With dual-band 802.11n WAPs, you can choose which band to put 802.11n traffic on, either 2.4 GHz or 5 GHz. In an area with overlapping signals, most of the traffic will be on the 2.4-GHz frequency, because most devices are either 802.11b or 802.11g. In addition to other wireless devices (such as cordless phones) microwaves also use 2.4-GHz frequency and can cause a great deal of interference. You can avoid any kind of conflict with

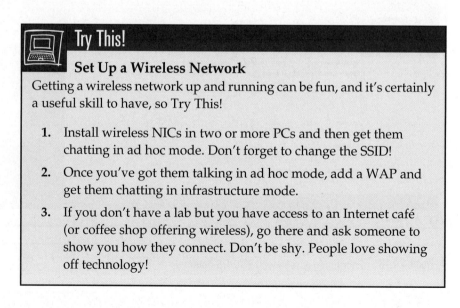

Try This!

Set Up a Wireless Network

Getting a wireless network up and running can be fun, and it's certainly a useful skill to have, so Try This!

1. Install wireless NICs in two or more PCs and then get them chatting in ad hoc mode. Don't forget to change the SSID!

2. Once you've got them talking in ad hoc mode, add a WAP and get them chatting in infrastructure mode.

3. If you don't have a lab but you have access to an Internet café (or coffee shop offering wireless), go there and ask someone to show you how they connect. Don't be shy. People love showing off technology!

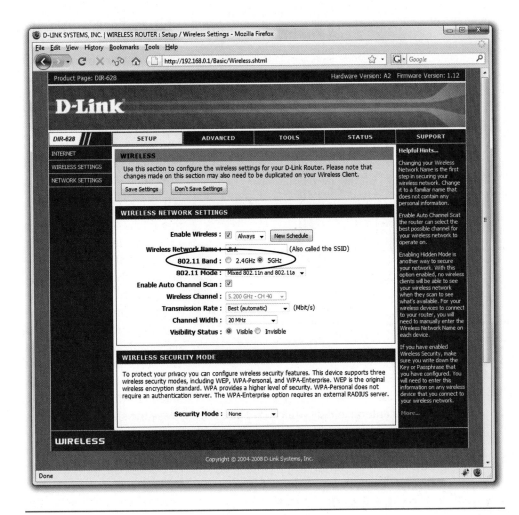

● **Figure 24.20** Selecting frequency

your 802.11n devices by using the 5-GHz frequency instead. Figure 24.20 shows the configuration screen for a dual-band 802.11n WAP.

Placing the Access Point(s)

The optimal location for an access point depends on the area you want to cover, whether you care if the signal bleeds out beyond the borders, and what interference exists from other wireless sources. You start by doing a site survey. A site survey can be as trivial as firing up a wireless-capable laptop and looking for existing SSIDs. Or it can be a complex job where you hire people with specialized equipment to come in and make lots of careful plans, defining the best place to put WAPs and which wireless channels to use. To make sure the wireless signal goes where you want it to go and not where you don't, you need to use the right antenna. Let's see what types of antennae are available.

Omni-directional and Centered   For a typical network, you want blanket coverage and would place a WAP with an omni-directional antenna in the center of the area (Figure 24.21). With an omni-directional antenna, the radio wave flows outward from the WAP. This has the advantage of ease of

use—anything within the signal radius can potentially access the network. Most wireless networks use this combination, especially in the consumer space. The standard straight-wire antennae that provide most omni-directional function are called **dipole antennae**.

Gaining Gain An antenna strengthens and focuses the radio frequency (RF) output from a WAP. The ratio of increase—what's called **gain**—is measured in decibels (dB). The gain from a typical WAP is 2 dB, enough to cover a reasonable area but not a very large room. To increase that signal requires a bigger antenna. Many WAPs have removable antennae that you can replace. To increase the signal in an omni-directional and centered setup, simply replace the factory antennae with one or more bigger antennae (Figure 24.22). Get a big enough antenna and you can crank it all the way up to 11!

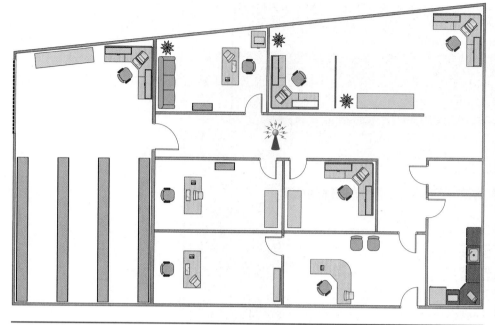

• **Figure 24.21**   Room layout with WAP in the center

• **Figure 24.22**   Replacement antenna on WAP

Cross Check

It's Still a NIC!

Just because you've gone wireless, don't think for a minute that any of the rules you learned in Chapter 23, "Local Area Networking," have changed. A wireless NIC works the same as a wired NIC. Keep in mind the rules for accomplishing things with wired NICs and see if you can answer these questions:

1. How do you access the TCP/IP settings for the wireless NIC?

2. What IP address is your wireless NIC set to use right now?

3. Can you enable and disable the wireless NIC?

Bluetooth Configuration

As with other wireless networking solutions, Bluetooth devices are completely plug and play. Just connect the adapter and follow the prompts to install the appropriate drivers and configuration utilities (these are supplied by your hardware vendor). Once they're installed, you have little to do: Bluetooth devices seek each other out and establish the master/slave relationship without any intervention on your part.

Connecting to a Bluetooth PAN is handled by specialized utility software provided by your portable device or Bluetooth device vendor. Figure 24.23 shows a screen of an older PDA running the Bluetooth Manager software to connect to a Bluetooth access point. Like their Wi-Fi counterparts, Bluetooth access points use a browser-based configuration utility. Figure 24.24 shows the main setup screen for a Belkin Bluetooth access point. Use this setup screen to check on the status of connected Bluetooth devices; configure encryption, MAC filtering, and other security settings; and use other utilities provided by the access point's vendor.

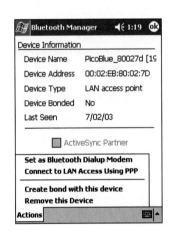

• **Figure 24.23** iPAQ Bluetooth Manager software connected to Bluetooth access point

 Bluetooth network access points are a rare sight out in the real world. Today small portables, PDAs, and smartphones almost certainly connect by using Wi-Fi or cellular network.

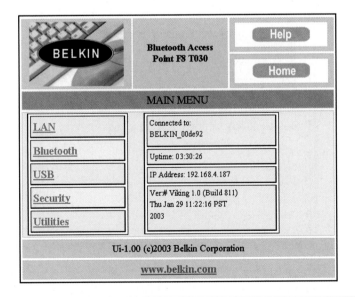

• **Figure 24.24** Belkin Bluetooth access point

• Figure 24.25   VZAccess Manager

Cellular Configuration

There is no single standard for configuring a cellular network card, because the cards and software vary based on which company you have service through. Fortunately those same cell phone companies have made the process of installing their cards very simple. All that is required in most cases is to install the software and plug in the card.

Once you've installed all of the correct drivers, simply plug in the card and start up the application. From here just follow the instructions that came with the software; in this case, double-click on the VZAccess network listed in the window (Figure 24.25). This initiates the connection to (in this case) Verizon's network. You can also go to the Options menu and select Statistics to see the specifics of your connection, as shown in Figure 24.26.

The key thing to remember about cellular Internet access is that it is almost completely configured and controlled by the cellular company. A tech has very little to do except to make sure the cellular card is plugged in, is recognized by the computer, and its drivers are properly installed.

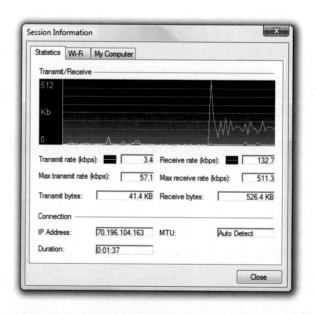

• Figure 24.26   Session statistics for VZAccess Manager

■ Troubleshooting Wi-Fi

Wireless networks are a real boon when they work right, but they can also be one of the most vexing things to troubleshoot when they don't. Let's turn to some practical advice on how to detect and correct wireless hardware, software, and configuration problems.

As with any troubleshooting scenario, your first step in troubleshooting a wireless network is to break down your tasks into logical steps. Your first step should be to figure out the scope of your wireless networking problem. Ask yourself *who*, *what*, and *when*:

- Who is affected by the problem?
- What is the nature of their network problem?
- When did the problem start?

The answers to these questions dictate at least the initial direction of your troubleshooting.

So, who's affected? If all machines on your network—wired and wireless—have lost connectivity, you have bigger problems than that the wireless machines cannot access the network. Troubleshoot this situation the way you'd troubleshoot any network failure. Once you determine which wireless nodes are affected, it's easier to pinpoint whether the problem lies in one or more wireless clients or in one or more access points.

After you narrow down the number of affected machines, your next task is to figure out specifically what type of error the users are experiencing. If they can access some, but not all, network services, it's unlikely that the problem is limited to their wireless equipment. For example, if they can browse the Internet but can't access any shared resources on a server, they're probably experiencing a permissions-related issue rather than a wireless one.

Finally, determine when the problem started. What has changed that might explain your loss of connectivity? Did you or somebody else change the wireless network configuration? For example, if the network worked fine two minutes ago, and then you changed the WEP key on the access point, and now nobody can see the network, you have your solution—or at least your culprit! Did your office experience a power outage, power sag, or power surge? Any of these might cause a WAP to fail.

Once you figure out the who, what, and when, you can start troubleshooting in earnest. Typically, your problem is going to center on your hardware, software, connectivity, or configuration.

Hardware Troubleshooting

Wireless networking hardware components are subject to the same kind of abuse and faulty installation as any other hardware component. Troubleshooting a suspected hardware problem should bring out the technician in you.

Open Windows Device Manager and look for an error or conflict with the wireless adapter. If you see a big yellow exclamation point or a red X next to the device, you have either a driver error or a resource conflict. Reinstall the device driver or manually reset the IRQ resources as needed.

If you don't see the device listed at all, perhaps it is not seated properly in its PCI slot or not plugged all the way into its PC Card or USB slot. These problems are easy to fix. One thing to consider if you're using an older laptop and PC Card combination is that the wireless adapter may be a CardBus type of PC Card device. CardBus cards will not snap into a non-CardBus slot, even though both new and old cards are the same size. If your laptop is older than about five years, it may not support CardBus, meaning you need to get a different PC Card device. Or, if you've been looking for a reason to get a new laptop, now you have one!

Software Troubleshooting

Because you've already checked to confirm that your hardware is using the correct drivers, what kind of software-related problems are left to check? Two things come immediately to mind: the wireless adapter configuration utility and the WAP's firmware version.

As I mentioned earlier, some wireless devices won't work correctly unless you install the vendor-provided drivers and configuration utility before plugging in the device. This is particularly true of wireless USB devices. If you didn't do this, go into Device Manager and uninstall the device; then start again from scratch.

Some WAP manufacturers (I won't name names here, but they're popular) are notorious for shipping devices without the latest firmware installed. This problem often manifests as a device that enables clients to connect, but only at such slow speeds that the devices experience frequent timeout errors. The fix for this is to update the access point's firmware. Go to the manufacturer's Web site and follow the support links until you find the latest version. You'll need your device's exact model and serial number—this is important, because installing the wrong firmware version on your device is a guaranteed way of rendering it unusable!

Again, follow the manufacturer's instructions for updating the firmware to the letter. Typically, you need to download a small executable updating program along with a data file containing the firmware software. The process takes only minutes, and you'll be amazed at the results.

Connectivity Troubleshooting

Properly configured wireless clients should automatically and quickly connect to the desired SSID. If this isn't taking place, it's time for some troubleshooting. Most wireless connectivity problems come down to either an incorrect configuration (such as an incorrect password) or low signal strength. Without a strong signal, even a properly configured wireless client isn't going to work. Wireless clients use a multi-bar graph (usually five bars) to give an idea of signal strength: zero bars indicates no signal and five bars indicates maximum signal.

Whether configuration or signal strength, the process to diagnose and repair uses the same methods you use for a wired network. First, check the wireless NIC's link light to see whether it's passing data packets to and from the network. Second, check the wireless NIC's configuration utility. Typically the utility has an icon in your system tray that shows the strength of your wireless signal. Figure 24.27 shows Windows XP Professional's

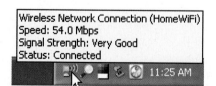

• Figure 24.27 Windows XP Professional's wireless configuration utility

built-in wireless configuration utility—called Wireless Zero Configuration (or just Zeroconf)—displaying the link state and signal strength.

The link state defines the wireless NIC's connection status to a wireless network: connected or disconnected. If your link state indicates that your computer is currently disconnected, you may have a problem with your WAP. If your signal is too weak to receive a signal, you may be out of range of your access point, or there may be a device causing interference.

You can fix these problems in a number of ways. Because Wi-Fi signals bounce off of objects, you can try small adjustments to your antennae to see if the signal improves. You can swap out the standard antenna for one or more higher-gain antennae. You can relocate the PC or access point, or locate and move the device causing interference.

Other wireless devices that operate in the same frequency range as your wireless nodes can cause interference as well. Look for wireless telephones, intercoms, and so on as possible culprits. One fix for interference caused by other wireless devices is to change the channel your network uses. Another is to change the channel the offending device uses, if possible. If you can't change channels, try moving the interfering device to another area or replacing it with a different device.

Configuration Troubleshooting

With all due respect to the fine network techs in the field, the most common type of wireless networking problem is misconfigured hardware or software. That's right—the dreaded *user error*! Given the complexities of wireless networking, this isn't so surprising. All it takes is one slip of the typing finger to throw off your configuration completely. The things you're most likely to get wrong are the SSID and security configuration.

Verify SSID configuration on your access point first, and then check on the affected wireless nodes. With most wireless devices you can use any characters in the SSID, including blank spaces. Be careful not to add blank characters where they don't belong, such as trailing blank spaces behind any other characters typed into the name field.

If you're using MAC address filtering, make sure the MAC address of the client that's attempting to access the wireless network is on the list of accepted users. This is particularly important if you swap out NICs on a PC, or if you introduce a new PC to your wireless network.

Check the security configuration to make sure that all wireless nodes and access points match. Mistyping an encryption key prevents the affected node from talking to the wireless network, even if your signal strength is 100 percent! Remember that many access points have the capability to export encryption keys onto a floppy disk or other removable media. It's then a simple matter to import the encryption key onto the PC by using the wireless NIC's configuration utility. Remember that the encryption level must match on access points and wireless nodes. If your WAP is configured for 128-bit encryption, all nodes must also use 128-bit encryption.

If you're lucky enough to have a laptop with an internally installed NIC (instead of a PC Card), your device may not have a link light.

Tech Tip

Windows XP and Zeroconf
One trick that works for wireless networks that seem a bit flaky with a Windows XP client is to disable the Wireless Zero Configuration service on the client. To do this, simply open the Services applet in Administrative Tools and change the Startup Type option from Automatic to Disabled. Document your change, of course, so you'll remember to turn Zeroconf back on in case it doesn't provide the fix you want.

Chapter 24 Review

■ Chapter Summary

After reading this chapter and completing the exercises, you should understand the following about wireless networking:

Discuss wireless networking components

- The wireless radio wave networks you'll find yourself supporting these days are those based on the IEEE 802.11 wireless Ethernet standard Wi-Fi and on the newer Bluetooth technology. Many cellular phone providers also provide Internet access through their networks. Wireless networks using infrared light use the IrDA protocol.

- Wireless networking capabilities of one form or another are built into many modern computing devices. Wireless Ethernet and Bluetooth are almost ubiquitous as integrated components or can easily be added by using USB, PCI, PCI Express, or PC Card adapters. Many handheld computers, smartphones, and PDAs have wireless capabilities built in or are available as add-on options.

- To extend the capabilities of a wireless Ethernet network, such as connecting to a wired network or sharing a high-speed Internet connection, you need a WAP. A WAP centrally connects wireless network nodes in the same way that a hub connects wired Ethernet PCs.

Analyze and explain wireless networking standards

- Wireless devices use the same networking protocols and client that their wired counterparts use, and they operate by using the CSMA/CA networking scheme, where nodes check before broadcasting. Wireless nodes also use the RTS/CTS protocol. When enabled, a transmitting node that determines that the wireless medium is clear to use sends an RTS frame to the receiving node. The receiving node responds with a CTS frame, telling the sending node that it's okay to transmit. Then, once the data is sent, the transmitting node waits for an acknowledgment (ACK) from the receiving node before sending the next data packet.

- You will need a utility to set parameters such as your SSID. Windows XP and up have built-in tools

for this, but otherwise you must rely on configuration tools provided by the wireless network adapter vendor.

- The simplest wireless network consists of two or more PCs communicating directly with each other without cabling or any other intermediary hardware (ad hoc mode). More complicated (and more common) wireless networks use a WAP to centralize wireless communication and bridge wireless network segments to wired network segments (infrastructure mode).

- Ad hoc networks are also good for temporary networks such as study groups or business meetings.

- Infrastructure mode is better suited to business networks or networks that need to share dedicated resources such as Internet connections and centralized databases.

- Out of the box, wireless networks have no security configured at all. Wireless devices want to be heard, and WAPs are usually configured to broadcast their presence to their maximum range and welcome all other wireless devices that respond. Further, data packets are floating through the air instead of safely wrapped up inside network cabling.

- Most WAPs support MAC address filtering, a method that enables you to limit access to your wireless network based on the physical, hard-wired address of the unit's wireless network adapter.

- Enabling WEP encrypts your data to secure it while in transit over the airwaves, but the WEP encryption standard itself is flawed and cannot be relied upon to protect your data against a knowledgeable and motivated attacker.

- WPA and WPA2 address the weaknesses of WEP and act as a sort of security protocol upgrade to WEP-enabled devices. WPA and WPA2 offer security enhancements such as an encryption key integrity-checking feature and user authentication through the industry-standard EAP.

- Depending on the standard used, wireless throughput speeds range from a measly 2 Mbps to a snappy 100+ Mbps. Wireless devices dynamically negotiate the top speed at which they can communicate without dropping too many data packets.

- Wireless networking speed and range are greatly affected by outside factors, such as interference from other wireless devices or solid objects. A wireless device's true effective range is probably about half the theoretical maximum listed by the manufacturer.

- 802.11a differs from the other 802.11-based standards in significant ways. Foremost, it operates in a different frequency range, 5 GHz, so 802.11a devices are less prone to interference. 802.11a also offers considerably greater throughput than 802.11 and 802.11b at speeds up to 54 Mbps, but its range tops out at only about 150 feet. 802.11a isn't widely adopted in the PC world.

- The 802.11b standard supports data throughput of up to 11 Mbps—on par with older wired 10BaseT networks—and a range of up to 300 feet under ideal conditions.

- The 802.11g standard offers data transfer speeds equivalent to 802.11a, up to 54 Mbps, with the wider 300-foot range of 802.11b. Because 802.11g is backward compatible with 802.11b, the same 802.11g WAP can service both 802.11g and 802.11b wireless nodes.

- 802.11n ups the speed even more to 100+ Mbps and extends the range to greater than 300 feet by using MIMO (multiple in/multiple out) with extra antennae. You can also configure it to use the less crowded 5-GHz band if you are using a dual-mode WAP.

- Wireless networking using infrared (IR) technology is enabled via the Infrared Data Association—IrDA—protocol stack, a widely supported industry standard, and has been included in all versions of Windows since Windows 95. IR is designed to make only a point-to-point connection between two devices in ad hoc mode of up to 4 Mbps, at a maximum distance of 1 meter.

- Bluetooth wireless technology is designed to create small wireless Personal Area Networks (PANs) that link PCs to peripheral devices such as PDAs and printers, input devices such as keyboards and mice, and even consumer electronics such as cell phones, home stereos, televisions, home security systems, and so on. Bluetooth is not designed to be a full-function networking solution.

- Cellular wireless networks enable you to connect to the Internet through a smartphone or portable computer with an access card with download speeds of around 1.5 Mbps. Cellular networks use various protocols, including GSM, GPRS, and CDMA. The current high-speed cellular network protocols are collectively called 3G.

Install and configure wireless networks

- The mechanics of setting up a wireless network don't differ much from a wired network. Physically installing a wireless network adapter is the same as installing a wired NIC, whether it's an internal PCI card, a PC Card, or an external USB device. Simply install the device and let plug and play handle detection and resource allocation. Unless you're using Windows XP or greater, you also need to install the wireless network configuration utility supplied with your wireless network adapter so you can set your SSID, communication mode, and so on.

- Wi-Fi networks support ad hoc and infrastructure operation modes. Which mode you choose depends on the number of wireless nodes you need to support, the type of data sharing they'll perform, and your management requirements.

- Ad hoc wireless networks don't need a WAP. The only requirements in an ad hoc mode wireless network are that each wireless node be configured with the same network name (SSID) and that no two nodes use the same IP address. You may also have to select a common channel for all ad hoc nodes.

- Typically, infrastructure mode wireless networks employ one or more WAPs connected to a wired network segment, a corporate intranet or the Internet, or both. As with ad hoc mode wireless networks, infrastructure mode networks require

that the same SSID be configured on all nodes and WAPs.

- WAPs have an integrated Web server and are configured through a browser-based setup utility. Typically, you enter the WAP's default IP address to bring up the configuration page and supply an administrative password, included with your WAP's documentation, to log in.

- Set up WEP encryption—if that's your only option—by turning encryption on at the WAP and then generating a unique security key. Then configure all connected wireless nodes on the network with the same key information. WPA and WPA2 encryption are configured in much the same way. You may be required to input a valid user name and password to configure encryption by using WPA/WPA2.

- As with other wireless networking solutions, Bluetooth devices are completely plug and play. Just connect the adapter and follow the prompts to install the appropriate drivers and configuration utilities. Connecting to a Bluetooth PAN is handled by specialized utility software provided by your portable device or Bluetooth device vendor.

Troubleshoot wireless networks

- As with any troubleshooting scenario, your first step should be to figure out the scope of your wireless networking problem. Ask yourself *who*, *what*, and *when*. This helps you focus your initial troubleshooting on the most likely aspects of the network.

- Hardware troubleshooting for Wi-Fi devices should touch on the usual hardware process. Go to Device Manager and check for obvious conflicts. Check the drivers to make sure you have them installed and up-to-date. Make certain you have proper connectivity between the device and the computer.

- Software troubleshooting involves checking configuration settings, such as the SSID, WEP, MAC address filtering, and encryption levels. Be sure to check configuration settings on both the WAP and the wireless NIC.

■ Key Terms

802.11a *(903)*
802.11b *(904)*
802.11g *(904)*
802.11i *(902)*
802.11n *(904)*
ad hoc mode *(900)*
Bluetooth *(906)*
carrier sense multiple access/collision avoidance (CSMA/CA) *(898)*
cellular wireless network *(907)*
dipole antennae *(914)*
gain *(914)*

IEEE 802.11 *(902)*
Infrared Data Association (IrDA) *(904)*
infrastructure mode *(900)*
MAC address filtering *(901)*
multiple in/multiple out (MIMO) *(904)*
personal area network (PAN) *(906)*
service set identifier (SSID) *(900)*
Wi-Fi *(902)*
Wi-Fi Protected Access (WPA) *(901)*
Wi-Fi Protected Access 2 (WPA2) *(902)*
Wired Equivalent Privacy (WEP) *(901)*
wireless access point (WAP) *(898)*

■ Key Term Quiz

Use the Key Terms list to complete the sentences that follow. Not all terms will be used.

1. A protocol for setting up wireless PANs and connecting to some peripherals is called _____.

2. Establishing a unique _____ or network name helps ensure that only wireless network devices configured similarly are permitted access to the network.

3. The wireless Ethernet standard that operates at a maximum of 54 Mbps on the 2.4-GHz frequency is _____.

4. Computers are in _____ when they connect directly together without using a WAP.

5. The 802.11 protocol is more commonly known as _____.

6. Of the three common wireless encryption protocols, _____ is the *least* secure.

7. The wireless Ethernet standard that runs at speeds up to 54 Mbps but has limited range because it uses the 5-GHz frequency is _____.

8. If you need to share an Internet connection or connect to a wired network through your wireless network, you would use _____.

9. The _____ feature enables devices on 802.11n networks to make multiple simultaneous connections, allowing for a theoretical throughput of 600 Mbps.

10. 802.11 implements _____, which proactively avoids network packet collisions rather than simply detecting them when they occur.

■ Multiple-Choice Quiz

1. Two wireless nodes that are communicating directly with each other, without any intermediary systems or hardware, are using what wireless mode?
   A. Ad hoc
   B. Bluetooth
   C. Infrastructure
   D. 802.11

2. What device centrally connects wireless network nodes in the same way that a hub connects wired Ethernet PCs?
   A. Bluetooth adapter
   B. Wireless NIC
   C. SSID
   D. WAP

3. What is the approximate range of an 802.11b/g network?
   A. ~1000 ft
   B. ~300 ft
   C. ~150 ft
   D. ~500 ft

4. Which encryption method used on wireless networks is the most secure?
   A. WEP
   B. Wi-Fi
   C. WINS
   D. WPA2

5. What can limit wireless connectivity to a list of accepted users based on the hard-wired address of their wireless NIC?
   A. Encryption
   B. MAC filtering
   C. NWLink
   D. WEP

6. Which wireless standard combines the longest range with the most throughput?
   A. 802.11a
   B. 802.11b
   C. 802.11g
   D. 802.11n

7. Personal area networks are created by what wireless technology?
   A. Bluetooth
   B. IrDA
   C. Wi-Fi
   D. Cellular wireless

8. What is the best technology if you need Internet access from anywhere in the country?
   A. Bluetooth
   B. IrDA
   C. Wi-Fi
   D. Cellular wireless

9. What standard gained a speed boost in its second version with Enhanced Data Rate technology?

   A. Bluetooth

   B. IrDA

   C. Wi-Fi

   D. Cellular wireless

10. Which of these Wi-Fi security protocols is the least secure and easily hacked?

    A. WEP

    B. WAP

    C. WINS

    D. WPA2

11. What is a cheap and easy way to extend the range of a WAP?

    A. Upgrade the antenna.

    B. Buy a WAP that advertises a longer range.

    C. You can't easily boost range.

    D. Upgrade the wireless NICs.

12. What is the technical name of a wireless network?

    A. SSID

    B. BSSID

    C. SSD

    D. WPA

13. What is the approximate range of a Bluetooth PAN?

    A. ~100 ft

    B. ~30 ft

    C. ~5 ft

    D. ~50 ft

14. Which of the following 802.11 standards can make use of both the 2.4- and 5-GHz bands?

    A. 802.11a

    B. 802.11b

    C. 802.11g

    D. 802.11n

15. Which of the following devices is a major source of interference for Wi-Fi networks?

    A. Cell phones

    B. Small FM radio transmitters

    C. Microwaves

    D. Fluorescent lights

■ Essay Quiz

1. Some friends of yours insist that wireless network standard 802.11a was available before 802.11b. They also say 802.11a is "better" than 802.11b. Find the pages in this chapter that discuss these standards, and jot down some notes to explain the facts.

2. You are enrolled in a writing class at the local community college. This week's assignment is to write on a technical subject. Write a short paragraph about each of the wireless standards that can reach theoretical speeds of 54 Mbps.

3. Prepare a short memo to your instructor (or friend) that outlines the basic differences between WEP and WPA encryption methods. Use any standard memo format you are familiar with. Include a company or school logo on the top of the page to make the memo appear to be printed on company stationery (or "letterhead").

4. Write a few paragraphs describing the pros and cons of both wired and wireless networks. Specifically, compare 100BaseT to the 802.11n standard. Then conclude with a statement of your own personal preference. You'll need to draw on information you found in this chapter and in Chapter 23, "Local Area Networking."

Lab Projects

• Lab Project 24.1

You just received a nice tax return and want to expand your home network. Your current wired home network setup consists of two Intel Pentium 4–class desktop PCs with 10/100-Mbps NICs and a relative's older laptop with both an RJ-45 port and 802.11b wireless built in. The main Internet connection coming into your home enters your more powerful desktop system first and then spreads out to a 100-Mbps switch from there. With your own money to be spent buying equipment, you seek a solution that will satisfy your needs for a long time.

You want to buy your new equipment locally so you can set it up right away. Use the Internet to explore prices and equipment in local stores. Also check out reviews of the items you are interested in obtaining. After you have done sufficient research, prepare an itemized price list with your choices arranged like the following table:

ITEM	STORE/MODEL	PRICE	QUANTITY	TOTAL
Wireless NICs, PCI				
Wireless NICs, PC Card				
Wireless Access Point				
Other				
TOTALS				

• Lab Project 24.2

You have been tasked with expanding your company's wireless network. Your IT Manager asked you to create a presentation that explains wireless routers and their functions. She specifically said to focus on the 802.11g and 802.11n wireless network standards. Create a brief, yet informative PowerPoint presentation that includes comparisons of these two technologies. You may include images of actual wireless bridges from vendor Web sites as needed, being sure to cite your sources. Include any up-to-date prices from your research as well.

The Internet

"The Internet is a great way to get on the Net."

— BOB DOLE

In this chapter, you will learn how to

■ **Explain how the Internet works**

■ **Connect to the Internet**

■ **Use Internet software tools**

Imagine coming home from a long day at work building and fixing PCs, sitting down in front of your shiny new computer, double-clicking the single icon that sits dead center on your monitor...and suddenly you're enveloped in an otherworldly scene, where 200-foot trees slope smoothly into snow-white beaches and rich blue ocean. Overhead, pterodactyls soar through the air while you talk to a small chap with pointy ears and a long robe about heading up the mountain in search of a giant monster.... TV show from the SciFi channel? Spielberg's latest film offering? How about an interactive game played by millions of people all over the planet on a daily basis by connecting to the Internet? If you guessed the last one, you're right.

This chapter covers the skills you need as a PC tech to help people connect to the Internet. It starts with a brief section on how the Internet works, along with the concepts of connectivity, and then it goes into the specifics on hardware, protocols, and software that you use to make the Internet work for you (or for your client). Let's get started!

■ How the Internet Works

Thanks to the Internet, people can communicate with one another over vast distances, often in the blink of an eye. As a PC tech, you need to know how PCs communicate with the larger world for two reasons. First, knowing the process and pieces involved in the communication enables you to troubleshoot effectively when that communication goes away. Second, you need to be able to communicate knowledgeably with a network technician who comes in to solve a more complex issue.

Internet Tiers

You probably know that the Internet is millions and millions of computers all joined together to form the largest network on earth, but not many folks know much about how these computers are organized. To keep everything running smoothly, the Internet is broken down into groups called **tiers**. The main tier, called *Tier 1*, consists of nine companies called *Tier 1 providers*. The Tier 1 providers own long-distance, high-speed fiber-optic networks called *backbones*. These backbones span the major cities of the earth (not all Tier 1 backbones go to all cities) and interconnect at special locations called *network access points* (*NAPs*). Anyone wishing to connect to any of the Tier 1 providers must pay large sums of money. The Tier 1 providers do not charge each other.

Tier 2 providers own smaller, regional networks and must pay the Tier 1 providers. Most of the famous companies that provide Internet access to the general public are Tier 2 providers. *Tier 3 providers* are even more regional and connect to Tier 2 providers.

The piece of equipment that makes this tiered Internet concept work is called a backbone router. *Backbone routers* connect to more than one other backbone router, creating a big, interwoven framework for communication.

Figure 25.1 illustrates the decentralized and interwoven nature of the Internet. The key reason for interweaving the backbones of the Internet was to provide alternative pathways for data if one or more of the routers went down. If Jane in Houston sends a message to her friend Polly in New York City, for example, the shortest path between Jane and Polly in this hypothetical situation is this: Jane's message originates at Rice University in Houston, bounces to Emory University in Atlanta, flits through Virginia Commonwealth University in Richmond, and then zips into SUNY in New York

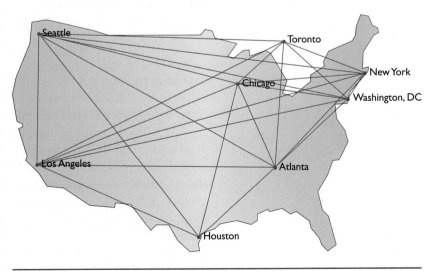

• **Figure 25.1**   Internet Tier 1 connections

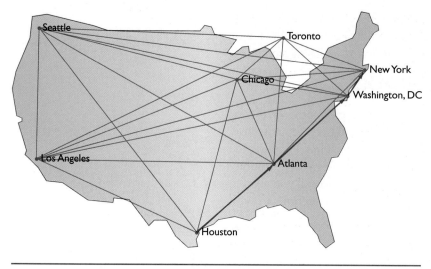

● **Figure 25.2**   Message traveling from Houston to NYC

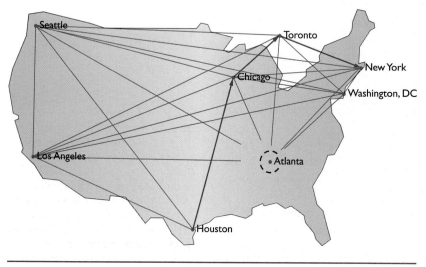

● **Figure 25.3**   Rerouted message from Houston to NYC

City (Figure 25.2). Polly happily reads the message and life is great. The Internet functions as planned.

But what happens if the entire southeastern United States experiences a huge power outage and Internet backbones in every state from Virginia to Florida go down? Jane's message would bounce back to Rice and the Rice computers. Being smart cookies, the routers would reroute the message to nodes that still functioned— say, Rice to University of Chicago, to University of Toronto, and then to SUNY (Figure 25.3). It's all in a day's work for the highly redundant and adaptable Internet. At this point in the game (2009), the Internet simply cannot go down fully—barring, of course, a catastrophe of Biblical proportions.

TCP/IP—The Common Language of the Internet

As you know from all the earlier chapters in this book, hardware alone doesn't cut it in the world of computing. You need software to make the machines run and create an interface for humans. The Internet is no exception. TCP/IP provides the basic software structure for communication on the Internet.

Because you spent a good deal of Chapter 23, "Local Area Networking," working with TCP/IP, you should have an appreciation for its adaptability and, perhaps more importantly, its extendibility. TCP/IP provides the addressing scheme for computers that communicate on the Internet through IP addresses, such as 192.168.4.1 or 16.45.123.7. As a protocol, though, TCP/IP is much more than just an addressing system. TCP/IP provides the framework and common language for the Internet. And it offers a phenomenally wide-open structure for creative purposes. Programmers can write applications built to take advantage of the TCP/IP structure and features, creating what are called TCP/IP services. The cool thing about TCP/IP services is that they're limited only by the imagination of the programmers.

You'll learn much more about TCP/IP services in the software and "Beyond A+" sections of this chapter, but I must mention one service that you've most likely worked with yourself, whether you knew them by that

term or not. The most famous service is the **Hypertext Transfer Protocol (HTTP)**, the service that provides the structure for the **World Wide Web** ("the Web," for short), the graphical face of the Internet. Using your **Web browser**—a program specifically designed to retrieve, interpret, and display Web pages—an almost endless variety of information and entertainment is just a click away. I can't tell you how many times I've started to look up something on the Web, and suddenly it's two hours later and I still haven't looked up what I started out wanting to know, but I don't actually care, because I've learned some amazing stuff! But then when I do go look it up, in just minutes I can find information it used to take *days* to uncover. The Web can arguably claim the distinction of being both the biggest time-waster and the biggest time-saver since the invention of the book!

At this point, you have an enormous, beautifully functioning network. All the backbone routers connect with fiber and thick copper cabling backbones, and TCP/IP enables communication and services for building applications for humans to interface across the distances. What's left? Oh, that's right: how do you tap into this great network and partake of its goodness?

Internet Service Providers

Every Tier 1 and Tier 2 provider leases connections to the Internet to companies called **Internet service providers (ISPs)**. ISPs essentially sit along the edges of the Tier 1 and Tier 2 Internet and tap into the flow. You can, in turn, lease some of the connections from the ISP and thus get on the Internet.

ISPs come in all sizes. Comcast, the huge cable television provider, has multiple, huge-capacity connections into the Internet, enabling its millions of customers to connect from their local machines and surf the Web. Contrast Comcast with Unísono, an ISP in San Miguel de Allende, Mexico (Figure 25.4). Billed as the "Best Internet Service in San Miguel," it services only a small (but delightful) community and the busy tourist crowd.

Connection Concepts

Connecting to an ISP requires two things to work perfectly: hardware for connectivity, such as a modem and a working cable line; and software, such as protocols to govern the connections and the data flow (all configured in Windows) and applications to take advantage of the various TCP/IP services. Once you have a contract with an ISP to grant you access to the Internet, the ISP gives you TCP/IP configuration numbers and data so you can set up your software to connect directly to a router at the ISP that becomes your gateway to the Internet. The router to which you connect at the ISP, by the way, is often referred to as the **default gateway**. Once you configure your software correctly, you can connect to the ISP and get to the greater Internet. Figure 25.5 shows a standard PC-to-ISP-to-Internet connection. Note that various protocols and other software manage the connectivity between your PC and the default gateway.

Microsoft calls the connections ISPs make to the Internet *access points*, which I think is a very bad name. You'd think we'd be able to come up with new terms for things! Instead, some folks in this industry continue rebranding things with the same phrases or catchwords, only serving to confuse already bewildered consumers.

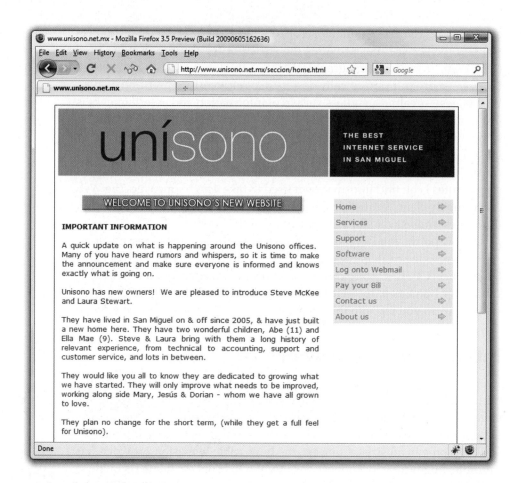

• **Figure 25.4** Unísono homepage

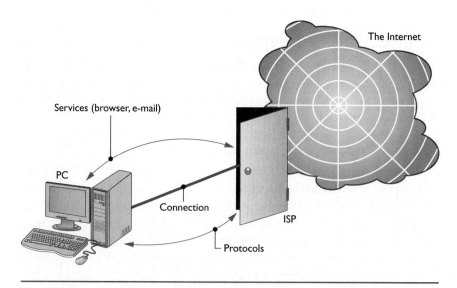

• **Figure 25.5** Simplified Internet connectivity

▓ Connecting to the Internet

PCs commonly connect to an ISP by using one of seven technologies that fit into four categories: dial-up, both analog and ISDN; dedicated, such as DSL, cable, and LAN; wireless; and satellite. Analog dial-up is the slowest of the bunch and requires a telephone line and a special networking device called a modem. ISDN uses digital dial-up and has much greater speed. All the others use a regular Ethernet NIC like you played with in Chapter 23, "Local Area Networking." Satellite is the odd one out here; it may use either a modem or a NIC, depending on the particular configuration you have, although most folks will use a NIC. Let's take a look at all these various connection options.

Dial-up

A dial-up connection to the Internet requires two pieces to work: hardware to dial the ISP, such as a modem or ISDN terminal adapter; and software to govern the connection, such as Microsoft's **Dial-up Networking (DUN)**. Let's look at the hardware first, and then we'll explore software configuration.

Modems

At some point in the early days of computing, some bright guy or gal noticed a colleague talking on a telephone, glanced down at a PC, and then put two and two together: why not use telephone lines for data communication? The basic problem with this idea is that traditional telephone lines use analog signals, while computers use digital signals (Figure 25.6). Creating a dial-up network required equipment that could turn digital data into an analog signal to send it over the telephone line, and then turn it back into digital data when it reached the other end of the connection. A device called a modem solved this dilemma.

Modems enable computers to talk to each other via standard commercial telephone lines by converting analog signals to digital signals, and vice versa. The term *modem* is short for modulator/demodulator, a description of transforming the signals. Telephone wires transfer data via analog signals that continuously change voltages on a wire. Computers hate analog signals. Instead, they need digital signals, voltages that are either on or off, meaning the wire has voltage present or it does not. Computers, being binary by nature, use only two states of voltage: zero volts and positive volts. Modems take analog signals from telephone lines and turn them into digital signals that the PC can understand (Figure 25.7). Modems also take digital signals from the PC and convert them into analog signals for the outgoing telephone line.

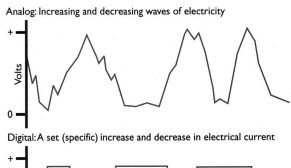

Analog: Increasing and decreasing waves of electricity

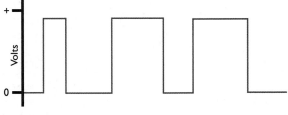

Digital: A set (specific) increase and decrease in electrical current

• **Figure 25.6**   Analog signals used by a telephone line versus digital signals used by the computer

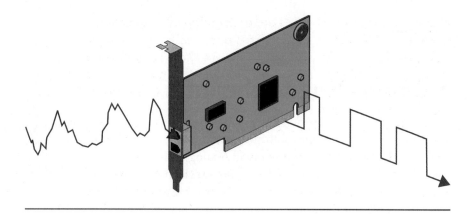

• **Figure 25.7**   Modem converting analog signal to digital signal

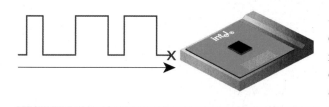

• **Figure 25.8**   CPUs can't read serial data.

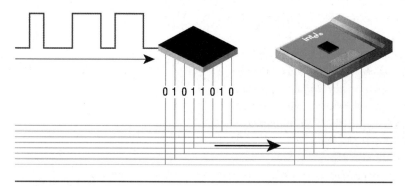

0 1 0 1 1 0 1 0

• **Figure 25.9**   The UART chip converts serial data to parallel data that the CPU can read.

A modem does what is called *serial communication*: It transmits data as a series of individual ones and zeros. The CPU can't process data this way. It needs parallel communication, transmitting and receiving data in discrete 8-bit chunks (Figure 25.8). The individual serial bits of data are converted into 8-bit parallel data that the PC can understand through the **universal asynchronous receiver/ transmitter (UART)** chip (Figure 25.9).

There are many types of UARTs, each with different functions. All serial communication devices are really little more than UARTs. *External* modems can convert analog signals to digital ones and vice versa, but they must rely on the serial ports to which they're connected for the job of converting between serial and parallel data (Figure 25.10). Internal modems can handle both jobs because they have their own UART built in (Figure 25.11).

Phone lines have a speed based on a unit called a **baud**, which is one cycle per second. The fastest rate that a phone line can

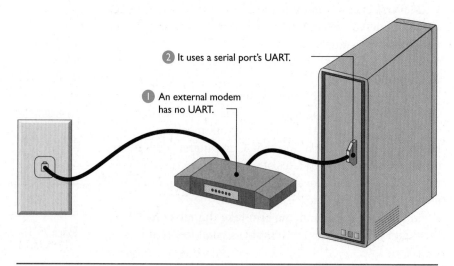

2 It uses a serial port's UART.

1 An external modem has no UART.

• **Figure 25.10**   An external modem uses the PC's serial port.

achieve is 2,400 baud. Modems can pack multiple bits of data into each baud; a 33.6 kilobits per second (Kbps) modem, for example, packs 14 bits into every baud: 2,400 × 14 = 33.6 Kbps. Thus, it is technically incorrect to say, "I have a 56 K baud modem." The correct statement is, "I have a 56 Kbps modem." But don't bother; people have used the term "baud" instead of **bits per second (bps)** so often for so long that the terms have become functionally synonymous.

Modern Modem Standards: V.90 versus V.92   The fastest data transfer speed a modem can handle is based on its implementation of one of the international standards for modem technology: the **V standards**. Set by the International Telecommunication Union (ITU), the current top standards are V.90 and V.92. Both standards offer download speeds of just a hair under 56 Kbps, but they differ in upload speeds: up to 33.6 Kbps for V.90, and up to 48 Kbps for V.92 modems. To get anywhere near the top speeds of a V.90 or V.92 modem requires a comparable modem installed on the other line and connecting telephone lines in excellent condition. In practice, you'll rarely get faster throughput than about 48 Kbps for downloads and 28 Kbps for uploads.

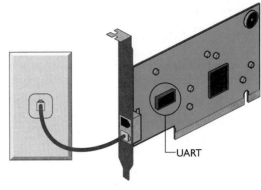

• **Figure 25.11**   An internal modem has UART built in.

Flow Control (Handshaking)   Flow control, also known as **handshaking**, is the process by which two serial devices verify a conversation. Imagine people talking on a CB radio. When one finishes speaking, he will say "over." That way the person listening can be sure that the sender is finished speaking before she starts. Each side of the conversation is verified. During a file transfer, two distinct conversations take place that require flow control: local (between modem and COM port) and end-to-end (between modems).

The modems themselves handle end-to-end flow control. PCs can do local flow control between the modem and COM port in two ways: hardware and software. Hardware flow control employs extra wires in the serial connection between the modem and the COM port to let one device tell the other that it is ready to send or receive data. These extra wires are called *ready to send* (*RTS*) and *clear to send* (*CTS*), so hardware handshaking is often called RTS/CTS. Software flow control uses a special character called XON to signal that data flow is beginning, and another special character called XOFF to signal that data transmission is finished; therefore, software handshaking is often called XON/XOFF. Software handshaking is slower and not as dependable as hardware handshaking, so you rarely see it.

Bells and Whistles   Although the core modem technology has changed little in the past few years, modem manufacturers have continued to innovate on many peripheral fronts—pardon the pun. You can walk into a computer store nowadays, for example, and buy a V.92 modem that comes bundled with an excellent fax machine and a digital answering machine. You can even buy modems that you can call remotely that will wake up your PC (Figure 25.12). What will they think up next?

Modem Connections   Internal modems connect to the PC very differently than external modems. Almost all internal modems connect to a PCI or PCI Express expansion bus slot inside the

• **Figure 25.12**   Some of the many features touted by the manufacturer of the SupraMax modem

PC, although cost-conscious manufacturers may use smaller modems that fit in special expansion slots designed to support multiple communications features such as modems, NICs, and sound cards (Figure 25.13). Older AMD motherboards used Audio/Modem Riser (AMR) or Advanced Communication Riser (ACR) slots, while Intel motherboards used Communication and Networking Riser (CNR) slots.

External modems connect to the PC through an available serial port (the old way) or USB port (Figure 25.14). Many older PCs came with 9-pin serial ports, whereas most external modems designed to connect to a serial port come with a 25-pin connector. That means you will probably need a 9-to-25-pin converter, available at any computer store, to connect your external modem. Serial ports are now quite rare as virtually all computers today have two or more USB ports.

Don't fret about USB versus serial for your modem connection, as the very low speeds of data communication over a modem make the physical type of the connection unimportant. Even the slow, aging serial interface more than adequately handles 56 Kbps data transfers. If you have the option, choose a USB modem, especially one with a volume control knob. USB offers simple plug and play and easy portability between machines, plus such modems require no external electrical source, getting all the power they need from the USB connection.

Dial-up Networking

The software side of dial-up networks requires configuration within Windows to include information provided by your ISP. The ISP provides a dial-up telephone number or numbers, as well as your user name and initial password. In addition, the ISP will tell you about any special configuration options you need to specify in the software setup. The full configuration of dial-up networking is beyond the scope of this book, but you should at least know where to go to follow instructions from your ISP. Let's take a look at the Network and Internet Connections applet in Windows XP.

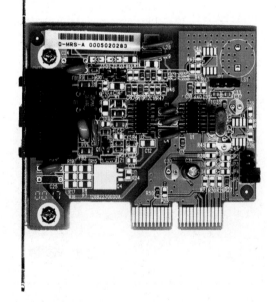

• **Figure 25.13** A CNR modem

• **Figure 25.14** A USB modem

Network Connections To start configuring a dial-up connection in Windows XP, open the Control Panel. Select Network and Internet Connections from the Pick a category menu and then choose *Set up or change your Internet connection* from the Pick a task menu The Internet Properties dialog box opens with the Connections tab displayed (Figure 25.15). All your work will proceed from here.

Click the Setup button to run the New Connection Wizard (Figure 25.16), and then work through the screens. At this point, you're going to need information provided by your ISP to configure your connection properly. When you finish the configuration, you'll see a new Connect To option on the Start menu if your system is set up that way. If not, open up Network Connections, and your new dial-up connection will be available. Figure 25.17 shows the option to connect to a fictitious ISP, Cool-Rides.com.

PPP Dial-up links to the Internet have their own special hardware protocol called **Point-to-Point Protocol (PPP)**. PPP is a streaming protocol developed especially for dial-up Internet access. To Windows, a modem is nothing more than a special type of network adapter. Modems have their own configuration entry in the Network Connections applet.

Most dial-up "I can't connect to the Internet"–type problems are user errors. Your first area of investigation is the modem itself. Use the modem's properties to make sure the volume is turned up. Have the user listen to the connection. Does she hear a dial tone? If she doesn't, make sure the modem's line is plugged into a good phone jack. Does she hear the modem dial and then hear someone saying, "Hello? Hello?" If so, she probably dialed

Cross Check

Installing a PCI Modem

Installing a PCI modem card involves pretty much the same process as installing any other PCI card. Refer to Chapter 8, "Expansion Bus," and cross check your knowledge of the process.

1. What do you need to guard against when installing a PCI card?

2. Any issues involving drivers, plug and play, or other hardware topics?

• **Figure 25.15** The Connections tab in the Internet Properties dialog box

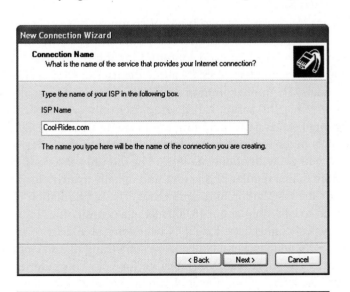

• **Figure 25.16** The New Connection Wizard

● **Figure 25.17**　Connection options in Network Connections

the wrong number! Wrong password error messages are fairly straightforward—remember that the password may be correct but the user name may be wrong. If she still fails to connect, it's time to call the network folks to see what is configured improperly in the Dial-up Networking settings.

ISDN

A standard telephone connection comprises many pieces. First, the phone line runs from your phone out to a network interface box (the little box on the side of your house) and into a central switch belonging to the telephone company. (In some cases, intermediary steps are present.) Standard metropolitan areas have a large number of central offices, each with a central switch. Houston, Texas, for example, has nearly 100 offices in the general metro area. These central switches connect to each other through high-capacity *trunk lines*. Before 1970, the entire phone system was analog; over time, however, phone companies began to upgrade their trunk lines to digital systems. Today, the entire telephone system, with the exception of the line from your phone to the central office, and sometimes even that, is digital.

During this upgrade period, customers continued to demand higher throughput from their phone lines. The old telephone line was not expected to produce more than 28.8 Kbps (56 K modems, which were a *big* surprise to the phone companies, didn't appear until 1995). Needless to say, the phone companies were very motivated to come up with a way to generate higher capacities. Their answer was actually fairly straightforward: make the entire phone system digital. By adding special equipment at the central office and the user's location, phone companies can now achieve a throughput of up to 64 K per line (see the paragraphs following) over the same copper wires already used by telephone lines. This process of sending telephone transmission across fully digital lines end-to-end is called **integrated services digital network (ISDN)** service.

ISDN service consists of two types of channels: Bearer, or B, channels and Delta, or D, channels. B channels carry data and voice information at 64 Kbps. D channels carry setup and configuration information and carry data at 16 Kbps. Most providers of ISDN allow the user to choose either one or two B channels. The more common setup is two B/one D, usually called a *basic rate interface* (*BRI*) setup. A BRI setup uses only one physical line, but each B channel sends 64 K, doubling the throughput total to 128 K. ISDN also connects much faster than modems, eliminating that long, annoying, mating call you get with phone modems. The monthly cost per B channel is slightly more than a regular phone line, and usually a fairly steep initial fee is levied for the installation and equipment. The big limitation is that you usually need to be within about 18,000 feet of a central office to use ISDN.

The physical connections for ISDN bear some similarity to analog modems. An ISDN wall socket usually looks something like a standard RJ-45 network jack. The most common interface for your computer is a device called a *terminal adapter* (*TA*). TAs look much like regular modems, and like

Another type of ISDN, called a primary rate interface (PRI), is composed of twenty-three 64-Kbps B channels and one 64-Kbps D channel, giving it a total throughput of 1.5 megabits per second. PRI ISDN lines are also known as T1 lines.

modems, they come in external and internal variants. You can even get TAs that are also hubs, enabling your system to support a direct LAN connection.

DSL

Digital subscriber line (DSL) connections to ISPs use a standard telephone line but special equipment on each end to create always-on Internet connections at blindingly fast speeds, especially when compared with analog dial-up connections. Service levels vary around the United States, but the typical upload speed is ~768 Kbps, while download speed comes in at a very sweet ~3+ Mbps!

DSL requires little setup from a user standpoint. A tech comes to the house to install the DSL receiver, often called a DSL modem (Figure 25.18), and possibly hook up a wireless router. The receiver connects to the telephone line and the PC (Figure 25.19). The tech (or the user, if knowledgeable) then configures the DSL modem and router (if there is one) with the settings provided by the ISP, and that's about it! Within moments, you're surfing at blazing speeds. You don't need a second telephone line. You don't need to wear a special propeller hat or anything. The only kicker is that your house has to be within a fairly short distance from a main phone service switching center, something like 18,000 feet.

> The two most common forms of DSL you'll find are *asynchronous* (*ADSL*) and *synchronous* (*SDSL*). ADSL lines differ between slow upload speed (such as 384 Kbps, 768 Kbps, and 1 Mbps) and faster download speed (usually 3–7 Mbps). SDSL has the same upload and download speeds, but telecom companies charge a lot more for the privilege. DSL encompasses many such variations, so you'll often see it referred to as *x*DSL.

• **Figure 25.18**   A DSL receiver

Cable

Cable offers a different approach to high-speed Internet access, using regular cable TV cables to serve up lightning-fast speeds. It offers faster service than most DSL connections, with a 1–10 Mbps upload and 6–50+ Mbps download.

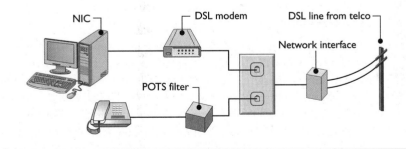

• **Figure 25.19**   DSL connections

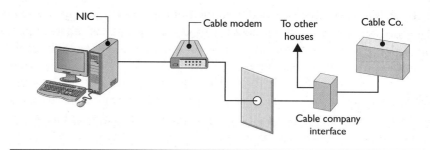

• Figure 25.20   Cable connections

Cable Internet connections are theoretically available anywhere you can get cable TV.

Cable Internet connections start with an RG-6 or RG-59 cable coming into your house. The cable connects to a cable modem that then connects to a NIC in your PC via UTP Ethernet cable. Figure 25.20 shows a typical cable setup. One nice advantage of cable over DSL is that if you have a TV tuner card in your PC, you can use the same cable connection (with a splitter) to watch TV on your PC. Both DSL and cable modem Internet connections can be used by two or more computers if they are part of a LAN, including those in a home.

LAN

Most businesses connect their internal local area network (LAN) to an ISP via some hardware solution that Network+ techs deal with. Figure 25.21 shows a typical small-business wiring closet with routers that connect the LAN to the ISP. You learned all about wiring up a LAN in Chapter 23, "Local Area Networking," so there's no need to go through any basics here. To complete a LAN connection to the Internet, you need to add a second NIC or a modem to one of the PCs and then configure that PC as the default connection. We'll revisit this idea in a moment with Internet Connection Sharing.

Wireless

Every once in a while a technology comes along that, once the kinks are smoothed out, works flawlessly, creating a magical computing experience. Unfortunately, the various wireless networking technologies out there today don't fulfill that dream yet. When they work, it's like magic. You walk into a coffee shop, sit down, and flip open your laptop computer. After firing up your Internet browser, suddenly you're quaffing lattes and surfing Web sites—with no wires at all.

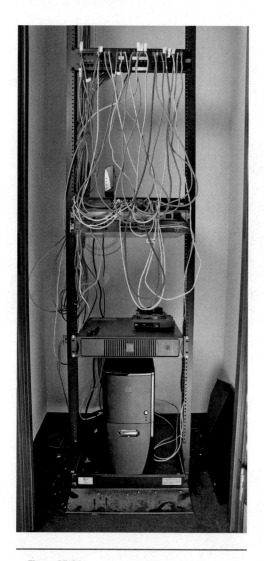

• Figure 25.21   A wiring closet

Suffice it to say that connecting to the Internet via wireless means that you must connect to a cellular network or to a LAN that's wired to an ISP. The local Internet café purchases high-speed Internet service from the cable or telecom company, for example, and then connects a wireless access point (WAP) to its network. When you walk in with your portable PC with wireless NIC and open a Web browser, the wireless NIC communicates with the *fully wired* DHCP server via the WAP and you're surfing on the Internet. It appears magically wireless, but the LAN to ISP connection still uses wires.

Cellular networking is even more seamless. Anywhere you can connect with your cell phone, you can connect with your cellular network–aware portable or laptop computer.

One form of wireless communication does not require local wires. For *Wireless broadband*, the ISP must put up a tower, and then any building within the line of sight (perhaps up to 10 miles) can get a high-speed connection.

Satellite

Satellite connections to the Internet get the data beamed to a satellite dish on your house or office; a receiver handles the flow of data, eventually sending it through an Ethernet cable to the NIC in your PC. I can already sense people's eyebrows raising. "Yeah, that's the download connection. But what about the upload connection?" Very astute, me hearties! The early days of satellite required you to connect via a modem. You would upload at the slow 26- to 48-Kbps modem speed, but then get super-fast downloads from the dish. It worked, so why complain? You really can move to that shack on the side of the Himalayas to write the great Tibetan novel and still have DSL- or cable-speed Internet connectivity. Sweet!

Satellite might be the most intriguing of all the technologies used to connect to the Internet today. As with satellite television, though, you need to have the satellite dish point at the satellites (toward the south if you live in the United States). The only significant issue to satellite is that the distance the signal must travel creates a small delay called the *satellite latency*. This latency is usually unnoticeable unless the signal degrades in foul weather such as rain and snow.

Windows Internet Connection Sharing

Internet Connection Sharing (ICS) enables one system to share its Internet connection with other systems on the network, providing a quick and easy method for multiple systems to use one Internet connection. Modern Windows versions (Windows 2000 through Windows 7) also provide this handy tool. Figure 25.22 shows a typical setup for ICS. Note the terminology used here. The PC that connects to the Internet and then shares that connection via ICS with other machines on a LAN is called the *ICS host* computer. PCs that connect via LAN to the ICS host computer are simply called client computers.

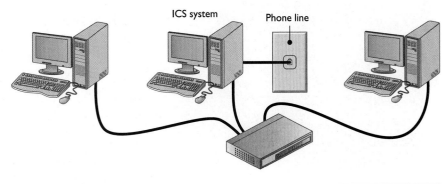

• **Figure 25.22**   Typical ICS setup

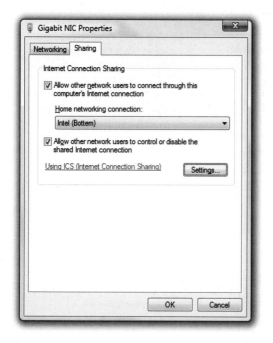

To connect multiple computers to a single ICS host computer requires several things in place. First, the ICS host computer has to have a NIC dedicated to the internal connections. If you connect via dial-up, for example, the ICS host computer uses a modem to connect to the Internet. It also has a NIC that plugs into a switch. Other PCs on the LAN likewise connect to the switch. If you connect via some faster service, such as DSL that uses a NIC cabled to the DSL receiver, you'll need a second NIC in the ICS host machine to connect to the LAN and the client computers.

Setting up ICS in Windows is very simple. If you are using Windows 2000 or XP, open the properties dialog for My Network Places. If you are using Windows Vista or 7, open the Network and Sharing Center and click on *Manage network connections* (Vista) or *Change adapter settings* (7) in the left-hand task list. Now access the properties of the connection you wish to share.

Click the Sharing tab (Windows 2000/Vista/7) or the Advanced tab (Windows XP), and select *Enable Internet connection sharing for this connection* (Windows 2000) or *Allow other network users to connect through this computer's Internet connection* (Windows XP/Vista/7, Figure 25.23). Clients don't need any special configuration but should simply be set to DHCP for their IP address and other configurations.

• **Figure 25.23**   Enabling Internet Connection Sharing in Windows Vista

Hardware Connection Sharing

Although Windows Internet Connection Sharing works, it has a major drawback—you must leave the computer running all the time so the other computers on the network can access the Internet. This is where the small home router fits perfectly. Several manufacturers offer robust, easy-to-configure routers that enable multiple computers to connect to a single Internet connection. These boxes require very little configuration and provide firewall protection between the primary computer and the Internet, which you'll learn more about in Chapter 26, "Securing Computers." All it takes to install one of these routers is simply to plug your computer into any of the LAN ports on the back, and then to plug the cable from your Internet connection into the port labeled Internet or WAN.

A great example of a home router is the Linksys WRT54G (Figure 25.24). This little DSL/cable router, for example, has four 10/100 Ethernet ports for the LAN computers, and a WiFi radio for any wireless computers you may have. The Linksys, like all home routers, uses a technology called **Network Address Translation**, or **NAT** for short. NAT performs a little network subterfuge: it presents an entire LAN of computers to the Internet as a single machine. It effectively hides all of your computers and makes them appear invisible to other computers on the Internet. All anyone on the Internet sees is your *public* IP address. This is the address your ISP gives you, while all the computers in your LAN use private addresses that are invisible to

• **Figure 25.24**   Common home router with Wi-Fi

the world. NAT therefore acts as a firewall, protecting your internal network from probing or malicious users from the outside.

Basic Router Configuration

These small routers require very little in the way of configuration if all you need is basic Internet connection sharing. In some cases, though, you may have to deal with a more complex network that requires changing the router's settings. The vast majority of these routers have built-in configuration Web pages that you access by typing the router's IP address into a browser. The address varies by manufacturer, so check the router's documentation. If you typed in the correct address, you should then receive a prompt for a user name and password, as in Figure 25.25. As with the IP address, the default user name and password change depending on the model/manufacturer. Once you enter the correct credentials, you will be greeted by the router's configuration page (Figure 25.26). From these pages, you can change any of the router's settings. Now look at a few of the basic settings that CompTIA wants you to be familiar with.

• **Figure 25.25**   Router asking for user name and password

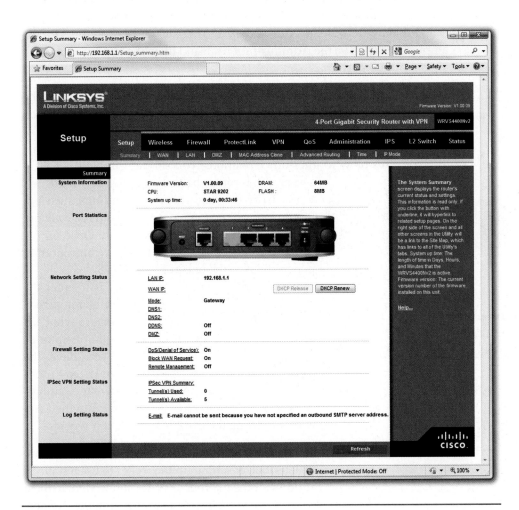

• **Figure 25.26**   Configuration home page

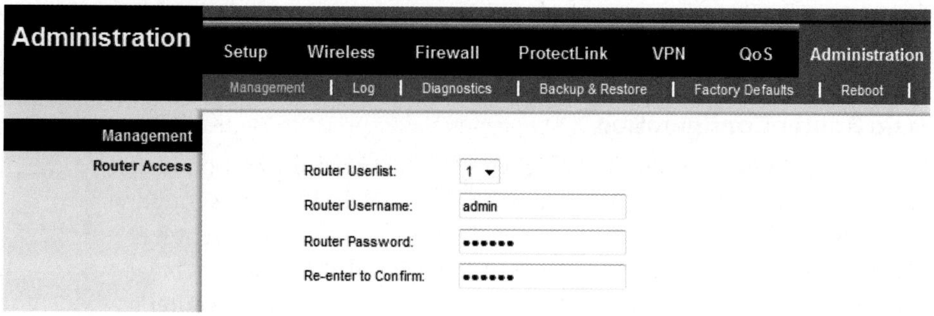

● Figure 25.27   Changing the user name and password

Changing User Name and Password   One of the first changes you should make to your router after you have it working is to change the user name and password to something other than the default. This is especially important if you have open wireless turned on, which you'll recall from Chapter 24, "Wireless Networking." If you leave the default user name and password, anyone who has access to your LAN can easily gain access to the router and change its settings. Fortunately, router manufacturers make it easy to change a router's login credentials. On this Linksys of mine, for example, I just click on the Administration tab and fill in the appropriate boxes as shown in Figure 25.27.

Disabling DHCP   If you are configuring a router for a small office, the router's built-in DHCP server might conflict with a domain controller on your network. These conflicts, although not dangerous, can cause a lot of frustration and shouting as everyone's network connections stop working. To avoid this blow to inter-office relations, you should disable the DHCP server in the router before you plug it into the network. To do this, use a separate computer such as a laptop, or unplug your computer from the wall and plug it into the new router to log in. Once on the configuration screen, you will see a configuration page similar to the one in Figure 25.28.

Once the DHCP server is disabled, the router will no longer hand out IP addresses, so you must make sure that the router's IP address is in the correct subnet of your office's LAN. If it isn't, you need to change it before you disable DHCP.

On my router, all that is needed is to enter the new address and subnet at the top of the screen shown in Figure 25.28. If you are unsure what address you need, ask your network administrator or CompTIA Network+ tech. Once you have the router's IP address taken care of, all you need to do is click the Disable radio button and save the settings. Now you can safely plug your router into the LAN without risking the ire of Internet-less coworkers.

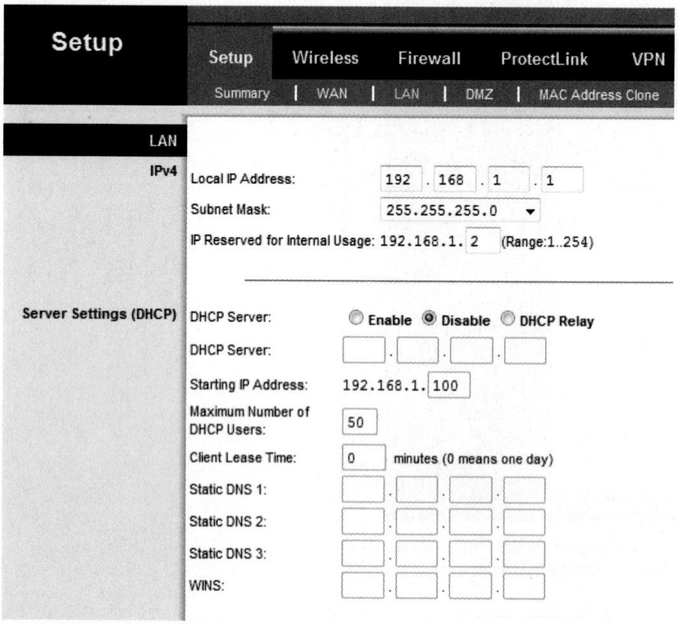

Setting Static IP Addresses   With that all taken care of, let's look at setting up the router to use a static IP address for the Internet or WAN connection. In most cases, when you plug in the router's Internet connection, it receives an IP address using DHCP just like

● Figure 25.28   Configuring the DHCP server

any other computer. Of course, this means that your Internet IP address will change from time to time, which can be a bit of a downside. This does not affect most people, but for some home users and businesses, it can present a problem. To solve this problem, most ISPs enable you to order a static IP. Once your ISP has allocated you a static IP address, you must manually enter it into your router. You do this the same way as all the previous changes you've just looked at. My router has a WAN configuration tab where I can enter all the settings that my ISP has provided me (Figure 25.29). Remember, you must change your connection type from Automatic/DHCP to Static IP to enter the new addresses.

Updating Firmware

Routers are just like any other computer in that they run software—and software has bugs, vulnerabilities, and other issues that sometimes require updating. The router manufacturers call these "firmware updates" and make them available on their Web sites for easy download. To update a modern router, you simply have to download the latest firmware from the manufacturer's Web site to your computer. Then you enter the router's configuration Web page and find the firmware update screen. On my router, it looks like Figure 25.30. From here, just follow the directions and click Update. A quick word of caution: Unlike a Windows update, a firmware update gone bad can *brick* your router. In other words, it can destroy the hardware and make it as useful as a brick sitting on your desk. This rarely happens, but you should keep it in mind when doing a firmware update.

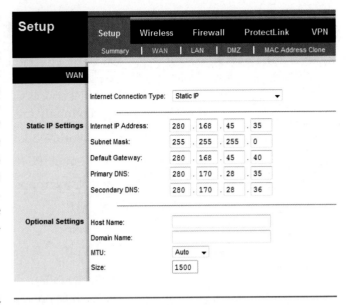

• **Figure 25.29**   Entering a static IP address

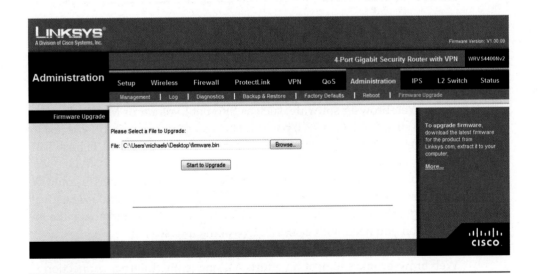

• **Figure 25.30**   Firmware update page

■ Internet Software Tools

Once you've established a connection between the PC and the ISP, you can do nothing on the Internet without applications designed to use one or more TCP/IP services, such as Web browsing and e-mail. TCP/IP has the following commonly used services:

- World Wide Web (HTTP and HTTPS)
- E-mail (POP and SMTP)
- Newsgroups
- FTP
- Telnet
- VoIP

Each of these services (sometimes referred to by the overused term *TCP/IP protocols*) operates by using defined ports, requires a special application, and has special settings. You'll look at all eight of these services and learn how to configure them. As a quick reference, Table 25.1 has some common port numbers CompTIA would like you to know.

Table 25.1	TCP/IP Service Port Numbers
TCP/IP Service	**Port Number**
HTTP	80
HTTPS	443
FTP	20, 21
POP	110
SMTP	25
TELNET	23

The World Wide Web

The Web provides a graphical face for the Internet. *Web servers* (servers running specialized software) provide Web sites that you access by using the HTTP protocol on port 80 and thus get more or less useful information. Using Web-browser software, such as Internet Explorer or Mozilla Firefox, you can click a link on a Web page and be instantly transported—not just to some Web server in your home town—to anywhere in the world. Figure 25.31 shows Firefox at the home page of my company's Web site, www.totalsem.com. Where is the server located? Does it matter? It could be in a closet in my office or on a huge clustered server in Canada. The great part about the Web is that you can get from here to there and access the information you need with a click or two of the mouse.

Although the Web is the most popular part of the Internet, setting up a Web browser takes almost no effort. As long as the Internet connection is working, Web browsers work automatically. This is not to say you can't make plenty of custom settings, but the default browser settings work almost every time. If you type in a Web address, such as the best search engine

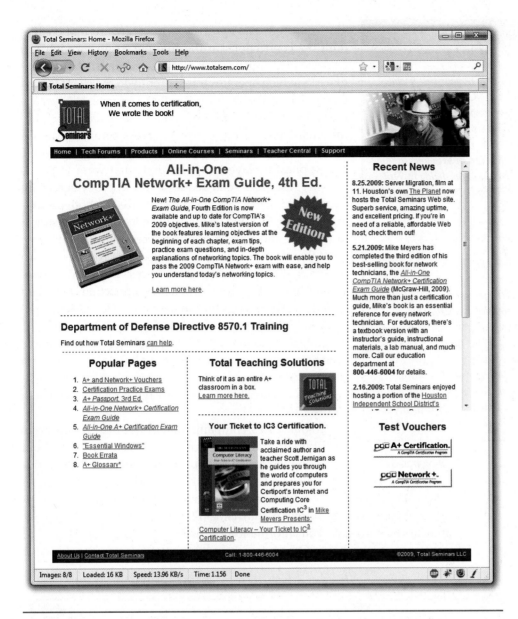

● **Figure 25.31**   Mozilla Firefox showing a Web page

on the planet—www.google.com—and it doesn't work, check the line and your network settings and you'll figure out where the problem is.

Configuring the Browser

Web browsers are highly configurable. On most Web browsers, you can set the default font size, choose whether to display graphics, and adjust several other settings. Although all Web browsers support these settings, where you go to make these changes varies dramatically. If you are using the popular Internet Explorer that comes with Windows, you will find configuration tools in the Internet Options Control Panel applet or under the Tools menu.

Proxy Server   Many corporations use a **proxy server** to filter employee Internet access, and when you're on their corporate network you have to set your proxy settings within the Web browser (and any other Internet software

PING

*The command-line tool PING may be your best friend for diagnosing TCP/IP errors. PING always works; you don't need to log on to a server or even log on to a system. Simply type PING followed by a DNS name or an IP address. To run PING, get to a command prompt (Start | Run | type **cmd** | click OK in Windows 2000/XP, or simply Start and type **cmd** in the dialog in Windows Vista/7) and type **ping** followed by a DNS name or IP address, like this:*

```
c:\>ping www.totalsem.com
```

Then press the ENTER key. If the Web server is up, you'll get a reply to that effect.

*You can even ping yourself: just type **ping 127.0.0.1** (127.0.0.1 is known as the loopback address). This can give you a quick check to make sure your NIC is functional. If you ping an address and get the famous "Request timed out" message, the device you are trying to ping is not available. Be aware, however, that "Request timed out" messages are fairly common when you use PING on the Internet because many servers turn off the PING reply as a security measure.*

you want to use). A *proxy server* is software that enables multiple connections to the Internet to go through one protected PC, much as ICS works on a home network. Unlike ICS, which operates transparently to the client PCs by manipulating IP packets (we say that it operates at Layer 3—the Network layer in the OSI model—see Chapter 23, "Local Area Networking"), proxy servers communicate directly with the browser application (operating at Layer 7, the Application layer). Applications that want to access Internet resources send requests to the proxy server instead of trying to access the Internet directly, both protecting the client PCs and enabling the network administrator to monitor and restrict Internet access. Each application must therefore be configured to use the proxy server. To configure proxy settings in Internet Explorer, choose Tools | Internet Options. Select the Connections tab. Then click the LAN Settings button to open the Local Area Network (LAN) Settings dialog box (Figure 25.32).

Note that you have three options here, with automatic detection of the proxy server being the default. You can specify an IP address and port for a proxy server by clicking the third checkbox and simply typing it in as shown in Figure 25.32.

In some cases, companies have different proxy servers for different programs, such as FTP. You can enter those proxy addresses by clicking the Advanced button and entering the individual addresses. You can also add addresses that should not go through the proxy servers, such as intranet sites. These sites can be added in the Exceptions box down at the bottom of the dialog (Figure 25.33). Your network administrator will give you information on proxy servers if you need it to configure a machine. Otherwise, you can safely leave the browser

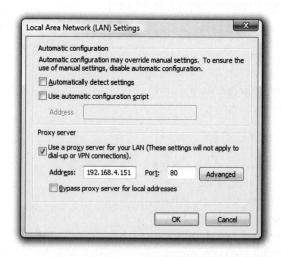

• **Figure 25.32**   The LAN Settings dialog box

• **Figure 25.33**   Specifying the proxy server address

configured to search automatically for a proxy server. If proxy servers are not used on your network, the automatic configuration will fail and your browser will try to connect to the Internet directly, so there is no harm in just leaving *Automatically detect settings* checked.

Security and Scripts While we're on the subject of configuration, make sure you know how to adjust the security settings in your Web browser. Many Web sites come with programs that download to your system and run automatically. These programs are written in specialized languages and file formats such as Java and Active Server Pages (ASP). They make modern Web sites powerful and dynamic, but they can also act as a portal to evil programs. To help with security, all better Web browsers let you determine whether you want these potentially risky programs to run. What you decide depends on personal factors. If your Web browser refuses to run a Java program (you'll know because you'll get a warning message, as in Figure 25.34), check your security settings because your browser may simply be following orders! To get to the security configuration screen in Internet Explorer, choose Tools | Internet Options and open the Security tab (Figure 25.35).

Internet Explorer gives you the option of selecting preset security levels by clicking the Custom level button on the Security tab and then using the pull-down menu (Figure 25.36). Changing from Medium to High security, for example, makes changes across the board, disabling everything from ActiveX to Java. You can also manually select which features to enable or disable in the scrolling menu, also visible in Figure 25.36.

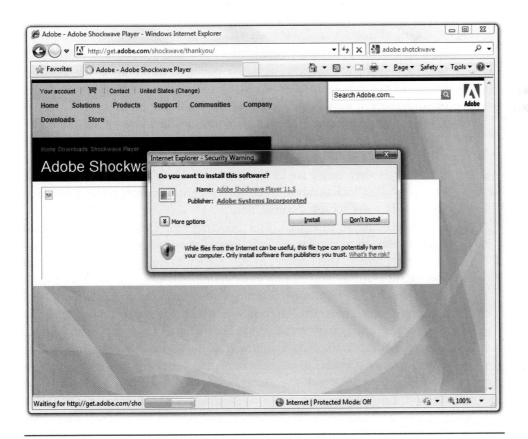

• **Figure 25.34**   Warning message about running ActiveX

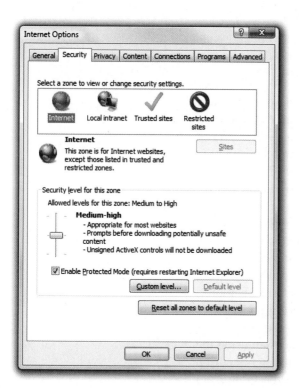

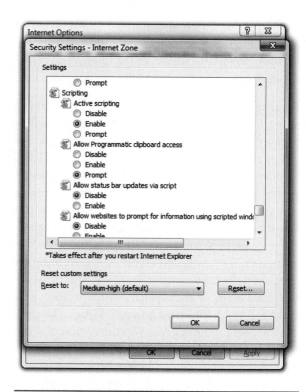

• **Figure 25.35** The Security tab in the Internet Options dialog box

• **Figure 25.36** Changing security settings

Depending on the Web site and your Web browser, you might also see a lock in the address bar or even different colors appearing on the address bar when accessing an HTTPS site. While these extras may vary from site to site and browser to browser, you can always count on seeing the lock in the bottom right-hand corner and the HTTPS in the address.

See Chapter 26, "Securing Computers," for the scoop on Trojans and other viruses.

Security doesn't stop with programs. Another big security concern relates to Internet commerce. People don't like to enter credit card information, home phone numbers, or other personal information for fear this information might be intercepted by hackers. Fortunately, there are methods for encrypting this information, the most common being **Hypertext Transfer Protocol Secure (HTTPS)**. Although HTTPS looks a lot like HTTP from the point of view of a web browser, HTTPS uses port 443. It's easy to tell if a Web site is using HTTPS because the Web address starts with *HTTPS*, as shown in Figure 25.37, instead of just *HTTP*. The Web browser also displays a lock symbol in the lower-right corner to remind you that you're using an encrypted connection.

There's one security risk that no computer can completely defend against: you. In particular, be very careful when downloading programs from the Internet. The Internet makes it easy to download programs that you can then install and run on your system. There's nothing intrinsically wrong with this unless the program you download has a virus, is corrupted, contains a Trojan horse, or is incompatible with your operating system. The watchword here is *common sense*. Only download programs from reliable sources. Take time to read the online documentation so you're sure you're downloading a version of the program that works on your operating system. Finally, always run a good antivirus program, preferably one that checks incoming programs for viruses before you install them! Failure to do this can lead to lockups, file corruption, and boot problems that you simply should not have to deal with.

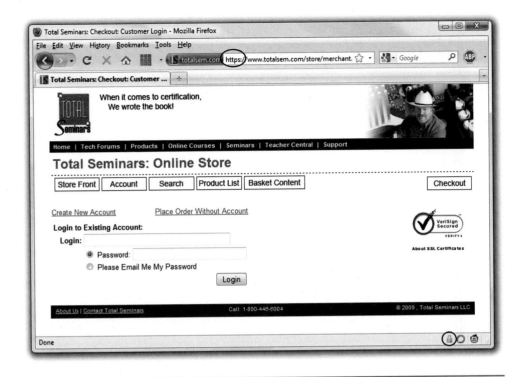

- **Figure 25.37**   A secure Web page

E-mail

You can use an e-mail program to access e-mail. The three most popular are Microsoft's Outlook Express, Windows Mail, and Mozilla's Thunderbird. E-mail clients need a little more setup. First, you must provide your e-mail address and password. All e-mail addresses come in the now-famous *accountname@Internet domain* format. Figure 25.38 shows e-mail information entered into the Windows Mail account setup wizard.

Next you must add the names of the **Post Office Protocol version 3 (POP3)** or **Internet Message Access Protocol version 4 (IMAP4)** server and the **Simple Mail Transfer Protocol (SMTP)** server. The POP3 or IMAP server is the computer that handles incoming (to you) e-mail. POP3 is by far the most widely used standard, although the latest version of IMAP, *IMAP4*, supports some features POP3 doesn't. For example, IMAP4 enables you to search through messages on the mail server to find specific keywords and select the messages you want to download onto your machine. Even with the advantages of IMAP4 over POP3, the vast majority of incoming mail servers use POP3.

The SMTP server handles your outgoing e-mail. These two systems may often have the same name, or close to the same name, as shown in Figure 25.39. Your ISP should provide you with all these settings. If not, you should be comfortable knowing what to ask for. If one of these names is incorrect, you will either not get your e-mail or not be able to send e-mail. If an e-mail setup that has been working well for a while suddenly gives you errors, it is likely that either the POP3 or SMTP server is down or that the DNS server has quit working.

Make sure you know your port numbers for these e-mail protocols! POP3 uses port 110, IMAP uses port 143, and SMTP uses port 25.

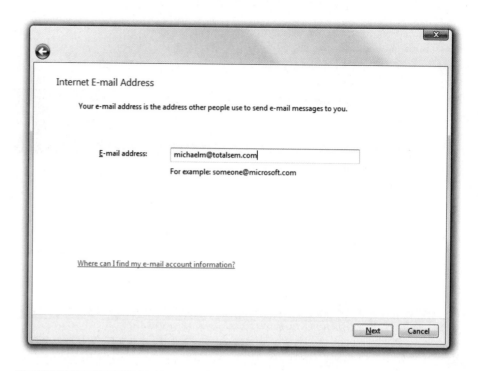

● **Figure 25.38**   Adding an e-mail account to Windows Mail

When I'm given the name of a POP3 or SMTP server, I use PING to determine the IP address for the device, as shown in Figure 25.40. I make a point to write this down. If I ever have a problem getting mail, I'll go into my SMTP or POP3 settings and type in the IP address (Figure 25.41). If my mail starts to work, I know the DNS server is not working.

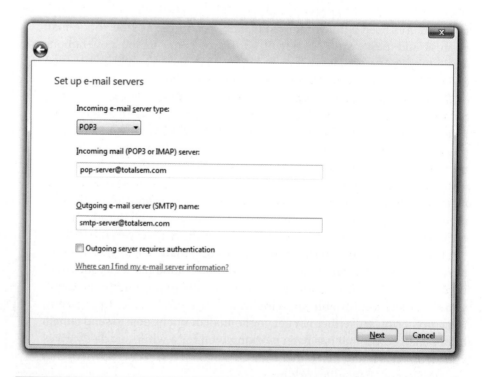

● **Figure 25.39**   Adding POP3 and SMTP information in Windows Mail

Mike Meyers' CompTIA A+ Guide to Managing and Troubleshooting PCs

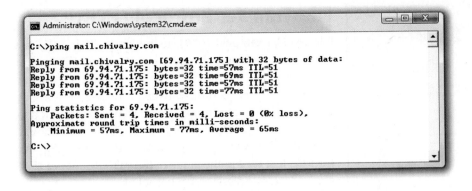

● **Figure 25.40**   Using PING to determine the IP address

Newsgroups

Newsgroups are one of the oldest services available on the Internet. To access a newsgroup, you must use a newsreader program. A number of third-party newsreaders exist, such as the popular Forté Free Agent, but Microsoft Outlook Express is the most common of all newsreaders (not surprising since it comes free with most versions of Windows). To access a newsgroup, you must know the name of a news server. *News servers* run the **Network News Transfer Protocol (NNTP)**. You can also use public news servers, but these are extremely slow. Your ISP will tell you the name of the news server and provide you with a user name and password if you need one (Figure 25.42).

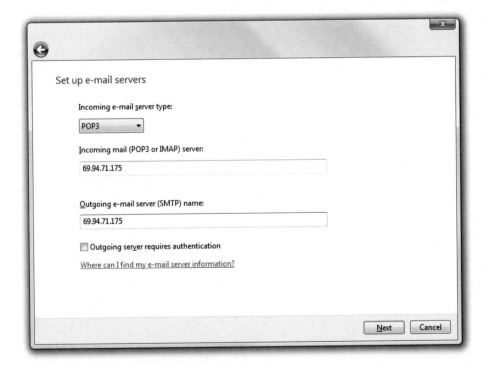

● **Figure 25.41**   Entering IP addresses into POP3 and SMTP settings

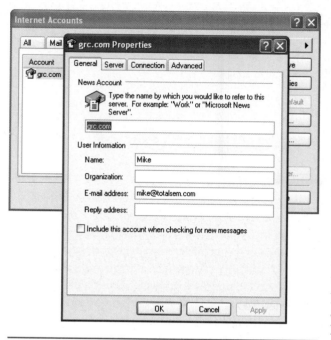

• **Figure 25.42**   Configuring Outlook Express for a news server

File Transfer Protocol (FTP)

File transfer protocol (FTP), using ports 20 and 21, is a great way to share files between systems. FTP server software exists for most operating systems, so you can use FTP to transfer data between any two systems regardless of the operating system. To access an FTP site, you must use an FTP client such as FileZilla, although most Web browsers provide at least download support for FTP. Just type in the name of the FTP site. Figure 25.43 shows Firefox accessing ftp.kernel.org.

Although you can use a Web browser, all FTP sites require you to log on. Your Web browser will assume that you want to log in as "anonymous." If you want to log on as a specific user, you have to add your user name to the URL. (Instead of typing **ftp://ftp.example.com**, you would type **ftp://mikem@ftp.example.com**.) An anonymous logon works fine for most public FTP sites. Many techs prefer to use third-party programs such as FileZilla (Figure 25.44) for FTP access because these third-party applications can store user name and password settings. This enables you to access the FTP site more easily later. Keep in mind that FTP was developed during a more trusting time, and that whatever user name and password you send over the network is sent in clear text. Don't use the same password for an FTP site that you use for your domain logon at the office!

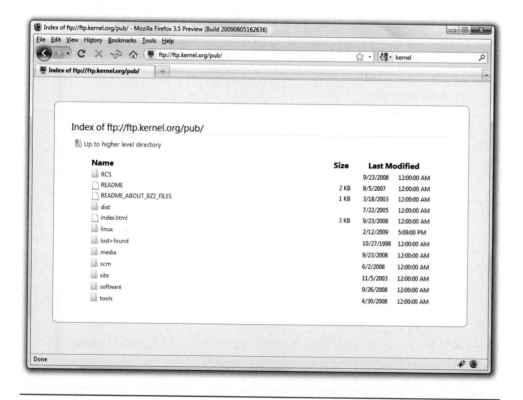

• **Figure 25.43**   Accessing an FTP site in Firefox

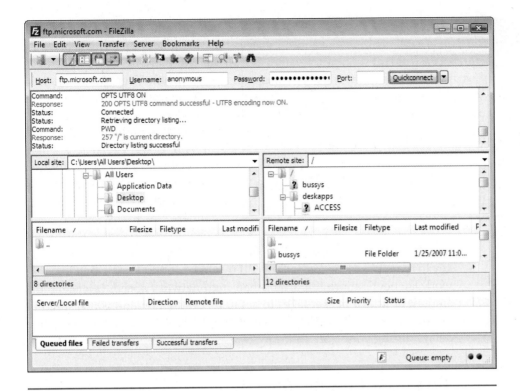

• **Figure 25.44**   The FileZilla program

Telnet and SSH

Telnet is a terminal emulation program for TCP/IP networks that uses port 23 and enables you to connect to a server or fancy router and run commands on that machine as if you were sitting in front of it. This way, you can remotely administer a server and communicate with other servers on your network. As you can imagine, this is rather risky. If *you* can remotely control a computer, what's to stop others from doing the same? Of course, Telnet does not allow just *anyone* to log on and wreak havoc with your network. You must enter a special user name and password to run Telnet. Unfortunately, Telnet shares FTP's bad habit of sending passwords and user names as clear text, so you should generally use it only within your own LAN.

If you need a remote terminal that works securely across the Internet, you need **Secure Shell (SSH)**. In fact, today SSH has replaced Telnet in almost all places Telnet used to be popular. To the user, SSH works just like Telnet. Behind the scenes, SSH uses port 22, and the entire connection is encrypted, preventing any eavesdroppers from reading your data. SSH has one other trick up its sleeve: it can move files or any type of TCP/IP network traffic through its secure connection. In networking parlance, this is called **tunneling**, and it is the core of a technology called VPN, which I will discuss in more depth later in the chapter.

> The CompTIA A+ certification exams test your knowledge of a few networking tools, such as Telnet, but only enough to let you support a Network+ tech or network administrator. If you need to run Telnet (or its more secure cousin, SSH), you will get the details from a network administrator. Implementation of Telnet falls well beyond CompTIA A+.

Voice over IP

You can use **Voice over IP (VoIP)** to make voice calls over your computer network. Why have two sets of wires, one for voice and one for data, going to

Try This!

Checking Latency with PING

Latency is the bane of any VoIP call because of all the problems it causes if it is too high. A quick way to check your current latency is to use the ever-handy PING, so try this!

1. Run PING on some known source, such as www.microsoft.com or www.totalsem.com.
2. When the PING finishes, take note of the average round-trip time at the bottom of the screen. This is your current latency to that site.

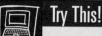

every desk? Why not just use the extra capacity on the data network for your phone calls? That's exactly what VoIP does for you. VoIP works with every type of high-speed Internet connection, from DSL to cable to satellite.

VoIP doesn't refer to a single protocol but rather to a collection of protocols that make phone calls over the data network possible. Venders such as Skype and Vonage offer popular VoIP solutions, and many corporations use VoIP for their internal phone networks. A key to remember when installing and troubleshooting VoIP is that low network latency is more important than high network speed. **Latency** is the amount of time a packet takes to get to its destination and is measured in milliseconds. The higher the latency, the more problems, such as noticeable delays during your VoIP call.

Terminal Emulation

All terminal emulation programs require separate server and client programs.

In Microsoft networking, we primarily share folders and printers. At times it would be convenient to be transported in front of another computer—to feel as if your hands were actually on its keyboard. This is called **terminal emulation**. Terminal emulation is old stuff; Telnet is one of the oldest TCP/IP applications, but the introduction of graphical user interfaces cost it much of its popularity. Today when techs talk about terminal emulation, they are usually referring to graphical terminal emulation programs.

Like so many other Windows applications, graphical terminal emulation originally came from third-party companies and was eventually absorbed into the Windows operating system. Although many third-party emulators are available, one of the most popular is the University of Cambridge's VNC. VNC is free and totally cross-platform, enabling you to run and control a Windows system remotely from your Macintosh system, for example. Figure 25.45 shows VNC in action.

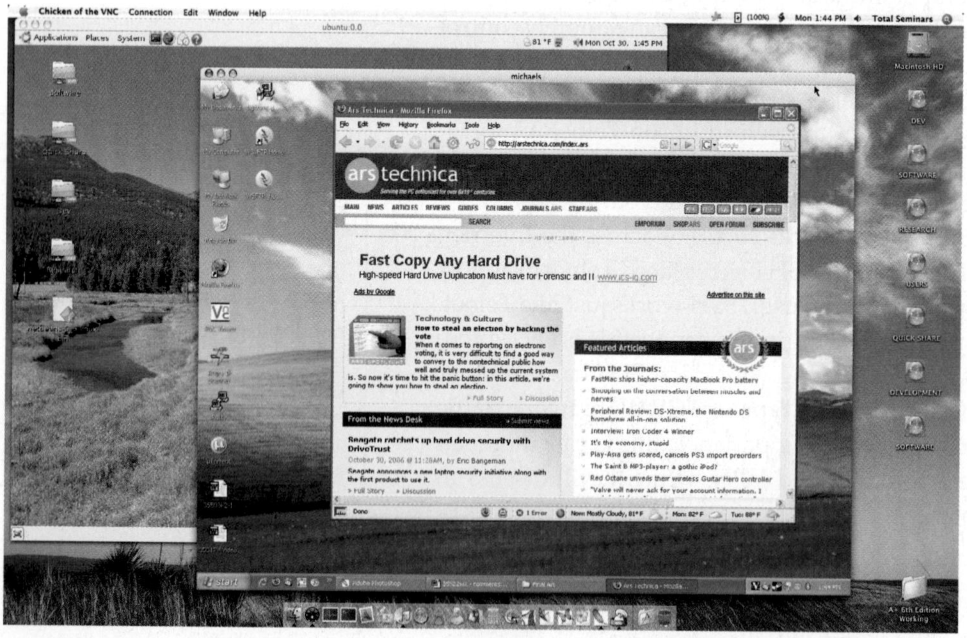

• **Figure 25.45** VNC in action

Windows 2000 Server (not Professional) was the first version of Windows to include a built-in terminal emulator called Windows Terminal Services. Terminal Services has a number of limitations: the server software runs only on Windows Server and the client software runs only on Windows—although the client works on *every* version of Windows and is free. Figure 25.46 shows Windows Terminal Services running on a Windows 2000 computer.

Windows XP and Vista offer an alternative to VNC: Remote Desktop. **Remote Desktop** provides control over a remote server with the fully graphical interface. Your

• **Figure 25.46** Old Terminal Services

desktop *becomes* the server desktop (Figure 25.47). It's quite incredible—although it's only for Windows XP and later.

Wouldn't it be cool if, when called about a technical support issue, you could simply see what the client sees? (I'm not talking voyeur cam here.) When the client says that something doesn't work, it would be great if you could transfer yourself from your desk to your client's desk to see precisely what the client sees. This would dramatically cut down on the miscommunication that can make a tech's life so tedious. Windows Remote Assistance does just that. Based on the Shared Desktop feature that used to come with the popular MSN Messenger program, **Remote Assistance** enables you to give anyone control of your desktop. If a user has a problem, that user can request support directly from you. Upon receiving the support request e-mail, you can then log in to the user's system and, with permission, take the driver's seat. Figure 25.48 shows Remote Assistance in action.

With Remote Assistance, you can do anything you would do from the actual computer. You can troubleshoot some hardware configuration or driver problem. You can install drivers, roll back drivers, download new ones, and so forth. You're in command of the remote machine as long as the client allows you to be. The client sees everything you do, by the way, and can stop you cold if you get out of line or do something that makes the client nervous! Remote Assistance can help you teach someone how to use a particular application.

• **Figure 25.47** Windows Vista Remote Desktop Connection dialog box

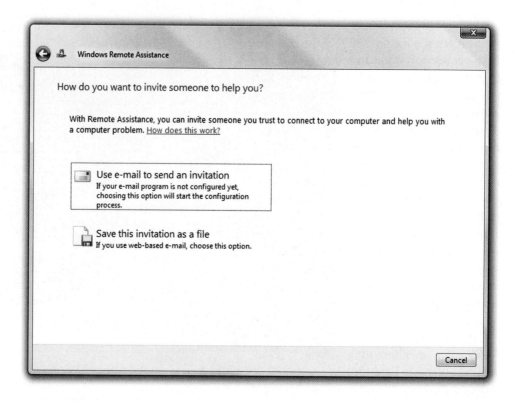

• **Figure 25.48**   Remote Assistance in action

You can log on to a user's PC and fire up Outlook, for example, and then walk through the steps to configure it while the user watches. The user can then take over the machine and walk through the steps while you watch, chatting with one another the whole time. Sweet!

The new graphical terminal emulators provide everything you need to access one system from another. They are common, especially now that Microsoft provides free terminal emulators. Whatever type of emulator you use, remember that you will always need both a server and a client program. The server goes on the system you want to access and the client goes on the system you use to access the server. On many solutions, the server and client software are integrated into a single product.

■ Virtual Private Networks

Remote connections have been around for a long time, long before the Internet existed. The biggest drawback about remote connections was the cost to connect. If you were on one side of the continent and had to connect to your LAN on the other side of the continent, the only connection option was a telephone. Or, if you needed to connect two LANs across the continent, you ended up paying outrageous monthly charges for a private connection. The introduction of the Internet gave people wishing to connect to their home networks a very cheap connection option, but with one problem: the whole Internet is open to the public. People wanted to stop using dial-up and expensive private connections and use the Internet instead, but they wanted to do it securely.

Those clever network engineers worked long and hard and came up with several solutions to this problem. Standards have been created that use encrypted tunnels between a computer (or a remote network) to create a private network through the Internet (Figure 25.49), resulting in what is called a **Virtual Private Network (VPN)**.

An encrypted tunnel requires endpoints—the ends of the tunnel where the data is encrypted and decrypted. In the SSH tunnel you've seen thus far, the client for the application sits on one end and the server sits on the other. VPNs do the same thing. Either some software running on a computer or, in some cases, a dedicated box must act as an endpoint for a VPN (Figure 25.50).

To make VPNs work requires a protocol that uses one of the many tunneling protocols available and adds the capability to ask for an IP address from a local DHCP server to give the tunnel an IP address that matches the subnet of the local LAN. The connection keeps the IP address to connect to the Internet, but the tunnel endpoints must act like NICs (Figure 25.51). Let's look at one of the protocols, PPTP.

PPTP VPNs

So how do we make IP addresses appear out of thin air? Microsoft got the ball rolling with the **Point-to-Point Tunneling Protocol (PPTP)**, an advanced version of a protocol used for dial-up Internet called PPP that handles all of this right out of the box. The only trick is the endpoints. In Microsoft's view, a VPN is intended for individual clients (think employees on the road) to connect back to the office network, so Microsoft places the PPTP endpoints on the client and a special remote access server program called Routing and Remote Access Service (RRAS), originally only available on Windows Server, on the server (see Figure 25.52).

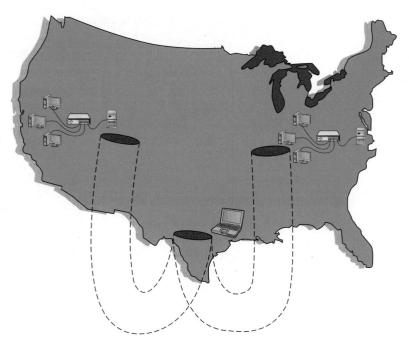

● **Figure 25.49**   VPN connecting computers across the United States

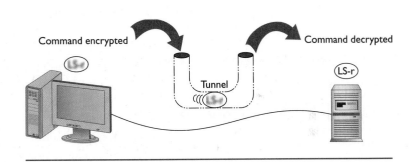

● **Figure 25.50**   Typical tunnel

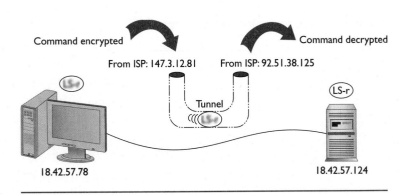

● **Figure 25.51**   Endpoints must have their own IP addresses.

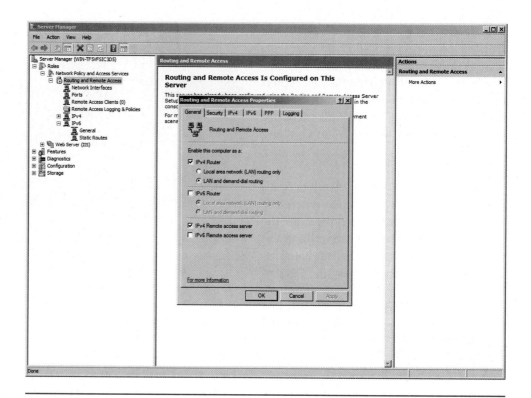

● Figure 25.52   RRAS in action

● Figure 25.53   VPN connection in Windows

On the Windows client side, you right-click on My Network Places and click on Create a New Connection (Windows 2000/XP) or right-click on Network and select *Set up a connection or network* (Windows Vista) from the Network and Sharing Center. This presents you with a dialog where you can enter all your VPN server information. Your network administrator will most likely provide this to you. The result is a virtual network card that, like any other NIC, gets an IP address from the DHCP server back at the office (Figure 25.53).

When your computer connects to the RRAS server on the private network, PPTP creates a secure tunnel through the Internet back to the private LAN. Your client takes on an IP address of that network, as if your computer were plugged into the LAN back at the office. Even your Internet traffic will go through your office first. If you open your Web browser, your client will go across the Internet to the office LAN and then use the LAN's Internet connection! Because of this, Web browsing is very slow over a VPN.

A system connected to a VPN looks as though it's on the local network but performs much slower than if the system were connected directly back at the office.

Beyond A+

The areas covered by the CompTIA A+ certification exams do a great job on the more common issues of dealing with the Internet, but a few hot topics (although beyond the scope of the CompTIA A+ exams) are so common and important that you need to know them: online gaming, chatting, and file sharing.

Online Gaming

One of the more exciting and certainly more fun aspects of the Internet is online gaming. Competing online against a real person or people makes for some pleasant gaming. Enjoying classics such as Hearts and Backgammon with another human can be challenging and fun. Another popular genre of online gaming is the "first-person shooters" format. These games place you in a small world with up to 32 other players. A great example is Valve Software's Counter-Strike: Source (Figure 25.54).

No discussion of online gaming is complete without talking about the most amazing game type of all: the massively multiplayer online role-playing game (MMORPG). Imagine being an elfin wizard, joined by a band of friends, all going on adventures together in worlds so large that it would take a real 24-hour day to journey across them! Imagine that in this same world, 2,000 to 3,000 other players, as well as thousands of game-controlled characters, are participating! Plenty of MMORPGs are out there, but the most popular today is World of Warcraft (Figure 25.55).

Each of these games employs good old TCP/IP to send information, using ports reserved by the game. For instance, the Quake series of games uses port 26000, while DirectX uses ports 47624 and 2300–2400.

• **Figure 25.54**   Counter-Strike: Source

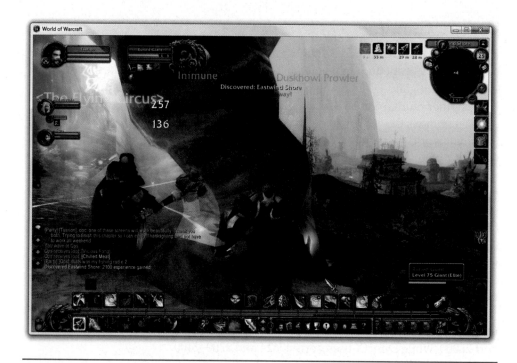

• **Figure 25.55**   My editor playing World of Warcraft

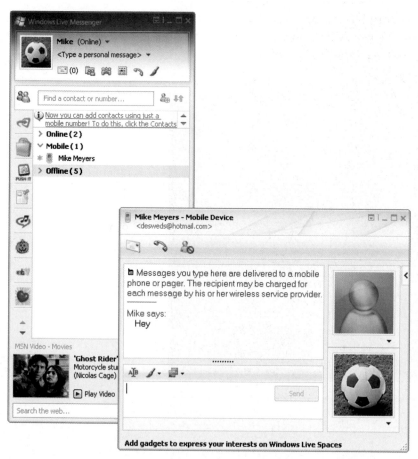

• **Figure 25.56**   Windows Live Messenger in action

Chatting

If there's one thing we human beings love to do, it's chat. The Internet provides a multitude of ways to do so, whether by typing or actual talking. Keep in mind that chatting occurs in real time. As fast as you can type or talk, whoever is at the other end hears or sees what you have to say. To chat, however, you need some form of chat software. The oldest family of chat programs is based on the Internet Relay Chat (IRC) protocol, and the single most common IRC chat program is probably mIRC. IRC protocols allow for a number of other little extras as well, such as being able to share files.

Today, companies such as AOL, Yahoo!, and Microsoft have made their own chat programs that not only provide text chat but also add features such as voice and video, turning your PC into a virtual replacement for your telephone! Figure 25.56 shows the popular Microsoft Windows Live Messenger software.

File Sharing

The last extra Internet function to discuss is also probably the most controversial: file sharing. File sharing basically consists of a whole bunch of computers with one program loaded, such as Napster or Kazaa. The file-sharing program enables each of the computers running that program to offer files to share, such as MP3 music files and MPEG movies. Once all of the file-sharing computers log on to the Internet, any of them can download any file offered by any other in the group.

File sharing through such *distributed* sharing software becomes almost anonymous and free—and that's the problem. You can share *anything*, even copyright-protected music, movies, and more. The music industry in particular has come out swinging to try to stop file-sharing practices. As a result, the music industry is working on a way to shut down those persons who share lots of files. But software developers have countered, creating Internet protocols such as BitTorrent to handle the distribution and make the file sharers much more difficult to find and punish. Figure 25.57 shows one of the more popular BitTorrent protocol programs called μTorrent (the μ is the symbol for "micro," so you pronounce it "micro torrent"). BitTorrent has many legitimate uses as well—its protocol is extremely efficient for the distribution of large files and has become the method of choice for distributing Linux distributions and large open-source applications such as Apache and OpenOffice.

These example programs just scratch the surface of the many applications that use the Internet. One of the more amazing aspects of TCP/IP is that its basic design is around 30 years old. We use TCP/IP in ways completely outside the original concept of its designers, yet TCP/IP continues to show its power and flexibility. Pretty amazing!

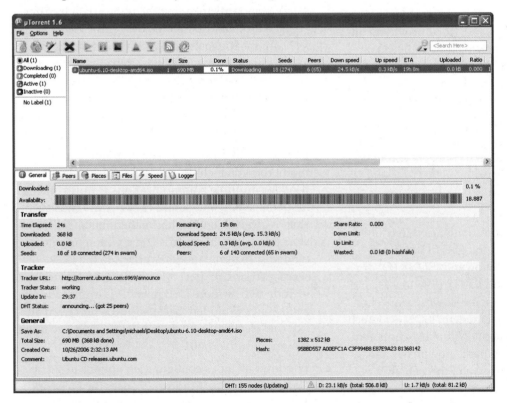

• **Figure 25.57** μTorrent

Chapter 25 Review

■ Chapter Summary

After reading this chapter and completing the exercises, you should understand the following about the Internet.

Explain how the Internet works

- A PC tech needs to know how PCs communicate with the world for two reasons: (1) to troubleshoot when a process or piece stops working, and (2) to communicate knowledgeably with a network technician who comes in to solve a more complex issue.

- The Internet is broken down into three tiers. Tier 1 providers own the fiber-optic backbones that interconnect at network access points. Backbone routers create an interwoven framework for redundant communications.

- TCP/IP provides the basic software structure for Internet communications. It provides IP addresses and the naming scheme for computers on the Internet. This protocol suite also offers a variety of other services, including HTTP, which provides structure for the Web.

- Internet service providers (ISPs) lease connections to the Internet from Tier 1 and Tier 2 providers. In turn, ISPs lease connections to allow individuals and companies to access the Internet. ISPs may serve customers nationwide, such as Comcast, or they may be limited to a small community of users.

- Connecting to the Internet requires hardware for connectivity and software to govern the connection and data flow. The router that connects you to your ISP is your default gateway.

Connect to the Internet

- Seven technologies are commonly used to connect a PC to an ISP. These technologies fit into four categories: (1) dial-up (analog and ISDN), (2) dedicated (DSL, cable, and LAN), (3) wireless, and (4) satellite. Analog dial-up, the slowest connection, uses a telephone line and a modem. ISDN is a much faster digital dial-up method. With the exception of satellite, which may use either a modem or a NIC, all the other technologies use an Ethernet NIC.

- A dial-up connection needs hardware, such as a modem or ISDN terminal adapter, and software, such as Microsoft's DUN.

- A modem converts digital signals from the PC into analog signals that travel on telephone lines, and vice versa. An example of serial communication, the modem transmits data as a series of ones and zeros. On the other hand, the computer processes data by using parallel communication or data in discrete 8-bit chunks. A UART chip converts serial to parallel and parallel to serial. An external modem uses the UART chip in the computer's serial port, while an internal modem has its own built-in UART.

- Phone lines measure speed in bauds, or cycles per second. However, the fastest baud rate a phone line can achieve is 2400 baud. Today's modems pack multiple bits of data into each baud. Although not technically correct, people use the term *baud* instead of *bps* so often that the terms have become synonymous.

- The International Telecommunication Union (ITU) sets V standards to define the fastest data transfer speed a modem can handle. Currently V.90 and V.92 are the highest standards, downloading data at just a little under 56 Kbps. Upload speeds differ, with 33.6 Kbps being the fastest for V.90 and 48 Kbps proving the fastest for V.92 modems.

- Modems may be internal or external. The less-expensive internal modems usually connect to a PCI or PCI Express expansion bus slot. Some motherboards include special expansion slots used for multiple communications features such as modems, NICs, and sound cards. AMD calls such slots ACRs, while Intel has named them CNR slots. Many motherboards come with integrated modems. External modems attach to the PC's serial port or USB port. Most motherboards today include two or more USB ports. It is a good idea to choose a USB modem because you won't need an external electrical source and it will likely include a volume control knob.

- Windows includes configuration options to set up dial-up networks. Windows XP uses the Network and Internet Connections applet, Windows 2000

calls this feature Network and Dial-up Connections, and Vista uses the *Set up a connection or network* wizard. To configure dial-up networking, you'll need information from your ISP. Dial-up links to the Internet use PPP streaming hardware protocol.

- If you can't connect to the Internet, look at the modem's properties to make sure the volume is turned up. Listen, too, for a befuddled voice on the other end that would indicate your modem is dialing the wrong number. Other things to check: Be sure the line is plugged into a good phone jack, and make sure the number and password are correct. If you still can't connect to the Internet, call the network technicians to check that the dial-up networking settings are correct.

- An ISDN consists of two types of channels: Bearer, or B, channels that carry data and voice at 64 Kbps, and Delta, or D, channels that transmit setup and configuration information at 16 Kbps. Users can use one or two B channels, but the most common setup is the BRI, consisting of two B channels and one D to provide a throughput total of 128 Kbps. Except for the steep cost of installation and equipment, ISDN lines are only slightly more expensive than regular phone lines, but this service is limited to an area within about 18,000 feet of a central office. ISDN uses a terminal adapter that looks like a regular modem and may be either external or internal.

- DSL modems connect to an ISP by using a standard telephone line and special connections on each end. Although service levels vary, typical upload speed is ~768 Kbps with a download speed of ~2+ Mbps. A tech usually comes to the house to install a DSL receiver (often called a DSL modem) as well as a NIC in the PC. DSL is usually limited to about 18,000 feet from a main phone service switching center.

- Cable TV companies offer high-speed Internet access, with an upload speed of about 1+ Mbps up and download transmission rates of 5+ Mbps. With a TV tuner card, cable enables you to watch TV on your PC.

- Wireless Internet service requires connecting to a LAN that's wired to an ISP. The other wireless option is a satellite connection. Although early satellite technology required uploads through a slow modem (26–48 Kbps) and fast downloads through the dish, newer technology uses the modem only for the initial setup, sending both downloads and uploads through the dish.

- ICS enables multiple systems to use one Internet connection. Included in all current Windows versions, ICS uses an ICS host computer connected to the Internet that then shares the connection via a LAN with client computers. The ICS host computer must have a NIC or modem to connect to the Internet and a NIC that plugs into a hub. The other PCs then connect to the hub.

- Small home routers allow multiple users to easily share a broadband connection without leaving a Windows computer running all the time. They provide NAT that allows you to share a single IP address while acting as an effective firewall. Configuration of small home routers is done through special Web pages built into the routers.

Use Internet software tools

- Applications provide TCP/IP services, including Web, e-mail, newsgroups, FTP, Telnet, and VoIP. Using Web browser software such as Internet Explorer or Mozilla Firefox, you can access Web sites and pages from Web servers throughout the world. If you are unsuccessful in connecting to a site, use the command-line tool PING to determine whether the server is up. Simply type **ping** followed by either the DNS name or the IP address. If the device you are trying to ping is not available, you'll see a "Request timed out" message. You can use the loopback address (127.0.0.1) to ping yourself.

- A proxy server is software that enables multiple connections to the Internet to go through one protected PC. Configure proxy settings through the Local Area Network Settings dialog box. Although automatic detection of the proxy server is the default setting, you can also specify an IP address for a proxy server.

- You should also know how to adjust security settings in your Web browser. In IE, choose Tools | Internet Options and open the Security tab. You can set different security levels or manually select the features you want to enable or disable.

- Security also includes encrypting information such as credit card numbers, home phone numbers, or other personal information. The most common method of encrypting this information is HTTPS. You'll identify Web sites using HTTPS by the *HTTPS:* that appears at the beginning of the Web address and the little lock icon located on the right side of the address bar or in the lower-right corner of the Web browser.

8. Which term describes hardware or software that protects your computer or network from probing or malicious users?

 A. Router

 B. Firewall

 C. Protocol

 D. Spyware

9. Liz can receive her e-mail, but she cannot send e-mail. Which of the following is most likely causing her problem?

 A. POP3

 B. SMTP

 C. IMAP

 D. UART

10. What is the name for the extremely fast networking connections through which Internet transmissions take place?

 A. Gateways

 B. Tier 1 providers

 C. Backbones

 D. ISPs

11. Which technology enables you to make voice calls over your computer network?

 A. Internet Voice Protocol

 B. Voice over IP

 C. Digital Telephony Subscriber Service

 D. Universal Asynchronous Receiver Transmitter

12. A user on Windows XP has asked you to teach her how to use a feature of Microsoft Word. What tool should you use?

 A. Remote Assistance

 B. Remote Desktop

 C. Telnet

 D. Secure Shell (SSH)

13. John walked up to a computer that couldn't connect to the Internet and immediately opened a command-line window and typed **ping 127.0.0.1**. Why?

 A. He wanted to test the connection to the default gateway.

 B. He wanted to test the connection to the nearest Tier 2 router.

 C. He wanted to test the NIC on the local machine.

 D. He wanted to test the NIC on the default gateway.

14. Where would you go first if you needed to configure a small Linksys router to use a static IP address?

 A. The router configuration applet in the Control Panel.

 B. The Router's configuration Web page.

 C. Plug in a Yost cable and start PuTTY.

 D. There is no way to give the router a static IP.

15. A new client lives in a rural area, outside the connectivity radius of the local cable company and definitely more than 20,000 feet away from the nearest switching center for the phone company. Which Internet option offers the client the best performance?

 A. Cable

 B. Dial-up

 C. DSL

 D. Satellite

■ Essay Quiz

1. With the rash of worms and viruses that attack computers connected to the Internet, how can you protect your computer?

2. Andrew's wife, Talena, collects pottery. Andrew found a shop on the Internet that has a piece she's been wanting. He'd love to get it for her birthday next week, but the only way it can arrive by then is if he pays for it with his credit card. He's a bit apprehensive about giving his credit card number over the Internet. He wants you to tell him whether you think the site is safe or not. How can you evaluate the site to determine whether it uses encryption for credit card numbers?

3. Sean is planning to take some distance education courses next term. He currently uses a regular phone line and a modem to connect to the Internet. He's consulted you to figure out what his options are for a faster connection. Review

his options, explaining the advantages and disadvantages, along with any restrictions that may prevent his receiving the service.

4. With a child in high school and another at a local college, it's always a struggle in Tom's house about who gets to use the computer to do Internet research. It's not feasible for Tom to have two DSL connections, but he does have a second computer. What solution can you offer to solve his problem?

5. You've become a regular columnist for your company's monthly newsletter. Everybody in the company uses e-mail and browses the Web, but you're convinced that the company would benefit if employees knew how to use some of the other Internet services. You've decided that this month's article will highlight three other Internet services. Which three will you discuss and what will you include about each?

Lab Projects

• Lab Project 25.1

Remote Desktop is a great feature of Windows. However, making it work when the computer you want to connect to is behind a router or firewall can be difficult. You need to consider and configure many things, such as the computer's public IP address and port forwarding or network address translation on the router. Using the Internet, find a tutorial or a step-by-step "how-to" article that guides you through configuring a remote computer and router to make a Remote Desktop connection possible.

• Lab Project 25.2

Remote Desktop provides the same functionality as some third-party software and services, such as the open source VNC software, Symantec's commercial pcAnywhere software, and the online service GoToMyPC.com. Each has its own benefits, such as no cost, ease of configuration, or cross-platform use. Research two other solutions that offer remote control functionality similar to Remote Desktop and compare and contrast the three. What are the similarities? What are the unique benefits of each? Which one would you be more likely to use yourself? Why?

• Lab Project 25.3

Have you heard of WebDAV? Web Distributed Authoring and Versioning is a set of extensions added to Hypertext Transfer Protocol to support collaborative authoring on the Web. While HTTP is a reading protocol, WebDAV is a writing protocol created by a working group of the Internet Engineering Task Force (IETF). WebDAV offers a faster, more secure method of file transfer than FTP, and some predict that it may make FTP obsolete. It's already incorporated into most current operating systems and applications. Some authors say that WebDAV will change the way we use the Web. Use the Internet to learn more about WebDAV and its features. Apple calls it "a whole new reason to love the Net." After learning about WebDAV, see if you agree.

• Lab Project 25.4

Are all high-speed Internet connections created equal? Test them to find out! Speakeasy.net hosts one of the best Internet sites for testing the speed of an Internet connection: www.speakeasy.net/speedtest/ Test three to five Internet connections that you can easily get to, such as your home, a friend's house, your school, a library, and an Internet café. How do the connections compare? If you can, find out which technology the connections use. Which one seems to offer the best connection in your area?

Securing Computers

"Strategy without tactics is the slowest route to victory. Tactics without strategy is the noise before defeat."

—Sun Tzu, *The Art of War*

In this chapter, you will learn how to

- **Explain the threats to your computers and data**
- **Describe key security concepts and technologies**
- **Explain how to protect computers from network threats**

Your PC is under siege. Through your PC, a malicious person can gain valuable information about you and your habits. He can steal your files. He can run programs that log your keystrokes and thus gain account names and passwords, credit card information, and more. He can run software that takes over much of your computer processing time and use it to send spam or steal from others. The threat is real and right now. Worse, he's doing one or more of these things to your clients as I write these words. You need to secure your computer and your users from these attacks.

But what does computer security mean? Is it an antivirus program? Is it big, complex passwords? Sure, it's both of these things, but what about the fact that your laptop can be stolen easily?

To secure computers, you need both a sound strategy and proper tactics. From a strategic sense, you need to understand the threat from unauthorized access to local machines as well as the big threats posed when computers go onto networks. Part of the big picture means to know what policies, software, and hardware to put in place to stop those threats. From a tactical in-the-trenches sense, you need to master the details, to know how to implement and maintain the proper tools. Not only do you need to install antivirus programs in your users' computers, for example, but you also need to update those programs regularly to keep up with the constant barrage of new viruses.

■ Analyzing Threats

Threats to your data and PC come from two directions: accidents and malicious people. All sorts of things can go wrong with your computer, from users getting access to folders they shouldn't see to a virus striking and deleting folders. Files can be deleted, renamed, or simply lost. Hard drives can die, and optical discs get scratched and rendered unreadable. Accidents happen and even well-meaning people can make mistakes.

Unfortunately, a lot of people out there intend to do you harm. Add that intent together with a talent for computers, and you have a deadly combination. Let's look at the following issues:

- Unauthorized access
- Data destruction, accidental or deliberate
- Administrative access
- Catastrophic hardware failures
- Viruses/spyware

Historical/Conceptual

Unauthorized Access

Unauthorized access occurs when a person accesses resources without permission. Resources in this case mean data, applications, and hardware. A user can alter or delete data; access sensitive information, such as financial data, personnel files, or e-mail messages; or use a computer for purposes the owner did not intend.

Not all unauthorized access is malicious—often this problem arises when users who are randomly poking around in a computer discover that they can access resources in a fashion the primary user did not intend. Unauthorized access becomes malicious when outsiders knowingly and intentionally take advantage of weaknesses in your security to gain information, use resources, or destroy data!

One of the ways to gain unauthorized access is through intrusion. You might imagine someone kicking in a door and hacking into a computer, but

more often than not it's someone sitting at a home computer, trying various passwords over the Internet. Not quite as glamorous, but still....

Dumpster diving is the generic term for anytime a hacker goes through your refuse, looking for information. This is also a form of intrusion. The amount of sensitive information that makes it into any organization's trash bin boggles the mind! Years ago, I worked with an IT security guru who gave me and a few other IT people a tour of our office's trash. In one 20-minute tour of the personal wastebaskets of one office area, we had enough information to access the network easily, as well as to embarrass seriously more than a few people. When it comes to getting information, the trash is the place to look!

Social Engineering

Although you're more likely to lose data through accident, the acts of malicious users get the vast majority of headlines. Most of these attacks come under the heading of **social engineering**—the process of using or manipulating people inside the networking environment to gain access to that network from the outside—which covers the many ways humans can use other humans to gain unauthorized information. This unauthorized information may be a network login, a credit card number, company customer data—almost anything you might imagine that one person or organization may not want a person outside of that organization to access.

Social engineering attacks aren't hacking—at least in the classic sense of the word—although the goals are the same. Social engineering means people attacking an organization through the people in the organization or physically accessing the organization to get the information they need. Following are a few of the more classic types of social engineering attacks.

> It's common for social engineering attacks to be used together, so if you discover one of them being used against your organization, it's a good idea to look for others.

Infiltration

Hackers can physically enter your building under the guise of someone who might have a legitimate reason for being there, such as cleaning personnel, repair technicians, or messengers. They then snoop around desks, looking for whatever they can find. They might talk with people inside the organization, gathering names, office numbers, and department names—little things in and of themselves but powerful tools when combined later with other social engineering attacks.

Dressing the part of a legitimate user—with fake badge and everything—enables malicious people to gain access to locations and thus potentially your data. Following someone through the door, for example, as if you belong, is called **tailgating**. Tailgating is a common form of infiltration.

Telephone Scams

Telephone scams are probably the most common social engineering attack. In this case, the attacker makes a phone call to someone in the organization to gain information. The attacker attempts to come across as someone inside the organization and uses this to get the desired information. Probably the most famous of these scams is the "I forgot my user name and password" scam. In this gambit, the attacker first learns the account name of a legitimate person in the organization, usually using the infiltration method. The

attacker then calls someone in the organization, usually the help desk, in an attempt to gather information, in this case a password.

Hacker: "Hi, this is John Anderson in accounting. I forgot my password. Can you reset it, please?"

Help Desk: "Sure, what's your user name?"

Hacker: "j_w_Anderson"

Help Desk: "OK, I reset it to e34rd3."

Certainly telephone scams aren't limited to attempts to get network access. There are documented telephone scams against organizations aimed at getting cash, blackmail material, or other valuables.

Phishing

Phishing is the act of trying to get people to give their user names, passwords, or other security information by pretending to be someone else electronically. A classic example is when a bad guy sends you an e-mail that's supposed to be from your local credit card company asking you to send them your user name and password. Phishing is by far the most common form of social engineering done today.

Data Destruction

Often an extension of unauthorized access, data destruction means more than just intentionally or accidentally erasing or corrupting data. It's easy to imagine some evil hacker accessing your network and deleting all your important files, but authorized users may also access certain data and then use that data beyond what they are authorized to do. A good example is the person who legitimately accesses a Microsoft Access product database to modify the product descriptions, only to discover that she can change the prices of the products, too.

This type of threat is particularly dangerous when users are not clearly informed about the extent to which they are authorized to make changes. A fellow tech once told me about a user who managed to mangle an important database when someone gave them incorrect access. When confronted, the user said: "If I wasn't allowed to change it, the system wouldn't let me do it!" Many users believe that systems are configured in a paternalistic way that wouldn't allow them to do anything inappropriate. As a result, users often assume they're authorized to make any changes they believe are necessary when working on a piece of data they know they're authorized to access.

Administrative Access

Every operating system enables you to create user accounts and grant those accounts a certain level of access to files and folders in that computer. As an administrator, supervisor, or root user, you have full control over just about every aspect of the computer. Windows XP, in particular, makes it entirely too easy to give users administrative access to the computer, especially Windows XP Home, which allows only two kinds of users: administrators and limited users. Because you can't do much as a limited user, most home and

small office systems simply use multiple administrator accounts. If you need to control access, you really need to use non-Home versions of Windows.

System Crash/Hardware Failure

As with any technology, computers can and will fail—usually when you can least afford for it to happen. Hard drives crash, the power fails—it's all part of the joy of working in the computing business. You need to create redundancy in areas prone to failure (such as installing backup power in case of electrical failure) and perform those all-important data backups. Chapter 16, "Securing Windows Resources," goes into detail about using backups and other issues involved in creating a stable and reliable system.

> CompTIA considers security to be an extremely important topic, whether you're at the Essentials level or at Practical Application. Unlike other chapters, almost every single topic covered in the rest of this chapter *applies equally to the Practical Application exam as it does to the Essentials exam.* In other words, you need to know everything in this chapter to pass either CompTIA A+ certification exam.

Essentials/Practical Application

Physical Theft

A fellow network geek once challenged me to try to bring down his newly installed network. He had just installed a powerful and expensive firewall router and was convinced that I couldn't get to a test server he added to his network just for me to try to access. After a few attempts to hack in over the Internet, I saw that I wasn't going to get anywhere that way. So I jumped in my car and drove to his office, having first outfitted myself in a techy-looking jumpsuit and an ancient ID badge I just happened to have in my sock drawer. I smiled sweetly at the receptionist and walked right by my friend's office (I noticed he was smugly monitoring incoming IP traffic by using some neato packet-sniffing program) to his new server. I quickly pulled the wires out of the back of his precious server, picked it up, and walked out the door. The receptionist was too busy trying to figure out why her e-mail wasn't working to notice me as I whisked by her carrying the 65-pound server box. I stopped in the hall and called him from my cell phone.

> **Me (cheerily):** "Dude, I got all your data!"
>
> **Him (not cheerily):** "You rebooted my server! How did you do it?"
>
> **Me (smiling):** "I didn't reboot it—go over and look at it!"
>
> **Him (really mad now):** "YOU <EXPLETIVE> THIEF! YOU STOLE MY SERVER!"
>
> **Me (cordially):** "Why, yes. Yes, I did. Give me two days to hack your password in the comfort of my home, and I'll see everything! Bye!"

I immediately walked back in and handed him the test server. It was fun. The moral here is simple: Never forget that the best network software security measures can be rendered useless if you fail to protect your systems physically!

Virus/Spyware

Networks are without a doubt the fastest and most efficient vehicles for transferring computer viruses among systems. News reports focus attention on the many virus attacks from the Internet, but a huge number of viruses still come from users who bring in programs on floppy disks, writable optical discs, and USB drives. The "Network Security" section of this chapter describes the various methods of virus infection and what you need to do to prevent virus infection of your networked systems.

■ Security Concepts and Technologies

Once you've assessed the threats to your computers and networks, you need to take steps to protect those valuable resources. Depending on the complexity of your organization, this can be a small job encompassing some basic security concepts and procedures, or it can be exceedingly complex. The security needs for a three-person desktop publishing firm, for example, would differ wildly from those of a defense contractor supplying top-secret toys to the Pentagon.

From a CompTIA A+ certified technician's perspective, you need to understand the big picture (that's the strategic side), knowing the concepts and available technologies for security. At the implementation level (that's the tactical side), you're expected to know where to find such things as security policies in Windows. A CompTIA Network+ or CompTIA Security+ tech will give you the specific options to implement. (The exception to this level of knowledge comes in dealing with malicious software such as viruses, but we'll tackle that subject as the last part of the chapter.) So let's look at three concept and technology areas: access control, data classification and compliance, and reporting.

Access Control

Access is the key. If you can control access to the data, programs, and other computing resources, you've secured your systems. **Access control** is composed of four interlinked areas that a good security-minded tech should think about: physical security, authentication, users and groups, and security policies. Much of this you know from previous chapters, but this section should help tie it all together as a security topic.

Secure Physical Area and Lock Down Your System

The first order of security is to block access to the physical hardware from people who shouldn't have access. This isn't rocket science. Lock the door. Don't leave a PC unattended when logged in. In fact, don't ever leave a system logged in,

Cross Check

Securing Windows Resources

Part of establishing local control over resources involves setting up the computer properly in the first place, a topic covered in depth in Chapter 16, "Securing Windows Resources." Check your memory of proper setup techniques from that chapter and see if you can answer these questions: How do you establish control over a computer's resources? What file system must you use?

Cross Check

Proper Passwords

So, what goes into making a good password? Turning once again to Chapter 16, "Securing Windows Resources," see if you can answer this question: What sorts of characters should make up a password? Should you ask for a user's password when working on that user's PC? Why or why not? If you're in a secure environment and know you'll have to re-boot several times, is it okay to ask for a password then? What should you do?

even as a limited user. God help you if you walk away from a server still logged in as an administrator. You're tempting fate.

For that matter, when you see a user's computer logged in and unattended, do the user and your company a huge favor and lock the computer. Just walk up and press the WINDOWS LOGO KEY-L on the keyboard to lock the system. It works in all versions of Windows.

 Users tend to make easy-to-crack passwords. Try a password generator Web site or program to make truly random passwords.

Authentication

Security starts with properly implemented **authentication**, which means in essence how the computer determines who can or should access it and, once accessed, what that user can do. A computer can authenticate users through software or hardware, or a combination of both.

Software Authentication: Proper Passwords   It's still rather shocking to me to power up a friend's computer and go straight to his or her desktop, or with my married-with-kids friends, to click one of the parents' user account icons and not be prompted for a password. This is just wrong! I'm always tempted to assign passwords right then and there—and not tell them the passwords, of course—so they'll see the error of their ways when they try to log in next. I don't do it but always try to explain gently the importance of good passwords.

You know about passwords from Chapter 16, "Securing Windows Resources," so I won't belabor the point here. Suffice it to say that you need to make certain that all of your users have proper passwords. Don't let them write passwords down or tape them to the underside of their mouse pads either!

It's not just access to Windows that you need to think about. There's always the temptation for people to hack the system and do mean things, such as changing CMOS settings, opening up the case, and even stealing hard drives. Any of these actions render the computer inoperable to the casual user until a tech can undo the damage or replace components. All modern CMOS setup utilities come with a number of tools to protect your computer,

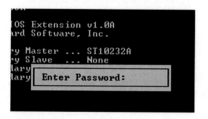

• **Figure 26.1**   CMOS access password request

such as drive lock, intrusion detection, and of course system access passwords such as the one shown in Figure 26.1. Refer to Chapter 7, "BIOS and CMOS," to refresh yourself on what you can do at a BIOS level to protect your computer.

• **Figure 26.2**   Keyboard-mounted smart card reader being used for a commercial application (*photo courtesy of Cherry Corp.*)

Hardware Authentication   Smart cards and biometric devices enable modern systems to authenticate users with more authority than mere passwords. **Smart cards** are credit-card-sized cards with circuitry that can identify the bearer of the card. Smart cards are relatively common for such tasks as authenticating users for mass transit systems, for example, but are fairly uncommon in computers. Figure 26.2 shows a smart card and keyboard combination.

People can guess or discover passwords, but forging someone's fingerprints is a lot harder. The keyboard in Figure 26.3 authenticates users on a local machine by using fingerprints. Other devices that will do the trick are key fobs, retinal scanners, and PC cards for laptop computers. Devices that require some sort of physical, flesh-and-blood authentication are called **biometric devices**.

Clever manufacturers have developed key fobs and smart cards that use radio frequency identification (RFID) to transmit authentication information so users don't have to insert something into a computer or card reader. The Privaris plusID combines, for example, a biometric fingerprint fob with an RFID tag that makes security as easy as opening a garage door remotely! Figure 26.4 shows a plusID device.

• **Figure 26.3**   Microsoft keyboard with fingerprint accessibility

NTFS, not FAT32!

The file system on a hard drive matters a lot when it comes to security. On a Windows machine with multiple users, you simply must use NTFS or you have no security at all. Not just primary drives but also any secondary drives in computers in your care should be formatted as NTFS, with the exception of removable drives such as the one you use to back up your system.

When you run into a multiple-drive system that has a second or third drive formatted as FAT32, you can use the *CONVERT* command-line utility to go from FAT to NTFS. The syntax is pretty straightforward. To convert a D: drive from FAT or FAT32 to NTFS, for example, you'd type the following:

```
CONVERT D: /FS:NTFS
```

You can substitute a mount name in place of the drive letter in case you have a mounted volume. The command has a few extra switches as well, so at the command prompt, type a */?* after the CONVERT command to see all of your options.

Users and Groups

Windows uses user accounts and groups as the bedrock of access control. A user account is assigned to a group, such as Users, Power Users, or Administrators, and by association gets certain permissions on the computer. Using NTFS enables the highest level of control over data resources.

Assigning users to groups is a great first step in controlling a local machine, but this feature really shines once you go to a networked environment. Let's go there now.

User Account Control Through Groups

Access to user accounts should be restricted to the assigned individuals, and those who configure the permissions to those accounts must remember the Principle of Least Privilege discussed

How's this for full disclosure? Microsoft does not claim that the keyboard in Figure 26.3 offers any security at all. In fact, the documentation specifically claims that the fingerprint reader is an accessibility tool, not a security device. Because it enables a person to log on to a local machine, though, I think it falls into the category of authentication devices.

plusID™

PRIVARIS™

• **Figure 26.4**   plusID (*photo courtesy of Privaris, Inc.*)

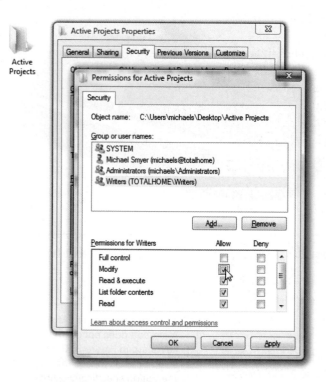

in Chapter 16, "Securing Windows Resources": Accounts should have permission to access only the resources they need and no more. Tight control of user accounts is critical to preventing unauthorized access. Disabling unused accounts is an important part of this strategy, but good user account control goes far deeper than that. One of your best tools for user account control is groups. Instead of giving permissions/rights to individual user accounts, give them to groups; this makes keeping track of the permissions assigned to individual user accounts much easier. Figure 26.5 shows me giving permissions to a group for a folder in Windows Vista. Once a group is created and its permissions set, you can then add user accounts to that group as needed. Any user account that becomes a member of a group automatically gets the permissions assigned to that group. Figure 26.6 shows me adding a user to a newly created group in the same Windows Vista system.

• **Figure 26.5** Giving a group permissions for a folder in Windows Vista

Groups are a great way to achieve increased complexity without increasing the administrative burden on network administrators, because all network operating systems combine permissions. When a user is a member of more than one group, which permissions does that user have with respect to any particular resource? In all network operating systems, the permissions of the groups are *combined*, and the result is what you call the **effective permissions** the user has to access the resource. As an example, if Rita is a member of the Sales group, which has List Folder Contents permission to a folder, and she is also a member of the Managers group, which has Read and Execute permissions to

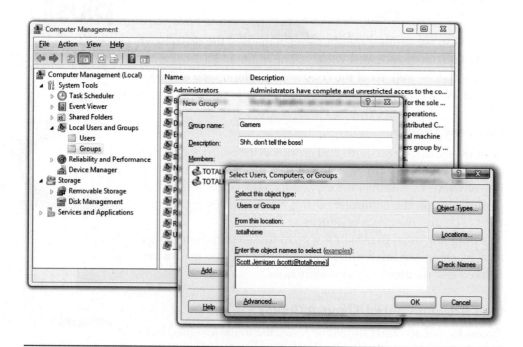

• **Figure 26.6** Adding a user to a newly created group in Windows Vista

Mike Meyers' CompTIA A+ Guide to Managing and Troubleshooting PCs

the same folder, Rita will have both List Folder Contents *and* Read and Execute permissions to that folder.

Watch out for *default* user accounts and groups—they can become secret backdoors to your network! All network operating systems have a default Everyone group that can be used to sneak into shared resources easily. This Everyone group, as its name implies, literally includes anyone who connects to that resource. Windows gives full control to the Everyone group by default, for example, so make sure you know to lock this down!

All of the default groups—Everyone, Guest, Users—define broad groups of users. Never use them unless you intend to permit all of those folks to access a resource. If you use one of the default groups, remember to configure them with the proper permissions to prevent users from doing things you don't want them to do with a shared resource!

All of these groups and organizational units only do one thing for you: They let you keep track of your user accounts, so you know they are only available for those who need them, and they can only access the resources you want them to use.

Security Policies

Although permissions control how users access shared resources, there are other functions you should control that are outside the scope of resources. For example, do you want users to be able to access a command prompt on their Windows system? Do you want users to be able to install software? Would you like to control what systems a user can log into or at what time of day a user can log in? All network operating systems provide you with some capability to control these and literally hundreds of other security parameters, under what Windows calls *policies*. I like to think of policies as permissions for activities as opposed to true permissions, which control access to resources.

A policy is usually applied to a user account, a computer, or a group. Let's use the example of a network composed of Windows XP Professional systems with a Windows 2003 Server system. Every Windows XP system has its own local policies program, which enables policies to be placed on that system only. Figure 26.7 shows the tool you use to set local policies on

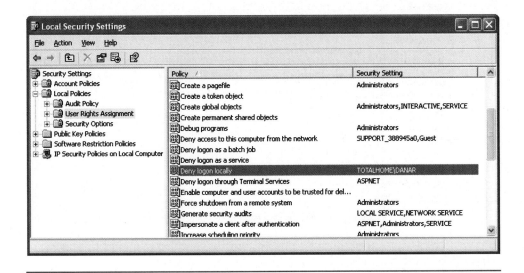

• **Figure 26.7**   Local Security Settings

an individual system, called **Local Security Settings**, being used to deny the user account Danar the capability to log on locally.

Local policies work great for individual systems, but they can be a pain to configure if you want to apply the same settings to more than one PC on your network. If you want to apply policy settings *en masse*, you need to step up to Windows Active Directory domain-based **Group Policy**. By using Group Policy, you can exercise deity-like—Microsoft prefers to use the term *granular*—control over your network clients.

Want to set default wallpaper for every PC in your domain? Group Policy can do that. Want to make certain tools inaccessible to everyone except authorized users? Group Policy can do that, too. Want to control access to the Internet, redirect home folders, run scripts, deploy software, or just remind folks that unauthorized access to the network will get them nowhere fast? Group Policy is the answer. Figure 26.8 shows Group Policy; I'm about to change the default title on every instance of Internet Explorer on every computer in my domain!

That's just one simple example of the settings you can configure by using Group Policy. You can apply literally hundreds of tweaks through Group Policy, from the great to the small, but don't worry too much about familiarizing yourself with each and every one. Group Policy settings are a big topic on most of the Microsoft certification tracks, but for the purposes of the CompTIA A+ exams, you simply have to be comfortable with the concept behind Group Policy.

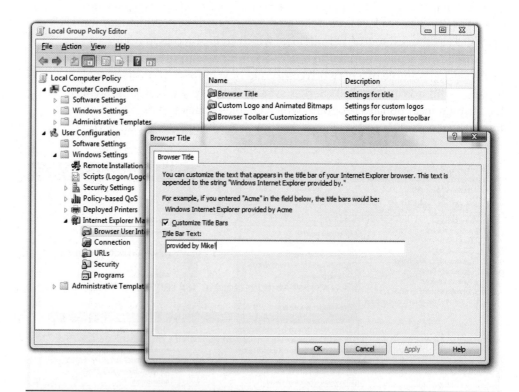

• **Figure 26.8**   Using Group Policy to make IE title say "provided by Mike!"

Although I could never list every possible policy you can enable on a Windows system, here's a list of some commonly used ones:

- **Prevent Registry Edits**   If you try to edit the Registry, you get a failure message.

- **Prevent Access to the Command Prompt**   Keeps users from getting to the command prompt by turning off the Run command and the MS-DOS Prompt shortcut.

- **Log on Locally**   Defines who may log on to the system locally.

- **Shut Down System**   Defines who may shut down the system.

- **Minimum Password Length**   Forces a minimum password length.

- **Account Lockout Threshold**   Sets the maximum number of logon attempts a person can make before being locked out of the account.

- **Disable Windows Installer**   Prevents users from installing software.

- **Printer Browsing**   Enables users to browse for printers on the network, as opposed to using only assigned printers.

Although the CompTIA A+ exams don't expect you to know how to implement policies on any type of network, you are expected to understand that policies exist, especially on Windows networks, and that they can do amazing things to control what users can do on their systems. If you ever try to get to a command prompt on a Windows system only to discover the Run command is dimmed, blame it on a policy, not the computer!

Data Classification and Compliance

Larger organizations, such as government entities, benefit greatly from organizing their data according to its sensitivity—what's called **data classification**—and making certain that computer hardware and software stay as uniform as possible. In addition, many government and internal regulations apply fairly rigorously to the organizations.

Data classification systems vary by the organization, but a common scheme classifies documents as public, internal use only, highly confidential, top secret, and so on. Using a classification scheme enables employees such as techs to know very quickly what to do with documents, the drives containing documents, and more. Your strategy for recycling a computer system left from a migrated user, for example, will differ a lot if the data on the drive was classified as internal use only or top secret.

Compliance means, in a nutshell, that members of an organization or company must abide by or comply with all of the rules that apply to the organization or company. Statutes with funny names such as Sarbanes-Oxley impose certain behaviors or prohibitions on what people can and cannot do in the workplace.

From a technician's point of view, the most common compliance issue revolves around software, such as what sort of software users can be allowed to install on their computers or, conversely, why you have to tell a user that he can't install the latest application that may help him do the job more effectively because that software isn't on the approved list. This can lead to some uncomfortable confrontations, but it's part of a tech's job.

The concepts behind compliance in IT are not, as some might imagine at first blush, to stop you from being able to work effectively. Rather they're designed to stop users with not quite enough technical skill or knowledge from installing malicious programs or applications that will destabilize their systems. This keeps technical support calls down and enables techs to focus on more serious problems.

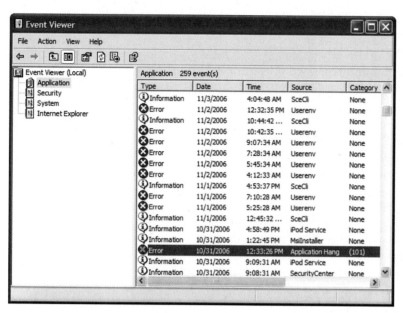

• **Figure 26.9**   Event Viewer

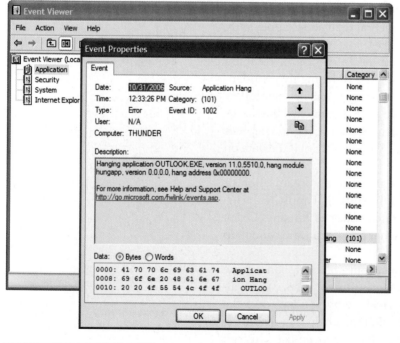

• **Figure 26.10**   Typical application error message

Reporting

As a final weapon in your security arsenal, you need to report any security issues so a network administrator or technician can take steps to make them go away. You can set up two tools within Windows so that the OS reports problems to you: Event Viewer and Auditing. You can then do your work and report those problems. Let's take a look.

Event Viewer

Event Viewer is Window's default tattletale program, spilling the beans about many things that happen on the system. You can find Event Viewer in Administrative Tools in the Control Panel. By default, Event Viewer has three sections: Application, Security, and System. If you've downloaded Internet Explorer 7, you'll see a fourth option for the browser, Internet Explorer (Figure 26.9). As you'll recall from Chapter 17, "Maintaining and Troubleshooting Windows," the most common use for Event Viewer is to view application or system errors for troubleshooting (Figure 26.10).

One very cool feature of Event Viewer is that you can click the link to take you to the online Help and Support Center at Microsoft.com, and the software reports your error (Figure 26.11), checks the online database, and comes back with a more or less useful explanation (Figure 26.12).

Auditing

The Security section of Event Viewer doesn't show you anything by default. To unlock the full potential of Event Viewer, you need to set up auditing. *Auditing* in the security sense means to tell Windows to create an entry in the Security Log when certain events happen, for example, a user

logs on—called **event auditing**—or tries to access a certain file or folder—called **object access auditing**. Figure 26.13 Shows Event Viewer tracking logon and logoff events.

The CompTIA A+ certification exams don't test you on creating a brilliant auditing policy for your office—that's what network administrators do. You simply need to know what auditing does and how to turn it on or off so you can provide support for the network administrators in the field. To turn on auditing at a local level, go to Local Security Settings in Administrative Tools. Select Local Policies and then click Audit Policies. Double-click one of the policy options and select one or both of the checkboxes. Figure 26.14 shows the Audit object access dialog box.

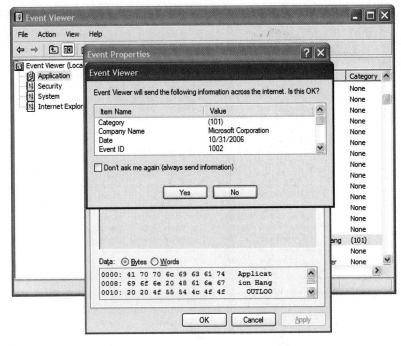

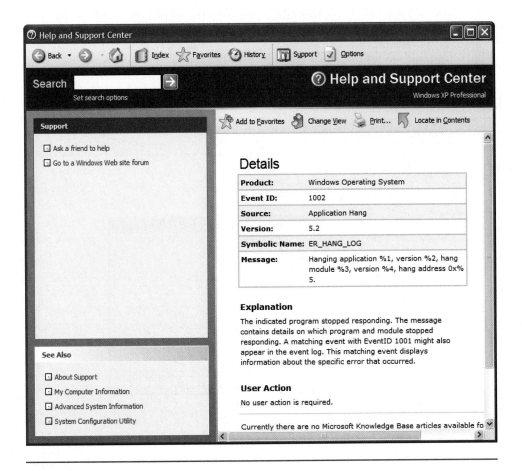

• **Figure 26.11**   Details about to be sent

• **Figure 26.12**   Help and Support Center being helpful

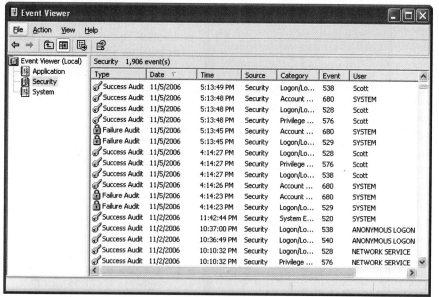

• **Figure 26.13**   Event Viewer displaying security alerts

Event Viewer stores log files in %SystemRoot%\System32\Config.

Incidence Reporting

Once you've gathered data about a particular system or you've dealt with a computer or network problem, you need to complete the mission by telling your supervisor. This is called **incidence reporting**. Many companies have pre-made forms that you simply fill out and submit. Other places are less formal. Regardless, you need to do this!

Incidence reporting does a couple of things for you. First, it provides a record of work you've accomplished. Second, it provides a piece of information that, when combined with other information you might or might not know, reveals a pattern or bigger problem to someone higher up the chain. A seemingly innocuous security audit report, for example, might match other such events in numerous places in the building at the same time and thus show that conscious, coordinated action was at work.

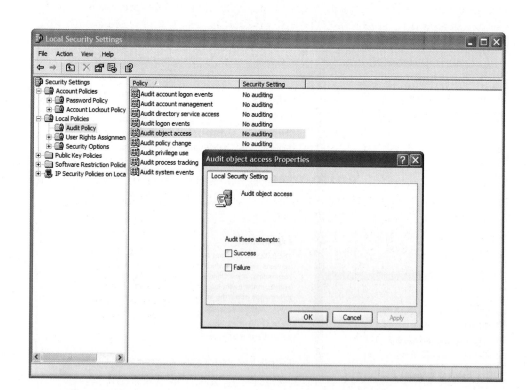

• **Figure 26.14**   Audit object access, with the Local Security Settings dialog box open in the background

Mike Meyers' CompTIA A+ Guide to Managing and Troubleshooting PCs

■ Network Security

Networks are under threat from the outside as well, so this section looks at issues involving Internet-borne attacks, firewalls, and wireless networking. This content is the security bread and butter for a CompTIA A+ technician, so you need to understand the concepts and procedures and be able to implement them properly.

Malicious Software

The beauty of the Internet is the ease of accessing resources just about anywhere on the globe, all from the comfort of your favorite chair. This connection, however, runs both ways, and people from all over the world can potentially access your computer from the comfort of their evil lairs. The Internet is awash with malicious software—*malware*—that is, even at this moment, trying to infect your systems. Malware consists of computer programs designed to break into computers or cause havoc on computers. The most common types of malware are grayware, spam, viruses, Trojan horses, and worms. You need to understand the different types of malware so you can combat them for you and your users successfully.

Grayware

Programs that intrude unwanted into your computing experience but don't actually do any damage to your systems or data—what's called **grayware**—can make that computing experience less than perfect. On most systems, the Internet Web browser client is the most often used piece of software. Over the years, Web sites have come up with more and more ways to try to get you to see what they want you to see: their advertising. When the Web first got underway, we were forced to look at an occasional banner ad. In the past few years, Web site designers have become much more sophisticated, creating a number of intrusive and irritating ways to get you to part with your money in one form or another.

There are basically three irritating grayware types: pop-ups, spyware, and adware. **Pop-ups** are those surprise browser windows that appear automatically when you visit a Web site, proving themselves irritating and unwanted and nothing else. **Spyware**, meanwhile, defines a family of programs that run in the background on your PC, sending information about your browsing habits to the company that installed it on your system. **Adware** is not generally as malicious as spyware, but it works similarly to display ads on your system. As such, these programs download new ads and generate undesirable network traffic. Of the three, spyware is much less noticeable but far more nefarious. At its worst, spyware can fire up pop-up windows of competing products on the Web site you're currently viewing. For example, you might be perusing a bookseller's Web site, only to have a pop-up from a competitor's site appear.

Pop-Ups   Getting rid of pop-ups is actually rather tricky. You've probably noticed that most of these pop-up browser windows don't look like browser windows at all. They have no menu bar, button bar, or address window, yet they are separate browser windows. HTML coding permits Web site and

advertising designers to remove the usual navigation aids from a browser window so all you're left with is the content. In fact, as I'll describe in a minute, some pop-up browser windows are deliberately designed to mimic similar pop-up alerts from the Windows OS. They might even have buttons similar to Windows' own exit buttons, but you might find that when you click them, you wind up with more pop-up windows instead! What to do?

The first thing you need to know when dealing with pop-ups is how to close them without actually having to risk clicking them. As I said, most pop-ups have removed all navigation aids, and many are also configured to appear on your monitor screen in a position that places the browser window's exit button—the little X button in the upper-right corner—outside of your visible screen area. Some even pop up behind the active browser window and wait there in the background. Most annoying! To remedy this, use alternate means to close the pop-up browser window. For instance, you can right-click the browser window's taskbar icon to generate a pop-up menu of your own. Select Close, and the window should go away. You can also press ALT-TAB to bring the browser window in question to the forefront and then press ALT-F4 to close it.

Most Web browsers have features to prevent pop-up ads in the first place, but I've found that these types of applications are sometimes *too* thorough. That is, they tend to prevent *all* new browser windows from opening, even those you want to view. Still, they're free to try, so have a look to see if they suit your needs. Applications such as AdSubtract control a variety of Internet annoyances, including pop-up windows, cookies, and Java applets, and are more configurable—you can specify what you want to allow on any particular domain address—but the fully functional versions usually cost at least something, and that much control is too confusing for most novice-level users.

Spyware   Some types of spyware go considerably beyond the level of intrusion. They can use your computer's resources to run *distributed computing* applications, capture your keystrokes to steal passwords, reconfigure your dial-up settings to use a different phone number at a much higher connection charge, or even use your Internet connection and e-mail address list to propagate itself to other computers in a virus-like fashion! Are you concerned yet?

Setting aside the legal and ethical issues—and there are many—you should at least appreciate that spyware can seriously impact your PC's performance and cause problems with your Internet connection. The threat is real, so what practical steps can you take to protect yourself? Let's look at how to prevent spyware installation and how to detect and remove any installed spyware.

How does this spyware get into your system in the first place? Obviously, sensible people don't download and install something that they know is going to compromise their computers. Makers of spyware know this, so they bundle their software with some other program or utility that purports to give you some benefit.

What kind of benefit? How about free access to MP3 music files? A popular program called Kazaa does that. How about a handy *e-wallet* utility that remembers your many screen names, passwords, and even your credit-card numbers to make online purchases easier and faster? A program called

Gator does that, and many other functions as well. How about browser enhancements, performance boosters, custom cursor effects, search utilities, buddy lists, file savers, or media players? The list goes on and on, yet they all share one thing: they're simply window-dressing for the *real* purpose of the software. So you see, for the most part, spyware doesn't need to force its way into your PC. Instead, it saunters calmly through the front door. If the graphic in Figure 26.15 looks familiar, you might have installed some of this software yourself.

Some spyware makers use more aggressive means to get you to install their software. Instead of offering you some sort of attractive utility, they instead use fear tactics and deception to try to trick you into installing their software. One popular method is to use pop-up browser windows crudely disguised as Windows' own system warnings (Figure 26.16). When clicked, these may trigger a flood of other browser windows, or may even start a file download.

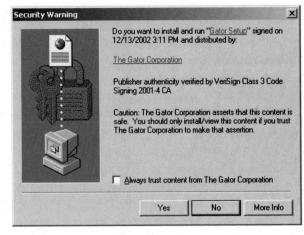

• **Figure 26.15**   Gator Corporation's acknowledgment warning

The lesson here is simple: *Don't install these programs!* Careful reading of the software's license agreement before you install a program is a good idea, but realistically, it does little to protect your PC. With that in mind, here are a couple of preventive measures you can take to keep parasitic software off of your system.

If you visit a Web site and are prompted to install a third-party application or plug-in that you've never heard of, *don't install it*. Well-known and reputable plug-ins, such as Adobe's *Shockwave* or *Flash*, are safe, but be suspicious of any others. Don't click *anywhere* inside of a pop-up browser window, even if it looks just like a Windows alert window or DOS command-line prompt—as I just mentioned, it's probably fake and the Close button is likely

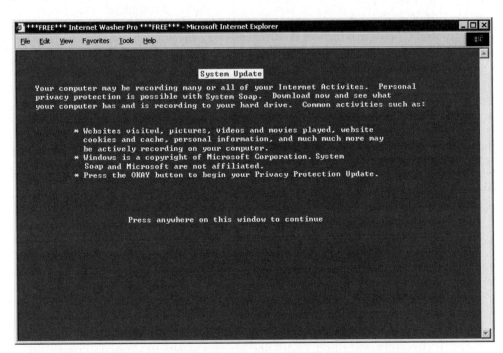

• **Figure 26.16**   A spyware pop-up browser window, disguised as a Windows alert

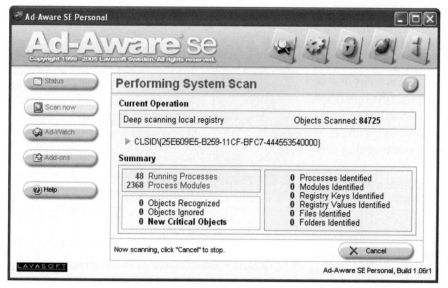

• **Figure 26.17**   Lavasoft's Ad-Aware

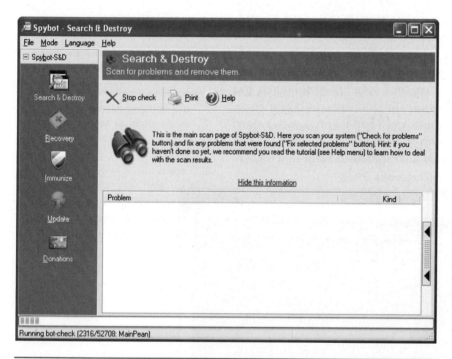

• **Figure 26.18**   Spybot Search & Destroy

a hyperlink. Instead, use other means to close the window, such as pressing ALT-F4 or right-clicking the browser window's icon on the taskbar and selecting Close.

You can also install spyware detection and removal software on your system and run it regularly. Let's look at how to do that.

Some spyware makers are reputable enough to include a routine for uninstalling their software. Gator, for instance, makes it fairly easy to get rid of their programs; just use the Windows Add/Remove Programs applet in the Control Panel. Others, however, aren't quite so cooperative. In fact, because spyware is so—well, *sneaky*—it's entirely possible that your system already has some installed that you don't even know about. How do you find out?

Windows comes with Windows Defender, a fine tool for catching most spyware, but it's not perfect. The better solution is to back up Windows Defender with a second spyware removal program. There are several on the market, but two that I highly recommend are Lavasoft's Ad-Aware (Figure 26.17) and PepiMK's Spybot Search & Destroy.

Both of these applications work exactly as advertised. They detect and delete spyware of all sorts— hidden files and folders, cookies, Registry keys and values, you name it. Ad-Aware is free for personal use, while Spybot Search & Destroy is shareware (Figure 26.18). Many times I've used both programs at the same time because one tends to catch what the other misses.

 **Try This!**

Spybot

If you haven't done this already, do it now. Go to www.spybot.info and download the latest copy of Spybot Search & Destroy. Install it on your computer and run it. Did it find any spyware that slipped in past your defenses?

Spam

E-mail that comes into your Inbox from a source that's not a friend, family member, or colleague, and that you didn't ask for, can create huge problems for your computer and you. This unsolicited e-mail, called **spam**, accounts for a huge percentage of traffic on the Internet. Spam comes in many flavors, from legitimate businesses trying to sell you products to scammers who just want to take your money. Hoaxes, pornography, and get-rich-quick schemes pour into the Inboxes of most e-mail users. They waste your time and can easily offend.

Try This!

Fight Spam Right!

Spam filtering software that you purchase and put on your computer can help, but you have to do some research to see which software offers the best performance. You want to avoid software that causes *false positives*—mislabeling acceptable e-mail as spam—because you miss legitimate e-mail messages from family and friends. So, fire up your trusty Web browser and do some searching.

Start by going to Google and searching for **anti-spam software reviews**. One of the first sites that should come up takes you to *PC Magazine*'s review list, which is kept up to date. What's the current Editor's Choice? What other options do you have?

You can use several options to cope with the flood of spam. The first option is defense. Never post your e-mail address on the Internet. One study tested this theory and found that *over 97 percent* of the spam received during the study went to e-mail addresses they had posted on the public Internet.

Filters and filtering software can block spam at your mail server and at your computer. AOL implemented blocking schemes in 2004, for example, that dropped the average spam received by its subscribers by a large percentage, perhaps as much as 50 percent. You can set most e-mail programs to block e-mail from specific people—good to use if someone is harassing you—or to specific people. You can block by subject line or keywords. Most people use a third-party anti-spam program instead of using the filters in their e-mail program.

Viruses

Just as a biological virus gets passed from person to person, a computer **virus** is a piece of malicious software that gets passed from computer to computer (Figure 26.19). A computer virus is designed to attach itself to a program on your computer. It could be your e-mail program, your word processor, or even a game. Whenever you use the infected program, the virus goes into action and does whatever it was designed to do. It can wipe out your e-mail or even erase your entire hard drive! Viruses are also sometimes used to steal information or send spam e-mails to everyone in your address book.

> Be sure to know the difference between viruses and spyware. Too many people use the terms interchangeably, and they're very different things.

Trojans

Trojans are true, freestanding programs that do something other than what the person who runs the program thinks they will do, much as the Trojan horse did in antiquity. An example of a *Trojan virus* is a program that a person thinks is an antivirus program but is actually a virus. Some Trojans are quite sophisticated.

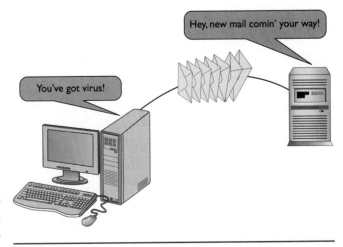

• **Figure 26.19** You've got mail!

It might be a game that works perfectly well, but causes some type of damage when the user quits the game.

Worms

Similar to a Trojan, a **worm** is a complete program that travels from machine to machine, usually through computer networks. Most worms are designed to take advantage of security problems in operating systems and install themselves on vulnerable machines. They can copy themselves over and over again on infected networks and can create so much activity that they overload the network by consuming bandwidth, in worst cases even bringing chunks of the entire Internet to a halt.

You can do several things to protect yourself and your data against these threats. First, make sure you are running up-to-date virus software—especially if you connect to the Internet via an always-on broadband connection. You should also be protected by a firewall, either as part of your network hardware or by means of a software program. (See the sections on antivirus programs and firewalls later in this chapter.)

Because worms most commonly infect systems through security flaws in operating systems, the next defense against them is to make sure you have the latest security patches installed on your version of Windows. A *security patch* is an addition to the operating system to patch a hole in the operating system code. You can download security patches from the Microsoft Update Web site (Figure 26.20).

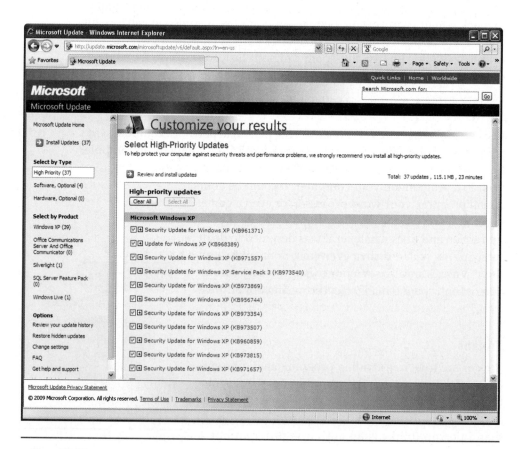

• **Figure 26.20** Microsoft Update

Microsoft's Windows Update tool is handy for Windows users as it provides a simple method to ensure that your version's security is up to date. The one downside is that not everyone remembers to run Windows Update. Don't wait until something goes wrong on your computer or you hear on the news that another nasty program is running rampant across the Internet. Run Windows Update weekly (or even better, automatically) as a part of your normal system maintenance. Keeping your patches up to date is called *patch management*, and it goes a long way toward keeping your system safe.

Virus Prevention and Recovery

The only way to protect your PC permanently from getting a virus is to disconnect from the Internet and never permit any potentially infected software to touch your precious computer. Because neither scenario is likely these days, you need to use a specialized antivirus program to help stave off the inevitable virus assaults. When you discover infected systems, you need to know how to stop the spread of the virus to other computers and how to fix infected computers.

Antivirus Programs

An **antivirus program** protects your PC in two ways. It can be both sword and shield, working in an active seek-and-destroy mode and in a passive sentry mode. When ordered to seek and destroy, the program scans the computer's boot sector and files for viruses and, if it finds any, presents you with the available options for removing or disabling them. Antivirus programs can also operate as **virus shields** that passively monitor your computer's activity, checking for viruses only when certain events occur, such as a program executing or a file being downloaded.

Antivirus programs use different techniques to combat different types of viruses. They detect boot sector viruses simply by comparing the drive's boot sector to a standard boot sector. This works because most boot sectors are basically the same. Some antivirus programs make a backup copy of the boot sector. If they detect a virus, the programs use that backup copy to replace the infected boot sector. Executable viruses are a little more difficult to find because they can be on any file in the drive. To detect executable viruses, the antivirus program uses a library of signatures. A **signature** is the code pattern of a known virus. The antivirus program compares an executable file to its library of signatures. There have been instances where a perfectly clean program coincidentally held a virus signature. Usually the antivirus program's creator provides a patch to prevent further alarms. Now that you understand the types of viruses and how antivirus programs try to protect against them, let's review a few terms that are often used when describing certain traits of viruses.

Polymorphics/Polymorphs   A **polymorph virus** attempts to change its signature to prevent detection by antivirus programs, usually by continually scrambling a bit of useless code. Fortunately, the scrambling code itself can be identified and used as the signature—once the antivirus makers become aware of the virus. One technique used to combat unknown polymorphs is to have the antivirus program create a checksum on every file in the drive. A *checksum* in this context is a number generated by the software based on the contents of

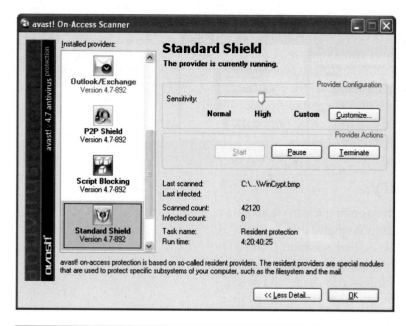

the file rather than the name, date, or size of that file. The algorithms for creating these checksums vary among different antivirus programs (they are also usually kept secret to help prevent virus makers from coming up with ways to beat them). Every time a program is run, the antivirus program calculates a new checksum and compares it with the earlier calculation. If the checksums are different, it is a sure sign of a virus.

Stealth   The term "stealth" is more of a concept than an actual virus function. Most **stealth virus** programs are boot sector viruses that use various methods to hide from antivirus software. The AntiEXE stealth virus hooks on to a little-known but often-used software interrupt, for example, running only when that interrupt runs. Others make copies of innocent-looking files.

• **Figure 26.21**   A virus shield in action

Virus Prevention Tips

The secret to preventing damage from a malicious software attack is to keep from getting a virus in the first place. As discussed earlier, all good antivirus programs include a virus shield that scans e-mail, downloads, running programs, and so on automatically (see Figure 26.21).

Use your antivirus shield. It is also a good idea to scan PCs daily for possible virus attacks. All antivirus programs include terminate-and-stay resident programs (TSRs) that run every time the PC is booted. Last but not least, know the source of any software before you load it. Although the chance of commercial, shrink-wrapped software having a virus is virtually nil (there have been a couple of well-publicized exceptions), that illegal copy of Unreal Tournament you borrowed from a local hacker should definitely be inspected with care.

Keep your antivirus program updated. New viruses appear daily, and your program needs to know about them. The list of virus signatures your antivirus program can recognize is called the **definition file**, and you must keep that definition file up to date so your antivirus software has the latest signatures. Fortunately, most antivirus programs update themselves automatically. Further, you should periodically update the core antivirus software programming—called the *engine*—to employ the latest refinements the developers have included.

Virus Recovery Tips

When the inevitable happens and either your computer or one of your user's computers gets infected by a computer virus, you need to follow certain steps to stop the problem from spreading and get the computer back up safely into service. Try this five-step process.

1. Recognize
2. Quarantine

3. Search and destroy

4. Remediate

5. Educate

Recognize and Quarantine The first step is to recognize that a potential virus outbreak has occurred. If you're monitoring network traffic and one computer starts spewing e-mail, that's a good sign. Or users might complain that a computer that was running snappily the day before seems very sluggish.

Many networks employ software such as the open source PacketFence that automatically monitors network traffic and can cut a machine off the network if that machine starts sending suspicious packets. You can also quarantine a computer manually, by disconnecting the network cable. Once you're sure the machine isn't capable of infecting others, you're ready to find the virus and get rid of it.

Search and Destroy Once you've isolated the infected computer (or computers), you need to get to a safe boot environment and run your antivirus software. You can try Windows Safe Mode first, because it doesn't require anything but a reboot. If that doesn't work, or you suspect a boot sector virus, you need to turn to an external bootable source, such as a bootable CD or flash memory drive.

Get into the habit of keeping around an antivirus CD-R—a bootable CD-R disc with a copy of an antivirus program. If you suspect a virus, use the disc, even if your antivirus program claims to have eliminated the virus. Turn off the PC and reboot it from the antivirus disc. (You might have to change CMOS settings to boot to an optical disc.) This will put you in a clean boot environment that you know is free from any boot-sector viruses. If you only support fairly recent computers, most have an option to boot to a USB flash drive, so you can put a boot environment on a thumb drive for even faster start-up speeds.

You have several options for creating the bootable CD-R or flash drive. First, some antivirus software comes in a bootable version, such as the avast! Virus Cleaner Tool (Figure 26.22).

Second, you can download a copy of Linux that offers a LiveCD option such as Ubuntu. With a LiveCD, you boot to the CD and install a complete working copy of the operating system into RAM, never touching or accessing the hard drive, to give you full Internet-ready access to many online antivirus sites. (You'll obviously need Internet access for those tools.) Kaspersky Labs provides a nice option at www.kaspersky.com.

Finally, you can download and burn a copy of the Ultimate Boot CD. It comes stocked with several antivirus programs, so you wouldn't need any other tool. Find it at www.ultimatebootcd.com. The only downside is that the antivirus engines will be out of date, as will their virus encyclopedias.

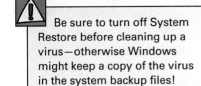 Be sure to turn off System Restore before cleaning up a virus—otherwise Windows might keep a copy of the virus in the system backup files!

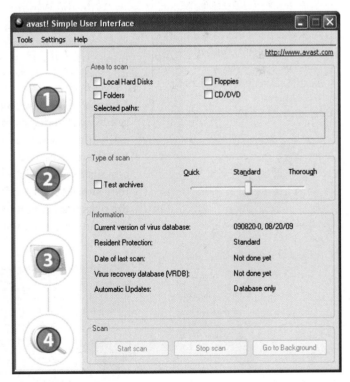

• **Figure 26.22** avast! Virus Cleaner Tool

Once you get to a boot environment, run your antivirus program's most comprehensive virus scan. Then check all removable media that were exposed to the system, as well as any other machine that might have received data from it or that is networked to the cleaned machine. A virus or other malicious program can often lie dormant for months before anyone knows of its presence.

E-mail is still a common source of viruses, and opening infected e-mails is a common way to get infected. Viewing an e-mail in a preview window opens the e-mail message and exposes your computer to some viruses. Download files only from sites you know to be safe, and of course the less reputable corners of the Internet are the most likely places to pick up computer infections.

Remediate Virus infections can do a lot of damage to a system, especially to sensitive files needed to load Windows, so you might need to remediate formerly infected systems after cleaning off the drive or drives. **Remediation** simply means that you fix things the virus harmed. This can mean replacing corrupted Windows Registry files or even startup files.

If you can't start Windows after the virus scan is finished, you need to follow the steps outlined in Chapter 16, "Securing Windows Resources," to boot to the Recovery Console in Windows 2000/XP, or boot into a repair environment in Windows Vista.

Once in the Recovery Console, you'll have access to tools to repair the boot sector (or *boot blocks*, as CompTIA calls them) through the FIXMBR and FIXBOOT commands. You can run BOOTCFG to rebuild a corrupted BOOT.INI file. EXPAND will enable you to grab any replacement files from the Windows CAB files.

With the Windows Vista repair environment, you have access to more repair tools, such as Startup Repair, System Restore, Windows Complete PC Restore, and the command prompt (Figure 26.23). Run the appropriate option for the situation and you should have the machine properly remediated in a jiffy.

Educate The best way to keep from having to deal with malware and grayware is education. It's your job as the IT person to talk to users, especially the ones whose systems you've just spent the last hour cleaning of nasties, about how to avoid these programs. Show them samples of dangerous e-mails they should not open, Web sites to avoid, and the types of programs they should not install and use on the network. Any user who understands the risks of questionable actions on their computers will usually do the right thing and stay away from malware.

Cross Check

System Recovery Options

You saw the Windows Vista System Recovery Options back in Chapter 17, "Maintaining and Troubleshooting Windows," so check your memory now. What's the major difference between System Restore and Windows Complete PC Restore? In what circumstances would you choose one tool over the other? What are the dangers, if any, in either tool?

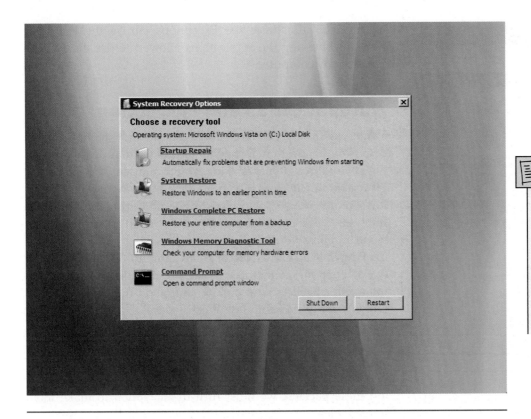

System Recovery Options
Choose a recovery tool
Operating system: Microsoft Windows Vista on (C:) Local Disk

Startup Repair
Automatically fix problems that are preventing Windows from starting

System Restore
Restore Windows to an earlier point in time

Windows Complete PC Restore
Restore your entire computer from a backup

Windows Memory Diagnostic Tool
Check your computer for memory hardware errors

Command Prompt
Open a command prompt window

Shut Down   Restart

Almost all routers come with built-in firewalls that enable you to create Access Control Lists (ACLs). An ACL might filter by port number, IP address, MAC address, time of day, day of the week, or even Web addresses.

● **Figure 26.23**   System Recovery options in Windows Vista

Finally, have your users run antivirus and antispyware programs regularly. Schedule them while interfacing with the user so you know it will happen.

Firewalls

Firewalls are an essential tool in the fight against malicious programs on the Internet. **Firewalls** are devices or software that protect an internal network from unauthorized access to and from the Internet at large. Hardware firewalls use a number of methods to protect networks, such as hiding IP addresses and blocking TCP/IP ports. Most SOHO networks use a hardware firewall, such as the Linksys router in Figure 26.24. These devices do a great job.

Windows XP and later come with an excellent software firewall, called the Windows Firewall (Figure 26.25). It can also handle the heavy lifting of port blocking, security logging, and more.

You can access the Windows Firewall by opening the Windows Firewall applet in the Control Panel. If you're running the Control Panel in Category view, click the Security Center icon (Figure 26.26) and then click the Windows Firewall option in the Windows Security Center dialog box.

● **Figure 26.24**   Linksys router as a firewall

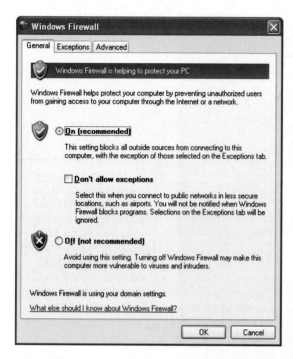

Windows Firewall is helping to protect your PC

Windows Firewall helps protect your computer by preventing unauthorized users from gaining access to your computer through the Internet or a network.

On (recommended)

This setting blocks all outside sources from connecting to this computer, with the exception of those selected on the Exceptions tab.

☐ **Don't allow exceptions**

Select this when you connect to public networks in less secure locations, such as airports. You will not be notified when Windows Firewall blocks programs. Selections on the Exceptions tab will be ignored.

Off (not recommended)

Avoid using this setting. Turning off Windows Firewall may make this computer more vulnerable to viruses and intruders.

Windows Firewall is using your domain settings.

What else should I know about Windows Firewall?

• **Figure 26.25**   Windows Firewall

Figure 26.27 illustrates the Exceptions tab on the Windows Firewall, showing the applications allowed to use the TCP/IP ports on my computer.

Authentication and Encryption

You know from previous chapters that the first step in securing data is authentication, through a user name and password. But when you throw in networking, you're suddenly not just a single user sitting in front of a computer and typing. You're accessing a remote resource and sending login information over the Internet. What's to stop someone from intercepting your user name and password?

Firewalls do a great job of controlling traffic coming into or out of a network from the Internet, but they do nothing to stop interceptor hackers who monitor traffic on the public Internet looking for vulnerabilities. Worse, once a packet is on the Internet itself, anyone with the right equipment can intercept and inspect it. Inspected packets are a cornucopia of passwords, account names, and other tidbits that hackers can use to intrude into your network. Because we can't stop hackers from inspecting these packets, we must turn to **encryption** to make them unreadable.

• **Figure 26.26**   Control Panel, Category view

Network encryption occurs at many levels and is in no way limited to Internet-based activities. Not only are there many levels of network encryption, but each encryption level also provides multiple standards and options, making encryption one of the most complicated of all networking issues. You need to understand where encryption comes into play, what options are available, and what you can use to protect your network.

Network Authentication

Have you ever considered the process that takes place each time a person types in a user name and password to access a network, rather than just a local machine? What happens when this *network* authentication is requested? If you're thinking that when a user types in a user name and password, that information is sent to a server of some sort to be authenticated, you're right—but do you know how the user name and password get to the serving system? That's where encryption becomes important in authentication.

In a local network, authentication and encryption are usually handled by the NOS. In today's increasingly interconnected and diverse networking environment, there is a motivation to enable different network operating systems to authenticate any client system from any other NOS. Modern network operating systems such as Windows and OS X use standard authentication encryptions such as MIT's **Kerberos**, enabling multiple brands of servers to authenticate multiple brands of clients. These LAN authentication methods are usually transparent and work quite nicely, even in mixed networks.

Unfortunately, this uniformity falls away as you begin to add remote access authentications. There are so many different remote access tools, based on UNIX/Linux, Novell NetWare, and Windows serving programs, that most remote access systems have to support a variety of authentication methods.

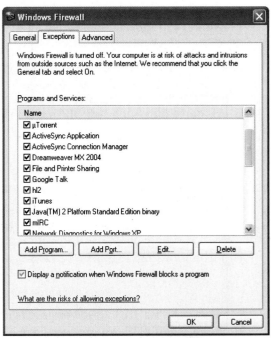

• **Figure 26.27** Essential programs (doesn't everyone need to run Half-Life 2?)

PAP Password Authentication Protocol (PAP) is the oldest and most basic form of authentication. It's also the least safe, because it sends all passwords in clear text. No NOS uses PAP for a client system's login, but almost all network operating systems that provide remote access service support PAP for backward compatibility with a host of older programs (such as Telnet) that only use PAP.

CHAP Challenge Handshake Authentication Protocol (CHAP) is the most common remote access protocol, by which the serving system challenges the remote client by asking the remote client some secret—usually a password. If the remote client responds appropriately, the host allows the connection.

MS-CHAP MS-CHAP is Microsoft's variation of the CHAP protocol, using a slightly more advanced encryption protocol. The version of MS-CHAP that comes with Vista is version 2 (MS-CHAP v2).

Configuring Dial-up Encryption

It's the server, not the client, that controls the choice of dial-up encryption. Whoever configures the dial-up server determines how you have to

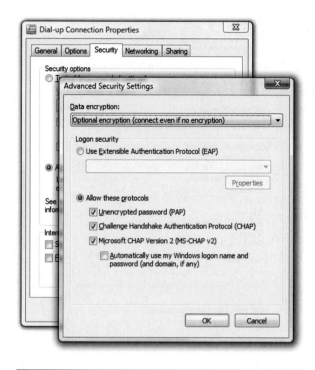

configure the dial-up client. Microsoft clients handle a broad selection of authentication encryption methods, including no authentication at all. On the rare occasion when you have to change your client's default encryption settings for a dial-up connection, you'll need to journey deep into the bowels of its properties. Figure 26.28 shows the Windows Vista dialog box, called Advanced Security Settings, where you configure encryption. The person who controls the server's configuration will tell you which encryption method to select here.

Data Encryption

Encryption methods don't stop at the authentication level. There are a number of ways to encrypt network *data* as well. The choice of encryption method is dictated to a large degree by the method used by the communicating systems to connect. Many networks consist of multiple networks linked together by some sort of private connection, usually some kind of telephone line such as ISDN or T1. Microsoft's encryption method of choice for this type of network is called **IPSec** (derived from *IP security*). IPSec provides transparent encryption between the server and the client. IPSec also works in VPNs, but other encryption methods are more commonly used in those situations.

● **Figure 26.28**   Setting dial-up encryption in the Windows Vista Advanced Security Settings dialog box

Application Encryption

When it comes to encryption, even TCP/IP applications can get into the swing of things. The most famous of all application encryptions is Netscape's **Secure Sockets Layer (SSL)** security protocol, which is used to create secure Web sites. Microsoft incorporates SSL into its more far-reaching **HTTPS** (HTTP over SSL) protocol. These protocols make it possible to create the secure Web sites people use to make purchases over the Internet. You can identify HTTPS Web sites by the *HTTPS://* included in the URL (see Figure 26.29).

A digital signature is similar to a digital certificate in that it verifies the sender of the data and assures the data's integrity. However, a digital signature lacks the third-party support of a digital certificate.

To make a secure connection, your Web browser and the Web server must encrypt their data. That means there must be a way for both the Web server and your browser to encrypt and decrypt each other's data. To do this, the server sends a public key to your Web browser so the browser knows how to decrypt the incoming data. These public keys are sent in the form of a **digital certificate**. This certificate is signed by a trusted authority that guarantees that the public key you are about to get is actually from the Web server and not from some evil person trying to pretend to be the Web server. A number of companies issue digital certificates to Web sites, probably the most famous being VeriSign, Inc.

Your Web browser has a built-in list of trusted authorities. If a certificate comes in from a Web site that uses one of these highly respected companies, you won't see anything happen in your browser; you'll just go to the secure Web page, where a small lock will appear in the lower-right corner of your browser. Figure 26.30 shows the list of trusted authorities built in to the Firefox Web browser.

• **Figure 26.29**   A secure Web site

However, if you receive a certificate from someone *not* listed in your browser, the browser will warn you and ask you if you wish to accept the certificate, as shown in Figure 26.31.

What you do here is up to you. Do you wish to trust this certificate? In most cases, you simply say yes, and this certificate is added to your SSL cache of certificates. However, an accepted certificate may become invalid, usually because of something boring; for instance, it may go out of date or the public key may change. This never happens with the "big name" certificates built in to your browser—you'll see this more often when a certificate is used, for example, in-house on a company intranet and the administrator forgets to update the certificates. If a certificate goes bad, your browser issues a warning the next time you visit that site. To clear invalid certificates, you need to clear the SSL cache. The process varies in every browser, but in Internet Explorer, go to the Content tab under Internet Options and click the *Clear SSL state* button (Figure 26.32).

● Figure 26.30   Trusted authorities

● Figure 26.31   Incoming certificate

Wireless Issues

Wireless networks add a whole level of additional security headaches for techs to face, as you know from Chapter 24, "Wireless Networking." Some of the points to remember or to go back and look up are as follows:

- Set up wireless encryption, at least WEP but preferably WPA or the more secure WPA2 and configure clients to use them.

- Disable DHCP and require your wireless clients to use a static IP address.

- If you need to use DHCP, only allot enough DHCP addresses to meet the needs of your network to avoid unused wireless connections.

- Change the WAP's SSID from default and disable SSID broadcast.

- Filter by MAC address to allow only known clients on the network.

- Change the default user name and password. Every hacker has memorized the default user names and passwords.

- Update the firmware as needed.

- If available, make sure the WAP's firewall settings are turned on.

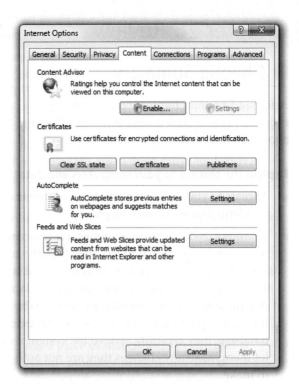

● **Figure 26.32**   The Internet Options Content tab

Cross Check

Securing Wireless Networks

Wireless networks are all the rage right now, from your local Starbucks to the neighbors around you. Securing wireless networks has, therefore, become an area that CompTIA A+ certified technicians must master. You read a lot about wireless networks in Chapter 24, "Wireless Networking," so turn there now and see if you can answer these questions.

What is the minimum level of encryption to secure a wireless network? What types of wireless will you find for connecting at your local coffee shop?

The Complete PC Tech

In this chapter, you will learn how to

- **Describe how computers work**
- **Implement a troubleshooting methodology**
- **Describe a technician's toolkit**

When a mission-critical computer goes down, regardless of the industry, people get upset. Workers can't work, so they feel guilty. Employers can't get product out on time, so they feel anxious. Supervisors blame employees for fouling things up, or at least the employees fear such blame, even if they did not break the machine.

Into this charged atmosphere comes the tech, ready to fix the computer and move on to the next challenge. Accomplishing this task, though, requires three things: First, a good tech must know the broken machine inside and out—how it's *supposed* to work when working properly. Second, the tech has to calm the workers and supervisors, and get answers to questions to gain relevant information about the problem. Third, the tech must troubleshoot the problem and fix the machine.

This chapter starts with an overview of how computers work and then dives into a section on dealing with customers and how to get them to tell you what you need to know and smile about it. The chapter wraps up with a proven troubleshooting methodology to help you figure out the source of problems and point you to the fix quickly.

Essentials

■ How Computers Work

You've spent a lot of time going through this book, reading about technologies and components in great detail. Each chapter contained troubleshooting information and methodologies for the components explained in that chapter. In Chapter 5, "Microprocessors," for example, you learned all about CPUs, from how they work to how to install them. You also learned about issues specific to CPUs, including the potentially difficult task of adding or removing the fan and heat sink assembly that all CPUs require. In Chapters 11, "Hard Drive Technologies," and 12, "Implementing Hard Drives," you dove into hard drives in gory detail. With each chapter, you added more and more information about the pieces that make up the personal computer today.

In this chapter, I want you to distill that knowledge, to think about the computer as a coherent machine. Each of the computer's components works together to enable people to produce some amazing things.

To master the art of troubleshooting as a PC tech, you need to approach a technical problem and answer one question: "What can it be? What can be causing this problem?" (Okay, that was two questions, but you get the idea.) Because every process involves multiple components, you must understand the interconnectedness of those components. If Jane can't print, for example, what could it be? Connectivity? Drivers? Paper jam? Slow network connection? Frozen application? Solar flares? Let's look at the process.

Way back in Chapter 3, "The Visible PC," you learned about the four parts of the computing process: input, processing, output, and storage. Let's take a moment to review the computing process, this time to see how you can use it to help you fix computers.

When you run a program, your computer goes through three of the four stages of the **computing process**: input, processing, and output (Figure 27.1). Input requires specific devices, such as the keyboard and mouse, that enable you to tell the computer to do something, such as open a program or type a word. The operating system (OS) provides an interface and tools so that the microprocessor and other chips can process your request. The image on the monitor or sound from the speakers effectively tells you that the computer has interpreted your command and spit out the result. The fourth stage, storage, comes into

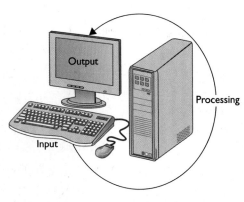

● **Figure 27.1**   Input, processing, and output

Cross Check

Printing Process

You learned all about the printing process in Chapter 22, "Printers," but now think in terms of the computing process. Does the computing process translate when applied to printers? How? If a user can't print, how does knowledge of the computing process help you troubleshoot the printing process?

play when you want to save a document and when you first open programs and other files.

Making this process work, though, requires the complex interaction of many components, including multiple pieces of hardware and layers of software. As a tech, you need to understand all the components and how they work together so that when something doesn't work right, you can track down the source and fix it. A look at a modern program reveals that even a seemingly simple action or change on the screen requires many things to happen within the computer.

Games such as Second Life (Figure 27.2) are huge, taking up multiple gigabytes of space on an Internet server. They simply won't fit into the RAM in most computers, so developers have figured out ways to minimize RAM usage.

In Second Life, for example, you move through the online world in a series of more or less seamlessly connected areas. Crossing a bridge from one island to another triggers the game to quickly update the information you're about to see on the new island, so you won't be out of the action and the illusion of being in the game world remains intact. Here's what happens when you press the W key on your keyboard and your character steps across the invisible zone line.

The keyboard controller reads the grid of your keyboard and, on discovering your input, sends the information to the CPU through the wires of the motherboard (Figure 27.3). The CPU understands the keyboard controller because of a small program that was loaded into RAM from the ROM BIOS on the motherboard when the PC booted up.

The CPU and the application determine what should happen in the game, and on discovering that your character is about to cross the zone line,

Second Life is a massively multiplayer online role-playing game (MMORPG) that offers a unique twist on the genre. You can create just about anything you can imagine, as far as your time and talent can take you. Second Life has a functioning economy that spills out into the real world, meaning you can buy and sell things within the game and turn that into real U.S. dollars, although the more common scenario is to spend real money to get virtual possessions.

• **Figure 27.2** Second Life

they trigger a whole series of actions. The application sends the signal to the OS that it needs a specific area loaded into RAM. The OS sends a signal to the CPU that it needs data stored on the hard drive plus information stored on the Second Life servers. The CPU then sends the commands to the hard drive controller for it to grab the proper stored data and send it to RAM, while at the same time sending a command to the NIC to download the updated information (Figure 27.4).

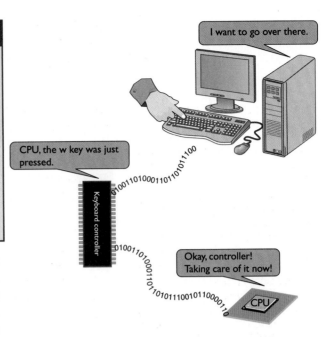

● **Figure 27.3**   Keyboard to CPU

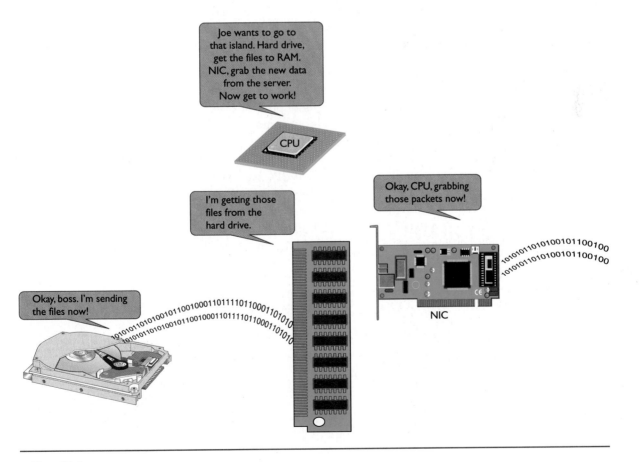

● **Figure 27.4**   CPU to hard drive and NIC

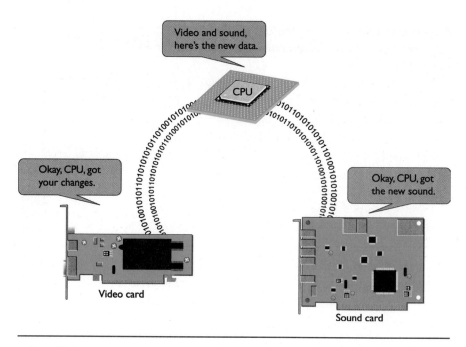

• **Figure 27.5**   CPU to video card and sound card

The hard drive controller tells the hard drive to cough up the data—megabytes worth—and then sends that data through the motherboard to the memory controller, which puts it into RAM and communicates with the CPU when it's finished. The network card and network operating system communicate with the Second Life servers and download the necessary updated information. The CPU then uses the application and OS to process the new data, sending video data to the video card and sound data to the sound card, again through the wires on the motherboard (Figure 27.5).

The video card processor puts the incoming data into its RAM, processes the data, and then sends out commands to the monitor to update the screen. The sound card processor likewise processes the data and sends out commands to the speakers to play a new sound (Figure 27.6).

For all of this to work, the PC has to have electricity, so the direct current (DC) provided by the power supply and the alternating current (AC) provided to the power supply must both be the proper voltage and amperage.

Finally, because Second Life is a network application, the OS has to send information through the NIC and onto the Internet to update everyone

Tech Tip

Video Counts

Windows Vista has raised the bar on video demands in a big way, so the video card in your users' systems can make a remarkable difference in their experience. Vista uses the video card to produce many of the cool visual effects of the interface. This means that a low-end video card in an otherwise serviceable machine can cause Vista to misbehave. Unless your client is gaming, there's no reason to drop $300+ on a video card, but assembling or recommending a system with yesterday's video is not necessarily a good thing!

Cross Check

Hard Drive Technologies

You learned about several hard drive technologies way back in Chapter 11, "Hard Drive Technologies," so turn there now and see if you can answer these questions. If an application stumbles or hesitates on the "load from the hard drive" section of the computing process, what could be the problem? Which of the available hard drive technologies offers better throughput? What would you recommend to a client who wanted to upgrade?

else's computer. That way, the other characters in the game world see you move forward a step (Figure 27.7).

What do you see or hear with all these electrons zipping all over the place? Out of a seemingly blank vista (Figure 27.8), a castle begins to appear, building itself piece by piece as your computer processes the new information and updates the video screen. You hear music begin to play from your speakers. Within a few seconds, with the data describing the new island fully downloaded and processed, the world on your monitor looks very different (Figure 27.9). That's when all goes well. Many megabytes of data have flowed from your hard drive and across the Internet, been processed by multiple processors, and sent to the monitor and the speakers.

To keep the action continuous and unbroken, Second Life, like many current online games, uses a process of continuous or **stream loading**: your computer constantly downloads updated information and data from the Second Life servers, so the world you see

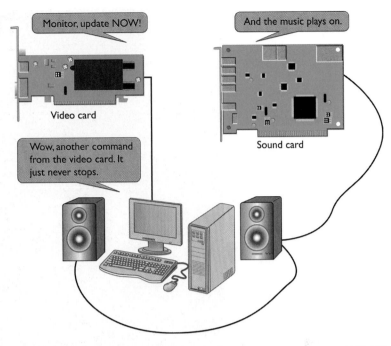

• **Figure 27.6** Updating the screen and speakers

changes with every step you take. When done right, stream loading can do some amazing things. In the GameCube game Zelda, for example, the game anticipates where you will go next and loads that new area into RAM before you take the step. You can be in one area and use a telescope to zoom in on

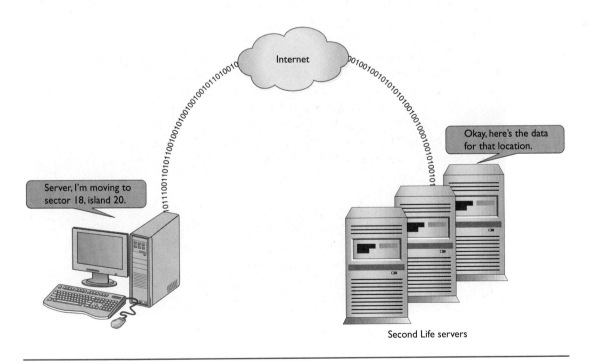

• **Figure 27.7** PC to Second Life servers

The CompTIA A+ certification exams assume that all techs should back up systems *every time* before working on them, even though that's not how it works in the real world.

Dead hard drives retain their data, so you can recover it—if you're willing to pay a lot of money. Having a good backup in place makes a lot more economic sense!

When taking a service call over the phone, first ask for the user's name and the problem!

Identify the Problem

There's a reason you're standing in front of a computer to repair it: something happened that the user of the computer has identified as "not good" and that's why you're here. The first step to **identifying any problem** is talking to the user. Get the user to show you what's not good. Is it an error code? Is something not accessible? Is a device not responding? Then ask the user that classic tech question (remember your communication skills here!): "Has anything recently changed on the computer that might have made this problem appear?" What you're really saying is: "Have you jacked with the computer? Did you install some evil program? Did you shove in a USB drive so hard you broke the connection?" Of course, you never say these things, simply ask nicely without accusing so the user can help you fix the problem (Figure 27.11).

In most troubleshooting situations, it's important to back up critical files before making changes to a system. To some extent, this is a matter of proper ongoing maintenance, but if some important bit of data disappears and you don't have a backup, you know who the user will blame, don't you?

If you run into a partially functional system where you might have to reinstall the OS but can access the hard drive, you should definitely back up essential data, such as e-mail, browser favorites, important documents, and any data not stored on a regularly backed-up server. Because you can boot to a copy of Windows and go to the Recovery Console, you should never lose essential data, barring full-blown hard drive death.

Establish a Theory of Probable Cause (Question the Obvious)

Now it's time to analyze the issue and come up with a theory as to what is wrong—a **theory of probable cause**. Personally, I prefer the word "guess" at this point because very few errors are so obvious that you'll know what to do. Fall back on your knowledge of the computing process to localize the issue based on the symptoms. Keep your guesses…err…theories…simple. One of the great problems for techs is their tendency to overlook the obvious problems in their desire to dig into the system (Figure 27.12).

Outside the Case

Take a moment to look for clues before you open up the case. Most importantly, use all your senses in the process.

What do you see? Is a connector mangled, or a plastic part clearly damaged? Even if that connector or part works fine, the physical abuse could provide extra information. If the user can't connect to a network, check the cable. Was something rolled over it that could have broken the thin, internal wires? Is that a jelly smear near the jammed optical drive door? (No pun intended, really!) A visual examination of the external computer is important.

When you put your hand on the system unit, does it feel hot? Can you feel or hear the vibrations of the fans? If not, that would be a clue to an overheating or overheated computer. Modern computers can run when overly hot, but generally run very sluggishly. If you run through basic malware fixes, but a computer still runs poorly, think about excessive heat as a potential problem.

If you spend a moment listening to the PC, you might get some clues to problem sources. As you'll recall from Chapter 12, "Implementing Hard Drives," a properly running hard drive doesn't make a lot of sound; just a regular hum from the spinning platters. If you hear clicking or grinding sounds from a drive, that's a very bad sign and a very important clue! Excessive thrashing or disk access can likewise lead to some potential problem areas, such as insufficient RAM or a badly fragmented drive.

Finally, don't forget your nose. If you smell the unmistakable odor of ozone, you know that's the smell electronic components give off when they cook or are simply running much too hot.

Inside the Case

Use all your senses when you go inside the system unit as well. Do you see any physical damage? Check the motherboard capacitors if you have a dead PC. Properly working capacitors should be nice and flat on top. They definitely shouldn't look like partly melted batteries or be bulging at the seams. Fans should be spinning. The power supply shouldn't be blistering hot. You should be able to localize sounds better with the case off, and any smell of cooking components will definitely be stronger.

● **Figure 27.12**   Ford the Tech misses the obvious.

As you do your inspection, both outside and inside the case, don't jump to conclusions too quickly. When you see a problem that looks obvious, stop and give yourself an "Are you sure?" moment. Consider the possibility that a problem you've seen 50 times before might *not* be the same thing. Of course, it probably *is* the same problem, but that moment of consideration might save you trouble later.

Okay, so you've decided on a theory that makes sense. It's time to see if your theory *is* actually the problem at hand—give it a test to see if it fixes the problem.

> Remember, many electrical components have risk. CRT monitors are under high vacuum and can implode if you drop them!

Test the Theory to Determine Cause

The biggest challenge to fixing a computer is that the theory and the fix pretty much prove themselves at the same time. Let's go back to the situation where the power plug isn't in the wall. You observe that nothing happens when the PC power button is pressed. You check the back of the power supply and see that the power cable is plugged in. You then look at the wall outlet...not plugged in! So you quickly plug it in and *tada*! It works! You're a

hero! In this simple case, your theory and your test are done in virtually the same move (Figure 27.13).

Of course, most problems aren't that easy. In many cases, **testing your theory** does nothing more than verify that something is broken. Let's say you install an update for your video driver. You reboot, log in to Windows, and suddenly the screen freaks out. Ah, a bad video driver, right? So to test, you reboot the computer and press F8 to get the boot options menu. You select VGA Mode (2000/XP) or Low Resolution Mode (Vista/7) and reboot. Now the computer boots up just fine. You know the problem, but how do you fix it? Roll back the video driver? Reinstall an older driver? Try downloading another copy of the new driver and installing the video driver again? Any of these solutions may be the right one. Choose one and go for it (Figure 27.14).

Uh oh, your first guess was wrong: the video is still messed up. No worries, just try another one of your theories. In most cases you'll just pick another and try again, but sometimes there's a point where the problem is bigger than you. It might be a problem on a server that you're not authorized to configure. It might be a problem with a user account, and techs in your company aren't allowed to change user accounts. It might be a

• **Figure 27.13**   Ford the Tech is a hero!

• **Figure 27.14**   Ford the Tech takes a chance!

problem with an in-house program and you don't have the skills to fix it. In these cases, you must *escalate* the problem.

Escalation is the process your company (or sometimes just you) goes through when you—the person assigned to repair a problem—are not able to get the job done. It's okay to escalate because no one can fix every problem. All companies should have some form of escalation policy. It might mean calling your boss. It might mean filling out and sending some in-house form to another department. Escalation is sometimes a more casual process. You might want to start researching the problem online; you might want to refer to in-house documentation to see if this problem has appeared in the past. (See "Document Findings, Actions, and Outcomes" later in this chapter.) You may want to call a coworker to come check it out (Figure 27.15).

• **Figure 27.15**   Ford the Tech asks for help from Scott.

Verify and Prevent

Fantastic! Through either your careful work or escalation, you've solved the problem, or so you think. Remember two items here. First, even though you think it's fixed, the user/customer might not think it's fixed. Second, try to do something to prevent the problem from happening again in the future, if possible.

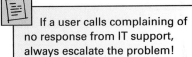

If a user calls complaining of no response from IT support, always escalate the problem!

Verify Full System Functionality   **Verifying** full system functionality is CompTIA's way to tell you to make sure the user is happy. Let's say a user can't print. You determine that the printer spool is stalled due to a locked-up laser printer. You reset the printer and the jobs all start printing. Job done, right? Well, during your theory testing, you switched the default printer to another laser printer on the third floor. The user doesn't know how to set the default printer back to the one you just fixed.

The best way to verify full system functionality is to have the user do whatever she needs to do on the repaired system for a few minutes while you watch. Any minor errors (such as incorrect default printers) will quickly become apparent, and you might learn some interesting aspects of how the user does her job. Knowing what your users do is critical for good techs to help them do their jobs better (Figure 27.16).

If Applicable, Implement Preventive Measures   A very smart tech once told me, "A truly good support tech's work goal should be to never have to get out of his chair." That's a pretty tall order, but it makes sense to me. Do whatever you can to keep this problem from repeating. For some problems, there are obvious actions to take, such as making sure anti-malware is installed so a computer doesn't get

• **Figure 27.16**   Ford the Tech sticks around and watches.

infected again. Sometimes there's no action to take at all: nothing can prevent a hard drive that decides to die. But you can take one more critical action in almost every case: education. Take advantage of the time with the user to informally train him about the problem. Show him the dangers of malware or tell him that sometimes hard drives just die. The more your users know, the less time you'll spend out of your chair.

Document Findings, Actions, and Outcomes

I think the famous historian George Santayana would have made a great PC technician when he said, "Those who cannot remember the past are condemned to repeat it." As a tech, the last step of every troubleshooting job should be documentation. This documentation might be highly formalized in some organizations, or it might just be a few notes you jot down for your own use, but you must document! What was the problem? What did you do to fix it? What worked? What didn't? The best guide to use for documentation is: "What would I have liked to have known about this problem before I walked up to it?" Good documentation is the strongest sign of a good PC tech (Figure 27.17).

Documenting problems helps you track the troubleshooting history of a machine over time, enabling you to make longer-term determinations about retiring it or changing out more parts. If you and fellow techs fix a specific problem with Mary's machine several times, for example, you might decide to swap out her whole system rather than fix it a fourth time.

Documenting helps fellow techs if they have to follow up on a task you didn't finish or troubleshoot a machine you've worked on previously. The reverse is also true. If you get a call about Frank's computer, for example, and check the records to find other service calls on his computer, you might find that the fix for a particular problem is already documented. This is especially true for user-generated problems. Having documentation of what you did also means you don't have to rely on your memory when your coworker asks what you did to fix the weird problem with Jane's computer a year ago!

Documenting also comes into play when you or a user has an accident onsite. If your colleague Joe drops a monitor on his foot and breaks both the monitor and his foot, for example, you need to fill out an *incident report*, just as you would with any kind of accident: electrical, chemical, or physical. An **incident report** should detail what happened and where it happened. This helps your supervisors take the appropriate actions quickly and efficiently.

■ Tech Toolkit

Way back in Chapter 2, "Operational Procedures," you learned the basic parts of a **tech toolkit**—a Phillips-head screwdriver and a few other useful tools, such as a Torx wrench and a pair of tweezers. Any good tech makes a

point to carry around at least these tools (Figure 27.18). Over time, you'll add more tools as your experience grows. But your toolkit won't stop at Phillips screwdrivers and Torx wrenches. You should include two other types of tools in your tech toolkit: utilities and field replaceable units (FRUs).

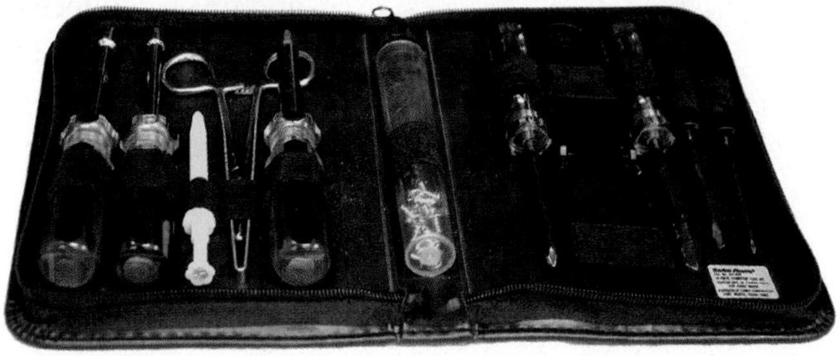

Utilities

Windows comes with plenty of handy utilities, but there are times when you need to use stronger tools than these. The PC industry has thousands of third-party utilities that techs might use to diagnose and repair PCs. Sadly, there is no single selection of tools I can tell you to get: the tools one experienced tech uses differ from the tools I use based on experience, skills, and job functions. That doesn't mean you haven't been hearing my opinions! Throughout this book you've seen quite a few third-party utilities, and many of them are on the CD that comes with your book for you to use right away. Given that you already have my opinion on so many tools, let's instead talk about the types of third-party tools you'll find in most tech toolkits.

Many techs like to challenge me on the idea of carrying around tools. They say, "I know what I like; I'll just download them!" Well, sometimes you don't have Internet access and sometimes you need tools ready to go (see the next section). Granted, there are a number of tools that I would never carry on me. For example, device drivers change so often that keeping a copy on disk is a waste of time. The tools I'm listing here are the ones I promise you want on disk, ready to go when you run into trouble.

• **Figure 27.18**   Typical technician toolkit

> **Tech Tip**
>
> **Tech Forums**
> The Tech Forums on the Total Seminars Web site (www.totalsem.com/forums) has an entire section dedicated to nothing more than what we call "Cool Tools." If you want an opinion on hundreds of tech utilities, come over to the Tech Forums and see what we like…and what we dislike.

Malware Cleaners

Ask any tech who works for Best Buy's Geek Squad, "What do you spend the most time doing on jobs?" and they will reply, "Cleaning malware." The first tech utilities you want in your toolkit are malware cleaners. To truly do it right, put your malware cleaners on a bootable optical disc because malware can sometimes attack a malware cleanup tool as you install. If you're not sure what to try first, grab a copy of the Ultimate Boot CD and try some of their fine cleanup tools.

Anti-Malware

After you clean the machine, make sure you have a copy of an anti-malware program that you can install so the user's machine doesn't get corrupted again. We talked about some of the popular freeware versions, but plenty of techs strongly prefer the pay versions and keep copies to sell to their customers.

Boot Tools

You need a tool that's better than the System Configuration utility at controlling what programs autostart on your Windows PC. OK, in this case, one tool stands out so strongly that you have to get it: Mark Russinovich's superb AUTORUNS. It's vastly superior to the built-in System Configuration utility

and gives you incredible control of everything that's autostarting. Sure there are others, but I love AUTORUNS. Get it at www.sysinternals.com.

Password Clearer

If you lose a Windows password, especially the Administrator password, and you can't log on to a system, you're in trouble. A number of tools let you reset any user's passwords. These programs don't let you *see* a password, only reset them, so if you have a user with encrypted folders, those won't be recoverable. None of these programs are easy to use, but when the alternative is not logging in, they will save you. Pretty much all of these programs run from a boot CD.

ZIP File Tool

Windows can read many compressed file formats (such as ZIP), but so many others are in use that it's often a good idea to have your own copy handy. I like 7-Zip (www.7-zip.org/), but there are plenty of equally popular alternatives.

Backup

Odds are good that from time to time you'll need to do a backup for a system. I keep an external hard drive with a backup tool so I can go in fast and make backups of the most critical files.

Don't Forget Your Thumb Drives!

I guess I'm showing my age when I talk about putting all these tools on CD media. Sorry, I'm old. Almost all of these tools work equally well on USB thumb drives. I keep my tools on CD media because I still run into the occasional system that doesn't have CMOS settings for a bootable thumb drive.

Field Replaceable Units (FRUs)

Always carry several **field replaceable units (FRUs)**—a fancy way to say *spare parts*—when going to a job site or workstation. Having several known good components on hand enables you to swap out a potentially bad piece of hardware to see if that's the problem. Different technicians will have different FRUs. A printer specialist might carry a number of fusers, for example. Your employer will also have a big effect on what is an FRU and what is not. I generally carry a couple of RAM sticks (DDR, DDR2, and DDR3), a PCI video card, a NIC, and a spare power supply.

The CompTIA A+ exams expect you to know that FRUs are computer components such as cards, memory, hard drives, processors, or power supplies that can be easily replaced in the field.

Tech Tip

Why PCI?

I keep a PCI video card in my kit because every computer made in the past ten years has PCI slots. If you run into a system with video problems, you can almost always simply slap in the PCI video card and discover quickly whether the AGP or PCIe video card or card slot is a problem. If the computer boots up with the PCI video card but fails on the PCIe card, for example, you know that either the PCIe card or the slot is causing the problem.

Chapter 27 Review

■ Chapter Summary

After reading this chapter and completing the exercises, you should understand the following about working as a tech.

Describe how computers work

- Good techs must know how their systems are supposed to work when working properly, must be able to calm workers and supervisors and get answers to relevant questions, and must be able to troubleshoot and fix computer problems. A question you must be able to answer is, "What can be causing this problem?"

- When you run a program, computers work through three stages of the four-stage computing process: input, processing, and output. Input requires special input devices such as a keyboard or mouse. The operating system provides the interface and tools so the CPU and other chips can process requests. The output devices, such as the monitor, speakers, and printer, tell you the computer has interpreted your commands. For all this to work, the PC must have electricity and proper AC/DC voltage and amperage.

- When you press a keyboard key, the keyboard controller reads the grid of your keyboard, discovers your input, and then sends the information to the CPU. The CPU understands the keyboard controller because of a small program that was loaded into RAM from the ROM BIOS on the motherboard when the PC booted up.

- Good techs understand the components involved in inputting, processing, and outputting, including the devices that store data, such as hard drives.

Implement a troubleshooting methodology

- The first step in fixing a computer problem is to identify the problem by talking to the client. To determine what the computer is doing or not doing, first allow the client to describe the situation; then ask leading questions to elicit answers.

- Most people feel defensive when asked to explain computer problems, so it is your job to put them at ease by asking the right kinds of questions. Questions such as "What did you do?" generally aren't much help. A better question might be, "When did it last work?" By taking the user explicitly out of the question, you show that you won't accuse them or judge their actions.

- Refrain from using computer jargon, acronyms, or abbreviations. Users are unlikely to be familiar with them and may get confused and think you are talking down to them. Ask simple questions that don't use technical lingo. Have the user physically show you the problem, demonstrating what is happening or what is not happening.

- Once you have ascertained the problem the user is having with the computer, it is important to back up critical data. Unless the hard drive is dead, you should have no reason to lose any data that was accessible before.

- Once you have secured the user's data, you need to establish a theory of probable cause. In other words, look at the machine and determine why it's not working correctly. Don't overlook the obvious, such as a disconnected power or network cable. Use all of your senses: look for damaged components, feel for excessive heat or lack of vibration, listen for any unusual or telltale sounds, and sniff the air for the unmistakable smell of ozone.

- If you run into something more complex than a disconnected cord, don't be afraid to try multiple solutions. Take a chance and see if it works. If you have run out of ideas, escalate the problem; no one person can solve all problems.

- After you have successfully solved the user's problem, have the user sit down and perform the task. This enables you to verify full system functionality with the user.

- Once everything is verified and the customer is happy, make sure to document your findings thoroughly. Keeping records is important. If you or a colleague encounters a similar problem in the future, the answer will be readily available.

Describe a technician's toolkit

- Troubleshooting is more art than science, and as such, there is no step-by-step list of actions to follow. You need to be flexible.

- A well-stocked tech toolkit consists of a Phillips-head screwdriver, flat-head screwdriver, Torx wrench, nut driver, tweezers, grabber tool, flashlight, magnifying glass, and anti-static wrist strap. You should also carry several FRUs. The FRUs you carry will depend on what kind of tech you are, but the FRUs most techs should carry include a few sticks each of DDR, DDR2, and DDR3 RAM, PCI video card, NIC, and power supply.

- Malware is the most common source of consumer computer problems today. Make sure your kit is well stocked with antivirus and other (preferably boot-time) malware removers.

- Lost logon passwords are a common problem, so your kit should include some form of password clearing utility. Remember, these just clear the existing password; they do not show it to you.

- Other handy tools to have are zip/archive extractors and backup utilities. Having these and the rest of your kit and a handy bootable thumb drive can make your job much easer onsite.

■ Key Terms

computing process *(1007)*
document *(1018)*
escalate *(1017)*
field replaceable unit (FRU) *(1020)*
identify the problem *(1014)*
incident report *(1018)*

stream loading *(1011)*
tech toolkit *(1018)*
test the theory *(1016)*
theory of probable cause *(1014)*
troubleshooting theory *(1013)*
verify *(1017)*

■ Key Term Quiz

Use the Key Terms list to complete the sentences that follow. Not all terms will be used.

1. A "spare part" you carry with you, such as an extra stick of RAM or a video card, is called a(n) _____.

2. A Phillips-head screwdriver and a few other useful tools should be in your _____.

3. Understanding the _____ enables you to troubleshoot problems more efficiently.

4. When asking questions to _____, remember to use a nonaccusatory tone.

5. Better online applications use _____ to download updated information and data constantly.

6. Once you have determined the problem with the machine and come up with probable causes, you should _____.

7. Once you have successfully repaired the machine, it is important to _____ with the user that everything is working correctly.

8. If you can't solve a troubleshooting problem, the next step is to _____ the problem to a higher-level tech.

9. A(n) _____ is your guess at what is wrong with the machine.

10. A(n) _____ gives the details about an accident on the job site.

■ Multiple-Choice Quiz

1. At what point during a repair should you escalate the problem?

   A. After the user describes the first problem

   B. As soon as you understand the problem

   C. As soon as you have a solution

   D. When you have tried all your theories and still can't resolve the problem

2. While working at the help desk, you get a call from a distraught user who says she has a blank screen. What would be useful follow-up questions? (Select two.)

   A. Is the computer turned on?

   B. Is the monitor turned on?

C. Did you reboot?

D. What did you do?

3. While working at the help desk, you get a call from Sharon in accounting. She's lost a file that she knows she saved to her hard drive. Which of the following statements would direct Sharon to open her My Documents folder in the most efficient and professional manner?

A. Sharon, check My Documents.

B. Sharon, a lot of programs save files to a default folder, often to a folder called My Documents. Let's look there first. Click on the Start button and move the mouse until the cursor hovers over My Documents. Then click the left mouse button and tell me what you see when My Documents opens.

C. Probably just defaulted to My Docs. Why don't you open Excel or whatever program you used to make the file, and then open a document, and point it to My Documents.

D. Look Sharon, I know you're a clueless noob when it comes to computers, but how could somebody lose a file? Just open up My Documents, and look there for the file.

4. What tool should be in every technician's toolkit?

A. Pliers

B. Hammer

C. Flat-head screwdriver

D. Phillips-head screwdriver

5. Al in marketing calls in for tech support, complaining that he has a dead PC. What is a good first question or questions to begin troubleshooting the problem?

A. Did the computer ever work?

B. When did the computer last work?

C. When you say "dead," what do you mean? What happens when you press the power button?

D. What did you do?

6. While working at the help desk, you get a call from Bryce in Sales complaining that he can't print and every time he clicks on the network shared drive, his computer stops and freezes. He says he thinks it's his hard driver. What would be a good follow-up question or statement?

A. Bryce, you're an idiot. Don't touch anything. I'll be there in five minutes.

B. Okay, let's take this one step at a time. You seem to have two problems, one with printing and the second with the network shared drive, right?

C. First, it's not a hard *driver*, but a hard *drive*. It doesn't have anything to do with the network share or printing, so that's just not right.

D. When could you last print?

7. Phoebe's computer was recently updated during the companywide patch push. Now all Phoebe gets is a black screen. What should you check first?

A. Take the monitor back to the maintenance room and check it with known good hardware.

B. Check to make sure the monitor is properly plugged into the system unit and is getting power.

C. Replace Phoebe's video card.

D. Take Phoebe's computer back to the maintenance room and reimage it.

8. You've just installed new printer drivers into Roland's computer for the big networked laser printer. What should you do to complete the assignment?

A. Document that you installed new printer drivers.

B. Tell Roland to print a test page.

C. Print a test page and go to the printer to verify the results. Assuming everything works, you're finished.

D. Print a test page and go to the printer to verify the results. Document that you installed new printer drivers successfully.

9. After examining Paul's computer, you think the problem has something to do with his video card but you are not certain. Should you try your uncertain fix, escalate the problem, or something else?

A. Escalate; you need to be 100% correct before you attempt a fix.

B. Stall for time and hope the problem fixes itself.

C. Calmly explain to Paul that his computer cannot be fixed.

D. Take a chance and try your first guess.

esponding to a coworker's request for
you find her away from her desk and
crosoft Excel on the screen with a spreadsheet
pen. How do you proceed?

   A. Go find the coworker and ask her to exit her
   applications before touching her computer.

   B. Exit Excel, save changes to the document, and
   begin troubleshooting the computer.

   C. Exit Excel without saving changes to the
   document and begin troubleshooting the
   computer.

   D. Use the Save As command to save the file
   with a new name, exit Excel, and begin
   troubleshooting the computer.

11. You have been working all afternoon on a user's
    workstation and you have finally fixed the user's
    problem. What should you do now?

    A. Tell the user the computer is fixed and leave.

    B. Invite the user to sit down and use the
    computer to make sure the problem is
    completely gone from the user's perspective.

    C. Tell the user the machine is fixed, go back to
    your office, and document the problem.

    D. As you leave for the tenth time, complain to
    the user that you are tired of always fixing
    his computer.

12. Which of the following makes a good field
    replaceable unit?

    A. Video card

    B. 20-inch CRT monitor

   C. Set of 2.1 speakers

   D. Printer

13. After replacing a keyboard a user has spilled
    coffee on for the fifth time, what should you say
    to the user?

    A. I can't guarantee the new keyboard will work
    if it gets dirty.

    B. I can't guarantee the new keyboard will work
    if you continue to spill coffee on it.

    C. These keyboards are expensive. Next time we
    replace one because you spilled coffee, it's
    coming out of your paycheck.

    D. You need to be more careful with your coffee.

14. When is it appropriate to yell at a user?

    A. When he screws up the second time

    B. When he interrupts your troubleshooting

    C. When he screws up the fifth time

    D. Never

15. Once you figure out what can be causing a
    computer to malfunction, what's your next step?

    A. Escalate the problem to a higher-level tech.

    B. Talk to the user about stream loading and
    other geeky things because your knowledge
    will put him or her at ease.

    C. Test your theory, starting with the obvious.

    D. Write an incident report to document the
    problem.

■ Essay Quiz

1. A friend is considering turning his computer
   hobby into a career and has asked your advice on
   outfitting himself as a freelance computer
   technician. What tools can you recommend to
   your friend?

2. A user phones you at your desk and reports that
   after pressing the power button on his computer

and hearing the hard drive spin up, his screen
remains blank. What questions can you ask to
determine the problem? Remember, avoid an
accusing tone.

3. Briefly explain the various steps in
   troubleshooting theory.

Lab Projects

• Lab Project 27.1

Think of items you would like to always have on hand as FRUs. Using the Internet, find prices for these items. Make a list of your items and their individual costs; then find the total cost for your equipment.

• Lab Project 27.2

Visit your local computer store or hardware store and purchase the items for a hardware tech toolkit. You may want to include a variety of screwdrivers, an anti-static wrist strap, tweezers, or other items.

• Lab Project 27.3

Create a software tech toolkit on CD or a USB flash drive loaded with a variety of drivers for NICs and video cards. Include free/open-source antivirus software, anti-spyware software, and any other software tools you think might be useful.

Mapping to the CompTIA A+ Objectives

appendix A

CompTIA A+ Essentials Objectives Map

Topic	Chapter(s)
Domain 1.0 Hardware	
1.1 Categorize storage devices and backup media	
FDD	3
HDD	3, 11
Solid state vs. magnetic	11
Optical drives	3, 13
CD/DVD/RW/Blu-ray	3, 13
Removable storage	11, 13, 17
Tape drive	17
Solid state (e.g. thumb drive, flash, SD cards, USB)	13
External CD-RW and hard drive	13, 11
Hot swappable devices and non-hot swappable devices	13
1.2 Explain motherboard components, types, and features	
Form factor	9
ATX / BTX	9
micro ATX	9
NLX	9
I/O interfaces	3, 18, 20, 22, 23, 25
Sound	3, 20
Video	3
USB 1.1 and 2.0	3, 18
Serial	3, 18
IEEE 1394 / Firewire	3, 18
Parallel	3, 22
NIC	3, 23
Modem	3, 25
PS/2	18
Memory slots	3, 6
RIMM	6
DIMM	3, 6
SODIMM	6
SIMM	6

Topic	Chapter(s)
Processor sockets	3, 5, 9
Bus architecture	5, 8
Bus slots	8, 9, 21
PCI	8, 9
AGP	8, 9
PCIe	8, 9
AMR	9
CNR	9
PCMCIA	21
PATA	11
IDE	11
EIDE	11
SATA, eSATA	3, 11
Contrast RAID (levels 0, 1, 5)	11, 12
Chipsets	5, 7, 9
BIOS / CMOS / Firmware	7
POST	7
CMOS battery	7
Riser card / daughterboard	9

1.3 Classify power supplies types and characteristics

AC adapter	10
ATX proprietary	10
Voltage, wattage and capacity	10
Voltage selector switch	10
Pins (20, 24)	10

1.4 Explain the purpose and characteristics of CPUs and their features

Identify CPU types	5
AMD	5
Intel	5
Hyper threading	5
Multi core	5
Dual core	5
Triple core	5
Quad core	5
Onchip cache	5
L1	5
L2	5
Speed (real vs. actual)	5
32bit vs. 64 bit	5

1.5 Explain cooling methods and devices

Heat sinks	5
CPU and case fans	5, 10
Liquid cooling systems	5
Thermal compound	5

Topic	Chapter(s)
1.9 Summarize the function and types of adapter cards	
Video	8, 19
PCI	8, 19
PCIe	8, 19
AGP	8, 19
Multimedia	20
Sound card	20
TV tuner cards	20
Capture cards	20
I/O	3, 11, 18, 22
SCSI	3, 11
Serial	3, 18
USB	3, 18
Parallel	3, 22
Communications	3, 23
NIC	23
Modem	23
1.10 Install, configure, and optimize laptop components and features	
Expansion devices	21
PCMCIA cards	21
PCI Express cards	21
Docking station	21
Communication connections	21, 23, 24, 25
Bluetooth	21, 24
Infrared	21, 24
Cellular WAN	21, 24
Ethernet	21, 23
Modem	21, 25
Power and electrical input devices	10, 21
Auto-switching	10
Fixed input power supplies	10
Batteries	21
Input devices	21
Stylus / digitizer	21
Function keys	21
Point devices (e.g. touch pad, point stick/track point)	21
1.11 Install and configure printers	
Differentiate between printer types	22
Laser	22
Inkjet	22
Thermal	22
Impact	22

Topic	Chapter(s)
2.4 Given a scenario, explain and interpret common laptop issues and determine the appropriate basic troubleshooting method	
Issues	21
Power conditions	21
Video	21
Keyboard	21
Pointer	21
Stylus	21
Wireless card issues	21
Methods	10, 21
Verify power (e.g. LEDs, swap AC adapter)	10, 21
Remove unneeded peripherals	21
Plug in external monitor	21
Toggle Fn keys or hardware switches	21
Check LCD cutoff switch	21
Verify backlight functionality and pixelation	21
Check switch for built-in WIFI antennas or external antennas	21
2.5 Given a scenario, integrate common preventative maintenance techniques	
Physical inspection	5, 11, 12, 22
Updates	4, 17
Driver	8, 17
Firmware	7
OS	17
Security	16, 26
Scheduling preventative maintenance	4, 17
Defrag	17
Scandisk	17
Check disk	17
Startup programs	4, 17
Use of appropriate repair tools and cleaning materials	5, 19, 21, 22
Compressed air	21, 22
Lint free cloth	19
Computer vacuum and compressors	5
Power devices	10
Appropriate source such as power strip, surge protector, or UPS	10
Ensuring proper environment	21
Backup procedures	16
Domain 3.0 Operating Systems and Software – Unless otherwise noted, operating systems referred to within include Microsoft Windows 2000, Windows XP Professional, XP Home, XP MediaCenter, Windows Vista Home, Home Premium, Business, and Ultimate.	
3.1 Compare and contrast the different Windows Operating Systems and their features	
Windows 2000, Windows XP 32 bit vs. 64 bit, Windows Vista 32 bit vs. 64 bit	4, 5
Side bar, Aero, UAC, minimum system requirements, system limits	4
Windows 2000 and newer – upgrade paths and requirements	14

Topic	Chapter(s)
Operating system installation options	12, 14
File system type	12, 14
Network configuration	14
Repair install	14
Disk preparation order	12, 14
Format drive	12, 14
Partition	12, 14
Start installation	12, 14
Device Manager	4, 7, 8
Verify	8
Install and update devices drivers	8
Driver signing	8, 17
User data migration – User State Migration Tool (USMT)	14
Virtual memory	4, 8
Configure power management	21
Suspend	21
Wake on LAN	21
Sleep timers	21
Hibernate	21
Standby	21
Demonstrate safe removal of peripherals	3, 21
3.4 Explain the basics of boot sequences, methods, and startup utilities	
Disk boot order / device priority	11
Types of boot devices (disk, network, USB, other)	11
Boot options	15, 17
Safe mode	15, 17
Boot to restore point	17
Recovery options	17
Automated System Recovery (ASR)	17
Emergency Repair Disk (ERD)	17
Recovery console	17
Domain 4.0 Networking	
4.1 Summarize the basics of networking fundamentals, including technologies, devices, and protocols	
Basics of configuring IP addressing and TCP/IP properties (DHCP, DNS)	23
Bandwidth and latency	25
Status indicators	23
Protocols (TCP/IP, NETBIOS)	23
Full-duplex, half-duplex	23
Basics of workgroups and domains	23
Common ports: HTTP, FTP, POP, SMTP, TELNET, HTTPS	25
LAN / WAN	23
Hub, switch and router	23
Identify Virtual Private Networks (VPN)	25
Basics class identification	23

Topic	Chapter(s)
5.2 Summarize the following security features	
Wireless encryption	24
WEPx and WPAx	24
Client configuration (SSID)	24
Malicious software protection	26
Viruses	26
Trojans	26
Worms	26
Spam	26
Spyware	26
Adware	26
Grayware	26
BIOS Security	7, 26
Drive lock	7
Passwords	7, 26
Intrusion detection	7
TPM	7
Password management / password complexity	16, 26
Locking workstation	4, 26
Hardware	26
Operating system	16
Biometrics	26
Fingerprint scanner	26
Domain 6.0 Operational Procedure	
6.1 Outline the purpose of appropriate safety and environmental procedures and, given a scenario, apply them	
ESD	2
EMI	2
Network interference	2
Magnets	2
RFI	2
Cordless phone interference	2
Microwaves	2
Electrical safety	10
CRT	19
Power supply	10
Inverter	19
Laser printers	22
Matching power requirements of equipment with power distribution and UPSs	10
Material Safety Data Sheets (MSDS)	22
Cable management	2
Avoiding trip hazards	2

Topic	Chapter(s)
Physical safety	2
Heavy devices	2
Hot components	2
Environmental – consider proper disposal procedures	22
6.2 Given a scenario, demonstrate the appropriate use of communication skills and professionalism in the workplace	
Use proper language – avoid jargon, acronyms, slang	2
Maintain a positive attitude	2
Listen and do not interrupt a customer	2
Be culturally sensitive	2
Be on time	2
If late contact the customer	2
Avoid distractions	2
Personal calls	2
Talking to co-workers while interacting with customers	2
Personal interruptions	2
Dealing with a difficult customer or situation	2
Avoid arguing with customers and/or being defensive	2
Do not minimize customers' problems	2
Avoid being judgmental	2
Clarify customer statements	2
Ask open-ended questions to narrow the scope of the problem	2
Restate the issue or question to verify understanding	2
Set and meet expectations / timeline and communicate status with the customer	2
Offer different repair / replacement options if applicable	2
Provide proper documentation on the services provided	2
Follow up with customer / user at a later date to verify satisfaction	2
Deal appropriately with customers' confidential materials	2

■ CompTIA A+ Practical Application Objectives Map

Topic	Chapter(s)
Domain 1.0 Hardware	
1.1 Given a scenario, install, configure, and maintain personal computer components	
Storage devices	11, 13
HDD	11
SATA	11
PATA	11
Solid state	11
FDD	13
Optical drives	13
CD/DVD/RW/Blu-ray	13
Removable	13
External	11, 13
Motherboards	3, 5, 7, 8, 9, 18, 20, 22
Jumper settings	9
CMOS battery	7, 9
Advanced BIOS settings	7
Bus speeds	8
Chipsets	7
Firmware updates	7
Socket types	3, 5, 9
Expansion slots	8, 9
Memory slots	6
Front panel connectors	9
I/O ports	9, 18
Sound, video, USB 1.1, USB 2.0, serial, IEEE 1394 / Firewire, parallel, NIC, modem, PS/2	3, 18, 19, 20, 22
Power supplies	10
Wattages and capacity	10
Connector types and quantity	10
Output voltage	10
Processors	3, 4, 5, 6, 8, 9
Socket types	3, 5, 9
Speed	5
Number of cores	5
Power consumption	5
Cache	5
Front side bus	5, 6, 8
32 bit vs. 64 bit	4, 5
Memory	6
Adapter cards	3, 8

Topic	Chapter(s)
Graphics cards	19
Sound cards	20
Storage controllers	3, 8, 9, 11, 12
RAID cards (RAID array – levels 0,1,5)	9, 11, 12
eSATA cards	3, 8, 11
I/O cards	3, 18
Firewire	3, 18
USB	3, 18
Parallel	3, 22
Serial	3, 18
Wired and wireless network cards	23, 24
Capture cards (TV, video)	20
Media reader	13
Cooling systems	
Heat sinks	5
Thermal compound	5
CPU fans	5
Case fans	5, 10

1.2 Given a scenario, detect problems, troubleshoot, and repair/replace personal computer components

Storage devices	11, 13
HDD	11
SATA	11
PATA	11
Solid state	11
FDD	13
Optical drives	13
CD / DVD / RW / Blu-ray	13
Removable	13
External	13
Motherboards	3, 5, 7, 8, 9
Jumper settings	9
CMOS battery	7, 9
Advanced BIOS settings	7
Bus speeds	8
Chipsets	7
Firmware updates	7
Socket types	3, 5, 9
Expansion slots	8, 9
Memory slots	3, 6, 9
Front panel connectors	3, 9
I/O ports	3, 18, 19, 20, 22
Sound, video, USB 1.1, USB 2.0, serial, IEEE 1394 / Firewire, parallel, NIC, modem, PS/2	3, 18, 19, 20, 22

Topic	Chapter(s)
Power supplies	10
Wattages and capacity	10
Connector types and quantity	10
Output voltage	10
Processors	2, 5, 6, 8, 9
Socket types	3, 5, 9
Speed	5
Number of cores	5
Power consumption	5
Cache	5
Front side bus	5, 6, 8
32 bit vs. 64 bit	5
Memory	6, 9
Adapter cards	8, 11, 13, 18, 19, 20, 22 23, 24
Graphics cards – memory	19
Sound cards	20
Storage controllers	8
RAID cards	11
eSATA cards	8, 11
I/O cards	
Firewire	18
USB	18
Parallel	22
Serial	18
Wired and wireless network cards	23, 24
Capture cards (TV, video)	20
Media reader	13
Cooling systems	5, 10
Heat sinks	5
Thermal compound	5
CPU fans	5
Case fans	5, 10
1.3 Given a scenario, install, configure, detect problems, troubleshoot, and repair/replace laptop components	
Components of the LCD including inverter, screen, and video card	19
Hard drive and memory	21
Disassemble processes for proper re-assembly	21
Document and label cable and screw locations	21
Organize parts	21
Refer to manufacturer documentation	21
Use appropriate hand tools	21
Recognize internal laptop expansion slot types	21
Upgrade wireless cards and video card	19, 21
Replace keyboard, processor, plastics, pointer devices, heat sinks, fans, system board, CMOS battery, speakers	21

Topic	Chapter(s)
1.4 Given a scenario, select and use the following tools	
Multimeter	10, 22
Power supply tester	10
Specialty hardware / tools	2, 10, 22
Cable testers	23
Loop back plugs	23
Anti-static pad and wrist strap	2, 3, 8
Extension magnet	2
1.5 Given a scenario, detect and resolve common printer issues	
Symptoms	22
Paper jams	22
Blank paper	22
Error codes	22
Out of memory error	22
Lines and smearing	22
Garbage printout	22
Ghosted image	22
No connectivity	22
Issue resolution	22
Replace fuser	22
Replace drum	22
Clear paper jam	22
Power cycle	22
Install maintenance kit (reset page count)	22
Set IP on printer	22
Clean printer	22
Domain 2.0 Operating Systems – unless otherwise noted, operating systems referred to within include Microsoft Windows 2000, Windows XP Professional, XP Home, XP MediaCenter, Windows Vista Home, Home Premium, Business, and Ultimate.	
2.1 Select the appropriate commands and options to troubleshoot and resolve problems	
MSCONFIG	17
DIR	15, 17
CHKDSK (/f /r)	12, 15, 17
EDIT	15
COPY (/a /v /y)	15, 17
XCOPY	15
FORMAT	15, 17
IPCONFIG (/all /release /renew)	23
PING (–t –l)	23
MD / CD / RD	15, 17
NET	23
TRACERT	23
NSLOOKUP	23
[command name] /?	15
SFC	15

Topic	Chapter(s)
Routers / Access Points	23, 24
Disable DHCP	23
Use static IP	23
Change SSID from default	24
Disable SSID broadcast	24
MAC filtering	24
Change default username and password	24
Update firmware	24
Firewall	26
LAN (10/100/1000BaseT, Speeds)	23
Bluetooth (1.0 vs. 2.0)	24
Cellular	24
Basic VoIP (consumer applications)	25
Basics of hardware and software firewall configuration	25, 26
Port assignment / setting up rules (exceptions)	26
Port forwarding / port triggering	25
Physical installation	23
Wireless router placement	23
Cable length	23
Domain 4.0 Security	
4.1 Given a scenario, prevent, troubleshoot, and remove viruses and malware	
Use antivirus software	26
Identify malware symptoms	26
Quarantine infected systems	26
Research malware types, symptoms, and solutions (virus encyclopedias)	26
Remediate infected systems	26
Update antivirus software	26
Signature and engine updates	26
Automatic vs. manual	26
Schedule scans	26
Repair boot blocks	26
Scan and removal techniques	26
Safe mode	26
Boot environment	26
Educate end user	26
4.2 Implement security and troubleshoot common issues	
Operating systems	4, 14, 15, 16, 26
Local users and groups: Administrator, Power Users, Guest, Users	16, 26
Vista User Access Control (UAC)	4, 16
NTFS vs. Share permissions	26
Allow vs. deny	16
Difference between moving and copying folders and files	15
File attributes	15

Topic	Chapter(s)
Shared files and folders	16, 26
Administrative shares vs. local shares	16
Permission propagation	16, 26
Inheritance	16
System files and folders	14
Encryption (Bitlocker, EFS)	4
User authentication	16, 26
System	7, 26
BIOS security	7, 26
Drive lock	7
Passwords	7, 26
Intrusion detection	7
TPM	7

About the CD-ROM

appendix B

Mike Meyers has put together a bunch of resources that will help you prepare for the CompTIA A+ exams and that you will find invaluable in your career as a PC tech. The CD-ROM included with this book comes complete with the following:

- A sample version of the Total Tester practice exam software with two full practice exams
- All the chapter review questions from the book
- A searchable electronic copy of the book
- A document from CompTIA with a list of acronyms that you should know for the CompTIA A+ exams
- A complete list of the objectives for both of the CompTIA A+ exams
- A copy of several freeware and shareware programs that Mike talks about in the book
- A sample of LearnKey's video training featuring Mike Meyers

The practice tests and video software are easy to install on any Windows 98/NT/2000/XP/Vista computer, and must be installed to access the Total Tester practice exams and LearnKey video sample. The eBook and CompTIA A+ acronyms and objectives lists are Adobe Acrobat files. If you don't have Adobe Acrobat Reader, it is available for installation on the CD-ROM.

System Requirements

The software on the CD-ROM requires Windows 98 or higher, Internet Explorer 5.0 or higher, and 50 MB of hard disk space for full installation. To access the video training from LearnKey, you must have Windows Media Player 9, which will be automatically installed when you launch the online training.

Installing and Running Total Tester

If your computer's optical drive is configured to Autorun, the CD-ROM will automatically start upon inserting the disk. If the Autorun feature does not launch the CD-ROM's splash screen, browse to the CD-ROM and double-click the Launch.exe icon.

From the splash screen, click the *Install A+ Practice Exams* button to install Total Tester. This will begin the installation process, create a program group named Total Seminars, and put an icon on your desktop. To run Total Tester, go to Start | Programs or All Programs | Total Seminars or just double-click the icon on your desktop.

To uninstall the Total Tester software, go to Start | Settings | Control Panel | Add/Remove Programs in Windows 2000/XP or Start | Control Panel | Uninstall a program in Windows Vista/7. Select the A+ Total Tester program. Select Remove, and Windows will completely uninstall the software.

About Total Tester

The best way to prepare for the CompTIA A+ exams is to read the book and then test your knowledge and review. The CD-ROM includes a sample of Total Seminars' practice exam software to help you test your knowledge as you study. Total Tester provides you with a simulation of the actual exam. There are three exam suites: 220-701, 220-702, and Chapter Review. Each numbered suite contains an exam that can be taken in either practice or final mode. Practice mode provides an assistance window with hints, references to the book, and the ability to check your answer as you take the test. Both practice and final modes provide an overall grade and a grade broken down by certification objective. The Chapter Review suite has seven exams. Each exam covers chapter review questions from several chapters. To launch a test, select Suites from the menu at the top and then select an exam.

Additional practice exams are available for both of the CompTIA A+ exams. Visit our Web site at www.totalsem.com or call 800-446-6004 for more information.

■ Accessing the eBook, CompTIA A+ Acronyms List, and CompTIA A+ Exam Objectives

You will find the eBook, CompTIA A+ acronyms list, and CompTIA A+ exam objectives useful in your preparation for the exams. To access these PDF documents, first be sure you have a copy of Adobe Acrobat Reader installed. If you don't have Acrobat Reader installed on your system, you can install it from the CD-ROM by clicking the *Install Adobe Acrobat Reader* button. Once you have installed Acrobat Reader, simply select the document you want to view from the CD-ROM's splash screen to open the document.

■ Shareware and Freeware

Mike has put together copies of some of his favorite freeware and shareware programs that are mentioned in this book. The CD-ROM includes a list with short descriptions of the programs. To use these programs, select the Shareware and Freeware option on the CD-ROM splash screen. The next menu lists each program. Select a program and follow the installation instructions to load the utility on your system.

■ LearnKey Video Training

If you like Mike's writing style, you will love watching him in his LearnKey video training. The CD-ROM includes sample videos of Mike covering several different topics. If you like them, you can purchase the full 20 hours of

interactive video training by contacting Mike's company, Total Seminars, at www.totalsem.com or 800-446-6004.

To check out Mike's video training, click the *Install LearnKey demo* button to launch a wizard to install the software on your computer. Follow the instructions in the wizard to complete the installation. To run the LearnKey demo, use Start | Programs | LearnKey or just double-click the icon on your desktop. Enter a user name and password to begin your video training.

■ Technical Support

For questions regarding the Total Tester software, visit www.totalsem.com or e-mail support@totalsem.com. For customers outside the United States, e-mail international_cs@mcgraw-hill.com. For questions regarding the content of the electronic book, visit www.mhprofessional.com/techsupport/.

LearnKey Technical Support

For technical problems with the LearnKey video training software (installation, operation, or uninstalling the software) and for questions regarding LearnKey video training, e-mail techsupport@learnkey.com.

GLOSSARY

10BaseT Ethernet LAN designed to run on UTP cabling. 10BaseT runs at 10 megabits per second. The maximum length for the cabling between the NIC and the hub (or switch, repeater, etc.) is 100 meters. It uses baseband signaling. No industry standard spelling exists, so sometimes written 10BASE-T or 10Base-T.

100BaseT Generic term for an Ethernet cabling system designed to run at 100 megabits per second on UTP cabling. It uses baseband signaling. No industry standard spelling exists, so sometimes written 100BASE-T or 100Base-T.

1000BaseT Gigabit Ethernet on UTP.

2.1 Speaker setup consisting of two stereo speakers combined with a subwoofer.

3.5-inch floppy drive All modern floppy disk drives are of this size; the format was introduced in 1986 and is one of the longest surviving pieces of computer hardware.

34-pin ribbon cable Type of cable used by floppy disk drives.

3-D graphics Video technology that attempts to create images with the same depth and texture as objects seen in the real world.

40-pin ribbon cable PATA cable used to attach EIDE devices (such as hard drives) or ATAPI devices (such as optical drives) to a system. (*See* PATA.)

5.1 speaker system Four satellite speakers plus a center speaker and a subwoofer.

8.3 naming system File-naming convention that specified a maximum of eight characters for a filename, followed by a 3-character file extension. Has been replaced by LFN (long filename) support.

80-wire ribbon cable PATA cable used to attach fast EIDE devices (such as ATA/100 hard drives) or ATAPI devices (such as optical drives) to a system. (*See* PATA.)

802.11a Wireless networking standard that operates in the 5-GHz band with a theoretical maximum throughput of 54 Mbps.

802.11b Wireless networking standard that operates in the 2.4-GHz band with a theoretical maximum throughput of 11 Mbps.

802.11g Wireless networking standard that operates in the 2.4-GHz band with a theoretical maximum throughput of 54 Mbps and is backward compatible with 802.11b.

802.11n Wireless networking standard that can operate in both the 2.4-GHz and 5-GHz bands and uses MIMO to achieve a theoretical maximum throughput of 100+ Mbps.

A/V sync Process of synchronizing audio and video.

AC (alternating current) Type of electricity in which the flow of electrons alternates direction, back and forth, in a circuit.

AC'97 Sound card standard for lower-end audio devices; created when most folks listened to stereo sound at best.

access control Security concept using physical security, authentication, users and groups, and security policies.

ACPI (advanced configuration and power interface) Power management specification that far surpasses its predecessor, APM, by providing support for hot-swappable devices and better control of power modes.

activation Process of confirming that an installed copy of a Microsoft product (most commonly Windows or a Microsoft Office application) is legitimate. Usually done at the end of software installation.

active matrix Type of liquid crystal display that replaced the passive matrix technology used in most portable computer displays. Also called *TFT (thin film transistor)*.

active partition On a hard drive, primary partition that contains an operating system.

active PFC (power factor correction) Circuitry built into PC power supplies to reduce harmonics.

ad hoc mode   Decentralized wireless network mode, otherwise known as peer-to-peer mode, where each wireless node is in meshed contact with every other node.

Add or Remove Programs   Applet allowing users to manually add or remove a program from the system.

address bus   Wires leading from the CPU to the memory controller chip (usually the Northbridge) that enable the CPU to address RAM. Also used by the CPU for I/O addressing. An internal electronic channel from the microprocessor to random access memory, along which the addresses of memory storage locations are transmitted. Like a post office box, each memory location has a distinct number or address; the address bus provides the means by which the microprocessor can access every location in memory.

address space   Total amount of memory addresses that an address bus can contain.

administrative shares   Administrator tool to give local admins access to hard drives and system root folders.

Administrative Tools   Group of Control Panel applets, including Computer Management, Event Viewer, and Reliability and Performance Monitor.

Administrator account   User account, created when the OS is first installed, that is allowed complete, unfettered access to the system without restriction.

Administrators group   List of members with complete administrator privileges.

ADSL (asymmetric digital subscriber line)   Fully digital, dedicated connection to the telephone system that provides average download speeds of 7 Mbps and upload speeds of 512 Kbps.

Advanced Startup Options menu   Menu that can be reached during the boot process that offers advanced OS startup options, such as boot in Safe mode or boot into Last Known Good Configuration.

adware   Type of malicious program that downloads ads to a user's computer, generating undesirable network traffic.

Aero   The Windows Vista desktop environment. Aero adds some interesting aesthetic effects such as window transparency and Flip 3D.

AGP (accelerated graphics port)   32/64-bit expansion slot designed by Intel specifically for video that runs at

66 MHz and yields a throughput of at least 254 Mbps. Later versions (2×, 4×, 8×) give substantially higher throughput.

algorithm   Set of rules for solving a problem in a given number of steps.

ALU (arithmetic logic unit)   CPU logic circuits that perform basic arithmetic (add, subtract, multiply, and divide).

AMD (Advanced Micro Devices)   CPU and chipset manufacturer that competes with Intel. Produces the popular Phenom, Athlon, Sempron, Turion, and Duron microprocessors; also produces video card processors under its ATI brand.

AMI (American Megatrends, Inc)   Major producer of BIOS software for motherboards, as well as many other computer-related components and software.

amperes (amps or A)   Unit of measure for amperage, or electrical current.

amplitude   Loudness of a sound card.

AMR (audio/modem riser)   Proprietary slot used on some motherboards to provide a sound inference–free connection for modems, sound cards, and NICs.

analog   Device that uses a physical quantity, such as length or voltage, to represent the value of a number. By contrast, digital storage relies on a coding system of numeric units.

anti-aliasing   In computer imaging, blending effect that smoothes sharp contrasts between two regions—e.g., jagged lines or different colors. Reduces jagged edges of text or objects. In voice signal processing, process of removing or smoothing out spurious frequencies from waveforms produced by converting digital signals back to analog.

anti-static bag   Bag made of anti-static plastic into which electronics are placed for temporary or long-term storage. Used to protect components from electrostatic discharge.

anti-static mat   Special surface on which to lay electronics. These mats come with a grounding connection designed to equalize electrical potential between a workbench and one or more electronic devices. Used to prevent electrostatic discharge.

anti-static wrist strap   Special device worn around the wrist with a grounding connection designed to equalize

electrical potential between a technician and an electronic device. Used to prevent electrostatic discharge.

antivirus program Software designed to combat viruses by either seeking out and destroying them or passively guarding against them.

API (application programming interface) Software definition that describes operating system calls for application software; conventions defining how a service is invoked.

APIPA (Automatic Private IP Addressing) Feature of Windows that automatically assigns an IP address to the system when the client cannot obtain an IP address automatically.

APM (advanced power management) BIOS routines that enable the CPU to turn selected peripherals on and off.

applet Generic term for a program in the Windows Control Panel.

archive To copy programs and data onto a relatively inexpensive storage medium (disk, tape, etc.) for long-term retention.

archive attribute Attribute of a file that shows whether the file has been backed up since the last change. Each time a file is opened, changed, or saved, the archive bit is turned on. Some types of backups turn off this archive bit to indicate that a good backup of the file exists on tape.

ARP (Address Resolution Protocol) Protocol in the TCP/IP suite used with the command-line utility of the same name to determine the MAC address that corresponds to a particular IP address.

ASCII (American Standard Code for Information Interchange) Industry-standard 8-bit characters used to define text characters, consisting of 96 upper- and lowercase letters, plus 32 nonprinting control characters, each of which is numbered. These numbers were designed to achieve uniformity among computer devices for printing and the exchange of simple text documents.

aspect ratio Ratio of width to height of an object. Standard television has a 4:3 aspect ratio.

ASR (Automated System Recovery) Windows XP tool designed to recover a badly corrupted Windows system; similar to ERD.

assertive communication Means of communication that is not pushy or bossy but is also not soft. Useful in dealing with upset customers as it both defuses their anger and gives them confidence that you know what you're doing.

AT (advanced technology) Model name of the second-generation, 80286-based IBM computer. Many aspects of the AT, such as the BIOS, CMOS, and expansion bus, have become de facto standards in the PC industry. The physical organization of the components on the motherboard is called the AT form factor.

ATA (AT attachment) Type of hard drive and controller designed to replace the earlier ST506 and ESDI drives without requiring replacement of the AT BIOS—hence, AT attachment. These drives are more popularly known as IDE drives. (*See* IDE.) The **ATA/33** standard has drive transfer speeds up to 33 MBps; the **ATA/66** up to 66 MBps; the **ATA/100** up to 100 MBps; and the **ATA/133** up to 133 MBps. (*See* Ultra DMA.)

ATA/ATAPI-6 Also known as ATA-6 or "Big Drive." Replaced the INT13 extensions and allowed for hard drives as large as 144 petabytes (144 million GBs).

ATAPI (ATA packet interface) Series of standards that enable mass storage devices other than hard drives to use the IDE/ATA controllers. Popular with optical drives. (*See* EIDE.)

ATAPI-compliant Devices that utilize the ATAPI standard. (*See* ATAPI.)

Athlon Name used for a popular series of CPUs manufactured by AMD.

ATTRIB.EXE Command used to view the specific properties of a file; can also be used to modify or remove file properties, such as read-only, system, or archive.

attributes Values in a file that determine the hidden, read-only, system, and archive status of the file.

ATX (AT eXtended) Popular motherboard form factor that generally replaced the AT form factor.

authentication Any method a computer uses to determine who can access it.

authorization Any method a computer uses to determine what an authenticated user can do.

autodetection Process through which new disks are automatically recognized by the BIOS.

compliance Concept that members of an organization must abide by the rules of that organization. For a technician, this often revolves around what software can or cannot be installed on an organization's computer.

component failure Occurs when a system device fails due to manufacturing or some other type of defect.

compression Process of squeezing data to eliminate redundancies, allowing files to use less space when stored or transmitted.

CompTIA A+ 220-701 (Essentials) One half of the CompTIA A+ exam, concentrating on understanding terminology and technology, how to do fundamental tasks, and basic Windows operating system support.

CompTIA A+ 220-702 (Practical Application) The other half of the CompTIA A+ exam, covering advanced troubleshooting and configuration.

CompTIA A+ certification Industry-wide, vendor-neutral computer certification program that demonstrates competency as a computer technician.

CompTIA Network+ certification Industry-wide, vendor-neutral certification for network technicians, covering network hardware, installation, and troubleshooting.

Computer (Vista) Default interface in Windows Vista and 7 for Windows Explorer; displays drives and network locations. (*See* My Computer.)

Computer Administrator One of three types of user accounts, the Administrator account has access to all resources on the computer.

Computer Management Applet in Windows' Administrative Tools that contains several useful snap-ins, such as Device Manager and Disk Management.

computing process Four parts of a computer's operation: input, processing, output, and storage.

Computing Technology Industry Association (CompTIA) Nonprofit IT trade association that administers the CompTIA A+ and CompTIA Network+ exams.

conditioning charger Battery charger that contains intelligent circuitry that prevents portable computer batteries from being overcharged and damaged.

connectors Small receptacles used to attach cables to a system. Common types of connectors include USB, PS/2, and DB-25.

consumables Materials used up by printers, including paper, ink, ribbons, and toner cartridges.

container file File containing two or more separate, compressed tracks, typically an audio and a moving picture track. Also known as a wrapper.

context menu Small menu brought up by right-clicking on objects in Windows.

Control Panel Collection of Windows applets, or small programs, that can be used to configure various pieces of hardware and software in a system.

controller card Card adapter that connects devices, such as a disk drive, to the main computer bus/motherboard.

convergence Measure of how sharply a single pixel appears on a CRT; a monitor with poor convergence produces images that are not sharply defined.

copy backup Type of backup similar to Normal or Full, in that all selected files on a system are backed up. This type of backup does not change the archive bit of the files being backed up.

COPY command Command in the command-line interface for making a copy of a file and pasting it in another location.

core Name used for the family of Intel CPUs that succeeded the Pentium 4.

counter Used to track data about a particular object when using the Performance console.

CPU (central processing unit) "Brain" of the computer. Microprocessor that handles primary calculations for the computer. CPUs are known by names such as Core i5 and Phenom.

CRC (cyclic redundancy check) Very accurate mathematical method used to check for errors in long streams of transmitted data. Before data is sent, the main computer uses the data to calculate a CRC value from the data's contents. If the receiver calculates a CRC value different from the received data, the data was corrupted during transmission and is re-sent. Ethernet packets have a CRC code.

C-RIMM or CRIMM (continuity RIMM) Passive device added to populate unused banks in a system that uses Rambus RIMMs.

crossover cable   Special UTP cable used to connect hubs or to connect network cards without a hub. Crossover cables reverse the sending and receiving wire pairs from one end to the other.

CRT (cathode ray tube)   Tube of a monitor in which rays of electrons are beamed onto a phosphorescent screen to produce images. Also a shorthand way to describe a monitor that uses CRT rather than LCD technology.

CSMA/CA (carrier sense multiple access with collision avoidance)   Networking scheme used by wireless devices to transmit data while avoiding data collisions, which wireless nodes have difficulty detecting.

CSMA/CD (carrier sense multiple access with collision detection)   Networking scheme used by Ethernet devices to transmit data and resend data after detecting data collisions.

cylinder   Single track on all the platters in a hard drive. Imagine a hard drive as a series of metal cans, nested one inside another; a single can would represent a cylinder.

daily backup   Backup of all files that have been changed on that day without changing the archive bits of those files. Also called *daily copy backup*.

daisy-chaining   Method of connecting several devices along a bus and managing the signals for each device.

data classification   System of organizing data according to its sensitivity. Common classifications include public, highly confidential, and top secret.

data structure   Scheme that directs how an OS stores and retrieves data on and off a drive. Used interchangeably with the term file system. (*See also* file system.)

DB connectors   D-shaped connectors used for a variety of connections in the PC and networking world. Can be male (with prongs) or female (with holes) and have a varying number of pins or sockets. Also called *D-sub, D-subminiature, or D-shell connectors*.

DB-15   A two- or three-row DB connector (female) used for 10Base5 networks, MIDI/joysticks, and analog video.

DB-25 connector   DB connector (female), commonly referred to as a parallel port connector.

DC (direct current)   Type of electricity in which the flow of electrons is in a complete circle in one direction.

DDR SDRAM (double data rate SDRAM)   Type of DRAM that makes two processes for every clock cycle. (*See also* DRAM.)

DDR2 SDRAM   Type of SDRAM that sends four bits of data in every clock cycle. (*See also* DDR SDRAM.)

DDR3 SDRAM   Type of SDRAM that transfers data at twice the rate of DDR2 SDRAM.

debug   To detect, trace, and eliminate errors in computer programs.

decibels   Unit of measurement typically associated with sound. The higher the number of decibels, the louder the sound.

dedicated server   Machine that is not used for any client functions, only server functions.

default gateway   In a TCP/IP network, the nearest router to a particular host. This router's IP address is part of the necessary TCP/IP configuration for communicating with multiple networks using IP.

definition file   List of virus signatures that an antivirus program can recognize.

defragmentation (DEFRAG)   Procedure in which all the files on a hard disk are rewritten on disk so that all parts of each file reside in contiguous clusters. The result is an improvement in disk speed during retrieval operations.

degauss   Procedure used to break up the electromagnetic fields that can build up on the cathode ray tube of a monitor; involves running a current through a wire loop. Most monitors feature a manual degaussing tool.

DEL (Erase) command   Command in the command-line interface used to delete/erase files.

desktop   User's primary interface to the Windows operating system.

desktop extender   Portable computer that offers some of the features of a full-fledged desktop computer but with a much smaller footprint and lower weight.

desktop replacement   Portable computer that offers the same performance as a full-fledged desktop computer; these systems are normally very heavy to carry and often cost much more than the desktop systems they replace.

device driver   Program used by the operating system to control communications between the computer and peripherals.

Device Manager   Utility that enables techs to examine and configure all the hardware and drivers in a Windows PC.

DHCP (Dynamic Host Configuration Protocol)   Protocol that enables a DHCP server to set TCP/IP settings automatically for a DHCP client.

differential backup   Similar to an incremental backup. Backs up the files that have been changed since the last backup. This type of backup does not change the state of the archive bit.

digital camera   Camera that simulates film technology electronically.

digital certificate   Form in which a public key is sent from a Web server to a Web browser so that the browser can decrypt the data sent by the server.

digital zoom   Software tool to enhance the optical zoom capabilities of a digital camera.

digitally signed driver   All drivers designed specifically for Windows are digitally signed, meaning they are tested to work stably with these operating systems.

DIMM (dual inline memory module)   32- or 64-bit type of DRAM packaging, similar to SIMMs, with the distinction that each side of each tab inserted into the system performs a separate function. DIMMs come in a variety of sizes, with 184- and 240-pin being the most common on desktop computers.

dipole antennae   Standard straight-wire antennae that provide the most omnidirectional function.

DIR command   Command used in the command-line interface to display the entire contents of the current working directory.

directory   Another name for a folder.

directory service   Centralized index that each PC accesses to locate resources in the domain.

DirectX   Set of APIs enabling programs to control multimedia, such as sound, video, and graphics. Used in Windows Vista to draw the Aero desktop.

Disk Cleanup   Utility built into Windows that can help users clean up their disks by removing temporary Internet files, deleting unused program files, and more.

disk cloning   Taking a PC and making duplicates of the hard drive, including all data, software, and configuration files and transferring it to another PC. (*See* image installation.)

disk duplexing   Type of disk mirroring using two separate controllers rather than one; faster than traditional mirroring.

Disk Management   Snap-in available with the Microsoft Management Console that enables techs to configure the various disks installed in a system; available in the Computer Management Administrative Tool.

disk mirroring   Process by which data is written simultaneously to two or more disk drives. Read and write speed is decreased but redundancy in case of catastrophe is increased.

disk quota   Application allowing network administrators to limit hard drive space usage.

disk striping   Process by which data is spread among multiple (at least two) drives. Increases speed for both reads and writes of data. Considered RAID level 0 because it does not provide fault tolerance.

disk striping with parity   Method for providing fault tolerance by writing data across multiple drives and then including an additional drive, called a parity drive, that stores information to rebuild the data contained on the other drives. Requires at least three physical disks: two for the data and a third for the parity drive. This provides data redundancy at RAID levels 3–5 with different options.

disk thrashing   Hard drive that is constantly being accessed due to lack of available system memory. When system memory runs low, a Windows system will utilize hard disk space as "virtual" memory, thus causing an unusual amount of hard drive access.

display adapter   Handles all the communication between the CPU and the monitor. Also known as a video card.

Display applet   Tool in Windows 2000 and Windows XP used to adjust display settings, including resolution, refresh rate, driver information, and color depth.

DMA (direct memory access) modes   Technique that some PC hardware devices use to transfer data to and from the memory without using the CPU.

DMA controller Resides between the RAM and the devices and handles DMA requests.

DNS (domain name system) TCP/IP name resolution system that translates a host name into an IP address.

DNS domain Specific branch of the DNS name space. First-level DNS domains include .COM, .GOV, and .EDU.

docking station Device that provides a portable computer extra features such as a DVD drive or PC Card, in addition to legacy and modern ports. Similar to a port replicator.

document Steps a technician uses to solve a problem: To record the relevant information. For a technician, this would be recording each troubleshooting job: what the problem was, how it was fixed, and other helpful information.

Documents folder Windows Vista/7 folder for storing user-created files. Replaces the My Documents folder previously used in Windows 2000/XP. (*See* My Documents.)

Dolby Digital Technology for sound reductions and channeling methods used for digital audio.

domain Groupings of users, computers, or networks. In Microsoft networking, a domain is a group of computers and users that share a common account database, called a SAM, and a common security policy. On the Internet, a domain is a group of computers that share a common element in their hierarchical name. Other types of domains exist—e.g., broadcast domain, etc.

domain-based network Network that eliminates the need for logging in to multiple servers by using domain controllers to hold the security database for all systems.

DOS (Disk Operating System) First popular operating system available for PCs. A text-based, single-tasking operating system that was not completely replaced until the introduction of Windows 95.

dot pitch Value relating to CRTs, showing the diagonal distance between phosphors measured in millimeters.

dot-matrix printer Printer that creates each character from an array of dots. Pins striking a ribbon against the paper, one pin for each dot position, form the dots. May be a serial printer (printing one character at a time) or a line printer.

double-sided RAM RAM stick with RAM chips soldered to both sides of the stick. May only be used with motherboards designed to accept double-sided RAM. Very common.

DPI (dots per inch) Measure of printer resolution that counts the dots the device can produce per linear (horizontal) inch.

DPMS (Display Power-Management Signaling) Specification that can reduce CRT power consumption by 75 percent by reducing/eliminating video signals during idle periods.

DRAM (dynamic random access memory or dynamic RAM) Memory used to store data in most personal computers. DRAM stores each bit in a "cell" composed of a transistor and a capacitor. Because the capacitor in a DRAM cell can only hold a charge for a few milliseconds, DRAM must be continually refreshed, or rewritten, to retain its data.

DriveLock CMOS program enabling you to control the ATA security mode feature set. Also known as *drive lock*.

driver signing Digital signature for drivers used by Windows to protect against potentially bad drivers.

DS3D (DirectSound3D) Introduced with DirectX 3.0, DS3D is a command set used to create positional audio, or sounds that appear to come from in front, in back, or to the side of a user. (*See also* DirectX.)

DSL (digital subscriber line) High-speed Internet connection technology that uses a regular telephone line for connectivity. DSL comes in several varieties, including asynchronous (ADSL) and synchronous (SDSL), and many speeds. Typical home-user DSL connections are ADSL with a download speed of 7 Mbps and an upload speed of 512 Kbps.

D-subminiature *See* DB connectors.

DTS (Digital Theatre Systems) Technology for sound reductions and channeling methods, similar to Dolby Digital.

dual boot Refers to a computer with two operating systems installed, enabling users to choose which operating system to load on boot. Can also refer to kicking a device a second time just in case the first time didn't work.

DualView Microsoft feature enbling Windows to use two or more monitors simultaneously.

dual-channel architecture Using two sticks of RAM (either RDRAM or DDR) to increase throughput.

dual-channel memory Form of DDR, DDR2, and DDR3 memory access used by many motherboards that requires two identical sticks of DDR, DDR2, or DDR3 RAM.

dual-core Dual-core CPUs have two execution units on the same physical chip but share caches and RAM.

dual-scan passive matrix Manufacturing technique for increasing display updates by refreshing two lines at a time.

dumpster diving To go through someone's trash in search of information.

DUN (Dial-Up Networking) Software used by Windows to govern the connection between the modem and the ISP.

duplexing Similar to mirroring in that data is written to and read from two physical drives, for fault tolerance. Separate controllers are used for each drive, both for additional fault tolerance and additional speed. Considered RAID level 1. Also called *disk duplexing* or *drive duplexing*.

Duron Lower-cost version of AMD's Athlon series of CPUs.

DVD (digital versatile disc) Optical disc format that provides for 4–17 GB of video or data storage.

DVD-ROM DVD equivalent of the standard CD-ROM.

DVD-RW Rewritable DVD media.

DVD-Video DVD format used exclusively to store digital video; capable of storing over 2 hours of high-quality video on a single DVD.

DVI (Digital Visual Interface) Special video connector designed for digital-to-digital connections; most commonly seen on PC video cards and LCD monitors. Some versions also support analog signals with a special adapter.

Dxdiag (DirectX Diagnostics) Diagnostic tool for getting information about and testing a computer's DirectX version.

dye-sublimation printers Printer that uses a roll of heat-sensitive plastic film embedded with dyes, which are vaporized and then solidified onto specially coated paper to create a high-quality image.

dynamic disks Special feature of Windows that enables users to span a single volume across two or more drives. Dynamic disks do not have partitions; they have volumes. Dynamic disks can be striped, mirrored, and striped or mirrored with parity.

EAX (Environment Audio eXtensions) 3-D sound technology developed by Creative Labs but now supported by most sound cards.

ECC (error correction code) Special software, embedded on hard drives, that constantly scans the drives for bad sectors.

ECC RAM/DRAM (error correction code DRAM) RAM that uses special chips to detect and fix memory errors. Commonly used in high-end servers where data integrity is crucial.

effective permissions User's combined permissions granted by multiple groups.

EFI (Extensible Firmware Interface) Firmware created by Intel and HP that replaced traditional 16-bit BIOS and added several new enhancements.

EFS (encrypting file system) Encryption tool found in NTFS 5.

EIA/TIA *See* TIA/EIA.

EIDE (enhanced IDE) Marketing concept of hard drive–maker Western Digital, encompassing four improvements for IDE drives, including drives larger than 528 MB, four devices, increase in drive throughput, and non–hard drive devices. (*See* ATAPI, PIO mode.)

electrostatic discharge (ESD) Movement of electrons from one body to another. A real menace to PCs, as it can cause permanent damage to semiconductors.

eliciting answers Communication strategy designed to help techs understand a user's problems better. Works by listening to a user's description of a problem and then asking cogent questions.

e-mail (electronic mail) Messages, usually text, sent from one person to another via computer. Can also be sent automatically to a group of addresses (mailing list).

electromagnetic interference (EMI)   Electrical interference from one device to another, resulting in poor performance of the device being interfered with. Examples: Static on your TV while running a blow dryer, or placing two monitors too close together and getting a "shaky" screen.

emergency repair disk (ERD)   Saves critical boot files and partition information and is the main tool for fixing boot problems in Windows 2000.

encryption   Making data unreadable by those who do not possess a key or password.

erase lamp   Component inside laser printers that uses light to make the coating of the photosensitive drum conductive.

Error-checking   Windows XP/Vista/7 name for the Checkdisk and ScanDisk tools.

eSATA   Serial ATA-based connector for external hard drives and optical drives.

escalate   Process used when person assigned to repair a problem is not able to get the job done, such as sending the problem to someone else.

Ethernet   Name coined by Xerox for the first standard of network cabling and protocols. Based on a bus topology.

Ethic of Reciprocity   Golden Rule: Do unto others as you would have them do unto you.

EULA (end-user license agreement)   Agreement that accompanies a piece of software, to which user must agree before using the software. Outlines the terms of use for the software and also lists any actions on the part of the user that violate the agreement.

event auditing   Feature of Event Viewer's Security section that creates an entry in the Security Log when certain events happen, such as a user logging on.

Event Viewer   Utility made available as an MMC snap-in that enables users to monitor various system events, including network bandwidth usage and CPU utilization.

EXPAND   Command-line utility program included with Windows used to access files within CAB files.

expansion bus   Set of wires going to the CPU, governed by the expansion bus crystal, directly connected to expansion slots of varying types (PCI, AGP, PCIe, etc.). Depending on the type of slots, the expansion bus runs at a percentage of the main system speed (8.33–133 MHz).

expansion bus crystal   Controls the speed of the expansion bus.

expansion slots   Connectors on a motherboard that enable users to add optional components to a system. (*See also* AGP and PCI.)

ExpressCard   Serial PC Card designed to replace CardBus PC Cards. ExpressCards connect to either a Hi-Speed USB (480 Mbps) or PCI Express (2.5 Gbps) bus.

extended partition   Type of non-bootable hard disk partition. May only have one extended partition per disk. Purpose is to divide a large disk into smaller partitions, each with a separate drive letter.

extension   Three or four letters that follow a filename and identify the type of file. Common file extensions are .ZIP, .EXE, and .DOC.

external data bus (EDB)   Primary data highway of all computers. Everything in your computer is tied either directly or indirectly to the external data bus. (*See also* frontside bus and backside bus.)

fast user switching   Account option that is useful when multiple users share a system; allows users to switch without logging off.

FAT (file allocation table)   Hidden table that records how files on a hard disk are stored in distinct clusters; the only way DOS knows where to access files. Address of first cluster of a file is stored in the directory file. FAT entry for the first cluster is the address of the second cluster used to store that file. In the entry for the second cluster for that file is the address for the third cluster, and so on until the final cluster, which gets a special end-of-file code. There are two FATs, mirror images of each other, in case one is destroyed or damaged.

FAT32   File allocation table that uses 32 bits for addressing clusters. Commonly used with Windows 98 and Windows Me systems. Some Windows 2000 Professional and Windows XP systems also use FAT32, although most modern Windows systems use the more robust NTFS.

FDISK   Disk-partitioning utility included with Windows.

fiber optics   High-speed channel for transmitting data, made of high-purity glass sealed within an opaque tube. Much faster than conventional copper wire such as coaxial cable.

file   Collection of any form of data that is stored beyond the time of execution of a single job. A file may contain program instructions or data, which may be numerical, textual, or graphical information.

file allocation unit   Another term for cluster. (*See also* cluster.)

file association   Windows term for the proper program to open a particular file; for example, file association for opening .MP3 programs might be Winamp.

file format   How information is encoded in a file. Two primary types are binary (pictures) and ASCII (text), but within those are many formats, such as BMP and GIF for pictures. Commonly represented by a suffix at the end of the filename; for example, .txt for a text file or .exe for an executable.

file server   Computer designated to store software, courseware, administrative tools, and other data on a local- or wide-area network. It "serves" this information to other computers via the network when users enter their personal access codes.

file system   Scheme that directs how an OS stores and retrieves data on and off a drive; FAT32 and NTFS are both file systems. Used interchangeably with the term "data structure." (*See also* data structure.)

filename   Name assigned to a file when the file is first written on a disk. Every file on a disk within the same folder must have a unique name. Filenames can contain any character (including spaces), except the following: \ / : * ? " < > |

firewall   Device that restricts traffic between a local network and the Internet.

FireWire (IEEE 1394)   Interconnection standard to send wide-band signals over a serialized, physically thin connector system. Serial bus developed by Apple and Texas Instruments; enables connection of 63 devices at speeds up to 800 megabits per second.

firmware   Embedded programs or code stored on a ROM chip. Generally OS-independent, thus allowing devices to operate in a wide variety of circumstances without direct OS support. The system BIOS is firmware.

Flash ROM   ROM technology that can be electrically reprogrammed while still in the PC. Overwhelmingly the most common storage medium of BIOS in PCs today, as it can be upgraded without a need to open the computer on most systems.

flatbed scanner   Most popular form of consumer scanner; runs a bright light along the length of the tray to capture an image.

FlexATX   Motherboard form factor. Motherboards built in accordance with the FlexATX form factor are very small, much smaller than microATX motherboards.

Flip 3D   In the Aero desktop environment, a three-dimensional replacement for ALT-TAB. Accessed by pressing the WINDOWS KEY-TAB key combination.

floppy disk   Removable storage media that can hold between 720 KB and 1.44 MB of data.

floppy drive   System hardware that uses removable 3.5-inch disks as storage media.

flux reversal   Point at which a read/write head detects a change in magnetic polarity.

FM synthesis   Producing sound by electronic emulation of various instruments to more-or-less produce music and other sound effects.

folders list   Toggle button in Windows Explorer for Windows 2000 and XP that displays the file structure on the left side of the window. In Windows Vista and 7, the folders list is active by default.

form factor   Standard for the physical organization of motherboard components and motherboard size. Most common form factors are ATX and BTX.

FORMAT command   Command in the command-line interface used to format a storage device.

formatting   Magnetically mapping a disk to provide a structure for storing data; can be done to any type of disk, including a floppy disk, hard disk, or other type of removable disk.

FPU (floating point unit)   Formal term for math coprocessor (also called a *numeric processor*) circuitry inside a CPU. A math coprocessor calculates by using a floating point math (which allows for decimals). Before the Intel 80486, FPUs were separate chips from the CPU.

fragmentation   Occurs when files and directories get jumbled on a fixed disk and are no longer contiguous. Can significantly slow down hard drive access times and can be repaired by using the DEFRAG utility included with each version of Windows. (*See also* defragmentation (DEFRAG).)

freeware Software that is distributed for free, with no license fee.

frequency Measure of a sound's tone, either high or low.

frontside bus Wires that connect the CPU to the main system RAM. Generally running at speeds of 66–133 MHz. Distinct from the expansion bus and the backside bus, though it shares wires with the former.

front-view projector Shoots the image out the front and counts on you to put a screen in front at the proper distance.

FRU (field replaceable unit) Any part of a PC that is considered to be replaceable "in the field," i.e., a customer location. There is no official list of FRUs—it is usually a matter of policy by the repair center.

FTP (File Transfer Protocol) Protocol used when you transfer a file from one computer to another across the Internet. FTP uses port numbers 20 and 21.

fuel cells Power source that uses chemical reactions to produce electricity. Lightweight, compact, and stable devices expected to replace batteries as the primary power source for portable PCs.

full-duplex Any device that can send and receive data simultaneously.

Full-Speed USB USB standard that runs at 12 Mbps.

fuser assembly Mechanism in laser printers that uses two rollers to fuse toner to paper during the print process.

gain Ratio of increase of radio frequency output provided by an antenna, measured in decibels (dB).

GDI (graphical device interface) Component of Windows that utilizes the CPU rather than the printer to process a print job as a bitmapped image of each page.

general protection fault (GPF) Error code usually seen when separate active programs conflict on resources or data.

geometry Numbers representing three values: heads, cylinders, and sectors per track; define where a hard drives stores data.

giga Prefix for the quantity 1,073,741,824 or for 1 billion. One gigabyte would be 1,073,741,824 bytes, except with hard drive labeling, where it means 1 billion bytes. One gigahertz is 1 billion hertz.

GPU (graphics processing unit) Specialized processor that helps CPU by taking over all of the 3-D rendering duties.

grayscale depth Number that defines how many shades of gray the scanner can save per dot.

grayware Program that intrudes into a user's computer experience without damaging any systems or data.

group Collection of user accounts that share the same access capabilities.

Group Policy Means of easily controlling the settings of multiple network clients with policies such as setting minimum password length or preventing Registry edits.

Guest/Guest groups Very limited built-in account type for Windows.

GUI (graphical user interface) Interface that enables user to interact with computer graphically, by using a mouse or other pointing device to manipulate icons that represent programs or documents, instead of using only text as in early interfaces. Pronounced "gooey."

HAL (hardware abstraction layer) Part of the Windows OS that separates system-specific device drivers from the rest of the NT system.

handshaking Procedure performed by modems, terminals, and computers to verify that communication has been correctly established.

hang When a computer freezes and does not respond to keyboard commands, it is said to "hang" or to have "hung."

hang time Number of seconds a too-often-hung computer is airborne after you have thrown it out a second-story window.

hardware Physical computer equipment such as electrical, electronic, magnetic, and mechanical devices. Anything in the computer world that you can hold in your hand. A floppy drive is hardware; Microsoft Word is not.

hardware protocol Defines many aspects of a network, from the packet type to the cabling and connectors used.

HBA (host bus adapter) Connects SATA devices to the expansion bus. Also known as the SATA controller.

HD (Hi-Definition) Multimedia transmission standard that defines high-resolution images and 5.1, 6.1, and 7.1 sound.

HDA (High-Definition Audio) Intel-designed standard to support features such as true surround sound with many discrete speakers.

HDD (hard disk drive) Data-recording system using solid disks of magnetic material turning at high speeds to store and retrieve programs and data in a computer.

HDMI (Hi-Definition Multimedia Interface) Single multimedia connection that includes both high-definition video and audio. One of the best connections for outputting to television. Also contains copy protection features.

heads Short for read/write heads; used by hard drives to store data.

heat dope See thermal compound.

hex (hexadecimal) Base-16 numbering system using 10 digits (0 through 9) and six letters (A through F). In the computer world, shorthand way to write binary numbers by substituting one hex digit for a four-digit binary number (e.g., hex 9 = binary 1001).

hibernation Power management setting in which all data from RAM is written to the hard drive before going to sleep. Upon waking up, all information is retrieved from the hard drive and returned to RAM.

hidden attribute File attribute that, when used, does not allow DIR command to show a file.

hierarchical directory tree Method by which Windows organizes files into a series of folders, called *directories*, under the root directory. (*See also* root directory.)

high gloss Laptop screen finish that offers sharper contrast, richer colors, and wider viewing angles than a matte finish, but is also much more reflective.

high-level formatting Format that sets up a file system on a drive.

high-voltage anode Component in a CRT monitor that has very high voltages of electricity flowing through it.

Hi-Speed USB USB standard that runs at 480 Mbps.

honesty Telling the truth—a very important thing for a tech to do.

host On a TCP/IP network, single device that has an IP address—any device (usually a computer) that can be the source or destination of a data packet. In the mainframe world, computer that is made available for use by multiple people simultaneously.

hot-swappable Any hardware that may be attached to or removed from a PC without interrupting the PC's normal processing.

HotSync (synchronization) Program used by PalmOS-based PDAs to synchronize files between a PDA and a desktop computer.

HRR (horizontal refresh rate) Amount of time it takes for a CRT to draw one horizontal line of pixels on a display.

HTML (Hypertext Markup Language) ASCII-based, script-like language for creating hypertext documents such as those on the World Wide Web.

HTTP (Hypertext Transfer Protocol) Extremely fast protocol used for network file transfers in the WWW environment.

HTTPS (Hypertext Transfer Protocol Secure) Secure form of HTTP used commonly for Internet business transactions or any time when a secure connection is required. (*See also* HTTP.)

hub Electronic device that sits at the center of a star topology network, providing a common point for the connection of network devices. Hubs repeat all information out to all ports and have been replaced by switches, although the term is still commonly used.

hyperthreading CPU feature that enables a single pipeline to run more than one thread at once.

I/O (input/output) General term for reading and writing data to a computer. "Input" includes data from a keyboard, pointing device (such as a mouse), or loaded from a disk. "Output" includes writing information to a disk, viewing it on a CRT, or printing it to a printer.

I/O addressing Using the address bus to talk to system devices.

I/O Advanced Programmable Interrupt Controller (IOAPIC) Typically located in the Southbridge, the IOAPIC acts as the traffic cop for interrupt requests to the CPU.

I/O base address First value in an I/O address range.

ICH (I/O controller hub) Official name for Southbridge chip found in Intel's chipsets.

icon Small image or graphic, most commonly found on a system's desktop, that launches a program when selected.

ICS (Internet Connection Sharing) Allowing a single network connection to be shared among several machines. ICS was first introduced with Windows 98.

IDE (integrated drive electronics) PC specification for small- to medium-sized hard drives in which the controlling electronics for the drive are part of the drive itself, speeding up transfer rates and leaving only a simple adapter (or "paddle"). IDE only supported two drives per system of no more than 504 megabytes each, and has been completely supplanted by Enhanced IDE. EIDE supports four drives of over 8 gigabytes each and more than doubles the transfer rate. The more common name for PATA drives. Also known as *intelligent drive electronics*. (*See* PATA.)

Identify the problem. To question the user and find out what has been changed recently or is no longer working properly. (One of the steps a technician uses to solve a problem.)

IEC-320 Connects the cable supplying AC power from a wall outlet into the power supply.

IEEE (Institute of Electronic and Electrical Engineers) Leading standards-setting group in the United States.

IEEE 1284 IEEE standard governing parallel communication.

IEEE 1394 IEEE standard governing FireWire communication. (*See also* FireWire.)

IEEE 1394a FireWire standard that runs at 400 Mbps.

IEEE 1394b FireWire standard that runs at 800 Mbps

IEEE 802.11 Wireless Ethernet standard more commonly known as Wi-Fi.

image file Bit-by-bit image of data to be burned on CD or DVD—from one file to an entire disc—stored as a single file on a hard drive. Particularly handy when copying from CD to CD or DVD to DVD.

image installation Operating system installation that uses a complete image of a hard drive as an installation media. Helpful when installing an operating system on a large number of identical PCs.

impact printer Uses pins and inked ribbons to print text or images on a piece of paper.

impedance Amount of resistance to an electrical signal on a wire. Relative measure of the amount of data a cable can handle.

incident report Record of the details of an accident, including what happened and where it happened.

incremental backup Backs up all files that have their archive bits turned on, meaning that they have been changed since the last backup. Turns the archive bits off after the files have been backed up.

Information Technology (IT) Field of computers, their operation, and their maintenance.

infrastructure mode Wireless networking mode that uses one or more WAPs to connect the wireless network nodes to a wired network segment.

inheritance NTFS feature that passes on the same permissions in any sub-folders/files resident in the original folder.

ink cartridge Small container of ink for inkjet printers.

inkjet printer Uses liquid ink, sprayed through a series of tiny jets, to print text or images on a piece of paper.

installation disc Typically a CD-ROM or DVD that holds all the necessary device drivers.

instruction set All of the machine-language commands that a particular CPU is designed to understand.

integrity Always doing the right thing.

interface Means by which a user interacts with a piece of software.

Interrupt 13 (INT13) extensions Improved type of BIOS that accepts EIDE drives up to 137 GB.

interrupt/interruption Suspension of a process, such as the execution of a computer program, caused by an event external to the computer and performed in such a way that the process can be resumed. Events of this kind include sensors monitoring laboratory equipment or a user pressing an interrupt key.

inverter Device used to convert DC current into AC. Commonly used with CCFLs in laptops and flatbed scanners.

IP (Internet Protocol) Internet standard protocol that provides a common layer over dissimilar networks; used to move packets among host computers and through gateways if necessary. Part of the TCP/IP protocol suite.

IP address Numeric address of a computer connected to the Internet. An IPv4 address is made up of 4 octets of 8-bit binary numbers translated into their shorthand numeric values. An IPv6 address is 128 bits long. The IP address can be broken down into a network ID and a host ID. Also called *Internet address*.

IPCONFIG Command-line utility for Windows servers and workstations that displays the current TCP/IP configuration of the machine. Similar to WINIPCFG and IFCONFIG.

IPSec (Internet Protocol Security) Microsoft's encryption method of choice for networks consisting of multiple networks linked by a private connection, providing transparent encryption between the server and the client.

IrDA (Infrared Data Association) Protocol that enables communication through infrared devices, with speeds of up to 4 Mbps.

IRQ (interrupt request) Signal from a hardware device, such as a modem or a mouse, indicating that it needs the CPU's attention. In PCs, IRQs are sent along specific IRQ channels associated with a particular device. IRQ conflicts were a common problem in the past when adding expansion boards, but the plug-and-play specification has removed this headache in most cases.

ISA (Industry Standard Architecture) Industry Standard Architecture design was found in the original IBM PC for the slots that allowed additional hardware to be connected to the computer's motherboard. An 8-bit, 8.33-MHz expansion bus was designed by IBM for its AT computer and released to the public domain. An improved 16-bit bus was also released to the public domain. Replaced by PCI in the mid-1990s.

ISDN (integrated services digital network) Standard from the CCITT (Comité Consultatif Internationale de Télégraphie et Téléphonie) that defines a digital method for communications to replace the current analog telephone system. ISDN is superior to POTS telephone lines because it supports up to 128 Kbps transfer rate for sending information from computer to computer. It also allows data and voice to share a common phone line. DSL reduced demand for ISDN substantially.

ISO 9660 CD format to support PC file systems on CD media. Supplanted by the Joliet format.

ISO file Complete copy (or image) of a storage media device, typically used for optical discs.

ISP (Internet service provider) Company that provides access to the Internet, usually for money.

jack (physical connection) Part of a connector into which a plug is inserted. Also referred to as ports.

Joliet Extension of the ISO 9660 format. Most popular CD format to support PC file systems on CD media.

joystick Peripheral often used while playing computer games; originally intended as a multipurpose input device.

joule Unit of energy describing (in this book) how much energy a surge suppressor can handle before it fails.

jumper Pair of small pins that can be shorted with a shunt to configure many aspects of PCs. Usually used in configurations that are rarely changed, such as master/slave settings on IDE drives.

Kerberos Authentication encryption developed by MIT to enable multiple brands of servers to authenticate multiple brands of clients.

kernel Core portion of program that resides in memory and performs the most essential operating system tasks.

keyboard Input device. Three common types of keyboards: those that use a mini-DIN (PS/2) connection, those that use a USB connection, and those that use wireless technology.

Knowledge Base Large collection of documents and FAQs that is maintained by Microsoft. Found on Microsoft's Web site, the Knowledge Base is an excellent place to search for assistance on most operating system problems.

KVM (keyboard, video, mouse switch) Hardware device that enables multiple computers to be viewed and controlled by a single mouse, keyboard, and screen.

LAN (local area network) Group of PCs connected via cabling, radio, or infrared that use this connectivity to share resources such as printers and mass storage.

laptop Traditional clamshell portable computing device with built-in LCD monitor, keyboard, and trackpad.

laser Single-wavelength, in-phase light source that is sometimes strapped to the head of sharks by bad guys. Note to henchmen: Lasers should never be used with sea bass, no matter how ill-tempered they might be.

laser printer Electro-photographic printer in which a laser is used as the light source.

Last Known Good Configuration Option on the Advanced Startup Options menu that allows your system to revert to a previous configuration to troubleshoot and repair any major system problems.

latency Amount of delay before a device may respond to a request; most commonly used in reference to RAM.

LBA (logical block addressing) Translation (algorithm) of IDE drives promoted by Western Digital as a standardized method for breaking the 504-MB limit in IDE drives. Subsequently adopted universally by the PC industry and now standard on all EIDE drives.

LCD (liquid crystal display) Type of display commonly used on portable PCs. Also have mostly replaced CRTs as the display of choice for most desktop computer users, due in large part to rapidly falling prices and increasing quality. LCDs use liquid crystals and electricity to produce images on the screen.

LED (light-emitting diode) Solid-state device that vibrates at luminous frequencies when current is applied.

Level 1 (L1) cache First RAM cache accessed by the CPU, which stores only the absolute most-accessed programming and data used by currently running threads. Always the smallest and fastest cache on the CPU.

Level 2 (L2) cache Second RAM cache accessed by the CPU. Much larger and often slower than the L1 cache, and accessed only if the requested program/ data is not in the L1 cache.

Level 3 (L3) cache Third RAM cache accessed by the CPU. Much larger and slower than the L1 and L2 caches, and accessed only if the requested program/data is not in the L2 cache. Seen only on high-end CPUs.

Li-Ion (lithium-ion) Battery commonly used in portable PCs. Li-Ion batteries don't suffer from the memory effects of NiCd batteries and provide much more power for a greater length of time.

limited account/user User account in Windows XP that has limited access to a system. Accounts of this type cannot alter system files, cannot install new programs, and cannot edit settings by using the Control Panel.

Linux Open-source UNIX-clone operating system.

Local Security Settings Windows tool used to set local security policies on an individual system.

local user account List of users allowed access to a system.

Local Users and Groups Tool enabling creation and changing of group memberships and accounts for users.

log files Files created in Windows to track the progress of certain processes.

logical drives Sections of a hard drive that are formatted and assigned a drive letter, each of which is presented to the user as if it were a separate drive.

login screen First screen of the Windows interface, used to log in to the computer system.

loopback plug Device used during loopback tests to check the female connector on a NIC.

Low-Speed USB USB standard that runs at 1.5 Mbps.

LPT port Commonly referred to as a printer port; usually associated with a local parallel port.

LPX First slimline form factor; replaced by NLX form factor.

lumens Unit of measure for amount of brightness on a projector or other light source.

Mac (Also **Macintosh**.) Apple Computers' flagship operating system, currently up to OS Xv10.6 "Snow Leopard" and running on Intel-based hardware.

MAC (Media Access Control) address Unique 48-bit address assigned to each network card. IEEE assigns blocks of possible addresses to various NIC manufacturers to help ensure that the address is always unique. The Data Link layer of the OSI model uses MAC addresses for locating machines.

MAC address filtering Method of limiting wireless network access based on the physical, hard-wired address of the units' wireless NIC.

machine language Binary instruction code that is understood by the CPU.

maintenance kits Commonly replaced printer components provided by many manufacturers.

mass storage Hard drives, CD-ROMs, removable media drives, etc.

matte Laptop screen finish that offers a good balance between richness of colors and reflections, but washes out in bright light.

MBR (master boot record) Tiny bit of code that takes control of the boot process from the system BIOS.

MCC (memory controller chip) Chip that handles memory requests from the CPU. Although once a special chip, it has been integrated into the chipset on all PCs today.

MCH (memory controller hub) Intel-coined name for what is now commonly called the Northbridge.

MD (MKDIR) command Command in the command-line interface used to create directories.

mega- Prefix that usually stands for the binary quantity 1,048,576 (2^{20}). One megabyte is 1,048,576 bytes. One megahertz, however, is a million hertz. Sometimes shortened to *Meg*, as in "a 286 has an address space of 16 Megs."

megapixel Term used typically in reference to digital cameras and their ability to capture data.

memory Device or medium for temporary storage of programs and data during program execution. Synonymous with storage, although it most frequently refers to the internal storage of a computer that can be directly addressed by operating instructions. A computer's temporary storage capacity is measured in kilobytes (KB), megabytes (MB), or gigabytes (GB) of RAM (random-access memory). Long-term data storage on disks is also measured in kilobytes, megabytes, gigabytes, and terabytes.

memory addressing Taking memory address from system RAM and using it to address nonsystem RAM or ROM so the CPU can access it.

Memory Stick Sony's flash memory card format; rarely seen outside of Sony devices.

mesh topology Network topology where each computer has a dedicated line to every other computer, most often used in wireless networks.

MFT (master file table) Enhanced file allocation table used by NTFS. (*See also* FAT.)

microATX Variation of the ATX form factor, which uses the ATX power supply. MicroATX motherboards are generally smaller than their ATX counterparts but retain all the same functionality.

microBTX Variation of the BTX form factor. MicroBTX motherboards are generally smaller than their BTX counterparts but retain all the same functionality.

microprocessor "Brain" of a computer. Primary computer chip that determines relative speed and capabilities of the computer. Also called *CPU*.

Microsoft Windows Logo Program Testing program for hardware manufacturers, designed to ensure compatibility with the Windows OS.

MIDI (musical instrument digital interface) Interface between a computer and a device for simulating musical instruments. Rather than sending large sound samples, a computer can simply send "instructions" to the instrument describing pitch, tone, and duration of a sound. MIDI files are therefore very efficient. Because a MIDI file is made up of a set of instructions rather than a copy of the sound, modifying each component of the file is easy. Additionally, it is possible to program many channels, or "voices" of music to be played simultaneously, creating symphonic sound.

migration Moving users from one operating system or hard drive to another.

MIMO (multiple in/multiple out) Feature of 802.11n devices that enables the simultaneous connection of up to four antennae, allowing for increased throughput.

mini-audio connector Very popular, 1/8-inch diameter connector used to transmit two audio signals; perfect for stereo sound.

mini connector One type of power connector from a PC power supply unit. Supplies 5 and 12 volts to peripherals. Also known as a floppy connector,

mini PCI Specialized form of PCI designed for use in laptops.

mini power connector Connector used to provide power to floppy disk drives.

mini-DIN Small connection most commonly used for keyboards and mice. Many modern systems implement USB in place of mini-DIN connections. Also called *PS/2*.

mirrored volume Volume that is mirrored on another volume. (*See also* mirroring.)

mirroring Reading and writing data at the same time to two drives for fault tolerance purposes. Considered RAID level 1. Also called *drive mirroring*.

MMC (Microsoft Management Console) Means of managing a system, introduced by Microsoft with Windows 2000. The MMC allows an Administrator to customize management tools by picking and choosing from a list of snap-ins. Available snap-ins include Device Manager, Users and Groups, and Computer Management.

MMX (multimedia extensions) Specific CPU instructions that enable a CPU to handle many multimedia functions, such as digital signal processing. Introduced with the Pentium CPU, these instructions are used on all ×86 CPUs.

mode Any single combination of resolution and color depth set for a system.

modem (modulator/demodulator) Device that converts a digital bit stream into an analog signal (modulation) and converts incoming analog signals back into digital signals (demodulation). Analog communications channel is typically a telephone line, and analog signals are typically sounds.

module Small circuit board that DRAM chips are attached to. Also known as a "stick."

Molex connector Computer power connector used by CD-ROM drives, hard drives, and case fans. Keyed to prevent it from being inserted into a power port improperly.

monaural Describes recording tracks from one source (microphone) as opposed to stereo, which uses two sources.

monitor Screen that displays data from a PC. Can use either a cathode ray tube (CRT) or a liquid crystal display (LCD) to display images.

motherboard Flat piece of circuit board that resides inside your computer case and has a number of connectors on it. You can use these connectors to attach a variety of devices to your system, including hard drives, CD-ROM drives, floppy disk drives, and sound cards.

motherboard book Valuable resource when installing a new motherboard. Normally lists all the specifications about a motherboard, including the type of memory and type of CPU that should be used with the motherboard.

mount point Drive that functions like a folder mounted into another drive.

mouse Input device that enables users to manipulate a cursor on the screen to select items.

MOVE command Command in the command-line interface used to move a file from one location to another.

MP3 Short for MPEG, Layer 3. MP3 is a type of compression used specifically for turning high-quality digital audio files into much smaller, yet similar sounding, files.

MPA (Microsoft Product Activation) Introduced by Microsoft with the release of Windows XP, Microsoft Product Activation prevents unauthorized use of Microsoft's software by requiring users to activate the software.

MPEG-2 (Moving Picture Experts Group) Standard of video and audio compression offering resolutions up to 1280 × 720 at 60 frames per second.

MPEG-4 (Moving Picture Experts Group) Standard of video and audio compression offering improved compression over MPEG-2.

MS-CHAP Microsoft's variation of the CHAP protocol, which uses a slightly more advanced encryption protocol. Windows Vista uses MS-CHAP v2 (version 2), and does not support MS-CHAP v1 (version 1).

MSCONFIG (System Configuration utility) Executable file that runs the Windows System Configuration utility, which enables users to configure a system's boot files and critical system files. Often used for the name of the utility, as in "just run MSCONFIG."

MSDS (material safety data sheet) Standardized form that provides detailed information about potential environmental hazards and proper disposal methods associated with various PC components.

MSINFO32 Provides information about hardware resources, components, and the software environment. Also known as System Information.

multiboot OS installation in which multiple operating systems are installed on a single machine. Can also refer to kicking a device several times in frustration.

multimedia extensions   Originally an Intel CPU enhancement designed for graphics-intensive applications (such as games). It was never embraced but eventually led to improvements in how CPUs handle graphics.

multimeter   Device used to measure voltage, amperage, and resistance.

multisession drive   Recordable CD drive capable of burning multiple sessions onto a single recordable disc. A multisession drive also can close a CD-R so that no further tracks can be written to it.

multitasking   Process of running multiple programs or tasks on the same computer at the same time.

Music CD-R   CD using a special format for home recorders. Music CD-R makers pay a small royalty to avoid illegal music duplication.

My Computer   Applet that allows users to access a complete list of all fixed and removable drives contained within a system.

My Documents   Introduced with Windows 98 and used in Windows 2000 and Windows XP, the My Documents folder provides a convenient place for users to store their documents, log files, and any other type of files.

My Network Places   Folder in Windows XP that enables users to view other computers on their network or workgroup.

native resolution   Resolution on an LCD monitor that matches the physical pixels on the screen. CRTs do not have fixed pixels and therefore do not have a native resolution.

NET   Command in Windows that allows users to view a network without knowing the names of the other computers on that network.

NetBIOS (Network Basic Input/Output System)   Protocol that operates at the Session layer (Layer 5) of the OSI seven-layer model. This protocol creates and manages connections based on the names of the computers involved.

network   Collection of two or more computers interconnected by telephone lines, coaxial cables, satellite links, radio, and/or some other communication technique. Group of computers that are connected and that communicate with one another for a common purpose.

Also, the name of Vista's version of the My Network Places folder.

network ID   Number that identifies the network on which a device or machine exists. This number exists in both IP and IPX protocol suites.

network printer   Printer that connects directly to a network.

NIC (network interface card)   Expansion card that enables a PC to physically link to a network.

NiCd (nickel-cadmium)   Battery that was used in the first portable PCs. Heavy and inefficient, these batteries also suffered from a memory effect that could drastically shorten the overall life of the battery. (*See also* NiMH, Li-Ion.)

NiMH (nickel-metal hydride)   Battery used in portable PCs. NiMH batteries had fewer issues with the memory effect than NiCd batteries. NiMH batteries have been replaced by lithium-ion batteries. (*See also* NiCd, Li-Ion.)

nit   Value used to measure the brightness of an LCD displays. A typical LCD display has a brightness of between 100 and 400 nits.

NLQ (near-letter quality)   Designation for dot-matrix printers that use 24-pin printheads.

NLX   Second form factor for slimline systems. Replaced the earlier LPX form factor. (NLX apparently stands for nothing; it's just a cool grouping of letters.)

NMI (non-maskable interrupt)   Interrupt code sent to the processor that cannot be ignored. Typically manifested as a BSOD.

NNTP (Network News Transfer Protocol)   Protocol run by news servers that enable newsgroups.

non-system disk or disk error   Error that occurs during the boot process. Common causes for this error are leaving a non-bootable floppy disk, CD, or other media in the drive while the computer is booting.

nonvolatile   Memory that retains data even if power is removed.

normal backup   Full backup of every selected file on a system. Turns off the archive bit after the backup.

Northbridge   Chip that connects a CPU to memory, the PCI bus, Level 2 cache, and AGP activities. Communicates with the CPU through the frontside bus. Newer CPUs feature an integrated Northbridge.

NOS (network operating system) Standalone operating system or part of an operating system that provides basic file and supervisory services over a network. Although each computer attached to the network has its own OS, the NOS describes which actions are allowed by each user and coordinates distribution of networked files to the user who requests them.

notification area Contains icons representing background processes, the system clock and volume control. Located by default at the right edge of the Windows taskbar. Most users call this area the system tray.

NSLOOKUP Command-line program in Windows used to determine exactly what information the DNS server is providing about a specific host name.

NTDETECT.COM One of the critical Windows NT/2000/XP startup files.

NTFS (NT file system) Robust and secure file system introduced by Microsoft with Windows NT. NTFS provides an amazing array of configuration options for user access and security. Users can be granted access to data on a file-by-file basis. NTFS enables object-level security, long filename support, compression, and encryption.

NTFS permissions Restrictions that determine the amount of access given to a particular user on a system using NTFS.

NTLDR Windows NT/2000/XP boot file. Launched by the MBR or MFT, NTLDR looks at the BOOT.INI configuration file for any installed operating systems.

NVIDIA One of the foremost manufacturers of graphics cards and chipsets.

object System component that is given a set of characteristics and can be managed by the operating system as a single entity.

object access auditing Feature of Event Viewer's Security section that creates an entry in the Security Log when certain objects are accessed, such as a file or folder.

ohm(s) Electronic measurement of a cable's impedance.

OpenGL One of two popular APIs used today for video cards. Originally written for UNIX systems but now ported to Windows and Apple systems. (*See also* DirectX.)

optical disc/media Types of data discs (such as DVDs, CDs, Blu-ray Discs, etc.) that are read by a laser.

optical drive Drive used to read/write to optical discs, such as CDs or DVDs.

optical mouse Pointing device that uses light rather than electronic sensors to determine movement and direction the mouse is being moved.

optical resolution Resolution a scanner can achieve mechanically. Most scanners use software to enhance this ability.

optical zoom Mechanical ability of most cameras to "zoom" in as opposed to the digital ability.

option ROM Alternative way of telling the system how to talk to a piece of hardware. Option ROM stores BIOS for the card onboard a chip on the card itself.

OS (operating system) Series of programs and code that create an interface so users can interact with a system's hardware, for example, DOS, Windows, and Linux.

OS X Current operating system on Apple Macintosh computers. Based on a UNIX core, early versions of OS X ran on Motorola-based hardware; current versions run on Intel-based hardware. Pronounced "ten" rather than "ex."

OSI seven-layer model Architecture model based on the OSI protocol suite that defines and standardizes the flow of data between computers. The seven layers are:
Layer 1 The Physical layer Defines hardware connections and turns binary into physical pulses (electrical or light). Repeaters and hubs operate at the Physical layer.
Layer 2 The Data Link layer Identifies devices on the Physical layer. MAC addresses are part of the Data Link layer. Bridges operate at the Data Link layer.
Layer 3 The Network layer Moves packets between computers on different networks. Routers operate at the Network layer. IP and IPX operate at the Network layer.
Layer 4 The Transport layer Breaks data down into manageable chunks. TCP, UDP, SPX, and NetBEUI operate at the Transport layer.
Layer 5 The Session layer Manages connections between machines. NetBIOS and Sockets operate at the Session layer.
Layer 6 The Presentation layer Can also manage data encryption; hides the differences between various types of computer systems.
Layer 7 The Application layer Provides tools for programs to use to access the network (and the lower layers). HTTP, FTP, SMTP, and POP3 are all examples of protocols that operate at the Application layer.

overclocking   To run a CPU or video processor faster than its rated speed.

P1 power connector   Provides power to ATX motherboards.

P4 12V connector   Provides additional 12-volt power to motherboards that support Pentium 4 and later processors.

P8 and P9 connectors   Provides power to AT-style motherboards.

packet   Basic component of communication over a network. Group of bits of fixed maximum size and well-defined format that is switched and transmitted as a single entity through a network. Contains source and destination address, data, and control information.

page fault   Minor memory-addressing error.

page file   Portion of the hard drive set aside by Windows to act like RAM. Also known as virtual memory or swap file.

PAN (personal area network)   Small wireless network created with Bluetooth technology and intended to link PCs and other peripheral devices.

parallel port   Connection for the synchronous, high-speed flow of data along parallel lines to a device, usually a printer.

parallel processing   When a multicore CPU processes more than one thread.

parental controls   Tool to allow monitoring and limiting of user activities; designed for parents to control the content their children can access.

parity   Method of error detection where a small group of bits being transferred is compared to a single parity bit set to make the total bits odd or even. Receiving device reads the parity bit and determines if the data is valid, based on if the parity bit is odd or even.

parity RAM   Earliest form of error-detecting RAM; stored an extra bit (called the *parity bit*) to verify the data.

partition   Section of the storage area of a hard disk. Created during initial preparation of the hard disk, before the disk is formatted.

partition table   Table located in the boot sector of a hard drive that lists every partition on the disk that contains a valid operating system.

partitioning   Electronically subdividing a physical hard drive into groups called *partitions* (or *volumes*).

passive matrix   Technology for producing colors in LCD monitors by varying voltages across wire matrices to produce red, green, or blue dots.

password   Key used to verify a user's identity on a secure computer or network.

Password Authentication Protocol (PAP)   Oldest and most basic form of authentication. Also the least safe, because it sends all passwords in clear text.

password reset disk   Special type of floppy disk with which users can recover a lost password without losing access to any encrypted, or password-protected, data.

PATA (parallel ATA)   Implementation that integrates the controller on the disk drive itself. (*See also* ATA, IDE, SATA.)

patch   Small piece of software released by a software manufacturer to correct a flaw or problem with a particular piece of software.

path   Route the operating system must follow to find an executable program stored in a subdirectory.

PC bus   Original 8-bit expansion bus developed by IBM for PCs; ran at a top speed of 4.77 MHz. Also known as the XT bus.

PC Card   Credit-card–sized adapter cards that add functionality in many notebook computers, PDAs, and other computer devices. Come in 16-bit and CardBus parallel format and ExpressCard serial format. (*See also* PCMCIA.)

PC tech   Someone with computer skills who works on computers.

PCI (Peripheral Component Interconnect)   Design architecture for the expansion bus on the computer motherboard, which enables system components to be added to the computer. Local bus standard, meaning that devices added to a computer through this port will use the processor at the motherboard's full speed (up to 33 MHz) rather than at the slower 8 MHz speed of the regular bus. Moves data 32 or 64 bits at a time rather than the 8 or 16 bits the older ISA buses supported.

PCIe (PCI Express)   Serialized successor to PCI and AGP, which uses the concept of individual data paths called *lanes*. May use any number of lanes, although

single lanes (×1) and 16 lanes (×16) are the most common on motherboards.

PCI-X (PCI Extended)   Enhanced version of PCI, 64 bits wide. Typically seen in servers and high-end systems.

PCL   Printer control language created by Hewlett-Packard and used on a broad cross-section of printers.

PCM (Pulse Code Modulation)   Sound format developed in the 1960s to carry telephone calls over the first digital lines.

PCMCIA (Personal Computer Memory Card International Association)   Consortium of computer manufacturers who devised the PC Card standard for credit-card–sized adapter cards that add functionality in many notebook computers, PDAs, and other computer devices. (*See also* PC Card.)

PDA (personal digital assistant)   Handheld computer that blurs the line between calculators and computers. Early PDAs were calculators that enabled users to program in such information as addresses and appointments. Modern PDAs, such as the Palm and PocketPC, are fully programmable computers. Most PDAs use a pen/stylus for input rather than a keyboard. A few of the larger PDAs have a tiny keyboard in addition to the stylus.

Pearson VUE   One of the two companies that administers the CompTIA A+ exams, along with Prometric.

peer-to-peer networks   Network in which each machine can act as both a client and a server.

Pentium   Name given to the fifth and later generations of Intel microprocessors; has a 32-bit address bus, 64-bit external data bus, and dual pipelining. Also used for subsequent generations of Intel processors—the Pentium Pro, Pentium II, Pentium III, and Pentium 4. Pentium name was retired after the introduction of the Intel Core CPUs.

pen-based computing   Input method used by many PDAs that combines handwriting recognition with modified mouse functions, usually in the form of a pen-like stylus.

Performance console   Windows tool used to log resource usage over time.

Performance Logs and Alerts   Snap-in enabling the creation of a written record of most everything that happens on the system.

Performance Options   Tool allowing users to configure CPU, RAM, and virtual memory settings.

peripheral   Any device that connects to the system unit.

permission propagation   Term to describe what happens to permissions on an object when you move or copy it.

persistence   Phosphors used in CRT screens continuing to glow after being struck by electrons, long enough for the human eye to register the glowing effect. Glowing too long makes the images smeary, and too little makes them flicker.

Personalization applet   Windows Vista/7 applet with which users can change display settings such as resolution, refresh rate, color depth, and desktop features.

PGA (pin grid array)   Arrangement of a large number of pins extending from the bottom of the CPU package. There are many variations on PGA.

Phillips-head screwdriver   Most important part of a PC tech's toolkit.

Phoenix Technologies   Major producer of BIOS software for motherboards.

phosphor   Electro-fluorescent material that coats the inside face of a cathode ray tube (CRT). After being hit with an electron, it glows for a fraction of a second.

photosensitive drum   Aluminum cylinder coated with particles of photosensitive compounds. Used in a laser printer and usually contained within the toner cartridge.

picoBTX   Variation of the BTX form factor. picoBTX motherboards are generally smaller than their BTX or microBTX counterparts but retain the same functionality.

pin I   Designator used to ensure proper alignment of floppy disk drive and hard drive connectors.

ping (packet Internet groper)   Slang term for a small network message (ICMP ECHO) sent by a computer to check for the presence and aliveness of another. Used to verify the presence of another system. Also the command used at a prompt to ping a computer.

PIO mode   Series of speed standards created by the Small Form Factor Committee for the use of PIO by hard drives. Modes range from PIO mode 0 to PIO mode 4.

pipeline Processing methodology where multiple calculations take place simultaneously by being broken into a series of steps. Often used in CPUs and video processors.

pixel (picture element) In computer graphics, smallest element of a display space that can be independently assigned color or intensity.

plug Hardware connection with some sort of projection that connects to a port.

plug and play (PnP) Combination of smart PCs, smart devices, and smart operating systems that automatically configure all necessary system resources and ports when you install a new peripheral device.

polygons Multi-sided shapes used in 3-D rendering of objects. In computers, video cards draw large numbers of triangles and connect them to form polygons.

polymorph virus Virus that attempts to change its signature to prevent detection by antivirus programs, usually by continually scrambling a bit of useless code.

polyphony Number of instruments a sound card can play at once.

POP3 (Post Office Protocol) Refers to the way e-mail software such as Eudora gets mail from a mail server. When you obtain a SLIP, PPP, or shell account, you almost always get a POP account with it. It is this POP account that you tell your e-mail software to use to get your mail. Also called *point of presence*.

pop-up Irritating browser window that appears automatically when you visit a Web site.

port (networking) In networking, the number used to identify the requested service (such as SMTP or FTP) when connecting to a TCP/IP host. Examples: 80 (HTTP), 20 (FTP), 69 (TFTP), 25 (SMTP), and 110 (POP3).

port (physical connection) Part of a connector into which a plug is inserted. Physical ports are also referred to as jacks.

port replicator Device that plugs into a USB port or other specialized port and offers common PC ports, such as serial, parallel, USB, network, and PS/2. By plugging your notebook computer into the port replicator, you can instantly connect the computer to nonportable components such as a printer, scanner, monitor, or full-sized keyboard. Port replicators are

typically used at home or in the office with the non-portable equipment already connected.

positional audio Range of commands for a sound card to place a sound anywhere in 3-D space.

POST (power-on self test) Basic diagnostic routine completed by a system at the beginning of the boot process to make sure a display adapter and the system's memory are installed; it then searches for an operating system. If it finds one, it hands over control of the machine to the OS.

PostScript Language defined by Adobe Systems, Inc. for describing how to create an image on a page. The description is independent of the resolution of the device that will actually create the image. It includes a technology for defining the shape of a font and creating a raster image at many different resolutions and sizes.

potential Amount of static electricity stored by an object.

power conditioning Ensuring and adjusting incoming AC wall power to as close to standard as possible. Most UPS devices provide power conditioning.

power good wire Used to wake up the CPU after the power supply has tested for proper voltage.

power supply fan Small fan located in a system power supply that draws warm air from inside the power supply and exhausts it to the outside.

power supply unit Provides the electrical power for a PC. Converts standard AC power into various voltages of DC electricity in a PC.

Power User(s) Group Second most powerful account and group type in Windows after Administrator/Administrators.

ppm (pages per minute) Speed of a printer.

PPP (Point-to-Point Protocol) Enables a computer to connect to the Internet through a dial-in connection and enjoy most of the benefits of a direct connection.

primary corona Wire located near the photosensitive drum in a laser printer, that is charged with extremely high voltage to form an electric field, enabling voltage to pass to the photosensitive drum, thus charging the photosensitive particles on the surface of the drum.

primary partition Partition on a Windows hard drive designated to store the operating system.

print resolution　Quality of a print image.

print spooler　Area of memory that queues up print jobs that the printer will handle sequentially.

printer　Output device that can print text or illustrations on paper. Microsoft uses the term to refer to the software that controls the physical print device.

printhead　Case that holds the printwires in a dot-matrix printer.

printed circuit boards　Copper etched onto a nonconductive material and then coated with some sort of epoxy for strength.

printwires　Grid of tiny pins in a dot-matrix printer that strike an inked printer ribbon to produce images on paper.

PRML (Partial Response Maximum Likelihood)　Advanced method of RLL that uses powerful, intelligent circuitry to analyze each flux reversal on a hard drive and to make a best guess as to what type of flux reversal it just read. This allows a dramatic increase in the amount of data a hard drive can store.

product key　Code used during installation to verify legitimacy of the software.

program/programming　Series of binary electronic commands sent to a CPU to get work done.

Programs and Features　Windows Vista/7 replacement for the Add or Remove Programs applet.

projector　Device for projecting video images from PCs or other video sources, usually for audience presentations. Available in front and rear view displays.

Prometric　One of the two companies that administers the CompTIA A+ exams, along with Pearson VUE.

prompt　A character or message provided by an operating system or program to indicate that it is ready to accept input.

proprietary　Technology unique to a particular vendor.

protocol　Agreement that governs the procedures used to exchange information between cooperating entities. Usually includes how much information is to be sent, how often it is sent, how to recover from transmission errors, and who is to receive the information.

proxy server　Device that fetches Internet resources for a client without exposing that client directly to the Internet. Usually accept requests for HTTP, FTP, POP3, and SMTP resources. Often caches, or stores, a copy of the requested resource for later use. Common security feature in the corporate world.

public folder　Folder that all users can access and share with all other users on the system or network.

queue　Area where objects wait their turn to be processed. Example: the printer queue, where print jobs wait until it is their turn to be printed.

Quick Launch toolbar　Enables you to launch commonly used programs with a single click.

QVGA　Video display mode of 320 × 240.

RAID (redundant array of inexpensive devices)　Six-level (0–5) way of creating a fault-tolerant storage system:
Level 0　Uses byte-level striping and provides no fault tolerance.
Level 1　Uses mirroring or duplexing.
Level 2　Uses bit-level striping.
Level 3　Stores error-correcting information (such as parity) on a separate disk, and uses data striping on the remaining drives.
Level 4　Level 3 with block-level striping.
Level 5　Uses block-level and parity data striping.

RAID-5 volume　Striped set with parity. (*See also* RAID.)

rails　Separate DC paths within an ATX power supply.

RAM (random access memory)　Memory that can be accessed at random; that is, which you can write to or read from without touching the preceding address. This term is often used to mean a computer's main memory.

RAMDAC (random access memory digital-to-analog converter)　Circuitry used on video cards that support analog monitors to convert the digital video data to analog.

raster image　Pattern of dots representing what the final product should look like.

raster line　Horizontal pattern of lines that form an image on the monitor screen.

RD (RMDIR)　Command in the command-line interface used to remove directories.

RDRAM (Rambus DRAM) Patented RAM technology that uses accelerated clocks to provide very high-speed memory.

read-only attribute File attribute that does not allow a file to be altered or modified. Helpful when protecting system files that should not be edited.

rear-view projector Projector that shoots an image onto a screen from the rear. Rear-view projectors are usually self-enclosed and very popular for TVs, but are virtually unheard of in the PC world.

Recovery Console Command-line interface boot mode for Windows that is used to repair a Windows 2000 or Windows XP system suffering from massive OS corruption or other problems.

Recycle Bin When files are deleted from a modern Windows system, they are moved to the Recycle Bin. To permanently remove files from a system, they must be emptied from the Recycle Bin.

REGEDIT.EXE Program used to edit the Windows Registry.

register Storage area inside the CPU used by the onboard logic to perform calculations. CPUs have many registers to perform different functions.

registration Usually optional process that identifies the legal owner/user of the product to the supplier.

Registry Complex binary file used to store configuration data about a particular system. To edit the Registry, users can use the applets found in the Control Panel or REGEDIT.EXE or REGEDT32.EXE.

Reliability and Performance Monitor Windows Vista's extended Performance applet.

remediation Repairing damage caused by a virus.

remnant Potentially recoverable data on a hard drive that remains despite formatting or deleting.

Remote Assistance Feature of Windows that enables users to give anyone control of his or her desktop over the Internet.

Remote Desktop Connection Windows tool used to enable a local system to graphically access the desktop of a remote system.

REN (RENAME) command Command in the command-line interface used to rename files and folders.

resistance Difficulty in making electricity flow through a material, measured in ohms.

resistor Any material or device that impedes the flow of electrons. Electronic resistors measure their resistance (impedance) in ohms. *See* ohm(s).

resolution Measurement for CRTs and printers expressed in horizontal and vertical dots or pixels. Higher resolutions provide sharper details and thus display better-looking images.

resources Data and services of a PC.

respect What all techs should feel for their customers.

response rate Time it takes for all of the sub-pixels on the panel to go from pure black to pure white and back again.

restore point System snapshot created by the System Restore utility that is used to restore a malfunctioning system. (*See also* System Restore.)

RET (resolution enhancement technology) Technology that uses small dots to smooth out jagged edges that are typical of printers without RET, producing a higher-quality print job.

RFI (radio frequency interference) Another form of electrical interference caused by radio-wave emitting devices, such as cell phones, wireless network cards, and microwave ovens.

RG-58 Coaxial cabling used for 10Base2 networks.

RIMM Individual stick of Rambus RAM. The letters don't actually stand for anything; they just rhyme with SIMM and DIMM.

RIP (raster image processor) Component in a printer that translates the raster image into commands for the printer.

riser card Special adapter card, usually inserted into a special slot on a motherboard, that changes the orientation of expansion cards relative to the motherboard. Riser cards are used extensively in slimline computers to keep total depth and height of the system to a minimum. Sometimes called a daughterboard.

RJ (registered jack) connector UTP cable connector, used for both telephone and network connections. RJ-11 is a connector for four-wire UTP; usually found in telephone connections. RJ-45 is a connector for eight-wire UTP; usually found in network connections.

RJ-11 *See* RJ (registered jack) connector.

RJ-45 *See* RJ (registered jack) connector.

ROM (read-only memory) Generic term for nonvolatile memory that can be read from but not written to. This means that code and data stored in ROM cannot be corrupted by accidental erasure. Additionally, ROM retains its data when power is removed, which makes it the perfect medium for storing BIOS data or information such as scientific constants.

root directory Directory that contains all other directories.

root keys Five main categories in the Windows Registry:
HKEY_CLASSES_ROOT
HKEY_CURRENT_USER
HKEY_USERS
HKEY_LOCAL_MACHINE
HKEY_CURRENT_CONFIG

router Device connecting separate networks; forwards a packet from one network to another based on the network address for the protocol being used. For example, an IP router looks only at the IP network number. Routers operate at Layer 3 (Network) of the OSI seven-layer model.

RS-232C Standard port recommended by the Electronics Industry Association for serial devices.

Run dialog box Command box in which users can enter the name of a particular program to run; an alternative to locating the icon in Windows.

S.M.A.R.T. (Self-Monitoring, Analysis, and Reporting Technology) Monitoring system built into hard drives.

S/PDIF (Sony/Philips Digital Interface Format) Digital audio connector found on many sound cards. Users can connect their computers directly to a 5.1 speaker system or receiver. S/PDIF comes in both a coaxial and an optical version.

Safe mode Important diagnostic boot mode for Windows that only runs very basic drivers and turns off virtual memory.

sampling Capturing sound waves in electronic format.

SATA (serial ATA) Serialized version of the ATA standard that offers many advantages over PATA (parallel ATA) technology, including thinner cabling, keyed connectors, and lower power requirements.

SATA bridge Adapter that allows PATA devices to be connected to a SATA controller.

SATA power connector 15-pin, L-shaped connector used by SATA devices that support the hot-swappable feature.

satellites Two or more standard stereo speakers to be combined with a subwoofer for a speaker system (i.e., 2.1, 5.1, etc.).

scan code Unique code corresponding to each key on the keyboard sent from the keyboard controller to the CPU.

SCSI (small computer system interface) Powerful and flexible peripheral interface popularized on the Macintosh and used to connect hard drives, CD-ROM drives, tape drives, scanners, and other devices to PCs of all kinds. Normal SCSI enables up to seven devices to be connected through a single bus connection, whereas Wide SCSI can handle 15 devices attached to a single controller.

SCSI chain Series of SCSI devices working together through a host adapter.

SCSI ID Unique identifier used by SCSI devices. No two SCSI devices may have the same SCSI ID.

SD (Secure Digital) Very popular format for flash media cards; also supports I/O devices.

SDRAM (synchronous DRAM) DRAM that is synchronous, or tied to the system clock and thus runs much faster than traditional FPM and EDO RAM. This type of RAM is used in all modern systems.

SEC (single-edge cartridge) CPU package where the CPU was contained in a cartridge that snapped into a special slot on the motherboard called Slot 1.

sector Segment of one of the concentric tracks encoded on the disk during a low-level format. A sector holds 512 bytes of data.

sector translation Translation of logical geometry into physical geometry by the onboard circuitry of a hard drive.

sectors per track (sectors/track) Combined with the number of cylinders and heads, defines the disk geometry.

serial port Common connector on a PC. Connects input devices (such as a mouse) or communications devices (such as a modem).

server Computer that shares its resources, such as printers and files, with other computers on a network. Example: Network File System Server that shares its disk space with a workstation that does not have a disk drive of its own.

service pack Collection of software patches released at one time by a software manufacturer.

SetupAPI.log Log file that tracks the installation of all hardware on a system.

Setuplog.txt Log file that tracks the complete installation process, logging the success or failure of file copying, Registry updates, and reboots.

SFC (system file checker) Scans, detects, and restores Windows system files, folders, and paths.

shadow mask CRT screen that allows only the proper electron gun to light the proper phosphors.

shared documents Windows pre-made folder accessible by all users on the computer.

shared memory Means of reducing the amount of memory needed on a video card by borrowing from the regular system RAM, which reduces costs but also decreases performance.

share-level security Security system in which each resource has a password assigned to it; access to the resource is based on knowing the password.

shareware Program protected by copyright; holder allows (encourages!) you to make and distribute copies under the condition that those who adopt the software after preview pay a fee to the holder of the copyright. Derivative works are not allowed, although you may make an archival copy.

shunt Tiny connector of metal enclosed in plastic that creates an electrical connection between two posts of a jumper.

SID (security identifier) Unique identifier for every PC that most techs change when cloning.

sidebanding Second data bus for AGP video cards; enables the video card to send more commands to the Northbridge while receiving other commands at the same time.

signal-to-noise ratio Measure that describes the relative quality of an input port.

signature Code pattern of a known virus; used by antivirus software to detect viruses.

SIMM (single in-line memory module) DRAM packaging distinguished by having a number of small tabs that install into a special connector. Each side of each tab is the same signal. SIMMs come in two common sizes: 30-pin and 72-pin.

simple file sharing Allows users to share locally or across the network but gives no control over what others do with shared files.

simple volume Volume created when setting up dynamic disks. Acts like a primary partition on a dynamic disk.

single-sided RAM Has chips on only one side as opposed to double-sided RAM.

slimline Motherboard form factor used to create PCs that were very thin. NLX and LPX were two examples of this form factor.

slot covers Metal plates that cover up unused expansion slots on the back of a PC. Useful in maintaining proper airflow through a computer case.

Smart battery Portable PC battery that tells the computer when it needs to be charged, conditioned, or replaced.

smart card Hardware authentication involving a credit-card-sized card with circuitry that can be used to identify the bearer of that card.

SmartMedia Format for flash media cards; no longer used with new devices.

SMM (System Management Mode) Special CPU mode that enables the CPU to reduce power consumption by selectively shutting down peripherals.

SMTP (Simple Mail Transport Protocol) Main protocol used to send electronic mail on the Internet.

snap-ins Small utilities that can be used with the Microsoft Management Console.

social engineering Using or manipulating people inside the networking environment to gain access to that network from the outside.

socket services Device drivers that support the PC Card socket, enabling the system to detect when a PC Card has been inserted or removed, and providing the necessary I/O to the device.

SODIMM (small outline DIMM) Memory used in portable PCs because of its small size.

soft power Characteristic of ATX motherboards, which can use software to turn the PC on and off. The physical manifestation of soft power is the power switch. Instead of the thick power cord used in AT systems, an ATX power switch is little more than a pair of small wires leading to the motherboard.

software Single group of programs designed to do a particular job; always stored on mass storage devices.

solid ink printers Printer that uses solid sticks of nontoxic "ink."

sound card Expansion card that can produce audible tones when connected to a set of speakers.

Southbridge Part of a motherboard chipset; handles all the inputs and outputs to the many devices in the PC.

spam Unsolicited e-mails from both legitimate businesses and scammers that accounts for a huge percentage of traffic on the Internet.

spanned volume Volume that uses space on multiple dynamic disks.

SPD (serial presence detect) Information stored on a RAM chip that describes the speed, capacity, and other aspects of the RAM chip.

speaker Device that outputs sound by using magnetically driven diaphragm.

sprite Bitmapped graphic such as a BMP file used by early 3-D games to create the 3-D world.

spyware Software that runs in the background of a user's PC, sending information about browsing habits back to the company that installed it onto the system.

SRAM (static RAM) RAM that uses a flip-flop circuit rather than the typical transistor/capacitor of DRAM to hold a bit of information. SRAM does not need to be refreshed and is faster than regular DRAM. Used primarily for cache.

SSH (Secure Shell) Terminal emulation program similar to Telnet, except that the entire connection is encrypted.

SSD (solid state drive) Data storage device that uses solid state memory to store data.

SSID (service set identifier) Parameter used to define a wireless network; otherwise known as the network name.

SSL (Secure Sockets Layer) Security protocol used by a browser to connect to secure Web sites.

standard account/user User account in Windows Vista that has limited access to a system. Accounts of this type cannot alter system files, cannot install new programs, and cannot edit some settings by using the Control Panel without supplying an administrator password. Replaces the Limited accounts in Windows XP.

standouts Small connectors that screw into a computer case. A motherboard is then placed on top of the standouts, and small screws are used to secure it to the standouts.

star topology Network topology where the computers on the network connect to a central wiring point, usually called a *hub*.

Start button Button on the Windows taskbar that enables access to the Start menu.

Start menu Menu that can be accessed by clicking the Start button on the Windows taskbar. Enables you to see all programs loaded on the system and to start them.

static charge eliminator Device used to remove a static charge.

static IP address Manually set IP address that will not change.

stealth virus Virus that uses various methods to hide from antivirus software.

stepper motor One of two methods used to move actuator arms in a hard drive. (*See also* voice coil motor.)

stereo Describes recording tracks from two sources (microphones) as opposed to monaural, which uses one source.

stick Generic name for a single physical SIMM, RIMM, or DIMM.

STP (shielded twisted pair) Cabling for networks, composed of pairs of wires twisted around each other at specific intervals. Twists serve to reduce interference (also called *crosstalk*)—the more twists, the less interference. Cable has metallic shielding to protect the wires from external interference.

streaming media   Broadcast of data that is played on your computer and immediately discarded.

stream loading   Process a program uses to constantly download updated information.

stripe set   Two or more drives in a group that are used for a striped volume.

strong password   Password containing at least eight characters, including letters, numbers, and punctuation symbols.

stylus   Pen-like input device used for pen-based computing.

subnet mask   Value used in TCP/IP settings to divide the IP address of a host into its component parts: network ID and host ID.

sub-pixel   Tiny liquid crystal molecules arranged in rows and columns between polarizing filters used in LCDs.

subwoofer   Powerful speaker capable of producing extremely low-frequency sounds.

super I/O chip   Chip specially designed to control low-speed, legacy devices such as the keyboard, mouse, and serial and parallel ports.

surge suppressor   Inexpensive device that protects your computer from voltage spikes.

SVGA (super video graphics array)   Video display mode of 800 × 600.

swap file   See page file.

switch   Device that filters and forwards traffic based on some criteria. A bridge and a router are both examples of switches.

SXGA   Video display mode of 1280 × 1024.

SXGA+   Video display mode of 1400 × 1050.

syntax   The proper way to write a command-line command so that it functions and does what it's supposed to do.

Sysprep   Windows tool that makes cloning of systems easier by making it possible to undo portions of the installation.

System BIOS   Primary set of BIOS stored on an EPROM or Flash chip on the motherboard. Defines the BIOS for all the assumed hardware on the mother-board, such as keyboard controller, floppy drive, basic video, and RAM.

system bus speed   Speed at which the CPU and the rest of the PC operates; set by the system crystal.

system crystal   Crystal that provides the speed signals for the CPU and the rest of the system.

system disk   Any device with a functional operating system.

system fan   Any fan controlled by the motherboard but not directly attached to the CPU.

System Management Mode (SMM)   Provided CPUs the ability to turn off high-power devices (monitors, hard drives, etc.). Originally for laptops; later versions are incorporated in all AMD and Intel CPUs.

System Monitor   Utility that can evaluate and monitor system resources, such as CPU usage and memory usage.

system resources   In classic terms, the I/O addresses, IRQs, DMA channels, and memory addresses. Also refers to other computer essentials such as hard drive space, system RAM, and processor speed.

System Restore   Utility in Windows that enables you to return your PC to a recent working configuration when something goes wrong. System Restore returns your computer's system settings to the way they were the last time you remember your system working correctly—all without affecting your personal files or e-mail.

System ROM   ROM chip that stores the system BIOS.

System Tools   Menu containing tools such as System Information and Disk Defragmenter, accessed by selecting Start | Programs or All Programs | Accessories | System Tools.

system tray   Contains icons representing background processes and the system clock. Located by default at the right edge of the Windows taskbar. Accurately called the *notification area*.

system unit   Main component of the PC, in which the CPU, RAM, CD-ROM, and hard drive reside. All other devices—the keyboard, mouse, and monitor—connect to the system unit.

Tablet PC   Small portable computer distinguished by the use of a touch screen with stylus and handwriting recognition as the primary modes of input. Also the

name of the Windows XP-based operating system designed to run on such systems.

tailgating Form of infiltration and social engineering that involves following someone else through a door as if you belong.

take ownership Special permission allowing users to seize control of a file or folder and potentially preventing others from accessing the file/folder.

Task Manager Shows all running programs, including hidden ones, accessed by pressing CTRL-SHIFT-ESC. Able to shut down an unresponsive application that refuses to close normally.

taskbar Contains the Start button, the system tray, the Quick Launch bar, and buttons for running applications. Located by default at the bottom of the desktop.

TCP/IP (Transmission Control Protocol/Internet Protocol) Communication protocols developed by the U.S. Department of Defense to enable dissimilar computers to share information over a network.

tech toolkit Tools a PC tech should never be without, including a Phillips-head screwdriver, a pair of tweezers, a flat-head screwdriver, a hemostat, a Torx wrench, a parts retriever, and a nut driver or two.

telephone scams Social engineering attack in which the attacker makes a phone call to someone in an organization to gain information.

Telnet Terminal emulation program for TCP/IP networks that allows one machine to control another as if the user were sitting in front of it.

tera- Prefix that usually stands for the binary number 1,099,511,627,776 (2^{40}). When used for mass storage, it's often shorthand for a trillion bytes.

terminal Dumb device connected to a mainframe or computer network that acts as a point for entry or retrieval of information.

terminal emulation Software that enables a PC to communicate with another computer or network as if the PC were a specific type of hardware terminal.

termination Using terminating resistors to prevent packet reflection on a network cable.

terminator Resistor that is plugged into the end of a bus cable to absorb the excess electrical signal, preventing it from bouncing back when it reaches the end of the wire. Terminators are used with coaxial cable and on the ends of SCSI chains. RG-58 coaxial cable requires resistors with a 50-ohm impedance.

Test the theory Attempt to resolve the issue by either confirming the theory and learning what needs to be done to fix the problem, or by not confirming the theory and forming a new one or escalating. (One of the steps a technician uses to solve a problem.)

texture Small picture that is tiled over and over again on walls, floors, and other surfaces to create the 3-D world.

TFT (thin film transistor) Type of LCD screen. (*See also* active matrix.)

theory of probable cause One possible reason why something is not working; a guess.

thermal compound Paste-like material with very high heat-transfer properties. Applied between the CPU and the cooling device, it ensures the best possible dispersal of heat from the CPU. Also called *heat dope*.

thermal printer Printers that use heated printheads to create high-quality images on special or plain paper.

thermal unit Combination heat sink and fan designed for BTX motherboards; blows hot air out the back of the case instead of just into the case.

thread Smallest logical division of a single program.

throttling Power reduction/thermal control capability allowing CPUs to slow down during low activity or high heat build-up situations. Intel's version is known as SpeedStep, AMD's as PowerNow!

throw Size of the image a projector displays at a certain distance from the screen.

TIA/EIA Telecommunications Industry Alliance/Electronic Industries Alliance. Trade organization that provides standards for network cabling and other electronics.

tiers Levels of Internet providers, ranging from the Tier 1 backbones to Tier 3 regional networks.

timbre Qualities that differentiate the same note played on different instruments.

toner A fine powder made up of plastic particles bonded to iron particles, used by laser printers to create text and images.

toner cartridge   Object used to store the toner in a laser printer. (*See also* laser printer, toner.)

touchpad   Flat, touch-sensitive pad that serves as a pointing device for most laptops.

touch screen   Monitor with a type of sensing device across its face that detects the location and duration of contact, usually by a finger or stylus.

TRACERT   Command-line utility used to follow the path a packet takes between two hosts. Also called TRACEROUTE.

traces   Small electrical connections embedded in a circuit board.

track   Area on a hard drive platter where data is stored. A group of tracks with the same diameter is called a *cylinder*.

trackball   Pointing device distinguished by a ball that is rolled with the fingers.

TrackPoint   IBM's pencil-eraser-sized joystick used in place of a mouse on laptops.

transfer corona   Thin wire, usually protected by other thin wires, that applies a positive charge to the paper during the laser printing process, drawing the negatively charged toner particles off of the drum and onto the paper.

transparency (Windows Vista Aero)   Effect in the Aero desktop environment that makes the edges of windows transparent.

triad   Group of three phosphors—red, green, blue—in a CRT.

Trojan   Program that does something other than what the user who runs the program thinks it will do.

troubleshooting theory   Steps a technician uses to solve a problem: identify the problem, establish a theory of probable cause, test the theory, establish a plan of action, verify functionality, and document findings.

TV tuner   Typically an add-on device that allows users to watch television on a computer.

TWAIN (technology without an interesting name)   Programming interface that enables a graphics application, such as a desktop publishing program, to activate a scanner, frame grabber, or other image-capturing device.

UAC (User Account Control)   Windows Vista feature that enables Standard accounts to do common tasks and provides a permissions dialog when Standard and Administrator accounts do certain things that could potentially harm the computer (such as attempt to install a program).

UART (universal asynchronous receiver/transmitter)   Device that turns serial data into parallel data. The cornerstone of serial ports and modems.

UDF (universal data format)   Replaced the ISO-9660 formats, allowing any operating system and optical drive to read UDF formatted disks.

UEFI (Unified Extensible Firmware Interface)   Consortium of companies that established the UEFI standard that replaced the original EFI standard.

Ultra DMA   Hard drive technology that enables drives to use direct memory addressing. Ultra DMA mode 3 drives—called *ATA/33*—have data transfer speeds up to 33 MBps. Mode 4 and 5 drives—called *ATA/66* and *ATA/100*, respectively—transfer data at up to 66 MBps for mode 4 and 100 MBps for mode 5. Both modes 4 and 5 require an 80-wire cable and a compatible controller to achieve these data transfer rates.

unauthorized access   Anytime a person accesses resources in an unauthorized way. This access may or may not be malicious.

Unicode   16-bit code that covers every character of the most common languages, plus several thousand symbols.

unsigned driver   Driver that has not gone through the Windows Hardware Quality Labs or Microsoft Windows Logo Program to ensure compatibility.

UPC (Universal Product Code)   Bar code used to track inventory.

Upgrade Advisor   The first process that runs on the XP installation CD. It examines your hardware and installed software (in the case of an upgrade) and provides a list of devices and software that are known to have issues with XP. It can also be run separately from the Windows XP installation, from the Windows XP CD. The Upgrade Advisor is also available for Windows Vista and Windows 7.

upgrade installation   Installation of Windows on top of an earlier installed version, thus inheriting all previous hardware and software settings.

UPS (uninterruptible power supply) Device that supplies continuous clean power to a computer system the whole time the computer is on. Protects against power outages and sags.

URL (uniform resource locator) An address that defines the location of a resource on the Internet. URLs are used most often in conjunction with HTML and the World Wide Web.

USB (universal serial bus) General-purpose serial interconnect for keyboards, printers, joysticks, and many other devices. Enables hot-swapping devices.

USB host controller Integrated circuit that is usually built into the chipset and controls every USB device that connects to it.

USB hub Device that extends a single USB connection to two or more USB ports, almost always directly from one of the USB ports connected to the root hub.

USB root hub Part of the host controller that makes the physical connection to the USB ports.

USB thumb drive Flash memory device that uses the standard USB connection.

User account Container that identifies a user to an application, operating system, or network, including name, password, user name, groups to which the user belongs, and other information based on the user and the OS or NOS being used. Usually defines the rights and roles a user plays on a system.

User Accounts applet Windows XP (and later versions) applet that replaced the Users and Passwords applet of Windows 2000.

user interface Visual representation of the computer on the monitor that makes sense to the people using the computer, through which the user can interact with the computer.

user profiles Settings that correspond to a specific user account and may follow users regardless of the computers where they log on. These settings enable the user to have customized environment and security settings.

User's Files Windows Vista's redux of the My Documents folder structure. It is divided into several folders such as Documents, Pictures, Music, and Video.

Users and Passwords applet Windows 2000 application that allowed management of user accounts and passwords.

Users group List of local users not allowed, among other things, to edit the Registry or access critical system files. They can create groups, but can only manage the groups they create.

USMT (User State Migration Tool) Advanced application for file and settings transfer of multiple users.

UTP (unshielded twisted pair) Popular type of cabling for telephone and networks, composed of pairs of wires twisted around each other at specific intervals. The twists serve to reduce interference (also called *crosstalk*). The more twists, the less interference. Unlike its cousin, STP, UTP cable has no metallic shielding to protect the wires from external interference. 1000BaseT uses UTP, as do many other networking technologies. UTP is available in a variety of grades, called categories, as follows:
Category 1 UTP   Regular analog phone lines—not used for data communications.
Category 2 UTP   Supports speeds up to 4 megabits per second.
Category 3 UTP   Supports speeds up to 16 megabits per second.
Category 4 UTP   Supports speeds up to 20 megabits per second.
Category 5 UTP   Supports speeds up to 100 megabits per second.
Category 5e UTP   Supports speeds up to 1000 megabits per second.
Category 6 UTP   Supports speeds up to 10 gigabits per second.

V standards Standards established by CCITT for modem manufacturers to follow (voluntarily) to ensure compatible speeds, compression, and error correction.

Verify Making sure that a problem has been resolved and will not return. (One of the steps a technician uses to solve a problem.)

vertices Used in the second generation of 3-D rendering, vertices have a defined X, Y, and Z position in a 3-D world.

VESA (Video Electronics Standards Association) Consortium of computer manufacturers that standardized improvements to common IBM PC components. VESA is responsible for the Super VGA video standard and the VLB bus architecture.

VGA (video graphics array) Standard for the video graphics adapter that was built into IBM's PS/2 computer. It supports 16 colors in a 640 × 480 pixel video display and quickly replaced the older CGA (Color Graphics Adapter) and EGA (Extended Graphics Adapter) standards.

video capture Computer jargon for the recording of video information, such as TV shows or movies.

video card Expansion card that works with the CPU to produce the images displayed on your computer's display.

video display *See* monitor.

virus Program that can make a copy of itself without your necessarily being aware of it. Some viruses can destroy or damage files. The best protection is to back up files regularly.

virus definition or data file Files that enable the virus protection software to recognize the viruses on your system and clean them. These files should be updated often. They are also called *signature files*, depending on the virus protection software in use.

virus shield Passive monitoring of a computer's activity, checking for viruses only when certain events occur.

VIS (viewable image size) Measurement of the viewable image that is displayed by a CRT rather than a measurement of the CRT itself.

voice coil motor One of two methods used to move actuator arms in a hard drive. (*See also* stepper motor.)

VoIP (Voice over Internet Protocol) Collection of protocols that make voice calls over a data network possible.

volatile Memory that must have constant electricity to retain data. Alternatively, any programmer six hours before deadline after a non-stop, 48-hour coding session, running on nothing but caffeine and sugar.

volts (V) Measurement of the pressure of the electrons passing through a wire, or voltage.

volume Physical unit of a storage medium, such as tape reel or disk pack, that is capable of having data recorded on it and subsequently read. Also refers to a contiguous collection of cylinders or blocks on a disk that are treated as a separate unit.

volume boot sector First sector of the first cylinder of each partition; stores information important to its partition, such as the location of the operating system boot files.

voucher Means of getting a discount on the CompTIA A+ exams.

VPN (virtual private network) Encrypted connection over the Internet between a computer or remote network and a private network.

VRM (voltage regulator module) Small card supplied with some CPUs to ensure that the CPU gets correct voltage. This type of card, which must be used with a motherboard specially designed to accept it, is not commonly seen today.

VRR (vertical refresh rate) The amount of time it takes for a CRT to draw a complete screen. This value is measured in hertz, or cycles per second. Most modern CRTs have a VRR of 60 Hz or better.

wait state Occurs when the CPU has to wait for RAM to provide code. Also known as pipeline stalls.

WAP (Wireless Access Point) Device that centrally connects wireless network nodes.

wattage (watts or W) Measurement of the amps and volts needed for a particular device to function.

wave table synthesis Technique that supplanted FM synthesis, wherein recordings of actual instruments or other sounds are embedded in the sound card as WAV files. When a particular note from a particular instrument or voice is requested, the sound processor grabs the appropriate prerecorded WAV file from its memory and adjusts it to match the specific sound and timing requested.

Web browser Program designed to retrieve, interpret, and display Web pages.

webcam PC camera most commonly used for Internet video.

Welcome screen   Login screen for Windows XP. Enables users to select their particular user account by clicking on their user picture.

WEP (Wired Equivalent Privacy)   Wireless security protocol that uses a standard 40-bit encryption to scramble data packets. Does not provide complete end-to-end encryption and is vulnerable to attack.

Wi-Fi   Common name for the IEEE 802.11 wireless Ethernet standard.

wildcard   Character used during a search to represent search criteria. For instance, searching for ***.doc** will return a list of all files with a .doc extension, regardless of the filename. The * is the wildcard in that search.

Windows 2000   Windows version that succeeded Windows NT; it came in both Professional and Server versions.

Windows 9x   Term used collectively for Windows 95, Windows 98, and Windows Me.

Windows Explorer   Windows utility that enables you to manipulate files and folders stored on the drives in your computer.

Windows Logo'd Product List   List of products that have passed the Microsoft Windows Logo Program and are compatible with Windows operating system. Formerly called the *Hardware Compatibility List* (or *HCL*).

Windows NT   Precursor to Windows 2000, XP, and Vista, which introduced many important features (such as HAL and NTFS) used in all later versions of Windows.

Windows sidebar   User interface feature in Windows Vista that enables users to place various gadgets, such as clocks, calendars, and other utilities, on the right side of their desktop.

Windows update   Microsoft application used to keep Windows operating systems up to date with the latest patches or enhancements. (*See* Automatic Updates.)

Windows Vista   Version of Windows; comes in many different editions for home and office use, but does not have a Server edition.

Windows XP   Version of Windows that replaced both the entire Windows 9x line and Windows 2000; does not have a Server version.

worm   Very special form of virus. Unlike other viruses, a worm does not infect other files on the computer. Instead, it replicates by making copies of itself on other systems on a network by taking advantage of security weaknesses in networking protocols.

WPA (Wi-Fi Protected Access)   Wireless security protocol that uses encryption key integrity-checking and EAP and is designed to improve on WEP's weaknesses.

WPA 2 (Wi-Fi Protected Access 2)   Wireless security protocol, also known as IEEE 802.11i. Uses the Advanced Encryption standard and replaces WPA.

WQUXGA   Video display mode of 2560 × 1600.

wrapper   *See* container file.

WSXGA   Video display mode of 1440 × 900.

WSXGA+   Video display mode of 1680 × 1050.

WUXGA   Video display mode of 1920 × 1200.

WVGA   Video display mode of 800 × 480.

WWW (World Wide Web)   System of Internet servers that support documents formatted in HTML and related protocols. Can be accessed by using Gopher, FTP, HTTP, Telnet, and other tools.

www.comptia.org   CompTIA's Web site.

WXGA   Video display mode of 1280 × 800.

x64   Describes 64-bit operating systems and software.

x86   Describes 32-bit operating systems and software.

XCOPY command   Command in the command-line interface used to copy multiple directories at once, which the COPY command could not do.

xD (Extreme Digital) picture card   Very small flash media card format.

Xeon Line of Intel CPUs designed for servers.

XGA (extended graphics array) Video display mode of 1024 × 768.

XPS (XML Paper Specification) print path Improved printing subsystem included in Windows Vista. Has enhanced color management and better print layout fidelity.

XT bus *See* PC bus.

ZIF (zero insertion force) socket Socket for CPUs that enables insertion of a chip without the need to apply pressure. Intel promoted this socket with its overdrive upgrades. The chip drops effortlessly into the socket's holes, and a small lever locks it in.